3/24/2016

Literature
of Developing
Nations
for Students

National Advisory Board

Literature
of Developing
Nations
for Students

**Presenting Analysis, Context, and Criticism on
Literature of Developing Nations**

Volume 2

Elizabeth Bellalouna, Michael L. LaBlanc, and Ira Mark Milne, Editors

GALE GROUP

Detroit
New York
San Francisco
London
Boston
Woodbridge, CT

Literature of Developing Nations for Students

Staff

Series Editors: Elizabeth Bellalouna, Michael L. LaBlanc, and Ira Mark Milne.

Contributing Editors: Elizabeth Bodenmiller, Reginald Carlton, Anne Marie Hacht, Jennifer Smith.

Managing Editor: Dwayne Hayes.

Research: Victoria B. Cariappa, *Research Team Manager.* Maureen Eremic, Barb McNeil, Cheryl Warnock, *Research Specialists.* Andy Malonis, *Technical Training Specialist.* Barbara Leevy, Tamara Nott, Tracie A. Richardson, Robert Whaley, *Research Associates.* Scott Floyd, Nicodemus Ford, Sarah Genik, Timothy Lehnerer, *Research Assistants.*

Permissions: Maria Franklin, *Permissions Manager.* Margaret A. Chamberlain, Edna Hedblad, *Permissions Specialists.* Erin Bealmear, Shalice Shah-Caldwell, Sarah Tomasek, *Permissions Associates.* Debra Freitas, Julie Juengling, Mark Plaza, *Permissions Assistants.*

Manufacturing: Mary Beth Trimper, *Manager, Composition and Electronic Prepress.* Evi Seoud, *Assistant Manager, Composition Purchasing and Electronic Prepress.* Stacy Melson, *Buyer.*

Imaging and Multimedia Content Team: Randy Bassett, *Image Database Supervisor.* Robert Duncan, Dan Newell, *Imaging Specialists.* Pamela A. Reed, *Imaging Coordinator.* Dean Dauphinais, Robyn V. Young, *Senior Image Editors.* Kelly A. Quin, *Image Editor.*

Product Design Team: Kenn Zorn, *Product Design Manager.* Pamela A. E. Galbreath, *Senior Art Director.* Michael Logusz, *Graphic Artist.*

Library of Congress Cataloging-in-Publication Data

Literature of developing nations for students / Michael L. LaBlanc, Elizabeth Bellalouna, Ira Mark Milne, editors.
    v.; cm.
    Includes bibliographical references and index.
    Contents: v. 1. A-L — v. 2. M-Z.
    ISBN 0-7876-4928-7 (set: alk. paper) — ISBN 0-7876-4929-5 (vol. 1) — ISBN 0-7876-4930-9 (vol. 2)
    1. Fiction—Stories, plots, etc. 2. Fiction—History and criticism. 3. Developing countries—Literatures—History and criticism. [1. Fiction—Stories, plots, etc. 2. Fiction—History and criticism. 3. Developing countries—Literatures—History and criticism.] I. LaBlanc, Michael L. II. Bellalouna, Elizabeth. III. Milne, Ira Mark. IV.Title.
    PN3326 .L58 2000
    809'.891724—dc21
                                    00-056023

Table of Contents

Introduction vii

Literary Chronology xi

Acknowledgments xv

Contributors xix

The Latin Deli: An Ars Poetica
    Judith Ortiz Cofer 1

The Law of Love
    Laura Esquivel 14

Leaving This Island Place
    Austin C. Clarke 27

Like Water for Chocolate
    Laura Esquivel 38

The Management of Grief
    Bharati Mukherjee 66

The Martyr
    Ngugi wa Thiong'o 84

The Middleman
    Bharati Mukherjee 107

No Sweetness Here
    Ama Ata Aidoo 123

Ode to My Socks
    Pablo Neruda 139

One Hundred Years of Solitude
Gabriel García Márquez 159

Petals of Blood
Ngugi wa Thiong'o 202

Pierre Menard, Author of the Quixote
Jorge Luis Borges 236

Prayer to the Masks
Léopold Sédar Senghor 265

A River Sutra
Gita Mehta 281

Seth and Samona
Joanne Hyppolite 304

Silent Wing
José Raúl Bernardo 319

So Far From God
Ana Castillo 333

So Long a Letter
Mariama Bâ 369

Studies in the Park
Anita Desai 400

The Switchman
Juan José Arreola 417

The Time of the Hero
Mario Vargas Llosa 436

Valley Song
Athol Fugard 470

The Village Witch Doctor
Amos Tutuola 491

Where the Air Is Clear
Carlos Fuentes 505

Wide Sargasso Sea
Jean Rhys 554

Glossary of Literary Terms 581

Cumulative Author/Title Index 593

Nationality/Ethnicity Index 595

Subject/Theme Index 597

Introduction

Purpose of the Book

The purpose of *Literature of Developing Nations for Students* (*LDNfS*) is to provide readers with a guide to understanding, enjoying, and studying novels by giving them easy access to information about the work. Part of Gale's "For Students" Literature line, *LDNfS* is specifically designed to meet the curricular needs of high school and undergraduate college students and their teachers, as well as the interests of general readers and researchers considering specific literary works. Each volume has entries on literary works by international authors (both men and women) of developing nations.

The information covered in each entry includes an introduction to the literary work and the author of the literary work; a plot summary, to help readers unravel and understand the events in a literary work; descriptions of important characters, including explanation of a given character's role in the literary work as well as discussion about that character's relationship to other characters in the literary work (please note that entries dealing with poems do not have descriptions of characters); analysis of important themes in the literary work; and an explanation of important literary techniques and movements as they are demonstrated in the literary work.

In addition to this material, which helps the readers analyze the literary work itself, students are also provided with important information on the literary and historical background informing each work. This includes a historical context essay, a box comparing the time or place the literary work was written to modern Western culture, a critical overview essay, and excerpts from critical essays on the literary work. A unique feature of *LDNfS* is a specially commissioned overview essay on each literary work, targeted toward the student reader.

To further aid the student in studying and enjoying each literary work, information on media adaptations is provided, as well as reading suggestions for works of fiction and nonfiction on similar themes and topics. Classroom aids include ideas for research papers and lists of critical sources that provide additional material on the literary work.

Selection Criteria

The titles for each volume of *LDNfS* were selected by surveying numerous sources on teaching literature and analyzing course curricula for various school districts. Some of the sources surveyed included: literature anthologies; *Reading Lists for College-Bound Students: The Books Most Recommended by America's Top Colleges;* textbooks on teaching dramas, novels, poems, and short stories; College Board surveys of dramas, novels, and poems commonly studied in high schools; National Council of Teachers of English (NCTE) surveys of dramas, novels, and poems commonly studied in high schools; and the Young Adult Library Services Association (YALSA) list of best books for young adults of the past twenty-five years.

Input was also solicited from our expert advisory board, as well as educators from various areas. Because of the interest in expanding the canon of literature, an emphasis was placed on including as wide a range of international, multicultural, and women authors of developing natiuons as possible. Our advisory board members—current high school and college teachers—helped pare down the list for each volume. If a work was not selected for the present volume, it was often noted as a possibility for a future volume. As always, the editors welcome suggestions for titles to be included in future volumes.

How Each Entry Is Organized

Each entry, or chapter, in *LDNfS* focuses on one literary work. Each entry heading lists the full name of the literary work, the author's name, and the date of publication of the literary work. The following elements are contained in each entry:

- **Introduction:** a brief overview of the literary work which provides information about its first appearance, its literary standing, any controversies surrounding the work, and major conflicts or themes within the work.

- **Author Biography:** this section includes basic facts about the author's life, and focuses on events and times in the author's life that inspired the literary work in question.

- **Plot Summary:** a description of the major events in the literary work. Lengthy summaries are broken down with subheads.

- **Characters:** an alphabetical listing of major characters in the literary work (except poems). Each character name is followed by a brief to an extensive description of the character's role in the literary work, as well as discussion of the character's actions, relationships, and possible motivation.

    Characters are listed alphabetically by last name. If a character is unnamed—for instance, the narrator in *Invisible Man*–the character is listed as ''The Narrator'' and alphabetized as ''Narrator.'' If a character's first name is the only one given, the name will appear alphabetically by that name.

    Variant names are also included for each character. Thus, the full name ''Jean Louise Finch'' would head the listing for the narrator of *To Kill a Mockingbird,* but listed in a separate cross-reference would be the nickname ''Scout Finch.''

- **Themes:** a thorough overview of how the major topics, themes, and issues are addressed within the literary work. Each theme discussed appears in a separate subhead, and is easily accessed through the boldface entries in the Subject/Theme Index.

- **Style:** this section addresses important style elements of the literary work, such as setting, point of view, and narration; important literary devices used, such as imagery, foreshadowing, symbolism; and, if applicable, genres to which the work might have belonged, such as Gothicism or Romanticism. Literary terms are explained within the entry, but can also be found in the Glossary.

- **Literary Heritage:** this section gives a brief overview of the literary tradition (or oral tradition, if a literary tradition is lacking) that lies behind and provides a context for a given work.

- **Historical Context:** This section outlines the social, political, and cultural climate *in which the author lived and the literary work was created.* This section may include descriptions of related historical events, pertinent aspects of daily life in the culture, and the artistic and literary sensibilities of the time in which the work was written. If the literary work is a historical work, information regarding the time in which the literary work is set is also included. Each section is broken down with helpful subheads.

- **Critical Overview:** this section provides background on the critical reputation of the literary work, including bannings or any other public controversies surrounding the work. For older works, this section includes a history of how the literary work was first received and how perceptions of it may have changed over the years; for more recent literary works, direct quotes from early reviews may also be included.

- **Criticism:** an essay commissioned by *LDNfS* which specifically deals with the literary work and is written specifically for the student audience, as well as excerpts from previously published criticism on the work (if available).

- **Sources:** an alphabetical list of critical material quoted in the entry, with full bibliographical information.

- **Further Reading:** an alphabetical list of other critical sources which may prove useful for the student. Includes full bibliographical information and a brief annotation.

In addition, each entry contains the following highlighted sections, set apart from the main text as sidebars:

- **Media Adaptations:** a list of important film and television adaptations of the literary work, including source information. The list also includes stage adaptations, audio recordings, musical adaptations, etc.

- **Topics for Further Study:** a list of potential study questions or research topics dealing with the literary work. This section includes questions related to other disciplines the student may be studying, such as American history, world history, science, math, government, business, geography, economics, psychology, etc.

- **Compare and Contrast Box:** an ''at-a-glance'' comparison of the cultural and historical differences between the author's time and culture and late twentieth-century Western culture. This box includes pertinent parallels between the major scientific, political, and cultural movements of the time or place the literary work was written, the time or place the literary work was set (if a historical work), and modern Western culture. Works written after the mid-1970s may not have this box.

- **What Do I Read Next?:** a list of works that might complement the featured literary work or serve as a contrast to it. This includes works by the same author and others, works of fiction and nonfiction, and works from various genres, cultures, and eras.

Other Features

A Cumulative Author/Title Index lists the authors and titles covered in each volume of the *LDNfS* series.

A Cumulative Nationality/Ethnicity Index breaks down the authors and titles covered in each volume of the *LDNfS* series by nationality and ethnicity.

A Subject/Theme Index, specific to each volume, provides easy reference for users who may be studying a particular subject or theme rather than a single work. Significant subjects from events to broad themes are included, and the entries pointing to the specific theme discussions in each entry are indicated in **boldface.**

Each entry has several illustrations, including photos of the author, stills from film adaptations (if available), maps, and/or photos of key historical events.

Citing Literature of Developing Nations for Students

When writing papers, students who quote directly from any volume of *Literature of Developing Nations for Students* may use the following general forms. These examples are based on MLA style; teachers may request that students adhere to a different style, so the following examples may be adapted as needed.

When citing text from *LDNfS* that is not attributed to a particular author (i.e., the Themes, Style, Historical Context sections, etc.), the following format should be used in the bibliography section:

> "Anowa." *Literature of Developing Nations for Students*. Eds. Elizabeth Bellalouna, Michael L. LaBlanc, and Ira Mark Milne. Vol. 1. Detroit: Gale, 2000. 72–4.

When quoting the specially commissioned essay from *LDNfS* (usually the first piece under the "Criticism" subhead), the following format should be used:

> Petrusso, Annette. Essay on "Anowa," *Literature of Developing Nations for Students*. Eds. Elizabeth Bellalouna, Michael L. LaBlanc, and Ira Mark Milne. Vol. 1. Detroit: Gale, 2000. 75–8.

When quoting a journal or newspaper essay that is reprinted in a volume of *LDNfS,* the following form may be used:

> Cohen, Derek. "Athol Fugard's 'Boesman and Lena,'" in *The Journal of Commonwealth Literature*, Vol. XII, No. 3 April, 1978, 78–83; excerpted and reprinted in *Literature of Developing Nations for Students*, Vol. 1, eds. Elizabeth Bellalouna, Michael L. LaBlanc, and Ira Mark Milne (Detroit: Gale, 2000), pp. 177–80.

When quoting material reprinted from a book that appears in a volume of *NfS,* the following form may be used:

> Myriam J. A. Chancy, "Lespoua fe viv: Female Identity and the Politics of Textual Sexuality in Nadine Magloire's 'Le Mal de Vivre' and Edwidge Danticat's 'Breath, Eyes, Memory,'" in *Framing Silence: Revolutionary Novels by Haitian Women* (Rutgers University Press, 1997), pp. 120–33; excerpted and reprinted in *Literature of Developing Nations for Students*, Vol. 1, eds. Elizabeth Bellalouna, Michael L. LaBlanc, and Ira Mark Milne (Detroit: Gale, 2000), pp. 195–201.

We Welcome Your Suggestions

The editors of *Literature of Developing Nations for Students* welcome your comments and ideas. Readers who wish to suggest novels to appear in future volumes, or who have other suggestions, are cordially invited to contact the editors. You may contact the editors via e-mail at:

mark.milne@galegroup.com. Or write to the editors at:

Editors, *Literature of Developing Nations for Students*
Gale Group
27500 Drake Road
Farmington Hills, MI 48331–3535

Literary Chronology

1889: Gabriela Mistral is born Lucia Goday Alcayaga in Vicuna, in the Elqui valley in northern Chile on April 7.

1890: Jean Rhys is born Ella Gwendolyn Rees Williams in 1890 in Dominica.

1896: Manuel Rojas is born in Buenos Aires, Argentina, on January 8.

1899: Jorge Luis Borges is born into an old, wealthy, Argentinean family in Buenos Aires on August 24.

1904: Pablo Neruda is born Neftalí Ricardo Reyes Basoalto in the town of Parral in southern Chile.

1906: Leopold Sedar Senghor is born in Joal, a village in Central Senegal.

1907: Rasipuram Krishnaswami Narayan is born in Madras (now known as Chennai), South India, on October 10.

1914: Octavio Paz is born Octavio Paz Lozano in Mexico City in the middle of the Mexican Revolution.

1918: Juan José Arreola is born on September 12 in Ciudad Guzman, in Jalisco, Mexico.

1920: Clarice Lispector, the youngest of three daughters, is born in Tchetchelnik, Ukraine, to Ukrainian parents on December 10.

1920: Amos Tutuola is born in Abeokuta, Western Nigeria, in 1920.

1924: Gabriela Mistral's poem about motherhood, "Fear," is published in her second collection of poetry.

1925: Rosa (Cuthbert) Guy is born in Diego Martin, Trinidad, on September 1.

1927: Manuel Rojas publishes one of his best known and most widely anthologized tales, "The Glass of Milk."

1928: Gabriel García Márquez is born March 6 in Aracataca, Colombia.

1928: Carlos Fuentes is born on November 11 in Panama City.

1929: Miriam Bâ is born.

1930: Chinua Achebe is born in eastern Nigeria on November 16.

1930: Derek Walcott is born January 23 in the capital city of Castries on the eastern Caribbean island of St. Lucia.

1932: Athol Harold Lannigan Fugard is born June 11 in Middelburg, a small village in the semi-desert Karoo region of South Africa.

1932: Manuel Puig is born on December 28 in General Villegas, in the pampas of Argentina.

1934: Austin C. Clarke is born on July 26 in St. James, Barbados.

1936: Mario Vargas Llosa is born in Arequipa, Peru.

1937: Anita Desai is born Anita Mazumdar on June 24 in Mussoorie, India.

1938: Ngugi wa Thiong'o is born James Thiong'o Ngugi, in Limuru, Kenya, on January 5.

1938: José Raúl Bernardo is born on October 3 in Havana, Cuba.

1939: ''Pierre Menard, Author of Quixote'' is first published.

1940: Ama Ata Aidoo is born Christina Ama Aidoo on March 23 in Abeadzi Kyiakor, Gold Coast (now known as Ghana).

1940: Bharati Mukherjee is born into an elite caste level of Calcutta society on July 27.

1941: Jorge Luis Borges establishes his reputation as a writer of fiction with the publication of his short story "The Garden of Forking Paths."

1942: Isabel Angelica Allende is born on August 2 in Lima, Peru.

1943: Gita Mehta is born in New Delhi, India.

1945: Gabriela Mistral receives the Nobel Prize for Literature.

1945: "Prayer to the Masks" is published in Senghor's first collection, *Songs of the Shadow*.

1947: First published in India in the newspaper *The Hindu*, R.K. Narayan's short story ''An Astrologers Day'' becomes the title story of a collection of short stories.

1949: Jamaica Kincaid is born in Antigua on May 25 as Elaine Potter Richardson.

1949: Victor Hernández Cruz is born in the barrio El Guanabano in the town of Aguas Buenas, Puerto Rico.

1951: Laura Esquivel is born in Mexico.

1952: Judith Ortiz Cofer is born February 24 in Hormigueros, Puerto Rico.

1952: "The Switchman" is published in the collection *Confabulario*.

1953: Ana Castillo, a leading voice in the Chicana/o movement, is born.

1954: Omar Sigfrido Castaneda is born on September 6 in Guatemala City, Guatemala, but grows up in Michigan and Indiana after his family moves to the United States.

1954: Octavio Paz publishes "Fable" after returning to Mexico from Paris.

1956: "Ode to My Socks" ("Oda a los calcetines") is published.

1957: Gabriela Mistral dies in Rosalyn Bay, Long Island, in January.

1958: Christina Garcia is born in Havana, Cuba, on July 4. Garcia moves to the U.S. with her parents when she is two years old.

1958: *Where the Air Is Clear* is published.

1959: Rigoberta Menchu is born to poor Native Indian parents in Guatemala.

1960: Clarice Lispector's story about personal relationships, "Family Ties," is published.

1962: Derek Walcott's poem about the Mau Mau Uprising in Kenya, "A Far Cry from Africa," is published.

1962: *The Time of the Hero*, Mario Vargas Llosa's first novel, is published in 1962.

1967: Nobel Prize-winning poet Derek Walcott publishes the play *Dream on Monkey Mountain*.

1967: *One Hundred Years of Solitude* is published.

1968: Gabriel García Márquez publishes "The Handsomest Drowned Man."

1969: Edwidge Danticat is born January 19 in Port-au-Prince, Haiti.

1969: Athol Fugard's *Boesman and Lena* premieres at the Rhodes University Little Theatre in Grahamstown, South Africa, on July 10.

1969: Joanne Hyppolite is born in Les Cayes, Haiti. Her family moves to the United States when she is four years old.

1970: Ama Ata Aidoo's *Anowa* is first published (although Aidoo had begun writing the play in the late 1960s), and later makes its British premiere in London in 1991.

1970: Aidoo's first collection of short stories, *No Sweetness Here*, is published.

1971: Pablo Neruda is awarded the Nobel Prize for Literature.

1973: Manuel Rojas dies in his adopted homeland of Chile on March 11.

1973: "Business" is one of a suite of five poems published in Victor Hernández Cruz's collection *Mainland*.

1973: Rosa Guy publishes the first of her trilogy of young adult novels, *The Friends*.

1973: Pablo Neruda dies of cancer in Santiago on September 23.

1974: The short story "The Martyr" by Kenyan novelist Ngugi wa Thiong'o, East Africa's leading writer, is first published in his collection *Secret Lives and Other Stories*.

1976: Manuel Puig publishes his best known novel, *Kiss of the Spider Woman*.

1977: Clarice Lispector dies on December 9.

1977: After six years of work, Ngugi wa Thiong'o publishes *Petals of Blood*.

1978: Jamaica Kincaid's short story "Girl" is first published in the June 26 issue of *The New Yorker*.

1978: Anita Desai's short story "Studies in the Park" is first published, in her collection *Games at Twilight*.

1979: Manuel Puig is awarded the American Library Association Notable Book Award for *Kiss of the Spider Woman*.

1979: Jean Rhys dies at the age of 88.

1980: Miriam Bâ publishes *So Long a Letter*.

1981: Miriam Bâ dies after a long illness.

1982: Isabelle Allende establishes her literary reputation with the publication of *The House of the Spirits*.

1982: Gabriel García Márquez wins the Nobel Prize for Literature.

1984: Rigoberta Menchú stirs international debate over the treatment of Native Indians with the publication of her autobiography *I, Rigoberta Menchú: An Indian Woman in Guatemala*.

1985: Jamaica Kincaid's second book, *Annie John*—comprised of short stories that first appeared in *The New Yorker*, is published.

1986: Jorge Luis Borges dies of liver cancer in Geneva, Switzerland.

1987: After a twenty-one-year hiatus from writing, Chinua Achebe publishes *Anthills of the Savannah* in Great Britain.

1988: Bharati Mukherjee's short story "The Middleman" is originally included in her second collection of short fiction, *The Middleman and Other Stories*, which won the 1988 Book Critics Circle Award for best fiction.

1989: Bharati Mukherjee's *Jasmine*, the story of a widowed Punjabi peasant reinventing herself in America, is published.

1989: Laura Esquivel publishes her first novel, *Like Water for Chocolate: A Novel in Monthly Installments, with Recipes, Romances and Home Remedies*, which becomes a bestseller in Mexico and is successful in the United States.

1990: Manuel Puig dies from complications following a gallbladder operation.

1990: Austin C. Clarke's short story "Leaving This Island Place" is published in the short story collection *From Ink Lake: Canadian Stories*.

1990: Octavio Paz is awarded the Nobel Prize in Literature.

1990: Amos Tutuola publishes *The Village Witch Doctor and Other Stories*.

1991: Omar S. Castaneda's *Among the Volcanoes*, a coming-of-age story written for young adults and set in a place far removed from the environments familiar to American readers, is published.

1992: Rigoberta Menchu is awarded the Nobel Peace Prize.

1992: Judith Ortiz Cofer first publishes "The Latin Deli: An Ars Poetica" in *Americas Review*.

1992: Derek Walcott is awarded the Nobel Prize in Literature for his poetry.

1993: Gita Mehta publishes *A River Sutra*.

1993: "Pierre Menard, Author of the Quixote" is published.

1993: *So Far From God* is published.

1994: Edwidge Danticat's *Breath, Eyes, Memory* is published. Danticat is hailed by *Publishers Weekly* as "a distinctive new voice with a sensitive insight into Haitian culture."

1995: Judith Ortiz Cofer publishes "Bad Influence" in *Stories of the Barrio: An Island Like You*.

1995: *Seth and Samona* is published in 1995.

1996: Laura Esquivel publishes her second novel, *The Law of Love.*

1996: *Valley Song* is published.

1966: *Wide Sargasso Sea* is published.

1997: Omar S. Castaneda dies of a heroin overdose in January.

1997: Cristina Garcia's *The Aguero Sisters* is published.

1997: Tutuola dies of diabetes and hypertension on June 8 in poverty and obscurity, having been unable to afford adequate medical attention for his ailments.

1998: Isabel Allende's literary celebration of sex and food, *Aphrodite: A Memoir of the Senses,* makes its way onto the *New York Times* best-seller list.

1998: *The Farming of the Bones* is published.

1998: Octavio Paz dies on April 19.

1998: José Raúl Bernardo publishes his historical novel *Silent Wing.*

Acknowledgments

The editors wish to thank the copyright holders of the excerpted criticism included in this volume and the permissions managers of many book and magazine publishing companies for assisting us in securing reproduction rights. We are also grateful to the staffs of the Detroit Public Library, the Library of Congress, the University of Detroit Mercy Library, Wayne State University Purdy/Kresge Library Complex, and the University of Michigan Libraries for making their resources available to us. Following is a list of the copyright holders who have granted us permission to reproduce material in this volume of *Literature of Developing Nations for Students (LDNfS)*. Every effort has been made to trace copyright, but if omissions have been made, please let us know.

COPYRIGHTED MATERIALS IN *LDNfS*, VOLUMES 1 & 2, WERE REPRODUCED FROM THE FOLLOWING PERIODICALS:

Américas, v. 45, July-August, 1993; v. 48, November-December, 1996. © 1993, 1996 Américas. Both reprinted by permission of Américas, a bi-monthly magazine published by the General Secretariat of the Organization of American States in English and Spanish.—*ARIEL: A Review of International English Literature*, v.29, October, 1998 for "Fables of the Plague Years: Postcolonialism, Postmodernism, and Magical Realism in 'Cien anos de soledad'" by Dean J. Irvine. Copyright © 1998 The Board of Governors, The University of Calgary. Reproduced by permission of the publisher and the author./ v. 24, April, 1993 for "Jean Rhys's Construction of Blackness as Escape from White Femininity in 'Wide Sargasso Sea'" by Maria Olaussen. Copyright © 1993 The Board of Governors, The University of Calgary. Reproduced by permission of the publisher.—*Belles Lettres: A Review of Books by Women*, v. 10, Fall, 1994. Reproduced by permission.—*Booklist*, v. 94, February 1, 1998; v. 94, July, 1998. Copyright © 1998 by the American Library Association. Both reproduced by permission.—*Christian Century*, v. 116, September 22, 1999. Copyright 1999 Christian Century Foundation. Reproduced by permission from The Christian Century.—*CLA Journal*, v. xxxvii, September, 1993. Copyright, 1993 by The College Language Association. Used by permission of The College Language Association.—*College Literature*, v. 19, October-February, 1992; v. 22, February, 1995. Copyright © 1992, 1995 by West Chester University. Both reproduced by permission.—*Commonweal*, v. 121, January 14, 1994. Copyright © 1994 Commonweal Publishing Co., Inc. Reproduced by permission of Commonweal Foundation.—*Comparative Literature*, v. 43, Fall, 1991 for "Myth, Contingency, and Revolution in Carlos Fuentes's La region mas transparente" by Maarten Van Delden. Reproduced by permission of the author.—*Confluencia*, v. 1, Fall, 1985. Reproduced by permission.—*Dallas Morning News*, October 20, 1996. © 1996 The Dallas Morning News. Reproduced by permission..—***Explicator***, v. 55, Winter, 1997. Copyright © 1997 Helen Dwight Reid Educational Foundation. Reproduced with permission of the Helen Dwight Reid Educational Foundation, published by Heldref Publications, 1319 18th Street, NW, Washington, DC 20036-1802.—***French Review***, v. 6, October, 1990. Copyright 1990 by the American Association of Teachers of French. Reproduced by permission.—***Hispania***, May, 1970 for "Aristotle and Vargas Llosa: Literature, History and the Interpretation of Reality" by Frank Dauster; v. 71, December, 1988 for "This is No Way to Run a Railroad: Arreola's Allegorical Railroad and Possible Source" by John R. Burt. © 1988 The American Association of Teachers of Spanish and Portuese, Inc. Reproduced by permission of the publisher and the author. © 1970, 1988 The American Association of Teachers of Spanish and Portuese, Inc. Both reproduced by permission of the publisher and the authors.—***Humanist***, v. 53, March-April, 1993 for "Nagugi wa Thiong'o and the Politics of Language" by Theodore Pelton. Copyright 1993 by the American Humanist Association. Reproduced by permission of the author.—***International Fiction Review***, v. 21, 1994. © copyright 1994 International Fiction Association. Reproduced by permission.—***Journal of Commonwealth Literature***, n. 5, July, 1968; v. xii, April, 1978; v. xvii, 1982. All reproduced with the kind permission of Bowker-Saur.—***Latin American Literary Review***, v. vi, Fall-Winter, 1977; v. xiv, January-June, 1986. Reproduced by permission.—***Latin American Perspectives***, v. 26, November, 1999. Reproduced by permission of Sage Publications, Inc.—***Literary Criterion***, v. xxvii, 1991. v. xxix, 1994. Both reproduced by permission.—***London Times***, September 18, 1997. Reproduced by permission.—***Los Angeles Times***, July 29, 1998; October 10, 1999. Copyright, 1998, 1999, Los Angeles Times. Both reproduced by permission.—***Maclean's Magazine***, v. 102, October 23, 1989 for "Jasmine" by Eleanor Wachtel. © 1989 by Maclean's Magazine. Reproduced by permission of the author.—***MELUS***, v. 22, 1997; v. 23, Spring, 1998. Copyright, MELUS: The Society for the Study of Multi-Ethnic Literature of the United States, 1997 Reproduced by permission.—***Modern Fiction Studies***, v. 26, Summer, 1980; v. 44, Winter, 1998. Copyright © 1980, 1998 by Purdue Research Foundation, West Lafayette, IN 47907. All rights reserved. Both reproduced by permission of The Johns Hopkins University.—***Multicultural Review***, v. 5, June, 1996. Reproduced by permission of Greenwood Publishing Group, Inc., Westport, CT.—

NACLA Report on the Americas, v. 32, March-April, 1999; v. 32, May-June, 1999. Copyright 1999 by the North American Congress on Latin America. Both reproduced by permission.—***Nation***, (New York), v. 246, April 16, 1988; v. 254, January 27, 1992; v. 262, January 29, 1996; New York, v. 264, May 19, 1997. © 1988; 1992; 1996; 1997 The Nation magazine/ The Nation Company, Inc. All reproduced by permission.—***New Literary History***, v. 24, Spring, 1993. Copyright © 1993 by New Literary History. Reproduced by permission of The Johns Hopkins University Press.—***New Statesman & Society***, v. 6, June 18, 1993. © 1993 Statesman & Nation Publishing Company Limited. Reproduced by permission.—***North American Review***, v. 281, March-April, 1996. Reproduced by permission.—***NWSA Journal***, v. 11, March 22, 1999. Reproduced by permission.—***Publisher's Weekly***, v. 237, December 21, 1990; v. 240, March 29, 1993; v. 241, January 24, 1994; v. 242, June 19, 1995; v. 245, January 19, 1998; v. 245, June 1, 1998. Copyright 1990, 1993, 1994, 1995, 1998 by Reed Publishing USA. All reproduced from Publishers Weekly, published by the Bowker Magazine Group of Cahners Publishing Co., a division of Reed Publishing USA., by permission.—***Research in African Literatures***, v. 23, Spring, 1992; v. 25, Summer, 1994. Copyright © 1992, 1994 Indiana University Press. Both reproduced by permission.—***Review of Contemporary Fiction***, v. 13, Summer, 1993. Copyright, 1993, by John O'Brien. Reproduced by permission.—***Romance Notes***, v. xxiv, Winter, 1983. Reproduced by permission.—***Romantic Review***, v. 86, January, 1995. Reproduced by permission.—***Studies in Short Fiction***, v. 29, Winter, 1992; v. 31, Summer, 1994; v. 32, Spring, 1995 Copyright 1992, 1994, 1995 by Newberry College. All reproduced by permission.—***Texas Studies in Literature and Language***, v. xix, Winter, 1977. Reproduced by permission.—***Times*** (London), August 21, 1997; April 30, 1998. © Times Newspapers Limited 1998. All reproduced from The Times, London by permission.—***Times Literary Supplement***, July 4, 1986; May 18-24, 1990. © The Times Supplements Limited 1986, 1990. Both reproduced from The Times Literary Supplement by permission.—***Twentieth Century Literature***, v. 39, Winter, 1993. Copyright 1993, Hofstra University Press. Reproduced by permission.—***UNESCO Courier***, November, 1989. Reproduced by permission.—***Washington Times***, May 15, 1997. Copyright © 1997 News World Communications, Inc. Reprinted with permission of The Washington Times.—***Women's Studies***, v. 22, March, 1993. © Gordon and Breach Science Publishers. Reproduce by permission.—*World Literature Today*, v. 52, Winter, 1978; v. 64, Summer, 1991; v. 69, Winter, 1995; v. 72, Winter, 1998; v. 73, Spring, 1999. Copyright 1978, 1991, 1995, 1998, 1999 by the University of Oklahoma Press. All reproduced by permission of the publisher.—*World Literature Written in English*, November, 1974; v. 28, Spring, 1988 © Copyright 1974 WLWE-World Literature Written in English. Reproduced by permission of the publisher.

COPYRIGHTED MATERIALS IN *LDNfS*, VOLUMES 1 & 2, WERE REPRODUCED FROM THE FOLLOWING BOOKS:

Chancy, Myriam J. A. From *Framing Silence: A Revolutionary Novels by Haitian Women*. Rutgers University Press, 1997. Copyright (c) 1997 by Myriam J. A. Chancy. All rights reserved. Reproduced by permission of Rutgers, The State University.— Cruz, Victor Hernandez. From *Mainland*. Random House, 1973. Reproduced by permission of Random House, Inc.—Evans, Jennifer. From *Annual Selected Papers of the ALA*. Edited by Stephen H. Arnold. Three Continents Press, 1983. Reproduced by permission.—Fulks, Barbara P. From *Reference Guide to World Literature, 2nd ed.* Edited by Lesley Henderson. St. James Press, 1995. Reproduced by permission.—Nagel, James. From *Traditions, Voices, and Dreams*. Edited by Melvin J. Friedman and Ben Siegel. University of Delaware Press, 1995. Reproduced by permission.—Neruda, Pablo. From *Neruda and Vallejo: Selected Poems*. Edited by Robert Bly. Beacon Press, 1971. Copyright © 1971 by Robert Bly. Reproduced by permission.—Ojo-Ade, Femi. From *Africana Literature Today*. Africana Publishing Company, 1982. Reproduced by permission in the U.S. by Holmes & Meier Publishers, Inc. In the world market by Heinemann Educational Books Ltd.—Paz, Octavio. From *Octavio Paz: Selected Poems*. Edited by Eliot Weinberger. A New Directions Book, 1984. Reproduced by permission.—Peters, Jonathan. From *A Dance of Masks*. Three Continents Press, 1978. Copyright © 1978 by Three Continents Press, copyright © 1996 by Three Continents Press/Lynne Rienner Publishers. Reproduced by permission of Lynne Publishers, Inc.—Reeve, Richard M. From Carlos Fuentes, *A Critical View*. Edited by Robert Broday and Charles Rossman. University of Texas Press, 1982. Copyright © 1982 by the University of Texas Press. All rights reserved. Reproduced by permission.—Tittler, Jonathan. From *Twyane's World Authors Series Online*. G. K. Hall & Co., 1999. Reproduced by permission.—Walcott, Derek.

From *Poetry for Students*. Edited by Mary Ruby. The Gale Group, 1999. Reproduced by permission of the author.—Willis, Robert J. From *Staging the Impossible: The Fantastic Mode in Modern Drama*. Edited by Patrick D. Murphy. Greenwood Press, 1992. Reproduced by permission of Greenwood Publishing Group, Inc., Westport, CT.

PHOTOGRAPHS AND ILLUSTRATIONS APPEARING IN *LDNFS*, VOLUMES 1 & 2, WERE RECEIVED FROM THE FOLLOWING SOURCES:

Achebe, Chinua, photograph. AP/Wide World Photos. Reproduced by permission.— Allende, Isabel, photograph. AP/Wide World Photos. Reproduced by permission.—Allende, Isabel, photograph. Archive Photos. Reproduced by permission.—Allende, Salvador (riding in car), photograph. UPI/Bettmann. Reproduced by permission.—Bernardo, Jose-Raul, photograph by Jerry Bauer. © Jerry Bauer. Reproduced by permission.—Borges, Jorge Luis (on couch, painting behind), photograph by Harold Mantell. Reproduced by permission.—Borges, Jorge Luis, photograph. The Library of Congress.—Bronte, Charlotte (engraved according to an act of Congress), 1873, engraving. Archive Photos/Kean. Reproduced by permission.—Castillo, Ana, portrait. Photograph by Barbara Seyda.—Cavazos, Lumi, (holding baby in arms), starring in Alfonso Arau's film "Like Water for Chocolate", photograph. The Kobal Collection. Reproduced by permission.—Clarke, Austin, photograph by John Reeves. Reproduced by permission.—Colombian Troops (line up on lawn), Bogota, Colombia, 1949, photograph. CORBIS/Bettmann. Reproduced by permission.—Colombian Troops (wearing various styles of military uniforms), Colon, Panama, 1902, photograph. CORBIS. Reproduced by permission.—Cortes, Hernan (approaching Aztec emperor Montezuma), Tenochtitlan, Mexico, engraving. The Library of Congress.—Cruz, Victor Hernandez (reading poetry outdoors), photograph. Arte Publico Press Archives, University of Houston. Reproduced by permission.—Danticat, Edwidge (hand on forehead), New York City, 1998, photograph by Doug Kanter. AP/Wide World Photos. Reproduced by permission.—Danticat, Edwidge, Ixel Cervera (Danticat singing her book for Cervera), New York City, 1998, photograph by Bebeto Matthews. AP/Wide World Photos. Reproduced by permission.—de Cervantes, Miguel, photograph.—Desai, Anita. Photograph courtesy of William Heinemann.—Eighth Street, Little Havana, Miami, Florida, c. 1981, photograph. Russell

Thompson/Archive Photos. Reproduced by permission.—Esquivel, Laura, photograph by Jerry Bauer. © Jerry Bauer. Reproduced by permission.—Esquivel, Laura, sitting wearing a flower print dews, photograph. © Jerry Bauer. Reproduced by permission.—Family near mealtime, Central Africa, photograph. United Nations. Reproduced by permission.—Fuentes, Carlos, photograph by Hugh Peralta. Archive Photos, Inc./Reuters. Reproduced by permission.—Fugard, Athol, photograph. AP/Wide World Photos. Reproduced by permission.—Fugard, Athol (seated on couch with Amy Irving), 1988, photograph. AP/Wide World Photos. Reproduced by permission.—Garcia, Cristina, photograph. AP/Wide World Photos. Reproduced by permission.—Garcia Marquez, Gabriel (looking right, in dark shirt), 1982, photograph. AP/Wide World Photos. Reproduced by permission.—Group of slaves disembarking (three-masted ship in distance), engraving. The Library of Congress.—Guy, Rosa, photograph by Jerry Bauer. © Jerry Bauer. Reproduced by permission.—Hurt, William and Raul Julia. From a scene from ''Kiss of the Spider Woman,'' photograph. The Kobal Collection. Reproduced by permission.—Mandela, Nelson and F.W. de Klerk, 1994, photograph. Reuters/Bettmann. Reproduced by permission.—Marti, Jose (arms folded across chest), photograph. The Library of Congress.—Menchu, Rigoberta, (hand raised, speaking), Tokyo, Japan, 1993, photograph. Reuters/Bettmann. Reproduced by permission.—Mistral, Gabriela, photograph. The Library of Congress.—Mukherjee, Bharati. © Jerry Bauer. Reproduced by permission.—Mukherjee, Bharati, photograph. AP/Wide World Photos. Reproduced by permission.—Muslim woman on beach, Senegal, 1978, photograph by Owen Franken. © Owen Franken/CORBIS. Reproduced by permission.—Narayan, R.K., photograph by Jerry Bauer. Reproduced with permission.—Neruda, Pablo, photograph by Jerry Bauer. © Jerry Bauer. Reproduced by permission.—Open boats along shore of Gold Coast, British West Africa, c. 1890-1910, photograph. © Corbis. Reproduced by permission.—Ortiz Cofer, Judith (seated), photograph. Arte Publico Press Archives, University of Houston. Reproduced by permission.—Paz, Octavio, photograph. AP/Wide World Photos. Reproduced by permission.—People being held in stadium (armed soldier standing guard), Santiago, Chile, 1973, photograph. CORBIS/Bettmann. Reproduced by permission.—Pinochet, Augusto (speaking into microphones, his right hand lifted, in uniform), 1978, photograph. AP/Wide World Photos. Reproduced by permission.—Puig, Manuel (wearing banned collar jacket), photograph by Jerry Bauer. © Jerry Bauer. Reproduced by permission.—Quiche/Mayan Indian woman weaving on backstrap loom, c. 1980, Guatemala, photograph. CORBIS/ Jack Fields. Reproduced by permission.—Rhys, Jean, photograph by Jerry Bauer. © Jerry Bauer. Reproduced by permission.—Schoolchildren, Dakar, Senegal, 1978, photograph by Owen Franken. © Owen Franken/ Corbis. Reproduced by permission.—Senghor, Leopold, photograph. AP/Wide World Photos. Reproduced by permission.—The July, 1970, Playbill for Athol Fugard's ''Boesman and Lena,'' Directed by John Berry, with James Earl Jones as Boesman, Ruby Dee as Lena and Zakes Mokae as Old African, at the Circle in the Square Theater, NY, Credit page, photograph. PLAYBILL (r) is a registered trademark of Playbill Incorporated, N.Y.C. All rights reserved. Reproduced by permission.—Vargas, Llosa (Jorge) Mario (Pedro), photograph. Jerry Bauer. Reproduced by permission.—Walcott, Derek, photographs by Jerry Bauer. © Jerry Bauer. Reproduced by permission.—Woman standing in ocean, watching ship in distance, a scene from the film version of Jean Rhys' novel ''Wide Sargasso Sea.'' The Kobal Collection. Reproduced by permission.

Contributors

Diane Andrews Henningfeld: Andrews Henningfeld is associate professor of English at Adrian College in Michigan; she has written extensively for a variety of educational and academic publishers. Entry on "The Garden of Forking Paths." Original essay on "The Garden of Forking Paths."

Cynthia Bily: Bily teaches writing and literature at Adrian College in Adrian, MI, and writes for various educational publishers. Entry on "Girl." Original essays on *Anthills of the Savannah*, and "Girl."

Adrian Blevins: Blevins, a poet and essayist who has taught at Hollins University, Sweet Briar College, and in the Virginia Community College System, is the author of *The Man Who Went Out for Cigarettes,* a chapbook of poems, and has published poems, stories, and essays in many magazines, journals, and anthologies. Original essay on "Girl."

Liz Brent: Brent has a Ph.D. in American Culture, specializing in cinema studies, from the University of Michigan; she is a freelance writer and teaches courses in American cinema. Entries on *Kiss of the Spider Woman*, "Leaving This Island Place," "The Martyr," "The Middleman," "No Sweetness Here," "Studies in the Park," and "The Village Witch Doctor." Original essays on *Anowa*, "Bad Influence," "Family Ties," "The Garden of Forking Paths," "Girl," "The Glass of Milk," "The Handsomest Drowned Man in the World," *Kiss of the Spider Woman*, "Leaving This Island Place," "Management of Grief," "The Martyr," "The Middleman," "No Sweetness Here," "Studies in the Park," and "The Village Witch Doctor."

Jennifer Bussey: Bussey holds a bachelor's degree in English literature and a master's degree in interdisciplinary studies; she is an independent writer specializing in literature. Entries on *Among the Volcanoes* and *Anthills of the Savannah*. Original essays on *Among the Volcanoes, Anthills of the Savannah*, "Management of Grief," and "Studies in the Park."

David Donnell: Donnell teaches at the University of Toronto, and has published seven books of poetry. His work is included in the *Norton Anthology of Modern Poetry*, and his volume *Settlement* has received Canada's prestigious Governor General's Award. Original essay on "A Far Cry from Africa."

Donald G. Evans: Evans is an adjunct professor at Hamilton College in Cedar Rapids, IA, as well as a free-lance writer for *Advertising Age* and editor for *Story Quarterly* . Entry on *Jasmine*. Original essay on *Jasmine*.

Darren Felty: Felty is visiting instructor at the College of Charleston, SC, and has a Ph.D. in literature from the University of Georgia. Entry on *Annie John*. Original essay on *Annie John*.

James Frazier: Frazier has an M.A. with a major in English literature from the University of Texas at Austin; he also teaches English and speech at Lytle High School, Lytle, TX. Entry on "The Management of Grief." Original essay on "The Management of Grief."

Lane A. Glenn: Glenn is an author, educator, director, and actor, located in Lansing, MI. Entries on *Boesman and Lena* and *Valley Song*. Original essays on *Boesman and Lena* and *Valley Song*.

Carole Hamilton: Hamilton is a freelance writer and an instructor at Cary Academy, Cary, NC. Entries on "Family Ties," *One Hundred Years of Solitude*, and "Pierre Menard, Author of Quixote." Original essays on "Family Ties," *One Hundred Years of Solitude*, and "Pierre Menard, Author of Quixote."

Jhan Hochman: Hochman holds a Ph.D. in English and an M.A. in cinema studies; his articles have appeared in *Democracy and Nature*, *Genre*, *ISLE*, and *Mosaic*. Entry on "A Far Cry from Africa." Original essay on "A Far Cry from Africa."

Jeremy W. Hubbell: Hubbell is a freelance writer, holds an M.Litt. from the University of Aberdeen, and is pursuing a Ph.D. in history at the State University of New York at Stony Brook. Entries on *Aphrodite: A Memoir of the Senses*, *The Time of the Hero*, and *Where the Air is Clear*. Original essays on *Aphrodite: A Memoir of the Senses*, *The Time of the Hero*, and *Where the Air is Clear*.

Elizabeth Judd: Judd is a freelance writer and book reviewer with an M.F.A. in English from the University of Michigan and a B.A. from Yale. Entry on *The Aguero Sisters*. Original essay on *The Aguero Sisters*.

Chelva Kanaganayakam: Kanaganayakam is an associate professor in the Department of English at the University of Toronto; his writings include *Structures of Negation: The Writings of Zulfikar Ghose*, *South Asian Writers and their Worlds*, and *Dark Antonyms and Paradise: The Poetry of Rienzi Crusz*. Entry on "An Astrologer's Day." Original essay on "An Astrologer's Day."

David J. Kelly: Kelly is a professor of English at College of Lake County, IL. Entries on "Fear" and "Seth and Samona." Original essays on "Fear" and "Seth and Samona."

Lydia S. Kim: Kim holds an M.S. Ed. from the University of Pennsylvania in Philadelphia, and teaches language arts and social studies at Cary Academy, Cary, NC. Entry on *I, Rigoberta Menchu*. Original essay on *I, Rigoberta Menchu*.

Rena Korb: Korb has a master's degree in English literature and creative writing, and has written for a wide variety of educational publishers. Original essays on "Family Ties," "The Friends," and "The Middleman."

Uma Kukathas: Kukathas is a freelance writer and a student in the Ph.D. program in philosophy at the University of Washington, specializing in social, political, and moral philosophy. Entries on "Fable," "Ode to My Socks," and *Petals of Blood*. Original essays on "Fable," "Ode to My Socks," and *Petals of Blood*.

Aviya Kushner: Aviya Kushner is the Contributing Editor in Poetry at *BarnesandNoble.com* and the Poetry Editor of *Neworld Magazine*. She is a graduate of the acclaimed creative writing program in poetry at Boston University, where she received the Fitzgerald Award in Translation. Her writing on poetry has appeared in *Harvard Review* and *The Boston Phoenix*, and she has served as Poetry Coordinator for *AGNI Magazine*. She has given readings of her own work throughout the United States, and she teaches at Massachusetts Communications College in Boston. Original essay on "A Far Cry from Africa."

Kimberly Lutz: Lutz is an instructor at New York University, and has written for a wide variety of educational publishers. Entries on *A River Sutra*, *So Long A Letter*, and *Wide Sargasso Sea*. Original essays on *A River Sutra*, *So Long A Letter*, and *Wide Sargasso Sea*.

Jennifer Lynch: Lynch teaches at the Potrero Hill After School Program and the Taos Literacy Program; she also contributes to *Geronimo*, a journal of politics and culture. Entries on "Bad Influence" and "The Switchman." Original essays on "Bad Influence" and "The Switchman."

Sarah Madsen Hardy: Madsen Hardy has a doctorate in English literature, and is a freelance writer and editor. Original Essay on "Girl."

Mary Mahony: Mahony has an M.A. in English from the University of Detroit and an M.L.S. from Wayne State University; she is an instructor of English at Wayne County Community

College in Detroit, MI. Entry on *The Friends*. Original essay on *The Friends*.

Sheri Metzger: Metzger is a freelance writer, has a Ph.D., and is an adjunct professor in the Department of English at the University of New Mexico in Albuquerque, NM. Entries on "The Handsomest Drowned Man in the World" and *House of the Spirits*. Original essays on "Bad Influence," "The Glass of Milk," "The Handsomest Drowned Man in the World," and *House of the Spirits*.

Tyrus Miller: Miller is an assistant professor of comparative literature and English at Yale University, where he teaches twentieth-century literature and visual culture; he has published a book entitled *Late Modernism: Politics, Fiction, and the Arts between the World Wars* . Entry on "Prayer to the Masks." Original essay on "Prayer to the Masks."

Carl Mowrey: Mowery has a Ph.D. in writing and literature from Southern Illinois University, Carbondale, IL. Entry on "The Glass of Milk." Original essays on "Fear" and "The Glass of Milk."

Wendy Perkins: Perkins is an assistant professor of English at Prince George's Community College, MD; she has a Ph.D. in English from the University of Delaware. Entries on "The Latin Deli," *The Law of Love*, and *Like Water for Chocolate* . Original essays on "The Latin Deli," *The Law of Love*, and *Like Water for Chocolate*.

Annette Petrusso: Petrusso is a freelance author and screenwriter, located in Austin, TX. Entries on *Anowa* and *Dream on Monkey Mountain*. Original essays on *Anowa* and *Dream on Monkey Mountain*.

Dean Rader: Rader has published widely in the field of American and Latin American art and literature. Original essays on "The Handsomest Drowned Man in the Wolrd," "Ode to My Socks," and "Pierre Menard, Author of Quixote."

Michael Rex: Rex is an adjunct professor at the University of Detroit-Mercy, MI. Entry on *So Far From God: A Novel*. Original essay on *So Far From God: A Novel*.

Chris Semansky: Semansky holds a Ph.D. in English from Stony Brook University, and teaches writing and literature at Portland Community College in Portland, OR. His collection of poems *Death, But at a Good Price* received the Nicholas Roerich Poetry Prize for 1991 and was published by Story Line Press and the Nicholas Roerich Museum. Semansky's most recent collection, *Blindsided*, has been published by 26 Books of Portland, OR. Entry on "Business." Original essays on "Business," "The Latin Deli," and "Prayer to the Masks."

Emily Smith Riser: Smith Riser has a master's degree in English literature, and teaches high school English. Original essay on *Among the Volcanoes*.

Christine Thompson: Thompson has an M.A., and is a part-time English instructor at Jefferson Community College, Watertown, NY. Entry on *Silent Wing: A Novel*. Original essay on *Silent Wing: A Novel*.

Karen D. Thompson: Thompson has done graduate work at the University of North Carolina, Greensboro, and has taught English at Asheboro High School (NC), Manor High School, Dripping Springs High School, and Dripping Springs Middle School (TX). Original essays on "The Friends" and "Studies in the Park."

Kelly Winters: Winters is a freelance writer, and has written for a wide variety of academic and educational publishers. Entries on *Breath, Eyes, Memory* and "The Farming of Bones." Original essays on *Breath, Eyes, Memory*, "A Far Cry from Africa," "The Farming of Bones," and *House of the Spirits*.

Paul Witcover: Witcover is a novelist and editor in New York City with an M.A. in creative writing and literature from the City University of New York. Original essay on "A Far Cry from Africa."

The Latin Deli: An Ars Poetica

Judith Ortiz Cofer

1992

Judith Ortiz Cofer first published "The Latin Deli: An Ars Poetica" in *Americas Review* in 1992. The poem later appeared in a collection of poems, short stories, and personal essays titled *The Latin Deli*. The collection received much critical acclaim. A reviewer in *Booklist* wrote that Ortiz Cofer's stories, essays, and poems are a "delicious smorgasbord of the sights, smells, tastes, and sounds recalled from a cross-cultural girlhood. Whether delineating the yearnings for an island homeland or the frustrations of a first-generation immigrant's struggles to grow up in 'el building' in a New Jersey barrio, Ortiz Cofer's work is rich in evocative detail and universal concerns." The poem "The Latin Deli" focuses on a place where Spanish immigrants meet to talk to each other in their native language and to buy food from their homelands. The deli, presided over by the owner, offers a respite from the culture clash they have experienced in America. As they walk down the aisles, reciting the names of Spanish food like poetry, they are able to hang on to the traditions of the past, in order to maintain a clear sense of their cultural heritage. Ortiz Cofer transfers her own experience as an immigrant to art and so establishes a link between herself and the deli owner. Ortiz Cofer suggests that through her poems and stories that center on the lives of Spanish immigrants, she, like the owner of the deli, offers comfort and a sense of identity to others who share her heritage.

Author Biography

Judith Ortiz Cofer was born on February 24, 1952, in Hormigueros, Puerto Rico, to J. M. and Fanny Ortiz. Her family immigrated to the United States in 1956 when her father joined the U.S. Navy. The family made several trips back to Puerto Rico from their home in Paterson, New Jersey. In an interview for *Melus* she describes her experience in both cultures:

> I write in English, yet I write obsessively about my Puerto Rican experience. . .That is how my psyche works. I am a composite of two worlds. . .I lived with. . .conflictive expectations: the pressures from my father to become very well versed in the English language and the Anglo customs, and from my mother not to forget where we came from. That is something that I deal with in my work all the time.

Ortiz Cofer received a B.A. from Augusta College in 1974, an M.A. from Florida Atlantic University in 1977, and studied at Oxford University in 1977. She held several teaching positions in Florida and Georgia before she gained her current position teaching English and creative writing at the University of Georgia. Ortiz Cofer began writing while she was a graduate student. She first wrote poems about Latina women and then broadened her literary endeavors to the novel, the short story, and the autobiography. Her work has gained her several awards including Scholar of English Speaking Union at Oxford University, 1977; fellow of Fine Arts Council of Florida, 1980; Bread Loaf Writers' Conference scholar, 1981; John Atherton Scholar in Poetry, 1982; a grant from Witter Bynner Foundation for Poetry, 1988, for *Letters from a Caribbean Island* (poetry); National Endowment for the Arts fellowship in poetry, 1989; Pulitzer Prize nomination, 1989, for the novel *The Line of the Sun*; Pushcart Prize for nonfiction, 1990; O. Henry Prize for short story, 1994; and Anisfield Wolf Award in Race Relations, 1994, for *The Latin Deli*.

Plot Summary

Title

The full title of the poem is "The Latin Deli: An Ars Poetica." "Ars Poetica" translates into "the art of poetry," which is the title of a poetical treatise by the Roman poet Horace (65-8 B.C.) and of a poem by Archibald MacLeish (1926). In Ortiz Cofer's poem the "art of poetry" could be interpreted in different ways. The deli itself could be like

a poem to the customers, as it provides them with meaning in their lives. Since the poem is the first piece of writing in *The Latin Deli*, Ortiz Cofer could also be suggesting that through her poems and stories that center on the lives of Spanish immigrants, she offers comfort and a sense of identity to others who share her heritage.

Lines 1-7

In these lines Ortiz Cofer introduces the poem's main character, whom she calls "the Patroness of Exiles"—what Ortiz Cofer could also be considered through her art. She delays her subject until the seventh line, after she has given a partial description of the deli. First she describes the Formica counter on which sits an "ancient register" with a "plastic Mother and Child magnetized to the top." This mixture of imagery reflects the reality of life for the Spanish-speaking immigrants who come into the store. The cheap countertop, the "ancient" register, and the "plastic" Mother and Child magnet reflect the lower economic status of the neighborhood. The register and magnet, however, take on a double meaning. The customers of the deli come there to connect with their heritage, and so these objects would comfort them. The "ancient" register keeps them in touch with the past. When Ortiz Cofer capitalizes the words "mother" and "child," she suggests these figures represent Mary and Jesus. Thus the magnet symbolizes the customers' strong religious beliefs that they have carried with them to the United States. Since these beliefs often clashed with the more secular American culture, the magnet helps them reinforce their sense of identity. In lines 4-6 Ortiz Cofer describes the "heady" smells of dried codfish and green plantains—food that also reflects the immigrants' culture. She reinforces the religious theme when she describes the plantain stalks hanging like "votive offerings." Line 5 finally introduces the owner, "the Patroness of Exiles" who as Ortiz Cofer notes in the first line "presides" over the deli. Ortiz Cofer gives her sacred status as she "opens" her food bins for her customers, providing them with a sorely needed cultural link. This Patroness watches over her customers like a Madonna, offering them comfort and a strong sense of self.

Lines 8-10

These two lines briefly describe the deli owner and begin a description of her interaction with her customers. Ortiz Cofer introduces her in a nondescript way as a woman of "no-age," suggesting that rather than being one specific person, she is an amalgam of all the women who run delis in ethnic neighborhoods. Her role in the neighborhood is to spend her days ''selling canned memories'' while listening to the inhabitants ''complain'' of their life in America and reminisce fondly of their past.

Lines 11-17

These lines describe their complaints and hopes in America as well as a nostalgia for their home. This passage also identifies the different groups that come together into the deli. Puerto Ricans ''complain'' about the deli's high prices and Cubans boast of ''a glorious return'' to Havana. In their determination to hold onto the past, they refuse to admit that life has continued in their homeland without them. Mexicans ''pass through'' the deli, looking to make their fortune in the New World. Ortiz Cofer uses internal rimes in these lines to highlight their hopes. For example, the Mexicans are ''ta*l*king lyrica*lly* of *dó*lares.''

Lines 18-23

This section returns the focus back to the deli owner, noting that her customers gain comfort from being able to speak Spanish to her. The image of maternal comfort is reinforced by her physical description: ''her plain wide face, her ample bosom resting on her plump arms, her look of maternal interest as they speak to her and each other of their dreams and their disillusions.'' These physical details help provide them with a sense of identity, since when they look at her, they ''gaze upon the family portrait.''

Lines 24-28

Here Ortiz Cofer continues the maternal image as she describes the owner's ''understanding'' smiles at the customers as they lovingly read the Spanish labels of the food in the deli's aisles. These names read aloud stir memories of their lost childhood. Ortiz Cofer reinforces this emotion when she employs alliteration in this passage with the soothing sounds of ''labels,'' ''aloud,'' ''lost,'' and ''lovers.''

Lines 29-37

This lengthy closing section first returns the focus to the owner, who personally wraps her customers' orders, and then to the customers themselves, whose shopping there becomes an integral part in their struggle to maintain their cultural identity. Ortiz Cofer notes that the food is more expensive in the deli, but the customers really do not

mind the extra cost. The food they would get from an American supermarket chain would not satisfy their ''hunger'' for a place where they can connect with each other and with their heritage. The Spanish-speaking people who come to her store have lost a clear vision of themselves in the difficult process of assimilation, as symbolized by ''the fragile old man lost in the folds of his winter coat.'' His love of his homeland emerges in the sounds of his language as he brings a shopping list ''that he reads to her like poetry.'' In the final lines Ortiz Cofer employs a touch of magic realism when she returns the focus to the owner and her almost supernatural powers as she ''divines'' her customers' needs. With the dual connotations of the word ''divine,'' the deli owner becomes a combination of a seer and an archetypal Madonna figure. She has the ability to ''conjure up'' products from her customers' homeland, ''from places that now exist only in their hearts.'' The poem closes with a focus on the difficult task of providing comfort to these transplanted people. Their hearts have become ''closed ports'' where memories of their heritage are moored. The owner's mission is to ''trade'' in these ports in order to enable her customers to reestablish a clear vision of self.

Themes

Culture Clash

The clash between American and Spanish culture becomes the impetus for the immigrants to come to the Latin deli. In an interview in *Melus* Ortiz Cofer notes that this theme predominates in all the stories and poems in *The Latin Deli*. Her work reflects her own experience with trying to reconcile the contradictions in her cultural identity. She explains, ''I write in English, yet I write obsessively about my Puerto Rican experience. . .That is how my psyche works. I am a composite of two worlds. . . .I lived with. . .conflictive expectations: the pressures from my father to become very well versed in the English language and the Anglo customs, and from my mother not to forget where we came from. That is something that I deal with in my work all the time.'' She continues, ''One of the things that is so dissonant about the lives of children in my situation is that I would go to school in Paterson and mix and mingle with the Anglos and Blacks, where the system of values and rules were so much different than those inside our apartment, which my mother kept sacred. In our apartment we spoke only Span-

Topics for Further Study

- Read other selections from Ortiz Cofer's *The Latin Deli: Prose and Poetry.* Do you find themes similar to those addressed in "The Latin Deli"?

- Research the psychological effects of cultural assimilation. How are the people in the deli affected by their immigration to the United States?

- Write a description of what you would miss about your culture if you moved to another country that did not have English as its dominant language.

---

ish, we listened only to Spanish music, we talked about *la casa* (back home in Puerto Rico) all the time. We practiced a very intense Catholic religion, with candles in the bathtub, pictures of the Virgin and Jesus everywhere." The customers in the deli, like Ortiz Cofer's parents, struggled to hang on to the traditions of the past, in order to maintain a clear sense of who they are and where they came from. There they see the symbols of their culture—the Mother and Child magnet and especially the food. They also can hear and speak their native tongue.

Identity

In an interview in *Callaloo* Ortiz Cofer explains how places like the Latin deli helped Spanish immigrants reestablish their cultural identity. She writes, "The book is called *The Latin Deli* because the centers, the hearts of the barrios in New Jersey were the bodegas, which were called delis by some of us. There were Jewish and Italian delis. So if you sold sandwiches, well, it was a deli and that was part of our language. . .[F]ood is important in its nurturing of the barrio. To my parents their idea of paradise was eating *pasteles* (pork meat turnovers)." The deli owner in "The Latin Deli" is similar to a woman in one of the collection's short stories, "Corazon's Café." Ortiz Cofer explains that this woman is "fully committed to nurturing the barrio, to bringing life to it, not by standing on a soap box, not by becoming a great philosopher, but

by keeping this bodega open. So that the people of 'el building' could have their *pasteles,* could have their cafe (coffee), could have a taste of what they needed to nurture them spiritually."

Art and Experience

The customers in the deli elevate the status of the items there to art as they read "the labels of packages aloud, as if they were the names of lost lovers." One "fragile old man lost in the folds of his winter coat" reads his lists of items "like poetry." The store items become poetry as they remind the customers of their culture and so reaffirm their sense of themselves.

This theme also emerges in the relationship Ortiz Cofer establishes between herself and the deli owner. Ortiz Cofer suggests that through her poems and stories that center on the lives of Spanish immigrants, she, like the owner of the deli, offers comfort and a sense of identity to others who share her heritage. In her *Callaloo* she notes, "The idea of staying alive by telling stories is something that has always fascinated me. . .I like the idea of the never-ending story that feeds one generation and then another. It's my own literary heritage; I am nourished by the stories that I heard and then I feed others, I hope. All my women—Corazon, Mama, all of them—rely on their imaginations to make their lives richer and to teach their daughters."

Style

Rhythm

Ortiz Cofer wrote "The Latin Deli: An Ars Poetica" in free verse, which varies line length and does not have an established meter. The poetic line becomes its basic rhythmic unit. Line breaks highlight important words in the poem. In "The Latin Deli" Ortiz Cofer frequently ends her lines with words that help convey the poem's themes. For example she ends lines 3-6 with "bins," "plantains" and "offerings," which reinforces the importance for the immigrants of the deli's Spanish food and the deli owner's position as "patroness," providing solace through food. Lines 18 and 19 end with "comfort" and "portrait," illustrating how the deli helps the customers reestablish comforting connections with their heritage.

Sound

Repetition of sounds in a poem can also emphasize key words and images and so create poetic structure. In addition, sounds can provide pleasure. Ortiz Cofer uses alliteration, the repetition of initial consonant sounds, in lines 26-27 in the words "labels," "aloud," "lost," and "lovers" to emphasize the joy the customers feel when they speak in their native language. She employs internal rime in lines 16-17 when she describes the Mexicans "talking lyrically of dóolares, which highlights their hopes in the New World. The importance of food becomes evident through examples of consonance, the repetition of final consonant sounds, in "bins" and "plaintains" (lines 4-5).

Literary Heritage

Magic realism is a fictional style, popularized by Gabriel García Márquez, that appears most often in South American literature. This style may have emerged from the mystification of Latin America that occurred during colonization, as many Europeans chronicled strange and supernatural occurrences in the new land. The term was first associated with the arts and later extended to literature. In the 1920s and 1930s, Latin American artists were influenced by the surrealist movement and so incorporated the style into their art. Authors who use this technique mingle the fantastic or bizarre with the realistic. Magic realism often involves time shifts, dreams, myths, fairy tales, surrealistic descriptions, the element of surprise and shock, and the inexplicable. Often something common converts into something unreal or strange in order to reveal the inherent mystery in life. The writer, however, usually creates a supernatural atmosphere without denying the natural world—a paradox characters appear to accept without question.

In an interview in *Callaloo*, Ortiz Cofer notes that Puerto Rican authors extend the definition of magical realism "to include a different way of looking at the world." She continues, "When you read *One Hundred Years of Solitude* by Gabriel García Márquez or *The House of the Spirits* by Isabel Allende, you are required to accept supernatural phenomena and to practice suspension of disbelief. When I write about espiritismo, I am writing about an ordinary, everyday thing that most Puerto Ricans live with. . .As I use espiritismo in my novel, there is nothing there that cannot be explained through natural law. I do not have any flying carpets or any other magical occurrences. . .My work reflects the reality that espiritismo. . .[is] for many ordinary people. . .an outlet for their emotions, a way to feel that they are in control of their world."

Historical Context

In an interview in *Callaloo* Ortiz Cofer comments on the cultural background of the poem as well as the collected works:

> The book is called *The Latin Deli* because the centers, the hearts of the barrios in New Jersey were the bodegas, which were called delis by some of us. There were Jewish and Italian delis. So if you sold sandwiches, well, it was a deli and that was part of our language. . .[F]ood is important in its nurturing of the barrio. To my parents their idea of paradise was eating *pasteles* (pork meat turnovers). All my stories, I feel, have political commitment, but in "Corazon's Cafe" there is a woman fully committed to nurturing the barrio, to bringing life to it, not by standing on a soap box, not by becoming a great philosopher, but by keeping this bodega open. So that the people of "el building" could have their *pasteles,* could have their cafe (coffee), could have a taste of what they needed to nurture them spiritually. It is a political story in that this woman supersedes her own personal needs in order to take care of the people of the barrio. This is the Puerto Rican experience that I know.

In a *Melus* interview with Edna Acosta-Belen, Ortiz Cofer comments on the tensions experienced by Spanish-speaking immigrants in the United States, which resulted from their experiences with conflicting cultures. Acosta-Belen comments that the writings of Latina authors like Ortiz Cofer "represent an excellent illustration of how issues of gender, race, culture, and class become intertwined, expanding the terms in which marginalized groups construe their identity in relation to the U.S. mainstream society." Ortiz Cofer adds, "One of the things that is so dissonant about the lives of children in my situation is that I would go to school in Paterson and mix and mingle with the Anglos and Blacks, where the system of values and rules were so much different than those inside our apartment, which my mother kept sacred. In our apartment we spoke only Spanish, we listened only to Spanish music, we talked about *la casa* (back home in Puerto Rico) all the time. We practiced a very intense Catholic religion, with candles in the bathtub, pictures of the Virgin and Jesus everywhere and I sort of felt (and I have a couple of ironic poems about this) that God was always watching.'' Establishments like the one described in ''The Latin Deli'' also became places where immigrants could experience the customs and cultures of their homeland.

Critical Overview

Judith Ortiz Cofer first published ''The Latin Deli: An Ars Poetica'' in *Americas Review* in 1992 and in 1993 in a collection of poems, short stories, and personal essays titled *The Latin Deli*. The work received overwhelmingly positive critical reviews. A reviewer in *Booklist* writes that Ortiz Cofer's collection of her stories, essays, and poems is a ''delicious smorgasbord of the sights, smells, tastes, and sounds recalled from a cross-cultural girlhood. Whether delineating the yearnings for an island homeland or the frustrations of a first-generation immigrant's struggles to grow up in 'el building' in a New Jersey barrio, Ortiz Cofer's work is rich in evocative detail and universal concerns.'' A reviewer in *Kirkus Reviews* finds the book ''a remarkably cohesive, moving collection—a tribute both to Cofer's considerable talent and her heritage.'' Kenneth Wishnia, in his *Melus* article, focuses on themes present in the poem. He notes that Ortiz Cofer ''works with many themes that are common to ethnic-American literature, for example, the feeling of being in exile in a strange land, where the sound of Spoken Spanish is so comforting that even a grocery list reads 'like poetry.'''

Criticism

Wendy Perkins

Perkins is an associate professor of English at Prince George's Community College in Maryland. In the following essay she examines one of the dominant themes in Judith Ortiz Cofer's ''The Latin Deli: An Ars Poetica''—the relationship between art and experience.

In his poetical treatise ''Ars Poetica,'' which translates into ''the art of poetry,'' Roman poet Horace writes of the importance of ''decorum'' in poetry, by which he means the appropriate connection between the parts of the poem and its whole. His principle of decorum emphasizes a concern with the relation of a poem to the reader—how the writer shapes the work to produce a pleasing experience for the reader. Judith Ortiz Cofer's ''The Latin Deli: An Ars Poetica'' also focuses on this relationship between reader and author. In the poem's description of the interaction between a Spanish deli owner and her customers, Ortiz Cofer establishes a connection between herself and the deli owner and herself and her readers. Ortiz Cofer suggests that through this poem that centers on the reality of Spanish immigrant life, she, like the owner of the deli, can offer comfort and a sense of identity to others who share her heritage. This effect, then, results from the art of her poetry.

In an interview in *Melus* Ortiz Cofer tells Edna Acosta-Belen about her personal vision of the relationship between art and experience: ''As I was growing up, I learned from [my female relatives'] very strong sense of imagination. For them storytelling played a purpose. When my *abuela* sat us down to tell a story, we learned something from it, even though we always laughed. That was her way of teaching. So early on, I instinctively knew storytelling was a form of empowerment, that the women in my family were passing on power from one generation to another through fables and stories. They were teaching each other how to cope with life.'' In an interview in *Callaloo* Ortiz Cofer adds that these women were ''powerful matriarchs'' for her: ''In my developing consciousness as a story-teller I saw that there was power there, power to influence.'' Commenting on her transfer of that oral tradition into literature, she explains, ''I like the idea of the never-ending story that feeds one generation and then another. It's my own literary heritage; I am nourished by the stories that I heard and then I feed others.'' Her poem ''The Latin Deli: An Ars Poetica'' opens her 1993 collection of stories, poems, and personal narratives, which focus on the daily struggles of Spanish immigrants as they cope with the difficult process of assimilation. Her works, like the offerings in the Latin deli, help ''nourish'' those who read them. Ortiz Cofer's careful shaping of ''The Latin Deli'' sets the tone of the collection and establishes the crucial relationship between art and reader.

In the *Melus* interview, Ortiz Cofer discusses her own assimilation experiences after she immigrated from her native Puerto Rico to Paterson, New Jersey: ''I write in English, yet I write obsessively about my Puerto Rican experience. . .That is how my psyche works. I am a composite of two worlds. . .I

What Do I Read Next?

- Santiago, Roberto, ed., in *Boricuas: Influential Puerto Rican Writings—An Anthology*, includes more than fifty selections of poetry, fiction, plays, essays, monologues, screenplays, and speeches from some of the most creative and lively Puerto Rican writers.

- Ortiz Cofer's 1995 collection of short stories, *An Island Like You: Stories of the Barrio*, is set in a New Jersey barrio; the stories focus on Puerto Rican teenagers.

- "The Latin Deli" was published in 1993 in a collection by the same name of poetry and prose by Judith Ortiz Cofer. The collection explores the lives of Latina barrio women.

- *Raining Backwards* by Roberto G. Fernandez looks at the lives of multiple generations of a family in Cuba and Miami. Like Ortiz Cofer, Fernandez focuses on the problems of assimilation in America.

lived with. . .conflictive expectations: the pressures from my father to become very well versed in the English language and the Anglo customs, and from my mother not to forget where we came from. That is something that I deal with in my work all the time." "The Latin Deli" exemplifies her maternal relatives' earnest desire to maintain a sense of cultural identity. The deli's customers respond to the challenge of living between two cultures by returning to the deli to experience the world of their homeland as they speak to each other and the owner in Spanish and as they sample the sights, aromas, and tastes of the offerings there. In the first few lines of the poem, Ortiz Cofer describes the deli, including the items that have a positive effect on the customers. First she notes the "plastic Mother and Child magnetized to the top" of an "ancient register." The customers of the deli come there to connect with their heritage, and so these objects comfort them. The "ancient" register keeps them in touch with the past. The capitalization of the words "mother" and "child" suggests these figures represent Mary and Jesus and highlights the spiritual nature of the deli. The magnet symbolizes the customers' strong religious beliefs that they have carried with them to the New World. Since these beliefs often clashed with the more secular American culture and their children's active assimilation efforts, the magnet helps them reinforce their sense of identity. In lines 4-6 food also becomes an important item in the deli. Ortiz Cofer describes the "heady" smells of dried codfish and green plantains—food that reflects the immigrants' culture. She reinforces the religious theme when she describes the plantain stalks hanging like "votive offerings."

Later in the poem, the customers read aloud the names of the foods on the shelves, which stirs memories of their lost childhood. Ortiz Cofer reinforces this emotion when she employs alliteration in this passage with the soothing sounds of "labels," "aloud," "lost," and "lovers." Their shopping there becomes an integral part in their struggle to maintain their cultural identity. Ortiz Cofer notes that the food is more expensive in the deli, but the customers really do not mind the extra cost. The food they would get from an American supermarket chain would not satisfy their "hunger" for a place where they can connect with each other and with their heritage. The Spanish-speaking people who come to her store have lost a clear vision of themselves in the difficult process of assimilation, as symbolized by "the fragile old man lost in the folds of his winter coat." His love of his homeland emerges in the sounds of his language as he brings a shopping list "that he reads to her like poetry." In her *Melus* interview, Ortiz Cofer notes her own connection to her native language and its influence on her art: "I use Spanish words and phrases almost as an incantation to lead me back to the images I need."

> The Spanish-speaking people who come to her store have lost a clear vision of themselves in the difficult process of assimilation, as symbolized by 'the fragile old man lost in the folds of his winter coat.' His love of his homeland emerges in the sounds of his language as he brings a shopping list 'that he reads to her like poetry.'"

In her interview in *Callaloo* Ortiz Cofer describes her own experience with the Latin delis in her neighborhood: "The hearts of the barrios in New Jersey were the bodegas, which were called delis by some of us. There were Jewish and Italian delis. So if you sold sandwiches, well, it was a deli and that was part of our language. . .[F]ood is important in its nurturing of the barrio. To my parents their idea of paradise was eating *pasteles* (pork meat turnovers)." The deli owner in the poem commits herself to nurturing her customers by offering them the products of their homeland. Ortiz Cofer reveals the deli owner's vital connection to the Spanish immigrants as she cuts her focus in the poem back and forth between them. She christens the owner "the Patroness of Exiles," who as Ortiz Cofer notes in the first line, "presides" over the deli. Ortiz Cofer gives her sacred status as she "opens" her food bins for her customers, providing them with a sorely needed cultural link. This Patroness watches over her customers like a Madonna, offering them comfort and a strong sense of self. This woman of "no-age" becomes an amalgam of all the women who run delis in ethnic neighborhoods. Her role there is to spend her days "selling canned memories" while listening to the inhabitants "complain" of their life in America and reminisce fondly of their past. Ortiz Cofer's physical description of her reinforces her nurturing image—"her plain wide face, her ample bosom resting on her plump arms, her look of maternal interest as they speak to her and each other of their dreams and their disillusions."

These physical details help provide her customers with a sense of identity, since when they look at her, they "gaze upon the family portrait."

In the poem's closing section, Ortiz Cofer reinforces her ties to the deli owner and her customers/readers. She employs a touch of magic realism when she notes the owner's supernatural powers as she "divines" her customers' needs. With the dual connotations of the word "divine," the deli owner becomes a combination of a seer and an archetypal Madonna figure. She has the ability to "conjure up" products from her customers' homeland, "from places that now exist only in their hearts." Through the construction of her poem, Ortiz Cofer "divines" the needs of her readers, "conjuring up" comforting images of their heritage. In the final lines of the poem, she notes the difficulties she and the deli owner face in their attempts to provide solace to these transplanted people whose hearts have become "closed ports" where memories of their heritage are moored. The mission for both Ortiz Cofer and the deli owner is to "trade" in these ports in order to enable their readers and customers to reestablish a clear vision of self. Thus the deli and the poem become a safe harbor for Spanish immigrants, like Ortiz Cofer, to reconnect with their cultural heritage and so find a respite for a time from the difficult process of acculturation.

Source: Wendy Perkins, in an essay for *Literature of Developing Nations for Students*, Gale, 2000.

Chris Semansky

A widely published poet, fiction writer, and critic, Chris Semansky teaches literature and writing at Portland Community College. In the following essay, Semansky explores the relationship between nostalgia and poetry in Ortiz Cofer's poem "The Latin Deli: An Ars Poetica."

In terms of population, the fastest growing segment of the United States is Hispanic. Hispanics constitute the second largest minority population in the country next to African-Americans, and Spanish is the most frequently spoken foreign tongue. Mexicans, Cubans, and Puerto Ricans make up the bulk of the Hispanic population. The Mexican population is largely concentrated in the West and Southwest, with states like California and Texas boasting the largest numbers. Cubans have a large presence in South Florida, and Puerto Ricans are heavily concentrated in New York City and northern New Jersey. The United States, or the "mainland," as it is known to Puerto Ricans, is considered a place of economic opportunity and freedom, and the rate of immigration to the states from Hispanic countries is very high. However, with opportunity also comes sacrifice. Those who leave home and come to America miss their homeland and a sense of belonging to a more homogeneous culture where family, neighborhood, and town often form the backbone of one's identity. Many immigrants becomes exiles of a sort, caught between cultures, not wholly belonging to their new home or their old. Judith Ortiz Cofer's poem, "The Latin Deli: An Ars Poetica," explores the nature of yearning for a place and a way of life that has been lost, linking it to the "stuff" of poetry itself.

The most profound feature of Romantic poetry and, arguably, modern poetry is the sense of loss: loss of love, loss of life, loss of identity. This loss is often couched in terms of nostalgia, a profound and insatiable desire for the past. Ortiz Cofer evokes this nostalgia in the opening lines of the poem, describing the Latin delicatessen:

> Presiding over a Formica counter, plastic Mother and Child magnetized to the top of an ancient register, the heady mix of smells from the open bins of dried codfish, the green plantains hanging in stalks like votive offerings, she is the Patroness of Exiles, a woman of no age who was never pretty, who spends her days selling canned memories while listening to the Puerto Ricans complain that it would be cheaper to fly to San Juan than to buy a pound of Bustelo coffee here, and to Cubans perfecting their speech of a "glorious return" to Havana—where no one has been allowed to die and nothing to change until then; to Mexicans who pass through, talking lyrically of *dolares* to be made in el Norte—

"Canned memories" is a figure of speech playing on the fact that delicatessens sell canned goods as well as produce and other items. Because this yearning and the attendant memories on which the yearning is based are repeated in almost ritualistic fashion, "canned" also means prepackaged, something which can be used time and time again with exactly the same effects. Canned laughter, or laugh tracks, a staple of television situation comedies, is one example of this effect. Nostalgia by its nature is always the same, a melancholic yearning for the past that can never be appeased. It repeats itself precisely because it cannot be appeased. The deli lends itself to feelings of nostalgia because its features and products are similar to those of the immigrants' homelands. The delicatessen is described as a cross between a church and a museum. Ortiz Cofer's description suggests that this is not one Latin deli, but *all* Latin delis. The food here and the Catholic knick knack, a Mary and Jesus magnet,

are staples of many Latin countries, most of which are heavily Roman Catholic, (Puerto Rico is 85 percent Catholic). Rather than satisfy the exiles' longing, however, the deli catalyzes it. These people are emotional exiles as well as physical ones. Though they have left their countries for a better life, they still long for the comfort of their homeland, as represented by foodstuffs such as plantains, a variety of banana that cannot be eaten raw, and Bustelo coffee, a particularly strong blend especially popular in Puerto Rico. The smells and sights of these items remind customers of their past and encourages them to act in particular ways. They become caricatures of exiles from their respective countries: the Puerto Ricans exaggerate and complain about how expensive goods are in the states; the Cubans beat their chests and brag of the day when they will overthrow Castro; the Mexicans are obsessed with making money to escape their impoverished lives. Stuck in the past, these cultural "interlopers" nonetheless must deal with the present. Their inability to do so forces them to live in a kind of purgatory, where the carrot of their homeland is dangled in front of them only to be pulled away the closer they get to it.

The proprietress of the deli is herself a combination of Mother Mary, museum curator, and muse. Like the exiles described and the deli itself, she is a type. Sexless and smiling, she embodies all of the characteristics of the stereotypical Latin mother with her "plain wide face, her ample bosom/ resting on her plump arms, her look of maternal interest." She symbolizes their heritage, the values of Latin culture, and stands for all that is good about the places they have left. In this way, she anchors the exiles in the past even though their hopes and dreams are also in the present and for the future.

Ortiz Cofer underscores the exiles' desire by focusing on language, visitors to the deli "wanting the comfort/ of spoken Spanish." Verbalizing the names of goods (for example, candy) takes the exiles deeper into their purgatory. The past is now like some unattainable lover, whose name they call but who will never answer. Ortiz Cofer once again highlights the ossified nature of the exiles' desire by calling these confections, "*Suspiros,/ Merengues,* the stale candy of everyone's childhood." Though the candies promise to be sweet, they only disappoint. They symbolize the static quality of impossible want.

The final images of the poem describe the extreme pathos of the exiles' situation. An old man, symbolizing all old men who are exiles, must have the ham and cheese sandwich from *this* deli, even though he could buy a less expensive sandwich elsewhere. The proprietress, in her role as patron saint of the exiles, attempts to satisfy this need by making the sandwich in the way that the man remembers it being made in his own country, ''slicing *jamon y queso* and wrapping it in wax paper/ tied with string: plain ham and cheese/ that would cost less at the A[and]P. . .'' The man's ''hunger'' is an appropriate metaphor, and the physical nourishment with which the deli supplies him only keeps his real hunger for his homeland alive. That she ''divines'' the needs of these exiles, and ''conjures'' up items from their past, suggests that she has powers, magical and religious. Her real trade is in desire. No doubt caught between cultures herself, this ''Patroness of Exiles'' presumably also keeps her own dreams of her homeland alive by trafficking in the hopes of others.

How can this description of a Latin delicatessen be called an ''Ars Poetica,'' or art of poetry? If readers consider the patroness a muse as well and consider the customers as poets this title can be better understood. Historically, patrons, both individuals and organizations, have materially and through encouragement supported poets. A good current example is the National Endowment of the Arts, which gives money every year to poets and artists to help them begin or complete projects. In return, poets acknowledge the support, sometimes in their verse itself. The ''Patroness of Exiles'' in the Latin deli offers customers emotional support and confirmation that their desires are ''real,'' even though it is ''canned memories'' that she sells. As muse, she inspires the exiles. In her store they find ''the comfort/ of spoken Spanish,'' mournfully recite the names of deli products, finding solace (and misery) in the act of naming itself. The promise that the patroness offers is the promise of poetry. Poetry, like the patroness, is able to ''conjure up'' things that exist only in the human heart. Poetry makes something out of nothing, and often originates in the imagination, the same place that gives birth to nostalgia and dreams. But there is something ironic in Ortiz Cofer's calling her poem an ''Ars Poetica,'' for if we understand the deli as a sad place, a ''stale'' place where heartbroken exiles are sold the same illusions over and over again, we must understand poetry, by extension, as something akin to the act of lying. This is similar to how Plato saw poetry in *The Republic*, when he argued for it being banned from his utopian community because it represented

no truth of its own, but rather provoked the emotions and kept humanity from knowing the real truth. In evoking the exiles feelings of hopelessness and despair Ortiz Cofer is not making anything up; rather, she is mining reality itself for the lies that we tell ourselves. The art of poetry for Ortiz Cofer, then, is the art of unmasking our own self-deceptions.

Source: Chris Semansky, in an essay for *Literature of Developing Nations for Students*, Gale, 2000 .

Kenneth Wishnia

In the following review of Ortiz Cofer's The Latin Deli: Prose and Poetry, *Kenneth Wishnia states that the writings of Ortiz Cofer ''defy convenient classification,'' though she addresses many common themes of ethnic-American writing, including the various sub-themes of culture clash such as sexuality, mores, and belief systems.*

Judith Ortiz Cofer's writing defies convenient classification, although she works with many themes that are common to ethnic-American literature, for example, the feeling of being in exile in a strange land, where the sound of Spoken Spanish is so comforting that even a grocery list reads ''like poetry.'' The daily struggle to consolidate opposing identities is perhaps most clearly exemplified by the tradition which determines that a latina becomes a ''woman'' at age 15, which means, paradoxically, not more freedom but more restrictions, since womanhood is defined as sexual maturity, which must then be contained at all costs. This leaves one of her characters feeling ''like an exile in the foreign country of my parents' house'' because of ''absurd'' rules that do not apply to her present reality in Paterson, New Jersey.

Another striking example of such cultural clash occurs in the story, ''Advanced Biology,'' in which a ninth grade Jewish boy tells the eighth grade narrator about both the Holocaust and reproductive biology. This leads her to doubt both God's ''Mysterious Ways'' and the Virgin Birth (and to have a screaming match with her mother on the topic), but concludes with her asking:

> Why not allow Evolution and Eve, Biology and the Virgin Birth? Why not take a vacation from logic? I will not be away for too long, I will not let myself be tempted to remain in the sealed garden of blind faith; I'll stay just long enough to rest myself from the exhausting enterprise of leading the examined life.

Indeed, Ortiz Cofer invites us to do the same when she presents the story of a young Puerto Rican girl's first disappointing attempt to date a non-latino

Catholic. In "American History," we get a fictionalized account of the girl living in a tenement in Paterson, who takes a liking to a "white" boy from Georgia named Eugene, only to have her mother warn her, "You are heading for humiliation and pain." Soon Eugene's mother tells her in a "honey-drenched voice" that it's "nothing personal," but she should "run back home now" and never try to speak to the boy again. In "The Story of My Body," a similar situation occurs, and her mother tells her, "You better be ready for disappointment." The warning is followed by the boy's father saying, "Ortiz? That's Spanish, isn't it?" as he looks at her picture in the yearbook and shakes his head No. In the poem "To a Daughter I Cannot Console," the narrator telephones her mother for advice on how to console her own lovesick sixteen-year-old daughter, and when her mother asks her "to remember the boy I had cried over for days. / I could not for several minutes / recall that face." The reader is left with the impression that such an event must have happened to Ortiz Cofer, or else why would she describe it three different ways in the same book? But it is precisely these "three different ways" that ask us—perhaps even compel us—to withdraw from "the exhausting enterprise" of examining too closely. Such events are common ethnic-American experiences, and thus all versions are in some way equally "true."

Other familiar themes treated in colorful and moving ways include the preparation of food (one character derives some fragment of solace after the death of her husband by entering her apartment building at dinnertime, and inhaling deeply "the aromas of her country," and there is a hilarious episode in which some furious adolescent petting is abruptly ended because the narrator has to go stir the red kidney beans before they get ruined), the untranslatability of certain culturally-bound concepts into English (nada can mean so much more than "nothing"), disappointment with fathers, men, and God, and the different standards of beauty between cultures. The essay "The Paterson Public Library" should be required reading in all high schools and colleges.

One especially provocative issue will have to serve for discussion: "The Story of My Body" begins, "I was born a white girl in Puerto Rico but became a brown girl when I came to live in the United States." This essay, about how our identities are often dependent upon how others define us, is followed by a poem appropriately called, "The Chameleon," and another essay, "The Myth of the

> Such events are common ethnic-American experiences, and thus all versions are in some way equally 'true.'

Latin Woman: I Just Met a Girl Named Maria," in which Ortiz Cofer exposes and rejects common stereotypes of latinas as "hot," "sizzling," etc., explaining that in Puerto Rico, women felt freer to dress and move "provocatively" because the climate demanded it, and they were more-or-less protected by "the traditions, mores and laws of a Spanish/Catholic system of morality and machismo whose main rule was You may look at my sister, but if you touch her I will kill you."

Yet, at the opening of "The Myth of the Latin Woman," Ortiz Cofer writes about how she coveted "that British [self-] control," and in the poem, "Who Will Not Be Vanquished?" she writes:

Morning suits us Spanish women.
Tragedy turns us into Antigone—maybe we
are bred for the part.

Perhaps an "insider" can write this, but does it not also suggest that we all have our own preferred stereotypes? (In a related issue, three of the reviewers who are cited on the back of the book don't seem to be familiar with the traditional Spanish system of naming, referring to the author as "Cofer," when she clearly identifies herself as "Ortiz Cofer.")

In "5:00 A.M.: Writing as Ritual," Ortiz Cofer describes a period in her life when motherhood and adjunct teaching freshman composition at three different campuses somehow failed to fulfill her completely, and she writes that "There was something missing in my life that I came close to only when I turned to my writing." There is a bit of this sentiment in all of us.

Source: Kenneth Wishnia, "The Latin Deli: Prose and Poetry," (book review) in *MELUS*, Vol. 22, No. 3, 1997, p. 206.

Michael J. O'Shea

In the following review of Ortiz Cofer's The Latin Deli: Prose and Poetry, *Michael J. O'Shea praises Ortiz Cofer's eclecticism, calling her writings "profound, poignant, funny, universal and*

❝ Cofer's writing is not 'about' being a Latina woman in America, nor is it 'about' what critics call 'marginality' or 'Otherness,' except to the extent that we are all marginal or Other to some degree. Who could be less 'Other' in U.S. society, for instance, than George Bush; but who has been more marginalized than he was in and since the last US presidential election?❞

---

moving." O'Shea suggests echoes of the writings of James Joyce in the works of Ortiz Cofer, but states that ultimately, it is her ability to weave autobiographical remembrances, humor, and general human concerns—as well as the interplay between fiction and non-fiction—that make her "an author worth knowing."

Judith Ortiz Cofer, author of fiction, poetry collections and essays, presents all three in her latest book, *The Latin Deli*. Some readers and reviewers might overlook the volume because of its eclecticism. (It might have escaped editorial notice in this journal, for instance, because about 60% of the volume is devoted to poetry and essays.) Others might ignore it because they incorrectly assume that its appeal is specifically "ethnic." The latter premise reminds me of a mid-Atlantic university administrator I knew whose office would not subscribe to the *New York Times* because "we don't care what's going on in New York." For the record, then, don't buy this book solely for the poems, solely for the stories, or solely for the essays; moreover, don't buy this book solely to read about the experiences of Puerto Rican characters in the continental US. Instead, buy this book for the profound, poignant, funny, universal and moving epiphanies between its covers.

Cofer's combination of essays and poems produces a sustained embroidery on the short stories (and vice versa). Indeed, the essays and personal poems (especially the poems "Absolution in the New Year," "Who Will Not Be Vanquished?," and "Anniversary," and the essays "Advanced Biology," "The Story of My Body," and "The Myth of the Latin Woman: I Just Met a Girl Named María") reveal some of the autobiographical materials that Cofer uses in her stories. Her characters include young Puerto Rican girls who, like her, grow up in Paterson, New Jersey, in or around a tenement known as "El Building." In "American History," the teenaged protagonist is so focused on her impending study "date" with the blond-haired Eugene that she is unable to respond to the other events of 22 November 1963. Her mother, offended by the daughter's failure to grieve over the Kennedy assassination, predicts that her infatuation with an Anglo boy will bring only "humiliation and pain." The prediction comes true immediately when Eugene's mother refuses to let the girl in the house. In a bitter epiphany recalling Joyce's "Araby" and "The Dead," the girl "went to my window and pressed my face to the cool glass. Looking up at the light I could see the white snow falling like a lace veil over its face. I did not look down to see it turning gray as it touched the ground below."

There are other echoes of Joyce, from the explicit allusions to *Ulysses* in the epistolary narrative "Letter from a Caribbean Island" to the homely character in "Nada" whose "long nose nearly touched the tip of his chin" (like Maria's in Joyce's "Clay"). On a more sustained level, Cofer's stories recall Joyce's *Dubliners* in their cumulative portrait of El Building's characters in different stages of maturity, from young Eva, who is baffled by the evidence of her father's marital infidelity in "By Love Betrayed," through the emotional powerhouse of "Corazon's Cafe," encapsulating two lives in the narrative frame of the hours following a young husband's sudden death. As the childless widow is surrounded in the embrace of her community, Cofer sketches that community's members with extraordinary economy and force.

Cofer's essays and poems are highly personal and as powerful as her stories. The interplay between her non-fictional commentary on the power of writing ("5:00 a.m.: Writing as Ritual") and the poems and stories that demonstrate that power constitute an implicit narrative structure tying the volume together. Several poems (among them "Saint Rose of Lima" and "Counting") evoke the power of Catholic symbol and mysticism recalled through some secular distance, yet retaining not only the power of vivid recollection but also that conferred by artistic transformation. The emotional range of the volume is impressive, from the moving posthumous reconciliation with a father in "Absolution in the New Year" (with its disarmingly witty yet powerful coda, "There is more where this came from") to the funny adolescent pangs of "The Story of My Body" ("Wonder Woman was stacked. She had a cleavage framed by the spread wings of a golden eagle and a muscular body that has become fashionable with women only recently.")

Cofer's writing is not "about" being a Latina woman in America, nor is it "about" what critics call "marginality" or "Otherness," except to the extent that we are all marginal or Other to some degree. Who could be less "Other" in U.S. society, for instance, than George Bush; but who has been more marginalized than he was in and since the last US presidential election? Judith Ortiz Cofer's work touches on human concerns that speak to none Other than all of us. She is an author worth knowing.

Source: Michael J. O'Shea, "The Latin Deli: Prose and Poetry," (book review) in *Studies in Short Fiction,* Vol. 31, No. 3, Summer, 1994, p. 502.

Sources

Acosta-Belen, Edna, review, in *Melus*, Vol. 18, No. 3, Fall, 1993, p. 15.

Ocasio, Rafael, "The Infinite Variety of the Puerto Rican Reality: An Interview with Judith Ortiz Cofer," in *Callaloo*, Vol. 17, No. 3, Summer, 1994, p. 730.

Review, in *Booklist*, September 15, 1993.

Review, in *Kirkus Reviews*, October 1, 1993.

Wishnia, Kenneth, review, in *Melus*, Vol. 22, No. 3, Fall, 1997, p. 206.

Further Reading

Review, in *Publishers Weekly*, Vol. 240, No. 45, November 8, 1993, p. 60.
    This reviewer praises the collection of works in *The Latin Deli* especially in their portrayal of the "complexities of Latina identity."

The Law of Love

Laura Esquivel

1996

When *The Law of Love* was published in 1996, Laura Esquivel was already a successful author. Her first novel, *Like Water for Chocolate: A Novel in Monthly Installments, with Recipes, Romances and Home Remedies*, published in 1989, became a bestseller in Mexico and the United States and has been translated into numerous languages. Her second novel, *The Law of Love*, however, did not receive the critical acclaim of the first. As in *Like Water for Chocolate*, in *The Law of Love* Esquivel focuses on the redemptive power of love. In this novel, which takes place in the twenty-third century and includes several ''regressions'' into past centuries, the main character, astroanalyst Azucena, struggles to reunite with her ''twin soul'' Rodrigo and, at the same time, restore peace to the universe by reinstating the Law of Love. This law states that when a person opens her heart enough to forgive all enemies, she will help perpetuate a Divine Will, a ''cosmic order'' that will bring peace and harmony to all. Esquivel's multimedia presentation, including color illustrations by Spanish artist Miguelano Prado and poetry and accompanied by a CD that contains arias by Puccini and Mexican danzones, results in a clever tale of love and understanding.

Author Biography

Laura Esquivel was born the third of four children of Julio Caesar Esquivel, a telegraph operator, and

his wife Josephina, in 1951 in Mexico. In an interview with Molly O'Neill in the *New York Times*, Esquivel explains, ''I grew up in a modern home, but my grandmother lived across the street in an old house that was built when churches were illegal in Mexico. She had a chapel in the home, right between the kitchen and dining room. The smell of nuts and chilies and garlic got all mixed up with the smells from the chapel, my grandmother's carnations, the liniments and healing herbs.'' In another *Times* interview, Esquivel told Marialisa Calta that her ideas for her first novel, *Like Water for Chocolate*, came out of her own experiences in the kitchen: ''When I cook certain dishes, I smell my grandmother's kitchen, my grandmother's smells. I thought: what a wonderful way to tell a story.'' Attention to the senses would also be one of the themes in her next novel, *The Law of Love*.

Esquivel grew up in Mexico City and attended the Escuela Normal de Maestros, the national teachers' college. After teaching school for eight years, Esquivel began writing and directing for children's theater. In the early 1980s she wrote the screenplay for the Mexican film *Chido One*, directed by her husband Alfonso Arau and released in 1985. Arau also directed her screenplay for *Like Water for Chocolate,* released in Mexico in 1989 and in the United States in 1993. First published in 1989, *Like Water for Chocolate* became a best-seller in Mexico and the United States and has been translated into numerous languages. The film version has become one of the most popular foreign films of the past few decades. In her second, less successful novel, *Ley del amor*, published in English in 1996 as *The Law of Love*, Esquivel again creates a magical world where love becomes the dominant force of life.

Plot Summary

The Law of Love mixes science fiction and magic realism with a sprinkling of New Age philosophy as it tells the story of Azucena, an astroanalyst in twenty-third-century Mexico City. Throughout the novel Azucena tries to help others as well as herself to remember and cope with their past lives. Along the way, she struggles to escape villains who threaten world peace and to reunite with her ''twin soul'' Rodrigo. Her multimedia story, interspersed with color illustrations by Spanish artist Miguelano Prado and poetry and accompanied by a CD that contains

Laura Esquival

arias by Puccini and Mexican danzones, ultimately asserts the unifying power of love.

The novel begins with the Spanish wresting control of Tenochtitlan, Mexico from the Aztecs in the sixteenth century and constructing a new city—which will eventually become Mexico City—upon its ruins. Rodrigo Diaz, one of Cortes's captains, demolishes a pyramid on a site where the Aztecs had conducted pagan ceremonies honoring a goddess of love, and builds his house there. As Rodrigo moves the stone that had formed the apex of the pyramid, he sees Citlali, one of his Aztec slaves, and rapes her on the spot. During the conquest of the city, Rodrigo had killed her son. Eventually, Citlali takes her revenge by killing Rodrigo's son. When his wife Isabel learns that after her son had died, her husband murdered Citlali and then took his own life, she does not have the strength to live.

The story then shifts to Mexico City in the twenty-third century and Azucena's pursuit of Rodrigo, her ''twin soul.'' Anacreonte, Azucena's Guardian Angel, explains the spiritual system of this future world, governed by a ''Divine Will'' or cosmic order that has been disrupted by ''Wreckoncilers'' who substitute ''lies for truth, death for life, and hatred for love inside our hearts.'' The Wreckoncilers are allowed to ''straighten out their screwups'' through several reincarnations "until finally they learn how to love." Anacreonte insists that Azucena and Rodrigo both still have "some outstanding debts to pay." The twin souls enjoy one blissful meeting with each other before Rodrigo disappears and Azucena begins a quest to be reunited with him. Isabel Gonzales, candidate for Planetary President, has exiled Rodrigo to the penal planet Korma, where he is unable to remember anything about his past. As she searches for Rodrigo, Azucena discovers someone is trying to kill her. With the help of Cuquita, her apartment building superintendent, she changes bodies in an effort to fool her pursuers. After Azucena spots Rodrigo on a newscast about Korma, she and Cuquita travel on an interplanetary spaceship to the planet. There she listens to music and regresses back to a past life during the Mexico City earthquake in 1985 that caused the death of her parents. She sees herself as a child who is killed by Isabel. Azucena then realizes that Isabel has hidden her violent past and probably has ordered her assassination. Rodrigo escapes the planet undetected after he exchanges bodies with Cuquita's husband. During the flight home, Azucena helps him regress into the past where he remembers that he was a pregnant woman raped by her brother-in-law, who was Citlali in a past life, and that he had raped her in the ruins of Tenochtitlan. Citlali and Rodrigo forgive each other for their past crimes.

After returning to the earth, police storm Azucena's building, Azucena and Cuquita's grandmother dies, and Azucena's soul takes her body. Teo, an undercover Guardian Angel, notices Azucena's acute jealousy over Rodrigo's attentions to Citlali and comforts her. Azucena regresses and discovers that she was Citlali's murdered child in a past life and that Rodrigo was the Conquistador who had killed her. During a televised debate between the two candidates for Planetary President, Azucena watches as Isabel's regressions become unblocked and projected on the screen. When Azucena then regresses, she realizes she was the daughter Isabel tried to have killed. She also discovers that Citlali had murdered Isabel's baby (Rodrigo's child), and Isabel had died hating her. In their next parallel lives, Isabel and she had been brothers. Citlali had raped her brother's wife (Rodrigo), and in return, Isabel had murdered her. Azucena decides that "then the Law of Love had come into play to balance the relationship between them, causing them to be born as mother and daughter, to see whether those ties could ease the hatred Citlali felt for Isabel. However, Isabel had never loved her

daughter. After she met Rodrigo and fell in love with him, Citlali and Rodrigo ran away together. Isabel finds them dead in the rubble of an earthquake and kills their child, her grandchild, who turns out to be Azucena.

During her trial, Isabel is found guilty of her past crimes. When Azucena offers her forgiveness, Isabel allows love to enter her heart. Rodrigo's memory returns and he recognizes Azucena as his twin soul. After he finds and replaces the capstone to the Pyramid of Love, the lost city of Tenochtitlan reappears and merges with Mexico City. Azucena is allowed to return to her original body and the reinstatement of the Law of Love creates harmony for all.

Characters

Anacreonte

Azucena's guardian angel, who tries to help her with her mission to reinstate the Law of Love. For most of the novel, however, Azucena refuses to communicate with him, preferring to work on her own. Anacreonte gets peevish when Azucena will not take his direction.

Azucena

Azucena is a "highly evolved" Super-Evo who gets preferential treatment in the novel's future society. As an astroanalyst in twenty-third-century Mexico City, she helps others regress to their past lives in order to provide them with harmony in their present lives. She is too proud to ask for Anacreonte's help on her quest to reunite with Rodrigo, her "twin soul," or with her mission to help bring peace to the planet through the reinstatement of the Law of Love. She, like Rodrigo, still has "some outstanding debts to pay," and so they are allowed to merge souls only on one occasion. "Her lack of self-confidence had prevented her from forming a stable relationship in the past. . .[D]eep down, she had always felt she didn't deserve happiness; yet she still had had a profound need to feel loved. It was in an effort to resolve these problems that she had decided to find her twin soul, thinking that with him she couldn't go wrong." Throughout the novel Azucena wavers between optimism and pessimism over her relationship with Rodrigo and the fate of the universe. Ultimately, with the help of her friends, she is able to stay on track and fulfill both of her goals.

Mr. Bush

The American candidate for Planetary President. Bush's assassination "presaged a return to an age of violence that everyone believed had been left behind" for more than a century, which makes Azucena's quest even more urgent.

Citlali

The novel opens with Rodrigo raping Citlali, an Aztec princess who had become his slave. Citlali's privileged upbringing helped develop her "great pride verging on defiance." Her sensuality causes Rodrigo to fall in love with her. Rodrigo earlier had killed her son, and as a result, Citlali vowed revenge. When she subsequently murders the son of Rodrigo and Isabel, she unwittingly starts a battle between herself and Isabel that is not played out until the end of the novel, several centuries later. In their next parallel lives, she and Isabel become brothers. After Citlali rapes Isabel's wife, Isabel murders her. The Law of Love influences their next reincarnation when Isabel becomes mother to her daughter Citlali. Azucena appears in the mix when Citlali and Rodrigo give birth to her. With Azucena's help, Citlali is able to forgive Rodrigo and Isabel for their past crimes against her.

Cuquita

The superintendent of Azucena's apartment building. In one of her past lives she was a film critic and so has "dubious credibility." Initially Azucena and Cuquita did not get along because Cuquita was "a social malcontent" who belonged to the Party for the Retribution of Inequities. Cuquita had always spied on Azucena, "trying to catch her at something. . .in order not to feel so inferior to her." When Azucena turns to Cuquita for help, however, Cuquita's compassionate nature emerges. Toward the end of the novel, Cuquita's desire to help Azucena is so strong that she becomes the ideal medium for Anacreonte to convey a message to his protegee.

Rodrigo Diaz

Azucena's soulmate and the object of her quest throughout the novel. The novel begins with Rodrigo as a Spanish conquistador in a past life and his rape of Citlali. "Rodrigo entered her body the same way he made his way through life: with the luxury of violence." He was, however, "not easy to fathom. Two people lived inside him. A gentle, loving side and a restless violent one." After a series of reincarnations, where he often commits violent acts against the other characters, he is reunited with Azucena.

Dr. Diez

Dr. Diez, Azucena's friend and her colleague at the clinic, invents a new device that photographs a person's aura and detects traces of others who have been in contact with that person. Isabel orders him killed after he plants a device in her head that will prevent anyone from learning about her past lives.

Divine Singer

See Teo

Ex-Azucena

One of Isabel's guards, who through a mixup now inhabits Azucena's old body. Ex-Azucena discovers he/she is pregnant with, as we later learn, Azucena Rodrigo's child. As a result, Isabel fires him/her. By the end of the novel, Ex-Azucena dies and Azucena returns to her body.

Carmela Gonzales

Carmela is Isabel's daughter. Carmela's obesity embarrasses her mother. Ex-Azucena's and Azucena's friendship and attention cause her self-image to improve, which enables her to lose weight. She fills in several details of her mother's villainous deeds during the trial, feeling no loyalty to her.

Isabel Gonzales

The merciless and ambitious villain in the novel, Isabel "eliminates whatever must be eliminated without a trace of remorse." She "provokes wars, practices corruption, and abuses the privileges of power. After she becomes a primary candidate for Planetary President, she becomes paranoid that everyone around her is an enemy. She orders her daughter disintegrated for one hundred years when she learns she will grow up with a strong will that might challenge her mother's. In past lives, she had murdered Citlali and Azucena and had been desperately in love with Rodrigo. After Isabel is pronounced guilty, Azucena forgives her, which results in Isabel's change of heart.

Grandmother

Azucena occupies the body of Cuquita's blind grandmother after her own dies. The elderly, disabled body takes some getting used to.

Ricardo Rodriquez

Cuquita's drunken husband who beats her and her grandmother. Rodrigo exchanges bodies with him during his escape from Korma, leaving Ricardo behind to deal with the planet's Stone Age inhabitants and Isabel's wrath.

Teo

Teo, an undercover Guardian Angel, notices Azucena's pain over Rodrigo's attentions to Citlali and comforts her. Their subsequent sexual encounters help return Azucena's optimism and enable her to carry on her mission. In an earlier reincarnation Teo had been the Divine Singer, who would dance small gods on the palm of his hand and speak through them. His hands and tongue were cut off after being arrested for disobeying the royal edict forbidding clay idols.

Themes

Meaning of Life

The meaning of life in *The Law of Love* involves a search for universal harmony and peace, which becomes Azucena's quest. In order to achieve harmony, individuals must open their hearts to Divine Love, which, Anacreonte explains, is "infinite. It is everywhere and entirely within reach at every moment." By the end of the novel, Azucena helps the inhabitants of Mexico City regain this peace: "The eyes of all present were able to look deep into the eyes of any other, without apprehension. No barrier existed. The other person was oneself. For a moment, all hearts harbored Divine Love equally. Everyone felt part of a whole. Like a mighty hurricane, love erased every vestige of rancor, of hatred."

Flesh vs. Spirit

Esquivel defines the Law of Love, which becomes the impetus in the novel for universal peace, as a fusion of the flesh and the spirit, involving a process of reincarnation: "The person who causes an imbalance in the cosmic order is the only one who can restore balance. In nearly all cases, one lifetime is insufficient to achieve that so Nature provides reincarnation in order to give Wreckoncilers the chance to straighten out their screwups. . .again and again they will be born near each other, until finally they learn how to love. And one day, after perhaps fourteen thousand lives, they will have learned enough about the Law of Love to be allowed to meet their twin soul. This is the highest reward a human being can ever hope for in life." When Azucena meets her twin soul, Rodrigo, their sexual encounter becomes a spiritual experience, as they "danc[e] through space to the rhythm of the music of the spheres." Azucena achieves a similar state when she has sex with Teo. Then, "the enjoyment Azucena was experiencing so opened her senses that she was able to perceive Divine Light. . .It was not until she was loved that she knew peace."

Anger and Hatred

The novel chronicles the characters' past crimes against each other, which fills them with anger and hatred and results in a disharmonious universe. As a result several of the characters seek revenge, which creates more suffering. After Rodrigo rapes Citlali and murders her son, she kills his and Isabel's child. In their next reincarnation, a male Citlali rapes a female Rodrigo. After observing this scene, Isabel kills Citlali. In another life, Isabel kills Rodrigo's and Citlali's child (her granddaughter Azucena), because she had been in love with Rodrigo and so was jealous of his love for Citlali.

Change and Transformation

The theme of change and transformation is closely linked to another theme in the novel: memory and reminiscence. Change can only occur when the characters force themselves to deal with their painful memories through regression into past lives. Azucena helps them face their suffering and release their anger as a first step in realizing a sense of peace and harmony.

Atonement and Forgiveness

The final step in the characters' growth process involves atonement and forgiveness. Through regressions, Azucena encourages Rodrigo, Citlali, and Isabel to give voice to their pent-up anger and so be ready to forgive those who have harmed them. This process also involves the recognition that they have caused others to suffer. In her session with Rodrigo, Azucena helps him regress to two past lives: when Citlali raped him when he was a woman and when he, as a Spanish conquistador, raped her. The first regression teaches him what it feels like to be raped. He is then able to release his feelings of powerlessness and rage. When he subsequently faces what he did to Citlali, he asks her forgiveness and is able to pardon her and himself.

Style

Structure

The Law of Love's innovative structure intersperses the story with color illustrations by Spanish artist Miguelano Prado and poetry. These pieces illuminate and intensify the action of the story. A CD containing arias by Puccini and Mexican danzones accompanies the novel, which periodically asks the reader to play different tracks. The music, like the illustrations and poems, is an effective tool for pulling the reader into the action of the story, especially one that relies on a fantastic style.

Style

Magic realism is a fictional style, popularized by Gabriel Garcia Marquez, that appears most often in South American literature. Authors who use this technique mingle the fantastic or bizarre with the realistic. Magic realism often involves time shifts, dreams, myths, fairy tales, surrealistic descriptions, the element of surprise and shock, and the inexplicable. Esquivel mixes New Age philosophy and science fiction with magic realism in *The Law of Love* as she explores the novel's themes. Regressions into past lives reveal important information about her characters that will help them find harmony in their present lives. Esquivel also uses futuristic inventions to aid her characters' discovery of themselves: Inanimate objects like glass have memories of events that can be projected onto a screen. When human's memories are projected, lies are unveiled. Bodies can easily be exchanged when one is in trouble. As a result of this type of body switch, characters can experience another's psyche and emotions and so are able to establish more sympathetic relationships with each other.

Imagery

The novel opens with the destruction of the dominant image in the novel, the Pyramid of Love, during the Spanish conquest of Tenochtitlan, Mexico. That act disturbs the "Divine Will" or cosmic order of the universe, which in turn disrupts the characters' lives. The narrator notes, "As long as the Temple of Love was not functioning, people would concentrate their love on themselves, not being able to see beyond their own image in the water's reflection." When the Pyramid's capstone is placed back on its apex, the lost city of Tenochtitlan reappears and merges with Mexico City, and harmony returns. Azucena engineers the return of the capstone through her devotion to the Law of Love.

Topics for Further Study

- Research the fall of Montezuma's Mexico. Explain how this takeover provides an effective backdrop for the tensions in *The Law of Love*.

- Examine the technological advances described in the novel. Which ones could become a reality in the twenty-first century?

- Investigate the term "magic realism." Read another work that employs this technique and compare it to *The Law of Love*.

- Research theories on reincarnation. How do they compare with the theories offered in the novel?

Anacreonte explains this law, noting that "when a person accumulates hatred, resentment, envy, and anger within, her surrounding aura becomes black, dense, heavy. . .To build up her energy level, and, with it, the level of her life, that negative energy must be released" and, as a result, love will fill her heart. Here Esquivel blends magic realism and New Age philosophy as she explores the novel's dominant theme: the redemptive power of love. The Pyramid of Love and the Law of Love focus attention on forgiveness and acceptance, which bring order and peace.

Literary Heritage

Magic realism is a fictional style, popularized by Gabriel Garcia Marquez, that appears most often in South American literature. This style may have emerged from the mystification of Latin America that occurred during colonization, as many Europeans chronicled strange and supernatural occurrences in the new land. The term was first associated with the arts and later extended to literature. In the 1920s and 1930s, Latin American artists were influenced by the surrealist movement and so incorporated the style into their art. Authors who use this technique mingle the fantastic or bizarre with the realistic.

Magic realism often involves time shifts, dreams, myths, fairy tales, surrealistic descriptions, the element of surprise and shock, and the inexplicable. Often something common converts into something unreal or strange in order to reveal the inherent mystery in life. The writer, however, usually creates a supernatural atmosphere without denying the natural world—a paradox characters appear to accept without question.

Historical Context

The Aztecs

The Aztecs dominated central Mexico at the time of the Spanish conquest. From their arrival in Mexico at end of the twelfth century until the founding of their capital, Tenochtitlan, in 1325, the Aztecs were a poor, nomadic tribe absorbing and adopting neighboring tribal cultures. However, during the fifteenth and early sixteenth centuries, they became powerful politically and developed their own distinct culture. They excelled in engineering, architecture, art, mathematics, and astronomy. Their art revealed innovations in sculpture, weaving, metalwork, ornamentation, music, and picture writing for historical records. When the Spaniards, under Hernan Cortes, arrived in 1519, the Aztec civilization was at its height. Many neighboring tribes who had suffered under Aztec conquests and so rebelled against Aztec rule aided the Spanish takeover of their lands. Cortes captured Montezuma II, the last of the independent Aztec rulers, and attempted to rule through him. After the Aztecs revolted in 1521, Montezuma was killed, and the Spanish destroyed Tenochtitlan.

Karma and Reincarnation

Karma is one of the basic concepts of Hinduism, Buddhism, and New Age philosophy. Karma is defined as a universal law of moral cause and effect that does not include a belief in a supreme power who punishes or absolves sinners. Those who believe in karma insist that individuals enjoy free will and so are fully responsible for their physical and mental actions. Those actions will determine their destiny in future incarnations. Thus, for example, those who cause others to suffer will experience feelings of guilt that they carry with them as they are reincarnated. During reincarnation, the soul occupies a new body after the old one dies. Some followers believe that the soul assumes the new body immediately, while others insist that this oc-

curs only after an interval of disembodiment. Although some religions teach that the soul may be reincarnated into a higher or lower form of life, most believe that the soul will inhabit the same species.

Critical Overview

When Margaret Sayers Peden's translation of Laura Esquivel's second novel, *The Law of Love*, was published in 1996, the reviews were mixed. Some critics argue that the novel does not live up to the promise of Esquivel's critically acclaimed first novel, *Like Water for Chocolate*. Others, however, like *Salon*'s A. Scott Cardwell, conclude that the novel "shows off, once again, Ms. Esquivel's romanticism, playfulness and bold ambition."

Many critics deem the book to be, at the very least, a partial success. A writer in *Kirkus Reviews* finds the novel "exuberant, hectic, [and] ultimately exhausting" and continues, "Whenever Esquivel is celebrating 'the hidden order of the world,' the salvational possibilities of love, she's engaging and persuasive. But the novel, which comes with a CD featuring arias and Mexican danzones (presumably to foster the right mood in the reader), and which includes several gaudy, comic-book-like sections illustrated by the artist Miguelano Prado, finally seems too anxious to overwhelm, too determined to entertain at any cost. There's enough here to demonstrate that Esquivel can write, and that she possesses considerable originality. Next time out, though, she needs to try a little less hard to astonish." *Library Journal* reviewer Barbara Hoffert echoes this review when she writes that the work "is at once wildly inventive and slightly silly, energetic and cliched."

Robert Houston in his article for the *New York Times Book Review* argues that "the CD. . .is a delight; and the illustrated panels by Miguelano Prado, though they contribute little, will surely please aficionados of that craft. The pre-Columbian poetry is welcome in any context." He concludes, however, that "no amount of razzle-dazzle can hide the fact that *The Law of Love* is seriously, perhaps even fatally, flawed. At times, Ms. Esquivel appears to ask a reader to take the book's characters and their troubles seriously, and at other times to see them only as the cardboard characters of farce or of Saturday morning cartoons. Nor can a reader be certain whether the novel is a sendup of New Age

Spanish adventurer Hernan Cortes approaches Aztec Emperor Montezuma in Tenochtitlan, the future site of Mexico City.

cliches or whether its narrator is truly an advocate for them. In trying to have it both ways, Ms. Esquivel has it neither.'' Commenting on the novel's structure, Houston writes, ''confusing, tediously plotted, marred by muddy philosophy and dubious verities, [the novel] strains far too hard to achieve its effects. It is, one hopes, only a brief detour for Ms. Esquivel. What was humor and charm in *Like Water for Chocolate* has become in this book simply silliness.''

Other reviewers find the novel to be a literary success. Donna Seaman in *Booklist* argues that while the novel ''gets off to a rocky start. . .[in its] sloppy opening sequence'' and ''gimmicky 'multimedia' presentation, Esquivel gets her bearings, and her narrative coalesces into a highly amusing mix of mysticism, science fiction, and her own brand of earthy and ironic humor.'' She finds the main character ''engaging'' and Esquivel's construction inventive. Seaman adds, ''Esquivel revels in clever futuristic speculation, imagining such things as an aura-reading computer, soul transplants into ''unregistered'' bodies, and intergalactic soccer matches. She also executes a number of inventive plot twists that keep Azucena and Rodrigo in suspense and danger and her readers in excellent spir-

its.'' Lilian Pizzichini in the *Times Literary Supplement* finds that this ''multimedia event. . .incorporates elements of magic realism, science fiction, and New Age philosophy.'' She concludes, ''Esquivel dresses her ancient story in a collision of literary styles that confirm her wit and ingenuity. She sets herself a mission to explore the redemptive powers of love and art and displays boundless enthusiasm for parody.''

Criticism

Wendy Perkins

Wendy Perkins, an associate professor of English at Prince George's Community College in Maryland, has published articles on several twentieth-century authors. In this essay she examines how the imaginative plot structure of The Law of Love *reinforces the novel's main theme.*

Reviews of Laura Esquivel's second novel, *The Law of Love*, were mixed when it was published in 1996. Robert Houston argues in the *New York Times Book Review* that the novel is ''confusing, tediously plotted, marred by muddy philosophy and dubious

What Do I Read Next?

- *House of the Spirits* by Isabel Allende (1986) is a magical story about a Latin American family that survives internal and external pressures.

- Esquivel's *Like Water for Chocolate*, first published in 1989, chronicles the life of Tita de la Garza in northern Mexico during the early part of the century as she struggles to win the right to be with the man she loves.

- *One Hundred Years of Solitude*, written by Gabriel Garcia Marquez and published in 1967, is considered the classic example of magic realism. This novel explores several generations of a Latin American family set against the age of revolution.

-

---

verities'' and ''strains far too hard to achieve its effects.'' However, Donna Seaman in *Booklist* admits that while the novel ''gets off to a rocky start. . .[in its] sloppy opening sequence'' and ''gimmicky 'multimedia' presentation, Esquivel gets her bearings, and her narrative coalesces into a highly amusing mix of mysticism, science fiction, and her own brand of earthy and ironic humor.'' While *The Law of Love* achieves neither the thematic depth nor the structural tightness of her critically acclaimed first novel, *Like Water for Chocolate*, it does provide another example of what *Salon*'s A. Scott Cardwell calls Esquivel's ''romanticism, playfulness and bold ambition.'' Ultimately, the novel succeeds in its inventive celebration of the redemptive power of love.

In the beginning of the novel, when Citlali plots revenge against the Spanish conquistador Rodrigo, who has killed her child and raped her, she meets his wife, Dona Isabel de Gongora. The narrator notes,

> neither of these women inhabited the same house. Isabel continued to live in Spain, Citlali in Tenochtitlan. Neither of them could recognize herself in the eyes of the other. Neither of the two shared a common landscape. Neither of the two could understand what the

other said. And this was not a matter of comprehension, it was a matter of the heart, for that is where words acquire their true meaning. And the hearts of both were closed. . .Both women would have to have been born with less arrogance to be able to set aside all that separated them and to discover the many things they had in common. . .While Isabel saw in Rodrigo the man she had dreamed of long ago in Spain, Citlali saw only her son's murderer. Neither of the two saw him as he really was.

This quote reflects the situation the characters find themselves in at the beginning of the novel. Each has closed his or her heart and, as a result, each has been unable to find happiness and fulfillment. Esquivel employs several creative plot devices that mix elements of magic realism, New Age philosophy, and science fiction to illustrate the novel's main theme—that one must open one's heart to others in order to find peace and establish harmony.

The opening scene in the novel sets the tone of disharmony that pervades for several centuries. The Spanish conquistadors raze the sixteenth-century Aztec city of Tenochtitlan and destroy sacred pyramids, including the Pyramid of Love. When Rodrigo rapes Citlali, his Aztec slave, on the Pyramid's former site, he begins a cycle of revenge that eventually erupts in universal chaos in the twenty-third century, when the novel's action takes place. Esquivel's employment of magic realism in this scene imaginatively illuminates the violence of Rodrigo's act and projects its devastating consequences for both Citlali and Rodrigo. The narrator suggests that the present-day trouble stems from the ''vexation of the pyramid'' beneath Rodrigo and Citlali, since the stones ''contain a truth beyond what the eye manages to see. . .a force of their own.'' After the rape Citlali begs ''the Gods for the strength to live until the day that this man should repent for having profaned not only her, but the Goddess of Love. For he could not have committed a greater outrage than to violate her on such a sacred site.'' This violent act disrupts not only Citlali's life, but also the cosmic order of the universe, which is ruled by the Law of Love. Anacreonte, Azucena's guardian angel, defines the process of this law: ''every action we take has repercussions in the Cosmos. . .When a person accumulates hatred, resentment, envy, and anger within, her surrounding aura becomes black, dense, heavy. . .To build up her energy level, and with it the level of her life, that negative energy must be released.'' After the release of this energy, the heart can prepare to receive and give love, and as a result, ''cosmic order in which we all have a place'' will be restored.

Anacreonte notes that when we find this order, "all is in harmony."

Esquivel's imaginative vision of the repercussions of such a violent act shifts to the twenty-third century and Azucena, who is charged with restoring the Pyramid of Love and thus the cosmic order. Here, Esquivel adds New Age philosophy to the narrative mix when she introduces Azucena, an astronanalyst who helps people regress back to their previous lives. Azucena thinks she is ready to be a "Reconciler," one who helps people "be in accord with Divine Will," but as Anacreonte notes, she is still too willful and stubborn to put others' needs before her own. When she refuses his guidance, Anacreonte insists, "Azucena never listens to reason. She is used to having her own blessed way." Since she has not yet gotten "some control over her emotions" and has "some outstanding debts to pay," she is allowed only one meeting with her "twin soul," Rodrigo—what all can attain if they follow the Law of Love. During their meeting, they "recognize each other's energy" and experience an ecstatic "mutual contemplation of souls."

Esquivel illuminates the devastating effects of anger and vengeance as Azucena helps the other characters in the novel regress to previous lives. Rodrigo, Citlali, and Isabel all have closed themselves off to others as a result of past injustices. Rodrigo was raped by Citlali after he had raped her in a previous life, and so the two become "Wreckoncilers substituting lies for truth, death for life, and hatred for love inside [their] hearts[;] they repeatedly dam the flow of the river of life." According to the New Age philosophy promoted by the characters,

> the person who causes an imbalance in the cosmic order is the only one who can restore balance. In nearly all cases, one lifetime is insufficient to achieve that so Nature provides reincarnation in order to give Wreckoncilers the chance to straighten out their screwups. . .Again and again they will be born near each other, until finally they learn how to love. And one day, after perhaps fourteen thousand lives, they will have learned enough about the Law of Love to be allowed to meet their twin soul. This is the highest reward a human being can ever hope for in life."

When Azucena helps them discover their past lives, she encourages them to release their pent-up anger as an initial step in restoring harmony. She then has Rodrigo tell Citlali that he had "to endure great pain to atone for [his] guilt." Rodrigo finally comes to terms with his past suffering as he tells Citlali, "I release you from my passion, from my desires. . .I release myself from your thoughts of

"Esquivel employs several creative plot devices that mix elements of magic realism, New Age philosophy, and science fiction to illustrate the novel's main theme—that one must open one's heart to others in order to find peace and establish harmony."

vengeance, for I have paid for what I did to you. . .I release you and I release myself. . .I pardon you and I pardon myself." When Citlali goes through a similar purging, she breaks the chain of vengeance and peace is restored.

Esquivel employs science fiction techniques in Azucena's process of evolution. She also experiences a sense of peace after regressing and purging herself of anger and jealousy, especially toward Citlali, who has been enjoying Rodrigo's attentions. She is able to open her heart to Citlali when she discovers that the woman had been her mother in a past life. Body transfer experiences also prompt Azucena's desire to connect with others. In the novel's futuristic society, one's soul can transfer to a new body, which is what happens to Azucena twice in the novel. The second time she takes over Cuquita's grandmother's body and learns what it feels like to be an old woman. The grandmother's blindness forces Azucena "to concentrate on herself, to look inward, to seek images from her past." A body exchange also forces the man who accidentally switched bodies with Azucena to experience what it is like to be pregnant.

The forging of sympathetic relationships with others from past lives and other bodies prompts Azucena to open her heart to all. Her friendship with Isabel's daughter fosters the girl's positive self-image, which results in her dramatic weight loss. Azucena can even, by the end of the novel, forgive the villainous Isabel, who had tried and sometimes succeeded to kill her in the present and in past lives. When she looks at Isabel with love, a response Isabel had never experienced before, Isabel breaks down, "her days of villainy. . .over." By the end of the novel, Azucena has rid herself of her anger and jealousies and so can complete her mission to restore the cosmic order. As a result, Rodrigo can now recognize her as his twin soul and so asks her to marry him. Esquivel symbolizes the harmony of their union through Rodrigo's discovery and replacement of the Pyramid's capstone, which causes the ancient city of Tenochtitlan and Mexico City to fuse, and "for a moment, all hearts harbored Divine Love equally. Everyone felt part of a whole."

In the *New York Times Book Review,* Houston complains that a reader cannot be "certain whether the novel is a sendup of New Age cliches or whether its narrator is truly an advocate for them. In trying to have it both ways, Ms. Esquivel has it neither." However, whether or not Esquivel promotes or parodies New Age philosophy as she mixes it with magic realism and science fiction is not the point of the novel. The characters' experiences with regressions, body exchanges, mystical stones, and cosmic order all come together in Esquivel's imaginative construction of the novel, which presents an effective and entertaining look at the law of love.

Source: Wendy Perkins, in an essay for *Literature of Developing Nations for Students*, Gale, 2000.

Barbara Mujica

In the following brief review of Esquivel's second novel The Law of Love*, reviewer Barbara Mujica gives a disfavorable overview of the novel's convoluted story and writes that while Esquivel's ability to use gimmicks in her prose were successful in her first novel* Like Water for Chocolate*, her use of multi-media gimmicks in* The Law of Love *ultimately can not save the novel.*

Laura Esquivel is a master of gimmickry. In *Como agua para chocolate* [*Like Water for Chocolate*] her device was the recipe. By beginning each chapter with instructions for the preparation of a delicious Mexican dish, she artfully constructed the metaphor at the center of her novel: Love is food. Love nourishes the ravenous spirit just as food nourishes the body; at the same time, love satisfies physical hunger just as a good meal enjoyed in delightful company can achieve a spiritual dimension. Since love and food satisfy human appetites, the preparation of marvelous meals becomes an expression of passion, which is exactly what happened in the book.

In *La ley del amor* the gimmick is music. A compact disc comes with each copy of the book, and

in the text Esquivel includes instructions telling when each segment is to be played. The idea is to give readers the opportunity to experience the same musical stimuli as the characters. Illustrated folios provide examples of the images the characters see when their memories are unlocked by the strains of Puccini. In addition the CD contains popular songs that set the mood for the upcoming chapters.

Unfortunately, the gimmick is not nearly as effective in *La ley del amor* as it was in *Como agua para chocolate*, partly because CDs are inconvenient, especially if you happen to be reading at, say, the beach or perhaps in the metro or the bathroom, and partly because the story is so tedious and convoluted that nothing—not even Puccini—can save it. The tale begins in the sixteenth century, when Rodrigo Diaz, one of Cortes's captains, rapes a beautiful Indian noblewoman named Citlali on the pyramid where the Aztecs worshiped the goddess of Love. The stones of the pyramid are, of course, magical, and so the act will have far-reaching consequences. When Citlali gives birth to a baby boy, Rodrigo tears the child from her and brutally murders him. The Indian woman takes revenge by killing the son Rodrigo has with his Spanish wife, Isabel.

According to the *Law of Love*, acts of brutality upset the cosmic order, which can only be restored when the perpetrators are purged of hatred and make amends. Since one lifetime is insufficient to achieve spiritual cleansing, reincarnation permits people who loathe each other to meet again over and over in successive lives until the process of purification is completed. Thus, Rodrigo encounters Citlali, Isabel, and the two murdered babies repeatedly throughout the centuries until at last, sometime around the year 2200, we find him in the arms of Azucena, his true love and kindred spirit (*alma gemela*).

Just when he and his loved one have finally found one another, Rodrigo is whisked away and sent to Korma, a distant planet inhabited by fierce, primitive beings. Disregarding the advice of Anacreonte, her guardian angel, Azucena, in search of Rodrigo, wheedles her way into a government office where she is outfitted with a virtual-reality headset. By listening to music, Azucena is able to relive a past life experience, during which she is a baby who is rescued from disaster by Rodrigo, who at that time (about 1985) was her father.

The power-hungry Isabel, who is running for World president, is in love with Rodrigo and has stolen him away from Azucena. Realizing that she is in imminent danger, Azucena finds her way to an unused body storage area and dons a new body just before her apartment is blown up by Isabel's goons. Unrecognizable in her new form, Azucena returns to her old apartment. Cuquita, a neighbor who is paying penance for misdeeds during a past life by living with an abusive husband, escapes from her own place and moves in with Azucena. The two are joined by Cuquita's grandmother, who comes in handy later when she dies, leaving her body available for Azucena, who is killed by Isabel, but receives permission of the gods to return and occupy the newly released body.

After a series of intergalactic spaceship chases, Azucena finally links up once again with Rodrigo, who doesn't recognize her and takes off with Citlati. By listening to music through virtual-reality headsets, Azucena witnesses scenes from past lives in which she was a baby murdered by Isabel, Citlali was a man who raped Rodrigo (a woman), and Isabel was Rodrigo's brother-in-law, who murdered Citlali in revenge. It is not until Azucena starts listening to Anacreonte and obeying the gods that things start falling back into place.

If all this sounds impossibly complicated and silly, it is, but the story is muddled even further by the appearance of an endless array of nonsensical characters—a highly maternal goon who occupies Azucena's former body and is known as Ex-Azucena, Cuquita's husband (whose body is later taken over by Rodrigo), Isabel's overweight daughter (who turns out to be Azucena's sister, which means, of course, that Isabel is really Azucena's mother).

While *Como agua para chocolate* touched readers with its clever weave of fantasy and reality, as well as its portrayals of a female-dominated family in revolutionary Mexico, a complex mother-daughter relationship, and a true love nourished by custards rather than kisses, *La ley del amor* offers readers little to relate to. At the end of *La ley del amor*, cosmic order is restored and Azucena gets her man, but the truth is, we couldn't care less.

Source: Barbara Mujica, "La ley del amor," in *Americas*, Vol. 48, No. 6, November-December, 1996, p. 61.

Louise Redd

In the following brief review of Esquivel's second novel The Law of Love, *reviewer Louise Redd gives us an overview of the novel's tangled story and writes that though the convoluted plotline may at times seem too soap-operaish (and the*

❝ At the end of *La ley del amor*, cosmic order is restored and Azucena gets her man, but the truth is, we couldn't care less."

multimedia packaged with the story too encumbering), its parallels to Mexico's shedding the aftereffects of the Conquest keep it from descending too far into parody.

In Laura Esquivel's first novel, *Like Water for Chocolate,* she wrote of potent dishes that wreaked strange effects, often acting as love potions, on those who ate them. Now in *The Law of Love,* her second novel, she again proves herself a talented literary chef, creating a delectable feast from ingredients as disparate as a 16th-century rape and a 23rd-century spaceship.

The *Law of Love* is an exuberant mix of science fiction, new age psycho-babble, fable and old-fashioned love story. Although its characters transport themselves from planet to planet by astro-telephone and can photograph each other's auras, they're still looking for love. And no one looks harder than Azucena, an astro-analyst who spends her days helping clients regress through past lives. After hours, and with the help of a bossy guardian angel, Azucena attempts to fulfill her life's mission: to reinstate the toppled capstone of the Pyramid of Love, on the site of ancient Tenochtitlan.

In addition to the absent capstone, she's also searching for a missing person: Rodrigo, her "twin soul" or ideal love. Her motivation to find Rodrigo is stoked by the memory of the one night of passion she enjoyed with him before he disappeared and incurred amnesia at the hands of the evil Isabel, the candidate for planetary president who has good reason to keep Rodrigo from spouting off about her past-life escapades.

Azucena must not only restore the pyramid but find Rodrigo and jolt him from his amnesia so he can recognize her as his twin soul. Both are hefty tasks, but Azucena has been prepping for them for many lifetimes.

> *The Law of Love,* her second novel, she again proves herself a talented literary chef, creating a delectable feast from ingredients as disparate as a 16th-century rape and a 23rd-century spaceship."

Her two missions are not unrelated. The law of love, as explained by Azucena's guardian angel, dictates that "as we displace hatred, we receive hatred in return. The only way around this is to transmute the energy of hatred into love before it leaves our body." The Pyramid of Love helped humans achieve this transmutation until Rodrigo, during a lifetime as a conquistador, knocked the top off the pyramid, raped a woman there and then built his home on the site.

And this is Azucena's "ideal love"? It seems that multiple lifetimes can cure even serious personality flaws; Rodrigo has spent seven centuries working off that nasty conquistador karma and earning the right to meet his twin soul. Both lovers suffer comic and cosmic transmutations along the paths to each other, until it is clear that the 23rd century's dazzling technology hasn't done much to improve the lot of the lovelorn.

Occasionally the gender and personality changes induced by the characters' multiple lifetimes lend *The Law of Love* an annoying soap-operatic quality. But there's a stubborn parallel between the characters' shedding of bad karma and futuristic Mexico's shedding of the trauma of the Conquest that keeps this light, sometimes silly novel grounded in serious concerns.

The *Law of Love* is being billed by its publishers as "the first multimedia novel," as it comes with illustrations and a CD of classical music and Mexican danzones. The reader is periodically instructed to take an "Intermission for Dancing," to listen to a certain track of the CD, or to study the illustrations. Ironically, the compelling nature of Ms. Esquivel's story renders the multimedia aspect of the novel somewhat intrusive; *The Law of Love* is such an enjoyable read that I resented being asked to step away from it to listen to a CD track or to look at some illustrations.

Ms. Esquivel has written a wild, romantic and often funny novel that needs no assistance from other media.

Source: Louise Redd, "Too Good for Such Fripperies: Reading Aids Distract from a Magical Novel," in *Dallas Morning News,* October 20, 1996, p. 8J.

Sources

Cardwell, A. Scott, review, in *Salon* [online].

Hoffert, Barbara, review, in *Library Journal*, January, 1996, p. 81.

Houston, Robert, "Karma Chameleons," in *New York Times Book Review*, November 17, 1996, p. 11.

Review, in *Kirkus Reviews*, July 1, 1996, p. 917.

Pizzichini, Lilian, review, in *Times Literary Supplement*, October 18, 1996, p. 23.

Seaman, Donna, review, in *Booklist*, August 19, 1996.

Further Reading

O'Neill, Molly, "At Dinner with Laura Esquivel: Sensing the Spirit in All Things, Seen and Unseen," in *New York Times Book Review*, March 31, 1993, pp. C1, C8.
   In this interview Esquivel discusses the magical nature of food and the "spiritual underpinnings of modern daily life."

Leaving This Island Place

Austin C. Clarke's short story "Leaving This Island Place" has been published in the short story collection *From Ink Lake: Canadian Stories*, collected by Michael Ondaatje, in 1990.

"Leaving This Island Place" is told from the perspective of a first-person narrator, the protagonist of the story, who is not named. The narrator is a young man preparing to leave his native Barbados ("this island place") in order to attend college in Canada. As the story opens, he is going to visit his father, who is dying in an almshouse. The narrator's mother and father were never married, and so he grew up in a home with his mother and stepfather and was not given his father's surname, making him a "bastard" child. Although his mother forbade the mention of his father's name throughout his childhood, the narrator occasionally sneaked off to visit his father. However, during the present time of the story, the narrator, who has made his way into the realm of the privileged social classes through his education, has become completely alienated from his father. His girlfriend, Cynthia, who is from a wealthy family, as symbolized by the Jaguar sports car her father has given her, does not even know he had a father. And, although she promises to see the narrator off at the airport, she does not show up. Throughout the story, the narrator repeats to himself the statement that he is "leaving this island," a step away from his family, friends, and native home about which he feels a mixture of guilt, anxiety, fear, and relief.

Austin C. Clarke

1990

This story centers on themes of family, paternity, death, socioeconomic class, and the significance of "leaving" one's homeland for a foreign culture. The narrator is aware that he is, to some extent, "out of place," as an illegitimate child of an underprivileged family who has worked his way into the realm of the privileged classes. His success as a cricket player represents both his connection to his father, who had been the captain of his village cricket team, and his own hard-earned success as a social climber.

Author Biography

Austin C. Clarke is best known for his Toronto Trilogy, a series of three novels about immigrants from Barbados living in Canada: *The Meeting Point* (1972), *Storm of Fortune* (1973), and *The Bigger Light* (1975). In addition, Clarke has written five novels and six short-story collections. Clarke's autobiographical works include *Growing Up Stupid under the Union Jack: A Memoir* (1980) and *A Passage Back Home: A Personal Reminiscence of Samuel Selvon* (1994).

Clarke was born on July 26, 1934, in St. James, Barbados. His father, Kenneth Trothan, was an artist, and his mother, Gladys Clarke, was a hotel maid. Clarke attended Coleridge-Parry Primary School in St. Peter, Barbados. He attended secondary school at Harrison College in Barbados. In 1955, Clarke entered Trinity College, of the University of Toronto, Ontario, in Canada, where he studied economics and politics. From 1959 to 1960, Clarke worked as a newspaper reporter in Timmins and Kirkland Lake, Ontario. In 1963, he became a producer and freelance broadcaster for the Canadian Broadcasting Corporation (CBC) in Toronto. From 1974 to 1976, he was a cultural and press attache for the Barbados Embassy in Washington, D.C. From 1975 to 1976, Clarke was general manager at the Caribbean Broadcasting Corporation, in St. Michael, Barbados. Clarke also worked as a freelance journalist for the *Toronto Globe* and the CBC. Clarke has held numerous positions as professor, lecturer, fellow and writer-in-residence at universities throughout the United States and Canada, including the positions as Hoyt Fellow and visiting professor of Afro-American literature and creative writing at Yale University from 1968 to 1971; professor of literature at Brandeis University from 1968 to 1969; visiting professor of literature at

Williams College in 1971; lecturer at Duke University from 1971 to 1972; visiting professor at the University of Texas, Austin, from 1973 to 1974; writer in residence at Concordia University in Montreal, Quebec in 1977; and writer in residence at the University of Western Ontario in 1978. Clarke also served on the board of trustees of the Rhode Island School of Design from 1970 to 1975, as vice-chairperson on the Ontario Board of Censors from 1983 to 1985, and on the Immigration and Refugee Board of Canada in 1988. Clarke's first marriage, to Trinity Collego, ended in divorce, and in 1957 he married Betty Joyce Reynolds, with whom he has three children: Janice, Loretta, and Jordan.

Plot Summary

The narrator of this story, who is not named, is preparing to leave his native Barbados in order to attend college in Canada. As the story opens, he is going to visit his estranged father, who is dying in an almshouse. The head nurse of the almshouse, Miss Brewster, shows the narrator to the room where his father lies dying. His mother and father had never been married, and so the narrator was born a "bastard" and was not given his father's surname. His mother then married another man, and he was raised in a house with his mother and stepfather. Although his mother forbade the mention of his father's name for the eighteen years of his childhood, the narrator occasionally risked punishment to sneak off and visit his father at his shack. The narrator was disturbed by the pornographic pictures of women hanging on his father's walls. The last time he visited his father, he had been so disturbed by these photos of naked women that he had run screaming away from his father's home. His father had been the captain of his village cricket team, but had been repeatedly arrested for drunkenness by a local policeman who seemed to have something against him. The narrator's relatives say that it was in jail that the father contracted the disease from which he is now dying, although the disease is not named. While he is visiting his dying father, the father asks that he have a nun from the Nazarene Church say a prayer for him before he dies, but the narrator ignores this request.

The narrator has made his way up in socioeconomic standing through his success in school, and as a cricket player. He is always aware, however, that he is "out of place" in the social world of his privileged friends, who throw him a going-away party the afternoon after he visits his father. His girlfriend, Cynthia, is from a wealthy family, and drives around in a Jaguar sports car her father has given her. After the party, he and Cynthia walk together on the Gravesend Beach. Cynthia insists that he write her every day from Canada. She claims that they should get married, but it is clear that she has not told her own father about their relationship, probably because of his lower social standing. When the narrator tells Cynthia that his father is dying, she laughs and says that she didn't even know he had a father. She promises him that she will see him off at the airport. But the following morning, as he boards the plane for Canada, he notes that Cynthia has not come. He wonders if his father is dead yet, and, if so, how he died, but realizes that he will never know. Although he feels guilty for leaving his dying father, the narrator reminds himself that he is "leaving the island" for better things. After the plane takes off, he looks down and sees nothing ahead of him but "the sea, and the sea, and then the sea."

Austin C. Clarke

Characters

Miss Brewster

Miss Brewster is the head nurse at the almshouse who shows the narrator to the room in which his father lays dying. The narrator's description of her evokes images of death which express his anxieties about his dying father: "She is old and haggard. And she looks as if she has looked once too often on the face of death; and now she herself resembles a half-dead, dried-out flying fish, wrapped in the grease-proof paper of her nurse's uniform."

Cynthia

Cynthia is the narrator's girlfriend. She is of a significantly wealthier family and higher socioeconomic class than the narrator. Her class status is symbolized by her Jaguar sports car. When the narrator tells her that his father is dying, she laughs and says she didn't even know he had a father. Cynthia promises the narrator that she will be at the airport to see him off when he leaves for college, but she does not show up. The narrator laments, "Cynthia is not coming through the car park in her father's Jaguar. She has not come, she has not come as she promised."

Narrator

The narrator of the story, who is not given a name, is the central protagonist. The story is told from his first-person point of view. The story centers on a period of time as he is preparing to leave his native Barbados to attend college in Canada. As the story opens, he is going to visit his estranged father, who is dying in an almshouse. Although the narrator comes from an underprivileged socioeconomic class, he has worked his way into the world of the privileged through his education and his success as a cricket player. His girlfriend, Cynthia, is from a wealthier family than he, as are his friends, who throw a going-away party for him. In addition to his class status, the narrator is aware of the fact that he is a "bastard"—a child born without a legally named father—and therefore carries his mother's last name. He feels guilty to be leaving for college while his father is dying—yet his desire to "leave this island place" and escape his family and cultural roots in pursuit of a higher education prevails and he boards the plane as planned. Nonetheless, the class differences between the narrator and his girlfriend also seem to prevail: she fails to see him off at the airport, as she had promised. As his plane takes off, the narrator reminds himself once again, "I am leaving the island"—a statement he has repeated throughout the story, which expresses a mixture of regret, guilt, alienation, and the overriding desire to escape his own background in order to start a new life in a foreign country.

Narrator's Father

As the story opens, the narrator's father lies dying in an almshouse, where the narrator goes to visit him. The narrator explains that his father and mother were not married, and so he does not carry his father's surname and was raised by his mother and stepfather. The narrator relates that his father had been the captain of the village cricket team, but had been broken down physically and in spirit from repeated arrests for drunkenness by a local policeman. Although his mother forbade the mention of his father's name for eighteen years, the narrator occasionally risked getting in trouble in order to visit him. The narrator feels guilty for leaving the island when he father is dying, but he also feels estranged from his father, and tries to comfort himself with the idea that he is leaving the island anyway and that it doesn't really matter that his father is dying.

Narrator's Mother

The narrator's mother became pregnant by his father out of wedlock, and so the narrator carries his mother's last name, rather than that of his father. His mother married a man who became his stepfather and forbade the mention of his biological father's name in the household.

Themes

Leaving

A central theme of this story is "leaving." The story follows the day prior to the departure of the narrator from his native Barbados to go to school in Canada. He mentions repeatedly that he is "leaving" the island of Barbados. The story focuses on the various implications for the narrator of "leaving" his home. Out of guilt, he goes to visit his dying father the day before he leaves. He is also leaving his girlfriend, Cynthia. Although she insists that he write every day, and that they should have run off to get married, and that she will be at the airport to see him off, her promises are hollow. She doesn't even show up at the airport to say goodbye to him. So leaving the island means not only abandoning his poor, dying father, but also forfeiting his relationship with Cynthia.

"Leaving" also functions symbolically in the story. "Leaving" symbolizes death. His father even describes his own imminent death by stating that his is "leaving." Furthermore, "leaving" the island, for the narrator, means leaving his family and his cultural roots. Throughout the story, the narrator expresses ambivalence about the fact that he is "leaving." At one level, the reminder that he is "leaving" is a justification for abandoning his father. "Leaving" also represents a fantasy of "escape" from both his troubled family history and his socioeconomic background. He tells himself that he is "leaving. . .for Canada. . .for hope. . .for glory." But he also feels the anxiety of leaving the home that he knows for the unknown, as represented by the image of the vast and endless sea which ends the story.

Social Climbing

One of the central anxieties expressed by the narrator is over his socioeconomic status. He is from an underprivileged background. The fact that he was born out of wedlock and is therefore a "bastard" is a constant reminder of his lower socioeconomic status in society: "The absence of [my father's] surname on my report card would remind me in the eyes of my classmates that I might be the best cricketer and the best runner, but that I was after all, among this cream of best blood and brains, only a bas-" His success at sports, particularly cricket, is a symbol for the narrator of his success as a social climber. He continually contrasts the world of the cricket field with the room in the almshouse where his father lies dying. Despite his success at school, and his association with his wealthy and privileged classmates, the narrator, at his farewell party, is constantly reminded that "I was out of place here, that I belonged with the beginning in the almshouse. Each giggle, each toast, each rattle of drunken ice cubes in the whirling glass pointed a finger back to the almshouse." One of the themes of the story, in relation to social climbing, is that, no matter how successfully one works one's way into the upper classes, no one can escape his or her roots.

Family and Paternity

This story is centrally concerned with the theme of family, and particularly with paternity. The narrator's parents were never married, and so he is an "illegitimate" child. His mother, who married another man, forbade the mention of his father's name throughout his childhood. Much of the narrator's

Topics for Further Study

- Clarke was born and grew up in Barbados, which is in the West Indies. Find a map of the West Indies, a grouping of many island nations. What other countries are part of the West Indies? Learn more about one of these countries, including its culture and history.

- Clarke can be categorized as a Canadian author, and therefore as part of the Canadian literary tradition. Learn more about Canadian literature. What historical trends and developments have characterized Canadian literature? Learn more about another Canadian author and his or her principal works. Read and discuss a story by this author.

- Clarke is a native of Barbados. Learn more about the history of Barbados and also about contemporary Barbados. What significant events or developments have occurred there?

- Clarke's fiction can be categorized in the literary tradition of the West Indies. Learn more about the history and significant developments in West Indian literature. Who are some other West Indian authors of note? Read and discuss a story by another West Indian author.

- Clarke's fiction is concerned primarily with the experiences, struggles, and achievements of immigrants from Barbados to Canada. Learn more about another population of immigrant to your own country or local area. What are and have been the immigration patterns of this group of people? What particular issues and concerns face immigrants from this particular nation or culture? What is the policy of your own nation toward immigration?

anxieties throughout the story revolve around this condition of alienation from his own father. Although he was forbidden, he did occasionally sneak off to his father's shack to visit him. And, although his mother assured him that his father "had come 'from no family at-all, at-all'" and "had had 'no background'" the narrator feels a strong sense of family in the presence of his father; he states that "to me in those laughing days he held a family circle of compassion in his heart." However, years before the story opens, the narrator had run away from his father's home and never again went to visit him. As the story opens, he is going to visit his father, who is dying in an almshouse. The narrator feels extremely ambivalent about his father, and about his father's death, but his overriding feeling is one of guilt for abandoning him as he is dying. The narrator tries to justify the fact that he is abandoning his own father in a time of need by telling himself that his father is already dead to him; he tries to relieve his conscience by reminding himself that he is "leaving the island" for a better life.

Style

Setting

This story is set in Clarke's native home of Barbados, the "island place" referred to in the story's title. Like the narrator and protagonist of his story, Clarke left Barbados as a young man in order to attend college in Canada. Thus, many of Clarke's stories are about immigrants who leave Barbados for North America. "This island place," in the story, represents not just home but the narrator's entire familial, ethnic, cultural, and socioeconomic roots. Thus, "leaving this island place" represents for the narrator the sense that he is abandoning his cultural roots in pursuit of socioeconomic success in the white-dominated Western world.

Point of View

This story is narrated from the first-person point of view. This means that the narrator is a character in the story, and that the reader is given only information, thoughts, or ideas available to that character. In this story, the narrator is not named, but is the protagonist of the story. First-person narration is important to this story because it concerns the narrator's inner conflicts as he prepares to leave his native island of Barbados to attend college in Canada. The reader is presented with the narrator's thoughts about his family and his socioeconomic standing. The first-person narration also presents impressions and descriptions of the protagonist as reflections of his own inner anxieties; for instance, when he is visiting his dying father, many of the people and objects he sees around him are described in terms which refer to death.

Dialogue

Clarke is celebrated among critics for his skillful rendering of the rhythms of speech of his Barbadian characters. Anthony Boxill, in the *Dictionary of Literary Biography,* makes note of his ''unerringly sharp ear for Barbadian speech patterns and rhythms'' which contribute ''much to the richness of his characterization.'' An example of this is the speech of Miss Brewster, who shows the narrator to the room in the almshouse where his father is dying:

> That man having fits and convulsions by the hour! Every day he asking for you. All the time, day in and day out. And you is such a poor-great, high-school educated bastard that you now acting *too proud* to come in here, because it is a almshouse and not a *private ward*, to see your own father! And you didn't even have the presence o' mind to bring along a orange, not even one, or a banana for that man, *your father!*

Repetition

This story makes use of repetition as a central narrative device. The title of the story, ''Leaving This Island Place,'' is echoed throughout the narrative. The narrator repeats phrases such as: ''But I am leaving''; ''I am leaving''; ''I am leaving this place''; ''I know I am leaving this island''; ''I am leaving this island place''; ''I am going to leave''; ''I was leaving''; and ''I am leaving the island.'' This serves in part to emphasize the theme of *leaving* as central to the story. In addition, the very fact of the excessive repetition of this phrase by the narrator implies that he is struggling with the fact that he is ''leaving'' and with its significance to his life. The phrase also takes on different implications at different points in the story. In some instances, the narrator reminds himself that ''I am leaving'' as a means of justification for the fact that he is abandoning his dying father. At other points, the

narrator reminds himself that ''I am leaving'' as an expression of his desire to escape his family and his uncomfortable social standing in Barbados. At other points, it is an expression of anxiety at the prospect of leaving his home, his family, and his girlfriend.

Literary Heritage

Clarke can be categorized according to two distinct literary heritages: he is both a Caribbean writer and a Canadian writer.

As a native of Barbados, which is part of the Caribbean, Clarke is grouped within this larger regional literary tradition. Because the Caribbean was colonized by Spain, France, Great Britain, and the Netherlands, the literature which has emerged from the island nations occupying it has been written in several different languages, corresponding to the language of the nation by which each island was colonized. Because the Spanish, who originally colonized the area, completely destroyed the people and culture native to the region, there is no record of the oral traditions which would have characterized the pre-Columbian era of Caribbean history. It was not until the 1920s that writers of the French- and Spanish-speaking Caribbean began to formulate a distinct literature emerging from black West Indian culture (rather than from European culture). The English-speaking Caribbean, which includes Barbados, did not develop along these lines until 1945. Early writers of the new tradition include George Lamming, V. S. Naipaul, and Louise Bennett.

Canadian literature has developed along two distinct lines: anglophone (written in English) and Francophone (written in French). Clarke is part of Canada's anglophone literary heritage. Clarke's story ''Leaving This Island Place'' has been collected in the anthology of Canadian literature entitled *Ink Lake,* edited by Michael Ondaatje.

Historical Context

Barbados

This story takes place in Barbados, an island nation in the Caribbean. As Clarke is originally from Barbados, many of his stories either take place there or are about immigrants from Barbados to the U.S. and Canada. Ninety percent of the population of Barbados is made up of people of African descent. The official language is English, but Bajan, a dialect of English, is also spoken. The capital of Barbados is Bridgetown. Barbados was colonized by the British from 1627, when they first established a settlement there, to 1966, when the island achieved national independence. In the seventeenth century, sugar plantations became the primary basis of the economy of Barbados. Africans were forcibly brought to Barbados to work as slaves on these sugar plantations. A slave rebellion was waged in 1816, but slavery was not abolished in the area until 1834. Nevertheless, Barbadians of African descent continued to be employed primarily on sugar plantations and continued to occupy the least privileged socioeconomic strata. Labor disturbances in the 1930s, however, led to various reforms in the 1940s, which made it possible for black political organizers in the region to gain power and influence. Barbados achieved complete internal self-rule in 1961, and national independence in 1966, although it remained part of the British Commonwealth. Throughout the 1980s, the political system of Barbados was considered one of the most stable in the English-speaking Caribbean.

West Indies

The island nation of Barbados is part of the West Indies. The West Indies are made up of twenty-three island nations occupying the Caribbean Ocean in the region between Florida and South America. The history of the West Indies is characterized by the colonization of British, Dutch, Spanish, French, and Danish, who fought back and forth over territories in the region in the seventeenth and eighteenth centuries. Thus the culture and language of the nations of the modern West Indies generally coincide with the culture of the nation by which it was colonized. The history of forcing enslaved Africans to work on the sugar plantations, however, characterizes the entire region. Many nations of the modern West Indies have organized around common economic interests through the formation of the Caribbean Community and Common Market, formed in 1973.

Cricket

The sport of cricket is important to the narrator's central concerns throughout the story. His father had been the captain of his village cricket team, and the narrator himself has become a cricket star in his own right. For the narrator, cricket represents his status as a social climber, for it is in the community of his wealthy, educated friends that cricket has become central to his identity. A game of cricket requires eleven members on each team, and is played with a bat and ball; each team is in a position to either "bat" or "bowl," and then switches between innings. The game of cricket began in the 1840s in New Zealand, but is derived from a game played by rural boys as far back as the thirteenth century. The formalization of cricket as an organized sport may in part be indicated by the founding of the New Zealand Cricket Council in 1894. In the West Indies, cricket was introduced in the early nineteenth century. Barbados was the first West Indian nation to participate in an inter-colonial match, in 1891, with what is now Guyana. An organized board for regulating cricket matches between islands of the West Indies, and with nations outside of the West Indies, was founded in 1927. In 1926, the West Indies joined the Imperial Cricket Conference, which was renamed the International Cricket Conference in 1965 and then the International Cricket Council in 1989. The first World Cup cricket competition was held in 1975. During the 1980s, the West Indies were a dominant force in international cricket competition. Although women played cricket beginning in the eighteenth century, the International Women's Cricket Council was not founded until 1958.

Critical Overview

Clarke received early encouragement in his writing in high school, and in college won prizes for several of his poems. Clarke went on to write as a journalist before settling on fiction as his preferred genre.

Clarke is known for his novels and short stories which focus on the struggles of black people attempting to succeed in white society. Anthony Boxill notes that Clarke "became the foremost recounter of the black West Indian immigrants' experience in Canada." Boxill describes the overriding tone of Clarke's fiction in regard to race relations: "Of his generation of West Indian novelists he is perhaps the most outspoken and bitter in depicting the experience of the poor black when confronted with the establishment, whether it is that of the white majority in Canada, the colonial expatriate, or the postcolonial ruling black middle class in Barbados."

Clarke's first novel, *The Survivors of the Crossing*, was published in 1964, ten years after his

Open air market in Barbados, Clarke's home country, before he emigrated to Canada in 1955.

arrival in Canada. It concerns the conditions of sugar plantation workers in Barbados. In this novel, the main character, Rufus, tries to organize sugar plantation laborers, but is discouraged both by the institutional powers of a white ruling class and also by members of the black middle class. His second novel, *Thistles and Thorns*, is also set in Barbados and centers on a boy, born illegitimate, who leaves the home of his mother in order to find his father. These novels were received by critics as flawed, but certainly the work of a promising author. As with most of Clarke's works, critics generally agreed on Clarke's talent for capturing the rhythms of Barbadian speech and for his depiction of comic scenes. However, as Boxill explains, "they are weakly structured and lack aesthetic distancing and tonal discipline." Clarke's characters also tend to fail to draw the reader in.

In his first two novels, Canada represents a promised land of escape from economic and social woes. His next three novels depict what immigrants from Barbados find when they reach Canada. His Toronto Trilogy is comprised of a series of three novels about immigrants from Barbados to Canada. These novels generally portray the condition of West Indian immigrants to Canada in terms of their struggles with racial prejudice and economic hardship. The first in the trilogy, *The Meeting Point*, was published in 1972. It centers on a woman who is a black immigrant from Barbados and who works as a maid for a Jewish family in Toronto. The second, *Storm of Fortune*, was published in 1973. It includes some of the same characters as the first, but after they have achieved a degree of financial success and harbor expectations of assimilating into mainstream culture. The third, *The Bigger Light*, was published in 1975. It centers on a man, an immigrant from Barbados, who becomes alienated from his family and his culture in the process of attempting to succeed in white society. While critics continued to admire Clarke's facility with the dialect of Barbados, his plot structures in the Toronto Trilogy were criticized as contrived to suit his social message.

Clarke's collections of short stories include *When He Was Free and Young He Used to Wear Silks* (1973), *Short Stories of Austin Clarke* (1984), *When Women Rule* (1985), *Nine Men Who Laughed* (1986), *In This City* (1992), and *There Are No Elders* (1993). His talents as a short story writer are indicated by the fact that in 1965 he won the University of Western Ontario President's Medal for the best story published in Canada that year.

Clarke's autobiographical work *Growing Up Stupid under the Union Jack: A Memoir* (1980) has been generally praised. Boxill states that in this work "Clarke is once again at his best. . .Full of humor and vigor, it recreates the world of his boyhood with much affection but without glossing over the injustice and brutality with which the society treated the poor and the black. One has the feeling that far from forcing his material into a predetermined rigid mold, the author has allowed this book to grow organically."

Criticism

Liz Brent

Brent has a Ph.D. in American Culture, with a specialization in film studies, from the University of Michigan. She is a freelance writer and teaches courses in the history of American cinema. In the following essay, Brent discusses the theme of death in "Leaving This Island Place."

As death is a central theme of this story, the narrative is filled with references, both direct and indirect, to death. Because the story is told from the first-person point of view of the narrator, these recurring references to death express his own inner psychological state and preoccupations. On a literal level, he is preoccupied with death because his father is dying. This fact, occurring just as he is preparing to leave Barbados for college in Canada, has brought up memories of his family circumstances and reminded him of his socioeconomic roots, in contrast to his current lifestyle as an educated, upwardly mobile young man. On a figurative level, the narrator's preoccupation with death symbolizes the theme of "leaving" and the various symbolic forms of death which accompany his imminent departure from his family and culture.

As the story opens, the narrator is visiting his dying father in an almshouse just across from the cricket field where he plays every Saturday. This is the narrator's first visit to his estranged father in many years. As he enters the almshouse and the head nurse shows him down the hallway to the room where his father lies dying, his perceptions of what he sees, hears, and smells around him are filled with associations to death. Everyone in the almshouse seems to him to be dying or already dead. "Something in those faces told me they were all going to die in the almshouse," he reflects. His own father's

impending death is first indicated in the story by the narrator's comment that he "would never live to see the sun of day again." The narrator's feelings of guilt and ambivalence toward his father are in part motivated by the knowledge that his father is dying, and in part palliated by the reminder that he is "leaving" and therefore does not need to get "involved" with his father. "I know it is too late now to think of saving him," he notes. "It is too late to become involved with this dying man."

Everyone there seems to him on the verge of death. The other men inhabiting the almshouse look to the narrator "half-alive and half-dead." Even the head nurse, Miss Brewster, seems to the narrator to be occupying the space of death: "She is old and haggard. And she looks as if she has looked once too often on the face of death; and now she herself resembles a half-dead, dried-out flying fish, wrapped in the grease-proof paper of her nurse's uniform." The impression that the almshouse is filled with masses of dying men is implied by the image that some of the men in the ward lie on their backs in bed, "like soldiers on a battlefield."

The narrator's impression that he is surrounded by death becomes transferred onto his own sense of himself, as if he were also dying; he feels that the men in the almshouse "all looked at me as if I were dying." When the narrator is finally in his father's room, he says, "I was alone with the dead." In his mind, his father is already dead. And his father's death again leads him to feel as if he himself were dead or dying, as he states that "there is death in this room and I am inside it." The narrator himself is nowhere near literally dying; symbolically, however, the imminent death of his father, and his imminent departure from the island, represent the death of his ties to his family and to his cultural roots. The death of his father symbolizes the disappearance of his only true connection to his personal and cultural history. And, while his father seems to him to represent his own death, his wealthy, educated friends, particularly his girlfriend Cynthia, are associated with life. In the room with his dying father, he tries to imagine Cynthia's face, as "I kept myself alive with the living outside world of cricket and cheers and 'tea in the pavilion.'" Thus, for the narrator, his desire to be associated with a wealthier socioeconomic class feels like a means of rescuing himself from death.

While in the room with his father, the narrator continues to evoke imagery symbolically associated with death. Echoing his claim earlier that his father

What Do I Read Next?

- *From Ink Lake: Canadian Stories*, edited by Michael Ondaatje and published in 1990, contains Clarke's story "Leaving This Island Place."

- Clarke's *The Meeting Point* (1967) is the first novel in his Toronto Trilogy. The novel is about a group of immigrants from Barbados to Canada.

- Clarke's *Storm of Fortune* (1973) is the second novel in the Toronto Trilogy, and follows the further experiences of the characters presented in the first.

- *The Bigger Light* (1975) is the third novel in Clarke's Toronto Trilogy.

- *Growing Up Stupid under the Union Jack: A Memoir* is Clarke's autobiographical story of his childhood in Barbados.

- *The Black Writer in Africa and the Americas* (1973), edited by Lloyd W. Brown, contains a piece contributed by Clarke.

---

will never again see the sun of day, his sees his father "in the sunset of this room." The sunset is a figurative image of death. The narrator repeatedly describes his father as not just dying but already dead. When his father speaks, he says that "it was the skeleton talking." And when his father holds out his hand to the narrator, the narrator perceives it as a "dead hand" and does not take it. In describing his father as if he were already dead, the narrator is attempting to justify the fact that he is going to be abandoning his own dying father when he leaves the island for Canada. By telling himself that the father is already dead, the narrator can imagine that there is nothing more he could be doing for the man, that he need not feel guilty for abandoning him. The narrator imagines that the physical distance of Canada will relieve his guilt over his abandonment of his father; later that day he imagines that, once in the airplane, he will be "bound for Canada, for hope, for school, for glory; and the sea and the distance had already eased the pain of conscience; and there was already much sea between me and the cause of conscience"—the "cause of conscience" being his dying father, about whom he feels so guilty.

It is the father who directly makes the connection between the narrator's plan for "leaving the island" and his own inevitable "leaving" when he dies. "I hear you going away," he says, "and that is a good thing. . .because I am going away. . .from this place." As he listens to his father's "words and

words and words" he continues to remind himself that, as far as he is concerned, his father is already dead. He thinks back to his childhood, when his mother forbade the mention of his father's name in the house, and concludes that "he had died before this present visit." And again, the narrator tells himself, "He was dead before this." Here the narrator is repeatedly trying to relieve his own sense of guilt by trying to convince himself that his father is already dead to him.

The narrator then uses the metaphor of his father's "claim" upon his life. A claim is an official document which proves legal ownership, usually of land. The narrator tells himself, "Let him die. I am leaving this island place. And let him die with his claim on my life. And let the claim be nailed in the coffin." This imagery implies that the narrator feels his father holds the rightful ownership to his own life. All of the narrator's efforts to tell himself that his father is already dead are thus in part an attempt to deny his father's "claim" upon his life, that is, to deny to himself that he has any duty to take care of his own father, even to help pay for something better than a pauper's funeral. Nonetheless, the narrator continues to feel that his father does indeed have a claim upon him. And this claim is in part the fact that the narrator belongs to his own family and his own culture. This claim is the proof that, although he can "leave the island," he can never escape his personal or cultural roots; they will always hold a claim upon him, no matter how successfully he makes his way into the privileged socioeconomic world.

When, after the farewell party thrown by his friends, the narrator walks on the beach with his girlfriend, he continues to perceive his surroundings in terms which make reference to death. The beach they walk on is called "Gravesend Beach," echoing his own guilt over the fact that his father will be buried in a pauper's grave. He hears "the laughter of crabs scrambling among dead leaves and skeletons of other crabs." Later, he describes the docked fishing boats as "lifeless," as they are "taking a breather from the deaths of fishing."

As he waits in the airport terminal for his plane, the narrator wonders, "My father, is he dead yet?" The degree of his alienation from his father is expressed through the fact that he considers looking in the obituary column of a newspaper in order to find out if his own father had died yet. Even his mother encourages him to think of "leaving the island" as a justification for abandoning his father; she tells him, "Look, boy, leave the dead to live with the blasted dead, do! Leave the dead in this damn islan' place!" But, despite his own, and his mother's, insistence that "leaving the island" is a legitimate excuse for abandoning his father, he continues to express guilt and sadness over this departure. However, rather than directly expressing his own sadness that he is leaving, the narrator projects this sadness onto the strangers he sees around him at the airport; he sees only "the fear and the tears and the handshakes of other people's saying goodbye and the weeping of departure."

While he has stated that "leaving the island" for him represents "hope . . .school. . .and glory," the final image of the story expresses his feelings of emptiness and loneliness upon "leaving" his family and his roots. As he looks down from the plane, he sees only, "the sea, and the sea, and then the sea."

Source: Liz Brent, in an essay for *Literature of Developing Nations for Students*, Gale, 2000.

> Symbolically, however, the imminent death of his father, and his imminent departure from the island, represent the death of his ties to his family and to his cultural roots."

Sources

Boxill, Anthony, "Austin C. Clarke," in *Dictionary of Literary Biography*, Volume 53: *Canadian Writers since 1960*, Bruccoli Clark, Gale, 1986, pp. 124-29.

Further Reading

Clark, Austin C., *Amongst Thistles and Thorns*, Heinemann, 1965; McClelland & Stewart, 1965.
    Amongst Thistles and Thorns tells the story of a young boy growing up in Barbados.

———, *The Bigger Light*, Little, Brown, 1975.
    The Bigger Light is the last of Clark's "trilogy" following the fortunes of characters introduced in *The Survivors of the Crossing* and *Storm of Fortune*.

———, *The Meeting Point*, Heinemann, 1967; McClelland & Stewart, 1967.
    The Survivors of the Crossing is the first in Clark's so-called "trilogy" of works exploring the unique problems of West Indian immigrants.

———, *Storm of Fortune*, Little, Brown, 1973.
    Storm of Fortune is the second of Clark's "trilogy" is the second of Clark's "trilogy", following the fortunes of characters introduced in *The Meeting Point*.

Like Water for Chocolate

Laura Esquivel

1989

First published in 1989, Laura Esquivel's first novel, *Como agua para chocolate: novela de entregas mensuales con recetas, amores, y remedios caseros,* became a best-seller in the author's native Mexico. It has been translated into numerous languages, and the English version, *Like Water for Chocolate: A Novel in Monthly Installments, with Recipes, Romances and Home Remedies,* enjoyed similar success in the United States. The film version, scripted by the author and directed by her husband, Alfonso Arau, has become one of the most popular foreign films of the past few decades. In a *New York Times* interview, Esquivel told Marialisa Calta that her ideas for the novel came out of her own experiences in the kitchen: ''When I cook certain dishes, I smell my grandmother's kitchen, my grandmother's smells. I thought: what a wonderful way to tell a story.'' The story Esquivel tells is that of Tita De la Garza, a young Mexican woman whose world becomes her family's kitchen after her mother forbids her to marry the man she loves. Esquivel chronicles Tita's life from her teenage to middle-age years, as she submits to and eventually rebels against her mother's domination. Readers have praised the novel's imaginative mix of recipes, home remedies, and love story set in Mexico in the early part of the century. Employing the technique of magic realism, Esquivel has created a bittersweet tale of love and loss and a compelling exploration of a woman's search for identity and fulfillment.

Author Biography

Esquivel was born the third of four children of Julio Caesar Esquivel, a telegraph operator, and his wife Josephina in 1951 in Mexico. In an interview with Molly O'Neill in the *New York Times*, Esquivel explained, "I grew up in a modern home, but my grandmother lived across the street in an old house that was built when churches were illegal in Mexico. She had a chapel in the home, right between the kitchen and dining room. The smell of nuts and chilies and garlic got all mixed up with the smells from the chapel, my grandmother's carnations, the liniments and healing herbs." These experiences in her family's kitchen provided the inspiration for her first novel.

Esquivel grew up in Mexico City and attended the Escuela Normal de Maestros, the national teachers' college. After teaching school for eight years, Esquivel began writing and directing for children's theater. In the early 1980s she wrote the screenplay for the Mexican film *Chido One,* directed by her husband Alfonso Arau and released in 1985. Arau also directed her screenplay for *Like Water for Chocolate,* released in Mexico in 1989 and in the United States in 1993. First published in 1989, the novel version of *Like Water for Chocolate* became a best-seller in Mexico and the United States and has been translated into numerous languages. The film version has become one of the most popular foreign films of the past few decades. In her second, less successful novel, *Ley del amor,* published in English in 1996 as *The Law of Love,* Esquivel again creates a magical world where love becomes the dominant force of life. The novel includes illustrations and a compact disc of music to accompany it. Esquivel continues to write, working on screenplays and fiction from her home in Mexico City.

Laura Esquivel

old, and ending with her death at thirty-nine. Each chapter also includes a recipe that Tita prepares for her family during this period. After her mother refuses to allow her to marry the man she loves, Tita channels her frustrated desires into the creation of delicious meals that often have strange effects on her family. Through the expression of her culinary art, Tita learns to cope with and ultimately break free from her mother's domination.

Tita is born on her family's kitchen table, amid the fragrant and pungent odors of cooking. Since Tita's mother, Mama Elena, is unable to nurse her, Nacha, the family's cook, takes over the task of feeding her. "From that day on, Tita's domain was the kitchen" and "the joy of living [for her] was wrapped up in the delights of food."

When she is a teenager, Pedro Muzquiz comes to the family's ranch and asks for Tita's hand in marriage, but Mama Elena refuses his request. Ignoring Tita's protestations, Mama Elena forbids her to marry, insisting that she abide by the family tradition that forces the youngest daughter to stay home and care for her widowed mother until her mother dies. Mama Elena suggests that Pedro marry Rosaura instead and Pedro agrees, deciding that a marriage to her sister is the only way he can stay close to Tita.

Plot Summary

Chapters 1-4: Under Mama Elena's Rule

In Esquivel's *Like Water for Chocolate* the narrator chronicles the life of her great-aunt, Tita De la Garza, who lives in northern Mexico during the early part of the century. The novel's twelve chapters, written one per month in diary/installment form, relate details from over two decades of Tita's life, beginning in 1910, when she is fifteen years

Mama Elena orders Tita to cook the wedding feast. As she prepares the cake, her sorrow over the impending marriage causes her tears to fall into the batter and icing. Nacha later tastes the icing and immediately is "overcome with an intense longing" as she thinks about her fiancé, driven away by Mama Elena's mother. The next morning Tita finds the elderly Nacha lying dead, "a picture of her fiancé clutched in her hands."

Tita now becomes the official cook for the ranch. Soon after the wedding, Pedro gives Tita a bouquet of roses to ease her depression over Nacha's death. She clasps them to her so tightly that the thorns cut her and she bleeds on them. When her mother forbids her to keep them, Tita mixes the petals in a dish that acts as an aphrodisiac for all who eat it, except Rosaura. Her eldest sister, Gertrudis, becomes so aroused by the meal that she runs to the outside shower, but the heat emanating from her body causes the wooden shower walls to burst into flames. Her body also exudes the scent of roses, which attracts a passing revolutionary. He sweeps her up on his horse, still naked, and rides away with her. When Mama Elena discovers that Gertrudis started to work at a brothel soon after her disappearance from the ranch, she disowns her.

The following year, Tita prepares the celebration feast for the baptism of her nephew Roberto, son of Pedro and Rosaura. Tita had been the only one present at Roberto's birth, which left Rosaura precariously ill. Since Rosaura had no milk after the birth, Tita tried to feed him tea, but he refused it. One day, frustrated by his crying, Tita offers him her breast and is surprised to discover that she can nurse him. When Pedro observes Tita nursing his son, their secret moment together further bonds them. Tita's celebration feast generates a sense of euphoria in everyone who shares it—except Mama Elena, who suspects a secret relationship between Tita and Pedro. Her suspicions lead her to send Rosaura, Pedro, and Roberto to her cousin's home in San Antonio, Texas.

Chapters 5-8: Tita's Rebellion

After they leave, Tita loses "all interest in life," missing the nephew that was almost like her own child. One day rebels ride up to the ranch and ask for food. Mama Elena tells them they can have what they find outdoors, but they are not permitted in the house. Finding little, a sergeant decides to search inside. Mama Elena threatens him with her shotgun, and the captain, respecting her show of strength, stops him. Tita becomes even more de-pressed when she realizes the men took the doves that she had enjoyed caring for. Later that day as Tita prepares the family's meal, a servant appears and announces Roberto's death because "whatever he ate, it didn't agree with him and he died." When Tita collapses in tears, her mother tells her to go back to work. Tita rebels, saying she is sick of obeying her mother's orders. Mama Elena smacks her across the face with a wooden spoon and breaks her nose. Tita then blames her for Roberto's death and escapes to the dovecote. The next morning, Tita refuses to leave the dovecote and acts strangely. Mama Elena brings Dr. John Brown to remove her to an insane asylum, but, feeling sorry for her, he takes her to his home instead.

Tita is badly shaken and refuses to speak. As she sits in her room at John's home, she sees an old Native American woman making tea on the patio. They establish a silent communication with each other. Later she discovers the old woman is the spirit of John's dead grandmother, a Kikapu Indian who had healing powers. John tells Tita stories about how his family had ostracized his grandmother and about her theory that all people need love to nourish their souls. When John asks her why she does not speak, she writes, "because I don't want to," which becomes her first step toward freedom.

One day Chencha, the De la Garza family's servant, brings some soup for Tita, and the food and her visit return her to her senses. Chencha then tells her that Mama Elena has disowned her. She also gives Tita a letter from Gertrudis, who writes that she is leaving the brothel because "I know that I have to find the right place for myself somewhere." Later, Tita accepts John's marriage proposal. When Chencha returns to the ranch, bandits break in, rape her, and attack Mama Elena, who is left paralyzed. Tita returns to care for her mother, who feels humiliated because of her need for Tita's help. Tita carefully prepares meals for her, but they taste bitter to Mama Elena, who refuses to eat them. She accuses Tita of trying to poison her so that she will be free to marry John.

Within a month Mama Elena dies, probably due to the medicine she was secretly taking to try to counter the effect of the poison she thought she was being given. Sorting through her mother's things, Tita finds letters hidden in her closet that tell of a secret love affair with a man of black ancestry, and of the birth of their child, Gertrudis. At her funeral Tita weeps for her mother's lost love. Pedro and Rosaura return for the funeral and Pedro is angry that Tita and John are engaged. While at the ranch, Rosaura gives birth to Esperanza, who like Roberto must be cared for by Tita, since her mother has no milk. Rosaura determines that her daughter, like Tita, will care for her and never marry, which angers Tita. When John leaves to bring his aunt to meet Tita, she and Pedro consummate their love.

Chapters 9-12: Tita's Fulfillment

Later, when Tita suspects that she is pregnant, Mama Elena's spirit appears, warning her to stay away from Pedro. Gertrudis, now married and a general in the revolutionary army, returns for a visit. After Tita relates her fears for her future, Gertrudis insists she must follow her heart and thus find a way to be with Pedro. One night Pedro gets drunk and sings love songs outside Tita's window. A furious Mama Elena soon appears to Tita and threatens her. When Tita tells her mother she hates her, her mother's spirit shrinks to a tiny light. The apparent reduction of Mama Elena's control relieves Tita, which brings on menstruation and her realization that she is not pregnant. However, the tiny light begins to spin feverishly, causing an oil lamp to explode and engulf Pedro in flames. As Tita tends to his burns, Rosaura and John note the strong bond that still exists between them. Upset, Rosaura locks herself in her bedroom for a week.

John has returned with his aunt, wanting to introduce her to his fiancée. Tita prepares a meal for them, knowing she will have to disappoint them by calling off the wedding. When Pedro argues with her because she is taking such care with John's feelings, Tita is angered that he doubts her love. "Pedro had turned into a monster of selfishness and suspicion," she muses. That same morning Rosaura finally emerges from her room, having lost sixty-five pounds, and warns Tita not to make Rosaura look like a fool by carrying on with her husband in public. That afternoon Tita receives John and his Aunt Mary, and confesses that she has lost her virginity and cannot marry him. She also tells him that she does not know which man she loves best, as it changes depending on which man is nearer. John tells Tita that he still wants to marry her, and that she would live a happy life if she agreed to be his wife.

The narrative jumps to twenty years in the future as Tita is preparing a wedding feast. However, it is to celebrate the union of Esperanza and Alex, John's son. The death of Rosaura a year ago had freed Esperanza and Tita, making it possible for both to openly express their love. Tita's wedding

meal again stirs the passions of all who enjoy it. Pedro's feelings for her, however, have been repressed too long; when he is finally able to acknowledge his passion freely, it overwhelms him and he dies. Devastated by his death, Tita eats candles so she can light the same kind of fire within her, and soon joins him in death. The sparks the lovers give off burn down the ranch. When Esperanza returns from her wedding trip she finds Tita's cookbook and passes it down to her daughter, the narrator of the story, who insists that Tita "will go on living as long as there is someone who cooks her recipes."

Characters

Juan Alejandrez

Juan is a captain in the revolutionary army when he first sees Gertrudis. He is known for his bravery, but when he smells the scent of roses emanating from Gertrudis's body after she eats one of Tita's magical dishes, he leaves the battlefield for the ranch. Juan sweeps Gertrudis up on his horse and carries her away from her home and her mother's tyranny. The two later marry and return for a visit to the ranch as generals.

Alex Brown

He is the son of Dr. John Brown; his mother died during his birth. He marries Esperanza Muzquiz, daughter of Pedro Muzquiz and Rosaura De la Garza, at the novel's end.

Dr. John Brown

The family doctor who lives in Eagle Pass. When he comes to attend Rosaura after Roberto's birth, he is astounded by Tita's beauty as well as her ability to assist her nephew's difficult birth. He returns to the ranch when Mama Elena De la Garza calls him to take Tita to an insane asylum. He instead takes Tita to his home and nurses her back to health. Tita responds to his kindness and patience and agrees to marry him. His understanding of her dilemma after she confesses her infidelity with Pedro leads her to reconsider her decision to call off the wedding: "What a fine man he was. How he had grown in her eyes! And how the doubts had grown in her head!" At the last minute, however, she realizes that her love for Pedro is stronger than her affection for John.

Gertrudis De la Garza

Gertrudis De la Garza is Tita's strong-willed, free-spirited sister. The eldest of the sisters, she is a passionate woman who takes sensual pleasure from life. Tita's cooking arouses such strong emotions in her that she runs off with a soldier in the revolutionary army and thus away from her mother's oppression. When Mama Elena discovers that Gertrudis is working at a brothel soon after her disappearance from the ranch, she disowns her. It is only after Mama Elena's death that Tita ironically discovers that Gertrudis was the product of their mother's illicit affair with a half-black man. Gertrudis returns to the ranch after Mama Elena's death, now married and a general in the revolutionary army. She advises Tita to follow her heart as she has done.

Mama Elena De la Garza

Mama Elena De la Garza is the tyrannical, authoritarian, middle-class matron who runs her daughters' lives along with the family ranch. She not only enforces the tradition that compels the youngest daughter to care for her widowed mother for the remainder of her life, she compounds Tita's suffering by forcing her to prepare the wedding feast for Pedro and her sister. Suspecting a secret relationship between Pedro and Tita, she sends Rosaura, Pedro, and Roberto to her cousin's in San Antonio. When Roberto subsequently dies, Tita blames her mother because she separated the child from Tita, who fed and nurtured him. Mama Elena doles out severe beatings and/or banishment from the family in response to any acts of rebellion. She beats Tita after the wedding guests eat Tita's meal and become ill, and breaks her nose with a wooden spoon when Tita blames her for Roberto's death. She banishes Tita from the ranch after Tita shows signs of madness and banishes Gertrudis for working in a brothel. Her need for control over her daughters is so strong that it does not end with her death. Her spirit appears to Tita to warn her to stay away from Pedro. When Tita refuses, Mama Elena becomes so angry that she causes Pedro to be severely burned. Her proud and stubborn nature also emerges after the bandits who raid the ranch injure her health. She feels humiliated by her need for Tita's assistance and thus cannot accept her daughter's offer of food and comfort—a rejection that ultimately leads to her death. Mama Elena does appear more human, however, when Tita discovers letters in her closet that reveal a secret passionate love affair from her past. After her lover and her husband died, Mama Elena suppressed her sorrow and never again was able to accept love.

Rosaura De la Garza

The middle of the three sisters, Rosaura De la Garza marries the man Tita loves. Maria Elena de Valdes, in her article in *World Literature Today,* notes that Rosaura tries to model herself after Mama Elena in her treatment of Tita and Esperanza. She becomes, however, ''an insignificant imitation of her mother. She lacks the strength, skill, and determination of Mama Elena.'' She also lacks her mother's passion. Tita discovers that Mama Elena has suffered from the loss of her true love and suppressed her emotions. Rosaura, on the other hand, never seems to display any capacity for love. Rosaura does, however, share some similarities with her mother. Like Mama Elena, she is unable to provide nurturance for her children. Tita must provide sustenance for both of Rosaura's children, just as Nacha had done for Tita. Also, Rosaura dies as her mother did, because of her inability to accept nurturance in the form of food from Tita.

Tita De la Garza

Tita De la Garza is the obedient but strong-willed youngest daughter of Mama Elena. On the surface she accepts her mother's dictates, even when they cause her to suffer the loss of the man she loves. Yet, she subtly rebels by rechannelling her feelings for him into the creation of delicious meals that express her passionate and giving nature. She obeys her mother's order to throw away the roses Pedro has given her but not before she creates an exquisite sauce from the petals. Through her cooking, she successfully communicates to Pedro her love for him. Tita's caring and forgiving nature emerges as she takes over the feeding of Rosaura's two children when their mother is unable to nurse them and as she tends to her mother after being banished from the ranch. Even after Mama Elena accuses Tita of trying to poison her so she will be free to marry John, Tita patiently prepares her meals. When Rosaura suffers from severe digestive problems, Tita also comes to her aid. Even while Rosaura rails against Tita about her feelings for Pedro and threatens to send Esperanza away to school, Tita serves a special diet to help her sister lose weight and ease her suffering. Tita does, however, have a breaking point. Her strength crumbles when Mama Elena sends Pedro, Roberto, and Rosaura away and later she hears the news of Roberto's death, which pushes her into madness. After she regains her sanity, she seems to redouble her will. She stands up to Mama Elena's spirit and thus refuses to be influenced by her. She also holds her own with Rosaura, and works out an arrangement where she can continue to have a relationship with Pedro and Esperanza. Her passion, however, is her most apparent characteristic. For over two decades, her intense feelings for Pedro never fade. Tita ultimately sacrifices her life for him when she lights herself on fire after his death so that their souls can forever be united.

Paquita Lobo

The De la Garzas' neighbor, who has unusually sharp senses. She is able to tell something is wrong with Tita when she is overcome by Pedro's presence at their first meeting. She also suggests that Tita appears pregnant at the very time when Tita suspects the same thing.

Morning Light

John Brown's grandmother, a Kikapu Indian whom his grandfather had captured and brought back to live with him. Rejected by his grandfather's proud, intensely Yankee family, Morning Light spent most of her time studying the curative properties of plants. After her medicines saved John's great-grandfather's life, the family and the community accepted her as a miracle healer. While at John's home, Tita sees her, or her spirit, making tea on the patio. As Tita spends time with her, they establish a silent communication with each other. Her spirit helps calm Tita. Later John tells Tita about his grandmother's theory that we all need love to nourish our souls: "Each of us is born with a box of matches inside us but we can't strike them all by ourselves. . . . Each person has to discover what will set off those explosions in order to live." Tita comes to accept and live by this theory.

Esperanza Muzquiz

Pedro's and Rosaura's daughter. Tita insists that they name her Esperanza instead of her own name, Josefita, because she does not want to "influence her destiny." Nevertheless, her mother tries to impose the same kind of fate that her grandmother imposed on Tita, but Rosaura's death frees Esperanza to marry Alex Brown, the man she loves.

Pedro Muzquiz

Pedro Muzquiz marries Tita's sister Rosaura only so he can stay close to Tita. He loves Tita, but shows little strength of character. He allows Mama Elena to run his life and separate him from the woman he loves. He also observes Tita's suffering under Mama Elena's domination and does little to intervene on her behalf. At one point Tita berates

him for not having the courage to run off with her instead of marrying Rosaura. Marisa Januzzi, in her article in *The Review of Contemporary Fiction,* claims that "Pedro sometimes seems so unimaginative that only in fantasy . . . could such an underdeveloped male character and magical ending satisfy Tita."

Roberto Muzquiz

First child of Pedro and Rosaura. Tita establishes a mother-child bond with him when his mother is too ill to feed him. When Pedro observes Tita nursing his son, their relationship is further strengthened. After Roberto's death, Tita is unable to cope with the sorrow and descends into madness.

Nacha

Nacha cooks for the De La Garza family and their ranch. Soon after she is born, Tita establishes a close relationship with Nacha. Since Tita's mother is unable to nurse her, Nacha takes over the task of feeding her and exposes her to the magical world of the kitchen. During her childhood, Tita often escapes her mother's overbearing presence and finds comfort in Nacha's company. Nacha becomes Tita's surrogate mother and the kitchen her playground and schoolhouse as Nacha passes down traditional Mexican recipes to her. Unfortunately, Tita loses Nacha's support when, after tasting the icing Tita has prepared for Rosaura's wedding cake, Nacha is "overcome with an intense longing" for her lost love, and she dies of a broken heart. Her spirit continues to assist Tita after her death, however, coming to her aid when she is delivering Rosaura's first baby.

Narrator

Esperanza's daughter and Tita's grandniece. The narrator explains that her mother found Tita's cookbook in the ruins of the De la Garza ranch. Esperanza told her daughter the story of Tita's life as she prepared the cookbook's recipes. The narrator has combined those recipes and the stories her mother told her about Tita, explaining that Tita "will go on living as long as there is someone who cooks her recipes."

José Trevio

José Treviño was the love of Mama Elena's life. Because he was mulatto—half-black—her parents forbade her to see him and forced her to marry Juan De la Garza instead. Mama Elena continued a relationship with him, however, and Gertrudis is his daughter. Tita only discovers this secret relationship after her mother's death.

Themes

Duty and Responsibility

The first chapter begins the novel's exploration of the theme of duty, responsibility, and tradition as it presents Tita's main conflict. Family tradition requires that she reject Pedro's marriage proposal so she can stay at home and take care of her widowed mother for the rest of her life. If she turns her back on this tradition, she will not fulfill what society considers her responsibility to her mother. Rosaura decides that she also will enforce this tradition for her daughter Esperanza and so prevent her from marrying Alex Brown. Tita recognizes, however, that the tradition is unfair; if she cannot marry and have children, who will support her in her old age? She tells Rosaura that she will go against tradition as long as she has to, ''as long as this cursed tradition doesn't take me into account.'' Nevertheless, she and Pedro respect his duty toward his wife and child, for they remain discreet in their love as long as she lives.

Obedience

In order to fulfill her responsibilities toward her mother, Tita must obey her—a difficult task, given Mama Elena's authoritative nature. Mama Elena makes harsh demands on Tita throughout her life and expects her to obey without question. Tita has never had the ''proper deference'' towards her mother, Mama Elena feels, and so she is particularly harsh on her youngest daughter. Even when Tita sews a ''perfect creation'' for the wedding, Mama Elena makes her rip out the seam and do it over because she did not baste it first, as Mama instructed. After Mama Elena decides that Pedro will marry Rosaura, she insists that Tita cook the wedding feast, knowing how difficult that task will be for her. When Nacha dies, Mama Elena decides Tita must take full responsibility for the meals on the ranch, which leaves Tita little time for anything else. Tita's struggle to determine what is the proper degree of obedience due to her mother is a major conflict in the novel.

Cruelty and Violence

Mama Elena often resorts to cruelty and violence as she forces Tita to obey her. Many of the responsibilities she imposes on Tita, especially those relating to Pedro and Rosaura's wedding, are blatant acts of cruelty, given Tita's pain over losing Pedro. Mama Elena meets Tita's slightest protest with angry tirades and beatings. Even when she just suspects that Tita has not fulfilled her duties, as when she thought that Tita intentionally ruined the wedding cake, she beats her. When Tita dares to stand up to her mother and to blame her for Roberto's death, Mama Elena smacks her across the face with a wooden spoon and breaks her nose. This everyday cruelty does not seem so unusual, however, in a land where a widow must protect herself and her family from bandits and revolutionaries.

Victim and Victimization

When Mama Elena coerces Tita into obeying her cruel dictates, she victimizes her. Tita becomes a victim of Mama Elena's obsessive need for power and control. Mama Elena confines Tita to the kitchen, where her life consists of providing for the needs of others. She rejects Tita's individuality and tries to force her to suppress her sense of selfhood. Tita's growth as an individual depends on her ability to free herself from the role of victim.

Sex Roles

The novel closely relates Tita's victimization to the issue of sex roles. When Tita's mother confines her to the kitchen, she relegates her to a limited domestic sphere. There Tita's role becomes a traditionally female one—that of selfless nurturer, placing the needs of others before her own. In this limited role, Tita struggles to find a sense of identity. When Tita is taken to Dr. Brown's house, she marvels at her hands, for she discovers ''she could move them however she pleased.'' At the ranch, ''what she had to do with her hands was strictly determined.'' She learns of Dr. Brown's grandmother, Morning Light, who experimented with herbs and became a respected healer.

Love and Passion

The forces of love and passion conflict with Tita's desire to fulfill her responsibilities toward her mother. In obeying her mother, Tita must suppress her feelings for Pedro. Her sister Gertrudis, on the other hand, allows herself to express her passion freely when she runs off with Juan and soon begins work at a brothel. Tita's and Gertrudis's passionate natures also emerge through their enjoyment of food. Both relish good meals, although Tita is the only one who knows how to prepare one. At one point, Gertrudis brings the revolutionary army to the De la Garza ranch so she can sample her sister's hot chocolate, cream fritters, and other recipes. This parallel of passion for love and passion for food can be carried over to the love of John Brown for Tita. Although he is captivated by her beauty, he feels no passionate jealousy over her relationship with Pedro. He comes from a North American family where the food, as Tita finds, "is bland and didn't appeal."

Sanity and Insanity

As the need to obey her mother clashes with her own desires, Tita begins to lose her sanity. When Mama Elena sends Rosaura, Pedro, and Roberto away, Tita loses all interest in life. The news of Roberto's death pushes her over the edge and she escapes to the dovecote, refusing to come out. When John removes her from the oppressive atmosphere her mother has created, and he and Chencha offer her comfort and love, her sanity returns. Mama Elena never questions her own state of mind, although she is obsessive in her need to dominate her daughters. When Tita is found in the dovecote, Mama Elena ironically states that "there's no place in this house for maniacs!"

Creativity and Imagination

Through Tita's creativity in the kitchen, she finds an outlet for her suppressed emotions. Thus, ironically, while Mama Elena tries to control Tita by confining her to the kitchen and forcing her to prepare all of the family's meals, Tita is also able to strengthen her relationship with others and to gain a clearer sense of herself. She pours all of her passion for Pedro into her meals, which helps to further bond the two. Her cooking also creates a bond with Pedro's two children, easing the pain over not being able to have children of her own with him. Tita's imaginative cooking is also a way for her to rebel against her mother; she recalls that whenever she failed to follow a recipe exactly, "she was always sure . . . that Mama Elena would find out and, instead of congratulating her on her creativity, give her a terrible tongue-lashing for disobeying the rules."

Supernatural

The final important element of the novel is Esquivel's use of the supernatural. Tita's magical dishes, which produce waves of longing and uncontrollable desire, become a metaphor for creativity and self-expression. Like an artist, Tita pours herself into her cooking and produces works of art that evoke strong emotions in others. Her careful preparation of her family's food also reveals her loving nature. Another supernatural aspect, the spirits of the dead that appear to Tita throughout the novel, suggest that one's influence does not disappear after death. Nacha's spirit helps give Tita confidence when she needs it, much like Nacha had done while she was alive. Mama Elena's spirit tries to control Tita from the grave, making her feel guilty about her passion for Pedro.

Style

Point of View

In fiction, the point of view is the perspective from which the story is presented. The unique point of view in *Like Water for Chocolate* helps convey the significance of the narrative. Esperanza, Tita De la Garza's niece, finds her aunt's cookbook in the ruins of the De la Garza ranch. As she recreates the recipes in her own home, she passes down to her daughter the family stories. Her daughter becomes the novel's narrator as she intersperses her great-aunt's recipes, remedies, and experiences into one book. She justifies her unique narrative when she explains that Tita "will go on living as long as there is someone who cooks her recipes."

Setting

The turbulent age of rebellion in Mexico provides an appropriate setting for the novel's focus on tyranny and resistance. Soldiers, bandits, and rebels are regularly mentioned in the novel, and often make actual appearances important to the narrative. It is a bandit's attack, for instance, which compels Tita's return home after her mother has disowned her. As Pancho Villa's revolutionary forces clash with the oppressive Mexican regime, Tita wages her own battle against her mother's dictates.

Structure

The narrative structure, or form, of the novel intersperses Tita's story with the recipes and remedies that figure so prominently in her life. By placing an actual recipe at the beginning of each chapter, the author is reinforcing the importance of food to the narrative. This structure thus attests to the female bonding and creativity that can emerge within a focus on the domestic arts.

Symbolism

A symbol is an object or image that suggests or stands for another object or person. Food provides the dominant symbol in the novel, especially as expressed in the title. "Like water for (hot) chocolate" is a Mexican expression that literally means water at the boiling point and figuratively means intense emotions on the verge of exploding into expression. Throughout the novel, Tita's passion for Pedro is "like water for chocolate" but is constantly repressed by her dictatorial mother. An incident that symbolizes Mama Elena's oppression occurs when Tita is preparing two hundred roosters for the wedding feast. As she castrates live roosters to insure that they will be fat and tender enough for the guests, the violent and gruesome process makes her swoon and shake with anger. She admits "when they had chosen something to be neutered, they'd made a mistake, they should have chosen her. At least then there would be some justification for not allowing her to marry and giving Rosaura her place beside the man she loved." Food becomes a symbol of Tita's love for Pedro as she uses it to communicate her feelings. Even though Tita remains confined to the kitchen, her creative preparation of the family's meals continues to serve as the vehicle of her love for Pedro and his children, and thus as an expression of her rebellion against her mother's efforts to separate them.

Style

Magic realism is a fictional style, popularized by Colombian author Gabriel García Márquez, that appears most often in Latin American literature. Authors who use this technique mingle the fantastic or bizarre with the realistic. Magic realism often involves time shifts, dreams, myths, fairy tales, surrealistic descriptions, the element of surprise and shock, and the inexplicable. Examples of magic realism in *Like Water for Chocolate* occur when Tita's recipes have strange effects on those who eat them, when spirits appear to her, and when she cries actual rivers of tears. The fantastic element in Tita's cooking is that it produces such strong emotions in her family. The art of cooking, however, does reflect the patience and talent of the cook—qualities that are appreciated by those who enjoy the results. The spirits who appear to Tita symbolize the long-lasting effects of those who influence our lives and our own feelings of responsibility and guilt.

Foreshadowing

Foreshadowing is a literary device used to create an expectation or explanation of future events. In *Like Water for Chocolate,* foreshadowing occurs when John tells Tita about his grandmother's theory of love and life. She said that "each of us is born with a box of matches inside us but we can't strike them all by ourselves." We need the breath of the person we love to light them and thus nourish our souls. She warns, however, that lighting the matches all at once would be fatal. This process occurs at the end of the novel when Pedro's suppressed passion for Tita is finally "lit," and the intense flame is too much for him to bear.

Paradox

A paradox is a statement or situation that seems contradictory or absurd, but is actually true. The kitchen becomes a paradoxical symbol in the novel. On the one hand, it is a place where Tita is confined exclusively to domestic tasks, a place that threatens to deny her a sense of identity. Yet it is also a nurturing and creative domain, providing Tita with an outlet for her passions and providing others with sustenance and pleasure.

Literary Heritage

Magic realism is a fictional style, popularized by Gabriel Garcia Marquez, that appears most often in South American literature. This style may have emerged from the mystification of Latin America that occurred during colonization, as many Europeans chronicled strange and supernatural occurrences in the new land. The term was first associated with the arts and later extended to literature. In the 1920s and '30s, Latin American artists were influenced by the surrealist movement and so incorporated the style into their art. Authors who use this technique mingle the fantastic or bizarre with the realistic. Magic realism often involves time shifts, dreams, myths, fairy tales, surrealistic descriptions, the element of surprise and shock, and the inexplicable. Often something common converts into something unreal or strange in order to reveal the inherent mystery in life. The writer, however, usually creates a supernatural atmosphere without denying the natural world—a paradox characters appear to accept without question.

Historical Context

The Mexican Revolution

Although Mexico had been independent from Spain since the early nineteenth century, their governments were continually beset by internal and external conflicts. In the early part of the twentieth century, revolution tore the country apart. In November 1910, liberal leader Francisco Madero led a successful revolt against Mexican President Porfirio Díaz after having lost a rigged election. Díaz soon resigned and Madero replaced him as president in November 1911. Considered ineffectual by both conservatives and liberals, Madero was soon overthrown and executed by his general, Victoriano Huerta. Soon after the tyrannical Huerta became president, his oppressive regime came under attack. Venustiano Carranza, Francisco "Pancho" Villa, and Emiliano Zapata led revolts against the government. In 1914 Carranza became president as civil war erupted. By the end of 1915, the war ended, but Villa and Zapata continued to oppose the new government and maintained rebel groups for several years.

A Woman's Place

Richard Corliss, in his *Time* review of *Like Water for Chocolate,* writes that "Laura Esquivel brought Gabriel García Márquez's brand of magic realism into the kitchen and the bedroom, the Latin woman's traditional castle and dungeon." Traditionally, a Latin woman's place was in the home. In the patriarchal society of the early part of the twentieth century, Mexican women were expected to serve their fathers and brothers and then when married, their husbands, sons, and daughters. These women often turned to the domestic arts—cooking, sewing, and interior decoration—for creative outlets, along with storytelling, gossip, and advice. As a result, they created their own female culture within the social prison of married life.

Maria Elena de Valdes, in her article on *Like Water for Chocolate* in *World Literature Today,* notes that little has changed for the Mexican woman. She defines the model Mexican rural, middle-class woman: "She must be strong and far more clever than the men who supposedly protect her. She must be pious, observing all the religious requirements of a virtuous daughter, wife, and mother. She must exercise great care to keep her sentimental relations as private as possible, and, most important of all, she must be in control of life in her house, which means essentially the kitchen and bedroom or food and sex."

Reading women's magazines became a popular pastime for many married Mexican women. These magazines often contained fiction published in monthly installments, poetry, recipes, home remedies, sewing and decoration tips, advice, and a calendar of religious observances. Valdes find similarities between the structure of *Like Water for Chocolate* and these magazines. She explains that "since home and church were the private and public sites of all educated young ladies, these publications represented the written counterpart to women's socialization, and as such, they are documents that conserve and transmit a Mexican female culture in which the social context and cultural space are particularly for women by women."

Critical Overview

When *Como agua para chocolate: novela de entregas mensuales con recetas, arores, y remedios caseros* was published by Editorial Planeta Mexicana in Mexico in 1989, it quickly became a best seller. The 1991 English version, *Like Water for Chocolate: A Novel in Monthly Installments, with Recipes, Romances and Home Remedies,* translated by Carol and Thomas Christensen, also gained commercial success. The novel has been translated into several other languages.

Critical reception has been generally strong, especially when noting Esquivel's imaginative narrative structure. Karen Stabiner states in the *Los Angeles Times Book Review* that the novel is a "wondrous, romantic tale, fueled by mystery and superstition, as well as by the recipes that introduce each chapter." James Polk, in his review in the *Chicago Tribune,* describes the work as an "inventive and mischievous romp—part cookbook, part novel." Marisa Januzzi similarly notes in her assessment in the *Review of Contemporary Fiction* that "this short novel's got more heat and light and imaginative spice than the American literary diet usually provides."

Few scholarly articles, however, have been published on the novel. Molly O'Neill, in her interview with Esquivel in the *New York Times,* notes that American critics often consign the novel to the "'charming but aren't we moderns above it' ghetto of magical realism." Scholars also may have avoided

Lumi Cavazos holds a small baby in Alfonso Arau's film adaptation of Like Water for Chocolate.

the novel because of what some consider its melodramatic tone. In a mixed review for the *Nation,* Ilan Stavans finds a "convoluted sentimentality" in the novel.

The articles that have been published praise the novel's cultural focus. Ilan Stavans, in the same *Nation* review, observes that the novel accurately "map[s] the trajectory of feminist history in Mexican society." Maria Elena de Valdes, in her article in *World Literature Today,* argues that the novel contains an intricate structure that serves as an effective parody of Mexican women's fiction. She also praises its main theme: "a woman's creation of space that is hers in a hostile world." Victor Zamudio-Taylor insists the work is one of those that "reactualize tradition, make different women's voices heard, and revitalize identity—both personal and collective—as a social and national cultural construction."

Esquivel's screenplay of *Like Water for Chocolate,* along with her husband Alfonso Arau's direction, helped the film become one of the most successful foreign films of the past few decades. Esquivel has also written the screenplay for the popular Mexican film *Chido One.* Her most recent novel, *The Law of Love,* again focuses on the importance

of love and incorporates the technique of magic realism. Reviews of the novel have been mixed. Barbara Hoffert argues in her *Library Journal* review that the novel "is at once wildly inventive and slightly silly, energetic and cliched." Lilian Pizzichini, however, writes in her review in the *Times Literary Supplement,* "Esquivel dresses her ancient story in a collision of literary styles that confirm her wit and ingenuity. She sets herself a mission to explore the redemptive powers of love and art and displays boundless enthusiasm for parody."

Criticism

Wendy Perkins

Perkins, Associate Professor of English at Prince George's Community College in Maryland, explores how Esquivel's use of magic realism in Like Water for Chocolate *reinforces the novel's celebration and condemnation of domesticity.*

In an interview with Laura Esquivel, published in the *New York Times Book Review,* Molly O'Neill notes that *Like Water for Chocolate* has not received

What Do I Read Next?

- Esquivel's second novel, 1996's *The Law of Love,* opens with the sixteenth-century Spanish conquest of Tenochtitlan, the future site of Mexico City. Many centuries later the reincarnations of this earlier drama confront each other as an astroanalyst, her missing soulmate, and a planetary presidential candidate.

- *The House of the Spirits* (1982) by Chilean Isabel Allende is a magical story about a Latin American family that survives internal and external pressures.

- Whitney Otto's 1991 novel *How to Make an American Quilt* focuses on women sharing the stories of their lives as they sit together and sew a quilt.

- *One Hundred Years of Solitude,* written by Colombian Nobel laureate Gabriel García Márquez in 1967, is considered the classic example of magic realism. This novel explores several generations of a Latin American family set against the age of revolution.

- The recipes in Ntozake Shange's 1982 novel, *Sassafras, Cypress & Indigo,* become part of the plot which focuses on the lives of three sisters.

- Shirlene Ann Soto's 1990 study *Emergence of the Modern Mexican Woman: Her Participation in Revolution and Struggle for Equality, 1910-1940* provides a good look at the varied roles of Mexican women during the time period of the novel.

---

a great deal of critical attention because it is "often consigned to the 'charming but aren't we moderns above it' ghetto of magical realism." Some critics, however, recognize the importance of the novel's themes: Ilan Stavans, in his review of the novel for *The Nation*, praises its mapping of "the trajectory of feminist history in Mexican society." In an article in *World Literature Today,* Maria Elena de Valdes argues that the novel reveals how a woman's culture can be created and maintained "within the social prison of marriage." Esquivel's unique narrative design is also worthy of critical attention. Her employment of magic realism, with its mingling of the fantastic and the real, provides an apt vehicle for the exploration of the forces of rebellion, submission, and retribution and of the domestic sphere that can both limit and encourage self-expression.

Tita De la Garza, the novel's central character, makes her entrance into the world in her mother's kitchen, and this female realm becomes both a creative retreat and a prison for her. As a site for the crucial link between food and life, the kitchen becomes the center of Tita's world. Here she gains

physical and emotional sustenance as Nacha, the family's servant and Tita's surrogate mother, teaches her the art of cooking. The kitchen also, however, becomes a site of oppression when Tita's mother forbids her to marry the man she loves and forces her into the role of family cook. The novel's public and private realms merge under the symbol of rebellion. As Pancho Villa's revolutionary forces clash with the oppressive Mexican regime, Tita wages her own battle against her mother's dictates. As Tita prepares magical dishes that stir strong emotions in all who enjoy them, the kitchen becomes an outlet for her thwarted passion. Thus the kitchen becomes a site for hunger and fulfillment. Yet Tita's cooking does not nourish all who sample it. In some instances her meals exact a certain retribution for her confinement to this domestic arena.

Throughout Tita's childhood "the joy of living was wrapped up in the delights of food." The kitchen was her domain, the place where Nacha taught her the domestic and communal rituals of food preparation and encouraged her creative input. Here she lovingly prepares meals for her family, including her sister's children, who thrive under her care. The narrative structure of the novel attests to the female bonding and creativity that can emerge within this domestic realm. The narrator, Tita's grandniece, intersperses Tita's story with the recipes that figure so prominently in her life.

The kitchen, however, soon becomes a site of repression for Tita when her mother, Mama Elena, refuses to allow her to marry. Here the mother-daughter relationship enacts a structure of political authority and submission when Mama Elena enforces the family tradition that compels the youngest daughter to care for her widowed mother for the remainder of her life. Thus the walls of the kitchen restrict Tita's life as she resigns herself to the role of cook for her mother as well as the other members of her family. An incident that symbolizes Mama Elena's oppression occurs when Tita is preparing two hundred roosters for the wedding feast. Mama Elena has compounded Tita's despair over losing Pedro by announcing that her sister, Rosaura, will marry Pedro instead, and that Tita will cook for the wedding party. One task Tita must complete is the castration of live roosters to ensure that they will be fat and tender enough for the guests. The violent and gruesome process makes Tita swoon and shake with anger, as she thinks "when they had chosen something to be neutered, they'd made a mistake, they should have chosen her. At least then there would be some justification for not allowing her to marry and giving Rosaura her place beside the man she loved."

Yet ironically, Tita's passion for Pedro, her lost love, and her independent spirit find a creative and rebellious outlet in this same domestic realm. While Mama Elena successfully represses Tita's public voice, she cannot quell the private expression of her emotion. Tita subconsciously redefines her domestic space, transforming it from a site of repression into one of expression when she is forced to prepare her sister's wedding dinner. This time her creativity results in an act of retribution. As she completes the wedding cake, her sorrow over Rosaura's impending marriage to Pedro causes her tears to spill into the icing. This alchemic mixture effects the entire wedding party: "The moment they took their first bite of the cake, everyone was flooded with a great wave of longing. . . . Mama Elena, who hadn't shed a single tear over her husband's death, was sobbing silently. But the weeping was just the first symptom of a strange intoxication—an acute attack of pain and frustration—that seized the guests and scattered them across the patio and the grounds and in the bathrooms, all of them wailing over lost love."

Thus Tita effectively, if not purposely, ruins her sister's wedding.

The kitchen also becomes an outlet for Tita's repressed passion for Pedro. After Pedro gives Tita a bouquet of pink roses, Tita clutches them to her chest so tightly "that when she got to the kitchen, the roses, which had been mostly pink, had turned quite red from the blood that was flowing from [her] hands and breasts." She then creates a sauce from these stained petals that she serves over quail. The dish elicits a unique response from each member of her family that reflects and intensifies hidden desires or the lack thereof: Pedro "couldn't help closing his eyes in voluptuous delight," while Rosaura, a woman who does not appear to have the capacity for love, becomes nauseous.

The most startling response comes from Tita's other sister, Gertrudis, who responds to the food as an aphrodisiac. Unable to bear the heat emanating from her body, Gertrudis runs from the table, tears off her clothes, and attempts to cool herself in the shower. Her body radiates so much heat, however, that the wooden walls of the shower "split and burst into flame." Her perfumed scent carries across the plain and attracts a revolutionary soldier, who swoops her up, naked, onto his horse and rides off with her, freeing her, if not her sister, from Mama Elena's oppression. Private and public worlds merge as Gertrudis escapes the confinements of her life on the farm and begins a journey of self-discovery that results in her success as a revolutionary general. The meal of rose petals and quail also intensifies the passion between Tita and Pedro and initiates a new system of communication between them that will help sustain their love while they are physically separated. Even though Tita remains confined to the kitchen, her creative preparation of the family's meals continues to serve as the vehicle of her love for Pedro, and thus as an expression of her rebellion against her mother's efforts to separate the two. Her cooking also continues to exact retribution against those who have contributed to her suffering.

When Rosaura and Pedro move away from the ranch, Tita's confinement to the kitchen drives her mad, and she leaves in an effort to regain her sanity. She later returns to the ranch and to the domestic realm, willingly, to care for Mama Elena, who has become an invalid. This willingness to return to the kitchen, coupled with her mother's need for her, empowers her, yet her mother continues her battle for authority. Even though Tita prepares her mother's meals carefully, Mama Elena cannot stand the taste and thus refuses to eat. Convinced that Tita intends to poison her slowly in order to be free to marry, she continues to refuse all nourishment and soon conveniently dies—suggesting the cause to be either her refusal to accept Tita's offer of love and nourishment, or the food itself. Esquivel leaves this question unanswered.

When Rosaura and Pedro return to the ranch after Mama Elena's death, Tita again resumes her role as family cook. Even though she has decided to stay in the kitchen and not run off with Pedro so as not to hurt her sister, she ultimately, albeit unwittingly, causes her sister's death. Tita confronts her sister over her part in aiding Mama Elena's efforts to separate Tita from the man she loves. Rosaura, however, refuses to acknowledge her role in her sister's oppression and threatens to leave with Pedro and her daughter, whom Tita has grown to love as her own. As a result Tita wishes "with all her heart that her sister would be swallowed up by the earth. That was the least she deserved." As Tita continues to cook for the family, Rosaura begins to have severe digestive problems. Tita shows concern over her sister's health and tries to alter her diet to ease her suffering. But Rosaura's severe flatulence and bad breath continue unabated, to the point where her husband and child cannot stand to be in the same room with her. Rosaura's suffering increases until one evening Pedro finds "her lips purple, body deflated, eyes wild, with a distant look, sighing out her last flatulent breath." The doctor determines the cause of death as "an acute congestion of the stomach."

Here Esquivel again, as she had after Mama Elena's death, leaves the question of cause open. Rosaura could have died from a diseased system, compounded by her inability to receive and provide love and comfort. Or she could have died as a direct result of Tita's subconscious efforts to poison her. Either way, Rosaura's death releases Tita from the oppressive nature of her domestic realm and allows her to continue to express herself through her cooking.

In *Like Water for Chocolate,* magic realism becomes an appropriate vehicle for the expression of the paradoxical nature of the kitchen as domestic space. This novel reveals how the kitchen can become a nurturing and creative domain, providing sustenance and pleasure for others; a site for repression, where one can be confined exclusively to domestic tasks and lose or be denied a sense of self; and a site for rebellion against traditional boundaries.

Source: Wendy Perkins, in an essay for *Literature of Developing Nations for Students*, Gale, 2000.

Ksenija Bilbija

In this excerpt, Bilbija examines traditional feminine and masculine roles as they are presented in Like Water for Chocolate.

When Virginia Woolf argues in *A Room of One's Own* for an appropriate and pertinent place for a woman, she never mentions the kitchen as a possible space in which her intellectual liberation from the patriarchal system could be enacted. At first glance, this area had always been assigned to a wife, servant, daughter, slave, mother, grandmother, sister or an aunt. For feminists, the kitchen has come to symbolize the world that traditionally marginalized and limited a woman. It represents a space associated with repetitive work, lacking any "real" creativity, and having no possibility for the fulfillment of women's existential needs, individualization or self-expression. . . .

A different, quite parodic and critical gender perspective has been presented in several recently published (cook)books by Latin American women writers. Laura Esquivel's *Como agua para chocolate: Novela de entregas mensuales con recetas, amores y remedios caseros* (1989) (*Like Water for Chocolate: A Novel in Monthly Installments with Recipes, Romances and Home Remedies*) and Silvia Plager's *Como papas para varenikes: Novela contraentregas mensuales, en tarjeta o efectivo. Romances apasionados, recetas judías con poder afrodisíaco y chimentos* (*Like Potatoes for Varenike: A Novel in Monthly Installments, Cash or Charge. Passionate Romances, Jewish Recipes With Aphrodisiac Power and Gossips*) (1994) have tried to revise stereotypical power relations and interpretations of male and female identity symbols. After all, alchemy and cooking probably did not always have rooms of their own, but may have shared the same transformative space.

In these novels the mythical, homogenized wholeness of Latin American identity posited by García Márquez, along with the exploration of its origins *vis-a-vis* Europe, becomes fragmented. The power of medieval alchemy, introduced by a vagabond tribe of gypsies who paradoxically bring the spirit of Western modernity, is parodically replaced by different ethnic cuisines: Aztec in the case of the Mexican writer and Jewish in the Argentine example. Both gastrotexts can be labeled as postmodern in the sense that they mimic mass-mediated explorations of gender identities. Their surprisingly similar subtitles replicate the format of a monthly magazine whose readers are housewives, or to use a more expressive, literal translation from the Spanish term *amas de casa*, mistresses of the home. *Like Water for Chocolate* is composed of twelve parts clearly identified by months and their corresponding dishes, with the list of ingredients heading the ''Preparation'' section. . . . By amalgamating the novelistic genre with cookbook recipes, Esquivel and Plager actualize a postmodern blurring of distinctions between high and low cultural values. Both writers insist on the cover that their respective books are actually novels, but they also subvert this code of reference by adding a lengthy subtitle that recalls and imitates the particular realms of popular culture that are associated with women. Although both of the books under consideration here are authored by women, I am not making the claim that recipe-writing is an archetypally female activity. As a matter of fact, by making a connection with alchemy, I would like to suggest that both activities have a common androginous origin in the past.

Esquivel's book was originally published in Mexico in 1989, became a national bestseller in 1990, continued its success with a movie version that garnered many international film awards, and in 1992 swept across the English speaking world—primarily the North American market—as a New York Times bestseller for several weeks. Plager's book came out in Argentina in April of 1994 and the public is still digesting it. Critics too. The editors' blurb on the jacket suggests that in *Like potatoes for varenike* the writer. . . 'shows us her culinary and humorous talents through an entertaining parody of the successful *Like Water for Chocolate*.' This statement is very significant for several reasons: first of all it represents the female writer *primarily* as a talented cook; second, it invokes the model, recognizes its success and appeals to the rights of cultural reproduction; and third, it claims that the book that the reader has in hand is actually a parody of that model.

Invoking the culinary expertise of the fiction writer, specially if the writer is a woman, fits all too well into the current, end of the century, wave of neo-conservativism. It also feeds into the postmodern confusion between reality and its simulation. Fiction is required to have the qualities of reality and reality is defined as what we see on television or read about in the newspaper; that ''reality,'' however, is physically and psychologically fragmented and can only offer an illusion of wholeness. The

avant garde insistence on the power of the imagination is giving way to research, ''objectivity'' and ''expertise.'' Personal confession and ''true stories'' are valued higher than ''imagined'' ones and experience—in this case the culinary one—becomes the basis of identity and the source of discursive production. No wonder that the genre of the nineties is testimonial writing!. . .

The gastrotexts that I am discussing deal with gendered identities in a truly postmodern fashion: by situating the female protagonist in the kitchen and by literally allowing her to produce only a ''kitchen table talk'' spiced with melodrama instead of grandiose philosophical contraptions, their authors ''install and destabilize convention in parodic ways, self-consciously pointing both to their own inherent paradoxes and provisionally and, of course, to their critical or ironic rereading of the art of the past'' [according to Linda Hutcheon in her book *A Poetics of Modernism*]. In that sense the feminist discourse becomes paradoxical: instead of insisting on the liberational dimension of feminism which wants to get woman out of the kitchen, the postmodernist return to the discourses of power leads Esquivel and Plager to reclaim the kitchen as a not necessarily gender exclusive space of ''one's own.'' Both writers rely heavily on traditional cultural practices and subvert the patriarchal values associated with masculinity and femininity. . . .

Esquivel and Plager construct texts that do not fit into the traditional discourse of maternity. *Like Water for Chocolate* is constructed around the mother, who by invoking social rules, requires her youngest daughter Tita to reject any prospects of independent life, and take care of her until death. After Tita's premature birth on the kitchen table. . . ''amid the smells of simmering noodle soup, thyme, bayleaves, and cilantro, steamed milk, garlic, and, of course, onion,'' Mamá Elena does not satisfy the baby's need for food, and Tita has to turn to Nacha, the cook, with whom she establishes the successful object relation. The proto object—the breast—determines the relationship that the individual will have with other objects in the course of life, is the foundation upon which the construction of individual subjectivity takes place. In this carnavalesque farce, the mother becomes a fairytale-like stepmother, while Tita, who will never feed her own child, becomes the nurturer for all in need. She appropriates the space of the kitchen, transforming it into the center of her power which alters the dominant patriarchal family structure. Hence, her emotions and well being determine the course of other's lives and she literally shares herself with the outside world: when she makes the cake for her sister's wedding to Pedro—with whom she was planning to get married—her tears of desperation mix with sugar, flour, eggs and lime peel. This later provokes melancholy, sadness and finally uncontrollable vomiting among the guests:. . .

> The moment they took their first bite of the cake, everyone was flooded with a great wave of longing. Even Pedro, usually so proper, was having trouble holding back his tears. Mama Elena, who hadn't shed a single tear over her husband's death, was sobbing silently. But the weeping was just the first symptom of a strange intoxication—an acute attack of pain and frustration—that seized the guests and scattered them across the patio and the grounds and in the bathrooms, all of them wailing over lost love. Everyone there, every last person, fell under this spell, and not very many of them made it to the bathrooms in time—those who didn't joined the collective vomiting that was going on all over the patio.

The somatic reaction provoked by Tita's bodily fluids actually shows how the daughter undermines the mother's authority and prohibition. Something similar happens with "Quail in Rose Petal Sauce": Tita decides to use the rose that Pedro gave her as a sign of his eternal love, and prepares a meal that will awake Gertrudis' uncontrollable sexual appetite. By introducing the discourse of sexuality without necessarily relating it to marriage and by nurturing without procreating, Esquivel opens for discussion the ever present topics of feminine self-sacrifice and subordination that have traditionally been promoted by patriarchal literature. . . .

By breaking the boundaries between body and soul and by showing that they are actually one, both Esquivel and Plager successfully undermine the duality so embedded in Western culture. They—latter day apprentices of Sor Juana Inés de la Cruz—go against Plato and his all too well known argument that the soul can best reflect if there are no distractions from the body. They dismantle that same duality that puts masculinity on one side and femininity on the other. *Like Water for Chocolate* and *Like Potatoes for Varenike* unlock the kitchen door and present us its most common inhabitants—women. Then, they leave this door wide open and invite man to share. In Esquivel's version Sergeant Treviño is the one who helps Gertrudis decipher the recipe for cream fritters and in Plager's book Saul and Kathy work together from the beginning in meal preparation. By going against the rigid patriarchal binary thinking they, in Derridean fashion, reveal that there is no "transcendental signified." There is no original recipe either, nor original cook.

It is all about transcending ego boundaries through dialogic, polyphonic texts, emphasizing the importance of nurturing, both for man and women, going against sexual oppression and connecting those "honey-tongued" people who are not only making their cake, but are ready to eat it too.

Source: Ksenija Bilbija, "Spanish American Women Writers: Simmering Identity Over a Low Fire," in *Studies in 20th Century Literature*, Vol. 20, No. 1, Winter 1996, pg. 147–61.

María Elena de Valdés

In the following essay on Esquivel's first novel Like Water for Chocolate, *author María Elena de Valdés studies the development of the female subject as it is manifested through language and visual cues in the context of time and place. She is careful to preface her comments on the novel with the note that both the novel and the movie are, to some extent, parodies of the genre of Mexican women's magazines in their use of short installments (recipes, tips, home remedies, etc.) and that this framework of traditional "women's (socio-cultural) space" sets the tone for the structuring of the female characters in the novel.*

Como agua para chocolate is the first novel by Laura Esquivel (b. 1950). Published in Spanish in 1989 and in English translation in 1992, followed by the release of the feature film that same year, the novel has thrust this Mexican woman writer into the world of international critical acclaim as well as best-seller popularity. Since Esquivel also wrote the screenplay for director Alfonso Arau, the novel and the film together offer us an excellent opportunity to examine the interplay between the verbal and visual representation of women. Esquivel's previous work had all been as a screenwriter. Her script for *Chido Guan, el Tacos de Oro* (1985) was nominated for the Ariel in Mexico, an award she won eight years later for *Como agua para chocolate*.

The study of verbal and visual imagery must begin with the understanding that both the novel and, to a lesser extent, the film work as a parody of a genre. The genre in question is the Mexican version of women's fiction published in monthly installments together with recipes, home remedies, dressmaking patterns, short poems, moral exhortations, ideas on home decoration, and the calendar of church observances. In brief, this genre is the nineteenth-century forerunner of what is known throughout Europe and America as a woman's magazine. Around 1850 these publications in Mexico were called "calendars for young ladies." Since home and church were the private and public sites of all educated young ladies, these publications represented the written counterpart to women's socialization, and as such, they are documents that conserve and transmit a Mexican female culture in which the social context and cultural space are particularly for women by women.

It was in the 1850s that fiction began to take a prominent role. At first the writings were descriptions of places for family excursions, moralizing tales, or detailed narratives on cooking. By 1860 the installment novel grew out of the monthly recipe or recommended excursion. More elaborate love stories by women began to appear regularly by the 1880s. The genre was never considered literature by the literary establishment because of its episodic plots, overt sentimentality, and highly stylized characterization. Nevertheless, by the turn of the century every literate woman in Mexico was or had been an avid reader of the genre. But what has been completely overlooked by the male-dominated literary culture of Mexico is that these novels were highly coded in an authentic women's language of inference and reference to the commonplaces of the kitchen and the home which were completely unknown by any man.

Behind the purportedly simple episodic plots there was an infrahistory of life as it was lived, with all its multiple restrictions for women of this social class. The characterization followed the forms of life of these women rather than their unique individuality; thus the heroines were the survivors, those who were able to live out a full life in spite of the institution of marriage, which in theory, if not in practice, was a form of indentured slavery for life in which a woman served father and brothers then moved on to serve husband and sons together with her daughters and, of course, the women from the servant class. The women's fiction of this woman's world concentrated on one overwhelming fact of life: how to transcend the conditions of existence and express oneself in love and in creativity.

Cooking, sewing, embroidery, and decoration were the usual creative outlets for these women, and of course conversation, storytelling, gossip, and advice, which engulfed every waking day of the Mexican lady of the home. Writing for other women was quite naturally an extension of this infrahistorical conversation and gossip. Therefore, if one has the social codes of these women, one can read these novels as a way of life in nineteenth-century Mexico. Laura Esquivel's recognition of this world and

its language comes from her Mexican heritage of fiercely independent women, who created a woman's culture within the social prison of marriage.

Como agua para chocolate is a parody of nineteenth-century women's periodical fiction in the same way that *Don Quijote* is a parody of the novel of chivalry. Both genres were expressions of popular culture that created a unique space for a segment of the population. . . .

Obviously, for the parody to work at its highest level of dual representation, both the parody and the parodic model must be present in the reading experience. Esquivel creates the duality in several ways. First, she begins with the title of the novel, *Like Water for Chocolate*, a locution which translates as "water at the boiling point" and is used as a simile in Mexico to describe any event or relationship that is so tense, hot, and extraordinary that it can only be compared to scalding water on the verge of boiling, as called for in the preparation of that most Mexican of all beverages, dating from at least the thirteenth century: hot chocolate. Second, the subtitle is taken directly from the model: "A Novel in Monthly Installments, with Recipes, Romances, and Home Remedies." Together the title and subtitle therefore cover both the parody and the model. Third, the reader finds upon opening the book, in place of an epigraph, a traditional Mexican proverb: "A la mesa y a la cama / Una sola vez se llama" (To the table or to bed / You must come when you are bid). The woodcut that decorates the page is the typical nineteenth-century cooking stove. The fourth and most explicit dualistic technique is Esquivel's reproduction of the format of her model.

Each chapter is prefaced by the title, the subtitle, the month, and the recipe for that month. The narration that follows is a combination of direct address on how to prepare the recipe of the month and interspersed stories about the loves and times of the narrator's great-aunt Tita. The narration moves effortlessly from the first person to the third-person omniscient narrative voice of all storytellers. Each chapter ends with the information that the story will be continued and an announcement of what the next month's—that is, the next chapter's—recipe will be. These elements, taken from the model, are never mere embellishments. The recipes and their preparation, as well as the home remedies and their application, are an intrinsic part of the story. There is therefore an intricate symbiotic relationship between the novel and its model in the reading experience. Each is feeding on the other.

In this study I am concerned with the model of the human subject, specifically the female subject, as it is developed in and through language and visual signification in a situated context of time and place. The verbal imaging of the novel makes use of the elaborate signifying system of language as a dwelling place. The visual imagery that at first expands the narrative in the film soon exacts its own place as a nonlinguistic signifying system drawing upon its own repertoire of referentiality and establishing a different model of the human subject than that elucidated by the verbal imagery alone. I intend to examine the novelistic signifying system and the model thus established and then follow with the cinematic signifying system and its model.

The speaking subject or narrative voice in the novel is characterized, as Emile Benveniste has shown, as a living presence by speaking. That voice begins in the first person, speaking the conversational Mexican Spanish of a woman from Mexico's north, near the U.S. border. Like all Mexican speech, it is clearly marked with register and socio-cultural indicators, in this case of the land-owning middle class, mixing colloquial local usage with standard Spanish. The entry point is always the same: the direct address of one woman telling another how to prepare the recipe she is recommending. As one does the cooking, it is quite natural for the cook to liven the session with some storytelling, prompted by the previous preparation of the food. As she effortlessly moves from first-person culinary instructor to storyteller, she shifts to the third person and gradually appropriates a time and place and refigures a social world.

A verbal image emerges of the model Mexican rural, middle-class woman. She must be strong and far more clever than the men who supposedly protect her. She must be pious, observing all the religious requirements of a virtuous daughter, wife, and mother. She must exercise great care to keep her sentimental relations as private as possible, and, most important of all, she must be in control of life in her house, which means essentially the kitchen and bedroom or food and sex. In Esquivel's novel there are four women who must respond to the model: the mother Elena and the three daughters Rosaura, Gertrudis, and Josefita, known as Tita.

The ways of living within the limits of the model are demonstrated first by the mother, who thinks of herself as its very incarnation. She interprets the model in terms of control and domination of her entire household. She is represented through a filter of awe and fear, for the ostensible source is Tita's diary-cookbook, written beginning in 1910, when she was fifteen years old, and now transmitted by her grandniece. Therefore the verbal images that characterize Mamá Elena must be understood as those of her youngest daughter, who has been made into a personal servant from the time the little girl was able to work.

Mamá Elena is depicted as strong, self-reliant, absolutely tyrannical with her daughters and servants, but especially so with Tita, who from birth has been designated as the one who will not marry because she must care for her mother until she dies. Mamá Elena believes in order, *her* order. Although she observes the strictures of church and society, she has secretly had an adulterous love affair with an African American, and her second daughter, Gertrudis, is the offspring of that relationship. This transgression of the norms of proper behavior remains hidden from public view, although there is gossip, but only after her mother's death does Tita discover that Gertrudis is her half-sister. The tyranny imposed on the three sisters is therefore the rigid, self-designed model of a woman's life pitilessly enforced by Mamá Elena, and each of the three responds in her own way to the model.

Rosaura never questions her mother's authority and follows her dictates submissively; after she is married she becomes an insignificant imitation of her mother. She lacks the strength, skill, and determination of Mamá Elena and tries to compensate by appealing to the mother's model as absolute. She therefore tries to live the model, invoking her mother's authority because she has none of her own. Gertrudis does not challenge her mother but instead responds to her emotions and passions in a direct manner unbecoming a lady. This physical directness leads her to adopt an androgynous life-style: she leaves home and her mother's authority, escapes from the brothel where she subsequently landed, and becomes a general of the revolutionary army, taking a subordinate as her lover and, later, husband. When she returns to the family hacienda, she dresses like a man, gives orders like a man, and is the dominant sexual partner.

Tita, the youngest of the three daughters, speaks out against her mother's arbitrary rule but cannot escape until she temporarily loses her mind. She is able to survive her mother's harsh rule by transferring her love, joy, sadness, and anger into her cooking. Tita's emotions and passions are the impetus for expression and action, not through the normal means of communication but through the food she prepares. She is therefore able to consummate her love with Pedro through the food she serves. . . .

> It was as if a strange alchemical process had dissolved her entire being in the rose petal sauce, in the tender flesh of the quails, in the wine, in every one of the meal's aromas. That was the way she entered Pedro's body, hot, voluptuous, perfumed, totally sensuous.

This clearly is much more than communication through food or a mere aphrodisiac; this is a form of sexual transubstantiation whereby the rose petal sauce and the quail have been turned into the body of Tita.

Thus it is that the reader gets to know these women as persons but, above all, becomes involved with the embodied speaking subject from the past, Tita, represented by her grandniece (who transmits her story) and her cooking. The reader receives verbal food for the imaginative refiguration of one woman's response to the model that was imposed on her by accident of birth. The body of these women is the place of living. It is the dwelling place of the human subject. The essential questions of health, illness, pregnancy, childbirth, and sexuality are tied very directly in this novel to the physical and emotional needs of the body. The preparation and eating of food is thus a symbolic representation of living, and Tita's cookbook bequeaths to Esperanza and to Esperanza's daughter, her grandniece, a woman's creation of space that is hers in a hostile world.

Source: María Elena de Valdés, ''Verbal and Visual Representation of Women: *Como agua para chocolate / Like Water for Chocolate*,'' in *World Literature Today*, Vol. 69, No. 1, Winter 1995, pp. 78–82.

Marisa Januzzi

In the following brief review of Esquivel's first novel Like Water for Chocolate, *reviewer Marisa Januzzi criticizes Esquivel's American publisher for attempting to ''buffer'' the novel for American audiences though, she argues, Esquivel's novel is ''spacious and gracious'' enough that it needs no such authentication. Januzzi calls Esquivel's novel a magical-realist narrative in which supposedly useless emotions and drama are rendered as mythic and historic sources of power.*

Jacket copy reveals Doubleday's amusing attempts to buffer this accomplished first novel for its American market: ''Evocative of *How to Make an American Quilt* in structure . . . and *Heartburn* in its irony

and wit, it is a lively and funny tale of family life in turn-of-the-century Mexico.'' An appreciative blurb from Diana Kennedy, an American expert on Mexican cooking, completes the scatter-brained introductory picture. (Just imagine reading a physician's authenticating remarks on the cover of *The Death of Artemio Cruz*, if you don't see my point.) Fortunately, this 1990 Mexican best-seller by screenwriter Laura Esquivel doesn't need the authentication, and it is spacious and gracious enough to accommodate these trivializing accolades. The reader who makes it past the comparisons and into the book will be taken by surprise—it's sort of like getting a really good *cafe con leche* when you'd been led to expect Sanka. This short novel's got more heat and light and imaginative spice than the American literary diet usually provides.

The narrator uses the device of a cookbook, found under the ashes of her ancestral home, as a means of telling the story of its author, her great-aunt Tita. Tita's sensitivity and affinity for the kitchen are depicted as prenatally established facts; on the first page of the novel, she is born early on a tide of her own tears into a mess of onions and spices on the kitchen table. She has no need of the usual slap on the bottom, because she is already crying. Perhaps, the book suggests, this is because of the onions. Or perhaps it is because Tita already knows she is fated to uphold a host of parasitical family traditions, most notably the custom of keeping youngest daughters unmarried to care for their mothers. When the salt residue from the tears is swept up, it fills a tenpound sack, which will be used for years of cooking. That detail, reminiscent of various odd storms in Garcia Marquez, sweeps the reader into a magical-realist narrative in which supposedly futile emotions are shown to have mythic and historic power.

It also introduces us to this author's gift of showing and telling her story: food is everywhere in this crafty book. References to it are tucked into the narrative like chocolate Easter eggs. (My favorite sentence: ''Wrapped up like a taco, the baby was sleeping peacefully.'') Tita's recipes, one per section, serve as mechanisms for and sometimes as commentaries on the plot. And for every reader who ever wished she could read letters through their blank sides in Jane Austen, this novel details ingredients. Interestingly, some of the foods and techniques called for, as well as the metric amounts, are among the untranslated elements in the text, leaving me to conclude that maybe recipes are even less translatable, in their way, than poetry.

Occasional bad moments in this book betray what seems, from an American point of view, to be an unsophisticated side of its author. For instance, the illegitimate mulatta sister is praised for her unusual gift of "rhythm," and her temporary career in a brothel is called, by the otherwise sensible Tita, a "liberation." Also, Pedro sometimes seems so unimaginative that only in fantasy, I thought, could such an underdeveloped male character and magical ending satisfy Tita . . . but of course this is fantasy, and maybe his better qualities are simply lost in cultural translation. In any case I was fated from birth to have these quarrels with Ms. Esquivel's novel, and I'd rather simply savor it. You will too.

Source: Marisa Januzzi, "Like Water for Chocolate: A Novel in Monthly Installments, with Recipes, Romances, and Home Remedies," (book review) in *The Review of Contemporary Fiction*, Vol. 13, No. 2, Summer, 1993, p. 245.

Barbara Mujica

In the following brief review of Esquivel's first novel Like Water for Chocolate, *Barbara Mujica outlines the plot of what she calls a "delightful" novel and writes that Esquivel's prose is direct, unencumbered, and fun to read, incorporating Mexican folklore, social realism, and fantasy without straying too far into the Magical Realism genre.*

If you loved the movie based on *Like Water for Chocolate* but haven't read the novel, run out and buy the book. Tita is even more captivating, Pedro more dashing, Nacha more nurturing, Gertrudis more outrageous and Mama Elena more odious on the page than on the screen.

Laura Esquivel's delightful first novel, a love story spiced with recipes and home remedies, pokes fun at romantic potboilers and at "serious," overly self-conscious magical realism alike. The heroine is Tita, third daughter of a well-to-do Mexican family that lives on a ranch near the U.S.-Texas border. Soon after her birth, Tita's father suffers a heart attack, causing her mother, Mama Elena, to lose her milk. As a result, Tita is raised in the kitchen by Nacha, the family cook, who feeds her nourishing gruels and teaches her not only to prepare delicious meals, but to communicate through food.

According to family tradition, the youngest girl is never to marry, but must devote her life to caring for her mother. However, Tita was not born for spinsterhood. The first time she lays eyes on handsome young Pedro Muzquiz at a party, she understands "how dough feels when it is plunged into boiling oil. The heat that invaded her body was so

> **This short novel's got more heat and light and imaginative spice than the American literary diet usually provides."**

real she was afraid she would start to bubble . . . like batter . . . and be unable to endure his gaze." When Pedro asks for her hand in marriage, the domineering Mama Elena convinces him to marry Tita's elder sister instead, a proposition that Pedro accepts in order to remain close to his beloved Tita.

This, of course, is a recipe for disaster, for Tita cannot help but express her true emotions through food. While preparing Pedro's and Rosaura's wedding cake, she cries into the icing. When the members of the wedding party eat the cake, they suddenly remember their past true loves and, as though there had been an emetic in the batter, they all wind up vomiting in the patio. Nacha dies clutching a picture of her long-lost fiance, whom the mother of Mama Elena prevented her from marrying. When Pedro brings flowers to Tita to celebrate her having completed one year as Nacha's replacement in the kitchen, Mama Elena orders her daughter to throw them away. Instead, Tita cooks a delicious quail in rose petal sauce. Through the food, her love enters into Pedro's body. Gertrudis, the middle sister, becomes so aroused after eating the dish that she dashes to the shower to cool off. However, her body heat is so intense that the stall catches fire. Running naked from the flames, Gertrudis comes upon one of Pancho Villa's captains, who sweeps her up and carries her away, making love to her on horseback. After working a stint in a brothel, Gertrudis becomes a general in the revolutionary army and eventually marries Juan, the handsome captain to whom she lost her virginity.

Even after she dies, Mama Elena continues to haunt Tita. When Tita thinks she is pregnant by Pedro, the ghost of her mother appears at the window and accuses her of indecency. But Tita has learned that her mother's behavior was not always so exemplary. Gertrudis was born of an affair that Mama Elena had with a mulatto man who later died. Tita had decided never to reveal the truth about her sister's father, but when Gertrudis has a mulatto

> "...unlike some young Latin American writers who seem hellbent on stuffing as many chimerical episodes as possible into their prose in order to prove themselves worthy perpetuators of magical realism, Esquivel combines elements of social realism and fantasy with total spontaneity."

baby and Juan accuses her of infidelity, Tita is forced to set the record straight. Knowing her mother's secret enables Tita to feel a certain compassion for her, for Tita recognizes that Mama Elena was a bitter, frustrated woman. At the same time, it empowers her to defy her mother, for she realizes that Mama Elena's aura of perfection is a sham. It is Tita's rejection of her mother that finally sets her free, but not free to marry Pedro.

Rosaura, who has a child named Esperanza (Hope), knows about Pedro's and Tita's romance but, instead of granting her husband a divorce, insists on pretending to be happily married in order to keep up appearances. Furthermore, she intends to follow the old family tradition: She destines Esperanza, her only daughter, never to wed, but to care for her until she dies. Tita, enraged over her sister's selfishness, vows to liberate her niece from this oppressive custom. In the end true love triumphs. Tita not only gets her man, but dances at Esperanza's wedding. However, the surprise finale is more reminiscent of Renaissance romantic tragedies and Mexican B-movies than of Hollywood's happy-ever-after endings.

Esquivel's writing is vivid, direct and fun to read. Each chapter begins with a recipe, segments of which are integrated into the plot. Narrated by Esperanza's daughter, the story incorporates bits of folk culture in such a natural way that, in spite of Esquivel's many obvious conceits, the writing never seems contrived. And, unlike some young Latin American writers who seem hellbent on stuffing as many chimerical episodes as possible into their prose in order to prove themselves worthy perpetua-

tors of magical realism, Esquivel combines elements of social realism and fantasy with total spontaneity.

Although one might quibble occasionally with the translators' wording, Carol Christensen and Thomas Christensen have done an excellent job of capturing Esquivel's verve and style. In either Spanish or English, *Like Water for Chocolate* is the perfect summer read.

Source: Barbara Mujica, ''Like Water for Chocolate,'' (book review) in *Americas,* Vol. 45, No. 4, July-August, 1993, p. 60.

Janice Jaffe

In the following essay on Esquivel's first novel Like Water for Chocolate, *author Janice Jaffe examines the traditional roles of Mexican women within the context of Esquivel's novel, and sees women's traditional domestic roles not as devaluing, as some feminists may, but rather as vehicles for creative and powerful expression in their own cultural context. She notes, however, that it is key to the novel's unique perspective that the protagonist also acts outside of the domestic (kitchen) sphere.*

During the same era that inspired the suspicion of women's activities in the kitchen cited in my epigraph, the Mexican nun Sor Juana Ines de la Cruz boldly celebrates the phenomena of the kitchen as worthy of philosophical observation:

> And what shall I tell you, lady, of the natural secrets I have discovered while cooking? I see that an egg holds together and fries in butter or in oil, but, on the contrary, in syrup shrivels into shreds; observe that to keep sugar in a liquid state one need only add a drop or two of water in which a quince or other bitter fruit has been soaked; observe that the yolk and the white of one egg are so dissimilar that each with sugar produces a result not obtainable with both together. I do not wish to weary you with such inconsequential matters, and make mention of them only to give you full notice of my nature, for I believe they will be occasion for laughter. But, lady, as women, what wisdom may be ours if not the philosophies of the kitchen? Lupercio Leonardo spoke well when he said: how well one may philosophize when preparing dinner. And I often say, when observing these trivial details: had Aristotle prepared vituals, he would have written more.

While sor Juana's ironized self-mockery for commenting on ''these trivial details'' reflects her frustration both at the confinement of women to this domestic sphere and at others' belittling of life in the kitchen, her culinary literary analogy at the end offers a tantalizing invitation. I begin with sor Juana because the recent novel couplings of culinary and literary creation which are the subject of this paper echo, at times deliberately, sor Juana's words.

Three centuries after sor Juana decried the forced relegation of women to the domestic sphere, represented by the kitchen, Rosario Castellanos denounced more emphatically the assumption that women's domain is the kitchen. In her story "Cooking Lesson," the narrator, an educated newlywed woman untrained in cooking announces sarcastically, "My place is here. I've been here from the beginning of time. In the German proverb woman is synonymous with Kuche, Kinder, Kirche." That Rosario Castellanos' feminist messages to Mexican women have taken root finds affirmation in Jean Franco's conclusion in *Plotting Women* that the goal of rejecting patriarchal domination has compelled "contemporary women novelists not only in Mexico but all over Latin America to move beyond the confines of domesticity." Yet, surprisingly, a number of Hispanic American and Latina women writers seem to be reclaiming the kitchen, perhaps affirming seriously the declaration which Castellanos' new bride offers sarcastically.

In Laura Esquivel's *Como agua para chocolate* (novela de entregas mensuales con recetas, amores y remedios caseros), *Like Water for Chocolate* (Novel of monthly installments with recipes, loves and home remedies), the recipes for twelve sumptuous Mexican dishes form the narrative frame, and the protagonist learns and teaches "los secretos de la vida" "the secrets of life" in the kitchen. The popularity of Esquivel's 1989 novel—into its eighth printing by October of 1991—seems to have resuscitated heirs to the Dominican friar's wariness of women in the kitchen, such as a critic who, dismissing *Como agua para chocolate* and its peculiar use of recipes as entirely lacking in literary merit, declares that, "no tiene otra aspiracion que ser novedosa" "it has no aspiration but to be novel." However, the novelty of Esquivel's enterprise, bringing together two supposedly incompatible companions for women today, the kitchen and writing, does have its ancestry, as does a certain skeptical response it evokes. Admittedly, Esquivel's concoction, which unabashedly mimics the form of a serialized romance or folletin while doubling as a cookbook, may incur criticism for uniting two literary forms notoriously and pejoratively associated with Cortazarian lectores-hembra or "female-readers." But I find enormously suggestive the popular appeal of this recent lighthearted blending of ingredients from the kitchen and the folletin, far transcending the "female-reader" audience of serial

> A taste of some of this literature may reassure concerned readers; none of this plethora of new works advocates a return to the proverbial state of 'barefoot, pregnant and in the kitchen,' or 'la mujer honrada, la pierna quebrada y en casa.'

fiction and popular romances. Specifically, I see in Esquivel's narrative a particularly liberating revival of sor Juana's analogy, whose timeliness today is evident in a veritable buffet of recipes for writing by Latin American and Latina women. A taste of some of this literature may reassure concerned readers; none of this plethora of new works advocates a return to the proverbial state of "barefoot, pregnant and in the kitchen," or "la mujer honrada, la pierna quebrada y en casa."

In 1984 the organizers of a conference dedicated to the writings of Latin American and Latina women proclaimed the importance of the kitchen for women writers when they published the conference proceedings under the title *La sarten por el mango, The Frying Pan by the Handle*. Editor Patricia Elena Gonzalez summarizes their discussions of women's writing with a metaphoric call to take up their pots and pans: "We could say that as we cut the onion, we cried; but upon peeling off the layers superimposed artificially over our identity as Latin American women, we found a center. Alright now, time to take the frying pan by the handle and start cooking." Pointing to the correspondences between cooking and writing, at this conference the Puerto Rican Rosario Ferre described her development as a writer in terms of the kitchen in an essay entitled "La cocina de la escritura" "The Kitchen of Writing." Sor Juana's assertion that, had he cooked, Aristotle would have written more, appears as the epigraph to this essay. Another work by Ferre, the story "El collar de camandulas" "The Rosary Chain," begins and ends with the whispered recitation of a family recipe for poundcake that evolves as a sign of the bond between the story's two female characters and, implicitly, a female reader. At the conclusion of the story the surviving, silenced female character employs the recipe to liberate herself from her male oppressors. When women writers of color in the United States, including several Latina writers, founded the Kitchen Table Press in 1981, providing a liberating voice for themselves, the name was chosen, "because the kitchen is the center of the home, the place where women in particular work and communicate with each other." Sharing this vision, the Latina writer, Helena Maria Viramontes, entitles her essayistic testimonial about her commitment to writing "'Nopalitos': The Making of Fiction" and likens her own creative process to that of her mother preparing nopalitos. Humbly, she acknowledges, "I have never been able to match her nopales, but I have inherited her capacity for invention," and, hence, learned to find "my space on the kitchen table" for writing. Each of these writers' kitchens or milieux as well as their cooking methods is unique and warrants individual study. Nonetheless, what links the works of all of these women writing after Rosario Castellanos is their reclaiming of the kitchen as a space of creative power rather than merely confinement, in literature which, like *Como agua para chocolate*, seems to address itself primarily to a complicit female audience.

"Como agua para chocolate" is a Mexican idiom which means extremely agitated or, in the English equivalent, boiling mad. But this title's culinary origin hints that to truly appreciate its meaning requires not only reading the novel but also preparing its recipe for chocolate. Similarly, from beginning to end, *Como agua para chocolate* foregrounds parallels between culinary and literary creation. This liaison is implicit on the novel's first page when the protagonist, Tita de la Garza, is born prematurely onto the kitchen table amid the ingredients of her art: "among the aromas of a noodle soup that was cooking, of the thyme, the bay leaf, the cilantro, the boiled milk, the garlic and, of course, the onion." A prototypical domestic literary form, Tita's diary cum recipe book, edited by her grandniece, comprises the serialized novel we read. Briefly, her story, the serial romance or novela por entregas surrounding Tita's recipes, is this. As the youngest daughter of the tyrannical Mama Elena, a widowed ranch owner living somewhere near the Mexican/U.S. border on the eve of the Mexican revolution, a mysterious family tradition dictates that marriage is forbidden her; instead she must remain at home to feed and care for her mother until the latter's death. The expression, "como agua para

chocolate," then, describes Tita's anger at her confinement to the kitchen as she endeavors to surmount the obstacles to her happiness. Tita's fate, which motivates the plot, rivals the most contrived of folletin stories, and her obedient intentions in the face of her mother's cruel domination reflect the polarized characterization typical of serialized fiction. However, in *Como agua para chocolate* the formulae of the folletin, including its episodic romantic plot and its melodramatic effects, are adapted to highlight the novel's recipes and the life of the kitchen.

Each chapter's title is that of the recipe to be recounted in it, a mouth-watering list of ingredients serves almost as a table of contents for each chapter, and the narrative begins with appetite-whetting instructions for preparing the recipe which Tita is engaged in making. Of course, because Tita is besieged with interruptions, like the women writers Virginia Woolf describes in *A Room of One's Own*, each recipe's narration is inevitably suspended to incorporate the incidents which intrude upon her cooking. Likewise, the anticipated meal necessarily returns to preempt other activities and their narration. These competing but complementary narratives reinforce one another in postponing the final denouement of the folletin, but the recipes and events narrated are also meant to mirror one another in eliciting nostalgic or erotic responses from their audience. Exemplifying this symbiosis, every chapter concludes, in folletinesque fashion, with a crisis resolved and a meal completed only to precipitate another unforeseen occurrence and accompanying dish, to be taken up in the following chapter. Consequently, a cliffhanging ellipsis and the promise "continuara" "to be continued," closes every chapter, followed by the name of the upcoming recipe, as if the recipe itself were part of the cataclysmic event whose narrative we anxiously awaited. And, in a sense this is so, because in this novelistic world the unique manner of preparing a recipe can unleash untold euphoria or despair. Tita's unintentional modification of the recipe for "Codornices en petalos de rosas" "Quails in rose petals," for instance, provokes such unbridled passion in her sister Gertrudis that she abandons the family and is catapulted into an erotic encounter on horseback with an unidentified villista. Similarly, when, true to folletin plotting, Tita's sister Rosaura betrays her by marrying Tita's true love, Pedro, and, to make matters worse, Tita has to prepare the wedding cake, our heroine's tears in the cake batter inspire a disastrous eruption of nostalgic weeping and vomiting among the wedding guests. No longer trivial or incidental, here the art of recipe-making determines the peripeties of plot. Furthermore, the narration of recipes itself works to define the relationship between reader, narrator and protagonist.

With a knowing wink to readers who enjoy the arts of recipe sharing and kitchen talk, the narrator initiates a conversation in the novel's first paragraph, on the significant topic of onions. Like Patricia Elena Gonzalez, whose words in *La sarten por el mango* I repeated earlier, Tita's grand-niece strays from the metaphoric image of an onion's layers to recall the more literal tear-jerking activity of chopping them. The narrator and Tita seem to unite in this gesture, as if to entice those who love the smell of onions and know the almost cathartic experience of chopping and sobbing. In addition, with the revelation of her own sensitivity to onions and of a family secret to avoid that inevitable flood of tears, the narrator exposes parallels between recipe sharing and narrative.

> The onion must be finely minced. I suggest you place a little piece of onion on your forehead to avoid the annoying tears that come when you're chopping it. The bad thing about crying when you chop onions isn't the simple fact of crying, but that sometimes you begin, as they say, you get an itch and you can't stop scratching. I don't know if this has happened to you, but to me, the simple truth is it has. Hundreds of times. Mom used to say that it was because I'm just as sensitive to onions as Tita, my great aunt.

The narrator, with her colloquial language and tone, simultaneously introduces three generations of women who have shared recipes, and invites the implied readers, ''Uds.,'' into the kitchen to participate in this activity. What makes a recipe especially appealing for a listener, she knows, is an accompanying story, in this case, as the narrator's admission of her and Tita's enormous sensitivity to onions suggests, a tear-jerking tale. The narrator is alluding to Tita's plight, and we are perhaps also meant to read in this an allusion to the norms of the folletin romance, comically adapted by Esquivel. More significant than the folletin here, however, is the ''embedded discourse'' of the recipe, which Susan J. Leonardi has explored as a predominantly feminine narrative strategy that, like recipe's root in Latin, recipere, ''implies an exchange, a giver, and a receiver.'' Her illustration, from cookbooks and novels incorporating recipes, of recipe exchange as a contract of trust or understanding between giver and receiver, narrator and listener aptly characterizes Laura Esquivel's culinary narrative. When the narrator in *Como agua para chocolate* introduces

herself, her mother and Tita in the opening paragraph she begins to construct the community described by Leonardi, ''a loose community of women that crosses the social barriers of class, race, and generation.''

Ignoring Mexican norms that prescribe familial allegiance while implicitly proscribing alliances across class and racial lines, this recipe-sharing community relies on different codes of female solidarity, read through characters' responses to recipes and the kitchen. Bonds of friendship form among characters who appreciate what sor Juana calls ''the natural secrets'' of the kitchen, the artistry in creating and preparing recipes, and also their restorative powers. The ranch's Indian cook Nacha, Tita, the maid Chencha, the family doctor's Kickapoo grandmother, and, peripherally, Tita's sister Gertrudis, compose this female community. In this regard, Esquivel's ''Novela de entregas mensuales'' ''Novel of monthly installments'' can be seen both to mirror the format of serialized fiction and to allude to a specifically female creative community, temporally oriented around a monthly (mensual) menstrual cycle.

Tita, born on the kitchen table into such a world, learns the secrets of life in the kitchen from Nacha, who feeds her as an infant and entertains her through childhood by inventing games related to cooking. Tita's childhood in the kitchen, including her play and conversation with Nacha, constitutes an apprenticeship in an artist's studio, which Tita directs after Nacha's death. ''Tita era el ultimo eslabon de una cadena de cocineras que desde la epoca prehispanica se habian transmitido los secretos de la cocina de generacion en generacion y estaba considerada como la mejor exponente de este maravilloso arte, el arte culinario'' ''Tita was the last link in a chain of cooks who since prehispanic times had been transmitting the secrets of the kitchen from generation to generation and was considered the finest practitioner of this marvellous art, culinary art.'' The tradition which Tita carries on is an oral one, learned experientially; however, with the death of Nacha Tita recognizes the fragility of a dying art, particularly recipes which Tita herself only vaguely recalls. These recipes, at the opportune moment for their use, are whispered by Nacha to Tita from beyond the grave. Gertrudis, perhaps the most devoted fan of Tita's recipes, fears that when her sister dies, ''moriria junto con ella el pasado de su familia'' ''the family's past would die along with her.'' Understanding both their evanescence in the absence of Nacha and their restorative function in Tita's daily life, Tita records the recipes, together with their accompanying story, because the situation of the recipe, such as Gertrudis' euphoria after tasting "Codornices en petalos de rosas" "Quails in rose petals," is inseparable in Tita's mind from the instructions for preparing the dish itself. Implicit in Tita's salvaging of Nacha's recipes in their context is a sense of the art of recipe narration as "embedded discourse." "Like a story, a recipe needs a recommendation, a context, a point, a reason to be" (Leonardi).

That reason to be, for Tita, resides especially in recipes' effects on their audience. Nacha's recipes are life sustaining for Tita; they inspire her to write her life to preserve the recipes, and, more literally, Nacha's soups restore Tita to health. Following a nervous breakdown, Tita yearns to remember any recipe, because this would mean "volver a la vida" "returning to life." Significantly, the word "recetas" in Spanish refers not only to recipes for food but to prescriptions for medicine. Likewise, the phrase "remedios caseros" in the novel's subtitle describes various home remedies interspersed through the narrative, but is also suggestive of the therapeutic character of the kitchen, specifically its recipes and accompanying conversation. Although the conversation centered on recipe-sharing and cooking in this kitchen falls short of that which the African American writer Paule Marshall heard as a child among "the poets in the kitchen," Marshall's description of these women's talk reflects its restorative quality. "There was no way for me to understand it at the time, but the talk that filled the kitchen those afternoons was highly functional. It served as therapy, the cheapest kind available to my mother and her friends. . . it restored them to a sense of themselves and reaffirmed their self-worth." In the kitchen with Nacha Tita experiences this therapy which both solaces and entertains.

The description of the kitchen, paradoxically symbolic of both confinement and escape, is suggestive of its dual role. The narrator purports to offer an image of the kitchen as an illustration of how it limits Tita's vision of the world, but the spatial imagery contradicts this message.

> It wasn't easy for a person who knew life by way of the kitchen to understand the outside world. This gigantic world which began from the kitchen door toward the inside of the house, because the one that lay adjacent to the back door of the kitchen and that overlooked the patio, the fruit garden, the vegetable garden, yes it belonged completely to her, she controlled it.

Even though the world denied to Tita is represented as "gigantesco" "gigantic" it seems to lead no farther than the inside of the house, while the world of the kitchen also comprehends a vast, open expanse outside the back door. Furthermore, the verbs employed to link this world to Tita, "le pertenecia" "belonged to her" and "lo dominaba" "she dominated it" are indicative of the protagonist's need for a space to control her own destiny, as she ultimately does through her recipes which transcend these confines. As the narrator explains, even Mama Elena cannot entirely repress Tita in the kitchen environment which inspires her creative expression, because "ahi escapaban de su riguroso control los sabores, los olores, las texturas y lo que estas pudieran provocar" "there the flavors, aromas, textures and what these might provoke escaped her rigorous control." Cruel rigor typifies Mama Elena's management of Tita's life, in and out of the kitchen. An unexcelled master at any skill concerning "partir, desmantelar, desmembrar, desolar, destetar, desjarretar, desbarratar o desmadrar" "splitting open, dismantling, dismembering, desolating, weaning, ham-stringing, destroying or separating a child from its mother (demothering)," one fundamental rule of culinary, or literary, art eludes Mama Elena, the need to adapt the rules to one's own creative talent. If Tita strays from the precise rules for a recipe, as with Rosaura's wedding cake and the "Codornices en petalos de rosas," she arouses Mama Elena's destructive fury. But Tita's creative spirit and its transformative power remain invincible. "Pero no podia evitar la tentacion de transgredir las formulas tan rigidas que su madre queria imponerle dentro de la cocina . . . y de la vida" "But she couldn't resist the temptation to transgress such rigid formulas as her mother wanted to impose on her inside the kitchen . . . and in her life." And, indeed, it is through the ingredients (ingredientes) of her recipes that Tita is ultimately able to transgress or cross over (transgredir) the tyrannical rules set by her mother.

When Tita convalesces in the home of the family's doctor following her breakdown, she enjoys her first experience of leisure and an accompanying recognition of the oppression she has lived. Staring fixedly at her now free hands, which in their idleness she barely recognizes as her own, Tita recalls how a rigid schedule of work in the kitchen has dominated all her days.

> At her mother's side, what her hands must do was coldly determined, there were no doubts. She had to get up, dress, light the fire in the stove, prepare breakfast, feed the animals, wash the dishes, make the

beds, prepare dinner, wash the dishes, iron the clothes, prepare supper, wash the dishes, day after day, year after year.

Although in spite of this recognition Tita later bows to familial obligation and returns home to care for her infirm mother, when Rosaura announces that her daughter Esperanza will carry on the family tradition, Tita takes up the cause of her niece's freedom with the zeal of a crusader. The aunt willingly instructs Esperanza in culinary artistry, but also takes advantage of their hours together to provide Esperanza with "otro tipo de conocimientos de los que su madre le daba" "other kinds of knowledge than what her mother offered her." Tita encourages her niece's intellectual curiosity and her right to decide her own destiny, and ensures that she attends school. Under Tita's dominion, then, the kitchen evolves as a space not only of domestic activity but of feminist rebellion. Esperanza comes to value the community and the creativity which the kitchen can foster, but as a result of Tita's rebellion, as an adult the niece enters the kitchen only when she chooses. Esperanza passes on to her daughter, the narrator, the legacy of Tita's embedded recipes but not the oppressive familial law.

In the last monthly installment, faithful to the norms of the folletin romance, Tita and Pedro are finally united, although contrary to most Catholic-oriented serial endings, not in wedlock. Instead, they find themselves "alone at last" when Tita's mother and Pedro's wife Rosaura die, victims of their own rejection of the social codes of the kitchen. Mama Elena perishes from a poisonous overdose of the emetic she takes to counteract the effects of the poison-laced food she believes Tita is preparing for her. Only after her death does Tita discover Mama Elena's letters from a forbidden romance with a mulatto. The man was murdered for their affair, during which Tita's sister Gertrudis was conceived. We can read Mama Elena's butcher-like mastery of the kitchen, then, as an angry response to the brutal imposition on her of societal conventions that forbade relations across racial and class lines. The recipe-sharing community consistently upsets these norms. Rosaura has rejected the society of the kitchen out of a desire for acceptance by "la crema y nata de Piedras Negras" "the cream of Piedras Negras society." Her death, of obesity and flatulence, therefore, is an act of poetic justice. With all obstacles removed, Tita and Pedro abandon themselves to the erotic euphoria induced by the wedding banquet Tita prepares for Esperanza. Their flames of passion not only engulf the lovers but burn the entire ranch. Magically, Tita's culinary literary creation survives intact amid the rubble.

On the novel's last page the narrator, who, significantly, appears to be speaking to us from the kitchen as she prepares the novel's first recipe, informs readers that we have been reading her great aunt's recipe book cum autobiography. The narrator's conclusion, that Tita will continue to live on as long as there is someone to prepare her recipes, constitutes an invitation to turn back, like the narrator, to the first chapter to read and prepare its recipe. In the process, Tita's story has revealed, the heirs of her recipes should make them their own, with the addition of their own stories. This ending offers an invitation to create, highlighting the recipe-sharing community in the folletinesque love story.

If Esquivel delights in imitating the contemporary serial romance, her pleasure derives in part from subverting its conventions, including the norm of ending with an opulent Catholic wedding, an exaggerated fascination with appearances measured in material abundance and a tendency to segregate characters according to race and class (Erhart). However, this novel hardly represents a denunciation of the folletin romance. More probably Esquivel chooses to mimic this fictional form, typical of women's magazines, which generally include recipes, because of her greater fascination with the creative possibilities of the discourse of recipes. In the process of inventing this recipe-sharing community, Esquivel's work displays its sharpest divergence from serialized fiction where "what is crucially missing . . . is any form of female solidarity."

The female community of the kitchen in *Como agua para chocolate* may reflect women's propensity to define their identity more relationally than men, as suggested by Nancy Chodorow. Yet, solidarity among Mexican women has historically been very difficult. Cherrie Moraga points to the perpetuation of the myth of la Malinche, the Indian woman accused of betraying her people by becoming Cortes' lover, to illustrate how women are encouraged to abandon one another in their search for male approval. This tendency is all the more pervasive in popular Latin American fictional forms like the serial romance and the novela rosa. Therefore, although *Como agua para chocolate* remains undeniably and unapologetically a romance, the creation in it of a community of women that defies these norms is of particular significance. Moreover, as has been observed reprovingly by the reviewer who criticized in Esquivel's novel an aspiration to novelty, ''Los personajes femeninos ocupan el primer plano de la novela'' ''The female characters occupy the foreground in the novel,'' and ''En *Como agua para chocolate* la presencia masculina es secundaria'' ''In *Como agua para chocolate* the masculine presence is secondary'' (Marquet). By locating the centric space of the novel in the kitchen, a primarily female setting, Esquivel has created an environment which promotes creative female community.

This is not to suggest that the novel supports a return of Mexican women to this domestic sphere, or that it should remain an exclusively female domain. The novel's title refers to a woman's anger at domestic imprisonment. Also, on repeated occasions in the novel men seem enticed to work in the kitchen. More tellingly, the fact that Tita's diary with her recipes emerges whole from the rubble of the ranch symbolizes both the liberation of the female artist from the oblivion of domesticity and the elimination of the patriarchal codes imaged by the ranch under the repressed and repressive dominion of Mama Elena. Key to the novelty of *Como agua para chocolate* is that the protagonist steps outside the kitchen without renouncing the creative force it embodies.

Yet this work also indicates that only after a woman is no longer confined to the space of the kitchen can she publicly celebrate its life. Tita, writing during the mythical time of the Mexican Revolution, records her recipes in her diary, but it remains in that private form until her grand-niece, the narrator, rewrites the diary and recipes as a novel. Sor Juana, an exception among women in the seventeenth century, can indulge in the pleasures of kitchen phenomena, because, as she proudly reminds an admiring poet in a romance, she is not forced to work there:

> Thanks be to God, that no longer do I have to beat Chocolate, nor must I be harassed by anyone who might visit me.

Writing in 1971, Rosario Castellanos felt compelled to denounce the perception that women's domain is the kitchen, because at that time under twenty percent of women worked in the paid labor force in Mexico and most who did performed jobs which they also performed at home. Furthermore, official recognition of literature by women in Spanish America remained an anomaly. As the contributions of male and female Hispanic American authors today become more equally represented, the challenge to speak to the great diversity of female experience opens the doors for new recipes for writing.

In answer to this appeal, Esquivel offers a liberating vision of a denigrated experience of ''dailiness'' in many women's lives. In *Como agua para chocolate*, although repressive societal traditions appear to dominate Tita's life, the specific manner of preparing a recipe actually determines the lives and destinies of the characters. Perhaps the suspicions of the seventeenth-century Dominican friar about the subversive goals of women in the kitchen were justified. By bestowing such transformative power on the creativity of the artist in the kitchen and by converting the creative metaphors of the kitchen into a narrative method, Esquivel answers Patricia Elena Gonzalez' metaphoric call to take up the weapons of the kitchen and start cooking, with a novel recipe for writing. Her work also suggests that the number and variety of possible recipes is infinite. The ingredients for this recipe include a recipe-sharing community, like Tita and her grand-niece whose voices unite to create the work we read; a kitchen, like the room for creative expression described long ago by Virginia Woolf; and the capacity for invention, which Helena Maria Viramontes finds in her mother's nopalitos. As for the ''Manera de hacerse'' ''Method of preparation,'' as Rosario Ferre expresses it:

> The important thing is to apply that fundamental lesson that we learned from our mothers, the first, after all, to teach us how to deal with fire; the secret of writing, like that of good cooking, has absolutely nothing to do with sex, but with the wisdom with which one mixes the ingredients.

Source: Janice Jaffe, ''Hispanic American Women Writers' Novel Recipes and Laura Esquivel's Como Agua Para Chocolate (Like Water for Chocolate),'' in *Women's Studies,* Vol. 22, No. 2, March, 1993, p. 217.

Sources

Calta, Marialisa, ''The Art of the Novel as Cookbook,'' in *New York Times Book Review*, February 17, 1993.

Corliss, Richard, review of *Like Water for Chocolate*, in *Time*, Vol. 141, No. 14, April 5, 1993, p. 61.

de Valdés, María Elena, ''Verbal and Visual Representation of Women: 'Like Water for Chocolate,''' in *World Literature Today*, Vol. 69, No. 1, Winter, 1995, pp. 78-82.

Hoffert, Barbara, review of *The Law of Love*, in *Library Journal*, July, 1996, p. 156.

Januzzi, Marisa, review of *Like Water for Chocolate*, in *Review of Contemporary Fiction*, Vol. 13, No. 2, Summer, 1993, pp. 245-46.

O'Neill, Molly, "At Dinner with Laura Esquivel: Sensing the Spirit In All Things, Seen and Unseen," in *New York Times*, March 31, 1993, pp. C1, C8.

Pizzichini, Lilian, review of *The Law of Love*, in *Times Literary Supplement*, October 18, 1996, p. 23.

Polk, James, review of *Like Water for Chocolate*, in *Tribune Books* (Chicago), October 8, 1992, p. 8.

Stabiner, Karen, review of *Like Water for Chocolate*, in *Los Angeles Times Book Review*, November 1, 1992, p. 6.

Stavans, Ilan, review of *Like Water for Chocolate*, in *Nation*, Vol. 256, No. 23, June 14, 1993, p. 846.

Zamudio-Taylor, Victor, and Inma Gulu, "Criss-Crossing Texts: Reading Images in 'Like Water for Chocolate,'" in *The Mexican Cinema Project: Studies in History, Criticism and Theory*, edited by Chon Noriega and Steven Ricci, The UCLA Film and TV Archive, 1994, pp. 45-52.

Further Reading

Batts Estrada, Mary, review of *Like Water for Chocolate*, in *Washington Post*, September 25, 1993, p. B2.
　　This review praises the novel for its mixture of culinary knowledge, sensuality and magic as "the secrets of love and life [are] revealed by the kitchen."

Kauffmann, Stanley, review of *Like Water for Chocolate*, in *New Republic*, Vol. 208, No. 9, March 1, 1993, pp. 24-25.
　　Kauffmann reviews the movie version of the novel and finds it "drawn-out" and "lacking in focus."

The Management of Grief

Bharati Mukherjee

1988

Bharati Mukherjee's story "The Management of Grief" tells the story of an Indian woman living in Canada whose husband and two sons are killed in a plane explosion. Through a process of deciding what parts of her culture to accept or reject and what parts of Western culture to adopt or reject, she works past her grief and begins rebuilding her life.

Mukherjee published the story in *The Middleman and Other Stories* in 1988, and the collection of short stories about immigrant experiences in the West won the National Book Critics Circle Award for fiction that year. "The Management of Grief" is unique in the collection because it is the only story about immigrants in Canada.

Based on the 1985 terrorist bombing of an Air India jet occupied mainly by Indo-Canadians (Indian immigrants living in Canada)—about which Mukherjee and her husband wrote the nonfiction book *The Sorrow and the Terror*—"The Management of Grief" is part of Mukherjee's effort to understand and communicate that catastrophe and its meaning.

Culture gives a person her primary tools and strategies for dealing with such universal human experiences as grief, and the title of the story encapsulates its basic themes. It is a story about the kind of grief that any human experiences, but it highlights the difficulties faced by immigrants in another country, namely, how to negotiate conflicting cultural demands and expectations, yet still

draw on the strengths of culture. Such a theme carries impact for the non-immigrant, too, who might want the freedom to reject inhumane elements of her own culture.

Author Biography

Born in Calcutta, India, on July 27, 1940, Muhkerjee is the second of three daughters of a wealthy chemist and his wife. In 1947, the year that India gained its independence from England, the Mukherjees moved to London where Mukherjee's father took a researching job. The girls attended private schools in London and Switzerland. In 1951, the family returned to Calcutta, and the girls attended the Loretto school, an elite private Catholic school run by Irish nuns. Thus all of their schooling emphasized Western values and traditions at the expense of Indian culture.

Mukherjee studied at Indian universities, earning a B.A. in English and an M.A. in English and ancient Indian culture, before coming to the United States in 1962 on a scholarship to the prestigious creative writing program at the University of Iowa. There she earned her M.F.A. in 1963, and would later earn her Ph.D. She also met Canadian Clark Blaise at Iowa, and married him on their lunch hour in 1963.

In 1966, Mukherjee and Blaise moved to Canada where she taught at McGill University and wrote her first and second novels, *The Tiger's Daughter* (1972) and *Wife* (1975). A year spent in India with Blaise in 1973 resulted in their collaboration on the nonfictional *Days and Nights in Calcutta* (1977). Despite her success, Mukherjee was generally unhappy in Canada, where she felt that the official policy of multiculturalism failed to address, and even exacerbated, the racism she frequently experienced.

So in 1980, hoping to find greater fulfillment in the cultural melting pot offered in the United States, she and Blaise moved to New York where she taught at several universities. The year 1985 was extremely important for Mukherjee's work. She published her first book of short stories, *Darkness*, and an Air India plane full of Indo-Canadians

exploded in a terrorist bombing. That event became the subject of her second collaboration with Blaise, *The Sorrow and the Terror* (1987), and of "The Management of Grief," published in *The Middleman and Other Stories* (1988). In 1989, she published her novel *Jasmine* and moved across the country to accept a distinguished professorship at the University of California at Berkeley, where she still teaches. Since then, she has published two more novels, *The Holder of the World* (1993) and *Leave It to Me* (1997).

Plot Summary

Mukherjee's "The Management of Grief" opens as the protagonist Shaila Bhave watches women moving around her kitchen quietly. The mood is somber for only the day before, Bhave's husband and two sons were killed in a plane explosion. Shaila talks with Dr. and Mrs. Sharma. One of the Sharma sons reports to them that officials are still uncertain about the explosion, "saying it could be an accident or a terrorist bomb." Most of the Indians there suspect that the plane was destroyed by a Sikh bomb. Shaila sits on the stairs talking with Kusum, her neighbor whose husband and daughter also died on the plane. Shaila expresses regret that traditional propriety kept her from telling her husband she loved him, and Kusum consoles her. Kusum's second daughter, Pam, interrupts the two. She wants her mother to look presentable for a reporter who is coming. Kusum and Pam fight bitterly, and Mrs. Sharma tries unsuccessfully to calm Pam down.

The scene shifts to what seems to be the next day, in Shaila's house. A government social worker named Judith Templeton visits and wants her to help provide services to the rest of the Indian community affected by the plane explosion. Judith, who is having difficulty because she lacks understanding of Indian culture and language, approves of Shaila's calm coping with the tragedy and wants to use her as an example. Though Shaila is hesitant because she questions her own calmness, she gives Judith permission to call her again after her trip.

Four days after the news of the explosion, Shaila is on the coast of Ireland looking out at the sea where the airplane went down. She and many others have come to Ireland to identify the bodies of their relatives. She talks with Kusum, who relates

Bharati Mukherjee

her swami's advice for coping with the grief. The two women talk indirectly of suicide. Shaila looks for sources of hope that her family is alive. The two women are approached by Dr. Ranganathan, who has lost a large family in the explosion, and he feeds Shaila's hope by telling her a good swimmer could have made it to one of the many small islands in the sea and could have pulled others with him. He throws roses into the sea and offers two for Shaila to throw, but she throws personal items of her sons' and a poem to her husband. Dr. Ranganathan helps her over the rocks and they head back to the bus that brought them here from the hospital.

Back at the hospital, Dr. Ranganathan accompanies Shaila into a room with pictures of the recovered bodies where she is supposed to find one of her sons. Despite efforts by the police and a nun to help her identify one of the pictures as her son, she denies finding him. She leaves the room with the others.

Shaila and Kusum fly together to Bombay, India, where they are stopped at customs because of Kusum's coffins. The officer there suspects they are smuggling contraband. Shaila screams at him, prompting a reflection that she has changed from the traditional Indian woman she once was.

Shaila spends the next four months in India with her parents and family friends. She feels trapped, unsure what to do with her life now. She and other Indians from Canada travel and entertain themselves, seeking distraction. The families of many of the widowers are arranging new marriages for them. Some of these men tell Shaila they do not want new wives. Yet many of them remarry anyway.

In an abandoned temple, over six months after coming to India, Shaila has a vision of her husband who sits next to a sadhu (holy man). He tells her ''You must finish alone what we started together.'' Shaila knows now that she will return to Canada.

Back in Canada, Shaila tries unsuccessfully to convince Kusum not to run away and join an ashram. Dr. Ranganathan has returned to Montreal and talks with Shaila often on the phone. He keeps his house, though he sleeps on a cot, not in the bed he shared with his wife before she died.

Judith Templeton continues to ask Shaila for help in reaching families that have not accepted her social services. Shaila goes with her to visit an elderly Sikh couple whose sons were killed in the plane crash. Since the sons took care of the bills and finances, the couple is in danger of losing utility services in their home. The government will take care of these tasks for them, even give them a pension, but out of fear and distrust they refuse to sign the requisite papers. Shaila talks with the two, who still believe, based on faith in God's providence, that their sons will return to care for them. ''God will provide, not government,'' the old man says. They refuse to sign Judith's papers. Later, in the car with Judith, headed to another survivor's house, Shaila realizes that these parents' hope is part of the culture she shares with them, that Judith's intolerance of their ''stubbornness'' is unacceptable, and she tells Judith to stop at the subway, where she gets out of the car despite Judith's objections.

Shaila begins to settle back into life. She writes to local papers and to the government, looking for answers about the explosion. She orders her finances, sells the house and takes an apartment, and contemplates how to complete what she and her husband started here in the West. She stays in touch with Kusum, who is now in an ashram in India, with Pam, who is working in Vancouver, and with Dr. Ranganathan, who has moved to Texas. Then one day in the park she hears the voices of her family tell her, ''Your time has come. Go, be brave.'' Unsure of what she will do next, she rises and starts walking.

Characters

Mithun Bhave

Shaila's younger son of ten years, he is also a good swimmer. Shaila throws into the sea a half-painted model airplane of his after he dies in the crash.

Shaila Bhave

Shaila Bhave is the thirty-six-year-old protagonist and first-person narrator of the story. She is repressed through most of the story and outwardly shows only subtle emotions. Much of her character is revealed by what she wants to say, but does not. Yet under all the repression of emotion, she wants to talk. She first begins to open up to Dr. Ranganathan, partly because he seems to understand her and encourages her hope. Shaila regrets not telling her husband that she loved him, and when she writes an expressive poem to him and throws it in the sea, she begins to gain an authentic voice for herself.

She also becomes more assertive as the story progresses. She screams at the customs officer in India, noting that she is no longer acting like the proper Indian woman. When she realizes that talking with Judith is pointless since Judith cannot hear her voice, Shaila abandons her. Shaila's numb, quiet, anxious calm in the beginning of the story grows into a more self-assured, accepting calm by the end.

Shaila flutters, as she says, ''between worlds,'' between the progressive, rational world of her parents and of Judith, and the more spiritual and traditional world embodied in her grandmother and India. Like many of the other characters, she is trying to find between the two a balance that will allow her a fulfilling life. In the end, she and Dr. Ranganathan seem to be on a similar path, one that embraces the West and the freedom of more progressive ideas while also acknowledging the strength to be drawn from their Indian culture and people.

Vikram Bhave

Vikram is Shaila's husband. At work, to help his colleagues, he anglicized his name to ''Vik,'' a detail which shows his efforts to remake himself in the new world. He dies in the crash with his two sons. When Shaila is in India, he appears to her in a vision and encourages her to continue the life they started together.

Vinod Bhave

Shaila's son, fourteen years old, dies in the plane crash. He had won swimming medals, and she and Dr. Ranganathan entertain the hope that he swam to safety with his brother and father. The authorities in Ireland think they may have found his body and bring Shaila to look at the pictures, but she denies that he is in them.

Elderly Couple

Judith Templeton takes Shaila to see an elderly Sikh couple who are refusing the government's social services. They have moved to Canada from a Punjabi village only weeks before the plane explosion which kills their sons. Simple survival tasks such as writing checks are beyond their ability, and soon they will lose utility service. Still, they distrust Judith and the government, preferring to put their faith in God's providence and in the hope that their sons will return. To them, accepting the government's help is also accepting its ways, its version of reality. Shaila reads the message in the man's eyes: ''I will not pretend that I accept.''

Though Shaila believed that, since they are Sikhs, they will refuse to open up to her, a Hindu woman, she and the elderly couple are able to relate through the loss of their sons, and rather than persuading them to accept the help Judith offers, their encounter with Shaila changes her, and their integrity moves Shaila to abandon Judith.

Kusum

Shaila's neighbor Kusum loses her husband, Satish, and her youngest daughter in the plane crash. She responds to her grief by consulting a swami and at the end of the story is living on one of his ashrams in India. Comfortable with her cultural traditions, Kusum, in the form of her swami, embraces the authorities of her culture. On the advice of her swami, she sees the deaths of the passengers as fated, and tells Shaila that depression over the loss is selfish.

Pam

Though a minor character, Pam represents the worst of Western commercial culture. The oldest daughter of Kusum and Satish, she feels that Kusum wishes she would have died instead of her younger "good-goody" sister. Pam clearly goes farther than any of the other characters in abandoning her own culture and adopting that of the West. She first appears in a McDonald's uniform, likes Canadian boys, and frequents the malls. She clings only to those parts of Indian culture that give her knowledge she can sell, namely, yoga and makeup hints for Indian and Asian girls.

Dr. Ranganathan

Dr. Ranganathan, who lost all of his family in the plane explosion, serves as a model to Shaila of how to deal with her grief while maintaining personal and cultural integrity. An electrical engineer who "knows important secrets of the universe, things closed to" Shaila, she thinks, he is well-adjusted to life in the West, yet retains important links with his Indian culture and its values. He believes that "it's a parent's duty to hope," a belief that helps Shaila relate to the elderly Sikh couple she visits with Judith.

Shaila's Parents

Shaila's ailing parents still live in India. They are progressive, liberal thinkers who put little stock in religion and who treat people as individuals without stereotyping. But their attitudes alienate Shaila from them somewhat. When Shaila has her vision of Vikram in the Himalayan temple, she is not comfortable telling her mother, who is impatient with such "prophetic dreams."

Dr. Sharma

Directly following the death of Shaila's husband and sons, Dr. Sharma, a fellow member of the Indo-Canada Society, helps her take care of the practical concerns of life, what his wife calls "mundane details." He talks with Shaila about finances and deals with phone calls. In one call, he notes that the Valium given to Shaila is "having the necessary effect," revealing his practical approach even to grief.

Mrs. Sharma

The wife of Dr. Sharma, Mrs. Sharma is pregnant with their fifth child. At the gathering in Shaila's house, she scolds Dr. Sharma for bothering Shaila with "mundane details" and scolds Pam for her insensitive comments to her mother, Kusum. Her main goal is to help the women manage, without interference, emotions of grief.

Judith Templeton

The Canadian government sends social worker Judith Templeton to help the Indo-Canadians whose family members died in the plane explosion. She is young and inexperienced, but has a master's degree in social work. Though she intends well, Judith is unable to transcend her book-learning and grows impatient with the Indian people who fail to fit into her Western paradigm. When Shaila abandons Judith after the interview with the elderly couple, thus rejecting the Western bureaucratic response to grief management that Judith represents, the best response Judith can give is, "Let's talk about it."

Themes

Religion

Religious conflict sets the scene for the plot of "The Management of Grief". The men and boys at Shaila's house as the story opens, mostly Hindus, believe that Sikh activists planted the bomb that killed Shaila's husband and two sons.

Religion and religious issues shape much of Shaila's consciousness. In India, Shaila realizes that she is somewhat repelled by the Sikhs she sees, even old family friends, despite her progressive upbringing by parents who "do not blame communities for a few individuals." Though her grandmother was a devout Hindu, her parents are not religious, and Shaila "flutter[s] between worlds." When helping Judith Templeton communicate with grieving families, Shaila says "I stiffen now at the sight of beards and turbans," the traditional look of Sikh men. Shaila's husband Vikram appears to her in a vision as she worships in a tiny temple in the Himalayas. He is with a holy man who recites Hindus prayers, and he tells Shaila to "finish alone what we started together," part of which was to go "halfway around the world to avoid religious and political feuding."

Culture Clash

The clashes of differing cultures create the tensions in "The Management of Grief," and much of Shaila's growth as a character takes the form of her learning to negotiate these tensions, especially within herself. The Sikhs who bomb the plane are pursuing their own nation and culture apart from the predominantly Hindu nation of India. In dealing with her grief, Shaila struggles against a newfound repulsion to Sikhs, noticing the difference between herself and her progressive, rationalist parents who never "blame communities for a few individuals," a difference that has always left her suspended between their world and the devout Hindu world of her grandmother, a different clash that informed Shaila's childhood.

The Indian culture clashes with Western culture especially as the latter is embodied in the social worker Judith Templeton. She measures the Indo-Canadians' grief with the charts, numbers, and techniques of Western psychology and social science, becoming impatient with individuals who do not fit her schema. Though she pushes "reconstruction" on the survivors, "she's a little surprised, even shocked, over *how* quickly some of the men have taken on new families" in response to the pressures of the Hindu culture. She grows impatient with the elderly Sikh couple's hope, but in their culture—in the culture of Dr. Ranganathan and Shaila—"it is a parent's duty to hope." Judith's failure to understand these cultural differences keeps her from transcending the situation and truly helping the people she has devoted her life to serving.

The contrasts between other characters further emphasize the theme of clashing cultures. Kusum's daughter, Pam, embraces the West, especially its consumer culture of malls and McDonald's, while Kusum returns to India to live in an ashram—a Hindu commune—with her swami. Dr. Ranganathan, though in many ways loyal to his Indian sensibilities, refuses to take another wife like many of the other men, despite enormous pressure from his family, and he returns West to start anew in Texas. The forces of cultural clash partly define all of the characters who engage that clash, while those who fail to acknowledge these forces fail to forge genuine identities.

Search for Self

Before her husband's death, Shaila has so little sense of self that she can hardly raise her own voice. After his death, she becomes more aware of her own silence. "I never once told him that I loved him," she regrets. "I was too much the well brought up woman. I was so well brought up I never felt comfortable calling my husband by his first name."

But as the story progresses, Shaila begins to assert her voice and with it her selfhood. At first, she does so chiefly symbolically, when she throws to the sea a poem she has written for Vikram: "Final-

Topics for Further Study

- Research and put on a debate about the desirability of Canada's policy of multiculturalism. Include a "representative" of Shaila Bhave in the debate. How does the policy compare to a "melting pot" policy like that of the United States? Does your answer to this question depend on your position in society?

- Gather information from psychology books on the ways that people experience and deal with grief. Do they accurately describe Shaila's experience in the story?

- Investigate the Sikh community of India. What is their stance now on the Air India bombing? What is the status of their fight for an independent state called "Khalistan"?

- Read several stories about the immigrant experience by other writers such as Bernard Malamud or V. S. Naipaul. How do their representations of the experience differ from Mukherjee's? How do their stories differ from the story we Americans like to tell ourselves about immigration to the United States?

ly, he'll know my feelings for him." Kusum reports that her swami says "depression is a sign of our selfishness," a selfishness that Shaila accepts, sensing that what some call "selfishness" is really a sense of one's own selfhood. Later, Shaila raises her voice at the customs officer in India, thus making her voice more public.

The climax of the story comes when Shaila finally asserts herself against the pushy Judith Templeton and thus accepts her own ways of negotiating culture and managing her grief. In the end, Shaila finds a sense of self in continuing the creation of a new identity that she began with her family years ago. After she has "tried to asses my situation, how best to live my life," she listens to the encouraging voices of her husband and sons once more and then strikes out on her own.

Style

Foil

Kusum serves as a foil to Shaila. A foil is a character whose qualities serve to contrast with and therefore emphasize the qualities of another character. Kusum holds to her traditions and their authority. When Shaila expresses regret that her traditional upbringing kept her from telling her husband she loved him, Kusum reassures her that this traditional way of married life is superior to that lived by "modern young girls" whose love is "fake." But this is not enough for Shaila, and she writes an expressive poem that she sends to her husband on the sea in Ireland, distinguishing herself from Kusum. When Kusum says "I have no right to grieve" and represses her grief on the authority of her swami who calls it selfish, Shaila runs down the beach calling herself selfish, thus resisting a traditional authority of her own culture. Kusum finally leaves Canada for an ashram run by her swami in Hardwar, India, despite Shaila's pleas not to "run away." At the end of the story, when Kusum writes to Shaila of the visions she has had of her dead daughter—while her living daughter wanders around North America—Shaila comments, slightly ironically, "I think I can only envy her." Though the two women have had to deal with very similar situations, Kusum's response helps Mukherjee show the courage and vitality in Shaila, who continues what she and her husband started in the New World and rebuilds from what she still has.

Point of View

Shaila Bhave tells her own story in her own words in the first-person point of view, an important stylistic feature since "The Management of Grief" is about a woman finding her own voice. The story moves smoothly between narration of events and dialogue, on the one hand, and Shaila's internal workings, on the other. A woman now alone in the world, wondering "how best to live my life" must tell her own story; there is no other who can tell it for her. Mukherjee believes that immigrants must tell their own stories, because no one "speaks for us, the new Americans from nontraditional immigrant countries," as she says in the *New York Times Book Review*. So her choice of first-person narration is also an enactment of her fictional project.

Jonathan Raban, also in the *New York Times Book Review*, says that Mukherjee's characters are "compulsively fluent talkers whose lives are too urgent and mobile for them to indulge in the luxury of the introspective past tense." Shaila's first-person present-tense narration shows her thoughts as she experiences them and this creates a mood of urgency in the face of the demands made by her different cultures. When she finally finds her own way of managing grief, she is a more independent, stronger person, writing her own story, in a sense, as she tells it.

Setting

The story, based on the historical bombing of an Air India jet in 1985, is set in three countries. It begins in Canada, moves to Ireland, then to India, and finally back to Canada. Place names permeate the story as the characters move from one city, airport, or village to the next.

The real events behind the story and the real geographical places clearly named throughout give the story a sense of urgency and reality. Furthermore, the movements in geographical setting reflect the changes in Shaila's sense of self and culture. She leaves Canada for Ireland, where she stands on the beach with Kusum, who will eventually return to India to live and embrace its culture, and Dr. Ranganathan, who will eventually return to the West and continue to create his new life there. In this scene the beach, itself a border between the clashing worlds of water and earth, provides the setting for a drama played out among three people trying to decide how and where they will set the stories of their own lives.

From Ireland, the setting shifts to India, where Shaila searches for ways to manage her grief, unsure whether to stay or return to Canada. But she has brought with her a history in the West, and she decides to return and continue her path there. But when she does, she brings to Canada what she experienced in India Thus the changes in setting instigate and reflect the changes in Shaila's attitudes and emphasize the uncertainty and fluidity possible in the immigrant life.

Literary Heritage

Though not particularly interested in being known as an Indian writer, Mukherjee has placed herself in the long tradition of immigrant writers such as V. S. Naipaul and Bernard Malamud. She claims to have learned much from their fiction. She dedicated *Darkness* to her friend Malamud and even named one of her sons after him.

The predominant mode of American fiction in the 1980s was a minimalism exemplified by such writers as Raymond Carver. Minimalism used short sentences, understatement, and very little elaboration. Mukherjee positioned herself against this style, preferring instead a more elaborate one that allowed her to explore the layers of meaning and significance in the layered lives of her immigrant characters. She believes that a writer's status as immigrant gives her a great subject about which to write, and the subject deserves a great style.

Historical Context

Postcolonial India

Great Britain began colonizing India in the middle of the eighteenth century and spent the next two hundred years trying to secure military and economic control of the area. The colonization was never peaceful, and in April 1919 British troops fired into a crowd killing or wounding over one thousand Indians. In 1920, Mohandas Gandhi began his famous campaigns of civil disobedience ending in 1947 with India's independence from Britain. The India of 1947 and after is referred to as postcolonial India. Mukherjee was seven years old when India gained her independence, so most of her life is the life of a postcolonial Indian.

Furthermore, Mukherjee, as well as most of the characters in "The Management of Grief," is part of the great Indian diaspora. A diaspora is a spreading out of a group of people, and, for most of this century, Indians have been leaving their native land to study, find jobs, and build lives elsewhere in the world, especially in the West. Mukherjee's father, for instance, worked in both London and Switzerland for several years (though he ultimately returned to India), and Mukherjee herself, by way of Canada, finally settled in the United States. Salman Rushdie, author of the famed *Satanic Verses,* is also part of this dispersion of Indian peoples.

Part of the postcolonial challenge for any country and its people is constructing an identity that can come to terms with the one the colonizing power imposed to serve its own ends. Thus Mukherjee, who grew up in Western schools and received her bachelor's degree in English, found much to value when she also studied ancient Indian culture in her

master's degree program in India. Mukherjee believes it is part of her mission to give non-European immigrants their own voices in her fiction, voices that rise above the clanging and clashing of cultures. This is particularly difficult for people who inherit a heritage that has been dominated by an outside power.

Sikhs and Hindus

While most Indian people adhere to the ancient religion of Hinduism, there arose in the fifteenth century a rival religion called Sikhism, which opposed itself to the caste hierarchy (social system of classes in India) of Hinduism and advocated social equality as well as monotheism. Today, Sikhs make up only about two percent of the Indian population and most of them live in the province of Punjab, where they share the Punjabi language. The region of Punjab was divided between India and Pakistan in 1947, and again divided between the Hindus and Sikhs in 1966. Since 1947, there has been talk, which gained momentum through the 1970s and 1980s, among some Sikhs of an independent Sikh state. Tensions exploded in 1984 when Indian Prime Minister Indira Gandhi sent the Indian Army to establish order and fighting broke out. Hundreds of Sikhs were killed. In October of 1984, two of Indira Gandhi's Sikh bodyguards assassinated her, prompting riots across India.

The feud between mainstream Hindu India and the Sikhs is part of the "religious and political feuding" Shaila and her husband "came halfway around the world to avoid." The elderly couple whom Shaila visits with Judith are Sikhs who left Punjab with their sons only weeks before. But political borders were not enough stop the feuds, and the violence and anger spilled over into Canada, erupting in Sikh and Hindu communities there. In 1985, the Sikhs claimed responsibility for the bombing of the Air India flight that crashed into the seas off Ireland killing hundreds of Indo-Canadians. Thus, Shaila's ambivalent feelings about the Sikhs she encounters have their roots in a long history of strife and disagreement.

Canada's Policy of Multiculturalism

Though in the past few decades it has come under attack, the idea of a cultural melting pot has always been a source of pride for the United States, a society where, in theory, people of differing cultures can come together into a single community, a nation of immigrants who live together in harmony. By contrast, Canada, in 1971, established an official policy of multiculturalism, which would strive not to melt the nation's cultures into one pot but to let them constitute a "mosaic of cultures" within Canada. Under such a policy, the Canadian government recognizes the autonomy of its many immigrant cultures and tries to adapt its services to their particular needs, allowing them, some critics say, to segregate themselves into smaller, homogenous communities. Judith Templeton, the social worker who visits Shaila, administers to the needs of the members of the Indo-Canada Society under the aegis of multiculturalism.

Mukherjee finds serious fault with the policy, and it contributed significantly to her decision to leave Canada for the United States in 1980. Herself the victim of severe racism in Canada, Mukherjee believes the policy of multiculturalism exacerbated Canada's racism and served as an excuse for the Canadian government to avoid involvement in the problems of its immigrant citizens. In fact, in *The Sorrow and the Terror*, she claims the policy allowed the Canadian government to ignore mounting tensions between Sikhs and other Indians by calling the problem an Indian concern, and that the government is therefore responsible for the 1985 Air India bombing. The debate over Canada's multiculturalism policy continues today.

Critical Overview

When *The Middleman and Other Stories*, the book of short stories that includes "The Management of Grief," appeared in 1988, it won the National Book Critics Circle Award for fiction and met with great critical success. In the *New York Times Book Review*, Jonathan Raban praised Mukherjee's style and her growth since *Darkness*, her first book of short stories. "Her writing here is far quicker," he wrote, finding "no slack in it." Dinah Birch, in the *London Review of Books*, wrote that *The Middleman and Other Stories* "presents a razor-sharp reflection of a world which is disconnected, but not without hope."

Critical commentary on the stories since then has centered on two issues, namely, Mukherjee's representations of gender and of the immigrant experience. Though critics Arvindra Sant-Wade and Karen Marguerite Radell, writing in *Studies in Short Fiction*, do not talk specifically about "The Management of Grief," they find in Mukherjee's stories a "sense of floating" that "is the key to the immigrant woman's experience," a sense that does

come through in "The Management of Grief." Suchitra Mathur, in *Feminist Writers*, sees a development in Mukherjee's fiction, "from an emphasis on the liberating potential of American individualism" to the ideas in *The Middleman and Other Stories* which explore "the possibilities of cross-national/cross cultural alliances that deconstruct rigid East/West oppositions and foster the construction of a self-affirming hybrid identity for women." Thus the woman immigrant has a certain freedom that allows her to assert herself in unique ways.

Much of what can be said of the woman immigrant can, of course, also be said of any immigrant, and most criticism on the stories has talked of immigration and the postcolonial experience with less attention to gender. Many have praised Mukherjee's work for its representation of the immigrant experience. But critics do not agree on whether Mukherjee has tried to go too far. Though her stories show "an awareness of the complex multiplicity of immigrant experiences," as Suchitra Mathur writes in *Feminist Writers*, critics such as Gail Ching-Liang Low, writing in *Women: A Cultural Review*, chide Mukherjee for "seeming not to be concerned with preserving cultural identities" and not wanting "to be labeled an 'Indian' writer."

If Low criticizes Mukherjee for not being "Indian" enough, Alpana Sharma Knippling, in an essay in *Bharati Mukherjee: Critical Perspectives*, scolds Mukherjee for trying to speak for the experiences of others. She reminds the critical world that Mukherjee led a privileged life as an upper-class Indian and has spent most of her life in the West. Therefore she does not, argues Knippling, have the right or the ability to speak for poor immigrants or immigrants from other cultures, as she tries to do in some of the stories in *The Middleman and Other Stories*. "She homogenizes her ethnic minority immigrant subjects, instead of calling attention to the actual heterogeneity of ethnic minority immigrant subjects in the United States."

Mukherjee, in her own defense against such attacks, emphasizes the American melting pot of culture, grouping herself among "the new Americans from nontraditional immigrant countries" in a *New York Times Book Review* article. "Each of us, mainstream or minority, is having to change. It's a two way metamorphosis," Mukherjee explained in an interview with Patricia Holt in the *San Francisco Chronicle*.

Though "The Management of Grief" may avoid some of the critical attacks made on

Mukherjee's story is based upon the 1985 terrorist bombing of an Air India jet.

Mukherjee's work as a whole, since Shaila is, like Mukherjee, an upper-class Indian woman, it still shows the immigrant trying to bridge two cultures. In so doing, it is part of a body of work that Gita Rajan, in *Writers of the Indian Diaspora,* calls "problematic," one that will continue to "demand a sustained inquiry by the reader into the issues that Mukherjee raises—personal, sociopolitical, and cultural."

Criticism

James Frazier

Frazier teaches high-school English in Lytle, Texas, and has a master's degree in English from the University of Texas. In the following essay, he discusses the elements of the journey structure in "The Management of Grief."

Odysseus, the hero of Homer's *Odyssey,* travels for over ten years trying to get home to his family and his community. When, at the end of the book, he finds his way home, it is the end of a long journey that lasted many years and confronted Odysseus with myriad challenges and threats. In this classic example of a journey story, he and the men on his ship are tempted by beauty, captured by a Cyclops, and whirled around an angry and treacherous sea. All of this makes for a good story, but behind the narrative there lies a complex journey structure, a structure critics such as Joseph Campbell, in his book *The Hero with a Thousand Faces,* have analyzed thoroughly and applied to literature, folklore, and religious narratives. This structure is also called the journey myth, since myth originally meant story or structure. Because the journey myth occurs so frequently in literary texts, it is a useful tool for comparing and analyzing them.

The main structure of Mukherjee's story "The Management of Grief" is a journey taken by the protagonist, Shaila Bhave. Put simply, in the beginning of the story she is in Canada. She goes away. She comes back, and the story ends with her in Canada. But in between, something has changed. A numb calm and a somber mood permeate her world before she leaves; she seems to be without will, passive, irresolute. At the end of the story, after her journey, the mood is calm, but more resolute, not at all numb. She still waits, but with open expectation, confident that she is doing the right thing and that she has made some sense of the confusion and pain caused by the death of her husband and two sons. She might not yet be happy or stable, but Shaila is

What Do I Read Next?

- *Darkness*, Mukherjee's first book of short stories, also focuses on the experiences of immigrants in the West.

- *The Sorrow and the Terror*, written by Mukherjee and her husband Clark Blaise, is a nonfiction investigation into the 1985 terrorist attack on the Air India plane that crashed off the coast of Ireland.

- In *Selling Illusions: The Cult of Multiculturalism*, Neil Bissoondath launches a controversial attack on Canada's policy of multiculturalism.

- *Jasmine*, a novel by Mukherjee based on the short story of the same name in *The Middle Man and Other Stories*, tells the story of a Trinidadian girl who illegally immigrates to the United States.

- *Where I'm Calling From*, a book of short stories by Raymond Carver, was published the same year as "The Management of Grief." Its minimalism provides a stark contrast to Mukherjee's style.

- *Days and Nights in Calcutta* is a memoir written by Mukherjee and her husband Clark Blaise based on a year they spent in India.

---

certainly better off emotionally. All journeys are to different extents successes or failures, and Shaila's seems to have been a success.

In a typical journey story, such as *The Odyssey,* a hero leaves his home with a clear purpose, even if it is not clear how he will achieve that purpose. When Odysseus leaves, it is to win a war with the Trojans. Likewise, when the knights of King Arthur's court leave Camelot, it is to find the Holy Grail. Shaila, as heroine, has the much darker task of going to Ireland to try to identify the bodies of her husband and sons. It is hard to imagine a successful journey for her. While Odysseus can return from the war victorious, and the knights might return with the Holy Grail, returning with the bodies of dead loved ones cannot carry the same sense of triumph. The extension of Shaila's trip beyond Ireland to India, however, reveals a deeper purpose behind the journey. There she will spend time with family and loved ones to help her cope with her loss. The title of the story emphasizes this need, which becomes the chief goal of Shaila's journey: how should she manage her grief?

This journey structure is further complicated in the story by the timing of Shaila's successes in this goal. While the Trojan War is won abroad, and the Holy Grail is found elsewhere than Camelot, Shaila's success with managing her grief seems to come after her journey is over. She has two moments of triumph at home in Canada. The first comes when she realizes her strength and abandons Judith Templeton, the pushy social worker. In doing so, Shaila also abandons the system of grief management that Judith would impose on her and the other Indo-Canadians. In most journey myths, the hero—in this case the heroine—must blaze his or her own path to the goal, and in quitting Judith's path, Shaila frees herself for her second triumph, the final hearing of her family's voices saying her "time has come," and the subsequent beginning of her new "voyage" on her own.

Yet while she is abroad, Shaila finds the sources of strength that she will later call on. The first such source comes in the character of Dr. Ranganathan. Judith preaches acceptance of grief. Kusum and her swami call the depression that accompanies grief selfish. But Dr. Ranganathan confirms in Shaila hope in the face of grief. This hope soothes her and gives her a positive emotion on which to focus. Shaila will continue to build off of it—even as she transforms it—throughout the story. Dr. Ranganathan's words—"It's a parent's duty to hope"—echo in Shaila's mind as she, with Judith, drives away from the elderly Sikh couple who refused to accept Judith's help. When Shaila sees that she shares this conviction of hope with the couple, she believes it to be part of ''our culture.'' Upon this realization, Shaila sees that Judith's impatience with what she calls ''stubbornness and ignorance'' reveal Judith's character and her implicit rejection of Shaila's own ways. This prompts her rejection of Judith and of Shaila's own complicity in Judith's project.

Shaila receives other empowerment on her journey in the form of her family. Her hope is rewarded for, in a sense, her family lives and supports her. She has the vision of Vikram in India, and back home in Canada she says ''my family surrounds me'' though ''they've changed shapes.'' She clings to the ''voices and the shapes and the nights filled with visions.'' In this spirit of hope, she waits and listens and prays, and receives the final communication from her family expressing their faith in her.

If what she learned from Dr. Ranganathan provided her first source of power, the vision of Vikram offers a second. In the vision, Vikram gives Shaila what she needs most: a sense of will and a purpose. ''What are you doing here?'' he asks, and Shaila does not know at this point. ''You must finish alone what we started together,'' he tells her. Both the fact that Shaila has this experience in a village temple in the Himalayas and that Vikram appears in a scene full of Hindu imagery emphasize Shaila's cultural roots. She seems to need a return to them to regain her bearings in life. Also, the episode feeds Shaila's general sense of hope and brings the mood of hope back into the story since what she and Vikram ''started together,'' namely moving ''halfway around the world'' and starting over, was an immensely hopeful project. Shaila returns to Canada with this mood which is essential to her growth there.

The final paragraph adds another complication to the journey structure of the story, for it takes the narrative a step beyond the typical elements of the journey myth. The basic elements are there—leaving home for a journey which ends on the return home—but here, after the return, Shaila begins a new journey, prompted not by the summons of the morgue, as in the beginning of the story, but by the pleas of her family who urge her to go. ''I do not know where this voyage I have begun will end. I do not know which direction I will take. I dropped the package on a part bench and started walking.'' So the story ends, and so Shaila's journeys are layered: the journey she makes in ''The Management of

> Put simply, in the beginning of the story she is in Canada. She goes away. She comes back, and the story ends with her in Canada. But in between, something has changed.''

Grief'' is necessary for her to continue the larger journey she began before this story began. The proper management of her grief turns out to be an obstacle in that larger journey, a journey that could have failed had Shaila remained in India rather than returned to Canada. Even if she had learned to manage her grief there, and thus succeeded in that challenge, she would have failed in the bigger journey that frames ''The Management of Grief.''

With that last paragraph, then, Mukherjee draws attention back to the bigger story she, as an immigrant writer, wants to tell through her writing, namely, the story of the challenges immigrants face and the tools they have for overcoming those obstacles. Other journeys in ''The Management of Grief'' help define the success of this immigrant, for they show other characters succeeding or failing in various degrees. Since Shaila returns to the West, resisting the temptation to stay in India, she establishes the West as her home within the structure of the journey myth. On the other hand, because Kusum forsakes what she and her husband started in the West, Kusum seems to fail. Her journey begins in her home country of India, takes her and her husband to the house across the street from Shaila, but ends back in India, thus establishing India as her home, and her journey abroad as something of a failure.

Kusum's daughter Pam fails in a different way than her mother. She adopts the culture of the West wholesale, never even venturing far from her home in Canada, and in so doing she forsakes the strength offered her by her deeper heritage. Dr. Ranganathan, on the other hand, meets with a success similar to Shaila's, and this understanding is facilitated by their friendship, while at the same time it solidifies and deepens that friendship. Shaila and Dr. Ranganathan are the beginning of a new community founded on the hopes embodied in the West as well as a faithfulness to the meaningful relationships of the past.

As Fakrum Alal points out in *Bharati Mukherjee*, ''The Management of Grief'' is unique among the stories of *The Middleman and Other Stories*, because it is the only one dealing with immigrants in Canada rather than in the United States or Central America. While Mukherjee's first book of stories, *Darkness*, dealt more with Canadian experiences, ''The Management of Grief'' is the last story Mukherjee has written about the experience of the immigrant in Canada. In this respect, it is a departure point for her, just as the end of the story—which is also the last page of *The Middleman and Other Stories*—is a departure point for Shaila. Jonathan Raban, in the *New York Times Book Review*, noted a common thread in the stories of *The Middleman and Other Stories*: ''Every story ends on a new point of departure. People are last seen walking out through an open door, planning an escape, or suspended on the brink of a blissful sexual transport,'' wrote Raban. ''For these birds of passage, America is a receding infinity of fresh beginnings; they keep aloft on luck and grace.'' Mukherjee seems to be saying that the start of Shaila's new journey at the end of the journey narrated in the ''The Management of Grief'' is typical of the immigrant experience.

Source: James Frazier, in an essay for *Literature of Developing Nations for Students*, Gale, 2000.

Liz Brent

Brent has a Ph.D. in American culture, with a specialization in film studies, from the University of Michigan. She is a freelance writer and teaches courses in the history of American cinema. In the following essay, Brent discusses themes of the rational and the irrational in Mukherjee's ''The Management of Grief.''

Mukherjee's short story ''The Management of Grief'' focuses on the character of Shaila Bhave, an East Indian immigrant to Toronto, Canada, whose husband and two sons have just died in a plane crash. The relatives of many of her friends and neighbors were also killed in the same crash. This story is concerned with the ways in which Mrs. Bhave, as well as those around her, deal with death. Throughout the story, rational versus irrational approaches to dealing with grief over their personal losses are contrasted. In addition, the culture gap between the Indian immigrants and the Canadian government

authorities assigned to help the survivors of the plane crash is also highlighted.

The story's title, ''The Management of Grief,'' highlights the contradiction Mrs. Bhave feels between rational approaches to ''managing'' the process of grief and the irrational ways in which the survivors actually experience their mourning. The Canadian government represents the epitome of rationalism in assigning a social worker, Judith Templeton, ''an appointee of the provincial government,'' to ''manage'' the survivors. In addition, the Canadian government demonstrates a lack of understanding of Indian culture as it affects the various ways in which the survivors grieve. Judith Templeton calls on Mrs. Bhave to help bridge the cultural gap between the government and the Indian immigrants. Templeton is specifically aware of the ways in which the government's rational approach to helping the survivors of the plane crash are lacking in terms of the cultural and emotional factors involved. Templeton tells Mrs. Bhave, ''We have interpreters, but we don't always have the human touch, or maybe the right human touch.'' Templeton's inability to appreciate the ways in which the survivors grieve their losses is attributed to her rationalized textbook approach to ''the management of grief.'' Mrs. Bhave presents this approach as dry and insensitive, leaving out the irrational ways in which each individual grieves in their own way: '''In the textbooks on grief management. . .there are stages to pass through: rejection, depression, acceptance, reconstruction.' She has compiled a chart and finds that six months after the tragedy, none of us still reject reality.''

The surviving family members are sent to Ireland, where the plane crashed, in order to identify bodies. There, the authorities provide them with factual information in an attempt to make them feel better. Mrs. Bhave comments with skepticism that they seem to think this rational approach will be helpful to the survivors: ''The police, the diplomats, they tell us things thinking that we're strong, that knowledge is helpful to the grieving and maybe it is.'' She, on the other hand, thinks that many of them do not find such rational information is helpful, that they ''prefer ignorance, or their own versions.'' Dr. Ranganathan, one of the survivors who has lost a large family in the plane crash, seems to be among those who find comfort in the rational. He is himself a scientist whose career is based on rational thinking, an electrical engineer whose ''work is famous around the world, something about the place where physics and electricity come together.''

Mrs. Bhave notes that, in learning that the plane crashed in an area of shark-infested water, Dr. Ranganathan is able to accept the fact that the bodies may have been eaten by sharks by perceiving it in rational terms: "In his orderly mind, science brings understanding, it holds no terror. It is the shark's duty. For every deer there is a hunter, for every fish a fisherman."

By contrast, many of the survivors rely on irrational ways of "managing" their grief. Mrs. Bhave's friend Kusum turns to her swami, a religious mentor, for consolation and wisdom. Kusum thus deals with the death of her family in part by the wisdom of her swami, who attributes the tragedy to "fate." She tells Mrs. Bhave that, "we can't escape our fate. He says that all those people. . .were fated to die together off this beautiful bay." Mrs. Bhave herself, however, does not find the wisdom of a swami, or the notion of "fate," to be any comfort; she thinks to herself that, instead of a swami, "I have my Valium." Kusum eventually deals with the loss of her family by moving, on her swami's advice, to his ashram in Hardwar. She tells Mrs. Bhave that she is "pursuing inner peace," but Mrs. Bhave seems to be skeptical about the value of such a pursuit.

Dr. Ranganathan, although a scientist and a rationalist, also draws on spiritual conceptions in his experience of grief. Unlike some of the others, he cannot bring himself to sell his house, because his house has become for him a site of spiritual devotion: "The house is a temple, he says; the king-sized bed in the master bedroom is a shrine. He sleeps on a folding cot. A devotee."

Mrs. Bhave herself feels caught between a rational and an irrational perspective on the loss of her family. Her mother's mother had been excessively superstitious, thinking the fact that her husband had died of diabetes at the age of nineteen was a sign that she herself was "a harbinger of bad luck." As a result of this belief, Mrs. Bhave's grandmother had neglected her own daughter for a life of self-deprivation. In reaction against this unpleasant upbringing based on superstition, Mrs. Bhave's mother "grew up a rationalist," and both of her parents "abhor mindless mortification." Mrs. Bhave thus feels caught between the rationalism of her parents and the irrational thinking involved in "faith," spirituality and religion. As she explains, "The zamindar's daughter kept stubborn faith in Vedic rituals; my parents rebelled. I am trapped between two modes of knowledge. At thir-

> " Mrs. Bhave herself, however, does not find the wisdom of a swami, or the notion of 'fate,' to be any comfort; she thinks to herself that, instead of a swami, 'I have my Valium.'"

ty-six, I am too old to start over and too young to give up. Like my husband's spirit, I flutter between two worlds."

Mrs. Bhave does, while in Ireland, take comfort in the irrational hope that, because one of her boys is a champion swimmer, he must have survived the plane crash into the ocean and swum with his little brother to an island where they are still alive and await rescue. Because she clings to this hope, Mrs. Bhave does not want to identify her son among the photographs of recovered bodies. While spending six months with her parents in India after the crash, Mrs. Bhave is confronted with numerous offers of spiritual assistance in her grieving. She and her parents travel to "the holy spots" in India: "In Varanasi, Kalighat, Rishikesh, Hardwar, astrologers and palmists seek me out and for a fee offer me cosmic consolations." Mrs. Bhave, nonetheless, is uninterested in these spiritual or "cosmic" approaches to "managing" her grief. However, she unexpectedly has an "irrational" experience in "an abandoned temple in a tiny Himalayan village." She states that "as I make my offering of flowers and sweetmeats to the god of a tribe of animists, my husband descends to me." In this vision, her husband takes her hand, smiles, and tells her, "*You must finish what we started.*" Because her mother "has no patience with ghosts, prophetic dreams, holy men, and cults," Mrs. Bhave lies to her about having experienced anything out of the ordinary in the temple. Back in Toronto, Mrs. Bhave finds that her incredible "calm" over the tragedy is in part due to the fact that she does not yet experience it as a loss: "How do I tell Judith Templeton that my family surrounds me, and that like creatures in epics, they've changed shapes?" Her sense that her husband and sons are still with her is so strong that "my days, even my nights, are thrilling."

The story culminates in a visit Mrs. Bhave makes as a translator for Judith Templeton to the home of an older Indian couple, newly arrived in Canada, whose adult sons were killed in the plane crash. In this situation, Mrs. Bhave becomes keenly aware that Judith Templeton's "management" approach to helping the grieving survivors of the crash is completely insensitive both to the cultural nuances of the Indian families, and to the irrational ways in which "we all grieve in our own way." The older couple seem to be in complete denial of the death of their sons, and Mrs. Bhave secretly understands this feeling; she thinks, "I want to say, my boys and my husband are with me too, more than ever." The older man sums up their resistance to the machine-like, rational, "management" approach of Mrs. Templeton through an indirect reference; because they have not left their sons' apartment or paid any bills, Judith Templeton explains to them, the water and electricity are going to be shut off; the old man's response is, "Who needs all this machinery?" This question symbolically expresses Mrs. Bhave's feeling that the "machinery" for "managing" grief, which the government has imposed upon the surviving families, is completely unhelpful to them in dealing with their personal losses. Upon leaving the apartment of the older couple, Mrs. Bhave, fed up with Judith Templeton and the Canadian government's attempt to rationalize the grieving process, spontaneously walks out on Judith Templeton in exasperation, and without explanation.

Mrs. Bhave is only able to move on with her life when the spiritual presence of her husband and sons leaves her. Toward the end of the story, she says, "The voices and the shapes and the nights filled with visions ended abruptly several weeks ago." Although not following the advice of a swami or any other organized religion, Mrs. Bhave makes sense of her experience of grief in her own way. She interprets the disappearance of these visions as "a sign." After one final vision of her family, Mrs. Bhave is able to genuinely begin her life again without them: "I heard the voices of my family one last time. *Your time has come, they said. Go, be brave.*"

Source: Liz Brent, in an essay for *Literature of Developing Nations for Students*, Gale, 2000.

Jennifer Bussey

Bussey holds a master's degree in interdisciplinary studies and a bachelor's degree in English literature. She is an independent writer specializing in literature. In the following essay, she describes

Mukherjee's use of distance (familial, emotional, psychological, geographical, and cultural) in the story "The Management of Grief."

Much of Bharati Mukherjee's fiction reflects her experiences in diverse cultures. She was born and reared in India, attended the University of Iowa, and then lived in Canada with her new husband. The couple returned to the United States, however, due to the racism Mukherjee faced in Canada. Her admirers are intrigued by the ways she works these unusual experiences into the lives of her characters as she depicts separation and confusion among differing cultures. In the short story "The Management of Grief," Bharati's main character is Shaila Bhave, a recently widowed Indian woman living in Canada. Shaila encounters separation and distance in many forms—familial, emotional, psychological, geographical, and cultural. What makes the story particularly interesting is that Mukherjee demonstrates the dynamic nature of distance. It is not fixed, which means that Shaila can expand and close various kinds of distances as she desires and as she is able. She is subject to changes that are beyond her control, such as the loss of her husband and sons in an airplane crash. But she discovers that, although the physical separation of her family has been forced on her, she can choose to maintain emotional and spiritual closeness to them.

The story's title is a reference to distancing emotionally and psychologically from the deep pain of grief; the businesslike word "management" implies that the pain of losing a loved one can be regulated and controlled. And this Shaila and the other characters attempt to do, using various forms of distance. In the first lines of the story, the reader senses distance between Shaila and the women in her kitchen. Shaila says, "A woman I don't know is boiling tea the Indian way in my kitchen. There are a lot of women I don't know in my kitchen, whispering, and moving tactfully." As she sits in her own home, Shaila is surrounded by strangers with whom she feels no desire to connect. She watches with detachment as the women prepare tea and food, trying to help with what is, at this point in the story, an unclear but ominous situation. Aware of her own odd calmness and composure, Shaila thinks, "I wonder if pills alone can explain this calm. Not peace, just a deadening quiet. I was always controlled, but never repressed. Sound can reach me, but my body is tensed, ready to scream. I hear their voices all around me. I hear my boys and Vikram cry, 'Mommy, Shaila!' and their screams insulate me, like headphones.'' A few pages later, a government official commends her ability to cope with the loss of her family, and Shaila thinks to herself, ''I am a freak. No one who has ever known me would think of me reacting this way. This terrible calm will not go away.'' She realizes that she is completely numb to the feelings she ought to be experiencing, and powerless to change this.

The first few pages of the story leave the reader questioning; it is clear that something tragic has happened, and that it affects many Indian people in Canada, but the horror of the plane crash is not revealed until several pages later. This technique creates confusion and curiosity, which draw the reader into the narrative. At the same time, it creates distance between the reader and the storyteller. Shaila, as the narrator, seems to be holding the reader at arm's length until ready to reveal the specifics of the awful tragedy. Shaila's emotional numbness and her unwillingness to reveal herself to the reader suggest that she is suffering the pangs of survivor's guilt. (Survivor's guilt is often felt by people who survive a tragic accident, or by the families of those killed.) Shaila comments that the lucky ones in the crash are the ''intact families with no survivors.'' Clearly, she feels that it is she, not her husband and sons, who has been ''cut off,'' or put at a distance; they are ''intact,'' together.

Shaila's trips to Ireland and then to India signify geographical distance, and each place has special meaning in Shaila's life. Her family's plane crashed over Ireland, which embodies her profound loss and holds the key to her ability or inability to say goodbye. On her trip to India, she must bury her husband and sons, and reconnect with the rest of her family in hopes of finding strength. On the surface, Shaila's journey to Ireland is for the purpose of identifying her loved ones, but the real reason she must go is to cast tokens of her love for them on the water and bid them farewell. In a very real sense, by traversing physical distance she is trying to close some of the distance between herself and her lost family. This is especially true for her husband. She explains to Kusum, another Indian woman who was widowed by the crash, ''I never once told him that I loved him. I was too much the well brought up woman. I was so well brought up I never felt comfortable calling my husband by his first name.'' In Ireland, she tosses a poem she has written for him into the water, thinking to herself, ''Finally he'll know my feelings for him.'' Clearly, the emotional distance between Shaila and her husband was great while he was alive, and only now that the distance is widened

> **❝** Shaila comments that the lucky ones in the crash are the 'intact families with no survivors.' Clearly, she feels that it is she, not her husband and sons, who has been 'cut off,' or put at a distance; they are 'intact,' together."

by his death does she take steps to draw closer to him.

Shaila's travels to Ireland and India also represent her impulse to close an expansive gap within herself, so she can feel the feelings she should be experiencing, and so she can discover who she is on her own and what she should do. Although crossing geographical distances does not literally bring her closer to the answers she seeks, the journey helps her understand that those answers are only to be found by forging her own identity. When Shaila has the vision of her husband telling her to finish the work they started and later hears the voices of her family telling her to be brave, she realizes that she has done the seemingly impossible—achieved emotional closeness to her family, even across the divide of death. She also understands that her husband respects her strength and wants her to be independent and fully alive. Early in the story, Kusum asks Shaila, ''Why does God give us so much if all along He intends to take it away?'' Shaila's story shows that while gifts sometimes are taken away, when something is taken away, something else is also given; endings are also beginnings.

Mukherjee shows that people often maintain a safe psychological distance between their vulnerability and the truth. Forced to cope with an unspeakable tragedy, Kusum and Shaila keep the truth of their losses away from their hearts until they are ready to face it. Kusum begins to see a swami, who tells her that she should not be depressed, because her family is now in a better place than Kusum herself. He adds that being depressed over their loss is selfish. Believing this allows Kusum to postpone—to manage—her grief. Shaila accomplishes the same end by holding onto the hope that, by some miracle, her sons survived the crash and are waiting on a nearby island to be rescued. She contends that because her older son was an accomplished swimmer, he could have swum to safety. Since he would not leave his younger brother to drown or be devoured by sharks, he would have pulled him to the island, too. She reasons, "No wonder my boys' photographs haven't turned up in the gallery of the recovered dead." This thought brings relief, as does viewing a number of bodies that do not turn out to be those of her sons. She is ecstatic and thinks of her suitcase full of dry clothes for her boys. Later, she rationalizes her seemingly irrational hopefulness when she thinks, "In our culture, it is a parent's duty to hope." Not until she has a vision of her husband's spirit does she begin to accept that she is alone in the world, at which point she closes the gap between her wishes and the truth.

The story also depicts a wide gap between Indian and Canadian culture. The bureaucrat Judith Templeton personifies the government's misguided efforts to help people it does not understand. Judith is a social worker, yet she is grossly unequipped to handle the trials of the people she is trying to help. Her goal is to force them to accept the kind of help the government can offer, but when they resist, she makes no effort to understand why. Instead, she views them as difficult and ignorant. Rather than educate herself about Indian culture, she spouts textbook research about grief management, assuming that this information applies universally to anyone suffering the loss of a loved one. She then categorizes the bereft according to which stage of grieving they have reached, using this is a measure of her own success or failure. Like Shaila and Kusum, Judith tries to control grief. Shaila tries to help Judith by acting as a translator, but Judith's insensitivity becomes too much, and Shaila leaves her on her own. Shaila chooses, finally, to accept the distance between herself and the social worker.

The story ends on a hopeful note. Throughout the story, Shaila is caught between the known and the unknown, between feeling and numbness, and between fear and confidence. She says, "At thirty-six, I am too old to start over and too young to give up. Like my husband's spirit, I flutter between two worlds." In this state of mind, Shaila actually inhabits distance. She exists between two worlds until she hears her family telling her, "Your time has come. Go, be brave." She then chooses to live fully. She accepts that she is beginning a new journey, and although she does not know where it

will take her, she is ready to "start walking." She accepts that she is not too old to start over, and, more importantly, that she is not afraid to start over. She steps out of the gap and begins the arduous task of creating a new life. Through a process of creating and closing various distances, Shaila has navigated, and perhaps even managed, her grief.

Source: Jennifer Bussey, in an essay for *Literature of Developing Nations for Students*, Gale, 2000.

Sources

Birch, Dinah, "Other People," in *London Review of Books*, Vol. 11, No. 13, July 6, 1989, pp. 18-19.

Ching-Liang Low, Gail, "In a Free State: Postcolonialism and Postmodernism in Bharati Mukherjee's Fiction," in *Women: A Cultural Review*, Vol. 4, No. 1, 1993, pp. 8-17.

Mathur, Suchitra, "Bharati Mukherjee: Overview," in *Feminist Writers*, edited by Pamela Kester-Shelton, St. James Press, 1996.

Mukherjee, Bharati, "Immigrant Writing: Give Us Your Maximalists!," in *New York Times Book Review*, August 28, 1988, pp. 1, 28-29.

Raban, Jonathan, review of *The Middleman and Other Stories*, in *New York Times Book Review*, June 19, 1988, pp. 1, 22-23.

Rajan, Gita, "Bharati Mukherjee," in *Writers of the Indian Diaspora*, edited by Emmanuel S. Nelson, Greenwood Press, 1993, pp. 235-42.

Sant-Wade, Arvindra, and Karen Marguerite Radell, "Refashioning the Self: Immigrant Women in Bharati Mukherjee's New World," in *Studies in Short Fiction*, Vol. 29, No. 1, Winter, 1992, pp. 11-17.

Sharma Knippling, Alpana, "Toward an Investigation of the Subaltern in Bharati Mukherjee's *The Middleman and Other Stories* and *Jasmine*," in *Bharati Mukherjee: Critical Perspectives*, edited by Emmanuel S. Nelson, Garland Publishing, 1993, pp. 143-59.

Further Reading

Alam, Fakrul, *Bharati Mukherjee*, Twayne Publishers, 1996. Alam surveys all of Mukherjee's work up to 1996 and places it within the context of her life. This is an excellent introduction to Mukherjee and contains a fine bibliography.

Campbell, Joseph, *The Hero with a Thousand Faces*, Princeton University Press, 1949.

In this classic mythology text, Campbell explores the journey myth in all its complexity, drawing on widely varying sources, both Eastern and Western.

Dhawan, R. K., *The Fiction of Bharati Mukherjee: A Critical Symposium*, Prestige (New Delhi, India), 1996.
Dhawan provides a critical overview of the unique work of Mukherjee as an Indian author writing in English.

Nelson, Emmanuel S., ed., *Bharati Mukherjee: Critical Perspectives*, Garland Publishing, 1993.
This group of essays by various critics sprung out of an academic convention at which Mukherjee herself was present. The essays include discussions of most of Mukherjee's work.

————, *Reworlding: Literature of the Indian Diaspora*, Greenwood Press, 1992.
This collection of essays by various critics and edited by Nelson includes essays on Mukherjee. It is a good introduction to the critical issues and writers of the Indian diaspora.

Parameswaran, Uma, "A Review of *The Middleman and Other Stories*," in *World Literature Today*, Vol. 64, No. 2, Spring, 1990, pp. 363-65.
In this book review, the critic commends Mukherjee's collection as a whole and devotes close to half the review discussing "The Management of Grief."

The Martyr

Ngugi wa Thiong'o

1974

The short story ''The Martyr'' by Kenyan novelist Ngugi wa Thiong'o, East Africa's leading writer, was first published in 1974, in his collection *Secret Lives and Other Stories*. ''The Martyr'' takes place in colonial Kenya, during a time of rebellion amongst the native Kikuyu people against the white European settlers and plantation owners. News of the murder of two white settlers by their own African ''houseboy'' initiates the events of the story. Mrs. Hill, a white plantation owner, is visited by her friends Mrs. Hardy and Mrs. Smiles to discuss the murder. Njoroge, an African man who works as the ''houseboy'' of Mrs. Hill, has plans to kill Mrs. Hill that night, with the help of the Ihii (Freedom Boys). While Mrs. Hill prides herself on her generosity to the Africans who work for her and the loyalty of her ''houseboy,'' Njoroge in fact deeply resents her for her ''smug liberalism'' and her ''paternalism'' in these matters. In his small hut that night, Njoroge thinks of his own wives and children, and then of Mrs. Hill's children, who are away at school. Seeing her ''humanized'' in this light, he is unable to conceive of killing her. He runs to her house to warn her before the Freedom Boys arrive to murder her. Alarmed and suspicious, Mrs. Hill incorrectly believes he is knocking at her door to kill her—and she shoots him in what she believes is self-defense. Thus, ''she had in fact killed her savior.''

''The Martyr'' addresses several concerns central to Ngugi's fiction and nonfiction writing. It takes place at a time of social and political upheaval

in Kenyan history. The oppressive nature of the European colonial presence in Kenya is portrayed from the perspective of a native Kenyan. The typical colonial attitude in Africa—that the African people are "savages" who benefit from the "civilization" of the white colonists—is expressed through the opinions of the white characters in the story. The Christian imagery of the "martyr" draws on Ngugi's Christian upbringing and his later renunciation of Christianity as a tool of colonialism. Finally, Ngugi explores the complexity of African and European relations in the colonial era, thus "humanizing" both sides of the conflict.

Author Biography

East Africa's most prominent writer, Ngugi wa Thiong'o, was born James Thiong'o Ngugi, in Limuru, Kenya, on January 5, 1938. In order to shed his colonial Christian namesake, Ngugi dropped "James" from his name in favor of his traditional name. As a result of his eventual international recognition as a novelist, short-story writer, playwright, and essayist, he is often referred to simply as Ngugi. Ngugi was one of twenty-eight children; his father, a peasant farmer who could not own his own land, had four wives, and Ngugi was the fifth child of the third wife. Ngugi first received primary education beginning in 1946, in a school established by colonialist missionaries. Two years later, he was transferred to a school run by members of his native Kikuyu tribe, which provided a more Afrocentric education. Beginning in 1955, Ngugi attended Alliance High School at Kikuyu. He was strongly affected by the Mau Mau Rebellion, which lasted from 1952 to 1960. Returning to his village from his high school, Ngugi found that his home and village had been burned to the ground through government efforts at dissipating the rebellion. Ngugi attended Makerere University College in Kampala beginning in 1959, from which he earned a B.A. in English, with honors, in 1963. In 1964, he earned a second B.A. from Leeds University in Yorkshire, England. He began graduate work at Leeds, but chose not to pursue a master's degree, making his fiction-writing a priority. From 1964 to 1970, he taught at several schools in East Africa and was a lecturer in English literature at the University of Nairobi in Kenya from 1967 to 1969. During this time, he and other faculty transformed the English department into a Department of African Languages and Literature. It was about this time that he changed his

name. From 1970 to 1971, he was a visiting lecturer at Northwestern University in Evanston, Illinois. He served as department chair of literature at the University of Nairobi from 1972 to 1977.

In 1977, Ngugi decided to write in the African languages of Kikuyu or Swahili, rather than English. He co-wrote a play in his native Kikuyu language, entitled *Ngaahika Ndeenda* (*I Will Marry When I Want*), which was first performed in 1977. As a result of the political message of the play, Ngugi was arrested and imprisoned without trial for a year; his experience of imprisonment is recorded in *Detained: A Writer's Prison Diary* (1981). Upon release from prison in 1978, Ngugi had lost his position at the University of Nairobi. In 1982, his theater group was banned by the government in a time of social rebellion and government repression, and Ngugi chose to live in exile. He subsequently lived and worked primarily in England, and later in the U.S. as a professor at Yale University and New York University. His 1986 novel *Matigari ma Njiruungi*, written in Kikuyu and translated in 1989 as *Matigari*, inspired such social unrest in Kenya that it was banned by the government. Although in exile, with his work unavailable to the Kenyan audience he most cherishes, Ngugi is considered the foremost East African novelist of his time. He remains best known for his novels, set at various points in Kenyan colonial and post-colonial history, including *Weep Not, Child* (1964), *A River Between* (1965), *A Grain of Wheat* (1967), *Petals of Blood* (1977), and *Devil on the Cross* (1980).

Plot Summary

The story begins with the announcement of the murder of Mr. and Mrs. Garstone, European settlers in Kenya, by their own "houseboy," a native of Kenya who had worked for them. The news of this act of rebellion by "unknown gangsters" is widespread. Mrs. Hardy and Mrs. Smiles, European settlers in the area, visit Mrs. Hill, also a European settler, to discuss the news. Mrs. Hill, one of the first settlers to the area, owns vast tea plantations. Her husband has died, and her children are at school in England. She prides herself on her fair and generous treatment of the Africans whom she employs. She is especially proud of her generosity in building the huts of her employees with real bricks. Mrs. Hill believes that the Africans can be "civilized" with the proper patience and understanding. Mrs. Hardy and Mrs. Smiles, on the other hand, see the African people as "savages" who will never be civilized. Mrs. Hill calls for Njoroge, an African man who has been employed as her "houseboy" for over ten years, to bring tea to her guests. Mrs. Hill boasts of the loyalty and love Njoroge has for her. That evening, Njoroge finishes work at the house of Mrs. Hill and returns to his brick hut. He feels disdainful of the tiny brick hut Mrs. Hill is so proud of providing for him and his family; he has sent his two wives and several children to live elsewhere because they cannot all fit into the little hut. Njoroge has planned this night to kill Mrs. Hill as an act of rebellion, with the aid of the Ihii (Freedom Boys). As he sits in his hut, thinking of his own family, he begins to think of Mrs. Hill's family—her deceased husband and her children in England. Thinking of her as a mother, Njoroge loses the heart to kill her; as a member of a family, she is humanized in his mind. He decides to run to her house and warn her before the Freedom Boys come to kill her. Meanwhile, Mrs. Hill, influenced by the conversation with her friends earlier in the day, readies a gun in order to protect herself. When she hears Njoroge knocking at her door, she incorrectly assumes that he has come to kill her, and she shoots him in what she believes to be self-defense. Thus, Mrs. Hill has "in fact killed her savior." The news of Njoroge's death celebrates Mrs. Hill for her bravery in fighting "a gang fifty strong." Her friends, Mrs. Hardy and Mrs. Smiles, visit her to congratulate her for this act. Mrs. Hill, however, remains reserved in her reaction to the situation, for "the circumstances of Njoroge's death worried her. The more she thought about it, the more of a puzzle it was to her." Mrs. Hill concludes with a sigh, saying, "I don't know." Mrs. Hardy and Mrs. Smiles, however, agree with one another that "all of them should be whipped."

Characters

Mr. and Mrs. Garstone

Mr. and Mrs. Garstone are white colonial settlers of Kenya, whose murder in their home by rebellious "unknown gangsters" initiates the events of the story. The news of this murder "was all on the front pages of the daily papers and figured importantly in the Radio Newsreel." Their murder is significant because of its political implications: "Perhaps this was so because they were the first European settlers to be killed in the increased wave of violence that had spread all over the country. The

violence was said to have political motives." The widespread news and "talk" of their murder and betrayal by their own "houseboy" is significant because it creates an atmosphere in which Mrs. Hill becomes afraid of Njoroge, her own "houseboy." It is this suspicion that ultimately leads her to shoot and kill him in what she believes to be an act of self-defense.

Mrs. Hardy

Mrs. Hardy is one of the white settlers who, along with Mrs. Smiles, visits Mrs. Hill to discuss the murder of Mr. and Mrs. Garstone. She is described as "of Boer descent and had early migrated into the country from South Africa. Having no opinions of her own about anything, she mostly found herself agreeing with any views that most approximated those of her husband and her race." Mrs. Hardy represents the closed-minded, ignorant white settler who does not bother to question the racism inherent to the European presence in Africa. Her tendency to adopt the opinions of those around her, and of her "race" in general, exemplifies the ways in which a racist social and economic system is perpetuated.

Mrs. Hill

Mrs. Hill is a white European settler. As her husband has died and her children are in school in England, she lives alone, without family. Mrs. Hill holds the social status among the white settlers of being one of the first, and most prominent, of the plantation owners in the region: "Being one of the earliest settlers and owning a lot of land with big tea plantations sprawling right across the country, she was much respected by the others if not liked by all." Mrs. Hill is a liberal, who takes pride in what she considers to be her generous and fair treatment of the African people who work on her plantation. Her "smug liberalism, her paternalism," however, is resented by Njoroge, her "houseboy." The limits of her self-perceived kindness toward Njoroge are tested when she assumes he has come to her house to kill her—and shoots him in what she believes to be her own self-defense. Although the reader knows that Njoroge has in fact come to rescue her from his fellow brethren, who themselves plan to kill her, Mrs. Hill remains ignorant of his true intentions in knocking on her door at night: "She did not know that she had in fact killed her savior." Nonetheless, her fellow white settlers perceive her act of murder as one of bravery and heroism: "On the following day, it was all in the papers. That a single woman could fight a gang fifty strong was bravery unknown. And to think she had killed one too!'' Mrs. Hill, however, seems to be disturbed by her own conscience in the matter; while her friends are congratulating her on her act of ''bravery,'' ''Mrs. Hill kept quiet. The circumstances of Njoroge's death worried her. The more she thought about it, the more of a puzzle it was to her.''

Njoroge

Njoroge is the man who ultimately becomes the ''martyr'' of the story's title. He has worked as Mrs. Hill's ''houseboy'' for over ten years. He is described as ''a tall, broad-shouldered man nearing middle age. . .He wore green trousers, with a red cloth-band round the waist and a red fez on his head.'' Njoroge first appears when Mrs. Hill calls him to bring tea. At the end of the day, Njoroge returns to his hut. Although he has two wives and several children, they have been sent to live elsewhere. He resents Mrs. Hill's ''smug liberalism'' and ''paternalism'' toward him. He has planned that night, with other Ihii (Freedom Boys), to kill Mrs. Hill as an act of rebellion against the settlers. However, as he awaits the arrival of his fellow rebels, he begins to think of Mrs. Hill's children; seeing her in the light of her role as mother to a family, Njoroge finds that he cannot bring himself to kill her. He decides instead to run to her house and warn her before the Freedom Boys arrive. Mrs. Hill, however, incorrectly interprets his knock at her door as an attempt to gain entrance and kill her-and she shoots him in what she believes is self defense. Njoroge, as Mrs. Hill's would-be ''savior,'' thus symbolically becomes a ''martyr'' in the Christian sense of the word—he becomes a Christ figure who dies for the sins of the white settlers against the African people.

Mrs. Smiles

Mrs. Smiles is a European settler who, along with Mrs. Hardy, discusses the murder of the Garstones with Mrs. Hill at the beginning of the story. Mrs. Smiles is the most aggressively racist of the three women. The opinions she holds of the African population are associated with the ''missionary'' attitude most typically held by Europeans in Africa: ''Mrs. Smiles was a lean, middle-aged woman whose tough, determined nose and tight lips reminded one so vividly of a missionary. In a sense she was. Convinced that she and her kind formed an oasis of civilization in a wild country of savage people, she considered it almost her calling to keep

on reminding the natives and anyone else in fact, by her gait, talk and general bearing.''

Themes

Colonialism

The most central theme in all of Ngugi's work is the effect of colonialism and post-colonialism on the African people. ''The Martyr'' takes place during a time of rebellion among Africans working on plantations against the European plantation owners. Through the characters of Mrs. Hardy, Mrs. Smiles, and Mrs. Hill, the narrator touches on widespread attitudes of the ''settlers,'' or colonialists, regarding the African people who work for them. Mrs. Hardy is the most outspoken of the three women regarding her racist attitude toward the Africans. She considers them to be ''savage,'' without hope of becoming ''civilized.'' In the final lines of the story, both Mrs. Hardy and Mrs. Smiles agree that ''all of them should be whipped.'' Mrs. Hill, on the other hand, holds ''liberal'' values in regard to her African employees. She prides herself on her generosity toward them, and adopts a patronizing attitude of patience toward them. Njoroge, an African man who works as Mrs. Hill's ''houseboy,'' provides an African perspective on the European colonists. Njoroge resents Mrs. Hill's ''smug liberalism'' and her ''paternalism'' toward him. While he is described as ''nearing middle age,'' Mrs. Hill still refers to him as ''boy.'' Furthermore, the brick huts which she feels she has so generously provided her employees are regarded by Njoroge as so small as to be unfit to house his family. The atmosphere of violent rebellion in which the story is set is justified by the degree of oppression practiced by the European plantation owners against their African employees.

Public Opinion

The events of Ngugi's story are in part narrated through gossip, hearsay, and the news media, which collectively constitute the public opinions of the white European colonialist settlers. The alleged murder of Mr. and Mrs. Garstone by their ''houseboy'' is the news event with which the story begins, and which sets off the subsequent action of the story. The story begins by reporting a reputedly factual event in the language of newspaper journalism: ''When Mr. and Mrs. Garstone were murdered in their home by unknown gangsters. . .'' However, within the same sentence, the narrator states that

Topics for Further Study

- Ngugi's life has spanned both colonial and post-colonial Kenyan history. Learn more about Kenya during the period of British colonization. What were the conditions of the people native to Kenya during the colonial period? During the post-colonial period (after gaining national independence in 1963)?

- Ngugi was deeply affected by the events of the Mau Mau Rebellion in Kenya, which lasted from 1952 to 1956. Learn more about the events of the Mau Mau Rebellion. How was the region affected by these events? What were the results of the rebellion?

- Kenya is located in the region of the African continent known as East Africa. Find a map of Africa. Where is Kenya located? What nations surround Kenya in East Africa? Learn more about the history of other nations in East Africa. In what ways has the development of these nations mirrored or differed from Kenya's development?

- Learn more about recent history and current events in Kenya over the past 5 to 10 years. How have the social, political, and economic conditions of the nation changed since the 1970s, when "The Martyr" was written?

"there was a lot of talk about it," implying that the "facts" of the incident, as reported, take on a life of their own within the realm of public opinion and gossip. The narrator continues, "It was all on the front pages of the daily papers and figured importantly in the Radio Newsreel." The implication is that the supposed murder of the European couple is a media event, regardless of whether or not the incident is accurately reported. The narrator goes on to mention the circulation of this news item through hearsay and rumor: "The violence was said to have political motives. And wherever you went, in the marketplaces, in the Indian bazaars, in a remote African duka, you were bound to hear something about the murder." Note that the narrator is careful to distance himself from any statement of fact about the incident; rather, the public opinion itself is reported in a tone of neutrality. This opening passage is important to an interpretation of the media event which occurs toward the end of the story—the killing of Njoroge by Mrs. Hill. The death of Njoroge is reported by the narrator in a similar manner—through a statement of the media reportage and the public opinion expressed by the Europeans: "On the following day, it was all in the papers. That a single woman could fight a gang of fifty

strong was bravery unknown. And to think she had killed one too!" The gross inaccuracy and distorted perception of the incident among the Europeans functions as a commentary on the workings of public opinion, and particularly the demonization of the Africans in the generally held opinion of European colonists.

Style

Narration and Tone

This story is narrated in the *third person*, meaning that the narrator is not a character in the story. However, this does not mean that the narrator's tone is completely objective. In fact, this particular narrator adopts a tone of almost exaggerated sarcasm in conveying the racist attitudes of the white European settlers. For instance, in describing Mrs. Hill's sense of herself as generous and kind toward the Africans who work for her, the narrator uses sarcasm to emphasize the self-congratulatory attitude of the "liberal" settlers, who felt themselves to be doing a favor for the Africans:

Not only had she built some brick quarters (*brick,* mind you) but had also put up a school for the children. It did not matter if the school had not enough teachers or if the children learnt only half a day and worked in the plantations for the other half; it was more than most other settlers had the courage to do!

The narrator's sarcasm is particularly apparent in the mocking tone of the parenthetical comment, "(*brick,* mind you)"; the emphasis on the word "brick" indicates the extent to which Mrs. Hill considers herself generous to her African employees above and beyond all duty. When Njoroge thinks with disdain of the inadequacy of his "brick" dwelling to house his family, the sarcasm of this earlier comment is justified. Thus, the narrator, though not a character in the story, adopts a perspective which is in keeping with Njoroge and other Africans—using sarcasm to mock and express disdain for the racist treatment of the white settlers toward the Africans.

Setting

Although it is not stated specifically in the story, it is clear to the reader familiar with Ngugi's background that it is set in Kenya during a time of rebellion among the Kikuyu people against the white plantation owners who exploit their labor. This is significant to the story because the Kikuyu were the first group of Africans in Kenya to launch an organized resistance against colonialism, beginning in the 1920s and 1930s. The Kikuyu were primarily concerned with the European ownership of land that was rightfully theirs; the Kikuyu were also the primary source of labor on the white plantations. Njoroge recalls that his father was killed for his participation in the "struggle" of the Kikuyu against the colonists: "He had died in the struggle—the struggle to rebuild the destroyed shrines. That was at the famous 1923 Nairobi Massacre when police fired on people peacefully demonstrating for their rights." Furthermore, the outright theft of land on the part of the colonists from the rightful Kikuyu owners is given direct reference; Njoroge recalls, "A big portion of the land now occupied by Mrs. Hill was the land his father had shown him as belonging to the family. They had found the land occupied when his father and some of the others had temporarily retired to Muranga owing to famine." Thus, although the characters in this story are fictional, the historical and cultural circumstances of the story are based on actual historical conditions and events in the history of the Kikuyu people.

Christian Iconography

Indirect references to Christian iconography are central to the symbolic meaning of this story. Ngugi, though he later renounced Christianity, had originally been educated in schools run by missionaries. The influence is apparent in the references to Christian iconography and symbolism in many of his stories. In this story, the "martyr" of the story's title refers to the image of Christ as a martyr. The character of Njoroge is thus symbolically represented as a Christ figure. His decision to save, rather than kill, Mrs. Hill is an act of what could be considered Christian charity. Njoroge's death at the hands of Mrs. Hill thus renders him a martyr to the cause of the Kikuyu struggle against the colonists. The narrator makes clear the symbolic role of Njoroge as a Christ figure in the line stating that Mrs. Hill "did not know that she had in fact killed her savior." The word "savior" to describe Njoroge clearly connects him with the image of Christ as savior.

Literary Heritage

Kenya is a country of dramatic variety, both in terms of its varied topography and cultural makeup. The land itself includes tropical coastline, largely uninhabited inland desert areas, and high fertile farmland bordered by the two tallest mountains in Africa. While nearly ninety-nine percent of the people are black Africans, there are broad ethnic and linguistic divisions that divide the native population into more than forty ethnic groups. The largest of these groups, the Gikuyu, of which Ngugi is a member, makes up twenty percent of Kenya's population of 32 million people. Other large ethnic groups include the Kalenjin, Kamba, Luhya, and Luo, all of whom can be distinguished by their unique languages or dialects. The remaining one percent of the population is made up of East Indians, Europeans, and Arabs. Many Kenyans are able to overcome language barriers between groups by communicating in Swahili, the national language, or English, the official language.

Traditional Kenyan literary forms are largely oral. Oral stories, dramas, riddles, histories, myths, songs, proverbs, and other expressions are used to educate and entertain as well to remind the community of ancestors' heroic deeds, the past, and the precedents for customs and traditions. Folktale tellers often use call-response techniques in which a praise accompanies a narrative with music. In Ngugi's *Petals of Blood*, Nyakinyua is one of the keepers of the cultural heritage. She is the village bard who tells stories and leads the community in song. During the circumcision she sings a witty, ribald song with Nguguna, which is seen in contrast to the vulgar verses sung by Chui and his modern friends. In the novel, Ngugi's use of different points of view and the recounting of events in the form of stories may be seen as his acknowledgment of traditional oral literary practices. In a 1980 essay, the author remarks that although the African novel uses a borrowed form, its great debt to the native oral tradition is narrative. Ngugi's 1977 play *I Will Marry When I Want*, which led to his arrest, was apparently most offensive to the government because of its use of songs to emphasize its messages. The play struck a chord with the Gikuyu-speaking audience because of its use of traditional literary techniques. After his imprisonment, Ngugi made a conscious decision to switch to writing in his native Gikuyu. He felt he must do this in order to more effectively reach the people for whom his writings are concerned—the peasant and working classes in Kenya.

Historical Context

Kenya

The history of this region during the late 19th and the 20th centuries is characterized by European colonization and exploitation of members of the tribes native to the area, such as the Massai and the Kikuyu. Britain, Germany, and France all had a hand in colonizing the area. The Imperial British East Africa Company dominated these efforts, beginning in the 1880s. In 1894, the British government declared the area the East Africa Protectorate. In the 1890s, British military forces were employed in order to quell resistance by African tribes to European rule. A railway, built between 1895 and 1903, was a key factor in encouraging European settlement and cultivation of the East Africa Protectorate in the early 1900s. During this time, members of the native African tribes were restricted to reservations and forced into labor on European plantations. In 1920, the region was renamed the Kenya Colony, after the region's highest mountain. Throughout the 1920s, Africans, such as members of the Kikuyu tribe, organized to press for their rights. In the 1940s, a small number of Africans were allowed to sit on the Legislative Council. In 1960, a conference in London led to an African majority on the legislative council for the first time. In 1963, the Republic of Kenya was created, under a new constitution that allowed for self-rule and national independence.

The Mau Mau Rebellion

In the decade preceding Kenya's national independence, large-scale protest, organized by members of the Kikuyu tribe, referred to as the Mau Mau Rebellion, was waged between 1952 and 1960. The primary issue was European ownership of farming land and plantations, as well as colonial rule in Kenya. The government thus declared a state of emergency. Jomo Kenyatta was arrested in 1952 as an organizer and instigator of the rebellion and was not released from prison until 1961—after he had already been elected president of the newly independent Kenya in 1960.

The Kikuyu

Ngugi's ethnicity is Kikuyu, one of the most populous tribes in Eastern Africa, representing approximately 20 percent of the entire population of Kenya. The Kikuyu, also known as Giguyu, Gekoyo, or Agekoyo, were at the forefront of African rebellion against British colonialism beginning in the 1920s and 1930s. In 1921, the Young Kikuyu Association was formed (renamed the Kikuyu Central Association in 1925). It was the Kikuyu who organized the Mau-Mau Rebellion in 1952. The first prime minister (1963-64) and first president (1964-78) of the independent Republic of Kenya, Jomo Kenyatta, was also Kikuyu.

African Languages

In the 1970s, Ngugi announced that he would write only in Bantu or Swahili, his native languages, rather than English, which is the official language of Kenya. The Bantu language is widespread throughout the African continent. Swahili is a Bantu language and is still spoken in many African nations, including Uganda, the Congo, and Tanzania, as well as Kenya.

Compare & Contrast

- **Early 20th Century:** Kenya is a Protectorate of Great Britain until 1963.

  Late 20th Century: After 1963, the Republic of Kenya is an independent, democratic nation.

- **1960s and 1970s:** When Ngugi's short story "The Martyr" is first published in the 1970s, Kenya's president is Jomo Kenyatta.

  1980s and 1990s: After Kenyatta's death in 1978, Daniel arap Moi becomes president of the Republic of Kenya.

- **1960s and 1970s:** When Ngugi's story "The Martyr" is first published, he is living and working in the Republic of Kenya, where his books are sold and read.

1980s and 1990s: As a result of political repression, Ngugi lives in exile from Kenya, where his works are banned.

- **Early 20th Century:** The typical Kikuyu man's household consists of a homestead surrounded by a hedge or stockade, with a separate hut for each wife.

Late 20th Century: As a result of the Mau-Mau Rebellion, beginning in 1952, many Kikuyu are moved from their homes by government forces. The resulting village settlement and land consolidation present economic advantages to the Kikuyu and are maintained in many cases even after the emergency ends.

Critical Overview

Ngugi has achieved international recognition as East Africa's leading novelist. His stories address the struggles of Africans in Kenya during the colonial and post-colonial eras. Critics have focused primarily on the political impetus in Ngugi's novels, stories, plays, and essays. G. D. Killam asserts, "Ngugi felt from the outset of his career as a writer that writing should serve social and political purposes." Ngugi himself, in an introduction to the story collection *Secret Lives*, states that his writing is "an attempt to understand myself and my situation in society and history." Charles Cantalupe, calling Ngugi "East Africa's greatest novelist and essayist," notes that Ngugi is "the most widely discussed and foremost African writer today in understanding the problems of postcolonial Africa." Cantalupe has also pointed out the international impact of Ngugi's work, despite the fact that it has been banned in his own country: "Since his exile from Kenya in 1982, the eloquence of Ngugi's novels, essays, and plays has rung out and echoed in nearly all the geographical and intellectual centers

in the world of arts and letters, with the tragic exception of Kenya itself." John Henrik Clarke refers to Ngugi as "a spokesman for African nationalism and for blacks and third world forces everywhere."

As described by Killam, the stories collected in *Secret Lives* "deal with the mature and moral worth of various aspects of original Gikuyu culture; of the effect of Christian teaching both in schools and the churches on the quality of African life; of the development of capitalism, class-consciousness, and human alienation as a new Kenya develops out of the independence struggle." Killam notes that in these stories, Ngugi "exploits the similarities between Gikuyu and Christian legends. . .Drawing on legends from the past to make a comment on the present Ngugi offers implicitly a plea for a return to basic human values." *Secret Lives* is divided into three sections: "Of Mothers and Children" (3 stories), "Fighters and Martyrs" (6 stories), and "Secret Lives" (4 stories). Killam explains that the stories in the second section, in which "The Martyr" appears, deal with "events in the period defined by the coming of the white man through his departure from Kenya," and with "aspects of the

Workers harvest tea leaves at an African plantation.

contact between Christianity and Gikuyu religions.''
In portraying these two cultures ''in collision,''
Ngugi demonstrates that ''decent values, usually
associated with original African values, suffer as a
result of coming into contact with imported ones.''
Killam asserts that ''The Martyr'' is ''perhaps the
best in the collection.'' He explains, ''The story is
centred in the human losses the independence struggle provoked. There was death and suffering and
ultimately everyone is made into a kind of martyr.''
Kimani Njogu points to the element of storytelling
itself in the political implications of the stories in
Secret Lives: ''At whatever vantage point these
stories are told or received, they have throughout a
combination of sharp social commentary with
storytelling as a way for characters to represent
their inner sufferings and anxieties. Apparently,
storytelling is for Ngugi not an addition to the spirit
of narrative, but an integral part of it.''

Ngugi has received the highest critical acclaim
for his novels. Killam notes that Ngugi's ''purposes
for writing are plain in the novels: each examines
the consequences of public, political events as they
affect the lives of individual members of the community.'' Killam adds that Ngugi ''can wed his
public vision to his artistic capacity and produce
novels which show how the lives of individuals are

given impetus, shape, direction, and area of concern
by the social, political and economic forces in the
society.'' His first published novel, *Weep Not, Child*
(1964), takes place during the Mau Mau Rebellion
against the European colonial presence in Kenya
and centers on a Kikuyu family. *A River Between*
(1965) is a love story about two people whose
relationship is doomed by the cultural divide between traditional and Christian beliefs. In *A Grain
of Wheat* (1967), the stories of four characters are
told in a series of flashbacks during and after the
fight for national independence for Kenya. *Petals of
Blood* (1977) is set in the era after Kenya achieved
national independence and offers a class-based critique of the conditions of peasants in Kenya due to
capitalist exploitation at the hands of foreign investors and the upper classes within Kenya. *Petals of
Blood* is Ngugi's most noteworthy, as well as his
most political, novel to date. *Devil on the Cross*
(1980) was written in both Kikuyu and English, and
takes an allegorical form in which the Devil is a
central character.

Ngugi's plays have received attention in part
due to their political impact in Kenya. Critics generally agree that his best play, co-written with Micere
Githae Mugo, is *The Trial of Dedan Kimathi* (1976).
Ngugi was arrested and imprisoned for a year upon

the production of the play *Ngaahika Ndeenda* (1977; *I Will Marry When I Want*), which criticizes the economic elite in Kenya.

Criticism

Liz Brent

Brent has a Ph.D. in American culture, specializing in film studies, from the University of Michigan. She is a freelance writer and teaches courses in the history of American cinema. In the following essay, Brent discusses the themes of family and betrayal in Ngugi's story.

In Ngugi's story, the themes of family loyalty and betrayal function as antitheses, or competing sets of values between which Njoroge, the main character, is caught. Njoroge works as the "houseboy" of Mrs. Hill, a white European colonial plantation owner. Njoroge is involved in an organized rebellion that involves the murder of individual white plantation owners by the Africans whose land they have stolen, and who have been forced to work for them. The historical significance of this setting is that the white European colonial settlers had first forced the Kikuyu (or Gekoyo) people of Africa off of their own land, and then forced them to work in slavery-like conditions for the profits of the Europeans on the very land which had been stolen from them.

Ngugi's fictional stories, often set in the historically real conditions of Kikuyu revolt against European colonialism, focus on the dilemmas and sacrifices of the individual in the face of the overwhelming forces of colonial racism and oppression. Ngugi's short story "The Martyr" is a strong example of this thematic focus. In exploring the themes of family loyalty and betrayal, Ngugi paints a landscape of colonial racism that dehumanizes both the oppressor and the oppressed.

The tensions created by European colonial dominance over African people are explored in this story through the theme of family. Family becomes the common denominator that "humanizes" Mrs. Hill in the eyes of Njoroge. At the same time, however, it is his concern for his family that causes Njoroge to particularly resent the insufficient housing Mrs. Hill has provided him; with two wives and many children, Njoroge is not able to house his family in the tiny hut in which he lives. Furthermore, Njoroge's sense of the displacement of his people from their rightful land combines themes of family and relig-

ion, as tied to the land. As he walks home at night and contemplates Mrs. Hill's house, the house represents for him the theft of land from his people: "Njoroge wanted to shout to the house all this and many other things that had long accumulated in his heart. The house would not respond." The image of "the immense silhouette of Memsahib's house-large, imposing" functions as a metaphor for the "imposing" and seemingly all-powerful white colonial domination over the Gekoyo people and land. Njoroge's anger at the theft of land by whites, and the subsequent effect on God-given familial rights, ties themes of family and spiritual belief to the land itself. Njoroge finds that "his whole soul rose in anger—anger against those with a white skin, those foreign elements that had displaced the true sons of the land from their God-given place. Had God not promised Gekoyo all this land, he and his children, forever and ever? Now the land had been taken away." The fact that Njoroge is literally employed on the very land that rightfully belongs to his family makes concrete the injustice of the historical conditions of colonialism: "A big portion of the land now occupied by Mrs. Hill was the land his father had shown him as belonging to the family. They had found the land occupied when his father and some of the others had temporarily retired to Muranga owing to famine. They had come back and *Nj'o!* the land was gone."

The "imposing" image of Mrs. Hill's house on the hill is contrasted with the tiny brick hut in which Njoroge is housed. The inadequacy of the housing is directly related for Njoroge to his ability to accommodate his family: "It was a very small room. . .Yet it was here, here, that he with two wives and a number of children had to live, had in fact lived for more than five years. So crammed! Yet Mrs. Hill thought she had done enough by just having the houses built with brick." It is in fact for the sake of family that Njoroge feels compelled to plot against Mrs. Hill's life, in order to "strike a blow for the occupied family land."

However, it is the thought of his own family that leads Njoroge to consider Mrs. Hill's family. She is a widow whose children are away at school in England. Imagining Mrs. Hill as the mother of children "humanizes" her in Njoroge's eyes, and he loses the will to kill her.

> He knew that she had loved her husband. Of that he was sure. She almost died of grief when she had learnt of his death. In that moment her settlerism had been shorn off. In that naked moment, Njoroge had been able to pity her. Then the children! He had known

What Do I Read Next?

- *Secret Lives and Other Stories* (1974) is Ngugi's first collection of short stories and includes "The Martyr".

- *Petals of Blood* (1977) is considered one of Ngugi's best, as well as most political, novels.

- *Detained: A Writer's Prison Diary* (1981) is Ngugi's memoir of his time spent in prison between 1977 and 1978.

- *An Introduction to the Writings of Ngugi* (1980) by G. D. Killam contains essays on key novels

and stories by Ngugi and includes a biographical outline of Ngugi's life.

- *Ngugi wa Thiong'o: Texts and Contexts* (1995), edited by Charles Cantalupe, is a collection of essays that place Ngugi's work in social, political, and historical context.

- *The World of Ngugi wa Thiong'o* (1995), edited by Charles Cantalupe, is a comprehensive collection of essays covering a wide spectrum of literary and historical themes in Ngugi's work.

---

them. He had seen them grow up like any other children. Almost like his own. They loved their parents, and Mrs. Hill had always been so tender with them, so loving. He thought of them in England, wherever that was, fatherless and motherless.

In fact, Njoroge comes to the conclusion that he wants to save her from murder by his fellow rebels.

Mrs. Hill, by contrast, knows nothing about Njoroge's family, although he has worked for her for over ten years.

> She thought of Njoroge. A queer boy. Had he many wives? Had he a large family? It was surprising even to her to find that she had lived with him so long, yet had never though of these things. This reflection shocked her a little. It was the first time she had ever thought of him as a man with a family.

The theme of betrayal runs throughout the story as an antithesis to the theme of family loyalty. The three European women who discuss the murder of Mr. and Mrs. Garstone are particularly disturbed by the fact that the couple were betrayed by their own "houseboy." In discussing the matter, Mrs. Hill assures her friends that her "houseboy," Njoroge, is "Very faithful. Likes me very much." Njoroge, in fact, does not like Mrs. Hill, and "had never liked" her. Mrs. Hill's perception that Njoroge is "very loyal" to her is thus shown to be another symptom of her paternalistic, colonial attitude. Mrs. Hill additionally claims of her other African work-

ers, "They all love me. They would do anything I asked them to!" Within the same conversation, Mrs. Smiles asserts the opinion that while "they look so innocent," they are in fact inherently treacherous, meaning full of betrayal. Mrs. Smiles utilizes a metaphor for betrayal in her comment: "Quite the innocent flower but the serpent under it." The mention of the "serpent" as symbolic of evil and betrayal hiding under the "innocent flower" invokes biblical implications of the serpent in the Garden of Eden.

Yet, Njoroge himself even sees his plan to murder Mrs. Hill that night, no matter how justified, as "treacherous." In thinking of Mrs. Hill, Njoroge finds that he cannot bring himself to see her in any other than human terms. This realization leads him to a decision that in fact betrays his fellow rebels; he ultimately acts "loyal" toward Mrs. Hill, and "treacherous" to his fellow Freedom Boys. "What was he to do now?" he asks himself. "Would he betray the 'Boys'?" Although he decides to betray the "Boys" and save Mrs. Hill, he must wrestle with his conscience over this new betrayal. He decides that, after saving her, he will go into the forest to fight as a rebel: "It would serve as a propitiation for his betrayal of the other 'Boys.'" Yet, on his way to her house to save her, he finds that "Again he hated himself for this betrayal" to the 'Boys'; he is also worried about the fact that "if the 'Boys' discovered his betrayal he would surely meet death.''

When he knocks at Mrs. Hill's door, she believes that he has betrayed her and led the gang to her house to kill her. Ultimately, however, it is Mrs. Hill who betrays Njoroge, by underestimating his loyalty to her as a fellow human being and member of a family, and thus assuming that his intentions are guilty and murderous—the result of which is her spontaneous decision to shoot him before finding out why he has come. Having killed him, the narration implies just a hint of guilt or remorse on the part of Mrs. Hill: "The circumstances of Njoroge's death worried her. The more she thought about it, the more of a puzzle it was to her.'' However, Mrs. Hill's worry and puzzlement do not lead her to seriously contemplate the possibility that Njoroge had come to save, rather than kill, her. She merely concludes these reflections with "a slow enigmatic sigh'' and the words "I don't know.''

Through juxtaposition of the opposing themes of family loyalty and betrayal, Ngugi explores the effects of colonialism and racist oppression on individuals and individual relationships. Njoroge comes to realize that, because of his conflicting loyalties to Mrs. Hill, as a fellow human being and member of a family, and to "The Boys,'' as a fellow Kikuyu organizing against racial oppression, he is, and will probably always be, "a divided man.'' Njoroge comes to hate this oppression not just because of its effect on the oppressed, but because of the ways in which it corrupts individual human relationships, such as that between Njoroge and Mrs. Hill. Njoroge comes to feel that, "For now it seemed an impossible thing to snap just like that ten years of relationship, though to him they had been years of pain and shame. He prayed and wished there had never been injustices. Then there would never have been this rift—the rift between white and black. Then he would never have been in this painful situation.'' This story ultimately suggests that family is a universal human concern which has the potential to "humanize'' the relationship between clashing cultures.

Source: Liz Brent, in an essay for *Literature of Developing Nations for Students*, Gale, 2000.

Theodore Pelton

In the following essay on Ngugi wa Thiong'o, Theodore Pelton discusses the Kenyan author's controversial use of his regional language, Gikuyu, as part of his active resistance against Western

> In exploring the themes of family loyalty and betrayal, Ngugi paints a landscape of colonial racism which dehumanizes both the oppressor and the oppressed.''

imperialism (an action which lead to his imprisonment in 1978). Pelton cautions that in order to properly approach Thiong'o's written work, the reader must also approach not only the man as activist and anti-imperialist, but also the mythic presence Thiong'o's actions have created.

> I am concerned with moving the
> centre . . . from its assumed
> location in the West to a multi-plicity
> of spheres in an the cultures
> of the world. [This] will
> contribute to the freeing of world cultures from the
> restrictive ways of nationalism, class, race,
>   and gender.
> In this sense I am an unrepentant universalist. For
> I believe that whlee retaining its roots in
>   regional and
> national individuality, true humanism with its
>   universal
> reaching out, can flower among the peoples of
> the earth. . . .
> - Ngugi wa Thiong'o, Moving the Centre: the
>   Struggle for Cultural Freedoms

The name Ngugi wa Thiong'o may be less recognizable to American audiences than those of Nobel Prize-winning African writers Nadine Gordimer and Wole Soyinka or even Nigerian novelist Chinua Achebe. And yet, the life and work of Ngugi provide an excellent starting point for people who wish to achieve some awareness of the many inter-related dilemmas—cultural, political, linguistic, developmental—that beset an entire continent of people and yet remain obscure even for the vast majority of educated Americans. In fact, Ngugi—the author of 19 books of fiction, nonfiction, drama, and children's literature—is as important today as any other single literary figure in understanding the problems of post, colonial Africa.

Ngugi wa Thiong'o was born James Ngugi in 1938 in Limuru, Kenya. In 1967, at the age of 29, Ngugi—already the author of three critically ac-

> At the end of the speech, a quavering old man approached the front of the auditorium, shaking a cane and denouncing Ngugi for blasphemy. 'And you are a Christian,' the man rather absurdly insisted. 'Your name, James, is a Christian name.'"

claimed novels—began an address to the Fifth General Assembly of the Presbyterian Church of East Africa by shocking his audience. ''I am not a man of the church,'' he stated. ''I am not even a Christian.'' Ngugi went on to censure the church for its role in the colonizing of his native land. At the end of the speech, a quavering old man approached the front of the auditorium, shaking a cane and denouncing Ngugi for blasphemy. ''And you are a Christian,'' the man rather absurdly insisted. ''Your name, James, is a Christian name.'' Perhaps as a result of this encounter, the next novel James Ngugi published bore his new Africanized name, Ngugi wa Thiong'o, formed by joining his mother's and father's family names. It is the name he has used ever since.

Thus, to approach Ngugi the writer, one must also confront this carefully cultivated mythic presence. Ngugi sees himself not just as a writer but also as a revolutionary continuing the fight against Western imperialism—particularly the sophisticated form of economic imperialsm that, he argues, has replaced traditional colonialism in his country. In his first three novels, *Weep Not, Child* (1964), *The River Between* (1965), and *A Grain of Wheat* (1967), he set out to develop a national literature for Kenya in the immediate wake of that nation's liberation from British rule. Setting his novels' plots against such historic events as the Mau Mau uprising and the subsequent day of Kenyan independence (or Uhuru) in 1963, Ngugi sought to create and establish historical legends for a nation less than half a decade old.

Ngugi was firm in his denunciation of any compromise with British colonialism—so much so,

in fact, that his personality and radicalism have become as important to his stature among African writers as his works. Stories of Ngugi's fiery literary and political activism now form a kind of oral literature among students of contemporary African culture. Ngugi himself has launched a second career telling these stories in subsequent nonfiction books, as well as in lectures and readings across Europe and North America.

One of the most famous of these stories concerns his experiences with the Kamiriithu theater project. Ngugi had been persuaded by the villagers in Kamiriithu, where he lived while teaching at the nearby University of Nairobi, to begin working with the local theater group on literacy projects. Since many of the villagers didn't speak English—the language of the former colonial administration, in which Ngugi had written his first four novels—and since he had an interest in exploring the traditions of pre-colonial African expression, Ngugi decided to write and produce a play in his own regional language, Gikuyu.

This was a bold initiative. Until 1970, theater in Kenya had been monopolized by the Kenyan National Theatre, a British-based company that produced largely Western plays, in English, with British actors. The Kenyan National Theatre had also altered the traditional ''space'' of African theater from a less formalized outdoor setting to a more formal and Westernized indoor one. Ngugi was interested in opening up the theater to the peasantry again; he wanted to make it not just an isolated aesthetic event for the cultural elite but ''part and parcel of the . . . daily and seasonal life of the community,'' as song and ritual had once been in the Kenyan countryside.

The play which resulted from Ngugi's experiments with the Kamiriithu Theatre, Ngaahika Ndeenda (*I Will Marry When I Want*), was wildly popular. Drawing from the experiences of theater participants who had been involved in the events of the time depicted—one man who made fake guns for the play had actually made real guns for the rebels—Ngugi allowed the audience themselves to feel a vital part of the artistic creation. The Kenyan government, however, was not as enthusiastic; it withdrew the license that allowed the ''gathering'' at the theater. Ngugi was arrested at the end of 1977 and ''spent the whole of 1978 in a maximum security prison, detained without even the doubtful benefit of a trial,'' as he noted in his book *Decolonizing the Mind: The Politics of Language in*

African Literature. Later attempts by others to resurrect the theater led first to a government ban on theatrical activities in the area and later to the razing of the open-air theater itself.

In cell 16 of Kamiti Maximum Security Prison, Ngugi began to write his fifth novel—and his first in Gikuyu. He had been raised as a speaker of the language despite attempts by the British colonial administration to install English as its language of instruction in Kenya (in the schools Ngugi attended, children were punished if they were caught speaking Gikuyu on the grounds). Until 1978, all of Ngugi's works had been written in English, but now he desired not the international audience English afforded but the local one reachable only through Gikuyu. This proved to be a formidable challenge; although British missionaries had developed a written form of the language in order to make the Bible more widely available to this audience, there was no formal literature written in Gikuyu, and native speakers were punished for attempts to write secular works in the language. By writing a novel, Ngugi was now stretching this written language system beyond any previous test, especially since it required him to standardize written Gikuyu and make it more accurately reflect the way native speakers practiced it.

As it turned out, an even more immediate challenge for Ngugi was how to actually write a book in prison when he was denied access to writing paper except for the purpose of making a confession. Ngugi solved this problem by writing on toilet paper—a seemingly impossible undertaking, but as Ngugi explained in *Decolonizing the Mind:* "Toilet paper at Kamiti was meant to punish prisoners. So it was very coarse. But what was bad for the body was good for the pen."

This novel, *Caitaani Mutharabainin (Devil on the Cross)*, was hugely popular, finding an audience even among the illiterate; it led, among other things, to the development of "professional readers," who sat in bars and read aloud to the clientele until a key passage, at which point they would stop and make sure their glasses were refilled before they continued the story. But after selling as well as any English-language novel ever published in Kenya, *Devil on the Cross* was banned by the government. A subsequent novel written in Gikuyu, *Matigari,* was published in that language by Heinemann of London but was seized upon arrival in Kenya; in fact, Ngugi's translation of this novel into English is the only version legally available in Kenya today.

Ngugi now lives in exile; he has taught at Yale University and Amherst College and was recently appointed professor of comparative literature and performance studies at New York University.

Why, the reader may be wondering at this point, did Ngugi's work so consistently run afoul of the Kenyan government? Ngugi contends that it was his choice of Gikuyu, more than any other single factor, which led both to his imprisonment and to his subsequent exile. A reader unfamiliar with African literature might be puzzled by this. Why wouldn't the Kenyan authorities wish to permit literary works written in an indigenous African language? One would think that the government of an independent African state, nearly 30 years after Uhuru, would seek both to champion its own languages as evidence of its cultural independence from the West and to celebrate its successful struggle against tyranny—in this case, the Mau Mau uprising which began its guerrilla war against Britain in 1952.

It is important to remember here that Kenya, like many other African states, is a nation whose boundaries were artificially drawn in Europe. Although the Kenyan government has never officially explained why Ngugi was detained, we can see in this an initial reason for its actions. Kenya relies upon English as a unifying force; the citizens of that country are in the paradoxical position of having as their only common language the one spoken by their former oppressors. Nor is this situation peculiar to Kenya; Nigerian novelist Chinua Achebe has written of this problem in Africa in general, and in his article "The Role of the Writer in a New Nation," published in a 1964 issue of *Nigeria Magazine,* he made clear his own opposition to the use of African languages for African literature:

> It is not that I underrate their importance. But since I am considering the role of the writer in building a new nation I wish to concentrate on those who write for the whole nation whose audience cuts across tribe or clan. And these, for good or ill, are writers in English.

Achebe has since modified his position, saying that he admires those writers who use African languages for their works but remains adamant about the use of English in his own. And it is important to remember that Achebe's credentials as a champion of literary Africanicity are impeccable. His first novel, *Things Fall Apart,* is probably the best-known African novel in the United States, and one that consciously seeks to show, in Achebe's words, that "African peoples did not hear of culture for the first time from Europeans; that their societies were not mindless but frequently had a philosophy of great depth and value and beauty, that they had poetry, and, above all, they had dignity.'' Moreover, Achebe's position on the use of European languages is more in keeping with the feelings of most African writers than Ngugi's.

Thus, the issue of which language should be used to compose a truly African contemporary literature is murky at best. Ngugi steadfastly maintains that writing in African languages is a necessary step toward cultural identity and independence from centuries of European exploitation. But, as critic David Westley has noted, the problem is historically complex: as a strategy to maintain apartheid—by definition the separation of defined racial groups—south Africa for many years encouraged African, language manuscripts, under the theory that the resulting problems of communication would make it harder for various groups to band together and collectively protest government policies.

Of course, discussions of language alone neglect the all-important issue of class, an issue to which Ngugi continually returns. The masses of peasants and workers in Kenya are largely illiterate in English, and it is precisely these people from whom the government wishes to keep Ngugi's writings. The reason is a simple one: Ngugi is an explicit and unabashed Marxist, and his works recall the revolutionary spirit of the Mau Mau rebellion which convinced the English to relinquish control of Kenya.

A little history is necessary here. While the origins of the term are controversial, Mau Mau seems to have originally been a British term to describe the small bands of guerrillas which sought to resist the domination of British settlers in the 1950s. At that time, the Mau Maus did not constitute an actual national movement. The British settlers, however, grew increasingly worried about their tenuous hold on the country; only 1 percent of the population, they nonetheless controlled all the best farmland in Kenya. Taking advantage of a change in colonial administration, the settlers began spreading horror stories of a nationwide revolution in the offing. The authorities responded with a crackdown; gradually, however, the measures taken—illegal detentions, the razing of villages, and the imposition of a 24-hour curfew had the ironic effect of provoking more and more people, particularly Gikuyu, to join the guerrilla bands.

Soon, the tiny force that the British tried to extinguish became a substantial guerrilla army (in Gikuyu, ''The Land and Freedom Army''). The national state of emergency that was supposed to last several weeks lasted for seven years; for four of these years, the so-called Mau Mau rebels fought a guerrilla war against British rule. Eventually, the British defeated this army, killing its leader, Dedan Kimathi, and establishing prison camps to ''rehabilitate'' captured rebels. In their attempts to make these prisoners confess their allegiance to Mau Mau (a step in the rehabilitation process), prison officials practiced horrible tortures—twisting mens' testicles, punching prisoners into incoherence, sometimes whipping them to death. When the British government itself, thousands of miles away, learned what was being carried out in its name, it decided to follow a new policy in Kenya and readied the country for independence.

However, the independence Britain had in mind was not the same as that which the Land and Freedom Army had fought for. If independence was to be granted, the British wished to yield control to a government they had themselves trained and installed—one that could be counted on to protect the landed interests in the nation. Thus, the colonial administration stepped down and a neocolonial administration—answerable not to the Kenyan people but to the economic interests that still retained actual control of the country—took its place. The Kenyan rebels returning from jail found, in the words of Anthony Howarth and David Koff in their 1973 documentary *Black Man's Country*, a nation that ''they had helped create, but which they had no place in.''

Ngugi asserts that the Kenyan government—and other neocolonial administrations like it in Africa—are fronts for ''U.S., led imperialism,'' a phrase he returns to again and again. He continually reminds us that the world is and always has been a linked unit, that the rich—be they nations or individuals—did not get that way on their own, but profited by the labor of the poor. ''Over the last 400 years,'' Ngugi said at a recent conference at Yale University, ''the developments in the West have not just been the result of internal social dynamics but also of the West's relationship with Africa, Asia, and South America.'' The so-called First World's privileged position did not come about simply by means of superior technical ingenuity or managerial skills (much as we like to laud ourselves for these things); it began with the stolen labor of slavery and continued with the enforced labor of colonial governments, working hand in hand with multinational corporations.

In sum, Ngugi argues, if today a nation enjoys wealth—particularly great wealth, as we do in the United States—it is directly linked to exploitation somewhere else in the world. This is why the Kenyan government, acting as the proxy of Western investment, will not tolerate the widespread dissemination of a revolutionary message by a fiercely committed Marxist who is also national hero (in 1964, Ngugi published the first novel in English by an East African), through a populist medium like drama or through structures designed to empower workers (written literature read aloud to the illiterate). In *Decolonizing the Mind*, Ngugi describes a revealing example of the type of self-discovery which occurred during his rehearsals of *Ngaahica Ndeenda* :

> I remember for instance how one group who worked in a particular department at the nearby Bata shoe factory sat down to work out the process and quantity of their exploitation in order to explain it all to those of us who had never worked in a factory. Within a single day, they would make shoes to the value of all the monthly wages for the entire work force of three thousand. . . . For whom were they working for the other twenty-nine days? They calculated what of what they produced went to wear and tear of the machinery and for the repayment initial capital, and because the company had been there since 1938 they assumed that the initial investment had been repaid a long time ago. To whom did the rest go? To the owners in Canada.

At a time when African governments do not wish to alienate large lender nations, such rhetoric represents a real threat to any neocolonialist regime. As Ngugi himself puts it:

> A writer who tries to communicate the message of revolutionary unity and hope in the languages of the people becomes a subversive character. It is then that writing in African languages becomes a subversive or treasonable offence with such a writer facing possibilities of prison, exile, or even death. For him there are no "national" accolades, no new year honors, only abuse and slander and innumerable lies from the mouths of the armed power of a ruling minority.

Ngugi's ear of imprisonment seems to have a marked impact on his writing. As he notes in *Detained: A Prison Writer's Diary*, he found himself analyzing the purposes of detention itself:

> Political detention, not disregarding its punitive aspects, serves a deeper, exemplary ritual symbolism. If they can break such patriot, if they can make him come out of detention crying "I am sorry for all my sins," such an unprincipled about-turn would confirm the wisdom of the ruling clique in its division of the populace into the passive innocent millions and the disgruntled subversive few. The "confession" and its corollary, "Father, forgive us our sins," becomes a cleansing ritual for all the past and current repressive deeds of such neocolonial regime.

But Ngugi abjured the "cleansing ritual." He is determined to keep the past alive, and *Detained* is ascrupulous record of the wrongs done against the Kenyan people: massacres, betrayals, abuses at the hands of the settlers (one of whom, incidentally, was Karen Blixen, whose own account of her time in Kenya, *Out of Africa*, would later become an Academy Award-winning movie starring Meryl Streep and Robert Redford), arrests and interrogations, including that of the author himself. Given the systematic attempt to break his will, the energy of Ngugi's response is astonishing. In *Detained*, he writes:

> I would remind myself that the . . . ruling class had sent me here so my brain would turn into a mess of rot. The defiance of this bestial purpose always charged me with new energy and determination: I would cheat them out of the last laugh by letting my imagination loose over the kind of society this class, in naked treacherous alliance with imperialist foreigners, were building in Kenya in total cynical disregard of the wishes of over fourteen million Kenyans.

When Ngugi emerged from jail, literature had a different purpose; since then, his works have had much less room for subtlety. It is as if the concentrated anger and moral outrage built up during his incarceration exploded upon his release—the blast revealing, in flood of sudden bright light, a stark vision in which all the ambiguity or shadowing we tend to value in creative works has been forever banished.

Take, for instance, *A Grain of Wheat* , Ngugi's last novel before his prison term. Published in 1967, this is a novel which cannily embraces ambiguity; at the moment of Uhuru, the Kenyans of a certain village seek out a hero to speak to them. Little by little, however, they realize that all the living have somehow been compromised, that war makes a person choose between life and heroism but rarely, if ever, allows both. When Mugo, the novel's central character, is finally forced to make a speech because the assembled masses think he is a hero, he instead tells them that he is the worst of all traitors, having sold out the village leader of the Mau Mau himself. He had wished only one thing, to be left alone; in war, this is a luxury.

Published 20 years later, Ngugi's most recent novel *Matigari* begins with Matigari ma Njiruungi, whose name in Gikuyu means "the patriot who survived the bullets," emerging from the forest, having finally killed Settler Williams and his assistant John Boy. The allegory is not subtle, nor is it meant to be: Settler Williams is the English oppressor; John Boy his aptly named Kenyan collaborator. Matigari roams the land seeking "truth and justice" and wishing also to reclaim the home he fought for against Williams and Boy. But Williams' and Boy's sons now own the house; they are Kenyan captains of industry who openly bribe the nation's leader, His Excellency Ole Excellence; the three of them constitute the nation's ruling authorities, who work to smash workers' strikes and suppress all dissent. Matigari's act of emerging from "the forest" recalls the Mau Mau rebels who emerged from colonial prisons; but his questions reveal him to be different from the contemporary citizens of his country, who bow silently to the friendly faced neocolonial oppression. Matigari had sworn himself to peace upon leaving the forest but begins to see that he must again pick up arms to fight for what is right.

A Grain of Wheat was a novel about a war that was presumed over. The final image of Matigari shows a young boy, Muriuki, arming himself with Matigari's weapons, readying to fight a war that is just beginning. If the earlier novel is more subtle, it must be remembered that Ngugi imagined it serving an evaluative function; a work that seeks to stir people to revolt has much less room for subtlety.

Nonetheless, such a purpose may be argued as creating not literature but propaganda. Writing in Gikuyu has undoubtedly changed the forms of Ngugi's fiction—there is more concentration on folk traditions, and the appeal is intended to be simpler and more direct. But there is a sense as well that the quality of Ngugi's fiction may have suffered. Ngugi's long, time readers were largely disappointed with Matigari; having become a political figure, some have argued, Ngugi has become less effective, perhaps even lazier, as a creative artist. Moreover, even Marxists have criticized Ngugi's politics; to many, the intellectual level at which he makes his pitch for socialism in Matagari is too simplistic, savoring too much of mere propaganda. Others have criticized his project as too naive and have accused Ngugi of willfully refusing to acknowledge the complexity of the African, languages controversy. At a conference in England, South African author Lewis Nkosi once responded to Ngugi's call for writers to use indigenous languages by shouting him down in Zulu; the point, of course, was that Ngugi could not understand what Nkosi was saying. Committed to the use of Gikuyu for his fiction, Ngugi has continued to use English for his books of "explanatory" prose, of which there were four in the last decade: *Detained: A Prison Writer's*

Diary (1981); a series of lectures published as *Writers in Politics* (1981); *Barrel of a Pen: Resistance to Oppression in Neo-Colonial Kenya* (1983); and *Decolonizing the Mind: The Politics of Language in African Literature* (1986). This seeming need to legitimate himself to his English, language readership (practically his entire readership), combined with the unfortunate fact that his novels, written in Gikuyu, do not usually get read in that language, renders Ngugi's choice of Gikuyu more a quixotic political gesture than an actual condition of existence for his fiction. This decision has led to some strange twists of fate: having declared himself a Gikuyu, language novelist, Ngugi has been required to become an even more prolific English-language essayist, turning out nonfiction in his colonial language faster than fiction in his native one.

Ngugi has also become the leading interpreter of his own works. Now all of his fiction is fringed with the author's own marginalia: "This is how I should be read"; "These are the conditions which produced this text"; "These are the issues my texts are concerned with." in this way, Ngugi wa Thiong'o, the writer, has become inseparable from Ngugi wa Thiong'o, the figure of the unfinished revolution. Mau Mau—which Ngugi was too young to join but which his older brother joined and died serving—has always been a constant presence in his works. Now the struggle which the rebels fought and lost, gaining independence yet finding themselves shut out of the government, has been picked up again by Ngugi. This time, each of his works seems to proclaim, we will be the victors in our struggle; this time we will get back what is rightfully ours—the land and wealth taken from us by foreign exploiters.

The five years since the publication of Matigari have been one of the longest periods of publishing inactivity in Ngugi's career. In many ways, the publication of that novel seemed to end a stage in Ngugi's career—one which began with his release from prison and saw the publication of two novels in Gikuyu and several works of nonfiction in English. According to Ngugi him, self, he said farewell for good to English six years ago with the publication of *Decolonizing the Mind*. "I have lost interest in the use of the English language," he remarked in a recent interview in Transition.

On January 18, 1993—Martin Luther King Day—James Curry/Heinemann published Ngugi's new collection, *Moving the Centre: The Struggle for Cultural Freedom*. The essays range from Ngugi's celebrated (some would say notorious) 1980 address to the Danish Library Association, *"Her Cook, Her Dog: Karen Blixen's Africa,"* to his 1990 salute to Nelson Mandela, *"Many Years Walk to Freedom,"* written in (and translated from) Gikuyu. Ngugi has also appeared in print as a spokes, person for Mwakenya, an underground movement which openly seeks "the establishment of a national economy, where all the resources of the land will go to the benefit of all Kenyans." The recent political news from Kenya, however, has not been good. On Wednesday, December 20, 1992, the nation held its first democratic elections in 26 years—and, as many people had predicted, the voting was marred by widespread irregularities and abuses. The election pitted President Daniel arap Moi and his Kenya African National Union against three main rivals: Oginga Odinga of the Forum for the Restoration of Democracy (FORD)/Kenya; Kenneth Matiba of FORD/Asili; and Mwai Kibaki of the Democratic Party. Moi, "who fought tooth and nail against multiparty democracy" (in the words of Canadian journalist Jonathan Manthorpe), won a bare plurality of the votes—nearly two million out of 7.9 million registered voters—but irregularities were reported at every polling station visited by journalists or international observers. (Even worse, three million Kenyans who had recently attained the age of majority were left off the rolls of eligible voters entirely; this, according to Manthorpe, in a country of 25 million people.) The victorious Moi has explained these irregularities as merely "administrative" glitches occasioned by a massive voter turnout, but it is unlikely that this election win quiet dissent against his government.

One wonders what the future has in store for Kenya. Although it appears to be one of the most stable nations in sub-Saharan Africa, Kenya is precariously situated. Famine and political chaos brought international military intervention in Somalia, its northeastern neighbor, and bands of Soma;i guninen have already been reported fleeing into Kenya. in Sudan, on the northwestern border, civil war and famine continue; in Angola, on the continent's western coast, free elections have been held after a 16-year civil war, but the new representative government is by no means stable; in the south, 1.5 million Mozambicans have fled that strife-ridden country during its civil war; and South Africa continues its own painful, convulsive transition from an apartheid nation.

One also wonders what the future has in store for Ngugi wa Thiong'o. Will he continue to write critical prose in that largely unread language, Gikuyu?

Will he write another novel in that language or in the more widely spoken Kiswahili (a language whose linguistic boundaries extend beyond Kenya)? Will he return to the theater? And, most poignantly, will he ever be able to return to Kenya?

Ngugi, as Kenya's leading cultural spokesperson, is a man dedicated to making the world aware of the oppressive regime that still rules his nation. But he is also committed to healing the continent itself of the long,standing injuries of colonization, and he believes that this healing can only come through cultural autonomy and self-determination. "I think the dividing line is really the issue of language," he repeats endlessly, tirelessly. He does not consider it an oversimplification to suggest that European languages themselves are the final, pervasive colonizing army that will not leave his homeland. So he repeats it again:

> We must avoid the destruction that English has wrought on other languages and cultures in its march to the position it now occupies in the world. The death of many languages should never be the condition for the life of a few. . . . A language for the world? A world of languages! The two concepts are not mutually exclusive, provided there is independence, equality, democracy, and peace among nations. Ngugi wa Thiong'o on cultural imperlalism:

Today the USA and the West in general control nearly all the news to and from Third World countries. . . . Most of the images on the cinema and television screens of the Third World are actuaffy manufactured in the USA. This dominance is likely to continue with the vast US investment in information technology. With the satellite TV, Cable TV, and the USA-based video productions, these images "made in the USA" will be received directly by many Third World families. We have already seen the devastating use of this technology in religious propaganda by the USA-based millionaire foundations who now promote idiotic illusions about the pleasures of the heaven to come on a mass hypnotic scale. Even such publicly discredited characters as [Jimmy] Swaggart and Oral Roberts will occupy regular spots running into prime television time in a number of African and Third World countries. . . .

The 1990s will therefore see even greater battles for the control of the minds and hearts of the exploited and the oppressed of the world, trying to mould them in the image of the neo-colonial father in the American heaven. The aim will still be what it has always been: to divide, weaken and scatter resistance. For how a people view themselves will affect how they view their values, their culture, their politics, their economics, and ultimately their relationship to nature and to the entire universe.

Source: Theodore Pelton, ''Nagugi wa Thiong'o and the Politics of Language,'' in *The Humanist,* Vol. 53, No. 2, March-April, 1993, p. 15.

Joseph Mbele

In the following essay on Ngugi wa Thiong'o, Joseph Mbele discusses how the Kenyan author's controversial use of his regional language, Gikuyu, raises questions and problems around the relationship of language to culture, questioning whether the author's use of his regional language functions as he intends to ''decolonize'' the African mind.

The subject of language is now central in discussions of African literature. Many issues have been raised. Is language the determining feature of African literature? Is it acceptable for the African writer to write in non-African languages? In the process of asking such questions, Ngugi wa Thiong'o has emerged as a key advocate of writing in African languages, and it has become almost unfashionable to challenge his views on the subject, but I believe it is necessary to examine what Ngugi has been saying and to consider the possibility of looking at the language question in new ways. Developments in literary theory enable us to pose new questions about the nature of language and the ways in which language mediates writing, authorial intentions, the reading process, and literary meaning. Such questions invite broader considerations of a political nature, involving the relationship among the social classes and the respective demands of nationalism and internationalism.

> Ngugi has expressed his views rather forcefully: An African writer should write in a language that will allow him to communicate effectively with peasants and workers in Africa; in other words, he should write in an African language. . . . Literature published in African languages will have to be meaningful to the masses and therefore much closer to the realities of their situation. (''On Writing'')

This statement is significant both for what it reveals and for what it conceals. It demonstrates great faith in the capacity of language to communicate ideas and sentiments intended by the writer. But we need to ask whether language is really such an efficient instrument of communication or if it is a more stubborn medium.

In discussing the nature of the word, Jurij Tynjanov illuminates the problematic nature of language in the following terms:

> A word does not have just one definite meaning. It is a chameleon and every time it occurs there appear not only various shadings but even various colors.

If the meanings of words are so indeterminate, the use of language poses serious problems for writers as well as readers. For writers, the essential problem is whether they can say, through language, what they desire to say. No matter how optimistic we might be about the power of language, we must concede that there are moments, as Heidegger explains, ''when we cannot find the right word for something that concerns us, carries us away, oppresses or encourages us. Then we leave unspoken what we have in mind. . . .'' Lewis Nkosi has suggested that, whatever language writers use, they cannot escape this problem:

> In a way, any writer always falls short of his true ideal: his struggle with his materials, the attempt to wrestle from language the true meaning of the world he seeks to depict, is always endless and incomplete. Incomplete, because in describing the true lineaments of what the writer sees with his inner eye language can only approximate the shapes and figures of his imagination. In this respect, therefore, the situation of the African writer is not unique. It is the same struggle with language.

The other problem concerns the reader. Like writing, reading is an active process. It is a dialogue, a struggle with language, and its outcome is far from certain. Even assuming that writers could say exactly what they intended to say, it is never certain that readers will receive the intended message. In proclaiming the need to ''communicate effectively with peasants and workers in Africa,'' Ngugi fails to recognize that the reading process is problematical. In discussing his experience in writing *Ngaahika Ndeenda* with the villagers, he clearly states his opinion about the transparency of language:

> And because there was no language barrier, the villagers could also comment on the content of the play. There was no mystification of the play's message. . . . They could now participate in correcting the content of the script. (''On Writing'')

But the reception of language is never so unproblematic that everyone agrees about its meaning.

Ngugi himself remains content to note the popularity of his Gikuyu-language works among the Gikuyu masses without asking himself what meaning they attach to these works. Concerning the reception of *Caitaani Muthara-ba-ini*, for example, he observes:

> The novel had an interesting kind of reception. At first it was read in families. When families gathered together in the evening, they would get one of their literate members to read for them. In this way the

novel was appropriated and became part of the community's oral tradition. It was also read in buses and matutus (sic) (small, crowded public transport vehicles); people would read for passengers between stops. Another example of the community's collective appropriation of the novel was the emergence of professional readers in bars. Someone would start reading the novel aloud while drinking his beer, and when the beer was finished, he would just put the novel down. And of course the other customers would have to offer him another round to get him started again. So he would read and drink, read and drink, until the glass was again empty and again refilled, and so on, through the evening. (''On Writing'')

Concerned about conveying what he regards as a revolutionary message, Ngugi assumes that the Gikuyu masses enjoy his works because they understand the message he intended to communicate. But if we can never be sure what readers see in a text, his assumption becomes even more dubious when we consider the probable responses of readers and audiences who are drinking beer.

Jonathan Culler has remarked that:

None would deny that literary works, like most other objects of human attention, can be enjoyed for reasons that have little to do with understanding and mastery—the texts can be quite blatantly misunderstood and still be appreciated for a variety of personal reasons.

Culler's point can be corroborated in the African context, where epics, folktales, and other oral genres often contain segments that neither performers nor audiences understand; nevertheless, this lack of understanding does not hamper their enjoyment of the performances. Thus, many of the Swahili who listen to the popular epic Rasi' LGhuli enjoy it without understanding what it is all about (Ridhiwani).

Under such circumstances, Ngugi's insistence that the African writer should write for peasants and workers is not as unproblematic as he assumes. Furthermore, African society is also comprised of other social groups, including intellectuals. Mao Tse Tung, one of the most influential champions of the peasants and workers, had a more realistic perspective on this question. While stressing that literature and art should be for the masses, he also pointed out that they are:

. . . needed by the cadres. The cadres are the advanced elements of the masses and generally have received more education; literature and art of a higher level are entirely necessary for them. To ignore this would be a mistake.

In other words, Mao recognized the importance of a literature that might be inaccessible to peasants

 This statement. . .demonstrates great faith in the capacity of language to communicate ideas and sentiments intended by the writer. But we need to ask whether language is really such an efficient instrument of communication or if it is a more stubborn medium."

and workers on account of its complexity or its existence in a foreign language. Not only Ngugi but also scholars such as Abiola Irele and Emmanuel Ngara, who rail against what they call elitist literature, are vulnerable to criticism on these grounds (Irele and Ngugi).

Mao was also ahead of Ngugi in another way. Although he recognized that the cultural level of the peasants and workers was low, he advocated that it should be continually raised. He would certainly have argued in favor of encouraging the peasants and workers to learn foreign languages. In contrast, Ngugi seems to assume that Gikuyu peasants will forever speak, write, and read only in Gikuyu. What benefits might Gikuyu peasants gain by learning English, French, or Russian? Anybody who espouses revolutionary causes, as Ngugi does, ought to address the question of foreign languages in a dialectical and forward-looking manner. The example of Karl Marx is worth noting in this respect. As Paul Lafargue points out:

Marx could read all European languages and write in three: German, French, and English, to the admiration of language experts. He liked to repeat the saying: ''A foreign language is a weapon in the struggle of life.

It would be neither accurate nor fair to charge Ngugi with having ignored internationalism. Although he champions writing in African languages and now writes only in Gikuyu, he has considered the question of how to reach readers outside. His answer has always been that they will be reached through translations:

Writing in Gikuyu does not cut me off from other language communities because there are always opportunities for translation. My Gikuyu novel, for example, has been translated not only into English and Kiswahili but also directly from Gikuyu into Swedish. A German edition is planned, and a translation directly from Gikuyu into Japanese may appear later. In other words, there is already a dialogue emerging with the rest of the world due to the translation of a piece of Gikuyu literature into foreign languages. This kind of dialogue has also occurred within East Africa with the publication of a translation into Kiswahili. Hopefully a situation will arise where this novel is translated directly into other African languages within and outside Kenya, so that once again there will be direct communication between two African language communities rather than indirect communication through an intermediary language such as English or French. (''On Writing'')

But something is always changed, added, or lost in translation. For this reason, there really can be no true translation; in fact, a translation is actually a new work of art. Ideally, works should be read in the original languages, and if we must have translations, we should acknowlege them as a necessary evil.

Since Ngugi appears to believe that the work remains the same in translation, why is it essential for him to write in Gikuyu first? If translation offers such an efficient bridge between languages, he could just as easily write in English and then have his work translated into Gikuyu. Irele is undoubtedly right when he argues that ''the literary artist will produce his best work in the medium that he most confidently controls.'' In light of this fact it is quite possible that Ngugi is capable of producing better work in English than in Gikuyu. By his own admission, he lacks the mastery of Gikuyu that would enable him to write his best work in it:

> And when we scripted the play in Gikuyu called *Ngaahika Ndeenda* (or *I Will Marry When I Want*), something happened which was very interesting. The people in the village of course knew their language much better than we did; so they began to offer their comments on the script. They would say, 'Oh, this image is wrong here, or that type of language is inappropriate there. An old man doesn't speak like this; if you want him to have dignity, he must use a different kind of speech. Oh my God, you are making him speak like a child! You university people, what kind of learning have you had?' ('' On Writing'')

Perhaps Ngugi can improve his mastery of Gikuyu, but he might also have abandoned English too soon.

In criticizing what he calls ''petty-bourgeois African writers'' who, while writing in foreign languages, misrepresent the African peasants, Ngugi actually undermines his own views on translation:

> Often the African peasant characters were made to appear naive and simple minded because of the kind of simplistic, distorted foreign languages through which they were made to articulate their feelings and world outlook. More often the peasant/worker characters were given the vacillating mentality and pessimistic world outlook of the petty bourgeois. But the final indignity was that even where the peasant/worker characters were given their due in terms of dignity and world outlook, they were made to express these awkwardly in foreign languages. Thus the tongues of millions of peasants were mutilated in the works of African writers, and in their stead the peasants were given plastic surgery in the literary laboratories of Africa and emerged with English, French and Portuguese tongues. (*Writers*)

However, he fails to cite a single work of African fiction in which peasants are portrayed in this way. Furthermore, one is tempted to ask what happens to Ngugi's own novels when they are translated into European languages. Do his Gikuyu peasants and workers escape the simple-mindedness and awkwardness that emerge when they are made to speak in an alien tongue? To save his peasants and workers from such indignities, Ngugi should perhaps refuse to allow any of his Gikuyu works to be translated into foreign languages.

Ngugi's decision to abandon English as a medium for expression for his creative work and to use only Gikuyu is intriguing because it seems to be based on a non-dialectical view of English and, for that matter, of other European languages as well. For him, these languages are simply the languages of the former colonial masters. Any African writer who uses them today thus becomes a victim of neocolonialism. Ngugi himself explains:

> There are other contradictions of a writer in a neocolonial state. For whom does he write? For the people? But then what language does he use? It is a fact that the African writers who emerged after the Second World War opted for European languages. All the major African writers wrote in English, French, and Portuguese. But by and large, all the peasants and a majority of the workers—the masses—have their own languages. Isn't the writer perpetuating, at the level of cultural practice, the very neo-colonialism he is condemning at the level of economic and political practice? For whom a writer writes is a question which has not been satisfactorily resolved by the writers in a neocolonial state. (*Writing Against Neocolonialism*)

However, if English, French, and Portuguese are the main languages of the former colonizers, they are also the languages of the working masses in England, France, and Portugal, and elsewhere. These languages were created by the masses and reflect their creative genius; they were not created by the imperialists, who only came onto the scene much later. It is an historical accident that they were used as the languages of colonialism, and this fact alone does not detract from their significance and value. Similarly, although Gikuyu is the language of Gikuyu peasants and workers, it is also the language of Gikuyu landlords and capitalists. If these capitalists and landlords had the power, they could easily use Gikuyu to dominate people of other language groups.

Ngugi has consistently argued that the colonialists downgraded African languages and promoted European languages; however, his views on this subject are rather simplistic. The colonialists' policies on African languages were not uniform throughout the continent, nor were they entirely negative. In fact, the colonialists and missionaries whom Ngugi castigates were instrumental in promoting many African languages. Even in Kenya, Ngugi's own country, they produced the orthographies, dictionaries, grammars, and readers that enabled large numbers of Africans to become literate in these languages. In many places in Africa, colonialists and missionaries started newspapers and publishing enterprises that enabled indigenous writers such as Thomas Mofolo of Lesotho and Shaaban Robert from Tanganyika to make names for themselves. That Ngugi can now write in Gikuyu and that he can be read by an appreciative Gikuyu audience result largely from the good work done by the colonialists and the missionaries.

In many ways, Ngugi's struggle against English appears to be fueled by psychological conflicts, anxieties, and guilt feelings. His situation is a variation on the Oedipal theme of the father-son conflict, for he is bent on killing the father, the former colonial master, who, through a process of displacement, is represented by the colonizer's language. But this language begot Ngugi as a writer. His struggle is all the more intense because the father is perceived as being intent upon emasculating and obliterating the son, by subjecting him to cultural institutions such as the language and the school. In this respect, Ngugi resembles all of us who were formerly colonized. Okot p'Bitek's Lawino has characterized our predicament quite well, embodying it in the metaphor of castration:

> Bile bums my inside!
> I feel like vomiting!
> For all our young men
> Were finished in the forest,
> Their manhood was finished

> In the classrooms,
> Their testicles were smashed
> With large books!

Ngugi's struggle to kill the father is at the same time a struggle to possess the mother, represented in this case as the mother tongue. The African writer who champions the mother tongue is haunted by a feeling of guilt at having betrayed her, as Chinua Achebe admits:

> Is it right that a man should abandon his mother tongue for someone else's? It looks like a dreadful betrayal and produces a guilty feeling.

But whereas Achebe has forged ahead and continued to use a European language, Ngugi criticizes this choice, calling it a manifestation of weakness:

> How did we arrive at this acceptance of the fatalistic logic of the unassailable position of English in our literature; [a phrase Achebe had used] in our culture and in our politics? ... How did we, as African writers, come to be so feeble towards the claims of our languages on us and so aggressive in our claims on other languages, particularly the languages of our colonization? (*Decolonising*)

References to aggressiveness and feebleness provide further proof, from a psychoanalytical perspective, that Ngugi is subject to a deep-seated anxiety. Feebleness is just another term for the condition that Lawino names, without mincing words, in the quotation cited above.

Ngugi's pronouncements about the use of languages in African literature are not completely unacceptable. Much of what he says is valid, but the subject is a complex one, and there are no easy solutions to the theoretical and practical problems that it implies. By pointing out the gaps and weak links in Ngugi's arguments, I hope to stimulate a rethinking of the crucial issues to which Ngugi has drawn our attention.

Source: Joseph Mbele, ''Language in African Literature: an Aside to Ngugi,'' in *Research in African Literatures,* Vol. 23, No. 1, Spring, 1992, p. 145.

Sources

Cantalupe, Charles, ed., *Ngugi wa Thiong'o: Texts and Contexts,* Africa World Press, 1995, p. x.

———, *The World of Ngugi wa Thiong'o,* Africa World Press, 1995, p. 5.

Clarke, John Henrik, "Introduction," in *Homecoming: Essays on African and Caribbean Literature, Culture and Politics*, by Ngugi wa Thiong'o, Lawrence Hill, 1972, p. viii.

Killam, G. D., *An Introduction to the Writings of Ngugi*, Heinemann, 1980, pp. 5, 17, 73-6, 78-9.

Njogu, Kimani, "Living Secretly and Spinning Tales: Ngugi's 'Secret Lives and Other Stories,'" in *Ngugi wa Thiong'o: Texts and Contexts*, Africa World Press, 1995, p. 340.

Further Reading

Booker, M. Keith, *The African Novel in English*, Heinemann, 1998.

Includes the chapter, "A Brief Historical Survey of the African Novel" as well as discussion of Ngugi's *Devil on the Cross* and works by Chinua Achebe, Ama Ata Aidoo, and Nadime Gordimer.

Jussawalla, Feroza, and Reed Way Dasenbrock, eds., *Interviews with Writers of the Post-Colonial World*, University Press of Mississippi, 1992.

Includes interviews with such prominent writers as Ngugi wa Thiong'o, Chinua Achebe, Anita Desai, and Sandra Cisneros.

Larson, Charles R., ed., *Under African Skies: Modern African Stories*, Farrar, Straus, 1997.

A collection of short stories by writers from a wide range of national and regional locales throughout Africa. Includes "A Meeting in the Dark" by Ngugi wa Thiong'o.

The Middleman

Bharati Mukherjee
1988

Bharati Mukherjee's short story *"The Middleman"* was originally included in her second collection of short fiction, *The Middleman and Other Stories*, which won the 1988 Book Critics Circle Award for best fiction. *"The Middleman"* is told from the perspective of Alfie Judah, an Iraqi immigrant to the U.S. who is a "middleman" for illegal arms deals to rebel armies in an unnamed Latin American country. Alfie is staying at the home of Clovis Ransome, a trader in illegal goods. When Ransome leaves for the day, Alfie is asked to drive Ransome's wife, Maria, on an errand. He takes her to the nearby headquarters of a group of guerilla fighters where Maria meets up with her lover Andreas. Alfie eventually becomes a "middleman" in a conflict between Andreas and Ransome over Maria, during which Maria shoots Ransome but spares Alfie.

"The Middleman" focuses on several themes common throughout Mukherjee's fiction. Alfie is an immigrant with a tenuous U.S. citizenship who has become caught up in the shadier side of American imperialism and capitalist enterprise. His lust for Maria is in part an attraction to a fellow dark-skinned person, although they are from two completely different cultures. Alfie is ultimately a character who survives in a multicultural setting in which he always finds himself as the "middleman" in business, political, and romantic conflicts.

Author Biography

Bharati Mukherjee was born on July 27, 1940, in Calcutta, India. Her father, a chemist, was the head of a pharmaceutical firm, and Mukherjee was raised in an upper-middle-class Brahmin Bengali family. She received a privileged education, attending schools in Britain and Switzerland as well as in India. In 1959, she earned a B.A. in English from the University of Calcutta. In 1961, she earned an M.A. in English and ancient Indian culture, also from the University of Calcutta. In 1961, Mukherjee went to the United States to participate in the Iowa Writers' Workshop, where she met Canadian writer Clark Blaise, whom she married in 1963. In 1963, Mukherjee also earned an M.F.A. from the University of Iowa. She held several teaching posts in universities in the United States, including Marquette University in Milwaukee, Wisconsin (1964-64), and the University of Wisconsin (1965). She moved with her husband to Canada in 1968, and in 1969 was awarded a Ph.D. In Canada, Mukherjee was a victim of racism; the experience had a profound affect on her personally as well as on her writing. She held a position as instructor and eventually associate professor at McGill University, Quebec (1966-78), but in 1978, fed up with the racism she encountered in Canada, she moved with her family to the U.S., where she held teaching positions at several different colleges and universities between 1978 and 1987. In 1987, she became a professor at the University of California at Berkley.

Mukherjee's writing career began with the publication of her first novel, *The Tiger's Daughter*, in 1972. Her second novel, *Wife*, was published in 1975. This was followed by two collections of short stories, *Darkness* (1985) and *The Middleman and Other Stories* (1988). *The Middleman and Other Stories* won the prestigious National Book Critics Circle Award for best fiction in 1988. Mukherjee published three subsequent novels: *Jasmine* (1989), based on a short story that appeared in *The Middleman*, *The Holder of the World* (1993), and *Leave It to Me* (1997). Mukherjee has written a number of nonfiction books, including *Kautilya's Concept of Diplomacy: A New Interpretation* (1976), *Political Culture and Leadership in India* (1991), and *Regionalism in Indian Perspective* (1992). In addition, she and her husband have co-written two nonfiction books: *Days and Nights in Calcutta* (1977), which recounts their differing perceptions of India during a visit there, and *The Sorrow and the Terror: The Haunting Legacy of the Air India Tragedy* (1987), about an Air India plane crash.

Plot Summary

The narrator is Alfie Judah, an Iraqi-born man with U.S. citizenship who works as a "middleman" in illegal arms deals. As the story opens, Alfie is staying at the home of Clovis Ransome, an American dealer in illegal goods, in an unnamed Latin American country. Alfie lusts after Ransome's wife, Maria, who is mostly Indian in origin. Bud Wilkins, a man in business with Ransome, pulls up in a pickup truck full of illegal merchandise. Ransome and Bud are going "fishing" for the day, although Alfie knows they are going out in a boat in order to pick up or drop off illegal merchandise. When Ransome and Bud leave, Maria asks Alfie to drive her to a nearby town to do some errands in Bud's pickup truck. Alfie, expecting a sexual affair with Maria, agrees to drive her. Maria, however, directs him to what turns out to be the headquarters of a group of guerilla rebel fighters. Much to Alfie's disappointment, Maria takes off with Andreas, one of the rebel fighters, leaving Alfie to fall asleep while waiting for her. Alfie also notes that Maria has brought the illegal arms in the back of Bud's truck for the rebels to unload and make use of. On the way back, Maria explains to Alfie that she had been kidnapped from her school at the age of 14 by the country's minister of education. She had then been "traded," like a piece of property, to Ransome as part of a business negotiation. When Alfie and Maria return to Ransome's home, Ransome is drunk. He tells them that Bud has been killed by rebels, although Alfie is sure Ransome himself ordered the killing. Ransome then passes out from drunkenness, and they carry him up to his room and lay him on the bed. Then Maria and Alfie spend the night together in Alfie's bedroom. When Alfie wakes up, a group of the guerilla rebels have entered Ransome's house and are in Ransome's bedroom. Andreas hands a gun to Maria, and she shoots Ransome. She then aims at Alfie but doesn't shoot him because, Alfie believes, "She had made love to me three times that night." Alfie has the insight, "Never has a truth been burned so deeply in me, what I owe my life to, how simple the rules of survival are." Maria then leaves with Andreas and the other rebels. Alfie stays in Ransome's house for a few days, after which he plans to call someone in the capitol in order to sell his information about the guerillas or the American arms dealers to whoever may be willing to pay him for the information. He concludes: "There must be something worth trading in the troubles I have seen."

Characters

Andreas

Andreas is a guerilla rebel fighter at the hideout to which Alfie drives Maria. Andreas and Maria are clearly lovers, and they leave Alfie for a tryst. That night, Andreas is among the rebels who enter Ransome's home. Andreas hands Maria the gun with which she shoots Ransome.

Eduardo

Eduardo is the "houseboy" at Ransome's house. He turns out to be one of the guerilla rebel fighters, who lets them into Ransome's house and leads them to his bedroom where he is shot.

Alfred Judah

Alfred Judah, the narrator of the story, is also referred to as Alfie. He is an Iraqi-born immigrant with a tenuous U.S. citizenship who works as a "middleman" in various illegal arms trades. As the story opens, he is staying at the home of Clovis Ransome, a dealer in illegal trades, in an unnamed Latin American country. Alfie lusts after Ransome's wife, Maria, and when Ransome leaves for the day, Maria asks Alfie to drive her on some errands. He believes she is intending to seduce him, but she has him drive her to the hideout of a group of guerilla fighters, where she leaves Alfie for a tryst with Andreas, one of the guerillas. However, on their way back, and that night, Maria and Alfie engage in their own tryst, while Ransome is passed out drunk and taken to his bedroom. In the middle of the night, the group of guerilla fighters enters Ransome's house and Maria shoots Ransome, but spares Alfie. Alfie ultimately plans on selling his knowledge of both the illegal traders and the guerillas to whomever might find the information valuable. Thus, Alfie remains a "middleman," in all of his economic, political, and romantic encounters.

Maria

Maria is the wife of Clovis Ransome and the object of Alfie's lust. Alfie notes, "With her thick dark hair and smooth dark skin, she has to be mostly Indian." Maria is aware of the fact that she is merely an object of exchange between a series of

Bharati Mukherjee

men in the course of their political and financial dealings. She was kidnapped at the age of 14 by the minister of education of her country, and then traded to Ransome as part of an illegal trade deal. When Ransome leaves for the day, Maria asks Alfie to drive her on some errands. She directs him to the hideout of a group of guerilla fighters, where she leaves Alfie for a tryst with Andreas, one of the fighters. In the process, she allows the rebel group to remove cargo that belonged to Ransome. That night, while Ransome is passed out drunk, she sleeps with Alfie. In the middle of the night, members of the rebel group are let into Ransome's house, and Andreas hands Maria a gun with which she shoots Ransome. She then aims the gun at Alfie, but spares him.

Clovis Ransome

Clovis Ransome is an American dealer in illegal goods who makes his home and runs his business in an unnamed Latin American country. He leaves for the day to go on a "fishing" trip with Bud Wilkins, although Alfie knows that they are making a pickup or delivery of illegal goods. When Alfie and Maria return to Ransome's house that night, Ransome is drunk. He explains that Bud Wilkins had been killed by rebels and then he passes out. It is clear to Alfie that Ransome had ordered the killing of Bud for unknown reasons. However, given Ransome's jealousy regarding Maria, there is an implication that perhaps Bud was killed for having an affair with Maria, similar to Alfie's recent affair with her. They carry him up to his room and lay him on the bed. In the middle of the night, the guerilla rebels enter Ransome's house and his bedroom. Andreas, one of the rebels, hands Maria a gun, with which she shoots Ransome.

Bud Wilkins

Bud Wilkins pulls up to Ransome's house with a pickup truck full of illegal goods. He and Ransome then leave to go "fishing" for the day. That night, Ransome informs Alfie and Maria that Bud has been killed by rebels—although it is clear Ransome himself ordered the murder of his business partner for reasons which are not specified.

Themes

The Middleman

The title of this story, "The Middleman," is also the title of the collection in which it was first published, *The Middleman and Other Stories*. The theme of the "middleman" is significant in terms of Mukherjee's concern with the immigrant experience in America. Alfie, the story's narrator and main protagonist, is a "middleman" both literally and figuratively in several ways. He makes his living as the "middleman" in illegal arms deals; although the precise nature of his work is not specified, it is clear that he works as a go-between in the sale of illegal merchandise. Alfie is also a "middleman" in terms of his cultural identity. He is Iraqi, with a tenuous and questionable American passport, doing work in an unnamed Latin American country. Thus, he is between two cultures and two cultural identities—that of his Iraqi origins, and that of his current, Americanized life. Alfie is also the "middleman" in the relationship between Maria and Clovis Ransome. Alfie has a sexual affair with Maria, who is Ransome's wife, and is thus caught in the middle of their tenuous marriage. In the final scene of the story, Maria is handed a gun by the rebel Andreas, and it is unclear at first whether she is going to shoot Ransome or Alfie or both. Thus, Alfie is again caught in the middle of a conflict between the rebels and Ransome; he holds no particular allegiance to either side, and yet finds himself in the midst of a deadly encounter. After Maria chooses to shoot Ransome and not Alfie,

Alfie once again plays the part of the "middleman"; he plans to sell or trade the inside information he has learned about both the American arms dealers and the rebel guerillas to whoever may be interested. Thus, Alfie, a man without strong ties to any particular nation, cultural identity, relationship, business partnership, or even political cause, remains a "middleman," a free agent motivated only by lust for women, greed for profit, and an instinct of self-preservation.

Americanization, Capitalism, and Immigrant Identity

A central theme of Mukherjee's fiction is the experience of immigrants, particularly Asian American and Middle Eastern immigrants in America. Alfie is an Iraqi-born immigrant, the legality of whose status as an American citizen is questionable. Alfie has chosen to pursue the proverbial American Dream through business transactions in the underworld of capitalist enterprise. Alfie is a "middleman" in illegal arms deals. The implication of this story is that Alfie's lifestyle as a "middleman" in illegal trades is a measure of the degree to which he has become Americanized. Alfie is often reminded of his own childhood experiences and his own culture in contrast to American culture and his life as an immigrant. Alfie recalls that he has always lusted after white, blonde women, the implication being that white women represent an American cultural ideal which he has internalized. However, the presence of Maria, who, dark-skinned and dark-haired, is mostly Indian, arouses Alfie's lust. He speculates that, beneath his surface level attraction to blonde white women, he finds that Maria's darkness arouses a sense of camaraderie and nostalgia for his own culture. Maria, in turn, functions as a unit of exchange in a whitewashed system of capitalism, whereby she is traded between men as part of their business negotiations. Thus, while American-style capitalism makes of Alfie a "middleman" with no ties or allegiances to any cultural identity, it similarly makes of Maria a type of "middleman" who is treated as a unit of exchange in a capitalist system.

Style

Narration

This story is told from the first person restricted point of view, which means that the events of the

Topics for Further Study

- All of Mukherjee's fiction focuses on the theme of immigrant identity and the immigrant experience in America. Read another one of her short stories. In what ways does it address themes similar to those of "The Middleman" in terms of the immigrant experience? In what ways does it address different themes?

- Mukherjee was born in India in 1940, less than a decade before India achieved national independence and self-rule. Learn more about the history of India before and after independence. What differences do you think Mukherjee saw during her childhood?

- Mukherjee's fiction focuses on immigrants to America from a variety of Asian and Middle Eastern regions. Learn more about past and current immigration patterns to the U.S. of one particular nationality of immigrant groups (such as Indian, Vietnamese, etc.). What is the history of immigration patterns and the immigrant experience of people to America from this particular region? What current issues face immigrants from this region?

- The main character of this story is a dealer in the sale of illegal firearms from the U.S. While the situation depicted in the story is fictional, what can you learn about such illegal trade practices in recent history?

---

story are presented to the reader from the perspective of one character in the story, in this case Alfie Judah. This first-person narrative is important to Mukherjee's concern with immigrant Americans struggling to formulate a sense of self and a sense of cultural identity within their new environment. As Fakrul Alam has pointed out, "In most of the stories collected in *The Middleman* and in her third novel, Mukherjee eschews the omniscient/superior perspective she had adopted earlier and attempts to allow her new Americans to tell their own stories."

Setting

This story is set in an unnamed or fictitious Latin American country in which guerilla rebels are attempting a revolution. However, the story's setting is clearly meant to evoke real historical locations and political struggles in such Latin American nations as Nicaragua. Passing reference to revolutionary leader Che Guevara, who was instrumental in the success of the Cuban Revolution, indicates the sense of realism Mukherjee wishes to convey. Furthermore, the setting in a Latin American country is significant to Mukherjee's concern with writing stories about immigrants from a broad range of

cultures who have moved into a broad spectrum of geographic and sub-cultural milieus throughout the Americas. In this case, the main character and narrator, Alfie, is Iraqi, holds an American passport, and is currently located in a Latin American country in the course of his work as a "middleman" in illegal arms deals. Fakrul Alam has pointed out that, in the collection of stories included in *The Middleman*, "Mukherjee's expanded range and confidence in her ability to write about old and new Americans being transformed by nontraditional immigration patterns can. . .be seen in her choice of settings. . . ." Alam goes on the say that "all the stories of *The Middleman* seem to be deliberately set all over North America to prove how the entire continent was being transformed by the influx of immigrants of Asian origin." Alam notes, "Mukherjee manages to assemble such a diverse gallery of characters from almost half the globe and makes use of such disparate settings in *The Middleman*. . ." In addition, Alam notes that in these stories Mukherjee "seems to be even going out of her way to draw on characters from relatively peripheral areas who have had diasporic experiences. Also, she appears in this volume to delight in putting her protagonists in extreme situations."

Tone

The tone of the narrator of this story includes a delightfully rich mixture of cynicism, humor, irony, and nostalgia. Alfie expresses nostalgia for his childhood experiences in and memories of Baghdad, Iraq. This tone of nostalgia is in keeping with Mukherjee's concern with the sense of loss of traditional culture experienced by immigrants who become integrated into American culture. Alfie's tones of irony and cynicism that permeate the story express his assessment of life in the world of American capitalism; he has accepted a world and a life in which every human interaction is a business transaction and a power game in which financial gain and self-preservation (''survival'') are the only goals. Alfie, who feels loyalty or allegiance to no person, culture, nation, political cause, or morality, is understandably cynical, accepting even his ''love-making'' with Maria as a business transaction in which he provided her with sex in exchange for her decision to spare his life. Finally, the irony and cynicism of this story are rife with humor. A minor example is when the narrator refers to his newly-acquired ability to open a bottle of beer without an opener as a ''New World skill.'' This phrase captures Alfie's sense of the triviality and meaninglessness of American culture, in which the ability to open a bottle of beer with one's teeth, for instance, achieves the status of a ''skill.''

Literary Heritage

Though not particularly interested in being known as an Indian writer, Mukherjee has placed herself in the long tradition of immigrant writers such as V. S. Naipaul and Bernard Malamud. She claims to have learned much from their fiction. She dedicated *Darkness* to her friend Malamud and even named one of her sons after him.

The predominant mode of American fiction in the 1980s was a minimalism exemplified by such writers as Raymond Carver. Minimalism used short sentences, understatement, and very little elaboration. Mukherjee positioned herself against this style, preferring instead a more elaborate one that allowed her to explore the layers of meaning and significance in the layered lives of her immigrant characters. She believes that a writer's status as immigrant gives her a great subject about which to write, and the subject deserves a great style.

Historical Context

Colonization and Independence in India

Mukherjee was born in Calcutta, India, just seven years before India became an independent nation. India had been a colony of the British empire for almost a century, from 1858 to 1947. The history of India during this period, therefore, is one of expansion of British power in conflict with organizations, protests, rebellion, and terrorist activism among the peoples of India. Before 1848, India had been colonized and ruled by the East India Company, but power was transferred to the British crown in 1858. Rebellion on the part of the Indians against European colonization was waged off and on throughout India's history of colonization. However, the first nationally organized Indian effort at achieving independence was formed in 1885, with the first meeting of the Indian National Congress. Nevertheless, Britain continued to expand its region of power in the area. In the years between World War I and World War II, Indian resistance to British rule continued, with the Indian National Congress inspired by the leadership of Gandhi. In 1947, when the British Parliament voted in the Indian Independence Act, British rule was finally ceded to Indian self-rule.

Modern Iraq

While many Americans are familiar with Iraq primarily in relation to the Gulf War of 1991 and its aftermath, this story was written several years before the Gulf War, and so a brief overview of Iraqi history is helpful in placing Mukherjee's character in a broader cultural context. In 1918, just after the end of World War I, Great Britain, which occupied Iraq, consolidated the three separate provinces of Mosul, Baghdad, and Basra into one nation, under British rule. Nationalist revolt of the Iraqi people against British rule began soon after, in 1920, and in 1921 Faysal was made king of Iraq under conditions of British parliamentary rule. In 1925, Iraq adopted a constitution while maintaining a monarchy. However, Iraq did not achieve full national independence from Britain until 1932. In 1958, the monarchy was toppled in a revolution and a republic was declared. In 1968, another revolution took place, during which Saddam Hussein was a leader in the revolt, and after which he was a top government official. In 1979, Hussein became president of Iraq. A border war between Iran and Iraq, referred to as the Iran-Iraq War, lasted from 1980 to 1988; the

U.S. supported Iraq. It was not until August of 1990, when Iraq invaded Kuwait, that the U.S. came into conflict with Iraq, sending military troops to the area beginning in August of that year, an action that erupted into a brief but decisive armed conflict early in 1991, referred to as the Gulf War.

Asian and Asian-American Women Writers

Bharati Mukherjee was born in India, became a Canadian citizen after marrying a Canadian man and living in Canada, and eventually settled in the United States, where she became a citizen in 1988. Mukherjee can thus be classified as an Indian writer, a Canadian writer, and an Indian-American or Asian-American writer. Other notable contemporary Indian and Asian-American women writers include Maxine Hong Kingston, best known for her autobiographical novel, *The Woman Warrior*; Amy Tan, best known for her novel (originally presented as a collection of short stories) *The Joy Luck Club* ; and Anita Desai, an Indian-born novelist and short story writer.

Critical Overview

"The Middle Man" was first published in 1988 as part of Mukherjee's second collection of short fiction, *The Middle Man and Other Stories*, which won the 1988 National Book Critics Circle Award for best fiction. *The Middleman* was, according to Fakrul Alam, "both a commercial and a critical success." "The Middleman" has also been anthologized in the 1997 collection *High Infidelity: 24 Great Stories About Adultery by Some of Our Best Contemporary Authors* (1997), edited by John McNally.

A central theme that runs through all of Mukherjee's fiction is that of the immigrant experience in America. Critics noted that this collection, comprised of stories written mostly after her move to America and published shortly after she became a U.S. citizen, is more optimistic in its view of the immigrant experience. In addition, Mukherjee maintains that immigrants from Third World cultures are not only changed by living in America, but also affect a change in American culture as a whole. According to Andrea Dlaska, "*The Middleman* thus not only emphasizes the extent and variety of Third World immigration to the United States, but above all charts the emergence of an America unsettled by the inevitable demographic changes of the late

twentieth century." Dlaska further explains, "The emphasis is on change as gain, not as loss. Uprooting oneself from the cultural registers of gender, class, and ethnicity is shown to be liberating for both old and new Americans. . .One clear advantage Mukherjee sees on the immigrant side is the newcomers' freedom to create new roles and futures for themselves." Dlaska points to "The Middleman" as one of the stories in the collection which "highlight characters who by choice or necessity have no ties of family or tradition to root them in any society." Dlaska remarks that, particularly in "The Middleman," "this freedom is shown to be transformed into the will to survive, an energy that is a gain and a match to the American pioneering spirit." The character of Alfie Judah, particularly, "has no dreams beyond financial gain, no cause or country to die for. The resulting lack of unassailable values and missionary zeal Mukherjee describes with amusing sarcasm."

Alam notes that the stories in this collection "represent a distinctive phase in Mukherjee's literary career. . .Mukherjee moves decisively away from the 'darkness' phase of her writing, where she dealt with expatriates trying to preserve their identities in a hostile world, to immigrants striving to transform their identities and stake out their claims to America." He states that, "Although her theme remains migrant lives, the angle of vision has changed radically. . . Her characters now are seen to be emerging from shadowy or marginal lives and putting out feelers to root themselves in a brave new world." Thus, Alam notes, "Mukherjee's theme in this phase of her literary career has become 'the making of new Americans.'"

Commenting on Mukherjee's use of language in *The Middleman and Other Stories*, S. K. Tikoo notes, "The writer's use of language is unconventional. The spoken language of the characters corresponds to their actual thinking process. Their speech is interspersed with words that may be familiar to the American ear but which must appear as slang to the non-American ear." Carol Ascher describes the effect of Mukherjee's use of language in these stories, noting that Mukherjee "writes with a rushed, rootless, naively cynical voice of Third World newcomers and those who get involved with them." Alam adds, "The writing is altogether more flexible, the idiom distinctively American, the tone no longer ironic or bitter." According to Alam, "Reviewers were almost unanimous in their praise of Mukherjee's handling of her subject matter and her skillful use of the American language."

Finally, Dlaska concludes that, through her characters in this set of stories, Mukherjee "impressively emphasizes" that "America's new immigrants are not a faceless, huddled mass to be pitied or feared but a diverse group of individuals who will share and shape the future of the nation." Tikoo summarizes the overall effect of the stories in this collection: "One gets the impression that the United States is bursting with life of all sorts." Furthermore, Mukherjee's stories "ultimately present a fascinating picture of what constitutes modern America and modern experience. The American society is multicultural and multiracial." Ascher summarizes the composite picture of America suggested by these stories in stating that, "Although Mukherjee's characters only participate in public life to advance their narrow private interests, in total they *are* the great social transformation affecting North America." Ascher concludes, "Finishing the collection, one senses that the strategy of these short stories has served her well. . .There is no other writer documenting these largely unseen immigrants." Alam concludes, "Indeed, it is not too much to say that with the publication of *The Middleman* Mukherjee had registered her claim to be considered one of the leading authors of contemporary America."

Criticism

Liz Brent

Brent has a Ph.D. in American culture with a specialty in film studies from the University of Michigan. She is a freelance writer and teaches courses in the history of American cinema. In the following essay, Brent discusses references to historically real people in Mukherjee's story "The Middleman."

Throughout Mukherjee's short story "The Middleman," the narrator, Alfie Judah, a "middleman" in the illegal arms trade, makes reference to several historical and media personalities, including Ted Turner, Che Guevara, and Miguel de Cervantes. In the following essay, I discuss each of these three historically real figures and their significance to the central themes of the story.

Alfie, the narrator, mentions several times throughout the story that most of the men in Clovis Ransome's employ wear Ted Turner baseball caps. Ted Turner (1938-) rose to power in the late twentieth century as a media mogul who pioneered the marketing of cable broadcasting. Turner purchased the UHF television station Channel 17 (broadcasting out of Atlanta) in 1970, and turned it into a profitable independent station within three years. Turner was among the first to broadcast via satellite to cable television subscribers. Channel 17 was eventually renamed the Turner Broadcasting System (TBS). Turner then launched the new cable broadcasting stations Cable News Network (CNN) in 1980 and Turner Network Television (TNT) in 1988 (the year in which Mukherjee's story was published). Turner also became the owner of sports teams, including the professional baseball team the Atlanta Braves in 1976 and the professional basketball team the Atlanta Hawks in 1977. Turner also caused controversy when, in 1986, he bought the MGM/UA Entertainment Company, which included the film studio Metro-Goldwyn-Mayer and its library of over 4,000 classic films; Turner met with protests from various artists, intellectuals, and members of the entertainment industry when he began to colorize many of the classic black-and-white films included in this library. In addition, Turner is a yachtsman who won the 1977 America's Cup yacht race. Many of these details are significant to Mukherjee's story as referred to in the narrator's discussion of Clovis Ransome's admiration for Ted Turner:

> He's a Braves man. Bud ships him cassettes of all the Braves games. . .It isn't love of the game, he told me last week. It's love of Ted Turner, man. His teams. His stations. His America's cup, his yachts, his network. If he could clone himself after anyone in the world, he'd choose Ted Turner. Then he leaned close and told me his wife, Maria. . .told him she'd put out all night if he looked like Ted Turner.

This mention of Ted Turner is significant to several central themes of the story. Clovis Ransome is a successful capitalist entrepreneur of the illegal underworld economy. Ted Turner is a consummate capitalist success story. Clovis's worship of Ted Turner indicates his business aspirations, according to which Turner would certainly be an impressive role model. Alfie, the narrator of the story, lives in a world in which every interaction is a business negotiation, and every thing—including another human being—is a commodity or unit of exchange. For instance, Maria, Ransome's wife, has been exchanged between men throughout her life as a commodity in the course of their business negotiations. Ted Turner as model entrepreneur and Maria as prime capital are thematically related in Alfie's interjection to the reader, during this exchange with Ransome, that he himself could not possibly "miss

What Do I Read Next?

- *The Middleman and Other Stories* (1988) by Bharati Mukherjee. Mukherjee's second collection of short fiction and winner of the 1988 Book Critics Circle Award for best fiction.

- *Jasmine* (1989) by Bharati Mukherjee. Mukherjee's third novel, based on the short story "Jasmine," which originally appeared in *The Middleman*.

- Mukherjee's fourth novel, *The Holder of the World* (1993), traces the lives of two women living in different centuries whose fates meet over a famous diamond called the Tear Drop.

- *Leave It to Me* (1997), Mukherjee's fifth and most recent novel to date, is about a woman's search for identity.

- *Days and Nights in Calcutta* (1977) by Bharati Mukherjee and Clark Blaise, traces Mukherjee and her husband's differing perspectives during a visit to India in 1973.

- *Charlie Chan Is Dead: An Anthology of Contemporary Asian American Fiction* (1993), edited by Jessica Hagedorn with an introduction by Hagedorn and a preface by Elaine Kim, is a collection of short stories by contemporary Asian-American writers and includes "A Father" by Mukherjee.

- *Imagining America: Stories from the Promised Land* (1991), edited by Wesley Brown and Amy Ling, is a collection of short fiction on the theme of immigration and the immigrant experience in America. It includes "A Wife's Story" by Mukherjee.

---

her charms, or underestimate their prices in a seller's market." So Ransome's admission that Maria would "put out all night" if he looked like Ted Turner suggests Maria's sense of herself as a unit of exchange and her sexuality as a bargaining chip; if Ted Turner is a successful business mogul, Maria would "put out all night" for him as a sound financial investment.

At one point in the story, Alfie, the narrator, takes note of the contents of the bedroom of Eduardo, Ransome's "houseboy," who turns out to be in league with the guerilla rebel fighters who eventually kill Ransome. Along with the "icons of saints" hanging on the walls, Alfie notices "posters of stars I'd never have heard of if I hadn't been forced to drop out." Along with many posters of women, Alfie comments that "the men have greater range. Some are young versions of Fernando Lamas, some are in fatigues and boots, striking Robin Hood poses. The handsomest is dressed as a guerilla with all the right accessories: beret, black boots, bandolier. Maybe he'd played Che Guevara in some B-budget Argentine melodrama." Alfie later notices that Maria's lover, the guerilla rebel fighter Andreas, is the man in this poster. Che Guevara (1928-1967) was a revolutionary thinker and leader in the Cuban revolution as well as in several other political struggles in South American and Central American countries. Guevara, who was born in Argentina, finished a medical degree in 1953. During his holidays from school, he spent time traveling in Latin America, and the poverty he witnessed strengthened his political convictions as a socialist. Guevara met the Cuban revolutionary Fidel Castro and fought with Castro's guerilla rebels to effect the overthrow of the Batista government in Cuba in 1959. Castro established a Marxist government in Cuba, with Guevara occupying various top government positions. Guevara was also committed to Marxist revolution and opposed to imperialism in nations throughout the world. Guevara was killed in 1967 while fighting with guerilla rebels in Bolivia. Guevara wrote the influential books *Guerilla Warfare* (first published in Spanish in 1960; translated into English in 1961), a manual for guerilla fighters, and *Reminiscences of the Cuban Revolutionary War*

> As Alfie and Maria are leaving the rebel headquarters, Andreas says, 'Viva la revolucion, eh?' to which the narrator replies, 'I have no feeling for revolution, only for outfitting the participants.'"

(first published in Spanish in 1963; translated into English in 1968).

The mention of Che Guevara is significant to Mukherjee's story in its reference to a Marxist revolutionary leader and guerilla fighter in Latin America. This story takes place in an unspecified Latin American country, in which guerilla rebel fighters and American traders in illegal goods negotiate business deals, vie for power, and betray and murder one another. The political, social, and national commitment of the guerilla rebels and their willingness to die for a cause are contrasted with Alfie, the narrator, who owes allegiance to no nation, cause, or political convictions. As a "middleman" in an economy of capitalist enterprise and exchange, Alfie represents the greed, selfishness, and a-morality of American-style capitalism. The degree to which Alfie functions as a free agent in the underworld is a measure of the extent to which he has become "Americanized" and drained of nearly all cultural ties. Throughout the story, Alfie contrasts his own valueless approach to life with the commitment of the rebels. As Alfie and Maria are leaving the rebel headquarters, Andreas says, "Viva la revolucion, eh?" to which the narrator replies, "I have no feeling for revolution, only for outfitting the participants." Alfie even figures his desire for Maria in terms of "margins"—how much it will "cost" him—again contrasting his own approach to life with that of a "hero" such as the rebel fighter Andreas (or Che Guevara): "I'm no hero, I calculate margins. I could not calculate the cost of a night with Maria, a month with Maria, though for the first time in my life it was a cost I might have borne." Again, in the final scene of the story, as Maria points the gun at Ransome, the narrator comments, "I know I am no hero. I know none of this is worth suffering for, let alone dying for." Alfie's insight, that Maria has decided to spare his life because "She had made love to me three times that night," again reinforces Alfie's perception that every human interaction is a business interaction. He finds that, "Never has a truth been burned so deeply in me, what I owe my life to, how simple the rules of survival are." Even his sexual encounter with Maria turns out to be a business transaction: he "owes" for sex, Maria has granted him the opportunity to live. Finally, even human "troubles" to Alfie are a potential commodity, an opportunity for financial gain; he concludes, "There must be something worth trading in the troubles I have seen." The passing mention of a committed revolutionary like Che Guevara functions to highlight Alfie's lack of commitment to anything or anyone but his own "survival" and financial gain.

In an exchange between Maria and Eduardo, the "houseboy" who works for Ransome, Alfie struggles to follow their dialogue in a dialect of Spanish:

He spits out, "He kills everything." At least, that's the drift. The language of Cervantes does not stretch around the world without a few skips in transmission. Eduardo's litany includes crabs, the chemicals, the sulfurous pool, the dead birds and snakes and lizards.

Alfie here refers to the Spanish writer Miguel de Cervantes (1547-1616). Cervantes is world renowned for having written the prototype for the European novel, *Don Quixote* (1605), and is considered by many to be the most important figure in Spanish literature. Furthermore, "owing to their widespread representation in art, drama, and film, the figures of Don Quixote and Sancho Panza are probably familiar visually to more people than any other fictitious characters in world literature." In the context of the above passage from Mukherjee's story, the reference to "the language of Cervantes" represents a highly respected form of the Spanish language, against which the narrator contrasts the local dialogue of Eduardo and Maria. Mukherjee's concern with cultural diversity throughout the Americas is expressed here through the implication that the (fictional) setting of this story is immersed in its own culturally specific dialect. The tone of the narrator's comment here is meant to be ironic in a slightly humorous way—suggesting that the local dialect represents a kind of butchering of the Spanish language proper—but, given Mukherjee's broader concerns with cultural specificity, it ultimately functions to make note of the broad range of cultural pockets within the Americas.

In conclusion, Mukherjee's story includes references to a broad range of historically real people, spanning current American mass culture (Ted Turner), Latin American history (Che Guevara), and world literature (Miguel de Cervantes). Knowledge of the significance of these references affords the reader a deeper appreciation of Mukherjee's central themes and a sense of the rich, dense, multi-layered texture of multicultural influences on the American landscape.

Source: Liz Brent, in an essay for *Literature of Developing Nations for Students*, Gale, 2000.

Rena Korb

Korb has a master's degree in English literature and creative writing and has written for a wide variety of educational publishers. In the following essay, she discusses the themes of identity, ethnicity, and foreignness in "The Middleman".

Bharati Mukherjee's collection of short stories *The Middleman and Other Stories* centers on the immigrant experience of new Americans coming from around the world—Asia, Africa, the West Indies. These immigrants, according to Fakrul Alam writing in his study *Bharati Mukherjee*, "are seen to be emerging from shadowy or marginal lives and putting out feelers to root themselves in a brave new world." In two essays that she wrote in the late 1980s, Mukherjee expressed the shift in her literary themes from the exploration of expatriates trying to preserve their identities to "the making of new Americans." Mukherjee writes of both of these experiences from a personal perspective. Born in Calcutta, she moved to Canada but she disliked that country's policy of multiculturalism, and she relocated to the United States in 1980, eventually becoming an American citizen.

The immigrant character in "The Middleman," Alfie Judah, is a Jew originally from Iraq, but he has also lived, at the very least, in India and New York City. Recently arrived in an unidentified Central American country ruled by corrupt officials, Judah has not left the United States by choice. "A modest provident fund I'd been maintaining for New Jersey judges was discovered," he explains. "My fresh new citizenship is always in jeopardy. My dealings can't stand too much investigation." Alfie, currently working as a middleman in arms-trading deals, has found himself in the company of like-minded colleagues: Clovis T. Ransome, a Texan who fled to Central America "with fifteen million in petty cash hours ahead of a posse from the SEC," and Bud

> " As the days pass, however, Alfie comes to appreciate Maria's 'lustrous browns, purple blacks.'"

Wilkins, another Texan and former CIA agent who was "forced into public life and made to go semi-public with his arms and transfer fees" and is now "entrenched" in the region.

These three men, all immigrants to Central America, maintain many characteristics inherent to the United States, both in actions they take and ways they look at the world. Ransome, though "he's spent his adult life in tropical paradises playing God," swills Jack Daniels whiskey, wears his Atlanta Braves baseball cap, watches all the Braves' games on tape, and would like nothing more than to emulate the Braves' owner, Ted Turner. Alfie notes this uniquely American love of baseball—"There are aspects of American life I came too late for and will never understand"— even though Ransome tells Alfie that "it isn't love of the game. . .It's love of Ted Turner, the man" and "his teams. His stations. His America's Cup, his yachts, his network." Turner's millions and the game of baseball are both pervasive American icons. The baseball team is yet another symbol of Turner's power in America, power that Ransome longs for.

Ransome, however, has little to bargain with. As Alfie reminds the reader at the beginning of the story, $15 million "doesn't buy much down here, a few thousand acres, residency papers, and the right to swim with the sharks a few feet off the bottom." Ransome must work his schemes, and work them hard, in order to become powerful and wealthy. The country's corrupt President Gutierrez is also involved with Ransome's schemes. A political whore, Gutierrez is "on retainer from men like Ransome, from the *contras*, maybe from the Sandinistas as well." Yet, the flexible nature of the president's allegiance—which aptly reflects the allegiance of the central characters in the story—is underscored by the fact that Maria, prior to becoming Ransome's wife, was Gutierrez's mistress. "Ransome partially bought and partially seduced [Maria] away from Gutierrez, so he's never sure if the president owes him one, or wants to kill him." Men without power in this Central America are vulnerable. Yet, men with power are not immune either; Gutierrez, ostensibly the top man in the country, "has enemies, right and left." In the high-stakes world of arms dealing and crime, no one is safe. The murders of Wilkins and Ransome will prove this truth before the story closes.

In lieu of higher chips, Ransome bargains with the beautiful Maria, prostituting his wife to Bud as incentive to the other man to let Ransome in on shady business dealings. Maria later reveals to Alfie other stories of "loaning her out, dangling her on a leash like a cheetah, then the beatings for what he suspects." Maria, however, is much more than a pawn in this game of power and munitions; she is also a guerrilla commander. She has Alfie drive Bud's truck to Santa Simona, a guerilla camp in the jungle. This is her birthplace, Maria tells Alfie. "'*This* is my house, Alfie,'" she says. The significance of this exchange relies on the disclosure that Maria is an immigrant to Ransome's world. Earlier, Alfie had equated Maria, though "dark, native," and clearly of Indian ancestry, as akin to the other women in Central America. As a physical representation of Latin America, Maria was not as desirable as "those European women" with "pale, thin, pink flesh" and "curly blond hair" whom he had desired when he was a boy in Iraq. Originally, Alfie had overlooked Maria—she was "in the background" and he deemed her unworthy of his attention, much as were the low-class prostitutes he had visited in Iraq, the "swamp Arabs from Basra and black girls from Baluchistan." As the days pass, however, Alfie comes to appreciate Maria's "lustrous browns, purple blacks." These imagistic details, especially their emphasis on color, again serve to underscore the theme of difference and foreignness, reminding the reader of the unique position a foreigner occupies in society and of the choices he or she must accordingly make.

One of the underlying truths about this Central American, crime-ridden world is no one can be trusted because no one truly belongs. Maria, a native, was betrayed at the age of 14 when Gutierrez came to her school and took her away and claimed her for his own, though she was engaged to another. The Indians who work for Ransome "hate gringos" and constantly recite a "litany of presidents' names, Hollywood names, Detroit names—Carter, *chop*, Reagan, *slash*, Buick, *thump*". Yet, all the while they busily hack away at their native landscape, "the virgin forests," to clear the land for Ransome; they wear his Atlanta Braves caps and demonstrate gestures learned from watching Ransome's baseball

tapes: "*we're Number One.*" The guerrillas who come to kill Ransome also wear Braves hats, implying that the men in Ransome's employ are actually in his wife's employ. No one, the story says, is part of one group. Even animal imagery throughout the story highlights this prevailing theme of alienation. Ransome's servant Eduardo beats crabs as they frantically "try to get by us to the beach where they can hear the waves." Alfie recognizes the extreme foreignness they present: "How do mating crabs scuttle their way into Clovis T. Ransome's kitchen?" he wonders. The bird that Alfie sees in the camp is "cramped and tortured" in its cage, and it is doomed to a life of entrapment, for "that boy broke its wings." No characters, not even animals, in the story are free to leave the life that has been created around them.

Alfie, as well, essentially has been an outsider wherever he goes, as the narration succinctly demonstrates. He lives in the "dog-eat-dog" world of crime, but according to his first wife, he is "a beagle." As a child, a family servant took him to see the stoning of a young Iraqi woman for committing adultery. "I realize I am one of the very few Americans who knows the sound of rocks cutting through flesh and striking bone," he says. Now in Central America, he wears sunscreen so he "won't turn black," that is, darken to the color of the native Indians. His skin color, however, saves him from the Indians' ire, for his "darkness exempts" him from classification as a gringo. When the guerrillas attack the Ransome ranch, the Indians ask if he is an *Americano* or a gringo. Maria answers that he is Jewish and that he comes from Israel. Although Alfie is Jewish, he comes from Iraq, a country in the Middle East that is predominantly Muslim, and as such is an inherent enemy of the Jews. Still, with this scene Alfie takes on yet another ethnic identity.

These themes of the inherent meaning of ethnicity and identity are at the heart of "The Middleman" and the other stories in the collection. Writes Amal, "Seen in the perspective of Mukherjee's literary career till this point, "The Middleman" is an unusual story for her to write, but as the first and titular story of the collection, it announces clearly her determination to venture as far away as possible from her milieu to write about all sorts of people caught up in a global diaspora." Mukherjee herself explained in a 1988 interview that she came to write the story of Alfie Judah "because he was a cynical person and a hustler, as many immigrant survivors have to be." Indeed, the end of the story affirms Alfie's character as he realizes that he has survived the attack on Ransome because of his affair with Maria. "Never has a truth burned so deeply in me, what I owe my life to, how simple the rules of survival are." The last paragraph of the story sums up Alfie's mindset and the way he gets through this world: "In the next few days when I run out of food, I will walk down the muddy road to San Vicente, to the German bar with the pay phone: I'll wear Clovis's Braves cap and I'll salute the Indians. . .Someone in the capital will be happy to know about Santa Simona, about Bud, Clovis. There must be something worth trading in the troubles I have seen."

Source: Rena Korb, in an essay for *Literature of Developing Nations for Students*, Gale, 2000.

Arvindra Sant-Wade and Karen Margeurite Radell

*In the following essay on Bharati Mukherjee's writings (*The Middleman and Other Stories, The Wife's Story, *and* Jasmine, *authors Sant-Wade and Radell examine Mukherjee's process of fashioning a literary identity for a female protagonist in alien cultures.*

The female protagonist in one of Bharati Mukherjee's prize-winning short stories, from the collection titled *The Middleman and Other Stories,* is shocked when her landlord lover refers to the two of them as "two wounded people," and thinks to herself that "She knows she is strange, and lonely, but being Indian is not the same, she would have thought, as being a freak." The Indian woman, Maya Sanyal, who is the central figure of the story, "The Tenant," recognizes her strangeness in America and her appalling loneliness, but she resists being recognized as a "freak." No doubt this term occurs to her when her current lover, Fred, a man without arms, refers to them both as wounded. She does not see herself as being as freakish as Fred, as bereft as Fred, though certainly the story makes clear that she has been wounded emotionally and spiritually by the struggle to come to terms with her new life in America. In one sense, Fred's assessment is accurate, for as the author indicates in all the stories in this collection, it is impossible to adapt to life in the New World without sustaining some kind of wound to one's spirit.

It is apparently a deeper wound for the women of the Third World, who are engaged in the struggle to fashion a new identity for themselves in an alien

> " The irony is that this refashioning of the self is both painful and exhilarating; hence, the terrible ambivalence of the women toward their own freedom—the freedom to *become* —an ambivalence expressed by these women in the midst of arduous change, in the powerful act of rejecting the past and moving energetically toward an unknown future."

culture. Perhaps this struggle results from their sudden freedom from the bonds of superstition and chauvinism that held them fast in their old, familiar cultures, freedom that seems to leave them floating, unbalanced, in the complex, sometimes treacherous air of this new and unfamiliar culture. The irony is that this refashioning of the self is both painful and exhilarating; hence, the terrible ambivalence of the women toward their own freedom—the freedom to *become* —an ambivalence expressed by these women in the midst of arduous change, in the powerful act of rejecting the past and moving energetically toward an unknown future.

In a *Massachusetts Review* interview, Mukherjee asserts that

> we immigrants have fascinating tales to relate. Many of us have lived in newly independent or emerging countries which are plagued by civil and religious conflicts. We have experienced rapid changes in the history of the nations in which we lived. When we uproot ourselves from those countries and come here, either by choice or out of necessity, we suddenly must absorb 200 years of American history and learn to adapt to American society. Our lives are remarkable, often heroic.

Mukherjee goes on to say that she attempts to illustrate this remarkable, often heroic quality in her novels and short stories. Her characters, she asserts, "are filled with a hustlerish kind of energy" and, more importantly, they take risks they wouldn't have taken in their old, comfortable worlds to solve their problems. As they change citizenship, they are reborn.

Mukherjee's choice of metaphor is especially apt with reference to the women in her fiction, for the act of rebirth, like birth itself, is both painful, and, after a certain point, inevitable. It is both terrible and wonderful, and an act or process impossible to judge while one is in the midst of it. So the women in Mukherjee's stories are seen deep in this process of being reborn, of refashioning themselves, so deep that they can neither extricate themselves nor reverse the process, nor, once it has begun, would they wish to. There is a part of themselves, however, that is able to stand back a little and observe their own reaction to the process, their own ambivalence. We know this because Mukherjee weaves contradiction into the very fabric of the stories: positive assertions in interior monologues are undermined by negative visual images; the liberation of change is undermined by confusion or loss of identity; beauty is undermined by sadness.

A close look at three stories from *The Middleman and Other Stories*, each with a female protagonist from the Third World, illustrates the author's technique and her success in conveying this theme of rebirth or refashioning of the self by immigrant women. The stories are ''The Tenant,'' ''Jasmine,'' and ''A Wife's Story,'' and in each of them, we encounter a different woman at a different stage in the subtle, complex, and traumatic process of becoming a new woman, one who is at home in the sometimes terrifying freedom of the new American culture. In each story, the exhilarating sense of possibility clashes with the debilitating sense of loss, yet the exuberant determination of the women attracts us to them and denies the power of pity.

Perhaps this attraction without pity derives from the women's avoidance of self-pity. In ''The Tenant,'' we first meet the protagonist, Maya, sitting over a glass of bourbon (the first one of her life) with a new colleague from her new job in the English Department at the University of Northern Iowa. The American colleague, Fran, is on the Hiring, Tenure, and Reappointment Committee, and is partly responsible for bringing Maya to the school. While Fran chats about her own life and gossips a little about Maya's landlord, Maya contemplates the immensity of her isolation and loneliness. And although she longs to be able to confide in someone, Fran even, she realizes that Fran is unable to receive these confidences because Fran cannot

see that Maya is a woman caught in the mingled web of two very different cultures. To Fran, ''a utopian and feminist.'' Maya is a bold adventurer who has made a clean break with her Indian past, but Maya understands, as the reader does, that there is no such thing as a ''clean'' break.

When Maya is invited to Sunday afternoon tea by another Bengali, Dr. Rabindra Chatterji, a professor of physics at her new university, she accepts with somewhat mixed feelings but dresses carefully in one of her best and loveliest saris. Once inside the Chatterji's house, in a raw suburban development that seems full of other Third World nationalities, Maya allows the familiar sights and smells of Indian high tea to take her back to that other world of ''Brahminness'':

> The coffee table is already laid with platters of mutton croquettes, fish chops, onion pakoras, ghugni with puris, samosas, chutneys. Mrs. Chatterji has gone to too much trouble. Maya counts four kinds of sweetmeats in Corning casseroles on an end table. She looks into a see-through lid; spongy, white dumplings float in rosewater syrup. Planets contained, mysteries made visible.

Maya's hostess begins to ask questions about Maya's distinguished family in Calcutta, and Maya thinks to herself that ''nothing in Calcutta is ever lost.'' She worries that the husband and wife may retreat to the kitchen, leaving her alone, so that they may exchange ''whispered conferences about their guest's misadventures in America.'' Apparently the story of her ''indiscretions'' (99) with various men, her marriage and divorce to an American, is known to the entire Bengali community in North America, which may be one of the reasons Dr. Chatterji both speaks and acts suggestively (he has one hand in his jockey shorts) when he drives her home that evening. Maya has been marked as a ''loose'' woman and as a divorcée, and therefore cannot ever hope to remarry respectably in the Indian (at least not the Brahmin) community: she is both in it and out of it, forever.

She occupies the same ambiguous position in the American community; although she has become an American citizen, she does not fully belong there either. She longs for a real sense of belonging, for the true companionship and love she dares to want, and eventually brings herself to answer an ad in the matrimonial column of *India Abroad*, the newspaper for expatriates. She answers the ad that declares:

> Hello! Hi! Yes, you *are* the one I'm looking for. You are the new emancipated Indo-American woman. You have a zest for life. You are at ease in USA and

yet your ethics are rooted in Indian tradition. . . . I adore idealism, poetry, beauty. I abhor smugness, passivity, caste system. Write with recent photo. Better still, call!!!

Maya does call the man who placed the ad, Ashoke Mehta, and arranges a meeting at Chicago's O'Hare airport, "a neutral zone" (109) they both prefer for this emotionally risky encounter. Until she meets Mehta, another immigrant who lives a life that bridges two worlds, she feels she lives in a "dead space" that she cannot articulate properly, even to herself. At the end of the story, after their courtship has entered its final phase, and she has decided to go to Connecticut to be with him, we know she will finally be able to repudiate her own accusations that her life is grim and perverse, that "she has changed her citizenship, but she hasn't broken through into the light, the vigor, the *bustle* of the New World." At the end, she does bustle off to meet the man who will make her whole again (and whom she will make whole) in this new life.

The next story, "Jasmine," also explores some of the more appalling, perhaps even "violent and grotesque aspects of [the] cultural collisions" Mukherjee writes about (Rustomji-Kerns). In this story, the protagonist is a young Trinidadian woman named Jasmine who has been smuggled illegally into the US, all paid for by her father ("Girl, is opportunity come only once"), and goes to work first in the motel of the Indian family who helped her get there, and later as a "mother's helper . . . Americans were good with words to cover their shame" for an American family. When her new American employers ask about her family and her home, Jasmine recognizes the need to deceive them:

> There was nothing to tell about her hometown that wouldn't shame her in front of nice white American folk like the Moffitts. The place was shabby, the people were grasping and cheating and lying and life was full of despair and drink and wanting. But by the time she finished, the island sounded romantic.

Jasmine must construct a suitable, tolerable narrative of her past and her roots, in the same way that she is attempting to construct a positive narrative of her life in the New World. She seems precariously balanced between what she once was and what she hopes to become. She is like other Mukherjee characters, who

> remind one of circus performers, a combination of tightrope walkers and trapeze artists, as they search for secure, even familiar, places they can claim as their home. . . . They try to transcend the isolation of being a foreigner not only in another country but also in their own cultures. (Rustomji-Kerns)

Jasmine tries hard to cut all ties with "anything too islandy" as she struggles to refashion herself in America. Though she cleans, cooks, and irons for the Moffitts, she never stops giving thanks for having found such "a small, clean, friendly family . . . to build her new life around." She is constantly thanking Jesus for her good luck. The irony is that through all the exuberance and energy we see how terribly she is exploited by the Moffitts, and how unaware she often is of this exploitation, though it is not something she could recognize, even if it were pointed out.

At Christmas time, Jasmine is taken by Bill Moffitt to see her only "relatives" in the country, the Daboos, the Indian family she had originally worked for. In her original interview, she had told Bill and Lara Moffitt that Mr. Daboo was her mother's first cousin because

> she had thought it shameful in those days to have no papers, no family, no roots. Now Loretta and Viola in tight, bright pants seemed trashy like girls at Two-Johnny Bissoondath's Bar back home. She was stuck with the story of the Daboos being family. Village bumpkins, ha! She would break out. Soon.

We never do get to see Jasmine "break out," but the sense that she is a survivor emanates from the story even when she weeps with homesickness on Christmas Day. However, Mukherjee undercuts Jasmine's enthralled sense of unlimited possibility with a poignant moment of epiphany at the end of the story. In the last scene, she is half-willingly seduced by Bill Moffitt:

> She felt so good she was dizzy. She'd never felt this good on the island where men did this all the time, and girls went along with it always for favors. You couldn't feel really good in a nothing place. . . . She was a bright, pretty girl with no visa, no papers, and no birth certificate. No, nothing other than what she wanted to invent and tell. She was a girl rushing wildly into the future. . . . it [the love-making] felt so good, so right that she forgot all the dreariness of her new life and gave herself up to it.

In "A Wife's Story," another immigrant woman has had her share of dreariness, loneliness, confusion, and anger in the effort to reshape her life in the land of opportunity. She too is weighed down by the burdens of two cultures and the hardship of trying to balance parts of her old life with the best of the new. The wife is a woman who has left her husband temporarily to pursue a graduate degree in New York, to break the cycle begun hundreds of years before. The narration is first person this time:

> Memories of Indian destitutes mix with the hordes of New York street people, and they float free, like

astronauts, inside my head. I've made it. I'm making something of my life. I've left home, my husband, to get a Ph.D. in special ed. I have a multiple-entry visa and a small scholarship for two years. After that, we'll see. My mother was beaten by her mother-in-law, my grandmother, when she registered for French lessons at the Alliance Française. My grandmother, the eldest daughter of a rich zamindar, was illiterate.

This woman has even gone so far as to befriend another lonely immigrant, a Hungarian named Imre, who also has a spouse and family back home in the old country. Their friendship, so necessary to her survival in New York, would be unthinkable in her own country; in India, married women are not friends with men married to someone else. But Imre helps her to survive assaults on her dignity and the hopelessness of not truly belonging. He comforts her after a David Mamet play (*Glengarry Glen Ross*) in which she must endure terrible lines about Indians, such as, "Their women . . . they look like they've just been f——ed by a dead cat." She feels angry enough and strong enough to write a letter of protest to the playwright, or at least to write it in her head.

The Americanized but still Indian wife surprises herself occasionally by literally breaking out in very un-Indian behavior (like the time she impulsively hugs Imre on the street), and when her husband arrives for a visit, she realizes how many of the changes in her own behavior she now takes for granted. She dresses in a beautiful sari and her heavy, ornate wedding jewelry to greet him at JFK Airport, but underneath the familiar costume she is not the same woman at all. She is not even sure whether she is unhappy about it, though she can tell her husband is disconcerted

The end of the story encapsulates both the strength of her spirited struggle to refashion herself and the difficulty of achieving wholeness when one is stretched between two cultures. On her way to bed with her husband, she stops to look at herself:

> In the mirror that hangs on the bathroom door, I watch my naked body turn, the breasts, the thighs glow. The body's beauty amazes. I stand here shameless, in ways he has never seen me. I am free, afloat, watching somebody else.

This sense of floating is the key to the immigrant woman's experience, whether it is the English professor in "The Tenant," the Indian girl from the Carribean in "Jasmine," or the PhD candidate in "A Wife's Story." Like Bernard Malamud, with whom Mukherjee compares herself in *The Massachusetts Review* interview, and other American writers of immigrant experiences, Mukherjee writes powerfully "about a minority community which escapes the ghetto and adapts itself to the patterns of the dominant American culture," and in her own words, her work "seems to find quite naturally a moral center." This moral center she speaks of comes quite naturally to her because she is attempting the nearly sacred task of making mysteries visible, to paraphrase an expression from "The Tenant."

Source: Arvindra Sant-Wade and Karen Margeurite Radell, "Refashioning the Self: Immigrant Women in Bharati Mukherjee's New World," in *Studies in Short Fiction,* Vol. 29, No. 1, Winter, 1992, pp. 11–17.

Sources

Alam, Fakrul, *Bharati Mukherjee*, Twayne, 1996, pp. 78-81, 86-87, 99.

Ascher, Carol, "After the Raj," in *Women's Review of Books*, Vol. VI, No. 12, September, 1989, p. 17.

Dlaska, Andrea, *The Making of New Americans in the Fiction of Bharati Mukherjee*, Braumiller, 1999, pp. 95-96, 117, 120-22.

Tikoo, S. K., "The American Dream: Immigration and Transformation Theme in *The Middleman and Other Stories*," in *The Fiction of Bharati Mukherjee: A Critical Symposium*, edited by R. K. Dhawan, Prestige, 1996, pp. 145-46.

Further Reading

Bloom, Harold, ed., *Asian-American Women Writers*, Chelsea House Publishers, 1997.
    A collection of excerpts from critical responses to a range of Asian-American women writers, including Maxine Hong Kingston, Amy Tan, and Bharati Mukherjee.

Dhawan, R. K., ed., *The Fiction of Bharati Mukherjee: A Critical Symposium*, Prestige, 1996.
    A collection of critical essays on the novels and short stories of Mukherjee.

Dlaska, Andrea, *The Making of New Americans in the Fiction of Bharati Mukherjee*, Braumiller, 1999.
    Discusses Mukherjee's major fictional works in terms of the immigrant experience in America.

Nelson, Emmanuel S., ed., *Bharati Mukherjee: Critical Perspectives*, Garland, 1993.
    A collection of critical essays on the writings of Mukherjee on a variety of themes and from a wide range of perspectives.

No Sweetness Here

Ama Ata Aidoo
1970

Ama Ata Aidoo's short story "No Sweetness Here" first appeared in 1970 as the title piece in *No Sweetness Here*, Aidoo's first collection of stories.

The story is narrated by a character known as Chicha, which is the local pronunciation of "teacher." Chicha is a Westernized woman who is the schoolteacher in the small Fanti village of Bamso. As the story opens, she is visiting Maami Ama, whose beautiful ten-year-old son Kwesi is Chicha's favorite pupil. Maami Ama tells Chicha of her seven-year-long marriage to Kodjo Fi; although she is his first wife, her husband has neglected her and shut her away from the rest of his family. The divorce proceedings between Maami Ama and Kodjo Fi take place the following day. As a result, Kwesi is to be taken away from his mother and placed in the custody of his father, who has taken no interest in him up to this point. Shortly after this decision is made, Kwesi is found bitten by a snake, and dies that night. After Kwesi's funeral, Chicha finds Maami Ama alone in her hut, clutching Kwesi's schoolbooks and uniform in agonized mourning.

This story concerns several themes central to Aidoo's works of fiction. It places an educated, Westernized African woman in the context of traditional village life. From this "outsider" perspective, the narrator is able to observe the unfair treatment of women in traditional marriage customs.

Author Biography

Novelist, playwright, and short story writer Ama Ata Aidoo was born on March 23, 1942, in Abeadzi Kyiakor, Gold Coast (now Ghana). Her mother was Maame Abba Abasema, and her father, a chief of Abeadzi Kyiakor, was Nana Yaw Fama. Aidoo attended the University of Ghana, graduating with a B.A., with honors, in 1964. She later attended Stanford University. From 1970 to 1982, Aidoo worked as a lecturer in English at the University of Cape Coast, Ghana. She was a consulting professor at the Phelps-Stokes Fund Ethnic Studies Program in Washington, D.C., from 1974 to 1975, and from 1982 to 1983, she held the post of Minister of Education in Ghana. She was writer-in-residence at the University of Richmond, Virginia, in 1989. In 1990 and 1991, Aidoo was the Chair of the African Regional Panel of the Commonwealth Writer's Prize. She has one child, Kinna Likimani.

Aidoo was first noted for her play *The Dilemma of a Ghost* (1965), which was first performed in 1964. This was followed in 1970 by the publication of her play *Anowa*. Aidoo's first collection of short stories, *No Sweetness Here*, was published in 1970. Her first novel, loosely autobiographical, entitled *Our Sister Killjoy; or Reflections from a Black-Eyed Squint*, was published in 1977. Aidoo has subsequently published several collections of poetry and a collection of stories for children. Her second novel, *Changes: A Love Story*, published in 1991, has received a generally positive response from critics, who see it as an improvement over her first novel. Aidoo has contributed stories to numerous anthologies, including *Modern African Stories* (1964) and *African Literature and the Arts* (1970). All of Aidoo's works are written in English.

Aidoo has become known for her fiction, which stresses the struggles of the modern African woman in an era of post-colonialism. Her works have been noted for their treatment of feminist concerns and their mixture of traditional African and Western literary styles.

Plot Summary

The narrator of this story is a Westernized woman working as the schoolteacher in the Fanti village of Bamso. She is known only as Chicha, the Fanti pronunciation of "teacher." As the story opens, she is visiting the hut of Maami Ama, whose ten-year-old son Kwesi is Chicha's favorite pupil. Chicha commends Maami Ama on Kwesi's physical beauty, teasing that she is going to kidnap Kwesi and take him away with her; Maami Ama appreciates the compliment, but also expresses her fear of losing her only child. Maami Ama explains that, although she is his first wife, she has been completely neglected by her husband of seven years, Kodjo Fi. She has been given his worst piece of land to farm, been personally ignored by him, and been shut out of the rest of his family; both his two sisters and his mother treat her badly. He has also taken no interest in their son Kwesi, who lives with Maami Ama. Maami Ama says to Chicha, "Our people say a bad marriage kills the soul. Mine is fit for burial." When Kwesi arrives home, Chicha observes the joy his arrival brings to his mother: "All at once, for the care-worn village woman, the sun might well have been rising from the east instead of setting behind the coconut palms. Her eyes shone."

On the following day, which is a festival day of Ahobaada, the divorce proceedings between Maami Ama and Kodjo Fi are conducted in the center of the village. During her students' recess, Chicha goes to observe the divorce and learns that Kwesi has been awarded to his father's custody. The people of the village seem to feel this is a fair decision. In addition, Kodjo Fi has not been made to pay Maami Ama a fee he officially owes her. The two sides of the family, Ama's and Kodjo Fi's, argue among themselves regarding the details of the divorce decision. Yet Maami Ama accepts these decisions with complete passivity, not attempting to fight for her rights to her son and the money she is owed.

When Chicha returns to the schoolhouse, all of the children are gone. She then finds them crowded in a circle around Kwesi, who is lying on the ground, having been bitten by a snake. Although Kwesi is attended to by both a traditional medicine man and a Western doctor, he dies that night. The next day, Chicha learns that Kwesi's family members are arguing among themselves as to who is responsible for his death. Chicha sits down and thinks of the ambitions she had had in mind for Kwesi—that he would leave the village to become highly educated and a world traveler. Chicha brings the schoolchildren to Kwesi's funeral and to the cemetery where he is buried. Both sides of Kwesi's family have set aside their differences in mourning the loss of this child. After the funeral, Chicha goes to Maami Ama's hut to find her in agonized mourning, clutching Kwesi's schoolbooks and uniform.

Characters

Chicha

Chicha (the local "Fanticized" pronunciation of the English word "teacher") is the village school-teacher and narrator of the story. She holds a unique position as a Westernized person who is living in the traditional Fanti village of Bamso. This narrator's "outsider" perspective on the events and traditions of the village provides the non-Fanti reader with a point of identification. Thus, the peculiarities of local traditions regarding marriage are questioned by this Western perspective. In the beginning of the story, Chicha is visiting Maami Ama at her house, discussing her son Kwesi and her unpleasant marriage. The next day, Chicha goes during her students' recess to observe the divorce proceedings. When she returns to the school, all the children are gone. She finds them surrounding Kwesi, who has been bitten by a snake. After Kwesi dies, Chicha finds Maami Ama in mourning in her home.

Kodjo Fi

Kodjo Fi is Maami Ama's husband. He is described as "a selfish and bullying man, whom no decent woman ought to have married." Although Maami Ama is his first wife, he has neglected her, given her his worst piece of land to farm, and isolated her from the rest of his family during their seven years of marriage. During the divorce proceedings, he is clearly favored over Maami Ama, given the rights to their only child and allowed to forego a fee he should have had to pay to her.

Kwesi

Kwesi, a ten-year-old boy, is Maami Ama's only child and a favorite of Chicha. He is repeatedly referred to as a beautiful child and described as "quite tall for his age. His skin was as smooth as shea-butter and as dark as charcoal. His black hair was as soft as his mother's. His eyes were of the kind that always remind one of a long dream on a hot afternoon." The narrator comments, "It is indecent to dwell on a boy's physical appearance, but then Kwesi's beauty was indecent." The result of his parents' divorce is that he is to leave his mother's house to live with his father's family. Shortly after the divorce proceedings, Kwesi is found lying on the ground, surrounded by the other school children, having been bitten by a snake. Although he is nursed for days by both a traditional medicine man and a Western doctor, he dies.

Maami Ama

Maami Ama is the mother of Kwesi, who is her only son. As the story opens, she explains to Chicha the unfortunate circumstances of her seven-year marriage to Kodjo Fi. Although she is his first wife, she has been given his worst piece of land to farm and has been shunned and isolated by the rest of his family. Although she loves her son dearly, she does not protest when, as a result of the divorce, his custody is granted to his father instead of her. She also does not protest not receiving the fee which her ex-husband is required to pay her. After Kwesi dies, Chicha finds her in mourning in her home. Maami Ama, from the perspective of Chicha, represents the extent to which women in this traditional culture passively accept unfair treatment by their community.

Themes

Marriage and Tradition

This story explores the perspective of the narrator, an "outsider," a Westernized African woman referred to as Chicha, on the marriage traditions of a small Fanti village. Maami Ama explains to Chicha that she has been unhappily married for seven years to a man named Kodjo Fi. Although she is his first wife, he has completely neglected her, as well as their son, and has allowed the rest of his family to shun and isolate her. In addition, Kodjo Fi is described as "a selfish and bullying man, whom no decent woman ought to have married." Maami Ama's "formal divorce" from Kodjo Fi exposes the narrator to traditional attitudes and practices of her culture which she had either not known or forgotten. The divorce proceedings take place at the home of one of the women of the village, and other members of the community attend for the sake of entertainment. When Chicha arrives on the scene, it has been decided that Kwesi will be taken away from Maami Ama, who has raised him, and given into the custody of his father, who has neglected him up to this point. In addition, Maami Ama is expected to pay a variety of fees to her husband which she cannot afford to pay. Finally, Kodjo Fi manages to shirk the paying of a fee he should traditionally have been required to pay to Maami Ama. Chicha observes the extent to which all of these traditions are unfair to the woman in the divorce. Maami Ama accepts the outcome passively, not even attempting to fight for the right to keep her son. As these various traditional rules of marriage and divorce are explained to her, Chicha

Topics for Further Study

- Learn more about the history of Ghana (called the Gold Coast prior to 1957). What were the region and its peoples like before the colonization by Europeans in the 15th century? What were the conditions of colonization which characterized the Gold Coast until 1957? How has the nation changed since achieving independence as the Republic of Ghana in 1957?

- Learn more about the cultural practices of Ghana and other African countries, in terms of the role of women in traditional African society. What traditions surround (or surrounded) courting, marriage, and family life in these regions?

- Aidoo's work is preceded in the history of West African literature by Amos Tutuola, best known for his novel *The Palm-Wine Drunkard* (1952), and Chinua Achebe, for his novel *Things Fall Apart* (1958). Learn more about these authors and their fictional works. In what ways are their concerns similar to, or different from, those of Aidoo? What similarities do they share in literary style, and their connection to the oral tradition of storytelling in Africa?

- The Republic of Ghana experienced various forms of national turmoil and social upheaval during the 1990s. Learn more about recent political events in Ghana. What types of conflicts have arisen within the nation, and how have these conflicts been resolved, or not?

---

recalls, "I sat there listening to these references to the age-old customs of my people of which I had been ignorant." The entire divorce process reminds Chicha of the distance between the traditional culture from which she comes and the Westernized perspective she has acquired through her higher education.

Gender and Beauty Standards

Chicha's admiration of Kwesi, the ten-year-old schoolboy, focuses above all on her observation of his sheer physical beauty. This highlights the teacher's outsider status to her own culture, in which it is considered inappropriate to dwell upon male physical beauty. The theme of male beauty thus develops Aidoo's central themes of gender roles in traditional culture and the perspective of the Westernized African on her own society. The story opens with a developed discussion of this theme: "He was beautiful, but that was not important. Beauty does not play such a vital role in a man's life as it does in a woman's, especially if that man is Fanti. If a man's beauty is so ill-mannered as to be noticeable, people discreetly ignore its existence. Only an immodest girl like me would dare comment on a boy's beau-

ty." The narrator again dwells on the physical details of the boy's beauty, acknowledging once again the extent to which such observations are contrary to traditional notions of gender: "His skin was as smooth as shea-butter and as dark as charcoal. His black hair was as soft as his mother's. His eyes were of the kind that always remind one of a long dream on a hot afternoon. It is indecent to dwell on a boy's physical appearance, but then Kwesi's beauty was indecent."

Maternal Love

The central relationship of the story is that between Maami Ama and her son Kwesi. The mother's love for her beautiful son is emphasized throughout the story, making his death all the more tragic. Kwesi is Maami Ama's only child and only real family, as she has been isolated from that of her husband. When Chicha jokes of kidnapping Kwesi to take him with her, Maami Ama expresses her "gnawing fear" of losing him: "'Please, Chicha, I always know you are just making fun of me, but please, promise me you won't take Kwesi away with you.' Almost at once her tiny mouth would quiver and she would hide her eyes in her cloth as if ashamed of her great love and her fears." Maami Ama goes on to plead, "'What will I do, Chicha, what would I do, should something happen to my child?' She would raise her pretty eyes, glistening with unshed tears." Maami Ama then insists that, should Kwesi misbehave in school, she herself would "willingly submit" to the punishment of caning in place of her child. These expressions of maternal love in the beginning of the story make all the more poignant and significant the mother's mourning of her son's death in the end. After Kwesi's funeral, Chicha finds Maami Ama in her hut, "kneeling, and like one who catches at a straw, she was clutching Kwesi's books and school uniform to her breast."

Style

Narration

This story is told from the perspective of the *first person restricted* point of view. This means that the narrator is a character in the story, and that the narrative point of view is limited to that of the narrator. The reader is given only information available to the narrator—in this case Chicha, the schoolteacher in the small Fanti village of Bamso. This narrative technique is effective for this story in that it allows the reader to identify with a woman who is an outsider to the traditional village culture in which she is living and working. Thus, her perspective on the characters and events around her, such as the conditions of the marriage and the traditions of divorce between Maami Ama and Kodjo Fi, is that of an outside observer. Although this is her culture of origin, she has been educated in a Western culture and so her own traditions are unfamiliar to her. This allows her, and the reader, both a privileged inside view of a traditional African culture and the vantage point of an outside perspective. This narrative technique allows for the exploration of themes central to much of Aidoo's fiction: the conflicts faced by the African woman who has been immersed in Western education and culture, as well as the unfair conditions of African women in traditional African culture.

Language

The use of language is central to Aidoo's story. Aidoo's fiction is written in English, but incorporates some elements of African languages and words, as well as hybridized terms that have grown out of the collision between African and Western culture.

For instance, the narrator is called Chicha, which, it is explained, is the "Fanticized" pronunciation of the English word "teacher." Another example of "Fanticized" English occurs in an exchange between Chicha and Nana, whom she passes on her way home:

> 'Kudiimin-o, Chicha.' Then I would answer, 'Kudiimin, Nana.' When I greeted her first, the response was 'Tanchiw', that is 'Thank you.'

The reader may guess that "Kudiimin-o" must be the Fanticized pronunciation of "Good morning."

Dialogue

Aidoo's first two literary publications were both stage plays. Critics have noted that her prose fiction, like a stage play, relies heavily on dialogue as a means of conveying character and developing the story. She thus allows the characters to speak for themselves, rather than telling the reader how to interpret them. This story makes use of dialogue between Maami Ama and Chicha in order to convey Maami Ama's feelings about her son and her relationship to her husband and his family. Dialogue is also central in the scene of the divorce proceedings, where Maami Ama's family members argue with Kodjo Fi's family members regarding the outcome of the divorce.

Description

While dialogue is central to developing character and building the story, Aidoo also uses vivid descriptive language in order to convey the daily life of a traditional woman in her village. During the conversation Chicha has with Maami Ama about her son Kwesi and her marriage, the description of Maami Ama's preparation of the food she has just brought in from her field captures a sense of her everyday life and work. The description, rich with mouth-watering details of the food itself and vivid with color, is worth quoting at length:

> . . .when I arrived at the hut, Maami Ama had just arrived from the farm. . .Oh, that picture is still vivid in my mind. She was sitting on a low stool with her load before her. Like all the loads the other women would bring from the farms into their homes, it was colourful with miscellaneous articles. At the very bottom of the wide wooden tray were the cassava and yam tubers, rich muddy brown, the colour of the earth. Next were the plantain, of the green colour of the woods from which they came. Then there were the gay vegetables, the scarlet pepper, garden eggs, golden pawpaw and crimson tomatoes. Over this riot of colours the little woman's eyes were fixed, absorbed, while the tiny hands delicately picked the pepper.

Literary Heritage

Like many African countries and cultures, each ethnic group in Ghana has a tradition of oral storytelling, including myths and legends on their religious figures and the beginning of the universe. Folktales are particularly important ways of both entertaining and imparting values. One type of folk story is the "dilemma tale," which presents social and moral issues in a way that provokes discussion of the topics raised. An example of this is Aidoo's *Anowa*.

While there is an emphasis on performance in the oral transmission of folktales, Ghana has a more modern theatrical tradition. Beginning in the late nineteenth century, commercial theater shows and troupes traveled throughout Ghana, coming into their own after World War II. Part of so-called "concert parties," three or more comedic actors in a troupe used stock characters to comment on social and familial problems while entertaining audiences. Primarily a nonurban phenomenon, these concert parties as a whole were rather like vaudeville in the United States in the late nineteenth and early twentieth centuries in form, and, to some degree, content.

Historical Context

Ghana

Aidoo was born in 1924, in the region of Africa now called Ghana. The history of Ghana, like that of many African nations, is that of colonization by Europeans, followed by national independence in the 20th century. The Portuguese first arrived in the region, by sea, in 1471. Their initial interest was in sources of gold, which they shipped to Europe. The area was thus known to Europeans as the Gold Coast until 1957. In the 1600s, Portuguese dominion in the Gold Coast ceded to the powers of Dutch, British, and Danish traders, who kidnapped Africans to be sold as slaves in the United States. In the early 1800s, these European nations outlawed slave trade. The British gradually increased their control in the Gold Coast during the 1800s, and in 1874 it was made a British colony. In the early 1900s, the primary trading resource of the Gold Coast became cocoa, from the development of vast cocoa plantations. In 1957, the region, renamed Ghana, achieved the right to self-government, although it remained a member of the British Commonwealth. In 1960, it became a republic. A military coup in 1972 resulted in an era of repressive policies; another military coup was carried out in 1981; in 1992, a new constitution was instituted, and in 1993 a fourth Republic of Ghana was established.

Education in Ghana

Chicha, the narrator of this story, is the schoolteacher in the small village of Bamso. Ghana enjoys a relatively high level of adult literacy, due in part to the government's establishment of a new system of education in 1974. There are three universities in Ghana, all of them owned and run by the government: The University of Ghana, the University of Science and Technology, and the University of Cape Coast.

West African Literature

M. Keith Booker has discussed Aidoo's works in the context of the development of the novel form in West African literature. Booker explains, "Writers from countries such as Nigeria and Ghana have been especially important in the development of the African novel, partially because Nigeria is the most populous country in Africa, and Ghana was the first African colony to achieve independence from British rule." Citing Amos Tutuola as a key figure, Booker adds, "Nigerian novelists can draw upon an especially strong tradition of oral storytelling." Tutuola's novel *The Palm-Wine Drunkard* (1952) was a seminal text in the development of West African literature in English. Booker claims that Tutuola "can be seen as a sort of bridge between traditional African oral narratives and the more conventionally literary African novels that began to be published soon after his work first appeared." Among other key West African novelists, according to Booker, is Chinua Achebe, particularly for his novel *Things Fall Apart* (1958); Booker states, "Achebe has been an inspirational figure for the generation of African writers who followed him, not only in West Africa, but in the entire continent."

Critical Overview

Aidoo is best known for her stories, which combine both Western literary and African oral storytelling traditions in exploring themes of feminism and colonialism pertinent to the modern African woman. Aidoo's first two publications were the stage plays *The Dilemma of the Ghost* ((1965) and *Anowa* (1970). Her third publication was the short story

Compare & Contrast

- **Late 19th-Early 20th Centuries:** From 1874 to 1957, the region now called Ghana was a colony of Britain known as the Gold Coast.

  Late 20th Century: In 1957, the Gold Coast achieved national self-rule, and was eventually renamed the Republic of Ghana.

- **1970s:** During the time Aidoo's early works were being published, Ghana experienced several military coups, resulting in various forms of repression within the nation.

  1990s: Beginning in 1994, Ghana experienced violent ethnic discord, as well as violent protest against new tax measures.

- **Early 20th Century:** Ghana, then called the Gold Coast, was no longer a major source of gold, but had developed cocoa plantations as a primary export.

  Late 20th Century: In 1997, new sources of gold were discovered in the Republic of Ghana, leading to the development of renewed mining operations.

- **1960:** The life expectancy in Ghana was approximately 46 years.

  1990: The life expectancy in Ghana had reached 55 years.

collection *No Sweetness Here* (1970). Aidoo's first novel, *Our Sister Killjoy*, was published in 1977. Her second novel, *Changes: A Love Story*, was published in 1991. Aidoo has also published collections of stories and poems for children, including *An Eagle and Chickens and Other Stories* (1986) and *Birds and Other Poems* (1987). She has also published two collections of poetry: *Someone Talking to Someone* (1985) and *An Angry Letter in January and Other Poems* (1992).

The short story "No Sweetness Here" was originally published in 1970 as the title story in Aidoo's first collection of short stories, *No Sweetness Here*. According to Naana Banyiwa Horne, in the *Dictionary of Literary Biography, No Sweetness Here* "includes Aidoo's most successful efforts at integrating African oral techniques and Western literary conventions." Horne goes on to say that Aidoo's "feminist concerns are most apparent" in this collection: "This gallery of female portraits offers perceptive images of womanhood, exposing sexism and degradation, and celebrating the physical and intellectual capabilities of women. In this panorama Aidoo covers a wide range of issues: budding girlhood and the identity crisis emanating from growing up female in a sexist environment. . .; modernization and its impact on both rural and urban women . . .; and transcendence over degradation, followed by the assertion of humanist values. . . ." Further, "Aidoo's interests are comprehensive and essentially tragic, with all the stories echoing the same theme: the absence of any quintessential sweetness in life."

Naana Jane Opoku-Agyemang, commenting on Aidoo's hybrid style, explains, "There is an experimental fusion of oral traditional forms, sharp dialogue and commentary, vivid imagery and adept use of language, which make [*No Sweetness Here*] a unique collection." Opoku-Agyemang points to Aidoo's narrative style, in which she "excels, principally, in her methods of narration and in the creation of powerful scenes. There are shifting points of view and narrative turns in *No Sweetness Here* that bear testimony to exciting and successful artistic innovations." Focusing on the dual narration in the story "No Sweetness Here", she states, "The absence of freedom for these women is seen through their point of view." Chicha is the story's principal narrator, while Maami Ama is a secondary narrator, as she tells her own story to Chicha: "Chicha is a narrator and commentator, while Maami Ama is a narrator of her own story, and an autobiographer. The close relationship between the two is important. It allows Chicha to take

Aidoo's stories offer perceptive images of African womanhood, exposing sexism and degradation, and celebrating the physical and intellectual capabilities of women.

over the narration of Maami Ama, when the death of Kwesi does not allow the latter to be sufficiently distanced emotionally to continue the narration.'' Opoku-Agyemang goes on to demonstrate that, using innovative narrative techniques, Aidoo creates strong female characters who must face their particular predicament within their own culture: *No Sweetness Here* ''confirms Aidoo's artistic talents as one who constructs her narratives by exploring various forms of the short story, and at the same time providing a variety of women in different contexts. These women are not superhuman. They are ordinary people who survive difficult circumstances. In using innovative forms to convey their plight, Aidoo shows artistic strength, pointing at possibilities and alternate ways of telling old tales to confront new problems.''

Linda Strong-Leek also praises Aidoo's creation of strong female characters in *No Sweetness Here* in illustrating issues facing the modern African woman: ''She is 'speaking about' many of the 'painful' situations faced by African women in her stories, such as being wives, mothers, prostitutes, cooks and children, or all these conditions combined, from the colonizers, and the Africans who replaced the colonizers after independence.'' Strong-

Leek elaborates on this point: ''The women in Aidoo's stories are strong, independent, and often willfully detached from society; yet they remain susceptible to the community's rules and definitions of womanhood. Although she seems to offer no final analysis or any definitive solution, Aidoo continually poses questions pertaining to how and why African women are subjugated, abused, neglected, and mistreated by post-colonial societies, and often by those they love.''

Ada Uzoamaka Azodo and Gay Wilentz point out that Aidoo's feminist perspective is a distinctly African woman's perspective; Azodo and Wilentz caution that Aidoo's fiction points out the differences in feminist issues facing African women from those of Western women. They explain that Aidoo's ''critical and creative writings have led to the development of a kind of African feminism based on the cultural traditions of the community and the region, which relates the political to the personal. She is one of the first women in African literature to address the fact that an acceptance of Western feminism, born from the patriarchal societies of Europe and the U.S., may not be what feminism has been set up to be for all peoples at all times; rather she turned to her own Akan cultural milieu, and began to examine what in that culture could direct an indigenous woman's movement that would make sense to the people.''

Criticism

Liz Brent

Brent has a Ph.D. in American culture, specializing in film studies, from the University of Michigan. She is a freelance writer and teaches courses in the history of American cinema. In the following essay, Brent discusses the role of the narrator and the theme of cultural tradition in ''No Sweetness Here.''

A central concern of Aidoo's fiction is the dilemma of the African woman who has received a Western education and returned to her native village and culture. Aidoo's story ''No Sweetness Here'' focuses on such a character. The story's narrator, referred to only as Chicha, is a Fanti woman who has been educated by the standards of Western culture, then returns to the Fanti village of Bamso as the area's only schoolteacher. Chicha's story merges with that of Maami Ama, whose son Kwesi is Chicha's favorite pupil. As Chicha learns more about Maami Ama's ill-fated marriage and subsequent divorce, she is confronted with the extent to which she finds that her own Westernized perspective on these events is far different from ''the age-old customs of my people of which I had been ignorant.'' In the following essay, I discuss several elements of Chicha's narration, which emphasize her encounter with these ''age-old customs,'' and her own place as both a native and a foreigner to her own culture. I focus discussion on the cultural differences she encounters in terms of gender and beauty standards as well as conceptions of time.

Central to the story are Chicha's perceptions of the child Kwesi and of his relationship to his mother. She becomes aware of her place as outsider to her own culture in terms of her ideas about gender and beauty. The importance of Chicha's feeling for Kwesi's physical beauty is indicated by the fact that the story opens with the statement, ''He was beautiful, . . .'' But Chicha's sense of the inappropriateness of the concept of male beauty is immediately indicated when, in the same sentence, she makes the disclaimer, ''. . .but that was not important.'' Chicha immediately goes on to explain the traditional Fanti

perspective on male beauty: ''Beauty does not play such a vital role in a man's life as it does in a woman's, especially if that man is a Fanti. If a man's beauty is so ill-mannered as to be noticeable, people discreetly ignore its existence.'' She then indicates her place as outsider to this Fanti perspective, admitting that ''only an immodest girl like me would dare comment on a boy's beauty.'' While she ''immodestly'' reminds Maami Ama that her son is ''so handsome,'' Maami Ama maintains the appropriate Fanti response to such a statement: ''You should not say such things. The boy is not very handsome really.'' However, Chicha detects beneath this surface propriety on the part of Maami Ama the true feeling she has for Kwesi's physical beauty: ''But she knew she was lying. 'Besides, Chicha, who cares whether a boy is handsome or not?' Again she knew that at least she cared, for, after all, ''didn't the boy's wonderful personality throw a warm light on the mother's lively though already waning beauty?''

Flying in the face of the traditions of her own culture, the narrator paints for the reader a rich, sensuous portrait of Kwesi's beauty: ''He was in Primary Class Four and quite tall for his age. His skin was as smooth as shea-butter and as dark as charcoal. His black hair was as soft as his mother's. His eyes were of the kind that always remind one of a long dream on a hot afternoon.'' Chicha again follows this description with a disclaimer: ''It is indecent to dwell on a boy's physical appearance, . . .'' However, she rejoins this disclaimer with an ironic mouthing of the traditional perspective on such excessive male beauty: ''. . .but then Kwesi's beauty was indecent.''

Chicha contrasts this cultural taboo regarding male beauty with the idle afternoon talk of the old men, who casually discuss the physical beauty of a woman:

> ''I say Kwame, as I was saying this morning, my first wife was a most beautiful woman,'' old Kofi would say. ''Oh! Yes, yes, she was an unusually beautiful girl. I remember her.''

By contrasting the taboo on the very idea of male beauty with the perfectly acceptable mention of female beauty, Aidoo suggests a critique of the traditional gender roles within Fanti culture. The narrator's status as both insider and outsider to this culture provides a perspective on these traditional gender roles, which puts them in question. On this issue, Aidoo implies that Chicha's semi-alienated status within her own culture makes possible a feminist critique of traditional Fanti gender roles.

What Do I Read Next?

- *Things Fall Apart* (1958), by Chinua Achebe, is considered the best known and most widely-read African novel.

- *Our Sister Killjoy: or, Reflections from a Black-Eyed Squint* (1966) is Aidoo's first novel.

- *Changes: A Love Story* (1991) is Aidoo's second novel.

- *No Sweetness Here* (1970) is Aidoo's first collection of short stories.

- *The Palm-Wine Drunkard* (1952) by Amos Tutuola is a seminal novel by the African writer who served as an inspiration for many writers who followed him.

Chicha's role as a non-traditional, Westernized outsider in her own culture is further emphasized through the repetition of a very different theme: time. At several points in the story, Chicha comments on the differences in her Westernized conception of time and the traditional Fanti conception of time. Chicha first mentions the Western conception of late afternoon by indicating, ''My watch read 4:15 p.m. . .'' She then contrasts this concrete, mechanized, Western conception of time with that of the Fanti. While the time according to the watch may be indicated in a brief statement, an explanation of the significance of this particular time of day for the Fanti requires a richer, more elaborate explanation:

> My watch read 4:15 p.m., that ambiguous time of the day, which the Fantis, despite their great ancient astronomic knowledge, have always failed to identify. For the very young and very old, it is certainly evening, for they've stayed at home all day and they begin to persuade themselves that the day is ending. Bored with their own company, they sprawl in the market-place or by their own walls. The children begin to whimper for their mothers, for they are tired with playing 'house'. Fancying themselves starving, they go back to what was left of their lunch, but really they only pray that mother will come home from the farm soon. The very old certainly do not go back on lunch remains but they do bite back at old conversational topics which were fresh at ten o'clock.

Thus, the Fanti conception of time is described in terms which evoke a particular mood shared by both young and old alike. However, Chicha identifies her own conception of the late afternoon with her regimented, Westernized education:

''But I was a teacher, and I went the white man's way. School was over.''

Throughout the story, Chicha mentions her watch and makes note of the time of various events and occurrences. As she walks toward Maami Ama's hut after school is out, she mentions, ''I had only my little clock in my hand.'' It is as if the presence of the clock in her hand is a constant reminder to both herself and her reader that she has been so immersed in Western education that she can rarely even let go of Western conceptions of time, even within the community of her own Fanti people.

A clash between Fanti cultural tradition and a Westernized system of education again occurs in the context of the day of the festival of Ahobaada. As the village teacher, Chicha is compelled to comply with a schedule based on Western cultural practice, for, as she explains, ''It had not been laid down anywhere in the Education Ordinance that schoolchildren were to be given holidays during local festivals.'' As a Fanti herself, however, she is painfully aware of the lack of provision for local cultural events and customs within this standardized system: ''And so no matter how much I sympathized with the kids, I could not give them a holiday, although Ahobaada was such an important occasion for them they naturally felt it a grievance to be forced to go to school while their friends at home were eating too much yam and meat. . .In the afternoon, after having gone home to taste the festive dishes, they nearly drove me mad.'' Chicha thus again finds herself caught between the dictates of a

Westernized education and the tug of cultural tradition upon the hearts and souls of her children.

Just as Chicha is not able to renounce a mechanized, Western conception of time, the implication here is that African children and parents must choose between the benefits of a Western education and the inevitable loss of cultural tradition attendant on such an endeavor. This loss of cultural ties that results from Western education is a central theme in much of Aidoo's fiction. Aidoo herself left her village of origin in order to receive a Western education, yet she expresses skepticism as to the value of this choice. As in the case of the character and story narrator Chicha, Aidoo questions the value of a choice that ultimately alienates the student from her or his own culture.

As in many of her stories, Aidoo's "No Sweetness Here" uses the narrative perspective of a character who is both outsider and insider to her own culture in order to launch a cultural critique on several levels. In this story, Chicha's Westernized perspective allows her to critique traditional Fanti gender roles, particularly regarding standards of beauty. On the other hand, however, Aidoo critiques the influence of Western culture, particularly education, on the African woman, as it ultimately works to alienate her from her own cultural traditions, such as the important festival of Ahobaada.

Source: Liz Brent, in an essay for *Literature of Developing Nations for Students*, Gale, 2000.

Ode Ogede

In the following essay on Ama Ata Aidoo's No Sweetness Here, *Ode Ogede describes Ata Aidoo's work as a defense of both culture and womanhood, and defends the use orality as a means of achieving a textual representation of the particular forms of orality that draws on the "aesthetics of orality."*

In her book *African Novels and the Question of Orality,* Eileen Julien bitterly attacks the notion that there is anything particularly African about orality or anything essentially oral about African culture. The "oral form," she contends, "is not the concrete literary simulacrum of African essence but is, rather, a manifestation of social consciousness, vision, and possibility allowed by particular moments and niches in African sociocultural life." Despite her doubts about the wisdom of associating orality with Africa, Julien does acknowledge that the manifestation of oral forms in the work of African writers is common, but rarely discussed. Indeed, her book is,

> " By contrasting the taboo on the very idea of male beauty with the perfectly acceptable mention of female beauty, Aidoo suggests a critique of the traditional gender roles within Fanti culture. The narrator's status as both insider and outsider to this culture provides a perspective on these traditional gender roles which puts them in question."

to date, the most detailed discussion of the major oral forms employed by such important African writers as Camara Laye, Ngugi Wa Thiong'o, and Sembene Ousmane. It is likely to remain the definitive study in the field for a long time.

Oral forms hold a special appeal for African writers, and Julien identifies a number of reasons why: "The art of speaking is highly developed and esteemed in Africa for the very material reasons the voice has been and continues to be the more available medium of expression, that people spend a good deal of time with one another, talking, debating, entertaining. For these very reasons, there is also respect for speech and for writing as communicative social acts." But because Julien would both sniff at the idea of associating the oral with Africa, while simultaneously acknowledging the fact that "there is a continuity in African verbal arts. . . . The artists are creatures of culture, their traditions are in them and inform their works," she engages in too much special pleading, betraying a defensiveness or protectionism toward Africa and the oral which is as objectionable as the Eurocentric prejudices that she attacks. If we are genuinely convinced that the oral is not an insignia of inferiority, we will hardly feel the need to conceal the fact that the African way of life is dominated by its oral culture.

One undeniable truth is that orality still serves as a badge of authenticity in the work of a number of African writers. But this tradition, which was first cogently elaborated in Chinua Achebe's famous

" If we are genuinely convinced that the oral is not an insignia of inferiority, we will hardly feel the need to conceal the fact that the African way of life is dominated by its oral culture."

words about his primary literary goal being to help his society "regain belief in itself and put away the complexes of the years of denigration and self-abasement," has been radicalized by younger writers, including Ayi Kwei Armah and Ngugi, among others. What these younger writers all have in common is an agenda that goes beyond Achebe's intention to lead his people to a recognition that African societies "frequently had a philosophy of great depth and value and beauty, that they had poetry and, above all, they had dignity" toward using oral forms as instruments for self-interrogation and as catalysts for revolutionary change in society. Ama Ata Aidoo, the only woman fiction writer of substance to come out of Ghana so far, reveals especially in her 1970 book of short stories, *No Sweetness Here,* that she was contemporaneous with Armah and Ousmane (and many years ahead of Ngugi) in using oral strategies in fiction both to subject her people to self-scrutiny and to suggest the means that could lead them to freedom.

Ironically, this all-important aspect of Aidoo's work has received scant attention. She is, for instance, omitted entirely in Julien's study. And despite the early attention Dapo Adulugba drew to the didactic element in *No Sweetness Here*—a feature borrowed from oral tradition—by remarking that Aidoo exhibits "the involved, sympathetic eye of a critical patriot," criticism of the oral quality in Aidoo's work has been deflected to her 1979 novel, *Our Sister Killjoy,* which, in fact, relies less on oral forms than do her short stories. And yet, as Craig Tapping has conceded, "to hear Aidoo read from this novel [*Our Sister Killjoy*], her short stories, plays, or poetry is to recognize that … Aidoo graphs the voice of an excited storyteller, marking intonations and emphases through the learned tech-

nical conventions of open or free verse and its denoted terminals.'' Nonetheless, the transposed oral form, on the one hand, and an actual oral event, on the other, are, of course, two entirely different activities. Cynthia Ward makes this distinction clear with a fine example: ''The value of the oral tale to the oral culture lies not entirely in the tale itself but, perhaps more significantly, in the discussion it generates after it is told, discussion that allows each participant to respond, whether by taking the center, presenting another illustrative fiction, or displaying his or her individual style.'' The oral performance is a live event that encourages communal participation, with gestures, mimicry, and body movement as its vital aspects. The difficulty in attempting to capture in print the key elements of performance is what makes Cynthia Ward remark, ''What is lost in … transcription—where spoken words are lifted from their immediate social context and deposited on a page, which tolerates no immediate response— is precisely the oral.''

But what about the different ways in which people in oral and literate cultures interpret phenomena? Ward opines that while there are differences, the idea popularized by Jack Goody and Ian Watt about the presumed simplicity of cognition in oral culture, relative to literate culture, is a myth. She believes that in writing cultures ''discourse takes on its dictatorial 'discursive universe'''; so here, unlike what obtains in oral cultures, ''words become objects with genealogies, subject to use in the service of establishing power and affirming an oppressive status quo.'' However, Ward goes on to observe how ''even in writing, the oral antiaesthetic makes a space for itself as writers who … insist on life outside the text take up the pen only to find that by writing they abrogate their own rights over direct semantic ratification.'' Although her argument is obviously overstated, due, understandably, to the perennial frustration researchers experience in capturing the oral material in cold print, Ward succeeds in exploring the oral as manifested in the work of the Nigerian woman writer Buchi Emecheta. My paper hopes to accomplish a similar task in the work of Aidoo, Ghana's foremost woman writer.

Aidoo's *No Sweetness Here* is, like Buchi Emecheta's *The Joys of Motherhood,* a defense of both culture and womanhood. It is a defense of culture in that it deals with the acculturation problems of Africans, portraying an idealistic view of the threatened values; feminist in that it deals most sympathetically with the experience—the longings, agonies, frustrations, and pain—of being a woman in a male-dominated society. Furthermore, Aidoo means in her stories to achieve a textual representation that draws on the aesthetics of orality. . . .

I have remarked earlier that the impact of all Aidoo's stories derives from her keen awareness that a story is not made interesting merely by its subject, but more importantly by its style, by how it is narrated. And although Odun Balogun in the essay cited above reasons that even a story with a thin theme can be redeemed by a good mastery of language, Aidoo's pieces like the title story ''No Sweetness Here'' and ''Two Sisters'' show that the best results are obtained from an intelligent balance of subject and style.

The theme of ''No Sweetness Here'' is the hardship African women encounter in polygamous households. This is in itself a subject of substantial interest but Aidoo adds pep to it by her choice of narrator: a teacher in a village school who knows her subject well, is objective, and is sensitive to suffering. She begins by recreating the daily routine of life in a typical village—the cycle of work and rest that typifies the life of ordinary women. Such a figure is Mami Ama, the central character of the story; a woman who has reasons to be happy but is not. Though she and her husband have been physically married for a long time, they have long been spiritually divorced. The object of abuse by her husband and his extended family and of the ridicule of her friends, Mami Ama's story frames the lives of many ordinary women who are victims of male brutality.

In the narrative design of the story, Aidoo is sensitive to the oral tradition of her culture, and the narrator's words capture well the rhythms of Ewe speech. She builds up Mami Ama's character charmingly—always dutiful, cheerful, hardworking; in short, doing all her best to get on in life. Ultimately, Aidoo designs Mami's story as a protest against women's lot. Now an orphan, Mami gives everything to her marriage so as to secure happiness, but she gains nothing. When the divorce takes place, she will be separated from her only son, who will automatically be given to his father for custody. To reflect how the child means everything in her whole life, Mami calls him ''my husband, my brother, my father, my all-in-all.''

Aidoo confirms the crucial interest she takes in her Ewe expressive heritage through the dramatic effect she strives for. In ''No Sweetness Here'' the sense of performance is heightened. The story builds up to a very emotionally charged level. An instance is the scene of reunion between Mami and her son, Kwesi. When Kwesi returns from school, we sense the filial bond, the love and affectionate care of a good mother. Even though, as we learn, Kwesi does not help his mother as other children do by bringing home firewood, water, or working on the farm, Mami is uncomplaining. A crucial irony that enhances the dramatic impact of the story is that the divorce happens on a festival day, so on the fated day when Kwesi will be separated for good from his mother, he is happily playing football, innocent of what is happening.

The divorce scene, which presents one of the most unkind and most brutalizing treatments of womanhood in the whole of African fiction, affords Aidoo an opportunity to launch an open attack on some of the injustices embedded in traditional African culture. To the monologue of the narrator—we seem to get most of the information from the narrator's reflections on Mami's plight—Aidoo adds dialogue, capitalizing effectively on its possibilities for both psychological penetration and dramatic representation. The reader witnesses the members of Mami's husband's family gang up with their son to humiliate a woman he once loved. The maltreatment that Mami receives is indeed pathetic; at the moment of separation she is branded foul names, abused, and then asked to refund her husband the dowry he paid on her. All her labors to feed and clothe her son, and to cater for his education without her husband's support, come to nothing—they take him away from her. The breakup involves two families, two communities that once were bonded by love. So hatred and animosity have replaced love and fellow feeling. The untimely death of Kwesi (from a snake bite) might belie a narrative design that reflects the author's desperation—a sort of an extreme and exaggerated reaction of pain to the injustices women suffer when polygamous marriages fail—but, in general, Aidoo's telling of this story embodies one of the attributes of the African writers who borrow from oral tradition: while acknowledging ''the power and charm of the African oral tradition [she] will have none of that social stratification that the tales put forward. . . .''

Unlike many an alienated Western-educated African, Aidoo takes a deep interest in her roots. Her achievement in the act of simulated oral performance that I have discussed in this essay confirms that the strategies and morals embedded in traditional oral literature can contribute meaningfully toward the redirection of all the shared patterns of cultural habits that govern contemporary African societies.

Source: Ode Ogede, ''The Defense of Culture in Ama Ata Aidoo's No Sweetness Here: The Use of Orality as a Textual Strategy,'' in *The International Fiction Review,* Vol. 21, No. 1 & 2, 1994, pp. 76–84.

Lloyd W. Brown

In the following essay on Ama Ata Aidoo's collection of short stories entitled No Sweetness Here, *Lloyd W. Brown examines the author's ironic perspective on the traditional roles of women, particularly rural women, in Africa.*

In ''No Sweetness Here'' the perspective on the rural woman shifts from the largely rural viewpoints, or self-images, of the village to the insights of a Western-educated young woman. The narrator is a school teacher through whose eyes we view Maami Ama, one of the vilage women. Maami is very attached to her son Kwesi who is also one of the narrator's pupils, but loses him, first to her estranged husband in a divorce hearing, and shortly after, to a fatal snake bite. The decidedly non-rural sources of the narrator's Western bearing and style are readily apparent in a mockingly scandalous candour about sex that evokes the notorious image of the sexually ''liberated'' Western, or Westernized, woman: ''He was beautiful, but that was not important. Beauty does not play such a vital role in a man's life as it does in a woman's or so people think. If a man's beauty is so ill-mannered as to be noticeable, people discreetly ignore its existence. Only an immodest girl like me would dare comment on a boy's beauty. 'Kwesi is so handsome,' I was always telling his mother. . . . His eyes were of the kind that always remind one of a long dream on a hot afternoon. It is indecent to dwell on a boy's physical appearance, but then Kwesi's beauty was indecent.''

On the surface, Aidoo seems to offer a fairly straightforward contrast between a narrator whose education and occupation effect the image of the self-sufficient outsider, and an older woman of traditional background. And this apparent contrast is the more marked when we consider the emphasis on Maami's vulnerability: her intense attachment to her son is as ambiguous as Mami Fanti's maternalism in ''A Gift from Somewhere'' in that this attachment both assures her claim to womanliness-through-motherhood and compensates for the limitations of her role (''a lonely mother and a lonely son'') in a

society of male prerogatives; and the male's prerogatives are underlined by the fact that the divorce proceedings that are modelled on tribal custom allow her no recourse against her husband's exclusive claims on *his* son. But looked at more closely, this contrast is less clear-cut. If Maami Ama's intense attachment to Kwesi compensates for her sense of isolation and vulnerability, so does the narrator's. For Kwesi's future education, career, and even sexual exploits have become a vicarious means of fulfilment for a woman whose education and occupation—albeit Western—have brought her a smaller degree of choice or mobility than her liberated rhetoric implies. Significantly, too, this vicarious self-fulfilment excludes the domineering male figure in the story, Kwesi's father, Kodjo Fi: ''In my daydreams . . . [Kwesi] would be famous, that was certain. Devastatingly handsome, he would be the idol of women and the envy of every man. He would visit Britain, America and all those countries we have heard so much about. . . . In all these reveries his father never had a place.'' On the whole, the narrator's insights into the ambiguous position of the rural woman reflect the ambiguities of her own situation. She too has a sense of personal vulnerability and limitations that she attempts to transcend through Kwesi's *male* future. Indeed, it is a major, and recurring, irony in Aidoo's work that the ''progressive,'' ''liberated,'' and ''sophisticated'' images of the Westernized woman are really masks: underneath there are the familiar vulnerability and a new, self-destructive insecurity in a time of conflicting cultural values. This is clear enough in the ''bad'' city women of ''In the Cutting of a Drink'' and in the narrator's uneasy sense of kinship with the isolated and victimized mother of ''No Sweetness Here.'' Hence the title of the latter work establishes a contextual irony for the narrative as a whole: on the one hand, it does imply a rebuttal of the notion that the situation of the rural woman is all sweetness, a notion that is fostered in the works of a writer like Nigeria's Oprian Ekwensi whose ''bad'' city women (especially Jagua Nana) usually retreat to unspoilt rural roots to re-discover a lost innocence; but, on the other hand, the title offers an even more personal reference, to the narrator's own individuality and to the lack of real ''sweetness'' (fulfilment behind her liberated Western image. Similarly, in ''Everything Counts'' the young university teacher who upholds her racial and sexual integrity by disdaining the national craze for European wigs still suffers from a sense of isolation—particularly since the Ghanaian ''brothers'' who have encouraged her in her militant African womanliness are still comfortably, and indefinitely, settled in Europe as perpetual students, with European girlfriends.

At the very least, however, the narrators of "No Sweetnees Here" and "Everything Counts" command respect because they are acutely aware of the irony of their situation as supposedly "liberated" and "independent" Western women. The doubledealing of her "brothers" overseas and its implication for her own isolation are not lost on the protagonist of "Everything Counts." And the narrator's conscious identification with Maami and Kwesi in "No Sweetness Here" attests to her awareness that her own situation is no less vulnerable than Maami's, and that conversely, her advantages as an "educated" woman are not necessarily superior to that resiliency of spirit that Aidoo invariably attributes to her rural women. There is no such awareness in the more intensely satiric "Two Sisters" where Aidoo ironically dons the style of the woman's magazine format in order to take a close survey of the urban middleclass woman. Her findings are not re-assuring. On the one hand, there is Connie, unhappily married to a compulsive philanderer, and on the other hand, there is her sister Mercy whose notions of "liberated" womanhood take the form of successive affairs with married politicians, their large cars, and with their healthy bank accounts. Aidoo's plot is pointedly hackneyed, for the ultimate irony of the sisters' lives is the essentially *deja vu* quality of their borrowed middleclass aspirations. As Aidoo's personified Gulf of Guinea muses, people are "worms" whose lives are both contradictory things and "repetitions of old patterns." Their tragedy as women, and the tragedy of their social milieu as a whole, consists of the fact that they are all living stereotypes whose experiences are a succession of second-hand clichés—Mercy's neo-Hollywood obsession with "sexy" clothes, uniformed chauffers, and vulgarly large American cars; Connie's desperate determination to be respectably, even happily, married, and her hackneyed conviction that the new baby will, somehow, restore the marriage.

With her usual fastidious attention to the thematic function of her short-story techniques, Aidoo embellishes this description of a Westernized middleclass with all the popular banalities of Western women's magazines. Unlike the acutely self-conscious narrators of "No Sweetness Here" and "Everything Counts," the vapidly Westernized Mercy thinks in unconscious clichés:

> As she shakes out the typewriter cloak and covers the machine with it, the thought of the bus she has to hurry

> **"** ...Kwesi's future education, career, and even sexual exploits have become a vicarious means of fulfilment for a woman whose education and occupation—albeit Western—have brought her a smaller degree of choice or mobility than her liberated rhetoric implies.**"**

to catch goes through her like pain. It is her luck, she thinks. Everything is just her luck. Why, if she had one of those graduates for a boy-friend wouldn't he come and take her home every evening? And she knows that a girl does not herself have to be a graduate to get one of those boys. Certainly, Joe is dying to do exactly that—with his taxi. And he is as handsome as anything, and a good man, but you know. . . .

Aidoo offers no easy solutions. Connie's baby effects a "magical" restoration of her failing marriage, a reconciliation that is suspect precisely because it is so sudden, so unfounded, and so obviously a mocking confirmation of Connie's wish-fulfilment. As for Mercy, having barely survived one "heart-breaking" liaison she is all set to embark on another at the story's end—and her prospects are no more favorable than before. Like the ironic techniques of the narrative itself, their lives have settled into a "repetition of old patterns." Once again, Aidoo has fused her narrative art with the perspectives and roles of her African women.

Source: Lloyd W. Brown, "Ama Ata Aidoo: The Art of the Short Story and Sexual Roles in Africa," in *World Literature Written in English,* November, 1974, p. 179.

Sources

Banyiwa Horne, Naana, *Dictionary of Literary Biography,* Volume 117: *Twentieth Century Caribbean and Black African Writers,* Gale, 1992.

Booker, M. Keith, *The African Novel in English,* Heinemann, 1998, pp. 30-32.

Opoku-Agyemang, Naana Jane, ''Narrative Turns in Ama Ata Aidoo's 'No Sweetness Here,''' in *Emerging Perspectives on Ama Ata Aidoo*, edited by Ada Uzoamaka Azodo and Gay Wilentz, Africa World Press, 1999, pp. 128-35.

Strong-Leek, Linda, ''Inverting the Institutions: Ama Ata Aidoo's 'No Sweetness Here' and Deconstructive Theory,'' in *Emerging Perspectives on Ama Ata Aidoo*, edited by Ada Uzoamaka Azodo and Gay Wilentz, Africa World Press, 1999, p. 146.

Uzoamaka Azodo, Ada, and Gay Wilentz, eds., *Emerging Perspectives on Ama Ata Aidoo*, Africa World Press, 1999, pp. xv-xvi.

Further Reading

Odamtten, Vincent O., *The Art of Ama Ata Aidoo: Polylectics and Reading Against Neocolonialism*, 1994.
    Odamtten includes critical essays on most of Aidoo's major works, interpreting them in the context of African history and culture.

Ode to My Socks

Pablo Neruda
1956

Neruda's straightforward but elegant poetic celebration of a pair of woolen socks is one of many odes he wrote to pay homage to the ordinary material objects of daily existence. The poem, written in short, irregular lines of free verse, is poetry at its most pure and elemental, as it communicates in words that all people can understand a simple message about the wondrous nature of the physical world. With no affectation nor any attempt at intellectualizing, the poem uses a series of unexpected and unusual images to sing praise to the beauty and extraordinariness of a mundane but useful object.

''Ode to My Socks'' (''Oda a los calcetines'') appeared in the second volume of a series of four collections of odes written between 1954 and 1959. The majority of the almost 250 odes praise common things, including a lemon, an onion, salt, wine, the sea, clothes, a watch, and laziness, but there are odes too to personages, from poets to literary critics. These poems marked a significant turning point in Neruda's career as an artist, as he moved away from the high style and overt politicizing of his works written in the late 1930s and 1940s to a plainer form and interest in the particulars of everyday life. However, despite this artistic shift, the odes also show Neruda's continued commitment to the political ideals seen in his other works. A devoted communist, he sought all his life to write poetry for common folk, to speak for and to the dispossessed and reflect their concerns in his poetry. The odes, with their simple language and celebration of ordi-

nary life, are indeed poetry for the people, a reconciliation of art and ideas with the concreteness life.

Author Biography

Neruda is one of the most-read poets in history. His collection *Twenty Love Poems and a Song of Despair* sold over a million copies in Spanish and has been translated into more than twenty languages, including Chinese and Russian. In addition to writing what is considered some of the greatest poetry of the twentieth century, Neruda was an essayist, translator, playwright, and novelist. He won the Nobel Prize for Literature in 1971. Neruda's career is divided into three periods, each of which shows a particular range of interests and artistic styles. The first period extends from 1921, when he began writing serious verse, to the beginning of the Spanish Civil War in 1936. The second is marked by the end of the war in Spain in 1939 to Neruda's return to Chile in 1952 after three years of exile for his political beliefs. The final period begins with his return to his homeland and ends with his death in 1973.

Pablo Neruda was born Neftalí Ricardo Reyes Basoalto in the town of Parral in southern Chile in 1904. His mother died a month after his birth, and the family eventually moved to Temuco, one of the last strongholds of the Araucanian Indians. One of the teachers at a girls' school in Temuco was Gabriela Mistral, who would later become a Nobel Prize-winning poet. She took a liking to Neruda, and introduced him to the classics. Neruda left Temuco at age seventeen to study French at the University of Santiago. In 1921 he won first prize in a student poetry contest. In 1922 he took the pen name Pablo Neruda (after the Czech writer Jan Neruda), declared himself a poet and activist, and left his formal studies. In 1923 he self-published *Crepusculario*. The following year the deeply erotic and lyrical *Twenty Love Poems and a Song of Despair* appeared and secured his reputation.

In 1927 Neruda obtained an appointment in the Chilean diplomatic service. He was posted to the Far East, where he suffered loneliness and isolation at being separated from his home and his cultural roots. The poems in the first volume of the collection *Residence on Earth* (1933), written during his time in Asia, use hallucinatory and sometimes surreal images to depict what he saw in the world around him. Back in Chile in 1933, he met the Spanish poet Federico García Lorca. In 1934 Neruda was sent to Spain as the Chilean consul, where he continued his friendship with Lorca and published the second installment of *Residence on Earth* (1935), which continues the inward-looking perspective of the previous volume. Neruda's life and outlook changed with the outbreak of the Spanish Civil War in 1936, during which he observed horrible violence and the execution of Lorca. Neruda's poetry thereafter became less personal and more directed at depicting social and political realities. Neruda had always been active politically, and his sympathy with the communist cause deepened during this time. After Spain, Neruda was posted to Mexico, where he was criticized after announcing his support for the Soviet Union. He returned to Chile in 1943, and wrote his epic poem *The Heights of Macchu Picchu* after visiting the Incan ruins. In 1949, Neruda's criticism of the right-wing government in Chile forced him to flee the country. While in exile, he finished the Marxist-inspired epic *Canto general de Chile* (1950), was awarded the Lenin Peace Prize, worked for the European Peace Party, and met his third wife, Mathilde Urrutia. Neruda returned to Chile in 1952, when the government eased its restrictions on the activities of left-wing activists.

The publication in 1954 of *Odas Elementales* (*New Elemental Odes*) marked a turning point in Neruda's poetry. With these simple verses he turned away from political concerns and the heroic tone of the epic to a humorous and sometimes ironic celebration of common objects and experiences. His language became plainer and free of overt political purpose. The use of an unaffected form and the celebration of simple objects was seen again in his second collection of odes, *Nuevas odas elementales* (*New Elemental Odes*) in 1956, in which "Ode to My Socks" appears. Neruda wrote prolifically for the next twenty years, producing works in a wide range of styles, from the simple and humorous to the politically didactic to the erotic. When Salvador Allende was elected President of Chile in 1970, he appointed Neruda as ambassador to France. Neruda was serving at the Chilean embassy in 1971 when he received word of his receipt of the Nobel Prize. Neruda returned to Chile in 1973 after being diagnosed with cancer, and lay ill when he heard of the violent military uprising in his country. He died in Santiago eleven days after the military coup that ousted Allende, on September 23, 1973.

Plot Summary

"Ode to My Socks"

Maru Mori brought me a pair of socks knitted with her own shepherd's hands, two socks soft as rabbits. I slipped my feet into them as if into jewel cases woven with threads of dusk and sheep's wool.

Audacious socks, my feet became two woolen fish two long gangly sharks of lapis blue shot with a golden thread, two mammoth blackbirds, two cannons, thus honored were my feet honored by these celestial socks. They were so beautiful that for the first time my feet seemed unacceptable to me, two tired old fire fighters not worthy of the woven fire, of those luminous socks.

Nonetheless I resisted the strong temptation to save them the way schoolboys bottle fireflies, the way scholars hoard sacred documents. I resisted the wild impulse to place them in a cage of gold and daily feed them birdseed and rosy melon flesh. Like explorers who in the forest surrender a deer to the spit and eat it with remorse, I stuck out my feet and pulled on the handsome socks, and then my shoes.

So this is the moral of my ode: twice beautiful is beauty and what is good doubly good when it is a case of two woolen socks in wintertime.

Pablo Neruda

Title

The title alerts us to its purpose: it is a poem in praise of socks. The ode is a poem of celebration or exultation. Originally odes were elaborate and stately compositions sung in public in honor of a great personage, event, or season. The form dates back to ancient Greece. The poet Pindar, who lived in the fifth century B.C.E., composed poems of praise or glorification in highly structured, patterned stanzas. The odes of the Roman poet Horace who lived in the first century B.C.E used a simpler lyric form. European Renaissance odists Pierre de Ronsard and Andrew Marvell wrote in both Pindaric and Horatian form. The odes of nineteenth-century English poets such as John Keats and Percy Shelley tended to be freer in form and subject matter than the classical ode. However, the ode in general is primarily formal in style and about a serious subject. "Ode to My Socks," like all the poems in Neruda's books of odes, announces itself as a poem of celebration and praise, but the objects that are the subject of glorification, surprisingly, are common, everyday things. Few people would expect that a humble pair of socks would be candidates for exultation in a poem, but this is what the title announces to readers will be done.

Lines 1-16

The poet explains that he received as a gift from Maru Mori (who, although this is not mentioned in the poem, was the wife of the distinguished Chilean painter Camilo Mori) a pair of woolen socks that she knitted for him. They are so soft that they feel like rabbit fur. Immediately the poet elevates the stature of these otherwise simple objects by likening them to jewel cases. But they are no ordinary cases; they seem to have magical yet earthy properties and he imagines them to be woven with "threads of / dusk / and sheep's wool."

Lines 17-45

The poet continues to exalt the socks by comparing them to various objects. He uses a series of images that would ordinarily never be used to describe a pair of socks. He says that clothed in the socks his feet became like woolen fish. They are two long sharks the color of a blue gemstone that are shot with a golden thread. The use of mixed metaphors emphasizes the wondrous nature of the socks. His feet in the socks he says are also two huge blackbirds, and two cannons. These unusual images, which are so unlike each other, call attention again to the extraordinary quality of these socks. The poet says they are celestial, again emphasizing their otherworldly nature. The socks are so beautiful that he feels his feet are not worthy of them. He compares his feet to two tired old firefighters and the socks to be made of woven fire. His feet are unacceptable to him because he thinks their plainness will put out the fire of the luminous socks.

Lines 46-78

Despite his feelings of inadequacy in the face of the beauty of these incredible socks, the poet resists the temptation not to wear them. He does not save them, he says, the way schoolboys keep fireflies in bottles or scholars store rare books on their shelves. He does not make the mistake of sacrificing their beauty and utility by preventing them from serving their function or allowing them to be enjoyed. He does not treat them like some precious animal that is placed in a gold cage and fed with birdseed and ripe melon, that is not allowed to do what it is supposed to do. With these images the poet again emphasizes the rare and exotic nature of these socks. The poet says he does not save the socks but rather wears them, but not without feelings of remorse. Indeed he feels a mixture of pleasure and pain, just as the explorer in the forest must do when he kills a rare deer and eats its tender and succulent young flesh. Despite all the feelings of admiration he has and the feeling that he is not good enough for these socks that perhaps should be kept as pristine as when he received them, he sticks out his feet resolutely and pulls on the socks and even covers them with his shoes.

Lines 79-88

There is a moral to the poem: Beauty and goodness are twice as beautiful and twice and good when they exist in two woolen socks in wintertime. Presumably they are doubly beautiful and good not only because they are two in a pair, but because they are beautiful and good, gorgeous and useful, and extraordinary and ordinary.

Themes

The Extraordinary in the Ordinary

As with the majority of the odes he wrote from 1954 to 1959, in ''Ode to My Socks'' Neruda exalts one of the basic things of daily existence. The poet describes the object of his celebration in such a way as to make it achieve an otherworldly status. It becomes clear that what normally might be taken for granted as being ordinary is actually quite extraordinary. The mundane objects described here, two socks, the poet in fact finds quite remarkable— soft as rabbits, like jewel cases, made of a nonmaterial substance (dusk) as well as wholly material sheep's wool. The socks transform the poet's feet, so that they become sharks, blackbirds, cannons. They are celestial, beautiful, luminous woven fire. The various similes used to describe the socks reinforce the idea of the enormous possibilities in the things of the world, and of grandeur and power (the poet's socked feet are compared to cannons) in unexpected places. The poem has the effect of turning readers' eyes outward to the world, to notice it in its detail, and to take a deeper enjoyment of the simple pleasures of life—to ''stop and smell the roses,'' as it were. There are things around us that often go unnoticed but which, when we stop for a moment to consider, it startles us to remember that they are essential to our daily existence and quite lovely in their own way. If we examine them closely we may in fact find that they are remarkable and extraordinary. The poem is very much a celebration not only of socks but of the very real objects of the material world that affect us deeply. The poet conveys this message of the wonder of the ordinary world with honest simplicity and a touch of whimsy, since it is indeed a mere pair of socks that arouses such emotion in him.

The Beauty of Utility

In the preface to *Nuevas odas elementales*, in which ''Ode to My Socks'' appears, Neruda says that he wants his poems to ''have a handle. . .to be a cup or a tool''—to be useful. His poems are intended to bear witness to the wonder of the everyday world. This injunction is beautifully borne out in this poem, which is useful of its own accord because of what it shows readers about the extraordinariness of life, and also because it celebrates the beauty in the usefulness of a pair of socks.

In the third stanza, after having glorified the socks by comparing them to blackbirds, fish, cannons, and fire and confessing that he feels unworthy of their greatness, the poet says that he resolved nonetheless to wear the socks. Wondrous, heavenly, and audacious as they are, he does not hide them in a drawer or admire them apart from their intended purpose. He explains in detail what he does *not* do with the socks. He doesn't save them like fireflies in a bottle, or keep them like sacred documents, or lock them up in a cage. To do so would be to not allow the socks to function as they were intended to.

These marvelous socks are, after all, still socks, and they are to be worn—to be *used*. They are certainly beautiful—celestial, in fact—but their purpose is to keep his feet warm. So he summons his courage to wear them, despite the remorse that tugs at him. He feels a sense of guilt at taking what will be a base, bodily pleasure rather than an aesthetic or intellectual enjoyment in the celestial socks. There is a tension here between the beauty and the utility of the sock. But still he sticks out his feet, and pulls them on.

At the end of the ode, the poet explains gently what the moral of the tale is. The statement of it is somewhat ambiguous, as he says merely that beauty is "twice beautiful" and goodness "doubly good" when one is talking about a pair of woolen socks in the wintertime. He stresses the dual function of the socks. They are doubly beautiful and doubly good because there are two of them—which is of course essential for socks to serve their purpose. And they are not only beautiful, they are good. The wonder of these socks is in their being objects to be admired *and* to be used. There is really no need for him to feel remorse because there is no tension between the beauty and utility of these objects; their beauty is also in their utility. Earlier in the poem the poet had praised the socks' incredible, otherworldly qualities, but at the end he pointedly refers to their goodness in wintertime, as useful objects that will keep his feet warm when this is most needed.

Topics for Further Study

- Research the literary form of the ode. In what sense does Neruda use the ode for its traditional purpose and to what extent does he revise its use? Does the traditional ode have a moral, as "Ode to My Socks" does?

- Investigate the post-World War II poetry of Neruda's contemporary, the Chilean poet Nicanor Parra (1914-). Examine the differences between Neruda's "impure poetry" as he uses it in his odes and Parra's "antipoetry."

- In "Ode to My Socks" Neruda compares his woolen socks to rabbit fur, jewel cases, sharks, blackbirds, and cannons. Compare his use of similes here to those used in his other odes or poems. Pay attention to the use of figurative and concrete language.

- Think of ordinary objects that can be celebrated in an ode. What poetic or literary devices are used to elevate the significance of common things?

Style

Style

"Ode to My Socks," like so many of Neruda's odes, is charming in its directness. There is an intimacy that is created immediately with the use of the first person. The poet begins by telling a personal story; these are socks that were given to him by a certain person, Maru Mori, that she knitted with her own hands, but which he finds to be endowed with an almost unbearable beauty. The entire tone of the poem is simple without being simplistic, direct without being artless, plain yet sophisticated. The moral offered at the end comes across as unaffected wisdom.

The simplicity of the poem is surprising considering that it is an ode, which traditionally is a solemn and elaborately structured poem. Choral odes of ancient Greece (so called because they were sung by the chorus during the performance of a drama) had a three-part structure of strophe (literally "turn"), antistrophe ("turning the other way"), and epode ("added song"). This structure marks a turn from one intellectual position to another and then a recounting of the entire ode subject. Neruda to some extent follows the conventions of the ode. He chooses a subject to praise (albeit one that is traditionally not the subject of such lavish exultation). His first "turn" is to celebrate the socks' beauty by comparing them to jewel cases, sharks, and so on. He "turns the other way" by saying what he did not do with the socks. Finally he offers a moral to the story by explaining obliquely why these socks are worthy of his admiration—and why he is in fact worthy of them.

In "Ode to My Socks," as again he does in his odes, Neruda uses very short, irregular lines. This emphasizes their simplicity, forcing a slower reading and making the poems sound more like natural speech and less artificially "poetic." But they are very clearly poems from their structure. This is in keeping with Neruda's desire to write poetry for those who did not normally read it, to represent life for "ordinary people" in a way that they could enjoy, to write as a poet of the people. Fernando Alegría, in his discussion of the odes, also points out that the short lines serve a function within individual poems. He says that Neruda does this not out of whimsy but "because he believes this type of line performs a definite functional purpose. . .These short lines are like the skeleton of a Baroque body. In its aerial structure, the Nerudian *Ode* is like a tall building made of glass and steel to support an invisible but formidable mass. . .In this poetic architecture every corner line becomes a live and resplendent fire of images which give birth to other images. . . ." The diction used in the odes is also straightforward. This is poetry that can be enjoyed by anyone, but has subtleties and artistry (including subtle internal rhymes that are not captured in translation) that make them interesting and textured.

Imagery

Neruda uses a great many images in his poem of very few words to describe a lowly pair of socks. The images are surprising and certainly not expected to be used of hosiery. The socks' softness is compared to rabbit fur. The shiny, dark bluish/black color of the socks is captured by comparing the poet's stockinged feet to blue sharks, blackbirds, and cannons. The socks are otherworldly, not quite material (they are made partly of dusk) and his feet are honored to wear them. Their luminosity is emphasized as they are likened to sharks the color of the lapis lazuli stone woven with gold thread and also to fire. That they are precious to the poet is noted as they are compared to jewel cases and even something he had a wild impulse to place in a gold cage. They are like a rare and exotic animal. All of these images that are used as comparison with the socks emphasize their extraordinary nature. They also contrast with the simple declaration at the end of the poem, where the poet describes them finally as simply as "two / woolen socks / in wintertime." The socks are all the things the poet has said; they are an aesthetic wonder. But their beauty lies also in their usefulness, and that is simply in being socks that make feet warm in wintertime.

Literary Heritage

Chile is a long, narrow country on the west coast of South America. It is about ten times as long as it is wide and stretches 2,650 miles from north to south. It has a varied climate and topography, from its deserts in the north to rugged, snow-capped central mountain ranges to its rainy south. For nearly 300 years, Chile was a Spanish colony. It gained independence in 1818, after which it has been ruled by mostly by democratically elected governments, with the exception of military dictatorships in the late 1920s and then from 1973 to 1989. About two-thirds of Chile's people are of mixed Indian and Spanish ancestry. The descendants of the original Araucanian Indians form a tiny minority. Spanish, the official language, is spoken by nearly all the population with the exception of some Indians, who retain their own tongues. About 76 percent of the population is Roman Catholic.

This small Latin American country has enjoyed a particularly rich literary heritage. Chilean writers who have reached international stature in the twentieth and early twenty-first centuries include the novelists and short story writers Joseé Donoso, Joaquin Edwards Bello, Manuel Rojas, Isabel Allende, and Nicanor Parra; the playwright Ariel Dorfman; and the cubist poet Vincente Huidibro. The poet Gabriela Mistral won the Nobel Prize for Literature in 1945, and Neruda won the prize in 1971.

Until the early nineteenth century, most of Latin American literature was indistinguishable from that of the Spanish conquerors. In the early twentieth century the literary movement called *Modernismo* (modernism), which had its roots in French and American poetry of the late 1800s, swept Chile and the rest of the continent. *modernismo* was influenced in part by French symbolism and the poetry of North American poets such as Edgar Allan Poe. Practitioners of *modernismo* tended to use elegant form and exotic images. When Neruda began writing in the early 1920s, the poetry of his Chilean contemporaries contained elements of late-nineteenth-century Spanish classicism as well as *modernismo*. Mistral was one of the few poets who rebelled against tradition and the elegant, mannered style of modernismo to take on a more authentically Chilean voice as she wrote of the suffering of children, peasants, and Indians. Neruda was certainly influenced by *modernismo* early in his career, but he too moved in the direction of Mistral, declaring that his artistic goal was to liberate Latin American poetry from the nineteenth century and bring it into the twentieth century by returning it to its cultural roots. Neruda's innovative techniques and contributions, including a concern with politics and social issues, attention to the sensuality of the present, use of tight metaphors, elaborate imagery, interior rhyme, repetition, and alliteration, and the use of multiple points of view, have had a revolutionizing influence on subsequent Chilean poetry and indeed all of Latin American literature.

Historical Context

Neruda was a political activist and a committed communist all his adult life, and historical events in Chile and around the world had a profound affect on his art. "Ode to My Socks" was written in 1956, four years after his return to Chile from political exile. Neruda published four books of odes from 1954 to 1959, and the verses in these collections show a profound shift in style and theme from his earlier work. Some critics have maintained that after the horrors of World War II and the political hardships he suffered in the late 1940s and early 1950s, Neruda sought to return to an examination and celebration of more elemental, human experiences. Others have contended that the odes reflect a time of simple happiness in the poet's life with his third wife, who inspired much of his later poetry. It is worth examining the historical context in which Neruda lived to get a sense of how history shaped his poetry and perhaps contributed to the style that characterizes "Ode to My Socks."

Chile in the Early Twentieth Century

When Neruda was born in 1904, Chile had been independent from Spain for eighty-six years. Neruda's life was little affected by World War I, during which Chile remained neutral and prospered economically because of wartime demand for nitrates, one of the country's chief natural resources. However, he grew up seeing considerable poverty in his home province. From early on, he was concerned with the plight of the peasants and workers around him, and he identified with the socialist cause that aimed at addressing the economic problems of Chile's poorest citizens. After World War I, Germany began to export synthetic nitrates, and the Chilean economy collapsed. Strikes erupted from all sectors of society, and conflict developed between liberal and conservative elements. The liber-

als gained power with the 1920 election of Arturo Alessandri Palma, but he was unable to pass his program of reform through Congress. During these turbulent years, Neruda lived in Santiago beginning his career as a poet and political activist. In 1924 a group of military figures launched a coup d'état in order to force liberal reforms. The dictatorship they formed was overthrown early in 1925 in another military coup. A new constitution was written that reformed the electoral system, reduced the power of the Congress, and conferred greater freedoms to individuals. Alessandri was restored to the presidency for less than a year. Emiliano Figueroa took over as president in 1926, and Carlos Ibáñez del Campo ruled from 1927 until 1931. It was during this time that Neruda obtained his first posting in 1927 as a diplomat. The worldwide depression that began in 1929 caused severe economic problems in Chile. After several more coups and changes in government, Alessandri was elected president again in 1932 and served until 1938.

The Spanish Civil War

Neruda did not escape political and social turmoil by living abroad. He was in Spain when the Civil War broke out in 1936. In this conflict, conservative forces in Spain overthrew the second Spanish republic. The war pitted Nationalists, led by the wealthy landowners and aristocracy, Catholic Church, military leaders, and fascist Falange party, against the Loyalists, which consisted of liberals, anarchists, socialists, and communists. Many of Neruda's close friends and associates, including the Spanish poet Federico García Lorca, were executed by Nationalist forces. Neruda aided in the Loyalist cause, organizing support for political refugees and helping them to find asylum in Chile. The events of the war had a profound effect on Neruda, and he wrote: "The world changed, and my poetry has changed. One drop of blood falling on these lines will remain alive in them indelible like love."

Chile in the 1940s and 1950s

In 1943 Neruda returned to Chile after a diplomatic posting in Mexico. The president in Chile at the time was Juan Antonio Ríos, a member of the Radical Party that was a part of a coalition of democratic groups united in a popular front. Ríos governed as a moderate as tensions escalated between factions of Chileans who supported the poli-

Compare & Contrast

- **1948:** The Communist Party is outlawed in Chile, and many left-wing intellectuals are imprisoned or forced into exile and hiding.

  1950s: U.S. Senator Joseph McCarthy announces that he has lists of Americans who are suspected communists, ranging from State Department workers to artists to businessmen. In 1954, the Senate holds hearings about these lists, which are televised nationally. Many suspected communists are blacklisted and are unable to find work.

  1970: Salvador Allende is the first communist to be elected democratically to head a nation in the Western Hemisphere.

  1973: Chilean military forces overthrow Allende's government. The United States' Central Intelligence Agency (CIA) supports those who oppose Allende, although U.S. involvement in the overthrow is not established. Chile is ruled by military leaders, headed by General Augusto Pinochet Ugarte, until 1989.

  1998: Pinochet is arrested in London at the request of a Spanish court, alleging that he had been responsible for the murder of Spanish citizens in Chile when he was president. He is later served with a second warrant alleging he was responsible for systematic acts in Chile of murder, torture, ''disappearance,'' illegal detention, and forcible transfers.

  1999: Human rights organizations reveal that documents declassified in 1998 indicated that the United States had not only paved the way for Pinochet to seize power but helped him keep it.

  2000: A communist party member runs for election in Chile.

  Today: The U.S. Communist Party is an active organization that continues to promote its vision of a socialist United States, despite the fact that the party has never won a significant political election.

- **1954:** Neruda begins composing his series of odes about common, everyday objects. The poems are written in simple, direct language so that they will reach people who are unfamiliar with poetry.

  1980s: Chicano poet Jimmy Santiago Baca writes and publishes poetry which he says is dedicated to the people on the streets rather than the elites in universities.

  Today: Many cities in the United States have programs called ''Poetry on the Buses,'' in which short, usually uncomplicated poems by people of all walks of life are displayed to reach a wide audience.

- **1949-52:** Neruda is forced into exile from Chile because of his commitment to communist ideas and his criticism of the Chilean government.

  1974-76: Nobel Prize-winning novelist Alexander Solzhenitsyn is arrested and tried for treason by his Soviet government in 1974 after the publication of *The Gulag Archipelago*. He is exiled from the Soviet Union for his criticism of the communist government. In 1976 he is given political asylum in the United States and settles in Vermont.

  1991: Chinese writer Yang Lian is forced into exile in Europe after his involvement in anti-government demonstrations in Tiananmen Square.

  1994: Wole Soyinka, winner of the Nobel Prize for Literature in 1986, is forced to flee Nigeria after a warrant is issued for his arrest for his criticism of the Abacha regime.

cies of the United States and those who supported the Soviet Union. Ríos entered the war on the side of the United States in 1944. During the war, the Communist Party emerged as one of the strongest political organizations in Chile, and Neruda was a prominent member. During this time, he continued to write poetry with a distinct sociopolitical message.

After the war the 1946 presidential election was won by Gabriel González Videla, a Radical Party leader who was supported by a left-wing coalition consisting mainly of the Radical and Communist parties. Videla's coalition lasted for less than six months. The Communists were removed from the cabinet in April 1947. In 1948 Neruda published an open letter denouncing Videla, and was forced into exile. The same year hundreds of other communists were imprisoned and the Communist Party outlawed. A military revolt led by former President Ibáñez was suppressed. Manifestations of social and labor unrest were frequent in the following years; in 1951 strikes occurred in almost every sector of the economy. A popular reaction against the traditional parties resulted in the election of General Ibáñez the following year.

In 1952 Neruda was permitted to return home, and he settled in Isla Negra, a seaside village on the Pacific coast of Chile, with his wife Mathilde. It was here in 1954 that he began composing his odes. "Ode to My Socks" appeared in 1956 in the second volume of these simple verses. The political voice that characterized his poetry of the earlier years is clearly softened in these direct poems that sing of the humble but extraordinary beauty of the everyday, praising such mundane things as an artichoke, clothes, fish stew, a tomato, girls gardening, and a fallen chestnut. Neruda declared that he wanted to write poetry for the people, for the peasants and workers who had helped him during his years in exile, for common folk who were unfamiliar with the conventions of sophisticated poetry. This aspiration seemed to stem from his lifelong commitment to communism and his desire to speak for and to the unrepresented. The poems also make clear the philosophical underpinnings of Neruda's position as a communist. Communism has its basis in the teaching of Karl Marx, who stressed the material (as opposed to immaterial, metaphysical, or spiritual) nature of the world and its effect on historical events. The things of the world and humans' place in it, according to Marxists, are what shape history. So then the odes, which celebrate the material

world, mark a turning point in Neruda's poetry because they move away from overt politicizing but reveal still the poet's enduring commitment to social justice and communist ideas. As Neruda himself said, "Poetry is like bread, and it must be shared by everyone, the men of letters and the peasants, by everyone in our vast, incredible, extraordinary family of man."

Critical Overview

Neruda wrote four volumes of odes from 1954 to 1959. *Nuevas odas elementales*, in which "Ode to My Socks" appears, was the second volume in the series and was released in 1956. Two more volumes followed in 1957 and 1959. Neruda apparently began writing the poems for a weekly column in a newspaper in Venezuela, which accounts for their simple, public style. Although his four books of odes were published separately, Neruda said that he thought of all his odes as making up a single work, as they tell "a history of the time, of diverse things, trades, people, fruits, and flowers, of life and my vision. . ." When the first collection, *Odas elementales*, appeared in 1954, it met with resounding success from all quarters in Chile, from ordinary readers to literary figures to academic critics. Even readers who were unsympathetic to Neruda's politics accorded them unequivocal praise. The conservative writer Hernán Diaz Arrieta wrote in the Chilean journal *El Mercurio* in 1955:

> Some say this clarity of expression was imposed by the Soviets so that Neruda would be able to reach the masses. If that were true, we would have to forgive the Soviets for an awful lot. . . Bitterness gone, complex obscurity banished, it was to fear that poetry would reach excessively down to the lowest common denominator and fall into prose. Well, never has the poetry of Neruda seemed more authentic. . . We would like to place a limit on its praise. It is said that no judgment is good without its reservations. But we can find none. We even forgive the poet his Communism.

The praise for the odes has continued almost unabated since their initial publication. René Costa, in his 1979 study of Neruda's works, mentions that some early critics did complain that the trivial subjects were not appropriate for the solemn form of the ode. The objects glorified—from flowers to fruit to clothes—seemed too trivial to be thus lauded.

With Neruda's fourth volume of odes, Costa also explains, some readers began to become concerned with what seemed to be the sameness of the odes, with their similar form and subject matter of the concrete things of daily existence. However, as might be expected of a great artist, just as the public began to tire of the odes, Neruda produced a new and very different work, the complex and politically infused *Estravagario* (1959).

All of Neruda's poetry has received tremendous critical attention in Spanish, and the odes are no exception. There has been less scholarly work done on them in English, but the many collections of Neruda's odes that have been published in English are an indication of their popularity. The release of the feature film *Il Postino* in 1996, about Neruda's stay on a small Italian island during his political exile and its effect on the humble villager who delivered his mail to him, raised interest in Neruda's poetry, including the odes. There are at least five collections of Neruda's odes translated in English, including *Odes to Common Things*, translated by Kenneth Krabbenhoft (1994); *Fifty Odes*, translated by George D. Schade (1997); *Selected Odes of Pablo Neruda*, translated by Margaret Sayers Peden (1990); *Neruda's Garden: An Anthology of Odes* (1995); and *Odes to Opposites* (1995).

Critics writing in English have admired the odes for the immediacy, simplicity, and unaffected beauty of the poems. Margaret Agosin remarks on the odes' perfect melding of theme and form. Fernando Alegría says that with the odes Neruda "inject[s] his readers the joy of living which springs from a profound understanding of the inner miracle of reality." And Salvatore Bizzarro comments on the odes' high lyricism. There have been no in-depth treatments of "Ode to My Socks" in English, but the critics who have remarked on the poem briefly see it as a fine example of Neruda odic art, with its vivid images, gentle philosophizing, whimsical tone, and concern for the beauty and utility in the everyday.

Criticism

Dean Rader

Rader has published widely in the field of twentieth-century poetry. In the following essay, he considers the didactic content of "Ode to My Socks."

"Ode to My Socks" is a poem about poetry. Or, at least it is a poem about Pablo Neruda's idea of what poetry is and what it should be. In some of his other odes, like "Ode to Salt," "Ode to a Watermelon," and "Ode to Laziness," he does what he does best—he shows us the magic in the mundane. He shows us how poetry is everywhere, and all we have to do is change how we look at the world. Neruda achieves this effect through his brilliant play with ekphrasis. An ekphrasis is a poem, usually an ode, dedicated or written about an art object. The most famous use of ekphrasis is probably John Keats's "Ode on a Grecian Urn." In "Ode to My Socks," he dedicates the ode, one of the most revered poetic forms, to a pair of socks knitted by a friend of his and shows us how wearing these socks transforms a typically routine gesture into an epiphanic moment, an almost holy engagement with the divine.

There is a funny rumor surrounding the genesis of Neruda's odes. According to legend, a literary critic made the claim that Neruda could write endlessly about abstractions and ideas, but he couldn't write about "things." So, to prove him wrong, in 1954 Neruda wrote a book entitled *Odas Elementales* (*Elemental Odes*) and another, *Nuevos Odas Elementales* (*New Elemental Odes*) in 1956. Robert Bly has translated the title as "Odes to Simple Things." And, the form of the poems conform to their subject. The lines are very short. Often, only one or two words appear on a line, and never are there more than four or five words per line. The form forces us to focus in on the individual word, the small unit, the thingness of the poem. In this way, Neruda's odes resemble Rainer Maria Rilke's *dinggedichte* or "thing poems." Also, it would appear that long after Ezra Pound's influence had lagged, Neruda had decided to take to heart some of Pound's imagist ideals, most notably the refusal to use any word that was not absolutely necessary. As William Carlos Williams would write later, "Not ideas but things."

What distinguishes Neruda's (and most Latin American) poetry from North American poetry is how they work with the image. Bly argues that Imagism should change its name to "Picturism," since the Imagists don't really use the image so much as they use the picture. Reality is not changed in Imagist texts, simply represented. In other words, there is a sense in which Imagism is little more than condensed, poetic realism. On the other hand, Bly suggests that real imagism is grounded in Surreal-

What Do I Read Next?

- *Twenty Love Poems and a Song of Despair* (1924), which launched Neruda's reputation, is one of the most widely read collections of Spanish poetry. The poems describe the poet's affairs with two women, and move from sensual passion to melancholy and detachment to bitterness.

- In a celebrated essay, "On Impure Poetry" (1935), Neruda calls for "a poetry as impure as old clothes, as a body with its foodstains and its shame, with wrinkles, observations, dreams, wakefulness, prophesies, declarations of love and hate, stupidities, shocks, idylls, political beliefs, negations, doubts, affirmations, and taxes."

- In *Poems and Antipoems* (1954), the Chilean poet Nicanor Parra practices the "impure poetry" called for by Neruda but without the gentleness or uplifting spirit of Neruda's verse. Parra's "antipoetry" is often ironic, savage, and iconoclastic.

- Josée Donoso's collection *Charleston and Other Stories* (1960) tackles questions of psycho-social identity, marginality, social caste, and the stifling codes of Chilean society.

- Neruda's posthumously published collection *The Book of Questions* (1974) poses questions in poetic form about all manner of subjects—from the meaning of life to what hell must be like for Adolf Hitler—with humor and pathos.

- Neruda's *Memoirs* (1974) offer insights into Latin American politics, art, and history with the poet's characteristic passion, breadth, and intimacy. The book includes portraits of such prominent figures as Lorca, Picasso, Gandhi, Mao Tsetung, Castro, and Allende.

- *Black Mesa Poems* (1989) by Chicano poet Jimmy Santiago Baca celebrates the elemental aspects of life and pays special tribute to the earth as well as the courage, tenacity, and dignity of the people of the *barrio*, or Mexican-American ghetto.

- *Eva Luna* (1988), a novel by Isabel Allende, the daughter of the slain Chilean President Salvador Allende, recounts the life of a poor young woman who finds friendship, love, and worldly success through her ability to tell stories. *The Stories of Eva Luna* (1991) is a collection of twenty-three passionate, human tales told by Eva to her European lover.

- Four famous practitioners of the ode from across cultures and centuries include the Greek lyricist Pindar (518-440 B.C.E.), the Persian Sufi mystic poet Rumi (1207-1273), the English Romantic John Keats (1895-1821), and the contemporary Mexican-American writer Gary Soto (1952-). Examples of their work can be found in *The Odes of Pindar* (1982), *These Branching Moments: Forty Odes by Rumi* (1996), *The Complete Poems of John Keats* (1994), and *Neighborhood Odes* (1994).

---

ism, in the subconscious, in the conflation of unlike ideas, such as when Neruda writes "my feet were / two fish made / of wool." Picturing Neruda's two feet as woolly fish is *much* different than picturing a red wheelbarrow glazed with rainwater beside the white chickens. So, another way to think of the distinction is to consider that the poetry of Pound, H. D. (Hilda Doolittle), and Williams is grounded in external images, whereas the poetry of Neruda is grounded in the internal image.

And oh, does Neruda give us some wonderful images in "Ode to My Socks." The poem begins in a typically narrative fashion; in fact, it is a sort of realist, autobiographical beginning. A woman, Maru Mori, brings Neruda a pair of socks that she knitted herself. However, as soon as Neruda describes the gift as "two socks soft as rabbits" the poem shifts from realism to surrealism, from the practical to the magical. Neruda animates the socks, almost to the point of personification. Note that he does not claim

> Picturing Neruda's two feet as woolly fish is *much* different than picturing a red wheelbarrow glazed with rainwater beside the white chickens."

they are as soft as rabbit fur but rabbits themselves. Already, the poet pulls us out of the realm of the rational by suggesting that the socks live. As is the case with most Neruda poems, he keeps pushing:

> I slipped my feet into them as though into two cases knitted with threads of twilight and goatskin. Violent socks, my feet were two fish made of wool, two long sharks sea-blue, shot through by one golden thread, two immense blackbirds, two cannons

Through these wild images and intense metaphors, Neruda makes his socks a kind of menagerie and a virtual arsenal. In the first part of the excerpt, we see Neruda linking the socks to magical treasure chests, woven chests, comprised of both real and metaphorical material. Then, with no warning, no explanation, the socks transform the poet's feet into various sea-creatures: woolly fish and blue sharks and back again to blackbirds. Students often want to attribute symbolic meaning to the rabbits or cases or fish or sharks or blackbirds; or they wonder if Neruda is referring to Wallace Stevens' poem "Thirteen Ways of Looking at a Blackbird." There is no evidence in this poem or in Neruda's opus that he is working on a symbolic level here. It is important to note that these images are not symbols; they are metaphors. Again, symbols usually refer to something external, whereas a metaphor is an internal, non-logical fusing of two unlike ideas. When he claims that the socks have turned his feet into two cannons, he is probably not suggesting that his body is armed for political revolution, rather that his feet have been "armed" through their immersion in enchanted socks.

So incredible are the socks, that at first the poet's feet seem unworthy of the socks, their "woven fire." This bizarre and powerful image seems to connote layers of meaning, yet makes little sense on a rational level. What if fire were material, cloth, thread? What if you could weave a flame? Through this image, we get a sense of how warm the socks

are through animation, not via simple description. Again, Neruda pushes how far he can take this motif. First, he likens the socks to fireflies, then birds. He wants to "put them / into a golden / cage" and "give them / birdseed / and pieces of pink melon." Notice how far the poetic imagination has brought us from the opening lines of the poem, even from the first metaphor of the socks feeling like rabbits. What's interesting about these images and metaphors is that they do not necessarily have anything to do with each other. The poem does not have a controlling metaphor the way a Shakespearean sonnet or a poem by John Donne might. Neruda leaps back and forth from image to metaphor to reality, then back into the world of the illogical and the irrational, where, for him, poetry resides.

But, poetry also resides in the external world, and on some level, this poem is not only about socks but about poetry as well. To be more precise, the poem might be a plea to the reader to think of the world in more poetic terms. What "Ode to My Socks" does share with Williams' "The Red Wheelbarrow" and "This Is Just to Say" is a belief that poetry exists everywhere. It exists in the most mundane, the most unnatural of places. It's simply a matter of looking at the world the way a poet does. Certainly, Maru Mori has knitted similar (even better) socks for other people who did not see them as rabbits but merely socks. Similarly, most people would not see the poetry in a red wheelbarrow or in frozen plums, but from the poetic perspective, poetry can happen anywhere. Thus, Neruda's poem continues its ekphrasistic energy because the world is art. Socks, books, watermelons, salt, clothes: all are art. Every object, every thing is a potential engagement with the artistic imagination. In the final stanza, Neruda tells us the theme of his poem: "The moral / of my ode is this: / beauty is twice beauty / and what is good is doubly / good / when it is a matter of two socks / made of wool / in winter." Notice how Neruda allots "good" and "beauty" their own lines, driving home the idea that beauty and goodness exist on the most "elemental" levels.

In the middle of the poem, Neruda compares his desire to safeguard his socks with the way "learned men / collect / sacred texts." The textuality of this image is no coincidence. Here, the poet wants to make a palpable connection between the socks, books, and the holy. For Neruda, poetry is sacred as life is sacred. Life is poetry, and we should read and engage our lives (and our poetry) the way one reads and engages a sacred, holy text. In the poem, two knitted socks are the sacred texts that Neruda engages; for you, Neruda's poem is another.

Source: Dean Rader, in an essay for *Literature of Developing Nations for Students*, Gale, 2000.

Uma Kukathas

Kukathas is a freelance writer and a student in the Ph.D. program in philosophy at the University of Washington, where she specializes in social, political, and moral philosophy. In the following essay, she explores the idea of utility in "Ode to My Socks" and other elemental odes.

"Ode to My Socks" is so simple and direct that it is hardly possible for a reader, even one not normally familiar with poetry, to not understand it from beginning to end. There are no subtle allusions, no poetic tricks, no metaphors that need unraveling here. The poet sings praise to a pair of woolen socks that he receives as a gift. The socks are beautiful, wondrous, celestial, and the poet is loathe to wear them because he feels he is not worthy of their grandeur. But he resists the temptation to hoard them, and he puts them on his feet to warm him against the cold. The poet then offers a short moral to his story. Each line and phrase of the poem is straightforward and presented in the rhythms of natural speech. It is poetry at its most basic: poetry as communication. In "The House of Odes," the opening poem in the collection *Nuevas odas elementales*, in which "Ode to My Socks" appears, Neruda makes very plain his intention with this and the rest of his "transparent" odes:

> I want everything to have a handle, I want everything to be a cup or a tool. I want people to enter a hardware store through the door of my odes.

> I work at cutting newly hewn boards storing casks of honey arranging horseshoes, harness, forks: I want everyone to enter here, let them ask questions, ask for anything they want.

With these simple poems, Neruda says, he intends to offer something useful to the world. These verses are not mysterious or complicated, but solid and utilitarian as a cup or a fork; they are tools to be used. But this is not to forget, however, that they are, first and foremost, *poems*. How does Neruda hope that his poems are to be considered something useful? What practical function can poetry play? "Ode to My Socks" can be seen to be a paradigm example of a Nerudian ode, and an examination of it makes it clear how Neruda's ode functions as a "tool," or how utility for him is tied up with art and poetic expression.

> Neruda's Marxist understanding of the material world as that that which transforms human life is communicated in this poem that draws close attention to the wonder of a concrete, physical thing."

On the most obvious level, the subject matter of "Ode to My Socks," as is the case with many of Neruda's odes, is something useful. In fact a pair of socks hardly seems like the sort of thing that one would praise in an ode *because* it isn't normally thought of as something other than useful. One doesn't think of socks apart from needing them to serve their function of clothing one's feet. But Neruda takes this staple object of daily existence (at least in the culture he is writing in) and describes it in such a way as to make it seem endowed almost with magical properties. As he celebrates his socks, this simple object of daily existence takes on a greater, deeper meaning. The reader is forced to look closely at something that ordinarily would be overlooked or ignored. Something that is taken for granted in everyday living becomes alive through the penetrating eye of the poet. It is worthwhile, the poem seems to say, to take a moment and consider carefully our material environment and the wonders in it. It is important to take notice of the beauty in things that serve human needs. Neruda's Marxist understanding of the material world as that which transforms human life is communicated in this poem that draws close attention to the wonder of a concrete, physical thing. Neruda says in a 1935 essay, "Toward an Impure Poetry," that this is in fact what he wants his poetry to do:

> It is well, at certain hours of the day and night, to look closely at the world of objects at rest. Wheels that have crossed long, dusty distances with their mineral and vegetable burdens, sacks from the coalbins, barrels and baskets, handles and hafts for the carpenter's tool chest. From them flow the contacts of man with the earth, like a text for all harassed lyricists. The used surfaces of things, the wear that hands give to things, the air, tragic at times, pathetic at others, of such

things—all lend a curious attractiveness to the reality of the world that should not be underprized.

The poem, then, is a useful tool as it reminds readers of the often forgotten presence and significance of the material world.

The idea of usefulness is also one of the central themes of the poems. The poetic voice of ''Ode to My Socks'' begins by explaining that he received these socks from Maru Mori, which she knitted with her own hands. The socks are the direct product of someone's intimate labor. The poet says he slipped them onto his feet as if into two jewel cases that have been woven with dusk and sheep's wool. He goes on to describe how wondrous these seemingly simple socks are. They transform his feet into two woolen fish, two lapis blue sharks woven with golden thread, two blackbirds. They are so beautiful that his feet seem unacceptable to him; he fears they diminish the glow of the socks. But yet he realizes that these socks must be used and worn. He resists the urge to save them the way schoolboys bottle fireflies or scholars hoard rare books, and resolves to wear them. He feels remorse that he must surrender these beautiful objects to his use, and feels guilty at the bodily pleasure he gets from wearing them. But, resolutely sticking out his feet, he does so.

The poet recognizes that the socks are not socks unless they are worn, and so, despite his guilt at sullying this beautiful creation, he puts them on. In the early part of the poem, the socks transform the poet's feet, making them into all manner of fantastic objects. But it is also his feet that transform the socks and turn them into these marvelous things. Art and utility are not two separate things, but inform each other somehow. *Using* the socks is what makes them the beautiful creations that they are. And using them is what makes them useful; a tool is not a tool unless it is used. The poet knows not to hoard the socks as schoolboys keep fireflies in glass bottles, for to do so would be to prevent them from serving their function. The firefly no longer shines when trapped in a bottle without air; books hoarded by scholars and not read and enjoyed by the rest of the world are lifeless. Similarly, socks that will not be worn are of no worth. Objects need to fulfill their purpose to truly be those objects. The poem, then, seems to offer the reader an exploration of the relationship between art and usefulness.

''Ode to My Socks'' is also a useful poem, a tool in its own right, because it has a clear didactic purpose. It offers a lesson to help the reader understand a practical problem. The ode presents a story of the poet's socks, his admiration of them, his ambivalence about wearing them, and then offers a clear moral at the end. The moral is that beauty and goodness are twice as beautiful and good when it comes to two woolen socks in wintertime. This moral reinforces the idea that the socks are both beautiful and useful, that they have a dual function of providing aesthetic pleasure and utility. The handsome woolen socks serve the very important function of warming the poet's feet in wintertime. And the poem has the function of explaining the lesson to be learned from the poet's ruminations about his splendid socks.

The ode, as seen thus far, is useful on several levels: it celebrates a useful object, it alerts the reader to the wonder of the material world, it explores the idea of the relationship between art and utility, and it serves a didactic function to explain with its moral that beauty and utility are united. The poem is also useful on a more general level. It is useful in that it is simple and can be easily understood. And because it is useful, it in fact reinforces its power and purpose as art and as poetry.

Neruda turned to the form of the ode after living abroad for many years and being involved in diplomatic, political, and literary activities. He was a committed communist, and most of his poetry written between 1936 and 1952 is clearly political. From his early days as a student activist and poet, Neruda envisioned himself as a voice of the people, as someone who would speak for those who could not speak for themselves. But much of his early poetry, even though it is written in his direct realistic style, is accessible only to a relatively sophisticated audience. Neruda uses a great many hermetic images and shifting perspectives, which makes much of his earlier poetry difficult reading for the unschooled reader. With the odes, however, poetry serves its elemental function as a means of communication. This is poetry—simple, direct, uncomplicated—that reaches all people. It speaks in the voice of those to whom Neruda all his life sought to speak for and to. Thus with the simple odes Neruda's poetry finally serves the function he meant it to throughout his career—to speak to the everyday concerns of the simple people of Chile.

Thus Neruda's ode is useful in the same way as the pair of socks in ''Ode to My Socks'' is useful. The ode is a tool of communication that only becomes a true tool—and a true work of art—once it is used. Poetry is not poetry when it fails to reach people because it is obscure or difficult or arcane; it becomes poetry not from being hoarded by scholars who understand it with erudition, or by being held up as an object of admiration, or by gathering dust on a bookshelf. Rather it becomes poetry by being read and understood—by being usable and by being used. With odes like ''Ode to My Socks,'' Neruda's poetry fulfills its intended purpose. This is a poem that can be read and understood by all people, that speaks in a voice that all can hear. With these poems, Neruda has produced beautiful and delicate works of art that are no less poetic or beautiful for their simplicity, but whose aesthetic delight is enhanced and extended by their utility.

Source: Uma Kukathas, in an essay for *Literature of Developing Nations for Students*, Gale, 2000.

Don Bogen

In the following review of the collection of poems entitled Selected Odes of Pablo Neruda, *Don Bogen gives an overview of the various phases and influences of Neruda's writing throughout his prolific writing career.*

Pity the poets of the New World. If Columbus et al. merely had to subdue the native flora and fauna long enough to set up shop here, the poets had to describe it all. They were stuck with the languages of the Old World—English, Spanish, French, Portuguese— but the literary traditions made about as much sense as a court ball at a trading post. No wonder many of them fell back on the hoariest text of all, the Bible, for a sense of the poet's role. The myth of Adam naming the creatures in the Garden was perfect for a world their languages had not yet touched. Not only did it simplify the task—if you don't know what to call this plant, river or group of people, make it up— it gave the poet a combination of innocence and importance that was hard to resist. In this country that vision ended with the closing of the frontier— Walt Whitman is the last successful exemplar—but it survived longer in Latin America. Describing South America in an interview published in Robert Bly's *Neruda and Vallejo: Selected Poems* (Beacon, 1971), Pablo Neruda noted ''rivers which have no names, trees which nobody knows, and birds which nobody has described. . . . Everything we know is new.'' The poet's task, as he put is, is ''to embrace the workd around you, to discover the new world.''

The Adamic poet, like his namesake, has a problem: If everything is new and you're the only one who determines what's what, how do you keep your pride at bay, and how do you know when to

> ❝ If everything is new and you're the only one who determines what's what, how do you keep your pride at bay, and how do you know when to stop?"

stop? Both Whitman and Neruda had enormous egos, and neither showed much restraint in output. Because Neruda wrote so much, including weak poems in almost all his more than forty books, it's advisable to start reading him in an edition of selected poems. The best of these, with translations by Anthony Kerrigan, W.S. Merwin, Alastair Reid and Nathaniel Tarn, has recently been reissued by Houghton Mifflin. The two new translations published by the University of California Press, Jack Schmitt's version of *Canto General* and Margaret Sayers Peden's *Selected Odes of Pablo Neruda*, provide a closer look at the poet's work of the 1940s and 1950s—both its glories and its excesses. This was a pivotal period for Neruda—the culmination of one phase of his career and the beginning of another—and these books are important additions to the body of work available in English translation.

With Neruda it's impossible to separate the poetry from the life. Both are huge, protean in their variety and ultimately political. Neruda, of course, has a sentimental appeal for anyone on the left. His commitment to the socialist cause and his death in the wake of the U.S.-sponsored Chilean coup can make him seem a literary martyr. But Neruda is more complex than this. While a single presence— expansive, passionate, directly personal—lies behind all his work, his career is marked by distinct changes in style and focus. The Adamic voice and political awareness we associate with him today are not strong elements in his early work. The volume that made him famous at 20, *Twenty Love Poems and a Song of Despair* (1924), is a hybrid of French Symbolist yearning for the ineffable, and earthy Latin American eroticism. In the two major books that followed, *Residence on Earth I* (1933) and *II* (1935), Neruda turned from a young love poet into a surrealist, capturing the alienation he felt as a diplomat in the Far East in bleak monologues with long, fluid lines and torrents of imagery. The end of this period of surreal despair came in the mid-thirties when Neruda was serving in the Chilean Embassy in Madrid. His firsthand encounter with fascism during the Spanish Civil War solidified the basic commitment to the left that infuses all his subsequent work. In 1945 he was elected senator in the Chilean legislature; that same year he joined the Communist Party.

Canto General (1950) is the flowering of Neruda's new political stance. This epic collection traces the history of Latin America from before the arrival of human beings, through pre-Columbian times, colonization, liberation from the European powers, and the Yankee imperialism of the twentieth century. Much of it was written while the poet was on the run from the dictator Gabriel Gonzalez Videla; Neruda escaped into exile in 1949. When he returned to Chile after Gonzalez Videla's government fell, Neruda transformed his poetry yet again, developing a shortlined, deliberately ''simple'' mode of looking at everyday things in three volumes of *Elemental Odes* (1954–57). Though he wrote in a variety of styles after the odes, there is a general unity of tone in the poems of his last twenty years. The confidence and openness of this work reflect the richness of the poet's life: his travels all over the world; his broad recognition, capped by the Nobel Prize in 1971; his wealth of friends, including Salvador Allende, who named him Ambassador to France; his domestic life at homes in Santiago, Valparaiso and the coastal village of Isla Negra, where Neruda had a rambling house full of everything he had collected over the years. The autumnal abundance of this period ended with Pinochet's seizure of power in 1973. Gravely ill with cancer, Neruda survived for eleven days after the coup, chronicling in his memoirs the murder of Allende and the destruction of the country he loved. After his death, soldiers ransacked his houses.

Written when Neruda was in his 40s, *Canto General* stands at the center of the poet's life and work. Jack Schmitt's translation—the first complete English version—gives us Neruda at his most Adamic and most overtly political. In this collection the poet's task is not only to name the geographic features and forms of life in Latin America but to examine this garden after the Fall, as it moves through history in the flawed human world of hope and exploitation. *Canto General* is a huge work, including some 300 poems collected in fifteen sections. The first half of the book is broadly chronological, with five sections extending from pre-Columbian times to the year before the book was published. The second half is a group of ten varied sections tracing Neruda's encounters with nature, recent history, people and himself. The kinds of work Neruda brings together in *Canto General*— verse letters to friends, satiric blasts, lists, chronicles, elegies, descriptions, autobiographical musings, exhortations, lyric interludes—show his astounding poetic fertility. What unifies this diverse material is his focus on the question of justice. On one level, all the poems are exhibits in a vast historical trial.

The main defendant in this trial is Gonzalez Videla, the leftist turned reactionary who ordered Neruda's arrest after the poet denounced him in 1948. A triggering device for the poet's rage, Gonzalez Videla gets more attention than other dictators in the book, but finally he is seen as just another lackey of twentieth-century imperialism, one of many Neruda attacks in the fifth section of *Canto General,* ''The Sand Betrayed.'' Our old friends Trujillo and Somoza crop up in this group as ''voracious hyenas,'' as Neruda calls them. Their brutality in the service of corporations like Standard Oil, the United Fruit Company and Anaconda Copper (each given its own skewering) echoes that of the conquistadors Neruda describes in the third section of his epic: the same pretext of respectability; the same official blessings, from U.S. presidents now rather than bishops; the same cruelty toward the populace; the same underlying drive for power and wealth. As Neruda traces the history of Latin America in the first half of *Canto General*, he sets up a basic alternating pattern of a just world and its destruction. The pre-Columbian harmony of people and nature celebrated in the beautiful opening section, ''A Lamp on Earth,'' is shattered by the Europen conquerors, then partially restored in a new form by the nineteenth-century liberators, then lost again in the neocolonialism of our time.

This pattern is fairly accurate, but it does raise two problems for the poet. The most obvious is repetition: Neruda's exhaustive catalogue of conquistadors, liberators and twentieth-century caudillos can at times become exhausting. The villains in particular tend to blur into one mass—which is obviously part of Neruda's point but nonetheless somewhat soporific. Some of my reaction may stem from general gringo ignorance of the intricacies of Latin American history—I confess I perked up when I saw Harry Truman come in for it in ''Puerto Rico'' or read about ''Wall Street heroes'' in ''Sandino (1926).'' Nonetheless, there are so many narratives of conquest and betrayal in the first 200 pages of *Canto General* that the various atrocities can begin to lose their punch. Neruda's tendency to slip into purple passages in some of the longer poems adds to this overstuffed quality.

The second problem is simplification. Again, Neruda's basic point is simple—there are good guys and bad guys in the history of Latin America—but sometimes the language is not lively enough to flesh out particular virtues and vices, and the figures end up as stereotypes. This happens most often when the poet is telling a story—narrative is generally the weakest element in *Canto General*. When Neruda abandoned his melancholy surrealism of the 1930s for the politically committed work that was to follow, he gave up some of the surprise and complexity that his plunges into the irrational had provided. Straight historical narrative doesn't always give him the oomph he needs to get his characters off the page. Fortunately, Neruda's restless technical inventiveness leads him to do more than just recount incidents, and many poems bring figures to life in bursts of sheer poetic energy, like the wacky run-on ironies at the start of ''Miranda Dies in the Fog (1816)''—

> If you enter Europe late dressed in top hat in the garden decorated by more than one Autumn beside the marble fountain while leaves of tattered gold fall on the Empire—

or the pounding list of accomplishments that defines the Araucanian Indian leader Lautaro in ''The Chiefs Training'':

> He drank wild blood on the trails. He wrested treasure from the waves. He loomed like a menacing god. He ate in every kitchen of his people. He learned the lightning's alphabet. He scented out the scattered ashes. He cloaked his heart with black furs. He deciphered the smoke's spiraling plume.

Neruda's masterpiece in *Canto General* is its second section, ''The Heights of Macchu Picchu.'' In this exquisitely paced group of a dozen poems occasioned by his visit to the ruins of the Inca citadel in 1943, Neruda finds the heart of his vision. Beginning the sequence in alienated wandering ''from air to air, like an/empty net,'' he concludes in a convincing solidarity with nameless exploited workers throughout history—''Juan Stonecutter,'' ''Juan Coldeater,'' ''Juan Barefoot''—who will ''speak through my words and my blood.'' The Adamic impulse here is fundamentally political, a matter of standing up for those whom history has buried, of naming crimes. The city of Macchu Picchu is central to the sequence, but not in the ways we might expect. Neruda doesn't praise it was a

symbol of pre-Columbian grandeur or even as a prototype of state socialism. Rather, the ruins serve as a locus for questions about basic human activities: work, survival in nature, community life. The stark majesty of this ''towering reef of the human dawn'' leads Neruda back to find its origins in punishing labor enforced by hunger and cold:

> Macchu Picchu, did you put stone upon stone and, at the base, tatters? Coal upon coal and, at the bottom, tears?

The deserted city has become ''a life of stone after so many lives.'' In his struggle to name those lives and define their meaning, Neruda develops a profound meditation on the glory and horror of human achievement.

Moving away from the history of Latin America, the last ten sections of Canto General are more personal in their approach. We see more of Neruda's life in the second half: his relations with friends in the rambling letter poems of ''The Rivers of Song'' his years as a senator from the poor mining provinces of northern Chile in ''The Flowers of Punitaqui''; and his days underground in ''The Fugitive,'' which includes one of his finest descriptive passages in this evocation of a poor quarter of Valparaiso:

> the high hills brimming with lives, doors painted turquoise, scarlet and pink, toothless steps, clusters of poor doors, dilapidated dwellings, fog, mist extending its nets of salt over things, desperate trees clinging to the ravines, clothes hanging from the arms of inhuman hovels, the hoarse whistle, abrupt creature of the vessels, the sound of brine, of the fog, the sea voice, made of strokes and murmurs.

It's not just the eye for sensory detail and the wealth of metaphor that dazzle here—readers of Neruda come to take these for granted—but the careful modulation that braids together houses, hills and sea fog as the images wind down the page. Topography, weather, social and economic conditions—Neruda catches the very texture of life in this district.

Other sections are less autobiographical, like Neruda's hymn and warning to the United States, ''Let the Woodcutter Awaken,'' or the dramatic monologues of ''The Earth's Name Is Juan,'' a poetic documentary on the struggles of Chilean workers. In ''America, I Do Not Invoke Your Name in Vain,'' Neruda takes on what might seem an unlikely mode for such an expansive poet: the lyric glimpse of one moment. Averaging a dozen short lines and often just one sentence long, these poems include some of the book's most haunting endings, as in "Youth" —"all adolescence becoming wet and burning/like a lantern tipped in the rain"—or "Hunger in the South":

> and just the winter cough, a horse moving through black water, where a eucalyptus leaf has fallen a dead knife.

The last two sections of *Canto General* wrap up Neruda's vast project with meditations on nature and death in "The Great Ocean" and a final grounding of his political vision in personal experience in "I Am." Nothing in Neruda is neat, but these two final units give a sense of closure like that in one of the bulkier Dickens novels: a kind of summary and goodbye that leaves you with a huge social canvas—eccentric, flawed in spots, but rich with imagination and human sympathy.

The sheer heft of *Canto General* makes me admire Jack Schmitt for his diligence. The literalness of his translation is both its virtue and its limit. While you never feel the need to have the Spanish on facing pages to check if Neruda really said that, Schmitt's texts don't always work well as poems in English. He has a tendency to rely on Latinate cognates, lending a certain abstract quality to the work, as in the opening lines of "The Great Ocean":

> Ocean, if I could destine my hands a measure, a fruit, a ferment of your gifts and destructions, I'd choose your distant repose, your steely lines, your extension guarded by air and night.

In translations from Romance languages the choice of whether to use a cognate or a different word that would avoid abstract overtones is a judgment call on any given line, but Schmitt's general procedure gives us a fairly Latinate and hence somewhat less physical Neruda. Great translations of a body of poetry—Richard Howard's Baudelaire, for example, or Stephen Mitchell's Rilke—reflect not only an affinity between translator and poet but a distinctive mastery of the original text, a transformation of the work into the translator's personal idiom. I wish Schmitt had seized Neruda in this way a little more. Though more accurate on a literal level, his translation of "The Heights of Macchu Picchu" lacks some of the flamboyant energy of Nathaniel Tarn's; and his versions of "Gold," "The Ships" and other individual poems are less lyrical than Anthony Kerrigan's. But Schmitt has produced a consistent, readable version of the entire *Canto General*, and this is a major achievement.

Margaret Sayers Peden's task is less monumental than Jack Schmitt's. Her *Selected Odes of Pablo Neruda* translates sixty-seven of the nearly 200 "elemental odes" Neruda collected in three major books of the 1950s. I suspect anyone familiar with the odes will find that Sayers Peden has left out a few favorites. I'd love to see a version of "Ode to the Potato," for instance, with its effortless movement from names for the food (South American *papa* versus Castilian *patata*), through its role in history, to the way it sings in a frying pan; or "Ode to Copper," which shows the human dimension behind the schoolbook concept of "natural resources." But Sayers Peden's collection is nonetheless rich and representative. Her translations bring out the sensuous quality of Neruda's odes well; there is little of the Latinate or abstract here. Neruda's distinctive tone in these poems—casual, self-conscious but direct, musing yet open to passion—is captured with great sensitivity. My only quibble is with Sayers Peden's enjambment. In these shortlined poems Neruda will occasionally use the line break to separate an article from a noun or a preposition from its phrase. But the translation does this about twice as often as the original, and the effect is to make some poems a bit less fluid in their movement than they might be.

After the bulk and stridency of *Canto General,* the odes give an immediate impression of ease. The drive to document oppression that pushes out the fairly blocky lines of *Canto General* and the fierce rhetoric that often accompanies it are replaced by skinny texts that lope down the page: speculative, funny at times, seemingly open to anything. The Adamic impulse has modulated. The odes are as expansive as *Canto General*, but Neruda is naming material things now rather than patterns in history. Instead of reaching for the "general" or universal, he turns to the basic, the "elemental." These poems have their designs on the reader—what work doesn't?—but they are deliberately user-friendly. As he puts it in "The House of Odes":

> I want everything to have a handle, I want everything to be a cup or a tool. I want people to enter a hardware store through the door of my odes.

Neruda's hardware store is not one of those spread-out franchises in a shopping plaza but the mom-and-pop operation squeezed into an urban lot that just happens to have everything you might ever need. And Neruda walks along with you as you browse, pointing out this and that, telling anecdotes, passing along a broad enthusiasm for everything that catches his eye. This is lively, accessible poetry. The odes combine a detailed specificity with an encyclopedic range of subjects: artichokes, atoms, chestnuts, his clothes—in the Spanish books Neruda even arranges them alphabetically. The danger in such abudance, of course, is prolixity. Neruda published three volumes of odes between 1954 and 1957, and the third collection shows him starting to run out of steam, with more passages that seem pulled directly from mere journal entries, more random meditations. And while the open-ended quality of these poems gives a sense of freedom and the possibility of surprise, the later odes occasionally fall back on vague moralizing to wrap things up, as at the end of "Ode to the Gentle Bricklayer": "Ah, what a lesson/I learned/from the gentle bricklayer!"

If there are a few duds in Sayers Peden's selection, her book also contains some of the best poems Neruda ever wrote. The ode format and the proposition of celebrating all elemental things clearly invigorated his work after the completion of *Canto General.* "Ode to a Watch in the Night" is among his most sensuous love poems, with a hushed richness of sound in both original and translation:

> A leaf falls, a droplet on the ground deadens the
> sound, the forest sleeps, waters, meadows, bells, eyes.

The pacing here and in other odes is masterful. Lines this short could easily ossify into predictability, but Neruda keeps them flexible by varying the line breaks and the syntax of phrases that run over them. At times his movement is light and rapid, a half-dozen lines for a single phrase. "Ode to Summer," "Ode to My Socks" and other take a kind of glee in this. Insouciant, almost occasional, they romp down the page. Elsewhere there's a more deliberate pace as Neruda keeps a single object in view, naming it with image after image. In "Ode to the Cranium" he describes his skull after a fall as "the one thing/sound as a walnut," invoking it in a list of metaphors:

> boned tower of thought, tough coconut, calcium dome
> protecting the clockworks, thick wall guarding treas-
> ures infinitesimal.

The combination of delight in abundance, curiosity and bemused self-mockery is typical of Neruda's tone in these engaging poems.

From the start of his career, Neruda was a poet of the senses, but in the odes he is at his most direct. Everything has not only a sound and a color but a smell, a taste, a texture, sometimes in startling combinations. In "Ode to the Birds of Chile," ocean light is "acid," parrots "metallic," the south-

ern swan a "ship/of silver/a mourning velvet." There is enough vibrant writing about food and drink in these poems to arouse the most jaded gourmet. Like great recipes, Neruda's odes to the lemon, tomatoes, wine, salt and maize unlock the possibilities in what might have seemed mundane. "Ode to Conger Chowder" actually is a recipe, with the poet inviting us to skin the eel, "caress/that precious/ivory" of garlic before tossing it in the pot, and savor the final product of this Chilean specialty so "that in this dish/you may know heaven."

The grace and humor of these food poems make them a real delight, but they are more than rich confections. As an "elemental" act, eating—along with working—is at the center of Neruda's political vision in the odes. In "Ode to Maize" he delves into the history of this most basic American crop, setting its promise of mass nutrition against the reality of inequality and hunger. When he looks at salt, the first thing he thinks about is the salt miner. For Neruda food and other pleasures are our birthright—not as gifts from the earth or heaven but as the products of human labor. As they celebrate the sheer wonder of being alive, the odes lead us back to origins. They are the clearest—and surely the most inviting—illustrations of Marxist materialism I know.

Neruda was a poetic Antaeus, constantly rejuvenated by making contact with the ground. The odes and *Canto General* draw their strength from a commitment to nameless workers—the men in the salt mines, the builders of Macchu Picchu—and the fundamental value of their labor. This is all very Old Left, of course. As the statues topple in the former Soviet republics and Eastern Europe, it may seem anachronistic to read what a faithful Communist had to say about Latin America and the world as a whole. But the collapse of the Second World hasn't ended the problems of the Third. If anything, it should make the pattern of oppression in Latin America—and the heavy hand of the colossus to the north in supporting it—even more clear. *Canto General* is an excellent corrective to the self-congratulatory versions of history we are hearing these days. The odes take us back to the elemental facts behind history. Both books are radical in the best sense of the term. They ask questions that get to the root of the matter: Where do things come from? Who suffers and who doesn't? Why?

Source: Don Bogen, "Selected Odes of Pable Neruda," (book review) in *The Nation,* Vol. 254, No. 3, January 27, 1992, p. 95.

Sources

Agosin, Marjorie, *Pablo Neruda*, Twayne Publishers, 1986.

Alegría, Fernando, "Introduction," in *The Elementary Odes*, by Pablo Neruda, translated by Carlos Lozano, Las Américas Publishing Company, 1961, pp. 9-17.

Bizzarro, Salvatore, *Pablo Neruda: All Poets and the Poet*, Scarecrow Press, 1979, 192 p.

Costa, René, *The Poetry of Pablo Neruda*, Harvard University Press, 1979, 208 p.

Belitt, Ben, ed., "Toward An Impure Poetry" (1935), reprinted in *Selected Poems*, by Pablo Neruda, Gove Press, 1991.

Sayers Paden, Margret, trans., "The House of Odes" (1956), reprinted in *Selected Odes of Pablo Neruda*, University of California Press, 1990, p. 171.

Further Reading

Alazraki, Jaime, "Pablo Neruda: The Chronicler of All Things," *Books Abroad*, Vol. 46, 1972, pp. 49-54.
  Offers a short discussion on the structure of the odes.

Bloom, Harold, ed., *Modern Critical Views: Pablo Neruda*, Chelsea House Publishers, 1989, 345 p.
  Representative selection of the best criticism available in English on Neruda's work; includes an essay by Walter Holzinger on the subject and form of the odes.

Teitelboim, Volodia, *Neruda: An Intimate Biography*, translated by Beverly J. DeLong-Tonelli, University of Texas Press, 1991.
  Biography written by a novelist and senator in the Allende government who was an intimate of Neruda's.

One Hundred Years of Solitude

According to Latin American novelist Mario Vargas Llosa, when *One Hundred Years of Solitude* was published, "Overnight, García Márquez became almost as famous as a great soccer player or an eminent singer of boleros." The novel is an epic saga of sex, fantasy, family, myth, and political history, replete with fantastic events told with a deadpan voice, and with self-reflexive allusions to the history of writing and the making of literature itself. Not only was the story compelling and humorous, but it showed that its author had a bold, new vision for modernist fiction. García Márquez once told a reporter, "I felt so happy writing when I was writing *One Hundred Years of Solitude*. In my dreams I was inventing literature." The story came to him as a whole while he was driving in Mexico with his wife. He said of his moment of epiphany, "I had it so completely formed, that right there I could have dictated the first chapter to a typist." Published in over thirty languages and having sold over ten million copies, *One Hundred Years of Solitude* is both a popular novel and an important work in the literary history of Latin America and an excellent example of modernist fiction. Not only a prominent example of "magic realism," the novel is also the work of a master storyteller, whose inventive expression and subtle humor have timeless appeal.

Gabriel García Márquez

1967

Author Biography

Gabriel García Márquez was born March 6, 1927 to Luisa Santiaga Márquez and Gabriel Eligio García in Aracataca, Colombia. His father, a telegraph operator, was unliked by his mother's family, so she gave her son to her parents and left to live with her new husband in another city. Gabriel García Márquez's maternal grandparents raised him until he was eight years old, when his grandfather, Colonel Nicolás Márquez, died, and the boy was sent back to his mother. The Colonel had had a profound influence on his grandson, taking young "Gabo" (the affectionate name by which Colombians now know him) to the circus, showing him ice, and telling him his about exploits as a liberal army general and the recent banana plantation strike (of 1929).

Gabo's grandmother, Tranquilina Iguardán was another veteran storyteller, whose tales mixed fact and fantasy seamlessly, and who talked with the living and the dead on equal terms. Like Ursula Iguardán in *One Hundred Years of Solitude*, Tranquilina Iguardán went blind in old age. A serious and non-athletic child, Gabo was writing verse at the age of ten, and attended a boarding high school for the gifted. He seldom lived with his parents or his fifteen siblings, one of whom was also named Gabriel. He went on to study law at the University of Bogatá, where he performed indifferently and switched to journalism, and then finally dropped out during the violent period following the assassination of Jorge Gaitán in 1948.

He found his niche in newspaper journalism, after transferring to college in Cartagena, writing first for *El Universal* and later for *El Heraldo*. In Barranquilla, he joined a group of young writers and artists known as the Barranquilla group, led by an old Catalonian book dealer, Ramón Vinyes. The silver-haired gentleman, like the old Catalonian book dealer in *One Hundred Years of Solitude*, steered the young scholars towards modernist books. When García Márquez contracted pneumonia, Vinyes sent him a package of modern books, including works by William Faulkner, Ernest Hemingway, James Joyce, and Virginia Woolf. At another point he tried "to find out what the hell had been done in the novel from the Bible on up to what was being written at the time," and so he dropped out of studying and spent six years reading.

Once fully steeped in his genre, García Márquez began writing novels by night while producing journalism by day. A stint overseas, in Europe, polished away the last traces of the provincial writer, although he struggled financially, having not yet received one penny from his published works. In 1958, he married Mercedes Borcha, a beauty of Egyptian origin he had met fourteen years earlier. He then accepted a brief assignment in New York City and traveled south through Faulkner's Mississippi to Mexico City to explore the world that gave birth to Yoknapatawpha County. In Mexico, sometimes collaborating with Carlos Fuentes, he wrote film scripts and experienced writer's block for a period. Then, the ending of *One Hundred Years of Solitude* came to him while he was driving, and he risked financial failure to spend the next eighteen months writing the novel. It was an overnight success, winning him numerous awards, including Italy's Chianchiano Prize in 1969, France's award for the best foreign book of 1969, and recognition among the top twelve novels of 1970 in the United States. García Márquez won the Nobel Prize for Literature in 1982. He continues to be an active journalist, and to produce a significant new work of fiction every few years. Although the political instability of Colombia makes it impossible for him to live there, he visits often and uses his pen in the fight for peace and human rights issues. He and his wife have two grown sons.

Plot Summary

There are twenty unnumbered chapters or sections of *One Hundred Years of Solitude* telling the story of six generations of the Buendía family. The patriarch José Arcadio Buendía has a fascination for the objects he buys from the traveling gypsy Melquíades. He abandons his domestic duties to toy unproductively with telescopes and alchemy, to the frustration of his more practical wife, Ursula. His avocation gets passed down to several generations, through his sons José Arcadio and Aureliano, in their town of Macondo.

Macondo was founded after José Arcadio Buendía won a cockfight, and the loser, Prudencio Aguilar, insulted his masculinity for not yet having consummated his marriage. He had been held off by Ursula who feared their union would result in a child with the tail of a pig, like their ancestors who likewise married cousins. Prudencio haunts the couple until they leave and found Macondo, a kind of simple paradise. The take in an orphan, Rebeca, who has a habit of eating dirt, and who will later marry their son. An insomnia plague requires José Arcadio Buendía to write the names of things and their uses on everything. After the plague ends, Melquíades returns from death, having been unable to bear the solitude. He will return again and again throughout the generations to guide the Buendías through the translation of his parchments. Now that Macondo is more than a simple frontier paradise, Don Apolinar Moscote comes with his seven daughters to act as magistrate.

War breaks out over a rigged Conservative party win, and Aureliano, who has busied himself making little silver fishes, joins the liberal army and becomes Colonel Aureliano Buendía. He organizes ''thirty-two armed uprising and los[es] them all.'' He also fathers seventeen Aurelianos with seventeen different women along his military trail. The Buendías are a lusty lot, with a penchant for incest that affects almost every male. Arcadio becomes obsessed with his own mother, but she substitutes Santa Sofía de la Piedad in her place. The women either indulge themselves at record levels of love-making or take pleasure in rebuffing their lovers, as Amaranta does with Pietro Crespi, to punish him for having loved Rebeca. José Arcadio marries Rebeca and steals land and levies the peasants for their living. They also fight and lose battles to the Conservative party, and several are executed by them, including Arcadio. Each generation has its José Arcadio ''type'' and each its Aureliano ''type,'' and to make things confusing for the reader, they are also named the same.

About midway through the novel, Colonel José Arcadio Buendía returns in defeat, captive, and in chains. He tells his mother that he is a wizard, and that when he was brought in he ''had the impression that [he] had already been through [it all] before.'' Ursula responds, ''What did you expect? Time passes.'' She has noticed a pattern in his offspring and their descendants, that ''While the Aurelianos were withdrawn, but with lucid minds, the José Arcadios were impulsive and enterprising, but they were marked with a tragic sign.'' The Aurelianos like to make little silver or gold fishes, to sell them, and then to use the money to buy materials to make more fishes; it is a metaphor for Latin American economy: going nowhere. The family has skills other than the Aureliano clairvoyance. When José Arcadio is killed, a trail of blood leads his mother to his dead body. No murderer is found, and the corpse cannot be scrubbed of the smell of powder. When the patriarch dies, Colonel José Arcadio Buendía

Gabriel García Márquez

somehow predicts it, and the death is accompanied by a flurry of tiny yellow flowers.

Aureliano José, who goes off to war with his father, develops another obsession for his aunt Amaranta. He asks a fellow soldier, ''Can a person marry his own aunt?'' The soldier replies, ''He can not only do that. . .but we're fighting this war against the priests so that a person can marry his own mother.'' War jades the ebullience of Colonel José Arcadio Buendía. He has become so effective a revolutionary leader that his commands are executed before he mouths them. The Colonel has lost his heart. He draws a chalk circle around himself, placing ''a distance of ten feet between himself and the rest of humanity.'' Even his aging mother does not move him. He surrenders in the shade of a giant ceiba tree outside of Macondo, signing the Treaty of Neerlandia. He is shot as a revolutionary, but, by some miracle, the bullet passes cleanly through his chest and he survives. The signing of the treaty becomes an occasion for celebration over the years. The seventeen Aurelianos fathered by the Colonel come, and are later easy targets for execution because Father Isabel has marked their foreheads with a permanent sign of the cross on Ash Wednesday.

A pair of twin sons of Arcadio and Santa Sofía de la Piedad, José Arcadio Segundo and Aureliano

Segundo, twist the normal pattern of Aurelianos and José Arcadios, perhaps because they played each other that they themselves forgot which is which. Aureliano Segundo carries on the task of deciphering Melquíades' manuscripts. José Arcadio Segundo becomes a Conservative, unlike the rest of the family. It is as though they have turned the family history back on itself. The two brothers share a young mulatto woman named Petra Cotes. Aureliano Segundo's first son by her is given to Ursula to raise to be a priest. He and Petra are so fecund that their lovemaking causes the proliferation of her farm animals, which she raffles off for money. By this time, all of Macondo is exceedingly prosperous, and the adobe huts of the early settlement are replaced with stately brick homes. To celebrate, the town has a festival, with Remedios the Beauty, a Buendía, as queen. A family from a faraway town sends its daughter as a rival queen, Fernanda del Carpia, and Aureliano Segundo marries her. They have a child, José Arcadio, whom Ursula raises to be "a Pope."

One of the seventeen Aurelianos, Aureliano Triste, starts an ice business (before he is shot as a child of rebel leader Colonel Aureliano Buendía) that is so successful that he has to bring in the railroad. Ursula gets the sense that time is going in a circle, because Aureliano Triste's schemes remind her of her husband's ventures. The yellow train bedecked in flowers brings in the gringos, too, and their establishment of banana plantations becomes a pestilence on the people who work there. When they strike (similar to the actual Colombian Banana Strike of 1928), the government mows down three thousand of the assembled people, and then lies about it. José Arcadio Segundo is thrown onto the train carrying the bodies off to the sea, but jumps off, haunted for the rest of his life by what he has witnessed. After the strike, it rains for "four years, eleven months, and two days." The rain rots everything, and the Buendía house begins to merge with the earth, until Amaranta Ursula returns from Europe to revive it. Ursula promises to die when the rain stops, and she does, after removing the decorations the children have put on her as they would a doll. Upon her death, at over one hundred fifteen years of age, birds die in droves. Amaranta Ursula and her lover Aureliano, a bastard grandchild of Fernanda, try to stave off "the voracity of nature" by planting oregano and begonias and setting out quicklime in "the age-old war between man and ant." She dies after giving birth to a child who fulfills the long-forgotten prophecy of being born with the tail of a pig. When Aureliano sees the baby

being dragged off by ants, he has an epiphany that allows him finally to understand the Sanskrit code of Melquíades' parchments, and he reads his own life as it is unfolding, "and he began to decipher the instant that he was living, deciphering it as he lived it, prophesying himself in the act of deciphering the last page of the parchments, as if he were looking into a speaking mirror." When he reaches the last line, Macondo and he are "wiped out by the wind and exiled from the memory of men."

Characters

Prudencio Aguilar

Prudencio loses a cockfight to his friend José Arcadio Buendía and insults him with the comment that perhaps Buendía's fighting bird might prevail with his virgin wife, where the man himself has failed. Killed by Buendía's spear, Prudencio haunts the family, with nightly appearances asking for water to moisten the asparto grass with which he attempts to plug his wound. He is the immediate cause of their leaving to found Macondo.

Alfonso

One of the drinking, carousing, and literary friends of the bastard Aureliano, named for a friend of the author's.

Alvaro

One of the drinking, carousing, and literary friends of the bastard Aureliano, named for a friend of the author's.

Aureliano Amador

The last of the seventeen Aurelianos fathered by Colonel Aureliano Buendía by seventeen different women during his war campaigns. Aureliano Amador (whose name connotes "love") shows up on the family doorstep, is repulsed by Aureliano and José Arcadio, and is shot.

Argénida

Argénida is Rebeca's servant and confidante.

Don Aureliano

See Aureliano Segundo Buendía

Aureliano Babilonia

See Aureliano Buendía

Mauricio Babilonia

Mauricio is young and sallow, "with dark eyes like a gypsy," an apprentice mechanic in the banana plantation garage. He seduces Meme in the movie theater, and continues their affair after her mother locks her in her room by stealing into her bathroom at night. A host of yellow butterflies always attends Mauricio, as though belying his tough exterior. He is paralyzed by a gunshot from an unknown assailant who presumably thought he was stealing chickens, and dies of old age, alone.

Mr. Jack Brown

Born in Prattville, Alabama, Mr. Brown arrives in Macondo by rail, in a silver-plated coach accompanied by fierce German shepherd dogs. As the supervisor of the banana company, he is called to court after the killings of the strike, but absconds and is replaced by Dagoberto Fonseca, who tries to masquerade as Mr. Brown.

Patricia Brown

The daughter of the banana plantation supervisor from Alabama, who befriends Meme.

Amaranta Buendía

The third child of José Arcadio Buendía and Ursula, Amaranta is "tight" and active, like her mother. Rebuffed by a visiting artist, Pietro Crespi, she vows to prevent her foster sister Rebeca's planned marriage to him, then burns her own hand and wears a black bandage in penance for hurting Rebeca. Amaranta, whose name connotes "love," is incapable of expressing love. She seduces Crespi only to rebuff him after he is fully smitten, causing him to kill himself. Out of sexual frustration, she plays kissing games with her nephew that end in seduction. The "smell of dead flowers" follows her till her death, for which she sews her own shroud. She offers to carry letters to the dead in her passing.

Amaranta Ursula Buendía

A strong character, like Ursula, who likewise cleans house and tries to revitalize Macondo, but fails. Like her ancestor José Arcadio Buendía, the patriarch, Amaranta Ursula breeds and releases caged birds (canaries), but they fly away the moment she releases them. She has the "hereditary vice of making something just to unmake it." Amaranta Ursula loves fashion and sews her own clothes. She returns from a boardinghouse in Brussels run by nuns with a husband, Gaston, whom she leads around on a silk leash. The bastard Aureliano (Babilonia) seduces her and they send the husband away to indulge in sexual fantasies, only to produce the fated child "with the tail of a pig" although the legend has long since been forgotten and they fail to understand its import. She bleeds to death after the birth.

Arcadio Buendía

Pilar's son by José Arcadio the younger, Arcadio learns silversmithing. To cure his obsession with her, his mother pays Santa Sofía de la Piedad fifty pesos to sleep with him. She marries him and they have twins, Aureliano Segundo and José Arcadio Segundo, and a seemingly retarded daughter, Remedios, known as Remedios the Beauty. Arcadio becomes a revolutionary like his uncle Aureliano, and is shot by a firing squad.

Aureliano Buendía (I)

The second son of José Arcadio and Ursula is born, like all of the family Aurelianos, with his eyes wide open. This trait presages his uncanny ability for prophecy, the first occurrence being his statement that a pot will spill. Unlike his boisterous brother, Aureliano is silent and withdrawn, imaginative, and contemplative. All of the Buendía Aurelianos are "withdrawn, with lucid minds." Also unlike his brother, Aureliano touches the ice, the pleasant memory of which he retains for the rest of his life. Aureliano falls in love with Remedios when she is only nine years old, and waits for her to grow old enough to marry. He becomes Colonel Aureliano Buendía and loses all thirty-two of his battles for the Liberal party. The power of leadership goes to his head and he becomes "lost in the solitude of immense power." He draws a chalk circle ten feet around himself and refuses to let anyone inside. His madness culminates in nearly murdering his friend Colonel Gerineldo Márquez for truthfully accusing Aureliano of betraying the Liberal cause through a compromising treaty. In a rare moment of remorse caused by his mother's intervention, Aureliano repents and invites his friend to continue the war. Aureliano does, however, assassinate a political rival with whom he has established a respectful friendship, the conservative general José Raquel Moncado; this time he ignores his mother's protests. When Moncado's widow proudly refuses him entry to her home when he visits to return Moncado's last personal possessions, he burns down her house. Ursula realizes that the Aurelianos have no soul. During the travels of his military campaigns, Aureliano fathered seventeen Aurelianos, each with different mothers. He is also the father of Aureliano José, by Pilar Ternara, with whom he loses his virginity after his brother's experience with her. The Colonel finally is shot by a firing squad, but the bullet passes through his chest and he survives. He finishes out his days making little gold fishes, and dies quietly one day when the circus comes back to town.

Aureliano Buendía (II)

The bastard son of Meme by Mauricio Babilonia is "delicate, thin, with a curiosity that unnerved adults." As a toddler he tortured insects. Ursula teaches him the art of silversmithing, and he has no interest in the world that rejects him for the manner of his birth. He takes up the family occupation of translating Mequíades'' manuscripts, cashing in the little fish he makes to buy books on Sanskrit, after discovering that it was the language of the manuscripts. Aureliano has an advanced case of the Aureliano prescience, and knows even things not written about in the encyclopedia he has read "like a novel." He says, "Everything is known." Ultimately, he abandons the parchments for Amaranta Ursula, with whom he begets a male child with the tail of a pig. Turning back to his translation, he discovers that the manuscripts form his family's life history, and he dies in the moment he reaches the present in the text, while a wind destroys the remains of Macondo.

Aureliano José Buendía

The love-child of Aureliano and Pilar Ternara, Aureliano José falls in love with Amaranta, his aunt, from her bathing of him as a child. She seduces him. He is shot (as one of the children of the rebel Colonel Aureliano Buendía) just before he was scheduled to make love to the beautiful virgin Carmelito Montiel. His dying words—"Bastards! Long live the Liberal party!"—are indicative of the typical Buendía dedication to the liberal cause.

Aureliano Segundo Buendía

One of the twin sons of José Arcadio and Santa Sofía de la Piedad, Aureliano Segundo so often switched identity markers with his twin brother as a joke that it is not certain whether he is Aureliano Segundo or José Arcadio Segundo. He has some of the trademark José Arcadio characteristics as well as those of the Aurelianos. Like the younger José Arcadio Buendía, Aureliano Segundo gets fat from debauchery and is addicted to lovemaking, but like Aureliano, he makes little gold fishes and studies

Melquíades' parchments. He also plays the accordion and reads the encyclopedia to his children, Renata Remedios, José Arcadio, and Amaranta Ursula. During his heyday of loving Petra Cotes, the pair become so wealthy that Aureliano Segundo papers their house in money, which Ursula has removed. Aureliano Segundo has the prescience of the other Buendía Aurelianos: he "remembers" Melquíades, even though he had never met him in life. He marries the northern beauty Fernanda del Carpio, who was "raised to be a queen," but has an ongoing, addictive affair with Petra Cotes that has the effect of making even her animals prolific. A throat ailment that feels like "crab claws strangling" him ultimately kills him at the same time his twin José Arcadio Segundo dies.

José Arcadio Buendía (I)

The patriarch of the Buendía family. He marries his cousin, Ursula Iguarán. There was an unfortunate precedent in this marriage, for his uncle had married her aunt, and the result of their union was a child born with the tail of a pig. José Arcadio has to threaten his wife with his grandfather's notched spear to consummate their marriage; none of their children bears the dreaded sign of incest, but five generations later, after further incestuous couplings, the monster is born. Because he kills his friend Prudencio Aguílar, who insults José after losing a cockfight to him, Buendía takes his pregnant wife away to found a new town, Macondo. There he abandons his domestic duties to study science, alchemy, and maps, inspired by the objects he buys from the itinerant gypsy, Mequíades. He also traps birds, to keep them in Macondo. He sinks into a spiral of solitude as his interests lead him to isolate himself in his study with his obsessions. His family ultimately ties him to a huge chestnut tree in the yard, where he dies, as a flurry of yellow flowers blankets the town.

José Arcadio Buendía (II)

The firstborn son of the patriarch José Arcadio and mother Ursula is strong like his father, but completely lacking his imagination. When the gypsies bring ice to the town, José Arcadio is afraid to touch it, though his younger brother Aureliano willingly does. José Arcadio mysteriously leaves Macondo with the gypsies, in shame for having lost his virginity to their housemaid Pilar Ternara. He returns years later tattooed from head to toe, with a string of rabbits over his shoulder. He has become a giant of a man, with a prodigious appetite for food and women. In fact, he is so well endowed that he gets women to pay him for his services. He seduces Rebeca and usurps nearby land to set up household with her, to which the Conservative government tacitly acceded. One day he is mysteriously killed, and the trail of blood from his ear travels throughout the town to Ursula's feet. No wound is ever found, and the mourners cannot scrub the smell of powder from him. The smell even permeates a concrete shell that the banana company engineers place over his hermetically sealed grave. All of the Buendía José Arcadios are "impulsive and enterprising, but. . .marked with a tragic sign."

José Arcadio Buendía (III)

The asthmatic, languid, and weepy son of Aureliano Segundo and Fernanda del Carpio, José Arcadio is going to become a pope, according to Ursula. She takes over the raising of this child as a pact with his father in return for allowing him to give his son the family name José Arcadio. This child is pampered with long baths and powderings, and admonished to fear the saints. Although he dutifully goes to Rome, the moment his mother dies he returns, dressed in taffeta and with a taste for being entertained by children. Four lascivious boys visit him daily and help him spend the three bags of gold they find hidden in a plaster saint that had been left by some passing men to be guarded by Ursula until their return. They return later and drown José Arcadio in his pool.

José Arcadio Segundo Buendía

One of the twin sons of José Arcadio and Santa Sofía de la Piedad, José Arcadio Segundo so often switched identity markers with his twin brother as a joke that it is not certain that he is not José Arcadio Segundo, since he has some of the José Arcadio characteristics as well as those of the Aurelianos. As a young boy, José Arcadio Segundo wanted to see an execution, but after he sees a man shot, he fears being buried alive. The twins both have an affair with Petra Cotes, who for a while fails to notice that she is serving two men, but José Arcadio easily gives her up. Like the patriarchal José Arcadio Buendía, José Arcadio Segundo buys fighting cocks, and like the warring Aureliano, he incites a banana strike and also studies the parchments of Melquíades. He has the misfortune of seeing the government fire into a crowd of people—strikers, wives, and children—and then being thrown onto the train taking three thousand dead bodies to dump into the sea. After this, he retires to read Mequíades' parchments.

José Arcadio Segundo dies reminding Aureliano (his young nephew) of the "more than three thousand" banana strikers and families killed and thrown into the sea. His mother cuts his throat, as promised, to prevent him from being buried alive.

Remedios The Beauty Buendía

Proclaimed queen of the festival celebrating the prosperity of Macondo, Remedios the Beauty is oblivious to her own charms and considers foolish the man who falls to his death trying to catch a glimpse of her naked body. She is considered almost retarded. The men are able to make her wear men's pants and climb a greased pole. Even shaving her head cannot decrease her appeal; "until her last moment on earth she was unaware that her irreparable fate as a disturbing woman was a daily disaster."

Renata Remedios Buendía

The only woman in *One Hundred Years of Solitude* with a nickname, Renata, daughter of Aureliano Segundo and Fernando, is like a second Amaranta. Meme attends a nunnery and studies to become a virtuoso on the clavichord. She brings home four nuns and sixty-eight classmates for a visit and they nearly destroy the house. When she returns home from the nunnery, she has a drinking habit and a taste for adventure. The latter she explores with an apprentice mechanic from the banana plantation, Mauricio Babilonia. After being caught, Meme pretends remorse, but her long evening baths are designed to allow Mauricio to scale the walls and spend time with her. A profusion of yellow butterflies every evening gives them away. After he is shot, she is sent to a convent to bear their bastard son, Aureliano. Meme dies in a hospital in Cracow.

Colonel Roque Carnicero

Colonel Carnicero (whose name means "meat butcher") has orders to shoot Colonel Aureliano Buendía. Carnicero draws lots to decide who will do the job (since retaliation is expected from the Liberal army), and he draws the slip himself. However, he does not shoot, because José Arcadio comes with a shotgun to save his brother. Carnicero and Colonel Aureliano Buendía go off to free the revolutionary general Victorio Medina, who is condemned to death in Riohacha.

Cataure

Cataure is a Guarjiro Indian, and Visitación's brother. He comes to announce that the patriarch

José Arcadio Buendía will die soon. After Cataure gives his news, tiny yellow flowers fall like rain.

Aureliano Centano

One of the seventeen Aurelianos fathered by Colonel Aureliano Buendía by seventeen different women during his war campaigns. Aureliano Centano helps Aureliano Triste in his ice business and spurs him to bring the railroad into Macondo.

Father Coronel

Father Coronel, "the Pup," replaces Father Nicanor after the latter dies of hepatic fever.

Petra Cotes

A beautiful mulatto with almond-shaped eyes who is for a time shared by the Segundo twins and then takes up with Aureliano Segundo. Their sexual fertility causes a proliferation of animals on her farm, so that she is able to become wealthy from raffling off the extra animals. Petra keeps Aureliano Segundo's boots that he wants to wear in his coffin as a way of keeping some measure of control over the man she shares with Fernanda. At first in spite and then with genuine generosity, Petra sends food anonymously to Fernanda for the rest of the latter's life. The years of rain "tame her eyes," age her, and destroy her property and animals, but she recovers enough to survive and fund her generosity.

Bruno Crespi

Bruno Crespi, husband of Amporo Moscote, owns the town toy shop and a theater that has two lion-headed ticket windows.

Pietro Crespi

An effete Italian pianola tuner with the "smell of lavender" about him, who wears tight trousers and dance slippers and teaches Amaranta and Rebeca to dance. He slits his wrists when Amaranta refuses him, having already frustrated his initial love for Rebeca.

Santa Sofía de la Piedad

Santa Sofía de la Piedad is the prostitute whom Pilar pays fifty pesos to sleep with her own son Arcadio to break him of his obsession with Pilar, his mother. Arcadio falls in love with Santa Sofía and they have the twins Aureliano Segundo and José Aureliano Segundo and Remedios the Beauty.

Fernanda del Carpio

Fernanda is raised by her northerner parents to "be a queen" and they sacrifice their house furnishings to realize this dream. After she returns from her education at a nunnery, they send her with a crown of emeralds to the festival celebrating Macondo's prosperity, and Aureliano Segundo falls in love with her, even though he has been happy with Petra Cotes. They marry, but her "heart of compressed ash" and her calendar of venereal abstinence which left only forty-two days available for lovemaking squelched his passion and he returned again and again to Petra Cotes. Fernanda represents the haughty northern Colombians, resented by the more passionate coastal Colombians. She complains like "the monotonous drone of a guitar" to her unhappy husband. In her loneliness, Fernanda continues to play at being queen, putting on her moth-eaten queen's dress even into old age, and is found lying on her bed wearing it after she has died.

The Elephant

See Camila Sagastume

Don Melchor Escalona

Teacher of the twins José Arcadio Segundo and Aureliano Segundo, whom he has difficulty telling apart, even with the identifying bracelets he has them wear, because they switch them.

Dagoberto Fonseca

A Spanish-speaking man who attempts to pass himself off as Mr. Brown during the trials following the strike massacre.

Francisco

An itinerant storyteller who acts as historian by telling the news and keeping track of events through his stories. It is he who announces to Ursula the death of her mother.

Gabriel

One of the drinking, carousing, and literary friends of the bastard Aureliano, named after the author.

Gaston

Amaranta Ursula's husband, whom she leads around on a silk leash. When he first arrives in Macondo, he is certain they will soon leave, but he has misjudged his wife's connections to Macondo. He entertains himself with his velocipede and works on starting an airmail service while he waits for her to come to her senses. When she and Aureliano announce their affair, he accepts it patiently.

Germán

One of the drinking, carousing, and literary friends of the bastard Aureliano, named for a friend of the author's.

Mr. Herbert

The first Anglo to arrive on Macondo, Mr. Herbert comes on the newly installed railroad line ''with the topaz eyes and skin of a thin rooster.'' After eating bananas, he hunts butterflies in the surrounding area, and then initiates a cultural transformation as scientists and colonists follow him to the area.

Ursula Iguaráran

Ursula resists her husband José Arcadio Buendía's sexual advances out of fear of producing a child with the tail of a pig. She is maternal and practical, a worker with ''the secret and implacable labor of a small ant.'' To support her household during her husband's obsessions with various scientific experiments, she makes a business of selling candy animals. She is resourceful in a way that the males in the family are not; she goes off to find her son José Arcadio and comes back years later having discovered another settlement of people on the swamp surrounding Macondo, thus establishing a source of trade for her town. When she goes blind, she continues to live so productively that no one guesses her affliction, having ''the lucidity of old age that allowed her to see.'' When she dies, at the age of 115 to 122 years, scores of dead birds are hurled to earth.

Father Antonio Isabel

The priest who succeeds ''the Pup'' and who allows José Arcadio Segundo to ring the church bells to ward off war. Father Isabel becomes senile. He is the priest who on Ash Wednesday puts the sign of the cross over the heads of the seventeen Aurelianos and a permanent ash mark makes them easy targets for Conservative assassins.

Gerineldo Márquez

An aged but surviving member of Colonel Aureliano Buendía's army (besides the Colonel), having ''escaped three attempts on his life, survived five wounds, and emerged unscathed from innumerable battles.'' Gerineldo falls in love with Amaranta, but she rebuffs him in the same manner she did Pietro Crespi, telling Gerineldo the reason is that he is so in love with his friend Colonel Aureliano Buendía. In fact, Gerineldo is the only one, besides Ursula, who dares to speak honestly with the Colonel, telling him on one occasion that he is ''rotting alive.'' Márquez dies of madness beneath Amaranta's window.

Melquíades

A ''heavy gypsy with an untamed beard and sparrow hands'' who wears a black hat like a raven and a velvet vest and who sells José Arcadio Buendía strange objects like a magnet, magnifying glass, telescope, maps, astrolabe, compass, and sextant. Whenever Melquíades visits he scribbles in Sanskrit on parchments which, at the very end of the novel, prove to be a prophecy of the Buendía family history for the next one hundred years. Melquíades becomes the first to die in Macondo, although he frequently reappears from the dead to guide and converse with later generations of Buendía men. His actual death is from a fever contracted in his worldwide travels to which he finally submits on a beach in Singapore.

Meme

See Renata Remedios Buendía

José Raquel Moncado

A conservative general who becomes mayor of Macondo when the conservatives win it. Even while they led opposing armies, José Raquel Moncado admired Colonel Aureliano Buendía and he teaches the Colonel to play chess when he holds him in captivity during one of the upswings of the conservative side. Moncado becomes an antimilitarist, rises to the title of magistrate, and effectively leads the town from its backward beginnings to incorporate it as a municipality. When the liberals retake the town, Colonel Aureliano Buendía ruthlessly has him shot, over the protests of the townswomen, including his own mother, Ursula.

Rebeca Montiel

Rebeca shows up at age eleven with the habit of eating dirt and carrying the bones of her (then unknown) parents in a canvas sack. Years later it is discovered that she is the daughter of Nicanor Ulloa and Rebeca Montiel. For a long time after her arrival in Macondo, she sits in a rocker without talking, sucking her finger, but finally, she grows to womanhood and sits sewing with Amaranta, who becomes her rival for visiting Italian Pietro Crespi. Crespi chooses Rebeca, but Amaranta spoils their plans, moths eat her wedding dress, and finally, José Arcadio, tattooed and returned from his stint with the gypsies, seduces and marries her. She lives to old age in the home he builds for her. The seventeen Aurelianos restore it to its original beauty when it becomes decrepit after the years of rain. She dies alone and bald from ringworm.

Amparo Moscote

The eldest daughter of Apolinar Moscote, she befriends Rebeca and they attend dances at the Buendía household. She later marries Bruno Crespi.

Don Apolinar Moscote

Apolinar Moscote, like the combined connotation of his godly given name (Apollo) and his lowly surname (the fly), has grand aspirations that do not come to fruition. Moscote comes to Macondo to serve as mayor and instantly earns the Liberal Buendía's resentment when he orders all doors to be painted blue, the color of the Conservative party. His seven daughters become his saving grace.

Remedios Moscote

Only nine years old when her family arrives in Macondo, she has to come of age before marrying Colonel Aureliano Buendía. She decorates their bedroom with her dolls, and dies of blood poisoning with twins crossed in her belly. A daguerreotype of her graces the Buendía home, lit by an eternal candle maintained by Ursula.

Nigromanta

''A large black woman with solid bones, the hips of a mare, teats like live melons, and a round and perfect head armored with a hard surface of wiry hair,'' Nigromanta makes chicken-head soup for the young bastard Aureliano and then falls in love with his lovemaking, which ''demanded a movement of seismic readjustment from her insides,'' after he seeks solace from his illicit love for Amaranta Ursula. A practical woman, Nigromanta makes Aureliano pay for her services after he tells her of his love for Amaranta Ursula.

Petronio

A sickly sexton, Petronio initiates José Arcadio Segundo into the rites of animal pederasty after the child asks him the meaning of the list of sins the priest has inquired about in his catechism.

Father Nicanar Reyna

Called in to officiate at the wedding of Aureliano and Remedios, Father Reyna stays on in Macondo. He is blessed with the skill of levitation—after drinking a cup of hot chocolate. He tries to convert the patriarch José Arcadio Buendía while the latter is tied to a tree, but fails. Father Reyna dies of hepatic fever.

Captain Aquiles Ricardo

Captain Ricardo is responsible for the shooting of Aureliano José, after which he himself is shot in retaliation.

Camila Sagastume

A dainty but huge woman who challenges Aureliano Segundo to an eating duel. She is the director of a school for voice.

Colonel Gregario Stevenson

A liberal general who disguises himself as a woman on a donkey in a last-ditch attempt to save the liberal army. He is killed bravely and competently defending a barracks almost single-handedly.

Pilar Ternera

''A merry, foul-mouthed, provocative woman'' who helps Ursula with her chores first seduces José Arcadio then his brother Aureliano, and bears them each a son, José Aureliano and Arcadio, respectively. She lives to be over 145 years old, having served as a prostitute for several generations of Buendías, and after having established a zoological brothel. She is buried sitting up in her rocking chair, according to her wishes.

Aureliano Triste

One of the seventeen Aurelianos fathered by Colonel Aureliano Buendía by seventeen different women during his war campaigns. Aureliano Triste is a mulatto who fulfills his grandfather's dream of setting up an ice factory. He also is responsible for bringing the railroad into Macondo.

General Téofilo Vargas

A full-blooded Indian Conservative general who takes refuge in Macondo. Colonel Aureliano Buendía refuses to kill him, but the Liberals hack him to death with machetes.

Magnífico Visbal

An army buddy of Colonel Aureliano Buendía who returns from years of losing thirty-two revolutionary wars, only to be killed during the days of violence. A brutal policeman chops his seven-year-old grandson to death for spilling a drink on him, and then decapitates Visbal for objecting.

Visitación

A Guarjiro Indian, Visitación tends to Amaranta and Arcadio when they are children, having fled the plague of insomnia raging in another town. When she dies, she sends her accumulated wages to Colonel Aureliano Buendía to carry on the Liberal revolution.

Themes

Solitude

Solitude is loneliness, whether truly alone or lost in the midst of strangers. It is the sense that the very world is foreign and uncaring. The theme of solitude appears throughout the novel, in each of six generations of the Buendía family, a family "marked by solitude" for the six generations that comprise one hundred years. When Colonel Aureliano Buendía draws a circle ten feet around himself and refuses to let anyone inside, his act epitomizes the "hard shell of his solitude," brought on by years of fruitless war. It is not enough, however, to blame his condition on the consequence of seeing men die, or losing thirty-two armed uprisings. The seeds of solitude were already within him, the legacy of both parents. José Arcadio Buendía chose to abandon his domestic duties to indulge himself in failed experiments proving facts already known and taken for granted by the rest of the world. He ate, slept, and worked in a private room attended only by the gypsy Melquíades, who returned from death because he was so lonely there. Ursula, who manages to keep the family fed and clothed, has her own strain of solitude, consisting of a prison of activity. She cannot prevent herself from fighting an endless battle against the ants marching into her home, herself a kind of worker ant who works and works without contemplation and with little real communication with the odd family members around her. She finds some solace in talking to her mute husband after he goes mad and has to be tied to a chestnut tree in the courtyard. At the end of the novel, the bastard Aureliano becomes so accustomed to his confinement away from the public that

Topics for Further Study

- Define "magic realism" in your own terms and describe its role in *One Hundred Years of Solitude*.

- What is the significance of the proliferation of the Buendías all bearing the same first name?

- Choose any two pairs of Buendía family members with the same name. Compare how they portray similar traits and note any differences between them. What is the significance of the similarities and differences?

- Research the United Fruit Company strike of 1928. Why is this an important event in Colombian history? In Latin American history?

- Trace the stages of Latin American history as outlined in the novel. What is García Márquez's attitude toward this history? Is he a reliable chronicler?

he is immune to the attractions of the world. For a time, his only friend is his uncle José Arcadio, a pederast, who returns from Rome having failed Ursula's design for him to become a Pope. No blame is assigned for the solitude of the Buendías. Their condition is merely reported by a deadpan narrator.

Family

It is so difficult to follow the relationships of the Buendía family, because of the "insistent repetition of names," that a family tree is printed in the front of the book and the reader must make constant reference to it. Like William Faulkner's Snopes and Compson families, the Buendía family has certain traits that carry through the generations, sometimes intensifying rather than dwindling out. Almost magically, naming a child Aureliano predetermines a man who has the power of clairvoyance and all of the José Arcadios are destined for tragedy. Ursula comments, "That's what they're all like. . .Crazy from birth." Also, like Faulkner's families, the theme of incest and fear of incest pervades the family. Often, this takes the form of an obsession by a male child for an older aunt or his own mother. The women at first yield, and then find a replacement; they seem to act more out of fear of giving birth to a child "with the tail of a pig" than out of distaste for incest itself. The family also has bonds that transcend the physical world. When the patriarchal José Arcadio Buendía is about to die, Colonel Aureliano sends word home to watch out for "Papa," because "he is going to die." When the son José Arcadio dies unexpectedly, a stream of blood travels throughout the town of Macondo from his head to finally end at Ursula's feet. In many ways, the Buendía family represents the Latin American family, but it is portrayed in extremes.

Style

Magic Realism

The term Magic Realism was first coined in 1925 by a German art critic, Franz Roh, to describe "magic insight into reality." Then Cuban novelist Alejo Carpentier used the term to describe fiction that contains elements of the fantastic blandly placed alongside the real. In *One Hundred Years of Solitude*, the characters accept these fanciful or wondrous events with the same seriousness and acceptance as they treat common, everyday occurrences. For example, Ursula is not shocked when a trail of blood leads her to her dead son; she simply follows it and begins to prepare the body for burial. Likewise, when Remedios the Beauty flies up into heaven, Ursula and the others accept this event as the natural destiny of a woman who seemed misplaced on earth. When other women step into the part of the courtyard where the miracle happened, they simply warn them to stay away, and avoid the fate of Remedios the Beauty. Some events seem to straddle reality and fantasy. Colonel Aureliano Buendía lives through his own execution because the bullet goes clean through him. Although this might be statistically possible, it seems more a part of the Colonel's other aspects of the magical. He is clairvoyant and knows when someone is coming, or, as in the case of his father, dying. He makes pots vibrate off the stove and spill. The non-utility and detailed specificity of some of the events adds a note of realism to them. Likewise, the priest levitates, but only after drinking hot chocolate. Whenever Mauricio Babilonia appears, a halo of yellow butterflies surrounds him. Dead birds hurl themselves against walls the day that Ursula dies.

Many of the events of magic realism echo myths and legends common in Latin America. As a boy, Gabriel García Márquez listened to his grandmother's tall tales. Years later, García Márquez realized that he wanted to reproduce her voice and tone in his writing: "She told things that sounded supernatural and fantastic, but she told them with complete naturalness." He also had to tell these things as she did, "with a brick face." These storytelling elements not only affected the tone of his stories, but also formed an underlying philosophical framework. There is an acceptance of wonder as a necessary and palpably present aspect of life. The world of nature invests life and meaning with powerful symbols that the patient and accepting person can comprehend. Studying it too intensely, as José Arcadio and his progeny did, leads to miscomprehension. Better off are those who, like Ursula, watch and listen to the world's wondrous events, using them as guides. In defense of his incorporation of magical elements into his fiction, García Márquez once quipped, "Reality is not restricted to the price of tomatoes!"

Symbolism

Symbolism is using objects to represent ideas. A symbol that recurs throughout the text is called a motif, and it acts like a refrain in music, amplifying and enhancing a theme. In *One Hundred Years of Solitude*, certain key images are associated with given people. Butterflies surround the garage mechanic Mauricio whenever he visits Renata, offsetting his brusque demeanor and lending credibility to Renata's fascination with him. They carry the symbolic meaning of temporality, of the brevity of life, and they also represent procreation, the intent and purpose of the butterfly's short summertime cycle. The ants, which most frequently are associated with Ursula's housekeeping activities, represent industry and nature, and thus symbolize man's war against nature, which in *One Hundred Years of Solitude* is the constant battle to drive back the jungle to protect civilization. In the end, the ants prevail, with their patient and relentless dedication to their tasks. Thus the ants also represent the petty concerns and futile efforts of humans to change nature's flow. In another case of symbolism, Remedios the Beauty flies up to heaven clutching in her hands a set of common, everyday bed sheets, for she had been in the act of folding clothes. Remedios the Beauty is like a saint, whose virtue is not piety, but beauty, and whose devotees are not religious, but lustful. The common bed sheet on one hand symbolizes everyday sexuality. On the other hand, it also corresponds to the holy shrouds of saints that are revered as holy relics. Remedios the Beauty takes her "relics" with her, as befits the ephemeral quality of physical, earthly beauty.

Literary Heritage

The literature of Latin America is often defined by it reliance on magical realism, sometimes referred to as symbolic mysticism. Much of the time, this means that the writer blends together naturalism and supernaturalism seamlessly. Often the literature of this area incorporates folktales and legends into the text, making the legends appear a natural part of the author's work. Magical realism erases the borders between the character's reality, the explicable and the inexplicable, and the natural world and the magical world.

Traditional Western literature has relied upon literary realism for more than one hundred years. This "realism" attempts to create a story and characters that are plausible, a representation of our everyday lives. Latin American literature attempts to portray the unusual, the spiritual, and the mystical, as ordinary facets of the character's lives. For the reader, magical realism requires an acceptance of the co-existence of the real and the imaginary. The author posits these magical events as authentic, with the supernatural events being interwoven seamlessly into the narration. For García Márquez, this element of mysticism is presented in an objective and unemotional voice. García Márquez also relies on a monosyllabic style of writing that puts the emphasis on the content, which is complex, while making the text itself accessible to the reader.

Historical Context

Colombia

Colombia is about twice the size of Texas, with varied terrain and a diverse range of biomes, from tropical jungle to mountains to arid desert. Approximately half of the country consists of savanna and the other half is amazon. The people vary in temperament as well: coastal peoples, including those like the Buendías, are carefree and show evidence of African cultural influences, while the inland "highlander" population, like the family of Fernanda del Carpio, is formal and more conservative.

The Spanish established a foothold in what was known as New Granada in 1510. In 1596, Francis Drake attacked Riohacha as recounted in *One Hundred Years of Solitude*. Indian populations were all but decimated; only one percent of today's population are Amerindian. Spain ruled the area for over three hundred years, until Simon Bolívar attained its independence in 1819. At that time, the Liberal and Conservative parties were established. Former slaves populated the coastal areas. During the nineteenth century, control passed back and forth between Liberal and Conservative leadership. The rivalry intensified during the "Thousand Days War" of 1899-1903, a period of seventy armed uprisings and eight civil wars that claimed over 100,000 lives and in which García Márquez's grandfather fought, culminating the period from 1821 to 1902 as one in which a war occurred every year and a half. In 1902, the Treaty of Neerlandia was signed by Liberal General Rafael Uribe, upon whom Colonel Aureliano Buendía is modeled.

The Liberal-Conservative contention is seen as endemic to the Colombian experience. According to Hernández Rodríguez, "among the most remote childhood memories of a Colombian are. . .those of political parties similar to two races which live side by side but which hate each other eternally." Feelings reached a peak after the assassination of a popular leftist leader, Jorge Gaitán, in 1948. The retaliation that followed claimed over 300,000 lives and was called "la Violencia." During this time land-grabbing, like that of José Arcadio Buendía, was rampant. The state of affairs could only be brought under control by dictatorship in 1953. Then, in 1957, the two parties agreed to a see-saw of power, in the interest of stabilizing the country. The "National Front" lasted until 1974 and provided for a politically balanced cabinet working with a president from a different party every four years. The idealistic system proved somewhat ineffective, for the hatred between the parties continued. Recently, however, the violence is situated between the cocaine cartels and civilian paramilitary guerrilla factions established because the government forces are outnumbered and their weapons cannot rival those of the criminal organizations. "The drug traffickers taught people that they were stupid to work," Márquez has said.

Compare & Contrast

- **1967:** In Colombia, the National Front, a coalition between the Liberal and Conservative parties, continued to share responsibility for government in a unique experience designed to give each party equal say by alternating president from one side to the other every four years. Although hostile feelings between the parties did not abate, the system was effective in getting legislation in place to stabilize the government. The resulting governmental structure mirrors that of the United States. Communist and Marxist groups were gaining power.

  Today: While the Liberal and Conservative parties remain the largest, other parties now are tolerated. However, Colombia continues to be torn by political violence, drug trafficking, and associated criminal activities and terrorism, along with widespread guerrilla fighting by cocaine cartels and paramilitary groups. In 1995 President Ernesto Samper Pizano was accused of accepting drug money in exchange for lenient sentencing of drug criminals.

- **1967:** The terror of *la Violencia*, a politically oriented civil conflict, was waning, while guerrilla conflict was rising, due to a sudden demand for cocaine on the world market. Ironically, the influx of money to drug cartels helped to stabilize the economy of Colombia.

  Today: While the drug trade has continued to bring money into Colombia, the countryside is torn apart by a near civil war between the drug mafiosi and the local landowners.

- **1967:** Modernist Latin American literature either sought social change or experimented with form, following the lead of Jorge Borges. Others concentrated on regionalism, the portrayal of local customs and colloquialism of an area, and on the use of myth and storytelling modes in fiction.

  Today: Postmodern literature has pushed into ever more radical experimentation in form, character, and plot. In addition, many works express the theme of relative values. At the same time themes of transcendence are on the increase, as writers reassert the presence of shared values and experiences.

The banana strike recounted in *One Hundred Years of Solitude* is based on the historical strike against the Boston-based United Fruit Company that occurred in 1928, a year after Gabriel García Márquez was born. The United Fruit Company employed over 15,000 men in the "banana zone" it had created in northern Colombia. The men were employed as contract workers, to avoid the Colombian laws requiring proper sanitation, medical care, and other benefits. The court ruling as recounted in *One Hundred Years of Solitude*, stating that the company had no obligations because it had "no workers," is based upon an actual court decision. The number of people killed when the government declared martial law and fired upon a crowd is not consistently reported. In some papers, none were killed; in others, around three hundred; García Márquez's version of 100,000 dead was reported in North American newspapers.

The "Boom"

In the 1960s, the world discovered Latin American fiction, mostly modernist, and sales of novels from Mexico, Chile, and Colombia enjoyed a boom in sales. The Boom coincided with and was pushed along by the creation of academic degrees in Latin American studies at major American and European universities, which was an indirect result of interest in Latin American affairs after Fidel Castro's Cuban Revolution of 1960. One writer, Carlos Fuentes of Mexico, played the midwife to many rising Latin American novelists, in his literary soirées in Mexico City and by putting new writers in touch with his publishers and literary scholars in Paris, London, and New York. Gabriel García Márquez was one of the first Latin American novelists to be able to support himself with his writing, expressly as a result of the popularity of *One Hundred Years of Solitude*.

Critical Overview

"In about the middle of 1967, the novel *One Hundred Years of Solitude* was published in Buenos Aires, provoking a literary earthquake throughout Latin America." So begins Mario Vargas Llosa's account of the phenomenon that resulted from the sudden appearance of Gabriel García Márquez on the Latin American literary scene. The novel has been translated into thirty languages and over ten million copies have been sold worldwide. It was a bestseller in Venezuela in 1969, when U.S. novelist Ron Arias was traveling there. He later wrote,

> I remember riding a crowded bus one day in Caracas, and two women who looked like secretaries were laughing over certain episodes they'd read in *One Hundred Years of Solitude*. I joined in; then it seemed half the bus did. This was in 1969 and it was the year's best seller. Everyone who had read it was bringing up his or her favorite character, and we were all howling together. The book as a whole had struck a common chord with us all, since historically we had all come from Macondo. . .we all had a *tío* [uncle] or two in a revolution, and I'm sure there were people in our lives chasing more than butterflies.

Arias's personal tribute to the popularity of *One Hundred Years of Solitude* attests to an appeal that still holds true thirty years later. Ian Bell, writing in 1995, attributes the popularity of the novel to García Márquez's ability to tap the human heart: "the author of *One Hundred Years of Solitude* is clearly an altogether more sensual and less starkly cerebral novelist than any of his Latin American contemporaries. Indeed, for all its playfulness, this entire book may be read as a tribute to the human power to love and endure, despite everything, to survive wars and tempests and hardships and yet retain the capacity to dream and to love."

Early critics also immediately noted the role of history in the novel. John Leonard's 1970 *New York Times* review stated, "it is not only the story of the Buendía family and the Colombian town of Macondo" but a "recapitulation of our evolutionary and intellectual experience." Writing in the same year, Michael Wood bespeaks the novel's multi-various tone, which is at once "elegant, iron-

ic, slightly complacent. . .[and] disciplined." Paul Edward Gray, writing for *The Yale Review* in 1970, praised "the fusion of the mundane and the magical, the real and the surreal" on the occasion of the English translation of the novel. In 1971, Gunther W. Lorenz, writing for the *Center for Inter-American Relations Review,* called it "the most unusual novel of our time." Richard Gullon's review in *Diacritics* noted the author's inventiveness and success at illuminating meaning: García Márquez "know[s] how to revitalize the ancient and almost forgotten art of storytelling."

In 1982, García Márquez received the Nobel Prize for Literature. Upon this occasion, Joseph Epstein wrote in *Commentary*, "no novelist now writing has a more enviable reputation." Gene H. Bell-Villada, writing for the *Latin American Literary Review* in 1985, noted that "García Márquez has done the most so far to save the novel from itself, to rescue it from the narrow impasses and byways into which it had taken refuge and set up shop." The 1990s brought about a shift in critical analysis of *One Hundred Years of Solitude* as politicized literary criticism was applied. In that vein, Irvin Solomon wrote in 1993 on the role of women in the novel, and perceived a marked gender bias: "As a whole, the women of Macondo are pictured as male-defined, biological reproducers or sexually pleasing objects who are treated thematically as accessories to the men who actually shape and control the world."

In his introduction to a 1989 anthology of scholarly essays on García Márquez, Harold Bloom complained of "aesthetic battle fatigue" brought on by a rereading of *One Hundred Years of Solitude*, yet despite certain literary limitations, Bloom attested to the novel's obvious and growing "canonical status." Ten years later, Raymond Williams made a similar assessment: "Master of magic realism, Nobel laureate, and the consequential practitioner of the right of invention since Borges, Gabriel García Márquez has become virtually the emblem of Latin American literature in recent years, particularly in the United States and Europe."

Criticism

Carole Hamilton

Hamilton is an English teacher at Cary Academy in Cary, North Carolina. In this essay she suggests that the elements of magic realism in One

Colombian troops in 1902, during the time of the War of a Thousand Days.

Hundred Years of Solitude *are more than simply exaggerations of fact, but are allegorical metaphors, or metaphors made real.*

García Márquez often wryly denies that his works are magical, fantastic, or surrealistic: "It always amuses me that the highest praise for my work comes for the imagination, while the truth is that there's not a single line in all my work that does not have a basis in reality." Latin America generally and Colombia specifically are lands of myth and wonder, where true accounts are as bizarre as fiction. The craziness of the United Fruit Company

banana strike, where the company circumvented the legal system by calling its workers "contractors," was a real event, based in history. The siring of seventeen Aurelianos by one man by seventeen different women could be real—García Márquez himself had fifteen siblings. However, that each of the seventeen Aurelianos was physically marked with ash can only be true in the metaphoric sense, as marked for death.

The magic realism of *One Hundred Years of Solitude* consists in just such metaphoric devices. With first a look at the variety of ways that the magic realism in *One Hundred Years of Solitude* has

What Do I Read Next?

- García Márquez reported being inspired by Franz Kafka's *Metapmorphosis* (1915), with its telling of "the wildest things with a completely natural tone of voice" in the same way that his grandmother used to tell stories.

- Virginia Woolf's *To the Lighthouse* (1937) has also been cited as a source of ideas for García Márquez.

- William Faulkner's family chronicles in *Absalom!*

Absalom! (1936) share similarities with those of *One Hundred Years of Solitude*.

- Other modern Latin American novels that blend historical elements with fiction include Carlos Fuentes' *Where the Air is Clear* (1985), Julio Cortázar's *Hopscotch* (1963), and Isabel Allende's *House of Spirits* (1982), which has been called a parody of *One Hundred Years of Solitude*.

---

been explained and analyzed, I will move on to describe how the magical or fantastic elements nearly always serve as "metaphors made real," as though García Márquez asked himself, "What if men really were 'marked for death'?" "What if men really lived for procreation, like the butterfly? Or, what if a woman really ascended to heaven? And what if her sacred quality was not religious and otherworldly, but its opposite—earthly, corporeal beauty?" These and questions like them seem to have driven García Márquez's creative project when he locked himself away for eighteen months, after having spent years preparing himself in the art of the novel by reading everything from the Bible to the latest modernist works for six years, and then dedicating himself to "inventing literature" anew. With the enthusiasm and idealism of the true novitiate, García Márquez became the "master of magic realism," generating his own brand of magical literature by pushing the limits of imagination to create metaphors made real.

George McMurray, writing in 1977, considered *One Hundred Years of Solitude* to be the best example of the Latin American phenomenon of "magic realism." Nearly every literary critic and scholar who has written about the novel is compelled to mention this aspect of it. Most often, they remark on what Gene Bell-Villada called the novel's "perfect integration of. . .unusual incidents into the everyday life represented in a text largely realistic." Writers like Raymond Williams note the

deadpan manner in which marvelous events are narrated: "García Márquez prohibits [fantastic events] being fantastic by dealing with them as if they were commonplace." García Márquez himself explained that he wanted to write "with the same expression with which my grandmother told [stories of the supernatural]: with a brick face." Fellow author Mario Vargas Llosa attributes the "prodigious enrichment" of wonders to the author's discovery "that the novelist is God," that literature "has not limits and that all excesses are permissible to the creator if he has the sufficient verbal power of persuasion to justify them." Magic realism infuses reality with imagination, by erasing the lines between daily life and dreams, between mortality and myth, and between the world and wonder at the world.

Critics and scholars also discuss the fittingness of the symbolism of García Márquez's fantastic events to the character associated with them. Gene Bell-Villada sees the swarm of butterflies surrounding Mauricio Babilonia as "representing a soft, 'poetic' side to his sensuality, making the apprentice auto mechanic more than just an aggressive stud, and thus more plausibly attractive to a girlish Meme Buendía." Morton P. Levitt points out that the "ship in the jungle serves as a metaphor of a way of life that will as suddenly appear and. . .as suddenly vanish, inexplicable, perhaps irrational, subject to the forces of nature if not to reason, at once beyond reason and thoroughly human, testimony both to the power of nature over history and to the

> "Magic realism infuses reality with imagination, by erasing the lines between daily life and dreams, between mortality and myth, and between the world and wonder at the world."

regenerative power of men within nature.'' Certainly the magic realism in *One Hundred Years of Solitude* enhances the rich meaning of its complex story, in metaphors that reach beyond the conscious level to affect the reader's phenomenological experience of the text. Metaphors serve to organize perceptions by providing a kind of framework through which a text is understood. Thus, the connotation of butterflies may not even reach the conscious level, but nevertheless shape the reader's understanding of Mauricio as having a lover's spirit, despite his gruff demeanor.

García Márquez has often been asked by interviewers to identify the sources of his ideas. Summarizing the commentaries of two other Latin American critics, Gene Bell-Villada reports that Remedios the Beauty ostensibly came from an urban legend about a young lady who ran off with the proverbial traveling salesman, and her parents made up the ascension story to hide their embarrassment, saying ''If the Virgin Mary could do it, so can our daughter.'' García Márquez added the bed sheets for additional credibility, he reports, after having seen a maid hanging up the wash. Fantastic stories, legends, myths, and exaggerations are commonplace in many areas of Latin America. In his preface to a recent anthology of criticism on García Márquez, Harold Bloom attests to the bizarre nature of Latin American life and politics, citing the example of Haiti's Papa Doc ordering all black dogs on the island destroyed because he feared that one of his enemies had ''transformed himself into a black dog.'' With such superstitious behavior occurring naturally in Latin America, it is no wonder that García Márquez chose to incorporate it into his stories, for these features are part of the texture of his culture. However, his artistic reworking of the metaphor, turning it so to speak on its end, is unique in literary history. It is the modernist parallel to

allegory, the creation of characters and traits based on abstract ideas—metaphors made real.

One of the simplest embodiments of metaphor made real can be seen in Ursula's blindness. She is the living epitome of ''blind faith.'' At the same time, she has, despite her physical blindness, acute vision into the hearts of others, seeing past superficialities to core truths. Nature gives her paths to follow, even before her loss of sight. When her son José Arcadio is killed, a path of blood leads her to her son's dead body, winding an impossible trail across the town. In old age, her vision into reality grows stronger while her sight grows weaker. It is ''the lucidity of old age'' that allows her to see that her son Aureliano has grown cold-hearted. She feels her way along the walls of her familiar home, ''the spirit of her invincible heart guid[ing] her through the shadows, as she feels her way along raising her children, grandchildren, great-grandchildren, and finally great-great-grandchildren, the last of whom she has to douse with perfume to track through the house. She is the only one in the family who sees the larger pattern of family fates. She notices that Aureliano Segundo is ''just like Aureliano. It's as if the world were repeating itself.'' She is the blind soothsayer who interprets the world, as she tells her husband, tied to his chestnut tree, news of her family. On a metafictional level, she also serves as story interpreter to the reader, with her occasional comments on the shape of her unfolding family history serving as plot guideposts.

Looking at specific incidents of the fantastic, Humberto E. Robles proposes that the ascent of Remedios the Beauty is a parody of the Virgin Mary's Ascension. Roberto González Echevarría comes to the same conclusion but notes an element of kitsch in the bed sheets making her ascension suggestive ''of the popular renditions of the event in religious prints.'' García Márquez's ascension comically juxtaposes the common bed sheets and everyday activity of folding clothes alongside the sacred. One can imagine García Márquez's imagination at work here, beginning with the ascension of a woman whose chief quality is not beatific, but its mundane cognate, the beautiful. García Márquez describes Remedios the Beauty using terms often used of saints: ''Remedios the Beauty was not a creature of this world.'' Words like ''miracle'' and ''magnificent'' are used in conjunction with her; she bears ''no cross on her back,'' yet she gives a ''pitying smile'' reminiscent of Christ or Mary just before her ascent. Like a saint, she is indifferent to fashion, malice, and sexual attraction, but her indifference is so extreme that she is considered retarded. She eats with her hands and is ''incapable of giving an answer that was not a miracle of simplemindedness.'' Nevertheless, as to a divinity, men sacrifice their lives, literally, to her. She herself is so unaware of her attractions that she cuts off her hair, a big inconvenience to her, ironically making herself all the more attractive. The cut tresses she uses ''to make wigs for the saints.'' In other words, she rids herself of an earthly possession that is more useful to the saints than to herself, as though they have more vanity than she. It is her earthly beauty, with or without her hair, that makes her divine. She exudes a unique natural odor, ''a tormenting breeze that was still perceptible several hours after she passed by.'' Taken altogether, the traits of Remedios the Beauty are those of a saint of beauty, an earthly saint whose palpable and sacred beauty emanates its own incense. Rather than just being described in metaphoric terms, Remedios the Beauty is the 'embodiment' of the metaphor of the idolized woman.

Rebeca is another metaphor made real: she is one of the living dead, a woman with a literal connection to the earth and to the grave. One connection is the sack of bones that go *clok-clok-clok*, her parents' bones. She cannot marry until they receive a proper burial—until they find their resting place in the earth. Another connection to the grave is Rebeca's favorite form of sustenance. While the first-generation José Arcadio and Aureliano nurse from their mother Ursula, their foster sister Rebeca eats dirt, physically nourished by it. Finally, she stays connected to death by living near the cemetery. When she and José Arcadio marry, they live across from the cemetery and wake the neighbors with their lovemaking as many as eight times a night. Rebeca is the embodiment of the human connection to the dead, and thus she can foresee, with an Aureliano-like prescience, that the shooting of Colonel Aureliano Buendía will take place against the cemetery wall. After the death of José Arcadio, Rebeca lives on in her home by the cemetery, completely forgotten by the family, as though she, too, is dead. Ursula in her blindness realizes how unfair they had been to reject her, since of them all, Rebeca alone ''had the unbridled courage that Ursula had wanted for her line.'' Amaranta, her lifelong enemy, the one who killed her soul by plotting against her wedding with Pietro Crespi, does not repent. She sews Rebeca's funeral shroud, consoling herself with a fantasy of restoring Rebeca's dead damaged face with paraffin and decking her with the hair of the saints. When Aureliano Triste brings news of having seen Rebeca, alive but aged, his description matches Amaranta's fantasy exactly, ''an apparition with leathery skin and a few golden threads on her skull.'' For most of her life, Rebeca is a living corpse, in reality as well as in Amaranta's hopes. Her house is like a rotting casket, entombing her but also slowly being taken over by the earth: ''the floor was broken by grass and wildflowers and in the cracks lizards and all manner of vermin had their nests, all of which confirmed that there had not been a human being there for at least half a century.'' Aureliano Triste easily pushes down the worm-eaten door. He finds Rebeca ''alive and rotting in her wormhole,'' haunted by memories of José Arcadio that Aureliano Triste awakens. When she finally dies, her head is bald from ringworm, as though decomposition has had a head start on her. In life, the grave is a part of her, returning to her the earth to which she has always been connected.

García Márquez has said that *One Hundred Years of Solitude* ''is a *metaphor for Latin America*.'' In several ways, this is so. The metaphor of solitude aptly speaks to a nagging sense of disconnectedness from both the Indian cultures and the conquistadors of its past, a violent sense of divisiveness resulting from numerous civil wars, and an embarrassed sense of backwardness in technology and cultural growth. Colombia and the other Latin American nations fit this description of national solitude. However, the art that García Márquez has created in *One Hundred Years of Solitude* at the same time asserts a pride in solitude, which is a pride in a complex and deeply ingrained set of Latin American identities. These identities are represented by characters like Ursula, Remedios the Beauty, and Rebeca, among the more than fifty others in the novel. Many of them are more than characters, for they also serve to represent the uniquely complex Latin American worldview. García Márquez has created Macondo and its population not merely as abstract representations of Latin American reality, but also has succeeded in creating the mirror image of mere metaphor. In this novel, García Márquez creates characters, events, and places that are fictional, physical entities as representations of metaphorical notions. It is as though he began with the metaphors of abstract ideas—blindness that can see, a saint of beauty, a life of living death—and used these notions as blueprints to design a town, its people, and its history. Just as the patriarch José Arcadio created science in response to the puzzling and wondrous gifts of Melquíades, Latin American itself has had to create itself, turning metaphors into reality.

Source: Carole Hamilton, in an essay for *Literature of Developing Nations for Students,* Gale, 2000.

Dean J. Irvine

In the following essay on Gabriel Garcia Marquez's One Hundred Years of Solitude, *author Dean J. Irvine examines the influences of postcolonialism and postmodernism as twin strands weaving the genre of magic realism as experienced in Marquez's novel.*

Akin to the strain of poststructuralist theory Jacques Derrida practices in his essay ''The Law of Genre,'' governed by ''a principle of contamination, a law of impurity, a parasitical economy'' and initiated as ''a sort of participation without belonging—a taking part in without being part of,'' the diagnostic method of this paper purports to enchain strains of postcolonialism and postmodernism as a model for the theory and practice of magic realism in Gabriel García Márquez's *Cien años de soledad* [*One Hundred Years of Solitude*]. The model of magic realism under construction here is a double-helix: postcolonialism as one genetic strand, postmodernism as the other. In this model, magic realism and the magic realist text are collocated in the twists and gaps of this double discourse, that is, the discursive of enchainment of postcolonialism and postmodernism.

In the essays collected by Lois Parkinson Zamora and Wendy B. Faris for the anthology *Magic Realism: Theory, History, Community* (1995), postmodernism and postcolonialism entwine as nonidentical theoretical discourses in the genealogy of magic realism. Like postmodernism and postcolonialism, magic realism is recognized as a historical product of the discourses of modernism and colonialism. It is accepted among commentators on magic realism that in 1925 the German art critic Franz Roh coined the term in reference to post-expressionist visual art. As well, critics generally observe an alternative concept of magic realism, though not the term itself, pioneered by the Cuban novelist Alejo Carpentier, who coined the phrase ''lo real maravilloso'' [''the marvelous real(ity)''] in his preface to *El reino de este mundo* (1949) in order to disengage his literary practice from that of European surrealism (Zamora and Faris; Connell). Critics often cite Carpentier's term ''the marvelous real(ity)'' in conjunction with Roh's

''magic realism,'' sometimes conflating the two terms. In parsing each term, Liam Connell underscores the problematic correlation: ''that Carpentier uses *maravilloso* rather than *magico,* and that critics who wilfully mistranslate Carpentier's phrase or, by not translating, imply a simple correspondence between 'the marvelous reality' and Magic Realism—not only obscure a genealogy which includes a Surrealist interest in the marvellous (Breton, *What Is Surrealism?*), but also invoke a number of cultural attributes which follow from the magical ... which are not, I think, similarly associated with the marvellous.'' The ''magic realism'' versus ''the marvelous real(ity)'' debate is now so widespread that I cannot detail it beyond its critical origins: in short, because Roh writes from a European, post-expressionist perspective and Carpentier from a Latin American, post-surrealist perspective, the debate inevitably invites antagonism among critics. Angel Flores's landmark essay ''Magical Realism in Spanish American Fiction'' (1995) recognizes neither Roh nor Carpentier as the starting point for what he names the ''new phase of Latin American literature, of magical realism,'' opting instead for Jorge Luis Borge's 1935 collection *Historia universal de la infamia.* Although Flores does not cite Borges's 1932 essay ''El arte narrativo y la magia'' as an originary moment in the theorization of magic realism, the widely acknowledged influence of Borges on García Márquez suggests that critics should also consider Borges's essay as a prototype. Moreover, to situate Borges in relation to García Márquez not only avoids the Roh versus Carpentier debate, but also diagnoses better the strain of magic realism in *Cien años de soledad,* especially in the context of Latin American postmodernism and postcolonialism.

Theo D'haen presents the history of the term magic realism as one coextensive with the history of the term postmodernism. For D'haen, magic realism is the progeny of the continental European avant-garde (post-expressionism, surrealism) and, as such, constitutes a discourse ''ex-centric'' to the ''privileged centre'' of Anglo-American modernism. Citing a consortium of international postmodern theorists (Douwe Fokkema, Allen Thiher, Linda Hutcheon, Brian McHale, Ihab Hassan, David Lodge, and Alan Wilde), D'haen locates the origin of the term postmodernism with the Latin American critic Frederico de Onís in the 1930s. D'haen suggests that the co-emergence of magic realism and postmodernism in the 1930s occurs when ''Latin America was perhaps the continent most ex-centric

Colombian troops take up positions in Bogota after President Mariano Ospina declares a state of emergency in November, 1949.

to the 'privileged centres' of power''; that the international acceptance of postmodernism would eventually absorb its "ex-centric" discourse into the "privileged centre" discourses of Europe and the United States; and that, at the same time, magic realism would establish itself as the province of "excentric" cultures including, but not limited to, Latin America. At present, D'haen determines, "in international critical parlance a consensus is emerging in which a hierarchical relation is established between postmodernism and magic realism, whereby the latter comes to denote a particular strain of the contemporary movement covered by the former.'' D'haen's reconciliation of the critical histories of magic realism and postmodernism leads him to conclude that postmodernism enacts "aesthetic consciousness-raising" and magic realism "political consciousness-raising . . . within postmodernism,'' or, to borrow from Fredric Jameson's *The Political Unconscious*, that their narratives perform "a socially symbolic act.'' D'haen does not propose an excavation of the Latin American roots of postmodernism in the same way he does the continental European origins of magic realism, but rather advocates a recognition of the dissemination of the theory and practice of postmodernism and magic realism in an international context.

To read the genealogies of postmodernism and magic realism D'haen constructs without skepticism, however, would be to contract the strain of historical amnesia experienced by the town of Macondo in *Cien años de soledad*. D'haen's genealogies infect us with postmodern strains of García Márquez's insomnia and banana plagues; they block our memory of the histories of colonialism and repress theories of postcolonialism designed to unblock our memory. The culturally specific location of the term postmodernism with the Latin American critic Onís is part of the history of colonialism; that is, the appropriation of *postmodernismo* by an international critical community clearly constitutes a kind of colonization of the Latin American term. In fact, to some Latin American critics, the current international application of the term postmodernism to Latin American fiction represents a type of discursive recolonization.

As a reaction to international postmodern theorists, the Latin American critic Iris Zavala decries "the uncritical, normative, univocal acceptance of '(post) modernism' . . . in order to object, from a Hispanic perspective, to some Anglo-American and French currents of the philosophical and meta-theoretical mainstream and their tendency to

> " The model of magic realism under construction here is a double-helix: postcolonialism as one genetic strand, postmodernism as the other."

apply the term (post) modernism globally and a-historically." Zavala reminds Anglo-American and continental European critics of the historical and cultural specificity of *modernismo* in Hispanic literature. In augmenting Onís, Zavala then posits a modified definition of *postmodernismo*:

> If one wants to conserve the term 'postmodernism' at least a somewhat more reliable point of reference from which to ask the question is needed. Going back to Onís, we must agree that modernism is the literary expression, and the stylistic motivation, of the entry of the Hispanic world into modernity, adding to his definition that it is the product of a severe rupture with past modes of production and of the emergence of industrialized societies. . . . This argument can be qualified if modernity is understood as an unfinished project in *some* societies and cultures, a program which constantly rewrites itself.

Bill Ashcroft offers an important corrective to the ahistorical and global applications of the term postmodernism to which Zavala objects. The discursive colonization and recolonization of *postmodernismo* is but one international incident in the long history of colonialism in Latin America. According to Ashcroft, "the colonization of Latin America obliges us to address the question of postcolonialism at its roots, at the very emergence of modernity." In this view, not only does modernity originate with European imperial expansion and colonization of Latin America, but also "postmodernity is coterminous with modernity and represents a radical phase of its development . . . in the same way postcolonialism is coterminous with colonization, and the dynamic of its disruptive engagement is firmly situated in modernity." "My contention" Ashcroft continues, "is that postcolonialism and postmodernism are both discursive elaborations of postmodernity, which is itself not the overcoming of modernity, but modernity coming to understand its own contradictions and uncertainties." Ashcroft's placement of the discursive category postmodernism at the

advent of postmodernity in Latin America obviously extends beyond the reach of postmodern theorists who locate the origin of postmodern aesthetics at the moment of Onís's coinage in the 1930s. Moreover, Ashcroft's conjunction of modernity and postmodernity and enchainment of postcolonialism and postmodernism in a Latin American context constitutes a double discourse analogous to the discursive code of magic realism in *Cien años de soledad*. For at the originary juncture of postcolonialism and postmodernism, *Cien años de soledad* narrates the "contradictions and uncertainties" that follow from imperial expansion, colonization, and modernization of Latin America.

Like postmodernism, magic realism is subject to colonial imperatives. For instance, those critics who limit the term magic realism to its first issue from the European avant-garde claim that "Latin American reality is colonized by the term" (Janes). Yet even in a Latin American context, Borges's attempt to reconcile the difference between magic and narrative realism promulgates a colonial imperative. The tacit colonialist project of Borges's essay "El arte narrativo y la magia" is made manifest in his explication of narratives of colonization: William Morris's *Life and Death of Jason* (1867), Edgar Allen Poe's *Narrative of Arthur Gordon Pym* (1838), and José Antonio Conde's *Historia de la dominación de los árabes en España* (1854–55). To interpret the law of cause and effect in narrative, Borges enjoins Sir James Frazer's reduction of magic in *The Golden Bough* to "una conveniente ley general, la del la simpatía, que postula un vínculo inevitable entre cosas distantes, ya porque su figura es igual—magia imitativa, homeopática—ya por el hecho de una cercanía anterior —magia contagiosa" ("El arte") ["a convenient general law, the Law of Sympathy, which assumes that 'things act on each other at a distance through a secret sympathy,' either because their form is similar (imitative, or homeopathic, magic) or because of a previous physical contact (contagious, or contact, magic)" ("Narrative")]. Rather than recognize difference, Borges intends "demonstrar que la magia es la coronación o pesadilla de lo causal, no su contradicción" ("El arte") ["to show that magic is not the contradiction of the law of cause and effect but its crown, or nightmare" ("Narrative")]. Borges's sense of the non-contradictory relation between the law of magic and the law of cause and effect betrays a colonialist tendency to assimilate the former (the premodern discourse of the colonized) to the latter (the modern discourse of

the colonizer). As a corollary, the colonizer's discourse is contaminated once it comes into contact
with the colonized's discourse, and vice versa; this
principle of discursive contamination is manifest, as
we will see, in the narratives of the insomnia and
banana plagues in *Cien años de soledad*. For at the
colonial juncture of the premodern and the modern,
narrative discourse functions according to "a principle of contamination, a law of impurity" (Derrida,
"Law"); this strain of narrative discourse inhabits
magic realism, which originates not with Borges
himself in the 1930s, but with the colonial narratives of the earliest explorers of Latin America.

Adopting this long historical view, Amaryll
Chanady identifies the colonial origins of magic
realist narratives in Latin America. Chanady represents and contests several different definitions of
magic realism: the portrayal of a supernatural indigenous world-view (magic) combined with the
description of contemporary political and social
problems (realism); the perception of Latin America as exotic; and the representation of an authentic
geographical, ideological, and historical expression
of Latin America. "In fact," Chanady posits, "magic
realism is often defined as the juxtaposition of two
different rationalities—the Indian and the European
in a syncretic fictitious world-view based on the
simultaneous existence of several entirely different
cultures in Latin America." Like Borges's "El arte
narrativo y la magia," Chanady's location of the
emergence of magic realism is coterminous with the
emergence of colonialism in Latin America, but
Chanady's recognition of difference between Latin
American cultures counters Borges's notion of the
noncontradictory relation between discursive worlds.
For Chanady, neither term in the self-contradictory
phrase magic realism is therefore reducible or sepa-
rable: "magic" cannot be reduced to a premodern
native world-view, nor "realism" to a modern
European world-view. As a discursive formation,
magic realism in the Latin American context elaborates those "contradictions and uncertainties" that
arise out of the co-existence of multiple cultures and
discourses, and that stem from the simultaneity of
imperial colonization and modernization.

Chanady cites Spanish exploration narratives
in order to illustrate the history of colonialism as a
metanarrative subtending Latin American magic
realism. Her first text, from Bernal Díaz del Castillo's *Historia verdadera de la conquista de la Nueva
España* on the discovery of the Aztec capital of
Tenochtitlán, speaks to colonial textual representations of the new world as fabulous: "[Éstas]

grandes poblaciones ... parecía a las cosas y
encantamento que cuentan en el libro de Amadís ...
y aun algunos de nuestros soldados decían que si
aquello que veían si era entre sueños. Y no es
maravillar que yo aquí lo escriba desta manera,
porque hay que ponderar much en ello, que no sé
como lo cuente, ver cosas nunca oídas ni vistas y
aun soñadas, como vimos" ["These great towns ...
seemed like an enchanted vision from the tale of
Amadís. Indeed, some of our soldiers asked whether
it was not all a dream. ... It was all so wonderful
that I do not know how to describe this first glimpse
of things never heard of, seen or dreamed of before" (*Conquest*; qtd. in Chanady)]. Her second
text, from Hernán Cortés s second *relación* to
Emperor Charles V in 1520, presents a colonial
encounter with the new world congruous with the
experience García Márquez ascribes to the inhabitants of Macondo: "son tantas y de tantas calidades,
que por la prolijidad y por no me ocurrir tantas a la
memoria, y aun por no saber poner los nobres, no las
expreso" (*Cartas*) ["there are so many," that is,
things in the New Continent, "and of so many
kinds, that because of the great number of them and
because I do not remember them all, and also
because I do not know what to call them, I cannot
relate them" (Chanady)]. García Márquez, in the
opening paragraph of *Cien años de soledad* , introduces a fictional world analogous to the "unnamed"
continent faced by Spanish explorers: "El mundo
era tan reciente, que muchas cosas carecían de
nombre, y para mencionarlas había que señalaras
con el dedo" ["The world was so recent that many
things lacked names, and in order to indicate them
it was necessary to point"]. This condition of
namelessness in *Cien años de soledad* predicates
the metanarrative of colonial history. The lack of
language necessary to name the colonized world
points to the formation and awareness of discursive
gaps, disruptive postcolonial sites of "contradictions and uncertainties" at the very origins of
colonization in Latin America.

Situating the concept of magic realism in a
postcolonial context, as Stephen Slemon proposes,
"can enable us to recognize continuities within
literary cultures that the established genre systems
might blind us to": continuities, that is, between
contemporary magic realist texts and texts written at
earlier stages of a culture's literary and colonial
history ("Magic Realism"). The magic realist text
enters into a dialogue with genres of colonial and
pre-colonial history and mythology; this dialogism
marks Latin American magic realism as postcolonial

discourse. For this reason, Slemon writes, there is "the perception that magic realism, as a socially symbolic contract, carries a residuum of resistance toward the imperial centre and to its totalizing systems of generic classification" ("Magic Realism"). Like D'haen's conception of magic realism as a postmodernist discourse, Slemon holds that magic realism as a postcolonial discourse performs "a socially symbolic act." According to Slemon, the agon between narratives and the decentering of dominant metanarratives of generic classification characterize the magic realist text as postcolonial:

> In the language of narration in a magic realist text, a battle between two oppositional systems takes place, each working toward the creation of a different kind of fictional world from the other. Since the ground rules of these two worlds are incompatible, neither one can fully come into being, and each remains suspended, locked in a continuous dialectic with the "other," a situation which creates disjunction within each of the separate discursive systems, rending them with gaps, absences, and silences. ("Magic Realism")

For García Márquez, the absence of language adequate to describe the phenomenal, unnamed world is signified through the "gaps, absences, and silences" in the magic realist text of *Cien años de soledad*. These silences and memory gaps are foregrounded in the insomnia plague, where precolonial and colonial discursive systems collide, and again in the banana plague, where neocolonial imperialist and judicial discourses delegitimate and erase the local political histories of the banana workers' revolt and of their massacre. But are such contestations between narratives and collisions between discursive worlds limited to magic realism as a postcolonial discourse?

Brian McHale argues in *Postmodernist Fiction* that one of the functions of the postmodern study of ontology as the "theoretical description of a universe" is to ask such questions as:

> What is a world? What kinds of world are there, how are they constituted, and how do they differ? What happens when different kinds of world are placed in confrontation, or when boundaries between worlds are violated; What is the mode of existence of a text, and what is the mode of existence of the world (or worlds) it projects? How is a projected world structured? And so on.

These questions lead McHale to propose the double thesis that "the dominant of postmodernist fiction is *ontological*," whereas "the dominant of modernist fiction is *epistemological*" and functions as if to ask such questions as:

> What is there to be known? Who knows it? How do they know it, and with what degree of certainty? How

is knowledge transmitted from one knower to another, and with what degree of reliability? How does the object of knowledge change as it passes from knower to knower? What are the limits of the knowable? And so on.

What I am forwarding here—as a heuristic strategy—is less the modernist or postmodernist status of *Cien años de soledad* than the notion that the novel, to import McHale's thesis, "dramatizes the shift of dominant from problems of *knowing* to problems of *modes of being*—from an epistemological dominant to an ontological one." In my view, the shift from questions of knowledge to questions of being is dramatized in the acts of reading embedded in *Cien años de soledad*. Melquíades's parchments—and the epistemological task of reading, interpreting, and translating them taken up by successive generations of the House of Buendía—are revealed in the final pages by Aureliano Babilonia, the last Buendía, to be the narratives of his own life and his family's history: the parchments, written prior to the events of the novel by Melquíades himself. Suddenly the embedded reader, Aureliano Babilonia, and the implied reader of *Cien años de soledad* are thrown, as Robert Alter puts it, into an "ontological vertigo." For Aureliano Babilonia, the world of the parchments he reads is indistinguishable from his world, the world of Macondo: for him, reading as a mode of interpretation gives way to a mode of being. So too, for the implied reader of the novel, a mode of interpretation is transformed into a mode of being. The text of *Cien años de soledad* therefore looks back upon both the implied and the embedded reader as "un espejo hablado" ["a speaking mirror"].

The ontological status of the implied reader is called into question in what Jon Thiem names a "fable of textualization":

> Not being literally in the text permits the reader to enjoy the exciting and dangerous fictional world without having to suffer the consequences of living in this world. . . . In a textualization this balance is upset. The world of the text loses its literal impenetrability. The reader loses that minimal detachment that keeps him or her out of the world of the text. The reader, in short, ceases to be reader, ceases to be invulnerable, comfortable in his or her own armchair, and safely detached, and instead becomes an actor, an agent in the fictional world.

But what is the ontological status of this displaced reader? If we consider the relationship between reader and text in terms of the hierarchized binary of "self" and "other," the displacement of the reader from the privileged position of "self" into the position of "other" performs what Linda Hutcheon in *A Poetics of Postmodernism* terms "aesthetic and political consciousness-raising." From a postcolonial perspective, Chanady argues that the exotic representations of Latin America in magic realist texts are "directed towards a reader who has little knowledge of certain aspects of Latin American nature and civilization. That reader need not be European—he can also live in a large Europeanized metropolis like Buenos Aires." Chanady's location of the (euro)centric reader in relation to the postcolonial, ex-centric text recalls Ashcroft, Griffiths, and Tiffin's construction of postcolonial theory and practice in *The Empire Writes Back*; this displacement of the magic realist text from privileged centres of imperial culture represents a postcolonial discourse writing back from a place "other" than "the" or "a" centre. While D'haen may theorize "the notion of the ex-centric, in the sense of speaking from the margin, from a place 'other' than 'the' or 'a' centre . . . [as] an essential feature of that strain of postmodernism we call magic realism," it is critically important to theorize writing back from a place "other" than the centre in that strain of postcolonialism we call magic realism.

The discursive enchainment of postmodernism and postcolonialism—the double-helix of magic realism in *Cien años de soledad*—is foregrounded in what I am calling fables of the plague years: the tales of the insomnia plague and the banana plague. The isolation of these fabulous tales in the text is perhaps analogous to the medical practice of quarantine; but it is, in keeping with my metaphor of the double helix, an attempt to isolate elements of a double code of postmodernism and postcolonialism in the generic code of magic realism. I will first isolate the insomnia plague in chapter three of *Cien años de soledad* as a kind of allegorical narrative, a fable in the broad sense of a fabulous tale, of the theoretical concerns of magic realism as a postmodernist and postcolonialist narrative discourse. Proceeding from the theoretical symptomology of the insomnia plague, I will then isolate the conditions of the banana plague beginning in chapter twelve of *Cien años de soledad* as an allegorical narrative of the sociopolitical concerns of magic realism and as a counter-colonialist and imperialist narrative discourse.

Prior to analysis of such theoretical allegories, however, an account of the insomnia plague itself is in order: an orphan—who is somehow related to Ursula and José Arcadio Buendía but remembered by neither, who is subsequently named Rebeca

(after her mother, so named in a letter of introduction), who refuses to speak until she is spoken to in the Guajiro native language by the servant Visitación, who actually speaks fluently in the Guajiro and Spanish languages, and who suffers from the vice of eating earth until she is cured by Ursula's homeopathic medicine—is revealed to be a carrier of the insomnia plague which infects the House of Buendía with the illness of insomnia. Visitación relates to the Buendías the critical manifestation of the insomnia plague—the loss of memory—which José Arcadio Buendía dismisses as a native superstition. The town of Macondo is then infected with the illness by eating Ursula's candied animals. In order to remedy the inevitable loss of memory, José Arcadio Buendía first marks every object in the town with its name and later appends a kind of instruction manual for each object, so transforming the town of Macondo into a text. He then embarks on the construction of "la mánquina de la memoria" ["the memory machine"]: an encyclopedic text in imitation of the marvelous inventions of the gypsies, "se fundaba en la posibilidad de repasar todas las mañanas, y desde el principio hasta el fin, la totalidad de los conocimientos adquiridos en la vida" ["based on the possibility of reviewing every morning, from beginning to end, the totality of knowledge acquired during one's life"]. Despite José Arcadio Buendía's attempts to forestall the decimation of the collective memory of Macondo with his strategies to inscribe and transcribe the totality of language-based knowledge, the insomnia plague ultimately effects the complete erasure of linguistic signifiers and signifieds: "Así continuaron viviendo en una realidad escurridiza, momentáneamente capturada por las palabras, pero que había de fugarse sin remedio cuando olvidaran los valores de la letra escrita" ["Thus they went on living in a reality that was slipping away, momentarily captured by words, but which would escape irredeemably when they forgot the values of the written letters"]. As an alternative system to José Arcadio Buendía's memory machine, the fortune teller Pilar Ternera conceives "el artificio de leer el pasado en las barajas como antes había leído el futuro. Mediante ese recurso, los insomnes empezaron a vivir en un mundo construido por las alternativas inciertas de los naipes" ["the trick of reading the past in cards as she had read the future before. By means of that recourse the insomniacs began to live in a world built on the uncertain alternatives of the cards"]. In the end, the panacea for the insomnia plague, restoring meaning to the meaningless yet textualized world of Macondo, is procured by the gypsy Melquíades. He returns as if from the dead, for it is believed that ''la tribu de Melquíades, según contraron los trotamundos, había sido borrada de la faz de la tierra por haber sobrepasado los límites del conocimiento humano'' [''Melquíades' tribe, according to what the wanderers said, had been wiped off the face of the earth because they had gone beyond the limits of human knowledge'']. While José Arcadio Buendía and Pilar Ternera face the problem of meaning in terms of interpretive or epistemological strategies, the problem of the insomnia plague is revealed to be ontological, a theoretical description of a world ''beyond the limits of human knowledge,'' an ontology of the magical real known only to Melquíades.

From the position of postmodernism, I interpret the insomnia plague in terms of what Thiem calls a ''fable of textualization,'' that is, a type of textualization which takes place when ''the world of the text literally intrudes into the extratextual or reader's world.'' Textualizations, Thiem writes, ''partake of a dreamlike quality which aligns them with a host of other magic realist devices and motifs. . . . [T]he oneiric resonance of textualization . . . , like so many other dream occurrences, . . . arises out of the literalization of a common metaphor.'' The literalization of common metaphors, such as plague and illness in *Cien años de soledad,* parallels the argument of Susan Sontag's book *Illness as Metaphor,* which opens with a kind of fable:

> Illness is the night-side of life, a more onerous [and oneiric] citizenship. Everyone who is born holds dual citizenship, in the kingdom of the well and in the kingdom of the sick. Although we prefer to use only the good passport, sooner or later each of us is obliged, at least for a spell, to identify ourselves as citizens of that other place.

Analogous perhaps to the manner in which we speak of ''master narratives,'' Sontag refers to ''master illnesses'': so in the phrase ''illness as metaphor,'' metaphor functions as a narrative in miniature. But Sontag urges the demystification of illness as a poetic figure. To argue that García Márquez literalizes the metaphor of ''plague'' or ''illness'' forces Sontag's point that ''illness is *not* a metaphor.'' In the textualized town of Macondo, the ''illness'' is literalized as a text inscribed upon a extratextual world. Thus in a ''fable of textualization'' such as ''la peste del insomnio'' [''the insomnia plague''], where ''the world of the text literally intrudes into the extratextual or reader's world,'' both *lector in fabula* (embedded reader) and (perhaps more tentatively) *lector ex fabula* (implied

reader) literally become contaminated with the illness of insomnia.

For the oneiric citizen of Macondo, the insomnia plague also stages the exhaustive possibilities of postmodernist metafiction:

> Those who wanted sleep, not from fatigue but because of the nostalgia for dreams, tried all kinds of methods of exhausting themselves. They would gather together to converse endlessly, to tell over and over for hours on end the same jokes, to complicate to the limits of exasperation the story about the capon, which was an endless game].

The fictions developed by the insomniacs of Macondo recall John Barth's theorization of postmodernist fiction as '''the literature of exhausted possibility'—or, more chicly, 'the literature of exhaustion''' (''Literature of Exhaustion''). The metafictional implication, of course, is the theorization of a ''literature of replenishment'' (Barth, ''Literature of Replenishment''): the restoration of dream narratives, that is, the metanarratives of the unconscious. But postmodernist metafiction in the insomnia plague does not deliver the panacea; it theorizes the deferral of sleep, the endless game of exhaustion, the automation of insomnia.

Reading the insomnia plague in the context of a magic realist strain of postmodernism, subtended by Lyotard's definition of the postmodern condition as ''incredulity toward metanarratives,'' demonstrates a corrosion of the semiotic chains of signifier and signified, a collapse of metalinguistic systems of referentiality, and a world without access to legitimation of knowledge based on metanarratives about knowledge. Yet meaning is restored to the world by way of Melquíades's panacea, a magical remedy perhaps for the postmodern condition. But the ontology of the panacea is, of course, but a nostalgia for what Derrida calls the *pharmakon* (*Dissemination*).

Reading the insomnia plague in the context of a magic realist strain of postcolonialism requires attention to the specific history of a marginal character—Visitación. That the insomnia plague is the same one which exiled Visitación and her brother Cataure from ''un reino milenario en el cual eran príncipes'' [''an age-old kingdom where they had been prince and princess''] suggests that one mutation of the insomnia plague is the history of European imperialism and colonialism in which the critical manifestation of amnesia (loss of memory) effects the violent erasure and expulsion of indigenous people and their cultures. For Visitación, ''su corazón fatalista le indicaba que la dolencia letal había de perseguirla de todos modos hasta el último rincón de la tierra'' [''her fatalistic heart told her that the lethal sickness would follow her, no matter what, to the farthest corner of the earth'']. For José Arcadio Buendía, ''se trataba de una de tantas dolencias inventadas por las supersticíon de los indígenas'' [''it was just a question of one of the many illnesses invented by the Indian's superstitions'']. Documentation of lethal sickness in colonial history would support Sontag's point that illness is not a metaphor and give evidence to prove that for colonized people illness is neither a metaphor nor a superstition. Yet the fabled representation of ''an age-old kingdom'' foregrounds the fabulous origins of the illness of insomnia and the fabulous narrative of the insomnia plague itself. The dialogic form of magic realism in a postcolonial context, then, incorporates the genre of the fable from an immemorial time in Visitación's age-old indigenous culture. According to Chanady, the incorporated genre of the fable in magic realism also originates in the fabulous tales of explorer narratives. To reiterate Chanady's point, ''magic realism is often defined as the juxtaposition of two different rationalities—the Indian and the European in a syncretic fictitious world-view based on the simultaneous existence of several entirely different cultures in Latin America.'' The double code of the insomnia plague in a postcolonial context thus enlists magic realism in what Rawdon Wilson calls the ''analysis of postcolonial discourse as the mode of a conflicted consciousness, the cognitive map that discloses the antagonism between two views of culture, two views of history . . . and two ideologies.'' Wilson's analysis occasions one final speculation on the double cultural, historical, and ideological code of the insomnia plague: that is, while a colonial strain of the insomnia plague effects Visitación's exile from ''an age-old kingdom,'' it could be argued also that a postcolonial strain of the insomnia plague effects the temporary erasure of the colonial imperialist system of naming. If only for a short spell, as it were, the world of Macondo is suspended in a fabled primordial narrative of namelessness.

Given the strain of colonial imperialism evident in the insomnia plague, the magic realist narrative of ''la peste del banano'' [''the banana plague''] exhibits the exposure of the inhabitants of Macondo to the sociohistorical epidemic of *neo* colonial imperialism. After the construction of the railroad into Macondo by one of Colonel Aureliano Buendía's illegitimate sons, Aureliano Triste, ''no sólo para la modernización de su industria, sino para vincular la

población con el resto del mundo'' [''not only for the modernization of his business but to link the town with the rest of the world''], the town is exposed to what is, in effect, a modern plague of industrialization and neocolonial imperialism. The railroad, as an effective and historically precedented vehicle for neocolonial imperialism, is the catalyst for the banana plague. Moreover, the narrative of the banana plague and the modernization of Macondo by railroad evidences Jameson's definition of magic realism, which ''depends on a content which betrays the overlap or the coexistence of precapitalist with nascent capitalist or technological features.''

As a conduit to multinational corporations, the railroad first brings about the ''invasión'' [''invasion''] and recolonization of Macondo by ''los gringos'' [''the gringos''], which provokes the town-dwellers to speculate on the relation between recolonization and their past experience of the catastrophic effects of civil war:

> There was not much time to think about it, however, because the suspicious inhabitants of Macondo barely began to wonder what the devil was going on when the town had already become transformed into an encampment of wooden houses with zinc roofs inhabited by foreigners who arrived on the train from halfway around the world. . . . Endowed with means that had been reserved for Divine Providence in former times, they changed the pattern of the rains, accelerated the cycle of the harvest, and moved the river from where it had always been and put it with its white stones and icy currents on the other side of the town, behind the cemetery. . . . So many changes took place in such a short time that eight months after Mr. Herbert's visit the old inhabitants had a hard time recognizing their own town].

That the droves of foreigners coming to Macondo by the railroad and occupying the town are described as ''una invasión tan tumultuosa e intempestiva'' [''a tumultuous and intemperate invasion''] invokes a discourse signifying a neocolonialist invasion; this invasion of Macondo, therefore, is a recolonization of colonial space. When the authors of *The Empire Writes Back* argue that ''the construction or demolition of houses or buildings in postcolonial locations is a recurring and evocative figure for the problematic of postcolonial identity,'' it suggests that the neocolonialist invaders settle in Macondo and so transform it into a postcolonial location. For a definition of the postcolonial in such a context, Slemon proposes that ''the concept proves most useful not when it is used synonymously with a post-independence historical period in once-colonized nations but rather when it locates a specifically anti- or *post*-colonial *discursive* purchase in culture, one which begins in the moment that colonial power inscribes itself onto the body and space of its Others'' (''Modernism's Last Post''). Taken together, the invasion of Macondo, the construction of encampments, the rerouting of the river, and the magical alteration of meteorological and seasonal cycles thus signify the inscription of neocolonial imperialism on an already colonial location. The invasion of Macondo even extends into the Buendías' home when ''la invasión de la plebe'' [''the plebeian invasion''] of foreigners comes to inhabit and transform the house into ''un alboroto de mercado'' [''a marketplace''], and thereafter recolonize the home of the ancestral colonizers of Macondo, the House of Buendía. However, as a counter-narrative strategy, García Márquez's defamiliarization of the historical representation of a neocolonial invasion through the narrative discourse of magic realism serves to destabilize rather than monumentalize the history of neocolonial imperialism represented by the invasion of Macondo.

The invasion is only a preliminary symptom of the banana plague, not the plague itself. Instigated by the Buendías' hospitable offer of bananas to Mr. Herbert, who arrives in Macondo as a hot-air balloon businessman and amateur entomologist, the subsequent ''plebeian invasion'' by rail and later land survey by ''un grupo de ingenieros, agrónomos, hidrólogos, topógrafos y agrimensores que durante varias semanas exploration los mismos lugares donde Mr. Herbert cazaba mariposas'' [''a group of engineers, agronomists, hydrologists, topographers, and surveyors who for several weeks explored the places where Mr. Herbert had hunted his butterflies''], leads to the banana company's invasion of Macondo. The banana plague lies dormant for a year following the arrival of Mr. Herbert, after which the invasion of Macondo comes to fruition: ''Había pasado más de un año desde la visita de Mr. Herbert, y lo único que se sabía era que los gringos pensaban sembrar banano en la región encantada que José Arcadio Buendía y sus hombres habían atravesado buscando la ruta de los grandes inventos'' [''More than a year had gone by since Mr. Herbert's visit and the only thing that was known was that the gringos were planning to plant banana trees in the enchanted region that José Arcadio Buendía and his men had crossed in search of the route to the great inventions'']. Just as the great inventions, the products of capitalist industrialization and ideology, arrive by rail, so too do the banana company and the banana plague, the producers and products of neocolonial

imperialism and its ideology. They invade Macondo by the same route. The colonization of ''the enchanted region,'' the barrier isolating the town from the industrial world, thus signifies the exposure of Macondo and its inhabitants to a particular ideological strain of neocolonial imperialism, that is, the banana plague.

The invasion and settlement, exploration and mapping, and later martial government of Macondo by the banana company and its plebeian workers work through the ideology and militant practice of colonial imperialism, though in the modern guise of multinational industrial capitalism. Colonel Aureliano Buendía's planned armed resistance to this neocolonial hegemony—''una conflagración mortal que arrasara con todo vestigio de un régimen de corrupción y de escándalo sostenido por el invasor extranjero'' [''a mortal conflagration that would wipe out the vestiges of a regime of corruption and scandal backed by the foreign invader'']—gestures toward a postcolonial resistance narrative, but remains unrealized for the reason that his ideological position, as a militant civil revolutionary, is virtually powerless against the multinational and anonymous forces backing the new colonizer, the banana company. Colonel Aureliano Buendía's dream of ''la guerra total'' [''the total war''] against the unspecified and unspecifiable ''foreign invader'' is a nostalgic remnant of an outworn ideology. The imperialist ideology of the new world colonizer, symbolized by the House of Buendía, is absorbed and then displaced by the neocolonial imperialist ideology of multinational industrial capitalism, symbolized by the banana company. Hence the naturalization of this neocolonial imperialist ideology in Macondo is signified by its penetration into the quotidian routines of the House of Buendía:

> La fiebre del banano se había apaciguado. Los antiguos habitantes de Macondo se encontraban arrinconados por los advenedizos, trabajosamente asidos a sus precarios recursos de antaño, pero reconfortados en todo caso por la impresión de haber sobrevido a un naufragio. En la casa siguieron recibiendo invitados a almorzar, y en realidad no se restableció la antigua rutina mientras no se fue, años después, la compañía bananera. [The banana fever had calmed down. The old inhabitants of Macondo found themselves surrounded by newcomers and working hard to cling to their precarious resources of times gone by, but comforted in any case by the sense that they had survived a shipwreck. In the house they still had guests for lunch and the old routine was never really set up again until the banana company left years later].

Like a latent disease, the ''banana fever'' settles into remission; its narrative recedes but does not disappear because its carrier is the House of Buendía, whose narrative is *Cien años de soledad*. Diagnosed by his wife Fernanda to be a carrier of "la sarna de los forasteros" ["the rash of the foreigners"], José Arcadio Segundo, who is later employed as a foreman with the banana company, not only infects the House of Buendía with the neocolonial imperialist ideology of banana plague, but also realizes the narrative of resistance against the same ideological strain.

"Illnesses have always been used as metaphors to enliven charges that a society was corrupt or unjust," Sontag writes in the introduction to her analysis of sociopolitical disease metaphors. For instance, Colonel Aureliano Buendía's metaphor of militant resistance that "would wipe out the vestiges of a regime of corruption and scandal backed by the foreign invader" at once deploys the figurative language of a plague, but it simultaneously redeploys the figure in order to attack it, as it were, using the plague metaphor to counteract the sociopolitical conditions of neocolonial imperialism embodied by the banana plague. As a figure of postcolonial discourse, the banana plague carries a politicized narrative of invasion and resistance; it is a socially symbolic narrative of neocolonial imperialist ideology and postcolonial resistance to this ideological strain. However, the enactment of resistance to the sociopolitical corruption and injustice signified by banana plague is, significantly, not carried out by Colonel Aureliano Buendía, but by an actual carrier of the plague, José Arcadio Segundo.

While the former fable of the plague years, the insomnia plague, presents a positive condition of namelessness, a utopian moment of the deinscription of colonial imperialist power, the latter, the banana plague, presents a negative act of erasure, a dystopian moment of the disempowerment and later depopulation of the banana workers. Like the narrative of the insomnia plague, the banana plague narrates a crisis of representation, but in the context of judicial and political discourse, and a loss of referential meaning, in the context of the banana workers' legal demands against the banana company. Reaper-like harbingers of the death of referentiality in the discursive arena of the court, "[l]os decrépitos abogados vestidos de negro que en otro tiempo asediaron al coronel Aurelano Buendía, y que entonces eran apoderados de la compañía bananera, desvirtuaban estos cargos con arbitrios que parecían cosa de magia" ["[t]he decrepit lawyers dressed in black who during other times had besieged Colonel Aureliano Buendía and

who now were controlled by the banana company dismissed those demands with decisions that seemed like acts of magic"]. Masters of illusion and the deferral of meaning, the lawyers represent deft poststructuralist practitioners of judicial discourse; their professional capacity, absorbed into the neocolonial imperialist power structure of the banana company, serves to exercise a sociopolitical hegemony over postcolonial subjects, namely, the banana workers. That the lawyers' "acts of magic" can cloak the neocolonial imperialist reality of the banana company speaks to the danger of discursive fabulation as a rhetorical and narrative device; that is, the reappropriation of magic realism into the judicial discourse of neocolonial imperialism strategically erases and ineffectuates the oppositional narrative discourse of postcolonialism. This discursive erasure of persons through the operations of fabulous judicial processes is evident in the concatenation of events prior to the massacre of the banana workers:

> [The mournful lawyers showed in court that that man had nothing to do with the company and in order that no one doubt their arguments they had him jailed as an impostor. . . . Tired of that hermeneutical delirium, the workers turned away from the authorities in Macondo and brought their complaints up to the higher courts. It was there that the sleight-of-hand lawyers proved that the demands lacked all validity for the simple reason that the banana company did not have, never had had, and never would have workers in its service because they were all hired on a temporary and occasional basis. . . . [A]nd by a decision of the court it was established and set down in solemn decrees that the workers did not exist].

For Slemon, one of the ways in which the postcolonial is distinguished from the postmodern depends upon the different theorization of the referentiality of language. While the postmodern text "necessarily admits a provisionality to its truth-claims," the postcolonial text maintains "a mimetic or referential purchase to textuality," a claim which admits "the positive production of oppositional truth-claims" ("Modernism's Last Post"). However, if the textual referents (contracts, degrees, laws) are governed by a judicial and political system which is controlled by a neocolonial power such as the banana company, the postcolonial purchase to textuality is rendered meaningless and powerless. On the one hand, then, the positive production of oppositional truth-claims subtends the banana workers' contestation of the banana company as a postcolonial resistance narrative; on the other hand, the provisionality of truth-claims underlies the sleight-of-hand lawyers' proof of the non-existence of both Mr. Jack Brown and the banana workers. The lawyers' poststructuralist language games, as a postmodernist strain of magic realist narrative discourse, thus overpower the banana workers' resistance narrative, as a postcolonial strain of magic realist discourse. This double-handed discursive logic ultimately effects the "real" massacre and disappearance of three thousand banana workers who "did not exist."

The prognosis for the banana plague is that of terminal illness. As a historiographic realist narrative—that is, a narrative based on textualized versions of history—the massacre of the banana workers might have terminated with the dissemination of "un bando nacional extraordinario, para informar que los obreros habían obedecido la orden de evacuar la estación, y se dirigían a sus casas in caravanas pacíficas" ["an extraordinary proclamation to the nation which said that the workers had left the station and returned home in peaceful groups"]. Such a narrative, an official record of history sanctioned by the neocolonial imperialist agenda of the banana company, would have erased the other narrative of three thousand banana workers, massacred, then stacked and exported "en el orden y el sentido en que se transportaban los racimos de banano" ["in the same way in which they transported bunches of bananas"]. The collision between these two narratives, one of official neocolonialist history and the other of unofficial postcolonialist history, creates a discursive situation in which both of the separate narratives are rent by silences, absences, and gaps in that each is negated by the existence of the other. Magic realist narrative discourse allows for the coexistence of such contradictory narratives of history. In the postmodernist strain of magic realism, Linda Hutcheon would describe this crisis of representation as "historiographic metafiction"—insofar as the banana massacre narrativizes the construction of historical narratives (although this designation would be dependent upon the textual referent of official history, that is, the neocolonial imperialist textualization of history). In the postcolonial strain of magic realism, conversely, I would posit José Arcadio Segundo's unofficial account of the history of the banana company as a postcolonial resistance narrative. José Arcadio Segundo, the only survivor of the massacre, lives to pass on to Aureliano Babilonia, the last Buendía, "una interpretación tan personal de lo que significó para Macondo la compañía bananera, que muchos años después, cuando Aureliano se incorporara al mundo, había

de pensarse que contaba una versión alucinada, porque era radicalmente contraria a la falsa que los historiodores habían admitido, y consagrado en los textos escolares" ["such a personal interpretation of what the banana company had meant to Macondo that many years later, when Aureliano became part of the world, one would have thought that he was telling a hallucinated version, because it was radically opposed to the false one that historians had created and consecrated in the schoolbooks]. What the foregoing attests is how the magic realist text stages a crisis of representation in which the double discourse of postmodernist and postcolonialist narratives, official and unofficial histories, acts out its contestations and contradictions.

Turning back to the final pages of *Cien años de soledad,* which I have already interpreted in terms of a postmodernist code of textualization, an alternate thesis presents itself and a reading in terms of a postcolonial decoding of historical, colonial narrative. In these final pages Aureliano Babilonia deciphers Melquíades's parchments to reveal the historical conditions of colonialism, that is, the absurd history of Sir Francis Drake attacking Riohacha and hunting alligators with cannons and stuffing them as trophies for Queen Elizabeth, which predicates the narrative of the House of Buendía: "Sólo etonces descubrió que Amaranta Ursula no era su hermana, sino su tía, y que Francis Drake había asaltado a Riohacha solamente para que ellos pudieran buscarse por los labernitos más intrincados de la sangre, hasta engendrar el animal mitológico que había de poner término a la estirpe" ["Only then did he discover that Amaranta Ursula was not his sister but his aunt, and that Sir Francis Drake had attacked Riohacha only so that they could seek each other through the most intricate labyrinths of blood until they would engender the mythological animal that was to bring the line to the end"]. In brief, Aureliano Babilonia's decipherment of the parchments decodes both the *arche* (origin) and *telos* (terminus) of the historical narratives of the House of Buendía and of colonialism. Beyond the code of colonialism hovers the postcolonial possibility, beyond the threshold of the magic realist text, as it were, in the unwritten absence, gap, and silence left after the decoding of the colonial code and the eradication of the House of Buendía: "Sin embargo, antes de llegar al verso final ya había compredido que no saldría jamás de ese cuarto, pues estaba previsto que la ciudad de los espejos (o los espejismos) sería arrasada por el viento y desterrada de la memoria de los hombres en el instante eu que Aureliano Babilonia acabara de descifrar los pergaminos, y que todo lo escrito, en ellos era irrepetible desde siempre y para siempre, porque las estirpes condenadas a cien años de soledad no tenían una segunda oportunidad sobre la tierra'' [''Before reaching the final line, however, he had already understood that he would never leave that room, for it was foreseen that the city of mirrors (or mirages) would be wiped out by the wind and exiled from the memory of men at the precise moment when Aureliano Babilonia would finish deciphering the parchments, and that everything written on them was unrepeatable since time immemorial and forever more, because races condemned to one hundred years of solitude did not have a second opportunity on earth'']. As both *arche* and *telos,* the final paragraph of the novel reflects upon the unnamed world in the opening paragraph: *Cien años de soledad* is indeed a city of mirrors, a *mise en abíme.* As the colonial narrative of the House of Buendía, Melquíades's parchments (and *Cien años de soledad*) mirror the colonial narrative of Melquíades's tribe, for the Buendías (''exiled from the memory of men'') are likewise ''borrada de la faz de la tierra for haber sobrepassado los limites del conocimiento humano'' [''wiped off the face of the earth because they had gone beyond the limits of human knowledge'']. After Aureliano Babilonia's final act of decoding Melquíades's parchments, the ''exile'' of the House of Buendía and the erasure of colonial history impose closure upon one narrative and open the possibility for postcolonial narrative.

To rearticulate Slemon's theorization of the confrontation between two oppositional discourses—that is, an encounter in which ''each remains suspended, locked in a continuous dialectic with the 'other,' a situation which creates disjunction within each of the separate discursive systems, rending them with gaps, absences, and silences'' (''Magic Realism'')—also reiterates the agon I have tried to mediate between the strains of postcolonialism and postmodernism and the gaps between their separate discursive systems. Because of the very difficulties theorists have with the term magic realism, it has often been considered a ''theoretical void'' (González Echevarría, ''Isla a su vuelo fugitiva''). But magic realism read through a double code of postmodernism and postcolonialism facilitates, if not a unilateral agreement between oppositional discourses, then an arbitration of aporias and theoretical voids.

Source: Dean J. Irvine, ''Fables of the Plague Years: Postcolonialism, Postmodernism, and Magical Realism in 'Cien anos de soledad,''' in *ARIEL,* Vol. 29, No. 4, October, 1998, pp. 53–80.

Wayne Fields

In the following essay on Gabriel Garcia Marquez's One Hundred Years of Solitude, *author Wayne Fields explores the ideal of the American epic in the context of Mircea Eliade's ideas of the sacred and the profane* (Cosmos and Chaos), *and suggests that Marquez's* One Hundred Years of Solitude *illustrates and fulfills the quest for the epic literature of the ''paradise of disaster.''*

1.

Mircea Eliade begins *Cosmos and Chaos,* his study of archaic ontology, with a discussion of archetypes and repetition. Premodern societies, he claims, validate their own world and experience by seeing them as repeating elements consecrated by ''gods, ancestors, or heroes'' in some ancient past.

> The world that surrounds us, then, the world in which the presence and the work of man are felt—the mountains that he climbs, populated and cultivated regions, navigable rivers, cities, sanctuaries—all these have an extraterrestrial archetype, be it conceived as a plan, as a form, or purely and simply as a ''double'' existing on a higher cosmic level. But everything in the world that surrounds us does not have a prototype of this kind. For example desert regions inhabited by monsters, uncultivated lands, unknown seas on which no navigator has dared to venture, do not share with the city of Babylon, or the Egyptian nome, the privilege of a differentiated prototype. They correspond to a mythical model, but of another nature: all these wild, uncultivated regions and the like are assimilated to chaos; they still participate in the undifferentiated, formless modality of pre-Creation. This is why, when possession is taken of a territory—that is, when its exploitation begins—rites are performed that symbolically repeat the act of Creation: the uncultivated zone is first ''cosmicized,'' then inhabited.

In other words, a place must first be made a *place* before it can be occupied, and that act of location is itself a calling out of chaos like the biblical creation. But for Americans, even late Twentieth century Americans, such views of the world and such founding rituals lie nearer at hand than ancient cultures. In a culture replete with ''cosmicizing'' efforts—rituals of opening shopping centers, dedicating public buildings, and ground breaking for future housing developments—we know ''the innumerable gestures of consecretion,'' and can affirm Eliade's conviction that, at the center of it all, lies the need for a center.

The act of centering has endless analogies in human experience, contemporary as well as ancient, but its fundamental value whether supplied by household gods or Mecca or political ideology is that it

> "This is why, when possession is taken of a territory—that is, when its exploitation begins—rites are performed that symbolically repeat the act of Creation: the uncultivated zone is first 'cosmicized,' then inhabited."

allows us to be someplace in a world of flux. It is that around which the cosmos radiates, assumes shape; it is the artifice which makes things meaningful. Even though in Eliade's schema each act of "consecration" declares, in one sense, another center, it more profoundly aligns this site with the *one* center that transcends space as ritual transcends time, affirming that all sacred space is central just as all sacred time is eternal.

> Thus the reality and the enduringness of a construction are assured not only by the transformation of profane space into transcendent space (the center) but also by the transformation of concrete time into mythical time. Any ritual whatever. . .unfolds not only in a consecrated space (i.e., one different is essence from profane space) but also in "sacred time," "once upon a time" (*in illo tempore, ab origine*), that is, when the ritual was performed for the first time by a god, an ancestor, or a hero.

This assumes validation from outside: human actions receive their meaning (and sacred in Eliade's construct implies meaningful while profane designates meaningless, like their companion terms cosmos and chaos) from the gods, and earthly locations become located by aligning them with transcendent geography. The consecrating priest declares the investment of meaning based on imitation and repetition. Authority lies behind that repetition in the god or hero who was its primary author.

2.

Few challenges are so great as that of being some place, being centered, in a new world. The inventiveness with which our European ancestors addressed this dilemma is at once the most impressive and the most outrageous aspect of the entire impressive and outrageous American experience.

Having fallen off the edge of their maps, old explorers rarely admitted to being lost but instead found themselves in the most remarkable of non-places, or rather—to be more precise—on the road to these non-places. Defying both geography and cosmology they proudly declared themselves only so many days march from the Amazon women, or the cities of gold, or the fountain of youth, or the Northwest Passage, or the earthly paradise. As a general rule they died or returned home convinced that they had, in fact, approached that magical place which could locate them and their ambitions in a significant context. Thus were established two enduring patterns in new world behavior: the first, having gotten hopelessly lost—whether geographically or politically—to declare oneself only so many days from the place of the heart's desire; and the second locate oneself through narrative rather than surveying equipment. The old myths took on new possibilities here: the old epics, Israel's as well as Rome's, could be reenacted once more. The first instinct then was to declare this a new world and then center it in terms of the old. But the struggle to be somewhere in America, to find a center, has been and continues to be an issue of great import. Yet for a variety of complicated reasons, dislocation persists as a new world problem. Economic and political ideologues, religionists and believers in any number of truths, compete with the most enduring of the old myths, offering a variety of expressions of the sacred by which we may locate ourselves and our countries. There is no shortage of people willing to tell us not only *where* we are but *who* we are.

Early in the Nineteenth century, literary nationalists in the United States cried out for an American epic that would legitimize this small collection of people scattered along the Eastern seaboard of North America by portraying a heroic future for them. The United States was less than impressive in the years after revolution and independence, and the literary nationalists demanded a story which told where they were going, and that established their significance in terms of what lay ahead. But typically they insisted this be at once a uniquely American literary creation, and one that satisfied all the tastes and expectations of smug Europe: an *Aeneid*, preferably, with a Columbus, or perhaps even a Washington or a Jefferson as its hero (though Columbus was the early favorite). This new world Aeneas, or so the most enlightened of them thought, was to be directed by personal vision rather than manipulated blindly by gods and could thus reveal the history that lay ahead, could project the America wich now awaited in time rather than geography. Ironically they longed for an epic with the future not the past as its subject matter. The appeal of the literary nationalists, while sometimes answered by poets, gained its most dramatic response from politicians all too eager to serve as national visionaries and to claim the destined American as the authority for their careers and as the answer to these persistent new world questions, where are we and who are we, the center being their political doctrine, their party or even their person. Too, there were increasingly the champions of the Self, the individual who as "the American, this new man," himself a liberated and liberating god, could act as his own center, ordering all that he surveyed. Daniel Boone, Cooper's Leatherstocking, and the transcendentalists "I" are all versions of this response.

But even as visionary politicians orated and Emerson lectured, another literature persisted in the United States, a literature rooted in the ironic distance separating the grandiose claims of American boosters and hucksters—starting with Columbus—and the everyday realities of life in this place. In this literature there was a good deal less certainty that a "center" was so close at hand, and, not surprisingly it was most prominent along the frontier where the discrepancy between a romantic view of America collided most violently with brutal facts of life at the edge of dislocation. When stories from this tradition began to appear in print, they were in many respects parodies of the more famous new world accounts which preceded them, and by the 1840s and the 1850s, they often presented full blown repudiations of orthodox renderings—political, philosophical, and literary—of the American experience. Two elements, apparently contradictory, thus provide essential ingredients for these stories: a sense of the outrageous and an overriding emphasis on physical reality.

In its most extreme form this literature has often been labeled the tall tale, a designation encouraged by the matter of fact use of exaggeration. This "tallness" is directly related to the grandiose claims that have been made on America's behalf since the first voyages of discovery and serves two quite different ends. On the one hand, it mocks those boastful voices, the voices of new world enthusiasts, whether grandiloquent politicians, exuberant land developers, or romantic philosophers, and, on the other celebrates the capacity of a real frontier people to live with a minimum of illusion. The America of these stories is neither the new Eden nor the new Rome. It is a world stripped down to essentials, a world where the real with all its rough edges is not concealed, a world in which, apart from the conventions of polite society, people are tested by a radical disorder. In so much as these people prevail, it is not because they become nature's nobility, nor because they are so brutish as not to be troubled by the kind of world they live in or because they find some source of amusement, order, even redemption in this context.

The literary antecedents so influential on the work of Twain and Faulkner are the writings of a group of frontier circuit lawyers and newspaper editors usually identified as Southwestern humorists. The settings for their stories were backwoods Georgia, Alabama, Mississippi, and Arkansas, and their central characters were the confidence men and storytellers who plied their trade in the new settlements of those regions. In this landscape, the first wave of civilization fronts directly on the disorder of a wilderness—cosmos fronts against chaos—a wilderness that is both physical and psychological, and the literature of the Southwestern humorists gains its subject matter from that confrontation. The confidence man Simon Suggs—whose motto is "it's good to be sneaky in a new country"—and the trickster/storyteller Sut Lovingood (who, along with Suggs, provides the genealogy of Faulkner's Snopes tribe) lack all the illusions of genteel society and are themselves, at least in their social relationship, agents of disorder. They overcome the first tentative representatives of authority—judges, politicians, land developers, and ministers—manipulating the pretension of the lofty and undoing the very order those dignitaries were meant to affirm. As Kenneth Lynn has remarked in *Mark Twain and Southwestern Humor* (Boston, 1959): "...when we view men and events through the glittering eye of the confidence man, we are 'in his world,' where no moral reference point exists; seen through the glass of the Suggsian consciousness, humanity has not the slightest dignity, while such terms as harmony, unity, stability...are exposed as empty mockeries."

This is literature from the edge of the world, where no center has yet been discerned or imposed—American in the most radical application of that term. A promiscuous literature made up of persons, actions, even language that would be discarded or repressed in proper society, it flaunts rather than conceals the low whether in bodily functions or in social types. It strives to get to the bottom line, to burrow under everything, the politicians' smug words, the minister's abstract morality, and the women's skirts. Or to make quicker work of it all, the trickster of Southwestern humor doesn't burrow under but blows up and then watches as the world flies out from beneath its pretensions and reveals its truest nature.

The only principle of order that does not break down in the trickster's explosive presence is that of story itself, and it is significant that he is often (as in Lovingood's case) teller as well as trickster, holding in himself the violent tension that lies at the heart of new world experience. He is the fool killer as the American in one guise always claims to be destroying all that is grandiose and self-righteous in America itself. But at the same time he also suggests (but only suggests) the very fragile power of story to provide, in place of the false "truths" he exposes, some other basis for coherence, some other basis for community.

It is this possibility that Mark Twain expands in his best stories. In "Jim Blaine's Grandfather's Old Ram," for example, Twain combines the effort of the fool killer with a celebration of the storyteller's art, but in contrast with the creators of Lovingood and Suggs, with greater emphasis on the latter. The subjects of these tales are inevitably people who live without either grand illusions or despair. Typical is Miss Wagner, the old woman who we are told is missing an eye but who borrows her neighbor's glass substitute whenever she entertains. The glass eye is too small and so has to be packed in cotton when used for formal wear by Miss Wagner. And being blind on that side, she tends to get the eye in wrong side outward as often as not, presenting the green backside to the world. But even when she gets it in properly, because it is yellow, it never matches her own blue eye. As the storyteller continues describing Miss Wayne matter of factly—as though there were nothing unusual in any of this—he in turn informs us that she is also missing a leg and is forced to borrow the artificial limb of a much shorter neighbor, and is bald, relying on yet another neighbor for the loan of a wig. If there are elements here of the grotesque that mark Southwestern humor's elaborate descriptions of physical infirmity, there is none of its mocking of the victims, none of the humiliation that serves as its primary goal. Rather, there is about Miss Wagner—and the many similar folk that move through Twain's best stories—an attractiveness, a nobility that is more impressive than the outrageous afflictions they have suffered. If under the clothing of the self-righteous minister or the pompous politician or the inflated banker there is a repulsive body, emblematic of a repulsive character, behind the false eye and beneath the borrowed wig, the mutilated Miss Wagner admirably endures, borrowing all those spare parts that she might continue to live as fully as possible. The outrageous fortune that has maimed her is absurd, but not Miss Wagner; it is fortune, or life itself, and not the old woman that is the butt of Twain's comedy.

In the other anecdotes that make up "Jim Blaine's Grandfather's Old Ram," only the undertaker, death's surrogate, is personally humiliated. The others—the man who rises up at his own funeral to complain about the coffin, Uncle Lem, on whom the Irish laborer falls, and the widow of the man nipped up by a carpet-making machine—these, like Miss Wagner, do the best they can in an outrageous world. The violence in their stories does not come from a fool killer, though it may in fact have killed many forms of foolishness, but from life, and the best of them respond by muddling through as well as they can rather than by surrendering. The widow, who buys the fourteen yards of three ply carpeting containing the mortal remains of her late husband, does so in an effort to prevent the indignity from going any farther, keeps the carpet from being cut and presents it for the funeral unfolded, unspindled and without further mutilation. If her effort to do the best she can by her husband only increases the absurdity, *she* nonetheless reclaims what she can from an absurd world.

The only heroic activity available to Twain's characters is to make do under the outrageous circumstances in which they find themselves. Inevitably, then, the only work of promise is that of making—and ultimately the making of stories—not for ethereal stuff, but from the awful and apparently insignificant matter that makes up real human life. Storytelling in this context takes on new significance and becomes a means of living without an absolute center, of living without the "sacred." Strange as it may seem for a teller of tall tales to speak indignantly against literary liars, when Twain levels his attacks, as he regularly does, against the Sir Walter Scotts and James Fenimore Coopers, he does so because he is convinced they have misrepresented the basic terms on which people must live, that they offer illusions of a world that intrinsically makes sense, when, for Twain, all sense is the hard won and transitory victory of craft, in particular, that of the storyteller. The teller he respects is the one who redeems something from life, much as Miss Wagner does, without misrepresenting it. The exaggerations of the tall tale, according to Twain, only confirms the basic absurdity of human experience whereas narratives in which righteousness is predictably victorious and wickedness predictably punished are offences against ''real'' life in the world. Jim Blaine, like Twain's other storytellers, manages to create memorable stories from characters who conventionally would be dismissed as insignificant, laughter out of what invites despair, and more remarkably, beauty from a language rejected by educated and polite society as vulgar and offensive. Denied the sacred he adopts the human and declares it sufficient to his own needs. This is the challenge to one line of new world act: denied the earthly paradise, the shining cities, to make something of what has in fact been found, all the corrupt, innocent, ugly, beautiful chaos of an uncentered new world.

3.

When, midway in *One Hundred Years of Solitude*, Aureliano Segundo searches for Fernanda, ''it was,'' we are told, ''an act of impossible fate, because in the confusion of her indignation, in the fury of her shame, she lied to him so that he would never know her real identity.'' Still he searches unceasingly, with the same unswerving zeal with which all generations of Buendias pursue their hearts' desires, their own ''centers.''

> When he asked for the most beautiful woman who had even been seen on earth, all the women brought him their daughters. He became lost in misty byways, in times reserved for oblivion, in labyrinths of disappointment. He crossed a yellow plain where the echo repeated one's thought and where anxiety brought in premonitory mirages. After sterile weeks he came to an unknown city where all the bells were tolling a dirge. Although he had never seen them and no one had ever described them to him he immediately recognized the walls eaten away by bone salt, the broken down wooden balconies gutted by fungus, and nailed to the outside door, almost erased by rain, the saddest cardboard sign in the world: ''Funeral Wreaths for Sale.''

There he finds the object of his search, of his desire, and says the narrator, ''For Aureliano Segundo it was almost simultaneously the beginning and the end of happiness.''

It is striking how similar the journals of New World explorers are, and how completely the many quests and searches of *One Hundred Years of Solitude* evoke those older accounts that begin in exultant hope, proceed with almost inconceivable tenacity, and end in mourning. Pursuing the center which will at last prove definitive and absolute, which will finally free them, the explorers either

stop short, still so many days march away, or, finding the center, as Aureliano Segundo does, discover it will not hold. These ''labyrinths of disappointment'' lie at the heart of new world experiences—not because disappointment is unique to this landscape, but because the American has carried all the old hope for a place beyond disappointment. Nor is it because there has been only disappointment here, but because when the old aspiration (one not altogether yielded even by the best of us) was for the earthly paradise, all else seems diminished by comparison. Columbus promised the Garden of Eden; it is hard to settle for Disneyland.

One Hundred Years of Solitude is at last the only appropriate response to that old plea for an American epic. It seems to be, even as the literary nationalists had hoped, a new world version of the *Aeneid*. It begins in an effort, familiar in our America, to undo history, to escape ghosts of past failure, to leave behind death, and to begin afresh, not merely in a new house or a new job but in a new age and as a new civilization—inevitably as a new world. So the party led by the original Jose Arcadio Buendia enters a terrain still in the throes of creation, a great swampy universe covered by ''an eternal vegetable scum,'' a primordial world awaiting shape, the ''uncosmocized'' realm of Eliade's chaos. In this expedition Buendia's party passes through ''enchanted'' regions, ''a universe of grief,'' a world of ''eternal sadness'' even as they seem both to escape from and to be captured by history. ''The men on the expedition,'' the narrator tells us, ''felt overwhelmed by their most ancient memories in that paradise of dampness and silence, going back to before original sin, as their boots sank into pools of steaming oil and their machetes destroyed bloody lilies and golden salamanders.'' So many voices of other travelers echo through this passage, as throughout the whole novel, voices of the ancient voyagers as well as of the new world explorers who enter enchanted regions and found in them a paradise of despair. The lush promise of Columbus' Eden, the wonders of Montezuma's kingdom are present here but brilliantly combined with the threat of ultimate dislocation which haunts early accounts of America: Coronado contemplating the prairie, an environment in which men on horseback are quickly lost to one another except for shouts and the clatter of metal; or, even more appropriately, Cabeza de Vaca lamenting a Florida in which it is possible to be someplace only in death. The passage, too, recalls those individuals and families in Fenimore Cooper's stories, who seek a neutral territory, free from old constraints, and, even more poignantly, the long line of frontier mystics, like the mythologized Boone, who knew they were in Kentucky (or some other fabled place) only because they were no longer any place else. Note as well how similar the landscape here is to the place in which the hero of Faulkner's *The Bear* sees Old Ben for the first time. This is *terra incognita*. Having eluded at last the old (even original sin), the Buendia party finds itself in the oldest, the primal, as it cuts its way through flora and fauna of an unfallen world. And, of course, it is here that the Spanish galleon, freighted with flowers, appears: the ultimate icon of the new world. "When they woke up," and it is as though they have been born anew to enter the world Adam-like,

> . . . with the sun high in the sky, they were speechless with fascination. Before them, surrounded by ferns and palm trees, white and powdery in the silent morning light, was an enormous Spanish galleon. Tilted slightly to the starboard, it had hanging from its intact masts the dirty rags of its sails in the midst of its rigging, which was adorned with orchids. The hull, covered with an armor of petrified barnacles and soft moss, was firmly fastened into a surface of stones. The whole structure seemed to occupy its own space, one of solitude and oblivion, protected from the vices of time and the habits of birds. Inside, where the expeditionaries explored with careful intent, there was nothing but a thick forest of flowers.

Beautiful and useless—it is four days removed from the sea—the galleon is set apart in "its own space" and removed from "the vices of time," is no more a part of America's world than of Europe's. It is vision brilliant and fragile, but one which cannot "center" us, for it only reminds us of how centerless everything in fact is. That it, itself, will be corrupted by discovery is verified when many years later, lying beside a "regular mail route," the ship is only a burned out frame in a field of poppies.

But these passages quoted from *One Hundred Years of Solitude* bear little stylistic resemblance to the writings either of Mark Twain or the Southwestern humorists. Rather the descriptions of the galleon and of the regions surrounding Macondo are reminiscent of a much older form of storytelling, the fairy tale—a genre whose influence on García Márquez is abundantly clear in "A Very Old Man with Enormous Wings" and "The Handsomest Drowned Man in the World." Like the Lovingood stories and "Jim Blaine's Grandfather's Old Ram," this is a tradition rooted in an oral folk culture, but unlike the latter it is primarily a literature of enchantment, indulging the regular cadences, the polished phrases, the hypnotizing tone which Twain

and his predecessors regarded as dangerous, the romancer's seductive devices, too far removed from real talk and real life to be trusted. The angular dialect of a narrator like Jim Blaine, by conventional standards, is anti-literary, but the discursive, disjointed, and rough metered Southwestern humor consciously repudiates fairy stories—championing a new world, disenchanted in tongue as well as vision.

The great strength of Twain's stories comes from their preoccupation with particularity. Suspicious of all abstractions, their author focuses on the specific, the idiosyncratic both of character and dialect. Thus his finest creations, Huck Finn most of all, seem fully realized and unique. But at its extreme this preoccupation with the particular threatens any effort at coherence, wholeness, just as the trickster threatens all social and moral order. It regards anything large or epic with suspicion and whittles it down to less intimidating size. The most significant of Southwestern humor is, therefore, its ability to overturn presumption, to free us from the grandiose schemes to which Americans have always been dangerously susceptible. As a consequence, apart from his celebrations of the Mississippi River, Twain found it impossible to speak of any grandeur. That which was conventionally thought noble, he debunked—old world masters, the ruins of Rome, Shakespeare's plays, United States' foreign policy. Other Western travelers praised the grizzly bear and giant sequoias. Twain spoke for the jackass rabbit and sagebrush. Others praised Sir Walter Scott. Twain upheld the illiterate storytellers of Nevada mining camps.

But jackass rabbits and sagebrush are not golden salamanders and bleeding lilies. Nor is there anything else allowed in Twain's work which suggests the America of enticement, the America that has led so many so far. In part because that enticement—in some of its most corrupt and corrupting forms—had enormous power over his own life, Twain turned away from all grandeur, adhering to the principle proclaimed in *Roughing It* that nothing that glitters is gold, and fixed his eyes on the common as much for safety as for principle. In this way he refused to pander to the literary nationalists' call for an American epic that would declare us a new race creating a new history, but he also made it impossible to fully explore the new world experience by turning away from the visions and dreams which, though they may have lacked validity, have lacked neither power nor consequences.

The Columbiad that the first generation of United States intellectuals so desperately desired comes, ironically, from Columbia, but as the Buendiad, an epic that recreates the history of the new world in Macondo, a history that is a fiction, or rather an elaborate anthology of fictions, of endless recurrence in which the deepest and most impossible desires become obsessions of such all-consuming strength that everything else—including "reality"—becomes unreal. The world of the Buendiad is radically new, requiring the rediscovery of the earth's roundness, and the reinvention of time, and that one great Edenic task that Americans reenact with an apparently inexhaustible delight—naming things. This is a world owing as much to the alchemist's shop as to expeditions of discovery, and which, without the golden salamanders, the bleeding lilies, the clouds of butterflies, the dazzling birds, could never convincingly suggest all the yearnings that have called America into being. In this regard the Southwestern humorists and Twain can only make us seem petty and foolish in our corruption, but *One Hundred Years of Solitude* realizes the terrible depth of our longings and generates a profound and terrifying vision of our aspirations and of the folly to which they will lead.

With the Buendias we enter first a world of enchantment, for that is the true beginning of America, and it is precisely because this world is fully realized that we move painfully and wonderfully into the world of disenchantment (though these are not, finally, discrete or sequential movements).

The young man who watches Remedios the Beauty as she bathes illustrates the danger of enchantment, a danger that has not changed since the time when people lived in fairy tales. Having crawled out on the thinnest edge of his obsession, the young man falls, breaking his head on the reality of the bathroom floor. In a book which provides an endless succession of centers, a virtual catalogue of human aspirations, Remedios the Beauty's would-be lover is only one of the many who are entranced and undone, like the sailors ruined by those "soft-skinned cetaceans" with the heads and torsos of women. Many of these obsessions, dreams, visions, illusions—call them what you will—are familiar to students of the new world: a new city, gold, a technological breakthrough, reform, beauty, power—the promised rewards of conquistadores, political savants, land developers, romantic philosophers, even academic grant seekers, all the visionaries who move through our past and our present, representing the truth that will set us free, the vision that will

make all things clear. Only in the history of the new world offered in *One Hundred Years of Solitude*, like that portrayed by Twain and his predecessors in the United States, all these betray us, the grandest of them, as well as the meanest. No progress is apparent. When Jose Arcadio, equipped with his new science, goes out to look for gold, he unearths the rusted armor of a Fifteenth-century gold seeker, and it rings most hollow when struck. At last the man who chases many dreams is tied to a tree, a grotesque parody of the centering act.

Every element of Southwestern humor's disenchantment is contained in *One Hundred Years of Solitude*, is made—incredibly—more outrageous, more inflated. In Macondo the flatulence is "flower withering," the vomit "leech filled," the fornication pursued with an energy beyond the wildest aspirations of a Lovingood. The insects and lizards that force the pompous out of their clothing in Sut's tricks here come in swarms undermining foundations and invading, not clothing alone, but flesh itself, and beyond that, the soul. Even the explosions of the earlier literature, the greatest accomplishment of the Southwestern fool-filler, cannot compare with Aureliano Segundo's slaughter yard—"an eternal execution ground of bones and innards, a mud pit of leftovers" where "they had to keep exploding dynamite bombs all the time so that the buzzards could not pluck out the guest's eyes." And of course Aureliano Segundo's efforts cannot compare with the obscene violence of economics and politics: the twice murdered 3000. When the machine guns open fire it seemed at first, we are told, "a farce."

> It was as if the machine guns had been loaded with caps, because their panting rattle could be heard and their incandescent spitting could be seen but not the slightest reactions was perceived, not a cry, not even a sigh among the compact crowd that seemed petrified by an instantaneous invulnerability. Suddenly, on one side of the station, a cry of death tore open the enchantment...

But in fact the enchantment is never broken and that is the genius of the book; just as *One Hundred Years of Solitude* is simultaneously nearly every new world story, it is simultaneously enchanting and disenchanting. The cry of death, "Aaaagh, Mother," may for a moment cut through rhythms of enchantment just as the anti-poetic voice of a Lovingood or a Twain narrator does with its discordant sounds, the locating power of a particular voice, but the narration of the novel remains unchanged and the cry is swallowed up by the powerful, impersonal incantation of the enchanter/narrator. "A seismic voice, a volcanic breath, the roar of a cataclysm broke out in the center of the crowd with a great potential for expansion. Jose Arcadio Segundo barely had time to pick up the child while the mother with the other one was swallowed up by the crowd that swirled about in panic." So it is with Aureliano Babilonia who, reading what we are reading, is overwhelmed by the cries of disenchantment which run through the text but is, nonetheless, hopelessly enchanted by the gypsy's book.

We get in the letters of Columbus both the garden and the chains, but they come at different moments and in different contexts. In *One Hundred Years of Solitude* they are contained in the same moment, every moment, the paradise always a "paradise of disaster." All the promises of the first New World explorers—the first of America's tall tale artists—are kept here, even the most incredible. This is Columbus' garden but its most Adam and Eve-like occupants are the incestuous aunt and nephew who appear at the end rather than the beginning and who recognize in themselves the cannibals Columbus in un-Edenic moments feared might inhabit these regions. Here too is Montezuma's wonderful palace, sometimes hinted at in the labyrinth of rooms in which the Buendias live, whose most remarkable feature, the chambers filled with birds and animals, are perpetuated in Macondo's zoological brothel.

Near the end, when what was future when the Spanish galleon first appeared has become the past, the burden becomes unbearable. For the last Aureliano what lies behind us in the book is a "past whose annihilation, consuming itself from within, ending at every moment but never ending its ending." All is at last being undone. The town deserted by the Catalonian who dismisses his once-loved books as "all that shit" and abandons them, then by the others who gathered in the bookstore across from the house where dreams were interpreted when the town still held dreamers. Even as Macondo is depopulated, reports come from Alvaro of other Americas where people go on as though nothing were happening, like the girl in the red sweater sitting beside a lake in Michigan, waving "out of hope, because she did not know that she was watching a train with no return passing by"—not Alvaro's train alone but her own as well.

At last there is only the final Aureliano reading the Gypsy's book, the book which we are reading and in which he is a character, reading toward his own annihilation which only we can prevent by not reading on to the end. But we read on—on through the final disillusionment, to the final line and ultimate dislocation.

Nothing is left. Not the Catalonian's library, not the Buendia house, not friends, not ideologies or theologies or theories of history, all those familliar touchstones that can locate us somewhere and declare us someone. We are told "it was foreseen that the city of mirrors (mirages) would be wiped out by the wind and exiled from the memory of men at the precise moment when Aureliano Babilonia would finish deciphering the parchments and that everything written on them was unrepeatable since time immemorial and forever more, because races condemned to one hundred years of solitude did not have a second opportunity on earth."

If *One Hundred Years of Solitude* is, as I have suggested, an epic of the new world, then it is an apocalyptic one, Macondo—America—destroyed by the absence of a center just as the cyclone, which has as its heart a vacuum, pulls everything apart. But this is, as we are reminded at every turn, a story and—like the other new world epic *Moby Dick* (which it resembles down to its cyclonic close)—more than that, a story built on innumerable other stories. Here the violence surpasses anything the Southwestern tricksters ever invented, and yet the story holds together, coheres as everything else unravels. Its echoes of fairy tales, the most obviously storied of all our fictions, its elaborate patterns that dance in intricate spirals from beginning to end, insist on an order even in apocalypse. Akin to Twain's stories, the demand in *One Hundred Years of Solitude* is that we live without illusion. And, with Twain's stories, there is amusement and delight even as we approach the last terrible word. But here, where the news is worse than anything poor Miss Wagner ever confronted the crafting must be exquisite. Nothing here is real, nothing unreal. All is story.

How do we live in a world that is uncentered, that has no truth by which things may be ordered? We tell stories, just as new world people at their wisest and most desperate have done from the beginning. It would be, and has often been, a terrible mistake to believe our stories, to make them truths, but it would be equally mistaken to give them up. In contrast to myth as Eliade describes it, story comes in the absence of the sacred authenticating presence. When the gods have fallen silent and men no longer have a single other worldly truth to validate and locate them, then the storytelling begins, finding its authority in the human rather than the divine. In this act the teller becomes a center—not *the* center for if such a thing existed we would need only priests and not stories—his story radiating out from him, anchored in this world only by his human presence. In the same way his audience clusters around him, pulling those in the radius of his voice into a kind of temporary community, a temporary order. In contrast to myth, storytelling is a human acivity that, as Walter Benjamin has suggested, gains its authority from the transient nature of human existence. The centering it offers may resemble that attributed by the ancients to their deities but the resemblance is only superficial since story finally celebrates human meanings rather than divine truths. Story is, as Twain understood, a way of making do in the absence of certainty; its center marks not the location of a divine action, but the artificial and arbitrary creation of a being always on the verge of dislocation, even extinction. It does not altogether assert cosmos, but nonetheless it is a calling out of chaos. It does not piously mark an already existing center, but creates one that did not previously exist, one that endures only so long as the story itself is being told.

The conclusion to *One Hundred Years of Solitude* can be read as the ultimate dislocation, the final outcome of living in a world that lacks a center. But the delight in shaping that informs every turn of the novel has not been a false pleasure. Nor has everything disappeared in the apocalypse, for the book remains, its ending no truer or more real than its beginning, though just as meaningful. The only reality is the teller's voice, the greatest affirmation the telling—the haunting voice of the gypsy alchemist who has at last found the gold in America. This is not the truth but an exquisite example of what honest tellers can make in a new world, a culmination of a long search carried on through an American literature and an American history.

Source: Wayne Fields, ''One Hundred Years of Solitude and New World Storytelling,'' in *Latin American Literary Review,* Vol. XIV, No. 27, January–June, 1986, pp. 73–88.

L. Robert G. Vela

In the following essay on Gabriel Garcia Marquez's One Hundred Years of Solitude, *Stevens and Vela discuss how the novel resolves the paradox of illusion versus reality by consciously not distinguishing between the two. In breaking the boundaries of the sacred and profane, they state, the novel presents the reader with a mythopoeic epic which condenses and retells the history of humankind.*

The technical difficulty of distinguishing between illusion and reality is one of the oldest and most important problems faced by the novelist in particular and by mankind in general. In art, philosophy, or politics, western man has traditionally made great conscious efforts to keep illusion separated from fact while admiring and longing (at least superficially) for a transcendental way of life. The irony of this longing resides in the fact that western man's scientific and technological achievements are in great part due to his ability to separate fact from fiction, myth from science, and illusion from reality. It is a paradox of western culture that it draws its psychological strength from a spiritual-mythical well while its muscle is drawn largely from science and technology.

In *One Hundred Years of Solitude,* Gabriel García Márquez deals with the paradox very successfully by not trying to solve it at all. That is to say, the perceptions of reality which appear in the novel are all *prima facie* perceptions and, as a consequence, become indistinguishable from reality. For example when Meme falls in love with Mauricio Babilonia she finds herself attended ever after by a swarm of yellow butterflies. The question whether they are real or imaginary butterflies is the wrong question. Márquez makes it evident that he places little value on such questions and that there is, in a way, no inherent value in real butterflies as opposed to imaginary butterflies in the world which he describes and, by extension, perhaps in our world as well.

The butterflies are there, *prima facie,* and the distinction between symbol and actuality is broken down and declared void by the lyrical fiat of his style. The technical result of this method and the value of this view is that the conventional distinction between figurative and literal language is impossible to make and pointless beside. Conventional literary terms are inadequate to describe the fusion of both literal and metaphorical language. We who are trained to compartmentalize our minds into fact and fancy, business and God, myth and science, are prone to wonder over the nature of these butterflies, their origin, and their significance. In reality, however, the question is presumptuous and has validity only in our narrow-minded world with its forty-hour work week and our constant, energy-consuming, watchful stand to keep fancy and reality separated in our minds.

When we are told that it rained for four years, eleven months, and two days, we need not ask

" We who are trained to compartmentalize our minds into fact and fancy, business and God, myth and science, are prone to wonder over the nature of these butterflies, their origin, and their significance."

ourselves whether this could be so; rather we soon come to accept it as a given quantity and eventually, through the art of García Márquez, we come to accept all things in the novel as they are. This, we are soon convinced, is also a workable view of reality. Multiplying such details with profound ingenuity, Márquez gradually brings the reader's skeptical biases into harmony with the spiritual and intellectual life of his townsfolk. When José Arcadio is shot.

> A trickle of blood came out under the door, crossed the living room, went out into the street, continued on in a straight line across the uneven terraces, went down steps and climbed over curbs, passed along the Street of the Turks, turned a corner to the right and another to the left, made a right angle at the Buendía house, went in under the closed door, crossed through the parlor hugging the walls so as not to stain the rugs . . . and came out in the kitchen, where Ursula was getting ready to crack thirty-six eggs to make bread.

There is no question as to how this episode is to be taken, only the simple declaration that it happened. This blood which defies the laws of physics is neither symbolical, miraculous, nor scientifically credible. It is simply a fiat of reality in Macondo. Are such events also possible in our own world? Perhaps they are more real in the Colombian *cienega grande,* yet, on the other hand, people who believe in the day of judgment and the resurrection of the dead, except for a certain narrowness of mind, should have little trouble with a stream of blood that does not coagulate in one minute and that travels uphill.

One of the elements constituting this poetic vision of things is the mythopoeic. The village of Macondo is a microcosm and the one hundred years recounted in the novel is a compression of the whole history of man. The village begins *ex nihilo,* rises to

a golden age, and falls away into oblivion. Everything that can happen in our world happened there. A village was founded, children begotten, revolutions spawned, technology developed, lust, love, death, and beatitude were all enacted with the luxuriant and unending variety that suggests the inexhaustibility of the individual experience of human events. Márquez's myth has its own cosmology, "going back to before original sin" (*OHYS = One Hundred Years of Solitude*). The world began the "day that Sir Francis Drake attacked Riohacha" (*OHYS*), and it is of no consequence that Drake set sail and lived a lifetime prior to this day. In the golden age of Macondo nobody died, and all men lived in a sacred and eternal present tense. As time passed knowledge accumulated, but wisdom was still the property of the few, and political power belonged, even as in our world, to the cheat and the liar. As the world aged, it was overtaken by a great insomniac sickness which resulted in a loss of memory. In fear that their loss would bring chaos, the people of Macondo put up signs to remind themselves of the identity of things; "table, chair, clock, door . . . ," and on main street they placed the largest of all the signs against their forgetfulness. *DIOS EXISTE* . In giving things names, they also gave them reality; in having José Arcadio Buendía to give things their names, Garcia Márquez gives him the function of Adam, the first man, and he simultaneously seems to tell us that anything which may be forgotten by man may lose its existence and, perhaps, its *reality.*

Márquez gives a sort of sacredness to all experience by breaking down the wall between the sacred and the profane, as he has broken down the wall between fact and fiction, and by refusing to intellectualize his characters. Remedios the Beauty, for instance, remains utterly chaste—not because she is pious, but because she is simple and does not know the thoughts of men. But what does it matter whether her innocence came by piety or ignorance? In either case, she ascends into heaven while hanging sheets in the backyard, and who is to gainsay her ascension? Márquez, whose point of view in the novel is somewhat like God's, has declared it so. In short, the writer has created in Remedios a natural piety which may be thought of as pure without puritanism—simultaneously sacred and profane.

Time also has mythopoeic significance in the novel. Everything ages and moves toward its own end. Life, regardless of its particular reality, is a transient condition, at best. Márquez's point of view in the novel is the point of view of God: all time is simultaneous. The story of Macondo is at once complete from beginning to end, and, at the same time, it is the story of only one out of an infinite number of worlds each with its own story. More than that, it is the story of José Arcadio Buendía, one out of an infinite number of men but one who is more the father of man than Adam himself, for if Adam's sin was to eat the fruit of the tree of knowledge, José Arcadio's was to live too much and too long. He lived from the beginning of time until the world became old. One has the feeling that if the world had not become old, José Arcadio would not have died —but he and his descendants would never have deciphered the parchments of the ancients, never have acquired knowledge. "What's happening," Ursula notes, "is that the world is slowly coming to an end . . ." (*OHYS*). ". . . *El tiempo pasa*" (*CAS = Cien Annos de Soledad*). When the great apocalypse does befall Macondo however, it falls not in fire or flood, but rather it creeps in as the rot and decay of antiquity. When Aureliano Babilonia deciphers the parchments of Melquíades which contain all the knowledge and all the secrets of the ancients, he finds that "Melquíades had not put events in the order of man's conventional time, but had concentrated a century of daily episodes in such a way that they co-existed in one instant." The simultaneity of all time cannot be achieved literally by the novelist, and therefore he must create the illusion of it. This Márquez does by creating a microcosm of Macondo and giving it a microhistory while the individuals involved are as real as we.

In the last analysis, "time" is one of the major themes of the novel, as its title suggests. By setting all things in the context of their mortality, by dramatizing the apocalyptic nature of antiquity and decay (some say the world will end in flood, some say in fire, Márquez says it will die of old age), Márquez induces in us a rich reverence for all of his characters and events. There are great depths of bitterness in this novel—bitterness for the death of the old woman stabbed to death by the soldiers' rifle butts, for the treachery of the government and the North American fruit company, for the trainload of massacred townsfolk whose corpses "would be thrown into the sea like rejected bananas" (*OHYS*). Yet time and decay spread over these bitter incidents in such a way as to mellow and sanctify them. All of history occurred in Macondo, and it became holy through Melquíades's recitation of it in the sacred parchments; in like manner Márquez transforms the common experience of our world into something magical by his telling of it in the novel. Time bestows its blessing; all things are made holy because they have existed.

A second element of Márquez's view of life, beyond the mythopoeic, is the concept that man is naturally a scientist. The wisdom of the people who live in Macondo is a composite of folk wisdom, hearsay, legend, superstition, and religion—all indiscriminately mixed. And yet Márquez builds into the novel a dear sympathy for a certain quality of knowledge. We might think of this sympathy as an instinct for science. José Arcadio Buendía has it, as do each of his descendants who, in successive generations, lock themselves away in Melquíades's room to search for knowledge and truth. This science itself is a mixture of alchemy and occultism, but in it there is a feature which separates it from the popular wisdom of the town: its profound belief that reality is infinitely more wondrous than the most inventive of illusions. It is true that in José Arcadio the love of science exists in undisciplined comradeship with the folk wisdom:

> Mediante un complicado proceso de exposiciones superpuestas tomadas en distintos ??ares de la casa, estaba seguro de hacer tarde o temprano el daguerrotipo de Dios, si??, o poner termino de una vez por todas a la suposición de su existencia. (*CAS*)

José Arcadio was crude and ignorant in his methodology, but a true scientist in his heart. His fascination with magnets, ice, the sextant, and the geography of the world make it clear that in spite of his own inability always to separate superstition from science, the great yearning of his heart was to *know* things. In many ways García Márquez sees him as the archetype of all scientists, for do they not all share his dilemma? Which scientist could ever truly separate his own illusions from his empirical knowledge? Which scientist could ever know that his methodology is pure and perfected? How much of modern science is old illusion given a new name? The common characteristic shared by true scientists, however, is their great wonder at the profound mystery of reality. And if this be so then to the brotherhood of Copernicus, Galileo, and Newton, old José—with his poor sextant and his undeterred will to find a system for identifying the exact stroke of noon—eternally belongs.

It is this instinctive awe of reality that separates the first from the second generation of gypsies. Melquíades—a combination of Wandering Jew, picaro, Mephistopheles, and God—is a huckster, true enough, but beyond his slight-of-hand and his alchemy he is a man of great wisdom. It is easy from the vantage point of a highly developed technological culture, to think of Melquíades and José Arcadio as being naive, having too many gaps in their learning to be true scientists. There are loose ends in their knowledge which make them seem provincial. Should we judge them thus, however, we would betray only our own provinciality, for all science has loose ends. There must have been something of the gypsy too in Albert Einstein, for his paradox of the clock is really not different from Buendía's visualizing the air and hearing the buzzing of sunlight. García Márquez perceives it all as a vital and organic whole, as though the jungle itself where a Gothic artifact, creating, nourishing, destroying, and regenerating in great, broad brush strokes and in infinitely delicate detail. Márquez's way of seeing things is compatible with both myth and science, but it is neither thing in itself. It has the analytical curiosity of science coupled with the synthetic method of myth. The result is a technique which puts him in the tradition of Unamuno, Gallego, and Lorca, and it may reveal him as one of the most inventive novelists of our day—not because others have failed to explore the artistic fusion of myth and science, symbol and surface, but because of Márquez's ingenuity and the profusion of his imaginative details.

The view of Gabriel García Márquez is a view of life as it is—complex changing, indefinite, and difficult to understand. It is a view of reality richer and more exciting than any cross-section of any of its parts could ever reveal.

Source: L. Robert G. Vela, "Jungle Gothic: Science, Myth, and Reality in One Hundred Years of Solitude," in *Modern Fiction Studies,* Vol. 26, No. 2, Summer, 1980, pp. 262–66.

Sources

Bell-Villada, Gene H., *García Márquez: The Man and His Work*, University of North Carolina Press, 1990, pp. 5, 70-71, 108, 111.

Bloom, Harold, ed., introduction to *Gabriel García Márquez*, Modern Critical Views Series, University of Minnesota Press, 1990, p. 231.

de Gullon, Ricardo, "Gabriel García Márquez & the Lost Art of Storytelling," in *Diacritics*, Vol. 1, No. 1, Fall, 1971, pp. 27-32.

Epstein, Joseph, "How Good Is Gabriel García Márquez?" in *Commentary*, Vol. 75, No. 5, May, 1983, pp. 59-65.

Fau, Margaret Eustella, and Nelly Sfeir de Gonzalez, eds., *Bibliographic Guide to Gabriel García Márquez 1975-1985*, Greenwood Press, 1992, 1986, pp. 75, 153.

González Ecchevarría, Roberto, "*Cien anos de soledad*: The Novel as Myth and Archive," in *Gabriel García Márquez*, edited by Harold Bloom, Modern Critical Views Series, University of Minnesota Press, 1990, pp. 107-23.

Janes, Regina, "Liberals, Conservatives, and Bananas: Colombian Politics in the Fictions of Gabriel García Márquez," in *Gabriel García Márquez*, edited by Harold Bloom, Modern Critical Views Series, University of Minnesota Press, 1990, pp. 125-46.

Levitt, Morton P., "From Realism to Magic Realism: The Meticulous Modernist Fictions of García Márquez," in *Gabriel García Márquez*, edited by Harold Bloom, Modern Critical Views Series, University of Minnesota Press, 1990, pp. 227-42.

Sfeir de González, Nelly, ed., *Bibliographic Guide to Gabriel García Márquez, 1986-1992*, Greenwood Press, 1994, p. 347.

Solomon, Irvin D., "Latin American Women in Literature and Reality: García Márquez's *One Hundred Years of Solitude*," in *Midwest Quarterly*, Vol. 34, No. 2, Winter, 1993, pp. 192-206.

Vargas Llosa, Mario, "García Márquez: From Aracataca to Macondo," in *Gabriel García Márquez*, edited by Harold Bloom, Modern Critical Views Series, University of Minnesota Press, 1990, pp. 5-19.

Williams, Raymond, *Gabriel García Márquez*, Twayne Publishers, 1984, p. 1.

———, *The Modern Latin American Novel*, Twayne Publishers, 1998, p. 94.

Further Reading

Bell-Villada, Gene H., *García Márquez: The Man and His Work*, University of North Carolina Press, 1990.
    Traces García Márquez's development as a writer and analyzes his major stories and novels.

Bloom, Harold, ed., *Gabriel García Márquez*, Modern Critical Views Series, University of Minnesota Press, 1990.
    Scholarly essays on his work.

de Valdéz, María Elena, and Mario J. Valdéz, eds., *Approaches to Teaching García Márquez's One Hundred Years of Solitude*, Modern Language Association, 1990.
    Essays that discuss how to incorporate the novel into various kinds of class curricula.

Janes, Regina, *One Hundred Years of Solitude: Modes of Reading*, Twayne Publishers, 1991.
    Analyzes the novel from the perspectives of various reading strategies, including mythic, political, and metaphysical.

McMurray, George, *Gabriel García Márquez*, Ungar, 1977.

A brief introduction to his life and works, with very traditional criticism of selected texts.

McNerney, Kathleen, *Understanding Gabriel García Márquez*, University of South Carolina Press, 1989.
Contains a chapter on *One Hundred Years of Solitude* and his two other major novels with introductory materials for the English reader.

Williams, Raymond, *Gabriel García Márquez*, Twayne Publishers, 1984.
A biographical account of the literary work of García Márquez, with analysis of the major novels and stories.

———, *The Modern Latin American Novel*, Twayne Publishers, 1998.
Individual chapters on major Latin American novelists and their works, before, during, and after the Latin American literary Boom.

Wood, Michael, *Gabriel García Márquez: One Hundred Years of Solitude*, Cambridge University Press, 1990.
Approaches García Márquez through related historical and literary events, with analysis of *One Hundred Years of Solitude* .

Petals of Blood

Ngugi wa Thiong'o

1977

Petals of Blood is the fourth novel written by Ngugi wa Thiong'o, who is more commonly known simply as Ngugi. The novel describes the inequality, hypocrisy, and betrayal of peasants and workers in post-independence Kenya. As with Ngugi's other works, many of the events depicted in the novel have their basis in historical and social fact. The work is a damning indictment of the corruption and greed of Kenya's political, economic, and social elite who, after the struggle for freedom from British rule, have not returned the wealth of the land to its people but rather perpetuate the social injustice and economic inequality that were a feature of colonial oppression. In addition to criticizing this neocolonialism, the novel is also a bitter critique of the economic system of capitalism and its destructive, alienating effects on traditional Kenyan society.

The deeply political novel takes the form of a detective story. Three prominent industrialists in the town of Ilmorog in north-central Kenya have been murdered, and four suspects are questioned by the police. These four are the protagonists of the novel, whose interrelated stories are recounted against the background of Kenya's past and present. The shifting perspectives and timeline of the novel reinforce the sense of dislocation and disorientation of the once proud community of villagers who now struggle against the indignities of the neocolonial world.

The publication of *Petals of Blood* disturbed many of Kenya's leaders when it appeared in 1977, but the government did not formally denounce the novel. However, less than a year after it appeared Ngugi was imprisoned for his play *I Will Marry When I Want*. That work makes even more explicit the comparison between post-independence Kenyan leaders and British rulers.

Some commentators have faulted Ngugi for the novel's heavy-handed treatment of its message, the intrusive authorial voice, and the outdated socialist solution he offers for his country's ills. However, critics agree that *Petals of Blood* is an important contribution to world literature. Its admirers view it as an ambitious work that presents with artistic integrity Ngugi's statement of his social and political philosophy, and find it to be a realistic portrayal of the postcolonial experience in Kenya.

Author Biography

Ngugi was born James Ngugi in 1938 in Limuru in the Gikuyu Highlands of Kenya. Like many of the dispossessed peasants in *Petals of Blood*, his father worked as a laborer on the estate of an African landowner. Ngugi's mother was one of his father's four wives, and Ngugi was one of about twenty-eight children in the family. After his primary school education at independent Kenyan schools, Ngugi attended Alliance High School, an institution that had many similarities to his fictional Siriana, with its western-biased curriculum and Christian teaching. During his high school years, many of his family members were involved in the Mau Mau uprising and the resistance movement. During the struggle, Ngugi's parents were arrested and his stepbrother was killed by government forces.

In 1958, Ngugi moved to Uganda to attend Makerere College, the only institution in East Africa at the time that conferred degrees. While at Makerere he began a marriage partnership with Nyambura, with whom he had five children. Also during his undergraduate years, he wrote his first novel, *Weep Not, Child*, and worked on what would later be published as his novel *The River Between*. He also wrote and produced a play, edited the student creative writing journal, and wrote newspaper articles. He completed a degree in English in 1963.

After a brief stint as a journalist in Nairobi, Ngugi went to Leeds University in England to take an M.A. There he associated with radical fellow students and moved in circles that encouraged critical thinking on political, social, literary, and academic issues. He also spent much of his energy working on his novel *A Grain of Wheat*. Ngugi left Leeds in 1967 without completing his thesis on Caribbean literature, and took a job as a lecturer at Nairobi University. There he advocated for a change in the structure and syllabus of the English department. He resigned from his post in 1969 in protest of the administration's poor handling of a crisis between the student body and the university government. He took a job at Makerere, where he helped to reorganize the syllabus from a traditional British structure to one based primarily on African literature. In 1970, Ngugi moved to Evanston, Illinois, to teach at Northwestern University. He returned to Kenya and to a job at the University of Nairobi in 1971, eventually becoming chair of the English department. He took it as his project to reorganize the focus of the department, and to place Kenya, East Africa, and Africa at the center of the curriculum.

After the publication of *Petals of Blood* in 1977, which took him six years to complete, Ngugi changed his name from James Ngugi to Ngugi wa Thiong'o. At the end of that year, after the highly successful staging of his Gikuyu-language play, in which he criticized the inequalities of the economic and social system in his country, he was detained without charges or trial for a year. After his release he ceased writing in English and began to write in Gikuyu only. His first Gikuyu-language novel, translated into English as *Devil on the Cross*, appeared in 1981. While in London for the launching of that book, he learned that if he returned to Kenya he would be arrested, and remained in exile abroad, traveling widely and lecturing. Since the late 1980s Ngugi has taught at American universities. He continues to write and to work with organizations promoting freedom and equality in Kenya.

Plot Summary

Petals of Blood opens with each of the four protagonists, Munira, Abdullah, Wanja, and Karega, being taken to the New Ilmorog Police Station for questioning. They are suspects in the murder of the three directors of Theng'eta Breweries and Enterprises—Chui, Kimeria, and Mzigo—who have been burned to death. Police Inspector Godfrey, from Nairobi, has been summoned to solve the case. Within this structure of a detective novel, Ngugi explores the interrelated lives of his main characters and the people around them as well as the transformation of Ilmorog and Kenya in the years following independence. The main action of the novel is not recounted chronologically, but is revealed in a series of flashbacks and confessions by various characters as well as by an omniscient narrator. The timeline shifts back and forth from the present to various times in the past, as far back as pre-colonial days. The present-tense action, in which the suspects are questioned and the murders solved, spans about ten days. The story of Munira's stay in Ilmorog, during which he meets the other principle characters, takes place over a period of twelve years. Narratives by other characters reveal events in their pasts as well as that of the land, back to the original founding of Ilmorog. Ngugi uses the broken chronology, shifting perspectives, and interrupted accounts to reveal very gradually the novel's events and the characters' psychological backgrounds. By the end of the novel a complex picture has unfolded of the characters' development and motives. The novel is divided into four parts, which correspond with major changes in the lives and attitudes of the protagonists, but again the action of each part again is not chronological and moves back and forth in time.

Part One: Walking

In the first flashback of the novel, Munira is seen arriving in Ilmorog to teach at the primary school. He meets Abdullah, the owner of the village shop and bar, and his adopted brother, Joseph. They are soon joined by Wanja, who has left her life as a bargirl to join her grandmother, Nyakinyua, on their ancestral land. Some time later comes the Karega. In various confessional narratives, the characters reveal important facts about themselves. Both Munira and Karega had, at different times, been expelled from elite Siriana High School for their involvement in strikes. The leader of the strike during Munira's tenure at Siriana was the charismatic and brilliant Chui. Wanja recounts her relationship with an older man who seduced her while she was still a schoolgirl and abandoned her when she became pregnant. It is also revealed that Karega's mother, Miriamu, has worked as a laborer on the land of Ezekiel Waweru, Munira's father. Also during the first part of the novel Wanja convinces Abdullah to send Joseph to school. Munira and Wanja have a brief affair before Wanja leaves to return to the Highlands. Karega also leaves Ilmorog to find his way in the world.

Another important episode in the first part of the novel is the "Tea Party" that Munira attends. He is lured to a covert meeting of the Kamwane Cultural Organisation (KCO) during which participants are asked to take an oath to protect the property of rich Gikuyus from the envy of other tribes. At the end of Part One, Munira meets Wanja and Karega in Kamiritho township, and the three travel back together to Ilmorog on Munira's bicycle. Munira hires Karega to work as an untrained teacher in the school. Ilmorog suffers a severe drought, and with no other resources, the villagers face the possibility of a famine. Part One closes with the villagers preparing to load up Abdullah's donkey cart and journey to the city on foot, on the advice to Karega, to seek help from their Member of Parliament to improve their living conditions.

Part Two: Toward Bethlehem

During the trek to Nairobi, Abdullah emerges as a brave warrior who has fought valiantly to win independence for Kenya, and is the hero of the journey. He entertains the village children with stories and procures food with his catapult. Also during the walk to the city Nyakinyua tells her people of Ilmorog's glorious past "when all Africa controlled its own earth" as well as of the British occupation and Kenyans' brave resistance to foreign rule. Wanja recounts the terrifying details of her experiences in the city as a bargirl. After the third day of walking, the villagers' food supplies almost exhausted, Joseph falls ill. The travelers seek help from the Reverend Jerrod Brown, who turns them away after telling them they do not need physical but spiritual nourishment. They go to the next house, which Munira discovers is the house of Chui, who is having a party with his modern, urban friends. The crowd is disrespectfully singing the "juicy" parts of traditional circumcision songs. One of the guests at his party, a woman with bright red lips and a huge "Afro wig," faints at the sight of the villagers, and Munira flees without asking for help for Joseph. Desperate, the villagers stop at the next house, where Karega, Wanja, and the villager Njuguna are imprisoned for trespassing. It turns out to be the house of Wanja's former lover Kimeria, who forces her to sleep with him in exchange for his aid. After the travelers arrive in Nairobi, they are offered assistance by a lawyer, but receive no help from their Member of Parliament, Nderi wa Riera. But the publicity following their trek to the city brings donations and aid from around the country. Also in the course of Part Two Karega reveals that after the strike at Siriana against the English headmaster Cambridge Fraudsham, Chui had been brought in to replace the ousted Englishman. The protest against Chui's policies, which were not much different from those of Fraudsham, was the cause of Karega's expulsion.

Part Three: To Be Born

Despite the failed mission to the city, the village enjoys some sense of renewal in the third part of the novel. Karega begins a correspondence with the lawyer, seeking to learn more about what African intellectuals are writing about the present struggle against economic inequality. He is disappointed and disillusioned by their abstract treatment of people's very real problems. The rains fall again, and a good harvest is gathered. The villagers celebrate their fortune with ancient songs and dances. The old woman Nyakinyua brews an ancient drink that had been banned by the British, Theng'eta, which the villagers partake of during a circumcision rite. Their consumption of the brew is followed by detailed confessions by the main characters. Abdullah reveals that he fought in the resistance with Karega's brother, Nding'uri, and that they were both betrayed by Kimeria. Karega tells of his love for Mukami, Munira's sister, and her suicide after her father's disapproval of their union. Munira is overcome with jealousy at Wanja's and Karega's growing love, and eventually has him dismissed from the school. Wanja confesses to Karega that the man she was forced to sleep with during the trek to the city was Hawkins Kimeria, the same person who had made her pregnant many years before and who Karega now knows is responsible for his brother's death. During the course of the third part Joseph is also shown as excelling at school, and Abdullah is increasingly proud of his younger brother's success. Part Three ends with the crash of an small plane carrying surveyors who have come to scope out the area for the building of the Trans-African Highway. The plane crash heralds a new age for Ilmorog. But for Wanja and the villagers, far more significant than the influx of new visitors into the town are the death of Abdullah's donkey and Karega's departure from Ilmorog.

Part Four: Again . . .La Luta Continua!

The final part of the novel sees the transformation of old, rural Ilmorog to a sprawling town of concrete, iron, stone, and glass. The Trans-Africa Highway linking Nairobi and Ilmorog is built and cuts the village in half, razing the old priest Mwathi's place to the ground. Abdullah's place, which eventually becomes Wanja's place, caters to the many new visitors by serving them roasted meat and drink. Wanja's and Abdullah's business booms. They build an extension to their bar and begin brewing Theng'eta, the ritual drink, and selling it to the workers and peasants of the New Ilmorog. Their success is short-lived, however, as Wanja is forced to sell her business to save her grandmother's land from being possessed by the bank. Mzigo, the new owner of her premises, with the help of Chui, Kimeria, and foreign financiers, transforms her business into a major brewery that employs over six hundred workers. Abdullah and Wanja are unable to obtain a license to brew their own Theng'eta, and lose everything. Abdullah is forced to sell oranges in the street and Wanja becomes a high-class prostitute serving the new rich of New Ilmorog. Abdullah and Wanja's relations become strained, but they are eventually reunited when Abdullah learns that Joseph is doing well at Siriana and goes to Wanja to tell her the good news. He finds her in her old hut, not in her brothel, and she is crying. He comforts her and they make love.

During this time, Munira turns increasingly to drink, and then to religion, becoming a member of an extreme Christian cult. Karega returns from his travels through the country, where he has been working with and educating the exploited underclass, and begins to organize the workers at the brewery. He sees the great changes to Ilmorog and what the people have lost. Many villagers, including Nguguna, have been forced off their land and into degrading jobs. A new tourist center has opened up in town, as well as a shantytown for the new poor. Munira meets Karega when he returns and takes him to see Wanja at her brothel. During that visit she reveals to them what she had done with the baby she had by Kimeria all those many years ago: she threw it down a drain and killed it. In the final pages of the novel, the details of the murder of the three brewery directors becomes clear and Inspector Godfrey solves his ''jigsaw puzzle.'' The three men had been in Wanja's house when the fire broke out. She had lured them there to humiliate them by rejecting them for Abdullah. However, it not Wanja who set the house on fire, but Munira. Munira explains that he wanted to burn down Wanja's whorehouse to save Karega from her immoral influences. Only Wanja knows that she had stabbed Kimeria before the fire actually broke out. As he waits in jail before his trial for the murder, Munira's father and Father Jerrod come to see him, and Munira criticizes their hypocrisy at not helping him earlier. The novel ends on several notes of hope, despite all that has transpired. Joseph visits Abdullah and expresses his ideals of constructing a new Kenya based on the values of his adopted brother. Wanja is pregnant with Abdullah's child. Karega learns that his mother is dead but also that the workers of Ilmorog are planning a rebellion, and so he sees possibilities in the future for the Kenyan working and peasant masses.

Characters

Abdullah

As the novel opens Abdullah, a former freedom fighter who has lost a leg in the struggle for Kenyan independence, runs a *duka*, or shop, where he sells provisions and drinks to the townsfolk of Ilmorog. Like the other protagonists, Abdullah has come to Ilmorog to flee his former life, its painful memories, and its responsibilities. He had been one of the bravest and most active participants in the movement for independence, joining the Mau Mau rebellion and fighting in the forest with the charismatic leader Ole Masai. During the uprising he and Karega's brother, Nding'uri, had been betrayed by Kimeria. Abdullah managed to escape, but Nding'uri had been hanged. After independence, Abdullah returns to his hometown, Limuru, expecting to see the fruits of his struggle—the redemption of the land for the people. But he finds that his heroism is not acknowledged, and he and other peasants are unrewarded for their sacrifice while those—including Kimeria—who have not fought for their country turn the economic system to their advantage. Abdullah moves with his donkey—his "second leg"—and his "brother" Joseph, whom he has rescued from a life on the streets, to Ilmorog "where I could have no reminder of so bitter a betrayal." At the beginning of the novel Abdullah is bitter and surly, barking orders to Joseph and making sarcastic remarks to Munira about his work at the school. But a transformation begins when Wanja convinces him to send Joseph to school. During the villagers' journey to the city, which is made possible by his donkey and cart, Abdullah inspires the travelers—reminding them of the independence struggle, singing patriotic songs, and procuring food for them. Abdullah is betrayed again by the end of the novel when his shop is forced to shut down to serve the interests of the economic elite, and he is reduced to selling oranges by the roadside. Abdullah's stump is one of the important symbols in the novel, a remind-

er of the betrayal of the peasantry. His mixed ancestry (he is the son of an African mother and an Indian father) underscores his struggle with a divided self. Abdullah's brief union with Wanja results in his fathering her child, which is a symbol of hope and possibility at the end of the novel.

Chui

Chui is an educator and one of the three African directors of the Theng'eta Breweries. We learn about his past from both Munira and Karega. Chui is an example of the potential and idealism of his country gone terribly wrong. While a student at Siriana High School, Chui led the students, including Munira, in strike against the policies of the new headmaster Fraudsham, advocating for better social conditions. He was expelled from Siriana and continued his education abroad. Years later, while Karega is a student there, Chui is called to Siriana to replace Fraudsham after he is ousted in another strike in protest of alienating, un-African school curricula. But it turns out that Chui outdoes his predecessor in promoting foreign values. He is a symbol of the corruption of Kenyan leaders who betray their people by implementing the colonial values and systems that had been fought against in order to gain personal power. Chui leads a decadent life, and he is shown as dishonoring his people's values as he sings bawdy versions of traditional songs with his wealthy urban friends. In Kiswahili, "Chui" means "leopard," perhaps an indication of the way he changes his spots to suit his own purposes.

Cambridge Fraudsham

The English headmaster at Siriana High School who is ousted after a student strike, and whose twisted values reveal him to be the "fraud" and "sham" that his name indicates.

Inspector Godfrey

Inspector Godfrey is the Nairobi police officer who is in charge of the murder investigation of Chui, Mzigo, and Kimeria. He sees it as his duty to protect the status quo of post-independence Kenya, although he himself is not a wealthy man. He approaches solving the murders with detachment, viewing it as a "criminal jigsaw puzzle" and does not concern himself with the moral questions of how and why.

J. M.

See The Lawyer

Reverend Jerrod

The hypocritical Reverend Jerrod, a well-to-do priest, turns away the weary Ilmorog travelers as they seek aid for the sick child Joseph during their journey to the city. The villagers need food, but he tells them to feed on "the food of the spirit, the bread and fish of Jesus."

Julia

Munira's estranged wife.

Karega

Karega is a student activist who becomes a union leader fighting for the workers in the developing industries of the New Ilmorog. After his expulsion from Siriana High School he is forced to take a series of jobs to make a living, and moves to Ilmorog in search of his old teacher, Munira, who hires him to work at the school. His spirit of action and reform is shown as he organizes the villagers' trek to see their Member of Parliament and voice their concerns about the drought. Munira dismisses Karega from his post after finding out about his affair with Wanja and his former relationship with his sister, and Karega wanders the country again continues to advocate for workers' rights. He returns to aid workers in their struggle against the owners of the Theng'eta Breweries. Karega is a member of the oppressed poor who, despite having had few advantages, maintains a vision for a more just society. He does not accept blindly what he is taught at school, nor even what the lawyer, whom he deeply respects, teaches him about how to right the wrongs of the existing social order. He sees the only way to reform the ills of society is to destroy the corrupt elite, and seeks to lead his people in their struggle against oppression. He is a sensitive and caring man, as seen in his relationship with his first love, Mukami, and later with Wanja. Karega's optimism and youthful idealism see a positive transformation in the novel as he channels his energies and dedicates his life to reconstructing Kenyan society.

Hawkins Kimeria

Hawkins Kimeria an industrialist and one of the three African directors of the Theng'eta Breweries whose murders are being investigated as the novel opens. He is painted as a despicable, almost inhuman character as the facts of his past are revealed: he became wealthy during the independence movement by transporting the dead bodies of the Mau Mau killed by the British, he betrayed Abdullah and

Karega's brother during the rebellion, and he made Wanja pregnant when she was just a schoolgirl. During the journey to the city, Kimeria humiliates Wanja once again by forcing her to sleep with him in order to help her companions and the sick child, Joseph.

The Lawyer

The lawyer is an activist who understands and tries to reform the corrupt economic and social system. He is educated and from a well-propertied family but his allegiances are with the people. A politically astute but compassionate man, he aids the villagers when they arrive in the city to air their grievances about their living conditions to their political representatives. Karega works for him after the lawyer is elected to political office, and finds that he is sincere but perhaps misguided in his hope of achieving radical reform through the mechanisms of the corrupt system. He is eventually brutally murdered by his political enemies.

Lillian

A bargirl-turned-Christian fanatic who eventually turns Munira to religion.

Miriamu

Karega's mother, a peasant farmer who has been forced to work on Munira's father's land.

Mukami

Munira's younger sister Mukami, a sensitive and unusual girl and the only member of the family for whom Munira feels any affection, killed herself several years before the action of the novel begins. Munira later finds out that her suicide was prompted by their father's disapproval of Mukami's love affair with Karega.

Godfrey Munira

Munira, a schoolteacher and the headmaster of Ilmorog Primary School, is one of the four principal characters who have been accused of murder. Munira is a complex individual. He is seen by himself and his middle-class family to be a failure, and he tries unsuccessfully to overcome his poor sense of self. His desire to bring education to the dusty village of Ilmorog seems to be the action of an idealist, but in fact his motives are to flee from his family and responsibilities. Like Karega, Munira was expelled from Siriana High School, but the event does not inspire him to action but rather to inaction. He has a narrow understanding of education, and does not encourage his students to think for themselves. He wants to be revered but has little interest in the situation of the people of the village. His jealousy at Karega's and Wanja's relationship prompts him to dismiss his former friend from his teaching post. Munira turns increasingly to drink to mask his unhappiness, and by the end of the novel embraces a fanatical brand of Christianity, insisting that his world cannot be changed and the only hope is in the next. However, despite his inaction for most of the novel, he performs *the* decisive act in the novel in committing the murders of the brewery directors. Munira's name means ''stump,'' which speaks to his enfeebled state and contrasts his weakness to the heroism of the lame Abdullah.

Muturi

An Ilmorog villager. His name means ''black'' in Gikuyu.

Mwathi wa Mugo

Mwathi is Ilmorog's occult priest, the mentor of the clan. His sacred compound is eventually bulldozed to make room for the Trans-African Highway, cleaving Ilmorog into two and forcing it into the modern age.

Mzigo

Mzigo is a school administrator and one of the three murdered directors of the Theng'eta Breweries. His character is not well fleshed out; he is presented as a one-dimensional figure whose only concerns are money and power. He represents the corruption of education in neo-colonial Kenya with its interests in supporting the established economic and social order and stifling real critical inquiry.

Nderi wa Riera

Nderi is the member of parliament for the people of Ilmorog. He ignores the villagers' concerns when they appeal to him for help after journeying to the city, and is seen as an opportunistic politician who seeks power for his personal ends. and ignores his electorate unless an election is approaching. In Gikuyu his name means ''vulture son of air.''

Nding'uri

Karega's older brother, a freedom fighter who lost his life during the Mau Mau rebellion.

Nedmi

The semi-legendary founder of Ilmorog.

Nguguna

An Ilmorog villager who is imprisoned with Karega and Wanja when the villagers seek help at Kimeria's house during the journey to the city. His name is allegorical and means ''common man'' in Gikuyu.

Joseph Nijraini

Abdullah's ''brother'' Joseph is transformed during the novel from a homeless vagabond eating rubbish in the streets to the star pupil at the elite private high school Siriana.

Njogu

An Ilmorog villager.

Nyakinyua

Wanja's grandmother, who is in a sense the mother of the community of Ilmorog. She is a storyteller who offers insights into Ilmorog's past, from pre-colonial times to her husband's brave struggle against the British.

Ruoro

An Ilmorog villager.

Wanja

Wanja is the central female character in the novel, a bargirl-turned-prostitute who is one of the four murder suspects. She moves to Ilmorog to escape life in her native Limuru and Nairobi, where she worked as a bargirl, and join her grandmother on her plot of land. As a schoolgirl Wanja was seduced by the wealthy Kimeria, who abandoned her when she became pregnant. During the course of the novel she reveals that she disposed of her baby in a drain, and has carried the guilt of her action with her for many years. In Ilmorog Wanja works at Abdullah's shop and eventually begins a successful distillery. When her business is not allowed to continue she makes herself into a high-class prostitute servicing the urban elite who have transformed Ilmorog. Wanja is at once an innocent and wise woman, a temptress and protector of the downtrodden. She is a woman of action, as she convinces Abdullah to send Joseph to school and rescues her grandmother's ancestral land from being repossessed by the banks. She is intelligent and remarkably resilient, and has a sensuality and physical presence that makes her desirable to all the principle male characters of the novel. She also exerts a strong psychological influence on the villagers of Ilmorog, and they assume that her name comes from ''Wanjiku,'' the mother of the nine clans of the Gikuyu people. Her name also means ''stranger or outsider,'' which is appropriate as she moves from city to city and town to town trying to find her place in the New Kenya.

Ezekiel Waweru

Ezekiel Waweru, Munira's father, is a wealthy landowner who uses his Christianity to advance his material interests. He forbids the relationship between his daughter Mukami and Karega, which results in her suicide. Waweru is concerned with money and success, and sees his son Munira as a failure.

Themes

Alienation of the Land

Petals of Blood is an overtly political novel, and the author's intention is to present readers with a portrait of the economic, social, and other ills of post-independence Kenya. As he makes clear in his writings, Ngugi does not think that his role as a writer is to change society, because only people can change society. However, as he says in a 1979 interview in *African Report*, he thinks writers can point out where things are wrong and also that ''fiction should embody the aspirations and hopes of the majority—of the peasants and workers.'' Clearly the main concern in *Petals of Blood* is to draw attention to the plight to the dispossessed peoples of Ilmorog, and by extension, of Kenya. The novel shows that after decades of colonial rule, many of the poorer segments of Kenyan society have been alienated from the land, the source of life for centuries. Even after independence, this separation continues. Karega's mother, Miriamu, is forced to work as a laborer on Munira's father's land. The villagers are helpless in the face of a drought that threatens their life. The landscape of Ilmorog changes forever when the Trans-Africa Highway is built, dividing the village into two. With the transformation of Ilmorog to an industrial center, peasants are forced to pawn their land to obtain bank loans, which they cannot pay, and their ancestral homelands are seized by financiers. The land of the people becomes just another commodity in the hands of economic rulers as Ilmorog is transformed

Topics for Further Study

- Research the history of Kenya from the first European settlements in the 1800s to the present day. Compare the political situation in Kenya today with that depicted in *Petals of Blood*.

- Examine the economic theories of capitalism and socialism. Explain why some people, like Karega in the novel, think that a socialist system would eradicate the economic inequalities that exist in a capitalist society.

- Investigate the role of women in traditional and modern Kenyan society, and compare it to that of women in the United States today.

- Research the independence movement in Kenya and the overthrow of the British rule. Compare the Kenyans' struggle for political freedom with that of other colonized peoples, including those in the Americas.

from a bucolic rural village to a polluted industrial development.

Critique of Capitalism

Related to the theme of the people's alienation from their land is Ngugi's critique of capitalism. Capitalism is an economic system in which the means of producing wealth are privately owned. The novel denounces such a system that has created unequal classes of rich and poor by dramatizing its effects on the people of Ilmorog. The capitalists in the novel—including Kimeria, Chui, Mzigo—are seen as ruthless men who are unconcerned with the misery that their greed creates. They seek to suppress the workers' union and refuse to raise their wages. They drive expensive cars and want for nothing, while the villagers travel on foot to seek help in the face of famine. They take from the people of Ilmorog the recipe of their traditional alcoholic brew, Theng'eta, and make millions from it, forcing the townspeople to work in the factory under poor conditions. The novel also presents these entrepreneurs as working in collusion with

Western corporations that continue to exploit the labor of the uneducated Kenyan masses. The revolutionary Karega, who some critics have viewed as presenting Ngugi's opinions, sees that the only way to reconstruct a just society is to do away with the elite who amass riches at the expense of the people. He presents a vision of a socialist system in which the working classes, those who create the wealth, have access to the fruits of their labor by owning the means of production and so are no longer exploited and oppressed by corrupt businesspeople.

Village versus City

The contrast drawn between village and city in the novel serves to underscore the damaging effects of capitalism as well as to make clear the difference in values between traditional and modern Kenyan society. The village of Ilmorog had once been a thriving place set against a ridge that the novel's narrator says must have been "one of the greatest natural beauties in the world." Founded by a courageous herdsman, Ndemi, who began cultivation of the lands, it was once a place of peace, beauty, and dignity. After independence, Ilmorog has become a dusty and backward place, but the people still uphold their integrity. The community is close-knit and hold onto their values and beliefs, participating in communal rites and helping each other. Their values are seen in contrast to those of the urban elite, whose sole interest is money and power. The city is seen as a place of corruption and decay, with tall buildings and gardens as well as shantytowns and bars. Over the course of the novel Ilmorog is transformed from a rural village to an industrial center, and with it comes a disintegration of its values. Wanja, who has been forced to give up her successful business and turn to prostitution in order to avoid being exploited in other ways, says of the values of the city and the "New Kenya": You eat somebody or you are eaten. You sit on somebody or somebody sits on you."

The Struggle for Independence

The novel details the heroic struggles of the freedom fighters, many of whom gave up their lives to achieve independence, or *Uhuru*, for Kenya. The village elder Nyakinyua recounts her husband's exploits and his proud refusal to be humiliated by the British. Karega's brother, Nding'uri, gave up his life for the cause as a Mau Mau rebel. And Abdullah, who has lost his leg during the resistance, is a reminder of the sacrifices made by the common people in the struggle for freedom from colonial rule. Now that independence has been achieved, however, the people who fought so bravely for their country are not rewarded. Rather, they are dispossessed by the wealthy few who did not participate in the struggle at all. Those like Mzigo and Kimeria who stayed in school or were involved in business during the movement have reaped the rewards of independence. With their money they have appropriated the land of the peasants who bought the country's freedom, leaving them dispossessed and without a means of livelihood. These entrepreneurs are seen as continuing the practices of the British oppressors, as they force peasants to work at subsistence wages on land that was traditionally theirs.

Christianity

Although the critique of Christianity in the novel is not as overt as are its social and political indictments, it seems clear that Ngugi means to point out the hypocrisy that attends many forms of Christian religious practice. There are no sympathetic portrayals of Christians in the novel. Ezekiel Waweru and the Reverend Jerrod Brown are seen as using Christianity to further their own material interests. Both have adopted the Christianity of the colonial masters and perpetuate the inequality of their system of values. When the villagers first encounter Reverend Jerrod Brown they assume he must be a white European because of his name. He offers them no help with the sick child, Joseph, nor does he give them food, and tells them they need only eat "the food of the spirit, the bread and fish of Jesus." Waweru has adopted the Christianity of the missionaries because it is more profitable for him to do so, but shows no Christian compassion to his son, daughter, or the laborers on his land. The Christian Lillian is also presented as a crazed fanatic who ignores the problems of this world by emphasizing life in the next, a strategy which she eventually gets Munira also to adopt.

Oppression

One of the persistent themes of *Petals of Blood* is oppression—social, economic, political, racial, and sexual. By oppressing them, or controlling the direction of people's lives, colonial and neocolonial rulers prevent ordinary Kenyans from reaching their full potential. The treatment of social, economic, and political oppression is tied in with the novel's critique of capitalism and the alienation of the people from their traditional work. Racial oppression is explored in attitudes of Europeans to Kenyans during colonial rule, particularly those of people like Fraudsham who view Africans as having to conform to a standard of behavior set by the British. The concern with sexual oppression becomes clear in the figure of Wanja, a woman of great energy, intelligence, and sensitivity whose only recourse in the face of economic failure and exploitation is to turn to prostitution and to serve the interests of men. Throughout the novel, peasants and workers are prohibited from prospering because of the oppressive external forces of colonialism and capitalism. In the figures of Joseph and Karega it is seen that it is possible for the Kenyan peasantry to flourish if, like flowers, they are exposed to nourishment and light and not prevented from shaping their own destiny.

Education

There is a great deal of discussion and action in the novel surrounding education. Four important characters—Munira, Chui, Karega, and Mzigo—are teachers. Munira, Chui, and Karega attended Siriana High School and were expelled for their revolutionary activities, which did much to determine how they would view their futures. Joseph earns a scholarship to Siriana also, and seems to exhibit the same idealism as that shown by the others. The future of the country seems to lie in what he will make of his experience there. Cambridge Fraudsham, the English headmaster of Siriana, represents the arrogance of the colonial school system, with its irrelevant curriculum that is forced upon Africans and its systematic degradation of its students because of their race. Like Ngugi, Karega and the other students who strike want the Kenyan educational system to reflect the contributions and experiences of Africans and not simply those of white Europeans. The hope for reform at Siriana is dashed when Chui, "a black replica of Fraudsham" takes over and forces students to conform to the same principles as those of the British. With this theme Ngugi again emphasizes that the new leaders in Kenya follow the same path as the oppressors they have just overthrown. Education also serves to contrast the characters of Munira and Karega. Munira has come to Ilmorog to be a teacher but he is not concerned with the welfare of his students as much as to be revered himself. He thinks the pupils should be given "simple facts" so they can pass their exams. Karega sees his students as thinking beings and he takes it as his duty to help them shape their future and their lives. As a union organizer he continues to teach workers and others about the truth—of the destructive powers of capitalism and the possibility for a better socialist society.

Style

Point of View

One of the most striking features of *Petals of Blood* is its narrative style that uses multiple points of view to weave together the stories of the protagonists and those around them. In the opening pages of the novel, events are seen through the eyes of each of the four protagonists. As the novel progresses, an omniscient, third-person voice enters and recounts parts of story. This narrator sometimes comments upon and interprets the events, but on occasion offers a more detached perspective. There is also a second narrative voice, which seems to be a collective one of the villagers of Ilmorog. In the early chapters of the novel, as Munira remembers his arrival in Ilmorog, his voice almost merges with that of the omniscient narrator. Indeed as each other character tells his or her story—whether old Nyakinyua or the lawyer, Karega or Wanja—the reader is drawn in and made to see the world from that personal standpoint. However, the reader must decide which voice and which version of the story to trust. In the context of a detective novel, the multiple points of view, overlapping timelines, and interrupted narratives make it difficult to piece together the "jigsaw puzzle" that will reveal the truth about the murders.

The fact that the story is told from very personal standpoints, often as confessions, also allows readers to understand characters not only as they are seen but as they see themselves. The revelations of characters also seeks to show how their lives are interrelated even as they speak from positions of isolation—it is in the retelling of their past lives Munira learns of his sister's affair with Karega, that Karega finds out that Abdullah fought with his brother in the resistance, etc. It is interesting that Ngugi never allows his villains to offer their perspectives; we learn only from the protagonists and the villagers of these men's horrible deeds.

Setting

Most of the action in *Petals of Blood* takes place in the north-central Kenyan town of Ilmorog. The town is in many ways one of the key characters in the novel. Its transformation parallels the transformation of the lives of its inhabitants and that of post-independence Kenya. None of the four protagonists comes from Ilmorog; all have fled to this dusty "wasteland" to escape their troubled pasts.

Like the characters of the novel and like Kenya itself, Ilmorog is a complex place—it has been ravaged by colonial exploitation but still reflects communal values. Its traditional spirit is seen in stark contrast to the concern with money and power that is a feature of the city. The building of the Trans-Africa Highway through the town cleaves it into two and ushers in what seems to be its final destruction, as with the new influx of people and money it adopts shallow, urban materialistic values. However, at the end of the novel Karega offers hope for a reconstruction of Ilmorog—and Kenya—by calling for a revolution of the people to take back the land that was traditionally theirs.

Symbolism

The title of the novel is taken from a poem, "Spawn," by the West Indian writer Dennis Walcott. The poem describes a huge tree preventing a little flower from reaching out into the light. According to Ngugi in a 1977 interview in the Nairobi *Sunday Nation*, the contemporary situation in Kenya and the effects of colonialism and neocolonialism similarly prevent the peasants and workers in Kenya from "flowering in dignity and glory." In the novel, the flower represents the repression of workers, peasants, and students from reaching out and achieving their potential. One of Munira's students shows him a flower that has "petals of blood." Munira smothers the student's imagination by correcting him, saying "there is no color called blood," and throughout the novel the education system is seen as being repressive and stifling of students' idealism and curiosity. Joseph, once given the opportunity, does begin to grow and flower, and one of the questions of the novel is how he will respond to the challenges that his education brings.

The "petals of blood" figure again during the circumcision ceremony as Nyakinyua cooks up the traditional brew, Theng'eta. The secret ingredient in the recipe is the blood-colored flower petal. However, again the evil hand of capitalism and its collusion with foreign interests and corporations reaches out and appropriates what traditionally belonged to the people—the traditional drink is mass-marketed as a soporific to keep peasants and workers in check and uncomplaining of their exploitation.

Another symbol related to the petals of blood of the title is fire. Fire is used repeatedly in the novel as an agent of destruction but also as a mysterious and purifying force. There are many other powerful symbols in the novel that reinforce its central ideas. The Trans-Africa Highway, which is a subject of discussion from the beginning of the novel, finally splits the village in half and allows in the predators that transform the land. Its arrival is heralded by the airplane, another symbol of progress and negative transformation. The airplane at first scares Abdullah's donkey and finally kills it. The symbol of the journey in the novel points to positive transformation: the villagers' journey strengthens their communal spirit and Karega's travels around the country help him to find his calling. Many of the characters or their features are also symbolic. Abdullah's stump leg can be seen as a physical symbol of the psychological maiming that is a feature of so many of the characters. The murdered brewery directors are clearly symbols for the evils of capitalism, the villagers are symbols of traditional (although sometimes unenlightened and misguided) values, and Fraudsham is a symbol of the warped ideologies of British rulers.

Literary Heritage

Kenya is a country of dramatic variety, both in terms of its varied topography and cultural makeup. The land itself includes tropical coastline, largely uninhabited inland desert areas, and high fertile farmland bordered by the two tallest mountains in Africa. While nearly ninety-nine percent of the people are black Africans, there are broad ethnic and linguistic divisions that divide the native population into more than forty ethnic groups. The largest of these groups, the Gikuyu, of which Ngugi is a member, makes up twenty percent of Kenya's population of 32 million people. Other large ethnic groups include the Kalenjin, Kamba, Luhya, and Luo, all of whom can be distinguished by their unique languages or dialects. The remaining one percent of the population is made up of East Indians, Europeans, and Arabs. Many Kenyans are able to overcome language barriers between groups by communicating in Swahili, the national language, or English, the official language.

Traditional Kenyan literary forms are largely oral. Oral stories, dramas, riddles, histories, myths, songs, proverbs, and other expressions are used to educate and entertain as well to remind the community of ancestors' heroic deeds, the past, and the precedents for customs and traditions. Folktale tellers often use call-response techniques in which a praise accompanies a narrative with music. In *Petals of Blood*, Nyakinyua is one of the keepers of the cultural heritage. She is the village bard who tells stories and leads the community in song. During the circumcision she sings a witty, ribald song with Nguguna, which is seen in contrast to the vulgar verses sung by Chui and his modern friends. In the novel, Ngugi's use of different points of view and the recounting of events in the form of stories may be seen as his acknowledgment of traditional oral literary practices. In a 1980 essay, the author remarks that although the African novel uses a borrowed form, its great debt to the native oral tradition is narrative. Ngugi's 1977 play *I Will Marry When I Want*, which led to his arrest, was apparently most offensive to the government because of its use of songs to emphasize its messages. The play struck a chord with the Gikuyu-speaking audience because of its use of traditional literary techniques. After his imprisonment, Ngugi made a conscious decision to switch to writing in his native Gikuyu. He felt he must do this in order to more effectively reach the people for whom his writings are concerned—the peasant and working classes in Kenya.

Historical Context

In *Petals of Blood*, Ngugi comments on the effects of colonial and post-colonial rule on the lives of the Kenyan people. The narrative begins with events in the early 1970s, twelve years after Kenya gained independence, or *Uhuru*, from the British colonial government, but the legacy of colonialism is still felt as a strong presence by the villagers in Ilmorog. In the novel key periods and events in Kenyan history are recalled, from the early days of British colonists to the Mau Mau Uprising to the social struggles following independence.

Beginnings of Colonialism

In 1887 a private British company attempted to start a trading business near the Kenyan coast, modeling itself after the British East India Company which had for years monopolized highly profitable European trade in India. While the Imperial British East Africa Company, as it was known, soon went bankrupt, the British government itself took over

the territory in 1895, and over the next decade gradually gained administrative control of most of modern Kenya. The British government encouraged English "settlers" to move to the fertile highland regions, where they created gigantic plantations while displacing hundreds of thousands of native Kenyans, mostly ethnic Gikuyus, from their traditional lands.

The Years Leading to Independence

For the next sixty years the economic, political, and social disparities between European settlers and native Kenyans gave rise to growing antagonism and conflict. It is estimated that by 1945 nearly twenty percent of Kenyan land (and clearly the most fertile) was owned by no more than 3,000 Europeans. Native Kenyans were used as laborers on these gigantic European plantations, or they were left to eke out a living on the remaining land that the Europeans found worthless. To make matters worse, the native peoples were treated by the ruling British as second-class citizens in their own land, forced to carry passports to travel from one section of the country to another, often restricted to certain areas of the land, barred from political office, and prohibited from voting and enjoying equal judicial rights.

The Gikuyu began organized protests against the British annexation of their traditional lands in 1924 with the formation of the Kikuyu Central Association (KCA). Throughout the 1920s the KCA organized peasants to demand that the discriminatory passport laws be dropped, and by the late 1930s led increasingly militant protests against the forced sale of their farm animals to the British government. The colonial government tried to squash these protests by banning the KCA in 1940, but by 1944 growing resentment among a broader spectrum of disenfranchised Kenyan ethnic groups came together to form the Kenya Africa Union (KAU). In 1947 Jomo Kenyatta was named the leader of the new KAU, and he soon came under the watchful eye of the British government for his demands that Kenyans gain greater political representation.

Revolution and Independence

By the early 1950s a growing segment within the KAU began to espouse violent revolt as the only means of freeing themselves from the tyranny of British colonialism. At the same time, the British government began to hear rumors of a covert association known as the Mau Mau. The group, they

Compare & Contrast

- **1930:** Few Kenyans are given opportunities to study in the English colonial schools. Those who do are forced to accept a curriculum heavy on European classics and short on African traditions or texts.

  1963: The newly independent Kenyan government responds to popular demand by building many new schools, including some in remote areas. Private citizens also found schools to meet the demand.

  1969: Students at Nairobi University protest in opposition to the western bias in the educational curriculum.

  Today: There are three national universities in Kenya. While schooling is not compulsory, eighty percent of children receive at least an elementary-level education. Works by African authors and scholars are featured in the curriculum.

  Today: Education is compulsory up to age sixteen for children in the United States. Schools respond to a growing demand for a multicultural curriculum to reflect the diversity of the population.

- **1900:** European settlers control twenty percent of all Kenyan land, which is most of the rich agricultural land suitable for farming. Native Kenyans are forced to work as laborers on European farms. They do not enjoy rights as full citizens under the law.

  1965: The newly independent Kenyan government takes over many farms and businesses owned by non-Africans, and sells or rents them to non-Africans. Non-Africans who become Kenyan citizens are allowed to keep their property. Many Kenyan peasants continue to work on land owned by Europeans or wealthy Africans to eke out a living.

  Today: About forty-five percent of the total area under cultivation in Kenya is occupied by large farms that employ laborers who earn low wages. Most of the rest of the land is held by cooperatives or subsistence farmers. Three-quarters of Kenya's population lives in rural areas and most people are employed in agriculture. Meanwhile, the United States Constitution guarantees the rights to private property. However, almost half of all Native Americans, the original inhabitants of the country, still live on reservation land, where unemployment, birth, and death rates are high, and suicides occur at twice the national rate.

- **1776:** The United States gains independence from Britain.

  1895: Kenya becomes a colony of Britain.

  1965: Kenya achieves independence from Britain.

  Today: There are still countries under direct or indirect control of foreign powers and whose people (although not always unanimously) call for self-rule. For example, Tibet calls for independence from China, Ireland from Britain, Puerto Rico from the United States, and East Timor from Indonesia.

---

learned, was rapidly gaining converts who gave oaths of their determination to wipe out the British settlers and government from Kenya. At first the British banned the secret Mau Mau organization, but this seemed only to add fuel to the revolutionary fire. British settlers became more concerned when in 1951 a white farmer was murdered, followed in 1952 by the assassination of Senior Chief Waruhiu Kungu, a Kenyan who was known for his denunciation of violent revolution. The settlers then demanded that the government take quick and decisive action to put down the revolt. In October 1952, a state of emergency was declared, and leaders of the KAU were rounded up and put on trial. Kenyatta himself was given seven years hard labor, although there was little evidence to support the colonial government's allegation that he advocated Mau Mau violence.

The jailing of their movements' leaders only intensified Kenyans' nationalism and the desire for revolution. Over the next four years rebel armies used acts of terrorism and guerrilla warfare to harass and intimidate the British administration as well as their Kenyan supporters. The British responded by reinforcing their troops, tightening restrictions on Kenyan movement, enforcing curfews, establishing holding camps, and executing Kenyans found guilty of carrying a weapon or taking the Mau Mau oath. By 1956 the last of the Mau Mau strongholds had been overrun, and in 1960 the state of emergency was ended.

The British colonial government came under considerable criticism both domestically and internationally for its tactics in ending the Mau Mau Uprising. Many Kenyans believed that the final deathcounts (11,503 insurgents and 590 British security force members) clearly showed the British to be the offending party, and an even broader range of Kenyans banded together to call for the end of British colonial government. The British agreed to these demands, and in February 1961 allowed Kenyans to vote for a new parliament. Kenyatta's party, the Kenya African National Union, won, but refused to take office until Kenyatta was released from prison. Six months later Kenyatta was finally freed, and when new elections were held after the country gained its formal independence on December 12, 1963, KANU easily won and named Kenyatta as the first president.

After Independence

Kenyan enthusiasm for a future freed from colonial exploitation soon became tempered by new issues, however. Within months of independence Kenya began a three-year war with neighboring Somalia over their common border. Domestically, the new government struggled to extend the school system to more rural communities and to redistribute some of the land and businesses that had been owned by Europeans and East Indians (many of whom were allowed to keep their property in exchange for taking Kenyan citizenship) to those Kenyans who had fought for independence. Increasingly, however, a large number of Kenyans began to believe that independence had done little to improve their lives, as a new set of rulers had simply taken over the few positions of power and wealth

vacated by the British administration. The new government also grappled with how to build national unity out of a country of so many fragmented ethnic and social groups.

In 1969 Kenyatta alarmed many citizens when he dissolved the Kenya People's Union, an opposition party that had formed in 1966, claiming that their leaders engaged in antigovernment activities. The Kenyatta government's fear of dissent was also made clear with Ngugi's arrest in 1977. After Kenyatta died in 1978, the vice-president, Daniel T. arap Moi, became president. In 1982 Moi made it constitutionally illegal to form any opposition party to the KANU. Although protests finally reestablished the legality of the multi-party system in 1991, Moi used his considerable power base to be reelected to new five-year terms in 1992 and 1997. The Moi government has been harshly criticized by international human rights organizations for its silencing of various political dissidents using violent means.

Critical Overview

Petals of Blood was officially launched by the Kenyan government in July 1977, in a show of the Kenyatta government's commitment to the principles of free speech. However, it was clear that the ruling elite and many members of the upper classes in Kenya were disturbed by Ngugi's harsh criticism of the established social and economic order. In reaction to the novel as well as to his play *I Will Marry When I Want*, after his release from detention in 1978 Ngugi was not reinstated in his job at Nairobi University, was arrested on trivial charges on several occasions, and received death threats.

Despite its status as a controversial work, the novel was received warmly by most readers and critics. An anonymous early review in Kenya's *Weekly Review* entitled "Ngugi's Bombshell" said that the Kenyan reader might feel as though Ngugi had been "walking all over your soul" because of the way he portrayed the results of independence. The reviewer went on to call the work Ngugi's "crowning achievement" but also noted the work's lack of humor and the people's unconvincing absorption in socialism. Joe Khadi, writing in the *Daily Nation*, another Kenyan publication, declared that "no writer has yet been able to expose the evils of such a system in as bold and fearless a manner." Other early African reviewers noted the novel's political impact, praised its narrative richness, and often criticized its use of Marxist principles.

Many western critics were also complimentary of the novel when it appeared. Christopher Ricks in the *Sunday Times* of London hailed it as "remarkable" and "compelling" for its presentation of political issues and innovative use of language. Novelist John Updike, however, writing in the *New Yorker*, was not as generous, saying that "Whatever else political fervor has done for Ngugi, it has not helped his ear for English."

The novel has enjoyed considerable scholarly attention, and many critics have echoed the sentiments of early reviewers, acknowledging the novel's considerable strengths while pointing out its weaknesses. One persistent criticism has been that the novel's political message is too overt. In his discussion of Ngugi's writings, the scholar G. D. Killam, for example, says also that the novel "is open to the charge of political attitudinizing in places." He says the call to right the injustices done to peasants and workers with colonial and postcolonial rule is treated at times with a heavy hand. However, Killam finds that the political attitudes and questions examined in the book are tempered by Ngugi's humanism, as throughout the novel his pressing concern is not with the putting forth of a political ideology but to draw attention to the degradation of human beings.

Other critics, however, have seen the novel's didacticism, or effort to teach and put forward a particular viewpoint, as detracting from its power as a work of art. Simon Gikandi faults Ngugi for his "authorial intrusiveness," saying that it often forces situations and characters to fit into a "predetermined ideological position." He says, for example, that the character of Joseph is not given any psychological development but emerges as a symbol of the ideals of reform that are central to the work. Gikandi suggests that this is a result of the novel being viewed by Ngugi as a means to "interpret, judge, and pattern the everchanging African reality" and as a useful social tool, much like traditional oracles, whose main purpose is to confront people with meanings and values. Gikandi does not criticize Ngugi's purpose, but finds that the authorial voice in the novel is often jarring. David Cook and Michael Okenimpke also notes the false notes in the

novel when putting forward a social and political message, but conclude that the novel is a "bold and powerful attempt to combine the intimacy of the traditional novel with a public rhetorical manner in a new and perhaps itself artistically and revolutionary amalgam in order to analyze social injustice and the human dilemmas it creates, and to mark out a practicable path to social change."

Critics have paid a great deal of attention to the complex narrative style of the novel. Many reviewers have viewed it as a powerful device, despite the author's occasional intrusiveness, as has been discussed. However, Stewart Crehan considers that the technique is confusing and that it is difficult to follow the "bewildering threads" of the narrative. He complains that with each new perspective, "an expected sharpening of focus does not materialize." Crehan also criticizes the novel for its failure to live up to the standards of an epic, its stilted style with its use of stock phrases and "over-reliance of commonplace word," and the muffled political message.

Petals of Blood has also been criticized by some feminist writers for its one-dimensional portrait of women. Elleke Boehmer, for example, points out that while most male critics and Ngugi himself has have pointed out the presence of strong female figures in this and his other novels, there is a strong patriarchal cast to his ideas. She says that his discussion of the rights of workers in *Petals of Blood*, for example, Ngugi seems to assume that true "work" is the productive labor of men, and that women are excluded from this arena. Boehmer does point out, however, that Ngugi's female characters, such as Wanja and Nyakinyua, are pioneers in the field of African writing in English.

While many analyses of *Petals of Blood* point out its limitations, the general view by critics is that the novel is a significant work of modern fiction, and an important contribution to the debate about colonial and postcolonial conditions in Kenya. It is Ngugi's work that is seen as most representative of his radical political views and his humanist commitment to social reform.

Criticism

Uma Kukathas

Kukathas is a freelance writer and a student in the Ph.D. program in philosophy at the University

What Do I Read Next?

- The novels *Things Fall Apart* (1958) and *No Longer at Ease* (1960) by the Nigerian writer Chinua Achebe depict Nigeria's experience with colonialism, from first contact with the British to the 1950s.

- The West Indian poet Derek Walcott, from whose poem "Swamp" Ngugi takes the title of his novel, discusses the conflict between his loyalties to Africa and to Britain in his poem "A Far Cry from Africa" (1990).

- In Ngugi's novel *The River Between* (1965), Christian missionaries attempt to outlaw the female circumcision ritual and create a rift between two Gikuyu communities, and people are torn between accepting Western and Christian ideas and holding on unquestioningly to their traditional ways. The growing conflict brings tragedy to a pair of young lovers who attempt to bridge the chasm between the people.

- *A Grain of Wheat* (1967) is Ngugi's compelling account of five friends who make different choices when the Mau Mau Rebellion erupts in colonial Kenya.

- *Detained: A Writer's Prison Diary* (1981) records Ngugi's thoughts and experiences while in prison, where he was held by the Kenyan government for a year without being charged for a crime.

- Ngugi describes *Decolonising the Mind* (1986) as "a summary of some of the issues in which I have been passionately involved for the last twenty years of my practice in fiction, theatre, criticism and in the teaching of literature." In the book Ngugi explains why he stopped writing in English in favor of his native Gikuyu.

- *I Will Marry When I Want* (1982) is Ngugi's translation of his 1977 Gikuyu-language play that he staged at his hometown of Limuru. The play, about the appropriation of land from peasants by wealthy landowners and the struggle of workers at a factory, was hugely popular with the people and led to Ngugi's detention without trial at the end of 1977.

- In stark contrast to the protest literature of African and Asian authors, the poem "White Man's Burden" (1899) by Rudyard Kipling expresses the common nineteenth-century view that white Europeans had a duty to "civilize" the "less enlightened" inhabitants of the non-Western world.

- The novel *Out of Africa* (1937) by Isak Dinesen, a Danish aristocrat who lived on a coffee plantation in Kenya, presents a portrait of the land and people in British East Africa before World War II from the point of view of a wealthy European woman.

---

of Washington specializing in social, political, and moral philosophy. In the following essay, she examines how the narrative technique of Petals of Blood *is used to underscore its theme of alienation and soften the didacticism of its political message.*

Many critics who have offered analyses of *Petals of Blood* have called attention to the novel's unusual narrative structure. In the work Ngugi uses multiple points of view to weave together the tales of his four main characters and the people around them. Fragmentary bits of information are revealed by two narrators and persons of varying backgrounds, and the reader must fit together characters' confessions, reminiscences, reports, musings, and sometimes dim remembrances to understand the truth of the story. The cumulative effect of the many-sided narration is that the reader must decide what and who to believe, but at the same time is presented with a quite clear social and political message. This narrative technique seems at least to some degree to be Ngugi's nod to the Kenyan oral tradition, in which tellers recount stories—often in the form of an exchange with others—for the moral education of their audience.

Some commentators, notably Stewart Crehans, have found Ngugi's style in the novel to be aesthetically unsatisfying. Crehans says that the threads in the novel are not well tied together, that the text "never rests, pinpoints, or focuses attention. . .[I]t has a kind of fugitive, alienated, almost neurotically anxious quality. . ." While Crehans seems to be right about the disjointed and sometimes strained tone of the novel, what he seems wrong not to allow is that the tangled web of narration serves important purposes in the work. The disparate viewpoints, interrupted accounts, and shifting sense of time in *Petals of Blood* produce an effect of confusion and dissonance that underscores the sense of alienation and dislocation of the Kenyan peasantry that is at the heart of the novel. The narrative method is also an effective device in this mystery story where the pieces of a "jigsaw puzzle" must be fit together to solve the crime. And the multiple perspectives that are used to express the ideas in this deeply political novel may be seen as warning against unquestioning acceptance of any one point of view.

The feeling of dislocation is apparent from the beginning of the novel. It opens with the arrests of the four protagonists, in four different places, in quick succession. This back-and-forth movement continues throughout the book. The first voice that is heard is that of a third-person narrator, but others soon chime in. In addition to the voices of the characters that tell their personal stories, there is another unnamed narrator, the collective voice of the villagers of Ilmorog. This "we" voice stands above the characters and judges their actions from the point of view of the community and the values it embodies. The "we" voice expresses bemusement at the new teacher Munira, surprise at the appearance of the first car in Ilmorog carrying Wanja's belongings, and joy at the singing and dancing at the festival before harvest time. The other, omniscient, narrator is more detached and authorial, and offers judgments of a different sort: sometimes factual, sometimes ironic, sometimes damning. It explains, for example, the cycles of rains on the land and comments on Munira's father's "holy trinity" of Bible, Coin, and Gun.

The four protagonists of the novel, the school-teacher Munira, the shopkeeper and ex-freedom fighter Abdullah, the bargirl Wanja, and the activist Karega, reveal the details of their lives not only in their confessions to others but in their musings to themselves. The confessions in the novel are powerful and again reminiscent of tales told by oral storytellers, drawing listeners in and creating a heightened expectation of a dramatic revelation. Through the confessions readers learn of the remarkable events in the characters' past and also discover how their lives overlap. The characters' private thoughts also are revealed as they meditate to themselves. Munira, in particular, as he recounts the details of his twelve years in Ilmorog to the police (in a combined public and private disclosure) allows readers into his singular world. By juxtaposing each of the characters' private thoughts about themselves with the narrators' and the other characters' perceptions of them, Ngugi presents complex portraits of these often very troubled human beings.

Indeed, one of the striking features of the novel is the complexity of the four protagonists, all of whom turn out to be quite different than they at first appear and who in many ways remain enigmas to the end. Munira is not an idealist who comes to teach at this rural outpost, it becomes clear, but a weak and fearful man who has escaped from the derision of a cruel father. He shies away from action throughout the novel, but it is he who performs the final, decisive act. Abdullah, it turns out, is not the insignificant shopkeeper of the early chapters of the novel, but a brave man of action who fought for his country in its greatest time of need. Wanja, whose unswerving energy seems to bring the possibility of positive change to Ilmorog, is both temptress and savior, dreamer and practical-minded businesswoman. Karega is an idealistic young man carrying scars of the tragic loss of his first love and in search of an outlet for his intellectual and political energies. Detailed pictures of all four characters emerge not from a third-person description of their lives, but from the multiple perspectives that shed light on their most public actions as well as their private self-deceptions.

Other characters in the novel also add to the narrative richness with their descriptions of events and situations. The old bard Nyakinya recites to the Ilmorog's grand past and tells of her husband's heroic struggle against the British. The lawyer explains to Karega what he thinks to be the political situation in Kenya and the best means to remedy it. All the viewpoints are, again, presented in quick succession, one following the other, sometimes with little or no indication of the narrative shift. The back-and-forth movement of the novel, the varied voices, and the explorations of Kenya's situation past and present have a sometimes dizzying effect. This sense of instability mirrors masterfully the alienation and disorientation in the lives of the villagers in the novel. Subjected to colonial rule, stripped of their land, forced to answer to corrupt governments unconcerned by their plight, their past values corroded by a new culture of money and power, this is a community in turmoil. The disorder in their lives is expressed not only through the details but in the telling of their story.

The narrative structure using multiple points of view also fits appropriately with the work as a detective story. At the beginning of the novel it is learned that three prominent businessmen have been murdered, and the four suspects are called in for questioning. Inspector Godfrey, in charge of the case, means to solve the problem like a ''jigsaw puzzle.'' The details of the crime slowly unfold, with the various reports and revelations that are offered by the different characters and narrators, but readers, like the inspector, must be careful whose account to believe. It is interesting to note that Godfrey leaves Ilmorog thinking that he has in fact solved the case even though he is missing a crucial piece of the puzzle. He has learned that it was Munira who burned down the house with the three brewery directors in it. However, he does not know that Wanja in fact killed one of the three men before fire broke out. This information is only gleaned because readers are allowed insight into Wanja's private thoughts.

Many critics have faulted *Petals of Blood* for its overtly political message and for the didactic voice that emerges from the narrators as well as individual characters. They find that the damning tone of the book, as it criticizes capitalism, colonialism, and neocolonialism, detracts from the work's artistic integrity. It is also assumed by many commentators, including Eustace Palmer and Simon Gikandi, that the voice of Karega is the voice of consciousness in the novel, and that Ngugi endorses Karega's socialist analysis and solution. They find this to be a shortcoming for a piece of an imaginative literature in which the reader should not be *told* what to believe. However, it should be noted that although Karega is a character who is portrayed very sympathetically, he is not the most prominent figure in the novel. Most of the events are not seen through his eyes, but rather through Munira's. Also, interestingly, although Karega seems to be the voice that echoes that of the author, he in fact issues a warning against taking any person's viewpoint too seriously. When Munira insists that what children in the

> " The disorder in their lives is expressed not only through the details but in the telling of their story."

school should learn are ''simple facts,'' Karega disagrees, saying:

> I cannot accept that there is a stage in our growth as human beings when all we need are so-called facts and information. Man is a thinking being from the time he is born to the time he dies. He looks, he hears, he touches, he smells, he tastes, and he sifts all these impressions in his mind to arrive at a certain outlook in his direct experience of life. Are there pure facts? When I am looking at you, how much I see of you is conditioned by where I stand or sit; by the amount of light in this room; by the power of my eyes; by whether my mind is occupied with other thoughts and what thoughts. Surely the story we teach about the seven blind men who had never seen an elephant is instructive. Looking and touching, then, do involve interpretation. Even assuming that there were pure facts, what about their selection? Does this not then involve interpretation?

So then even if the author does sympathize with the solution offered by Karega, he in fact uses the voice of this character to point out to readers that any solution must be scrutinized closely by those who are presented with it. And, he says, at all stages in humans' lives they are equipped to learn the truth for themselves. Karega himself, in searching for a solution to the pressing social problems he sees all around, does not unquestioningly accept the position of the activist lawyer, but seeks out his own understanding and answer. This emphasis on different interpretations, again underscored by the use of varying perspectives in the narration, seems to urge readers not to take at face value any political viewpoint but to sift through the different impressions and think through possible solutions. This appeal seems to soften the otherwise didactic thrust of the novel.

Of course the fact that Ngugi in his novel uses his unusual narrative device to achieve certain effects does not mean that the technique is without flaws. Certainly in some parts of *Petals of Blood* the language is stilted and ideas put into the mouths of certain characters jarring. But despite these failings,

Ngugi's work offers a bold and original style that is eminently suited to its subject matter, and the unusual method of storytelling in *Petals of Blood* adds richness and depth to this ambitious and complex novel.

Source: Uma Kukathas, in an essay for *Literature of Developing Nations for Students*, Gale, 2000.

K. L. Goodwin

In the following essay on Ngugi's Petals of Blood, *K.L. Godwin examines the genre of Commonwealth literature and the politicization of fiction in the quest for a balance between "national affection and intellectual pan-Africanism".*

Commonwealth literature is not everyone's notion of a viable or useful category, and some may think that it smacks of postcolonial cultural imperialism, but it is a wider (if less precise) category than 'world literature written in English' and has the advantage of admitting regional and national literatures that would otherwise have to find shelter under the not-necessarily appropriate umbrellas of the 'third world', 'black', 'Asian', or 'Pacific' writing. One does not have to approve of British (or Australian, New Zealand, or United States) colonial rule to recognise that its effects on education, legal systems, writing, and culture generally continue to be evident, so that there are still useful comparisons to be made between the literature of one former British colony and another. That does not mean, of course, that the comparisons are necessarily very important ones; certainly it does not mean that they constitute the most interesting features of the literatures. It does mean, though, that 'Commonwealth literature' still makes sense as a category, somewhere between national literature or the literature of one language and world literature (of necessity partly in translation).

One of the questions much debated over the past three decades has been 'How political should Commonwealth literature be?' To ask this question is to beg a great many more and to invite a multitude of glib, qualified, relativistic answers. 'What is the difference between literature and propaganda?'; 'Can we afford literature in desperate times and circumstances?'; 'Can worthwhile literatures be written in a corrupt society?' are some of the obvious questions. 'As political as the writer wants or the society needs'; 'As political as is compatible with literary (or permanent, or human, or social, or cultural, or. . . .) value': 'It doesn't matter' are some of the obvious answers. . . .

In studying the satirical allegory of Ngugi in *Petals of Blood, Devil on the Cross* and *Matigari* it would be possible to raise a number of rhetorical questions concerned with the blending of modes. It is sufficient at this stage to note that Ngugi moves effortlessly between realism, satire, farce, fantasy, and exhortation. Narrative fiction is not just for telling a story in a realistic mode; but can also discuss the telling of the story, raise questions about the reliability of the narrator or the speaker, and create spaces where the story is held while exhortation or discussion occurs. For Ngugi, fiction can both create its own illusion and strip away the illusion of others. That is why it is so dangerous to the authoritarian state. That is why, in *Matigari,* the Minister for Truth and Justice bans all dreams, desires, and songs (120, 125), why he attributes 'distortion' to fiction (103) and announces that 'All we are interested in here is *development*. We are not interested in fiction.' Ngugi's sense of irony makes him immediately follow that anti-fiction pronouncement with a fiction created by the Minister:

> '. . . Let us now forget that such people as Matigari ma Njiruungi ever existed. Let us with one accord, like loyal parrots, agree that Matigari ma Njiruungi was just a bad dream. That bid of history was just a bad dream, a nightmare in fact. We have qualified professors here who can write new history for us . . .'

Here is an example of the narrator creating a fictional character, the Minister for Truth and Justice, who creates the fiction that the fiction of which he is part does not exist. In putting things this way I am, of course, using 'fiction' in at least two different senses (narrative and falsehood), but the blurring of these two senses originates not with me but with Ngugi. It is, indeed, part of the fabric of his satire, for one of the major objects of satire in the novel is a government *Doublethink* or *Newspeak* that bears comparison with that found in *Animal Farm* or *1984* .

Satire, like metaphor, symbol, allegory, and myth, is a notoriously artful and intricate process. In this regard it is like *Newspeak*, one of its own targets. In other words, it partakes of the qualities of what it is condemning. This is an inescapable feature, because both the objects and the process of satire are conveyed by language, which is itself notoriously wayward and devious.

Ngugi's specific satirical purpose is made more intricate because he wants to condemn one kind of transnationalism while advocating another. He wants to condemn the transnationalism of the Theng'eta Breweries, which are foreign owned but to advocate a kind of trasnational romantic socialism based on small self-managed units, both rural and industrial. In such an ideal community of international socialism national boundaries would be transcended or atleast rendered inconsequential. The capitalist power struggle would be eliminated. It would be a world quite the converse of the one in which *Petals of Blood* is situated. In such a newly constructed world Wanja would no longer have to say 'This world. . . .this Kenya. . . .this Africa knows only one law. You eat somebody or you are eaten' (291).

The satiric target in *Petals of Blood* is a neo-colonialism that represents economic and intellectual bondage. The economy of Kenya is controlled by multinational corporations that provide local directorships to government ministers and other capitalists. The education is represented by Siriana Secondary School (mentioned also in *Weep Not, Child*) where Cambridge Fraudsham has been replaced as headmaster by Chui, 'a black replica of Fraudsham'. *Petals of Blood* presents, then, an indictment of 'development', multinational corporations, international finance, and neo-colonial education.

In the novel, Karega (the Gikuyu name meaning rebel, or he who refuses) is not prepared to accept that there is no alternative to the law that 'You eat somebody or you are eaten.' His answer to Wanja is that 'Then we must create another world, a new earth'. When interrogated by Inspector Godfrey, he explains how this might come about:

> 'I don't believe in the elimination of individuals. There are many Kimerias and Chuis in the country. They are the products of a system, just as workers are products of a system. It's the system that needs to be changed. . .and only the workers of Kenya and the peasants can do that.'

Karega has become disillusioned by the constitutional methods advocated by the compassionate lawyer who helped the people from Ilmorog when they came to Nairobi to petition their MP. According to Karega, the lawyer (who is subsequently murdered) placed too much faith in such institutions as parliament and private property. Karega is opposed to most sources of political and economic power. He abhors the venality and tribal manoeuvrings of parliamentarians; private ownership of land; the business-infiltrated trade unions; and the churches. Karega's final vision, at the very end of the novel, brings together most of these attitudes. Although cleared of complicity in the fire at Wanja's brothel, he is to be detained because 'I am suspected of being a communist at heart'. The young worker-girl who visits him in prison tells him

> **"** One of the questions much debated over the past three decades has been 'How political should Commonwealth literature be?'"

of rumours that there will be 'a return to the forests and the mountains' to complete the revolution that the Mau Mau leaders, Stanley Mathenge and Dedan Kimathi, began. Karega's mind reviews the situation:

> Imperialism: capitalism: landlords: earthworms. A system that bred hordes of round-bellied jiggers and bedbugs with parasitism and cannibalism as the highest goal in society. This system and its profiteering gods and its ministering angels had hounded his mother to her grave. These parasites would always demand the sacrifice of blood from the working masses. These few who had prostituted the whole land turning it over to foreigners for thorough exploitation, would drink people's blood and say hypocritical prayers of devotion to skin oneness and to nationalism even as skeletons of bones walked to lonely graves. The system and its gods and its angels had to be fought consciously, consistently and resolutely by all working people! From Koitalel through Kang'ethe to Kimathi it had been the peasants, aided by the workers, small traders and small landowners, who had mapped out the path. Tomorrow it would be the workers and the peasants leading the struggle and seizing power to overturn the system and all its prying bloodthirsty gods and gnomic angels, bringing to an end the reign of the few over the many and the era of drinking blood and feasting of human flesh. Then, only then, would the kingdom of man and woman really begin, they joying and loving in creative labour. . . .

The Christian Eucharistic imagery of eating flesh and drinking blood is consistently used here to convey predation and exploitation. God and angels are used as images for the demonic intentions and practices of capitalism.

For Karega and for Ngugi there is a particular reason for using Christian imagery with a demonic interpretation. Christianity, particularly in the charismatic form represented by Lillian's movement, is both a rhetorical and a political rival to socialism or communism. The school teacher, Godfey Munira, for instance, was obsessed by the notion of a new world, a notion expressed in the kind of language he had previously heard from his white Christian headmaster (Cambridge Fraudsham) and from his narrow, sanctiomonious, Christian mother and wife. Disillusioned with education, his work, and his whole life, he is a ready convert to Lillian's movement. The street evangelist preaches about a new earth, a new world, to be achieved through Christ.

For Karega and for Ngugi the apocalyptic imagery has to be recaptured for socialism. One of the best ways of discrediting the Christian interpretation and agenda is to appropriate and subvert basic Christian terminology about the Eucharistic feast and apply it to what is obviously evil.

The process of appropriation includes both subversion and re-direction. Some of the imagery (the signifiers) must be transferred from a favourable signification (or set of signifieds) to an unfavourable one. The primary example is that of the Eucharistic feast. Some must be retained with a favourable signification but transferred to a different set of referents. In other words, the connotation and ambience of the images have to remain auspicious and commendatory but what they refer to has to be shifted. The primary example is of the new heaven and the new earth, transferred from a Christian apocalypse to a socialist one. . . .

The delicacy of the manoeuvre that has simultaneously to subvert and retain well-known symbols is equally in evidence in the treatment of attitudes to nation, colour, class, and gender. Ngugi wants on the one hand to examine and criticise aspects of these cultural indicators, and on the other to re-direct them towards his utopian vision of a socialist world. There is, I believe, a latent theory in Ngugi that cultural expression is bound up with, and can be an index of the quality of social and political life. In a simple form this theory can perhaps be attributed to John Ruskin. In a more complex form, involving the circular or unevenly reciprocal process of 'over-determination', it might be attributed to such theorists of cultural production as Louis Althusser. The source is, however, of less interest than the fact of Ngugi's having such a belief. When *Petals of Blood* was launched in Nairobi, he stated, in rather Althusserian terminology, that

> Literature, as part of culture, is really a reflection of the material reality under which we live . . . I have come to realise that no people can develop a meaningful national culture under any form of foreign economic domination. (*Writers in Politics*)

Two other points can appropriately be made about the process of subversion and retention. The first is that, unlike parody, it does not—indeed must not if it is to succeed—destroy the efficacy of the

original model; the power must remain though its object is altered. The second is that Ngugi did not himself invent the process of re-directing Christian symbolism in this way. In his 1973 paper, 'Literature and Society' he draws attention to an identical process occurring among the Mau Mau revolutionaries in the 1950s:

> They [the Mau Mau] took Christian songs; they took even the Bible and gave these meanings and values in harmony with the aspirations of the struggle. Christians had often sung about heaven and angels, and a spiritual journey in a spiritual intangible universe where metaphysical disembodied evil and good were locked in perpetual spiritual warfare. Christians sang:. . . (*Writers in Politics*)

The example Ngugi gives is the Gikuyu version of the hymn 'Stand up! stand up for Jesus! Ye soldiers of the Cross'. He quotes the text from *Nyumbo cia K'uinira Ngia,* Hymn No. 115. Re-translated into English, one of the stanzas becomes:

> Young men arise
> Jesus calls you to
> Take up spears and shields and to
> Throw away your fears.
> For what's the point of fear?
> Go ye with bravery;
> Led by Jesus
> You'll be victorious.

In a song book published by Gakara Wanjau about 1952, the words of Song No. 41 represent a re-alignment of 'Stand up! stand up for Jesus!' towards the Mau Mau cause. The translation offered by Ngugi is as follows:

> Young men arise
> Mbiu calls you to
> Take up spears and shields
> And don't delay,
> Get out quickly
> Come help one another
> The white people are foreigners
> And they are very strong (i.e. well-armed).

This is clearly not a parody of the Christian hymn, but a reorientation of it to a different worthy object. In Ngugi's words:

> It was as if the people of Kenya did to the Christian universe and spiritual idealism what Marx did to Hegel's dialectics: made them stand firmly on the ground, our earth, instead of standing on their head. The aim, in other words, is to change a people's world outlook, it is to seize back the right and the initiative to define oneself.

Christianity is, then, ripe for the appropriation of its imagery, its re-direction to other ends. It has a powerful hold on the cultural thinking of the people; it is foreign and multi-national; it is, as Karega says in *Petals of Blood,* a 'a weapon against the workers'; and it has many adherents among the neocolonial classes of parliamentarians, civil servants, and business people. But some of Ngugi's objects of satire are not readily amenable to the re-direction of Christian imagery. The British concept of the rule of law, for instance, has been satirised through exaggeration and absurdity in its own terms, as it is in the speech of the Minister for Truth and Justice in *Matigari.* The Christian doctrine of quietism and obedience to civil authority ('Render unto Caesar what is Caesar's, and unto God what is God's') cannot be re-directed. It has, on Ngugi's principles, to be opposed and rejected, for the allegory of *Matigari* leads to the discarding of the belt of peace and the return to the weapons used in the war of liberation. In order to have its due place in this allegorical meaning Christian quietism must be made to seem irrelevant or inappropriate (except for hypocrites), and this is the effect when the doctrine is enunciated by the priest to the earnest seeker Matigari. At the beginning of Part 3 Matigari thus comes to the conclusion that

> one could not defeat the enemy with arms alone, but one could also not defeat the enemy with words alone. One had to have the right words, but these words had to be strengthened by the force of arms.

In this final part, Matigari comes to the conclusion that distinctions and discriminations through colour, gender, class, and nationality have been imposed by colonialism and continued by neo-colonialism. They must be abolished, an action which involves taking up arms against the privileged class of 'the imperialists and their retinue of messengers, overseers, police and military' by 'the working people'.

The status of one form of distinction is left ambiguous. Near the end of *Matigari* the children of the rubbish dump begin a chant against oppression, treason, the governmental doctrine of parrotology and parrotry, and 'nationality-chauvinism'. To what extent this is intended to be an anti-nationalist or pan-African slogan is unclear. It could be interpreted as that or it could be equally plausibly interpreted as a cry merely against jingoism and the equation of the national interest with the ruling party's interest. It may well be that Ngugi, in order to remain a credible alternative national leader, needs to obscure this point. It is just as ambiguous in *Petals of Blood* and *Devil on the Cross.* Perhaps the most succinct of the ambiguity occurs in *Petals of Blood,* where Karega, in one of his streams of consciousness, reflects on who should own the land:

> Why, anyw400, should soil, any soil, which after all was what was Kenya, be owned by an individual? Kenya, the soil, was the people's common shamba, and there was no way it could be right for a few, or a section, or a single nationality, to inherit for their sole use what was communal. . .

'Nationality' here primarily refers, of course, to the various peoples who inhabit Kenya—the Gikuyu, Luhya, Luo, Kamba, Kalenjin, and so on. But the statement does raise the question of how the boundaries of present-day Kenya were imposed and whether the European concepts of 'nationality' and 'nationhood' are appropriate. The dilemma of balancing national affection or acceptability with intellectual pan-Africanism affects not only Ngugi; it is the dilemma of many African patriots, whether pro-or anti-governmet.

Source: K. L. Goodwin, "Nationality — Chauvinism Must Burn!: Utopian Visions in Petals of Blood and Marigari," in *The Literary Criterion,* Vol. XXVII, No. 3, 1991, p. 1–14.

Ayo Mamudu

In the following essay on Ngugi's Petals of Blood, *Ayo Mamudu examines the narrative structures of the work as used to weave the past, present and futures of the characters into a portrait that illustrates the general history of human behavior.*

> *Time present and time past*
> *Are both perhaps present in the future,*
> *And time future contained in time past.*
> — *T.S. Eliot, "Burnt Norton"*

Considered with his earlier novels, Ngugi's *Petals of Blood* shows a relative complexity which is inseparable from the ambitiousness of its author's aim and scheme: to examine the tangle of human relationships (and identify an underlying principle), to make clear patterns comprehensively observed in the history of a people (and show the *wholeness* of that history), and, above all, to achieve these objectives in a way that captures the changeable, dramatic and often chaotic qualities of life or history as it unfolds. Consequently, *Petals of Blood* shows a greater attention to form than Ngugi's earlier novels, of which he has said, "I put a lot of emphasis on content and language, not so much on form" (Ngugi, "Making of a Rebel").

Ngugi takes care to elaborate his view of human relationships, to which is closely related his view of the history of his society. He demonstrates the complexity of human relationships, exploring the whirlpool effect of people's actions, social interactions and personal dreams and schemes. Then, out of the confusion emerges a clear pattern described

> " ...on the individual level, one life not only shows parallels to and repetitions of motions in another (past) life but also repeats aspects and moments of itself as it twists and turns in its career; on the national scale, the pattern of historical repetition and parallel all but acquires the qualities of cyclicalness, giving the impression of progression without progress."

by Wanja in the image of the Siamese twins of love and hate:

> Love and hate—Siamese twins—back to back in a human heart. Because you loved you also hated: and because you hated you also loved. What you loved decided what you would have to hate in relation to what you loved. What you hated decided the possibilities of what you could love in relation to that which you hated. And how did one know what one loved and hated?

Further explanation is provided by the view of history that in the life both of the individual and the community, the past, the present and the future are dynamically interrelated, each melding with the others. In Karega's words to Wanja—''To understand the present . . . you must understand the past. To know where you are, you must know where you came from, don't you think?''—there is the appreciation of the necessarily basic links between past and present—without, perhaps, awareness of the dynamic qualities of those links. The awareness, underscored by the scope and pattern of events in the novel, is implicit in Karega's demand for a ''critical'' study of the past, not as a museum piece but in order to secure '''a living lesson to the present''' (Awooner). Yet another view of history which the novel demonstrates is that in many ways the present (as by the force of logic, the future) tends to replicate the past. Thus, on the individual level, one life not only shows parallels to and repetitions of motions in another (past) life but also repeats

aspects and moments of itself as it twists and turns in its career; on the national scale, the pattern of historical repetition and parallel all but acquires the qualities of cyclicalness, giving the impression of progression without progress.

In *Petals of Blood*, the past is a living and very active reagent in the life and events of the present; in the affairs of individuals and of the community, past (immediate as well as distant) and present explain, complement, reinforce and comment on one another. It is to achieve these aims that the story of the novel is served, as Munira says of one month of his life, ''in broken cups of memory.'' And to give order to the lives of the leading characters as well as draw all into a pattern of unity and symmetry, Ngugi assigns a significant role in interpersonal relations to what may be described as the burdens of the past, what Munira refers to as the ''claims of some shadowy connections in our past.'' Thus, to reveal the characters fully, the novel focuses less on their present and more on their past; for the greater part, it digs into the past in trying to understand the present. Sometimes, of course, the present sheds a new light on the past just as most other times, the past illumines the present; consistently, both past and present serve to fill out, clarify or complete the character sketch. In the process the story takes on a quality of complexity and the method of its telling is *revelatory*, moving from a position of seeing darkly to one of seeing clearly: a method not incompatible with the nature and means of the detective-story frame which loosely but clearly girdles the events of the novel.

One consequence of the *revelatory* method or approach is that the story gains in interest as rather profuse patterns of repetitions, parallels and ironies emerge. Bit by bit, a number of things are revealed, exposed, even explained; often the effect is surprise. The life and career of Munira may serve to illustrate this method, which draws attention to the complexity of things yet seeks to resolve the complex totality into comprehensible strands, which tries to find recurrent patterns in the life of the individual, in his relations with others and within the larger context of his society. Considered a non-achiever by his father, Munira is burdened with guilt; the feeling of guilt explains his choice of Ilmorog, ''his rural cloister,'' as the place to settle down at as well as the devotion and enthusiasm he shows in working there. His feeling that he is part of the family without actually belonging to it is partly explained by, and says something for his admiration of his sister Mukami's rebellious spirit before her early death; and his attitude and moral position are implicitly commented on by the gradual disclosure of the dishonesty and mammonism which are the true foundations of his father's success. The notion of success or failure (real or apparent) provides the background to Munira's sense of achievement after setting Wanja's house on fire: "He, Munira, had willed and acted, and he felt, as he knelt down to pray, that he was no longer an outsider for he had finally affirmed his oneness with the Law." His willingness to surrender to "the Law" must be related to his youth with his over-zealous Christian father, to the influence of Lillian, the reformed prostitute (whom Munira himself patronized a number of times) and leader of a religious sect and, finally, his own persistent if unadmitted desire to evade responsibility. It is interesting to observe that it takes the religious activities of a one-time prostitute to imbue Munira with a religious fervour that makes him see in the burning of Wanja's whorehouse an act of purification. His action and the moral intention which prompts it reach back to Munira's schoolboy days when, after patronizing Amina the prostitute, he built an imitation of her house and set it on fire as an act of atonement; then, he "watched the flames and he felt truly purified by fire." Ironically, fire has never been far from the thoughts of Wanja herself; she finds in fire a continual threat to her family, citing her aunt's death by burning, her own narrow escape from the flames at the Kamiritho Heavenly Bar (the very place where Munira the schoolboy had patronized Amina) and the little fire which mars her celebration in Ilmorog. But, curiously, she has always also found in fire something similar to Munira's thoughts on the night he sets *her* house on fire; a symbol of purification—

> "—but I have liked to believe that she burnt herself like the Buddhists do, which then makes me think of the water and the fire of the beginning and the water and the fire of the second coming to cleanse and bring purity to the earth of human cruelty and loneliness."

There can be no over-emphasizing the sense of discovery which the revelatory approach creates in the reader as well as among the characters themselves; from past facts or actions and present knowledge, significances are built up and these draw further attention to the intricacy of the web of human relationships. There is something in the manner of telling which lends a startling quality to our knowing: that Karega is the son of Mariamu, a settler labourer on Munira's father's plantations whose other son Nding'uri was the friend and companion of Abdulla in the Mau Mau struggles; that the two of them were betrayed by Kimeria, who has since risen to become one of the three African directors of the Theng'eta Breweries; that Kimeria seduced and abandoned Wanja as a schoolgirl who, since coming to Ilmorog, loves Karega in preference to Munira, whose own sister Mukami had committed suicide when their father opposed her love for Karega; that Chui, another director of the Theng'eta Breweries, was as a boy expelled from Siriana together with Munira; that Munira taught Karega at Manguo, serving as referee when the latter applied for admission to Siriana; that Karega was later expelled from the school for leading a strike; that the Nairobi lawyer is himself a product of Siriana; that Abdulla, having found Joseph scavenging for food at a refuse dump (a thing Abdulla himself had done as a boy), will find part of his final satisfaction in life in Joseph's admission into Siriana, his fees paid by Wanja who makes the money as a prostitute from patrons who include Chui, Kimeria and Mzigo. . . . Thus utterances, actions and events which by themselves appear insignificant or ordinary are endowed with new meaning and new significance through the unravelling skein of the relationships between the individuals as well as through the interplay between the past and the present.

To achieve the interlacing of past and present, the separate worlds of memories and of present actions are mapped out, sometimes side by side and other times mounted one on the other; always, the strength of the links which bind the two worlds is clearly demonstrated. Occasionally, Ngugi draws attention to the concreteness of the realm of memories, this other world which is as physical and solid as the plains of Ilmorog. Munira may thus be shown "absorbed in thoughts he did not know he had, speaking from a past he should have forgotten, crossing valleys and hills and ridges and plains of time to the beginning of his death. . . ." Abdulla seems to suggest, on one occasion, that to revisit that world is an exertion which registers on the features or that he is able to recall that world with a freshness which leaves its mark on his mood:

> Abdulla cleared his throat. His face changed. He suddenly seemed to have gone to a land hidden from them, a land way back in a past only he could understand.

Indeed, recognizable signposts are put up in the shape of face, the turn of thought or the sound of voice, pointing the way from the present to the past, from the world of the present to that of memories. In all, these signposts emphasize internal space as the ground for much of the action of the novel. Thus, recalling his school days in Siriana, Munira's voice could "become more and more faint with the progress of the narrative. But it retained the weight and power of a bitter inward gaze''; similarly drifting into the past, Wanja ''lowered her voice a little as she said the last words and Munira could somehow imagine a tortured soul's journey through valleys of guilt and humiliation and the long sleepless nights of looking back to the origins of the whole journey.'' A character's transport from the one to the other world is easily recognized by the reader when the charcter becomes ''absorbed in himself'' or dwells ''alone within that inward gaze'' or when adverbs such as ''thoughtfully'' and ''dreamily'' occur in the narrative. The occasions or reasons for the frequent journeys into the world of the past do not always have to do with introspection or thoughtfulness; sometimes a face, a situation or an event may remind a character of something similar, analogous or explicatory, just as a story or an account of events offered by a member of a group may set off another member on such a journey. There is, besides, the unique night at Nyakinyua's when the drinking of Theng'eta seems particularly to sharpen the memory, shed inhibitions and loosen the tongue.

For the larger purpose of *Petals of Blood* the interconnections of past, present and future on a communal scale are stressed. Narratively, this purpose dictates the use of multiple points of view so that the vast expanse (in terms of time and place) of events either as lived out or filtered through the individual minds and memories can be adequately and convincingly reported and so as to emphasize the entwined complexities of the realities, facts or events which cumulatively constitute the history of a people. Although events are seen through the eyes of a number of other characters, there is the voice of a chief narrator whose role ought perhaps to be more properly regarded as that of a presenter. The absence of a clear definition of that role explains why the chief narrator, in relating communal events and developments, is sometimes an individual observer/participant (''I''), sometimes a member of the participant group (''we''); at other times, he is the observer, aloof, omnipresent and omniscient; yet other times, he is the invisible recorder of folk history, the disembodied voice of the group.

Literally and symbolically the main characters relate to different generations and periods of the history of the people, in broad terms, the past, the present and the future. The very old characters— Njuguna, Ruoro, Muturi, Nyakinyua, etc. —are in the novel not as ''decorative'' background or even because they provide the nostalgia which hovers about the fringes of the novel. In their persons these characters make the distant past live and through their reminiscence and occasional use of legends the novel in effect encompasses the history of the Kenyan people right from the legendary founding patriarch Ndemi through the period of ''the Arab and Portuguese marauders from the Coast.'' Abdulla advances the history through the ''Mau Mau'' struggles, bridging the past and present when the main actors are younger: the lawyer, Wanja and Karega, with the last two pointing the way to the future when the child Wanja is expecting alongside the unnamed children daily being born (''New Mathenges . . . new Koitalels . . . new Kimethis . . . new Piny Owachos . . . these were born every day among the people . . .'') will take up the continual struggle.

The people's spirit to fight, to struggle, to reject what is objectionable in the social institutions represents in a deeper, less physical sense the continuity between the past, the present and the future. This fact supplies one rather subtle dimension to the description of Nyakinyua: ''The old woman, strong sinews forged by earth and sun and rain, was the link binding past and present and future.'' Nyakinyua's husband, it must be remembered, had come back from the jungles of the Second World War a changed man, carrying with him the mysterious knowledge of the significance of the fire emitted by the fabulous creature that he and others had encountered in the jungles; in his words:

> ''. . . When it spat out the light, I thought I saw sons and daughters of black people of the centuries rise up as one to harness the power of that light, and the white man who was with us was frightened by what would happen when that power was in the hands of these black gods . . .''

Part of that ''power'' glimpsed by Nyakinyua's man was to be demonstrated during the Kenyan struggle against the British colonial government. And because the ''black gods'' of the vision turned out after independence to be considerably less than divine, even human, the struggle once again was taken up, to stop ''the gigantic deception being played on a whole people by a few who had made it, often in alliance with foreigners.'' Nyakinyua plays a leading role as a member of Old Ilmorog people's delegation to the city; much older and much weaker in body, she demonstrates the same spirit in New Ilmorog when her land is in danger from the grasping hooks of the new economic forces. She summons her old spirit and courage, tries to rouse and rally similarly placed peasants and is let down; but she decides to fight alone: ''I'll go alone . . . my man fought the white man. He paid for it with his blood . . . I'll struggle against these black oppressors . . . alone . . . alone. . . .''

Abdulla also symbolizes continuity in the history of a people through the spirit of struggle; but his significance is not confined to this role. A living, maimed testimony of the people's struggle in the past when Kenyans took the oath—of which the new KCO oath is a perversion—Abdulla helps by association to extend temporally and spatially the history of struggle and resistance, recalling and evoking Ole Masai, Dedan Kimathi, Chaka, Toussaint, Nkrumah, Nasser, Cabral. Abdulla in addition demonstrates the cohesive force of the epic journey in the structure of the novel: besides its obvious symbolic signification of a search into the kingdom of knowledge (where Munira for one discovers ''that man's estate is rotten at heart,'' the journey affords Abdulla an opportunity to relive his past as a battler, on the same old plains and valleys. Because of his activities on this journey, which parallel, recall and reinforce his activities during the nation's struggles in the past, he is ''transformed'' in the eyes of the people; every member of the delegation appreciates his courage, and

> Wanja, sitting just behind Nyakinyua and Abdulla, was particularly happy: she had always felt that Abdulla had had a history to that stump of a leg. Now it was no longer a stump, but a badge of courage indelibly imprinted on his body.

Even before Nyakinyua and Abdulla are dead, Karega proves to be an insurance that the spirit of struggle in the land is not about to die. He rejects the lawyer's liberalism as the answer to the problems of the land because of its inherent contradictions, contemptuously disregards Munira's (and Lillian's) offer of religious piety or even moral purity as the means of establishing justice on earth or of preparing the self for a future life after death, shares Wanja's rejection of the role of victim (but rejects what she sees as the solution, to join the exploiters if one cannot beat them) and believes firmly in the collective struggle as the one path to a New World, a New Earth. If the New Jerusalem is not reached today, Karega feels sure, the fighters among the children daily being born will struggle through into its walls tomorrow.

Because struggle has always remained one of the permanent realities of the history of the people, *Petals of Blood* may arguably be considered a celebration of the spirit of struggle and of the people's heroes who lead such struggle. Indeed, the impression is created that the fact of struggle can in itself be an end worth celebrating; because a single struggle or an act of defiance must send reverberations down the corridors of history, that struggle or defiant act easily acquires larger-than-life dimensions in the minds of the people. Hence the ''epic journey'' to the city is soon incorporated into popular history through songs so that, for instance, in singing about it, Nyakinyua is careful to emphasize the representative aspects and the timeless qualities of the experience:

> it was no longer the drought of a year ago that she was singing about. It was all the droughts of the centuries and the journey was the many journeys travelled by people even in the mythical lands of two-mouthed Marimus and struggling humans. She sang of other struggles, of other wars—the arrival of colonialism and the fierce struggles waged against it by newly circumcised youth.

Yet, the truth is that if the fact of struggle and the act of heroism have consistently recurred in the history of the people, it is in part precisely because oppression, social injustice and disaffection have been also recurrent in the community. In other words, if the people can proudly point to a pantheon of heroes, past and present, it is because the community has known the presence of the Arab slave traders, the marauding Portuguese, the European settlers and colonial administrators—each group needing and obtaining the services and collaboration of some members of the community—and now (worse still) the new African elite, enjoying a disproportionate share of the wealth of the land. It is the fact of failure in the past, the respected past, as in the present which has always necessitated the act of struggle—and created the fabled and living heroes. In the description of the present state of the nation which Wanja gives in terms of Ilmorog countryside, the *past* she refers to is that of the period about the time of political independence; Munira's contribution to the discussion draws attention to the fact that there is nothing exactly new in the present disappointments:

> ''So green in the past,'' she said. ''So green and hopeful . . . and now this.'' ''A season of drought . . . so soon . . . so soon!'' echoed Karega, remembering past flowers of promise. ''It's the way of the world,'' said Munira. . . .

The disappointments (past and present) which constitute a major focus of interest in the novel always bear the marks of betrayal. Recalling her husband's observations about the struggle for political freedom, Nyakinyua remarks: '''There were a few traitors among them, those who wanted to remain porters at the gate, collectors of the fallout from the white man's control of that power . . . .''' Ezekieli, formerly Waweru, the father of Munira, is a surviving member of that group, living on as a materially bloated Christian. In general, the quality of life of most members of the community and the socio-economic structures which are accountable for the way things are turn Karega's thought to "'Massacres of hopes and dreams and beauty.'" To prove the point, there is Abdulla who in old age moved about in "the wilderness of his bitterness, of his consciousness of broken promises, of the wider betrayal of the collective blood of the Kenyan fighters for land and freedom."

One reliable piece of evidence that failure or disappointment betrayal (like victory and the feeling which attends it) is a self-repeating thing is Ngugi's frequent recourse, in reference to hopes, yearnings and desires in persons and social situations in the present as in the past, to phrases such as "new hopes," "new beginnings," "new horizons," even "new world" or "new earth." Obviously the frequent appearance of these phrases means clearly that a gap has frequently separated attainment and expectations. In frequently promising herself new starts in life and entertaining fresh hopes, Wanja's life becomes a metaphor for the career of the nation. Her coming to Ilmorog to settle, for example, is the result of one such promise: "Wanja had made a pact with herself. She would have a completely new beginning in Ilmorog." Her discovery later in life is equally interesting as a metaphor for the conclusions to be drawn from a survey of the national history: "Maybe life was a series of false starts, which once discovered, called for more renewed efforts at yet another beginning." Additionally, of course, the discovery is significant because it helps to clarify and to make acceptable Karega's conviction that "There are times . . . when victory is defeat and defeat is victory." Together Wanja's discovery and Karega's conviction (itself a discovery for Karega) make possible the final vision of the novel which in turn allows the mood of optimism to predominate over that of despair.

In order to summarize comprehensively the cyclical patterns he observes in the history of Kenya (as well, of course, as to add local colour to events) Ngugi often turns his attention to the seasons and the human activities related to the different seasons; from these he draws images and metaphors. It is appropriate for instance that the people of Ilmorog (mostly peasants and herdsmen) live and feel in accordance with the rain-drought cycle; besides, in the prevalent season Ngugi finds metaphors with which to make statements about the quality of life of the people. In periods of drought Ilmorog is fre-

quently described in terms such as "this wasteland" and "desert place"; in the rains, the metaphorical, even symbolic, possibilities multiply. For example, there can be the simple, direct descriptions of the peasants "busy putting seeds in the soil" and the combination of fact and symbol in a statement such as:

> At the beginning of April it started raining. The eyes of the elders beamed with expectation of new life over Ilmorog. . . .

The process by which the fact takes on symbolic significance is illustrated in the linking of the journey to the city with rain and crop (in the sense of hopes and expectations):

> Yes, it will rain. Crops will grow. We shall always remember the heroes in our midst. We shall always sing about the journey in the plains.

Steadily and cumulatively the significance of the cycles of the seasons is compressed into the symbols of seeds, flower and harvest.

These symbols are used with such freedom and flexibility that complications, if not confusion, could be the reward of the unwary reader. It is easy enough to see the relationship between effort and achievement in terms of seed-time and harvest-time—as, on a personal level, Munira comes to Ilmorog in the hope of finding "a safe corner in which to hide and do some work, plant a seed whose fruits one could see . . ." It is also easy to understand the flower in terms of the period leading up to, or the expectations of, crop or harvest. It is not as easy to see or accept the flower in *Petals of Blood* as a symbol, among other possibilities, of disappointed hopes. The comments made by Munira, for instance, to his pupils reveal the startling use of the symbol of flower, the relevance of Munira's words to the social realities touches on hopes and disappointment and, by implication, the necessity to fight the oppressive agents who produce among the suffering masses a state of etiolated existence:

> "Right. This is a worm-eaten flower . . . It cannot bear fruit. That's why we must always kill worms . . . A flower can also become this colour if it's prevented from reaching the light."

From this level, the mental leaps required of the reader become relatively easy: the flower as the state of promise actually or potentially unfulfilled, as when Karega remembers "past flowers of promise"; the flower as a symbol of destruction, spiritual or physical, as when Munira acknowledges his role as "a privileged witness of the growth of Ilmorog from its beginnings in rain and drought to the present flowering in petals of blood"; and the flower as the symbol of the means of achieving moral and social purification, as when Munira has set Wanja's whorehouse on fire:

> He walked away toward Ilmorog Hill. He stood on the hill and watched the whorehouse burn, the tongues of flame from the four corners forming petals of blood, making a twilight of the dark sky.

Thus the promising state, even when unfulfilled—now or in the past—and the means by which social or moral cleansing is or is thought to be carried out in order to build new hopes, are suggested in the flower, linking seed-time with harvest-time, and as recurrent as the seasons.

As with *flower, harvest*—together with its associated ideas such as harvest-time (a culmination of both seed-time and flowering), fruit and crop—is variously pressed into symbolic service. The love relationship between Karega and Wanja is, for example, on one occasion described in direct reference to the ''new crops'': ''Their love seemed to grow with the new crops of the year.'' Besides, the anticipation of the happy rewards of a promising relationship can see the harvest in the flower. So, Munira, after arranging a tryst with Wanja, thinks: ''Beautiful petals: beautiful flowers: tomorrow would indeed by the beginning of a harvest''; and when the rewards are anticipated in the form of the flesh, they produce a ''trembling'' in the body:

> Her pleading voice had startled Munira out of his thoughts. He too wanted to stay the night. He would stay the night. A joyous trembling courses through his body. Aah, my harvest

—a description which, in a suggestion of the equality of all creatures great and small, is applied to cattle attempting to mate: ''Sometimes the male would run after a young female, giving it no rest or time to eat, expecting another kind of harvest'' — another kind because the narrator has just shifted his gaze from women harvesting peas and beans. Yet another kind of harvest is the discovery of the significance of intertwined memories, such as dawns on Karega after drinking Theng'eta and making love to Wanja: ''So many experiences, so many discoveries in a night and a half. Harvest-time for seeds planted in time past.'' A moment, any moment in the history of the individual or the community, may thus be seen as a harvest, the flower or the seed, but it may also be seen in terms of any one of the three states relative to the other two; the reference may be to the seed, for example, in the sense that the seed looks forward to the flower which bears expectations of or hopes or potential for harvest which will itself look forward to the beginning of another season when the harvest provides the seed, etc.

Such are the cycles and the seasons that Ngugi traces in the history of the Kenyan people, bound apparently to a course in which successive waves of hope must crash on the shingles of disappointment. Of course, some achievements have been made even if these are generally more apparent than real and even when attainment has been far less fulfilling than anticipation. These achievements, for what they are worth, are the result of the people's struggles, the result of what Ngugi refers to as ''the spirit of the land''; this spirit is the one guarantee of a better future for the people.

In brief then, *Petals of Blood* demonstrates not a cleavage but an integration of form and content in many ways. The telling of the story is convoluted because the properties of the story are; the complexity of human relationships and the tortuousness of the path of Kenyan history impose on Ngugi the manner of their telling. If that path, as Ngugi sees it, is far from resembling the trajectory of an archer's arrow (in a windless tunnel), it is not that of a mill either, it would seem to be a winding stair, meaning for the climber repetitive, circular motions at ever-increasing levels linking the point of departure to that of arrival. Hence, even though Kenya's today may appear in essence the same as its yesterday, unhappy, unsatisfactory and prompting struggle among the people, yet both today and yesterday provide, through the spirit of struggle evinced, the basis for the expectations of a changed, happier tomorrow. To underline the ever-present links between past, present and future and to emphasize the necessarily repetitive motions of progression through them, Ngugi interweaves present and past, now and then, here and there, finding in the cycles of nature, the seasons and human activities related to them a reservoir of metaphors and symbols.

Source: Ayo Mamudu, ''Tracing a Winding Stair: Ngugi's Narrative Methods in Petals of Blood,'' in *World Literature Written in English,* Vol. 28, No. 1, Spring, 1988, pp. 16–24.

Jennifer Evans

In the following essay, Jennifer Evans examines the development and portrayal of female characters in Ngugi's Petals of Blood. *Evans discusses how the African woman, so often sketched as a passive image, is in Ngugi's writing both repository of traditional values and active on the forefront of change; thus Ngugi's female characters act as the thread of historical continuity in his work.*

''The story of this heroic resistance: who will sing it ? Their struggles to defend their land, their wealth: who'll tell of it?'' asks the narrator in Ngugi's *Petals of Blood.* Ngugi himself, as poet-historian, has taken up the challenge to tell the people's history. In his novels he presents the lives of ordinary Kenyan men and women, seen in the context of the vital continuity of past, present, and future, as the real basis of Kenyan history. He seeks consciously to correct ''a history . . . distorted by the cultural needs of imperialism,'' which fosters the image of a weak people ''who had not struggled with nature and with other men to change their natural environment and create a positive social environment,'' and ''who had not resisted foreign domination.'' For Ngugi, struggle is the dynamic of history and society, and is central to his reappraisal of the African past. In *Petals of Blood* Karega, in his search for self-identity through black history, comes to the conclusion:

> The true lesson of history was this: that the so-called victims, the poor, the downtrodden, the masses, had always struggled with spears and arrows, with their hands and songs of courage and hope, to end their oppression and exploitation: that they would continue to struggle until a human kingdom came.

The African woman has particularly been the victim of a passive image since she suffers both colonial and male domination. Yet in Ngugi's novels women are shown to have a fundamental role in the struggle against oppression and exploitation, and often courage and hope are ultimately found in their hands. As Judith Cochrane has put it, Ngugi's women are ''guardians of the tribe.'' They are presented as the central strength of the Gikuyu people, custodians of traditional culture, and symbols of authentic Gikuyu identity.

While almost all of Ngugi's female characters are consistently endowed with traditional virtues and values, his female images are not reactionary or static. He shows that women and their lives are changing, and heroines such as Nyambura, Mumbi and Wanja are seen in the forefront of social change. At the same time it is through female images that Ngugi shows historical continuity most effectively, and reveals how qualities drawn from the traditional world find their expression in the contemporary world.

The post-independence society depicted in *Petals of Blood,* and in some of the sharp and poignant stories in *Secret Lives,* appears to be ruthless, immoral, and ruled by money. Discussing contemporary Kenyan capitalism in *Homecoming,* Ngugi says:

It is the height of irony that we, who have suffered most from exploitation, are now supporting a system that not only continues that basic exploitation, but exacerbates destructive rivalries between brothers and sisters, a system that thrives on the survival instincts of dwellers in a Darwinian jungle. The writer cannot be exempted from the task of exposing the distorted values governing such a jungle precisely because this distorts healthy human relationships.

Ngugi exposes the distorted values governing human relationships in *Petals of Blood* most vividly through his portrayal of Wanja, the barmaid-whore, a female figure more complex than the women in any of his previous works. In her role as a prostitute Wanja succinctly reveals the exploitative materialism that dominates people's lives. Her humanity is reduced to a market commodity, and her personal relationships to financial transactions. The prostitute does have a kind of independence and freedom, but Ngugi shows these to be as negative and illusory as the so-called independence of a neocolonial state. Wanja appears to reflect society's conflicts and contradictions, strengths and weaknesses. Her career illustrates the very real dilemmas facing many Kenyan women in a rapidly changing society, but it can also be seen as a metaphor for the fate of Kenya, even of the African continent as a whole. The venerated image of Mother Africa is now found as a whore, abused and exploited by the men of the new black elite.

Ngugi's criticism is aimed not so much at individuals, as at the political and economic system in which, to quote Karega, ''one could only be saintly and moral and upright by prostituting others.'' Certainly men such as Kimeria, Chui and Mzigo are corrupt opportunists who deserve little sympathy, but it would be a mistake to see Wanja simply as an innocent victim. Her potential is wasted and she is exploited, but she also exploits others, most obviously in running her own whorehouse. Her ''eat or be eaten'' philosophy is an expression of the destructive rivalry of capitalism, and is no more moral than the self-serving greed of the Kimerias. It is in this loss of innocence and idealism that Wanja differs from the heroines of Ngugi's earlier novels.

Female characters in Ngugi's first three novels have tended to be idealized. *A Grain of Wheat* presents a wider range of characters than the innocent young women and noble enduring mothers of *The River Between* and *Weep Not Child,* but the prevailing female image remains virtuous. We are never led to doubt that the heroines are motivated by anything other than idealism, and a desire for truth and justice. They remain innocent of any evil or destruction unwittingly resulting from their actions. Even Mumbi, the most fully realised woman in the earlier novels, despite her unfaithfulness to Gikonyo, retains a certain incorruptible purity. Perhaps it is this kind of female virtuousness that provokes Adrian Roscoe's criticism that the women characters do not receive "tough handling."

In *Petals of Blood* Wanja is not placed on such a pedestal. She is less perfect an more human than her predecessors. She has a generous warm personality, but can at times be selfish, callous and vindictive. Nevertheless Wanja's strengths are her dominant characteristics, and in these she resembles Ngugi's previous heroines. She does possess the admirable qualities Ngugi associates with the true Gikuyu woman. As Eustace Palmer points out:

> She belongs to that remarkable breed of Ngugi women—Mwihaki, Nyambura, Muthoni, Mumbi, Wambuku—all of them brave, resilient, resourceful and determined.

Palmer's further assertions that none of these women are "really feminine," and that "it is more the masculine aspects of Wanja's character that are stressed," appear to lack justification, unless the women's remarkable qualities and lack of passivity are regarded as essentially masculine traits. Women such as Muthoni, Nyambura, Mumbi and Wanja are involved in creating new feminine roles and changing attitudes to womanhood. The "new" Mumbi who demands respect and equality in her relationship with Gikonyo at the end of *A Grain of Wheat,* is very much a kindred spirit to Wanja, whose life is a constant struggle for respect and independence as a woman. As Wanja puts it:

> If you have a [c——]excuse my language, but it seems the curse of Adam's Eve on those who are born with it—if you are born with this hole, instead of it being a source of pride, you are doomed to either marrying someone or else being a whore.

Mumbi's is the protest of the subordinate wife, Wanja's that of the whore. Both feel they are entitled to expect something more from life. If we can see the hopeful and ardent Mumbi as an image of the new nation in 1963, then Wanja can be seen as the rather tarnished version of that image in the late sixties and seventies.

Although Mumbi and Wanja can both be described as new types of women, they do not represent a denial of their traditional heritage, but its modern expression. The close and harmonious relationship each of these young women enjoys with an older woman who is the epitome of tradition, ex-

> " He shows that women and their lives are changing, and heroines such as Nyambura, Mumbi and Wanja are seen in the forefront of social change. At the same time it is through female images that Ngugi shows historical continuity most effectively, and reveals how qualities drawn from the traditional world find their expression in the contemporary world."

presses their identification with a feminine heritage. The nature of these relationships between women derives from traditional notions of community, and appears as saving and exemplary in the contemporary context of developing capitalism. In *A Grain of Wheat* the quality of feminine cooperation, solidarity and understanding between Mumbi and Wangari shows mother-in-law and daughter-in-law not as contrasting figures, but as complementary images of two ages of Gikuyu womanhood. In *Petals of Blood* the close relationship between Wanja and her grandmother Nyakinyua has a similar function.

Critics have commented on Nyakinyua as the embodiment of traditional values. As traditional woman *par excellence,* Nyakinyua's portrayal strongly refutes the stereotype of the traditional woman as the silent passive burden-bearer. This is a woman who makes her protest by [sh——ing] a mountain in Munira's schoolyard, who excels in the poetry of "erotic abuse" in circumcision songs, who leads the women in attacking KCO officials, who convinces the elders they should support the march to Nairobi, and who takes an enthusiastic part in it. Even her death can be seen as a final protest against the loss of her land. Wanja has inherited Nyakinyua's courageous and defiant spirit, but whereas Nyakinyua appears a woman of the past, acting throughout the novel as the voice of the people's history, Wanja is very much a woman of the present. She intrigues the people of Ilmorog when she arrives by car with her modern possessions, among them the first pressure lamp to be seen in the village. Wanja initiates action and brings changes. She revives Abdulla's shop, sends Joseph to school, and sparks off Ilmorog's economic growth by selling Theng'eta. She is praised in popular songs for turning ''a bedbug of a village into a town.'' Not only does Wanja change the things around her, she is also constantly changing herself. Part of her complexity is that she is both the ''city woman'' that the villagers initially take her to be, and the rural daughter of the soil. As Abdulla jokingly puts it, she is a ''barmaid farmer.''

It is through working in the fields that Wanja and Nyakinyua come together most closely, and Wanja's enthusiasm and involvement in this practical labor show her affinity with the earth, the basis of the people's tradition and identity. A short period with the soil entirely changes Wanja's bearing and appearance. Karega observes on the march to the city:

> Over the past few weeks he had witnessed the gradual withering away of her earlier calculated smoothness, the practised light in her eyes, and the birth of a broken-nailed lean beauty.

After the return to Ilmorog, Wanja is strongly involved with the women's farming cooperative, the Ndemi-Nyakinyua group. At times such as this, when Wanja is giving of herself to the community and not selling her body to men, she appears most beautiful and most fulfilled. Both Munira and Abdulla wonder at her ''utter transformation.''

The climax of this period of transformation is Wanja's love affair with Karega. This has an idyllic, pastoral quality and is shared with delight, with the exception of Munira, by the whole of Ilmorog:

> But we were soon intrigued, fascinated, moved by the entwinement and flowering of youthful love and life and we whispered: see the wonder-gift of God. Crops will sprout luxuriant and green. We shall eat our fill and drink Theng'eta at harvest-time.

The involvement of Karega and Wanja dominates the village, and in turn reflects a new mood of communal confidence and optimism. Yet the promise of these halcyon days is not fulfilled. The untimely departure of Karega and the death of Abdulla's donkey mark the beginning of the end for the community of the old Ilmorog, and the dissolution of Wanja's identity as daughter of the soil.

Ironically, Wanja's further transformation to wigged and painted whorehouse madam finally turns upon her redemption of Nyakinyua's land.

Following Nyakinyua's death, Wanja sells her share of the new business with Abdulla in order to get the land back. This gesture is meant to serve Nyakinyua's memory and somehow honor the family tradition of resistance for which Wanja's grandfather had died, but Wanja builds on her land a whorehouse to service the needs of the new black masters such as Chui, Mzigo and Kimeria, the betrayers of the people. Outside ''Sunshine Lodge'' the grass is cut to bear the words ''Love is Poison,'' as if Wanja must carve in the earth itself the poison that is eating her heart. This is a perverse display of her estrangement from the soil, which earlier had brought her happiness when she had sowed and harvested with Nyakinyua, and loved Karega.

Only after Karega's return to Ilmorog does Wanja come to understand the meaning of Nyakinyua's dying words:

> he will return, only I fear that you may not be *there* to receive him. . .

Wanja, the daughter of the soil, is not ''there.'' She has betrayed Nyakinyua's spirit and her grandfather's heroism. Rejecting her true Gikuyu heritage, Wanja is following instead in the steps of her cowardly, greedy father. In opening her whorehouse she seeks revenge against men and a society that has failed her. Yet her prostitution of herself and others is not a challenge to corrupt capitalism, but an accommodation to its values. She becomes cynically committed to financial profit and self-interest, ''Wanja first'' as she calls it. Abdulla feels at this stage that Wanja has ''lost that firm grasp, that harmony with the invisible law.'' She no longer contributes to the well-being of the community, but grows wealthy at its expense. In Karega's terms Wanja has ''chosen sides.'' She has joined the world of the Kimerias and Chuis, those who rob the people.

Govind Narain Sharma contends that

> Karega's chief failure, hardened as he is by unhappy experiences and his doctrinaire rigidity, lies in his inability to understand Wanja and to return her love.

Karega does possess a certain moral righteousness of the young and innocent, but his critical attitude towards Wanja is perhaps a virtue rather than a failure. It is only through the confrontation with Karega in her old hut that Wanja honestly confronts herself, and comes to terms with what she is doing and what she has become. She is then able to take responsibility for the choices and actions she has made throughout her life, to see that ''at least she could have chosen to fight differently,'' and that

to destroy, and to create. This action goes
t a basic tenet of Gikuyu womanhood stated
Grain of Wheat —"a child from your own
is never thrown away." Wanja comes to feel
choosing to murder her own child that she
murdered her own life." Her barrenness is not
physical, but expressive of a far deeper
al and emotional lack of fulfillment. At the
of her affair with Karega, Wanja feels she is
t to flower," but is deprived of her opportuni-
is only after the fire that this finally comes
Having positively renounced her exploitative
Wanja approaches the world with a new con-
ness. Her pregnancy and her reunion with her
r, while a little contrived and melodramatic,
eaningful expressions of her new flowering.
a is no longer the "outsider" the meaning of
ame implies. She experiences a homecoming
eaffirms her identity with her Ilmorog origins.
heeding the voice of Nyakinyua, Wanja is
ed as her mother's daughter and daughter of
il, and regains her life-giving potential. Like
nage of the pregnant woman Gikonyo plans to
in *A Grain of Wheat*, Wanja's pregnancy is a
ol of hope and regeneration, a promise for the
e. Mumbi and Wanja, as fertile female images,
sent Mother Earth, Mother Africa, and the
val of the people, both in body and soul.
ne exemplary female fighter and mother, the
nan, in *The Trial of Dedan Kimathi*, says of
thi's spirit:

mathi was never alone . . . will never be alone. No
llet can kill him for as long as women continue to
ar children.

It is fitting that the father of Wanja's child
ld be Abdulla, the unsung Mau Mau hero who
ht with Kimathi, a man whom Karega comes to
rd as "the best self of the community, symbol
enya's truest courage." In terms of the changes
Wanja, it is significant that Abdulla sees his
ionship with her in images of an elemental
n with the earth:

nly that for him now, a woman was truly the other
orld: with its own contours, valleys, rivers, streams,
dges, sharp turns, steep and slow climbs and de-
cents, and above all, movement of secret springs of
fe . . . A woman was a world, the world.

The exact nature of the future relationship
ween Abdulla and Wanja is left undefined. Con-
tional marriage is not offered as a facile solution
Wanja's predicament as a whore. Her liberation
ot to be achieved through her union with a man,
through her fulfillment as an independent woman. In reply to her mother asking whose child she is
bearing, Wanja does not give a straightforward
answer, but draws a picture in which the image of
Abdulla is merged with other images of the people's struggle:

For one hour or so she remained completely absorbed
in her sketching. And suddenly she felt lifted out of
her own self, she felt waves of emotion she had never
before experienced. The figure began to take shape on
the board. It was a combination of the sculpture she
once saw at the lawyer's place in Nairobi and images
of Kimathi in his moments of triumph and laughter
and sorrow and terror—but without one limb. When it
was over, she felt a tremendous calm, a kind of inner
assurance of the possibilities of a new kind of power.

Through her drawing Wanja feels for the first
time the exhilaration of her creative power, expressed both in her artistry and her pregnancy. Her
confidence no longer comes from the cynical manipulation of the power of her body over men, but
from a new sense of worth and self-respect. The
sculpture Wanja mentions had puzzled the marchers
from Ilmorog because it was a figure that possessed
both male and female features, "as if it was a man
and a woman in one." Nyakinyua eventually settles
the argument about it:

"A man cannot have a child without a woman. A
woman cannot bear a child without a man. And was it
not a man and a woman who fought to redeem this
country?"

The allusions inherent in Wanja's reference to
the sculpture suggest that she has come to understand that men and women must stop exploit-
ing each other, and instead work together to destroy capitalism's "Darwinian jungle" and realize
Karega's socialist "human kingdom": "The kingdom of man and woman, joying and loving in
creative labor."

The hopeful image of a new life resulting from
the union of Abdulla and Wanja is complemented
by the beginnings of a new united workers' movement in Ilmorog. Karega learns of this development
from Akinyi, a factory girl who has been sent by the
workers to visit him in jail. The girl's optimism
rescues Karega from the depression and despair
caused by the news of his mother's death, and
revives his hopes for the future. His vision is restored in a series of female images in the closing
words of the book:

"You'll come back," she said again in a quiet affirmation of faith in eventual triumph.

He looked hard at her, then past her to Mukami of
Manguo Marshes and again back to Nyakinyua, his

her revenge and her financial success have been no victory at all.

Wanja, like Gikonyo in *A Grain of Wheat,* becomes wealthy at the cost of losing whatever real value there was in her life. Munira describes the new wealthy Wanja as "that bird periodically born out of ashes and dust," but it is not until the burning of the whorehouse that the image of Wanja as phoenix, continually associated as she is with fire and new beginnings, reaches its cathartic culmination. After this fire Wanja appears as if born again, purified and bearing new life within her. Munira had intended to save others from Wanja, but she is the one who is saved. All three men, who in some way seek personal salvation in Wanja, are finally instrumental in her redemption. Karega brings her to an intellectual understanding of her invidious position, Munira satisfies her spiritual craving for purification by fire, while Abdulla physically drags her body from the burning house.

Munira watching the whorehouse fire from Ilmorog Hill sees

the tongues of flame from the four corners forming petals of blood, making a twilight of the dark sky.

Wanja's identification with fire is part of the complex pattern of imagery that associates her with the title phrase "petals of blood." Wanja makes her first appearance in the novel immediately after the first explicit reference to "petals of blood" when a red flower is discovered during a nature lesson, and Munira is left to wonder about questions provoked by the "flower with petals of blood" and the visit of the "stranger girl." One flower found by the school children does not have full color, and because it is worm-eaten has no stigma or pistils. Munira explains that this flower "cannot bear fruit," and that "a flower can also become this color if it's prevented from reaching the light." The condition of the flower indirectly reveals the condition of Wanja, who in her life of wasted talent is like a flower kept from the light, and has come to Ilmorog to try and regain her procreative powers. At another level both Wanja and the flower reveal the condition of a corrupt, unhealthy society. Only later in the novel is the "flower with petals of blood" shown to by Theng'eta, which again is strongly associated with Wanja. Significantly it is her idea that Theng'eta is brewed for circumcision day, a ritual time for shedding blood and fertility rites. This first brewing, made possible by Wanja's energy and Nyakinyua's skill and knowledge, produces the visionary "holy

water" of legend. [...]
into a cheap, comm[...]
numbs the senses, [...]
into whoredom.

Munira's attract[...]
contradictory, but fr[...]
by a sense of sin. [...]
Wanja taking him on[...]
pleasure." The ambig[...]
of her charm, as she ap[...]
in terms of a pervers[...]
"petals of blood":

Munira felt her even m[...]
touched her: her taunt h[...]
the beckoning coquetry [...]
only by deflowering h[...]
flowering in blood. A [...]
couldn't she carry an ad[...]
Drive a VW: Ride a Vi[...]
Interesting Prostitute.

Munira's thwarted [...]
later seems to be convert[...]
which she remains a domi[...]
spiritual and sexual passi[...]
Munira's "conversion," [...]
aroused by the preaching o[...]
formerly used as a sexual [...]
also seen in the strange n[...]
sexual motives that lead hi[...]
house. The fire itself is a re[...]
earlier ritual burning of the[...]
Amina, the prostitute with w[...]
ty. Apart from being attempt[...]
world, both fires are attempt[...]
guilt, and overcome his fe[...]
inadequacy. Munira's vengean[...]
grim kind of poetic justice t[...]
the man who had flowered [...]
meets a bloody death at her ha[...]
fire destroys all evidence of [...]
same evening Abdulla had bee[...]
idea that he must kill Kimeria[...]
manhood, but it is Wanja who k[...]
her womanhood.

Although Karega protests tl[...]
sinations are pointless and w[...]
system, the way in which the d[...]
presented suggests that justice has[...]
act of violence in this instance is[...]
liberation, a kind of cleansing[...]
Fanonist violence. Wanja's earl[...]
new-born child is, by contrast, an[...]

mother, and even beyond to Akinyi to the future! And he smiled through his sorrow.

"Tomorrow ... tomorrow ..." he murmured to himself.

"Tomorrow ..." and he knew he was no longer alone.

This "affirmation of faith" echoes the tone of tempered optimism found in the "Acknowledgments" at the very beginning of the novel, where Ngugi gives thanks to:

Many others
One in the struggle
With our people
For total liberation
Knowing that
However long and arduous the struggle
Victory is certain.

The female images employed in *Petals of Blood* suggest that in this struggle for total liberation women have a vital role to play.

Source: Jennifer Evans, "Mother Africa and the Heroic Whole: Female Images in Petals of Blood," in *Annual Selected Papers of the ALA,* Series Ed. Stephen H. Arnold, Three Continents Press, 1983, pp. 57–66.

Sources

Boehmer, Elleke, "The Master's Dance to the Master's Voice: Revolutionary Nationalism and the Representation of Women in the Writing of Ngugi wa Thiong'o," in *Postcolonial Literatures,* edited by Michael Parker and Roger Starkey, Macmillan Press, 1995, pp. 143-53.

Cook, David, and Michale Okenimpkpe, "Petals of Blood," in their *Ngugi wa Thiong'o: An Exploration of His Writings,* Heinemann Educational Books, 1983, pp. 87-112.

Crehan, Stewart, "The Politics of the Signifier: Ngugi wa Thiong'o's *Petals of Blood,*" in *Postcolonial Literatures,* edited by Michael Parker and Roger Starkey, Macmillan Press, 1995, pp. 101-26.

Gikandi, Simon, "The Political Novel," in his *Reading the African Novel,* Heinemann Kenya, 1987, pp. 111-48.

Killam, G. D., "Petals of Blood," in *An Introduction to the Writings of Ngugi,* Heinemann, 1980, pp. 96-118.

McLaren, Joseph, "Ideology and Form: The Critical Reception of *Petals of Blood,*" in *Paintbrush: A Journal of Poetry, Translations, and Letters,* Vol. 20, Nos. 29-30, Spring/Autumn, 1993, pp. 73-91.

"Ngugi interviewed by Magina Magina," in *African Report,* No. 90, February, 1979, pp. 30-31.

Further Reading

Chileshe, John, "*Petals of Blood*: Ideology and Imaginative Expression," in *Journal of Commonwealth Literature,* Vol. 15, No. 1, 1980, pp. 133-37.
  Explores the conflict of authorial ideology and literary mode of expression in *Petals of Blood* and says that it is in part due to historical factors.

Killam, G. D., "A Note on the Title of *Petals of Blood,*" in *Journal of Commonwealth Literature,* Vol. 15, No. 1, 1980, pp. 125-32.
  Discusses how Ngugi uses the resources of Walcott's poem "Swamp" in *Petals of Blood.*

Kozain, Rustum, "Form as Politics, or the Tyranny of Narrativity: Re-Reading Ngugi wa Thiong'o's *Petals of Blood,*" in *Ufahamu,* Vol. 18, No. 3, 1990, pp. 77-90.
  Offers a reading of *Petals of Blood* analyzing its form in relation to its political content.

Ogude, James, *Ngugi's Novels and African History: Narrating the Nation,* Pluto Press, 1999, 183 p.
  Discussion of Ngugi's novels placing them in their contemporary historical and social contexts; includes a detailed discussion of women as victims in *Petals of Blood.*

Palmer, Eustace, "Ngugi's *Petals of Blood,*" in *African Literature Today,* Vol. 10, 1979, pp. 152-66.
  Critical overview of the novel that sees it as Ngugi's most ambitious work, noting the novel's strengths and weaknesses.

Sicherman, Carol, *Ngugi wa Thiong'o: The Making of Rebel: A Source Book in Kenyan Literature and Resistance,* Hans Zell Publishers, 1990, 486 p.
  A source book that traces the historical, political, and cultural background of Ngugi's work, with a chronology of his career as well as documents that provide insight into Kenya's history.

Smith, Craig V., "'Rainbow Memories of Gain and Loss': *Petals of Blood* and the New Resistance," in *Paintbrush: A Journal of Poetry, Translations, and Letters,* Vol. 20, Nos. 29-30, Spring/Autumn, 1993, pp. 92-108.
  Says that the revolutionary desire in *Petals of Blood* revises the past.

Stratton, Florence, "Cyclical Patterns in *Petals of Blood,*" in *Journal of Commonwealth Literature,* Vol. 15, No. 1, 1980, pp. 116-24.
  Sees the novel as an interpretation of history that is applicable in all times and places.

Pierre Menard, Author of the Quixote

Jorge Luis Borges

1939

The *Oxford Book of Latin American Essays* (1997) calls ''Pierre Menard, Author of the Quixote'' ''the most influential essay ever written in Latin America.'' Typical of Borges' style, the work does not fall neatly into the genre of narrative story or of essay—it is a fictional essay. Borges wrote it to test his mind after recovering from a head injury that gave him hallucinations and was complicated by a dangerous case of septicemia. In the form of a scholarly article, it tells of one Pierre Menard, a French symbolist recently deceased, who had undertaken the absurd task of rewriting Cervantes' *Don Quixote* as a product of his own creativity. Menard wanted his version to ''coincide with'' the original—word for word. The narrator applauds and legitimizes the act as academic heroism. Because of Borges' erudite reputation, the publication of this story sent scholars scrambling to discover the obscure author from Nimes, Pierre Menard. They unearthed a minor essayist, with a forgettable published essay on the psychological analysis of handwriting. The narrator of the Borges story, himself a fussy pedagogue, explains that Menard succeeded in indoctrinating himself so thoroughly in Cervantes' culture, thoughts, and language that the finished portions of his *Quixote* exactly match the Cervantes text. Furthermore, the narrator calls Menard's achievement ''infinitely richer'' than that of Cervantes, due to its modern philosophical perspective and the obstacles Menard overcame to produce it. The narrator means that the modern context imbues the same words with differ-

ent meanings, presaging postmodernism reader-response theories. As Donald Yates points out in his introduction to a collection of Borges' fiction, "Pierre Menard, Author of the Quixote" "quite subtly anticipated critical literary theory that would emerge a quarter of a century later." The story would be included in *Ficciones* (1944), a widely translated collection and the first Latin American work to achieve international acclaim.

Author Biography

Jorge Luis Borges unintentionally helped to found Postmodernism through his blurring of the lines of genre and the borders between fiction and reality. Borges was born in 1899 in Buenos Aires, Argentina to middle-class parents. His father, a lawyer and psychology teacher, taught Borges philosophy and encouraged his love of reading and thinking. His mother came from a long line of freedom fighters, and taught him perseverance. Both parents spoke and read English, as did Borges' paternal grandmother, who lived with them, and the nanny she procured for the family. Ultimately, Borges would be fluent in Spanish, English, French, and German; he learned to read Italian and Latin. He grew to adolescence in Palermo, playing fantasy games in the library and garden with his younger sister Norah, who was his only friend. Jorge (or "Georgie" as his mother called him), translated Oscar Wilde's "The Happy Prince" into Spanish when he was nine years old. With thick glasses and no interest in sports, the young Borges fell victim to local school bullies. But his luck changed in 1914 when he was fifteen, for his family moved to Geneva, Switzerland (where the family, naive about the severity of European tensions, was stranded for all of World War I) to seek medical help for his father's blindness. In Europe, Borges began his intellectual life in earnest, encouraged by fellow intellectual students. After returning to Buenos Aires in 1921, he worked as an assistant librarian for nine years, reading and writing in his spare time. In 1938, a bump on the head that got infected and led to septicemia nearly killed him, but his hallucinations inspired a turn toward fantasy in his writing. To test his mind, he wrote "Pierre Menard, Author of the Quixote", which was well received. Borges lost his library post when the Fascist Juan Peron came to power in 1946. However, his literary achievements were recognized through his appointment as President of the Sociedad Argentian de Ecritores (Society of

Argentine Writers, or SADE) in 1950. By now, Borges was fighting blindness, to which his father had succumbed years earlier. He dictated poems to his mother, who read to him in Spanish, English, and French and took dictation from him for years. After the 1955 Cordoba Revolution, Borges was named Director of the National Library. Now completely blind, he quipped, "I speak of God's splendid irony in granting me at one time 800,000 books and darkness."

Love played a minor role in Borges' life. He would not marry the love of his youth, Elsa Astete Millan, until forty years later, after her first husband died. Their marriage then lasted only three years, after which Borges returned to his mother's home, where he stayed until her death in 1973. Later, in 1986, he married his secretary, Maria Kodama, on his deathbed.

Octavio Paz noted that for Borges, the lines of genres are blurred, "his essays read like stories, his stories are poems, and his essays make us think, as though they were essays." In 1961, Borges was awarded the Formentor's International Publisher's Prize jointly with Samuel Beckett. He continued to write, speak, and travel widely for the next twenty-five years. He died of liver cancer in 1986 in Geneva.

Borges also wrote under the pen names B. Lynch Davis, B. Suarez Lynch, F(rancisco) Bustos, and H(onorario) Bustos Domecq.

Plot Summary

The story takes the form of a scholarly article about a recently deceased novelist. The novelist's name, Pierre Menard, does not appear until the third sentence. The narrator of the article establishes credibility by citing literary ladies with unfamiliar names, then presents a catalogue of writings found among Menard's private papers. The narrator asserts that this list is more accurate than one published earlier by a Madame Henri Bachelier in a newspaper with Protestant leanings. The list encompasses an unusually wide range of interests, from love sonnets to Boolean logic. Many are esoteric and strange, such as an invective against the French poet Paul Valery which is really "the exact reverse of Menard's true opinion of Valery," and an article on the elimination of one of the pawns in the game of chess, wherein Menard "proposes, recommends, disputes, and ends by rejecting this innovation." These and

Jorge Luis Borges

other poems and essays represent the "visible" part of Menard's works.

Now the narrator turns to Menard's crowning achievement, which the narrator deems "subterranean, interminably heroic, and. . .inconclusive." The rest of the essay concerns itself with Menard's re-authoring of just over two chapters of *Don Quixote*. This was the result of a project partially inspired by a theory of "total identification" with an author. Menard undertook "to know Spanish well, reembrace the Catholic faith, to fight against Moors and Turks, to forget European history between 1602 and 1918, and to *be* Miguel de Cervantes."

In a serious tone, the narrator extols Menard's ambitious project and acknowledges his accomplishment of having completed the ninth and thirty-eighth and a portion of the twenty-second chapters of Part One of *Don Quixote*. Although the task was "complex in the extreme and futile from the outset," Menard succeeded in producing these segments literally word for word.

The narrator considers Menard's achievement far greater than that of Cervantes, because for a Spaniard of the early seventeenth century to write in his own language of contemporary events was not as significant an effort as Menard had to make to write in archaic Spanish about events he knew only through research into history. The narrator quotes several long passages from a letter he says he received from Menard, in which the Frenchman justifies his project. In the letter, Menard explains that he chose *Don Quixote* because he had read it at age twelve and had forgotten it to the point where his memory of the text paralleled the "anterior image of a book not yet written." Thus he could begin with similar ideas to those of Cervantes when he began to write *Don Quixote*. The narrator asserts that even though Menard never completed his project, he sometimes imagines that he did, and that while reading the Cervantes version, he further imagines that he detects the Frenchman's style of writing.

To demonstrate the significance of Menard's achievement, the narrator juxtaposes two identical passages, first Cervantes' and then Menard's. The reader is directed to notice the subtle shift in interpreting the phrase "truth, whose mother is history." In Cervantes' text, the phrase is mere rhetoric, praising truth. However, in Menard's identical version, "truth, whose mother is history" carries the syntactic weight of the modern consciousness of history's remaking of the past, with its concept that history creates truth. The narrator explains, "Historical truth, for him, is not what took place; it is what we think took place." The narrator draws the reader's attention to differences in acculturation that affect the reader's expectation and interpretation. The meanings of the words change over time. The appreciation of style also changes, for whereas the language sounds suitable for a seventeenth-century Spanish author, it seems affectedly archaic and stiff when it comes from a modern French author.

The story ends with the narrator's commendation of Menard for having "enriched the art of reading" through his use of "deliberate anachronism and fallacious attribution." These are the devices that Borges himself uses in his story.

Characters

Madame Bachelier

A literary lioness who supposedly published a "fallacious" catalogue of Menard's works in a Protestant newspaper. Madame Bachelier, like the other literary personages in this story, is little more than a footnote. As observed by Borges' biographer Martin Stabb, "believable flesh-and-blood people are almost entirely absent in his [Borges'] work.'' Borges himself said in a 1971 interview, ''As to characters, I don't think I have evolved a single character. I think I'm always thinking in terms of myself, of my limitations, and of the possible lives I should have lived and haven't.''

Simon Kautsch

A philanthropist married to the Countess de Bagnoregio who has been slandered by those to whom he gives.

Pierre Menard

Pierre Menard is the subject of the fictional essay ''Pierre Menard, Author of the *Quixote*,'' but he is hardly a character in the true sense of that word. Rather, Pierre Menard offers the narrator a reason to expound on his theories of language, memory, reading, and historical context. A historical Pierre Menard did live in Nimes, France, at the time of which Borges writes, though his published essay on the psychoanalytical analysis of handwriting (1931) was unremarkable. A Louis Menard (1822-1901), possibly Pierre's father or grandfather, had attempted to rewrite the *Odyssey*. Borges' Menard is either a fictional composite or a spin-off, changed by the context into which Borges writes him. According to the narrator, Menard, a French symbolist, decided to write *Don Quixote*, again, from his own creative mind. To do so, Menard had ''to know Spanish well, to reembrace the Catholic faith, to fight against Moors and Turks, to forget European history between 1602 and 1918, and to *be* Miguel de Cervantes.'' The narrator cites a letter from Menard to himself in which the French author justified his project and described its inherent problems. For one, Menard has to reconstruct what Cervantes wrote spontaneously. For another, ''it is not in vain that three hundred years have passed'' between Cervantes' composition and his. Nevertheless, Menard chooses to ''arrive at *Don Quixote* through the experiences of Pierre Menard'' rather than attempting somehow to ''be'' Cervantes. Thus, Menard's text can be read as a twentieth-century work, and its words connote contemporary meanings. As to his choice of texts, Menard considered *Don Quixote* an ''unnecessary'' work (unlike Poe's *Bateau Ivre*, a work he sees as a cornerstone of literary history). In addition, Menard had read the book as an adolescent, and his hazy memory of it would serve the same function as ''the imprecise, anterior image of a book not yet written.'' Unfortunately, Menard's words are compromised by his

''resigned habit of propounding ideas which were the strict reverse of those he preferred.''

Don Quixote

The main character in Miguel Cervantes' 1605 picaresque novel, *Don Quixote*, a novel that Pierre Menard partially rewrote. Don Quixote is the idealistic hero of Cervantes's novel. In Chapter 38 of the novel that bears his name, the inveterate soldier Quixote presents his preference for arms over letters. The innocent Don Quixote spends his days looking for damsels in distress, and falls in love with a commoner whom he mistakes for a noble and fair lady.

Monsieur Edmond Teste

Monsieur Teste is the title character of a collection of sketches attempting to express pure consciousness written by French poet and writer Paul Valery (1871-1945), a protege of Symbolist poet Stephane Mallarme (1842-1898). Edmond Teste is considered to be Valery's alter ego.

Baroness de Bacourt

A lady at whose social gatherings held each Thursday (her *vendredis*) the narrator allegedly met ''the late lamented poet,'' Pierre Menard, the subject of his story. In his catalogue of Menard's ''visible'' works, the narrator cites ''a cycle of admirable sonnets'' written for the Baroness. In a footnote, he adds that the Baroness is currently ''sketching a portrait'' of Menard.

Countess de Bagnoregio

A minor writer who has granted her consent for the narrator to present his research on Pierre Menard. The Countess, he adds, has ''one of the most refined minds in the principality of Monaco'' and is now married to Simon Kautsch, a misunderstood philanthropist.

Miguel de Cervantes

Author of *Don Quixote* (1605) and contemporary of William Shakespeare. They died on the same day: April 23, 1616.

Themes

Memory

Memory is what is retained (or created, in Borges' terms) in the mind from experience. The

Topics for Further Study

- Is "Pierre Menard, Author of the Quixote" a short story or an essay?

- Explain the difference between the interpretations of Cervantes' version and Menard's version of the passage from *Don Quoxote*. How does the passage of time affect the meaning of words?

- Of what significance is knowing whether or not Pierre Menard is a fictional character?

- What purpose does the catalogue of Menard's works serve?

- The phrase "merely astonishing" is an oxymoron. Find another oxymoron in the story. How does it contribute to the story's meaning?

theme of memory fascinated Borges, who wrote "Pierre Menard" as a test of his own mental ability after a minor head injury turned serious and gave him hallucinations. Borges' concept of memory roughly parallels that of Marcel Proust, a writer whom Borges introduced to literature circles in Argentina. Proust's landmark seven-volume novel about memory, *Remembrance of Things Past* (1917), exemplifies the theory of French philosopher Henri Bergson that humans do not experience life when events happen, but later, in forming memories of those events. The processing of memories, Bergson postulated, takes place in the *duree* [duration], deep in the mind, where the superficial constraints of clock time do not interfere. Bergson's theories of time and memory inspired the Symbolist poets, Marcel Proust, and also Borges among others.

Like Proust, Borges attempted to express his own conception of memory and time in his fiction. At the end of his story "Tlon, Uqbar, Orbis Tertius" the narrator writes, "Already in memory a fictitious past takes the place of the other past, of which we know nothing, not even that it is false." In "Pierre Menard," the narrator postulates memory as a creative act. He compares memory, an act of recon-

structing the past from the parts retained in the mind, with creation, which also constructs a whole from parts. Pierre Menard had read *Don Quixote* long ago, and had forgotten parts of it. His faded memory corresponds to "the imprecise, anterior image of a book not yet written." In other words, Menard's hazy memory resembles the germ of an unborn idea, one that has not yet fully formed into a creative vision.

Meaning and Interpretation

In a 1967 interview with Richard Burgin, Borges said that "every time a book is read or reread, then something happens to the book. . .and every time you read it, it's really a new experience." A reader comes to a story with a set of culturally shaped experiences and values that influence the way the reader understands the meaning of the words on the page. As the reader matures and gains new experiences, new perspectives, these meanings may change, because the reader's core beliefs and values have changed. The reader also responds to, or pays attention to, different aspects of the story depending on his or her status in life and personal interests. As in life, an older person pays attention to different issues in a text than a younger person does. A woman may interpret the same scenes differently than would a man. A person who has recently lost a friend or relative to death may notice different details than one who has never experienced such a loss. Differences between readers and between reading sessions also occur on a cultural level, as societies and cultures change over time. Readers of each new era pay attention to new details, as they experience shifts in values, beliefs, and perspectives. Things once taken for granted are questioned. Consciousness is raised on new issues and old ones pass into obscurity. Though the words of a passage remain the same, over time, connotations associated with the words impart new meanings and resonate to new values.

Even within a given time and place, the same phrase can take on different meanings according to different contexts. Literary critic Stanley Fish explains this phenomenon in his 1980 essay, "Is There a Text in This Class?" According to Fish, no sentence can be understood outside of context. In other words, the reader can only interpret the meaning of a sentence by mentally connecting the words to previously held beliefs and knowledge. These beliefs and knowledge derive from the person's social context: all readers are "situated" within a particular culture and history. A sentence is written or uttered in a given "situation" that impacts the way it will be interpreted. The phrase from Fish's essay "Is there a text in this class?" could refer to assigned books to read or a text left behind. Fish explains,

> . . .within those situations, the normative meaning of an utterance will always be obvious or at least accessible, although within another situation that same utterance, no longer the same, will have another normative meaning that will be no less obvious and accessible. . .This does not mean that there is no way to discriminate between the meanings an utterance will have in different situations, but that the discrimination will already have been made by virtue of our being in a situation (we are never not in one) and that in another situation the discrimination will also already have been made, but differently.

Reader-response theorists debate over whether meaning derives solely from the reader's awareness and creation or whether the author prescribes meaning in the form of words on a page that invoke connotations. The difference is significant, and lies at the heart of "Pierre Menard."

The two identical passages of text, one by Cervantes and one by Menard, demonstrate how the act of reading imbues a text with meaning. The second interpretation of the phrase "history, the mother of truth" becomes Borges' own understanding of William James' philosophy of pragmatism. Thus his own beliefs and knowledge reflect his interpretation of Menard's passage, which he attempts to pass on to the reader. According to Stanley Fish, how the reader "gets" that meaning is another thing altogether.

Style

The Literary Hoax

In a 1976 interview, Borges admitted that "Pierre Menard" is "what we might call a mystification, or a hoax." A hoax is an attempt to present a text as authentic, either for monetary gain or as a joke. A literary hoax often takes the form of a text that the author presents as authentic, perhaps as translation of a recently discovered scroll or long-lost manuscript. In one of the chapters of *Don Quixote* rewritten by Menard, chapter IX of Book I, the narrator tells of having purchased by chance an old Arabic scroll at the silk market, and mentions that the scroll just happened to contain a missing fragment of the history of Don Quixote of La Mancha. Having found the missing piece, the narrator continues his story. Borges parodies the found manuscript with

Menard's re-invented manuscript. Rather than finding a lost work, however, Menard writes a work all over again, publishing a story that is not lost, but already published and extant.

Borges' literary hoax echoes another idea from *Don Quixote*. In Cervantes' prologue, a friend tells the narrator to fabricate bits of Latin and throw in random historical references, so that he "may perhaps be taken for a scholar, which is honorable and profitable these days." The friend also advises including several notable authors in the beginning, to give the book authority. Borges takes his cue from Cervantes. He begins with two testimonials that authorize his essay and he lists an impressive catalogue of Menard's writings to authenticate Menard as a viable writer. Borges creates a character with a fictitious list of works (paralleling the discovered long-lost texts), but they are trivial, personal writing whose discovery is nearly meaningless. These works, which the narrator presumably found among Menard's personal effects after Menard's death, are quirky and contrived. Perhaps Borges' narrator takes comfort in the assurances provided to the narrator of *Don Quixote* by the "intelligent" friend that there is no reason to fear discovery in this deceit, for "no one will take the trouble to ascertain whether you follow your authorities or not."

Literary hoaxes have existed since ancient Egyptian times, when merchants offered large sums for Greek manuscripts to sell to the Ptolemaic rulers. With such a reward, many false replicas of Greek documents were fabricated and sold at a profit. "Pierre Menard." in its own way, has also succeeded very well as a literary hoax. Scholars continue to conjecture who might be the original Menard, and one Borges expert, Daniel Balderston, has devoted fifteen years to studying and recreating all of the historical and literary knowledge that Borges drew upon to write his essays, including the story "Pierre Menard." In the introduction to his 1993 work, *Out of Context*, Balderston remarks that his years of research have given him new insight into the "fun Borges had at the time of writing ["Pierre Menard"].

Ambiguity and Oxymoron

Ambiguity is openness to interpretation; it is writing that allows—or forces—the reader to contrive meaning independently. Ambiguity comes in degrees, and Borges' stories lie at the high end of the scale. His stories cause the reader to puzzle over their meaning. Usually, when a story, poem, essay, or other piece of writing contains a phrase that is difficult to comprehend, the story's context gives pertinent clues. However, many Borges stories resist interpretation because the context also remains mysterious. Sometimes even knowing the facts does not help. Of how much use is knowing whether Pierre Menard existed or not? Or whether he actually tried to rewrite *Don Quixote*? Does it really matter who the Baroness de Bacourt was? In other places the narrator frustrates the reader with oxymoronic sentences, such as when he attributes to Menard the notion that ''all times and places are the same, or are different.''

In ''Pierre Menard,'' the narrator proclaims that ''Ambiguity is a richness.'' The narrator's story contains dozens of high-sounding but ambiguous statements, such as ''merely astonishing'' and ''pointless travesties.'' In both of these phrases, the words ''astonishing'' and ''travesties'' are rather vague, but the modifiers ''merely'' and ''pointless,'' rather than clarifying their referents, qualify them beyond sense into nebulous oxymorons. ''Astonishing'' means something extraordinary, while ''merely'' connotes something commonplace, its opposite or near opposite. Somehow a sense of quiet surprise comes through the oxymoron in spite of its self-contradiction. Likewise in the phrase ''swept along by the inertia of language and the imagination,'' inertia means staying on a given path, thus lacking the creativity of imagination. Yet, the phrase manages to carry the sense of being at the mercy of language and imagination, as of a force outside of oneself. The process of deriving the meaning of Borgesian oxymorons requires the reader to reconcile the opposing terms. Jaime Alazraki, in an article called ''Oxymoronic Structure in Borges' Essays,'' explains how the incongruity ''is only illusory. The two components clash on a conventional level only to reach a deeper level of reality. Like any other trope, it represents an effort to correct through language the deficiencies of language itself.'' Borges' stories demand that the reader create meaning by discerning it from his rich but ambiguous prose, by navigating between opposing terms; it is not just Menard who has ''enriched the slow and rudimentary art of reading by means of a new technique,'' but Borges himself.

Bricolage

''Bricolage'' is something made out of whatever is at hand, of available bits and pieces, or trifles. It comes from the French verb *bricoler*, meaning to putter about. A short story that employs bricolage uses details that do not contribute to what Edgar Allan Poe termed the ''single effect'' sought by early modernist short story writers. Following Poe, conventional modernist wisdom had it that, due to the brevity of the short story, each of its elements must contribute to the story's theme and meaning. As Elizabeth Bowen said in her preface to *The Faber Book of Modern Short Stories*, a short story ''must have tautness and clearness; it must contain no passage not aesthetically relevant to the whole.'' The modern short story was meant to be lyrical, to have the concise intensity of a poem. Bricolage resists lyricism by using a motley arrangement of symbols that evoke various responses and disrupt the possibility of a holistic, lyrical meaning. Bricolage is a postmodern device, exemplified in the works of novelists Thomas Pynchon and Don DeLillo and short story writer Bobbie Ann Mason. In ''Pierre Menard'' Borges employs bricolage in the catalogue of the ''visible product of Menard's pen.'' The list includes works on chess, sonnets, and symbolic logic, an assortment that was not unusual for intellectuals of the early modern period such as Menard (and also Borges). The list contributes to the story a sense of everyday reality and of the triviality of Menard's life.

Literary Heritage

The literary heritage of Borges' fiction can be understood in the broader context of Latin-American literature, and more specifically, Argentine literature. Before conquest and colonization by European forces, the native Indian cultures of Latin-America had a well-developed tradition of written and oral literature. Latin-American literature since colonization emerged from the narratives of the conquered native Indian peoples as well as the European conquerors themselves. Later, the literature sprang from the Native Indian's struggles against colonial domination, which became known as a ''literature of oppression.'' Latin-American literature in the latter half of the twentieth century developed a concern with literary and linguistic form, as exemplified by the experimental short stories of Borges, first published in the late 1940s. Borges also imported the avant-garde poetic movement of ''Ultraism'' (*Ultraismo*, named for the literary journal *Ultra*, to which he was a regular contributor) from Spain to Buenos Aires, Argentina, in 1921. Although Borges later moved away from Ultraist principles, revising much of this early poetry, his influence upon other Argentine and Latin American writers remained significant.

Historical Context

Between the World Wars in Argentina

It is not without significance that one of the chapters of the Quixote rewritten by Pierre Menard concerns a debate between "arms and letters." In 1939, Hitler was moving a substantial army into Poland and Czechoslovakia and 7,500 Jewish businesses were destroyed in Germany on Kristallnacht (Night of Crystal, named for the broken storefront windows) on November 9 and 10, 1938. Borges had been trapped in Zurich during World War I, his father having made the mistake of taking his family with him to Europe in 1914 in order to seek treatment for advancing blindness. The Borges family had ties to Europe, as did (and does) Argentina itself, since at that time roughly one-third of Argentines were European immigrants, some of them Jews who had left Hitler's Germany. The military armament and sense of impending disaster in Europe would have been apparent to Borges as he wrote. He courageously denounced Hitler and his program of a "final solution" of exterminating all Jews in the pages of the Argentine literary magazine *Sur*, where "Pierre Menard" would later be published.

Having had a history of political instability, Argentina found itself during the inter-War years with numerous thriving Fascist organizations, and frequent shifts occurred between democratic to Fascist leadership. Harboring German agents and generally supportive of the pro-Axis Powers, Argentina maintained neutrality long into World War II, even after the attack on Pearl Harbor by Japan. In 1945, it joined the Allies just in time to be counted among the winning nations for the final victory.

Modernism and Postmodernism

Modernism was an early-twentieth-century reaction against the movements of naturalism and Romanticism of the nineteenth century. It retained elements of the Symbolist movement of the late nineteenth century, especially the Symbolist interest in metaphor and in human consciousness. Borges was not just a modernist writer but a transitional one whose work began in modernism and helped to shape postmodernism as he moved from his *gaucho* (Argentine cowboy) stories and mysteries into his metaphysical experiments.

Although Borges claimed to have no personal philosophy, his works demonstrate the influence of several eighteenth-century philosophers whose theories inspired modernist thought. Borges admired Hume and Berkeley for their notions of the self as a motley and ever-changing collection of different perceptions, and he spoke frequently of Schopenhauer's concept of a universal will that can only be contained through the intellect. Borges found literary inspiration in the essentially pessimistic stories of Henry James and Franz Kafka, noting that neither of these authors developed characters, but rather wrote parables composed of intricate plots. The Borgesian turn from storytelling toward philosophy and metaphysics became pivotal in launching the postmodern movement, in which authors, in a sense beginning with Borges, challenged the separation between reality and fiction by blurring these lines in their stories. Postmodern literature, presaged by Borges' style and interests, self-consciously destabilized traditional conventions of character, genre, and plot.

Critical Overview

Early criticism about Borges centered on his poetry, and when he began to write essays, most critics preferred his poems. His works appeared primarily in the literary magazine *Sur*, which was a fledgling venture when he first contributed to its pages, but which later emerged as one of South American's most important venues for new Hispanic literature. Surprisingly, Borges gained national attention despite his apparent disinterest in his nation's turbulent political scene, in an era when Argentine writers proved their courage through polemical writing. He was also criticized for his literary games, and the fact that certain of his key phrases, themes, and devices tended to crop up again and again. Fellow Argentine writer Ernesto Sabato facetiously asked, "Will he be condemned from now on to plagiarize himself?" At least one compatriot recognized Borges' groundbreaking technique; Cesar Fernandez Moreno called him "a premature phenomenon of our culture" under whose tutelage the country would one day gain the literary acumen to vie with European writers. An early work of criticism by Ana Maria Barranechea (1957) viewed Borges through the lens of "irreality," thus placing him firmly within the

Compare & Contrast

- **1939:** In Argentina, President Robert M. Ortiz tried to establish democracy in a mostly Fascist country, partly to remedy its economic difficulties.

  Today: Since 1989, Carlos Saul Menem, elected president of Argentina, has successfully pulled Argentina back from the brink of economic despair. He has balanced the budget and imposed an austerity program to curb inflation, which had been running at 900 percent in the 1980s. With diplomatic relations restored with Great Britain after a falling-out over the Falkland Islands in 1982, Argentina is well on its way to establishing itself as a positive economic power in South America.

- **1939:** Europe mobilized for inevitable war with Germany. Hitler invaded Poland and Czechoslovakia.

  Today: Although the Balkan area remains a military hot spot, decisive action on the part of NATO has prevented the conflict from intensifying and spreading to other countries.

- **1939:** Modernist literature expressed a sense of pessimism and exhaustion through flat characters who move relentlessly through a complex and absurd world.

  Today: Postmodern literature attempts to express the uniqueness of the individual through the theme of relative values. At the same time, however, a sizable and growing number of writers are turning back to transcendent values, aware that, despite diversity, the human condition shares many values and experiences in common.

---

modernist movement. Her view of him is rather dark, seeing in him "the horrifying presence of the infinite and the disintegration of substance into reflections and dreams." It was the European expatriots living in Argentina who ensured that Borges' works were translated into French, Italian, and German, thus exposing him to international criticism with the result in 1961 that he shared the Formentor International Publisher's Prize with Samuel Beckett. John Updike, in his capacity as book reviewer for the *New Yorker*, hinted in 1965 that in Borges might be found a proposal for "some sort of essential revision in literature itself." In 1967, Colombian novelist and liberal Gabriel Garcia Marquez said of Borges, "He is one of the writers. . . I have read most, and yet he is perhaps the one I like least" because he "writes about mental realities, he is sheer evasion." However, in the same year, John Barth found in Borges the inspiration for his essay "The Literature of Exhaustion," published in the *Atlantic*. Barth's theory comprised the "death of the author," the consequence of all stories having already been told. Barth called this state of affairs "the used-upness of certain forms or the felt exhaustion of certain possibilities." Barth cites the story "Pierre Menard" as an example of "the difficulty, perhaps unnecessity, of writing original works of literature." Borges, according to Barth, offered a new literary agenda, to self-consciously imitate what has been written already. Barth himself adhered to this agenda by writing his "Lost in the Funhouse," also published in the *Atlantic* in 1968. The Borges theme of the labyrinth serves as the central organizing metaphor for Barth's short story.

The sixties saw Borges responding to international interest in his writing, and he traveled worldwide on lecture and reading tours. However, in Argentina as well as abroad, Borges was often seen as an anomaly in contrast to writers committed to social change, such as civil rights and feminist advocates. Argentine critics and fellow writers accused him of solipsism, alone and impotent in his narrow world of dreams and labyrinths. Mexican critic Jaime Garcia Terres called him "a sort of self-sufficient vacuum." Reader-response theories of the eighties brought about a shift in valuing this aspect of Borges, such that Jean Marco applauded his ''context-free paradigm which can be reactivated through reading at any time and under any circumstances.'' In other words, Borges' lack of social ''commitment'' (context), his interest in surfaces and the artifice of writing, is now considered significant and relevant. This revaluation derives from the shift over the last twenty years from political writing to interest in issues of reading and interpretation. The concern over the sources for his numerous allusions to minor authors (whether apocryphal or historical) now resonates to the postmodern sense that the context has no pertinence. If, on one hand, he made up certain allusions, then his works parody reality; if, on the other hand, his allusions are real, yet unimportant, then his works, again, parody reality. Thus, recent criticism, encouraged by the appearance of three new centenary editions (commemorating the hundredth anniversary of his birth in 1899) of his poems, stories, and essays, respectively, has responded favorably to the Borgesian irony.

In Pierre Menard, *Borges creates an imaginary author who decides to write a pre-existing work, namely Miguel de Cervantes's* Don Quixote.

Criticism

Carole Hamilton

Hamilton is an English teacher at Cary Academy in Cary, North Carolina. In this essay she examines the theme of reading in the literary project of ''Pierre Menard, Author of the Quixote.''

''Pierre Menard, Author of the Quixote'' is metafiction about the overlap between essay writing and story writing. Writing certainly lies at the center of the story, beginning with the title. However, ''Pierre Menard'' is also ''metareading,'' a story that concerns itself with the relationship between writing and reading.

References to writing abound in this story. The narrator establishes Pierre Menard's credibility as an author by listing a catalogue of his written work, his ''visible *oeuvre*.'' The works represent a range of types, from sonnets and letters to monographs, manuscripts, and translations. The last item of the list, handwritten, is about one of the elements unique to writing: punctuation. The breadth of topics treated by the writings in the catalogue testifies to Menard's intelligence and worth; his writing identifies him as an erudite and prolific writer. His most impressive work is a project to ''produce a number

of pages which coincided—word for word and line by line—with those of Miguel de Cervantes.'' The narrator applauds this act of re-envisioning an entire novel, calling the finished product ''perhaps the most significant writing of our time.'' Menard himself, in a letter quoted by the narrator, equates his undertaking with ''the final term of a theological or metaphysical proof'' or to God. Menard assures the narrator in his letter that ''The task I have undertaken is not in essence difficult. . .If I could just be immortal, I could do it.'' Thus, the creative act of writing is placed on a divine level. Menard is also legitimized in a chain of biblical-sounding ''begats,'' as a descendent of a line of writers beginning with Poe. He is following an honored tradition. The novel that Menard chooses to re-create, Miguel de Cervantes' *Don Quixote*, also carries a theme of writing, being a new written genre (the picaresque novel) and having many authorial intrusions that constantly remind the reader of the act of writing that produced the novel. The difference between the author's goals is that while Cervantes' work views writing as a means to the end of narration, Menard's project centers on how writing affects the act of reading, and not on writing as an end in itself.

What Do I Read Next?

- On the theme of memory, see Borges' "Shakepeare's Memory", in which the German narrator is possessed by the bard's thoughts, and also Borges' "Funes, His Memory", about a man who could forget nothing. For other Borgesian fictional essays, "Parable of Cervantes and the *Quixote*" is a brief commentary on the fate of literary works, "An Examination of the Work of Henry Quain" presents notes on an unwritten novel, and "The Approach to Al-Mu'Tasim" is a quasi-serious treatise on a non-existent novel very similar to "Pierre Menard".

- Colombian Gabriel Garcia Marquez's short story parable "A Very Old Man with Enormous Wings" concerns differing interpretations of reality.

- Borges often acknowledged the influence of Franz Kafka on his own work. *The Trial* is representative of Kafka's themes and style.

- Frederick Crews' *The Pooh Perplex* and Vladimir Nabokov's *Pale Fire*, like "Pierre Menard", also parody the self-importance of literary scholars.

The crowning moment of "Pierre Menard" occurs when the narrator places the excerpt from Cervantes' novel alongside the excerpt from Menard's identical version. The narrator's analysis then proves that reading, the flip side of writing, depends upon its audience to be appreciated. In the last paragraph of "Pierre Menard", the narrator summarizes the impact of Menard's having re-written the *Quixote* as a contribution to reading: "Menard (perhaps without wishing it) has enriched, by means of a new technique, the hesitant and rudimentary art of reading." Given that the final product matches the original Quixote word for word, how can a second Quixote, an identical twin text of the first, have any bearing on reading, if the words are exactly the same? The answer lies in the "rudimentary art" of reading itself, which is an act not of translation, but of interpretation and putting into other words. Reading, as Borges' story illustrates, is *always* an act of interpretation, for although the texts appear the same on the page (though begotten by a different process), they "mean" differently. Reading is a complex art that can be accomplished on many different levels.

In "Pierre Menard" Borges presents many kinds of reading, of varying levels of complexity, that might be arranged in a "hierarchy of reading" corresponding roughly to psychologist Abraham Maslow's hierarchy of needs, a system of organizing human goals. On the bottom of Maslow's pyramid are the most basic human requirements for survival: food, water, air, sleep. At the top, Maslow placed the human need for self-actualization. In Borges' hierarchy, the basic "survival" reading skill is simple cataloguing, the librarian's skill that Borges practiced as an assistant librarian. The narrator of "Pierre Menard" proves his skill of cataloguing early in the story, when he carefully lists all of Menard's writings, correcting omissions of earlier lists. The next level up on Borges' hierarchy of reading would be comprehension. In the narrator's annotations of the catalogued items, he demonstrates his skill of comprehension, for the topic of each item is succinctly summarized. Comprehension is a relatively simple tool used by the high school student to learn parts of a text. However, comprehension lacks depth; one might comprehend the essence of a well-known book (such as *Don Quixote*) simply because it has become an icon of culture. Regarding *Don Quixote* the narrator points out that "fame is a form—perhaps the worst form—of comprehension."

On a slightly more complex level would be interpretation, an act of inferring meaning between the lines and taking other information into consideration. The narrator proves his astuteness as a reader at this level of Borges's hierarchy of reading when he points out that Menard's diatribe against Paul Valery "states the exact reverse of Menard's true opinion of Valery." Here, the narrator has read Menard's life against his written opinions in order to arrive at a more thorough understanding of his subject than a casual reader might derive. The narrator has taken Menard's personal context—his habits of mind—into consideration in his interpretation. Borges, whose father had gone blind and who very early in his life began to have vision problems that would lead to blindness, had personal reasons to value the skills of comprehension and interpretation in reading. With his weak eyesight, it was important for Borges to grasp what he read quickly, so as not to need a second reading. In this Borges became quite successful, developing his memory to retain ideas, languages, and whole passages of favorite texts. Almost everyone who met Borges remarked on his uncanny ability to recall passages from books he had read years ago in the course of conversation about other books. Interpretation requires memory as well as understanding.

One of Menard's inspirations involves an even higher level of reading than interpretation—"total identification" with the author. To accomplish total identification with a sixteenth-century Spanish author, the French Menard had to "learn Spanish, return to Catholicism, fight against the Moor or Turk, forget the history of Europe from 1602 to 1918" all in order to "*be* Miguel de Cervantes." As daunting an undertaking as this might seem, Menard dismissed it as "too easy." Rather than read his way to a total identification with Cervantes, Menard wanted to come to the *Quixote* "*through the experiences of Pierre Menard.*" In other words, Menard wanted to retain his own identity while absorbing Cervantes' world view thoroughly enough to reproduce his writing. Menard's project is similar in some ways to the goals of the university literature professor, who tries to understand authors in enough depth to explain their work. Borges, writing "Pierre Menard" as a young man, had no way of knowing that he would later become a university professor of English literature too! Soon literature professors were approaching Borges himself in this fashion. One of them, Borges scholar Daniel Balderston, spent fifteen years on the Menardian task of trying to read and learn everything that Borges would have read and known when he wrote his stories, including "Pierre Menard." Balderston wanted "to re-

> " The difference between the author's goals is that while Cervantes' work views writing as a means to the end of narration, Menard's project centers on how writing affects the act of reading, and not on writing as an end in itself."

cover the fullness of Borges's knowledge of his historical knowledge at the time of [composing]." Like Menard, Balderston chose to retain his own identity, knowing that he could not create the innocence of Borges' knowledge, since intervening history affects his understanding. Balderston's research is a rehistoricization of Borges. The postmodern term "rehistoricization" also applies to Menard's goal, because he ostensibly succeeded in understanding Cervantes' world, his historical context, while maintaining the identity of Menard. Menard and Balderston are ideal readers, who do not lose their own selves through "total identification." They understand the writer's words within their historical context as well within the contemporary context, with different values and beliefs.

The second inspiration for Menard was "anachronism," an idea he gleaned from "one of those parasitic books that set Christ on a boulevard." Since Borges has not supplied a specific title and author of such a "parasitic book," critics have debated what book he had in mind. Balderston suggests Joyce's *Ulysses*, where Leopold Bloom is a quotidian Christ, while Emilio Carilla suggests a 1922 Argentine novel called *Jesus en Buenos Aires.* However, the question is irrelevant in the context of reading Borges' story, for the point is not the specific allusion but the concept behind it, in this case, the placing of a famous character into a radically unexpected context. Such allusions, nearly impossible to trace, appear throughout "Pierre Menard" and they catapult the reader into the highest category of the Borges hierarchy of reading, to create meaning from deliberate ambiguity. This is where the craft of writing merges with the art of reading. Whether or not the reader can verify the story's "fallacious attributions," he or she is forced to create a meaning. This is a form of joke played by Borges upon his readers, to frustrate coherence as a way to "enrich the slow and rudimentary art of reading." As critic John Frow put it, "Borges's 'Pierre Menard, Author of the *Quixote*' is a perfectly serious joke that we are still learning how to take seriously." The casual (who takes Borges' word for it) as well as the inquisitive reader (who hunts down every reference) approach the text from different angles, but in either case must fabricate their own sense of his "deliberate anachronism and fallacious attributions." By considering "Pierre Menard, Author of the Quixote" an essay/story about reading, the oxymoron of the two inspirations for Menard's project begins to make sense, too. One of the texts that inspired Menard was the Novalis "philological fragment" on total identification with the author—in other words, a "perfect" reading. The other was a "parasitic book" that played with context—in other words, it disrupted the reader's expectations. Taking the two opposing concepts together, Borges seems to suggest that full understanding, epitomized by "total identification" and perfect understanding, is undesirable and inadequate, because the reader has to negotiate context, epitomized by the example of Christ taken out of his expected context. Borges could not have intended "Pierre Menard" to spawn the postmodern idea of the "death of the author," the concept that nothing new can be written. On the contrary, Borges meant the readers of "Pierre Menard" to discover the "birth of the reader," the idea that it is readers who make the text, and not authors alone.

Source: Carole Hamilton, in an essay for *Literature of Developing Nations for Students*, Gale, 2000.

Dean Rader

Rader has published several articles on twentieth-century American and Latin American literature. In this essay, he discusses Borges' innovative style and his postmodernist tendencies, despite the fact that he was engaging in postmodernist techniques before the term was ever coined.

Unfortunately, when scholars and readers think of Jorge Luis Borges, they do not think of a funny man. Typically, people characterize Borges and his work as abstract, philosophical, difficult, enigmatic, labyrinthine, but rarely humorous and playful. In "Pierre Menard, Author of the Quixote," Borges is at his best because while the story meets all of the standard Borges criteria mentioned above, it is also one

of his funniest pieces. Its utter absurdity, its creative form, its textuality, and its lack of traditional narrativity mark it as a classic postmodern text; however, the concept of postmodernism had yet to be articulated when Borges was working on the story in the early 1950s. In this way, the story is a pioneering text, one way ahead of its time, in part because of its awareness of itself as a text. At no point are we ever to believe that the text is "reality." We are always certain that the document before us is just that, a document, a description, not a representation of events. In fact, Borges has established his career on writing short stories that are not really stories—they don't have a traditional plot. There is no beginning, middle and end; no rising action, no denouement. In fact, many of his pieces are mock scholarly articles, fiction, but not stories. Such is the case with "Pierre Menard." The story is, in fact, a giant trick, a ruse, a parody of the kind of literary criticism that the narrator of the story is himself engaging in, a prophetic parody of exactly the kind of article you are reading at this very moment.

In his essay for the *Dictionary of Literary Biography*, Alberto Julian Perez identifies the "creation of stories whose principal objective is to deal with critical, literary, or aesthetic problems" as one of two traits that distinguish Borges' art. Without question, this motif is the primary engine driving "Pierre Menard." The other, according to Perez, is the "development of plots that communicate elaborate and complex ideas that are transformed into the main thematic base of the story." In other words, Borges makes his ideas the central character in his works, not human beings. Even though the story deals with a fictional writer named Pierre Menard, Borges' text does not engage the life of Menard; it's really not about him. Rather, it is a reading of his most intriguing work, an unfinished manuscript copy of *Don Quixote*. Of course, Menard is not the original author of *Don Quixote*; Miguel de Cervantes wrote that lengthy tome over 300 years ago. Yet, in 1934, Menard sets out to write the *Quixote* as well: "He did not want to compose another *Quixote*—which is easy—but *the Quixote itself*. . .[h]is admirable intention was to produce a few pages which would coincide—word for word and line for line—with those of Miguel de Cervantes." Through his narrator, a Menard apologist, Borges proceeds to explain how Menard achieved this peculiar and somewhat ridiculous feat and to argue why Menard's version, though identical to Cervantes', is superior. Thus, the story brings into its own textuality all of the literary critical apparatus one would use to analyze, classify, explicate and explain it. In other words, Borges shows the reader how to be a literary critic of one of his own stories.

In his overview of ''Pierre Menard'' for *Short Stories for Students*, Greg Barnhisel claims that Borges ''is a writer of ideas, and it is ideas that drive his fictions.'' Borges' idea in ''Pierre Menard'' is that a text accumulates the ideas and movements and philosophies and cultural weight of the era in which it was written. In one of the most famous passages of all of Borges' work, the excited narrator compares Menard's *Quixote* with Cervantes' *Quixote*:

> It is a revelation to compare Menard's *Don Quixote* with Cervantes'. The latter, for example, wrote (part one, chapter nine):
>
> ''. . .truth, whose mother is history, rival of time, depository of deeds, witness of the past, exemplar and adviser to the present, and the future's counselor.''
>
> Written in the seventeenth century, written by the ''lay genius'' Cervantes, this enumeration is a mere rhetorical praise of history. Menard, on the other hand wrote:
>
> ''. . .truth, whose mother is history, rival of time, depository of deeds, witness of the past, exemplar and adviser to the present, and the future's counselor.''
>
> History, the *mother* of truth: the idea is astounding.

This is a hilarious passage. The excerpts are identical. Yet, because they were written at entirely different moments in history, each text is imbued with the various events and concepts that have informed that moment. Borges notes that Menard was a contemporary of William James and links Menard's text with the provocative and influential ideas generating from James' philosophy of pragmatism. Knowing this history, one is forced to read Menard's text in that light. No such philosophical movements existed when Cervantes was writing; thus, as the narrator informs us, ''Menard's fragmentary *Quixote* is more subtle than Cervantes'.'' According to the narrator, Cervantes' text is mired in the rather dull history of Spain around 1600 and cannot evoke or signify anything that has happened since. However, because Menard is a genius, and because his text appears in the early part of the twentieth century, then his words resonate with the hum of modernity, the inspiration of psychology, the radical dicta of Nietzsche.

Not only does the content of the texts alter from author to author, so does the impact of the style. Our narrator finds Menard's style affected, archaic. The language is mired in the past and seems alien. On the other hand, Cervantes' Spanish is easy and

''. . .the story brings into its own textuality all of the literary critical apparatus one would use to analyze, classify, explicate and explain it. In other words, Borges shows the reader how to be a literary critic of one of his own stories.''

reflects the tone and vocabulary of the Spanish of his time. Still, despite this setback, the narrator boldly asserts that even though ''Cervantes' text and Menard's are verbally identical. . .the second is almost infinitely richer.'' Borges is often criticized for writing a literature that does not speak to the political and social events of his time, and while some of these charges are warranted, in his own cryptic way, he suggests in this story that literature is an extension of the time and culture in which it was written. One cannot separate a text from the culture that produced it, and though Borges never addresses the repressive politics of the Peron government, he is aware of the ways in which history is as much an author of a text as the person whose name is attached to the text—not surprisingly, a stance also held by Menard in his version of the *Quixote*.

Traditionally, students, writers, scholars and teachers have distinguished between ''creative'' writing and literary criticism. One is artistic, the other, scholarly. One is art, the other comments on art. Borges complicates these distinctions in ''Pierre Menard'' not so much through Menard's project but through his project, ''Pierre Menard, Author of the *Quixote*.'' A former librarian and scholar, Borges published many essays that employed the same language and analytical tools that our nameless narrator employs in the story, and that both you and I are employing in an attempt to make sense of Borges' text. For instance, the narrator provides us with a very detailed bibliography (19 entries) of Menard's work. No doubt, you have had to construct such a bibliography; however, in this case, every single entry is a fiction. None of the texts mentioned exists. What's more, the story is complete with footnotes, adding to the legitimacy of the scholarship of the piece. This obsession with textuality (the notion of texts within texts) is a classic characteristic of postmodernism, of which Borges was perhaps the most important precursor. Another way in which ''Pierre Menard'' predicts postmodernism lies in its implicit critique of tenets of the New Criticism. For the New Critics, the author, his or her era, political and social events, biography and intertextuality were anathema. The only thing that mattered was the text itself, the text's autotelism. In fact, the New Critics wanted to remove the author from the text altogether. Of course, Borges' text suggests just the opposite. The text's very meaning is dependent on the author and the culture in which the text is produced. Finally, Borges engages in a double parody in the story, another important aspect of postmodernism. He not only parodies *Don Quixote*, he parodies the act of interpreting all literary texts. The most postmodern of gestures is to call your own project into question. Borges does this brilliantly here.

Though Barnhisel and others question Borges' use of ''piggybacking''—Menard latches on to Cervantes, Borges latches on to ''Menard,'' critics, including myself, latch on to Borges, and you, perhaps, latch on to us—he reminds us of the degree to which all texts and all projects are interconnected. In a lecture toward the end of his life, Borges claimed that the audience was the true author of his stories. By that he meant that through our own individual interpretation of a text, we ''create'' the nuances of that text. Thus, it would make Borges happy to know that in some way, we are all authors of the *Quixote*.

Source: Dean Rader, in an essay for *Literature of Developing Nations for Students*, Gale, 2000.

Michael J. Wreen

In the following essay on Jorge Luis Borges's Pierre Menard, Author of Quixote, *Michael J. Wreen argues that Borges's story is a sustained parody presenting an ironic commentary on the process of creative activity as a necessary but ultimately impossible task.*

In a recent article, ''Once Is Not Enough?'', I argued that a book word-for-word identical with Cervantes' *Quixote* wouldn't be a new *Quixote*, numerically distinct from Cervantes', if it were produced in the manner described in Borges' short story ''Pierre Menard, Author of the *Quixote*.'' Menard's novel would simply be Cervantes', I tried

to show, although admittedly produced in a very odd way. But philosophical issues (such as the individuation of works of art) are one thing, literary interpretation quite another. In this paper, I'll be offering a comprehensive interpretation of Borges' story and arguing, against a number of critics, that ''Pierre Menard'' is philosophically correct, i.e., that the correct interpretation of Borges' story doesn't have Menard as the author of a new *Quixote*. Even more importantly, I'll be arguing that the story is an extremely penetrating one, with philosophical depths as yet unexplored, although its main interest, metaphysical and otherwise, lies in a direction other than the individuation of works of art. These being my main theses, let me also issue an advance warning that my approach is itself more than a little philosophical.

I

Given my purely philosophical examination of the duplicate *Quixote* case, the most direct way to approach Borges' story would be to ask, Why on earth would anyone ever reproduce Cervantes' novel in the way that Menard does? But the more indirect route, and the one I'll be traveling here, is to marshal evidence bit by textual bit, all the while proceeding with the aim of constructing a unified and comprehensive interpretation. That methodology begs no critical questions, as the first one evidently does.

Structurally, ''Pierre Menard'' has three parts. In the first, the setting, dramatic voice, and mode of narration are established; the main character, Pierre Menard, is introduced; the prevailing tone is set; and a number of themes are broached. The story is cast in the form of an elaborate literary obituary and memoir written by an unnamed friend and admirer of Menard. Supposedly, it's an official, formal assessment and appreciation of the great man, an intellectual and a figure of stupendous, even revolutionary, but unfortunately unknown, literary achievement. Superficially, the piece resembles the sort of literary honorarium found not so much in professional journals as in the self-appointed flagships of high art, i.e., in literary magazines with pretensions to high culture. We soon discover, however, that the narrator's assessment may be somewhat biased and skewed—that he may be, in other words, an unreliable narrator. His first few sentences show him to be patronizing and bullying, and within two paragraphs his political conservatism, hauteur, and condescending attitude toward any and all who don't share his convictions are made evident. After first taking an altogether gratuitous snipe at Protestants and Masons, he proceeds to name-drop a title or two, in order, he says, to establish his authority to write an assessment of Menard and his oeuvre, but actually to call attention to himself and his aristocratic connections. Moreover, his prose style is pretentious, bombastic, and affected, and smacks more than a little of the fourth-rate symbolist:

> One might say that only yesterday we gathered before his [Menard's] final monument, amidst the lugubrious cypresses, and already Error tries to tarnish his Memory. . . . Decidedly, a brief rectification is unavoidable (Borges).

Clearly, this is not an assessment to be trusted. But even more clearly, and even more importantly, this is fiction, not non-fiction, despite the obituary/literary-memoir format. No piece of non-fiction would ever be as blatantly prejudiced, arrogant, or inflated as "Pierre Menard." Moreover, given only what has been said so far, it's quite probably a parody of a certain kind of litterateur and literary document, and quite probably a story whose prevailing tone is ironic. If that is so, what we should be on the lookout for is exactly the opposite of what we see glittering brightly on the surface. In fact if that's the case, if we don't look any farther than the surface, we're liable to miss what the story is really all about. Taking the story to be an argument for the numerical distinctness of Menard's *Quixote* would be to be blind to the story's pervasive irony, in particular that regarding Menard's creative activity.

II

Part one of the story concludes with a slightly annotated list of Menard's "visible" work. From the list we learn that Menard is a very minor symbolist poet and an intellectual with a number of disparate, narrow, and highly idiosyncratic interests. Menard has published a sonnet and written a sonnet cycle "for the Baroness de Bacourt," and has done extensive work in literary theory and criticism. In addition to writing "an invective against Paul Valery," an invective which expresses "the exact opposite of his true opinion of Valery," he has

> written a monograph on the possibility of constructing a poetic vocabulary of concepts which would not be synonyms or periphrases of those which make up our everyday language, "but rather ideal objects created according to convention and essentially designed to satisfy poetic needs."

He's also examined the "essential metric laws of French prose," as well as replied to "Luc Durtain (who denied the existence of such laws), [using] examples [culled] from Luc Durtain['s own work]."

"...the more indirect route, and the one I'll be traveling here, is to marshal evidence bit by textual bit, all the while proceeding with the aim of constructing a unified and comprehensive interpretation."

His other achievements include having fashioned a "determined analysis of the 'syntactical customs' of Toulet," having translated Quevedo's *Aguja de navegar cultos* and Ruy Lopez's book on chess, *Libro de la invencion liberal y arte del juego del axedrez*, and having transposed the maligned Valery's *Le Cimetiere marin* into alexandrines. But various obscure corners of philosophy were also peeking places for Menard. He composed work sheets for a monograph on George Boole's symbolic logic, and wrote "a monograph on 'certain connections or affinities' between the thought of Descartes, Leibniz and John Wilkins," a monograph on Leibniz's *Characteristica universalis*, a monograph on Raymond Lully's *Ars magna generic,* and a book, *Les problemes d'un probleme,* on the different solutions to the problem of Achilles and the tortoise. Rounding out the list of Menard's "visible" achievements are a number of other odd items: "a technical article on the possibility of improving the game of chess [by] eliminating one of the rook's pawns," an article in which Menard "proposes, recommends, discusses, and finally rejects the innovation"; "a preface to the *Catalogue* of an exposition of lithographs by Carolus Hourcade"; "a 'definition' of the Countess de Bagnoregio, in the 'victorious volume'. . . published annually by this lady to rectify the inevitable falsifications of journalists"; and "a manuscript list of verses which owe their efficacy to their punctuation."

The picture drawn here is both consistent and complete: Menard is a precieux, a turn-of-the-century decadent, a symbolist, and a snobbish cultivator of social connections. So far, then, he's a man rather like the narrator. But he's a decadent and symbolist of a rather more complex sort than the narrator, since he's also a poet and a very peculiar and desiccated academic as well. Moreover, while academics and poets are known for their eccentricities and narrow and peculiar interests, Menard's quantitative differences from other poets and academics in these respects make for a qualitative difference. For the list is little more than an extended catalogue of arrant academic twaddle, of intellectual pettiness without a point. It thus shows that Menard, unlike other poets and academics, has completely lost sight of what is truly important and interesting about poetry and intellectual matters, and thus lost contact with the real world, the world that gives poetry and academic matters their value in the first place. His, instead, is an autotelic universe, a universe circumscribed and defined by interests fabricated by his own exhausted intellect. His vitality, as a real man and a thinker, has diminished to the point that his studies are well-nigh useless, and he himself simply a curious life form, culturally speaking. No wonder Borges said that the list is "a diagram of [Menard's] mental history" and thus that "il y a chez lui [Menard] un sens de l'inutilite de la litterature." The theme that Barrenechea finds in so many of Borges' works, that of the writer as noncreative, is present in "Pierre Menard" from the start, in both the narrator's introduction and the catalogue of Menard's "achievements."

III

The second part of the story is a description and explanation of what the narrator regards as far and away Menard's greatest accomplishment, invisible though it may be. "I turn now," he says, "to [Menard's] other work: the subterranean, the interminably heroic, the peerless. And—such are the capacities of man!—the unfinished." Yes, such are the capacities of man that men don't finish their work. But small ironies such as this aside, what is perhaps the "most significant [work] of our time," the narrator tells us, "consists of the ninth and thirty-eighth chapters of the first part of Don Quixote and a fragment of chapter twenty-two." Menard has written a *Quixote*, or at least part of a *Quixote*, that is word-for-word identical with Cervantes' but not identical with Cervantes'. To say as much is to affirm an absurdity, the narrator admits, but Menard is capable of the absurd, capable of achieving the impossible.

Here, for the first time, another major theme is introduced, that of literary creation as necessarily an impossible task, a theme consistent with but stronger than the uselessness of literature. In addition, one of the themes hinted at earlier, the logical inseparability of the man of letters—whether reader or writer—from the literary work—whether fictional or nonfictional—is explicitly drawn out and underscored. For since Menard symbolizes the man of letters, literature and litterateur fuse in Borges' story: the man, Menard, has no more reality than the performance of the literary task. Indeed, he lives within the task, Borges tells us, since he lives within books alone. The written word eventually makes those who live by it part of it, Borges seems to say—probably not a little a propos of himself. As I'll try to show below in section XII, even this strong thesis will eventually need strengthening.

Menard was inspired by two very different sources to undertake his "impossible" task: a "philological fragment by Novalis [whoever he might be, if anyone at all]. . .which outlines the theme of total identification with a given author, [and]. . .one of those parasitic books which situate Christ on a boulevard, Hamlet on La Canebiere or Don Quixote on Wall Street." Literature draws upon literature, both in Novalis and in the parasitic book, and thus the theme of the autotelic nature of literature and the literary life, here again represented by Menard, is reinforced. Menard's life-literature's life—is not only essentially parasitic upon the extraliterary world; at its worst, in the terminal stages of its inevitable decline, it is parasitic upon itself, unable to draw inspiration from anything other than itself. The result is an anemic and decadent literature, both uninspired and uninspiring. In the case of Menard, in fact, the disease has spread even further: he was "inspired" by two pieces of literature, one a fragment of an essay, one probably a novel, which are themselves already parasitic pieces of literature, dependent for their existence on the prior existence of literature in general (the essay fragment) and specific literary works (the novel). Menard's undertaking, to replicate—"duplicate" would be more accurate—an already existent literary work, the Quixote, was itself inspired by two pieces of literature already parasitic on literature. Hence once again, but at a new level, the theme of the autotelic nature of literature—or, what is the same thing, Menard's autotelic world and the autotelic nature of his mind. But hence also a new thesis: this is a world in which, in the long run, the distinction between author and fictional character is only a nominal distinction, only a distinction of words—which, of course, is the only kind of distinction there could be in such a world.

IV

Following a statement of Menard's intended project, the narrator lets Menard speak for himself, quoting a letter he supposedly wrote him. "'My intent is no more than astonishing,'" Menard wrote, "'The final term in a theological or metaphysical demonstration—the objective world, God, causality, the forms of the universe—is no less previous and common than my famed novel. The only difference is that the philosophers publish their intermediary stages of their labor in pleasant volumes and I have resolved to do away with those stages.' In truth," as the narrator says, continuing the story where Menard left off, "not one worksheet remains to bear witness to his years of effort."

This is parody once again, only this time concerning the inflated self-images of artistes and assorted defenders of the intellectual realm. It's also a send-up of the sort of Manifesto of Grand Artistic Purpose that self-righteous guardians of high culture are usually only too glad to issue. "Manifesto of Grand Delusion" would be more accurate in most cases, though, but especially apt in this one, because the parody and irony here are particularly pointed: whether he knows it or not, Menard's "famed novel" is famed for no other reason than that it is Cervantes'. I say this because (1) to intend to produce a novel word-for-word identical with one that already exists; (2) to use word-for-word identity with it as the standard for completion of your task; and (3) to rely, as Menard evidently did, on his memory of that novel in producing his text—for not only had he read Cervantes' book (admittedly, many years past), he had to look at Cervantes' text in order to make sure that his 'rough drafts' were indeed rough drafts (that is, not word-for-word identical with the relevant parts of Cervantes') and thus undoubtedly re-approached his job with some memory of Cervantes' text in mind—to do all of that is just to reproduce Cervantes' text in a very roundabout, strange way. Given the context, then, the irony is more pointed than a mere parody of the sort of person or document in question would otherwise be. Menard is a ridiculous figure not only because of his inflated self-image, self-congratulatory and self-satisfied manner, and pompous prose posing, but because his studious seriousness is put in the service of a logically impossible task. Again, this is the theme of literary creation as an impossible task, but again there is an enrichment: here the task really is literally impossible.

That, of course, didn't deter Menard. Various plans to accomplish his objective occurred to him.

Rejected as too easy was to "know Spanish well, recover the Catholic faith, fight against the Moors or the Turk, forget the history of Europe between the years 1602 and 1918, be Miguel de Cervantes." But since doing that is logically impossible, Menard's proposed modus operandi is, with an irony that is perhaps too heavy, hardly too easy: being numerically distinct people is logically impossible, just as squaring the circle, or writing a *Quixote* numerically distinct from Cervantes' while exactly duplicating the book, intending to so duplicate it, and checking your production for accuracy against it is. This, however, the unnamed narrator readily admits: "[But being Cervantes is] impossible! my reader will say. Granted, but the undertaking was impossible from the very beginning and of all the impossible ways of carrying it out, this was the least interesting." That the method and task itself are impossible is conceded by the narrator, but being the spiritual kin of Menard, he rejects the plan because it's not interesting, not because it's not possible. That is the sort of solipsistic and autotelic universe that the narrator and Menard inhabit.

V

The plan that Menard decided upon was "to go on being Pierre Menard and to reach the *Quixote* through the experiences of Pierre Menard." "'My undertaking is not difficult, essentially,'" Menard wrote to the narrator. "'I should only have to be immortal to carry it out.'" But this self-absorbed posturing conceals yet another contradiction. Since it's impossible—physically, not logically this time—to be immortal, the "undertaking" is just the opposite of "essentially easy," and Menard, like the narrator, is anything but rational for brushing aside the contradiction as of little moment. Besides, it's not at all clear that immortality would guarantee completion of the task. If the task is logically impossible (given Menard's methods), then eternity guarantees only never-ending frustration.

The narrator is not essentially different from Menard. He shares his delusions of literary grandeur, and prefers specious but personally satisfying rationalization to common sense. Again like Menard, he prefers a world of pleasant literary fantasies to one of cold literary—and literal—facts. "Some nights past," he says,

> while leafing through chapter XXVI [of the *Quixote*]—never essayed by him—I recognized our friend's style and something of his voice in this exceptional phrase: "the river nymphs and the dolorous and humid Echo." This happy conjunction of a spiritual and a physical adjective brought to my mind a verse

by Shakespeare which we discussed one afternoon: ''Where a malignant and turbaned Turk . . . .''

But to interpret passages not written by someone as if they were and to delight in the thoughts and emotions thereby evoked is to abandon hard, cold reality—including the hard, cold reality of literary interpretation—for a dream world of delicious delusions, and to do so, in this case, in an especially bizarre and fatuous fashion. For what the narrator is implicitly doing here is attributing a style to Menard and then reading Cervantes against the backdrop of that style. He is, in other words, reading Cervantes as a logically posterior writer and stylist. Philosophically speaking, this is worse than interpretation turned inside out. There is no logically independent style of Menard that can act as a backdrop, because no logically independent work of his exists. The only work there is is Cervantes'. Hence it is logically impossible to read Cervantes the way the narrator does, much less to savor, as he evidently does, that reading. Cervantes is not the logically posterior writer because there isn't, and couldn't be, any logically anterior one.

Icing for the cake here, adding to the perversity of the narrator's delight, is his aesthetic insensitivity. To quote Shakespeare's line ''Where a malignant and turbaned Turk . . .'' with approval is to love The Bard not wisely but too well. The line is undoubtedly one of the thousand that Jonson would have blotted, for the conjunction of the adjectives is anything but delicate or aesthetically subtle. Rather, it's ludicrous and unintentionally humorous, the literary kin, aesthetically speaking, of Dickens' famous line about leaving the room in a flood of tears and a sedan chair. Drawing attention to Menard's—really, Cervantes'—''exceptional phrase'' regarding ''dolorous and humid Echo'' by comparing it with Shakespeare's blunder is to draw attention to its obvious defects, two of which, in addition to the one already hinted at in regard to the line from Shakespeare, are its decadent languidness and vapidity. Unlike Othello, the narrator is easily wrought, both logically and aesthetically; but like Othello, being wrought, he's perplexed in the extreme.

Recovering from the listless digression regarding Menard and Shakespeare he's fallen into, the narrator asks, Why did Menard choose to re-create the *Quixote*? Why the *Quixote* rather than some other book? Menard himself provided the answer, the narrator tells us, in a letter he wrote him. The *Quixote* is '''not. . . inevitable,''' he said there; it's '''a contingent book; the *Quixote* is unnecessary. I

can premeditate writing it, I can write it, without falling into a tautology.'''

This is simply philosophical confusion. Strictly speaking, as I've already argued, Menard can't write the *Quixote* at all—not without falling into a (logical) contradiction. In that sense, of course, he can certainly avoid ''falling into a tautology,'' contradictions being just the opposite of tautologies. But writing the Quixote—or anything else—and actually falling into a tautology? What would it be like to do that? What, in other words, does Menard mean by ''tautology''? The context here is replete with philosophical terms, ''contingent,'' ''unnecessary,'' and ''inevitable'' among them, and that fact, in conjunction with Menard's documented philosophic interests and background, would make it seem that the term is also being used in a philosophical sense. Philosophically speaking, tautologies are logically compound statements which are truth-functionally true, that is, true under all assignments of truth values to their component parts. Tautologies in this sense are necessarily true, and therefore true in every possible or imaginable universe. They're not contingently true, not true in this but not every possible or imaginable universe. Menard's dichotomy of tautologies, necessity, and the inevitable on the one hand, and contingencies and what he can imagine the universe not containing—such as the *Quixote*—on the other, thus seems secure and well founded.

But it isn't, not really. Remember, in this sense a tautology is a statement, and no statement of the form ''X wrote Y'' or ''Y exists,'' where X is a person and Y a book, is truth-functionally true, or even analytically true (true solely in virtue of the meanings of the terms found in it). Every statement of either form couldn't be anything but non-tautologous, and thus contingently true, if true at all. There's simply nothing on the other side of Menard's implied contrast, then, no statement concerning the existence of a book or authorship that's tautologous. Consequently, the statements ''The *Quixote* exists'' and ''Cervantes is the author of the *Quixote*'' are non-tautologous, just as Menard has them. That's hardly enlightening or surprising, however, and the truth of Menard's claim, given the similar non-tautologous nature of all statements of the same form, thus provides no reason for choosing the *Quixote* over any other book.

But maybe this way of reading Menard, a technical and highly philosophical one, isn't the right way to read him. Menard does say that he can't imagine the universe without Poe's line, ''Ah, bear in mind this garden was enchanted!'' or without the *Bateau Ivre* or the *Ancient Mariner,* and the statement ''The *Quixote* exists'' is supposed to contrast with them. But how? ''Poe wrote the line 'Ah, bear . . .''', ''The *Bateau* lure exists,'' and ''The *Ancient Mariner* exists'' are one and all non-tautologous and contingent. But once again, so is ''The *Quixote* exists.'' And though it's easy to imagine the universe without the statement about the *Quixote* being true, it's equally easy to imagine the universe without the others being true as well, contrary to what Menard says. Besides, soon after making his remarks about the *Quixote*'s being contingent and contrasting Cervantes' work with other ''inevitable'' ones, Menard goes on to say that ''to compose the *Quixote* at the beginning of the seventeenth century was a reasonable undertaking, necessary and perhaps even unavoidable,'' thus flatly contradicting himself. No master of logic he, Menard.

Perhaps, though, despite the philosophical context he himself has established, and despite his own philosophical interests and background, Menard doesn't intend ''tautology'' in a philosophical sense at all; perhaps he means it simply in its everyday sense, as a needless repetition of something, whether a statement, a question, a command, or whatever. Menard's main idea, then, would be that he wouldn't be needlessly repeating Cervantes in undertaking a new *Quixote,* though repeating him he would certainly be. Now, however, the notion of inevitability can come into play—and can come to Menard's rescue, even. ''Inevitable'' similarly doesn't mean necessary in any logical or causal sense, or any other sense common to philosophical discourse, Menard could say; rather, it means aesthetically necessary. Menard's claim would then be that he wouldn't be repeating Cervantes needlessly, in that he wouldn't be repeating him in an aesthetically unnecessary way. There's room, aesthetically speaking, for a new *Quixote,* Menard thinks, and that's why Cervantes' work is contingent—and that, in fact, is what he, Menard, means by ''contingent'': aesthetic possibility. According to him, Cervantes' *Quixote* has made new aesthetic possibilities possible, including the possibility of a work word-for-word identical with it but numerically and aesthetically distinct from it. By way of contrast, the aesthetic possibilities of romantic literature have been exhausted, the death knell having been sounded by the decadents. That's why Menard mentions Poe's line, the *Ancient Mariner*, and the *Bateau Ivre* all in the same breath. No new aesthetic possibilities

remain for romantic literature, for its successor has exhausted them all. Hence, for his crowning literary achievement the *Quixote* is perfect, while romantic literature not even possible.

While this generous interpretation of Menard is consistent with his remarks and, moreover, is in keeping with what we know of the man—I think in particular of the aesthetic sensibilities revealed in the catalogue of his ''visible achievements''—it's as problematic as the others. The central difficulty is not so much the obviously vague and unexplained concept of aesthetic possibility as the claim that it's possible for Menard to create an aesthetically distinct *Quixote* but not an aesthetically distinct *Ancient Mariner.* Numerical distinctness may ensure aesthetic distinctness, but aesthetic distinctness—itself bound up with the concept of aesthetic possibility, it would seem—is predicated on the logically prior notion of numerical distinctness, and not vice versa. Thus aesthetic distinctness presupposes numerical distinctness, and so even on this interpretation of Menard's remarks, it must be possible for him to create a numerically distinct *Quixote* but not a numerically distinct *Mariner.* Even waiving the objection that creating the former isn't really possible in this case, why isn't the latter possible if the former is? If it's possible to create a new *Quixote* in the way Menard envisages, why not a new *Mariner*? He supplies no reason for distinguishing the cases as far as the individuation of works of art is concerned, and logically and ontologically they certainly seem on a par. That's a very good reason for thinking that they can't be distinguished. As far as the main issue is concerned, then, the conclusion that should be drawn is that if there is a reason for Menard's choosing the *Quixote* over every other book—and I think there is, and will be discussing it in due course—it has nothing to do with the argument Menard himself supplies, regardless of how generously it's interpreted. Instead, the passage about his choice of the *Quixote* should be read in light of what we already know about Menard himself. So read, it doesn't function philosophically, since its purpose isn't to provide us with insights on the nature of the aesthetic; rather, it functions literarily, so to speak, since its purpose is deepen our understanding of the precieuse and provide yet another ironic fix on the pathetic, illogical, solipsistic, and academic, in the worst sense of the word, character that he is.

VII

The third major section of the story is partly a critical evaluation of Menard's *Quixote*, partly a panegyric of the man, and partly a theoretical reflection on the aesthetic lessons taught us by him. Panegyric and theoretical reflection are inextricably bound up with each other, however, and thus will be considered together below. Also, the third section is far and away the richest of the three, from a philosophical point of view, and so a fair amount of space will need to be devoted to it in order to do it justice. First, then, the narrator's critical assessment of Menard's magnum opus.

Having detailed how difficult it was to pull off the trick of writing a new *Quixote* at all, the narrator proceeds to argue that the new *Quixote* is aesthetically superior to the original. Menard's book is "more subtle" than Cervantes', for instance, because Menard doesn't

> oppose . . . to the fictions of chivalry the tawdry provincial reality of his country; Menard selects as his 'reality' the land of Carmen during the century of Lepanto and Lope de Vega. . . . He neglects altogether local color. This disdain points to a new conception of the historical novel [and] condemns Salammbo, with no possibility of appeal.

But even if Menard's were a new *Quixote* I doubt that it would be quite so easy to "condemn" Flaubert's novel. Salammbo's place in the historical record is a little too secure to be dislodged by any single event in the literary world, even the mysterious appearance of the *Quixote* (or a new *Quixote*). But the narrator's remark here is probably just critical hyperbole, not intended to be taken literally. He may just mean that Menard's achievement casts a new light on Flaubert's work, locating it in the historical development of the novel in an altogether new and unexpected fashion. To which the proper reply is, True enough—but only if Menard's book is indeed a new one. If it's not and the reader is intended to know as much, the narrator's remark will need to be reinterpreted in the context of the story as a whole. Independent evidence I've already marshalled in fact suggests all three: (1) that the novel wouldn't be a new one; (2) that the reader is intended to know as much; and thus (3) that the narrator's critical remarks should be understood ironically. We have a fairly complete mental history of Menard and a slightly annotated bibliography of his published work to draw upon in interpreting just what his literary capacities are, and we have something similar, first hand, in the case of the narrator, namely the evidence provided by his own prose in the story. All such evidence, from the first paragraph of the story onwards, suggests an ironic reading of the argument for Menard's greater subtlety.

So does the passage itself. For at least two reasons, to argue for Menard's greater subtlety on the basis of his having selected the land of Carmen during the century of Lepanto and Lope de Vega as his "reality" is just the sort of nonsense that is an strong indication of irony. First, since Menard's overarching intention was simply to produce a text word-for-word identical with Cervantes', he didn't select, in the sense the narrator seems to have in mind, namely intend to write about, the land of Carmen. . . . Even if, as is very likely, Menard knew that the country and century depicted in Cervantes was the land of Carmen. . . , that doesn't entail that he intended to write about the land of Carmen. . . . (When I walk home from school, I know that my shoes will wear down a little bit, but that doesn't mean that I intend that they wear down a little bit.) On the contrary, the odds are very high that, wrapped up in his imitative task as he was, concentrating on reproducing Cervantes' text word-for-word, thoughts, much less intentions, respecting the land of Carmen. . . never crossed his mind. The narrator's saying that Menard selected the land of Carmen. . . , in the sense of intending to write about, is merely another instance of his abandoning a person in reality for a pleasant projection in a dream world.

Second, contrary to the narrator's suggestion, the "A selects B" construction is what contemporary philosophers would call referentially transparent. Roughly speaking, a sentence is referentially transparent if and only if codesignative terms can be substituted for each another in it salva veritate, that is, without change of truth value. If "Menard selected the land of Carmen." is true, and the land of Carmen. . . is Spain in the 17th century, then "Menard selected Spain in the 17th century" is true. So if Spain in the 17th century is the land and time that Cervantes selected and wrote about—which it certainly is—then Menard and Cervantes selected and wrote about the same land in the same century— they selected and wrote about the same thing, in other words. Thus philosophical analysis upholds the commonsense conviction that, despite the narrator's evident delectation, Menard can't be distinguished from Cervantes on the basis of what he selected to write about. The argument for Menard's greater subtlety is a sham, then, and the narrator merely spinning wheels in a fantasy land of his— and Menard's—own creation. The literary effect of this, given the immediacy of its impact and given the narrator's stilted and overly cultured means of expression, is pitched but merry irony. But the acme of irony is yet to come.

VIII

Before it does, though, an ironic flourish of a different sort is cleverly drawn. "It is well known," says our bombastic narrator,

> that Don Quixote. . . decided the debate [on arms and letters] against arms and in favor of letters. Cervantes was a former soldier: his verdict is understandable. But that Pierre Menard's *Don Quixote*—a contemporary of *La Trahison des clercs* and Bertrand Russell— should fall prey to such nebulous sophistries!

But the nebulous sophistries are in the passage itself, not the *Quixote* —or even any *Quixote*, including, arguendo, the one written by Menard. If Don Quixote decided the debate in favor of arms, it certainly doesn't follow that Cervantes did, though the narrator asserts as much without argument. Considered per se, inferences from what a fictional character says to what the author of the fiction believes, are notoriously shaky and unreliable. More importantly, the inference the narrator makes here is facilitated by the fact that he identifies Cervantes and Quixote, and thus blurs the distinction between reality and fiction, a distinction he and Menard have been attacking, consciously or not, since the advent of their literary careers. As I'll try to show below, in the long run Borges himself is attacking the same distinction, though not unwittingly, and with deliberate literary and philosophical purpose in mind. Recognition of gorges' intentions in this regard is essential to understanding his overarching purpose in the story.

For the present, however, we need only note that the narrator's attempted removal of the barrier between fact and fiction, implicit in his identification of Cervantes and Don Quixote, is continued in his remark about "Menard's *Don Quixote*." Even granting for the sake of argument that Menard's is not Cervantes' *Quixote*, the claim that his *Quixote* is a contemporary of Bertrand Russell is still, on many philosophers' views, simply a category mistake: the former is a fictional character, and thus in one logical category; the latter is a real man, and thus in quite another. That being the case, it's nonsense, strictly speaking, these philosophers would maintain, to regard the two as existing within the same time frame, and thus nonsense to regard them as contemporaries. Again, the narrator assimilates fact to fiction—or vice versa; it makes no difference within the bounds of the story itself. The concept of a category mistake being a much disputed one, however, the charge of nonsense probably shouldn't be pressed. Still, the narrator is far from off the logical hook. For even if comparing fictional char-

acters and real people is sometimes possible, in this case the comparison remains logically egregious. Menard's *Quixote* is obviously not a contemporary of Russell: Russell was born in 1872; Don Quixote, even, by the narrator's admission, in Menard's "new" story, lived in the late 16th and early 17th centuries. Rather, Menard's *Quixote* is a contemporary of Cervantes' *Quixote*. Since Menard, from what we can infer from the story, was born in approximately 1870, he and not his Quixote is the true contemporary of Russell. Once again—and irrespective of the contestable charge of a category mistake—there is a logical, indeed a metaphysical, confusion of the fictional and the factual, of character and author. The narrator identifies Menard with the fictional character he created, just as he previously identified Cervantes with the fictional character he created.

But the confusion is compounded and thus enriched here, in the second case, for Menard's *Quixote* is not only said to be a contemporary of Russell but of a book, *La Trahison des clercs*. The notion of a category mistake thus begs to be granted admission for the third time, but even if the request is again denied, the idea of people and books being contemporaries is an inherently odd one—until, that is, the idea is coupled with an understanding of the narrator's and Menard's persistent inability to distinguish fact from fiction. Given an open door between the two realms, the most natural comparison is with the door itself, namely a book. The supreme irony topping the whole thing off, of course, is that the conflation of the distinction between the real and fictional exists only within a piece of fiction itself, Borges' story.

But to return to the main issue: since the narrator's argument for an evaluatively important difference between the "two" *Quixotes* —a difference concerning the aesthetic quality of the passages favoring arms over letters—rests on a number of logical and metaphysical confusions, there is no good reason for thinking the two different in that respect. There is thus no difference that needs to be explained—and what the narrator does next is tender an explanation—and thus also no basis for thinking that the conclusion that he immediately draws from his "finding" concerning arms versus letters, the conclusion that Menard's text is "infinitely richer" than Cervantes', is anything but wishful thinking. Indeed, even if the narrator had made a good case for his claim respecting arms versus letters, the argument would still be poor one, the inductive leap from a single piece of evidence to an outrageously strong conclusion respecting infinite richness being one of several light years.

IX

But the narrator has other arguments to offer. Compare, he says, the following passage from Cervantes:

> . . . truth, whose mother is history, rival of time, depository of deeds, witness of the past, exemplar and adviser to the present, and the future's counselor. . .

with this one from Menard:

> . . . truth, whose mother is history, rival of time, depository of deeds, witness of the past, exemplar and adviser to the present, and the future's counselor. . . .

Since Cervantes wrote in the 17th century, his passage is "mere rhetorical praise of history." The passage from Menard, on the other hand, originating in the 20th century as it did, is "astounding." Menard takes history to be the mother of truth, not "an inquiry into [truth's] origin. Historical truth, for him, is not what has happened; it is what we judge to have happened. The final phrases—exemplar and advisor to the present, and the future's counselor—are brazenly pragmatic." Vast differences of an evaluative nature exist between the two books, then.

But it's hard to shake the feeling that the argument here is itself more sophistical than any of the "nebulous sophistries" found in the Quixote. The narrator telling us that two passages of very distinctive prose, passages which are word-for-word identical, differ radically in their aesthetic properties—that beggars comparison with Ionesco's psychotic professor telling his pupil that instead of saying "The roses of my grandmother are as yellow as my grandfather who was Asiatic" she is saying "The roses of my grandmother are as yellow as my grandfather who was Asiatic" (Ionesco). There has to be something wrong with the argument.

And there is. The imputed differences between the passages doesn't really depend so much on their being products of different time periods—though, admittedly, their being such could warrant interpreting them differently, even differently in aesthetically important ways—as on an equivocation in the narrator's reading of them. The crucial terms in both his glosses are "history" and, though only implicit in his reading of Cervantes, "truth." Depending on why the narrator thinks that the passage from Cervantes is mere rhetorical praise of history—he doesn't tell us—the first and possibly the second of these terms are equivocated on.

One way to understand his claim about Cervantes is with "history" taken to denote those actual, concrete, (in the main) non-linguistic events and facts that occur or exist out there in the world. With "truth" being taken in its usual sense to denote a property of propositions, namely their correspondence with (again, in the main) extra-linguistic event or fact, history is the mother of truth in that events and facts are logically prior to, and the metaphysical determinates of, the correspondence relation. Events and facts make, metaphysically, true propositions true. The other way to understand his claim about Cervantes is with "truth" taken in its common and colloquial sense of knowledge: "truth" is what we know to be true, in the first sense of the term. "History," then, understood in the sense just mentioned, would be the mother of truth in that our knowledge of what is the case would be logically and ontologically dependent upon the existence of those actual concrete events and facts out there in the world. "History" could even be taken in a second sense, in the sense of an oral or written record of history in the first sense of the term, and slightly weaker remarks of a similar nature would still hold good. Our knowledge of events and facts is dependent, as a matter of contingent fact, on "history" in the sense of an oral or written record. Any of these readings of Cervantes makes sense, but none will help the narrator escape the charge of equivocation.

The reason is that his reading of Menard takes "history" and/or "truth" in an altogether different sense (or senses). In claiming that Menard defines history as the origin of reality, and then going on to say that for Menard, historical truth—that is, history, in the first of the senses just identified—is what we judge to have happened, the narrator gives evidence for his claim that Menard's remark is astounding, no mere rhetorical praise of history. Why is it astounding? Because Menard's passage is budding pragmatism: what we judge to have happened determines, ontologically, what did happen. That's what the claim that history is the mother of truth amounts to. But notice that "history" here has to be understood in terms of what we judge to be the case—basically, the written or oral record—and not extra-linguistic, out-there, concrete reality. "History," then, is not to be understood in the sense that it probably should be in the passage from Cervantes, for there it had to do with extra-linguistic fact. Even on the reading of Cervantes on which "history" is taken as the written or oral record, an equivocation remains, since in his reading of Cervantes, "truth" has to be understood in the sense of knowledge, and the claim that history is the mother of truth read as a contingent claim which basically states that our knowledge of extra-linguistic events and facts is dependent, as a matter of contingent, causal fact, on the oral and written record. Obviously, the narrator means something much more philosophically significant than that in his reading of Menard, since he reads him as propounding a central tenet of pragmatism, that what is the case is determined by what we judge to be the case. An equivocation of some sort thus remains, no matter how the narrator's remarks are read, and no matter what argument is imputed him respecting his claim about Cervantes; and the most natural way to read him is with an equivocation on ''history.''

''What of that, though?'' someone might object. ''What is pejoratively identified as an equivocation might be simply reading one passage one way and another another, that's all. Even if the two passages are verbally identical, that doesn't necessarily mean that the narrator misinterpreted anything. Said on one occasion, 'I went to the bank' might mean that I took a trip to the financial institution; said on another, that I headed for the local fishing hole. No equivocation there, just correct interpretation. Why isn't the narrator doing just the same thing? After all, Cervantes lived way back when, Menard at the turn of this century, and that seems to be the basis for his different interpretations. So what's really wrong with reading the passages as he does?''

In principle, this is a good objection—indeed, I've already agreed that two passages could be verbally identical yet differ markedly in meaning and aesthetic significance. I don't think that it'll do here, however. Without doing anything more than dipping my big toe into the murky waters of the theory of interpretation, I can at least say that the burden of proof lies on those who would give different readings to verbally identical texts. True, my critic and the narrator make some effort to shoulder that burden, since both mention the life-dates of our authors, and the narrator the pragmatism of William James. Mere passage of time doesn't ensure difference of meaning, however (else language would be extremely unstable, probably impossible), and even assuming that Menard's *Quixote* isn't Cervantes', the putative reference to James remains just that, putative, unless the passage in question can be tied to James in some way. If an allusion isn't clear from a passage, the usual way to establish its presence is to consult the surrounding

verbal environment. Since Menard's prose is from first to last orthographically identical with Cervantes', though, no help from that quarter can be expected here. For the same reason, the passage from Menard actually has to be understood in exactly the same way as the corresponding passage from Cervantes, a fact reinforced if the circumstances surrounding the production of Menard's work are considered. The equivocation charge, then, is not out of place. The narrator once again willfully interprets as he chooses, never bothering with such matters as consistency if it doesn't suit him.

A more important objection, at least to my way of thinking, concerns not the ''whether'' of my analysis, but the ''why.'' ''Why make such heavy weather about it? Isn't it obvious that something's wrong, that his remarks are ludicrous? Why go on to explain the joke—for that is what it is—when it's obvious? That's just to kill it, and taking it in without detailed analysis is essential to appreciating it, and also essential to the story.''

Yes and no, on that last point. Many times jokes, like stories in general, have to be read with a pair of glasses, and not a microscope, when first encountered in order for the reader to be properly affected. Future readings and complete understanding, however, often require a pains-taking analysis of elements whose nature and interactions aren't at all obvious, even if their effects are. Here, my aim is not only to explain what underlies our sense of the ludicrous in reading the narrator's remarks, but also to provide evidence for my more global thesis that the story is misunderstood unless read as ironic through and through. That last point is hardly obvious.

X

The narrator's last point respecting his critical assessment of Menard can be more briefly considered. According to the him, there is a vast difference in style between Cervantes' and Menard's works. This time the advantage is Cervantes', however.

> The archaic style of Menard—quite foreign, after all [since Menard is French]—suffers from a certain affectation. Not so that of his forerunner, who handles with ease the current Spanish of his time.

But this is absurd. Menard steeped himself in the Spanish of Cervantes' time, and may well have written 17th century Spanish with ease—one suspects that he did, given his determination and seriousness. The fact that he didn't live in 17th-century Spain certainly doesn't entail, in and of itself, that his style is affected, any more than Cervantes' living in 17th century Spain entails that his isn't. In fact, even if Menard did write in the 20th century, and even if he, in contrast to Cervantes, didn't handle 17th-century Spanish with ease, that doesn't entail that his style was affected, and Cervantes' not. Psmith, a character in a number of P.G. Wodehouse's novels, handles the particular brand of English he speaks with ease, but his speech is affected nonetheless. And even if Psmith didn't handle it with ease but with great and grave difficulty, his speech would still be affected. People who have trouble expressing themselves don't ipso facto speak in an affected manner. The prominent factors that go into making speech affected include vocabulary, syntax, paragraph construction, and so on, such factors perhaps being relativized to (usually unstated) vocabulary, syntax, paragraph construction, and so on, that are taken as normative, i.e., taken as natural, not affected. Ease or difficulty of production and historical placement per se have nothing to do with it. A denizen of the 25th-century France who wrote the sort of English found in this paper wouldn't be writing in an affected manner. The narrator's argument concerning style is thus as shoddy as all his other arguments, and his delight in difference once again nothing more than demonstration of duncery. It is thus, in the context of the story's studied tone, further demonstration of Borges' superb irony, as well as his uncanny ability to parody prose that is itself affected. In this case, the result of the latter is an additional layer of irony, since because affectation here turns on itself, mocks and parodies itself, the narrator's apotheosis of Menard's "achievement"—duplicating another's exact words and claiming not just (numerical) difference but superiority—is itself a similar duplicative and dubious achievement: the prose of praise exemplifies the very affectation it denigrates. The narrator once again shows himself the spiritual kin of Menard.

XI

Praise of a man is a natural concomitant of praise of his achievement, and so Menard's alter ego proceeds to heap effusive praise on him. Beginning with the world-weary and intellectually dispiriting, if not condescending, remark that "there is no exercise of the intellect which is not, in the final analysis, useless," and illustrating his dolorous thesis with a comment to the effect that the eventual fate of entire philosophies is to pass into mere paragraphs or names in a history of philosophy, the narrator thus eases into his true topic: Menard, the man who transcended such *fin de siecle* truths, the artist who truly did create ex nihilo—or almost, anyway. His praise of the man, however, is as odd and unintentionally condemnatory as his claims respecting his achievement. Menard

> derived from these nihilistic verifications [a] singular . . . determination. He decided to anticipate the vanity awaiting all man's efforts; he set himself to an undertaking which was exceedingly complex and, from the beginning, futile. He dedicated his scruples and his sleepless nights to repeating an already extant book in an alien tongue. He multiplied draft upon draft, revised tenaciously and tore up thousands of manuscript pages. He did not let anyone examine these drafts and took care [that] they should not survive him. In vain have I tried to reconstruct them.

Taken seriously, this is praise that unwittingly damns both its object and itself. If all is for nought and Menard is deliberately imitating the universe, then he is deliberately pursuing nothing, and must be judged accordingly. Similarly, if the book he plans to write already exists and his aim is to repeat it, his task is indeed futile, as the narrator says, but not for any grand metaphysical reason having to do with the transient nature of all things. A much more mundane reason concerning actions which merely duplicate part of our intellectual history will do in this case. Sleepless nights, copious drafts, and efforts to cover one's artistic tracks are, in the light of the duplicative nature of Menard's task, its evident futility, and the lack of any artistic value of its end product, no grounds on which to praise the "artistic genius" behind them. Rather, they're good reasons to think that the so-called genius is mad, and that he prefers personally gratifying ego-projections to decidedly less gratifying encounters with reality. Ironically, the only fictional world Menard succeeds in creating is not one he himself would recognize, since it's the one he lives in, and mistakes for reality. The same goes for the narrator, of course. Thus the narrator's further remarks on Menard's creative efforts—

> [the] "final" *Quixote* [is, or can be seen as] a kind of palimpsest, through which the traces—tenuous but not indecipherable—of our friend's "previous" writing should be translucently visible . . . unfortunately, only a second Pierre Menard, inverting the other's work, would be able to exhume and revive those lost Troys

—reinforce previous themes. Ironically, even on the narrator's and Menard's own principles, nothing, neither the final *Quixote* nor the discarded drafts nor anything else, could be counted as a "Troy." Nihilism doesn't allow that, and our two principals are, by their own admission, nihilists. In fact, of course, their entire philosophy of literature, whether of its creation (as with Menard) or its criticism (as with the narrator), is founded on a self-contradiction. Nihilism can be used neither as a theoretical support for artistic creation—there would be nothing to aspire to—nor as a theoretical underpinning for value judgments—all such judgments would contradict their philosophical foundation. The narrator's praise of Menard's work, and so also of Menard, thus undermines itself.

Last and probably funniest of all, however, is praise of Menard because he "enriched . . . the halting and rudimentary art of reading" by adding a new "technique" to the usual repertoire,

> that of . . . deliberate anachronism and . . . erroneous attribution. This technique, whose applications are infinite, prompts us to go through the *Odyssey* as if it were posterior to the *Aeneid* and the book *Le Jardin du Centaure of Madame Henri Bachelier* as if it were by Madame Henri Bachelier. This technique fills the most placid works with adventure.

Menard not only created a masterpiece; he taught us something new about the nature of artistic creation, namely that it's futile, but that one can nonetheless accomplish great things by repeating extant works. The fact that the lesson is self-contradictory is of no moment, apparently. And Menard, we now learn, not only added to literature and to the fundaments of the theory of artistic creation; he also taught us something about the theory of reading and added to the fundaments of the philosophy of interpretation. Now when we read we can attribute what we like to whom we like, and proceed accordingly. "Deliberate anachronism" and "erroneous attribution"—this is such stuff as the new reading (proto-deconstruction?) is made on. But it is also such stuff as illusions are made on. Since the applications of this new technique are, as the narrator rightly says, "infinite," what has really been issued is a crypto-invitation to make all interpretations equally valid, because all equally well founded. The fact that the theory thus undermines itself, because it allows itself to be read anachronistically, and with anyone as its author, ironically escapes the narrator's notice. It, too, like his theory of value, is built on a self-destructive premise. Thus nihilism in the evaluative realm meets its theoretical counterpart, anarchy, in the interpretive. The result is further immersion in the dream world of Borges' ironic tale.

XII

If the above is even roughly correct, Borges' story is a multi-leveled parody, thoroughly ironic in tone, and from first to last deadly serious in the way that only a sophisticated piece of humor can be. The very claim registered in its title, "Pierre Menard, Author of the *Quixote*," is a focal point for the pervasive irony found throughout. But there is another level of enveloping irony not yet explored. Three routes lead to it, one from the *Quixote* itself, one from an essay of Borges on the *Quixote*, and one from elements within the story itself.

Consider first the *Quixote*. The story of the *Quixote* is basically quite simple. Don Quixote, an otherwise sane man, has had his wits scrambled by an inordinate devotion to literature, in particular, romances of chivalry. He imagines himself to be called upon to roam the world in search of adventures, ill-fitted though he undoubtedly is for trying encounters of any kind. Initially luring Sancho Panza, his loyal and credulous sidekick, with the prospect of governorship of an island, Quixote proceeds to wander the countryside and seek adventures befitting a grand knight. In his distorted mind everyday objects are transformed into things threatening, romantic, or noble, and he is thus plunged into absurd misadventure after absurd misadventure, always with unfortunate consequences for himself. He is finally "rescued" when one of his old friends disguises himself as a knight, overthrows him, and requires him to refrain from chivalrous exploits for a year. Soon after returning to his village, however, Don Quixote falls ill and dies.

My thesis is that the story of Don Quixote is, *mutatis mutandis*, the story of "Pierre Menard." Menard is the new Quixote, not the new Cervantes.

Consider now Borges' piece on the *Quixote*, "Partial Magic in the *Quixote*." "The form of the *Quixote*," Borges writes there, "made [Cervantes] counterpose a real prosaic world to an imaginary poetic world. . . . For Cervantes the real and the poetic were antinomies." The same real and prosaic world is counterposed to an imaginary and poetic world in "Pierre Menard," although in that world letters has won over arms, and the chief battleground is thus the page, not the plain. Just as, in Borges' words, "the plan of [Cervantes'] book precluded the marvelous [that is, the magical and the physically and logically impossible], [although] the latter had to figure in the novel, at least indirectly, as crimes and mystery [have to figure] in a parody of a detective story," so, too, the marvelous, the physically or logically impossible, has to figure in a parody of artistic creation, literary criticism, and creative genius. Like Cervantes, Borges could not "resort to talismans or enchantments, but [rather had to] insinuate . . . the supernatural in a subtle—and therefore more effective—manner." In his "intimate being," Borges tells us, "Cervantes loved the supernatural." So did he, Borges. He showed his love by eventually resolving the antinomy between the poetic and the prosaic, and doing so without contradiction. The resolution can be found, in fact, in "Pierre Menard" and other of his fictional works.

If "Cervantes takes pleasure in confusing the objective and subjective, the world of the reader and the world of the book," so, once again, does Borges. But so, too, do Menard and the narrator! There are crucial difference between the cases, however. Menard and his Sancho Panza have no initial fix on the difference between reality and illusion, and act, like Quixote and his Sancho Panza but unlike Cervantes and Borges, in dead but parodic earnest. The one fictional pair mistake barbers' basins for helmets, the other minuscule and useless academic studies for intellectual achievements. Our authors, on the other hand, are fully cognizant of the difference between reality and illusion, but delight in deliberately blurring the boundaries between them. They do so in order to achieve a number of artistic effects and, always in the case of Borges, sometimes in the case of Cervantes, to explore certain logical and metaphysical problems. To cite one important instance: Cervantes explicitly introduces himself into the *Quixote* as a character, introduces the *Quixote* into the *Quixote* as a book, and, in one chapter, slyly, playfully, and ironically advances the idea that he is not the author of the *Quixote*. Parallels with paradoxes of self-reference, for instance, Bertrand Russell's concerning the class of all classes not members of themselves, immediately suggest themselves. Borges introduces himself into his *Quixote* more subtly. On my reading, "Pierre Menard" is a scaled-down mock heroic parable set in the 20th century, with Menard as the 20th century equivalent of Don Quixote. Borges occupies—at least initially—Cervantes' position in relation to the story. But that changes; he like Cervantes, enters into his own story as a character. How he does this is complex, so I hope that the explanation which follows does justice to its complexity.

Menard is a 20th century knight-errant, that is, an academic. He's thus a 20th century figure in a profession held in high esteem but also frequently the object of ridicule, the latter because of the well-known tendency of academics to foist their own particular brand of high falutin' and pretentious nonsense on other academics and unsuspecting members of the general public. Menard tilts at the windmills of erudition with learned-sounding but effectively pointless monographs and articles until he succumbs to his final and grandest delusion, that of writing a new book word-for-word identical with one he knows already exists, the *Quixote*. Here is the point at which Borges enters into the explanation. Borges is himself an academic *par excellence* and more than a little given to such fanciful, if not high falutin', nonsense as the denial of the existence of material objects. He's also and more than a little given to writing in a style that borders on the pretentious—as he himself well knows.

Simply in re-writing, in a very transformed fashion, the Quixote as "Pierre Menard," Borges undertakes a task parallel to that—artistically identical with that—of his protagonist. He introduces himself into the story, in other words, as his own failed author, Menard, in his attempt to create a new a story which is identical with one that already exists, one found in the *Quixote*. Unlike Cervantes, he identifies with his own very confused protagonist, all the while knowing that he's not him and doesn't suffer his delusions or mania. Yet, like Menard, he continues his efforts at creation, thinking all the while that all he's doing is repeating the work of another man. And, in a sense, he is. The laughable incidents, the grandiose scheme, the self-delusion, the misdirected attempts for the highest value that man can attain, the loyal companion, above all the parody and ironic tone—all are there in both Cervantes and Borges. Borges doesn't succumb to his Menard's delusion, of course, in trying to write a book word-for-word identical with Cervantes, but he comes as close as possible while managing to avoid stepping over the psychotic edge. Thus we see that Menard is Quixote, suitably modernized and intellectualized, and Menard also Borges, suitably fictionalized and exaggerated. But since Borges himself is Cervantes, suitably modernized and intellectualized, Cervantes is Borges is Menard is Quixote. The antinomy between the prosaic and the poetic, the real and the magical, fact and fiction, is ultimately resolved by Borges, then, in thoroughly blurring the distinction between them: in essence, at the metaphysical depths, there is no difference between them, or at least none that is discernible by us. That is one of Borges' philosophical insights, an insight that is ontological in nature. A second is actually meta-philosophical and methodological. It's that one important way to write metaphysics is to write metaphysical fiction, and that one way to write metaphysical fiction is to write meta-fictional fiction. In this case, that involves writing fiction ("Pierre Menard") about fiction

(*Don Quixote*) that is, in the sense of the "is" of identity, the fiction written about. But if these are Borges' philosophical insights, he's also left us with at least three residual paradoxes to ponder and delight in. As might be expected, all are paradoxes of self-reference.

The first is that Borges pokes fun at himself—and all other creative artists, too, of course, Cervantes and Menard included—and yet understanding the folly of the creative endeavor requires simultaneously understanding that it is serious business, hardly folly, and anything but laughable. To get Borges' point we have to take him and his story seriously; but to get his point we also have to see that he and his story, and so by implication all authors and stories, are not to be taken seriously. Authors are self-deluded fools, and writing a worthwhile story an impossible task. But to understand that, we have to interpret the author as anything but a self-deluded fool and his story as anything but worthless.

The second paradox concerns the fact that proper interpretation of Borges' story requires us to realize that Menard's *Quixote* won't be numerically distinct from Cervantes'. Menard's *Quixote* simply is Cervantes', even though it's thought by him to be a new and important work. Much of the story's irony, and so worth, depends on the fact that Menard failed and had to: reproducing another's work while knowing it and using it as a standard for the creation of your own necessarily means that nothing new has been achieved, no new object of worth has come into existence. Yet if Borges created "Pierre Menard" by intentionally reproducing another's work, all the while knowing it and using it as a standard for the creation of his own, then on the grounds just mentioned, grounds implicit in Borges' story itself, Borges himself failed to produce anything new and valuable. In other words, if Borges' story is good, that is at least in part because Menard didn't create a new and valuable work; but on the same grounds that condemn Menard, neither did Borges create a new and valuable work. The novelty—numerical distinctness—and value of the story depend, internally, on grounds that, applied externally, condemn the story itself.

The third paradox is akin to the second but fully external. It's that "Pierre Menard" is an essentially parasitic work, well-nigh a reproduction of the essential features of Cervantes' *Quixote*. As such, it would seem to be the *Quixote*, or at least share its fate and have no value apart from it, no value not shared with it. But that's just not so. "Pierre

Menard"'s existence is its own, and its value, as I hope to have shown, likewise its own. The paradox, quite simply, is how, contrary to the seemingly impeccable argument that duplication means identity, duplication can sometimes make for difference; or, equivalently, how Don Quixote can ride again, even though his spurs have long been on the rack. (1.) For instance, Andre Maurois, in his "Preface" to Jorge Luis Borges, *Labyrinths*, p. xi. Maurois doesn't get the descriptive details of the story right, either. (2.) Georges Charbonnier, *El escritor y su obra* (Veintiuno Editores, Mexico: 1967), p. 75; as reported by Gene H. Bell-Villada, p. 122. (3.) George Charbonnier, *Entretiens avec Jorge Luis Borges* (Paris 1967), p. 161; as reported by D. L. Shaw, p. 23. (4.) The notion of a category mistake is explained in the first chapter of Gilbert Ryle's *The Concept of Mind*. (5.) The term "historical truth" has to be read in the way indicated, or the narrator's claim respecting Menard's pragmatism would be baseless. (6.) Since it might not be evident why such a doctrine is central to a philosophy known as "pragmatism," I should add that on pragmatism, one of the central, and justifiable, determinants of what we believe is cognitive convenience. In addition, the pragmatist holds that in the long run it's impossible to draw a distinction between what we justifiably believe to be the case and what is the case. This doesn't mean that for a pragmatist anything goes, i.e., that we can judge anything we like to be the case and it thereby will be so. Experience sets relatively strict constraints on what we can justifiably believe, as do other factors, such as consistency and coherence. For the pragmatist, though, justifiable belief is underdetermined by all such factors, and that necessitates the use of an additional criterion. According to him, that criterion is cognitive convenience. (7.) I hope. (8.) My thanks to Walter L. Weber for his comments, dogmatic though even he admits they were, on an earlier draft of this paper.

Source: Michael J. Wreen, "Don Quixote rides Again!," in *Romantic Review*, Vol. 86, No. 1, January, 1995, p. 141.

Sources

Alazraki, Jaime, "Oxymoronic Structure in Borges' Essays," in *The Cardinal Points of Borges*, edited by Lowell Dunham and Ivar Ivask, University of Oklahoma Press, 1971, pp. 51-52.

Balderston, Daniel, *Out of Context: Historical Reference and the Representation of Reality in Borges*, Duke University Press, 1993, p. 21.

Barth, John, "The Literature of Exhaustion," in *Atlantic*, August, 1967, pp. 29-34.

Berley, Marc, review of *Collected Fictions* , edited by Andrew Hurley, in *Commentary*, July, 1999, p. 89.

Bowen, Elizabeth, preface to *The Faber Book of Modern Stories*, Faber, 1937, p. 14.

Burgin, Richard, *Jorge Luis Borges: Conversations* , University Press of Mississippi, 1998.

Fish, Stanley, "Is There a Text in This Class?," in *Critical Theory Since 1965*, edited by Hazard Adams and LeRoy Searle, University Press of Florida, 1986, p. 526.

Iser, Wolfgang, "The Reading Process," in *Reader-Response Criticism: From Formalism to Post-Structuralism*, edited by Jane P. Tompkins, Johns Hopkins University Press, 1980, p. 55-56.

Stabb, Martin S., *Jorge Luis Borges*, Twayne, 1970, p. 117.

Stein, Gordon, *Encyclopedia of Hoaxes*, Twayne, 1970, p. 117.

Updike, John, "Books: The Author as Librarian," in *New Yorker*, October 30, 1967, pp. 223-46.

Further Reading

Alazraki, Jaime, "Oxymoronic Structure in Borges' Essays," in *The Cardinal Points of Borges*, edited by Lowell Dunham and Ivar Ivask, University of Oklahoma Press, 1971.
Alazraki analyzes the linguistic and thematic oxymorons in Borges' essays, concluding that they serve as a form of conciliation between contradictory terms.

Alifano, Roberto, *Twenty-four Conversations with Borges: Including a Selection of Poems*, Lascaux Publishers, 1984.
A series of interviews with an aging Borges conducted from 1981 through 1983, arranged by topic.

Balderston, Daniel, *Out of Context: Historical Reference and the Representation of Reality in Borges*, Duke University Press, 1993.
Balderston researched extensively the sources for seven Borges works to conclude that his seemingly apocryphal details are mostly factual and therefore do represent reality.

Barrenechea, Ana Maria, *Borges: The Labyrinth Maker*, New York University Press, 1965.
The first serious scholarly work on Borges. Although Barrenechea ignores Borges' humor and irony, her analysis remains convincing and important.

Cohen, J. M., *Jorge Luis Borges*, Barnes & Noble Books, 1973.
A brief analysis of Borges' works juxtaposed with a summary of his life.

di Giovanni, Norman Thomas, *The Borges Tradition* , Constable, 1995.
Fives commemorative lectures on Borges by leading scholars published on the occasion of the lifting of a trade embargo between Britain and Argentina.

Fishburn, Evelyn, and Psiche Hughes, *A Dictionary of Borges*, Duckworth, 1990.
An alphabetically arranged list of allusions found in Borges' works with a brief description for each entry.

Lusky Friedman, Mary, *The Emperor's Kites: A Morphology of Borges' Tales*, Duke University Press, 1987.
An examination of Borges' stories through the structuralist lens, following the approach of Vladimir Propp's 1928 *The Morphology of the Folktale*.

Stabb, Martin S., *Jorge Luis Borges*, Twayne, 1970.
A standard though dated Twayne survey of Borges' life and works.

Woodall, James, *Borges: A Life*, HarperCollins, 1996.
Woodall's recent work is considered by many to be the best general biography of Borges.

Prayer to the Masks

Léopold Sédar Senghor
1945

Over the course of his long career as a writer, philosopher, and statesman, the Senegalese poet Léopold Sédar Senghor has inspired countless young writers throughout the French-speaking world. Along with Aimé Cesaire and Léon Damas, he founded the *négritude* movement, which argued that the black people of colonial Africa and the Caribbean should take pride in their African roots and find in their native traditions an inspiration for a new literature and a new way of life. Senghor went on to put these ideas into practice in his wide field of activity. He wrote voluminously as a poet and as a philosopher of the new culture and politics of African independence from colonial rule. In the political arena, he was one of the major architects of independence for his own country, Senegal, and for French West Africa more generally. He served as president of Senegal for two decades.

''Prayer to the Masks'' is typical of Senghor's writing throughout his long career, although it comes from his first collection, *Songs of the Shadow*, published in 1945. It exhibits clearly the features that would characterize his poetic writing: the use of African themes and settings, the highly rhythmic long lines reminiscent of the Bible and Walt Whitman, the evocations of music and song, and the contrast of the vitality of a mythic (and future) Africa with the present of both Europe and Africa under colonialism. It is the poem of a young man seeking to connect with a past he senses will give him inspiration to struggle past the damaged life of

the present to forge a better future for himself and his people.

Author Biography

Senghor was born in Joal, a village in Central Senegal, in 1906. His father was a successful merchant dealing with the French in goods for the export trade. After one year of elementary education in Joal, he was sent to a missionary school in Ngasobil and a Catholic high school in Dakar, where he was educated in the French language and French culture. Although he had originally wanted to enter the priesthood, Senghor was sent on scholarship to France in 1928, where he pursued the study of literature at the Lycée Louis le Grand and the Sorbonne. In the preparatory class at the lycée, Senghor befriended his classmate Georges Pompidou, who later became president of France. Senghor earned the License-ès-lettres (equivalent to a bachelor's degree), the Diplôme d'études supérieures (equivalent to the master's), and the agrégation (like a Ph.D.). He was the first African from the French colonies to earn the latter degree.

The 1920s and 1930s were decades of developing political and cultural consciousness on the part of American, Caribbean, and African-born blacks. Relatively large urban communities of blacks developed in such world cities as New York and Paris, and previously separate groups such as African-Americans, Caribbean-Creoles, and Africans from French colonies such as Senegal began to encounter one another, form friendships and organizations, and collaborate in cultural and literary publications. Their response was to found a literary and cultural movement, affirming the unique value of blackness and the black cultures of Africa and the Americas, under the banner of "negritude." The founding figures were Senghor, Aimé Césaire, and Léon Damas, all three students in the early 1930s in Paris and participants in a series of reviews and journals. The term "negritude" itself was coined by Aimé Césaire in his book-length poem *Notes on a Return to the Native Land*. Later, in 1947 and 1948, Damas and Senghor published anthologies that further gave shape to the literary movement.

Senghor served in the French army during World War II and was confined for several months in a German prisoner-of-war camp. After the war, he was actively involved in Senegalese and African politics. He served in the cabinet of the French prime minister Edgar Faure in 1955 as Secretary of State. In 1960, he was closely involved in attempts to form a multi-state federation of West African states, and in that same year, he was elected president of the newly independent Republic of Senegal. He served as president until 1980, when he stepped down from office. In 1984, he was appointed to the prestigious Académie Francaise for his literary and humanistic achievements.

Plot Summary

Lines 1-4

The poem begins with an "apostrophe," an address to an object or spirit. Here, as the title indicates, this address is a prayer to the masks, which appear in the poem both as works of African art and as more general spirits of African culture, society, and history. The poet lists the colors of the masks as black, red, black-and-white, thus also suggesting the reference of the masks as symbols of race and skin color. In the third line, Senghor suggests that these masks are also spirits of nature, linked to the winds that blow from the four directions of north, south, east, and west. As spirits that blow, they also imply that the masks are related to the poet's breath and poetic inspiration. As the fourth line indicates, he greets them with silence, as if listening to what the mask-spirits will whisper to him on the wind.

Lines 5-7

The poet introduces his family's guardian animal, the lion, symbol of aristocratic virtue and courage. Traditionally these animals were thought to be the first ancestor and the protector of the family line. In mentioning his lion-headed ancestor, Senghor refers to the name of his father, Diogoye, which in his native Serer language means lion. In ceremonies where masks would be used, the family might be represented by a lion mask. In lines 6 and 7, Senghor further reinforces the implications of long tradition and patriarchal power. The lion guards the ground that is forbidden to women and to passing things, in favor of values, memories, and customs that stretch back into mythic antiquity.

Lines 8-10

These lines develop a complex relation between the faces of the ancestors, the poet's face, and the masks. Line 8 speaks of the masks as idealized representations of previously living faces. The masks eliminate the mobile features and signs of age in the faces of the living ancestors, but in doing so outlive their death. In turn, they are able to give shape to the face of the poet bent over the page and writing his prayer to the masks. He appeals to them to listen to him, for he is the living image of those masks to whom he is writing a prayer.

Lines 11-12

These lines contrast the glorious past of Africa, when vast black-ruled empires spanned the continent, and the present, in which the peoples of Africa have been subjugated by the imperial conquests of European nations. The "pitiable princess" symbolizes the nobility of traditional Africa, and her death represents both the general suffering and decline of traditional African culture and the loss of political power of blacks to rule themselves. Yet the relation to Europe is not presented solely in a negative way. The image of the umbilical cord suggests that the European conquest has nourished a new Africa soon to be born, but one that will eventually have to sever its ties with its European "mother" if it is to live and grow.

Lines 13-14

The masks are called to witness the sad history of modern Africa, and they look on, god-like with their changeless faces. Yet Senghor also suggests that the traditional customs and values have apparently not been able to respond to the great changes that history has brought about. The poem implicitly comes to a question and a turning point: do the masks represent a valuable longview from which the present can be seen in its proper perspective, or are they merely relics of a past that have nothing to say to those who are exploited and suffering in the present?

Lines 15-16

The poet prays to the magic spirits of the masks to help speed the rebirth suggested by the image of the umbilical cord connecting Africa to Europe in line 12. Implicitly, reviving the ancestral spirits of the masks will help sever the ties of dependence. In turn, a reborn African creativity can help Europe to a more life-affirming use of its material and scientific wealth, just as the brown yeast is necessary for making bread from white flour.

Leopold Senghor

Lines 17-19

These lines further develop the idea that Africa will provide the life-impulse to a Europe that is oriented toward mechanical values, materialist gain, and war. It is the rhythm of African music and dance that can change the thud of machines into something better. A reborn Africa will lend its youthful energy to a senile Europe, bringing joy and hope where there has been isolation, exhaustion, despair, and death.

Lines 20-21

In the imagery of "men of cotton, of coffee, of oil," Senghor refers to the exploitation of Africa for its raw materials and to European conceptions of black Africans as merely a source of cheap labor and economic profit. Looking back to the figures of death and rebirth in the previous lines, he ironically notes how "they," the Europeans, view the black African as a fearful image of death, "the waking dead."

Line 22

But rather than allowing their humanity to be reduced to the economic value of the agricultural goods listed in line 20, the African of the future will have a different, creative relation to the soil and the natural world. Like the participants in a traditional ceremony in which masks are used, these new Africans absorb the powers of the natural spirits through the rhythm of dance, music, and poetry.

Themes

Relation to the Ancestors

The figure of the mask is Senghor's central image in the poem of the traditional past and the ancestors for whom it was a living reality. He uses the word "mask" as a kind of incantation to call up the ancestral spirits who in the present, implicitly, are hidden and hard to hear. The "silence" to which the poet refers suggests the need to greet the ancestors with attention and respectful awe. He also notes that the masks are the way that he can access the "breath of my fathers," that is, the living spirit of the ancestors who will inspire the poet to his song. His own face, he writes, resembles the face of the masks, because the masks bear the idealized features of the real faces of the poet's ancestors. The latter part of the poem admits that the ancestral past is in danger of being lost to the forces of modernity, which have come to Africa in the form of the colonial conquests of the French, British, Dutch, and Belgians. The "princess" of line 12 refers to the aristocratic past of the African empires, and in line 14 the "immutable eyes" of the masks suggest both the god-like tranquillity of the ancestors and their inability to do more than witness the sufferings of the present. The poem as a whole wrestles with the question of whether the appeal to the ancestral spirits will be able to help the African overcome the present state of subjugation and hopelessness.

Connection to the Land

Senghor refers to the protected ground of the lion-headed ancestor, a sacred space in which the poet can link himself to the line of "fathers" leading all the way back to the mythic first ancestor, the lion. In the last line, it is the soil itself that transmits its power to the feet of the dancer and by implication, too, to the metrical feet of the poet in writing his poem.

Contrast of Africa and Europe

Africa appears in the poem in a dual light. It is the suffering victim of oppression, economic exploitation, and violence, wrenched from its traditional beliefs and ways of life and forced to serve a foreign master. And it is an irrepressible source of life, creativity, and positive relation to the natural world. Europe, too, is ambivalently presented. It is a kind of cruel mother, on which modern Africa is dependent, yet whose embrace is crushing rather than sustaining. In the questions that make up lines 16-18, the world of Europe appears to be the bleak ground of mechanized industry and war, a space of death, hopelessness, and oblivion. Presently, Africa depends on Europe, while Europe exploits the labor and natural riches of Africa. Yet what Europeans see disdainfully as the African's closeness to nature and the land, seemingly a lack of higher spirituality, the African knows to be a profound spirituality and artistic creativity as symbolized in the final line by the dance.

The Synthesis of African and European Culture

Senghor projects a future overcoming of Africa's subordinate position, through which not only the colonized people of Africa but also the European colonizer stands to benefit. The central image in which this theme is developed is that of bringing the brown yeast of African culture to the white flour of European civilization to make a bread that is higher and more nourishing than either element taken separately. Similarly, lines 16-18 suggest that Africa can become a revitalizing force for European societies that have grown cold, weary, and decadent. It is by embracing the life-affirming aspects of African culture that European culture can refresh itself.

Style

Apostrophe

Senghor often uses the figure of "apostrophe," a term in rhetoric referring to a direct address to an object, a place, an abstraction or ideal, or an immaterial entity such as a god or spirit. In "Prayer to the Masks," he addresses his poem to the masks, which in turn are figures of the ancestors and repositories of mythic powers. Apostrophe characteristically is used to imply the power of the poet's word or voice to wake hidden powers in nature or to bring the dead to life. Thus, in the latter half of "Prayer to the Masks," Senghor implores the masks to join with him in pushing forward the rebirth of Africa, but at the same time implying that it is his poetic "cry" that can compel the cooperation of the masks.

Topics for Further Study

- Discuss how Senghor depicts the past, present, and future in his poem. How does the present relate to the traditional African past? What role will the tradition play in the future of Africa?

- Senghor's poem draws strongly on a patriarchal myth that evokes his father's name and the masculine totemic animal of the lion, while excluding women from this sacred "ground" protected by the lion-mask. Yet he also uses feminine imagery of the "dying princess" of traditional Africa and the umbilical cord attaching Africa to the colonial "mother" of Europe. How does "Prayer to the Masks" relate gender to his vision of the Africa of the past, present, and future? How do you think the poem might have differed if it had been written by an African woman?

- Senghor was a central participant in the "Negritude" movement, a literary and cultural movement that asserted pride in being black and in the traditions of Africa and of the African peoples brought to the Americas as slaves. Other important participants included the Martiniquean poet Aimé Césaire and the Guyanese poet Léon Gontran Damas. In what ways might the idea of Africa and African roots be different for Senghor, who grew up in a small village in Senegal, and the "New World" Negritude poets, who had never been to Africa when they began writing?

- Senghor was educated in French schools and universities, and he wrote in French. Yet he also uses French, the language of the colonizer, to criticize colonialism and to assert the value of African traditions, history, and beliefs. What sorts of problems do you think his literary use of

French might have posed for Senghor in writing his poems? What did he gain by writing in French? Would it have been better for him to have written his poetry in Serer, his native language? What does Senghor bring to French literature and language from an African perspective? How does Senghor's use of the French language relate to his vision of future relations between Africa and Europe?

- Senghor puts at the center of his work a form of African art and spirituality, the mask. Find another poem that takes off from a work of art and compare how it functions in that work with the role of the masks in Senghor's poem.

- The African-American scholar and writer W. E. B. Du Bois argued that being both a highly educated American citizen and a man subject to American racial prejudice caused him to possess a "double consciousness" typical of the experience of blacks in America. He was compelled to think of himself both as a legally equal citizen of the United States and as a socially stigmatized black man, to live his life as a man aware of his superior education and accomplishments and as a man viewed by many of his fellow citizens as inferior because of his race. In what ways does Senghor's poem, which negotiates a relation between his pride in his "negritude," his aspirations for African independence, and his French education, exhibit a similar "double consciousness"? How do the particular circumstances of Africa and French colonialism differ from the American racism and legacy of slavery to which Du Bois was responding?

Rhythmic Repetition and Musicality

Senghor uses a strongly cadenced verse, with the rhythm marked by frequent and strongly accented repetitions. Indeed, several of his later poems carry subtitles indicating musical accompaniment

by "jazz orchestra with trumpet solo"; by such traditional African instruments as the khalam, tama, gorong, talmblatt, and mbalakh; or by such combinations as flutes and balafong or organs and a tom-tom. The opening lines of "Prayer to the Masks," in which the word "mask" is repeated six times, is typical of Senghor's chant-like use of rhythm. The final line, with its evocation of dancing feet beating the ground, is another image of the rhythmic character of the poem itself, a dance of the words across the page.

Use of Analogy

Through his use of analogy, the poet sets in resonance the human and natural worlds, and the historical present with the mythic past. Thus, in the third line, the mask becomes a map that in turn relates to the territory across which the wind blows. The figure of the lion refers at the same time to the father's name, to the mythic lion who was said to be the first ancestor of the family line, to the mask that represents the ancestor's spirit, and to the noble qualities that have communicated themselves through the blood. The image of flour, yeast, and bread in line 16 refer both to the colors associated with Europeans and Africans (white flour and brown yeast) and suggest a future cooperation that will be beneficially "nourishing" to everyone. The image of the "men of cotton, of coffee, of oil" in line 20 brings together the features of the hair and skin of the African with the typical products of his labor.

Contrasts and Oppositions

A steady alternation of opposed lines is a key device in "Prayer to the Masks" and many other poems by Senghor. In the first half of "Prayer to the Masks," for example, Senghor contrasts the ephemeral or frivolous sphere that he associates with women to the serious, eternal ground connected with the lion, the spirit of the fathers. The latter half contrasts Africa as the dying princess with Europe as the mother from which a new Africa will have to separate itself. Similarly, the vitality and life-giving creativity of a future Africa is opposed to the mechanical, death-seeking hopelessness of Europe. The final lines reverse the valuations of the black man by the European. If the European sees the African as an exploitable extension of material goods such as cotton, coffee, and oil, the African knows himself to stand in a creative, joyful, artistic, and religious relationship to the natural riches of Africa.

Literary Heritage

Senegal's literary and artistic traditions are connected to the rich heritage of the great African empires of the pre-colonial past, to Islamic culture, and to the oral cultures of the several peoples that occupy its different regions. In his poetry, Senghor refers to the rituals and beliefs associated with masks and other forms of traditional art, to the dance, and to troubadour storytelling accompanied by a wide variety of instruments and drums. Yet the legacy of colonialism also strongly marked this native heritage with the influence of French language and culture. The French colonial administrations placed a particular emphasis on the educational system as a way of spreading the French language and civilization into its colonial territories. Thus, when Senghor entered the French schools, he would have found himself taught the history of a country which he had not even visited, while learning that Africans were inferior and had no proper culture of their own. This division of his cultural heritage between the native land and language of his childhood and the adopted language and learning of his manhood would become a central issue for Senghor in his poetry, politics, and thought. While a student of French and classical literature in Paris in the early thirties, he sought to regain contact with the African culture from which he had been cut off and he took up the study of ethnography and African languages. His entry into political life, which would eventually lead him to the presidency of independent Senegal, was as an investigator and speaker on educational policy, especially about the problem of how best to balance French and native culture in the education of French-African colonial subjects.

Historical Context

French Colonialism in Africa

French colonial settlement in Africa dates back to the seventeenth century, when the French were involved in the slave trade both on the African side and in the Caribbean. The trade reached its heights in the middle decades of the eighteenth century and then fell off rapidly with the French Revolution, the wars that rocked Europe in the late eighteenth century, the successful slave revolts in Haiti and elsewhere, and the efforts of humanitarians and enlightenment intellectuals to abolish this ugly denial of human freedom.

Compare & Contrast

- **1903:** W. E. B. Du Bois publishes *The Souls of Black Folk*, declaring that the problem of our epoch is the problem of the ''color line.''

  1928: Claude McKay publishes his novel *Banjo*, which champions Caribbean ''folk'' cultures and raises important issues about tensions between blacks in the Caribbean and Africans. The novel was intensely discussed among the African and Caribbean students in Paris, including the founders of the ''Negritude'' movement.

  1934: Parisian poet-students Senghor, Césaire, and Damas found the journal *L'Etudiant Noir* (*The Black Student*), widely seen as the first important landmark in the Negritude cultural movement.

- **1916:** Marcus Garvey arrives in Harlem from his native Jamaica and declares that the future of the black people of the world lies in rejecting the barriers to greatness set down by white society and entreats them to return to Africa. His Universal Negro Improvement Association (UNIA) has a membership ranging from 2 to 4 million people.

  1933: Adolf Hitler and his National Socialist Party come to power in Germany. Hitler propagates a viciously racist ideology that views the white, Nordic ''Aryan'' race as superior and those Jewish, Slavic, and black descent as inferior, subhuman races, worthy of enslavement and extermination. These views become the official policy of the German state, which begins preparations for war and conquest.

  1955: Rosa Parks refuses to move to the back of a bus in Montgomery, Alabama, beginning a year-long bus boycott and launching the movement to desegregate all public facilities in the southern United States.

  1968: Civil Rights leader Martin Luther King is assassinated.

  1990: Nelson Mandela, leader of the anti-apartheid African National Congress in South Africa, is released from prison after twenty-seven years of incarceration. Four years later he is elected the first president of South Africa following the fall of apartheid, and serves for five years.

- **1919:** British soldiers in India massacre large numbers of unarmed protesters at the Jallianwala Bagh in Amritsar.

  1931: Nine young black men are arrested in Scottsboro, Alabama for the alleged rape of two white girls, one of whom later withdraws her accusation. Eight are sentenced to death and the ninth, a thirteen-year-old, to life in prison. The case, thought by many to be fabricated and a shameful expression of white racism, drags on for years, leading to several mistrials and the eventual dropping of charges or paroling of the defendants.

  1945: The Nazi concentration camps are liberated by the Allies, revealing to the world the military-industrial system in which six million Jews and hundreds of thousands of other peoples considered racially or politically ''inferior'' were exterminated.

  1960: Police kill sixty-seven young black protesters and wound 186 in Sharpesville, South Africa.

  1994: Between April and July 1994, more than 800,000 mostly Tutsi civilians in Rwanda are massacred by their Hutu neighbors. Despite extensive media reporting, the international response is slow and does little to stop the killing.

- **1961:** Senegal gains independence, with Léopold Sédar Senghor as its first president.

  1975: Mozambique and Angola gain independence from Portugal.

  1980: Senghor retires from the presidency of Senegal.

A second wave of colonization occurred in the latter half of the nineteenth century, with the scramble of the European powers to conquer the territories of Africa, Asia, and Latin America for European colonial empires seen as sources of cheap raw materials, cut-rate labor, and new markets for expanding industrial societies. At the same time, new ideologies began to emerge that "scientifically" justified imperial conquest on grounds of natural and immutable differences of intelligence between the races. French colonialism oscillated between two contradictory sets of values. Convinced of the universal value and legitimacy of French civilization, based on the enlightenment principles that animated the French Revolution, France aggressively sought to "assimilate" the native populations of the colonies. The French language, culture, and history were taught, and the rights and institutions of French politics were extended to the colonized peoples. Yet at the same time, both "scientific" racism and modern ethnography, with its emphasis on the specificity and organic unity of individual cultures, tended to undermine the universalist outlook.

Senghor's personal experience in many ways exemplifies the rather contradictory ways in which these two opposed ideas of how French and native African cultures were related. On the one hand, he was allowed access to the French educational system, in which he excelled, gaining a measure of prestige and respect even within the ordinary channels of French society. He mastered the French language and academic curriculum and eventually earned the equivalent of a Ph.D. in Classics and Literature, going on to teach for a time in a high school outside of Paris. Yet at the same time, as an African born outside the "French" enclaves of Senegal, he had to argue several times for special exceptions to be made to allow him to continue on to higher stages of his education. The more recent ideas about what level and what kind of education was right for the African had led to obstacles to an African's "assimilation" through education in the French system.

Vichy France and World War II

With the outbreak of World War II, men from all over the French empire, including black Africans such as Senghor, were called up or volunteered to fight for France against the threat posed by Hitler's German army. The French army, however, was quickly defeated, and on July 14, 1940, the Nazis entered Paris. The government fled south to the resort of Vichy; and on the 17th of July, the World War I war hero Marshall Pétain called an armistice that split France between the northern two-thirds under German occupation and a southern piece under the nominally French but collaborationist Vichy regime. Following the Allied invasion of North Africa in November 1942, the Nazis moved in to occupy the rest of France, ending even the thin premise that the Vichy government was anything but an instrument of the occupiers. With the D-Day invasion and the pushing back of the German army towards the Rhine and across, the liberation of France became the true turning point of the war. Paris was liberated on August 25, 1944, and the leader of the free French forces, General Charles de Gaulle, began the task of rebuilding France's government at home and in the colonies.

Decolonization and Independence

Following World War II, there were broad stirrings throughout the colonized world for independence. Several factors contributed to this movement. The wartime demonstration of the vulnerability of the colonial powers during the German and Japanese occupations and postwar attempts to revive the old colonial hierarchy despite the courageous sacrifices of many natives during the war played a key role. Similarly, the partisan struggle, in which the Communist parties had gained great prestige, and the victory of Mao Zedong's revolutionary army in China helped inspire similar guerrilla movements. The successful struggle for independence from British colonialism in India, led by Ghandi and Nehru, further fueled the sense of colonized peoples that their long-suppressed hopes for self-rule might soon come to fruition. Outright warfare broke out in Vietnam shortly after the war, leading to the defeat of the French army at Dien Bien Phu in May 1954. Anti-French riots occurred in Madagascar, Tunisia, and Morocco, and most decisively, in November of 1954 the insurrection in Algeria broke out, a conflict that would lead to the engagement of half a million French soldiers and nearly provoke civil war in France itself. In 1958, in order to stave off a coup attempt by the French army in Algeria, General de Gaulle returned to power and introduced a new constitution. Among the features of the constitution was a referendum of the colonial member states of the French empire allowing them to ratify the constitution or to vote "no" and effectively choose immediate independence. Of the African states, only Guinea chose to vote against the constitution and paid a high price when the French immediately withdrew its resources, expertise, and administrative structure from the newly founded country. The other states sought to form an African federation that would move towards independence, but on friendly terms with France. The Federation failed to take shape, but Senghor's skillful political work and his efforts in finding a third, more moderate road to decolonization allowed Senegal to become independent, with French support, in 1961. Senghor was elected as the first president and governed for the next two decades.

Critical Overview

Critics have tended to discuss Senghor's "Prayer to the Masks" along two lines. It is seen as an assertion of the value of African traditions and the African past, including Senghor's own childhood experience; it has also been discussed as Senghor's most hopeful vision of Africa's potential contribution to a new synthetic, global culture that will supersede colonial domination.

Its assertions of the African's spontaneous joyfulness and his attunement to the rhythm of the land and nature, qualities that Senghor opposes to the coldness and despair of the European, are seen as early expressions of the Negritude philosophy that would achieve its greatest influence after World War II. The more hopeful tone of "Prayer to the Masks" connects it with other works in *Chants d'ombre* (*Shadow Songs*) and contrasts with the somber note of the next volume, *Hosties noires* (*Black Hosts* or *Black Victims*), many of the poems of which date from the same period as those collected in the earlier volume.

Criticism

Tyrus Miller

In the following essay, Miller considers the problem of an African writer educated in French who wishes to address African themes in his writing.

Senghor's poem "Prayer to the Masks" appeared in his first book, *Chants d'Ombre* (*Shadow Songs*), which collected his poems written during the 1930s and early 1940s. These poems reveal the influence of Senghor's original displacement from his home-

land to study in France, and their tone oscillates between a melancholic view of Europe as it descended towards war and fascism and an often nostalgic conjuration of the Africa of Senghor's childhood. Yet Senghor's evocation of African traditions, customs, beliefs, and settings should not be seen merely as the nostalgic fantasy of an expatriate poet for his homeland. Behind Senghor's poetic Africa lies a much more comprehensive program for the cultural, educational, and political, the ideal of "negritude" that he would pursue with other black poets of the Caribbean and African colonies. Senghor's early poetry, "Prayer to the Masks" included, explore the predicament of the colonial intellectual trained in the language and culture of the colonizer, while seeking to turn his sense of cultural alienation into a perspective from which to look on his homeland with new eyes.

Within this broader cultural predicament, moreover, lies a more focused artistic problem for the French-African poet: how to relate his acquired artistic medium of expression, the poem written in the French language and European verse forms, to the African content he seeks to express. Senghor addresses this artistic challenge by referring his poem to the traditional African art form of the mask. The African masks, as the object of his "prayer" and the native corollary of his French poetry, serve as an ideal image in the poem, for they allow Senghor to claim that his poetry is not something foreign and artificial, a break with the traditions of Africa, but an extension of those traditions into new expressive media. In a sense, his poem claims to be another form of mask, a mask made wholly of words, but performing the same function as the more typical mask carved from wood or ivory. Senghor suggests that it is the spirit that occupies the art work and not the material that it is made of that invests it with its power. The test of the carved object and of the shaped words of a poem are their fidelity to the ancestors, the source of their sacred energies. Similarly, in his conclusion to the poem, Senghor rejects the colonialist's image of the black African as "men of cotton, of coffee, of oil." Just as with the traditional and modern works of art, for Senghor it is not the materials, but the spirit that dwells in the material that shows the true value of these men. The vital forces they manifest in the dance, their musical and rhythmic relation to their land, are the genuine measure of their worth, not the narrowly economic standard of profits and payments.

Although the image of the mask in the poem is comprehensible without any deeper knowledge of

What Do I Read Next?

- Senghor's *On African Socialism* collects three important essays outlining his vision of nationhood and the special nature of African societies on the road to national development and socialism. These works are considered classics of modern African political philosophy.

- *Ujaama: Essays on Socialism*, by the Tanzanian leader Julius Nyerere, is a useful point of comparison to Senghor's political thought.

- Janet G. Vaillant's biography of Senghor, *Black, French, and African: A Life of Léopold Sédar Senghor*, offers extensive context for Senghor's education, political activities, and friendships with writers and statesmen. It is clearly and accessibly written.

- Aimé Césaire's *Notebook of a Return to the Native Land* is a book-length poem, partially in prose and partially in verse, that recounts the homecoming to Martinique of this poet, friend of Senghor, and comrade in the negritude movement. Symbolically, it enacts the rebirth of the black poet beyond the partial, damaged self-

images he had taken over from both black and white perceptions of him.

- *The Negritude Poets*, edited by Ellen Conroy Kennedy, presents a wide selection of poets from Africa, the Caribbean, and the French-speaking island nations of the Indian Ocean, Madagascar and Mauritius, who were inspired by the negritude movement. The volume provides a useful context for the founding poets—Senghor, Césaire, and Damas—and shows the wide influence of their example and ideas.

- Franz Fanon's *Black Skins, White Masks* is a brilliant and influential exploration of the problem of personal identity in a racially divided, colonial society. Written while he was studying psychiatry in Paris after World War II, Fanon's book gives a very powerful, poetic account of his confrontation with French racism, but also with his own false self-conceptions as a French-educated colonial subject from Martinique. The analogies and differences of Senghor's and Fanon's experiences as students in Paris are instructive.

African thinking about masks, this background of belief, which Senghor could assume in at least his African readers, enriches the symbolism still further. Masks are utilized in a few specific contexts such as initiations, funerals, or the beginnings and endings of seasonal agricultural labor. They tend to be connected primarily with rural, agrarian peoples and places, such as Senghor's native village, Joal. Ceremonies involving masks are means by which these agrarian communities call up and display for themselves the events of the mythic past, like the founding of a family line, the settlement of an area, or the defeat of an enemy. By representing and repeating the mythic event in the framework of the present, the masks function to bind the community to its past and to allow its present representatives to draw strength and legitimacy from that past. Masks also serve to channel spiritual forces, coming out of

the world of the ancestors and the mythic past into the work of daily life. In this function, they play a dual role, that of trapping energies from the spirit world and that of protecting living humans from the powers of the ghosts, spirits, and demons that surround them. The mask, as it is used in the ritual, allows the dancer to impersonate the spirit and be invested with the spirit's power, but also to trick the spiritual beings and be able to control and manipulate them. In sum, they play a crucial role in helping those societies that use masks to maintain a delicate equilibrium between the world of the living and the world of the ancestors, between present and past, between life and death. To fail to recall the ancestors and their glorious deeds would be to lose touch with the life-giving wellsprings of tradition; yet to grant the dead too much power over the living would be dangerous as well.

While in his poem Senghor generally celebrates the African traditions represented by the masks, this background helps the reader to understand better how this celebration is qualified and ambivalent in ways similar to the cautious attitude towards the dead expressed by the dual function of the mask. Senghor writes a poem about masks in which he claims an analogy between his poem and the traditional mask and a bond between himself and the mythic ''lion-headed'' ancestor of his father's family line. Clearly, in this respect, Senghor seeks to recall and reactivate the spiritual powers of the ancestors, the dead, the mythic and magical traditions of African ritual. More difficult to perceive, however, is the other, protective face of his poem-prayer. This aspect can be seen in Senghor's *difference* from the traditions and ritual art forms that he appears to be celebrating. His poem, one might say, is a mask that mimics the African past and its ritual forms rather than the undiminished presence and power of that traditional past. For after all, Senghor has chosen to write a poem (and a poem in French at that!) rather than actually carve a mask. His poem is printed on the two-dimensional flatness of paper rather than etched into the rugged graininess of the wood. And it is meant to be read aloud or even silently, so that its lines conjure up the feeling and sense of a ritual, not literally chanted on a ceremonial occasion such as a funeral or seeding of the ground. The drummed and danced rhythms to which his poem alludes are never physically sounded in the poem, however much its metrical accents allow a reader to imagine them. Senghor's poem thus calls upon the strength of the ancestral spirits for its inspiration, but it purposefully weakens the power of these spiritual forces over the poet by reducing them to paper, ink, and words.

Senghor's poetic mask, however, may be turned not only towards the African past, but also towards the French colonial present. In other words, in writing his poetry, Senghor not only mimics the traditional mask of African ceremony, seeking to tap and control its energies, but also adopts the prestigious mask of the French writer and intellectual. This act of masking allows him to show that the cultural power of the French intellectual is not a ''natural'' result of some essential Frenchness but rather a role for which they and he have been trained to perform. It also enables him to draw upon the formidable power of the colonizer's culture, while maintaining his separate identity intact and hidden behind the countenance his writing displays in public. In a manner of speaking, Senghor tricks the

> Senghor suggests that it is the spirit that occupies the art work and not the material that it is made of that invests it with its power. The test of the carved object and of the shaped words of a poem are their fidelity to the ancestors, the source of their sacred energies.''

powerful French ''spirit'' (or its representatives in the university, the colonial administration, the government) into acting benevolently toward him.

In composing his poem-prayer, then, Senghor is metaphorically donning a kind of paper mask to mimic the carved and ornamented masks of traditional ritual. As a French-African poet, he captures something of the power of African tradition and of French cultural prestige, while not being totally absorbed into either. He needs the ancestral spirits to inspire him, and he fulfills his obligation to them in recalling them in the artistic place of his poem. Yet it is not from the village society and according to the standards of traditional African values that he, the French-educated poet living in Paris, is seeking recognition. Rather, those who will grant him recognition are urban, literate, French speakers, men and women reading him in large cities such as Paris, Dakar, Tangiers, and New York. To succeed as a poet, he must be ''African, but not too African,'' ''French, but French with a difference.'' He must manage the difficult act of expressing a local content and feeling, rooted in his rural Senegalese childhood, in a cosmopolitan form learned through his French education and residency in Paris.

This complex relation of resemblance and difference is captured most explicitly in the difficult eighth, ninth, and tenth lines: ''Masks of unmasked faces, stripped of all dimples, all wrinkles, / Who have formed this image, my face bent over the altar of blank paper / In your image, hear me!'' The simplified features of the masks are mirrored by the concentrated expression of the poet's own face as he performs his own form of artistic worship, the ritual of sitting down to write poetry. The poet's relation to the ancestral spirits of the mask is not, however, simply a reflection. It is rather a *translation*, a difficult and risky movement between artistic media, between the Serer and the French language, and between the cultural idiom of villages such as Joal and the European cosmopolitan dialect spoken by Parisian intellectuals.

Senghor's poem expresses the wish that this translation of the past into the present might be possible rather than fully convincing the poet or his readers that the wish can bring its promise to life. It is in this sense that it is properly titled a ''prayer.'' Its attitude is prospective, seeking a better, brighter future, and pointing to itself as anticipating a time when African energies and French forms might work in cooperative concert. At present, however, Senghor acknowledges that Africa is suffering the loss of her traditions while the painful and traumatic process of rebirth, which will convulse both Africa and Europe, has not yet occurred. Africa remains bound by the umbilical cord of dependency to Europe, in a state of latency and infancy, unable to separate itself, speak, move, and grow.

Ultimately, Senghor offers his ''Prayer to the Masks'' as a token of hope, as a single example of all that might be brought to life out of the two cultures that have shaped his life, through their exchanges, cooperative efforts, and mutual translations. Yet he also recognizes that this wishful dream at present remains unfulfilled for both him and his people, and that, like other dreams deferred and opportunities lost, it might still founder on historical realities. It is thus not with complacent surety, but an urgency haunted by the presence of danger, that Senghor asks: ''For who would teach rhythms to a world blasted by machines and guns? / Who would carry the joy-cry to waken the dead and the orphaned at dawn? / Say, who would bring life's memory back to the men of gutted hopes?'' His poem uses all the power that Senghor can muster from both cultures to answer: it is our task to try.

Source: Tyrus Miller, in an essay for *Literature of Developing Nations for Students*, Gale, 2000.

Chris Semansky

A widely published poet, fiction writer, and critic, Chris Semansky teaches literature and writing at Portland Community College. In this essay, Semansky argues that the locale of ''Prayer to the Masks'' is Senghor's Parisian flat, a lodging transformed through writing the poem.

Perhaps one of the first questions occurring to readers contemplating ''Prayer to the Masks'' by Leopold Sedar Senghor is where the poem occurs, more specifically, what is indicated by the sixth line's ''this place.'' A possible answer is Senghor's apartment in Paris. This theory comes from ''In Memoriam,'' the first poem in Senghor's first poetry collection, *Shadow Songs* (1945), the volume also containing ''Prayer to the Masks.'' ''In Memoriam'' portrays the exiled black African Senghor anxiously considering venturing out of his Paris apartment on a Sunday that also happens to be All Saints Day, a doubly sacred occasion. The poet is in the process of summoning the courage necessary to walk down and into the Parisian streets, meet those ''faces of stone'' with ''blue eyes,'' those people with ''hard hands'' who are at once brothers and historical enemies. Senghor writes that his ''glass tower,'' (that is, his apartment building) is filled with ''impatient Ancestors'' and ''Forefathers'' whom the poet calls on. Throughout Africa, masks are multifunctional, one of their functions being to breathe life into myths that attempt to explain the origins of daily customs.

> Guard my dreams as you did your thin-legged migrant sons! O Ancestors! Defend the roofs of Paris in this dominical fog, The roofs that protect my dead. Let me leave this tower so dangerously secure And descend to the streets, joining my brothers

''In Memoriam'' is an earlier, and one might say, a more immature poem than ''Prayer to the Masks'' since ''In Memoriam'' shows the poet asking for *personal* help, entreating the Ancestors to guard his dreams and embolden him enough to join the Parisians outside.'' Prayer to the Masks,'' on the other hand, has Senghor calling on the Masks/Ancestors to save *the world,* specifically from the incusions of Europe. As a result of this progress from self-centeredness toward altruism, a theory might be ventured: the longer Senghor remained apart from his homeland, the more religiously mature he became.

While ''In Memoriam'' shows the poet gazing down upon the roofs and streets of Paris, ''Prayer to the Masks'' allows readers—those pedestrians strolling along lines of words instead of boulevards of buildings—to look back and up into the poet's apartment, likely a small space, probably a room serving as both living space and study. Looking up, the pedestrian is able to see only the masks on the walls, but upon entering the building, the poet's room might look this way: on each of the four walls hangs a mask representing one of the four cardinal points. On a table or desk is the "Ancestor with the lion head," perhaps a statue or a mask like the others.

Throughout Africa, masks are multifunctional, one of their functions being to *breathe* life into myths that attempt to explain the origins of daily customs. According to Jean Laude, "masked" ceremonies are

> cosmogonies enacted to reinvigorate time and space. By their means an attempt is made to restore humanity and the forces entrusted to mankind to the pristine which all things lose when subject to time. However, they are also truly cathartic displays, during which human beings take stock of their place in the universe and see life and death depicted in a collective drama which gives them a meaning (quoted in Chevalier 639-40).

Like the African cosmogonic ceremony described above, the poet calls upon the masks and the "Ancestor with the lion head" to reinvigorate the time and space of white-dominated Africa and restore the meaning of human existence—if not to its pristine state—to a state reinvigorated through imagining the pristine. When Senghor calls upon the "four cardinal points where the Spirit blows" to save a dying Africa and animate a "deadened" Europe, his invocation can be imagined as a call to hot African winds—ghibilis, samiels, and simooms—to warm a Europe grown chilly with civilization. But the appeal to the masks can also be interpreted as the private ritual of a writer-in-exile calling upon his four masks to inspire him with the spirit of homeland, to breathe inspiration into the ritual of (his) writing, a ceremony, by the way, often dear to exiles. The poet calls upon the African masks because in them ancestors and (home)land are fused. Ancestors buried in the land decay into and become part of the *ancestral land* from which the masks are presumably made (whether they be of wood, clay, or metal). The masks "exude the immortal air," "the breath of my Fathers," which the poet will inhale. For those less inclined to believing in spirits, the masks can be imagined as in possession of an odor rich with the remembered smell of ancestral land, an emanation the poet inhales as inspiration. In sum, the elaborate complex whereby resurrection of the buried dead into Ancestral masks inspires continuance of the living world can be seen as a poeticization blowing beyond the four borders of a page of poetry, advancing outward into the world's four cardinal points.

Senghor's invocation to the masks can also be seen in the light of African initiation ceremonies where the masked mystagogue incarnates a spirit with whom he initiates an inexperienced youth into adulthood. On the one hand, the poet, separate from the mask, can be said to be an initiate yearning for the ability to harness the magic of words, and, on the other hand, the poet is the masked mystagogue himself, initiating readers, especially Western readers, into the mystery of words and poetry. Senghor also depicts himself as either split between Africa and Europe or having a double identity as both African and European. In other words, Senghor might at times be torn between his African and French identities, and at other times, attempt to be part of both Africa and Europe, even to reconcile them. Indeed, such characterizations correspond with what is written about Senghor's life.

Masks are also apotropaics, charms to ward off evil, like a crucifix or bulb of garlic to protect against vampires. In terms of masks-as-apotropaics, the poet calls upon the masks (as protector Spirits or Ancestors) to guard his lodgings from laughter and his African brethren from the suffering caused by European invasions and colonizations. In addition, the poet calls upon the masks to transform his poem into an apotropaic to protect the "oppressed children" and the "sorrowful princess" of Africa from the harm caused by a Europe "tied to us at the navel" ("tied to us at the navel" could indicate Europe as Africa's parent, especially if the "oppressed children" are African, but it is more likely Europe is to be understood as Africa's child, Africa usually considered home to humanity's ancestors). Apotropaic masks, are in fact, often worn by dancers to harness invisible Spirits for the protection of society. Because such Spirits are powerful, laying hold of them can be dangerous. And so the mask must also protect its wearer from being overwhelmed when channeling the Spirits' power into the community. While Senghor does not specifically call upon his masks to protect him in the same way as he did in "In Memoriam," the masks, or at least, the "Ancestor with the lion head," are thought to be already protecting his room/study "from women's laughter/ and any wry, profane smiles."

The meaning of the "Ancestor with the lion head," is multiple. Senghor's father's name is Basile Diogoye Senghor, Diogoye meaning "the lion" in Senghor's native Serer language (both people and language are known as *Serer,* pronounced "seer-ear"). In addition to this paternal connection to the lion-headed ancestor, there is the rich cultural symbology associated with lions, meanings differing little between Africa and Europe. For example, among the Bambara, a people dwelling in and just south of Senegal, the lion symbolizes divine knowledge and occupies a rank in the Bambara tradition-al social hierarchy only one step below that of priest-sage. The lion, then, can be viewed as a tight complex of identities: Ancestor, source of divine knowledge, protector against frivolousness, guardian of the sacredness of Senghor's study, and as inspiration. The characterization is of a seri-ous parental God for whom divine knowledge is no laughing matter. These Masks/Ancestors/Gods "stripped of every dimple," are *grounded,* are serious chthonic Ancestors, not frivolous Olympian mischief-makers. And though grounded, these An-cestors are still idealized, are eternally unchanging Gods "stripped . . . of every wrinkle." These are dead ancestors resurrected and elevated into God-like Ancestors who in turn transform the poet into priest, his "face leaning/ On an altar of blank paper," writing his prayer/poem, and chanting his prayer/song.

The origin of gods is thought by some to have been an apotheosis of dead ancestors conceived to live on and guard the living. Senghor builds on this apotheosis by symbolically elevating the status of his room/study into a sanctuary, his desk into an altar, himself (as poet) into priest, and the poem ("Prayer to the Masks") he is writing into a sacred document or prayer. Typical of prayer, Senghor's "Prayer to the Masks" is an entreaty to the Masks/Ancestors/Gods to save Africa from Europe and grant Africa the role of leavening the "white flour" of Western civilization, inspiring it to rise to new heights by, paradoxically, bringing it back to earth, back to expressions of joy, rhythm, and dance, back to poem, psalm, and prayer. In the same way Senghor recognizes that "white flour" must be leavened by black African influence, "Prayer to the Masks" shows how empty *white* paper can be "leavened" into poem, prayer, psalm, and possibly into scrip-ture by black ink.

Source: Chris Semansky, in an essay for *Literature of Developing Nations for Students,* Gale, 2000.

Jonathan Peters

In the following brief essay on Senghor's A Dance of Masks, *Jonathan Peters examines the artistic, spiritual and political implications held by the traditional piece of African art, the mask.*

In "Prière aux Masques" Senghor, as poet of Negritude, shows his concern with the white world. The title suggests that the poem is a prayer to the gods and spirits who watch over his race. It is more than just a prayer, however, for it contains a basic statement of Senghor's poetic credo.

An obvious distinction of "Prière aux Masques" is that unlike "Femme noire" and "Masque nègre" not one but several masks are involved and their summons from the four cardinal points stresses the importance of the occasion:

Black mask, red mask, you black-and-white masks
I greet you in silence!
Masks of the four points from which the
      Spirit breathes
(PO)

Senghor scrupulously follows the alphabetic order in his salutation to the masks—"*B*lack mask, *r*ed mask, you *b*lack-and-*w*hite masks"—as he paints them in black, red and white, the colours of tradi-tional Africa. His greeting is a silent one of rever-ence in a place whose very air smacks of eternity in its isolation from all contact with the profane.

Although the primary intent of the invocation is a plea to the masks, something of their character is revealed in the last lines of the preliminary address which takes up half the poem:

You distill this air of eternity in which I breathe
      the air of my Fathers.
Masks with faces without mask, free from all
      dimples and wrinkles
You who have composed this portrait, this face of
      mine bent over the altar of white paper
In your own image, hear me!
(PO).

In these lines is something of the paradox inherent in the African mystique, at least from a Western standpoint. In African art the mask is a symbolic representation of the human face, which is, in Senghor's words, "the most faithful reflection of the soul." Far from hiding or disguising the identity beyond it, the sacred African mask reveals in its form and texture the character of the deity it represents. The sacred masks in this poem are therefore "without mask" because they illumine the presence of the very founders of the race. There is on the one hand an image-analogy between the face of the suppliant and the sacred mask-Fathers who have modelled his face, and on the other a contrast between his own face and the "altar of white paper," which is consecrated because it is used to record the prayer to the masks.

Following the appeal for the masks' kindly audience, Senghor proceeds to the prayer proper. The subsequent six lines of the poem present black Africa and white Europe as objective correlatives:

See the Africa of empires dying—it is the agony
    of a pitiful princess
And Europe too to whom we are linked by
    the navel.
Fix your immobile eyes on your children who
    receive orders
Who give away their lives like the poor man his
    last garment.
Let us answer "Present!" at the rebirth of
    the world
As the leaven that the white flour needs.
  (*PO*).

The future of the two continents is inextricably linked because they have the same life line. Thus the death of Africa, the proud and pitiful princess, also spells doom for Europe. The African empires which held sway up to the nineteenth century have been disintegrating under European influence and the Second World War threatens the life of Europe torn by an inward struggle, a struggle in which the black man has been called upon to sacrifice his life for peace. But after this physical death, a new world will be born in which Africa will again have a key function, "[a]s the leaven that the white flour needs."

This last phrase suggests that the black man will be charged with the task of infusing a spiritual essence into a world that is for all practical purposes white—and sterile. There ensues an elaboration of the black man's role in a question and answer situation followed by an affirmation of that role:

For who will teach rhythm to the world laid low
    by machines and cannons
Who will shout with joy to wake up the dead and
    the orphans at the dawn?
Say, who will give back the memory of life to the
    man with eviscerated hopes?
They call us cotton men, coffee men oily men
They call us men of death.
We are the men of the dance, whose feet regain
    force by drumming on the hard earth.
  (*PO*).

The implication here is that only the black man who has maintained a constant connection with the world of nature and the world of spirits can fulfil this vital task, for the Caucasian, in his preoccupation with a machine civilization, has brought the world to ruin by this very machine. The Negro, who has up till the present been the downtrodden of the earth will then become the hero and the apostle of the dawn of tomorrow's world. He will make it rise, phoenix-like, from its own ashes.

The assertion of the black man's contribution is made with full awareness of his current existential position. He has many stereotypes, all of them revealing a bias above all against his colour, which

> His greeting is a silent one of reverence in a place whose very air smacks of eternity in its isolation from all contact with the profane."

forces on him a myth of inferiority. Ironically Senghor reverts to a European myth, that of the Greek Antaeus, to make his final postulate about the black man's identity as well as about his role: "We are the men of the dance, whose feet regain force by drumming on the hard earth."

The Messianic note of much poetry of Negritude is present in the questions that are posed in "Prière aux Masques." The apocalyptic day of destruction caused by the machines of white culture is to be followed by a day of resurrection achieved through the rhythmic flow of sap from a "civilisation sans machine." Inasmuch as rhythm is the correlative principle of death and life and similar dualities only beings endowed with it can infuse the vital sap into the deadened nerve centre of occidental civilization. According to Senghor, the Negro reigns supreme in the domain of rhythm; consequently, it will be his duty to teach the resuscitated world the rhythm of life and to announce the Good News in the impending dawn—an honour he has by virtue of his retention of the vital link with the cosmic forces ruling the universe as he dances the dance of the world.

What Senghor seems to have done in "Prière aux Masques" is to accept part of the Negro stereotype which he then modifies at the same time as he tacitly rejects the other half. The physical characteristics of the Negro ("cotton men coffee men oily men") which also refer to his humble or peasant status have been sublimated in "Femme noire" and "Masque nègre." What cannot be accepted here is that black is the colour of death; for Senghor, black is the colour of life, and the blackness of the Negro has this special significance for him in marked contrast with the Caucasian's identification of black with death. In any event death and life are twin aspects of the same reality. In particular, in Africa "there is no irreducible opposition between life and death." As "men of the dance," therefore, the black race engages in a dance celebrating the renewing cycle of life and death. . . .

Source: Jonathan Peters, in *A Dance of Masks,* Three Continents Press, 1978, pp. 28–31.

Sources

Bâ, Sylvia Washington, *The Concept of Negritude in the Poetry of Léopold Sédar Senghor*, Princeton University Press, 1973.

Hymans, Jacques Louis, *Léopold Sédar Senghor: An Intellectual Biography*, Edinburgh University Press, 1971.

Sartre, Jean-Paul, ''Orphée Noir,'' in his *Situations III*, Gallimard, 1949, pp. 229-86.

Senghor, Léopold Sédar, *The Foundations of ''Africanité'' or ''Négritude'' and ''Arabité,''* translated by Mercer Cook, Presence Africaine, 1971.

————, *Selected Poems / Poésies Choisies*, translated by Craig Williamson, Rex Collings, 1976.

Spleth, Janice, *Léopold Sédar Senghor*, Twayne Publishers, 1985.

Further Reading

Bâ, Sylvia Washington, *The Concept of Negritude in the Poetry of Léopold Sédar Senghor*, Princeton University Press, 1973.
> Bâ discusses Senghor's poetry using the concept of negritude and the background of African philosophy as her focus.

Hymans, Jacques Louis, *Léopold Sédar Senghor: An Intellectual Biography*, Edinburgh University Press, 1971.
> Very good historical and biographical study that discusses Senghor's work and thought within the broader tendencies of African and negritude philosophy.

Sartre, Jean-Paul, ''Orphée Noir,'' in his *Situations III*, Gallimard, 1949, pp. 229-86.
> This essay was Sartre's controversial introduction to Senghor's 1948 anthology of negritude poets.

Senghor, Léopold Sédar, *Anthologie de la nouvelle poésie nègre et malgache de langue française*, Presses universitaires de France, 1948.
> Senghor's celebrated and influential anthology of negritude poets.

————, *The Collected Poetry*, translated by Melvin Dixon, University Press of Virginia, 1991.
> A full edition of Senghor's poetry in English translation.

————, *The Foundations of ''Africanité'' or ''Négritude'' and ''Arabité,''* translated by Mercer Cook, Presence Africaine, 1971.
> A lecture given by Senghor in Cairo in 1967 in which he discusses the shared roots of North and Sub-Saharan Africa and the potential cooperation between Arab and Black Africans.

————, *Selected Poems*, edited by Abiola Irele, Cambridge University Press, 1977.
> An edition of the poems in the original French, with an informative introduction and annotations to the poems.

————, *Selected Poems / Poésies Choisies*, translated by Craig Williamson, Rex Collings, 1976.
> A bilingual facing-page selection of Senghor's poem, with a helpful introduction.

Spleth, Janice, *Léopold Sédar Senghor*, Twayne Publishers, 1985.
> A basic survey of all the poetry and the personal and intellectual context of Senghor's writing.

A River Sutra

Gita Mehta
1993

In *A River Sutra*, Gita Mehta took a new direction in her writing. In her previous works, *Karma Cola* (1979) and *Raj* (1989), Mehta had focused on the interactions between India and the Western world. In *A River Sutra*, Mehta changes focus and explores the diversity of cultures within India. To accomplish this, Mehta presents seemingly unconnected stories in her novel, stories about Hindu and Jain ascetics, courtesans and minstrels, diamond merchants and tea executives, Muslim clerics and music teachers, tribal folk beliefs and the anthropologists who study them. What binds these stories together are two things: the Narmada River and a "sutra." "Sutra," as Mehta explains in the glossary to her novel, means "literally, a thread or string." In the case of her novel, the "sutra" is the theme of love that runs through all the stories, threading them loosely together. The Narmada River stands for another type of "sutra." This river, known as the holiest in India, threads together the diverse people who live on its shores or who come to worship at its waters. The term "sutra" also refers to an Indian literary form, so in the novel, each story is in itself a "sutra" that presents a message. Every time the nameless narrator tries to tease out the meaning of one "sutra," he encounters another pilgrim or lost soul with another story to tell.

Critics have responded positively to *A River Sutra*. They remark on both the simplicity of the storytelling style—a style as old as India—and the complexity of the themes the novel explores. As the

reviewer from the *Washington Post Book World* noted, the stories leave the reader with "the sense that things are richer and more meaningful than they seem, that life is both clear and mysterious, that the beauty and the horror of this world is both irreducible and inexplicable." Critics further praise how Mehta introduces Western readers to a world they have not fathomed. *A River Sutra*, however, suggests that the "sutra," or the theme of love, running through the stories can connect all people together.

ples—have been interwoven. The India she writes in this novel seems foreign and strange to Western readers. Sensing this, Mehta included a glossary of terms to aid the uninitiated. In 1997, Mehta published *Snakes and Ladders: Glimpses of Modern India*, a work of nonfiction. In this collection of essays, Mehta explores the collisions between technological modernism and ancient traditions in present-day India. Mehta currently divides her time among New York, London, and India.

Author Biography

Gita Mehta was born in New Delhi, India in 1943 to parents who were very involved in the movement for Indian independence. In 1943, India was still a British colony. Three weeks after Mehta was born her father was jailed for supporting the nationalist cause. At the age of three, Mehta was left to be raised in a convent in Kashmir so that her mother could better aid her jailed husband. After India gained its independence, Mehta's father went into politics.

Unlike her traditionally educated mother, Mehta earned a university degree at Cambridge in England. There she met her husband, Sonny, who is currently the editor-in-chief at the publishing house Alfred A. Knopf in New York City. As a journalist, Mehta covered such events as the Bangladesh war of 1971. Mehta has written and filmed several television documentaries. Her first novel, *Karma Cola*, published in 1979, was an answer, in part, to Westerners' insistence that as a woman in a sari Mehta was an expert on India. The book humorously examines India's enchantment with American materialism and America's attraction to Indian mysticism. The quest for either, said Mehta in an interview for *Harper's Bazaar*, is a "kind of lobotomy." Her next book, *Raj*, a historical novel, was published in 1989. In this novel, Mehta documents the divisions between Hindu, Muslim, and Sikh Indians and their struggle against British rule. The novel spans almost 100 years of Indian history, from 1897—the height of British imperial power—to 1970, the year that India, by breaking with the tradition of rulership, became more truly democratic. In 1993, Mehta published *A River Sutra*. In this novel, Mehta pays scant attention to how India has interacted with Western traditions. Rather, she focuses on how the stories and traditions of diverse Indians—Muslims, Jains, Hindus, and tribal peo-

Plot Summary

The Narrator's Story

The loose collection of stories that comprises Gita Mehta's *A River Sutra* are connected by three things: the Narmada River, the theme of love, and the narrator's inability to understand the various tales of the human heart he hears. Mehta gives very little information about this narrator. The reader never knows his name, much less the secrets of his heart. It is through this nameless man that the reader learns the stories of uncommon pain and joy that the narrator has collected during his tenure as the manager of a government rest house on the banks of the Narmada River.

The Monk's Story

Ashok is the first of many people to tell the narrator his story of love. The monk is probably only thirty years old, and yet he has already tired of a world that offered him anything he wanted: extreme wealth, a loving family, and the opportunity to better other people's lives through charity. The monk has willingly decided to become a monk in a religion where, as other monks tell him, he will suffer almost constant pain. Ashok believes these sacrifices are worthwhile because in his renunciation, as the same monks tell him, he "will be free from doubt."

The narrator cannot understand Ashok's adherence to a religious order where the highest level of enlightenment will probably come, as Ashok's father says, from "starving himself to death." The narrator shudders to think that one day he will see Ashok's body, just as he has seen so many other priests' bodies, as a corpse floating down the Narmada River. After listening to the monk's story, the story's meaning is still a mystery to the narrator. The old Muslim mullah Tariq Mia must finally explain that the Jain monk's story was about "The

Gita Mehta

human heart. . .Its secrets.'' His frozen heart thawed by ''compassion. . .for the human helplessness that linked us all,'' the monk finally feels connected to the world. His renunciation of the world, paradoxically, is his celebration of that connection.

The Teacher's Story

As Tariq Mia seeks to enlighten the narrator about the true meaning of the monk's story, he offers him another story, one of a teacher's love for his student. This story, like the monk's, is meant to show the secrets of the human heart. A music teacher, Master Mohan fell in love with the sound of a blind pupil's perfect voice. Imrat's music represented a haven to Master Mohan whose own life had been filled with disappointment. Braving the wrath of his family, who despise him, he adopts the boy and nurtures his gift. He selflessly helps to further the boy's singing career, seeking no financial gain for himself. Master Mohan's greedy wife is outraged by her husband's actions. Out of revenge and greed she arranges for the boy to sing for a wealthy patron. Wary of the man's motives and seeking to protect the boy, Master Mohan had refused the rich man's request for a private concert. Tragically, Master Mohan's instincts were correct. As Imrat sings his devotional Muslim songs in front of the wealthy man, the man slits the boy's throat. Hearing

Master Mohan's tale, Tariq Mia can only assume that the ''great sahib'' killed the boy so that Imrat could share his voice with no one else. Devastated, Master Mohan makes his pilgrimage to the Muslim saint Amir Rumi's tomb, where Imrat had dreamed of singing. Instead of going back to his wife and children, Master Mohan throws himself in front of a train. If the rich man killed the boy so that no one would hear his voice again, Master Mohan kills himself because he cannot imagine life without the boy. A world without the boy's purity of soul and voice is not worth living in.

The Executive's Story

Soon after hearing this story, the narrator meets Nitin Bose, a young tea executive. Apparently insane, Nitin hands the narrator his diary and implores him to read it. Once a careless executive living the high life in Calcutta, Nitin had accepted the stewardship of a tea plantation nestled in the Himalayan foothills. Isolated, he began reading and rereading the legends of the Puranas, collections of legends dating from between the first century B.C. to the sixth century A.D. He was delighted to learn of the ''mythological tales dealing with the very area in which my tea estate was situated, legends of a vast underground civilization stretching from these hills all the way to the Arabian Sea, peopled by a mysterious race half human, half serpent.'' As he confided to his diary, however, he didn't for a moment believe the legends.

After two years, however, the legends Nitin had read began to merge with his real experience. Night after night he imagined that one of the half-serpent women seduced him. For a long time, Nitin was unable to make sense of the mysterious Rima who visited his bed each night: "I did not know whether I had fashioned her from the night and my own hunger.'' When he finally learned that she was not mythical, but merely a coolie's wife, Nitin explains how "Waves of disgust engulfed me and I wanted to vomit with shame.'' Rejecting Rima, Nitin determined to go back to Calcutta. But playing on his beliefs in the legends, Rima plotted a just revenge. Luring Nitin into the moonlight, Rima followed the folk beliefs and caught Nitin's soul between two halves of a coconut shell. Believing in the magic, Nitin lost his mind. According to a tribal priest, "If your sahib wants to recover his mind he must worship the goddess at any shrine that overlooks the Narmada River.''

At the government rest house, Nitin finds villagers who worship the same ancient goddess as the people of the Himalayan foothills. Following their rituals, Nitin is finally cured. After he has left the rest house, the narrator learns that the village children are singing his story. Nitin has become another of the many tales about the Narmada River.

The Courtesan's Story

Next, the narrator meets an old courtesan, trained in the arts of love, who has had to survive by turning into a common prostitute. She describes the height of her skills and art in great detail, and longs for the days when such delicacy was appreciated. This woman taught her daughter the art of the courtesans and tried to protect her from the sexual advances of men. Despite her care, the daughter is kidnapped by a notorious criminal, Rahul Singh. Searching for her daughter, the courtesan has come to the Narmada River. When she finally finds her daughter, however, it is too late. The daughter fell in love with her captor, believing in his belief that the two had spent all their past lifetimes together. When Rahul Singh is killed by the police, the courtesan's daughter despairs and loses the baby she is carrying. Her plots to avenge her husband's death are thwarted. Convinced that Rahul Singh did not want his bride to adopt his life of crime, the courtesan's daughter does not know how she will live. After comforting her mother one last time, the girl jumps off a cliff

into the waiting Narmada River below. Believing her child to be cleansed of her sins, the old courtesan begins the long walk home.

The Musician's Story

When the narrator first sees the musician, he believes she must be a beautiful woman. Her sari reveals a graceful form. However, when she turns to face the narrator, he is struck by the ugliness of her features. Her ugliness had played a large role in her life. Her father, a famous musician, took her under his wing, in part to protect her from her mother's sighs at the girl's homeliness. Under her father's tutelage, the daughter learned how to become a great musician in her own right. But she followed the traditional beliefs that her music, and all women's music, should complement a man's stronger notes. After it becomes apparent that no one will want to marry this girl, her father strikes a deal with an aspiring musician. He will teach the young man all he knows if the young man will agree to marry his daughter. The two pupils begin to play music together. The harmonies they create are so beautiful that the girl is convinced in the power of their love. She perfectly complements this man's music. As her mother begins the wedding preparations, however, the family learns that the young man has abandoned his teacher and his bride. He intends to marry another. Heartbroken, the musician vows to never play music again. Her father has taken her to the Narmada River so that she can "understand that I am the bride of music, not a musician.'' But she thinks there is no hope: "it is an impossible penance that he demands of me, to express desire in my music when I am dead inside.''

The Minstrel's Story

Tariq Mia tells the narrator of a Hindu ascetic, Naga Baba, who taught him the song of the river. This man, who Mia guesses was highly educated before he renounced the world, wandered along the banks of the Narmada with a small girl, Uma, in tow. Mia has not seen the Naga Baba in years, but his story had touched him.

In his travels, the Naga Baba, who dressed in rags, washed in the ashes of the cremated, and begged for food, had found a little girl in a brothel. Threatening to curse the house of ill repute, the Naga Baba had convinced its owner to relinquish the girl. Uma, as he renamed her, had been sold to the brothel by her father. Repeatedly raped by customers, Uma was frightened of all men. To nourish her spirit, the Naga Baba dedicated her to the Narmada River, in a sense baptizing her in its waters. Saying that the river was her new mother, the Naga Baba began to teach Uma the songs of the river. For years they traveled together, but one day the ascetic abandoned his charge in search of further "enlightenment." Alone, Uma became a river minstrel who traveled between religious festivals, keeping the legend of the river alive in song.

The Song of the Narmada

In the novel's last chapter, Uma comes to the narrator's rest house. She says she has been sent to sing to him the song of the river. The narrator is shocked to learn that the respected professor, Dr. Shankar, who has been staying with him, was the one who summoned Uma. He is even more shocked to learn that the well-dressed and thoroughly modern Dr. Shankar is none other than the Naga Baba himself. The road to enlightenment, as Dr. Shankar explains, led him back to the world of men. As he tells the narrator, "I have no great truths to share. . .I told you, I am only a man." Unsatisfied with this revelation, the narrator demands a further explanation. But Dr. Shankar persists, "Don't you know the soul must travel through eighty-four thousand births in order to become a man?. . .Only then can it reenter the world." As the novel closes, the narrator wonders what he would do if he ever left the rest house. The reader is left to wonder if the narrator will follow the Naga Baba's path and reenter the world, or, like so many of the people whose stories he heard, jump into the river that he has begun to worship.

Characters

Asha

One of Professor Shankar's young female assistants.

Ashok

Ashok, a Jain monk, has renounced his billionaire lifestyle to become an ascetic. As Mehta explains in the glossary to *The River Sutra*, Jain is an "Indian religion of extreme antiquity." The Jains, who follow the teachings of Mahavira, a religious reformer who lived in 500 B.C, broke with the Hindus over the rigid caste system that divided people into distinct classes. The monks of the Jain religion seek to lose all sense of themselves by following strict ascetic principles. In self-mortification, which includes begging for food and cutting off all ties with friends and family, they seek enlightenment. Living by the doctrine of "ahimsa," or nonviolence, these monks vow not to hurt a single living creature. To this end, they wear muslin masks over their mouths, lest they accidentally kill an insect that would fly into their mouths.

The monk is probably only thirty years old, and yet he has already tired of a world that offered him anything he wanted: extreme wealth, a loving family, and the opportunity to better other people's lives through charity. The monk has willingly decided to become a monk in a religion where, as other monks tell him, he "will experience cold. Hunger. Heat. Thirst. Sickness." Ashok believes these sacrifices are worthwhile because in his renunciation, as the same monks tell him, he "will be free from doubt. . .delusion. . .extremes." The monk takes the drastic step of becoming an ascetic because once his frozen heart is thawed by "compassion. . .for the human helplessness that linked us all," he feels connected to the world for the first time. His renunciation of the world, paradoxically, is his celebration of that connection.

Naga Baba

The narrator is floored to learn that the learned expert on the Narmada River, Professor Shankar, is the same person as the ascetic hermit Naga Baba. As an ascetic, Naga Baba had renounced the world. He wandered the countryside, bathed in the ashes of the cremated, and begged for sustenance. Professor Shankar, a stylish expert on the Narmada River, seems thoroughly modern. His skepticism about the mythology surrounding the river contrasts to the Naga Baba's holy purpose. But as Professor Shankar explains, he has reentered the world, learning that the greatest enlightenment comes from being a man and part of the rush of life. His search for enlightenment that led him to become an ascetic has led him back to the world he once renounced. It seems that the girl Uma, whom the Naga Baba had rescued from a brothel, probably taught him this lesson. Tariq Mia muses that the ascetic could find no higher enlightenment than his relationship with the abused girl. In many ways, the mullah's assessment is correct. In loving and caring for her, the Naga Baba abandoned his solitary wanderings. Teaching her the songs and traditions of the river led him back to his old profession of archaeologist. Through love, the Naga Baba regained the world and became once again the famous Professor Shankar.

Nitin Bose

This tea merchant is sent by his uncle to recuperate at the narrator's Government rest house. Apparently insane, Nitin Bose first claims to authorities that he is a woman. Once a young executive in Calcutta, Nitin Bose has seemingly lost his mind while governing a tea plantation in the isolated Himalayan foothills. Having immersed himself in the folk tales of the region, Nitin Bose can no longer distinguish reality from the mythological stories. After years of celibacy he imagines that a serpent-like woman comes to his bed each night. He is not sure if she is real or a fantasy. After realizing that he has been sleeping with Rima, a peasant woman, Nitin is repulsed by the love affair. Disgusted by her low caste, Nitin declares that the spell she had cast over him is broken. Enough of the fantasy remains, however, for Nitin to believe that Rima has captured his soul. Clinging to this belief he has come to the rest house, hoping that the tribal people will use their ancient religion to free him. His sin was not that he rejected Rima, but that he rejected the power of desire. By sacrificing to the goddess of desire, Bose can become sane and whole once more.

Mr. Chagla

Mr. Chagla, the narrator's clerk, must ride 19 kilometers from his town of Rudra to the Government rest house each day. Mr. Chagla's bustling activity contrasts to the narrator's detached observation. Frequently Mr. Chagla enlightens the narrator about tribal customs and the villagers' way of life. Despite his inferior work and social position, Mr. Chagla seems much more aware of the meaning of life than his boss. As he explains to the narrator, "But, sir, without desire there is no life. Everything will stand still. Become emptiness. In fact sir, be dead." This a lesson the narrator has yet to learn.

The Courtesan

This elderly woman describes how she was traditionally trained in the art of love. Taught "to teach nobleman good manners," the courtesan's job differed from that of the common prostitute. As this woman explains, learning to be a courtesan enabled her to become "more accomplished than any woman in India." With a changing culture, however, the art of love lost value. Courtesans instead became prostitutes: "Trained as scholars, artists, musicians, dancers, we are only women to [vulgar men], our true function to heave on a mattress and be recompensed by some tawdry necklace flashing its vulgarity on a crushed pillow."

Still loving her art, this courtesan trained her daughter in the art of love but protected her from men. When her daughter is kidnapped, it is as though this woman has lost her art for the second time.

The Courtesan's Daughter

This beautiful young woman who was kidnapped by a criminal fell in love with her captor. Trained in the art of love like her mother, this girl's delicacy and refinement clash with the infamous bandit who has taken her. The bandit, Rahul Singh, however, believes that they were fated to be together and have spent many past lifetimes tragically in love with each other. She falls passionately in love with him, but shortly afterward he is killed by police and she loses the child she is carrying. The narrator is very attracted to this woman, but he is repelled by her courtesan nature. She seems manipulative, as though she can act out love without feeling it. The narrator's not sure whether or not he should feel sorry for her or believe her tale of love. But when he learns that she had plotted to kill her husband's killers, and when he sees that "all the artifice had dropped from her demeanor. Now her eyes had the desperation of a trapped animal," he believes her veracity. When she jumps into the Narmada River to end her own life, he can hope, with her mother, that "she would be purified of all her sins."

The Great Sahib

This unnamed rich music lover offers Master Mohan 5000 rupees to hear Imrat sing. Master Mohan does not trust the great sahib's servant who comes to solicit the boy's services, so he refuses. Master Mohan's wife, however, greedy for money, arranges for the boy to sing. Seemingly enraptured by the boy's voice, the great sahib asks, "Such a voice is not human. What will happen to music if this is the standard by which god judges us?" Then he, inexplicably, slits Imrat's throat. As a rich man, he faces no repercussions.

Imrat

The blind boy sings devotional Muslim songs with the voice of an angel. While his life has been marred by tragedy—his father died in a flood and his sister has had to leave him behind—the boy seems to find ecstasy in singing. He dreams of singing a song his father taught him at the tomb of the Muslim Saint, Amir Rumi, and of making enough money to be reunited with his sister. Murdered by a rich maniac, who, as Tariq Mia surmises killed his "object of worship so no one but himself

can enjoy it,'' Imrat seems a symbol of both innocence and love. His innocent desires collide with a
corrupt world, and the most perfect voice his loving
music master ever heard is snuffed out.

Imrat's Sister

Unable to take care of her blind brother, Imrat's
sister leaves Calcutta to become a maid servant. She
entreats Master Mohan to watch after Imrat and
hopes to soon make enough money to retrieve
her brother.

Master Mohan's Wife

The shrewish wife of Master Mohan blames her
husband for their poverty. Born to wealth, she lets
her husband know that she is ashamed of him. Her
greed and spite lead her to send Imrat to the unnamed ''great Sahib'' who murders the boy. Rather
than return home from Tariq Mia's mosque to his
wife and the children who also hate him, Master
Mohan commits suicide.

Tariq Mia

An old Muslim mullah, or teacher, who meets
regularly with the narrator to play chess and phil-
osophize. Tariq Mia lives in a Muslim village
within walking distance of the narrator's Government rest house. He teaches his friend about the
music of Amir Rumi, the Muslim Saint whose tomb
adjoins Tariq Mia's mosque. In their long chess
games, Tariq will frequently break into song and try
to explain to the narrator the meaning of life. Time
and again, he returns to the theme of love. In his
stories, he shows how the ''capacity to love'' is the
most important of life's gifts. At the end of the
novel, the narrator shuns the friendship of Tariq
Mia, believing the man and his village to be ''frozen
in time, untouched by the events of the larger
world.'' However, Tariq Mia's own capacity to
love, as evidenced in his teaching and his devotion
to spiritual musical, suggests that he is more truly
part of the world than the narrator. As he says to the
narrator, ''How can you say you have given up the
world when you know so little of it?''

Misfortune

See Uma

Dr. Mitra

Dr. Mitra, the cynical local doctor, left a prestigious career to work in relative obscurity. He delights in the stories about the Narmada River. According to the narrator, Dr. Mitra ''maintains that he

encounters more interesting patients here than he
could hope to find in Delhi or Bombay, and whenever he describes a pilgrim brought to him with only
one-third of a body or some particularly horrifying
form of elephantiasis, his eyes shine with excitement as if he is describing a work of art.''

Mohammed-sahib

He accompanies Master Mohan to the music
festival where he meets Imrat. He encourages Master Mohan to brave his wife's wrath and bring home
the boy prodigy. The paanwallah cynically thinks
little of Mohammed-sahib's advice: ''It is easy for
him to give advice when it costs him nothing.'' The
paanwallah's cynicism seems apt when later Mohammed-sahib, fearing his own wife's temper, refuses to let Imrat stay at his house.

Master Mohan

A music teacher from Calcutta who sought out
the tomb of the Muslim Saint Amir Rumi, which
adjoins Tariq Mia's mosque. As he is obviously
emotionally tormented, Tariq has him relate his
problems. Years later, Tariq Mia tells Master
Mohan's story, another tale of love, pain, and loss,
to the narrator. This henpecked music teacher who
had failed to reach fame in his own life, finds joy,
love and fulfillment when he adopts a blind boy
with a magnificent voice. Master Mohan feels connected to the world once more through the child's
music. The boy's brutal murder leaves him in despair. He has come to the mosque to offer the boy's
recorded voice to the Muslim Saint, since Imrat was
not able to fulfill his dream of singing at Amir
Rumi's tomb. Afterward, he throws himself in front
of a train, killing himself. When the narrator wants
to know why, Tariq Mia answers, ''Perhaps he
could not exist without loving someone as he had
loved the blind child. I don't know the answer, little
brother. It is only a story about the human heart.''

The Monk

See Ashok

The Monk's Father

The unnamed wealthy diamond merchant tries
to persuade his son to stay in his world and not
become a Jain monk. His son, though, is partly
drawn to Jain's asceticism because of what he views
as his father's hypocrisy. His father says that he
follows the doctrine of ahimsa, and has become a
merchant so as not to harm, like a farmer must, any
living thing. However, the monk sees the squalor in

which the diamond workers live and holds his father responsible. Even as he rejects his father, though, the monk comes to fully understand the meaning of ahimsa. His father's anguish over the loss of his son is what he says "melted the numbness that froze my heart." That his father does not understand Ashok's decision is evident in the lavish celebrations he throws to mark his son's renunciation of the world. Throwing diamond chips and pearls into the crowd who has come to witness his son's initiation into the Jain sect, the monk's father feels that he is doing good. He fails to foresee the result of his action: riots as the peasant clamor to get more.

Moonlight

See Uma

The Musician

This female musician has a beautiful figure but an abnormally ugly face. Attracted by the music her father makes, this woman is delighted to become his pupil at the age of six. She describes how she learned to view the world through music, understanding the Hindu gods and nature as makers of music. Years later she understands that "Through music, [my father] tried to free me from my own image so I could love music wherever it was to be found, even if it was not present in my own mirror." When it seems apparent that no one will want to marry the ugly girl, her father explains that he "will be giving [her] as wife to. . .the gods of music." But the musician does fall in love with her father's pupil as the music they make together transcends the physical and unites them in a spiritual world of sound. Her music complements the male pupil's. The two become engaged—it is her father's condition for taking the man as a student—and they seem on the verge of true happiness. The pupil abandons the musician, however. Distraught, the musician turns away from her music. She feels betrayed by the harmony that failed to sustain her love.

The Musician's Father

A hard task-master, the musician's father will not let his daughter begin to make music until she can see and hear the music of the natural and spiritual world. A patient teacher, he instills in his daughter his own passion for music. When his daughter's heart is broken by her fiance, the father tries to make her fall in love with music once more. He takes her to the Narmada River to heal her soul, but his loving efforts seem futile. His daughter was betrayed by more than just love, but by the music her father had taught her to trust and worship.

The Musician's Fiance

This music student becomes betrothed to the musician so that he can study with her father. He seemingly falls in love with the musician, despite her homeliness, because her music so perfectly compliments his own. He betrays the power of their music and love by abandoning the musician for another bride.

The Musician's Mother

This traditional mother is distressed by her daughter's ugliness. She fears she will not be able to find a husband for her daughter.

The Narrator

The nameless narrator had been a high-ranking bureaucrat before the death of his wife. Adrift without a wife or family, he decides to exit the world. Not believing that he has the strength to become a true Hindu hermit and renounce the world and all comforts, he instead takes over the management of a Government rest house on the banks of the Narmada River. In his relative isolation, the narrator becomes an observer, collecting stories of human love and suffering, but not really feeling these emotions for himself. With every story he hears, of religious love, familial love, sexual love, and eternal love, he realizes his own incapacity to connect with the world through love. Watching the Narmada River, the holiest River in India said to be the daughter of the Hindu god Shiva, the narrator watches life go by but seems powerless to become part of it.

The Paanwallah

This street vendor (he sells the Indian digestive paan) encourages Master Mohan to find a little happiness, suggesting that the music teacher attend a music festival. Later he takes credit for Master Mohan's patronage of the blind singer Imrat. He keeps the money Imrat makes so that Master Mohan's wife cannot take it.

Rima

Rima is the serpent-like woman who comes to Nitin Bose's bed at night. Well-versed in the legends of the Himalayan foothills, this peasant woman, the wife of a coolie, enchants Nitin with her stories as well as her lovemaking skills. After he rejects her, Rima lures Nitin into the moonlight and tells him that she has captured his soul in a coconut shell. Her lower caste and tribal heritage make her both attractive and repulsive to Nitin.

Mr. Sen

An overseer on the tea plantation, Mr. Sen translates the peasants' songs for Nitin Bose.

Dr. V. V. Shankar

See Naga Baba

Ashok

A member of the board for a tea company, Ashok tries to persuade Nitin Bose to leave his tea plantation and return to Calcutta. When Nitin refuses, Ashok tells him, "You are definitely going mad." Though Ashok comes across as a boor, his words are prophetic.

Shashi

Shashi, an old school friend of Mr. Chagla's, is a police officer from the town of Rudra.

Sheela

One of Professor Shankar's young female assistants.

Rahul Singh

An infamous bandit, Rahul Singh hides out with his band in an uninhabited forest on the banks of the Narmada River. He kidnaps the Courtesan's daughter because he believes she was his wife in a previous lifetime. The power of his love seduces her. He is killed by the police.

Uma

Uma is sold by her father, who calls her "Misfortune," to a brothel when she is just a child. Repeatedly raped by male customers, Uma is frightened of men and dreads the world. Instantly sensing her pain, the Naga Baba makes the brothel's owner give him the girl by threatening to curse the establishment if the woman does not comply. Taking Uma to the Narmada River, the Naga Baba declares that the river is now her mother. As a handmaiden to the river, Uma will learn its legends and songs. Through the Naga Baba's care and love, Uma is healed, and free of the hideous fate that awaited her as a child prostitute. She becomes a river minstrel, keeping the stories of the river that saved her alive.

Topics for Further Study

- In *A River Sutra*, Mehta describes the many diverse ethnic and religious groups that inhabit modern-day India and suggests that a common heritage and geography link them together despite their differences. Research the various ethnic and religious groups that live in India today. What traditions do they share?

- Investigate how modern culture has impacted traditional Indian beliefs. How does Mehta present this culture clash?

- Explore the Indian folk and religious stories about the Narmada river. How do these ancient tales compare to Mehta's river stories?

- A number of the women depicted in *A River Sutra* have very little power. What opportunities do women have in India today? How are these opportunities affected by traditions such as arranged marriages?

Themes

Love

The most obvious theme in *A River Sutra* is that of love. The Narmada River itself is described as a lover, flowing to meet her bridegroom, the Lord of the Oceans. In each story that the nameless narrator hears he learns more about what his friend Tariq Mia calls the secrets of the human heart. The varieties of love that touch the heart are as endless as the stories of the Narmada River. The narrator learns of a monk's love for all living creatures. Trying to live by the doctrine of "ahimsa" or nonviolence, this Jain monk tries to empathize with the suffering of everything from the smallest insect to his own wealthy father. In attempting to utterly deny his own feelings and to take on the pain of the world, the Jain monk finds that his frozen heart has melted. Master Mohan falls in love with a blind boy singer through the purity of the boy's voice. In caring for this boy, Master Mohan is selfless. Acting as a true father, Master Mohan forgets his own needs, putting the boy's happiness above all things. When the boy is murdered, it seems logical for Master Mohan to take his own life. So too does the courtesan's daughter commit suicide after her lover dies. Some love, the narrative suggests, is so all encompassing that life without that love becomes impossible to bear. Other manifestations of love, however, offer sustenance for continuing to live and persevere. The love that the ascetic Naga Baba feels for his ward Uma helps him to decide to rejoin the world and abandon his ascetic ways. Once Nitin Bose has recovered from the insanity brought on by his strange desire for a mystery woman and his renunciation of that desire, he is free also to rejoin the modern world. The narrator himself seems to have never searched for his own capacity to love. A bystander, he seems only able to listen to the stories and watch the Narmada River flow past.

Renunciation

As the narrative begins, the reader learns that the narrator has decided to renounce the modern world. Deciding not to pursue promotion within the bureaucracy for which he works, the narrator chooses instead to become the caretaker of a government rest house. Renunciation is a major tenet of the religions of India, and thus a major theme of the novel. The narrator admits that his renunciation of the world is minor compared to the true "vanaprasthi," those who have "retired to the forest to reflect." As he explains, "I knew I was simply not equipped to wander into the jungle and become a forest hermit, surviving on fruit and roots." But this is exactly what many of the people he meets have decided to do. The Jain monk was a fabulously wealthy man, the son of a diamond merchant, and yet he renounced this lifestyle to search for enlightenment. The Naga Baba was a renowned archaeologist who chose to dress in rags and wash in the ashes of the cremated. Both of these men in choosing the humiliations and hardships the world has to offer are a bit incomprehensible to the narrator. Mehta does not judge these ascetics harshly, but the narrative suggests that true enlightenment comes from love. And to truly love, one must connect with the world. The Naga Baba's eventual path, rejoining the world as Professor Shankar, seems perhaps a better destiny than the one most likely to befall the Jain monk. The narrator imagines that one day he will see the monk's emaciated corpse floating down the Narmada River. To reach his enlightenment, the monk will neglect his body's needs and potentially will starve to death.

Isolation

Closely related to the theme of renunciation is isolation. However, the truly isolated in the novel have not chosen their fate as the Jain monk and the Naga Baba did. The musician, for instance, is isolated by her ugliness. Her face repels possible suitors, and the man she loves abandons her. Forced to be alone, her fate is especially difficult. As a female musician she learned to be "the bride of music," her delicate chords are meant to complement the more masculine sounds of a male musician. Having found the perfect harmony with her fiance, she cannot imagine being able to play with anyone else. Her plaintiff sounds remind her of what she has lost, so she gives up her music. Similarly, the courtesan is isolated when her art no longer has meaning in the modern world. Trained in the "art of love," the courtesan dreams of a world long since past where she was able to perform before appreciative audiences. Changing times have changed her into a prostitute, forced to have sex with vulgar men. She lives without hope that the former world will ever return. Isolated from love and happiness by circumstance, these women do not have the power to renounce the world. It has renounced them.

Style

Point of View

A nameless narrator describes his life and experiences in the first person. However, unlike most first-person narrators, this man reveals very little about himself. Rather, the reader gets to know this character through what he does not say. He seems to have no life story, no main event that made him choose to live a retired life on the banks of the Narmada River. In contrast, the people the narrator meets and the stories he hears reveal the tumultuous nature of truly living. Without exception, the narrator meets or hears tales of extraordinary people, people who have made enormous sacrifices for love or who have been treated cruelly by life. The narrator's very lack of story, however, makes him an everyman. The readers eavesdropping in on the stories told by the exceptional relate more to the man who seems so ordinary. A narrator without a narrative, this man seems like most people—he is still searching for his own life story. Through him the stories of the courtesan, the tea executive, the musician, the monk, the Naga Baba, and Master Mohan are filtered. As the narrator retells these characters' stories, the readers, along with the narrator, struggle to understand these characters' choices. Questioning their motives and their sanity, the readers also wonder whether they are like the narrator, only observers afraid to embrace the love and disappointment that the world offers.

Sutra

The word "sutra," as Mehta explains in the glossary to her novel, means literally a "thread." But a "sutra" is also a type of story, one that contains a message or moral. The novel *A River Sutra* is arranged as a set of seven "sutras." The narrator and the reader hear seven separate stories that all contain a similar thread or theme. Each story contains another message about the secrets of the human heart and the capacity to love. This theme unites together the disparate stories. The river itself is another "sutra," and Mehta shows how the myths of the river connect together the diverse people who converge on its shores. The narrator's voice and the flow of the river he watches over tie up the stories into one continuous stream. Eventually, it seems that these new "sutras" will join the billions of stories connected to the Narmada River, becoming, like the legends of old, part of Indian culture.

Symbolism

Despite the deceptively simple language that Mehta uses and the folktale-like way she tells the stories, Mehta employs a sophisticated symbolism throughout *A River Sutra*. Like the Narmada River with which she begins the novel, most things stand for something else. Thus the holiest river in India is named with the Sanskrit word for "whore." Similarly, the river represents the cure for madness to the tribals who live beside it, and is the dancing daughter of Shiva, the God of Destruction, to the Hindus who worship at the river's side. But less consequential things in the novel also have a double meaning. The valley that separates the narrator from the Muslim mullah, Tariq Mia, is metaphorical as well as physical. A gulf exists between them, separated as they are by religious difference and variant world views. In an almost funny twist at the end of the novel, the narrator who has sought aimlessly for enlightenment begins to find it. As the ex-ascetic wanderer Professor Shankar drives away, the narrator describes how "The jeep doors slammed shut and headlights pierced the jungle, throwing strange shadows across the bamboo groves. Sudden arcs of light raked the darkness as the jeep roared down the twisting path that led to Rudra. I stared at the flashes

of illumination." It is only at this moment that the narrator looks inward, trying to find the secrets in his own heart, as he's left "wondering for the first time what I would do if I ever left the bungalow." Instead of finding illumination in the teachings of a religious man, the narrator finds it in the headlights of a jeep. The light that pierces the jungle finally pierces his own heart.

Literary Heritage

A River Sutra is a very textual novel. In almost every section, traditional Indian literary texts and art forms are referred to. This is important because in many ways *A River Sutra* is modeled on these other works. The very word "sutra" in the novel's title refers to an Indian literary form, that Mehta describes as "usually aphoristic in nature." An aphorism is a short statement that contains a general truth. In other words, "sutras" usually contain a moral or a message intended to enlighten the reader.

Many Western readers of *A River Sutra* may recognize the term "sutra" from the famous Indian book of exotic love, *Kama Sutra*. This encyclopedic work, written in the fifth century A.D. by the Indian Vatsayana, is referred to in Mehta's novel. The theme of *Kama Sutra* as well as its form are significant to *A River Sutra*. Mehta's novel explores many different types of love, including sexual love. The theme of love is common in many Indian works. Mehta also mentions the Bengali poet Chandidas (c. 1350-1430), whose songs, as Mehta explains, "dealt with every form of human love." Similarly, one part of the *Mahabharata*, an ancient Hindu epic poem central to the Hindu religion, describes how, as Milton J. Foley explains, "there is the bliss of seeing God and loving God in all things." This work, as well as the poems of Mirabi (c. 1450-1520), a female Hindu poet who wrote worshipful songs to the god Krishna, are referred to in *A River Sutra* and help to suggest the timelessness of Mehta's theme.

Another Indian text central to *A River Sutra* is the *Purana*. This collection of folktales tells the story of India's mythological past. One character in *A River Sutra* becomes so entranced by these legends that he has a hard time distinguishing fact from fiction. But in many ways *A River Sutra* shows how such stories are collected. This novel, after all, is a collection of stories that add to the mythology of the Narmada River. The "sutras" of the river all contain a similar moral: nothing is more powerful than love.

Historical Context

When India is in the American news, it is often to document another conflict between the Hindu majority and the Muslim minority. As a reporter, Mehta covered the Bangladesh War of 1971, a war that highlighted the conflicts between the ethnic and religious groups of the Indian sub-continent. Her life was also shaped by the conflicts between Indian nationalists and British imperialists. Her father was arrested for treason to the British Empire shortly after her birth. The ability to grow up in a free India was not an option for her parents. India's cultural ties to Britain, however, remained strong, as evidenced by Mehta's decision to attend university in Britain. Today, she lives on three continents— Europe, North America, and Asia—as she divides her time among London, New York, and India. Mehta drew on the perspective of all three cultures in her earlier works, exploring the clashes and connections between these different worlds. In *A River Sutra*, however, Mehta turns her authorial gaze inward to examine not the diversity of the modern world, but the diversity of India.

To understand the India Mehta describes in *A River Sutra*, one must understand the history of the country. Tracing the divisions of the Indian people back 4,000 years, Mehta describes how Aryan nomads invaded the Indian sub-continent, decimating the tribal people they found. The stories of these people survived, however. The tea executive Nitin Bose is reading the ancient legends of these pre-Aryan people as he peruses the volumes of the Puranas, the collection of folk tales that date as far back as the first century B.C. The Narmada River, sacred to the Hindus and worshipped as the daughter of their god, Shiva, was holy also to these tribal people. Worshipping their goddess under a Banyan tree by the banks of the river, "the tribals believe they once ruled a great snake kingdom until they were defeated by the gods of the Aryans." Believing that they were "Saved from annihilation only by a divine personification of the Narmada River," these remainders of an ancient people believe that the river can cure snakebite and madness. Despite that the Aryan invasion occurred thousands of years ago, the novel suggests that the divisions it created were never healed. The tribal people by the river's

edge are described again and again by the narrator as "illiterate." The tribal people Nitin Bose encounters in the Himalayan foothills are described as racial others of low caste. In her novel, Mehta seeks to rectify these differences by showing the common culture that these diverse people share, how the legends of each have become interwoven as they have lived for centuries by the river's edge. Similarly, the novel highlights the similarities between the Muslim and Hindu faithful who worship by the river. The Hindu narrator seeks to learn from those of a different background, whether from the Muslim mullah or the Jain monk. The mullah, Tariq Mia, also refers to their shared heritage, asking the narrator to meditate on "Kabir, the man whose poems made a bridge between your people and mine." This religious reformer, as Mehta explains in her glossary to the book "was vastly popular with the masses and persecuted by the ruling classes," as well as by the leaders of the Hindu and Muslim faiths. Evoking his name, Tariq Mia suggests that the common ground between the religions—the search for love and enlightenment—can create a bridge. Writing at a time when India is still divided by religion and by a rigid caste structure that deems some people "untouchable," Mehta offers the interwoven stories of the Narmada River, as another possible bridge.

Critical Overview

Critics have responded positively to *A River Sutra*. A reviewer in *Publisher's Weekly* described how "this novel of India beautifully embodies the art and craft of storytelling as Mehta portrays diverse lives touched by the river Narmada, a holy pilgrimage site 'worshipped as the daughter of the god Shiva.'" The same reviewer praises Mehta for "not avoid[ing] the controversies of life in her homeland, including the caste system and political/religious rivalries," noting that "she willingly exposes its complexities." Rahul Jacob of the *Los Angeles Times* applauded how "every yarn begins the lazy circle again, another variation on the novel's central themes. Each story ends with a beguiling turn into the next one. The simplicity of Mehta's writing nicely complements the novel's profound concerns."

Reviewers of *A River Sutra* especially appreciate the form of the novel and how it ties into ancient storytelling traditions. The reviewer at the *Denver Post*, for one, likened Mehta to "Scheherazade,"

A ruined place on the banks of the Narmada River, which is considered India's holiest river and is featured in each of Mehta's interconnected stories that comprise A River Sutra.

and the book to *Arabian Nights*. The tempo of the book, however, seems in sharp contrast to Mehta's other works. Her first book, *Karma Cola* (1979), humorously examined the misconceptions Americans hold about Indian culture, and the naivety with which Indians exalt American capitalism. Mehta's historical novel, *Raj* (1989), also looked at India in relation to Western culture. In it, Mehta explored the effect that British imperialism had on Indian nationalism. Her latest work, *Snakes and Ladders: Glimpses of Modern India*, a collection of essays, returns to the themes of her earlier works. In this 1997 work of nonfiction, Mehta once again examines the collision of cultures in India. She concentrates especially on the clash between the burgeoning technological industries in India and the ancient religious traditions. *A River Sutra*, by contrast, is a much more internal novel, as Mehta explores both the rich traditions of India and the mysteries of the human heart. The novel was such a departure that Mehta did not think it was appropriate for her original publisher, Simon and Schuster. As Mehta said in an interview with Wendy Smith, of *Publishers Weekly*, ''I wrote *A River Sutra* privately; I didn't tell anyone I was doing it, and I genuinely didn't think it would get published out-

side of India. It astonishes me that that's the one people have responded to most.''

Criticism

Kimberly Lutz

Lutz is an instructor at New York University and has written for a wide variety of educational publishers. In the following essay, she explores how A River Sutra *translates both the culture of India and the experiences of love for the uninitiated.*

The India of Gita Mehta's *A River Sutra* is foreign, exotic, and unexpected. She describes an India that is ethnically, geographically, and religiously diverse. What binds the people of this country together, Mehta suggests, is both the Narmada River and the importance of love. However, what the Narmada and love mean to the various characters of the book is as various as the characters themselves. Mehta's job is to translate their experiences, to reveal the ''sutra,'' or thread, that runs through their stories. The translation helps to bind together a people whose differences, historically, have split them

What Do I Read Next?

- In Mulk Raj Anand's 1935 novel *Untouchable*, the author explores the Hindu caste system through the eyes of a man deemed an "Untouchable" by Indian society.

- *Kim*, Rudyard Kipling's 1901 novel about an Irish boy growing up in India, describes the diversity of India through a particularly English perspective.

- Gita Mehta's 1997 collection of essays, *Snakes and Ladders: Glimpses of Modern India*, docu-

ments the clash of modernity and ancient traditions in present-day India.

- *Mahabharata*, the ancient epic poem of the Hindus, has been attributed to the Hindu sage Vyasa. The form and themes of this poem are drawn upon in Mehta's *A River Sutra*.

- Salman Rushdie's controversial novel *The Satanic Verses* (1988) imaginatively describes the Islamic tradition in India.

---

apart. But Mehta is also translating for a Western audience. If the banks of the Narmada River shelter 400 billion sacred places that span the centuries and millennia of an ever-changing India, the Western reader indeed needs a guide to begin to navigate the river and its meaning.

The characters of *A River Sutra* can literally not understand each other. Throughout the novel, characters must find translators to make sense of the world around them. Nitin Bose, the young tea executive, ends up living among Himalayan peasants whose features, culture, and language are all foreign to him. The songs the peasant women sing in the fields are sung in a language unknown to Nitin Bose. He must turn to the overseer Mr. Sen for a translation. Similarly, when the Muslim mullah, Tariq Mia, first meets the Hindu ascetic Naga Baba, he can listen to the river song Baba sings, but the words hold no meaning for Mia. The Naga Baba must translate the Sanskrit lyrics. Even words that are known need to be translated in *A River Sutra*. The narrator is shocked to learn that in Sanskrit the word "narmada" means "whore." He argues, "That's impossible. The Narmada is the holiest river in India." It is possible because in India, and on the Narmada River itself, as the cynical Dr. Mitra suggests, there are layers of meaning. One could as soon uncover the significance of the Narmada River to India's history and mythology as know the 400 billion stories the river has spawned. Within even

simple words, like the religious incantation "Om," there are layers of meaning. The ugly musician teaches the narrator that the word "Om" is in fact multisyllabic, and that each syllable of the chant has meaning: "Om is the three worlds. / Om is the three fires. / Om is the three gods. / Vishnu, Brahma, Shiva." Reciting the word, she explains, takes one from the world of "waking consciousness" to "dreaming consciousness" to "dreamless sleep." To hear the subtle differences between the sounds of the chant, the narrator must be guided. The world (and the word) is too complex to understand alone.

If Indians speak more than fifteen languages, they also practice a variety of religions. In *A River Sutra*, the reader learns of Jains, Hindus, Muslims, and ancient tribal religions. Throughout the novel, the narrator seeks guides who can explain these diverse religions to him. However, he can never really get to the heart of religions he does not understand. He listens to his guides, but he continually judges their motivations and beliefs. His resistance suggests the extent to which another's experience can only be understood on a surface level. For instance, the narrator patiently listens to the Jain monk's story, but never comprehends his meaning. The monk describes in detail—a reader completely unfamiliar with the Jain religion can grasp the religion's principles—his decision to renounce the world. Particularly, the monk is eloquent on the principle of "ahimsa," or nonviolence. Forced to wear a mask so as not to unknowingly hurt an insect that could fly into his mouth, laboriously brushing a rock with a soft brush before he sits down to, again, not unknowingly harm an insect, and fearing to pluck a banana because ''who knows what small creatures live in the leaves or trunk of a banana free,'' the monk seems obsessive. But once the principle of ahimsa is understood on a larger scale, his attention to minutiae makes sense. In desiring not to hurt a single living creature, the Jain monks try to open themselves up to the world through empathy. Empathizing with the pain an insect would feel upon being crushed, they also empathize, as this monk describes, with the emotional loss a father feels when his son renounces the world and turns ascetic. This ability to get inside the skin of all living things leads, the Jain monks believe, to perfect enlightenment. Yet even as he listens to the monk's story of religious love and renunciation, the narrator cannot get inside the monk's spiritual skin. Rather, he imagines the starvation the young man will undergo and his likely fate: ''At this time I have sometimes seen the dull glow of something being swept downstream and known that it was the corpse of an ascetic thrown into the river with a live coal burning in its mouth. I cannot stop myself from wondering if some day while I am sitting here in the dark I will see the monk's body floating beneath the terrace.'' The narrator truly is in the dark. Focusing on the possibility of seeing the young monk's wasted and emaciated corpse floating down the Narmada River, he misses the larger meaning behind the monk's story. To understand that, he must seek out another guide, this time Tariq Mia. Listening to the story second hand, Tariq Mia figures out that the monk was explaining how he found ''the capacity to love.'' For the narrator, who has never found this capacity for himself, no amount of guides will be able to unravel the secrets of the human heart.

Interestingly, when the narrator walks to Tariq Mia's mosque, he describes ''the valley that separates us.'' This valley is physical, as well as metaphorical. Throughout the novel, the reader learns how the people of India are divided by geography. The tea executive who moves from Calcutta to the Himalayan foothills sees the difference as one between the ''inescapable humanity'' of the hot and crowded city and the unpopulated solitude of the cool mountain range. Pilgrims who walk the length of the Narmada River and back again traverse a varied landscape. The landscape, however, is only as varied as the beliefs of those who inhabit India. Time and again, the narrator is presented with

> "The heart, like the Narmada River, contains at least 400 billion stories. A native guide can help to tease out the meaning behind a few of the stories, but the secrets of the heart resist complete comprehension."

different ways of looking at the world. He recoils from the ''savagery'' of Muslim spiritual lyrics as well as from the ''artifice'' and ''the manipulations of the courtesan.'' The two courtesans he meet are skilled in the ''art of love.'' Understanding love as an art, however, indicates that it is a skill to be learned, that these women can play men as musicians play sitars. The narrator's life may have been untouched by love, but he rejects this manifestation of it. In his search for meaning he cannot understand those who completely renounce the world to become ''forest hermit[s], surviving on fruit and roots,'' but he also fights against the cynicism of Dr. Mitra who ''shakes his head in disbelief at the extremes to which religious folly could take men.'' Dr. Mitra may ''delight in unraveling the treads of mythology, archaeology, anthropology in which the river is entangled,'' but the narrator hopes to find enlightenment in the stories. He is not interested in simply deconstructing them. Despite the power of the river stories, the narrator is dismissive of the animist beliefs of the pre-Aryan people who populate the Narmada's shores. He hopes that his aide, Mr. Chagla, has not ''been infected by this foolishness'' of ''illiterate villagers'' who worship a snake as a goddess. Many valleys indeed separate the narrator from those around him.

Gita Mehta understands that the picture of India she paints will be unfamiliar to her readers. She provides a glossary of terms most likely unknown to the Western reader. The glossary, while extensive, is not comprehensive. Mehta does not attempt to serve as a guide to all of India in its diversity. The religious differences of Sikhs or Christians (some of whom are descendants of 16th Century Portuguese colonists) are not touched upon, nor is the impact of Great Britain's imperialism and how the English carved out a nation in a land where before there were separate kingdoms and tribes. The India she describes is too vast and diverse for a single guide. For ultimately, the India of *A River Sutra*, the India that can be experienced through the stories of the Narmada River, is a metaphor for the human heart. The heart, like the Narmada River, contains at least 400 billion stories. A native guide can help to tease out the meaning behind a few of the stories, but the secrets of the heart resist complete comprehension.

Source: Kimberly Lutz, in an essay for *Literature of Developing Nations for Students*, Gale, 2000.

James Christopher

In this brief review Parables without Purpose, *James Christopher reviews the National Theatre Studio/Indosa's staging of Gita Mehta's* A River Sutra *and finds that this production fails to express the wealth of religious diversity, which the novel so wonderfully captured.*

You can't miss the sense of event that hovers like joss-stick incense over the National Theatre Studio/Indosa staging of Gita Mehta's *A River Sutra*. The venue is largely to blame. Finding this strange 18th-century warehouse on an island in the East End proves as much a pilgrimage as the Narmada River is to the characters of Mehta's novel.

Rosa Maggiora's 90ft set taps superbly into the atmospherics. A river of lights sparkles against the brickwork. A rocky bank, framed on either side by a guesthouse and a temple, dominates the space. The audience are scattered on cushions; a lucky few hog benches at the back; the unlucky many, out on wings, have terrible sightlines.

What unfolds is a series of stories that hinge around Sam Dastor's retired civil servant who owns the guesthouse. Having renounced the city in search of peace he puzzles over the mystic grip of the river, a symbol of lust and absolution. Never has renunciation seemed such a middle-class sport. Dastor's benign Hindu makes chaste small-talk with Scott Ransome's unconvincing postman. One expects cucumber sandwiches to start appearing. Instead, a Jain monk (Andrew Mallett) happens by, and we see his life story enacted as a dreamy sketch.

The monk, it transpires, has abandoned his diamond fortune to "live in the world". Suitably horrified, Dastor's civil servant consults the local wise man (Talat Hussain), who tells him the story of an impoverished musician, his nagging wife, and the discovery of a blind beggar boy with the voice of

an angel. So it goes: small parables sprouting organically from the compost of Tanika Gupta's wholesome adaptation.

The Roald Dahl twists, which inspire spiritual angst in the civil servant, did little for me. It's all very pastoral, slow-moving and unbelievable. The actors rarely succeed in inhabiting their parts and the mixed casting sometimes makes Indhu Rubasingham's production look like the last days of the Raj rather than the intended celebration of religious diversity.

Source: James Christopher, ''Parables without Purpose,'' in *The London Times,* September 18, 1997, p. 38.

The Literary Criterion

In the following essays on Gita Mehta's A River Sutra, *the reader is presented with two views on Mehta's novel. C.N. Ramachandran examines how Mehta's novel deviates from the context of traditional Indian literature narrative style and function. A.G. Khan also examines the text with regard to Mehta's narrative style and functioning as they work to frame the two categories of characters Khan sees, 'steadfast' and 'fugitive'.*

C. N. Ramachandran

1

A River Sutra is Gita Mehta's third novel, the other two being *Karma Cola* and *Raj*. While the first two novels are in the well-known comic-ironic mode, this novel can be said to be, roughly, in the allegorical mode. Further, one wonders whether *A River Sutra* can be called a novel at all. Having the Western *Don Quixote* and the Indian *Dasakumara Charitha* as its models *The River Sutra* exploits the formal possibilities of the genre to the fullest. It is a framed narrative. It is the story of an I.A.S. Officer, who, after retirement, chooses to be the manager of a Guest House, on the banks of the Narmada river in the Vindhya range. Since at this spot, there are pilgrimage centres of Hindus, Jains, Buddhists and Muslims, the manager constantly comes across many pilgrims; and, occasionally, the pilgrims tell him their strange/tragic tales. The novel, after the preamble, begins with ''The Monk's Story'', and ends with ''The Song of the Narmada''. In all there are seven inset-stories.

Although ancient Indian aestheticians were content to distinguish between *Katha* and *Akhyayika* on the basis of who the narrator is, and didn't explore the narrative further, if we bring together such long narratives as *Kathasaritsagara*, *Panchatantra*, *Kadambari* and *Dasakumara Charita*, we can construct an Indian narrative tradition and identify its constituents. To start with, all Indian narratives—be they epics like *Mahabaratha*, fiction such as *Kadambari*, or folk-narratives like *Vethal Panchavimshati*—are framed narratives. In fact, the strategy of 'framing' seems to be essentially oriental, which reached Europe during the Middle Ages through Arabic. Many of Boccaccio's and Chaucer's tales have been traced back to India. Often there is a 'double or triple framing'. Secondly, the narrative mode in the Indian (or Oriental) tradition is non-realistic and fantastic. Thirdly, the framed stories are often variations of certain broad human experiences, no attempt being made to particularise either the characters or incidents in time and space. In fact, almost all narratives can be said to be variations played on a few archetypal patterns of human behaviour.

In a framed narrative, the frame could be passive or dynamic. A passive frame is one which functions only as a mechanical link among the diverse stories (as in *Decameron*). On the other hand, in a dynamic frame, there is constant mediation between the frame and the inset stories; each qualifying and commenting on the other (as in Chaucer's *Canterbury Tales*). Again, a dynamic frame may function as a counterpoint to the inset stories, providing the work multiplicity of point of view or polyphony to use Bakhtin's term (as in Boll's *The Lost Honour of Katherina Bloom*.) Or, the frame may provide a specific spatio-temporal context, as A. K. Ramanujan argues, to the inset story/stories (as in *The Hand Maid's Tale*.)

Generally, frames in Indian narratives are passive; they just serve to bring together assorted stories. Only in the case of *Panchatantra*, the frame has some dynamism in it: the five princes who are told the various stories learn something from each story and at the end their maturation is complete. From this point of view the frame in *A River Sutra* is both functional and dynamic.

The narrator in the frame, the retired bureaucrat, isn't a know-all wise man. Often, he doesn't either understand a tale told him or only partially understands it. After listening to the first tale ('The Monk's Story') he is 'disturbed'; and discusses the meaning of the story with his older friend Tariq Mia. Even Tariq Mia's explanation (that "the human heart has only one secret, the capacity to love") is beyond his comprehension. Similarly,

> Never has renunciation seemed such a middle-class sport."

after listening to the second story, the frame-narrator is perplexed and angry. He tells the readers: "I was upset by the old Mulla's accusation that I did not understand the World." Sometimes, even Mr. Chagla, his assistant, appears to be more knowledgeable. When Mr. Chagla states, as if he is stating the obvious, that "without desire there is no life", the frame-narrator is baffled. "I stared at him in astonishment", he adds.

The point to be noticed here is that the frame-narrator also grows as the novel progresses. In fact, from one point of view, he could be considered the centre around whom and whose process of perception and understanding of men and society, the entire novel revolves. When the novel begins, he is a 'Vana prasthi', and he is determined to be totally detached from the world, from the elevated position of self-assumed wisdom. But at the end, his older friend, Tariq Mia tells him: "Destiny is playing tricks on you. Don't you realize you were brought here to gain the world, not forsake it?" The retired bureaucrat is annoyed and claims that he knows the world well enough. Later, however, he realizes that still he is groping in the dark: "I stared at the flashes of illumination, wondering for the first time what I would do if I ever left the Bungalow".

More importantly, what is to be stressed in the structuring of the novel is its multiple focalisation. Tariq Mia, the friend-philosopher of the main narrator, is also limited in his grasp of men and matters. In fact, there is no single character in the novel whose knowledge of the world is not imperfect. Each tale, narrated from a limited point of view, is later discussed, analysed and commented upon, again in their limited comprehension, by the two frame characters, who share a sort of teacher-pupil relationship. In other words, the novelist here, consciously, seems to adapt the framework of the *Upanishads*—the pupil sitting close to the teacher and entering into a dialogue with him. In the very beginning of the novel, the writer underscores this point, making her principal narrator say: "Do you know what the word Upanishad means? It means to

" Naga Baba's transformation from a fossilised ascetic to a compassionate person who cares for the child and after rescuing her from brothel becomes her teacher and guardian is subtle. The teacher, in this process, himself learns to be kind and considerate. The enlightenment he attains enables him to realise that to shun people is not as challenging as to love and rear man."

sit beside and listen. Here I am, sitting, eager to listen.''

Now, coming to the framed tales, each of the seven tales is designed as a variation on the single theme of 'attachment.' While the frame-narrator is one who has renounced the world, the first inset-story is of the heir to an international diamond merchant, who also resolves (following the model of Mahavira) to renounce the world, yearning to be free from the world. But, after becoming a Jain Monk, having renounced every possession, he realises he has newer bonds with the world. After narrating his tale, he states, he has to hurry and join his brother monks. ''I am too poor to renounce the world twice'', he admits. And this admission bewilders the principal narrator. The succeeding tales also, similarly, play off the themes of 'attachment-detachment.' Whereas passionate attachment leads to tragic consequences in the 'Teacher's Story' and 'The Executive's Story', 'The Musician's Story' and 'The Minstrel's Story' uphold detachment. But again, the last story— 'The Song of the Narmada' —registers the futility of detachment. The Naga Baba returns to the world as an archaeologist and undertakes Narmada excavations. In other words, each tale either contradicts or qualifies the implications of the earlier tale/s (as in *Canterbury Tales*); and all the inset-tales are qualified by the frame.

Consequently, what we get at the end of the novel is a multiple vision of the 'many-coloured dome'—Life.

The vision of life implied by the totality of the text is a paradoxical position of both 'attachment-detachment.' The frame and a few inset-stories mount a serious critique of attachment to the world in the form of wealth, power and sensual indulgence. While the principle narrator is sick of a highly placed bureaucrat's life and voluntarily becomes a 'Vanaprastha', the narrator of the 'Executive's Story' is even more critical. He observes in his diary that he and his 'estate boys', in their drinking, gambling and wenching, indulged in ''Careless self-destruction.'' Similarly the singer in ''The Musician's Story'', transforms her unrequited love to the love of divine music.

However, the novel rejects the concept of total detachment as well. At one point, Mr. Chagla gravely states to the frame-narrator: ''But, Sir, without desire there is no life. Everything will stand still. Become emptiness. In fact, Sir, be dead.'' Prof. Shankar alias Naga Baba declares towards the end, dismissing the divinity of the river Narmada: ''If anything is sacred about the river, it is the individual experiences of the human beings who have lived here.''

Such profound affirmation of life and human experiencee is reinforced by repeated motifs of love and rebirth. The allusions to the penance of Uma to achieve Shiva's love, to the five arrows of Kama (Panchasayaka) which none can withstand, to the death of Kama (Kamadahana) which makes Kumara's birth possible, to the origins of Veena created by Shiva to immortalize Uma's immortal beauty, to the seven notes of music which are all drawn from Nature—all these allusions indirectly uphold the divinity of love, and conjugal bliss. The lyrics of the great Sufi poet Rumi, quoted here and there appropriately, again strengthen this motif—of love, both human and divine. In fact, the entire novel, *The River Sutra*, is a fascinating mosaic of rich and repetitive images, motifs, and allusions.

What places the novel at the centre of Indian narrative tradition is that each inset story seems to have been selected and elaborated with an awareness of the Indian Rass theory. For instance, the Monk's story, based on renunciation, has 'Shanta' as its Sthayi, and Karuna as Sanchari rasas. The Teacher's story, centred on greed and jealousy, evokes Bhibhatsa and concommitant Karuna. While the Courtesan's story evokes Sringara and Vira, the Executive's story Adbhuta and Hasya. While

Vipralambha Sringara and Karuna are communicated through the Teacher's story, Adbhuta and Karuna dominate the Minstrel's story. It is appropriate from this point of view that the novel's title is partially Indian: the River 'Sutra'.

The all-pervasive central symbol in the novel is the river Narmada. The novel captures her varied moods from varying angles. The river, born in the Vindhyas and flowing westwards, is the meeting point of all the central characters in the climatic moments of their lives. She is the "Delightful one", "forever holy, forever inexhaustible." If sometimes she appears as a bride, flowing to meet her bridegroom, the oceean with all ardour, some other times she has the allurement of a whore. In fact, as Dr. Mitra explains to the bureaucrat, 'narmada' in Sanskrit, also means 'a whore.' What interests Dr. Shankar, the archaeologist, in Narmada is not that it is a 'holy' river but that it is an immortal river. That is, "the Narmada has never changed its course. What we are seeing today is the same river that was seen by the people who lived here a hundred thousand years ago. To me such a sustained record of human presence in the same place—that is immortality." The cave drawings in the vicinity of Narmada are among the "oldest evidence of human life in India." The ancient Alexandrian geographer, Ptolemy, wrote about the Narmada. Vyasa is supposed to have dictated his Mahabharatha on this river bank and Kalidasa's works graphically describe the river and the nearby Vindya range. "It is as if reason and instinct are constantly warring on the banks of the Narmada. I mean, even the war between the Aryans and the pre-Aryans is still unresolved here."

Obviously, Narmada symbolises Life in general, and Indian culture and society in particular. The river, with Shiva and Supaneshwara temples on one side, the Muslim mosque and the tomb of the Sufi poet, Rumi, on the other and many Jain, Buddhist and tribal temples and shrines scattered over its course, symbolises the culture that is both ancient and modern, both monotheistic and theistic, and both Aryan and non-Aryan. In fact, *The River Sutra* could as well have been titled 'Bharath Sutra'.

2

Gita Mehta blazes a new trail after her *Karma Cola*'s "entertaining account of the consumerist West struggling to gobble up Hinduism and choking itself in process." The enlightenment she tried to pass on to the West must have prompted her to probe deep into the intricacies of Hinduism that needs reinterpretation in a language that the modern world can comprehend. Her *A River Sutra* is, in contrast to her *Karma Cola*, a serious probe not only in the mythology but also in the psychic depths of the conscious/sub-conscious/unconscious. It was no surprise that scholars tried to vie with one another in examining it at the Sixth International Commonwealth Conference held at Hyderabad (Oct. 93). Another Conference on Indian Writing in English held at Indore (Dec. 93) also evoked interest in the book.

While campaign to "Save Narmada" has already been launched by environmentalists and social activists like Medha Patkar, Baba Amte, Shabana Azmi; interest in Narmada as a river acquires great significance. It would be in the fitness of things to examine first what Gita has to say about Narmada.

A. G. Khan

I

Shankaracharya's poem on the river is a sublime hymn to Siva's daughter. She is Siva's *kripa* [(Grace)]. *Surasa* [(cleanser)], Rewa [(dancing deer)]. She is Delight and at the same is also the evoker of *Narma* (lust). She is twice-born, first of penance and then of love. If she evokes desire she also soothes. The serpent of desire is tamed on her banks. Though suicide is a sin it is a release from the cycle of rebirth if it is on the banks of Narmada. Because of its eroding power every pebble assumes the shape of a *lingam* as goes the proverb along her banks *Har Kankar ek Shankar* (every pebble is an object of worship). In order to attain Moksha one has to take a dip in the holy Ganges; but mere sight of the river ensures salvation. The devotees call her "Narmade Har!" (Cleanse us, Narmada, the Mother). The novel in this sense is not *A RIVER SUTRA* but *A RIVER STOTRA (STUTI)*: An eulogy to the great river.

In addition to the mythical probe that Gita brings to her work she also substantiates it with scientific data. Mr. Shankar, the archaeologist, explains why he loves Narmada:

"I'm afraid I only care for the river's immortality, not its holiness."

"It has a very fast current, which erodes the river bed, cutting deeper and deeper into the rock. But the Narmada has never changed its course.—To me such a sustained record of human presence in the same place—that is immortality."

"This river is an unbroken record of the human race. That is why I am here."

"You have chosen the wrong place to flee the world, my friend"—"Too many lives converge on these banks."

At this juncture we have to remind ourselves that if mythologically Narmada is Siva's daughter; here is a Shankar trying to explain its archaeological significance. By her choice of "Mr. Shankar" Gita Mehta has lent the narrative a subtle nuance.

From the literary point of view the river is not a *sutra* but a *sutradhar*. No, the narrator is not the real *sutradhar*. It is the river that unifies all the episodes into a great human drama. It integrates the tales into a coherence that several scholars fail to notice when they examine it from the narrator's perspective. Not only this, the river integrates Assam with the valleys of Vindhyas, the plains of Malwa. The tribal belief of Assamese folk-lore integrates Himalayas with the Vindhyas through Narmada—her capacity to cure the "possessed". There might seem an inner contradiction when we find that the two banks have different racial cultures, calendars, histories. Ved Vyas dictated *The Mahabharat* on the banks of this river. People still search for *Abhimanyu* , the elephant in the valleys of the Vindhyas. The Immortal Warrior of Supnaswara gives an indication of the legend. Though we are told that "instincts and reason" are warring here, yet people came here to seek solace and salvation. In this way, the title and the novel have an artistic relationship that establishes itself superbly.

II

If Melville's *Moby Dick* can be regarded as a *whale of books* in context of the Whale it describes, *A River Sutra* has several *sutras* to lead to myriad interpretations. It can be explored in terms of narrative technique, psychological insight in probing the unconscious/sub-conscious as well as the racial consciousness; sociological, archaeological, mythological explorations could also be fascinating. Equally fascinating would be the philosophy of music as enunciated in two separate tales.

From the narrative point of view the fifteen chapters flow from the origin to its final destination in a natural gush with frequent detours yet returning again and again to the main current: flowing placid sometimes but quite often with gusto.

While the narration by Narrator-1 is removed once from the actual participants, those by Narrator-2 (Tariq Mia) are distanced twice from the actual actors.

This paper, after such lengthy digression, seeks to study the characters under two categories: the fugitives and the steadfast. One must remember the fate of the fugitives in search of peace and serenity in the *Karma-Cola,* though in this case Gita Mehta begins a healing touch and grants them the desired enlightenment. The steadfast after their initial convulsions are rooted firmly and chase none; whereas the fugitives escape from some evil/fear to grasp some sheetanchor. The steadfasts are optimistically and confidently adhering to their piece of land. Their vision has reached beyond the horizon and have neither fear nor envy.

It must be noted that the characters are complementary. One can identify the mirror-images; the "other self" which when juxtaposed together can give fulness of character lending them the much desired symmetry. . . .

It is in the union of these opposites that we have a fuller view—the narrator-I who shuns society and abhors all mundane human activities (as mere *Maya*); Tariq Mia has the Sufi's wisdom to recognise "Don't you realize you were brought here to gain the world, not forsake it". Similarly, the Monk in Search of *Nirvana* has yet to reconcile to the idea that Naga Baba could grasp:

"Is this your enlightenment? Is this why you endured all these penances?" . . .

"Don't you know the soul must travel through eighty four thousand births in order to be a man?" Having earned life as man he does not want to squander it by renouncing. Hence as soon as wisdom dawns on him "Only then can it re-enter the world". Escape does not behove a man—the crown of creation, *Ashraful Makhluqat* (as the Muslims regard man). One cannot attain enlightenment through asceticism but through action—rational and benevolent. It is at this juncture that we discover the significance of the couplet from Chandidas' love song that acts as the foreword to the novel:

Listen, O brother.
Man is the greatest truth.
Nothing beyond.

Hence any sect that secludes man is myopic. This is what Tariq Mia was trying to convince the narrator.

Master Mohan, who failed as musician, tries to see rays of redemption in the blind disciple he adopted and yet was deprived of fulfilment of his ambition; the old father had his shock when his chosen disciple "escapes" and marries some other girl in place of the ugly daughter of the maestro. In one case the teacher was the failure, the disciple a success; in other, the teacher was a genius but the disciple a mediocre. If in one case there was a greedy and cantankerous nagging wife, in another, a patient and tolerant daughter. . . .

We see that these steadfasts are no longer goaded by any quest. Their patience, forbearance has been amply rewarded . . . banks of a river like Narmada. Her magic presence radiates the cure that can be an antidote to snake bite, or malevolent effect of the Saturn.

The old musician's daughter, the courtesan's daughter and the Naga Baba could act as nature and balanced person only because of the serenity that the river radiates on to people. Ugliness of body was compensated by nobility of soul. She is trying to become what her father wants her now to be:

"—that I must meditate on the waters of the Narmada, the symbol of Shiva's penance until I have cured myself of my attachment to what has passed and can become again the ragini to every raga".

"I must understand that I am the bride of music, not of a musician".

That love, the noblest passion, should drive the bandit to risk his life to please his beloved is a fact that the 'socialities' will find difficult to swallow. The world where "drink, shoot, and f——" reigns supreme; adoration for a woman might seem ridiculous. But having appreciated the sincerity and warmth of his love, the Courtesan's daughter forgets her "royal" expectations. Theirs became a companionship in which "we could be together for ever, and sometime we set to search for the warrior but never found him, distracted by our desire for each other". After her husband's death instead of returning to society's luxurious life as a Courtesan, she willingly drowned herself so that their love could remain untarnished.

The Naga Baba through his penances in the Himalayas and the deserts had developed capacity to conquer the limitations of the body. But his real *diksha* began when he was enjoined by his guru to beg at the houses of those who were untouchables, unclean or profane. This discipline to respect the humblest, to hate none, to find divinity even in the most depraved is initiation to wisdom. It is during such an errand that he rescues a child from a brothel resulting in a transformation of "chand" into Uma.

The "moonlight" was transformed into "peace of night".

By the serenity they have attained. We are reminded of Milton's line: "They also serve who stand and wait."

The three persons who emerge out of the trial and painful experience undergo a process of transmutation. The stage that the Brahmin is asked to attain through Yoga, where grief and joy no longer disturb the soul, has been attained by them. Such alchemy is possible only on the . . .

The message is crystal clear. None can triumph by negating the MAN. The first step towards enlightenment is to be humble:

you will be a social outcast.
you will be insulted.
you will be hounded.

But this is only the beginning. One cannot renounce the world so long as there are teeming millions in agony. One cannot afford to leave the toiling and suffering humanity to its fate and achieving Nirvana/Moksha only for oneself.

Naga Baba's transformation from a fossilised ascetic to a compassionate person who cares for the child and after rescuing her from the brothel becomes her teacher and guardian is subtle. The teacher, in this process, himself learns to be kind and considerate. The enlightenment he attains enables him to realise that to shun people is not as challenging as to love and rear man. While the monk was unwilling to renounce the world twice; Naga Baba returns to the world he had renounced.

Tariq Mia, the mullah of a small village seems to the narrator "frozen in time untouched by the events of a larger world" but this is the stage that Yogis aspire to. He has "games for older men" because the ignorant is the most certain of his wisdom, "the young believe they understand the world."

Not only these three but even the fugitives do not miss their cup of bliss! The narrator and the executive become wise and more mature, balanced, calm and serene when they are brought to the proximity of primitive life: folk dance, nature's abundant austerity teach them the bliss of solitude.

Taken as a whole the novel is a significant contribution to Indian writing in English—specially to the feminine writing which has all of a sudden in its aggressive stance resorted more to libido than to good sense. In addition, having debunked the conmen

> Mehta made her name with 'Karma Cola', a caustic reportage on the charlatans who milked the hippie-era fascination with Indian mysticism. Here, she unearths the wisdom buried by such folly."

of India in *Karma Cola* an attempt to restore the real saints to their pedestal was a necessity long felt. She has done her penance in a dignified manner.

Source: C. N. Ramachandran and A. G. Khan, "Gita Mehta's A River Sutra: Two Views," in *The Literary Criterion,* Vol. XXIX, No. 3, 1994, pp. 1–15.

The following brief review calls Gita Mehta's A River Sutra, *an embodiment of the art and craft of Indian storytelling, seamlessly weaving separate stories together into a wider framework, producing compelling narratives which do not shy away from the socio-political complexities of the geographical setting.*

This novel of India beautifully embodies the art and craft of storytelling as Mehta (*Karma Cola; Raj*) portrays diverse lives touched by the river Narmada, a holy pilgrimage site "worshipped as the daughter of the god Shiva." At the heart of the work is an unnamed retired civil servant, the narrator, who desires only the peace and quiet of a contemplative life on the river. His neighbor, a religious teacher, comments: "Don't you realize you were brought here to gain the world, not forsake it?" That world shows up in the form of various seekers—among them, a monk, an executive, a courtesan—whose stories occupy separate chapters but are seamlessly woven into the main narrative for our delight and edification (as the "sutra" of the title implies). Perhaps the most beautiful vignette is "The Musician's Story," in which an 18-year-old sitar player, daughter of a famous musician and teacher, comes to the river seeking relief from the ache of unrequited love. The music of India, the raga, figures prominently in other chapters too. As characters reveal the pleasure and pain that have shaped their lives, Mehta discloses the wonders of this coun-

try—the Jain religion; savory samosas and pickled mangoes; bazaars where one can choose from "glass bangles," "clouds of spun sugar" or "a bar of soap with a film star's face on the wrapping." Mehta does not avoid the controversies of life in her homeland, including the caste system and political/religious rivalries; rather, she willingly exposes its complexities. A charming and useful glossary of foreign terms makes a second journey through the fascinating text irresistible.

Source: "A River Sutra," (book review) in *Publisher's Weekly,* Vol. 240, No. 13, March 29, 1993, p. 33.

Boyd Tonkin

In the following brief review of Gita Mehta's A River Sutra, *Boyd Tonkin praises the novel as didactic and refreshing prose, part of an Indo-British wave of writers who confirm that the "cultural passage between south Asia and the west can still yield fresh perspectives."*

The stumbling nonentities who pass these days for cabinet ministers love to invoke the glories of our language. As if, with their ghastly off-the-peg cliches about village greens and warm beer, they had any right to act as its custodians. In fact, English as a literary medium has been rescued by regular shots of alien talent: Irish, American, Carribean and Asian. Most of its present glory comes from authors who would fail the Tebbit "cricket test" with flying colours.

Among them, the tribe of Indo-British writers conspicuously thrives. Two new works—both second novels—confirm that the cultural passage between south Asia and the west can still yield fresh perspectives. "A River Sutra" by Gita Mehta unfolds within a wholly Indian world of fable and folklore; but its implied reader is western and it reflects a cosmopolitan intellectual's rediscovery of roots. Mehta made her name with "Karma Cola", a caustic reportage on the charlatans who milked the hippie-era fascination with Indian mysticism. Here, she unearths the wisdom buried by such folly.

A civil servant retires to what he imagines will be a time of contemplation, as warden of a guest house beside a holy river. Soon, unbidden visitors arrive with stories that disclose the deep structure of Indian art and myth. A music teacher's tale explores the Sufi spirituality that softened Islam in India; a sexually obsessed executive pays unwilling tribute to Kama, god of love; and so on. "Adrift in the strangeness of other people's lives," the bureaucraft undergoes a refresher course in subcontinental civilisation. Mildly didactic it may be, but the compelling prose of "A River Sutra" flows as swiftly as the sacred stream. . . .

Source: Boyd Tonkin "A River Sutra," (book review) in *New Stateman & Society,* Vol. 6, No. 257, June 18, 1993, p. 41.

Sources

Foley, Milton J., "The Hero's Quest: Heroic Visions in *The Bhagavad Gita* and the Western Epic," in *English*, 1993, pp. 89-100.

Review in *Publishers Weekly*, Vol. 240, No. 13, March 29, 1993, p. 33.

Smith, Wendy, "Gita Mehta: Making India Accessible," *Publishers Weekly*, Vol. 244, No. 19, May 12, 1997, p. 53.

Worthington, Christa, *Harper's Bazaar*, 1989, p. 73.

Further Reading

Beck, Brenda, *The Three Twins: The Telling of a South Indian Folk Epic*, Indiana University Press, 1982.
    This book gives insight into the oral epic tradition in Indian culture and allows the reader to see how Mehta borrowed from such traditions in *A River Sutra*.

Mehta, Gita, *Karma Cola*, Simon & Schuster, 1979.
    In her first book, Mehta explores the humorous ways in which Americans try to understand India and Indians try to understand America.

———, *Raj*, Simon & Schuster, 1989.
    In this historical novel, Mehta presents a poignant picture of India under British imperialism and the struggle for freedom.

———, *Snakes and Ladders: Glimpses of Modern India*, Doubleday, 1997.
    This collection of essays documents the hardships and successes of Indians adapting to the technological advances of the modern world.

Smith, Wendy, "Gita Mehta: Making India Accessible," in *Publishers Weekly*, Vol. 244, No. 19, May 12, 1997, p. 53.
    In this article, Smith explores Mehta's development as a writer.

Vatuck, Ved Prakash, *Studies in Indian Folk Traditions*, Manohar, 1979.
    In this book, Vatuck provides background on the Indian folklore that Mehta describes in *A River Sutra*.

Seth and Samona

Joanne Hyppolite

1995

At the center of Joanne Hyppolite's novel for young adults, *Seth and Samona*, is the idea of having faith in human beings, of accepting differences and hoping for the best from others. The novel is narrated by Seth Michelin, an eleven-year-old boy whose family has immigrated from Haiti to Boston, Massachusetts. Seth's parents, grandmother, and numerous aunts and uncles still follow many of the cultural practices that they followed in the old country, while Seth and his brother and sister are faced with blending their cultural tradition into the world where they live now. Samona Gemini is Seth's classmate and his closest friend, even though he goes out of his way to pretend that he is embarrassed by her. Like Seth, Samona does not exactly fit into the social atmosphere of their fifth grade class. While Seth is quiet and withdrawn, Samona is loud and outgoing, given to lying, bragging, and drawing attention to herself. Seth repeatedly calls Samona ''crazy'' and he pretends to pity her because she will never have friends until she acts ''normal.'' Still, it is obvious from the way he acts toward her that, despite what he says, he admires her for the freedom that he lacks. *Seth and Samona* was the winner of the second annual Marguarite de Angeli Prize, and has won critical and popular acclaim for Hyppolite.

Author Biography

Seth and Samona is Joanne Hyppolite's first book, published when she was twenty-six years old. Hyppolite was born in Les Cayes, Haiti, in 1969, but her life in that country was brief: like Seth in the novel, her family moved to the United States when she was young, just four years old. She grew up in Dorchester, a predominantly Haitian area of Boston, which is where the novel takes place. After earning a bachelor's degree in creative writing from the University of Pennsylvania, she went on to study at the University of California at Los Angeles, where she earned her master's degree from the Department of Afro-American Studies. *Seth and Samona*, which was published in 1995, was awarded the Second Annual Marguerite de Angeli Prize from Delacorte Press, which published the book. Hyppolite's second novel, *Ola Shakes It Up*, is about a nine-year-old girl who moves from the city to a placid suburban community and tries to make it as lively as her old Boston neighborhood. Currently, Joanne Hyppolite lives in Miami, Florida, where she teaches and writes and is studying for her doctorate degree in Caribbean literature. Asked what her inspiration for writing is, she responded, "Life. It continually surprises one. If you can capture a piece of that in your writing, then you've accomplished something."

Plot Summary

Mrs. Fabiyi's House

This book is about the begrudging friendship between the narrator, Seth Michelin, who lives in Dorchester area of Boston, and a schoolmate of his, Samona Gemini. They are both eleven years old and in fifth grade. Seth's family is from Haiti, and Samona's mother, who is raising the children by herself, is a poet and an undercover reporter for a disreputable magazine. After a short background about how they met two years earlier, the first of their adventures begins. It happened, as Seth's narration explains, "last Wednesday," when Samona raced up to him on the sidewalk, insisting that he accompany her to Mrs. Fabiyi's house. Mrs. Fabiyi is a strange neighborhood lady from Nigeria who threw cold soup on them the previous Halloween. She has not be around for more than a week, and Samona says they should go and see if she is ill,

although when pressed she explains that her real reason for wanting to go is because her cat has gone over there and she wants to make sure it is all right. To get Seth to go, she reminds him that Mrs. Fabiyi's house is a mystery to all of the children at school, and entering it would make them "the coolest kids in the fifth grade."

They take food to Mrs. Fabiyi, but at first they find her house empty. As they are walking down a dim, deserted corridor, a panel opens in the wall and the weird old woman comes out waving a piece of wood at them. Samona explains that they brought the food for her, in case she was sick, and Mrs. Fabiyi thinks this is funny. She was just away visiting her sister in Nigeria, she explains. She threw cold soup on them on Halloween as part of the Trick or Treat fun. She invites them in and they see her house decorated with African art and find the cat playing with Mrs. Fabiyi's cat. At the end of the second chapter, Samona stuns Seth by announcing that she is going to participate in the Little Miss Dorchester pageant.

The Wake

Returning home from Mrs. Fabiyi's house, Seth encounters the strange sight of several of his aunts and uncles gathered in his parents' living room, with the lights dim and the curtains drawn. One aunt who never drinks is drinking, an uncle who always laughs is not laughing, and an aunt who always prays is praying. Seth feels panicky before they tell him that his grandmother's sister, Matant Margaret, has died. She is a distant relative who lived in a nursing home, and Seth hardly knew her. His older brother and sister, Jean-Claude and Chantal, go about their normal lives—especially Chantal, who talks on the phone with her boyfriend Jerome and is disappointed because she will have to miss a date with him because of the wake. Still, Seth's grandmother is so overcome with sorrow that she takes to her bed. Seth does not know what to make of all of this sorrow, and he does not know what a wake is, only that he will miss school later in the week to attend one.

The next day Samona tells Seth and his younger cousin Enrie that her brothers had been to a wake for her aunt Delia the year before. When Seth points out that Aunt Delia is still alive, she explains that it is because the wake was successful, that the mourners prayed so hard that Aunt Delia rose up from the dead. Seth does not accept her explanation, but the whole time at the wake he is alert, in case Matant Margaret should rise up, shaking everybody's hands.

At the wake, Seth observes his relatives who have come from all over the country and from Haiti and Canada, and their respect for Matant Margaret makes him feel sorrow for her death. The day after the funeral he goes to Samona's house with food left over from the funeral and he observes the chaotic situation of her family. Returning home, he talks to his father about how strange the people in the Gemini household are, and his father explains that, "Different doesn't mean bad. It just means different."

Jerome

The following Sunday Seth hears his brother and sister fighting again: Jean-Claude does not approve of her dating Jerome, especially since she sneaks out to see him without their parents' permission. She does not like the way her family casts her into the traditional female role, expecting her to do all of the cooking and cleaning and to grow up to be a nurse, when she has higher aspirations, and Jean-Claude thinks that Jerome put these ideas in her head. He leaves the house after saying, "I could kill Jerome for all of the trouble he's making for her," and mentioning that he is going to see Reggie, a tough, gun-toting gang member. Seth cannot get away to follow Jean-Claude until he has taken his grandmother to church, but then he sneaks away and goes to the Baptist church where the Gemini family worships, to ask Samona's older brother Anthony for help in finding Reggie.

Anthony takes Seth and Samona in his car to where he thinks Reggie might be staying, and he orders the children to stay in the car while he goes in. While he is gone, though, they see Reggie walk by, so they run after him. Samona calls out his name, and Reggie turns on them with his gun drawn, but Anthony stops him before he shoots. Reggie tells them that Jean-Claude had been there but already left for the 7-Eleven, where Jerome works.

They find Jean-Claude outside of the store, and he explains that he came to fight with Jerome but that he could not bring himself to do it. He still feels guilty, though, for having thought about it. When they go home, Chantal says that she is going to tell their parents that she is dating Jerome, and about her plans for the future.

The Beauty Contest

When Seth tells his family that Samona plans to enter the Little Miss Dorchester beauty pageant, he is surprised that they are supportive of her. Chantal is glad that someone with talent is going to be in the contest, while Jean-Claude doubts that the judges will be able to appreciate her beauty because she is black. The more people mention her attributes, the angrier Seth becomes, because he refuses to admit that she is either good-looking or talented.

To prepare for the competition, Samona practices with Bessie Armstrong, another girl in their class who is popular. She goes to Seth's house and has her hair and makeup done by his sister, mother and grandmother. She begins going over to Mrs. Fabiyi's house, but Seth cannot tell why. He begins to worry that she will lose her individuality if she changes too much in order to win the competition.

All of the members of both families attend the Little Miss Dorchester pageant. Samona creates a stir when she comes out on stage with a Nigerian dress and a colorful headdress. For the talent portion, she wears a worn old shirt and carries a basket on her head. When it is time to perform, though, she freezes with stage fright. In order to help her loosen up, Seth, who throughout the book acts embarrassed by Samona's behavior, stands in front of the stage and does the "funky chicken" dance that Samona often did. Laughing at him eases her stage fright, and Samona gives a rendition of Sojourner Truth's famous "aren't I a woman?" speech. She wins second place and the approval of a teacher who had disliked her previously, and Seth, who has always grumbled about her antics, congratulates her. In response, she sticks out her tongue at him, comforting Seth that being in the contest has not changed her completely: "That's when I knew for sure that the old Samona was still there."

Characters

Bessie Armstrong

Bessie is a pretty girl in Seth and Samona's class at school. When she talks to Seth, admiring him for having the nerve to go to Mrs. Fabiyi's house, he is flustered and unable to talk. Later, when she is preparing for the beauty competition, Samona becomes friends with Bessie. She tells Seth that Bessie's mother does not like noise, so she has to play quietly, and that there is no fun around her house, and they both pity her.

Mrs. Fabiyi

In the beginning of the book Seth and Samona fear Mrs. Fabiyi, a strange old Nigerian woman who lives on their block. The previous Halloween, she had thrown a pot of cold vegetable soup on them, and all of the children are afraid of the strange things she keeps in her house. Samona talks Seth into skipping his piano lesson and going to Mrs. Fabiyi's house, using the excuse that they are worried because she has not been around for some time but actually because Samona is worried that the old woman has stolen her cat. They find out that she had been away visiting her sister, that the cat was visiting Mrs. Fabiyi's cat, and that the soup was her attempt to play a trick on Halloween, to have some fun with them. Later in the book, Samona visits Mrs. Fabiyi in preparation for the Little Miss Dorchester contest, and Seth visits on his own to find out what Samona is up to, learning to relate to her as a person and not as a witch.

Anthony Gemini

Samona's older brother used to be involved with gangs, but he quit that after being arrested and spending a short time in the juvenile detention center. He has a scar on his face from a gang fight. Now he works on drawing because he wants to be an architect. Anthony is a friend of Reggie, the tough street gang leader whom Seth thinks his brother is going to see for help against Jerome, and so Seth goes to Anthony for help in finding Reggie before his brother can. They take Anthony's convertible and race over to where Reggie is staying, and Anthony acts as a mediator between Reggie and the kids.

Binta Gemini

Samona's mother is a poet of some accomplishment, having once been featured on a Public Broadcasting System special about poets from the Black Power movement of the 1960s. Because she cannot make much money writing poems, she also does undercover investigative reporting for a news magazine, the *Intruder*. The date whom she brings with her to the Little Miss Dorchester beauty pageant, Mr. Biggs, is an ex-minister from the Nation of Islam that she is investigating for the magazine. Mrs. Gemini calls Seth ''Young King'' because ''she always says I look like I have the burden of a kingdom on my shoulders.'' She was never married to Samona's father, who left them shortly before they moved to Boston two years earlier.

Leticia Gemini

When Leticia found out that her boyfriend Tyrone was cheating on her, Samona tells Seth, she invited him over and baked him a meatloaf with dog food, to point out that he had behaved like a dog. Samona's older sister runs a psychic hot line from the phone, and when she is busy she has Samona talk to her customers. On the day that Seth visits her family, Leticia is busy practicing opera singing, having seen Leontyne Price on the television. Before Chantal started dating Jerome, Leticia and she were best of friends, and when it is feared that Jean-Claude has gone to fight with Jerome Leticia's first reaction is to go to Chantal for support.

Nigel Gemini

Samona's other older brother, Nigel, is the one who has never been in trouble. He is studying at Boston College to be an engineer, and at home he is an inventor. He has had his family crushing grapes in a plastic swimming pool so that they can make Gemini Wine, but he later admits that this was a bad idea because wine has to sit for about fifty years before it is any good, and so even though their children will someday become rich off of the idea it won't help in the present. While Seth is over at the Gemini house Nigel comes up with the idea of making a love potion out of vegetables, and he and Anthony race out into their mother's garden to steal what he hopes will be the necessary ingredients before she finds out.

Samona Gemini

Samona is a strong-willed individualist, unafraid to speak her mind and willing to try out new clothes and new ideas without fear of embarrassment. She sells shampoo that has manure in it door-to-door, she takes a wrong turn at the zoo and ends up in the middle of Monkey Paradise, and she leads Seth to Mrs. Fabiyi's house spreading the wild story that the old lady stole her cat and ate it. Samona's overactive imagination and her impetuousness are reflected in her home life, in her mother's creativity as a poet and as an investigative journalist and her siblings' various schemes to make money. In the last section of the book, readers are made to worry for Samona because she looks headed for embarrassment at the Little Miss Dorchester competition. This concern is heightened by the fact that, as Seth points out, so much of Samona's identity involves acting without self-consciousness, so that embarrassment would change her completely: ''Samona couldn't do anything because she was trying to be somebody normal. Only this somebody normal didn't have Samona's guts or her attitude.'' Seth is so concerned about what would be lost by Samona becoming "normal" that he embarrasses himself in order to make her laugh and feel at ease.

Granme

Seth's grandmother lives with his family and shares a room with his sister Chantal. She does not speak English, only Kreyol, the combination of French and English that is the dialect of Haiti. When her sister dies, relatives come from all over the United States and Canada to pay homage to Granme—"It was a real big deal that she was the oldest living person in the family," Seth explains. Granme is steeped in tradition and sometimes confused by American ways, such as when she complains about Samona's hairstyle.

Manmi

Seth's mother is a nurse at the hospital. She has a new hairstyle and she likes it, even though it did not seem that she would: as Seth once pointed out to Samona's mother, "Haitians *like* to be old-fashioned." Seth's mother holds strongly to Haitian tradition and the Catholic church.

Chantal Michelin

Seth's sister has one of the hardest roles in her family. Because of the sexist traditions of Haitian culture, she is treated as if she is only good for menial labor, even though as an American citizen she is fully aware that she can accomplish much more than she is allowed to. According to tradition, she should grow up to be a housewife or a nurse, but Chantal wants to work in politics and help people. Added to her quest for independence is the age-old problem of her family being protective of her as she reaches the age where she wants to go out with boys. Her relationship with Jerome is secret until the episode where Jean-Claude goes out to fight with him; after that she decides that it is best to be honest and tell her parents about Jerome, but they still decide that she is too young to start dating.

Jean-Claude Michelin

Seth's older brother is a pacifist, well respected in the streets for stopping fights and for working with gang members who want to make their lives better. He is concerned with his identity as a black man and rejects traditional American concepts of "beauty" as a way of excluding black people and making them feel inferior. Jean-Claude is somewhat old-fashioned in his views: when Chantal develops the idea of being an independent woman, Jean-Claude assumes that the idea was put into her

head by her boyfriend Jerome, and he becomes so angry about it that he almost gets into a fight with Jerome, in spite of the fact that fighting goes against his deepest beliefs. He comes to his senses in time, though, and the fact that he nearly committed such a rash action makes him reconsider his beliefs and realize that he was treating his sister in a sexist way instead of letting her be her self.

Seth Michelin

The narrator of the novel, Seth is in fifth grade, the son of Haitian immigrants. His exploits in this novel include confronting the old neighborhood woman that all of the children fear, attending his first wake, and trying to keep his older brother out of a fight, but the main focus, that keeps all of these different stories together, is Seth's development of a sense of who he is. Like many children of immigrants, Seth practices the customs of the old country when he is at home, including speaking French and eating Haitian food. When he goes to school, though, he is like the other American kids, playing basketball with his friends, shy around girls. The novel strongly implies that, even though he often complains about Samona's strange behavior, he actually admires it, going out of his way to find out what she is up to even while he is complaining that he would like her to leave him alone. Since Seth is so conscious of his family's old-world ways, his attraction to Samona seems to be the way that she can be comfortable with her position as a social outcast. The fact that the members of his family and Bessie Armstrong think well of Samona raises suspicions about whether she is really the social outcast Seth tells readers she is, or if he just emphasizes her bad points in order to help himself deny his attraction to her.

Papi

Seth's father once dreamed of being an airplane pilot, but he could not afford lessons and could not join the Air Force to learn to fly, so he works at the airport, in the baggage section of Air France. He plays on a soccer team, the Mighty Spiders, on weekends.

Reggie

Reggie is a gang member well-known in the neighborhood. He has been in jail twice already, even though he is only sixteen. Jean-Claude works with Reggie, trying to keep him out of trouble. He has taught Reggie how to read, with the hope that he could better himself. When Jean-Claude races out of the house, angry at Jerome, he says that he is going to see Reggie, and Seth worries that he might ask Reggie to beat Jerome up or even kill him. When Anthony helps him find Reggie, Seth runs after him with Samona, and she calls out Reggie's name. He pulls his gun on the children before Anthony arrives and prevents him from shooting.

Tone

See Anthony Gemini

Themes

Racism

The main characters never experience racism directly within this story, but the effects of life within a racist society surround them. One clear example of this is shown in Jean-Claude's fatalism about how the Little Miss Dorchester competition will turn out: Some light-skinned, long-haired little girl that conforms to the judges' twisted concepts of beautiful will win as usual,'' he says sarcastically. ''When people say 'Black is Beautiful,' they usually mean the brighter the black the more beautiful.'' He ends up being wrong—although people are upset when Samona does not win, no one suggests that the judges were motivated by racism. Because Seth and Samona interact only with other black characters in this story, and because they understand their social discomfort to be unique to their personalities (Samona's because she is a free spirit, Seth's because of his Haitian background), they do not dwell on the pressures of racism. The older characters recognize the social disadvantages caused by racism, but they do not make much of this burden when understanding their own potential.

Death

A child's first experience of death is always an important event, and Hyppolite features Seth's brush with death in an extended segment of this story. The mystery of death is dealt with calmly and with humor, by having Seth half-believe Samona's tall tale about the deceased person coming back to life at the wake if the mourners pray hard enough. This explanation serves a higher purpose than just providing readers with laughs at Seth's expense, though: it helps to focus his attention on the intensity of the grief felt by those around him. Although he is not very familiar with the dead woman, his grandmother's sister, and he does not know the out-of-town mourners who have come to stay with his family, still he recognizes their sadness. He is able to accept the strangeness of a formal wake because he expects even worse supernatural strangeness. Thinking about the deceased, Matant Margaret, Seth recalls a story he once heard about her loving relationship with her own grandfather, and the fact that she did not cry at his wake, even though they were very close. This helps him deal with his fear and concentrate on the good things he has heard about Matant Margaret's life.

Culture Clash

Both Seth and Samona have problems fitting into society. For Samona, the problem is caused by being and individualist and non-conformist, which are traits that her mother seems to encourage in her children. Seth repeatedly makes a point of how unpopular Samona is and how he thinks he should stay away from her, even though he always finds some reason, however weak, to go and see her. ''You'll get a terrible reputation,'' he tells her at one point, regarding her lying. ''That's why I don't like to hang around with you—.'' Still, when he sees her dressed up for the beauty pageant he realizes how bad she feels about being an outcast from the dominant culture, and he thinks of what a shame it would be for Samona to change her unique personality just to fit in. With his own family, Seth and his brothers and sisters have to struggle against their parents' Haitian traditions, because they understand American society better than their parents ever will. Jean-Claude is admired in the streets as someone who can bring peace to violent situations—''Everybody trusts Jean-Claude''—but in his parents' house he is talked about derisively because of his new, modern haircut and the earring he wears. For Chantal it is worse: she knows what women can accomplish and she has high expectations for herself, but her family assigns her the traditional role for a woman, to clean and cook.

Difference

At the end, when he does Samona's ''funky chicken dance'' to get her to loosen up and forget her stage fright, Seth shows that he is accepting the parts of her personality that he always tried to keep away from. Even though he admits that he likes the new look that his grandmother, mother and sister give Samona, he worries that changing her exterior will change what is unique inside. When she becomes friends with Bessie Armstrong, Seth's values are confused. He previously admired Bessie for her

Topics for Further Study

- Explore the stories of some famous women whose families came from countries that did not encourage women's independence, and report on how they overcame the difficulties put in their way.

- Are American beauty contests becoming more open to people who look like Samona, or are they still steeped in the European concept of beauty, favoring girls with fair skin? Provide evidence to support your answer.

- After Christianity, voodoo is the most common religion practiced in Haiti. Read about voodoo cultural practices, and explain what aspects of his family's background may have helped Seth believe Samona's story about what goes on at a wake.

- Chantal expresses the wish to go back to Haiti and help the people there who are politically oppressed. Report on the situation in Haiti in 1995, when this novel was published, and what it is like today.

- Find a recording of James Brown's song "Superbad," and choreograph your own funky chicken dance to it.

- In this book, Jean-Claude teaches Reggie, a gang member, to read, and Anthony returns to school after a stay in the juvenile detention center. Explore the statistics on gang members who reform, and report on the programs that show the most success.

---

good looks, but now Samona looks like Bessie; he had wished Samona was not so different from the other girls, and Samona had become more average for the competition; still, he panics at the thought of Samona losing her uniqueness. Even though the talent that Samona chooses to display for the sow—a dramatic rendition of Sojourner Truth's speech—is a personal, individual choice, it is not one that she is entirely comfortable with, or she would not freeze up as she does. By making her laugh with his parody of her old, goofy style, Seth shows how much he appreciates what is unique about her.

Style

Point of View

Seth Michelin is the narrator of this story, and as a result the events that readers see are filtered through the mind of this eleven-year-old boy. For the most part, this is what makes the story interesting. He comes from a Haitian family and lives in the working-class section of a big city during the 1990s,

and this is a perspective that is not often shown in books. Readers find that their expectations about the types of people who live in Seth's world are overturned by reading this story. Not only does Mrs. Fabiyi, the strange old lady, turn out to actually be nice, which is a standard turn of events in many children's stories, but *Seth and Samona* breaks stereotypes with characters like Anthony, a former gang member who had gone on to college; Reggie, a current gang member who is learning to read and is slowly breaking away from the culture of violence; Chantal, who is respectful of her parents' Haitian and also rebellious; and Bessie Armstrong, who is pretty and popular but who can also be seen with pity because of her joyless home life. Readers come to understand these characters and others because of Seth's interaction with them, and their unique qualities make perfect sense because Seth accepts them so casually as part of his world.

As a narrator, though, Seth cannot be trusted entirely. Like most typical eleven-year-old boys, he is not willing to admit that he likes a girl, especially a girl who is as unique and exotic as Samona. As a result, he often makes a point of complaining about her and he puts her down with mild insults. This is clear from the book's first page, telling of their first encounter. Seth is captivated by Samona because he can see her underwear, and he cannot stop staring at her, but rather than admit any attraction, as he tells the reader, "Right then and there I thought, 'That Samona Gemini is one crazy girl and I plan to stay away from her.'" Of course, he does not, and the rest of the book is about adventures that they have together, with Seth weakly making excuses about how fate throws them together time and again in spite of his "lifelong plan of avoiding her."

Episodic Plot

Unlike most novels, which follow one story from beginning to end, *Seth and Samona* is told as a series of episodes. The story of their visit to Mrs. Fabiyi's house is completely finished before the episode about the wake for Matant Margaret begins; the next story, about Jean-Claude and Jerome, begins just after the visitors who came to town for the funeral leave; and the plans for the Little Miss Dorchester contest are only seriously discussed after that plot line is finished. There are some overlapping points between these stories, so that none of them could actually stand alone without having a few sentences edited out. For instance, the beauty contest is mentioned as early as the end of Chapter 2, and Mrs. Fabiyi, who Samona learned not to fear in the first section, helps Samona in the last. Chantal's relationship with Jerome is just mentioned in the section about the wake, preparing readers for the time a few chapters later when it will be at the center of the plot. And the fact that Mr. Biggs, who is Mrs. Gemini's date for the beauty pageant, is an ex-Nation of Islam minister is referred to back in chapter 5, when she says that she has a magazine assignment to investigate an ex-minister. The plot is easy to follow because it consists of four short stories instead of one long, complex one, but it also connects those stories together smoothly.

Climax

Even though this novel consists of four stories, the end of the final one is clearly the high point of the book. Each of the individual stories has something to tell readers about courage, about family, about meeting social expectations and going beyond them, but it is Samona's triumphant performance at the Little Miss Dorchester competition that summarizes what the book is all about. For one thing, it strikes a balance between Samona's goofy,

childish behavior of earlier escapades and the "new Samona," the one with curled hair and makeup, which Seth fears will erase all of the individuality from her. Also, the finale shows Seth changing, loosening up from his attitude about Samona's youthful fun. His chicken dance in front of the entire auditorium shows that, when it comes down to it, despite his complaining, he will do what he has to do to help his friend Samona, and also that her oddball behavior is more important to him than social acceptance. It is telling that Samona's performance at the book's climax is Sojourner Truth's speech, which supports the rights of blacks, women and the poor, who have in the past been made outcasts in American society. Samona is striking a blow for individuality by using the intellectual approach of history, while Seth supports individuality with unique behavior. In this moment they both reverse roles and come to see the world from the other person's perspective.

Literary Heritage

Haiti has always been one of the poorest countries in the Western Hemisphere, and as a result literature has not been a high priority for its inhabitants. To this day, between twenty and forty-five percent of the country's inhabitants are unable to read, and those who have been able to attain an education have used it to fight against the country's debilitating poverty. In addition to this, women have been abandoned to a secondary position in Haitian society, as is seen in *Seth and Samona* by Chantal's struggle against her parents' expectations that she will be a housekeeper or take a menial job. As a result of these conditions, there is not a very large canon of writing by Haitian women.

The first novels by Haitian women began appearing around 1934, at the end of the U.S. occupation of the country. As with many cultures, the first female authors wrote romances, writing to an audience of other women, not taken seriously as literary artists. For the following decades, Haitian writers in general, and women in particular, were virtually ignored by American and European literary establishments. It was only during the 1960s, with the ascendancy of the Civil Rights movement and the Women's Rights movement, that individual writers from Haiti began to make their mark. By the 1990s, when the excessive violence and repression if the Duvalier government and its military successors became international news, the world was hungry for information about Haiti. In response to the repressive government, a literature of social consciousness and rebellion had grown up among the people who had escaped Haitian poverty but could not forget it. Most of the Haitian writers who have established any degree of fame are, like Joanne Hyppolite, emigrants who have left the country and are looking back on the life that they once knew.

Historical Context

Haiti

The country that Seth's family comes from, Haiti, is an island in the Caribbean Sea. It is part of a string of islands known as the West Indies, which stretches from the Yucatan peninsula of Mexico to the coast of Florida. There are about 7.2 million people in Haiti, of which roughly seventy-five percent live in poverty (by comparison, the U.S. poverty rate was fourteen percent in 1995). The country has a history of poverty, which has itself caused even worse poverty. There is no industry, and only about one-fifth of the land can be used for farming because careless farming techniques in the past have leeched all of the nutrients out of the soil. Diseases, from AIDS to tuberculosis, run rampant because the country has no resources for an effective public health policy. The country has little hope of keeping up with the technological boom, since only forty to forty-five percent of the population knows how to read. Newspaper circulation is three per one thousand people; there is one telephone per 164 people, and one television for every 260 people. The life expectancy for men is 47 years of age, and for women it is 51, while in the United States it is 73 for men and 79 for women.

The main reason for Haiti's poverty is its economic development throughout history. European culture came to Haiti in 1492, when Christopher Columbus landed there. It was a base for the slave trade in the 1700s, which has led to a population descended from African heritage and to the country's French influence, which is evident in the *kreyol* language Seth's grandmother speaks (*kreyol*, commonly spelled *creole*, is a mixture of French, English and African dialects). In 1801 Haiti declared itself free from France, but its history had been a struggle to hold onto its freedom. From 1915 to 1934 the country was occupied by the United States in order to keep France and Spain from establishing forces in the Western Hemisphere.

After World War II Haiti came under the control of the Duvalier family. François Duvalier was elected in 1957, and by 1958 he declared absolute rule, outlawing his political rivals. When he died in 1971 his son Jean Claude Duvalier took control. Popular unrest drove him into exile in 1986, after which chaos ruled, with a quick succession of governments. In 1990 Jean-Bertrand Aristide, a Roman Catholic priest and advocate of the poor, was elected, but the military refused to let him rule, and he was driven into exile. Aristide's supporters continued to stand up to the government, and in return the government fought the people, committing numerous atrocities and human rights violations. In 1994 United States diplomatic forces forced the military leader to let Aristide return to the office that was rightfully his. He ruled until his successor was elected in 1996.

Sojourner Truth

The speech that Samona recites for the talent part of the Little Miss Dorchester competition is one of the most famous speeches in American history. It was given by former slave Sojourner Truth at the 1851 Women's Rights Convention in Akron, Ohio. She as born with the name Isabella in 1797 or 1798 in upstate New York. She was a slave from the time of her birth until slavery was abolished in New York in 1828. After that, she became a Protestant preacher and worked with the poor in New York City. She changed her name to Sojourner Truth in 1843 and took off preaching across the country. She became involved in the movement to abolish slavery, and then later in the Women's Rights movement.

There is some doubt about the actual wording of her famous "Ain't I A Woman?" speech because the person who is said to have written it down, Frances Gage, who was president of the convention, did not publish it until twelve years later. Still, there is no doubt about the powerful effect of the speech. It was given after the convention had been addressed by several male ministers on the subject of male superiority, claiming that God meant men to be superior because Jesus was a man and because men were intellectually superior. Sojourner Truth's response was not rehearsed or in any way planned: she just walked to the podium and spoke to the audience.

For the next twenty years, Sojourner Truth traveled the country, speaking and preaching. She met with President Lincoln in 1864 to encourage him to go ahead with his plans to free the slaves. In 1875 she retired to Battle Creek, Michigan, where she died in 1883.

Critical Overview

Since its first publication in 1995, *Seth and Samona* has been lavished with critical praise, with its admirers only infrequently able to find small points to question. The book's publisher, Delacorte Press, awarded it the second annual Marguarite de Angeli Prize for that year. It has become a staple on lists of books that offer multicultural views to school children and among books concerned with bringing the Haitian experience to readers of all ages. Most reviewers have felt that this novel offers compelling characterizations, realistic situations and a look at the lives of blacks in America, Haitian-Americans in particular, that looks at important social issues without preaching. As the review in the *School Library Journal* explained it for library purchasing boards that were considering this book for their collection, "the dialog and characterizations combine flawlessly to give Seth a loud, clear voice; through him, readers come to know Samona, who is a special person indeed." A similar publication, *The Horn Book Magazine*, which reviews children's books for parents and educators, proclaimed that "Seth's narration rings true in this laudable first novel."

The few weaknesses that reviewers have been able to find in the novel have never been considered cause to give it a bad overall review, and their disappointments are seldom consistent from one reviewer to the next. For instance, while the *School Library Journal* commends the books' use of Seth as a narrator, Martha Merson, of Boston's Adult Literacy Resource Institute, wondered whether, given, the events portrayed here, Seth is really the best character to have tell the story. "I keep wondering if Hyppolite made the right decision in choosing

Seth's perspective," she wrote. Merson then went on to consider the consider the book's requirements: the different aspects of this particular corner of Dorchester that Hyppolite wanted to examine and the fact that the novel would be less fun if readers had Samona's view of life told directly by her. Her conclusion was that "only a peer of Samona's situated on a Haitian family could give us such a broad view"—in other words, Seth was the right narrator after all. Merson's review begins with noting that the book is "beautifully written," but ends with the observation that "I felt vaguely dissatisfied with the book.

Another reviewer who felt just slightly displeased was Hazel Rochman, who examined it for *Booklist* when it was published. Overall, she was impressed, but she did express one slight twinge of regret over the fact that the book's social message was not integrated more throughout the story. "Some of the episodes are contrived," Rochman noted, "and the messages about black pride are sometimes too spelled out, but they aren't simplistic messages." As with Merson, she recognized that the things she liked least about the story might be necessary to convey the things she liked the most.

Bob Corbett, former publisher of a magazine about Haiti called *Stretch*, reviewed the book from the perspective of an immigrant from Haiti, and found that *Seth and Samona* examined the problems of being the first generation n a family to grow up in a new country "with sensitivity, insight, and engaging characters." Like all of the book's other reviewers, Corbett was impressed with Hyppolite's ability to write about Seth's life and situation with such honesty, and his added perspective made him even more enthusiastic about this novel: "certainly any Haitian-American family facing these sorts of immigrant issues would be well advised to introduce the book to pre-teens and teens of their household, and read it themselves in the bargain."

Criticism

David Kelly

David Kelly is an instructor of creative writing and composition at the College of Lake County and

What Do I Read Next?

- Edwidge Danticat was born in Port-au-Prince, Haiti, in the same year that Joanne Hyppolite was born. Her collection of short stories about Haitians and Haitian-Americans, titled *Krik? Krak!*, was published the same year as *Seth and Samona* and was nominated for the National Book Award.

- *Taste of Salt* is a novel of modern Haiti by Frances Temple, capturing local traditions and customs. It was written at about the same reading level as *Seth and Samona*. Published in 1991 by Orchard Books, New York.

- Joanne Hyppolite's other novel to date is *Ola Shakes it Up* (1998), about a child, Ola, who moves from the city to an all-white, rules-and-regulations controlled suburb, and proceeds to initiate her own "Operation Shake 'Em Up" to bring a little life to the place.

- Nine-year-old Gillian and her best friend Hank are the main characters in Amy Hest and Jacqueline Rogers' *Getting Rid of Krista*. Tired of the attention always given to her older sister, Gillian schemes to have her discovered by producers and taken away to Broadway.

- Fans of the unusual aspects of Samona's family might appreciate the even more eccentric family in Sid Hite's *Those Darn Dithers*, published in 1996. It is the story of a family of entertainers and inventors, less realistic than this book but just as imaginative.

- Famed actor Ossie Davis has written a novel about the Civil Rights Movement for young adults, called *Just Like Martin*, about a fourteen-year-old straight-A student and pastor at his church, Isaac Stone, and his relationship with his Korean War-veteran father during the turbulent 1960s.

- A more sinister view of the urban experience is seen in *Fast Talk on a Slow Track*, by Rita Williams-Garcia, about eighteen-year-old high school valedictorian Denzel, who decides to pass up his opportunity to go to Princeton and instead becomes a door-to-door salesman. The book chronicles his competition with a rival salesman, Mello, who is an unwed father, illiterate and a drug user.

- Anne-Christine d'Adesky's novel *Under the Bone* is an acclaimed, but disturbing, novel about life in Haiti in the 1990s, with the social turmoil and resultant violence that is only alluded to by Hyppolite.

Oakton Community College. In this essay he traces the evolution of Seth's family away from the sexist Haitian tradition by focusing on the character of Jerome, who never actually appears in the novel.

It is obvious that the most important character in Joanne Hyppolite's novel *Seth and Samona* is Seth, the book's narrator. The second most important character is his friend Samona, although, if her name had not been in the title, this would not be so obvious. If her name were left out of the title, readers might be inclined to miss her importance, interpreting her as a strong comic relief and a character who shows Seth something about himself in the end, but not completely crucial if one reads this book as the tale of an immigrant family's period of adjustment to contemporary American society. Even though Samona is close to Seth, his immediate family is closer—at least, in the beginning of the story.

Seth's family is a typical immigrant family in the way that they have a closer understanding of each other than of the people in the world around them. Little is said of their parents' social relations outside of their immediate family, but through Seth's eyes readers come to know Seth's relationships with Samona and her family, with his male friend Skid and with Samona and Bessie Armstrong. His brother Jean-Claude has social relations outside of the family with Reggie, a street tough. And his sister Chantal has an American boyfriend, Jerome. It is only natural that all of these relationships would act to bring the close-knit Michelin family apart, not in any tragic way, but in a way that is necessary in order to integrate their Haitian family into their new society. Various Haitian customs are mentioned, from foods to folktales, but the strongest element of Haitian culture affecting this family is its attitude toward women and their place in society. For Boston in the 1990s, the Michelins' attitude toward women is quite noticeably narrow. The character that does the most to change it, and consequently to change Seth's family from Haitians living in America to actual Haitian-Americans is not Samona but Jerome, the one character who never appears in the book.

Unlike Samona, Jerome is taken by members of Seth's family as a threat. Jean-Claude and his parents feel the need to protect Chantal from Jerome's corruptive influence. To some extent, this is not a reaction based in Haitian culture or any other culture, it is just the age-old struggle of parents and siblings looking out for their own. On the other hand—from the perspective which Chantal sees it—their rule against her dating anyone is excessive in American culture and too steeped in the Haitian tradition of keeping girls at home, where they could train to be good housekeepers or to work menial jobs until they are ready to marry. At the end of the book, when Seth's parents have learned that Jerome's intentions are probably honorable and that Chantal is probably sensible in her ambitions, they still keep a close reign on her social life, prohibiting her from dating in a way that few modern American families would.

For Jean-Claude, Jerome represents more than the general threat of what might happen when Chantal starts to date. He dislikes Jerome for who he is, not just as a potential suitor to Chantal—at least, so he says. His hatred is so intense that his family and friends believe Jean-Claude, who ordinarily stops violence in the neighborhood, could do something out of character, may even commit murder. Though he is from the younger generation, Jean-Claude's view of Jerome is colored by the old Haitian prejudices.

Early in the novel, Seth explains that Jean-Claude sees Jerome as "a lost brother with no future." Jerome has dropped out of high school and he works full-time at the 7-Eleven. Since he obviously isn't lazy—he works full-time at his job—

> The character that does the most to change . . . Seth's family from Haitians living in America to actual Haitian-Americans is not Samona but Jerome, the one character who never appears in the book."

Jean-Claude's anger would appear to stem from the fact that Jerome is not pursuing an education. There is little about him that marks him as lost, though. There is no sign that he dislikes learning, and he in fact seems intelligent, if intelligence is to be measured by curiosity. Seth, who is as uneasy about Jerome as his brother, is most disturbed by his eyes, which he says "always seemed to be looking at everything like he was trying to take it apart and understand it." Jerome is not lazy, he is not unintelligent, and he is not selfish—Samona finds out that the reason he is working is to support his mother. There is no clear reason for Jean-Claude to dislike Jerome except for the fact that he is dating his sister—if that is all, then his anger is a bit intense.

It is ironic that Jean-Claude should think so badly about Jerome, considering that he does not hold anything against Reggie, who seems a truly "lost brother." Reggie has been in jail twice, he has no real address and he carries a gun, but Jean-Claude accepts him, offering him help and hope. Jean-Claude can cope with gangster and criminals on a social basis, but he cannot cope with someone who he feels is a threat to his sister, and so he ends up imagining Jerome to be the real criminal. It is ironic that Seth explains that "Jean-Claude did not have a good reason not to like Jerome" just before explaining his brother's religious mission toward society's toughest elements: "They call Jean-Claude 'the savior' out on the streets 'cause he's always the one to step in and stop a fight or of he hears about something going down, he'll go and try to talk people out of making trouble. Everybody trusts Jean-Claude." In dealing with Jerome, 'the savior' (or, as he's later called, J.C., the initials he shares with Jesus Christ) is not only incapable of preventing trouble, but he starts it himself.

Late in the book, when tension between Chantal and her family is at its height, Jean-Claude offers the closest thing he is to give for a reason for hating Jerome: "Chantal doesn't know what's good for her. I could kill Jerome for all the trouble he's making for her." He is redirecting his anger toward Chantal, assuming that she is not responsible for her actions, seeking, in a sexist way, the nearest man around to bear the brunt of the anger he feels for her. From an earlier scene in which she explained herself to Seth, readers know that Chantal in fact does know what is good for her. What Jean-Claude interprets as "trouble" is her wish to break away from the role assigned to females in the traditional Haitian household, and the reason he assumes that Jerome is making it for her is that he cannot, in keeping with the tradition of sexism, believe that she is capable of making her own trouble. His parents may be too cautious in refusing to let their daughter date, but Jean-Claude, as a member of the generation that is growing up in America, should be able to tell his sister's thoughts from those her boyfriend has planted in her mind. His worldview is centered around the ideas of males, though, from the Haitian ways of previous generations, so that Jean-Claude, who can see that beauty contests treat blacks as inferiors, does not see that he is treating women as incapable of making intelligent choices independently. When he finally does realize the truth about Chantal, how she feels suppressed by her family and how she aspires to greatness in the service of humanity, Jean-Claude learns from Jerome that the whole problem has been caused by underestimating his sister. "He was telling me stuff I should have already known about Chantal," he explains.

Jerome is not the cause of Chantal's desire for independence, but he is linked to it, and this makes him a very important element to the story. The violations that Seth and Jean-Claude link to him, such as her lying to her parents, her staying out late, and her dissatisfaction with her role in the household, are nobody's responsibility but her own. "He listens to me," Chantal explains, when Seth wants to know why she is attracted to Jerome: there is no dizzy talk of love, no spiteful glee about teaching her parents a lesson, just relief that someone, finally, is taking the time to understand her and to take her ideas seriously.

Samona's family is anything but typical, but it is a good model in this story for a family setting where males and females are treated equally. While Seth's sister Chantal is expected to clean and cook, Samona's sister Leticia, who is Chantal's age, has her own business, a horoscope phone line. She runs it poorly, leaving her customers to the mercy of an eleven-year-old, but at least the business is hers to run foolishly if she wants to, and no one has forbidden her to pursue it. When Seth talks to Chantal about her dreams, he remembers once when the entire class laughed at Samona's dream of being an astronaut, how she went home at lunch time and brought back her mother to show that she had support. Chantal's dream to be a politician and someday help the impoverished and oppressed people of Haiti is realistic, noble. . .and forbidden in her household. In Samona's household, they may have dreams that are unlikely, but at least Leticia's plan to be an opera star is considered to be of equal importance to Nigel's plan to be an inventor.

The resolution of the crisis over Jerome's influence comes when Jean-Claude realizes that, not only is Jerome not a threat, but that he was wrong to pay such little attention Chantal. He realizes that Chantal has been treated poorly, that there is much more to her life than cooking and cleaning: it is an important breakthrough for Jean-Claude, bringing him into the modern American way of thought, breaking from his Haitian past. It just as much a moment of revelation for Seth, who understands that his understanding of women as secondary citizens will not suffice to explain the world anymore. "Jean-Claude thinks he knows what's best for everybody," Seth muses. "He tries to change people and usually it's for the better, but he was wrong about Jerome and Chantal. They don't need changing. It was Jean-Claude who needed to do some listening."

There are several results from this. One is that Seth, seeing himself reflected in Jean-Claude's sexist attitude toward Chantal, begins to wonder about his own relationship with Samona, and whether he has failed to take her as seriously as he should. "Was I being like Jean-Claude?" he thinks, feeling guilty about constantly dismissing her ideas as "crazy." The complexity of Seth's relationship with Samona has less to do with gender roles than with his constant repression of his attraction to her as a woman (as is made clear by his nervousness when matters of sex or beauty come up), but his self-awareness is nonetheless a good sign for his chance at a relatively stable future with her.

The other result of all of this is that, at the command of their grandmother, the member of the household most firmly entrenched in Haitian tradition, Seth and Jean-Claude are forced to scrub the bathroom. For males in a Haitian home to do any household chores represents a severe break with tradition, but the bathroom has special significance in this story. When he had to wait while Chantal scrubbed the tub, Jerome muttered, just loud enough for Seth to hear, a judgment that cursed the sexist tradition of the whole family: "typical Caribbean." Now, with boys taking part in the cleaning, the family is more typically American.

Source: David Kelly, in an essay for *Literature of Developing Nations for Students*, Gale, 2000.

Lyn Miller-Lachmann

In the following review of Joanne Hyppolite's first novel Seth and Samona, *Lyn Miller-Lachmann gives an favorable overview of the novel's plot and its well-sketched characters, but notes that the weakness of the novel may be it's overabundance of subplots and secondary characters, leaving the work feeling less unified than a novel should feel.*

Seth Michelin is a proper Haitian-American boy, studious and serious. His sixth-grade classmate, Samona Gemini, is an African-American girl, the child of an artist and a brilliant prankster who is always getting Seth caught up in her schemes. Yet when Seth's older brother, Jean-Claude, goes ballistic over their sister's boyfriend, Seth convinces Samona and her older brother to follow Jean-Claude and stop him before someone gets hurt. To compound Seth's worries, Samona is changing. On a whim, she signs up for a neighborhood beauty pageant. Pretty soon, she is hanging out with a prissy, feminine girl she used to hate, wearing a fluffy hairdo, and stewing over the right dress.

Hyppolite's principal characters are well drawn as they deal with each other and with the changes of early adolescence. The Haitian-American author portrays Seth's family and his working-class Boston neighborhood in a convincing and affecting manner. Though there is the hint of danger and violence, she presents characters who genuinely care about each other and about their own futures. The theme of pride in one's heritage is evident throughout. If there is one flaw in this generally well-written work, it is the overabundance of secondary characters and subplots, which threaten to make this first novel more a series of vignettes than a unified story.

> Though there is the hint of danger and violence, she presents characters who genuinely care about each other and about their own futures. The theme of pride in one's heritage is evident throughout."

Source: Lyn Miller-Lachmann, "Seth and Samona," (book review) in *Multicultural Review,* Vol. 5, No. 2, June, 1996, p. 90.

Publisher's Weekly

In the following review, Joanne Hyppolite's novel, Seth and Samona, *is called an unusually ambitious first novel about a Haitian-American family, showing promise for Hyppolite as a writer though at times the novel is overly burdened with subplots and complications.*

An unusually strong cast populates this ambitious first novel, set in Boston. Narrator Seth Michelin, the youngest of a closely knit Haitian American family, has spent two years trying in vain to distance himself from Samona Gemini, the kooky, flamboyant daughter of a free-spirited poet who happens to be a friend of Mrs. Michelin. The warmth—and the strict codes of honor and propriety—that bind Seth's family prove a powerful attraction to Samona, just as they will to the reader, while Seth's fresh voice adds witty counterpoint. Hyppolite errs, however, in adding too many complications. Seth's older brother, for example, serves essentially as a mouthpiece for observations on being a person of color in America; there's also a brief foray into a neighborhood of gun-toting youths and some discussion of women's roles in traditional families. The plot wobbles under so much baggage, and the final story lines, about Samona's participation in a girls' beauty pageant, lose their force. Even with these flaws, Hyppolite's promise is unmistakable, and readers will hope for encore appearances from her characters.

Source: "Seth and Samona," (book review) in *Publisher's Weekly,* Vol. 242, No. 25, June, 19, 1995, p. 60.,

Sources

Campbell, Elaine, and Pierette Frickey, eds., *The Whistling Bird: Woman Writers of the Caribbean*, Lynne Rienner Publishers, 1998.

Review in *Horn Book*, 1995.

Further Reading

Chancey, Myriam J. A., *Framing Silence: Revolutionary Novels by Haitian Women*, Rutgers University Press, 1997.

When Haitian politics is discussed, the role of female artists is usually underrepresented. This book takes a strongly feminist approach toward events and literature. This is one of the few books that addresses the history of radicalism in Haitian women's literature and the way that the political history of the country throughout the twentieth century affected it.

Rochman, Hazel, review, in *Booklist*, May 1, 1995.
This collection is very non-political, choosing examples that celebrate life over those that are meant to promote an agenda.

Rotberg, Robert I., *Haiti: The Politics of Squalor*, Houghton Mifflin, 1971.
This dated history does not have the most recent information about the country, but it does give a good and thorough background of what life was like up to the 1970s.

Silent Wing

José Raúl Bernardo

1998

It was with favorable expectations that *Silent Wing* was received in 1998. Coming into the market just two years after *The Secret of the Bulls*, a novel set in pre-Revolutionary Cuba, which won positive attention from the *Los Angeles Times* as one of the best works of first fiction for 1996, could not hurt. Although critics had mixed feeling concerning *Silent Wing*, readers have offered favorable remarks. The most frequent comment concerns their appreciation of Bernardo's writing about Cuba's famous poet patriot, Jose Julian Marti. One reader stated that the book ''brought much reflection and analysis of internal conflicts.'' Another reader remarked that he preferred his history ''embedded in a good story.'' Further comments focus on the relevance of Marti's thoughts and deeds to today's turbulent political situations. Wherever there is inequality there is need for individuals with integrity. Bernardo's novel suggested that many leaders pause to contemplate before taking action. Readers seem to appreciate a protagonist who has many unanswered questions concerning life and making the right decisions.

Author Biography

Born in Havana, Cuba, October 3, 1938, Bernardo is the son of Jose Bernardo and Raquel Perez. He studied at the Havana Conservatory, Cuba, where

he received a Bachelors of Music in 1958. He attended Miami University in Florida where he received a Masters in Music in 1969. He received his Ph.D. at Columbia University in 1972. An architect, playwright, composer, and writer, Bernardo was a planner for the Havana City Hall, Cuba, in 1959. After moving to the United States, he was an architect of Harrison and Abramovitz, 1964-1967, the vice-president of Museum Planning Incorporated, 1967-69, and an architect of Joyner/Bernardo, 1969 until the present.

Of his musical accomplishments, he wrote an opera, "La Nina de Guatemala", in 1974, a work based on the poem by the same name of the Cuban poet and patriot Jose Marti. He also wrote "Sonata for Amplified Piano" and "Canciones Negras" in 1973 and published *Poemas Misticos* in 1979. He composed the operas "Something for the Palace" in 1981 and "Unavoidable Consequences" in 1983. Yet, perhaps his most significant work in opera is "The Child" first produced in 1974 and the antecedent for Bernardo's historical novel *Silent Wing*. He was the Composer in Residence at the Cent City Opera, Denver, Colorado, during the summer of 1981. He also wrote "That Night of Love" for the film score for the movie *Fat Chance*. Bernardo received awards in the form of production grants for his work on "The Child" as early as 1974. He is a member of the National Opera Institute and the New York Council on the Arts and American Music Center. He was made Honorary Citizen of Guatemala in 1975.

Perhaps the events in Cuba during 1957-1958, at the time Bernardo was completing his bachelor's degree, made an impact on him. Fidel Castro had emerged as a rebel leader in opposition to the Batista movement. When Castro forces fought Batista's army and took Santiago on January 2, 1959, the war ended. Warcrimes trials followed in which 600 were executed. Whether Bernardo directly felt any of the fear or concern other Cuban citizens experienced is unknown; yet, it is important to remark upon Bernardo's exposure to the rich literary heritage of his homeland. Bernardo learned of the works of Cuba's Jose Marti. Bernardo's historical novel *Silent Wing*, published by Simon [and] Schuster in 1998, is a story of the challenge and passionate times of Marti's life. Cuba was not yet liberated from Spain and its citizens, Marti among them, faced imprisonment and exile for expressing opinions concerning politics and independence.

Bernardo lives in the Catskill Mountains of New York State and is a United States citizen. Bernardo's first novel, *The Secret of the Bulls*, published by Simon [and] Schuster in 1996, was named one of the best works of first fiction by the *Los Angeles Times*. A cassette version of the book published in 1996 and read by actor Lou Diamond Phillips is available through Audioscope. The novel *The Secret of the Bulls* has been translated into five languages including Greek.

Plot Summary

Part 1

Jose Bernardo's *Silent Wing* portrays the life and loves of Cuban poet and revolutionary hero Jose Julian Marti. The novel begins in Guatemala City, Guatemala, in the year 1877 and concludes twenty-two years later in Dos Rios, at the east end of Cuba in the year 1895. This is the story of a man compelled to speak, write, and take action on behalf of freedom, even if that means sacrificing his own true love and life in the process.

The narrative begins with Sol, "a beautiful young woman with dreamy dark eyes and long golden hair." She is seventeen, of marrying age, uninterested in any of the young men she has met. She converses with her nursemaid Xenufla, a Mayan Cakchiquel Indian woman. Xenufla intimates that "men can be a lot of fun." Sol is embarrassed but listens closely to her advice. Following Xenufla's instructions carefully, she visits a church in Jocotenango and speaks to the statue of Santa Rita.

Sol records in her diary the details of the saint's advice:

> Then, all of a sudden, I felt a tremor under my feet. I thought we were going through an earthquake, so I looked around me. But not a thing was moving, and yet I was shaking badly. I got so scared. I did not know what to do. It was then I looked up at the Saint again and noticed that her eyes were changing form and color, little by little becoming dark blue instead of brown until they became the dark blue eyes of a handsome man with dark, thick eyebrows.

Sol returns home and describes to Xenufla what has happened. Xenufla is happy for the "wondrous sign." She is convinced that the man has been chosen by the gods "to always be by her nina's side" and that he is "on his way to her. Now all there was to do was to wait for him."

Part 2

Julian is a young man of 26 traveling on board a small steamship named El Futuro heading for Guatemala. Exiled from his homeland of Cuba for nearly nine years, he has constantly moved with "no country" and "no job." He wonders when he will be able to return to his homeland.

Ten years before, he had lived in Mexico City with a job writing political essays for La Revista Universal. After a coup d' tat, he was encouraged to leave and travel to Guatemala. Senor Fermin has written a letter to Professor Saavedra, the principal of the Escuela Central in Guatemala City on Julian's behalf. He has given Julian money and a letter of introduction to Gualterio Rubios, the new liberal president of Guatemala. Although Julian has few possessions, his books are the most precious:

> His books are his friends-the friends who talk to him.
> Just as his diaries are his friends-the friends who listen.

Before leaving Mexico City, Julian proposes to Lucia, the daughter of an exiled Cuban lawyer. Her acceptance surprised him, yet, "what was done was done."

Upon his arrival in the small Mayan village of Puerto Dulce, Julian makes his way over the mountains to Guatemala City. The journey is exhausting but Julian enjoys the nights in the jungle. He writes his diary, "I slowly fall asleep, dreaming of love."

Julian arrives in Guatemala City, finds an inexpensive place to stay, and makes plans to contact Professor Saavedra. Julian meets Professor Saavedra and immediately impresses him. Already Saavedra wishes to introduce Julian to Don Manuel, the general who led the Guatemalans to independence.

On his way to his room one evening, Julian meets an organ grinder and a little monkey called Chirilingo. The man tells Julian that the monkey will bring him "a little bit of wisdom about the future." He is given two messages: "When honor and truth are at odds, let truth prevail" and "Don't give up hope. The girl you've been waiting for is just around the corner."

Part 3

Julian and Lucia continue to correspond through letters. Julian is hired as an instructor and requested to examine the new civilian codes for Guatemala. Gabriela, the younger sister of Sol, is one of Julian's pupils. She begs her father to invite Julian to Sol's "coming-of-age" party. Don Manuel agrees. An invitation is sent.

Jose-Raul Bernardo

During a local, passionate, and erudite debate in the school's auditorium, Julian has an opportunity to speak on the subject of which is mightier, the pen or the sword? Julian presents a stirring speech in which he concludes, "It is up to each of us to make that world [of peace] come true. Today." Later that evening, his Mayan friend Panoplo remarks cryptically, "It's painful, very painful to be chosen by the gods."

Julian goes with Professor Saavedra to meet Don Manuel. Don Manuel is immediately impressed with Julian and treats him like a son. Later, at Sol's party, Julian keeps to himself. Then he sees Sol, "the most beautiful girl he has ever seen in his life." He is completely swept up by emotion. Sol is equally as swept up. Julian, however, realizes that he will never have a chance to fulfill his dream:

> And as Julian weeps for joy, he finds himself also weeping at the devastating realization that, as close as he has been to the woman of his dreams, the woman of his poems, he must learn to forget her, he must not-ever-see her again. His most sacred word of honor has been given to Lucia. And once a Cuban criollo man gives his word of honor, it is never to be broken. Never.

Julian writes a letter to Lucia declaring they will be married and "live the life" of her "dreams." He intends to keep his pledge. During a conversation with Panoplo, Julian learns of a Mayan belief.

Julian confesses he has found his love and has lost her. Panoplo explains, "if you really found the woman the gods mean for you to have, then she will always be by your side, no matter what.

Part 4

Julian spends every free moment in the company of Don Manuel and as many "private" moments as he is allowed with Sol. Lucia makes wedding plans and spends Julian's money as quickly as she receives it. Their wedding date is set. Julian plans to leave for Mexico City. Lucia, in the meantime, wonders if she loves Julian. She thinks:

> She would like to love him. She wants to. She needs to love him. She needs to let the passionate woman she hides inside to come out and fully experience that kind of love, the kind she has heard so much about, whatever that kind of love is like. All she knows about that kind of love is through her lady friends.

Julian and Sol part.

Part 5

Lucia and Julian, now married, journey to Guatemala where a position of full professor awaits him. They arrive in Guatemala City and meet with Professor Saavedra. Shortly after their arrival, Don Manuel invites them to his home. Julian arrives with Lucia to discover that there are rumors that President Rubios has "gone crazy" and has imprisoned several suspected traitors. They return to their hotel where Julian announces they will be leaving Guatemala. This stuns Lucia. She informs him that she is pregnant and accuses him of not thinking of her.

A doctor visits Sol and finds her feverish. In her mind, she sees Julian in the white gazebo where they used to meet and talk. She runs to him and gives herself to him completely. That same night, Julian goes to the gazebo where he and Sol often met. There he finds Xenufla and learns that Sol has died. He writes in his journal, "Shaded by a silent wing I must write of a love in full bloom."

Part 6

After several years of traveling from Guatemala, Venezuela, Honduras, Mexico, and Florida, Julian, Lucia, and their son Ismaelillo live in Brooklyn, New York. It is the winter of 1883. Julian is unhappy. Lucia is embittered by the life they lead. Lucia confronts Julian about a worn photograph. Julian denies nothing. Less than a week later, Julian returns to an empty apartment. Lucia has left with their five-year-old son. Upon reading Lucia's letter,

he vows: "My son will not die in an enslaved Cuba."

It is now May 19, 1895. Julian is in a small encampment in Dos Rios, Cuba with his army at the ready. He receives a report that the enemy is close and gives the order to attack. As he "leads his men in a fearless charge," he is bringing his dreams to fruition. He is shot and killed. His last thoughts are of Sol.

Part 7

The USS Maine is destroyed while anchored in the bay of La Habana. The United States enters into war with Spain. The result of the war is liberation of Cuba on May 20, 1902.

Characters

Anacleto

Anacleto is one of the muleteers Julian hires to take him through the jungle to Guatemala City. He is half-Mayan and half-white.

Cholito

Cholito is the half-white, half-Latino barber in Guatemala City who dresses in white and takes pride in his light, white-man's skin.

Colonel Corrientes

Colonel Corrientes is a tall, impressive man who has a thick black mustache and a pointed goatee. He appears at the debate in full dress uniform with a chest filled with medals and gleaming sword. He is as stunning a speaker as his appearance implies.

Doña Rosaura

Doña Rosaura is the loving wife of Don Manuel. She presents herself with dignity and social grace. She has tried to raise her three daughters in kind. However, she is often at odds with her middle daughter Gabriela who obviously has Don Manuel wrapped around her finger. She will stand behind her husband and loves him deeply. Upon meeting her husband, she fell deeply in love with him, not unlike Sol's response to Julian. She is a person who Don Manuel will always be able to rely upon. She is steadfast.

Don Manuel

Don Manuel is a man who married late in life for love. His wife Doña Rosaura is twelve years younger. He is fifty-seven years old. He has a short, gray beard and is balding. He carries the scars of battle caused by arrows, bullets, and knives. He is a survivor who is much more interested in petitions of peace than in fighting wars. He is proud, however, of his accomplishment. He has been instrumental in beginning and ending the war for Guatemalan independence. Yet, he has a weakness. Although he has been a man who has "controlled armies of rebellious men, subjugated armies of enemies, and fought armies of bureaucrats," he cannot say "no" to his middle daughter Gabriela. He is taken by Julian and secretly hopes that he will marry his daughter Sol. He had once had a son who died at the age of three of Galloping Malaria. It has been something that haunts him. Only when he met Julian did he begin to believe that he could have another "son" in his life.

Señor Fermín

Señor Fermin is a Guatemalan man who befriended Julian in Mexico City and teaches him the proper means of introduction. He is Julian's connection to Professor Saavedra. He gives Julian money for the journey as well as a letter of introduction. He claims to be a former schoolmate and personal friend of Gualterio Rubios. His advice: "Being in the right political circles can never hurt a young man."

Gabriela

Gabriela is the nearly fourteen-year-old daughter of Don Manuel. She is pushy, rude, spoiled, and has the favor of her father. She is a hopeless romantic who discovers some of Julian's poetry as well as introduces her father to the idea of inviting him to their home. Without her insistence Julian would not have Sol.

Ixhula

Ixhula is Anacleto's Mayan wife who is as cruel a taskmaster as she is beautiful. She travels with her husband and takes Julian to Guatemala City.

Julián

Julian is twenty-six years old at the time the novel begins. Born in Cuba, he was exiled at the age of seventeen after serving some years at hard labor for writing political essays for *La Revista Universal*, an "ultra liberal" publication. He has dark, unruly, curly hair with dark blue eyes. During his exile from Cuba he wrote a booklet entitled "Life of a Political Prisoner in Cuba." During his nine years of exile, he has traveled to Isla de Pinos, Madrid, Zaragoza, Paris, London, Progreso, Ciudad Mexico, Veracruz, Contoy, Isla Mujeres, Belize, and Guatemala. He is a teacher and writer whose father is a former Spanish army Lieutenant living on an army pension. Strong, muscular, broad-shouldered, his body chiseled by hard labor, he is enroute to a promised job in Guatemala City. He is leaving behind in Mexico City his fiancee Lucia, the daughter of a well-to-do Cuban lawyer. Julian is journeying to Guatemala hopeful to acquire work that will make him a good and successful husband to Lucia. He vows not to return to her until he has found success. He travels with only a very few items, scholarly books and his personal diaries. He writes his observations, feelings, speeches, and poems within the pages of those journals. He is never without them.

Julian is haunted by his experiences in Cuba as a political prisoner and dreams of one day making a difference and freeing his homeland and its people from the tyranny of the Spanish crown. While in Guatemala City Julian meets Sol, the eldest daughter of Don Manuel and faces yet another personal challenge. He falls in love with the young woman and fights with himself to choose honor over love. He is betrothed to Lucia and will not break his promise of marriage to her. He considers this betrayal no less heinous than allowing tyranny to exist in Cuba. For Julian nothing is simple. He is torn by his love of country and his passionate, deep love for Sol who seems to feel as he does. He discovers through his conversations with her that she is just as passionate toward the welfare of the Cuban people as Julian.

Julian is a man on the verge of greatness. In an open debate at the town hall in Guatemala City he is the third person to speak after two distinguished men have argued whether the pen or the sword is mightier. It is during Julian's remarks that one sees his potential to be a dynamic, powerful leader. This does not go unnoticed by members of the audience. Forever torn between his love of Sol and his love of country, Julian faces his deepest fears and changes the history of Cuba.

Lucía

Lucia is a twenty-nine-year-old spinster at the beginning of the novel. She has glossy black hair, hazel eyes, a distinguished nose, elegant thin lips, a trim body, and a flawless complexion. She is a stunning beauty who does not see herself as beautiful. The daughter of a successful exiled Cuban lawyer, she has lived for a number of years in Mexico City. She has had the tutelage of two spinster aunts while living there. She has felt left out of the best of society because of her father's exile. She hates her life in Mexico City and yearns to marry a man who will give her the station she so desperately needs. She is as shallow as she is beautiful. She does not share her father or Julian's love of her homeland. She has no interest in politics unless it might serve to improve her standing in social circles. Upon hearing that Julian had been appointed a full professor in Guatemala City, she builds her trousseau, spending nearly all of the money Julian sends to her. Once married she grows to resent Julian's passion and patriotism. This will eventually lead her to leave him and take their child with her.

Organ Grinder

The organ grinder and his monkey Chirilingo offer Julian two statements of wisdom on two different colored pieces of paper.

Panoplo

Panopla is a wrinkled old Mayan bartender at the Ultimo Adios. He tells Julian about the Mayan gods called the "Chacs" who are the four great dogs of the coast which is where Panoplo's home is located. He teaches Julian about food, drinking, and politics. He is deeply concerned about the plight of Indians and wonders how the current political situation will affect them.

Rabbi Mordecai

Rabbi Mordecai is thin and short and has a full white beard. He dresses for the debate in a simple frock coat with a black silk yarmulke on his head. He is an eloquent and impassioned speaker and is every bit a match for Colonel Corrientes. He is marked to be one of the president's political "victims."

Gualterio Rubios

President Rubios is a secretive man who stays removed from the public eye except in auspicious occasions such as the public debate. It is at the debate that he is first seen in the novel. He has come as "a citizen" and not "president." He wears no uniform during the event and sits with his family in a back row. Yet, he is the man who can wield terrible power with a moment's notice. He claims to be of a liberal mind but becomes suspicious of the existence of subversive efforts. He declares his own form of Marshall Law and has several people arrested. He has them executed without accusation and trial. It is at this juncture that Julian realizes that he has not truly escaped the tyranny he knew so well in Cuba. It is cause for despair and for gathering one's conviction and going forward with altruistic plans. President Rubios much to everyone's surprise does not arrest Julian.

Professor Saavedra

Professor Saavedra is an exiled "old" Cuban professor who is the principal of the Escuela Central, an exclusive girls school in Guatemala City. It is to Professor Saavedra that Señor Fermin who is a personal friend of the president of Guatemala directs Julian. Professor Saavedra is enthusiastic, encouraging, and genuinely friendly. Julian quickly impresses him and dreams that one day Julian will be able to "free" Cuba. He is instrumental in arranging public debates at the school and prides himself on his liberal mind and sincere love for his homeland.

Soledad

Sol is the eldest daughter of Don Manuel, the general who began the Guatemalan revolution and succeeded. She has golden blond hair, is slender, has a long neck and a creamy complexion. As the novel begins, she is seventeen. During a conversation with her nursemaid Xenufla, Sol is directed to journey to a small church in Jocotenango named after Santa Rita to ask the saint for guidance in choosing a husband. Sol follows Xenufla's precise instructions and has a vision of a dark-haired man with dark blue eyes. She returns to Xenufla and is told the Mayan saying, "Souls woven together by the gods can never be unraveled." With youthful exuberance Sol shares her nursemaid's apparent joy over the vision she has had. It will be months before she meets the man of her vision. That man is Julian.

Sol is an well-educated young woman, an exception for her time. It is under her father's guidance that she has learned the violent past of her homeland of Cuba. Her general father who loves all his children and his wife has told her of war and brutality. When Sol meets Julian, there is more to their relationship than the chemistry of attraction. She truly seems his "soul-mate." Despite her youth she acts much older and wiser than her years. When Julian leaves to honor his promise, she believes he has left to help Cuba become free. Even after learning of Julian's obvious betrayal of her love, she is not angry. She has only sympathy for him for she knows he lives a lie every day of his life. She will endure because he does. She will go to her death with the purest love intact.

Doña Lucrecia Suárez-Villegas

Doña Lucrecia is a tight-lipped, skinny old woman who wears the tightest corset to show how straight and strict a life she leads. She is a malicious, gossipy old lady who has the "ear" of President Rubios. She is "respected" and feared by many in the city. At the public debates she sits in "her chair" and views the event. She is instrumental in turning the president against the populous of Guatemala City, particularly Colonel Corrientes and Rabbi Mordecai, the two gentlemen who debated the might of sword versus pen.

Xenufla

Xenufla is an older Mayan Cakchiquel Indian woman who "raised" Sol, so named by her when she was born. She informs Sol of the Indian custom of a maid going to the church of Jocotenango to visit Santa Rita and seek a "sign" concerning who she might marry.

Yubirio

Yubirio is an older Cuban sailor who works on the steamship El Futuro that takes Julian closer to Guatemala. He teaches Julian the "power of music" as they work.

Themes

Love and Honor

A central theme of the novel centers on affairs of the heart. Questions constantly arise for Julian as he searches for justice and peace of mind. It is love of his country that has caused him to be exiled. He journeys to Guatemala in hopes that he can do the honorable thing and become successful so that he can marry Lucia. However, everywhere he travels he meets people who have been affected by dishonorable acts, people who are victims like he is. People exiled for expressing their thoughts concerning honor. Julian wrestles with love as well. Should he choose to share his life with Sol who loves him deeply and completely? Or, should he keep his promise to Lucia and do the honorable thing even though he is sentencing himself to a lifetime of

Topics for Further Study

- Research the life of Cuban patriot and poet Jose Julian Marti and compare events in his life with events in the novel.

- Compare and contrast Julian's and Lucia's impressions of Guatemala City.

- Investigate the revolutionary history of Cuba since the early 1800s until the present day. Decide if there are common elements or events shared by both eras.

- Translate one of Jose Marti's poems from Spanish to English.

- Describe the nineteenth-century "coming-of-age" party. Explain how this custom did or did not change during the twentieth century.

- Define the meaning of the following Spanish words and relate them to events in the story: "criollo," "habanero," "ninas," "chirilingo."

misery? On the evening that Julian realizes that he has met the woman of his dreams, he "weeps for joy." Yet, "he finds himself also weeping at the devastating realization that, as close as he has been to the woman of his dreams, the woman of his poems, he must learn to forget her." He knows now the truth of the dilemma: "His most sacred word has been given to Lucia. And once a Cuban criollo man gives his word of honor, it is never to be broken. Never."

The Pen and the Sword

Closely connected to honor is the question: which is mightier, the pen or the sword? Julian speaks at the debate and discovers a means to bridge the gap between two compelling sides. He says, "Separately. . .either pen. . .or sword. . .can help us conquer the world." He adds, "But united. . .pen and sword, checking and balancing each other, like mind and heart, like body and soul. . .United. . .pen and sword make each of us into that ideal poet-warrior the ancient Greeks dreamed about." The sword changes circumstance swiftly, such as in a revolution. Yet, does not the pen carry action into law? A few words spoken can move hundreds. Can a sword be used in as constructive a fashion? Julian concludes, "It is up to each of us to make that world of tomorrow come true. Today."

Freedom and Slavery

Don Manuel had hoped to affect further change, to free all who inhabit Guatemala but there is a division of class between people of Indian descent and of Spanish descent. Even within the boundlessness of Freedom there seem to be restrictions. Panoplo, the old Mayan bartender listens to Julian's observations about the debate. He listens and nods and all the while he is thinking. As the narrator emphasizes, "He [Panoplo], like Julian, also fervently dreams of liberty, not only for his own people, but for himself as well. What would it be like to be free, he asks himself, free to speak again in his own language, free to practice his own religion, free to be proud again of being who he is, a Mayan man living on Mayan land?" The question is raised: how free are a people if part of their population is still enslaved? On a whim the president of Guatemala arrests individuals and has them executed without benefit of trial. Assumed freedom is a fragile as glass. It can shatter under the blow of tyranny.

Sacrifice for the Greater Good

Several characters in the novel face the choice of sacrifice over personal gain and choose sacrifice. Julian chooses to keep his word and marry Lucia even though it means that he will not have Sol in his life. Sol "gives away" Julian, choosing to acknowledge that he is a man who must keep his word and therefore his integrity. In the future he will be able to keep a greater promise, that of freeing Cuba from the oppressive force of Spanish rule. Rabbi Mordecai goes to prison rather than apologize for his views and the free expression of them. His choice seals his fate, ends his life.

Style

Point of View

The point of view in *Silent Wing* is that of third-person omniscient, the all-knowing narrator. The reader is given information concerning the inner-

most workings of the heart. The reader learns not only of Julian's journey to Guatemala but of his first stirring impressions of Guatemala City. The use of present tense "calls, sees, talks," invites intimacy. It is as if the reader is listening to a close friend relating the story. When Julian approaches Guatemala City, he sees strange objects breaking out of the oppressive heat of the jungle and encounters what seems to be a vision: "The valley is shrouded by a thick, pale gray mist that hovers over it, moving very languidly. . .piercing through that mist there appear to be dozens of tall, white, pointing spires, almost obelisks. Julian shakes his head." Traveling nearer, he sees more of the city "lying on a high plateau, up in the mountains, close to the clouds; a magnificently beautiful place where spring is said to be perennial." Through the omniscient narrator, the reader learns what is thought and felt and rarely spoken.

Foreshadowing

Foreshadowing is a detail in a story that hints at the eventual outcome of events and helps create mood or sustain a tone. In the novel Julian has a moment of intense clarity after meeting with Professor Saavedra. He thinks of the Cuban cigar that Saavedra offered and equates it with the struggle for freedom. Julian is thinking he does not want to sit behind a desk and have a comfortable life. The narrator informs the reader of Julian's thoughts: "If it is true that only the blood of martyrs feeds dreams, well then, Lord, please, let me feed dreams, even if that means that I'd have to become a martyr myself." Several years later, in the midst of one of the first battles for Cuban independence Julian will be killed. Shortly after this scene, Julian joins a celebration and is asked by an organ grinder whether he wishes to have a "bit of wisdom." The first message is, "When honor and truth are at odds, let truth prevail," and the second is "Don't give up hope. The girl you've been waiting for is just around the corner." Both pieces of advice apply to Julian's life yet it is the next event that serves as another foreshadowing. Julian tucks the notes inside his pocket but one falls to the ground, the note that speaks of honor and truth: "But as he does, the first piece of paper. . .the pale cream one, falls out of his pocket without him realizing it. . .that tiny piece of paper now lies on the surface of the sidewalk next to dozens of trampled pale cream petals of the wonderfully scented magnolia flowers. Unnoticed. Totally unnoticed. Forgotten." It is shortly after this scene that Julian meets Sol and his life changes in ways he could not have imagined.

Symbolism

Silent Wing is a novel that contains numerous objects and places that offer more than their literal meaning. The towers of Guatemala City are white and seem to pierce the canopy of the jungle. Julian reacts as if he has seen something akin to a vision. He has heard that Guatemala City is eternally Spring. The color white repeats with the description of the gazebo near Sol's home. The gazebo is a place where Sol feels safe with her deepest emotions. It is near the gazebo that she enters the river to be renewed. Within the confines of the cemetery there is a statue of an angel, a white marble angel. White often means purity of thought, word and deed. White can also symbolize renewal or cleansing. In this novel white means all those things as well as its opposite. No matter how hard either Sol or Julian tries to hide their feelings for each other, they cannot conceal them. Although few words are spoken between the two of them, so much is communicated. The most significant symbol, however, are the angels. In the cemetery "everywhere inside are white marble angels, frozen in time and space, some of them kneeling, some of them standing, atop elaborate marble crypts, looking up with hopeful eyes toward the sky above them, now dark blue, while their silent wings, lit by the nascent moon, cast long dark blue shadows on the surface of the Earth." "Silent wings" become those thoughts, prayers, hopes, dreams left unspoken. This novel is a story of unspoken, unrequited dreams and love. Angels, intending to lighten a mortal's burden, cannot, after all, help others for they cannot help themselves, mute as they are standing motionless and silent in the graveyard.

Literary Heritage

Cuba is a country whose literary heritage revolves around a rich legacy of song, poetry, and storytelling. Descendants from Spanish, African, and Native American populations and cultures, Cubans enjoy a deep and passionate interest in music, dance, and theater. Cuba has a national system of libraries, a chain of theaters, a movie industry, a jazz orchestra, touring ballet companies, and folk music groups. In Cuba there is a National Council of Culture and The Book Institute. Writers of the Americas is a conference held in Cuba at which thirty-five emerging American writers are given the opportunity to engage in an intensive cultural, literary, and intellectual exchange with Cuban counterparts.

Bernardo studied at the Havana Conservatory receiving a Bachelors of Music in 1958. Bernardo writes about a part of the life of Jose Marti, the national poet of Cuba, in his historical novel *Silent Wing* . Song, poetry, and music add to the literary texture of that novel.

Historical Context

The Castro Movement

Although the Castro Movement did not occur until seventy years after the setting of *Silent Wing*, José Raúl Bernardo was living in Havana, Cuba and attending university during one of that country's most turbulent times. During the late 1950s Fidel Castro fought against overwhelming odds to oust the dictator Batista who had been in power since the 1930s. During 1957 and 1958 Castro gained more support from the public and in January 1959 defeated Batista and took Santiago. It was during this upheaval that Bernardo was completing his degree in music. Perhaps one might argue that a writer is the sum of his or her experiences. Significant political events can impact our lives and make lasting impressions.

The Life of Jose Marti

Considered one of the greatest writers of the Hispanic world, Marti devoted his life's work to ending Spanish rule of his homeland Cuba. Bernardo in his historical novel *Silent Wing* offers fictionalized glimpses of the private struggles of Marti. Born in Havana in 1853, he was exiled to Spain at the age of seventeen. While there he published a pamphlet exposing the horror of imprisonment at a political figure in Cuba, something he experienced himself. Bernardo incorporates Marti's life experiences in the text of his novel. By 1895 he was actively leading opposition efforts to overthrow Spanish rule. He died during one of the first battles of that war, another historical item that is included in the novel.

Critical Overview

The historical romance *Silent Wing* is author José Raúl Bernardo's second novel. Upon publication it was well-received, especially by those readers who have an appreciation for the depth and complexity of the life of Jose Julian Marti. Concerned with such themes as Honor and Truth, Freedom and Tyranny, Love and Promises Made, Bernardo views a story hardly removed by time. The political questions raised could be applied today in several parts of the world, including modern Cuba. Yet, Bernardo does not limit his narrative to such compelling themes. He touches upon passion and desire as well. Brad Hooper, a contributor in *Booklist* called it a "greatly atmospheric historical novel" which "opens with a heartwarming scene." That is the brief scene in which Sol is instructed to go to the small church and implore a vision of her future love. Hooper recommended the novel, describing it as "compelling" from the first to last page. Although a contributor in *Publishers Weekly* considered Marti's life "more dramatic and eventful" than Bernardo's novel, a contributor in *Library Journal* noted its "sentimental romance" qualities. The latter contributor also pointed out that the novel was published during the "centenary year of Cuban sovereignty." Thomas Curwen, a contributor in the *Los Angeles Times* emphasized Bernardo's focus on a "moment in Marti's life" has "turned a political life into a love story, making it clear that only a thin line separates the two. One leads to misery, the other to an early grave." Curwen summed up the tone of Bernardo's novel when he stated, "More than the life of Jose Marti, we get a glimpse of his poetry and a touch of his anguished soul."

Criticism

Christine Thompson

Thompson has a M. A. degree and is a part-time English instructor at Jefferson Community College, Watertown, New York. In the following essay, she explores the significance of the imagery and foreshadowing of Silent Wing *and how they communicate the novel's theme of love and honor.*

Affairs of the heart are the central focus of this historical fiction based on the true life of Jose Julian Marti, Cuba's national poet and revolutionary hero. Heroes, by definition, may seem larger than life and nearly perfect. They may appear to be fearless, confident, self-satisfied, never filled with self-doubt. Julian is a "hero" plagued by self-doubt, fear, and a never-ending list of questions. These questions re-

volve around ideals such as keeping one's word, honoring promises and pledges made, and being true to one's dreams no matter the personal cost.

Despite being exiled from his homeland of Cuba, Julian endeavors to "get a job, to marry Lucia and start a family". Yet, Julian quickly realizes that he has a more important dream: "Freeing my homeland is my dream. My life's ambition, my life's cause. My destiny". It is that dream that has brought him to Guatemala City. The city in the jungle upon first encounter seems to draw him in: "The valley is shrouded by a thick, pale gray mist that hovers over it, moving very languidly. And piercing through that mist there appear to be dozens of tall, white, pointing spires, almost obelisks". He soon discovers they are bell towers, dozens of them. He feels at once that this is the place for him to renew his dreams. He has traveled through the jungle and has acquired an appreciation for Guatemala and its people. He does not cease thinking about his homeland but the poet/writer in him is enticed by the beauty that he sees all around him to languish for a brief time.

Enroute to the haven of Guatemala City, he had stopped for a time in Puerto Dulce, arriving on Good Friday afternoon. Mayan Indians had gathered for their yearly procession through the village streets. It was said that the display was to "pacify two gods they fear most: the god who spurts tongues of fire from the mountaintops and the god who shakes the earth". Julian watched three life-sized statues be carried past. There were two white women statues with "pale blue glass eyes and long curly wigs of real blond hair" that were "kneeling down, their polychromed wooden faces weeping carved tears". But it was the third statue that had caught Julian's attention. It was a "standing figure of a tired white man with a long curly beard and with the saddest eyes Julian had ever seen". There was "something" about the statue that did not "look right." Julian did not figure this out until after he arrived in Guatemala City and was meeting Professor Saavedra for the first time.

Julian was thinking about how complacent Professor Saavedra, a fellow Cuban exile, seemed as he smoked his Cuban cigar and explained the responsibilities of an instructor to Julian. Julian's thoughts drifted to questions. He wondered if that was how he was "going to end." He thought about having been born a "doer." Then he thought about dreams: "But dreams have to be made into reality, at whatever the cost. At whatever the sacrifice. Or else they remain nothing but dreams. I am not going to dry up, if it is true that only the blood of martyrs feeds dreams, well then, Lord, please, let me feed dreams, even if that means that I'd have to become a martyr myself. There is a saying that one should be careful what one wishes for. This is the case with Julian. He is destined to be a "doer." He will be instrumental in gathering an army that he will lead on Cuban soil to fight and die for the cause of freedom. It is at this moment that he discovers what he had thought "wrong" about the statue in the Good Friday procession: "His eyes. That was what was wrong with the image of that man. His eyes—the eyes of the man carrying the cross would not *could not* have been the saddest eyes in the world, but on the contrary, they would have been the most exultant eyes in the world, enraptured with joy. Because, by his action, that man was feeding dreams. And by feeding dreams, he was making his own dreams come true and fulfilling his own destiny".

On his way home from his visit with Professor Saavedra, Julian walks next to an outer wall of the cemetery of Guatemala. It is a "large complex partly hidden behind high, white, stuccoed walls; everywhere inside are white marble angels, frozen in time and space, some of them kneeling, some of them standing, atop elaborate marble crypts, while their silent wings, lit by the nascent moon, cast long dark blue shadows on the surface of the Earth". Again, Julian thinks of sadness as he enters a cantina. His sadness is that of his "last good-bye" to Cuba. The good-bye he hopes will not be his last. But there is more he will lament before he leaves Guatemala to pursue his pledges. He has not counted on meeting the "love of his life" that will give him pause and challenge both his sense of honor and his depth of commitment.

This struggle is foreshadowed in the unlikeliest of places. Julian encounters an organ grinder and his monkey entertaining a local crowd. He stops to watch and listen. The organ grinder suggests that his monkey, his Chirilingo can tell Julian "a little bit of wisdom about the future". This "wisdom" is two fold. The first message is "When honor and truth are at odds, let truth prevail" and the other is "Don't give up hope. The girl you've been waiting for is just around the corner". Julian smiles and ignores the significance of the two "truths". Yet, they will foreshadow both his triumph and his downfall. The monkey, though colorfully dressed, is wearing a white shirt and pants. Again the color white is mentioned. White may represent purity, innocence, integrity, and clarity of mind. Julian will

Jose Marti, Cuban patriot and poet.

soon meet someone who will test all of his moral fortitude and cause him to question promises made.

Sol is a young woman who follows the suggestion of her Mayan nursemaid and seeks a vision from Santa Rita concerning the "right man" who will come into her life and "always stay by her side". This man has dark hair and dark blue eyes. This man is Julian. Though she has not met him yet, she fervently believes in the vision. It is not by accident that Julian attends her "coming-of-age" party. It seems the gods have plans for both of them. When Julian first sees Sol, he is mesmerized by her golden hair that is "decorated with the tiniest of white flowers" and where it falls on her "white as alabaster" shoulders. Julian thinks he sees wings on her shoulders like those "beautifully carved white wings of the white marble angels" in the cemetery. Sol needs no further proof that Santa Rita is watching over her. She now knows she has met the man of her "vision". Julian is the "man the gods mean for her to have always by her side".

This meeting is a foreshadowing of Julian's fall from honor. He speaks with Panoplo and tells him that he has met the woman of his dreams. Julian begins to weep, first "for joy", then because of the "devastating realization that, as close as he has been to the woman of his dreams, the woman of his

> But it was the third statue that had caught Julian's attention. It was a 'standing figure of a tired white man with a long curly beard and with the saddest eyes Julian had ever seen'. There was 'something' about the statue that did not 'look right."

poems, he must learn to forget her, he must not *ever* see her again. His most sacred word of honor has been given to Lucia. And once a Cuban criollo man gives his word of honor, it is never to be broken. Never". But however profound the "wave" of elation and joy the Mayan gods may send to someone, there is a price to be paid. Julian "breaks" his promise and spends as much time as he can with Sol. When he meets her and sees her before him, he cannot do anything but "ride the wave of the gods as high and for as long as the gods will let him" (137). This "wave of joy" will crest and crash. Julian and Sol will not cease loving each other; but Julian will keep his word and marry Lucia. He will say good-bye to the one woman he truly loves not matter the heartbreak. Sol will send him away with the wish that he remain true to his pledge to free his homeland and its people.

The most potent of the many "white" symbols in this novel is the gazebo on Sol's property: "a small white gazebo by the river, a tiny pavilion the family calls El Mirador, The Lookout, because the views from it are outstanding". This is Sol's "place of power," her "katok," a Mayan word meaning a "magical place that allows the soul to travel ahead and move forward". Before Julian leaves for Mexico City and his life with his fiancee Lucia, he recognizes that it is Sol who represents the Spirit of Guatemala and not the "cold white marble statues" of the cemetery. After Julian departs Guatemala, Sol falls ill with malaria. In her mind and heart she travels to the gazebo and there she experiences a "joining" with Julian on the "soul-level". Once completed, she dies. Upon his return to Guatemala,

Julian feels compelled to visit Sol in the middle of the night and hurries to the gazebo. It is here that he discovers Sol has died. He cries out for her believing that this is where her spirit remains. Words of encouragement come to mind: Sol had told him before his departure to "always let the love of freedom guide your life".

Years later, after moving to Brooklyn, New York, and living in a loveless marriage with Lucia, he tells his wife the truth. She leaves him, taking their son with her. It is several years later when Julian has his "day in the sun". He is leading an attack on Spanish forces on his homeland and there dies in battle. Not only had he lived the dream, his dying thoughts were filled with the only other *true* love in his life, Sol.

Source: Christine Thompson, in an essay for *Literature of Developing Nations for Students*, Gale, 2000.

Thomas Curwen

In the following review, Thomas Curwen describes Silent Wing *as a torrid love story on its surface, but with moving echoes of Cuban poet Jose Marti's life.*

As Cuba edges toward the great unknown—life after Castro, that is—everyone, it seems, wants a piece of the 19th century poet and patriot Jose Marti. The pope quoted him in his January sermons to the Cuban people, and Castro puts him before Marx and Lenin in his revolutionary pantheon. Some ideologies make strange bedfellows and even stranger novels.

At first blush, "Silent Wing" is a torrid love story based on Marti's life, so filled with troubled sighs and quiet yearnings that you have to wonder what Jose Raul Bernardo is up to. His new novel comes as close to bodice-ripping as you can without popping buttons or tripping over cliches.

When we first meet Marti, here renamed Julian, the year is 1877. He is 25. The "burning passion of individual freedom" runs wildly through his veins, but it is a passion incompatible with a world shaking from a century of revolution. Already he has endured two years of hard labor in a stone quarry and six years in exile.

Engaged to a Cuban woman in Mexico City, he plans to marry once he gets settled in his new home, Guatemala, but then he meets Soledad, oldest daughter of the country's most famous general. They fall in love, and Julian is racked by duty to his fiancee, his love for Sol and his desire to free Cuba from Spanish tyranny.

By focusing on this moment in Marti's life, inspired by the autobiographical poem "La Niña de Guatemala," Bernardo has turned a political life into a love story, making it clear that only a thin line separates the two. One leads to misery, the other to an early grave.

Marti was 42 when he was killed in a skirmish with Spanish soldiers in Cuba in 1895, seven years before the country won its independence. He had spent the previous 15 years raising money to defeat the Spanish, working as a journalist in New York City and, most important for Bernardo, enduring a loveless marriage that lasted until his wife left him, returning to Cuba with their son, knowing he would never follow.

Tormented by a life he dreamed of but never knew, Marti neither reunited with his son nor saw his country free. He did, however, return with a band of rebels. Leading a charge atop a white horse at Dos Rios and getting fatally clipped by a bullet might have been an accident of fate, or it might have been the wish of a man unable to live with disappointment, the greatest of which, according to Bernardo, was a love he lost.

"She has the shiniest hair," thinks Julian when he first sees Sol, "golden hair that frames her head as if it were a resplendent halo that in the light of the myriads of flickering candles surrounding her, seems to glimmer. . . . On her shoulders, are those wings? White wings?"

Credit Bernardo, who was widely praised for his first novel, "The Secret of the Bulls," for keeping some distance from the lovers, even mocking Julian in his rapture. Yet the sentimentality of the novel, the poetic conceits and even the title come from Marti himself, the poet who wrote without any irony:

> On the darkest nights I've seen
> Rays of the purest splendor
> Raining upon my head
> From heavenly beauty.
> I've seen wings sprout
> From handsomest women's
> shoulders,
> Seen butterflies fly out
> Of rubbish heaps.

"Silent Wing" is written—as if in tribute to the man some believe to be Latin America's greatest writer—with lush and indiscriminate colors. Guatemala City is "dotted by dozens, hundreds of bell

> " 'Silent Wing' is a lovely story, doing what historical fiction does best. More than the life of Jose Marti, we get a glimpse of his poetry and a touch of his anguished soul."

towers, proudly standing erect, their bronze bells singing softly in the faraway distance, scintillating like sparklingly bronze stars whenever they catch and reflect the light of the setting sun," and Julian's torment is exquisitely rendered.

At the moment of truth, alone in a riverside gazebo with Sol, he must turn away. "To survive. To avoid rushing to her and grabbing her in his arms, then kissing her feet, her hands, her entire body, every single strand of her glorious hair, her eyes, her mouth."

Even though the melodrama overtakes the story and the political gets lost in a sea of sentiment, the writing is assured, and the themes are grand. The revolutionary battles the bourgeois, the radical fights the status quo, and the plight of love, caught in the middle, makes for high, if not histrionic, drama.

At second blush, "Silent Wing" is a minor but altogether likable cousin to such 19th century novels as "The Red and the Black" and "The Sentimental Education." Let Marti and Julian's tragedy be portrayed in rather potboiled terms—reckless choice and brash honor—but Bernardo still makes us care about him. "Silent Wing" is a lovely story, doing what historical fiction does best. More than the life of Jose Marti, we get a glimpse of his poetry and a touch of his anguished soul.

Source: Thomas Curwen, "Silent Wing," (book review) in *Los Angeles Times,* July 29, 1998, p. 5.

Brad Hooper

In the following review, Brad Hooper gives a brief description of Jose Raul Bernardo's novel Silent Wing, *calling it a "delicious romance" that follows a young hero's struggles between duty and desire.*

This greatly atmospheric historical novel opens with a heartwarming scene. In late-nineteenth-century Guatemala, Soledad, the lovely young daughter of the national liberator, hears from her old Indian nanny that "the man meant by the gods to be always by her side . . . was on his way to her." And, sure enough, he appears—in the form of Julian, a handsome young Cuban writer exiled from his homeland because of his liberal views concerning Cuban independence from Spain. Julian has come to Guatemala to assume a teaching position. He is engaged to a young lady back in Mexico, where he has lived, and he plans to earn sufficient funds to send for her. But when he meets Soledad ("How does one describe the sun?"), his heart is torn between duty and desire. Duty wills out, yet it is Soledad who is on his mind on the day several years later when he gives his life for Cuban independence. Deliciously romantic as well as resonantly political, Bernardo's novel is compelling from first page to last.

Source: Brad Hooper, "Silent Wing," (book review) in *Booklist,* Vol. 94, No. 21, July, 1998, p. 1856.

Publisher's Weekly

In the following brief review, Bernardo's Silent Wing *is negatively compared with historical, manner-bound novels of the 19th century.*

Following on the heels of last year's much praised *The Secret of the Bulls* Bernardo returns to colonial Cuba in a disappointing, fictionalized version of the life of Jose Marti, here depicted as the poet and revolutionary Julian. Just before setting out to seek his fortune as a writer, teacher and activist in Guatemala, idealistic Julian proposes marriage to Lucia, a frivolous Cuban woman who desires a trousseau more than political freedom for her country. A man of his word, Julian feels he must honor his vow even after he meets the girl of his dreams in Guatemala; the woman who shares his passion for freedom is clearly the counterpart to Marti's "Nina de Guatemala." The choice to portray Marti's life as fiction seems a lamentable error, since the patriot's real life was more dramatic and eventful than

this conventional historical novel conveys. And Bernardo's attempt to sketch a 19th-century society bound by manners, a la James or Wharton, but simultaneously stressed by the tumultuous and violent political situation, is thwarted by a text that reads like a screenplay filled out with stage directions. This rushed, awkwardly written work does not do justice to the complexities of Marti's life. Readers would do better with one of many biographies dealing with the Cuban hero.

Source: "Silent Wing," (book review) in *Publisher's Weekly,* Vol. 245, No. 22, June 1, 1998, p. 47.

Sources

Thomas Curwen, "At the Intersection of Passion, Politics, and Poetry," in *Los Angeles Times,* July 29, 1998, p. 6.

Brad Hooper, review in *Booklist,* July 19, 1998.

Review in *Library Journal,* June 1, 1998, p. 149.

Review in *Publishers Weekly,* June 1, 1998, p. 47.

Further Reading

Bernardo, Jose Raul, *The Secret of the Bulls*, Scribner: 1997.
    Sweeping family chronicle set in Cuba from the turn of the century to the mid-1930s, emphasizing Cuban machismo, family struggles and passions.

Ripoll, Carlos, *Jose Marti Thoughts*, Endowment for Cuban American Studies: 1994.
    Anthology of writings and thoughts on American society from Cuban writer Jose Marti, posing the central question, how to achieve a functional accomodation of truth, self-interst and reason.

Stendahl, Ann Jefferson, editor, *The Red and the Black*, Everyman Paperback Classics: 1997.
    A young man nurtures dreams of glory in a post-Revolutionary world. Stendhal, one of France's greatest novelists, fashions this story with riveting psychological accuracy and a passionate awareness of political exigency.

So Far From God

Ana Castillo

1993

When *So Far From God* was published in 1993, it was heralded as the newest masterpiece from one of the most elegant voices in the Chicana movement. Julia Alvarez and Sandra Cisneros both favorably reviewed the book as true to the Chicana experience and brilliantly funny. The novel revolves around the life of Sofi, a wife, a mother, and a Chicana who discovers what it means to be a woman. Through the deterioration of her marriage, the deaths of her daughters, and the awakening of her social activism, Castillo produces an image of a Mexican-American woman who endures all and comes out stronger than ever before. Castillo mixes religion, supernatural occurrences, sex, laughter, and heartbreak in a novel unlike anything previously seen in American Literature. *So Far From God* is a funny novel than does not have a happy ending; a novel dominated by tragedy, yet full of the victory of the human spirit; a novel that is highly entertain while still thought provoking. Castillo wants to expose the joys and realities of contemporary Mexican-American life on the edge of American culture. Castillo said, in an interview with Simon Romero, that she wanted to use humor in her fiction because the themes she explores are so dense, that without the humor, her point would get lost. She wanted her novel to challenge the status quo in terms of expectations of women, religion, language, and medicine.

Author Biography

Ana Castillo, a leading voice in the Chicana/o movement, was born in 1953. Although her novels, nonfiction, and poetry are all set in the American Southwest, Castillo was raised and educated in her native Chicago, where she earned a B.A. degree in Studio Art and Secondary Education (1975) and an M.A. in Latin American and Caribbean Studies from the University of Chicago (1979). In the late 1970s, Castillo moved to southern California where she taught English as a second language and developed her style and distinctive voice. Always an activist, she uses her fiction, poetry, and nonfiction as tools to illuminate the plight of Hispanics, especially women, in contemporary American culture. She cofounded the journal *Third Woman* and also serves as a contributing editor to *Humanizarte Magazine* .

Her international fame, following the publication of *The Mixquiahuala Letters* (fiction; 1986), and poetry such as *Otro Canto* (1977), *The Invitation* (1979), *Women Are Not Roses* (1984), and *My Father Was a Toltec* (1988) led to a teaching opportunity at France's Sorbonne University and a Ph.D. in American Studies from the University of Bremen, Germany, in 1991. Since then, Castillo has continued to lecture, read from her works, and publish fiction and poetry about the lives of Hispanic women.

Like most public intellectuals, among whom she numbers herself, Castillo has donated her papers, workbooks, and personal memorabilia to a major university. The Castillo Collection, the largest major collection of a Hispanic woman writer, is at the University of California at Los Angeles and is open to all students and scholars. The collection contains material, both personal and public, dating from 1973 to 1990 and is continually being updated by Castillo. The table of contents for the collection is available from UCLA's website.

Castillo has won numerous awards including the Before Columbia Foundation's American Book Award in 1987 and two National Endowment for the Arts awards. *So Far From God* won both the Carl Sandburg Literary Award in Fiction of 1993 and the Mountains and Plains Bookseller Award of 1994. Castillo's diverse publications, activism, and continued popularity make her one of the leading voices in a revitalized feminist Chicana/o movement along side other artists like Sandra Cisneros, Julia Alvarez, and Denise Chávez.

Plot Summary

Episode 1

Ana Castillo's So Far From God is written in a structure similar to a tele-novella, the Latino version of a soap opera, in that the novel is a series of "episodes." The first episode introduces the six major characters: Sofi, her daughters, and her husband. Sofi is introduced by describing her function within her society. Her daughter, Loca, dies at age three and the community helps Sofi mourn. Everyone comes to the wake except Sofi's husband, Domingo. None of Sofi's family had approved of their marriage and even the local priest had refused to perform the wedding ceremony. Domingo had left Sofi soon after Loca's conception.

At the baby's funeral, all of Sofi's neighbors are astonished when the seemingly dead child pushes open the lid of her coffin and flies onto the roof of the church. She argues with the priest and claims to have gone to Hell and come back. Because she seems to see things on a different level and because of her odd behavior, the townsfolk start calling the baby La Santa Loca (The Crazy Saint), which quickly becomes simply La Loca (The Crazy One). She cannot stand people other than her family, so she does not go to school or interact with the community.

Sofi's three other daughters are introduced in this first part as well. Esperanza is the "smart" one, Caridad the "pretty" one, and Fe the "normal" one. Esperanza, the college-educated reporter, joined a Chicano rights organization and discovered that the men were only interested in sex. She is jilted by Ruben and finds a job at a local television station as a broadcast journalist. Caridad hated school and works as an orderly in a hospital only to afford to go out, get drunk, and have sex. Caridad's three abortions, all performed by her sister La Loca, and her failed marriage right out of high school contribute to her weakness for men and alcohol, leading to tragedy later. Fe has a respectable job at the local bank and is engaged to Tom Torres, manager of a mini-mart.

Gradually, misfortunes begin to befall the characters. Esperanza's college boyfriend returns, divorced from his Anglo wife, and he wants to use Esperanza for sex again. She goes along with it for a while, but decides that he is not what she wants and that working in Washington, DC, is her dream. She leaves the security of her family and moves across the country. Fe's seemingly perfect relationship

Ana Castillo

ends with a Dear Jane letter: Tom breaks the engagement without even talking to her. Fe suffers a mental breakdown and spends a year screaming and beating her head against the walls. At the same time, Caridad is sexually assaulted, badly beaten and mutilated, and left for dead on the side of the road. Sofi spends the year tending to Fe and Caridad while La Loca takes care of the house and Esperanza takes care of Sofi. The first episode ends with the recovery of Caridad, who miraculously bears no scars, and of Fe, who is left with severe damage to her vocal chords. Domingo returns as well, not because he has missed his family but because the

community has insulted his honor by suggesting that he had married another woman. A lout, gambler, and deserter he is, but a bigamist he is not.

Episode 2: Esperanza

Esperanza never seems at ease with her life. She is torn between her love for Ruben and her desire for a career. When her mother criticizes her for sleeping with Ruben, suggesting that Ruben is not going to "buy the cow if he gets the milk for free," Esperanza answers that she is not a cow. She turns down a job in Houston, Texas, because that is where Ruben's ex-wife will be living. She begins seeing Ruben again, but realizes that he only wants sex and not a relationship; she breaks it off before he has a chance to. She then takes a job at a national network in Washington, DC.

Esperanza is soon assigned to the Persian Gulf to cover the war there. She is killed on the job, but her body is never recovered. Sofi and Domingo are invited to Washington, DC, to receive a medal in her honor. Later Esperanza appears as a ghost to comfort her mother and play with her sister, La Loca.

Episode 3: Caridad

Caridad's life is rich in both events and spirituality. After she recovers from her attack, she moves out of the family home and begins her spiritual training at the hands of Dona Felica, an elderly healer. Dona Felica and Caridad go on several pilgrimages to local shrines that tend to mix Pagan ritual with Catholic Christian symbolism and theology. At one of these shrines, Caridad falls in love with another woman, not so much in a sexual way but more in a spiritual way. She and this young woman eventually become friends, after Caridad has spent a year meditating in a cave, and her abilities to heal and channel spirits greatly increase. She meets Dona Felica's godson, Francisco, a devoted sculptor. He becomes fixated on Caridad, both as a spiritual holy woman and as a target of lust. Just as Caridad finds happiness with Woman-on-the-Wall, Francisco's urge to remove her influence from his life becomes unbearable. He pursues Caridad and her lover, threatening them both with rape and murder. Caridad chooses to leap to her death from a pueblo rather than risk being murdered by her stalker. Like Esperanza's, Caridad's body is never found.

Episode 4: Sofi's Turn

At this point in the novel, Castillo uses flashback to describe the relationship between Sofi and Domingo, thus setting the stage for the rest of the story. Sofi and Domingo met at her cousin's *quinceañera*, a traditional Latin American coming-out party marking a girl's fifteenth year. Domingo was charming and gorgeous, and Sofi fell in love with him. He crashed Sofi's *quinceañera* the next year and they danced all night long. Three years later they married and had a baby girl once every three years until Domingo had gambled away all the land that Sofi had inherited from her father. He abandoned her soon after La Loca's conception and did not return until the child was a teenager. Although Domingo tries to straighten himself out, he

can't; he loses even the house Sofi lives in. At that point, she divorces him and decides to live for herself. She organizes the laborers into unions and cooperatives, then runs for mayor of the unincorporated area. She puts her energies into making her community better, bringing in a real hospital instead of the clinic where her daughter had been declared dead after an epileptic seizure, attracting real grocery stores, and improving the roads, sewer system, and water supply system. She also comes to terms with the deaths of Esperanza and Caridad.

Episode 5: Fe

Fe never really recovers from her year of screaming after Tom canceled the wedding, but she does manage to get on with her life. She was always more grounded than any of her sisters, and she soon returns to work at the bank. She falls in love with (or settles for) her cousin Casimiro, an accountant. They eventually marry and try to start a family. However, soon after her wedding, Fe leaves her job at the bank to work at a parts cleaning factory. She hears that workers can make good money and if they do as they are told, there are bonuses as well. Fe is a very good and careful worker. She is soon promoted and given more special assignments with various chemicals. No one ever explains the dangers to Fe and she does not think to ask because she cannot believe that her bosses would not care about her health. Fe discovers that she has terminal cancer when she fails to get pregnant and she seeks help from a fertility specialist. While the company offers to pay a small amount, Fe hires a lawyer to sue the company which is now under investigation by the government. Fe's illness makes her research the chemicals that she used and her horror and shock at what these chemicals do to human tissue is real and terrifying. Like her sisters, she dies unfulfilled; her body, or what is left of it, is cremated and buried next to the tombstones of Esperanza and Caridad.

Episode 6: Loca

Sofi and Domingo's youngest child has no better luck that her sisters. Her seeming death as a young child, which was actually an epileptic seizure that left her with no vital signs, and her miraculous return from the dead made her special. She spends her time talking to the animals, birds, and ghosts of the neighborhood. She is able to talk to both Esperanza's and Caridad's ghosts, and this comforts her mother. However, as the years go by, she becomes weaker and more withdrawn. Two faith healers, Dr. Tolentino and Dona Felica, could not cure her, although both tried for many months. Tolentino tries to psychically remove numerous growths from her stomach and intestines, while Felica gives her teas to improve her strength and appetite, but nothing works. In actuality, La Loca has AIDS, although the story does not reveal how she got it. Soon La Loca dies—a true death this time—and is buried with her sisters. Sofi mourns yet again.

Episode 7

In a very real way, *So Far From God* revolves around the search of one woman for the meaning of life. After La Loca's death, Sofi gives up trying to be a good daughter, wife, and mother. She asks herself, "What's the use? Christalmighty!" When Sofi decides that she no longer has to care for her parents, her husband, her daughters, her land, her shop, or her community, she finds out that she herself is the most important person in her life. She founds an organization dedicated to the mothers of children who have been killed or died young.

Characters

Caridad

Caridad is the third and most beautiful of Sofi's daughters. She is vibrant, sensual, and sexually active. She loved one man and when he broke her heart by cheating on her after their wedding, Caridad turned her back on love. For several years, she gets involved with dangerous men, heavy drinking, and lots of sex. She has three abortions, all performed by her sister, La Loca, and is severely beaten by a supernatural beast. Following a year in a coma, the same year Fe is screaming, Caridad discovers a new side to herself in her "holy recovery." She realizes that she has the potential to be a spiritual healer and channeler. She begins to train with Dona Felicia and her year of wilderness solitude only enhances her reputation. Unfortunately, Caridad becomes the object of a stalker's attentions. Her stalker, Francisco el Penitente, is mentally unbalanced and believes that the only way to get Caridad out of his mind is to kill her. Caridad, rather than be murdered, jumps to her death off an ancient Pueblo Indian cliff dwelling. Her death represents the cultural forces working on women to suppress their sexuality and remove their control over their own lives.

Domingo

Domingo is Sofi's husband and the father of her children. He is also a gambler. He abandons the family soon after La Loca's birth because he cannot stay in one place. He returns immediately after Caridad's "holy restoration"—a twenty-year absence. Sofi allows him to stay and they are happy for a while. He builds Caridad a house with his winnings from the Illinois lottery and continues to gamble without Sofi's knowledge. When he loses Sofi's house and four-acre lot to a Federal judge in an illegal card game, Sofi finally divorces her husband. He moves into the house that he built for Caridad and leaves the narrative.

Dona Felicia

Dona Felicia, much like Sofi, is an older woman whose life has been anything but peaceful. Married, widowed, and abandoned several times, Felicia has buried all of her children and lost any faith in organized religion. She is a spiritual healer who trains Caridad as a channeler. She feels responsible for Caridad's death since it is Felicia's godson who stalks her. She tries to save La Loca, but her skills are useless against AIDS. Dona Felicia tries to help Sofi cope with the loss of all of her children.

Esperanza

Esperanza is the eldest of Sofi's daughters. She is the only one to complete college and to "discover" her ethnicity. Esperanza was a bit of an activist in college, marching and picketing for the cause of Hispanic Brotherhood. She became a journalist, working at a local television station before accepting a national job based in Washington. She accepted the job only after both of her sisters recovered and she felt no longer needed. Esperanza went to cover the 1991 Persian Gulf War and was killed in action. The hypocrisy surrounding the U.S. military and American treatment of Hispanic women becomes obvious in the way the authorities treated her death and their patronizing attitude toward her parents.

Fe

Fe is Sofi's second daughter, often considered the "normal" one. She worked at the local bank since graduating from high school and was engaged to a nice, normal guy, Tom Torres. Fe is embarrassed by her family and tries very hard not to invite her friends over or to involve her family in her professional life. When Tom breaks off their engagement, Fe goes crazy, screaming and beating her head against the walls of the family home for one year. After her recovery, which is just as sudden as her screaming fit, she returns to work, not realizing the damage her screaming has done to her voice. She marries her cousin and goes to work in a parts-cleaning plant for more money. She volunteers to do hazardous work duty, not knowing that the chemicals were hazardous, and eventually dies from cancer. Like Esperanza's death, Fe's death exposes the dangers and terrible working conditions faced by Hispanic women, as well as the callous attitudes white corporate American holds towards its workforce.

La Loca

Although readers never learn her real name, Sofi's fourth daughter, La Loca, is aptly named. La Loca gets her name from events surrounding her first death and funeral when she was three years old. After an epileptic fit leaves her comatose, La Loca's family believes that she is dead and plans to bury her. She awakes just as the priest is muttering over her casket. The child ''flies'' to the roof of the church and tells everyone that she has been to Hell and has come back. La Loca changes greatly: she can no longer stand people touching her, nor can she handle the smell of any people other than her family, she talks to animals, ghosts, and other spirits. La Loca is considered a saint at first, but her odd behavior soon makes the townspeople drop the ''Santa'' part and refer to her as La Loca, the Crazy One. Like her sisters, La Loca does not live a long and happy life. Soon after Fe's and Caridad's deaths, she is diagnosed with AIDS. How she contracted the disease is never revealed, but since she never had a boyfriend or a blood transfusion, her illness becomes as supernatural as her life. La Loca's death inspired her mother to form Mothers of Martyrs and Saints (M.O.M.A.S.), an organization dedicated to keeping alive the memories of people killed when young.

Sofi

Sofi is one of the major characters in *So Far From God*. She is the mother of four daughters and towards the end of the novel, she becomes the unofficial mayor of the town. Her devout Catholicism and her personal strength are the things that allow Sofi to survive her husband's behavior and desertion and the deaths of all her children. Sofi grows from a dependent, superstitious woman to a strong, dominant political force in southern Arizona. Throughout the novel, Sofi works to keep her family together. As the novel's title suggests, Sofi is always just beyond the touch of the divine. Only when she stops trying to be the perfect wife and mother does she realize and embrace herself as a woman and becomes free.

Themes

Woman as Daughter, Wife, and Mother

One of the major themes in *So Far From God* is the idea of a woman's role in society. Traditionally, Hispanic women are taught to serve three people: father, husband, and child. These roles can be confining, particularly for modern women, and Castillo challenges this image of woman in her novel. The daughters, Esperanza, Fe, Caridad, and La Loca all try to be dutiful daughters and wives, yet they are unsuccessful in these roles. Esperanza's boyfriend leaves her for another woman, while Fe's husband drives her to a job that kills her. Caridad's marriage falls apart as do all of her other relationships, while La Loca's hatred of people effectively rules out romance. Even Sofi acts like a dutiful daughter and passes up the chance for true love. However Castillo complicates this theme by making the alternatives to the traditional role just as unsuccessful. Esperanza puts her career ahead of family and is killed, while her three sisters all choose paths that lead away from the traditional wife and mother syndrome and they all die childless as well. Castillo suggests that until women can see themselves as human beings first, they will be ultimately unsuccessful. Sofi loses everything her culture tells her is important: her husband, her children, and even her home. Only when she has nothing left to lose does Sofi realize that she must live her life for herself as a woman, not as someone's daughter or wife or mother.

Exploitation of Women

The idea of exploitation runs throughout twentieth-century American literature, and *So Far From God* is no different. Here the exploitation extends to women at home as well as work. Esperanza gives her life for her job as does Fe, but Fe's experience is much harsher. Her employers at the bank and the factory do not really care about her as a human being. In fact, the factory manager takes advantage of Fe's willingness to do whatever job to make a good impression and earn a bonus. She soon discovers that the chemicals she has been using are lethal and the company couldn't care less. Her death is painful and extended as the cancer eats away at her body. Sofi, too, falls victim to emotional and illegal exploitation. Her husband continues to gamble and loses her house and property in a card game. Even though the judge, who won Domingo's bet, knows that his actions were illegal since Domingo neither owned the land, nor could the judge take it, he still forces Sofi to pay rent on her own home. She cannot sue him because of his status as a judge and so, he exploits her ignorance and fear for his own benefit. Caridad is exploited as well, both before and after her "holy recovery." She allows herself to become a sexual plaything using sex as a way to forget her pain. After she becomes aware of her spirituality, she allows Dona Felicia and others in her community to use her talents, her struggles, and her faith to their own ends. Caridad's exploitation also costs her her life. Castillo seems to be arguing that exploitation of any kind is unavoidable for women.

Religion

Religion and devotion to a faith causes most of the problems in this novel. The major flash-points deal with how women are supposed to interact with a sexist religion and still remain women. Catholicism, as described in *So Far From God*, does not allow the female characters any way out. They must submit to male authority or die. Dona Felicia and, at the end, Sofi both reject this kind of religion and are freed from its constraints, but both have lost everything that they hold dear. Caridad tries to rework her religious beliefs, but she cannot escape the effect she has on other people. They mill around her, invade her privacy, and, in the end, force her leap to her death as the only means of escape. Castillo casts religion as a fundamental part of human existence, but argues against the confining rules of organized religion and its evil effects on society at large.

Family Space

Family, traditionally, invokes ideas of warmth, security, and safety. Much as she does with religion, Castillo turns this idea on its head. Family space becomes a place where pain, death, and fear dominate. Fe learns that her life, as she knows it, is over at home when Tom sends her a "dear Jane" letter, while Sofi loses her home to her husband's gambling problem. Even Caridad's home (the trailer she rents from Felicia and the house her father builds) become sites of pain and victims of theft. Family

Topics for Further Study

- After researching the effects of gambling addiction and its prevalence in states with lotteries, race tracks, and casinos, compare the way gambling addiction works to Domingo's situation in the novel.

- Compare the spiritual and psychic healing methods practiced by Dona Felicia and Dr. Tolentino to both more traditional forms of Western medicine and faith-healing.

- How do Fe's work experiences and Sofi's local activism compare to the more national program of labor and social reformers of the Hispanic and African-American communities?

- Considering how the Chicano/a movement began in the U.S., how does the novel illustrate the difficulties of being female and Hispanic in American culture?

- Research and view some Spanish language "tele-novellas," (Hispanic soap operas). Compare the narrative structure of these "tele-novellas" to *So Far From God*.

and family space become sites of loss and pain, forcing readers to rethink their own ideas about security and peace.

Spiritual vs. Physical

Along these same lines, Castillo presents the conflict between spiritual and physical identities. For the women in the novel, spiritual needs are subdued to the needs of the physical. Fe and Esperanza neglect their spiritual needs and are killed for their troubles. However, living totally in the spiritual realm is not an option either. Both Caridad and La Loca choose to ignore the physical world for the spiritual and they, too, die. Castillo seems to suggest that extremes are unhealthy and fatal, but that moderation does not come easily. The conflict between the physical and the spiritual realms is one fought and re-fought by every generation.

Style

Point of View

So Far From God is told by a third-person fully omniscient narrator who intrudes in the text as almost a separate character. She is funny, witty, and irreverent. Each chapter begins with a lengthy title similar to the "argument" before each canto of an epic poem. The narrator then enters the text with a funny summary of the coming action. However, all this plot preview in no way detracts from the novel's excitement or the reader's enjoyment. Rather, it builds anticipation by letting readers know what is going to happen and then letting them sit back and enjoy the ride.

Language

In her interview with Simon Romero, Castillo explains that though she did not grow up or live in the New Mexico area, she wanted to capture the style of language spoken there. She suggests that the English and the Spanish are highly localized and unlike the language spoken in California or Chicago. She mixes Spanish phrases into the text with great regularity and tries to elongate the sentences, to mimic the conversation style of the peoples of the area. In her use of Englished Spanish and Spanished English, Castillo attempts to create a new language, one that all her readers can understand and enjoy.

Epic Fiction

So Far From God is written as a kind of satirical prose epic in the tradition of Cervantes's *Don Quixote*. Castillo's use of the supernatural, high language, episodic structure, and the witty narrator all contribute to this form. Sofi's tragedies and triumphs are described in epic terms and the story of a no-name woman in the middle of a tiny Hispanic New Mexico town takes on great themes and ideas. Sofi rises from being an abandoned wife to the head of an international organization. Castillo's novel is full of wit, humor, and a sadness that challenges her readers to redefine what being great and successful means.

Historical Context

The Feminist Chicana Movement

The Chicano/a Movement was born in the wine-growing region of California in the early 1970s when Cesar Chavez organized the mainly Hispanic migrant farmworkers into an effective, vocal labor union. Within a few years authors, poets, actors, and politicians were demonstrating and demanding equal rights for Americans of Hispanic descent in terms of language recognition, cultural integrity, and political power. As the movement grew, many women within the movement began to feel left out or misunderstood. Writers like Sandra Cisneros, Josaphina Lopez, and Gloria Anzaldua argued for a pro-female wing to the movement, saying that the concerns of Hispanic women were being ignored by the traditional macho attitude of the male leaders. Ana Castillo enlivened the debate by casting doubts on both the traditional definitions of womanhood and the newer "liberated" Hispanic woman put forward by the Feminist Chicana Movement.

OSHA/EPA Enforcement

So Far From God also criticizes the lack of enforcement of the federal government's rules in the workplace (Occupational Safety and Health Administration) and the environment (Environmental Protection Agency). Castillo subtly argues, through the tragic death of Fe, that most of this enforcement comes too little, too late. OSHA is a federal agency that is supposed to monitor working conditions and the health of America's workers. In the late 1980s and early 1990s, OSHA's policies were relaxed and the numbers of inspectors was reduced. The federal government of the period preferred a more business-friendly policy and so did not rigorously enforce OSHA regulations. The EPA was run in a similar manner. Castillo's novel attacks this "hands-off" approach as being deadly and dangerous.

Critical Overview

The 1993 publication of *So Far From God* was met with great applause. Castillo had already made her critical and popular reputation with her previously published poetry collections and her novel *The Mixquiahuala Letters*. The *Washington Post Book World* and the *San Francisco Chronicle* claimed it was a novel of great power and worth. While Chicana/o literature, as a whole, has not really penetrated the national reading market, leading intellectuals of the Chicana/o Movement also praised the novel as lyrical, moving, and authentic in tone, voice, and characterization. Scholars such as Theresa Delgadillo, Carmela Delia Lanza, Kamala Platt, and Roland Walter have investigated various aspects of Castillo's novel, mainly focusing on the use of language and family.

Theresa Delgadillo, in her article "Forms of Chicana Feminist Resistance: Hybrid Spirituality in Ana Castillo's *So Far From God*," argues that Castillo's use of spirituality and feminism are unique in Chicana literature. She explores how the novel reconciles the ideas of a patriarchal religion (Catholic Christianity) with ideas of equality, feminism, and the "special" role of Hispanic women as wives and mothers. Kamala Platt, on the other hand, sees Castillo's great achievement as the ability to define elements of environmentalism as integral to feminism. Platt suggests that in order for women, or men for that matter, to be truly concerned about equality between the genders, then they must also, according to her reading of Castillo, be concerned with balance and equality between nature and humanity.

The other major area of scholarly interest in Castillo's novel deals with how she manipulates ideas of home and family. Both Carmela Delia Lanza and Roland Walter explore how Castillo uses language and family to produce disharmony and discomfort with traditional ideas of domestic life. Working from bell hooks's ideas of domestic space, Lanza argues that Castillo "constructs the home as a 'site of resistance' for the woman of color living in a racist and sexist world" thus "deconstructing physical, political, and spiritual boundaries." Walter argues that Castillo creates characters who are borderline people, not comfortable in either mainstream American or Hispanic culture.

Castillo's reputation for creating readable, witty, thought-provoking fiction advances to a higher degree in *So Far From God*. She uses the tragedies in the lives of a single family to create a novel that, as Sandra Cisneros says, is "wacky, wild, y bien funny."

Criticism

Michael Rex

Rex discusses the development of Sofi as a human being outside of the traditional roles for Hispanic women of daughter, wife, and mother.

Ana Castillo's 1993 novel, *So Far From God*, explores the relationship between family members and their community in a traditional Hispanic community, making this community more accessible to non-Hispanic cultures. While critics like bell hooks and Theresa Delgadillo have argued that the home in this novel is a place where spirituality and selfhood get reworked and re-organized, the idea that Sofi rebels against the traditions of daughter, wife, and mother have generally been under-examined and have not been explored in the context of Sofi's "failed" yet successful rebellion.

Sofi's resistance to the patriarchal attitudes of her culture begins early in her life, but comes as a flashback in the novel. Sofi attends her cousin's coming-out party and meets Domingo. He is universally disliked by her middle-class Hispanic family, but Sofi is in love. She challenges the rules and her family by marrying him over her family's and her community's objections. Even the local priest refuses to perform the ceremony. From a traditional feminist point of view, Sofi's rebellion is a powerful act of independence. However, Castillo seems to cast it in a much more negative light. From the very beginning of the novel, Castillo paints Domingo as a loser, a gambler, and a player. In the flashback episode, Domingo is young and suave and just a bit dangerous. By rebelling against the social order, Sofi is opening herself up to a dangerous man. While Castillo seems to be suggesting that women should remain in the traditional role as dutiful daughters who always do what Daddy says, the subtext of the novel makes it clear that it is Sofi's family's fault that she ends up with Domingo. Castillo is critiquing Hispanic (and American) culture by suggesting that if Sofi's family had not been so dead-set against Domingo, she would not have fallen so hard for him and ruined her life.

Sofi herself realizes what she has given up after her daughter Caridad's death. She realizes that her duty to her parents should not supersede her duty to herself, but at the same time, her parents failed in their duty to her by making life with Domingo so attractive. These same ideas about family duty are illustrated in the ways Sofi's daughters behave as daughters. Unlike their mother, Esperanza, Caridad, Fe, and La Loca are free to do what they want with their lives, marry whomever they please, find their own career paths, and do everything that Sofi did not. Yet here, too, Castillo shifts the terms of the feminist debate by making the outcomes of these daughters' actions just as painful and ultimately unsuccessful as Sofi's own choices.

Sofi's behavior as a wife again goes against the traditional role of Hispanic wife and therefore the

Some critics have noted Castillo's novel as a parody of the Spanish-speaking telenovelas, or popular soap operas that attract millions of viewers in Latin America. Depicted here, soap opera star Lima Duarte performs with fellow actors on the set of Rocky Santiero.

definition of a ''good'' Hispanic woman. For most of her married life, Sofi did follow the traditional path. She married Domingo instead of just sleeping with him; she took care of the house and her husband, and even welcomed him back after a fifteen-year absence. In feminist terms, Sofi is a victim of patriarchal rage because she does not do anything for herself. She allows Domingo to leave and then accepts him back with no questions asked. However, she does start to stand up for herself when Domingo loses the house and butcher shop in a card game. Sofi makes the decision to divorce her husband. While divorce is common in American culture and many Hispanic women do divorce every year, the idea of divorce is not culturally accepted in Chicana/o culture. Due in part to the overwhelming influence of Catholicism, divorce is a fate to be avoided at all costs. Sofi displays her understanding of this by having not divorced Domingo when he left her the first time. However, her reason for not divorcing Domingo had nothing to do with any love she had for him; it was merely to keep up appearances. Sofi worries more about how she appears than whether or not she is happy. Happiness is not part of the equation for a wife in Sofi's mindset.

Sofi is finally able to break this pattern when she finds out that Domingo has lost her land and her house. She has been the long-suffering wife. She put up with his gambling, his desertion, his broken promises, and his lies. She sacrificed everything to play the role of a good wife. Domingo bet her house—the house was hers, not his, a gift from her father—on the turn of a card. He lost. And like a traditional Hispanic wife, she lost right along with him. Sofi had finally had enough. She divorced Domingo and forced him to sign over his half of the house he had built for Caridad so that La Loca would have a place to live when Sofi died. She completely wrote him out of her life. It is in her rejection of the role of wife that Sofi acts most like a feminist heroine.

Sofi's rejection of the traditional roles for Hispanic women comes to it fullest expression in the way she mothers her four daughters: Esperanza, Caridad, Fe, and La Loca. Throughout the novel, Sofi never encourages her daughters to be anything, not even traditional Hispanic women. She does not discourage them either, but she does not raise her daughters the way she was raised. She allows all of

What Do I Read Next?

- Gloria Anzaldua's *Borderlands: La Frontera* (1987) is a collection of personal essays and poetry from one of the major authors of the Chicana/o movement. The first half of the work (personal essays) deals with how Anzaldua sees herself as a woman, an Hispanic, and a lesbian. The second half is a collection of poetry written from Anzaldua's soul which speaks of heartbreak, joy, lost, and triumph. The text is written in English with a large amount of Spanish without an attempt at translation. Anzaldua argues that her use of Spanish in an English text makes her non-Spanish readers feel just like Hispanic people do in an English only world.

- *The House on Mango Street* (1989) and *Woman Hollering Creek* (1991) are the two major works by Sandra Cisneros, perhaps the most recognized writer of the Chicana/o Movement. Both works, the first a novel, the second a collection of short stories, deal with the problems of being female and Hispanic in Anglo-America. *The House on Mango Street* is a coming of age novel about a Chicago girl named Esperanza, who through coming to grips with the poverty, class hatred, and ethnic stereotypes, creates a world of her own. *Woman Hollering Creek* is a collection of stories dealing with a vast array of Hispanic women from the young girl discovery sex to a professional woman trying to break the chains of Hispanic wifedom and motherhood.

- Gabriella Ibieta's 1993 collection of short stories by Latin American writers, contains thirty stories by twenty-two authors from a variety of countries and cultures. The stories are all translated or written in English and display the wide range of themes, similarities, and differences within the Latin community. There are stories by world renowned authors like Jorge Luis Borges and Juan Rulfo as well as lesser known authors like Luisa Valenzuela and Augusto Roa Bastos.

- Ana Castillo's novel *The Mixquiahuala Letters*

(1986) and collection *Goddess of the Americas: Writings on the Virgin of Guadalupe* (1997) explore issues of femininity, family, and spirituality. *The Mixquiahuala Letters* is a novel written in letter or epistolary form telling the story of a friendship between two artists. One is Anglo, the other Hispanic. The novel traces their friendship over twenty years in a kind of odd-couple pairing of opposites who find that they need each other after all. Castillo's collection of essays, stories, and poems dealing with the Virgin of Guadalupe explores similar ground as her novels, but in a different way. Here, she is exploring the way spirituality makes identity and how the use of a ''native'' saint makes Hispanic spirituality different from other forms of Catholicism.

- Mexican author Laura Esquivel's 1992 *Como Agua Para Chocolate* (translated by Carol and Thomas Christensen as *Like Water for Chocolate*) took America by storm in the early 1990s. This novel, told in a series of monthly installments with recipes and romances, explores rural life in turn of the twentieth century Mexico. The heart-breaking story of Tita and her lover Pedro, captures the hearts and minds of readers. The 1993 film version became the highest grossing foreign film in American history and the novel won the 1994 ABBY award from the American Booksellers Association.

- The idea of womanist prose was defined in Alice Walker's *In Search of Our Mothers' Gardens.* This collection of essays, put together in 1983, explores the meaning, lives, and troubles of being female and Black in modern-day America. Much like what Castillo does for Hispanic women in her novel, Walker does in her essays and the 1981 Pulitzer Prize-winning novel, *The Color Purple.* Walker's works strive to complete the picture of American life by opening the doors to the Black female experience.

> She allows all of her daughters room to express their sexuality, their talents, and their realities. But it does not do her any good. All four of her daughters die in tragic circumstances, leaving Sofi more devastated and alone each time."

her daughters room to express their sexuality, their talents, and their realities. But it does not do her any good. All four of her daughters die in tragic circumstances, leaving Sofi more devastated and alone each time.

Esperanza has never been Sofi's favorite, but Sofi does care for her eldest daughter. She tries to advise her on sex without being overbearing and does not voice objections to her career decisions. It is only after Esperanza's death during the Gulf War that Sofi starts to question her parenting methods. She realizes that she hardly knows her daughters, but, at the same time, feels that it is too late to do anything about it. Sofi did exactly what her culture told her to do in all such situations.

When Tom breaks off his engagement to Fe, Sofi's third daughter, she suffers a breakdown and spends an entire year screaming and banging her head against the walls of her house. Sofi behaves like the "good" mother. She does not interfere, but tries to get Fe to eat and come to her senses. Sofi is much more active in Fe's life because she knows about love. She approaches Tom and his mother and accuses him of destroying her daughter. She attacks him verbally as only a mother can and relishes her part in the drama. Yet, she goes back home without seeing Tom himself and lets her daughter scream her head off. Sofi does not try to end Fe's behavior, but then neither does she punish her for it. After Fe recovers, she is still welcome in her mother's house and no mention is made about the way she speaks or behaves. Sofi does not encourage Fe's engagement to Casimiro, but neither does she stand in the way of Fe's chance at happiness. Sofi seems almost detached from her daughters' lives after Esperanza's

death, afraid that getting too close will bring bad luck. She deals with Fe's death in this stoic fashion. Sofi is still caught up in her public appearance and cannot see what her daughters need from her.

Perhaps her most traditional yet unconventional expression of motherhood is the way Sofi deals with Caridad and La Loca. Caridad seems to be her favorite child and throughout the novel, Sofi is either excusing her behavior or finding ways to justify it. After Caridad is attacked and beaten, Sofi dedicates all of her energy to nursing her daughter, yet she can do nothing more than sit by her bedside and pray. After Caridad's "miraculous" recovery, Sofi plays down her maternal role by letting her daughter move out of the house and into a trailer of her own. Even the death of Caridad's horse and her own year-long disappearance in the mountains cannot shake Sofi's determination to play the good mother. As tragedies mount around her, Sofi gives up more and more of her own self to be the good mother that society tells her she must be. Even after Caridad's death, Sofi feels that she must continue to play the good-mother role. She turns her attention to her remaining daughter and her community.

Sofi's relationship with her youngest daughter, known as La Loca, the Crazy One, is complicated at best. She witnessed her daughter's "death" at age three, was prepared to bury her, and smothered her with mothering after she rose from the dead at her own funeral. Sofi never tries to make La Loca fit into society; she never takes her to school or church nor does she push her to socialize in any way. La Loca is her crazy one, her eternal baby. Yet, she does express genuine concern for her strange daughter. Sofi questions her daughter's relationship with the ghosts and the animals and insists that she wear clean clothes. Sofi tries to make her daughter's last months comfortable and realizes that she is not in control of events but is merely an observer to the unfolding of her family's lives.

In this characterization, Castillo seems to be condemning the traditional role of motherhood as one that cannot really affect how people or things turn out. Yet, in a blast of heavy-handed sarcasm, Castillo creates a character who turns her failed role of mother into a successful national role as the president and founder of an organization devoted to memorializing children who have died or been killed young. Sofi also takes on the role of mothering her entire community; she is able to do for her town what she cannot do for her children. Sofi is able to provide ways of getting living wages for the farm hands, providing better food through a co-op program, and provide better medical and utility services through a real hospital and decent sewer and water systems.

It is only when Sofi has lost everything that she realizes that she, as a person, must matter before she can do anything worthwhile. "Sofi had devoted her life to being a good daughter, a good wife, and a good mother, . . . and now there was no mother to honor, no father to respect, no 'jitas (children) to sacrifice for, no rancho to maintain, and no land left to work." It is through the characterization of Sofi, a woman who loses everything that her society says makes her a woman, that Castillo argues most passionately for a new definition of womanhood both for Hispanic women and women all over the world.

Source: Michael Rex, in an essay for *Literature of Developing Nations for Students*, Gale, 2000.

Roland Walter

In the following essay on Ana Castillo's novel So Far From God, *Roland Walter examines the politics of dislocation and relocation as a "locus of possibility" for Castillo's female characters, who, he argues, relocate their consciousness from separateness to collective, radical mestiza-based consciousness which allows them a strategy of "empowerment and liberation".*

In *So Far From God* Castillo creates community-defined by Tomas Rivera as "place, values, personal relationships, and conversation" by means of a "speakerly" magico-realist narrative texture. The driving forces of this process are women: women who think, dream, act and relate in what Anzaldua has called a "pluralistic mode," transcending binary oppositions, a rational "dualistic thinking in the individual and collective consciousness," in an effort to heal "the split that originates in the very foundation of our lives, our culture, our languages, our thoughts" (Borderlands). The keyword of this worldview, carried as in Sapogonia by a discourse in which the natural and supernatural categories of reality are harmoniously intertwined, is faith: a faith that facilitates a dynamic relationship between human beings and their surroundings and an implicit magico-realist conception of the world in which the imaginary is regarded as factual reality. Faith is the fundamental principle which underlies La Loca's resurrection, Caridad's miraculous recovery and predictions, Felicia's holistic treatments, and the appearance of living (mythical) spirits. This pecul-

iar type of faith, which is revised and actualized through female agency, is the driving force behind the collective activism and the implicit alternative mode of living and relating outlined in the novel; a counter-hegemonic mode conceived as possible solution to the postmodern fragmentation and dislocation experienced in the borderlands.

This magico-realist worldview, whose fundamental essence resides in "the interconnectedness of things", is expressed by means of a "speakerly" texture in which a skaz-like discourse, being at work in and acting on the actual discourse, an unnamed narrator, who as a storyteller represents both a communal and an individual voice, and the use of multiple points of view and perspectives re-create and interweave individual and collective experiences as the novel's political unconscious. A telling example of this fluid dialogical texture is the episode in which Sofi, La Loca's mother, announces to a comadre her plan to run for mayor of Tome. On entering Sofi's house just before the actual dialogue between the two women, the comadre, whose namelessness suggests her collective identity, is lost in thoughts about Sofi and her family. Introduced by the phrase, ". . .for when she repeated the story later to the other in the Chicano borderlands through an affirmation of otherness—an otherness not imposed but recreated: an identity based on difference with the capacity to relocate, a "differential consciousness"—whose nature shifts from individual separateness to collective multiplicity that posits no "ultimate answers, no terminal utopia. . .no predictable final outcomes" but transcends hegemony via concrete utopia, a strategic use of deconstructive differance that traces the necessity for change and anticipates the possibility of an alternative lifestyle. By locating the agency of change in the mestiza—the re-creation of woman as creator who has a vision, is not "afraid to speak that vision" (Saeta Interview), and, most importantly, acts accordingly. And by restoring their indigenous roots, Castillo invests her female characters with a historicized and politicized consciousness—a nonessentialized consciousness based on a radical mestiza subjectivity, that is, a subversive position of intelligibility and mode of knowing necessary for the transformation of cultural practices—as strategy of empowerment and liberation. For that reason I read her politics of dislocation and relocation as resistance Xicanisma that envisions the mestiza consciousness as "a crossroads sin fronteras," (Borderlands) a "locus of possibility" (Sandoval), a motivating force behind "the development of an alternative social

> "...By restoring their indigenous roots, Castillo invests her female characters with a historicized and politicized consciousness—a nonessentialized consciousness based on a radical mestiza subjectivity, that is, a subversive position of intelligibility and mode of knowing necessary for the transformation of cultural practices...."

system'' (Castillo Massacre). The deconstructive nature of this undertaking resides in the revelation of the necessity for insurgency/activism without legitimating the envisioned results as transcendental truths: a ''talking back'' whose echos do not spiral down into abyme but create a ''real state of emergency'' (Benjamin) that carries the possibility of ''new life and new growth,'' (Hooks) or to use Heidegger's phrase, ''something begins its presencing'' in the Chicano borderlands (Bhabha).

Source: Roland Walter, ''The Cultural Politics of Disclocation and Relocation in the Novels of Ana Castillo,'' in *MELUS,* Vol.23, No. 1, Spring, 1998, pp. 81–97.

Carmela Delia Lanza

In the following essay, Carmela Delia Lanza examines author Ana Castillo's deconstruction of women's physical, political, and spiritual boundaries within her novel So Far From God *and explores how both the author and her characters seek to merge these arenas, connecting their domestic and public lives.*

In the nineteenth century, Louisa May Alcott made subjects of objects when she wrote her domestic novel *Little Women*, which centered on four sisters and their mother during the American Civil War. Alcott created a home for the March girls that was removed from the world of war and male supremacy. In the twentieth century most critics who have devoted their attention to home space and domestic

ritual have concentrated on white, middle-class homes (Matthews). It is necessary, however, to begin including working-class homes and the homes of women of color in this dialectic. The subject of home space has not gone unnoticed by some women of color, like cultural theorists bell hooks and Gloria Anzaldua, and novelist Toni Morrison. Each of these writers is re-visioning the home space and its significance regarding gender roles, racism and spirituality in the homes of working-class women of color. For example, in her essay, ''Homeplace: a Site of Resistance,'' bell hooks is not interested in further exploration of the ''white bourgeois norms (where home is conceptualized as politically neutral space).''Instead, she uses her theory to examine the ''homeplace'' of African American women, a space she defines as a ''site of resistance and liberation struggle.''

bell hooks's theory on ''the homeplace'' can be used to explore the domestic world that Ana Castillo has created in her novel, *So Far From God*. In this novel, Castillo, like hooks and other women writers of color, constructs the home as a ''site of resistance'' for the woman of color living in a racist and sexist world. Deconstructing physical, political and spiritual boundaries, Castillo takes on the role Gloria Anzaldua describes in her book, *Borderlands/La Frontera*, as ''the new mestiza.'' With its playful and ironic style, and its insistence on ambiguity and contradictions, So Far From God offers a postmodern inversion of Alcott's *Little Women*. Both works are American novels dealing with the primary relationships of four sisters; however, Castillo's novel is concerned with four Chicana sisters and a mother living a working class life in Tome, New Mexico. According to Cordelia Chavez Candelaria, Castillo is ''one of the earliest Chicana voices to articulate a sexual politics through textual poetics,'' and this is clearly seen in *So Far From God*. Unlike Alcott's created home space that for the most part is politically neutral, the home space in Castillo's novel is infused with political resistance. It is a place where women of color have an ''opportunity to grow and develop'' spiritually and politically, which is not always possible or allowable in a ''culture of white supremacy.''

The daughters in *So Far From God* are dealing with power relations that the March girls in nineteenth century middle class America did not even have to think about. The March girls, despite their own oppression in a patriarchal culture and their own sympathy for the poor and destitute, were part

An army medic assists a wounded soldier during the Persian Gulf War. In Castillo's novel, Esperanza, a TV news anchorwoman, visits her family as a ghost after getting killed covering Operation Desert Storm.

of the hegemony of white culture. The sisters in *So Far From God*, on the other hand, must construct a home space that will offer them sustenance, security and spirituality in order to move into a white world as subjects. This is crucial, for according to hooks, "when a people no longer have the space to construct homeplace, we cannot build a meaningful community of resistance." The daughters in *So Far From God* are given the opportunity to "reconceptualize ideas of homeplace, once again considering the primacy of domesticity as a site for subversion. . ." (hooks).

I am sitting at my kitchen table, thinking about the anger in Ana Castillo's novel—and how it is masked in humor. A narrator's voice disguising rage with flippancy, telling the story of four daughters who cannot live their entire lives in their mother's home, womb, female space. My baby starts to cry—he is angry because he's hungry, and I have to stop thinking about why Caridad is wearing Fe's wedding gown when she floats across the room in her healing vision. I get a bottle for the baby and it is love in action; it is a political act; it is a moment when my private sphere, my home space is directly connected to the growth of another human being. I

think about what Louise Erdrich said regarding mothering and how that relates to my home, my so-called private life:

> One reason there is not a great deal written about what it is like to be the mother of a new infant is that there is rarely a moment to think of anything else besides that infant's needs. Endless time with a small baby is spent asking, "What do you want? What do you want?"

It is the opposite of war. The ego is put aside; ideas, philosophies, theories all shrink down in the chthonic force of sustaining life—feeding another person.

It is in this continuous state of childbirth, moving into grace with all my resistance that I want to say, "Leave me alone, I'm busy." But I don't. According to Clarissa Pinkola Estes "There is a saying, 'You can't go home again.' It is not true. While you cannot crawl back into the uterus again, you can return to the soul-home. It is not only possible, it is requisite." I wash and sweep within the four walls and create stories; and like Ana Castillo, Toni Morrison, Gloria Anzaldua, and Louise Erdrich, I want to give voice to the "cultural silence of the domestic sphere" (Wright). Writing a poem while writing a poem in my home space.

> "... According to Christianity and most major religions, woman is carnal, animal, and closer to the undivine, she must be protected. Protected from herself. Woman is the stranger, the other. She is man's recognized nightmarish pieces, his Shadow-Beast. The sight of her sends him into a frenzy of anger and fear."

In the first chapter of *So Far From God*, the voice of the matriarchy is clearly heard through the mother, Sofi, when her daughter, La Loca, comes back from the dead. After Loca awakens from her other state of consciousness (whether she actually dies or suffers from epilepsy is irrelevant), opens her coffin and flies up to the church roof, the priest immediately declares his judgement by asking, "'Are you the devil's messenger or a winged angel?'" He is embodying the voice of institutions-Christianity, patriarchy. La Loca can either be a devil or an angel, a virgin or a whore according to his linear thinking. Sofi, however, will not allow this destructive language of dichotomy to continue. She demands in the voices of Coatlicue, Hestia, Demeter, Guadalupe:

'Don't you dare!. . .Don't you dare start this about my baby! If our Lord in this heaven has sent my child back to me, don't you start this backward thinking against her; the devil doesn't produce miracles! And this is a miracle, an answer to the prayers of a brokenhearted mother. . .'

Sofi is the head of her home, a home she has created for her daughters. For one daughter, Loca, the home is the only space she can call her own. She stays home, not playing the role of angel or devil, and is "without exception, healing her sisters from the traumas and injustices they were dealt by society-a society she herself never experienced firsthand." As for the other daughters, they "had gone out into the world and had all eventually returned to their mother's home." They become trapped in the "quest-pattern that has dominated Western litera-ture" (Romines). They are unwilling to accept what Kathryn Allen Rabuzzi describes in her book about spirituality and domesticity, *The Sacred and the Feminine: Toward a Theology of Housework*, as the "positive face of chaos, a letting go into possibilities that freedom from externally fixed routine allows" and that external routine is the world of male domination and the world of racism. In the novel, the daughters can only face chaos when they reenter their mother's home and re-discover their identity, their spirituality, and their strength. Eventually all of the daughters, including La Loca, experience loss in the collision of their need to create a home space with the destructive forces outside.

where I am born, I fall
in the snow you and I cannot open our mouths
to the ice house of rules and minutes,
quick thoughts of before buildings and I
feel muscles in every brick, steel girder,
I cannot breathe and try to explain what it feels
like to live in a world as an alien.
What is our place in the universe at a time
that goddess and poet have both made
     their excuses
leaving us biting our nails in the dark trying to
turn the highway into a bowl,
melting another iceberg with our tongues,
"Suck on this,"
"housework doesn't suck
 because if it did, men would love it,"
From a greeting card that was given to a friend.
We wait inside Emily's poem,
the freezing people walking in circles
making our tombstone from a home and we can
     no longer
resign or revision or remember our honey moon.

The first daughter to move away from the home and into the perilous and destructive outside world is Esperanza. She enters her "quest-pattern" when she chooses to leave home and work as a television anchorwoman in Washington, D.C. On the surface, her decision appears sensible: "'. . .it was pretty clear to her that there was no need of her on the homefront. Her sisters had recovered" from their encounters with physical and emotional abuse. Esperanza also believes her mother no longer needs her because her father has returned home years after abandoning the family. Esperanza, however, mis-judges her own position and the source of power within her family. In turning away from her home, her mother, her sisters, she is turning away from "the great and terrifying mother earth from whom all life emerges, but to whom it likewise all returns" (Rabuzzi). Her sisters continue to need her and her father is as ineffective now as he has always been.

Esperanza is deceived by the male values that dominate the outside world in the novel; in turning from the female world of her home space (which her mother and sisters created) to the male world of war, she is moving towards self-destruction and can only return home after she is dead, in the form of a spirit. At first she speaks through La Llorona, who is described in the novel as "a loving mother goddess." La Llorona is a messenger who informs La Loca (they were on a "first-name basis") that Esperanza has died. After that, Esperanza is seen by all the members of the family including the father who is a bit disturbed by his "transparent daughter." Sofi sees Esperanza as a little girl who "had had a nightmare and went to be near her mother for comfort." Caridad has one-sided conversations with Esperanza talking mostly about politics, and La Loca sees and talks to her by the river behind their home.

As a spirit, Esperanza returns to the home space to be comforted by her mother and sisters and to also teach them. Once Esperanza becomes a spirit, she is no longer a victim or an object of the white world. She belongs to a world that Anzaldua boldly asserts exists, a spiritual world that "the whites are so adamant in denying." It is no accident that the dead Esperanza communicates with La Llorona, "a woman who had been given a bad rap by every generation of people since the beginning of time..." (Castillo). While she lived, Esperanza was also given a "bad rap." But in death, La Llorona is revisioned and so is Esperanza. Both are liberated from the boundaries of white culture. Both can finally return home-and the home can be a river or a mother's arms.

After Esperanza accepts her job in Washington, D.C., she is assigned to Saudi Arabia, a place about to erupt in war. Esperanza accepts this fate because she desires to move away from the home where the "mothers are the ones who actually have to change, feed, and connect with children for all their bodily functions," and move towards the "male saviors" whose "relative absence...from homelife automatically places them in a privileged position" (Rabuzzi). It is ironic (or maybe not so ironic) that Esperanza, in choosing the male hero as her model-leaving home, participating in a patriarchal institution, war, because "'it's part of my job'"—is really choosing torture and death. Esperanza is experiencing what Anzaldua aptly describes in La Frontera as "shutting down." She is living with the fear of rejection from the outside culture and she is also living with the fear of losing her home, her mother,

"La Raza." Esperanza experiences this psychic paralysis. She is a woman of color who is:

> Alienated from her mother culture, 'alien' in the dominant culture, the woman of color does not feel safe with the inner life of her Self. Petrified, she can't respond, her face caught between los intersticios, the spaces between the different worlds she inhabits.

It is only after Esperanza has died that she can return to her "mother culture."

> Smoothing the sheets down on the bed,
> stroking a window pane,
> carrying a book to the table
> and I think of hands making him soup,
> carrying dirty underwear to the washing machine,
> ripping lettuce under cold water,
> stretching the chicken legs apart,
> slamming the ice tray against the table,
> holding, pushing, patting, kneading,
> punching the pillow down under my stomach and
> looking at the light spilling out to the street,
> "you are not my mother and you never will be,"
> tasting my blood with honey
> on my finger, around the corners of my mouth
> and I wonder how I have lasted another
>   moon cycle
> in this place.

Fe is another one of the daughters in *So Far From God* who chooses a patriarchal institution that moves her away from her home space and eventually destroys her. Fe chooses marriage and in a literal and symbolic way, it poisons her to death.

The daughter who chooses marriage, chooses to create a new domestic environment echoes the myth of Demeter and Persephone. Persephone does leave her mother but she eventually returns to her for at least some of the year's cycle:

> Persephone therefore has two homes: her home of origins with her mother and her present adult home with her husband. Because the story is told from the perspective of her mother, Persephone's homecoming is her ascent to Demeter, not her descent to Hades. (Rabuzzi)

Anzaldua discusses her own separation and return to her origins which involves the dance of rebelling, celebrating, and defending aspects of her own Chicana culture. She asserts that it was necessary for her to leave home in order "to live life on my own." Yet she concludes, "in leaving home I did not lose touch with my origins because lo mexicano is in my system. I am a turtle, wherever I go I carry 'home' on my back." Fe, in marrying Casimiro and moving to the land of "the long-dreamed-of automatic dishwasher, microwave, Cuisinart and the VCR," is trying in her own way to return to her mother but she cannot truly find her way back because of her inability to view her home and her culture in all of its complexity. She can only look at her mother's home and her sisters as a source of embarrassment or pity:

> As it was, while Fe had a little something to talk to Esperanza about, she kept away from her other sisters, her mother, and the animals, because she just didn't understand how they could all be so self-defeating, so unambitious.

Fe wants desperately to re-vision her mother's home by making it sterile, shiny, closer to the definition of home by mainstream white culture. She cannot see the spiritual richness in her home. In fact, Fe describes one of her sisters, La Loca, as "a soulless creature" because she always wears the same clothes and doesn't bother with shoes. For herself, Fe insists on imitating the mainstream culture with a considerable amount of effort: "Fe was beyond reproach. She maintained her image above all-from the organized desk at work to weekly manicured fingernails and a neat coiffure." Anzaldua points out that fear is the cause of this denial of home, a kind of "homophobia." She states:

> We're afraid of being abandoned by the mother, the culture, la Raza, for being unacceptable, faulty, damaged. . .To avoid rejection, some of us conform to the values of the culture, push the unacceptable parts in the shadows. Which leaves only one fear—that we will be found out and that the Shadow-Beast will break out of its cage.

At the beginning of the novel, Fe embraces mainstream white culture; she wants to be like the white women she works with. She chooses "three gabachas" from her job to be her bridesmaids instead of her sisters. But instead of gaining any power, she ends up wrapped in the shower curtain, screaming her way back to the matriarchal circle of her mother and sisters. Her first boyfriend, Tom, decides he isn't ready for intimacy and commitment. And it is her mother and her sisters who become the healers and nurse, who clean and pray over Fe. Fe loses her voice as a result of her constant screaming yet she still does not learn how to integrate her home space with the world outside.

Eventually, Fe marries one of her cousins, Casimiro. She still desires to live in a suburb in a house that does not smell the way her mother's house smells.

Fe's journey does end back at home and she is finally able to see her home as a source of comfort, wisdom and spirituality but it is only after the outside world has done its best to destroy her. After being exposed unknowingly to a very toxic chemical, Fe goes home to die:

> A year from the time of her wedding, everything ended, dreams and nightmares alike, for that daughter of Sofi who had all her life sought to escape her mother's depressing home-with its smell of animal urine and hot animal breath and its couch and cobijas that itched with ticks and fleas; where the coming and goings of the vecinos had become routine because of her mom's mayoral calling. . .Despite all this and more, Fe found herself wanting to go nowhere else but back to her mom and La Loca and even to the animals to die just before her twenty-seventh birthday. Sofia's chaotic home became a sanctuary from the even more incomprehensible world that Fe encountered that last year of her pathetic life.

In Fe's chase for the American Dream, she only finds infertility, deception, and ultimately a death that unlike her sisters' deaths, offers no spiritual transformation or resurrection: "Fe just died. And when someone dies that plain dead, it is hard to talk about."

Caridad, the other sister who leaves, like Fe and Esperanza also finds violence and ultimate destruction in the world outside the home. Early in the novel Caridad is physically attacked. It is a brutal sexual invasion, an attack on the female body:

> Sofi was told that her daughter's nipples had been bitten off. She had also been scourged with something, branded like cattle. Worst of all, a tracheotomy was performed because she had also been stabbed in the throat.

Caridad's attack is treated by her society as merely a cause for prayer, because "the mutilation of the lovely young woman was akin to martyrdom." And it is treated with contempt by the police department who felt she deserved what she got because of her sexual promiscuity. In the end Caridad is "left in the hands of her family, a nightmare incarnated." Caridad's attack is an attack on the female, on what is closest to home—death, birth, blood. According to Anzaldua in *Borderlands/ La Frontera* :

> The female, by virtue of creating entities of flesh and blood in her stomach (she bleeds every month but does not die), by virtue by being in tune with nature's cycles, is feared. Because, according to Christianity and most major religions, woman is carnal, animal, and closer to the undivine, she must be protected. Protected from herself. Woman is the stranger, the other. She is man's recognized nightmarish pieces, his Shadow-Beast. The sight of her sends him into a frenzy of anger and fear.

Caridad becomes "the stranger, the other" when she is attacked, and she is only healed through her sisters and mother at home. She floats through the living room wearing Fe's wedding gown and is beautiful again; her wounds all vanish because La Loca prays for her. She moves into a transcendent world by no longer existing as an object for the world. Instead, Caridad meets an older woman, Dona Felicia, a surrogate mother who teachers her to become a healer. Dona Felicia is the one who points out the power that Caridad and her family possess:

> All they did at the hospital was patch you up and send you home, more dead than alive. It was with the help of God, heaven knows how He watches over that house where you come from. . . .

Therefore, it is through the rituals of the home that Caridad enters into a spiritual life. Caridad's renewed life "became a rhythm of scented baths, tea remedies, rubdowns, and general good feeling." She makes particular chores like dusting her altar and her statues and pictures of saints, taking baths, and cleaning her incense brazier part of her spiritual life. She takes on the role of a priestess, who "enacts her purification rites primarily for her own benefit" (Rabuzzi).

In the outside dominant culture where "We've been taught that the spirit is outside our bodies or above our heads somewhere up in the sky with God" (Anzaldua), Caridad's actions may be perceived as "cultlike" or even superstitious. But for women of color, her actions not only contradict what hooks identified as "white bourgeois norms (where home is conceptualized as politically neutral space)," they re-connect and re-member the home to the body to the spirit.

Caridad's mentor, Dona Felicia, creates a home in her trailer that is overflowing with the smells of beans cooking and incense burning. She is creating in her home "the spiritual life and ceremonies of multi-colored people" (Anzaldua) and is moving out of the "consciousness of duality" (Anzaldua). There is nothing neutral about her home (as there is nothing neutral about Sofi's home, filled with the smells of animals). They do not imitate the white culture with the "white sterility they have in their kitchens, bathrooms, hospitals, mortuaries and missile bases" (Anzaldua). Instead, Caridad and Dona Felicia's homes echo Anzaldua's words on institutionalized religions and home:

> Institutionalized religion fears trafficking with the spirit world and stigmatizes it as witchcraft. . . . In my own life, the Catholic Church fails to give meaning to my daily acts, to my continuing encounters with the 'other world.' It and other institutionalized religions impoverish all life, beauty, pleasure.

Anzaldua also writes about her own home rituals and how they are strongly connected to her creative and spiritual life:

> I make my offerings of incense and cracked corn, light my candle. In my head I sometimes will say a prayer— an affirmation and a voicing of intent. Then I run water, wash the dishes or my underthings, take a bath, or mop the kitchen floor.

Despite Caridad's rejection of institutionalized religions and her attempts to create a protective home space for herself, whether it is in a trailer or in a cave, she is again terrorized by the outside world. The woman she loves, Esmeralda, is raped by Francisco, a man who is obsessed with Caridad. Because of this man's desire to own a woman at any cost, because of his "machismo," which Anzaldua defines as a need to "put down women and even to brutalize them" (a concept which Anzaldua connects to racism and shame), Caridad and Esperanza both commit suicide at Acoma. They go to Acoma after Esmeralda's attack, and when Caridad realizes that Esmeralda was violated, and that Francisco followed them, they hold hands and jump off the mesa and are taken by Tsichtinako, "the Invisible One who had nourished the first two humans, who were also both females." This spirit leads both women back to the womb, back to a safe home: not out toward the sun's rays or up to the clouds but down, deep within the soft, moist dark earth where Esmeralda and Caridad would be safe and live forever.

> we cannot talk,
> it is better to only hear
> the water running in the kitchen sink
> dreaming of rooms and you sitting
> across from me saying "yes, yes
> I will defend you, I know exactly what I will say"
> but after you leave your words change,
> you lie and eat food my dead grandmother
>   prepares and
> I know I must change all my poems now,
> throwing books at you in front of my par-
>   ents' house
> and you laugh and hold your breath waiting
> for the hysterical woman to stop so you can
> go on walking down the street,
> so you can go on driving in the car,
> so you can go on your horse
> to another town and fuck another woman
> with your words, your money and your gun.

As long as woman is put down, the Indian and the Black in all of us is put down. The struggle of the mestiza is above all a feminist one. As long as los hombres think they have to chingar mujeres and each other to be men, as long as men are taught that they are superior and therefore culturally favored over la mujer, as long as to be a vieja is a thing of derision, there can be no real healing of our psyches. We're halfway there—we have such love of the Mother, the good mother. The first step is to unlearn the puta/virgin dichotomy and to see CoatlapopeuhCoatlicue in the Mother, Guadalupe. (Anzaldua)

The two women in the novel who do not leave home are the mother, Sofi, and one daughter, La Loca. Both women look to their home space as a source for spiritual growth and as a reconnection between their own culture and the outside dominating culture. Neither Sofi nor Loca desire the objects, the static role or the sterile, domestic environment of mainstream white culture. They are rooted in their own history and at the same time, they accept their world in its playful state of constant change, and contradictions. This tension between rootedness and flexibility is observed by Anzaldua in *Borderlands/La Frontera:*

> Los Chicanos, how patient we seem, how very patient... We know how to survive. When other races have given up their tongue, we've kept ours. We know what it is to live under the hammer blow of the dominant norteamericano culture. But more than we count the blows, we count the days the weeks the years the centuries the eons until the white laws and commerce and customs will rot in the deserts they've created, lie bleached. Humildes yet proud, quietos yet wild, nosotros los mexicanos-Chicanos will walk by the crumbling ashes as we go about our business. Stubborn, persevering, impenetrable as stone, yet possessing a malleability that renders us unbreakable, we, the mestizas and mestizos, will remain.

Sofi was married to a gambler, Domingo, who was:

> little by little betting away the land she [Sofi] had inherited from her father, and finally she couldn't take no more and gave him his walking papers. Just like that, she said, 'Go, hombre, before you leave us all out on the street

Domingo returns years later and attempts to win back Sofi's affection but she has no desire to share a life with him again. She will no longer accept his perceptions as law: "'And don't call me 'silly Sofi' no more neither.' ... 'Do I look like a silly woman to you, Domingo?''' Sofi is participating in what Norma Alarcon describes as "the ironically erotic dance that Castillo's speaking subjects often take up with men"; however, Sofi is no longer allowing herself to be victimized by the dance.

Domingo makes the mistake of losing Sofi's house in a gambling bet and that is one mistake Sofi cannot forgive, for her identity, her history is her house:

> But the house, that home of mud and straw and stucco and in some places brick—which had been her mother's and father's and her grandparents', for that matter, and in which she and her sister had been born and raised—that house had belonged to her.

Domingo's insensitivity and carelessness concerning this loss is what finally pushes Sofi to file divorce papers. She also manages to hold on to her house. Like the matriarchal goddess, Hestia, who will not allow any god to "share her strictly matriarchal province," and who nurtures a fire in the hearth that was "the center of the earth," (Walker), Sofi cannot let the fires in her home go out or let the fires consume her in rage. In her book, *The Sacred and the Feminine,* Rabuzzi describes this balancing act of the housewife who must carefully dance between her own home rituals, which includes spirituality, and outside influence:

> ...all the domestic rites a housewife performs are designed to maintain Hestia's fire properly. If she allows the fire to go out, her house is no longer a home...if a homemaker allows the fire to rage out of control, her home will vanish along with its physical embodiment. (Rabuzzi)

Sofi balances her dedication to her home, her duty to "La Loquita, her eternal baby" and her devotion to herself when she decides to finally bring closure to her failed marriage. Sofi does not act in a fit of rage; in fact with a charitable and flexible nature, she offers him a small house in Chimayo (which was built for Caridad). She may not want to be married to Domingo but she refuses to see him homeless.

This balancing act is also evident when Sofi, despite the fact that her own grandparents built the house, accepts an arrangement with the judge who won the house in a cockfight. He allows Sofi to "reside in her own home after she agreed to pay him a modest rent."

Like her mother, La Loca uses the home space as a source of spiritual nourishment and a source of strength. Loca does all her work, whether it is healing her sisters or talking to La Llorona, within the domestic sphere. While living in her mother's home, Loca becomes a mythic force in her own right. She becomes a player in a scene far older and larger than her individual self. No longer does she participate in profane historical time; instead she is participating in mythic time (Rabuzza). Loca visits hell, heals her sisters Fe and Caridad, and can smell other people's agony. She participates in a "mortal collision between the rituals of a house'' (Romines) when she describes to Sofi how she can smell her father's spiritual pain:

> Mom, 'La Loca said, 'I smell my dad. And he was
>   in hell, too. . . .
> Mom, I been to hell. You never forget that smell.
>   And my dad. . .he was there, too.'
> 'So you think I should forgive your dad for
>   leaving me, for leaving us all those years?'
>   Sofi asked.
> 'Here we don't forgive, Mom. . . . Only in hell do
>   we learn to forgive and you got to die
>   first. . . . Mom, hell is where you go to
>   see yourself.
> This dad out there, sitting watching T.V., he was
>   in hell a long time.'

Loca, like Hestia, is a virgin who is ''the representative of pure homelife'' (Rabuzzi). Since her experience of death and resurrection at age three, Loca never leaves home, and she only allows her mother to come close to her. She never went to school, to mass, to any social activity. Her entire world is the house, the stalls, and the river by the house. She does not attempt to assimilate into the dominant culture like her sisters, Fe and Esperanza. She plays the violin without having to go to a teacher outside the home; she just learns using her own ability and talent. Loca doesn't rely on mainstream institutions for anything, whether it be to gain knowledge or spirituality in her life.

Yet the world comes to Loca in the shape of a disease, AIDS. Castillo does not explain how Loca contracts the disease, which adds to Loca's role in the novel as a character who is larger than her own self (Rabuzzi). The disease, which Castillo describes as the ''Murder of the Innocent,'' seeks Loca out.

In the end, like Caridad, Loca is taken away by a female deity, the Lady in Blue who is wearing a horsehair vest under her habit. The lady can be Guadalupe, La Llorona, ''My-Mother-Who-Gives'' Coatlicue—all aspects of the goddess who was ''usurped of ancient feminine prerogatives'' (Walker) by the outside culture but has found a voice within the home space. Loca, within her domestic sphere, is still disrupted by the racism and sexism of the patriarchy. She is the representative feminist healer and speaker operating from within the home. She is also the queer that Anzaldua speaks about when she says, ''People, listen to what your joteria is saying.'' And because of the disease she contracts, a disease of the postmodern world, she, like her sisters, Esperanza, Fe and Caridad, is a representative victim of the patriarchy. For only Sofi

remains at the end of the novel, as the president of Mothers of Martyrs and Saints, an organization that worships another symbol of the home, the womb.

> I wanted to write about this dream and call it
> ''peeling garlic'' smelling my fingers
> hours after I cooked
> and no, I do not believe women would start a war
> because they are not looking
> at the beginning or the end

What is home? Is it ''the space in which you feel secure enough to be most fully yourself'' (Rabuzzi)? Is domestic ritual only a private act? ''I am writing a book, performing a public act that seems a far cry from my turkey dressing,'' writes Romines. Is it? What do women learn in the home? Is the ''place where all that truly mattered in life took place-the warmth and comfort of shelter, the feeding of our bodies, the nurturing of our souls. There we learned dignity, integrity of being; there we learned to have faith'' (hooks). Anzaldua writes, ''I am a turtle, wherever I go I carry home on my back.'' I stand outside, bleeding. I watch the lunar eclipse, a heavy moon pulling on my womb; the moon is slowly disappearing above my house, and I hear my baby breathing under my skin. Five months ago, home for him was my body. I want to join the voices of the private and public that will not look at what is done in the home as disconnected to what is done outside the home, that will not disconnect the female body from the female spirit. I want to join the force ''making a new culture—una cultura mestiza—with my own lumber, my own bricks and mortar and my own feminist architecture'' (Anzaldua).

Source: Carmela Delia Lanza, ''Hearing the Voices: Women and Home and Ana Castillo's *So Far From God*,'' in *MELUS*, Vol. 23, No. 1, Spring, 1998, pp. 65–79.

Theresa Delgadillo

In her review of Ana Castillo's novel So Far From God, *Theresa Delgadillo describes how Castillo, through the voices of four Chicano women, presents ''women as agents of social change,'' challenging cultural, political, and religious forms of oppression.*

Ana Castillo's 1993 novel *So Far from God* counters a pervasive stereotype of Chicanas as passive individuals victimized by oppression or subordinated by a patriarchal church by presenting a cast of female characters who resist domination every day of their lives—though some days more successfully than others. The awakenings that these characters experience emerge from a continual battle against subjugation in which they shift the terms and tactics of their struggle as circumstances permit. The novel insists that the transformative effort of human life engaged in struggle also finds expression in the spiritual, metaphysical, and religious life of the oppressed. Through an emphasis on communities of women, a Chicana feminism fueled by a woman-centered spirituality emerges to challenge the subjugation of women within and without Chicana/o cultures, the marginalization of other sectors of U.S. society, and the destruction of the environment. Because it highlights the centrality of hybrid spirituality in the lives of characters engaged in cultural and political resistance, the novel challenges pervasive notions of religion as an obstacle to progressive action and perceptions of the sway of Catholicism in Chicana communities. It also asks us to see cultural resistance alongside political resistance, and to recognize women as agents of social change.

So Far from God tells the story of a family of women including Sofi, a single mother for much of her daughters' lives, and her four daughters: Esperanza, a political activist and broadcast journalist; Caridad, who is first a nurse's aide, then a battered woman, and, finally, a *curandera* (healer); Fe, a jilted bride whose job as a factory worker leads to her death by cancer; and Loca, a childhood saint, a recluse, and a healer.

Through its depiction of these lives the novel creates what Ramón Saldívar terms an "oppositional ideological form" that can serve "both a unifying communal function as well as an oppositional and differentiating end." Saldívar argues that Chicano narrative goes beyond realism to facilitate social change by systematically uncovering "the underlying structures by which real men and women may either perpetuate or reformulate" the "world of social hardship and economic deprivation." Castillo's novel embraces the creative and transformative truth-telling that Saldívar sees as characteristic of Chicano narrative.

The Native as Resistance

Central in this process is the recovery of the india/mestiza voice, what Norma Alarcón describes as the "recodification of the native woman" essential to a sense of self and communal identity that can combat cultural, political, social, and economic oppression. In many ways, this novel follows the lead established by Alarcón in her seminal article, "Chicana's Feminist Literature: A Re-Vision Through Malintzin/or Malintzin: Putting Flesh Back

on the Object," by retracing, albeit fictionally, a history of india/mestiza women's subjugation and resistance. For Loca and Esperanza, in particular, the hybrid spirituality they practice becomes one with their political action. The link between their faith and their action parallels the practice of liberation theology, as, for example, in Nicaragua, where Christians were inspired by their faith to participate in a revolution (Betto). As in the exercise of liberation theology, this hybrid spirituality makes concrete the connection between the spiritual and the material, and between the personal and the public—not only for Loca and Esperanza, but for Caridad, Fe, and Sofi as well. However, the radical nature of this hybrid spirituality's challenge to the status quo arises not from a reinterpretation of Christianity, but from its embrace of both indigenous and Christian elements. In the Americas, a sense of the abiding validity of native beliefs and practices springs both from existence in the materiality (topography, landscape) of these continents and their human communities, as well as from the uninterrupted insistence of native populations on defining the world and themselves, that is, from their history of resistance to oppression. Castillo's novel more specifically links itself to what Gloria Anzaldúa calls the "Indian woman's history of resistance," creating a narrative that corresponds to Arnold Krupat's conception of "anti-imperial translation" because, like Native American literature, it is "saturated with the worldviews and the performative conventions of traditional, oral, Native American expressive genres" (Krupat). The acceptance of Christianity and native beliefs allows for the incorporation of diverse ways of knowing and interpreting the world.

Although the novel offers examples of religious syncretism, which are inevitable where hybrid spirituality is possible, it does not take a syncretic view of spirituality. That is, it does not attempt to fuse divergent spiritual and religious practices into a unified whole. Instead, the novel emphasizes differing traditions and practices coexisting in the same world as aspects of the multiple subjectivities that define its characters. Though divergent traditions inform the lives of the characters in *So Far from God*, Castillo often takes the "heterodoxical stance" toward both indigenous- and Christian-inspired practices that Kimberly Blaeser notes is also a feature of much Native American fiction.

This novel asserts that indigenous cosmologies and perspectives that challenge not only Western conceptions of history as linear and teleological but also Western notions of progress form an essential component of resistance. It thereby challenges Western epistemology, particularly what Ashis Nandy terms the "unilinear pathway from primitivism to modernity, and from political immaturity to political adulthood, which the ideology of colonialism would have the subject society and the 'child races' walk." Because the hybridity that results is neither accomodationist nor assimilationist, but disruptive, the novel's religious interlacing becomes a site for radical change.

In the Americas that "unilinear pathway" became the doctrine of Manifest Destiny, and, as Castillo deftly conveys in relation to one community and one family in *So Far from God*, its achievements were far from progress for those whose suffering was their price. These accomplishments include the genocide and subjugation of indigenous peoples from New England to Hawaii, the institution of chattel slavery, the Mexican-American War, and the invasions of Nicaragua, Haiti, the Dominican Republic, Cuba, Grenada, and Panama.

The novel's stress on the harm caused by such notions of progress rests on both this negative history and the continued presence of Western conceptions of progress in the lives of its characters. Yet, the novel challenges those conceptions by emphasizing not one past but many, and by bringing these into the present. The narrative offers stories about past events, such as the Mexican Revolution and the Chicano student movement, that reveal the officially unrecognized role of women. Castillo's characters also occasionally become the figures of indigenous myths—new versions of old stories. Finally, Sofi and Esperanza both confront patriarchal views of their roles and lives only by remembering their own past. Homi Bhabha argues that in "redefining the signifying relation to a disjunctive 'present'" by "staging the past as *symbol*, myth, memory, history, the ancestral—but a past whose iterative *value as sign* reinscribes the 'lessons of the past' into the very textuality of the present," the postcolonial subject, the subordinated, the native, determines her "identification with" and "interrogation of" modernity. She has agency. Castillo's narrative undoubtedly creates Chicana characters who actively participate in the construction of their world, yet the text goes beyond questioning to confront, as Nandy has described it, the responsibility that Western conceptions of history, progress, and political economy bear for the "genocides, ecodisasters and ethnocides" that have affected the entire globe. From this perspective flows Nandy's "defence of non-modern cultures and traditions" as

> Because it highlights the centrality of hybrid spirituality in the lives of characters engaged in cultural and political resistance, the novel challenges pervasive notions of religion as an obstacle to progressive action and perceptions of the sway of Catholicism in Chicana communities."

integral to resistant hybridity, a position that Castillo's text also sustains.

Practitioners of the hybrid spirituality of *So Far from God* accept multiple forms and systems of knowledge, including the intuitive, mythical, native, psychic, folkloric, spiritual, material, and rational, as well as traditional practices and ceremonies. The novel's identification with indigenous cultural practices, beliefs, and traditions speaks to the complexity of the experience of the colonized and oppressed. Its hybridity expresses this life experience—not the genetic makeup—of subordinated groups, and in so doing it challenges the corruption, exploitation, and environmental destruction of the strictly rational center from its previously silenced margins.

In *Domination and the Arts of Resistance*, James Scott argues that subordinate or marginalized populations seek to improve or reverse the conditions of their subordination both covertly and overtly; his discussion clarifies the link between seeming submission and overt rebellion. As Scott explains, "relations of domination are, at the same time, relations of resistance." This continual negotiation of power reveals itself in both the public roles played by the powerful and powerless as well as the private roles and practices each group allows itself when "hidden" from view of others. Although Scott does not suggest that the privacy from which one critiques power necessarily requires a particular physical space, spatialization of resistance can be important. For example, domestic space—gendered

> "Through an emphasis on communities of women, a Chicana feminism fueled by a woman-centered spirituality emerges to challenge the subjugation of women within and without Chicana/o cultures, the marginalization of other sectors of U.S. society, and the destruction of the environment."

as the space of women—or barrio space can nurture covert resistance to domination, not because these are "safe" sites (they often are not), but because they are mostly hidden from the view of dominants. Scott's discussion of what he terms the "hidden transcript," the exchanges, communications, and actions of each group invisible to the others allows us to see subordinate group members not simply as victims who are not yet aware of their own oppression, but as actors engaged in a process of struggle that sometimes has room to erupt publicly. Scott sees in the religious practices of subordinate groups their imaginative capacity "to reverse or negate dominant ideologies." This ideological resistance is not limited to the locus of the hidden transcript, but also asserts itself in public and may influence a dominant group to accept a practice of subordinates in order to protect the public performance of their power. In this novel the home functions as the restricted space where the hidden transcript can unfold, while the community of Tome shifts between public and restricted space. Here we see women attempting, in myriad ways and with varying degrees of success, to deflect subordination and to effect changes that will gain them power.

Through an exploration of the experiences, perspectives, and imaginations of subordinated populations, Scott, Bhabha, and Nandy challenge notions of subjectivity and culture as static and unitary, and of culture as the terrain of dominants alone. Unlike the concept of syncretism, which emphasizes the reconciliation of diverse beliefs, systems, or practices in a new form, the conceptions

of cultural hybridity that these theorists offer allow us to recognize the heterogeneity and ongoing negotiations that constitute culture in general, and the unique way in which this is performed in Castillo's text.

Given the contentious history of the Chicana/o population in U.S., it is not surprising that much of its literature is politically charged or deals with political, economic, social, and cultural resistance to oppression. It is not unusual for the literature of this heterogeneous community to grapple with conflicting claims and demands, for its characters engage a discourse of identity in which issues of power and opposition to the dominant society are central. Consequently, Chicana/o literature has demonstrated a preoccupation with the multiplicity of subject positions that colonized and oppressed people must of necessity occupy in their experiences. In this respect, Castillo's novel is no exception, representing a virtual catalog of the subjectivities, often in opposition to one another, in Chicana communities. Alarcón suggests that this is one of Castillo's trademarks ("Sardonic Powers"), while Yvonne Yarbro-Bejarano notes that Castillo's characters perform what Anzaldúa terms mestiza consciousness, whereby individual subjects "speak from a multiplicity of positions." However, *So Far from God* also expands our definitions of what constitutes "resistance," of what is "political," and of who is capable of effecting social change by focusing on the defiance that characterizes the family of women at its center and the insurgency that erupts as they engage in ongoing battles.

La Loca's Resurrection

The death of the child La Loca and her funeral are powerful opening images that indicate clearly and strongly the direction of this story. From unexplained violence to Sleeping-Beauty-like death, then to rebellion, which transforms her to a living and respected female healer, La Loca's journey in the first few pages presages the journeys of each of her sisters and her mother in the rest of the novel.

Significantly, La Loca's journey is four-part and she is also one of four sisters/daughters—Loca, Fe, Caridad, and Esperanza. The number four is particularly important in many Native American cosmologies because it represents the earth's directions and air currents. It is symbolic of a balance of elements, including both the material and spiritual, as well as the links between them. In *The Sacred Hoop*, Paula Gunn Allen cites numerous examples of the prevalence of four as an organizing number in ritual and ceremony of many Native American nations. In *Literature of the American Indian*, edited by Sanders and Peek, documents, stories, and poems from diverse tribes also attest to the widespread use of the number four as an organizing principle in oratory and literature. In fact, Allen believes that the uses of the number four among Laguna and other nations indicates that ''four is a categorical symbol-statement about the primacy of female power in tribal ritual life'' (*The Sacred Hoop*).

The prevalence of fours in this text de-emphasizes the centrality of Catholic hierarchy, and yet coexists with the three of the Holy Trinity that Father Jerome represents. Despite his strict devotion, or perhaps because of it, the priest appears to be little more than a figurehead, unable to establish a relationship with La Loca, either at her resurrection or later in her life. Father Jerome is also notably absent from the Holy Friday procession in chapter 15 that melds spiritual with cultural and political resistance. His religion is a rarefied practice, divorced from the material, emotional, and social world around him. However, as the novel demonstrates, it is not the priest or the Catholic hierarchy who determine what faith is nor how it is practiced.

The opening scene of the novel frames the issue of woman-centered healing in opposition to the patriarchal church that predominates throughout the narrative. Loca's resurrection as well as her ability to fly to the top of the church confound Father Jerome, who asks her, ''Are you the devil's messenger or a winged angel?'' (Castillo). Father Jerome's words have several effects. Unsure about what he sees, he asks for clarification and thereby implicates Loca, a female, in deception. Second, his question calls attention to the possible presence of a dangerous power as well as a healing one, emphasizing a dualistic view of good and evil. Third, his question reflects a preoccupation with the institution and doctrine of the church rather than its adherents.

Father Jerome, ''a little concerned about the grieving mother,'' stops the funeral from proceeding into the church, despite the intense outdoor heat, because he wants to avoid a scene inside. Father Jerome's decision to detain the funeral procession outside, in 118—degree heat, for what, as our narrator tells us, is a lecture on ''funeral decorum'' reveals how, for him, doctrine comes before people. Sofi's intense grief is juxtaposed with this callous act of a representative of what he claims is a compassionate institution. Despite his sermon, Sofi cries out in agony over what is to her the inexplicable death of her daughter.

Sofi's cry challenges Father Jerome's sermon and insists on her own right and ability to ''know'' why her daughter has died. Her very human reaction of grief and the stir it creates could also well be the catalyst for waking Loca up from the ''dead,'' or what is later described as a type of epileptic coma. Hence, Sofi's action also has practical repercussions in changing the course of events because Loca does awaken, to the surprise and fear of all present, and ascends to the church roof, primarily to avoid contact with Father Jerome. This striking scene suggests that Castillo is engaged in revisionism on a small scale, substituting a Chicana resurrection for Christ's resurrection, and accordingly creating an alternate religious history or perhaps a new myth. La Loca's resurrection at the beginning of the novel indicates that this will be a story about the recovery of Chicana power and voice. Perhaps, in keeping with Jarold Ramsey's view of how myths tell their audience ''who they are,'' Loca's resurrection, and Sofi's role in bringing it about, speaks to Chicanas about their individual and collective qualities.

When Father Jerome suggests that Loca might be a messenger of the devil, Sofi defends Loca, and by extension herself and every other woman, and scolds the priest, rejecting his authority to name or define the phenomenon before him. Sofi's action here, while mildly censured by the surrounding crowd, is indicative of the kind of independence of spirit that her daughters inherit.

The third challenge to Father Jerome's authority to interpret faith occurs when the priest calls La Loca down from the roof of the building and tells her, ''we'll all pray for you.'' Loca does float down to the ground but corrects the father, saying, ''Remember, it is I who am here to pray for you.'' By insisting on the miraculousness of her experience and her communion with other realms, Loca insists on her spiritual power and agency. She is a character whose very presence refutes the Church's propositions that she is either merely a victim, offered by Father Jerome, or the product of an ignorant family and community, a position later taken by the Bishop.

The three challenges to the doctrine represented by Father Jerome comprise strong evidence of Castillo's revisionism. In this case, she has placed Father Jerome in the position of St. Peter, who denies his association with Jesus three times following the Last Supper. In the Bible, Peter realizes his error and repents, but Father Jerome experiences no such realization about the power or equality of women. After many unsuccessful attempts to bring La Loca into his flock, he decides to take "pity on her and finally dismisse[s] Loca as a person who [is] really not responsible for her mind."

Pilgrimage to Tsimayo/Chimayo

Loca's funeral procession is only one of several important public rituals in the novel. A second important procession is the pilgrimage to Chimayo or Tsimayo. The alternate spellings and different pronunciations of this sacred site—"ch" versus "ts"—highlight the distinction between Catholic and indigenous traditions of worship at this site: Castillo uses the "ch" spelling when describing *doña* Felicia's annual Lenten Week trip, but offers the "ts" spelling when locating the site within "the land of the Tewa." Embedded in each spelling of the word is a distinct cultural, social, political, and economic history of divergent populations defining the same space for themselves. Although the use of the Spanish sound "ch" may appear to be simply an attempt to render the sound of native pronunciation in Spanish, the effort to make the word part of the Spanish language becomes emblematic of the adoption of indigenous religious practice. The word, however, comes from a native language, although there have been varied opinions on its origin and meaning: "The word chimayo is seemingly Maya in origin. It meant the dark wood of a tree particularly favored by cabinet makers in their work. Others claim it to be a Tewa word meaning 'good flaking stone'" (Stanley).

Caridad, beginning her apprenticeship as a *curandera*, accompanies *doña* Felicia on the pilgrimage. The narrative informs us of the history of worship at Tsimayo/Chimayo as well as the later Catholic adoption of the site as sacred. Both the Catholic Our Lord of Esquipulas and the natural earth are worshipped at Tsimayo/Chimayo, but the narrative emphasizes this Catholic adoption of native practice when it describes the long lines of Catholics waiting to collect a little bit of the holy earth that heals from a small dirt well in the chapel. Historically, the worship of Our Lord of Esquipulas at this site began in the latter half of the eighteenth century, although native peoples had valued the "curing potentials of the mud and dirt" at Tsimayo/Chimayo since before the arrival of whites (Stanley), a resource embraced later by Catholics who

referred to the site as the "Lourdes of New Mexico" (Stanley).

Caridad, in making the pilgrimage, understands that "the Catholic Church endorsed as sacred what the Native peoples had known all along since the beginning of time" (Castillo). Her attitude toward the Church's adoption of the veneration at Tsimayo/Chimayo is ironic, meant to draw our attention to the social and economic reasons for such a gesture on the part of the Catholic Church. Her comment also points to the convergence of religious practices and beliefs in the site itself and among the people there—a syncretic rather than hybrid site for many who worship there (but not including Caridad) because it fuses two spiritual traditions.

The devotion at Tsimayo/Chimayo also suggests other instances of Catholic acceptance of native practice, especially Guadalupe worship. A common view of this practice, expressed by Saldívar, regards it as a manifestation of Catholic hegemony over Mexican women: "the holy mother Catholic Church has enforced on Mexican women a cultural model of passivity and guilt figured in the Virgin of Guadalupe to ensure their allegiance to a transcendental, phallocentric Logos." Castillo's novel, however, asks us to see in the worship of Our Lady of Guadalupe not the ever-brilliant colonizers duping those poor Indians, but instead the possibility that an indigenous practice continues under a different name: "Just like a country changed its name, so did the names of their legends change" (Castillo). Many have argued that the worship of Guadalupe is the Catholic version or name for "Tonantzin, the mother goddess of the Mexica, whose temple or center of devotion was at the hill of Tepeyac" (Poole), and who was "sometimes identified with two other mother deities, Coatlicue (serpent skirt) and Cihuacoatl (woman serpent)" (Poole).

Guadalupe-worship illustrates how a type of covert critique of domination by subordinates—the assertion of agency in maintaining one's ability to define the world that is inherent in the maintenance of native cosmologies and epistemologies by colonized populations—can become part of the public transcript of power relations. The sixteenth-century historian of pre-Hispanic life in Mexico, Bernardino de Sahagún, "considered the devotion itself to smack of neopaganism." (Poole). Instead of a clever ploy by the conquering Spaniards to convert the Indians, Guadalupe worship appeared to at least some of those conquering Spaniards to show that, in fact, the Indians had transformed one of their indigenous deities into an object of the Spaniards' worship.

Contemporary Chicana critical theory and Chicana visual and literary art have altered our view of the syncretism of Guadalupe worship, encouraging us to revalue the survival of native female power in this figure. Anzaldúa suggests that the veneration of Guadalupe may have origins in the matrilineal Azteca/Mexica culture that was overturned by Aztec centralization and forced into a covert existence, a view that problematizes any notion of a romantically unified indigenous past and expands our understanding of that past by identifying indigenous women's resistance. The analogy that Castillo's text creates between Caridad and La Virgen de Guadalupe brings the history of Indian women's resistance into the present: the dark-skinned Caridad who has suffered beating and mutilation, who has begun an apprenticeship as *curandera,* and who has rediscovered love for women, is taken for a saint and compared both to Guadalupe and the Apache woman warrior Lozen when discovered alone on the mountain to which she retreated.

Historically, Our Lady of Guadalupe has been deployed in the service of both accommodation, that is, to win Indian converts to the Church, and rebellion, to symbolize Mexican nationalism against Spanish domination in the revolution launched by Miguel Hidalgo in 1810 and to figure native claims to land and other rights for Emiliano Zapata's army a century later (Poole). In the 1960s, members and supporters of the United Farm Workers in California marched under banners of Guadalupe. Playwright Luis Valdez described the significance of this as follows: "The Virgin of Guadalupe was the first hint to farm workers that the pilgrimage [to Sacramento in the spring of 1966] implied social revolution" (qtd. in Chávez). Devotion to her, then, can hardly be characterized simply as an exercise in submission.

Even the seemingly harsh view of the Penitente Brothers becomes a complex exploration of the power relations and cultural values inscribed in the practices of this society:

> While it's not every day that you see a crowd following a Christ-like figure carrying a cross along the highway (unless your people are from Chimayo or Tome or similar places throughout the territory controlled by the Spanish queen and friars for centuries with such ferocity that neither Mexican nor U.S. appropriation diluted the religious practices of the

descendants of the Spaniards who settled there, including this procession that has been performed annually for two hundred years and will probably go on for two hundred more, such is their fervent devotion). (Castillo)

This passage emphasizes "control" over territory coupled with the historical facts of Spanish, Mexican, then U.S. appropriation, thereby suggesting that the cultural value of a group practice can shift relative to the political and economic power of that group. The practices of the Penitente Brothers are clearly cultural markers of a now less-powerful population. By also focusing on the "ferocity" of possession and linking it to the depth of cultural practice, the text demonstrates how seemingly contradictory cultural practices can exist side by side—because they become embedded in a social and material landscape. The text, therefore, qualifies the notion of complete conquest by revealing the complexity of the past and continued negotiation between dominants and subordinates from the perspective of the native, rather than that of the conqueror.

Female Power and Its Links to the Natural World

The affinity with the natural world and natural order characteristic of a native spirituality that these Chicana characters embrace leads to a site of female strength and power in this novel: "La Loca was only three years old when she died. Her mother Sofi woke at twelve midnight to the howling and neighing of the five dogs, six cats, and four horses, whose custom it was to go freely in and out of the house" (Castillo).

The sensitivity of the animals, the intensity of their attempts at communication, and their proximity to the members of the household are striking. Sofi listens, gets up to check the house, and discovers the baby in convulsions. The scene highlights the interconnection between human and animal, and communication between the two, a dialogue that continues throughout the novel, as, for example, when the animals signal that Caridad has fully recovered (Castillo).

Loca subsequently spends much time outdoors and with animals, rather than in the house, indicating her own individual affinity with the surrounding natural world. She is not, however, the only female character who places herself in the natural world instead of the man-made world. She and other women in this novel do so in a very distinct fashion. In a discussion of the relationship between the natural world and humans evident in contemporary women's writing, Alicia Ostriker notes Annette Kolodny's view that "the power of men's fantasies depends consistently on a vision of nature and woman, as alive, fecund, and essentially mindless. Women who identify their own bodies with earth, however, tend not merely to celebrate the concept of fecundity but to link earth's powers with a critical and subversive intelligence, or with the creative imagination itself." For many contemporary female writers "nature [. . .] is always that in which we are embedded rather than that from which we are divided" (Ostriker). The women of *So Far from God*, and in particular the *curanderas*, are examples of the phenomenon in contemporary writing of imagining a relationship to nature different from the one that predominates in our society and of linking this distinctive relationship with another kind of intelligence. This kind of writing eliminates the dichotomy between the individual and what Allen calls the "out there" (*Sacred Hoop*).

Caridad and Esmeralda's leap from the top of the mesa at Acoma poignantly illustrates the idea that humans are of nature, rather than above nature. When Francisco and others look over to see what happened to Esmeralda and Caridad, they don't see anything but hear "the spirit deity Tsichtinako calling loudly with a voice like wind, guiding the two women back, not out toward the sun's rays or up to the clouds but down, deep within the soft, moist dark earth where Esmeralda and Caridad would be safe and live forever." In this image, the earth is not a coffin, but "alive in the same sense that human beings are alive" (*Sacred Hoop*). This image stands in stark contrast to the Western view of earth as surface, as female body to be exploited.

At first, this scene might appear to minimize the demise of two women who have been stalked by an obviously disturbed man. The text conveys, however, the intertwining relationships between human and natural worlds in its vision of a world beneath ours. This scene suggests both the Laguna creation story of the four worlds beneath ours from which humans emerged (Silko) and versions of the *The Woman Who Fell from the Sky* (Sanders and Peek; Allen, *Spider*)—stories that challenge the single-minded conception of land as exploitable resource. In the Seneca story, the act of falling is not a metaphorical representation of destruction, but instead a birth into another world and therefore an act

of creation (Sanders and Peek). By linking Chicana characters with Native American worldviews, Castillo identifies and valorizes an indigenist aspect of Chicana/o identity. By refusing to sensationalize the demise of Caridad and Esmeralda, the text also counterposes the assumed importance of human death with the often unconsidered issue of destruction of the living earth.

Most importantly, the scene of Caridad and Esmeralda's death contrasts their way of living in this world with that of Francisco el Penitente. The two women share a perspective that helps them understand their world, a spirituality consistently grounded in the landscape and people around them, a religious practice that values their selves and their bodies, and a life dedicated to helping others—Esmeralda as a rape counselor and Caridad as a *curandera*. Both women also participate in hybrid worship at Chimayo/Tsimayo—where they first meet.

Francisco, on the other hand, follows another kind of faith. The text describes his initiation into the *santero* (a shaman/artist who creates religious figures and images, a sanctuary-keeper) practice as a move driven by his deep respect and love for the men of his family who had always been "devoted to their homes and land" (Castillo). When Francisco joins his *tío* (uncle) Pedro in the process of creating a *bulto* (a carved or sculpted image of a holy figure or saint)—carefully selecting a tree for wood, preparing and carving the wood, harvesting plants and soils for paint—he seems, like Caridad, Loca, and even Sofi, to combine contemplative silence and engagement with the surrounding world in his religious practice. Yet the text also suggests that the tradition of creating *bultos*, handed down through the generations, continues to embody the feeling of those first Spanish *santeros* in what is now New Mexico that they were in a "strange land" that was "so far from God."

Later, Francisco's faith becomes increasingly defined by abnegation, as, for example, when he mixes ashes with his food. While working on a *bulto* of San Isidro for a neighbor, his ritual repetition of prayer seems aimed not at focusing on the place where he is but at forgetting and denying that place and his own developing love interest in Caridad. Francisco's veneration of his deceased mother, coupled with his alternating disgust for and adoration of Caridad, comprise the dangerous extremes of the objectification of women—an attitude that is not simply a product of Penitente membership but has multiple sources—that will eventually lead him to violence against Caridad and Esmeralda. Francisco's religion is not entirely responsible for everything else in his life, although, at times, he clearly longs for such a situation. The text veers away from stereotyping Francisco as simply a fanatic Penitente by bringing other elements into the picture. His troubled state is, in part, attributable to his service in the Vietnam War, a life-and therefore also faith-altering experience. He also seems to have been the unwitting exotic foil for a privileged young white woman's sexual experimentation. Although we might attribute greater significance to Francisco's war experience in influencing his later behavior, the example of a short-lived relationship with a white woman serves to remind us of the numerous, perhaps even seemingly trivial, manifestations of his marginalization in Anglo society that affect his individual psyche.

By including a Penitente brother among a cast of characters who practice a home-centered faith, such as Sofi, Loca, and *doña* Felicia, the text offers us another example of an alternative religious tradition: what Anthony Stevens-Arroyo describes as the "indifference to the institutional church" yet "loyalty to Catholic heritage" that has characterized Latino experience over four centuries. Historically, the Penitente societies emerged to lead the communal practice of faith at a time when there were few priests in the region, and the *bultos, retablos* (religious altar pieces), and other religious decorative items they produced were not valued by the French and Mexican clergy (Wallis, Ortega, Stanley). Some analyses of Penitente traditions stress their origins in a conceptualization of religious life offered by early Franciscan missionaries in New Mexico (Hewett and Fisher, Wallis). However, Jose Amaro Hernandez cites evidence that suggests Penitente associations were native to New Mexico. A reading of Ramón Gutiérrez's *When Jesus Came, the Corn Mothers Went Away* reveals similarities between Penitente activities and some Pueblo religious practices. According to Hernandez, in addition to religious and spiritual activities, Penitente associations functioned as mutual aid organizations and agricultural cooperatives dedicated to maintaining communities. The traditional institutional schism between the Catholic Church and Penitente societies became even more pronounced in the post-1848 period, when the Catholic Church replaced the primarily Spanish-origin clergy throughout the Southwest with French and Anglo priests, exacerbating the cultural conflict. During this period, Penitente

associations were subjected to the combined prejudice of newly arrived Anglo and French Catholic clergy as well as Protestant ministers (Hernandez). Nonetheless, they were for a short time also able to exert some influence on the political events and legislation affecting the now-dispossessed population of Chicanos (Hernandez). Their history as a lay confraternity is, therefore, not devoid of conflict with the institutional Church or surrounding populations; in recent years, Penitentes have again faced discriminatory attacks, this time from hateful vandals. The Penitentes, too, are heirs to a history of resistance to social, political, and cultural domination.

Like the female characters in this novel—each of whom is defined not only by her spiritual practice, but also by her race, class, and gender, that is, by her place in the material world around her—Francisco is not simply a Penitente. Despite the fact that he carves a *bulto* for a neighboring farmer, his family history, economic opportunities, education, war experience, and social status all contribute to shaping a religious practice that is not primarily concerned with community, but with self-testing. Consequently Francisco leaves this world alone, while Caridad and Esmeralda accompany each other. Francisco's story challenges readers to consider, first, how culpable is religion in Francisco's action? And, second, has the resistant character of a traditional practice been altered through the generations? By bringing Francisco, Caridad, and Esmeralda together to illustrate the contradictions among divergent spiritual practices as they intersect with other aspects of existence, the text rejects a type of happy-ending fusion of all interests into a superior culture—a sentimental version of multiculturalism—and instead advocates a greater acceptance of the "American Indian universe" "based on dynamic self-esteem," in contrast to the more widely accepted "Christian universe" that is "based primarily on a sense of separation and loss" (Allen, *Sacred*). Yet it does so without rejecting those aspects of Christianity that have engendered resistance.

The voice that calls to Caridad and Esmeralda as they descend, Tsichtinako or Tse che nako, is Thought Woman in the Keres cosmology, the female spirit and intelligence that is everywhere and is everything, (Allen, *Sacred*), who "is the true creatrix for she is thought itself." The presence of an originary female spirit here, a common figure in Native American belief systems (Allen, *Sacred*), points to the "affirmation of tribal values, tribal thought, and tribal understandings," which "can result in a real decrease in human and planetary destruction and in a real increase in quality of life for all inhabitants of planet earth.'' In reclaiming a woman-centered spirituality in which women are also healers, Castillo constructs a feminist, indigenist cultural identity, and, as Alvina Quintana points out, deconstructs male cultural paradigms that oppress Chicanas—and everybody else, too (Quintana).

Hybrid and Mestiza Healers

The hybridity that Caridad and Esmeralda display in this text is even more pronounced in the figure of *doña* Felicia, who blends indigenous and Catholic beliefs in the vocations of living and healing. *Doña* Felicia's acceptance of Catholic holy figures and natural spirits parallels that of the Nahuas, who ''freely accepted other gods into their pantheon, where they were worshiped together with the ancestral gods'' (Poole). *Doña* Felicia's hybrid spirituality also suggests the new mestiza consciousness that Anzaldúa delineates as the hope of the future in an increasingly hybrid universe—a ''tolerance for contradictions'' fueled by ''continual creative motion that keeps breaking down the unitary aspect of each new paradigm'' and creates the possibility for change.

Doña Felicia's embrace of Catholicism comes late in life, and is ''based not on an institution but on the bits and pieces of the souls and knowledge of the wise teachers that she met along the way'' (Castillo). The narrator describes her faith as ''a compromise with the religion of her people'' that develops into a greater reverence for God and the Catholic saints. Key in this description of *doña* Felicia is her attentiveness to those around her, for in this way she learns not only about Catholicism, but also about indigenous healing. She later trains Caridad in the skills of observation and listening essential to the practice of a *curandera*, and schools Caridad in the natural elements that can be used in healing. Considering the life that Caridad previously led—drowning her sorrows in alcohol—and the brutal assault that ended this phase of her existence, *doña* Felicia's lessons would also appear to be immediate and sound advice for Caridad.

In this novel women (with the exception of Dr. Tolentino) practice natural medicine primarily in the home, where the hidden transcript unfolds. This space is revealed to be a center of survival, recovery, and self-knowledge. For example, Esperanza returns home after college and the break-up with Cuauhtemoc/Rubén. The sisters, together, help Fe recover from her broken engagement at home, and later, on a visit home, Sofi insists that Fe see a doctor about her poor health. Caridad experiences a miraculous recovery at home following the attack on her. Loca assists each of her sisters through these difficulties, but when her own health fails, she, too, is cared for at home by several pairs of loving hands. That these sisters support and nurture each other in times of need, yet remain childless, strengthens the novel's feminist positioning by replacing the tendency to biologize compassion and nurturance with a depiction of the active formation of solidarity among women who are oppressed. Although these women directly feel the effects of a sexist, racist, and exploitative society, they also manifest the power to heal themselves and their communities through prayer, the application of traditional *remedios* (cures) and action.

Stevens-Arroyo notes the centrality of the home in Latino religious practice, which he attributes to a form of ''popular religiosity'': ''the home-centered aspects of Catholicism are much stronger among Latinos than among Euro-American Catholics, assuming a primacy over clerically dominated and institutionally-based traditions like mass attendance and obedience to the clergy.'' Stevens-Arroyo maintains that this ''home-centered religion'' forms a ''resistance against imperialism,'' particularly in the late 60s and early 70s period of political upheaval. In *So Far from God*, Loca epitomizes what Stevens-Arroyo describes as a Latino variation of Catholicism, but as we have seen, Loca is only one of many healers, all of whom rely on both Catholic and traditional forms of healing, thereby transforming their homes into sites of hybrid healing practice.

Yet Caridad, Esperanza, Fe, and Loca die. Except for Loca's first miraculous resurrection, there are no quick fixes, no easy solutions, no sure cures. Neither the hybrid practice of faith nor indigenous medicine and spirituality can prevent their deaths. And this fact makes this aspect of the text all the more clear: faith, spirituality, and religion are also about how we live in this world, not just about what happens to us after we die.

By privileging indigenous culture and history, and indigenous women's healing practices, the novelist reclaims an aspect of the ancestral past that Ortega and Sternbach call the delineation of ''a matriarchal heritage'' common in Latina literary discourse, to create agency and subjectivity for her mestiza and native characters. An aspect of Castillo's embrace of this cultural heritage includes her attention to the centrality of the *curandera,* who as Tey Diana Rebolledo suggests, "has emerged as a powerful figure in the writing of women and men" and whose appearance "demonstrates not only her enduring representational qualities as myth and symbol but also the close identification of the culture with her mystic and spiritual qualities."

Overcoming Violence and Silence

In *So Far from God*, Caridad, who has fallen into a life of drink and one-night stands with men she meets in bars, suffers a brutal and overpowering physical attack. The narrator reports that some townspeople regard the attack as the natural outcome of what they consider Caridad's questionable behavior, and we are left with the impression that Caridad has learned "the bitter truth" about the violent enforcement of women's second-class status in this society (Ostriker). However, while Castillo shows us the real physical oppression that all women face in the figure of a beaten and mutilated Caridad, she does not simply point the finger at men.

Caridad, Loca, and *doña* Felicia know that

> it wasn't a man with a face and a name who had attacked and left Caridad mangled like a run-down rabbit. Nor two or three men. That was why she had never been able to give no information to the police. It was not a stray and desperate coyote either, but a thing, both tangible and amorphous. A thing that might be described as made of sharp metal and splintered wood, of limestone, gold, and brittle parchment. It held the weight of a continent and was indelible as ink, centuries old and yet as strong as a young wolf.

Rather than the all-too-familiar story of a woman's brutalization, Caridad's experience directs us to the purpose of re-visioning Chicana and Chicano lives, for what is so destructive and evil, always present yet not always easy to pin down, but the sexism of our society? Similar to the power of the state swooping down on an Indian family like a "thing coming out of the sky with barbs and chains" in Louise Erdrich's "American Horse," Castillo's *malogra* (evil spirit) metaphorically describes the force of the institutionalized patriarchal relations that foster disregard for women at every level of society. When these ideas take hold of individuals and then are practiced by them, they can create the kind of violence against women experienced by Caridad. By envisioning the violence against her-

self as one caused by the *malogra,* Caridad allows us to see it in all its systemic force—it represents the overarching hegemonic discourse of patriarchy to and from which, as Rosaura Sánchez points out, individuals either consent or dissent. Francisco, and even Caridad herself at this point in her life, consent. Castillo thereby illuminates both the real physical threats that women face and the ideological discourse that authorizes that violence.

This episode of Caridad's life, however, does not end with mutilation but with renewal. Sánchez's caution to remember that "human beings are both products and producers of the society they inhabit" speaks directly to Castillo's portrayals of women. Because Caridad shifts from a position of consent to one of dissent in relation to the ideology that endorses violence against her and other women, she demonstrates that both men and women can alter the underlying reasons for violence against women. The stages of her physical and spiritual transformation pose the challenges of engaging in this process. Looked down upon by the police who found her (Castillo) and "half repaired by modern medical technology" (Castillo)—both highly representative of the dominant power and the difficulty of undertaking to alter that power—Caridad returns home to experience a miraculous recovery while in the care of her sisters and mother. She then dedicates her life to helping others by learning how to become a *curandera.* But the realization that she finds herself attracted to another woman leads Caridad to a year of isolation and reflection; this experience strengthens her to such a degree that when she is discovered in the Sangre de Cristo Mountains she is literally immovable despite her small physical size. When Francisco and several other men attempt to relocate her from the cave where they find her, they are both angry and stumped by her amazing power (Castillo). Like her sister Loca, Caridad's *curanderismo* and spiritual life, combining attention to her own health with a vocation for healing others, allows her to challenge her own marginality and to assume agency. Her acceptance of love for women is a part of this change and contrasts sharply with her previous relations with men.

So Far from God confirms Rebolledo's observation that "silence, and overcoming it, are significant concerns in Chicana literature." In this novel several characters labor to overcome silence and testify to their own lives, a process that allows them to break out of their isolation and join together with other women. For Esperanza, Fe, and Caridad, silence leads to suffering and destruction. Esperanza, though a political activist and broadcast journalist, does not protest the way in which Rubén treats her, and consequently falls victim to his selfishness. Her inability to demand more from Rubén stems in part from societal constraints against female self-fulfillment that lead her to feel "like a woman with brains was as good as dead for all the happiness it brought her in the love department."

Similarly unhappy, Fe, shocked by the refusal of her fiancé Tom to go through with their wedding and plans for living the American Dream, unleashes an unending scream. Fe's overt expression of pain, rage, and frustration temporarily brings her closer to what is in her view an overly emotional and superstitious family from whom she had previously remained aloof. Her release, however, is only a partial escape from her dependence on dominant ideologies. When Fe finally stops screaming, her vocal chords are damaged, signaling that her recovery is incomplete. Though no longer dependent on Tom, she remains vulnerable to the consumerist American Dream of life, buying her way to happiness and then placing herself at the service of Acme International in her quest to get ahead, a company whose illegal and environmentally unsound practices kill her. Fe spurns her family, particularly her sister Loca, in her drive to assimilate. Embarrassed by what she sees as an odd family, she moves away from her home and neighborhood. Her uncritical acceptance of the hegemonic discourse of middle-class America imposes distance between Fe and a family not considered typically American in such discourses because of its gender composition, race, ethnicity, and culture (Sánchez). Fe's isolation contributes to a silence and passivity that eventually kills her. She recognizes this in her last visit to the Acme plant even if the realization comes too late to save her: "The whole plant had been completely remodeled . . . all the stations . . . which used to be open to everybody and everything, were partitioned off. Nobody and nothing able to know what was going on around them no more. And everybody, meanwhile, was working in silence as usual." In light of her newly acquired knowledge about the poisonous work environment at Acme and the company's practice of releasing toxic pollutants outside of the plant, Fe's graphic description of the physical divisions between silent workers indicates a developing class-consciousness that was previously blocked by her acceptance of dominant discourses. But her observation on the silence of the workers also speaks to a re-evaluation of her cultural, ethnic,

and racial consciousness as well. Previously, Fe considered Sofi, Loca, and Caridad "self-defeating" and "unambitious" because they were not interested in becoming wage-workers; she felt "disappointment and disgust" for Loca's condition; although she respected Esperanza's television job, she "had no desire to copy Esperanza's La Raza politics." Because her family did not fit the profile of the American Dream, Fe limited her interaction with them and maintained silence regarding her own life and plans. The scene of her return to the Acme plant represents her awakening to the many divisions that Fe has unwittingly allowed to dominate her life.

Sofi overcomes her own longstanding silence when she notices the disintegration invading her community. The people, and especially the men, on whom Sofi had always relied to keep things running smoothly seem unable to do anything to solve the town's problems. As unofficial Mayor of Tome, she organizes a town-wide cooperative project, involving both women and men, and wins the respect of her community. When her husband Domingo soon gambles away their income from the effort, Sofi finally remembers that twenty years before it was not he who had walked out on his family but she who had kicked him out.

The fact that this "one little detail" was "forgotten" by Sofi and everybody else in the community suggests that there were no other roles for women beyond wife/mother or abandoned wife/mother. Sofi could not, in a sense, truly speak her life until she had created new roles for women in which she and others could be appreciated for something other than being a wife/mother. When this happens, Sofi remembers this story of her breakup with Domingo. In the meantime however, she has, with difficulty, lived an independent life apart from this unsatisfying relationship, even if disguised in abandonment. Although for many years Sofi's effort to avoid the pattern of subordination forced on other women is covert, her resistance does eventually become a public effort to include women fully in communal governance.

These characters reveal the many ways that Chicanas have been silenced by the dominant society and by their communities, as well as the ways that Chicanas have struggled against this erasure. Although Fe's rejection of her sisters is most pronounced, both Caridad and Esperanza also distance themselves from a family of women that somehow shames them; yet for all three, and even for Sofi, too, that distance is bridged by the communal sharing of grief, caring, and healing that the women together provide for one in need.

A Holy Friday for Our Time

Though this novel focuses on Chicana characters, it does not do so at the expense of other women or other struggles. Manifesting a commitment to alliances with other marginalized groups, the text creates a bridge between the divergent populations it describes in the Holy Friday procession scene. The novel thereby fashions a creative and fictional counterpart to the voices of women united in the collection *This Bridge Called My Back: Writings by Radical Women of Color*, in which Audre Lorde says that joining with others in battle is essential to one's own freedom: ''Without community, there is no liberation, only the most vulnerable and temporary armistice between an individual and her oppression.'' In the foreword to the second edition of this collection both Gloria Anzaldúa and Cherríe Moraga underscore the urgency of building alliances globally and of doing this through action; Anzaldúa says, ''Caminante, no hay puentes, se hace puentes al andar (Voyager, there are no bridges, one builds them as one walks).'' The women of Tome do walk in the final Holy Friday ceremony, not just for themselves but for future generations, and not by themselves but in unison with others. The visit to each station of the cross in this procession symbolically creates the bridge between those in struggle. In contrast to earlier scenes of the Penitente ceremony that literally recreates Christ's suffering at Tsimayo/Chimayo, this ceremony exposes the widespread suffering caused by capitalist exploitation. Rather than accepting suffering as the route to salvation, the participants in this Holy Friday ceremony enact a protest against the destruction of the environment. As one Navajo woman says, ''[W]e are trying very hard now to save ourselves before it's too late. Don't anybody care about that?'' (Castillo).

La Loca, who has spent much of her life caring for her sisters, not only participates in this public event, but is figured as a central character of its drama. Weak from illness, Loca rides her horse in the procession, in effect presiding over it. The description of her attire alludes to the familiar folk wisdom regarding the garments to be worn on one's wedding day. Loca wears something borrowed—her father's suspenders and her mother's boots; something blue—her sister Esperanza's blue chenille robe; and something old—jeans with holes where there was a brand-name tag that Loca has cut off to honor a boycott of the company. Her outfit, significantly, is missing something new. In a ceremony that enacts a renewed commitment to struggle, Loca's garb highlights the old while the ceremony itself suggests that commitment to a community may be more important than commitment to an individual marriage. In fact, few of the marriages described in this novel endure.

The cultural and political activities of the women—linked throughout the novel—culminate in the Holy Friday procession, in which each station of the cross marks the contemporary suffering of working peoples and oppressed populations. Fe's presence is particularly felt in this scene. Her painful death from cancer illustrates the future awaiting a woman and a community who buy into the consumerist American Dream, who live only in the present and not also in the past and future. Her mother Sofi carries a picture of Fe in the procession. This act simultaneously honors Fe and joins her in struggle with all those participating in the Holy Friday march, a gesture reminiscent of the many declarations of ''*Presente!*'' (''Present!'') heard among the peoples of Latin America when honoring the martyrs and heroes of revolutionary battle.

Sofi's action testifies to her daughters' and her own struggle against oppression, which, as Rebolledo suggests, is an integral aspect of Chicana literature that is often personal and collective, often including the names and stories of mothers, grandmothers, sisters, aunts, and friends (Rebolledo). Castillo writes the lives not only of four sisters and their mother but also includes the stories of *doña* Felicia, Maria, Esmeralda, Helena, Rita de Belen, Mrs. Torres, *doña* Severa, garment workers on strike, workers suffering toxic poisoning at work, Navajo women trying to save future generations from uranium contamination, the many suffering from AIDS, and more. These characters exemplify the emergence of a Chicana subjectivity that defines itself within the context of community and in league with the struggles of others attempting to overcome marginality, subordination, and silence. This chapter embodies an idea that Sonia Saldívar-Hull articulates: ''For the Chicana feminists it is through our affiliation with the struggles of other Third World people that we find our theories and our methods'' The Holy Friday procession merges the concerns of Chicanas, working people, Native people, environmentalists, and antiwar activists, and in doing so it parallels the complex subjectivities in the community of Tome, particularly those of the five women whose lives are at the center of the novel. In the blend of Catholicism, native belief, self-respect, political action, and reflection, the procession epitomizes the power of a hybrid resistance.

Conclusion

Sofi's lament to her *comadre* (intimate female friend) that they are all ''so poor and forgotten'' echoes Francisco's sentiments (Castillo). Yet Sofi and her *comadre* both come to understand that they can get closer to ''God'' through their own actions. The efforts they initiate to improve the economic self-sufficiency of Tome for the benefit of everyone in the community also succeed in restoring communal social relations and dignity. Sánchez says that the ''concept of centering subjectivity in collectivities is an important cultural and political construct in Chicano literature.'' This novel allows us to see the multiple—sometimes competing, sometimes converging—interests in Chicana subjectivity through female characters who struggle to name, assert, and lead their complicated selves against societies that continually seek to categorize them with one-dimensional labels, such as single mother, jilted woman, slut, devil, Catholic, troublemaker, or loyal worker. What Sofi and her *comadre* accomplish in Tome results just as much from their religious faith as it does from their ethnic, gender, and class identifications, and it demonstrates that spirituality and religious faith both shape and are shaped by questions of gender, class, race, ethnicity, and sexuality. The strength of the women in this novel flows from their ability to embrace all aspects of themselves to effect such astonishing change. Like other characters, Sofi and her *comadre* are grounded in the multiple material, social, economic, political, and religious realities of their world.

By focusing on communities of women who engage in resistance, the text offers an alternative to the dominant literary paradigms wherein ''individualism often represents the strength of male power, while community becomes equated with female weakness'' (TuSmith). This novel attacks the individualism that fuels a chaotic live-for-the-moment mentality by showing us how that individualist ethic harms women, communities, and the environment.

Their spiritual hybridity is central to the process of self-discovery, assertion, and union with others in which Castillo's female characters engage.

Their practice of Catholicism represents endurance, survival, and sometimes conformity, but it is also a faith shaped by its practitioners into what they need. And yet, as Anita Valerio explains, ''Some would like to believe that the values of the Roman Catholic Church and the values of the Native American tribal religions are one and the same.'' They are not. A hybrid practice also maintains and recovers the knowledge of a spirituality wherein women partake and heal. Some women gain this knowledge directly, as in the case of Caridad, Loca, and *doña* Felicia, while others acquire it indirectly—for example, Sofi learns from her daughters—but all are empowered and fortified by it. When Sofi and her *comadre* enlist other women and men in revitalizing the town of Tome, they create a contemporary version of the Pueblo historical legacy of matriarchy, a system in which women shared equally with men the governance of the economic and spiritual life of their communities. Setting the novel in Tome, New Mexico, creates a textual link to a specific history of indigenous women that reminds us of the constructedness of patriarchal economic relations.

So Far from God illustrates the complexity of Chicana lives and the varied perspectives necessary to enact transformation because it depicts a community both defined and moved to action by diverse subjects. The novelist adds to an economic analysis the cultural resistance of oppressed nationalities and honors the role of women in this resistance. By doing so, she reveals a strength, not an obstacle, in her culture.

Source: Theresa Delgadillo, ''Forms of Chicana Feminist Resistance: Hybrid Spirituality in Ana Castillo's *So Far From God*,'' in *Modern Fiction Studies,* Vol. 44, No. 4, Winter, 1998, pp. 888–916.

Ilan Stavans

In this brief review, Ilan Stavans describes Ana Castillo's So Far From God *as a novel that attempts to be both a parody of well-known Spanish-speaking soap operas and a social satire but unfortunately fails to find a balance between these perspectives.*

The recent renaissance of Latino letters is led by a number of very accomplished women. This, of course, is good news. It has, after all, taken far too long to find Hispanic women a room of their own in the library of world literature. With the exception of Sor Juana Ines de La Cruz, a seventeenth-century Mexican nun who astonished the Spanish-speaking world with her conceptual sonnets and philosophical prose (Octavio Paz wrote a spellbinding biography, *Sor Juana Or, The Traps of Faith*, [see *Commonweal*, January 27, 1989]), women have rarely been read and discussed by mainstream Latino culture. Rosario Castellanos, Isabel Allende, Elena Poniatowska, and Gabriela Mistral—the latter received the 1945 Nobel Prize—are a few of the better-known women authors. Prominent among the new wave of Latino writers in English are Sandra Cisneros, Julia Alvarez, and Cristina Garcia. In opening a window across gender lines, each revisits the Hispanic's innermost fears and hopes.

On the very same list is Ana Castillo, a veteran novelist, poet, translator, and editor whose previous books were published by small presses in Arizona, Texas, and New Mexico. Unfortunately, Castillo remains relatively unnoticed by the media. She is the most daring and experimental of Latino novelists, and as American novelists Robert Coover and William Gaddis well know, experimentalism has its costs. Born in 1953 in Chicago and now living in Albuquerque, Castillo was educated at Northern Illinois University and the University of Chicago. She is the author of *Sapogonia: An Anti-Romance* in 3/8 Meter, published in 1989, and of the poetry collections *Women Are Not Roses*, *The Invitation* and *My Father Was a Toltec*. Her most memorable work, to my mind, is *The Mixquiahuala Letters* , an avant-garde epistolary novel published in 1986 and recently reissued by Anchor-Doubleday. *Letters* received a Before Columbus Foundation's American Book Award.

The novel concerns the friendship of two independent Hispanic women, Alicia and Teresa, whom we accompany, through the device of introspective letters, from their youthful travels to Mexico to their middle-years in the United States. Stylistically *Letters* is a tribute to Julio Cortazar, the Argentine master responsible for *Hopscotch*, a novel typical of the sixties' French nouveau roman, and is designed as a labyrinth in which the writer suggests at least two possible sequences for reading—two possible ways of ordering the chapters. Similarly, Castillo's book offers three alternative readings: one for the conformist, another for the cynic, and the last for the Quixotic. Among the very few people I know who have read *The Maxquiahuala Letters*, none (including me) has had the patience to attempt each of the three possibilities.

While Castillo's experimental spirit, much like Carlos Fuentes's, often strikes me as derivative and academically fashionable, her desire to find creative

> **"** Melodrama is indeed the key word here. Castillo is involved in a dramatic embroidery characterized by heavy reliance on suspense, sensational episodes, and romantic sentiment. Any parody works through a tacit agreement between writer and reader, who share the knowledge of the genre parodied and understand the rules of the game."

alternatives and to take risks is admirable. An accomplished parodist, Castillo's obsession, it seems, is to turn popular and sophisticated genres upside down—to revisit their structure by decomposing them. In recent years, however, her avant-garde ambitions seem to be fading. Lately, she has become a client of Susan Bergholtz, a powerful New York literary agent whose list includes such Latino writers as Cisneros, Alvarez, and Rudolfo A. Anaya. In many ways, Bergholtz is occupying a role similar to that of Carmen Balcells in Barcelona, who launched the careers of south-of-the-border luminaries such as Gabriel Garcia Marquez and Mario Vargas Llosa. Bergholtz is convincing major publishing houses to put big bucks into novels by and about Hispanics. Moving from the periphery to the center necessarily entails sacrifice, however. *So Far from God* is a case in point: the experimental spirit is absent here.

The novel's intent is original: to parody the Spanish-speaking telenovela, e.g., the popular television soap operas that enchant millions in Mexico and South America. Framed by two decades of life in Tome, a small hamlet in central New Mexico, the novel tells the story of a Chicana mother, Sofia, and her four daughters: Fe, Esperanza, Caridad (their names, as Spanish speakers can testify, recall a famous south-of-the-border melodrama), and La Loca. The terrain is overtly sentimental and cartoonish. Magic realism is combined with social satire: whores, miracles, prophecies, resurrections, and a visit to the Chicano activism of the late sixties intertwine.

Melodrama is indeed the key word here. Castillo is involved in a dramatic embroidery characterized by heavy reliance on suspense, sensational episodes, and romantic sentiment. Any parody works through a tacit agreement between writer and reader, who share the knowledge of the genre parodied and understand the rules of the game. Unfortunately, with an overabundance of stereotypes and its crowded cast of theatrical characters, *So Far from God* stumbles from the outset. Castillo loses control of her marionettes. Even more disturbing, Castillo is never quite sure whether to ridicule her characters or idealize them in spite of their superficiality. As a result, the novel is uneven, conventional, and often annoying.

Still, we must pay attention to Ana Castillo. In due time, her creativity will match her passion to experiment and the outcome will be formidable. In fact, of all the Hispanic writers in the firmament of the current Latino renaissance, she strikes in me as the most intellectually sophisticated and thus might end up producing the most intriguing books. Unlike most of her colleagues, a sense of tradition can be found in Castillo's approach to the novel. She is a deeply committed reader whose art, I'm afraid, is not necessarily for the masses. Her tastes are singular, but she has yet to write the book that will display her talent in its full splendor.

Source: Ilan Stavans, "And so close to the United States— *So Far From God* by Ana Castillo," in *Commonweal,* Vol. 121, Issue 1, January 14, 1994, p. 37.

Sources

Anzaldua, Gloria, *Borderlands: La Frontera, the New Mestiza*, Aunt Lute Books, p. 203.

Delgadillo, Theresa, "Forms of Chicana Feminist Resistance: Hybrid Spirituality in Ana Castillo's *So Far From God*," in *MFS*, Vol. 44, No. 4, Winter, 1998, pp. 888-916.

Lanza, Carmela Delia, "Hearing the Voices: Women and Home and Ana Castillo's *So Far From God*," in *MELUS*, Vol. 23, No. 1, Spring, 1998, pp. 65-79.

Platt, Kamala, "Ecocritical Chicana Literature: Ana Castillo's 'Virtual Realism,'" in Greta Gaard and Patrick Murphy's *Ecofeminist Literary Criticism: Theory, Interpretation, Pedagogy*, University of Illinois Press, 1998, pp. 139-57.

Romero, Simon, "An Interview with Ana Castillo," in *NuCity*, June 18-July 1, 1993.

Saeta, Elsa, "A MELUS Interview: Ana Castillo," in *MELUS*, Vol. 22, No. 3, Fall, 1997, pp. 133-49.

Walter, Roland, "The Cultural Politics of Dislocation and Relocation in the Novels of Ana Castillo," in *MELUS*, Vol. 23, No. 1, Spring, 1998, pp. 81-97.

Further Reading

Ferriss, Susan, Ricardo Sandoval, and Diana Hembree, editors, *The Fight in the Fields: Cesar Chavez and the Farmworkers Movement*, Harcourt Brace, 1997, p. 288.
    A recent biography of Chavez and the Farmworkers' Union. Discusses his role in starting the Chicano/a Movement.

Gonzalez, Maria, "Love and Conflict: Mexican American Women Writers as Daughters," in *Women of Color: Mother-Daughter Relationships in 20th-Century Literature*, edited by Brown, Guillory, and Elizabeth, University of Texas Press, 1996, pp. 153-71.
    Compares the work of Sandra Cisneros, Denise Chavez, and Ana Castillo in terms of family, language, and female identity.

Jones Hampton, Janet, "Ana Castillo: Painter of Palabras," in *Americas*, Vol. 52, No. 1, January/February, 2000, pp. 48-53.
    The article casts Castillo as a verbal and visual artist dealing with her ideas of turning forty.

McCracken, Ellen, "Rupture, Occlusion and Repression: The Political Unconscious in the New Latina Narrative of Julia Alvarez and Ana Castillo," in *Confrontations et Metissages*, edited by Benjamin Labarthe et al, Maison des Pays Iberiques, 1995, pp. 319-28.
    McCracken explores the narrative structure of Castillo's *So Far From God* and Alvarez's *How the Garcia Girls Lost Their Accents*.

Montabanc, William, "Latin America: A Quixotic Land Where the Bizarre Is Routine," in Marilyn Smith Layton's *Intercultural Journeys*, HarperCollins, 1991, pp. 107-10.
    A collection of true reports from Latin America makes Montabano explore and question the reality and the absurdity of life "south" of the border.

Sachez, Rosaura, "Reconstructing Chicana Identity," in *American Literary History*, Vol. 9, No. 2, Summer, 1997, pp. 350-63.
    Explores how Hispanic-American women writers have defined and redefined women in light of the Civil Rights Movement, the Feminist Movement, and the Labor Movement.

So Long a Letter

Mariama Bā

1980

So Long a Letter, Senegalese author Mariama Bâ's first novel, won the prestigious Noma Award for Publishing in Africa soon after its publication in 1980. The epistolary novel traces the story of Ramatoulaye Fall, a recent widow. She recounts how her husband, Moudou, betrayed their marriage by taking a young second wife. Ramatoulaye records her anger at both Moudou and the customs that allow polygamy in her long letter to her lifelong friend Aissatou. In her letter, she muses on how Aissatou's marriage was ruined, also by polygamy. Ramatoulaye and Aissatou, both highly educated women, seem victimized by the traditional customs that deny women status equal to that of men. However, as Ramatoulaye relates, each woman is able to become successfully independent; neither accepts the position of submissive wife. Even while railing against her fate, Ramatoulaye also takes comfort in many traditional values. She hopes for a world where the best of old customs and new freedom can be combined. While well received, *So Long a Letter* has been the subject of some critical controversy. Some critics question Bâ's feminism, noting that women are pitted against each other in this novel. Others are put off by what they call class elitism in Bâ's novel: They find her portrayals of lower-class characters unsympathetic. Most critics, however, believe that Bâ accurately describes the social, religious, and gender differences that can divide a people even as they strive to forge a strong new nation. They find Bâ sympathetic to all women,

even the perceived enemies in the novel—the youthful new wives who displace the middle-aged women. In letting one woman eloquently tell the anguish of her heartbreak, Bâ suggests that all women have important stories to tell and that their plight should be given voice.

Author Biography

Mariama Bâ's first novel, *So Long a Letter*, features two female characters—Ramatoulaye Fall and Aissatou Bâ—whose lives follow trajectories similar to the author's own. Like these women, Bâ was educated in a Western-type school in her native Senegal. She, again like her heroines, not only witnessed Senegal's transformation from a French colony to an independent country, but as a teacher was active in easing her country through the transition. However, while Bâ's heroines seek personal fulfillment after their marriages fail, Bâ herself became an advocate for women's rights. Divorced, like her character Aissatou, Bâ joined several feminist organizations in Senegal. Particularly, Bâ pointed out the problems women face in polygamous marriages.

Bâ, who was born in 1929, lived a somewhat privileged life. She was given the opportunity to study at the Ecole Normale at a time when many Africans, and especially women, did not have access to education. Raised by her maternal grandparents because her mother had died, Bâ was also schooled in traditional Muslim values. As her father, to whom she was close, worked as a politician and civil servant, Bâ learned early the importance of civic duty. This is reflected in her own choice of careers. Upon graduating, she became first a teacher and then an inspector of schools. Bâ's character Ramatoulaye may be speaking for the author when she proudly reflects on teaching: "Teachers . . . form a noble army accomplishing daily feats, never praised, never decorated. An army forever on the move, forever vigilant. . . . This army, thwarting traps and snares, everywhere plants the flag of knowledge and morality." Bâ also married a powerful man, Obeye Diope, Senegal's Minister of Information. The couple had nine children before divorcing.

In 1980, Bâ published *So Long a Letter*. Praised by reviewers, the novel won the Noma Award for Publishing in Africa. This novel was soon followed by *Scarlet Song* in 1981. Bâ, however, would not live to see her second novel's publication. She died after a long illness in 1981.

Plot Summary

So Long a Letter, Mariama Bâ's first novel, is literally written as a long letter. As the novel begins, Ramatoulaye Fall is beginning a letter to her life-long friend Aissatou Bâ. The occasion for writing is Ramatoulaye's recent widowhood. As she gives her friend the details of her husband's death, she sets off on a journey of remembering the major events in her and Aissatou's lives.

Ramatoulaye's husband, Moudou Fall, died suddenly of a heart attack. Following the strictures of her Muslim faith, Ramatoulaye must remain in seclusion for a long period of time. This seclusion is broken, however, by the ritualized visits of relatives and friends of the dead man. During the first days, Ramatoulaye must share her home with Binetou, her co-wife. This young woman, who is the same age as Ramatoulaye's oldest daughter, and Ramatoulaye sit in state to welcome the visitors. The visitors bring money to these women out of respect for the dead, but ultimately their family-in-law, Moudou's siblings and parents, take the money away from the widows. In her letter, Ramatoulaye muses about why Moudou forced her into the awkward position of co-wife after 25 years of marriage and 12 children. But before telling the story of Binetou's elevation from shy schoolgirl to wealthy wife, Ramatoulaye recalls her own courtship years before.

Ramatoulaye and Aissatou were well-educated young women, having attended a French-run school in a time when few Senegalese women were given this opportunity. Sought after in marriage by multiple suitors, both women married for love. Ramatoulaye's mother disapproved of her choice—Moudou Fall, the young rising lawyer from a less elite family. Aissatou's in-laws looked down their noses at her. The daughter of a goldsmith, Aissatou was considered an unfit bride for the doctor Mawdo Bâ, the son of a tribal princess. But both women followed their hearts and with their husbands set out to forge new traditions to match their country's new independence.

But after recollecting their happy pasts, Ramatoulaye records in her long letter the problems that destroyed the two couples' tranquillity. Aissatou, now a divorced woman living in the United States, left Mawdo after he took a co-wife. Still in love with Aissatou, Mawdo was pressured by tradition and his mother's demands to take a wife who shared his same noble blood. His mother, Aunty Nabou, had never truly accepted Aissatou or her four sons. Years of planning her "revenge" on Aissatou, however, finally paid off. Aunty Nabou had adopted her niece and namesake, young Nabou, years before. After training this girl to be a perfect wife for her son, Aunty Nabou told Mawdo "I will never get over it if you don't take her as your wife. Shame kills faster than disease." To save his mother from shame, Mawdo agreed to the wedding. He planned to continue living with Aissatou and only to visit young Nabou as often as is required by the Islamic laws governing polygamy. But Aissatou, refusing to share her husband, defiantly divorced him and took their sons. She refused to be bound by a tradition that she saw as humiliating.

Ramatoulaye took a very different approach after her husband abandoned her for the young and beautiful Binetou. Without Ramatoulaye's knowledge, Moudou had fallen in love with his daughter's friend. Ramatoulaye and her daughter, Daba, were aware that an older "sugar daddy" was courting Binetou, but they didn't realize that the man was Moudou. Binetou didn't hide her disdain for this man, but admitted that she would become his second wife. Her own impoverished family needed the wealth Moudou could provide. Binetou's mother basically sold her daughter for a trip to Mecca, a new house, and increased social standing. While Ramatoulaye and Daba bemoan Binetou's fate, they have no idea that her "promotion" will cause the breakup of their family. On the day Moudou married Binetou, he gave Ramatoulaye no warning. Instead he sent his brother, his cleric, and his best friend to tell Ramatoulaye what he had done. Ramatoulaye's friends and family are shocked when she decides to accept her position as co-wife and not divorce Moudou. But Moudou really has no intention of honoring his vows to Ramatoulaye. He stops providing for her and their twelve children and instead showers gifts on Binetou.

Ramatoulaye explains to Aissatou how she pulled her life together after this abandonment. She had always worked, and she learned to act as both mother and father to her children. It is after she has adjusted to this life that Moudou dies. Widowhood brings her new opportunities, but she decides to carry on as a working single mother. Moudou's older brother offers to make Ramatoulaye his fourth

A Muslim woman stands on a beach in Senegal.

wife. At this point, though, Ramatoulaye finally discovers her strength and anger. She had never forgiven Tasmir for serving as his brother's ambassador by telling her of Moudou's marriage to Binetou. Now she sees through his proposal of marriage. He does not care about her or her children's well-being; he only wants to get his hands on her money. For very different reasons Ramatoulaye also turns down another offer of marriage. Her old suitor, Daouda Dieng, had never fallen out of love with her. Now a powerful politician, he wants to share his life with Ramatoulaye and her children. However, Ramatoulaye realizes that she does not love him. Esteem, she feels, is not enough to sustain a marriage. Further, Daouda Dieng is married. Ramatoulaye decides that she could never cause pain to another woman by usurping her place. Polygamy destroyed her happiness, and Ramatoulaye would hate to destroy the happiness of Dieng's wife.

Towards the end of the novel, Ramatoulaye describes how her family is being affected by changing traditions. One of her sons rails against the inequities of a racist teacher who refuses to treat a black Senegalese as an equal. Her oldest daughter, Daba, is in a true marriage of equals. Three of her younger daughters defiantly smoke. She reflects on what this means: "Suddenly I became afraid of the flow of progress. Did they also drink? Who knows, one vice leads to another. Does it mean that one can't have modernism without a lowering of moral standards?" As if in answer to her question, Ramatoulaye learns that her daughter Aissatou (named for her friend) is pregnant out of wedlock. In the past, this would have been a tragedy. A strict Muslim family would reject their daughter. But now, Ramatoulaye decides to love her daughter and try to make the most out of a tricky situation. She laments that boys can hide evidence of their "transgressions" while girls often have to pay a high price. Luckily the family, along with Aissatou's lover, work out a plan that will allow Aissatou to remain in school and to eventually marry the father of her child. As the novel ends, Ramatoulaye looks forward to a visit from the friend to whom she is writing the letter. She envisions that they both will be able to search for future happiness.

Characters

Abou

Daba Fall's husband, Abou, believes in equality between spouses. He helps Daba recover some of her father's possessions after Moudou Fall's death.

Amy

See Aminata Fall

Aissatou Bâ

Ramatoulaye's best friend, Aissatou, is also an educated woman. When her husband took a second wife, Aissatou refused to condone his actions. She divorced him and sought power in her own right. When Ramatoulaye writes to her, Aissatou is working for the Senegalese embassy in the United States, overseeing her sons' education, and proving her independence. The daughter of a goldsmith, Aissatou had always been defiant. She married Mawdo Bâ, a man of a higher caste, despite the disapproval of his family. Later, she refuses to listen to the naysayers who claim that her sons will be irretrievably hurt by her divorce. She believes, correctly, that her sons can only be strengthened by her resolve.

Mawdo Bâ

Aissatou's husband and Moudou's best friend, Mawdo Bâ is a renowned doctor. He married Aissatou despite his family's objections. His mother, a tribal princess, thought that her son and family would be tarnished by his marriage to a goldsmith's daughter. Years later, to appease his mother, Mawdo takes a second wife who shares his noble lineage. He claims to still love only Aissatou, but following the dictates of Muslim law, he routinely has sex with his new wife. Ramatoulaye and Aissatou are disgusted that Mawdo can separate emotional love from physical love. When Aissatou divorces him, Mawdo is despondent. But as his new wife continually gets pregnant, Ramatoulaye has little sympathy for him.

Jacqueline Diack

Ramatoulaye recalls the story of her friend Jacqueline, a black Protestant woman, as an example of the pain women can suffer in marriage. A native of the Ivory Coast, Jacqueline is never accepted into Senegalese society. She suffers a nervous breakdown as a result of her husband's many infidelities. Ramatoulaye calls Jacqueline's story "happy" because in the end she recovered, and her husband, "touched by his wife's breakdown," became more loving. By retelling the story, Ramatoulaye admits that she did not divorce her husband because she too was hoping for a happy ending.

Samba Diack

Samba Diack is Jacqueline's husband. His frequent affairs cause her to sink into a deep depression.

Daouda Dieng

Daouda Dieng, a doctor and politician, was Ramatoulaye's first suitor. While she always respected him, and he was her mother's first choice, Ramatoulaye knew she could never love him. Thirty years after his thwarted courtship, Daouda still loves Ramatoulaye. After Moudou dies, he proposes. His feelings unchanged, he is willing to care for her and her twelve children. However, Ramatoulaye still cannot return his love. Further, Daouda has taken a first wife and Ramatoulaye refuses to cause her hurt by becoming Daouda's second wife.

Farba Diouf

Farba Diouf is Aunty Nabou's brother and young Nabou's father. He gives young Nabou to Aunty Nabou to raise.

Aissatou Fall

Ramatoulaye's second-oldest daughter, Aissatou, becomes pregnant out of wedlock.

Ramatoulaye describes Aissatou as a caring and motherly girl who had helped her immeasurably during her seclusion. She is shocked that Aissatou could have engaged in premarital sex. However, Ramatoulaye decides that her love for Aissatou is stronger than the custom that would have her disown her daughter. Together with Aissatou's lover Iba, they plan how to make the best of the situation.

Alioune Fall

Alioune is one of Ramatoulaye's sons.

Aminata Fall

Aminata, known as Amy, is one of Ramatoulaye's twin daughters.

Arame Fall

Arame, one of Ramatoulaye's daughters, is known as one of the "trio." The "trio" are three of the siblings who are inseparable from each other. The "trio" break Ramatoulaye's rules and defiantly smoke.

Awa Fall

Awa is one of Ramatoulaye's twin daughters.

Binetou Fall

Binetou, Moudou Fall's second wife, is described as a beautiful and intelligent girl. She is from an impoverished family, but through her school has made friends with the children of the elite. Best friends with Dada Fall, Ramatoulaye's oldest daughter, Binetou admits that her family is pressuring her to marry an older man whom she cannot love. Binetou tries to resist, but her mother finally persuades her that it is her duty to accept the elder suitor. Dada and Ramatoulaye are shocked to learn that Binetou's "sugar daddy" is none other than their father and husband, Moudou. After the marriage, Binetou is compelled to abandon her studies. She leads a life of dissipation, seeking happiness in nightclubs and fast cars. Unhappy in marriage, she persuades Moudou to stop seeing his first wife and twelve children. She flaunts her new wealth while Moudou's first family struggles to maintain a middle-class existence. But Binetou is portrayed as a victim of customs that make it hard for women to choose their own destinies.

Daba Fall

Ramatoulaye's oldest daughter, Daba, is a fiercely modern woman. She tries to convince her mother to divorce Moudou after he marries Binetou. Earlier, she had tried to convince Binetou to reject the proposal of her "sugar daddy." Daba marries for love, but believes that if she or her husband should fall out of love, no vows should keep them together.

Dieynaba Fall

Dieynaba, one of Ramatoulaye's daughters, is known as one of the "trio." The "trio" are three of the siblings who are inseparable from each other. The "trio" break Ramatoulaye's rules and defiantly smoke.

Malick Fall

Malick is one of Ramatoulaye's sons. His arm is broken when he is hit by a car.

Mawdo Fall

Mawdo, one of Ramatoulaye's sons, complains of a racist teacher: "The teacher cannot tolerate a black boy coming first in philosophy." Ramatoulaye has her daughter Daba try to deal with the ensuing conflict.

Moudou Fall

Moudou Fall is Ramatoulaye's errant husband. As the novel begins, he has just died unexpectedly. But Ramatoulaye describes his life history in her letter to Aissatou. A lawyer, Moudou had been educated in France. He rose in political power as the leader of trade union organizations. His practical realism allowed him to make significant improvements in the condition of workers. Five years before the novel begins, Moudou fell helplessly in love with Binetou, his daughter's best friend. Promising Binetou and her family material comforts, he convinces the girl, who is physically repulsed by him, to become his second wife. Without telling Ramatoulaye, Moudou weds Binetou. Ignoring the dictates of Islamic law, Moudou basically abandons Ramatoulaye and his twelve children. Spending all his money to try to make Binetou happy, Moudou stops caring, materially or emotionally, for his first family.

Omar Fall

Omar is one of Ramatoulaye's sons.

Ousmane Fall

Ousmane is Ramatoulaye's youngest son.

Ramatoulaye Fall

The author of the long letter to her friend Aissatou, Ramatoulaye is a recent widow. In her letter she records the many changes that have taken place in her life, and tangentially, in her country. An educated woman, Ramatoulaye follows the dictates of Muslim custom but seems flexible to change. Thus, she embraces the rituals that cause her, as a new widow, to remain secluded for forty days. Earlier she had accepted without protest her husband's decision to take a second wife. However, Ramatoulaye is also fiercely independent and strong. The mother of twelve children, she can financially support herself and her family through her work as a teacher. She sees her occupation as an important calling. As a teacher, she holds herself responsible for the future of her country. Most significantly, Ramatoulaye believes in the possibility of finding happiness. Therefore, she will not marry again unless she falls in love. She refuses to settle for the security and improved social standing that a new husband could bring. Instead, she lovingly marshals her family into the future, intent on weathering the storms, such as an unmarried daughter's pregnancy, that life will bring.

Tamsir Fall

Moudou Fall's eldest brother, Tamsir, is described as a despicable man. He first tells Ramatoulaye of her husband's betrayal. She never forgives Tamsir for acting as though such news would not be devastating to a loving wife. After Moudou's death, Tamsir, following the tenets of his Muslim faith, asks Ramatoulaye to marry him. He pretends that he asks out of respect. But Ramatoulaye knows that Tamsir covets her house and her wealth. Already he lives off of the occupations of his three other wives. They labor hard while he reaps the rewards. Spurning his proposal, Ramatoulaye tells Tamsir exactly what she thinks of him.

Yacine Fall

Yacine, one of Ramatoulaye's daughters, is known as one of the ''trio.'' The ''trio'' are three of the siblings who are inseparable from each other. The ''trio'' break Ramatoulaye's rules and defiantly smoke.

Farmata

A ''griot woman,'' which means according to the novel's footnotes that she is ''part-poet, part-musician, part-sorcerer,'' Farmata acts as a go-between for Ramatoulaye. Farmata carries Ramatoulaye's letter rejecting Daouda Dieng's marriage proposal to the spurned suitor. She also alerts Ramatoulaye to the fact of her unwed daughter's pregnancy. Farmata believes that Ramatoulaye should either throw her daughter out of the house or sue the baby's father for damages. As usual, Ramatoulaye ignores Farmata's advice.

Iba

See Ibrahima Sall

The Iman

The Muslim cleric comes to tell Ramatoulaye, along with Mawdo Bâ and Tamsir, that Moudou has married Binetou. Ramatoulaye is repelled by how he tries to sugar-coat the news, making it seem like she should welcome the intrusion of a co-wife. The Iman also accompanies Tamsir when he asks Ramatoulaye to marry him. In her outspoken rejection of Tamsir's unwanted proposal, Ramatoulaye feels that she gets her revenge on these men who support polygamy, a system that invariably harms women.

Lady Mother-in-Law

Binetou's mother, Lady Mother-in-Law is depicted as an avaricious and grasping woman. Of low social standing, she covets wealth and respect. To this end, she convinces her daughter to marry Moudou, a man Binetou cannot love. Moudou can provide his Lady Mother-in-Law with all she desires: a trip to Mecca, a new house, new clothes, and social connections. After Moudou dies his daughter Daba takes delight in stripping the Lady Mother-in-Law of the vestiges of wealth she gained by selling her daughter in marriage.

Aunty Nabou

Mawdo Bâ's mother, known as Aunty Nabou, is a tribal princess. Proud of her heritage, she is sorely disappointed when her son weds Aissatou, the daughter of a goldsmith. To take revenge on Aissatou for stealing her son, Aunty Nabou schemes to make Mawdo marry his cousin, young Nabou. Aunty Nabou is portrayed as a traditional Senegalese woman. She wields power through her position as a princess and a mother. Ramatoulaye believes that Aunty Nabou seduces the young Nabou to her way of thinking through the ancient folk stories she tells over and over. Through these stories, she teaches young Nabou how to be a ''proper'' wife to Mawdo.

Young Nabou

Young Nabou is raised by her aunt, Aunty Nabou, to become Mawdo Bâ's wife. A successful midwife, young Nabou is respected by Ramatoulaye. Despite the fact that she causes the breakup of Mawdo's marriage to Aissatou, Ramatoulaye considers young Nabou "one of us." In other words she is an intelligent and principled woman who can stand on her own. Raised to love Mawdo, she can't help but be a good wife. Young Nabou's prospects, however, are limited by the ancient customs she adheres to.

Ibrahima Sall

Aissatou Fall's boyfriend, Iba, is a college student. He impregnates Aissatou out of wedlock. His love for her is clear, however, in the plans he makes to secure their future. Ramatoulaye, who expects to hate the man who "ruined" her daughter, finds that he is a wonderful addition to her family.

Themes

European vs. African Traditions

As critic John Champagne has pointed out, *So Long a Letter* is filled with descriptions of the culture clash apparent in 1970s Senegal. Besides the "hybridity" of the novel's form and content, Champagne argues that the novel "combines a European genre—the epistolary novel—with indigenous oral gestures" and "presents us with a culture irrevocably altered by the colonial presence." Thus, Champagne notes how "one might find in proximity both cowries and Fiats, boubous and night clubs, safara (as the glossary explains, 'liquid with supernatural powers') and electroshock therapy." While at times it seems as though Bâ favors Western ways over African traditions, Bâ mainly shows how both exist side by side. Ramatoulaye is distressed that her daughters have begun to smoke and to dress like Western women. She hopes that a Western type of feminism will not lead to moral dissolution: "A profligate life for a woman is incompatible with morality. What does one gain from pleasures? Early aging, debasement." However, Ramatoulaye is also grateful to the white teacher who expanded her narrow horizons. Ramatoulaye rails against the injustice of polygamy, and seems to condemn Islam for allowing it. At the same time, she takes comfort in the rituals of Islam. Rather than seeing the enforced mourning time for widows as an inconvenience, she appreciates having time to reflect on her life. The

novel does show how the position of women varies under a Western or a traditional Senegalese system of values. Traditionally, women gained power through family connections. Ramatoulaye and Aissatou, on the other hand, have gained power through education and careers. Reconciling their roles as career women and as members of extended families causes each woman difficulties.

Relationships among Women

Related to the theme of African traditions versus European values is another important theme: the relationships of women to each other. Ramatoulaye describes in detail the ways in which female family members relate under time-honored traditions. The daughter-in-law must open her home to her husband's family. The family-in-law will take care of her in her widowhood based on her behavior during marriage. Ramatoulaye describes how her mother-in-law "would stop by again and again on her outings, always flanked by different friends . . . so that they might see . . . her supremacy in this beautiful house in which she did not live. I would receive her with all the respect due to a queen, and she would leave satisfied, especially if her hand closed over the banknote I had carefully placed there."

Topics for Further Study

- Investigate how African feminists are addressing the cultural and religious traditions, such as polygamy, that hinder their efforts at greater equality.

- Research Senegal's independence movement and look at how *So Long a Letter* depicts the change from French colony to independent nationhood.

- Explore the relationships of Senegalese women to their extended family members and compare those relationships to those Bâ describes in *So Long a Letter*.

- What challenges are the Senegalese facing today? How much has changed since Bâ wrote *So Long a Letter* in 1980?

Despite her success as a teacher, Ramatoulaye must be completely submissive to her husband's mother. Aissatou, however, cannot please her mother-in-law. Aunty Nabou refuses to accept Aissatou, the daughter of a goldsmith, as a suitable wife for her son. It is in Aunty Nabou's power, then, to destroy her daughter-in-law's happiness. She insists that her son take a second, more socially acceptable, wife. Women do not always look out for the best interests of other women. Binetou's mother forces Binetou to marry a man she does not love or esteem. Binetou, once married to Moudou, insists that he stop communicating with Ramatoulaye and their many children. But, *So Long a Letter* also celebrates the alliances women can make. Ramatoulaye and Aissatou draw emotional and material comfort from their long friendship. Aissatou provides the abandoned Ramatoulaye with a much-needed car. Ramatoulaye recalls with pride the lasting friendships she made at school with African women from many countries. Young Nabou works hard as a midwife to improve women's lives. Ramatoulaye decides, after Moudou's death, that she would never agree to become a man's second wife because she would not wish to inflict harm on the first wife. As the novel ends, Ramatoulaye says that her "heart rejoices each time a woman emerges from the shadows." In other words, she rejoices when any woman can overcome the obstacles placed in her path. Ramatoulaye seeks not only her own happiness, but happiness for all women.

Style

Epistolary Novel

One of the earliest forms of the novel was the epistolary novel. This means that the entire action of the narrative is conveyed through letters. In the case of *So Long a Letter*, the narrative is told through just one very long letter from Ramatoulaye to her friend Aissatou. Here the letter works almost as a diary. Ramatoulaye records both her feelings and the events that take place around her. She reflects on the past and looks forward to the future. She also transcribes letters within her one long letter. The reader hears her dead husband Moudou's voice through snippets of the letters he wrote to Ramatoulaye before they were married. The reader learns of Aissatou's indignation at her husband's betrayal through the letter she wrote to him. But for the most part, all information is filtered through Ramatoulaye's perspective. A first-person narrator,

she is not necessarily a reliable guide to the feelings of her extended family. She cannot get inside the head of her young co-wife, Binetou, or know for certain the motives of the Lady Mother-in-Law (Binetou's mother) or of Aunty Nabou (Aissatou's mother-in-law). Instead she shows the reader how she views the world. This means that questions are often left unanswered. Why did Moudou abandon Ramatoulaye? How was Aissatou able to bear the gossip when her husband took another wife? The reader does not know because Ramatoulaye can only accurately represent her own feelings. In writing down the story of her life, however, Ramatoulaye is also able to control it, to decide what events were important to her own development.

In Medias Res

In medias res means in the middle of things. In *So Long a Letter*, the novel really does begin in the middle of things. Ramatoulaye begins her story by describing her husband's death and funeral. She then takes a mental journey back in time to recall her education and courtship. Next she writes of how her husband abandoned her five years before his death. She writes to her friend of how she endured the abandonment. This takes her back to the present time. At this point, the narrative moves forward as she describes what happens in the months following her husband's death. As the novel ends, she is about to end the seclusion of her widowhood and rejoin the world. Starting in the middle is an important tactic. Ramatoulaye starts at a critical moment in her life—her husband's death. To see how this event will affect Ramatoulaye, the reader must understand what experiences have shaped her. By recalling the past, Ramatoulaye gives the reader a fuller sense of who she is and what she values. The rest of the novel is devoted to showing how she moves on from the critical event. This technique is employed in most epics. By using it to tell the story of one woman's life, Bâ suggests that a woman's personal history is, in a sense, an epic.

Literary Heritage

In *So Long a Letter*, Bâ moves between literary heritages. Educated in a French-run school in Africa and with full access to European culture, Bâ was well aware of Western cultural practices. Her character Ramatoulaye speaks of enjoying "intellectual films, those with a message, sentimental films, detective films, comedies, thrillers. . . . I learned from them lessons of greatness, courage and perseverance. They deepened and widened my vision of the world, thanks to their cultural value.'' Bâ further indicates what she has learned from Western narratives when Ramatoulaye extols the ''power of books.'' Recalling her own days at a French-run school, Ramatoulaye declares, ''Books knit generations together.'' Cognizant of a world beyond her own, a world opened through books and movies, Bâ was in a position to craft her story through the traditions that best suited it.

Some of these traditions were native to Africa. In the novel, Bâ tells of how a traditional woman, Aunty Nabou, finds power through the stories she tells. Writing about Aunty Nabou, critic Dorothy Grimes remarks that Ramatoulaye links the ''seductive power of voice'' to ''tribal education.'' Voice, in this case, means the power to move through words, and particularly through the oral storytelling tradition. The message comes from the way the stories are told rather than through the actual stories. ''Telling folk tales, late at night under the starlit sky,'' Aunty Nabou's ''expressive voice glorified the retributive violence of the warrior; her expressive voice lamented the anxiety of the Loved One, all submissive. She saluted the courage of the reckless; she stigmatized trickery, laziness, calumny; she demanded care of the orphan and respect for old age.'' These stories, and the way they are told, teach. Values are transmitted through both the folk ways and the new ways, represented by print culture and film. Bâ employs both ways in her novel. She begins the book with an invocation, ''My friend, my friend, my friend. I call on you three times.'' As the footnotes to the book explain, such an invocation, drawn from African traditions, ''indicates the seriousness of the subject to be discussed.'' The topic is serious because Bâ, like Aunty Nabou or the films that contain important lessons, wants to teach. In the preface to *So Long a Letter*, the editor writes, ''She believed that the 'sacred mission' of the writer was to strike out 'at the archaic practices, traditions and customs that are not a real part of our precious cultural heritage.''' The ''sacred mission'' of teaching is what Bâ found in the literary tools she drew upon in her work.

Historical Context

Senegal had been a French colony since the seventeenth century. In 1960, Senegal gained its independence and became a separate nation. Mariama Bâ, then, who was born in 1929, lived through the tumultuous years leading to independence and in the time of civic unrest that followed independence. These years also offered a few elite African women access to education. In *So Long a Letter*, Ramatoulaye records how she and Aissatou were able to go to school under the guidelines that divided French West Africa into autonomous (though not yet independent) countries. This division of the vast French Imperial possessions occurred after World War II. Ramatoulaye's white teacher recognizes the importance of these few African girls' education, and tells them that they have an '''uncommon' destiny.'' Considering that today, twenty years after Bâ's death, the literacy rates for Senegalese women are far lower than those for Senegalese men, their fate was uncommon indeed. Bâ's French education and her exposure to Africans from many countries caused her, in the words of her heroine, to be ''lift[ed] . . . out of the bog of tradition, superstition and custom, to . . . appreciate a multitude of civilizations without renouncing our own, to raise our vision of the world, cultivate our personalities, strengthen our qualities, to make up for our inadequacies, to develop universal moral values in us.'' This wider perspective, however, of the educated French African woman came into conflict with the social mores and traditions of Senegal. This is evident in *So Long a Letter* by Ramatoulaye's decision to choose Moudou as a husband over Daouda Dieng, her mother's preferred choice, and by Aissatou's defiance of the traditions that would prohibit her, a goldsmith's daughter, from marrying Mawdo, the son of a tribal princess. Despite their education, both women learn that even in ''New Africa'' it is not easy for a woman to determine her own destiny. The rituals that demand obedience to mothers-in-law and their husbands' family members contrast with the autonomy Ramatoulaye and Aissatou have in their classrooms. Additionally, they face the problem of their husbands' polygamy. Traditionally, polygamy was designed to provide for women in an area where women far outnumbered men. Further, polygamy ensured the birth of more children, also necessary in a traditionally agricultural economy. But the civic and religious laws that allow polygamy seem out of place in ''New Africa.'' Ramatoulaye and Aissatou are more than capable of meeting their own economic needs. Unwelcome co-wives, therefore, undermine the independence they have achieved through their education and careers. Both women view polygamy as an unnecessary vestige of the past.

Bâ also captures some of the other conflicts evident in post-independence Senegal. After Leopold Senghor, a poet/statesman, took office as the first president of Senegal in 1960, he had to contend with civic unrest and a dire drought that rattled Senegal's emerging economy. The character Moudou Fall in *So Long a Letter*, then, is overcoming great obstacles when as a union organizer he "checks the trade union revolt." The novel suggests that he may have acted corruptly in order to gain a high position within the Ministry of Public Works. During Bâ's lifetime, corruption was rife. Though in 1978 the government allowed multiparty elections, only the Socialist party wielded any true power until the year 2000 when a president from an opposing party was elected. In snippets, Bâ does criticize the monolithic power of the Senegalese government, a government that chooses to build expensive embassies in other countries for show while ignoring the needs of its citizens. The needs of the citizens appear great. Even Binetou, who has access to education, comes from a family where food was not plentiful. Young Nabou, a midwife, hopes to improve a healthcare system where too many infants die needlessly, but "she remained powerless, faced with the force of death." Mariama Bâ was writing from a position of relative privilege and comfort, but her calling as a teacher and a writer brought her face to face with the harsher realities faced by many Senegalese.

Critical Overview

So Long a Letter was an instant critical success, winning the Noma Award for Publishing in Africa. Despite her premature death, Bâ is seen as a major African writer. Her slender first novel, while popular (it was translated into sixteen languages), has also been at the center of controversy. Critics are not sure what to make of Bâ's politics. Some call her a feminist, but others think she betrays feminism. Some are proud of her distinctly African literary voice, but others think she caters to Western values. Some see her envisioning unity across the classes, but others find her novels elitist.

Much of the controversy surrounding Bâ's novel springs from the controversy surrounding Islam and polygamy in Africa today. Ramatoulaye, after all, as the narrator of *So Long a Letter*, presents herself as a victim of polygamy. This stance draws the critical attention of those who seek to defend polygamy and those who see, with Ramatoulaye,

polygamy as a violation of women's rights. Critic Ella Brown, for instance, sees the novel as a condemnation of Islam: "It is obvious that [Ramatoulaye's] religion is the cause of the many ills she complains of. Her life would be much happier in a society that gave greater consideration to the needs of women." Dorothy Grimes, however, argues that "it seems Mariama Bâ, in the persona of Ramatoulaye, would have women also seek to reclaim traditional custom and thus to redefine it." In other words, Grimes does not believe Bâ would want to abandon the old traditions but rather transform them for a changing world. Edris Makward, meanwhile, calls Mariama Bâ "the first African woman to stress unequivocally the strong desire of the new generation of Africans to break away from the age-old marriage customs and adopt a decidedly more modern approach based on free mutual choice and the equality of the two partners." Other critics, such as J. O. J. Nwachukwa-Agbada and Audee Tanumu Giwa, however, believe that Bâ does not present either Muslim religious beliefs or polygamy accurately.

In his article, "'A Feminist Just Like Us?': Teaching Mariama Bâ's *So Long a Letter*," John Champagne outlines some of the difficulties of teaching Bâ's novel in American classrooms. American students tend to identify with Ramatoulaye's outrage at her husband's polygamy. Seeing Ramatoulaye as "one of us," the students read the novel as a critique of Senegalese and Islamic traditions and as supportive of American values. But as Champagne argues, to read the novel this way ignores its foreignness and difference, for, as Champagne points out, "at times, *So Long a Letter* is virtually unintelligible to a Western audience unfamiliar with both the history of Senegal and Islam. This is particularly true of the opening sections of the novel, in which the rituals surrounding the burial and mourning of Ramatoulaye's husband are described." As Champagne argues, however, his students who ignore the historical specificity of Bâ's novel are no different that the many critics who "have in fact praised [the novel's] appeals to universalism and global feminism." The best way for a Western reader to approach this novel, according to Champagne, is to cultivate an awareness of "the hybridity of Senegalese postcolonial culture." In other words, the best reader of *So Long a Letter* will recognize Bâ's debt to the historical forces that have shaped modern Senegal. Champagne's article also suggests that the controversies surrounding *So Long a Letter* have as much to do with the critics' various

These Senegalese children are playing on the steps in front of a theater advertising a concert by an ensemble from France, former colonial ruler of Senegal. The photo captures how competing French and Senegalese cultures shaped the region.

subject positions—their nationality, gender, and religion—as with the novel itself.

Criticism

Kimberly Lutz

Lutz is an instructor at New York University and has written for a wide variety of educational publishers. In the following essay she discusses the differences among the polygamous marriages in *So Long a Letter*.

Two of the plot lines in Mariama Bâ's *So Long a Letter* center around the effect of polygamy. In a letter written to her friend Aissatou Bâ, Ramatoulaye Fall describes how her husband, Moudou Fall, fell in love with a young woman. Moudou eventually takes this woman, Binetou, as his second wife. In the course of this very long letter, Ramatoulaye also remembers the circumstances surrounding Aissatou's divorce of her husband, Mawdo Bâ. Mawdo, obeying the commands of his mother, had married Young Nabou, a woman who shared his noble heritage. Refusing to be relegated to the status of "co-wife,"

Aissatou chose to leave Mawdo. Ramatoulaye pointedly chooses not to follow her friend's example and decides to stay married to Moudou.

Not surprisingly, much of the criticism of *So Long a Letter* focuses on the problem of polygamy. In his article "'A Feminist Just Like Us?': Teaching Mariama Bâ's *So Long a Letter*," John Champagne, summarizing the critical response, notes that many feminist critics "equate Islam and polygamy" and believe that Bâ is writing about the problems of both. Some Muslim critics, meanwhile, according to Champagne, feel that Bâ misreads "both Islam and the Koran." These critics find Bâ's perspective too dependent on Western values, and they think that she stereotypically portrays polygamy in *So Long a Letter*.

Perhaps the problem with these readings, however, is that they equate Moudou's polygamy with Mawdo's. Critics such as Irene Assiba d'Almeida, in her article "The Concept of Choice in Mariama Bâ's Fiction," focus on how Ramatoulaye and Aissatou "have made different choices in similar situations." But are the situations really so similar? Indeed the novel describes three separate (and one potential) polygamous marriages. The motives be-

> **"** ...I would argue that the differences among the novel's polygamous marriages are a lot more significant to an understanding of post-Independence Senegalese culture than the mere fact that polygamy exists."

hind each are widely different. The experiences of the ''co-wives'' in each are also different. Certainly Mariama Bâ eloquently speaks against polygamy in her novel. But I would argue that the differences among the novel's polygamous marriages are a lot more significant to an understanding of post-Independence Senegalese culture than the mere fact that polygamy exists.

Islamic scholars debate about whether or not the Koran really supports polygamy. Leila Ahmed, for one, has argued that Koranic verses ''that admonish men, if polygamous, to treat their wives equally and go on to declare that husbands would not be able to do so—using a form of the Arabic negative connoting permanent impossibility—are open to being read to mean that men should not be polygamous.'' In other words, Ahmed shows that the Koran tells men that they are breaking the rules of Islam if they do not treat their wives uniformly and that the Koran then goes on to say that it is humanly impossible for men to obey this rule. Perhaps then, the Koran suggests that men would be wise to marry only one woman. Other scholars note that Mohammed himself did not engage in polygamous marriage until after his first beloved wife had died. His subsequent marriages were more about political alliances than love.

So Long a Letter clearly shows that Moudou Fall is breaking the tenets of Muslim faith in his second marriage. Ramatoulaye who decides that she loves her husband too much to divorce him, tells Aissatou, ''I had prepared myself for equal sharing, according to the precepts of Islam concerning polygamic life.'' But, she never gets a chance to see if she can endure the ''humiliation'' of sharing her

husband. Moudou abandons her and her children altogether. Ramatoulaye knows that Moudou has ''cut off all contact'' and that she was ''abandoned: a fluttering leaf that no hand dares to pick up.'' Binetou, unhappy in marriage, demands that Moudou relinquish all ties with his first family. Ramatoulaye's plight, especially to a Western reader, does not seem to result from the technical polygamy, but from the very real abandonment. It is the old story; after twenty-five years of marriage and twelve children, Moudou wants a ''newer model.'' Or as Ramatoulaye describes, she is being exchanged ''like a worn-out or out-dated *boubou*,'' the traditional Senegalese dress. She focuses on her middle-aged body: ''My stomach protruded from beneath the wrapper that hid the calves developed by the impressive number of kilometres walked since the beginning of my existence. Suckling had robbed my breasts of their round firmness. I could not delude myself: youth was deserting my body.'' In contrast, Binetou is ''incontestably beautiful and desirable.'' As Ramatoulaye notes, ''Her beauty shone, pure. Her shapely contours could not but be noticed.''

In many ways, Moudou manipulates the law of polygamy for his own purposes. He uses the law to justify his behavior, but he in no way follows the precepts of his Islamic faith. The novel suggests that the fault lies in Moudou's character. Ramatoulaye's mother, after all, never trusted Moudou's appearance, but found him ''too handsome, too polished, too perfect for a man.'' The little the reader learns about Moudou seems to support Ramatoulaye's mother's assessment. Moudou is overly concerned about physical appearance, both his and his wives'. He spends money foolishly for show and lives beyond his means. Most damning, he seems to have abandoned the values and ambitions that caused Ramatoulaye to fall in love with him in the first place. Ramatoulaye may say that it is only the ''spiteful'' who believe that Moudou sold out the workers he represented as a trade union leader so that he could gain high political office, but she seems to be a biased observer. Indeed, Moudou's need for more money so that he could buy Binetou cars and jewelry could very likely have caused him to become corrupt. Perhaps he did quell ''the trade union revolt'' to become the technical adviser in the Ministry of Public Works. He may have abandoned his commitment to improving the living conditions of workers just as he abandoned Ramatoulaye.

Another of the novel's polygamous characters, Tamsir Fall (Moudou's older brother), also seems to manipulate the laws that allow polygamy for his own selfish gain. Some scholars of African culture and polygamy believe that polygamy served an important purpose in pre-industrial Africa. In times when women outnumbered men, polygamy ensured the support of women in need. Additionally, some argue that polygamous relationships helped to produce the many children needed to effectively farm the land. Tamsir, however, has not taken three wives to help support their needs. Rather, as Ramatoulaye throws in Tamsir's face, he lives off of his wives: "Your income can meet neither [your wives'] needs nor those of your numerous children. To help you out with your financial obligations, one of your wives dyes, another sells fruit, the third untiringly turns the handle of her sewing machine. You, the revered lord, you take it easy." Tamsir comes to Ramatoulaye seeking her hand in marriage. He claims to do so out of respect for his dead brother and to provide for the widow. But Ramatoulaye knows that Tamsir is not altruistic. He wants to get his hands on her wealth. If, in Moudou's case, polygamy is an excuse to chase after a girl his daughter's age, in Tamsir's it is a calculated way to make money. The superfluous children (Moudou fathers sixteen before his premature death and Tamsir's are called "numerous") also seem unnecessary in industrial Dakar. Each child, needing to be educated (Ramatoulaye speaks of the great expense), does not add to the family's material wealth. Rather Tamsir seeks a fourth wife in part to support the children he already has. Tamsir's idea of polygamy perverts any cultural basis that might have justified it.

The novel's two remaining polygamists are much more sympathetic characters. Daouda Dieng (who tries to take a second wife but does not succeed), in Ramatoulaye's estimation, is "an upright man." A politician, "he would fight for social justice. It was not love of show or money that had driven him towards politics, but his true love for his fellow man, the urge to redress wrongs and injustice." Not content to work only in politics, Daouda also runs a medical clinic. Believing that his skills as a doctor are too valuable to the people to forsake, Daouda commits himself to the extra work. When he seeks Ramatoulaye's hand in marriage after Moudou's death, he does so because he has always loved her and he believes that he can help take care of her and her twelve children. He does not plan to abandon his first wife, but to live a polygamous life as established by Muslim law. Ramatoulaye refuses his proposal for two reasons. First, she does not love him. Second, as she tells him, "You think the

problem of polygamy is a simple one. Those who are involved in it know the constraints, the lies, the injustices that weigh down their consciences in return for the ephemeral joys of change." Daouda is not indicted for wanting a second wife. Rather Ramatoulaye believes that Daouda, like many men, simply does not realize the ramifications of polygamy. He needs to be taught the costs of polygamy so that he, as a moral man, can reject a system that Ramatoulaye (and Mariama Bâ) finds untenable. Daouda may see polygamy as a way of gaining the happiness—Ramatoulaye's love—that he has sought his entire life. But Ramatoulaye argues that the happiness could only come at a cost so high that it would destroy his conscience.

This is the cost that Mawdo Bâ, Aissatou's husband, learns only too well. His happiness is destroyed by his polygamy, mainly because his beloved wife Aissatou divorces him soon after he marries Young Nabou. Mawdo's reasons for polygamy are much different than Moudou's, Tamsir's, or Daouda's. He marries his cousin Nabou out of a sense of family obligation. His mother, Aunty Nabou, adopted the girl, raised her, and groomed her to be Mawdo's wife. After his mother has announced the wedding date, Mawdo feels cornered. He must marry Nabou to save his mother from humiliation. Aunty Nabou had planned the marriage, moreover, to punish Aissatou. The daughter of a goldsmith, Aissatou had never won the approval of Aunty Nabou, a tribal princess. In this plotline, Mariama Bâ really shows how two very different cultures collide in present-day Senegal. Aissatou, an educated woman, represents "New Africa," and the liberated woman. She and Mawdo marry as equals and out of love. Aunty Nabou, a princess and a renowned teller of ancient folktales, represents the older, ingrained customs. Young Nabou, Ramatoulaye explains, loves Mawdo as though he were a prince out of one of Aunty Nabou's stories. In the battle between old and new ways, the old seemingly win out. Aunty Nabou is able to force Mawdo to marry Young Nabou. Aissatou leaves Africa altogether and begins working for the Senegalese Embassy in America. But Mawdo's unhappiness in the second marriage indicates that the old traditions, the marriages based on noble bloodlines and the acceptance of polygamy, are riddled with problems.

At the end of the novel, Ramatoulaye remains hopeful about the power of love: "The success of the family is born of a couple's harmony, as the harmony of multiple instruments creates a pleasant symphony.'' She ties the future of nations to the future of families: ''The nation is made up of all families, rich or poor, united or separated, aware or unaware. The success of a nation therefore depends inevitably on the family.'' In these final musings, Ramatoulaye is perhaps wondering what Senegal's success as a nation will be. Her family and Aissatou's family in many ways did not work. Each woman in seeking to marry for love was tripped up by tradition, Ramatoulaye because her husband manipulated the laws of Islam to satisfy the lust born of a mid-life crisis, Aissatou because her husband followed the dictates of his mother. The educated woman and the industrial economy do not mix well with the culture of polygamy. In describing four different manifestations of polygamy, Mariama Bâ seeks to show why it cannot work. In *So Long a Letter*, the reader mainly learns of Ramatoulaye's heartbreak at her husband's betrayal. But Bâ also indicates how polygamy hurts men, women, and nations, even when the polygamist is a much better person that Moudou Fall.

Source: Kimberly Lutz, in an essay for *Literature of Developing Nations for Students*, Gale, 2000.

Ann McElaney-Johnson

In the following review, Ann McElaney-Johnson examines Mariama Ba's Une Si Longue Lettre, *a realistic story of a woman who struggles to define her place in the social order, and describes the novel's dual use of displacement.*

Until quite recently the woman's place in African francophone literature has been defined by the male writer. Christopher Miller speaks of the traditional image of the ''femme noire'' in African literature, an image that ''shows how francophone literacy constantly 'talks' about women and depends on women for allegorical fuel but excludes women from the process of literate creation.'' Male writers have traditionally presented female characters who often bear no resemblence to their real-life counterparts. Through their texts these writers have displaced the woman. They have imposed a speech on her that is not her own. They have placed her in what Florence Stratton refers to as the ''shallow grave'' where female characters are forced to accept restricting stereotypes created and promulgated by masculine societies.

Abena Busia, in her challenging and provocative article on the black women's rebellious voices,

hails the arrival of an era where women reject this displacement and reclaim their rightful place:

> We are not reaffirming our presence or ''actualizing'' ourselves as if we have been absent, we know we never left; we are simply, but quite radically, reclaiming our own *stories* which have for so long been told for us, and been told wrong.... [W]hatever our national roots or origins, the world has been transformed, and the twentieth-century nation states that we all live in seem fated to develop into bastions of paternalistic power in which both sacred and secular ideologies have worked to domesticate and disempower the female, a process which, in many cases (matrilineal African societies, in particular), has been achieved against the native structuring ideologies of the societies concerned.''

Women are indeed telling their own stories. They are speaking of their longstanding displacement, and through literature they are claiming their right to their own place. Mariama Bâ's *Une Si longue lettre* serves well as an example of a woman's story depicting more realistically female characters who struggle to define their place in the face of a social order which has for so long limited their sense of self. The displacement of women in this novel is two-fold. The initial displacement of the woman by a patriarchal society which usurps her rightful place is seen in the established social system and is expressed by spouses, family members, friends, and religious leaders. This paper argues that a second displacement is the central theme of the novel. Women consciously opt to distance, to displace, themselves from such stereotypes. This subsequent displacement is a challenge to the society portrayed in the novel.

The stories Ramatoulaye recounts in her letter to Aîssatou are stories of abandonment and isolation of different women by a patriarchal society most often represented by the figure of the husband. The most obvious usurpation of the woman's rightful place is seen in the institution of polygamy. Ramatoulaye and Aîssatou suffer abandonment as their spouses choose a second wife to purportedly share, not usurp, their place in the home. In her letter Ramatoulaye reflects on ''cette solitude et cette réclusion forcées''; she speaks of the many women ''méprisées, reléguées ou échangées, dont on s'est séparé comme d'un boubou usé ou démodé.'' Challenges to polygamy are silenced by facile justifications of the institution. The family of Ramatoulaye's husband defends Modou's decision to take a second wife as a divine imperative: ''Dieu lui a destiné une deuxième femme, il n'y peut rien.'' Polygamy is further justified as a uniquely male necessity

What Do I Read Next?

- In her second novel, *Scarlet Song* (1981), Mariama Bâ describes the difficulties faced by an interracial couple in Senegal.

- Ken Bugul, a Senegalese woman who studied in Belgium, wrote her autobiography, *The Mad Bâobab Tree* in 1982. In it she describes how she violated the traditions of her upbringing.

- In her 1975 autobiography, *A Dakar Childhood*, Nafissatou Diallo describes growing up in Senegal. *A Dakar Childhood* was one of the earliest works of literature by a Senegalese woman.

- In 1979, Aminata Sow Fall, a Senegalese teacher, wrote her second novel, *The Beggars' Strike*. The novel explores class conflicts in Dakar.

- In *The Wretched of the Earth* (1963), radical African nationalist Frantz Fanon describes the effect of European colonialism in Africa and proposes how to shake off the imperial cloak.

---

that women cannot understand but must accept. Aîssatou's husband, Mawdo, explains:

> On ne résiste pas aux lois impérieuses qui exigent de l'homme nourriture et vêtements. Ces mêmes lois poussent le ''mâle'' ailleurs. Je dis bien ''mâle'' pour marquer la bestialité des instincts. . . . Tu comprends. . . . Une femme doit comprendre une fois pour toutes et pardonner; elle ne doit pas souffrir en se souciant des ''trahisons'' charnelles.

It is interesting to note that the force behind Mawdo's polygamous marriage is, in fact, a woman. It is his mother who manipulates this marriage and ''devant cette mère rigide, pétrie de morale ancienne, brûlée intérieurement par les féroces lois antiques, que pouvait Mawdo Bâ?'' Mawdo accepts a second wife to please his mother and the ancient laws. It is not, then, simply a question of the victimization of women by men in this novel. The framework of Bâ's text is larger: it is the patriarchal society that serves as a backdrop. Women in this society, and female characters in the novel, are often strong proponents of this patriarchal polity. Educated in the ''old'' way, women are made an accessory in their repression. In preparing a second wife for her son, Mawdo's mother instills in the young girl the traditional image of the woman:

> L'empreinte de l'école n'avait pas été forte en la petite Nabou, précédée et dominée par la force de caractère de tante Nabou qui, dans sa rage de vengeance, n'avait laissé rien au hasard dans l'éducation qu'elle avait donnée à sa nièce. C'était surtout, par les contes, pendant les veillées à la belle étoile, que tante Nabou avait exercé son emprise sur l'âme de la petite Nabou, sa voix expressive glorifiait la violence justicière du guerrier; sa voix expressive plaignait l'inquiétude de l'Aimée toute de soumission.

The young woman is taught to be the submissive loved one in her relationship with the glorified warrior. The traditional term ''l'Aimée'' is quite revealing. The woman, identified by a past participle, is defined in relation to the man. Her value is determined by her husband. As in the case of the petite Nabou, it is the mother of Ramatoulaye's co-wife who subjects her young daughter, Binetou, to marriage with an older, married man. Even in her anger, Ramatoulaye recognizes that Binetou is ''un agneau immolé comme beaucoup d'autres sur l'autel du 'matériel.'''

Ramatoulaye's reflections on a woman's place, or lack thereof, in a polygamous marriage underline the cruelty of this social order: ''J'étais abondonnée: une feuille qui voltige mais qu'aucune main n'ose ramasser . . . .'' Her choice of metaphor is apt. Her place usurped, she is adrift. She must now find her own place. She must redefine herself if she is to escape the ''shallow grave.''

The necessity of this redefinition on the part of the woman is echoed in the words of Daouda, an older suitor of Ramatoulaye who once again proposes marriage to her. An active member of the National Assembly, he recognizes the need for women to speak for themselves, to reclaim their place at the center of society:

"Women are indeed telling their own stories. They are speaking of their longstanding displacement, and through literature they are claiming their right to their own place."

La femme ne doit plus être l'accessoire qui orne. L'objet que l'on *dé place* [my emphasis], la compagne qu'on flatte ou calme avec des promesses. La femme est la racine première, fondamentale de la nation où se greffe tout apport, d'où part aussi toute floraison. Il faut inciter la femme à s'intéresser davantage au sort de son pays.

This male figure's discourse is a challenge to the traditional representation of women in the literary corpus. Ramatoulaye and the many other women of whom she speaks must reject the image of the "femme noire," a stereotype internalized as young women. Ramatoulaye herself embraced this image when Modou used this traditional representation in his letters written from France during their courtship. These examples of male writing, the only representation of male text in the novel, are reminiscent of traditional male writers. Modou, far from home, writes to a young Ramatoulaye that "le teint laiteur des femmes" does not attract him. He writes instead: "C'est toi que je porte en moi. Tu es ma négresse protectrice. Vite te retrouver rien que pour une pression de mains qui me fera oublier faim et soif et solitude." The images can not but recall Senghor's "Femme noire":

Femme nue, femme noire
Vêtue de ta couleur qui est vie,
de ta forme qui est beauté!
J ai grandi à ton ombre;
la douceur de tes mains bandait mes yeux.

or his poem "Nuit de Sine," in which he asks the woman: "Pose sur mon front tes mains balsamiques." Modou has imposed the traditional and limiting stereotype of the woman/healer/mother on Ramatoulaye. The young Rama, although a strong woman who chooses her own husband and career, accepts this identity. It is only later, when her husband adopts other traditional perspectives on the place, or lack of place, of the woman, that she must react.

This novel, the writing of a long letter to a close woman friend who has suffered similar pain, is in fact this reaction. Although written in the form of a letter, the text resembles a journal. The ambiguous phrase that opens the text ("en guise de réponse") can be understood in two fashions. It can simply mean that this letter is Ramatoulaye's way of responding to previous letters written by Aîssatou, but it can also imply that in place of responding by letter, the author will open a "cahier" to record her feelings. This intimation of private writing is further enhanced by Ramatoulaye's frequent change of addressee in her writing. Although most of her thoughts are addressed to Aîssatou, Ramatoulaye directs her remarks to others as well: she speaks to Modou, to other "victimes d'un si triste sort" and to those male doctors who misunderstand the pain these women suffer. Furthermore, the letter/journal, written during the "Mirasse," a four-month and ten-day period of mourning and seclusion, is never sent. Aîssatou's imminent arrival at Ramatoulaye's home reduces the text's importance as a letter. Instead, the letter/journal derives its importance as an opportunity for Ramatoulaye to embark on an inner journey to better understand herself. The journey is an exploration of her past and her loss of place. Her recalling of the past becomes a search for her own place. She must "de-place" herself in order to be herself.

The struggle to achieve the dis-placement from the stereotypes inposed on Ramatoulaye is difficult. In her letter she recalls Aîssatou's similar pain as she tries to confront her own. At the time of her own husband's betrayal, Aîssatou cast off the identity society had imposed on her by rejecting her husband's duplicitous love and, significantly, his name. In a letter to her husband affirming her dignity, she wrote: "Je me dépouille de ton amour, de ton nom. Vtue du seut habit valable de la dignité, je poursuis ma route." In order for Aîssatou to "dis-place" herself, however, she was forced to leave her home. Finishing her education, she moved to the United States to work as an interpreter for the Senegalese embassy.

The fact that she was unable to remain in her society and occupy her own space as she defines it is very significant in Ramatoulaye's similar struggle in which cultures conflict. Ramatoulaye and Aîssatou were educated in Western schools. They are, therefore, the product of two cultures. While traditional thought claimed that "L'école transforma nos filles en disblesses, qui détournent les hommes du droit chemin," as young women they believed themselves "de véritables soeurs destinées à la même mission émancipatrice" and "libérées donc des tabous qui frustent." Yet, even at a young age, Ramatoulaye recognized the conflicts born of these changes:

> Nous étions tous d'accord qu'il fallait bien des craquements pour asseoir la modernité dans les traditions. Ecartelés entre le passé et le présent, nous déplorions les 'suintements' qui ne manqueraient pas. . . . Nous dénombrions les pertes possibles. Mais nous sentions que plus rien ne serait comme avant. Nous étions pleins de nostalgie, mais résolument progressistes.

As an adult, although Ramatoulaye commits herself to raising modern children, educated men and women who will not settle for a tradition that stifles them, she finds that she herself is marked by this tradition. She is not willing to cast it off as did Aîssatou. She is torn between two cultures. She rejects polygamy but implicitly accepts it by choosing to stay with Modou. She wishes that her children will receive a modern education yet is upset when her daughters defy tradition by wearing pants and smoking.

The end of the letter, the end of this journey, leads, however, to greater self-knowledge. In the last chapter she confides:

> Les irréverisibles courants de libération de la femme qui fouettent le monde, ne me laissent pas indifférente. Cet ébranlement qui viole tousles domaines, révèle et illustre nos capacités. Mon coeur est en fête chaque fois qu'une femme émerge de l'ombre. Je sais mouvant le terrain des acquis, difficile la suivie des conquêtes: les contraintes sociales bousculent toujours et l'égoîsme mâle résiste.

This letter, this journal, leads finally to a transformation. Ramatoulaye is ready to "dis-place" herself. Unlike her friend, she will not leave her culture: she will instead welcome Aîssatou's arrival in the traditional way, yet she is a woman "coming out of the shadows." She affirms that "malgré tout . . . l'espérance m'habite. C'est de l'humus sale et mauséabonde que jaillit la plante verte et je sens pointer en moi, des bourgeons neufs. Le mot bonheur recouvre bien quelque chose, n'est-ce pas? J'irai à sa recherche."

The novel does not end here, however. Ramatoulaye's final statement brings the reader back to the initial theme of the novel, the letter, when she speaks about writing: "Tant pis pour moi, si j'ai encore à t'écrire une si longue lettre. . . ." The act of writing has become the means to finding one's own place. It is through writing about herself

and her past that Ramatoulaye is able to reconstruct herself, to distance herself from disabling stereotypes.

Whereas women from past generations, the mothers and grandmothers of Ramatoulaye and Aîssatou, communicated only through oral means ("Nos grand'mères dont les concessions étaient séparées par une tapade, échangeaient journellement des messages. Nos mères se disputaient la garde de nos oncles et tantes"), this generation claims the written form as its own. In the same way that a Western education separated these women from a sometimes stifling tradition, it also gave them a powerful instrument that sets them off from the "femme noire" image. The claiming of writing, traditionally an exclusively masculine form of communication, as their own enables the women to dispossess themselves of the images imposed on them by the traditional male writer. The woman is no longer created through the man's text; she creates herself in her own text. Within the context of the story, writing oneself literally becomes a refusal to compromise. Aîssatou's rejection of a polygamous marriage is in the form of a letter to her husband. Through the experience of writing her story, Ramatoulaye progresses from a victim unable to reject polygamy in her marriage with Modou to a woman capable of using the written word in her letter refusing Daouda's proposal of a second polygamous marriage.

This written "prise de parole" does not represent a cultural conflict for Ramatoulaye. As Miller demonstrates, the women in the novel do not simply adopt a uniquely Western form of expression; they adapt it to their own culture, a culture based on orality rather than literacy (although she clearly rejects the exclusively oral education used to manipulate young women, she herself sees great value in the oral lessons of her grandmother as she struggles to raise her children in a changing world). Ramatoulaye's style of writing reflects this mixture of orality and literacy. She continually cites both conversations and written texts as she tells her story. This written account ends, in fact, in anticipation of a conversation with her friend upon her arrival the next day. Orality and literacy blend together.

Busia asserts that "the centrality of oral narrative, so important to African literary tradition, lends distinctive form to the rebellious writings of black women worldwide." Orality is indeed central in Bâ's novel. The familiar tone and the retelling of conversations particularize this style. Perhaps most striking is the inclusion of formulae that are used to announce conversation in Ramatoulaye's culture. Prefacing the actual account of her story, Ramatoulaye uses a well-known formula to indicate the gravity of the matter: ''Amie, ami, ami! Je t'appelle trois fois.'' Bâ insists on the importance of this formula by explaining its significance in a footnote. Tamsir's announcement of Modou's marriage is carefully transcribed with the formal axioms indicating a message of great importance. Finally, repetition of key phrases in the novel recalls the oral tradition of the griot. Ramatoulaye's recounting of her life after Modou's departure is rendered more dramatic, more piercing by repetition of structure and words. Throughout the account, the use of ''je'' with a verb in the imperfect tense creates a particularly haunting rhythm. Repetition of the phrases ''jétais abandonnée: une feuille qui voltige mais qu'aucune main n'ose ramasser, aurait dit ma grand'mère'' (2 times) and ''Je survivais'' (4 times) insists on the orality of this culture while integrating it with the written form.

Miller points out that even in the choice of genre, Bâ incorporates two traditions. She uses the epistolary form, a European genre rarely adapted to francophone literature, but deviates from this established form by writing a modified journal, a form used most often by male francophone writers. Miller proposes that in doing so ''the position that Mariama Bâ staked out for herself is unique, distinguishable from both the 'European' female point of reference and the 'African' male one. In effect she has broken down that opposition between, on the one hand, 'female' and 'feminist' as uniquely European, and on the other hand, the francophone literary tradition as uniquely male.'' Bâ has defined her own space. As a writer she has displaced herself in relation to both the European and masculine stereotypes. Like Ramatoulaye, her literary creation, writing defines her place.

Perhaps the writing of this novel can be considered Bâ's ''en guise de réponse'' to the oppressive displacement of women. Interestingly, there is no closure to the novel. Ramatoulaye's conclusion: ''tant pis pour moi si j'ai encore à t'écrire une si longue lettre . . .'' refuses to conclude. The act of responding through writing, a woman's deliberate displacement of herself as she frees herself from the shallow grave, will continue. The social order has been challenged; there will be no more silence; there will be no closure.

Source: Ann McElaney-Johnson, ''The Place of the Woman or the Woman Displaced in Mariama Ba's *Une Si Longue*

Lettre,'' in *CLA Journal,* Vol. XXXVII, No. 1, September, 1993, pp., 19–28.

Mildred Mortimer

In the following essay, Mildred Mortimer studies the Senegalese woman writer Mariama Ba's novel Une si Longue Lettre *and attempts to resolve whether Ba reinforces the idea that women social reformers are either sacrificed or remade by the patriarchal society or whether she expresses them as strengthening the female bond.*

Depicting the Dakar-Niger Railway strike of 1947 in his novel *Les Bouts de bois de Dieu,* Ousmane Sembène gives several female protagonists revolutionary scripts. When Penda delivers a fiery speech proposing that the women of Thiés march on Dakar, she is responding to a community crisis, the railway workers strike, by moving women into public space. Both her speech and the march challenge societal norms: ''De mémoire d'homme c'était la premiére fois qu'une femme avait pris la parole en public á Thiés.'' Although Sembène projects the women into the political arena, he concludes the novel on an ambiguous note. As the marchers near Dakar, Penda dies, killed by the police. At the conclusion of the demonstration the women return home to resume their former activities: ''Le soir venu, elles regagnaient la maison paternelle ou le toit conjugal.'' Women who have been catalysts for change either disappear or are recuperated by the patriarchal structure.

Sembène published *Les Bouts de bois de Dieu* in 1960, two decades before the emergence of Senegalese women writers Nafissatou Diallo, Aminatou Sow Fall, Mariama Bâ, Ken Bugul. Bâ, in particular, offers an important contrast to Sembène's text. I propose to study her *Une si longue lettre,* seeking a response to the following questions: Does Bâ's text reveal Sembène's same ambiguity? In other words, are women who appear as catalysts for change sacrificed or recuperated by the patriarchy? How does Bâ treat the conflict between the patriarchal tradition that confines African women to domestic space and women's struggle to claim public space?

In her first novel, Bâ chooses the letter as a vehicle for recounting episodes of her heroine's past. Following her husband's death, Ramatoulaye begins a long letter to her childhood friend, Aïssatou, in which she describes how she copes after Modou, her husband of twenty-five years, takes a second wife. Choosing a young woman the age of his oldest daughter, Modou abandons Ramatoulaye and their twelve children.

Bâ received the Noma prize for *Une si longue lettre*, acclaimed by the judges for its significant testimony and true imaginative depth (Zell). Given its strong attack on polygamy, however, the novel was evaluated primarily as a sociological statement. Critics who focus on the socio-political and cultural dimensions of polygamy in the work agree that Ramatoulaye, the heroine, is a victim of a society that endorses and encourages polygamy, but disagree as to whether she uses her energies heroically to overcome obstacles or to reproach bitterly the patriarchal structure.

Without neglecting the socio-political implications of the work, the present study focuses upon Ramatoulaye's journey to self-understanding, emphasizing the narratee's role in the novel. I shall argue that Ramatoulaye addresses her long letter (28 chapters) to Aïssatou because she is both an intimate friend and an important role model. The reader learns that Aïssatou faced the issue of polygamy in her own marriage, refusing it before the crisis occurred in Ramatoulaye's home. Aïssatou's revolt and subsequent ''escape'' to America makes her Ramatoulaye's ideal reader. Her success in the ''new world'' is convincing testimony that the journey outward is possible.

By writing to Aïssatou the narrator introduces the tension between enclosure and the outward journey. In Bâ's fictional world Senegalese men are most often offered the opportunity to make the journey outward, returning home with gained maturity, whereas Senegalese women are usually barred from this experience. Modou has been to France to study; Ramatoulaye has not. Given this context, Aïssatou's journey to the United States is a radical statement of revolt.

The death and funeral of Ramatoulaye's estranged husband result in enclosure for Ramatoulaye rather than the outward journey. Following the demise of Modou, Ramatoulaye is committed by Islamic tradition to spend four months in mourning and seclusion. Ramatoulaye uses this period to travel in time rather than space. She recalls the past in an attempt to understand herself better and to cope with the present. Annis Pratt states that women's escape through imagination is strategic, a withdrawal into the unconscious for the purpose of personal transformation. Indeed, Ramatoulaye turns to the inner journey to obtain knowledge, through

Leopold Sedar Senghor remained President of the Republic of Senegal for twenty years following its independence from France in 1960.

self-examination and maturity, through personal transformation. By examining her own thoughts, memories, and the collective experience of family and nation emerging from colonialism, Ramatoulaye attempts to gain a heightened sense of maturity.

The reader's task in this work is to evaluate Ramatoulaye's inner journey, bearing in mind a binary construct, the portrait and the mask. Does the novel conceal as much as it reveals? Let us refine the question. Does enclosure (brought about by the Islamic tradition of respectful mourning) lead to disclosure, or ironically, to concealment and therefore to the self-delusion of a protagonist who proposes an inner journey for the explicit purpose of lucidity and self-understanding?

The novel begins with a direct statement of purpose:

> Aïssatou, J'ai recu ton mot. En guise de réponse, j'ouvre ce cahier, point d'appui dans mon désarroi: notre longue pratique m'a enseigné que la confidence noie la douleur.

Having just received a letter from Aïssatou (which we later learn announces Aïssatou's forth-

> At the end of her journey, Bā's heroine, unlike Sembène's catalysts for change, is neither eliminated nor recuperated by the patriarchy. On the contrary, Ramatoulaye has learned to use the enclosure as her refuge and writing as a means of communication to strengthen female bonding."

coming visit to Dakar), Ramatoulaye announces Modou's death. At the same time, she expresses the need for this correspondence as support in time of crisis. This very long letter, ultimately a diary, will allow Ramatoulaye to express her intimate thoughts and justify her responses to life through the act of writing to her ideal reader, her closest friend.

Thus, the death of Modou, *not* his second marriage and ultimate abandonment of Ramatoulaye and their children, is the catalyst for the letter. The important subtext in the work, revealed in the opening paragraphs, is the importance of female bonding, presented as a legacy of traditional Africa. Ramatoulaye recounts the friendship between their grandmothers, mothers, and finally recalls their shared childhood: "Nous, nous avons usé pagnes et sandales sur le même chemin caillouteux de l'école coranique." Hence, at the beginning of her letter Ramatoulaye acknowledges that Aïssatou is her ideal reader because of common experiences: a shared Islamic past, a long sustained friendship, and a painful experience of polygamy—"Hier tu as divorcé. Aujourd-hui, je suis veuve." Later, she will come to terms with Aïssatou's decision, her choice to embark upon the journey outward to a new world and a new life.

Enclosure as an important structuring element of the novel must take into account the Islamic context; the latter influences both the narrative content and structure. The mourning period, an obligation of Islam, provides Ramatoulaye with the time frame in which to write the long letter. Open-

ing the notebook that becomes a 131-page novel, she explains:

> Mon coeur s'accorde aux exigences religieuses. Nourrie, dès l'enfance, à leurs sources rigides, je crois que je ne faillirai pas. Les murs qui limitent mon horizon pendant quatre mois et dix jours ne me gênent guère. J'ai en moi assez de souvenirs' à ruminer.

Islam as well provides the vehicle for disclosure. "Mirasse," an Islamic precept, calls for the disclosure of all possessions of the deceased for the purpose of inheritance. Ramatoulaye states: "Le Mirasse" ordonné par le Coran nécessite le dépouillement d'un individu mort de ses secrets les plus intimes. Il livre ainsi à autrui ce qui fut soigneusement dissimulé." Her religion thus encourages revelations of a deceased person's past so as to praise the individual. She reinterprets this practice to allow for the disclosure of Modou's financial and emotional treachery. She explains that upon his death she learned that he had taken a loan to pay for his second wife's home by putting a lien on his first wife's property (a residence that they had in fact paid for jointly). Subsequently, Ramatoulaye broadens the definition of disclosure to unveil Modou's emotional breach of faith in their marriage.

Ramatoulaye's reaction to the process of "mirasse" is crucial to her journey toward lucidity and the reader's understanding of the protagonist. By disclosing Modou's transgressions to the readers (Aïssatou, you, me), she, the betrayed individual, allows us to seek evidence of a healing process. We can then ascertain whether the victim remains victimized, blocked by his betrayal of their married life, or whether she proves capable of transcending the experience by word and deed, discourse and actions.

For the purpose of analysis, the novel can be separated into three sections. Announcing Modou's death and introducing the concept of *mirasse,* the first part (letters 1–4) puts forth the two structuring devices: enclosure and disclosure. The second part (letters 5–17), depicts Ramatoulaye's journey through time. By means of analepses (reaches into the past or flashbacks), the protagonist gathers information that prepares her for the present. In the final part of the novel (letters 18–24) Ramatoulaye, having spent forty days in mourning, forgives Modou. However, as a widow Ramatoulaye faces a series of moral and emotional challenges that test her judgment and values. These trials complete the protagonist's maturation process.

Hélène Cixous, a leading exponent of the women's movement in France, has written: "Woman must put herself into the text—as into the world and into history—by her own movement.'' Once Ramatoulaye concludes the description of the rituals surrounding Modou's burial, presenting ethnographic details as well as her open criticism of the crass materialism that spoils tradition, she encounters the difficulty of ''putting herself into the text.'' She begins with two false starts: a ''cri de coeur,'' in which she proclaims herself victim, followed by a letter to Modou, not to Aïssatou, in which she remembers with great sentimentality their first meeting. Although Ramatoulaye praises Modou's progressive views, as she recalls them, his words contradict her portrait; they reveal a young man locked into gender stereotypes. For example, calling Ramatoulaye his ''négresse protectrice,'' Modou languishes in Paris, missing ''le dandinement des négresses le long du trottoir.'' Hence, Ramatoulaye's acts of telling and showing contradict one another.

This analepsis, a flashback reaching thirty years into the past, poses the problem of the narrator's reliability. Shlomith Rimmon-Kenan, who considers personal involvement to be a main source of unreliability, defines a reliable narrator as one who provides the reader with ''an authoritative account of the fictional truth.'' Intense personal involvement in her own story leads Ramatoulaye, an autodiegetic or first-person narrator, to insert the story of Aïssatou's marriage into the novel. By writing *about* Aïssatou in addition to writing *to* her, Ramatoulaye restores the objectivity that will grant reliability to her narrative. Aïssatou serves not only as ideal reader and role model but as reality ''anchor'' as well. Thus, by using the structural device of doubling—parallel events or similar experiences that reinforce the sense of parallel lives—Ramatoulaye regains an authoritative voice.

The doubling begins in the first letter when she remembers their shared childhood. Later, she recalls that both young girls were inspired by the extraordinary vision of their European school director. Looking back on these formative years, Ramatoulaye views her school mistress as the one who freed them from tradition. She writes in the first person plural, emphasizing the school director's effect upon both of them:

> Nous sortir de l'enlisement des traditions, superstitions et moeurs; nous faire apprécier de multiples civilisations sans reniement de la nôtre; élever notre vision du monde, cultiver notre personnalité, renforcer nos qualités, mater nos défauts; faire fructifier en nous les valeurs de la morale universelle; voilà la tâche que s'était assignée l'admirable directrice.

The director's message is clearly subversive. Urging her students to break with tradition and to affirm their personality, she calls for revolt rather than submission. Ramatoulaye's act of rebellion is to reject the suitor chosen for her by her mother, and marry Modou Fall, a man of her own choosing. Similarly, Aïssatou, the daughter of a blacksmith, defies the traditional caste system by marrying a son of royalty. Their rebellion has further consequences; their choices prepare the way for polygamy. Ramatoulaye chooses a man whose propensity towards infidelity is immediately recognized by her mother. Aïssatou, who marries above her station, incures the vengeance of a scheming mother-in-law who succeeds in bringing a second wife into her son's household.

Although the doubling creates the dimension of parallel lives in the novel, the narrator reveals that Ramatoulaye and Aïssatou are not mirror images of one another. When their husbands enter into polygamous marriages for different reasons, one to please a scheming mother, the other to find the excitement of youth, the two women react to polygamy in very different ways. Aïssatou rebels; Ramatoulaye acquiesces. Aïssatou responds to Mawdo's announcement of his second marriage with an angry letter in which she states her refusal to remain within the marriage:

> Je ne m'y soumettrai point. Au bonheur qui fut nôtre, je ne peux substituer celui que tu me proposes aujourd'hui. Tu veux dissocier l'Amour tout court et l'amour physique. Je te rétorque que la communion charnelle ne peut être sans l'acceptation du cœur, si minime soit-elle.

Ramatoulaye, who quotes Aïsstou's entire letter, cannot bring herself at this point to follow her friend in revolt. Despite admiration for Aïssatou's refusal of polygamy, she turns the other cheek. The second section of the novel discloses not only Modou's treachery but Ramatoulaye's failed revolt. Both husband and wife lose touch with their earlier progressive selves. He becomes a caricature of an old fool trying to regain his youth: ''Modou s'essouflait à emprisonner une jeunesse déclinante qui le fuyait de partout.'' She, lacking courage, agrees to a polygamous union out of fear of loneliness. Only after he truly abandons her and she is forced to take on the role of single parent does she resume the rhetoric of revolt. Ramatoulaye arguably writes the ''long letter'' to Aïssatou upon Modou's death because she was unable to write the ''short letter,'' as Aïssatou had done, and thereby reject polygamy.

The second section can be characterized as failed revolt but it prepares the protagonist for the series of trials or challenges that result in her final transformation. This preparation takes the form of comforting past memories on the one hand, and acts of independence on the other. As she evokes memories of her youth and early adulthood, the narrator uses them as a source of happiness. Recalling the years when she was first married to Modou (as was Aïssatou to Mawdo), Ramatoulaye turns to nature for inspiration. She depicts the beach at Ngor:

> Sur le sable fin, rincé par la vague et gorgé d'eau, des pirogues, peintes naïvement, attendaient leur tour d'être lancées sur les eaux. Dans leur coque, luisaient de petites flaques bleues pleines de ciel et de soleil.

Viewed metaphorically, the boats waiting to be launched on the vast ocean correspond to the two idealistic couples whose lives, at that moment in time, are filled with boundless dreams. This optimistic phase occurs in the mid-1960s when the Senegalese nation was first emerging from colonialism. As Ramatoulaye faces adult responsibilities in her personal life, Senegal assumes the responsibilities of nationhood. Hence, the narrator establishes a direct link between the personal and the historical-political phase.

Although the mid-section of the novel depicts a protagonist who appears to have lost her earlier rebellious stance (and is therefore unable to revolt against her husband's abuse of power), two specific incidents toward the end of the section indicate that, despite her initial acquiescence, Ramatoulaye will recapture both the spirit and the language of revolt. First, Ramatoulaye recounts her experience of braving the curious stares of a public who wonders why she is alone at the cinema.

> On dévisageait la femme mûre sans compagnon. Je feignais l'indifférence, alors que la colère martelait mes nerfs et que mes larmes retenues embuaient mes yeux. Je mesurais, aux regards étonnés, la minceur de la liberté accordée à la femme.

Here Ramatoulaye finds the courage to venture alone into public space but at the same time masks her anger toward a hostile public. Then Aïssatou's gift of a new car allows her to travel more freely in the city. The Fiat proves to be a challenge. She conquers her fear of driving and obtains her driver's license. These experiences affirm her presence in public space. Occurring after Modou's departure but before his death, they attest to the protagonist's essentially independent spirit and foreshadow her final transformation.

The fortieth day of mourning marks the beginning of the third and final section of the novel. At this point, the widow forgives her late husband. In addition, suitors begin to ask for her hand. First Ramatoulaye's brother-in-law and then a former suitor propose marriage. Presented with a co-wife several years before, Ramatoulaye is now asked to become one herself. Refusing her brother-in-law (whose offer is motivated by the desire for her inheritance), she finally expresses her anger: "Ma voix connaît trente années de silence, trente années de brimades. Elle éclate, violente, tantôt sarcastique, tantôt méprisante." The woman who greeted the announcement of Modou's second marriage with a smile and feigned indifference now removes the mask of passivity and acquiescence. She finds the words to affirm her identity, expressing her conviction that marriage must be a choice between partners, not an arrangement between families:

> Tu oublies que j'ai un coeur, une raison, que je ne suis pas un objet que l'on passe de main en main. Tu ignores ce que se marier signifie pour moi: c'est un acte de foi et d'amour, un don total de soi à l'être que l'on a choisi et qui vous a choisi. (J'insistais sur le mot choisi.)

Later, rejecting the second suitor, Daouda Dieng, whose motivation is affection not avarice, Ramatoulaye writes him a letter to explain that she cannot enter into a polygamous marriage because she has suffered the consequences of one. Thus, Ramatoulaye finally writes a letter rejecting polygamy, although neither the tone nor the circumstances recall Aïssatou's angry words to her ex-husband, Mawdo.

Having learned to express her anger openly as she rejects polygamy, Ramatoulaye faces her final trials. Forced to cope with family crises as a single parent, she rises to each occasion: a son's motorcycle accident, then the pregnancy of an unmarried daughter.

As she writes her last letter to Aïssatou, Ramatoulaye eagerly awaits her friend's visit. The dual process of introspection and writing, of enclosure and disclosure, have led Ramatoulaye to cease questioning Modou's initial rejection. No longer a victim, she now expresses new hope in her future. "C'est de l'humus sale et nauséabond que jaillit la plante verte et je sens pointer en moi des bourgeons neufs." The epistolary novel that began with Modou's death ends in an expression of rebirth.

Ramatoulaye's journey leads to lucidity. She discovers that Modou abandoned her because of his weakness, vanity, and she learns a deeper truth, to believe in herself. By removing her mask, the smile of acquiescence, she recovers her earlier vitality and optimism. Moreover, the successful conclusion of the first journey prepares the protagonist for a second one, a new quest for happiness.

At the end of the novel Ramatoulaye awaits Aïssatou in the traditional manner, seated on a straw mat. Unlike Aïssatou, who chose the outward journey and left Senegal in order to begin a new life, Ramatoulaye decides not to leave her community. She avoids the risk of uprootedness in exile, the challenge that her friend assumes, and reaches a new beginning via a different route. Ramatoulaye creates an identity that blends traditional and modern elements. Rather than break with her society, she attempts to work from within.

An interesting parallel can be drawn between Bâ's novel and the orphan tale of oral narrative. For example, Bernard Dadié's ''Le Pagne noir'' recounts the adventures of Aïwa, sent by her stepmother to whiten a black cloth. As she travels in search of water in which to wash the object, the orphan courageously confronts danger and frustration. Finally, the ghost of her mother descends from heaven to replace the black cloth with a white one which the stepmother immediately recognizes as the winding sheet used to bury Aïwa's mother. Not only does the orphan accomplish the task, she teaches the wicked stepmother a lesson.

Both Bâ's novel and Dadié's folktale depict a vulnerable female protagonist. Ramatoulaye, like Aïwa, ventures forth unprotected in a hostile world. She has lost the protection of her husband (a variant of the orphan's loss of a parent), and is forced by a patriarchal society to grapple with a series of difficult tasks. One of her final tests is to reject her two suitors. By refusing a second marriage to which she is not committed by love, Ramatoulaye confronts and overcomes her fear of loneliness. The orphan's trials have been compared to initiation rites. Ramatoulaye's tests initiate her to a new stage of life: the role of a single person.

In Dadié's orphan tale, Aïwa, despite her hardships, never removes her mask, a smile: ''Elle sourit encore du sourire qu'on retrouve sur les lévres des jeunes filles.'' Ramatoulaye, on the other hand, discards the smile that has functioned as a mask and asserts her individuality and independence. As she assumes a dynamic identity, she reaffirms the rebellious spirt of her youth. Challenging the patriarchy that demands submission and obedience,

Ramatoulaye looks within herself to find the courage to break free.

When Aïwa accomplishes the impossible task, she is rewarded for her stoicism and obedience by receiving the help of her mother, a spirit of the dead. Ramatoulaye's intercessor, however, is not a spirit from the other world, but Aïssatou. The faithful friend and confidante offers Ramatoulaye two gifts, a car and a letter, and thereby provides her with tools of transformation. The Fiat allows Ramatoulaye to lay claim to public space by traveling freely in it, thus encouraging her to affirm a new identity. The letter, Aïssatou's declaration of separation from her husband, Mawdo, initiates Ramatoulaye to the act of writing as a process as well as a product of liberation.

In contrast to the winding sheet of the dead mother, a white cloth that puts an end to the orphan's quest in Dadié's narrative, the white sheets of Ramatoulaye's notebook propose a new beginning. Presented as a therapeutic activity in the early pages of the novel, writing subsequently results in liberation as well as in healing. Moreover, in Bâ's novel, the act of writing as a process of disclosure that promotes discovery and self-affirmation clearly reinforces female bonding. Hence, the two structuring devices, enclosure and disclosure, the one facilitating the journey inward, the other recording it, serve another important function; they strengthen communication between Ramatoulaye and Aïssatou. These bonds between narrator and narratee have made it possible for Ramatoulaye to put herself into the text.

At the end of her journey, Bâ's heroine, unlike Sembène's catalysts for change, is neither eliminated nor recuperated by the patriarchy. On the contrary, Ramatoulaye has learned to use the enclosure as her refuge and writing as a means of communication to strengthen female bonding. In Bâ's text the written word becomes a creative tool of self-expression and a weighty weapon against the patriarchy. By recording her journey to self-understanding, Ramatoulaye, in effect, writes her own revolutionary script.

Source: Mildred Mortimer, ''Enclosure/Disclosure in Mariama Ba's *Une Si Longue Lettre*,'' in *The French Review*, Vol. 64, No. 1, October, 1990, pp. 69–78.

Femi Ojo-Ade

In the following review, Femi Ojo-Ade discusses Mariama Ba's Une Si Longue Lettre, *a novel that expresses the writer's desire to showcase wom-*

en's role in a heavily patriarchal society and how they struggle against and within that structure while striving for a revolutionized future.

> 'Women are man's proletariat.' (*Karl Marx*)
> 'Woman is inferior to man and is his subject.'
>   (*The Koran*)
> 'The head of every man is Christ; the head of
>   every woman is man.' (*The Bible*)

Introduction

Since the first contact with the white world, black literature has remained a literature of the underprivileged, a voice of the victim, a mirror of man's inhumanity to man, a record of the revolt of the recalcitrant against the cultural rape perpetrated by the racist colonizer. Unfortunately, the community has emerged worse off than the individual. From the long drawn-out struggle came self-determination, self-satisfaction, self-aggrandizement: the self before the other; the élite before the masses; man before woman. Black literature underscores the continued colonization of the race; for authentic decolonization can be achieved only when the equation changes from self-independence to society-independence, from male-superior/female-inferior to male-female.

Like the near impossible dream of genuine black emancipation in a world where confusion, conflagration and ever-changing complexities and complexes draw people away from a real effort to solve basic problems, female liberation may remain just that, a dream frustrated by harsh, existential realities. The Bible gives us Adam and Eve. The Koran asserts male superiority. The twentieth century, the era of dynamism and progress, the age of decolonization and purification (some would quickly add decadence and pollution), presents a forum for feminism, even if the fad is viewed with a sneer by the chauvinistic community.

Feminism, an occidental phenomenon like many others, has spread ever so slowly but steadily to the forbidden land of Africa. Forbidden, because the continent where man supposedly first surfaced prides herself on her tradition and resilience against foreign cultural intrusion. Such 'aberrations' as feminism are abhorred by many who are, however, the very purveyors of the bastardization of that culture whose contents remain confusing to their civilized minds. Criticism does not stop feminism from rearing its head; for society is a dynamic entity condemned to change from within and without. The war between male and female is now a contempo-

rary constant, and new literary voices from among the once silent minority cry out to be heard, even if there is reason to doubt on whose behalf the revolt is being declared.

Grace Ogot, Efua Sutherland, Ama Ata Aidoo, Flora Nwapa, women writers all, constitute the 'old guard', steeped in the traditions of the land, complaining of their sufferings as subjects of the male master, but seeking solace in a society that has proclaimed woman the mother. That group's conciliatory position has been superseded by a current of revolt. Compromise is replaced by criticism and condemnation. Respect turns into repudiation. Devotion is buried by divorce. Buchi Emecheta, Nafissatou Diallo, Mariama Bâ, those are the voices currently crying out for the liberation of woman, the second-class citizen. Not an easy struggle, that; for the vocal female victim, born of the delicate wedlock of tradition and colonialism, and therefore imbued with the modernizing notions of intellectualism and equality, cannot shed the cloak of womanhood, that glorified niche carved out of the birth-pangs that constitute every mother's ever-lasting joy. Contradiction is indeed inevitable. Hard choices have to be made, and commitment could be destructive. *Une si Longue Lettre* is a study of those contradictions.

Mariama Bâ, the author, is Senegalese, an educated Senegalese, a member of several associations interested in enhancing the female position in a predominantly Moslem, male-oriented society. Her western education notwithstanding, she would like to be considered as an 'average Senegalese woman', 'a woman of the house'. *Lettre* is her first novel and it is filled with autobiographical elements, expressing as it does the novelist's desires and dilemma's, tracing her life in a society caught between the established order of the past and the exigencies of the present. A traditionalist at heart, Bâ aspires to be a revolutionary. A maternal retiring figure through and through, she aspires to be a pioneer in female emancipation. Her family upbringing and the Koranic training have imbued her with the absolute law of 'divine wish': man is woman's overlord. Added to that is Bâ's fatalism. Destiny is a fixed reality, impossible to avoid.

> Destiny seizes whoever he wants, when he wants. If his desire tallies with yours, he brings you an overabundance of bliss. But most often, he unbalances and brings conflict. You can only submit yourself to his laws.

However, such fatalistic tendencies are contradictory to the tenets of the white man's school where Bâ learned how to manipulate the French language. Submissiveness in the face of suffering is discouraged and the victim is told to demand total reform of the social order. Her 'letter' is written in the form of a notebook kept by the heroine named Ramatoulaye. Married for thirty years to Modou by whom she has twelve children, Ramatoulaye has been separated for five years from her husband who repudiated her and left her for a much younger woman. Her 'letter', ostensibly addressed to a bosom friend, a divorcee working as an interpreter in the Senegalese embassy in New York and due to return home very soon, is written immediately after Modou's death. It is a reflection of life in a psychological ghetto of mental torture and social disorder, where woman is a slave and a beast of prey. Divorce is a rarity but separation and infidelity are common. The life of the couple, far from being a haven of contentment and consideration, is a hell of conniving criminals and common cretins. According to Bâ, two camps are precisely delineated: the victimizer, the slave-master, the ruler of this hell on earth, is Man; the victimized, the slave driven at times to the point of mental exhaustion, is Woman.

The Male Victimizer

Man, the unfaithful husband; Man, the womanizer; Man, the victimizer—Bâ's novel describes him in all his negative forms, without an exception to console his pride. First, there is Ramatoulaye's spineless husband, Modou Fall, a successful lawyer, a trade-union leader turned company executive. Happily married for twenty-five years, he suddenly takes an interest in Binetou, a teenage schoolgirl and friend of his daughter, Daba. Before his first wife can sift through the maze of lies and manipulations, Modou has abandoned the matrimonial home to live with his new wife and her mother. Ramatoulaye is left forever with the question unanswered: 'Madness? Spinelessness? Irresistible love? What internal upheaval deranged Modou Fall to make him marry Binetou?' Definitely the fault is not Ramatoulaye's; as she makes the reader understand, she has made a thorough self-analysis and has come up with nothing to explain her husband's behaviour. Modou himself has the following explanation: God has destined him to have a second wife. To which the victimized heroine quickly responds with a sneer similar to that of a perfect angel ogled by a lecherous wolf but adamant to keep her innocence intact.

Yet, there are indications that Modou may not be a totally lost case of male monstrosity.

Ramatoulaye mentions the fact that Binetou, 'a bit timid, frail, ill-at-ease, visibly, in (the bourgeois) milieu', is a beautiful apple ripe for plucking by someone with eyes good enough to see. 'Her beauty shone, pure. The harmonious curves of her body could not pass unnoticed'. There she was, all aglow, a constant visitor to the Fall household, God's beauty there for appreciating by the clear-sighted, handsome Modou. Besides, Binetou, beautiful and appreciative of beauty around her, takes in the concrete elements of comfort in the Fall home. Bourgeois bountifulness conflicts with peasant poverty and the young girl's mother drives home the point, incessantly. She 'wishes so much to get out of her mediocre condition' and begs her daughter to give her 'a happy ending, in a real house'. So, the narrator depicts the mother as a materialistic, daughter-hawking monster while her daughter is the innocent victim.

Man is the symbol of evil. There is Modou's friend, Mawdo Bâ, an excellent doctor but an execrable husband. Like Modou, he is happily married to Aïssatou, intelligent daughter of a goldsmith. The wife does the husband proud by raising her status in society: she becomes a teacher, leaving behind her the banal existence of the uncivilized for the bourgeois life of the civilized. Mawdo falls prey to his mother's jealousy and vengeful sentiments over her only son's relationship with Aïssatou, the simple peasant, and her poor, lower-class family. The narrator writes:

> Your mother-in-law, who saw you glowing near her son, who saw her son frequent more and more your father's forge, who saw your mother become more robust and better dressed, your mother-in-law thought more and more of her vengeance.

The vengeance came in the form of a girl, the niece of Aunt Nabou, Mawdo's mother. She goes to her brother and brings back the young girl to live with Mawdo. Duty towards mother calls for devotion. Devotion to duty is concretely expressed in desire of the flesh. Little Nabou grows in girth quickly enough. A child is the natural outcome, and Aïssatou decides to put an end to her life with Mawdo. Her parting remarks to the irresponsible husband:

> You wish to dissociate love pure and simple from physical love. I hurl back at you the accusation that carnal knowledge cannot be without the acceptance of the heart, no matter how minimal it is. . . . Man is one: grandeur and animality confused. No gesture on his part is pure ideal. No gesture on his part is pure bestiality.

If Mawdo is guilty of failing to control the sexual beast in him, one wonders whether he is any more guilty than the mother who makes him marry his beautiful cousin; or more guilty than Ramatoulaye who helps Aunt Nabou to raise and educate the wife-to-be in full knowledge of the facts, while Aïssatou is kept in total ignorance.

There is no redemption for man, the monster. There is the Senegalese doctor, Samba Diack, married to the Ivoirian Jacqueline. A stunning beauty, she disobeys her parents, marries the foreigner in Abidjan and leaves with him for Dakar. Landed in a world strange to her, she becomes disoriented and disillusioned. She is harried for being a Protestant in a Moslem society, and is treated as a bushwoman by the hostile Senegalese. Diack makes life worse by his constant escapades with the alluring Dakarois girls that he had missed so much during his Ivoirian sojourn. Jacqueline falls into nervous depression and is on the brink of insanity. Fortunately, she is saved by a competent, humane psychiatrist who helps rid her of the dark shadow dogging her footsteps. And Diack? Not much is really said about him in the novel. The bare facts of his disdainful nature are put before us. Jugement has been made by the narrator: Man is guilty, as usual. However, all the episodes described by the narrator prove beyond doubt that the victimizer, no matter how vile he is, no matter how mean he is, is an ever-present figure in woman's life.

Aïssatou; Divorce, a Solution in Solitude

Man's basic guilt, the root cause for his vilification, the main element of his vicious behaviour, is polygamy. Polygamy, the estate revered by traditionalists as a function of Africanity. Polygamy, once supported and even suggested by African woman as a socioeconomic expediency. That, vows Aïssatou, is a thing of the past. Polygamy is now the bane of society. Polygamy is a vice to be dealt with not by procrastination but by divorce. So, Aïssatou Bâ leaves the beast called Mawdo.

Aïssatou is, like her friend Ramatoulaye, an intellectual, that rare breed especially among the female species. Excellent students in the white man's school, their intelligence is extolled by their peers, and they themselves set out to be pioneers in the emancipation of women. Ramatoulaye will forever remember the white woman who 'first wanted for [them] a destiny "out of the ordinary"'. She continues:

We were real sisters destined for the same emancipatory mission. To free us from the prison of traditions, superstitions and local mores; to make us appreciate multiple civilizations without denying ours; to raise our vision of the world, to cultivate our personality, reinforce our qualities, checkmate our faults; bring to fruition in us the values of universal morals; there is the task that the admirable headmistress took upon herself.

The civilizing mission of colonialism could not have succeeded better. Aïssatou and Ramatoulaye are, so to speak, among the select few, and the selectors are, naturally, the whites. Their light shines forth in all its splendour. The path is well traced out before them: to bring to reality the 'profound options of the new Africa, to promote the black woman', to liberate her from the frustrating taboos of traditional Africa. The lesson is taught with precision, and assimilated—the word is not used by chance—extraordinarily well: marriage is built on love. Parents have no right to choose a husband for a girl. Dowry is a materialistic institution. All that matters to the wife is her husband who belongs to her wholly and to whom she belongs wholly, irrespective of any family ties that he normally has. Polygamy underscores African savagery and man's dehumanization of woman.

Aïssatou has four children by Mawdo, but that is a secondary issue when the time of rupture arrives. Consideration for the children would be another example of the tenets of a society of treeclimbers. 'Innocent victim of an unjust cause and hardy pioneer of a new life', she rejects sharing her husband's vile existence. She prefers dignity to disgrace, chooses solitude instead of solidarity. Solidarity. The warmth of a touch, a smile, a gesture. The sound of human voices. The chatter of children playing under the tropical sun. The shouts of a shameless husband defending his sham cause. The anger of a tearful wife consoled by the presence of the human face near her late at night and in times of trouble. But such solidarity, without rhyme or reason, without logic, is unacceptable to the civilized, calculating mind. Aïssatou leaves Dakar for New York with her four children. The narrator leaves a lot of questions half-answered or unanswered, such as the following: is Aïssatou happy in her solitude? How does she survive through the cold, wintry New York nights? What is her present attitude to men? Ramatoulaye's story tends to imply that Aïssatou's departure is not an action taken in search of happiness; or if that is the motive, that the objective is never attained. The saving grace in Aïssatou's embattled existence is her career and, as any overworked administrator, or interpreter or intellectual, would admit, a career is aeons removed from human care; books, in the final analysis, beget boredom. In Ramatoulaye's opinion, Aïssatou is saved by her books. 'Having become [her] refuge, they supported [her]'.

> The power of books, marvellous invention of man's astute intelligence. Various signs, associated into sounds; different sounds moulding the word. Arrangement of words from which idea, thought, history, science, life, spring out. Unique instrument of relationship and culture, unequalled means of giving and receiving. Books knit together generations in the same continuous labour towards progress.

This ode to knowledge, powerful in its poetic fervour, overwhelming in its declaration of the birth of life through books, is far from convincing as far as happiness is concerned, however. Indeed, Aïssatou's rupture from her husband allows her to develop her skills and utilize her intelligence, although no clear statement is made by the narrator as to how those possibilities exist more outside the family home than within. The suggested reason is the lady's opportunity to travel abroad, although again we are not told that there was ever any problem in the nature of the husband's refusing to allow his wife room to breathe and travel. Anyway, Aïssatou travels to France—and the myth of the metropolis, centre of civilization, bursts forth in all its splendour—and then she goes to America. Ramatoulaye tells us what her friend's letters tell her: the sojourn in foreign lands and the immersion in her career help Aïssatou turn away resolutely from 'the searchers of ephemeral joy and of facile liaisons'. Still the questions already posed remain unanswered. To all intents and purposes, culture constitutes a mere consolation. The career has afforded the lady upward mobility. She makes a lot of money, enough to be able to buy a brand-new car for Ramatoulaye who feels greatly hurt by the sight of her husband's second wife dashing all over Dakar in her ever-changing Alfa Romeo sports cars. Now, a tendency to out-bourgeois the bourgeoisie is common among the lower classes. If Ramatoulaye is convinced that such is the case with her rival Binetou's mother, the same should be true for her friend Aïssatou.

The same Ramatoulaye who sees her friend's liberation through books, narrates to us a sad case of the search for knowledge, namely that of a French teacher in Dakar: 'Studies must have been the only distraction of her youth. Cross-grained, she must have blocked out all fits of passion. Her solitude no doubt made her seek change' (p. 66). The change

found is a teaching assistantship in Senegal. Older and wiser, the French woman, still a spinster, seeks solace in the colony. Her dreams of evasion end up unrealized. Her hopes in exotic lands are destroyed. Disillusionment sets in. She ends up on a hospital bed, beaten, nailed down by a throat infection, awaiting repatriation to the homeland that she fled. Before the chosen day arrives, death chooses her as his victim, thus completing her destiny of distress. Books, as we have stated, often beget boredom. Life is with human beings, in spite of the setbacks, the sadness, and the suffering. No doubt the same essential element is lacking in Aïssatou's life.

Besides, what originality exists in the vocation of an interpreter? Like the translator, and the secretary, the interpreter is a mere messenger of a message, a carrier of a cargo. A vehicle. A voice. A slave. A shadow. And the vehicle sometimes lacks communication; and the voice at times turns hoarse and misinterprets the message. The slave is used and discarded by the master; the shadow can never become the being. So, while achieving a goal worthy of the black bourgeoisie—they are all slaves of their borrowed civilization—Aïssatou remains what she has been: a sad slave, a loveless loser. She and her children will have a story to tell upon their return from America and, if others' experience is anything to go by, that story will be one of alienation, racism and solitude.

Ramatoulaye, or the Victim Turned Victimizer . . . and still Victim of Love and Life

If Aïssatou symbolizes female intransigence, Ramatoulaye represents compromise, or so it would appear. She is abandoned after twenty-five years of marriage. Her eldest daughter, the intrepid, revolutionary type named Daba, is totally in favour of divorce from her inhuman father. But Ramatoulaye hesitates, then decides against divorce. She stays in the family home with her children, while Modou moves to the new house with Binetou. A case of the victim accepting her situation? Not so, insists the heroine, because the 'letter' that constitutes the novel being studied, a 'point of support in [her] anguish', is a form of vengeance. The text is written after Modou's death; it therefore also represents, as the narrator affirms, 'confidential information that drowns distress'. Not for Modou the sweet memories of his widow, nor the valediction based on the departed soul's virtues. Modou had his way in life; in death, he becomes a victim of his wife's sharp idiomatic weapon.

However, that is only part of the story. Modou is not only one man, but all men. The narrator makes plenty of generalizations. All men are traitors. All are polygamous by nature. All are sexual animals. All are victimizers that must be victimized. Hence Ramatoulaye sets out to hurt all men. The way she chooses is to refuse all suitors. First, Tamsir, her husband's brother who, by tradition, has a right to her. She spits her venom at the ugly man:

> You forget that I have a heart, a mind, that I am not an object to be passed from hand to hand. You are ignorant of what marriage means to me: an act of faith and of love, a total gift of the self to the being that you've chosen and that has chosen you.

Thus the aspiring conqueror is destroyed by a deft move of the feminist tongue. The point is emphasized several times in the text: she chose to marry her husband; she chooses not to leave the family home; she chooses not to marry her brother-in-law, just as she chooses not to marry Daouda Dieng, the man of virtue and riches who was her first love.

But, as usual, certain questions remain unanswered: is it simply a matter of choice? Is Ramatoulaye's rejection of Tamsir not due to her desire for vengeance against a man who supported her husband's polygamy? Has her choice not to marry Dieng got something to do with his polygamous life and his age? Is her recalcitrant attitude symptomatic of her wish to be a trail-blazer? Her relationship with Dieng poses other questions, such as: is she really in love with the man? Is her decision not to marry him a result of her jealousy of his first wife? The affair shows that Ramatoulaye and Daouda are, indeed, in love. After her official mourning period, he visits her and proposes anew. She awaits his visit with anxiety. She is burning with love for the man's compliments. She is dying to be ogled, to be fawned upon. She exalts: 'To be a woman! To live like a woman! Ah, Aïssatou! That night, I was moved, pardon my feeling. The savour of life is love. The salt of life is again love'. And when Daouda asks for her hand in marriage that second time, she experiences a moment of ecstasy, of 'drunkenness'. The gentleness of his words inebriates her, and she says that she is not ashamed to confess it. One wonders then why the following statement, made at the moment of decision: 'My heart does not love Daouda Dieng. My mind appreciates the man. But the heart and the mind are often discordant'. Her letter to Daouda, in spite of its ambiguity and decorum—traits of bourgeois hypocrisy—is categorical on one score, that she abhors polygamy. Playing second fiddle is not her idea of marriage, yet she wishes to continue seeing the man. The latter rejects her offer of friendship.

The Dieng case is of the utmost importance in understanding the narrator's character. I have stated that all men are vilified by her, without exception. Daouda Dieng, to a certain extent, constitutes an exception, because he has all the virtues that the other men mentioned in the novel lack. Once that general assertion is made, however, we are once more confronted with the ambiguity that is present throughout the novel: what, in essence, is Dieng's virtue? The question is pertinent, and remains unanswered, because the man is guilty of the one sin that makes for the condemnation of all the others, namely, he is a polygamist. Ramatoulaye's softness towards him, her ability to see beyond polygamy for once, are proof of the love that binds them together. This critic's opinion is that the heroine decides not to marry Dieng because she stands a good chance of being accused of playing the destructive role filled by the likes of Binetou and little Nabou. That would be another element of the contradiction which is her life. Who knows, she might have found happiness and harmony with Daouda Dieng, even as one of his wives; but social constraints which she actually imposes upon herself, block her path. A case of the reactionary hidden in a revolutionary's clothing.

The unequivocal rupture with Dieng brings us back to the beginning: Ramatoulaye the would-be victimizer remains a loving, willing victim to the end. 'Excessively sentimental', she finds it very difficult to assume the role of a pioneer of feminism. Unlike Aïssatou, she cannot forget the first fire lit in her by the irrepressible, irresistible Modou:

> Modou Fall, the very instant you bent before me to invite me to dance, I was convinced that you were the one I was waiting for.

In spite of the later days of abandonment and harshness, she is definitively marked by the earliest qualities of the man:

> Above all, you knew how to be tender. . . . The discovery of your sharp intelligence, your engaging sensitivity, your usefulness, your ambition, that admitted no mediocrity.

In spite of the wishes of the adult children, she decides to stay. And the consequence? Times of suffering. Tears of solitude. Despair aggravated by the man's death. 'I lived alone in a monotony only cut short by the purifying baths and change of mourning clothes, every Monday and Friday'. In spite of everything, Ramatoulaye loves Modou, just as she has always loved Daouda Dieng. The picture that remains in the reader's mind is not that of the man packing and leaving the house; not that of the male brute sexually attacking the innocent Binetous and Nabous of Africa; not that of the wife vomiting her ire on the monstrous man and leaving Africa for healthier climes abroad. The engrossing picture is that of Ramatoulaye, suddenly called to her dead husband's hospital bed, overwhelmed by what she calls the 'atrocious tragedy', desperate in her desire to revive him, straining to take his lifeless hand but restrained by sympathizers, sincere and hypocritical ones alike. That love surpasses all class constraints and traditional taboos. Ramatoulaye's mother is reticent about her liaison with the 'too handsome, too perfect' Modou. The daughter insists, disobeys, goes with her man.

> Marriage without dowry, without pomp, under the disapproving looks of my father, before the painful indignation of my frustrated mother, under the sarcastic remarks of my surprised sisters, in our town silenced by astonishment.

And we might rush to state that all is a matter of love between the heroine and her man. But the ambiguity prevalent in the text exists here, too. Love in the colonial context—that society evolving toward the accepted zenith of materialistic civilization—is not detached from the material. Love of the man goes with love of his money. Love means care, and comfort—love of lovers, and the good life. Ramatoulaye's avowed engrossment in the metaphysical, soulful aspects of her marriage notwithstanding, her desires, her nature, her life, bear the indelible mark of the *évolué* woman. She can hardly stand her in-laws who, by their very existence, seem to constitute a threat to her oasis of plenty with Modou. And the reader remembers vividly the white colonial officer's wife up in the reservation; you must book an appointment before daring to go up there to disturb the peace of the master's *ménage*. The reader recalls encounters with his brother's foreign wife; blood does not absolve one from the sacrilegious act of visiting without warning or invitation. The black bourgeoisie and their white ways: Ramatoulaye, black as the night, sun-tans with pleasure on the beach of Ngor. 'The sea air incited us to good humour . . . discouragement and sadness went away replaced suddenly by feelings of plenitude and radiance'. The beach is the refuge of the rich. Escape in suburbia is the privilege of the sophisticated. The whole picture brings to mind the contrast between the privileged and the impoverished; the healthy air of the sea as against the hellish air of the city; the mansions of the middle-class as against the miserable structures in which the masses are imprisoned. Ramatoulaye claims that some in-laws unjustly envy her material power and the power of her mind, and she sees nothing wrong in her own situation as compared with that of the pauper. The fact is, she has a choice; the pauper does not. It is, indeed, that wish to exercise her freedom of choice that makes her marry Modou instead of Dieng. It is that love of freedom that makes her espouse western education, or is it? The freedom of feminism does not triumph totally, even when the feminist claims to hate man with all her heart:

> Some men called us crazy. Others called us little devils. But many wanted to possess us. How many dreams had we fed desperately, that could have been concretized in lasting happiness and that we have disappointed in order to embrace others that have pitiably blown up like soap-bubbles, leaving us empty-handed?

So love is not removed from lust, even in the psyche of our ardent feminists. Freedom is not far from imprisonment. Feminism cannot rid woman, African woman, of femininity. Ramatoulaye loves to be possessed; just as she finally, definitively, is possessed by Modou, Man.

If hate lies at the root of the autobiographical *Une si Longue Lettre*, love is ever-present too. Autobiography is itself a lesson in bitterness and scepticism in the face of the disappointments and failures of life. Bitterness is decidedly evident in the style of Bâ's novel. The omniscient, omnipresent narrator-heroine chooses her moments of perspicacity and paucity of knowledge rather dexterously, and always to the detriment of Man and mother-in-law. That technique raises questions of authenticity. How, for example, does Ramatoulaye know what goes on in the minds of others, besides those whom she talks to directly or those whom she learns about from others? Bitterness engenders bias. Extremism is the hallmark of this feminism even if, as partisans of any victimized group would quickly add, such a posture is often a necessity in the face of the all-too-powerful victimizer. Bitterness of the bourgeoisie: Ramatoulaye cannot comprehend 'the entrance of Modou, a personality, into that family of *ndol* [paupers]'. Binetou, Modou's second wife, deserves all the pity in the world however; innocent and sincere, 'she did not know Modou's overwhelming will-power, his tenacity before the obstacle, his pride to vanquish, his resistance inspiring new assaults at every failure'. The narrator asks the exculpatory question: 'What can a child do before a furious mother that howls her hunger and thirst for life?' However, we know that Binetou is more or less as old as Ramatoulaye was when, at the moment of marriage, she disobeyed her mother, chose

Modou and rejected the mother's choice. And if Binetou is 'a sacrificial lamb, as are many others, before the altar of material', it is no less of a truth that Ramatoulaye, and Aïssatou, are avid worshippers before that very altar.

Indeed, the innocent victim named Ramatoulaye is mean. And Ramatoulaye the critic is a cheat. She establishes a hierarchy even among the female species. Aïssatou is superior to little Nabou; Nabou is superior to Binetou; Ramatoulaye, naturally, is superior to all. The yardstick for comparison is the level of civilization. Civilization, as in western culture. Civilization, as in acculturation. Civilization, as in capitalism. For the reader must be clear about one fact: Ramatoulaye's middle-class origins are to her a source of pride and her commitment as a pioneer is, first and foremost, to that class.

Conclusion: Elements of a Colonized Literature

Now, my way of bringing together class stratification and commitment to female freedom might be viewed as a contradiction which, indeed, it could be but is not. Ramatoulaye's feminism as an expression of freedom constitutes only a partial aspect of the total reality of African life. Femininity is the virtue of the traditionalist; feminism, the veneer of the progressive striving to become a man. The latter feels insecure, unfulfilled, incomplete. Colonialism has taught her the lessons of civilization. Equality. Emancipation. Independence. In short, the African woman has a right to enjoy the privileges of the man who is now the new master. Like the man, the feminist lives on borrowed training and thoughts. But the questions remain: what is freedom in de-colonized Africa? Is African literature as a whole truly de-colonized from a borrowed life, a borrowed language? We may recall that the French language continues to give the privileged position to the masculine; to a borrowed life, a borrowed literature. It is true that the best-known African writers are still those able to manipulate 'without a trace of accent or cultural cleavage', the master's tongue. Bâ's feminism, especially as expressed by Aïssatou the interpreter, smacks of Beauvoirism: the traditional marriage is a deterrent to woman's promise. No marriage. No attachment. No master. The home becomes a transitory institution. Love is a passing sentiment secondary to other elements of existence. The emphasis is on the female self.

Simone de Beauvoir's existentialist stance is based upon concrete experiences within a particular Eurocentric context, which creates some problems for the European imitator, but grave difficulties for the African follower. Firstly, the European may find that her's is not an easy-to-generalize, true freedom. Secondly, the African finds that Beauvoirist liberation does not end up in real freedom for the woman; it engulfs the erstwhile victim in another abyss, solitude. The critic Albert Memmi is categorical about what the real objective of all oppressed beings ought to be: 'an oppressed person does not save himself all alone'. The irony, the aggressiveness behind the fatalism, the oppressive stand taken by the feminist, the African feminist, cannot save her from her communal background, unless she decides to go into permanent exile, which in itself would constitute a facile, sham solution. Solidarity, human, man-woman (couple), man-child-woman (family) solidarity, that is the essence of life. The couple remains perhaps the best solution to solitude. Lack of children is an abstraction, a mutilation of life. It is significant that the Ramatoulayes of Africa have not decided to live without children. Beauvoirism preaches a fake freedom, a liberty that is no less a lie than the cataleptic civilization passed on to the colonized by the colonizer.

Female emancipation is fraught with ambiguities. Ramatoulaye is caught between tradition and progress. Though her declared choice is the latter, her lived experiences prove her attachment to the former. The picture of her daughters in slacks is, for her, an eyesore. Life without marriage is death. When all the tears are shed, when the tension subsides, she affirms: 'I remain convinced of the inevitable and necessary complementarity of man and woman'. The harmony of the couple coalesces with the happiness of the country. The family is a microcosm of the nation. Success. Solidarity. It is symbolic that the narrator leaves to a man, Daouda Dieng, her feminist politician-friend, the last word on the female condition:

> Woman must no longer be the decorating accessory. The object that you displace, the companion that you flatter, or calm down with promises. Woman is the original, fundamental root of a nation where every contribution is established, from which every development emanates. Woman must be induced to be more interested in her country's destiny.

Ramatoulaye accepts the declaration like a silent goddess in the traditional setting, which goes to show that the woman still needs the male on many an occasion, even where proof of her freedom is concerned. Daouda Dieng, the politician, the feminist, is as much a colonized person as Ramatoulaye, a fact probably hard to take but a fact all the same. Earlier in the novel the narrator states that one of the aims of the 'new' African woman, that is the educated, is to 'appreciate multiple civilizations without denying ours'. Now, the problem that neither she nor Dieng has solved is, how to do just that. The age-old problem of the colonized: how to escape the colonial cage stifling black culture; how to remain black in a world becoming whiter every day. The black woman's problem, in the final analysis, is part of the bigger burden of being black in the world.

Marx has stated that woman is man's proletariat. A true statement, indeed, but only as far as western, or European, civilization is concerned. Therein lies the dilemma of Africa. She is caught between her own culture and the imported culture. Marx means economic enslavement, no doubt. But there is more to it: social and psychological alienation; cultural bastardization; a destiny of death. The black woman is confused; the black man too. She needs love and demands it from her man. Unfortunately, the burden of blackness and the confusion of his borrowed culture often prove too overwhelming to allow him time for love. He is too busy comparing himself to the white man and, ironically, the same self-destructive process is being desperately pursued by the woman. So, Ramatoulaye Fall, confused, civilized, committed, is still seeking solace somewhere. She will no doubt write 'such a long letter' again, to herself, to her sisters, to us her men. And she may find solace some day, and we may read her letter, or tear it up and throw it into the dustbin.

Source: Femi Ojo-Ade, ''Still a Victim? Mariama Ba's *Une si Longue Lettre*,'' in *African Literature Today,* African Publishing Company, No. 12, 1982, pp. 71–87.

Sources

Ahmed, Leila, *Women and Gender in Islam*, Yale University Press, 1992.

Assiba d'Almeida, Irene, ''The Concept of Choice in Mariama Bâ's Fiction,'' in *Ngambika: Studies of Women in African Literature*, edited by Carole Boyce Davis and Anne Adams Graves, Africa World Press, 1986, pp. 161-71.

Brown, Ella, ''Reactions to Western Values as Reflected in African Novels,'' in *Phylon*, Vol. 48, No. 3, 1987, pp. 216-28.

Champagne, John, '''A Feminist Just Like Us?': Teaching Mariama Bâ's *So Long a Letter*,'' in *College English*, Vol. 58, No. 1, January, 1996, pp. 22-42.

Grimes, Dorothy, ''Mariama Bâ's *So Long a Letter* and Alice Walker's *In Search of Our Mothers' Gardens*: A Senegalese and an African American Perspective on 'Womanism','' in *Global Perspectives on Teaching Literature*, edited by Sandra Ward Lott, Maureen S. G. Hawkins, and Norman McMillan, National Council of Teachers of English, 1993, pp. 65-76.

Makward, Edris, ''Marriage, Tradition and Women's Pursuit of Happiness in the Novels of Mariama Bâ,'' in *Ngambika: Studies of Women in African Literature*, edited by Carole Boyce Davis and Anne Adams Graves, Africa World Press, 1986, pp. 271-81.

Further Reading

Giwa, Audee Tanumu, ''*So Long a Letter*: A Feminism That Is Not,'' in *Kuka*, 1985-86, pp. 57-61.

Giwa finds Bâ's representation of the Muslim religion and the Koran's laws governing polygamy to be inaccurate.

Sarvan, Charles Ponnutharai, ''Feminism and African Fiction: The Novels of Mariama Bâ,'' in *Modern Fiction Studies*, Vol. 34, No. 3, Autumn, 1988, pp. 453-64.

In this article, Sarvan reads *So Long a Letter* in terms of Senegalese history, colonial education, and Islamic polygamy.

Studies in the Park

Anita Desai
1978

Anita Desai is widely recognized as one of India's leading English-language fiction writers. Her short story ''Studies in the Park'' was first published in 1978, in her collection *Games at Twilight*.

The story is told from the point of view of Suno, a young man whose family is continually pressuring him to study for a major exam which will determine his future educational track. But all of the members of his family—his mother, father, and uncle, as well as his brothers and sisters—make so much noise and interrupt him so frequently that he is unable to concentrates on his studies. In exasperation, Suno leaves his house to study at a cafe; but even the cafe is not without noise and interruptions. Finally, Suno discovers that many young men like himself study in the park near his house, and he too begins to study there every day. One day, shortly before his exam, Suno sees what he interprets as a ''vision'' in the park: a beautiful, but sickly, young woman lying on a park bench with her head in the lap of another man. Suno is so struck by this ''vision'' that he experiences a transformation, as a result of which he chooses not to take the exam after all, but to pursue life as an adventure, rather than as a race.

''Studies in the Park'' explores several themes which are central to the stories of Anita Desai. The narration is concerned with the internal consciousness of the central character, who struggles for a sense of individuality against the pressures from his

family to conform to societal expectations. The internal monologue of the narrative is characteristic of Desai's ''stream-of-consciousness'' style of writing, and the strongly descriptive language has earned Desai recognition as a leading ''imagist'' writer.

Author Biography

Anita Desai is recognized as one of India's leading novelists writing in English. She has been noted for her rich imagery and her focus on the interior world of her characters who struggle with finding meaning in their lives and often stray from the path of conformity to the values of their families. Desai was born Anita Mazumdar on June 24, 1937, in Mussoorie, India; she grew up in Delhi. Her mother was German and her father Indian (Bengali), and Desai was raised speaking Hindi and German as well as English. In 1957, she graduated from the University of Delhi with a B.A. in English. In 1958, she married Ashvin Desai, an executive, with whom she had four children. She began publishing short stories in the late 1950s. Because she was taught to write in English, it has remained her preference for fiction writing.

Desai gained recognition with her first novel, *Cry, the Peacock* (1963), in which an Indian woman, struggling with her role in her family, kills her husband and then commits suicide. Her next four novels were *Voices in the City* (1965), *Bye-Bye Blackbird* (1968), *Where Shall We Go this Summer* (1975), and *Fire on the Mountain* (1977). Her only collection of short stories, *Games at Twilight and Other Stories*, was published in 1978. She has subsequently written four more novels, *Clear Light of Day* (1980), *In Custody* (1984), *Baumgartner's Bombay* (1989), and *Journey to Ithaca* (1995). She has also written a children's story, *The Village by the Sea* (1982), which was made into a movie in 1992. In 1993, *In Custody* was also adapted to the screen in Hindi and Urdu with English subtitles and produced by Merchant and Ivory. Desai first came to the United States in 1987, where she has taught at Smith College (1987-88), Mount Holyoke College (1988-93), and the Massachusetts Institute of Technology, beginning in 1993.

Anita Desai

Plot Summary

This story is told from the point of view of Suno, a young man whose family is constantly pressuring him to study for a major exam which will determine his future educational track: ''Oh study, study, study, they all breathed at me.'' But Suno is constantly interrupted and distracted by each and every member of his family. Most of all, ''they don't know the meaning of the word Quiet.'' His father listens to the radio news in six different languages. From the kitchen he hears his mother frying foods and sloshing water around. When his brothers and sisters come home from school, they taunt him and then run away. In addition, his mother frequently interrupts him to insist that he drink milk with sugar in it, ''like a baby.'' In exasperation, Suno leaves his house to try studying at a cafe. But the cafe proprietor, and then the waiter, insist on talking to him. Leaving the cafe, he comes upon a *gram* vendor, who suggests he go to study in the local park. In the park, Suno finds that there are many young men studying, or attempting to study, for the same or similar exams. At first feeling out of place there, Suno begins to go to the park every day to study. Although ''it took me time to get accustomed to the ways of the park,'' he finds that, ''soon I got to know it as well as my own room at home and found I could study there, or sleep, or daydream, as I chose.'' Yet Suno hates everyone else who comes to the park, except the other students. When there is only one month to go before his exam, the pressure from his family increases. His father implores him to ''get a first'' on the exam: ''Get a first, get a first, get a first—like a railway engine, it went charging over me, grinding me down, and left me dead and mangled on the tracks.'' Then one day in the park, Suno sees something which he later calls a ''vision'': he sees a beautiful but sickly young woman lying on a park bench with her head in the lap of an older man. Struck by this sight, which he describes as ''Divine,'' or ''a work of art,'' or ''a vision,'' Suno runs home. He is so strongly affected by this sight that ''everything else had suddenly withered and died, gone lifeless and purposeless when compared with this vision. My studies, my family, my life—they all belonged to the dead and only what I had seen in the park had any meaning.'' When Suno returns to the park, he sees the world around him in a different way; whereas before he had resented all the other people, he begins to interact with them in a pleasant way. As a result of his ''vision,'' he decides not to take the exam after all, because ''life has taken a different path for me, in the form of a search, not a race'' as it is for his father and the others. Suno continues to go to the park, wondering ''if I shall ever get another glimpse of that strange vision that set me free. I never have, but I keep wishing, hoping.''

Characters

The Gram Vendor

The *gram* vendor is a street vendor who first calls Suno's attention to the park as a place of study. The gram vendor is described as having ''a crippled arm that hung out of his shirt sleeve like a leg of mutton dangling on a hook. His face was scarred as though he had been dragged out of some terrible accident.''

Suno

Suno is the narrator of the story. He is a young man whose entire family is continually pressuring him to study for a major exam which will determine his future educational track. Suno is extremely irritated and distracted by every noise and interruption caused by his family as he sits in his room trying to study. In exasperation, Suno leaves his

house to try studying in a cafe; but both the cafe proprietor and the waiter insist on talking to him. Giving up on the cafe, Suno wanders into the local park, where many young men such as himself are studying, or attempting to study, for similar exams. From then on, Suno returns to the park to do his studying. One day he sees a scene which he later thinks of as a ''vision'': a very sickly young woman is lying with her head on the lap of an older man; the two are so absorbed in one another that they do not notice anything around them. Something about this ''vision'' inspires a transformation in Suno. He decides not to take the exams after all, not to succumb to the pressure of his family, but to approach life as a ''search'' rather than a ''race.''

Suno's Father

Suno's father, like the other members of his family, is seen as someone who both pressures him continually to study for his exam and who distracts him from his studies by listening to the radio news in six different languages.

Suno's Mother

Suno mentions his mother primarily as one of several family members who continually pressure him to study for his exam, yet she is continually making noise, primarily from her cooking, or interrupting him to give him milk with sugar in it.

Young Woman on the Park Bench

One day while in the park, Suno comes across a young woman lying on a park bench with her head resting in the lap of an older man. He describes what he later thinks of as his ''vision'' in the following terms: ''She was a Muslim, wrapped in a black *borkha*. . .I saw her face. It lay bared, in the black folds of her *borkha,* like a flower, wax-white and composed, like a Persian lily or a tobacco flower at night. She was young. Very young, very pale, beautiful with a beauty I had never come across even in a dream.'' Although he never sees this woman again, Suno is inspired by the sight of her, his ''vision,'' to seek out a different path in life from that which his family had been forcing him onto.

Themes

Family

Like many of Desai's stories, this one focuses on the theme of the individual struggling to define her- or himself in the face of overwhelming family and societal pressures. Thus, the role of the family is central to the story. Suno is overwhelmed by his family's intrusions into his life. In the first place, it is his family that is putting so much pressure on him to study for the exam: "study, study, study," they tell him. Yet it is also the activities of the family members which make it impossible for Suno to focus on his studies. His father listens to the radio news in six different languages. His mother makes noise in the kitchen with the sizzling sounds of her frying and the sounds of water sloshing around. His younger brothers and sisters tease and harass him when they return home from school. Even the sounds of his father's shoes squeaking on the staircase interfere with Suno's powers of concentration. And his mother, in an effort to help him study, only further interrupts him to make him drink milk with sugar in it. Suno's first step in escaping the oppressive atmosphere of his family life is to leave the house in order to find a quieter place to study. In the process of physically stepping out from the family home, Suno eventually makes a symbolic break from the path they expect him to take in life.

Death in Life, Life in Death

Suno's "vision" of the young woman in the park allows him to truly experience life for the first time. However, before he reaches this point of personal transformation, Suno sees all around him images of death. The death he sees symbolizes the death-in-life he has been leading, studying night and day for an exam his parents are pressuring him to take. Suno first associates his life of studying for the exam with a living death when he speaks with another student whom he meets in the park. Suno notices that the other student's "face was like a grey bone." From this image of bone Suno makes a leap to images of death. "I felt as if we were all dying in the park, that when we entered the examination we would be declared officially dead." Suno thinks of the educational degrees for which he and the other students are studying as being "like official stamps— they would declare us dead. Ready for a dead world. A world in which ghosts went about. . . . Slowly, slowly we were killing ourselves in order to join them." Leaving the park, Suno comes across a beautiful dying girl on a park bench. This image of life on the verge of death jolts Suno into a realization about life. Suno thinks of the dying girl on the bench with the older man as belonging "to the dead," but he realizes that "now I had seen what being alive meant." With this "vision," Suno makes the choice to live his own life by refusing to

Topics for Further Study

- India was a colony ruled by Great Britain from 1858 to 1947. Learn more about the history of India during this period. In what ways did the Indians struggle against the domination of British rule? What are some of the major events in the history of this struggle?

- India became an independent nation, the Republic of India, in 1947. Learn more about India during the post-independence period.

- The two major religions of India are Hindu and Muslim. Learn more about one of these religions. What is their central belief system? What is the history of this particular religious group in India? Where else in the world is this a major religion?

- Education has been an important political issue throughout the history of modern India. Learn more about the history of the education system in India during the twentieth century. What significant developments occurred in the area of education during this period?

take the exam which for him would only be a stamp of death.

Style

Narrative Point of View

This story is told in the first person, which means that the narrator is a character in the story whose knowledge is restricted to that of his own point of view. The narrator in this story is Suno, a young man at odds with his family life. Suno's first-person narration is central to the story because it focuses on his internal monologue regarding the pressures his family has placed on him to study for the exam, and the distractions they cause which make it hard for him to study. Because the story is about Suno's internal transformation, as a result of his "vision" in the park, the internal monologue provides the reader with a view to Suno's inner struggles and his renewed sense of the meaning of his life.

Stream-of-Consciousness Narration

Characteristic of Desai's writing style is the stream-of-consciousness internal monologue of her main characters. A stream-of-consciousness writing style aims at representing the flow of thoughts which run through a person's mind; thus, it is often characterized by a disorganized jumble of ideas and images. Suno's stream-of-consciousness narration runs throughout the story, beginning with the opening sentence: "Turn if off, turn it off, turn it off!" It becomes clear that Suno is not actually telling his father to turn off the radio, but is merely thinking, in a frustrated and exasperated frame of mind. Listing the six different languages in which his father listens to the radio news, the narration continues in Suno's stream-of-consciousness thinking: "What next, my god, what next? Turn it off before I smash it onto his head, fling it out of the window. . . ." But of course Suno could never outwardly express this anger toward his father, and so the thoughts which quickly follow these violent thoughts within the same sentence are a warning to himself not to act on his rage: ". . . do nothing of the sort of course, nothing of the sort." Expressing both his rage and his efforts at calming himself within a single sentence presents the reader with a sense of urgency and exasperation which mirrors Suno's internal state. This stream-of-consciousness narration reappears throughout the story, in order to represent Suno's internal state of mind.

Tone

The tone of narration may change throughout a story. In this story, Suno's thoughts about his family while in his room trying to study are particularly sarcastic in tone, and therefore often humorous. While Suno the character is completely exasperated with his family, his descriptions of their activities are exaggerated to the point of satire. Early in the story, Suno describes the hissing sounds of his mother's cooking in the kitchen as a source of irritation in his attempts to study for the exam; yet what begins as description launches off into fanciful sarcasm and exaggeration: "What all does she fry and feed us on, for God's sake? Eggplants, potatoes, spinach, shoe soles, newspapers, finally she'll slice me and feed me to my brothers and sisters." Suno's sarcastic and exaggerated descriptions of the sounds

of his household which irritate and distract him continue in a humorous vein: "The bell rings. Voices clash, clatter and break. The tin-and-bottle man? The neighbors? The police? The Help-the-Blind man? Thieves and burglars? All of them, all of them, ten or twenty or a hundred of them, marching up the stairs, hammering at the door, breaking in and climbing over me—ten, twenty or a hundred of them."

Setting

The setting is a central element of this story. It is set in India, as are most of Desai's stories. More importantly, perhaps, this story is set in two primary locations: Suno's house and the park in which he studies. These two locations have very different effects on Suno. His home is a place of noise, irritation, and intrusion by various members of his family. When he is not being reminded by members of his family to "study, study, study," he is being interrupted in his studies by the various noises they make. The park, on the other hand, while still a reminder of his upcoming exam, is free of the oppressive intrusion of his family on his thoughts. Symbolically, the home represents a place where Suno is expected to conform to the expectations of his family and his culture—to "get a first" in the exam. The park, however, represents a space in which Suno ultimately discovers "life" and, as a result, a sense of "freedom" from these expectations—particularly the expectation to study for the exam.

Literary Heritage

Desai is one of the leading Anglo-Indian fiction writers of the 20th Century. Anglo-Indian places Desai with other Indian writers whose works are originally written in English (rather than Hindi, or any of India's regional languages). The first Anglo-Indian novel, *Rajmohan's Wife,* was written by Chandra Chatterjee, and the first modern Indian novelist was Bankim Chandra. According to R.K. Dhawan, "The Indian English novelist until the thirties wrote for a readership largely Indian and unmistakably nationalist." Writing in 1989, Dhawan explains that, "The Indian English fiction in post-Independent India has assumed over the preceding thirty years all kinds of colourful traditions. It is now free from the social and political overtones of a rabidly nationalistic variety." Dhawan concludes that "The Indian English novel has enjoyed its golden period during the last few decades.'' Desai is the most widely recognized of contemporary female Indian novelists, in the company of Kamala Markandaya, Ruth Jhabvala, and Nayantara Sahgail.

Historical Context

Colonization and Independence of India

India was a colony of the British empire for almost a century, from 1858 to 1947. The history of India during this period, therefore, is one of expansion of British power in conflict with organizations, protests, rebellion, and terrorist activism among the peoples of India. Before 1848, India had been colonized and ruled by the East India Company, but power was transferred to the British crown in 1858. In 1876, Queen Victoria of England took on the additional title of Empress of India. Rebellion on the part of the Indians against European colonization was waged off and on throughout India's history of colonization. However, the first nationally organized Indian effort at achieving independence was formed in 1885, with the first meeting of the Indian National Congress. Nevertheless, Britain continued to expand its region of power in the area. In 1886, Britain conquered Burma, which it added to its Indian territory. In 1906, the British government instituted a series of reforms ostensibly to increase Indian political influence. With the advent of World War I in 1914, many Indians willingly fought on the side of the British, with the expectation that their loyalty in war would result in further concessions of British power to Indian self-rule; but the disappointment of this expectation following the war only served to spark further protests. Throughout the inter-war years, Indian resistance to British rule continued, with the Indian National Congress inspired by the leadership of Gandhi. In 1947, when the British Parliament voted in the Indian Independence Act, British rule was finally ceded to Indian self-rule.

Bengal

Desai's father was of Bengali origin. The region of Bengal, primarily Muslim (as compared to a Hindu majority throughout India) was divided into two provinces by the British in 1905, without regard to the concerns of Bengali national identity. While the Bengali had previously been active in resistance to British power, the division of Bengal inspired massive protest. From 1908 to 1910, struggles be-

tween Bengali resistance movements and repressive measures on the part of the British government were particularly fierce. In 1911, Bengal was reunited, and the British capital of India was transferred from Calcutta (in Bengal) to Delhi.

Religions in India

In Desai's story, it can be assumed that Suno is from a Hindi family, as he notes that the young woman he sees on the park bench is Muslim. The major religions of India are Muslim and Hindu. During the years of protest against British rule, particularly in the inter-war period, Indians were internally divided in their political goals along these religious lines. Gandhi worked hard to unify the two religions in the cause for independence, but his efforts were ultimately unsuccessful. Thus, when the British ceded power in 1947, India was divided into two countries—Pakistan was to be Muslim, while India (to be called the Republic of India) would be Hindu. However, the process of instituting this national division was wracked by bloody civil war among Hindus and Muslims.

Languages of India

With the achievement of national independence in 1947, India officially recognized 14 different languages and dialects throughout the nation, while maintaining English as the language for government transactions. The national language was to be Hindi. Thus, while English is not the ''mother tongue'' of most Indians, many writers choose to write in English. Desai, for instance, has always written in English because, she has explained, it is the language she was taught to write in school. Other Indian writers and intellectuals, however, argue that a true Indian literature should be written in an Indian language.

Education in India

An important element of Indian protest against British rule included a call for various reforms and improvements in the area of education, and particularly for a system of national education. Gandhi's call for the boycott of British products eventually included a boycott of British schools and colleges. During this period, independent Indian schools were established, but were quickly dissolved with government suppression of the movement. Gandhi also pushed for increased educational opportunities for girls, and helped women to organize public protests on this issue. In the post-independence era, various efforts at reform have been instituted by the govern-

Compare & Contrast

- **Mid-Nineteenth to Mid-Twentieth Century:** Between 1958 and 1947, India is a colony under British rule.

  Late Twentieth Century: As of 1947, India becomes an independent nation called the Republic of India. Pakistan is created as an independent nation.

- **Mid-Nineteenth to Mid-Twentieth Century:** In 1947, the newly formed Republic of India officially recognizes 14 different Indian languages and dialects, as well as English.

  Late Twentieth Century: The Republic of India now officially recognizes 18 different Indian languages and dialects (as well as English).

- **Early Twentieth Century:** In the pre-independence era of Indian history, there is essentially no substantial body or output of Indian literature written in English, known as Anglo-Indian literature.

  Late Twentieth Century: A notable body of Anglo-Indian literature emerges in the 1950s and continues to develop.

---

ment in the area of education; major reforms were enacted in 1968, and again in 1986.

Critical Overview

Desai is widely recognized as one of the leading Indian novelists writing in the English language. R. K. Dhawan notes that Desai's novels ''have drawn worldwide attention and she stands in the forefront in the world of fiction.'' B. Ramachandra Rao refers to Desai as ''one of the most fascinating original writers in Indo-Anglican writing today.'' Both Seema Jena and R. S. Sharma state that Desai is ''one of the most promising novelists writing in English today in India.'' Usha Bande concurs that Desai is ''one of the most serious yet appealing novelists on the Indian-English firmament.'' Critics generally agree that, as Rao has said, Desai is ''one of the most significant of the Indo-Anglican novelists.'' Dhawan has stated that Desai ''has added a new dimension to the Indian English fiction.'' Dhawan explains that, whereas previous Anglo-Indian novelists (Indian novelists writing in English) have focused on the external world of Indian culture, Desai ''is interested in the psychic life of her characters and her novels reveal that her real concern is with the exploration of the human psyche.'' Rao points to Desai's focus on character over story, which, he says, ''makes her work something very unusual in Indo-Anglican fiction. It gives to the Indo-Anglican novel a poetic depth, a psychological sophistication which were lacking.'' Jena concurs that Desai ''has tried to introduce a modern psychological vein and projects a sensibility generally not encountered in other Indo-Anglican writers of fiction.'' Sharma notes that Desai's ''sensitive handling of the craft of fiction has brought her both popular appreciation and critical acclaim,'' and that she ''has established herself as one of the significant voices in Indo-Anglican fiction.''

Primarily a novelist, Desai has published one collection of short stories, *Games at Twilight* (1978), which includes ''Studies in the Park.'' Sharma explains that Desai's short stories ''show the same tendency towards a psychological exploration of states of 'being,' that we observe in her longer fiction, but they are more tightly organized and compact.'' Sharma notes that in most of the stories in *Games at Twilight* ''the protagonist happens to be a young adolescent struggling to come to grips with the adult world. The stories capture that moment in their life when reality intrudes in their world of innocence like a hot blast and destroys their complacent acceptance of what appears to them to be real.''

Two young men read in Pherozesha Metah Park, Bombay.

Sharma concludes that Desai's short stories "have a freshness that makes them a significant contribution to the art of short-story in Indian writing in English."

Desai is known for stories and novels which focus on the internal life of her characters rather than on plot or story. These characters struggle to forge a sense of individuality in the context of oppressive family and societal expectations. As Jena notes, "Her main concern is to depict the psychic state of her protagonists, at a crucial juncture in their lives." In discussing the short stories of *Games at Twilight*, Rao states, "These characters have secret inner lives which make them unique and

they react against the inane routine of everyday life." Rao goes on to say that the characters in these stories "are all struggling and sensitive individuals protesting against the drabness and dullness of a life of conformity. These characters are not creatures of habit and, although they differ from one another in degree, they are of the same kind. They are stubbornly unyielding and carefully protect the vision of the secret world of passion and beauty."

Critics also note Desai's use of language and description in conveying the internal monologues of her characters through a stream-of-consciousness flow of words. Jena explains that Desai "has forged a style supple and suggestive enough to convey the fever and fretfulness, the eddies and currents in the stream of consciousness of her characters. The grapple with thoughts, feelings and emotions is reflected in the language, syntax and imagery.'' Sharma points to Desai's rich imagery and her keen observation of the world around her, pointing out that Desai ''observes every sight and sound with an uncommon intensity. Nothing escapes her eyes, not even the legs of a spider.''

Rao describes the ''imagist'' style in Desai's use of language and description in the short stories as a ''technique of evoking a mood or atmosphere by carefully piling up innumerable details of the colours, the smells and the sights of Indian life.'' Rao notes, however, that ''this technique which is quite effective in the novels has obvious drawbacks when employed in the short story. Owing to its shorter length, the short story does not offer enough space for Anita Desai to build up the tempo or to evoke the mood as she does in her novels.'' Nonetheless, Rao's assessment of Desai's style in the short stories is primarily positive: ''Within these obvious limitations imposed by the short story as an art form, Mrs. Desai does succeed in giving us very poetic descriptions of the heat and the dust, the beauty and the sordidness of the environment in which her protagonists live. Mrs. Desai's gift for the telling phrase, and her uncanny ability to see the unusual and the unfamiliar are displayed in the short stories as well.''

Criticism

Liz Brent

Brent has a Ph.D. in American culture, with a specialization in film studies, from the University of Michigan. She is a freelance writer and teaches courses in the history of American cinema. In the following essay, Brent discusses descriptive language in Desai's story ''Studies in the Park.''

Desai's fictional style is known for its elaborate and detailed descriptive language, which effectively evokes the internal mood and landscape of a first-person narrator. In ''Studies in the Park,'' Suno is a young man whose family has put severe and incessant pressure on him to ''study, study, study'' for a major exam which will determine his future educational and career track. Although his parents have

attempted to maximize his study time by sending his uncle away temporarily and giving his room to Suno, and although his mother attempts to nourish his mind with tall glasses of sugared milk, Suno is incessantly disturbed and distracted by the sounds made by the activities of various members of his family in the course of their daily activities. ''Studies in the Park'' is written from the perspective of Suno's first-person narrative point of view. The narration, then, is itself a portrait of the landscape of Suno's mind; the richly descriptive language throughout the story is a reflection of Suno's internal state of mind. Because Suno's primary goal, at least in the beginning, is to find a quiet place to study, his descriptions of sounds—the sounds of human voices, as well as the various sounds they make in the course of their activities—take on extremely negative connotations. The descriptive language used throughout the story to describe a wide spectrum of human-generated noises is indicative of Suno's mood of extreme anxiety and agitation in the face of familial pressure to succeed on the exam. This essay covers a close analysis of descriptions of noises throughout ''Studies in the Park'' in order to highlight the ways in which Suno's perceptions of the world around him are a reflection of his internal state of mind.

The story begins with extensive descriptions of the noises Suno hears in his household. The setting of the story in a multilingual modern India allows for Suno's father to listen to the radio news in six different languages. Suno's description of these sounds takes on a tone of hysteria which he only keeps himself from acting upon by way of his own internal voice keeping him in check:

> Turn it off, turn it off, turn it off! First he listens to the news in Hindi. Directly after, English. Broom— brroom—brrroom—the voice of doom roars. Next, in Tamil. Then in Punjabi. In Gujarti. What next, my god, what next? Turn it off before I smash it onto his head, fling it out of the window, do nothing of the sort of course, nothing of the sort.

> Here Desai depicts Suno's perception of the noises around him using descriptive words such as ''roar,'' as well as nonsensical made-up sounds such as ''Broom—brroom—brrroom—.''

In next describing the sounds made by his mother in the kitchen, Suno focuses on the ''hissing'' sounds of deep fried foods being prepared. In describing the sounds of water flowing from the tap, Suno's description builds a rhythm of repetition meant to reproduce the monotonous and seemingly endless sounds of water flowing: ''Ah, now she's

What Do I Read Next?

- *Games at Twilight* (1978) is Desai's only collection of short stories to date. It includes "Studies in the Park".

- *Cry, the Peacock* (1963) was the first of Desai's novels to win her critical acclaim. It is about an Indian woman at odds with her family and her role in society.

- Desai's *Clear Light of Day* (1980) is a novel about two Indian sisters and their struggles with Indian culture.

- *Journey to Ithaca* (1995), Desai's most recent novel to date, focuses on a European couple's encounter with Indian culture.

- Desai's novel *Baumgartner's Bombay* (1988) concerns a German-Jewish Holocaust survivor living in India.

- *Anita Desai's Fiction: Patterns of Survival Strategies* (1992) by Mrinalini Solanki addresses philosophical issues raised by Desai's fiction.

- *Human Relationships in Anita Desai's Novels* (1995) by Shashi Khanna discusses themes of interpersonal relations in Desai's novels, in the context of the place of women in Indian society.

---

turned on the tap. It's roaring and pouring, pouring and roaring. . ." Suno continues the effect of this description through the use of exaggeration: ". . .into a bucket without a bottom." Later he combines these sound descriptions into one sentence which, along with the repetition of such a description, further conveys his irritation: "When my mother fills buckets, sloshes the kitchen floor, fries and sizzles things in the pan, she thinks she is being Quiet."

Suno's description of the household sounds continues, in an incessant manner meant to represent Suno's amplified perceptions of each and every sound throughout the household: "The bell rings. Voices clash, clatter and break." Again, Suno uses exaggeration in his descriptions of these sounds in order to indicate his heightened state of anxiety: "All of them, all of them, ten or twenty or a hundred of them, marching up the stairs, hammering at the door, breaking in and climbing over me—ten, twenty or a hundred of them." Descriptive language such as "marching" and "hammering" evokes images of violence and aggression. When his mother brings him an unwelcome glass of milk to help him study, and the glass tips over, it "clangs on the floor."

Suno's descriptions of human voices, particularly those of his family members, are especially evocative in their negative connotations. He states that his mother's voice "wheedles its way into my ear like a worm." The metaphor of his mother's voice compared to a worm evokes images of dirt, sliminess, and disgust, especially when one imagines it crawling directly into one's ear. When he pulls the ears of his younger brothers and sisters to punish them for disturbing him, they "screech," only to be quieted by another annoying sound when his mother "whacks" them. Suno's descriptions of the sounds made by his father are equally harsh and unpleasant. His father speaks "in a voice that came out of his nose like the whistle of a punctual train." The image of the train returns later in the story, and implies Suno's sense of being run down, as if by a train; the comment that it is a "punctual" train suggests Suno's negative attitude about the rigidity, structure, and discipline imposed on him by the impending exam. His father's shirt can be heard "crackling," and his father walks down the stairs "crushing each underfoot in turn."

Suno attempts to express his irritation and assert his own will in a voice designed to match those of the rest of his family for unpleasantness. In

> His father's shirt can be heard 'crackling,' and his father walks down the stairs 'crushing each underfoot in turn.'"

exasperation, Suno "raced out of my room, with my fingers in my ears, to scream till the roof fell down about their ears." But he is checked in this show of anger by the presence of his father. However, when Suno finally does assert his decision to leave the house and study elsewhere, he expresses it in a voice described as "croaking," "screaming," and "screeching." As a reminder of the family noises he is trying to escape, his family members break out in "howls" of protest.

Upon leaving his house, Suno first attempts to study at a cafe, as have many a famous writer. However, both the proprietor, Lala-ji, and the young waiter approach Suno and speak to him in tones described variously as "whining," "sighing," "murmuring," and "babbling," as well as "with an oath." Leaving the cafe and walking dejectedly along, Suno notes that even his posture makes his father "scream." However, Suno encounters the first pleasant sound of the story when he comes upon the gram vendor, whose voice is described variously as "friendly," "not insinuating, but low, pleasant," and "sympathetic." Even when the vendor begins to whistle—a sound which surely would have driven Suno over the edge coming from a member of his own family—Suno describes the sounds in pleasant, positive terms. Suno states that the man "began to whistle, not impertinently, but so cheerfully that I stopped and stared at him."

However, when he enters the park in a continued attempt to find a quiet place to study, Suno is assaulted with more sounds which are offensive to him. He notes the old men who sit in the park "mumbling through their dentures or cackling with that mad, ripping laughter that makes children think of old men as wizards and bogey-men." The women in the park "screamed, just as grey and fawn and black birds do," at their children. However, Suno, upon his first visit to the park, compares his discomfort there to "a visitor to a public library trying to

control a sneeze." Whereas he has come to the park to escape noise, he describes his feeling there in terms of an effort to control his own impulse to disrupt an imposed silence (as in a library). Suno notes other students, such as himself, sitting in the park, "reading aloud in turns." Suno himself soon opens a book as he strolls along, "reading to myself in a low murmur." The latter two descriptions, of himself and the other students, are at least neutral, if not pleasant and soothing in their connotations. At first, Suno continues to be distracted by the sounds in the park, such as another student "reciting poetry in a kind of thundering whisper." Suno's irritation throughout the story with the sounds of other human beings is extended to include the very presence of other human beings in the park, for he states that "I resented everyone else who came to the park." The sounds of the old men who have ventured out to get milk are described in terms of their milk bottles "clinking," and their conversation described as taking place in "argumentative, hacking tones." Suno most hates the athletes, who, almost naked, are given massages in the park. Suno's description of the sounds they make concentrate on his feeling of disgust for their bodily presence. The masseuses "huffed and puffed and cursed," with the athletes "groaning and panting in a way I found obscene and disgusting." Suno's disgust with the physical bodies of these men expresses his general feelings of disgust with life—both his own and that of other human beings. And, while Suno notes that afternoons in the park were "quiet," he goes on to describe the irritating noises of the evening visitors. Families sit together, "listening to a transistor radio," the mothers sit together "like flocks of screeching birds," while the young men sit around "moaning" and "the children's cries would grow more piercing with the dark. . ." As the date of the exam grows nearer, the students in the park "talked less" and "mumbled" to themselves. As his anxiety level is raised with the stepped-up pace of his study schedule, Suno notes that he "yelled at my mother," while his family members "made clicking sounds with their tongues."

However, after the "vision" which alters Suno's perception of himself and his life, changing his course from that of a "race" to that of a "search," Suno's perception of the sounds of other human beings in the park is also altered. Whereas before he could find no end of irritating noises emanating from everyone in the park except himself, Suno now finds himself engaging in pleasant verbal interactions with other people in the park.

Sometimes I stopped to rest on a bench and conversed with one of the old men, telling him who my father was and what examination I was preparing for, and allowing him to tell me about his youth, his politics, his philosophy, his youth and again his youth.

In addition, Suno begins to ''joke'' with the other students, and even ''exchanges a few words'' with the yoga teacher. Through this change in Suno's description of the sounds of other human beings, he expresses a change in his internal state of mind—from one of alienation from those around him to one of joy and harmony in the company of his fellow man.

Source: Liz Brent, in an essay for *Literature of Developing Nations for Students*, Gale, 2000.

Jennifer Bussey

Bussey holds a bachelor's degree in English literature and a master's degree in interdisciplinary studies. She is an independent writer specializing in literature. In the following essay, she explores Desai's use of sound in ''Studies in the Park'' as a way of depicting how Suno experiences internal and external reality.

One of the most prominent Indian authors writing in English, Anita Desai is known primarily for her novels. Her short fiction, however, displays many of the same techniques, such as her distinctive and evocative use of imagery. ''Studies in the Park'' is marked by Desai's masterful use of sensory images to create atmosphere and herald change. The result is a story with a strong sense of place, and one that shows how the main character's external environment profoundly impacts his internal struggle. Desai's detailed descriptions of the sounds of Suno's home and of the park show the reader what those places are like, and point up their negative and positive impacts on Suno. In addition, much of Desai's fiction centers on the personal struggles of Indian men and women trying to cope with the contemporary demands of family and society, and this short story is a variation on that recurring theme.

In ''Studies in the Park,'' Desai relies heavily on sounds—from family members' voices to kitchen noises—to describe Suno's surroundings and how he feels in those surroundings. At the beginning of the story, as he studies at home for the exam that will determine his options in the workforce, he feels like the world is closing in on him. He is under tremendous pressure from his family to study hard

> Up to this point, sounds have represented annoyance and distraction. But the rhythmic sounds of the park, in contrast to the chaotic ones at home, enable him to disconnect from the external world while sitting squarely in the middle of it.''

and do well. His father constantly reminds him, ''Remember Suno, I expect good results from you. Study hard, Suno.'' The pressure increases when his father says, ''You must get a first [the highest grade], Suno . . . must get a first, or else you won't get a job. Must get a job, Suno.'' In addition to his father's words, the chaotic sounds of Suno's home life include his mother's constant chopping and frying in the kitchen, and his siblings' running and screaming. Desai describes discordant sounds on every page to reflect how Suno experiences this environment. Her words and phrases include ''voice of doom,'' ''hissing,'' ''clash, clutter and break,'' ''screech,'' ''bawl,'' ''whine,'' ''howls,'' and ''croaked.'' Such words make clear that the sounds of the household are an assault on Suno's ears and psyche. In fact, the story begins with Suno's urgent desire for his father to turn off the radio news he listens to in various languages—''Turn it off, turn it off, turn it off!'' The noise around him is a manifestation of the insensitivity, confusion, and pressure of his demanding situation. Suno thinks to himself, ''What about the uproar around me? These people don't know the meaning of the word Quiet.''

When he leaves the house and find somewhere else to study, Suno stops in a cafe to have tea and review his textbooks. Because it is the middle of the day, he expects it to be quiet and virtually empty. He is forced to leave, however, when the waiter will not stop talking to him.

The first pleasant sound in the story is heard when Suno approaches the gate to the park, where a food vendor greets him and explains that many students go to the park to study. As Suno enters the park, he notices that the vendor begins ''to whistle, not impertinently but so cheerfully that I stopped and stared at him.'' The melodious sound and cheerful attitude are strange to Suno.

Once inside the park, Suno continues to notice unpleasant noises, but eventually falls into the rhythm of the park's sounds. He says, ''I fell into its routine, its rhythm, and my time moved in accordance with its time.'' Desai's use of the word ''rhythm'' reinforces the important role of sound in determining the atmosphere of the park. Here, Suno is able to become absorbed in his studies and his own thoughts, even amidst bustling activity. Up to this point, sounds have represented annoyance and distraction. But the rhythmic sounds of the park, in contrast to the chaotic ones at home, enable him to disconnect from the external world while sitting squarely in the middle of it.

When Suno happens upon a bench where two people are sitting together, he sees something of himself in them, yet at the same time he sees exactly what his life is missing. From their conversation, Suno gathers that the woman is dying. Whether or not this is accurate is of little consequence. What matters is that Suno sees two people who are, like him, completely absorbed in themselves. They even seem to be unaware of the two children playing right beside the bench. The difference is that these two people have found something meaningful—each other—in which to absorb themselves. While Suno feels that he has shut out the world for the sake of doing well on an exam and securing a good job (which is what his family and society expect of him), the people on the bench have shut out the world for the sake of each other. There is clearly a great deal of love between them, be it romantic or familial, and this is an experience unknown to Suno. The relationship between them seems devoid of selfishness, greed, or competition, and strikes Suno as almost divine. He witnesses a profound human connection, something Suno has resisted throughout the story up to this point. With his family, the yoga instructor, the elderly men in the park, and the athletes, Suno has responded with disdain and superiority to everyone around him. The yoga instructor invites Suno to join his group and Suno thinks, ''You won't catch me making an ass of myself in public. And I despise all that body-beautiful worship anyway. What's the body compared to the soul, the mind?'' When the elderly men look at Suno with a commiserating look, Suno thinks, ''As if he's been through exams, too, long ago, and knew all about them. So what?'' As for the athletes and

wrestlers who sunbathe and have massages in the park, Suno regards them as men who ''live in a meaty, sweating world of their own—massages, oils, the body, a match to be fought and won—I kicked up dust in their direction but never went too close.'' Suno's own thoughts have been as discordant as the sounds of his home.

The two people on the bench make Suno realize how misguided he has been in refusing to connect with the people around him. He comes to feel that because of isolating himself for the sake of the exam, he is himself dying, and that the vision of the man and woman on the bench has brought him to his senses—to health. Before he sees the people on the bench, he questions the meaning of studying for his exam: ''Why were we creeping around here, hiding from the city, from teachers and parents, pretending to study and prepare? Prepare for what? . . . Ready for a dead world. A world in which ghosts went about, squeaking or whining, rattling or rustling. Slowly, slowly we were killing ourselves in order to join them.'' His vision of the couple, then, is a blessing, and he believes that this turning point actually saves his life. Suno's trance-like state of observation is broken by the faint sound of the woman's laugh. To Suno, the sounds of the business world are ''squeaking or whining, rattling or rustling,'' but the faint laugh of the woman on the bench is the sound of life. Considering that he believes she is dying, this is somewhat ironic. But her laugh shows him that as long as there is still life, there is still the opportunity to embrace it. Suno thinks, ''I felt I could never open my books and study or take degrees after that. They belonged to the dead, and now I had seen what being alive meant.'' Until the small laugh, the scene is completely silent, a technique that demonstrates the uniqueness of the episode in relation to the rest of the story. The silence also creates an atmosphere of importance and sacredness.

Suno's seeing the two people is coincidental, yet his reaction to them changes the course of his life. He comes to view life as a search rather than a race; he understands that he has been fundamentally changed and is now wholly unlike the diligent students still immersed in their textbooks in the park. After Suno's metamorphosis, Desai continues to describe Suno and his surroundings with sound, but the nature of the sounds changes from harsh and imposing to soft and engaging. The park is filled with giggling, joking, conversation, and exchanges. Suno himself converses pleasantly with the yoga instructor, interacts with the elderly men in a meaningful way, and chats casually with students. While the reader is not shown Suno's new home life, we can infer that his parents' worries will not now affect Suno in the least. Ramachandra Rao of *Journal of Literature and Aesthetics* observed that Suno is like many of Desai's protagonists in that he ''acquires a new awareness and a new technique which enable him to protect his integrity as a human being.'' Suno has essentially exchanged one routine for another; instead of going to the park to escape humanity and its noise, he goes to immerse himself in it. The new routine is one that he believes will lead him to fulfillment and happiness as he connects with, rather than withdraws from, the people around him.

Source: Jennifer Bussey, in an essay for *Literature of Developing Nations for Students*, Gale, 2000.

Karen D. Thompson

In the following essay, Thompson places ''Studies in the Park'' in context as compared to other coming-of-age stories.

''Studies in the Park'' by Anita Desai is a richly symbolic coming-of-age story. In it Suno, a young man preparing for exams at the academy, leaves behind his awkward adolescence and enters adulthood in the span of three months. Unlike those in many coming-of-age stories, Suno's transition into adulthood is not marked by a religious ceremony, a civil promotion, or a secret ritual. Neither is Suno's rite of passage defined, as many are, by a single or a series of tragic events. Instead, his metamorphosis is initiated by his finding in the park a place to study, furthered by his accidental discovery, and completed by his finding within himself a balance of mind, body, and soul.

In another important aspect, Suno's allegorical journey, complete with its startling epiphany, diverges slightly from other stories in this genre. In many coming-of-age stories the protagonist faces a crisis—the death of a loved one or a challenge that requires maturity or courage—that pulls the protagonist from the security of youthful innocence into the difficulties of adulthood. In these stories the crisis constitutes the climax, and the resolution lies in surviving the crisis. Readers invest neither time nor thought in predicting what adulthood holds for these characters. In this aspect Desai's tale transcends the standard coming-of-age story, for in her allegory readers are allowed to see, even encouraged to consider, the hopeful future that awaits Suno.

> When he later returns to the park, he is no longer a boy but a man whose life now strikes a previously missing balance.''

As the story begins, Suno lives a crowded life in a crowded home with his family. Readers are first introduced to Suno's mother, a woman who tends her family almost fanatically. She is constantly cutting and frying, monitoring her youngest children, checking in on Suno, and offering milk. She is probably uneducated given the setting of the story, and she is a disciplined woman who adheres to a strict schedule of preparing meals, sending her husband to work, and sending her younger children to school.

Suno's father enters into the story from the bedroom where he has just listened to the news in six different languages. In this way he serves as a foil to Suno's mother because he represents the educated individual whom Suno is destined to become. Yet, like his wife, he also represents discipline. He checks his watch as he enters the kitchen and asks for his meal, and readers have the impression that he is as regular as the cuckoo that comes out to announce the hour and no more effectual. He goes off to work, but we do not know where or to what job. When he exhorts Suno to pass his exams so that he can get a job, the father mentions nothing of what type of job this should be. The younger children are, in Suno's words, ''wild.'' They are noisy and messy, throwing their school satchels into his room and leaving their greasy fingerprints on his books. Figuratively, Suno stands atop the fulcrum between the extreme discipline of his educated father and laboring mother on one end and his unruly younger siblings on the other. Though he is studying for his exams when he is first introduced, he is not an adult—he hasn't passed his test. Unlike his disciplined parents, he is compliant only to the extent that he is participating in the program that has been chosen for him without open rebellion. He is also unlike his siblings in that he is not a wholly undisciplined child who plays at school and everything else as they do.

In setting the scene for this story, Desai focused on the sights, sounds, and even smells that fill Suno's apartment. The effect of her attention to sensory detail is that readers easily understand why Suno, whose hypersensitivity approaches illness, flees his apartment for a calmer place to study. In his search for such a place, he first stops at a tea shop where he witnesses a scenario that could become his future if he does not pass his exams. Confronted by the tea shop's bored proprietor who speaks of the cost of sugar as if it is more important than the war that has caused the rationing of sugar, and a young waiter who failed school at the sixth level and yet is proud that he has a job and can figure a bill, Suno realizes that he cannot study there. On a figurative level, readers understand that neither the shop proprietor's misdirected societal concern nor the waiter's ignorance represent Suno's lot in life.

Suno leaves the tea house and finds himself confronting the iron gates of a city park. The iron bars at the park entrance symbolize that something of value, or something not easily accessible to everyone, lies within the park. As he stands before the gate, Suno is addressed by the *gram* seller. "I'm glad I was never sent to school," the vendor says, and then continues whistling a song about living in paradise. All Suno sees of the *gram* seller is his crippled arm and his scarred face, and Suno's preoccupation with the man's injuries hints that this encounter is meant for symbolic consideration. Perhaps he is a maimed veteran of the war, and his scars serve notice that an education may be valuable if only to save one from the military.

Eventually, Suno enters the park, and he enters as a child. He remembers the times he has been here after running away from school "to lie on a bench, eat peanuts, [throw] stones at the chipmunks that came for the shells, and drink from the fountain." He acknowledges that he never liked the park as much as he liked the streets where boys played marbles or the vacant lot behind the movie house where he and his friends threw rocks at rats. Although his young boy's mind does not grasp the connection, what Suno dislikes about the park is its imposed order. It is like "an hotel, or an hospital, belonging to the city but with its own order and routine, enclosed by iron rails, laid out according to prescription in rows of palms, benches and paths." The park symbolizes Suno's own life, a life seemingly owned by people other than himself and moving forward according to prescribed paths. Looking now at the park as one searching for a place to study rather than as one running from studies, Suno

employs a critical eye. He disdains the old men sitting on green benches and "cackling with that mad, ripping laughter that makes children think of old men as wizards and bogey-men." Likewise he rejects the women screaming at their disorderly children and the madmen dancing around and "scratching like monkeys." He does not feel at home with the other students, either, thinking that they belong in the park while he is a "gatecrasher." At this point in the story, Suno's transformation begins. He starts to notice the park's particular rhythms and becomes comfortable enough to "study there, or sleep, or daydream." While acclimating himself thus to the park, however, Suno is not happy with all he encounters. He despises those participating in the "body-beautiful worship" of yoga and describes their movements as "contortions that would embarrass an ape." When asked to participate he declines, thinking to himself that the body does not compare to the soul, the mind. He likewise criticizes the old men going to gather Government dairy rations. Observing them carrying on philosophical conversations, he guesses that "Certainly it was the mind above the body for these old coots," but still he ridicules them and their passionate theological discourse. The most despicable of all the people in the park, he believes, are the wrestlers who are pampered and massaged and oiled. According to Suno, "They lived in a meaty, sweating world of their own—massages, oils, the body, a match to be fought and won."

Suno's reflections on the yoga participants, the old men, and the wrestlers carry importance because they stress Suno's focus on his intellect, his studies, at the expense of his body and his soul. His disdain for the "contortions" of those practicing yoga and for the wrestlers symbolizes his rejection of the physical part of himself. His contempt for the old men and their philosophical and theological musings illustrates that he is likewise at odds with his spiritual self. In effect, as Suno pursues his studies and rejects his physical and emotional needs, he becomes more and more unbalanced and less and less a whole, healthy individual.

As Suno's exams approach and loom only a month away, his mental state begins to deteriorate. He fantasizes that his books are rooted to his palms as he studies and that they are feeding off of him. He insists that the books "were parasites and, like parasites, were sucking us dry." He speaks to another young man studying for exams and discovers the young man to be little more than a walking specter. "Wait till you do your B.A.," the specter announces, and this statement has the same effect on Suno as the Grim Reaper saying, "I'll come for you soon."

Suno slinks from the park, trying to escape the death that he sees ever-present there, and while trying to escape, stumbles upon the scene that saves him. He encounters a young woman, beautiful and dying, with her head resting in the lap of an old man. Readers do not know exactly why this vision so stirs Suno. Maybe it is the paradox—the irony—of a young, beautiful woman's untimely death that touches him profoundly. Perhaps the vision stuns him because he interprets the young woman as a representation of his own life and the old man, in whose arms she lies dying, as the academic pursuits that are leading him toward an early figurative and literal death. This interpretation makes sense in light of Suno's describing the old man's beard as being "like a goat's, or a scholar's." Most probably what moves Suno is the way the couple looks into each other's eyes, completely alive and absorbed in each other and the moment, a luxury Suno has never experienced and never will without making changes.

Whatever goes through Suno's mind, the scene shakes him. It provides the friction necessary to stop his momentum, and from his resting place he is finally able to look around and consider all the possible directions open to him. That night Suno finally allows himself to sleep after being first confronted by his father's anger and then soothed by his mother's nurture.

When he later returns to the park, he is no longer a boy but a man whose life now strikes a previously missing balance. Whereas before he had disdained both the body, as evidenced by his dislike for the yoga practitioners and the wrestlers, and the soul, as evidenced by his contempt for the old men and their philosophy and theology, he now values their experiences. He stops to talk with the old men, and more importantly to listen, and he flirts with the possibility of participating in yoga exercises. He states quite clearly that he will not take his exams and, therefore, will not fill the role mandated for him by his father and higher powers. He has learned his most important lesson: he can exercise his free will.

"Studies in the Park" diverges pleasantly from the typical coming-of-age story. In most, the protagonist's survival, especially if physical and mental health accompany the survival, provides both climax and resolution; readers are not encouraged to consider the protagonist's future. In Desai's story, however, while readers are *aware* of Suno's passage into adulthood, they are additionally *intrigued* by the possibilities now before him. They might wish to run into Suno in the park in five, ten, even twenty years and ask him how he's been.

Source: Karen D. Thompson, in an essay for *Literature of Developing Nations for Students*, Gale, 2000.

Sources

Bande, Usha, *The Novels of Anita Desai: A Study in Character and Conflict*, Prestige Books, 1988, p. 11.

Dhawan, R. K., *The Fiction of Anita Desai*, Bahri Publications, 1989, pp. 10-15.

Jena, Seema, *Voice and Vision of Anita Desai*, Ashish Publishing House, 1989, pp. 9, 11.

Ramachandra, Rao B., *The Novels of Anita Desai*, Kalyani Publishers, 1977, pp. 7-8, 62.

———, "Themes and Variations in the Novels and Short Stories of Anita Desai," in *Journal of Literature and Aesthetics*, Vol. 2, Nos. 2-3, April-July, 1982, pp.74-9.

Sharma, R. S., *Anita Desai*, Arnold-Heinemann, 1981, pp. 5, 149-50, 165-66.

Further Reading

Bellioppa, Meena, *The Fiction of Anita Desai*, Writers Workshop, 1971.
> From technique to critical reception around the world, this book includes a variety of essays designed to lend insight into Desai's writing.

Choudhury, Bidulata, *Women and Society in the Novels of Anita Desai*, Creative Books, 1995.
> Critical discussion of Desai's novels in terms of the roles of women in Indian society.

Dash, Sandhyarani, *Form and Vision in the Novels of Anita Desai*, Prestige, 1996.
> Critical discussion of language and themes in Desai's novels.

Gopal, N. R., *A Critical Study of the Novels of Anita Desai*, Atlantic Publishers, 1995.
> Critical analysis of Desai's novels to date.

Parker, Michael, and Roger Starkey, eds.,*Postcolonial Literature: Achebe, Ngugi, Desai, Walcott*, St. Martin's Press, 1995.
> Parker and Starkey review how the aftermath of colonialism is reflected in the literature of various countries.

Pathania, Usha, *Human Bonds and Bondages: The Fiction of Anita Desai and Kamala Markandaya*, Kanishka Publishers, 1992.

By comparing the works of two Indian women writers, Pathania explores themes of oppression and perseverance.

Sharma, Kajali, *Symbolism in Anita Desai's Novels*, Abhinav Publications, 1991.

Critical discussion of recurring symbolic images and themes in Desai's novels.

Sivanna, Indira, *Anita Desai as an Artist: A Study in Image and Symbol*, Creative Books, 1994.

Critical analysis of the elements of visual description in Desai's fiction.

Solanki, Mrinalini, *Anita Desai's Fiction: Patterns of Survival Strategies*, Kanishka Publishers, 1992.

This book discusses the many manifestations of Desai's survival theme in her novels and short stories. Solanki shows how Desai's characters struggle to overcome the pressures and hardships of modern life.

The Switchman

Juan José Arreola

1952

"The Switchman" was published in 1952 in the collection *Confabulario*. Ten years later it was re-released, along with the rest of his published work at the time, in the collection *El Confabulario total*. Arreola invented the word "Confabulario," meaning a collection of fables, and his ability for invention is apparent from the stylistic originality of "The Switchman" as well as the broad range of his other work.

"The Switchman" is a dialogue between an anonymous traveler and a switchman on the railroads, in which the railroader details the horrors of the sub-operational rail system. He describes areas where one or no rails exist, facades of stations designed to trick passengers into disboarding, and the slim odds of the stranger ever reaching his destination. On one level the story operates as a satire on the Mexican transportation system, while on another the railroad is an analogy for the hopeless absurdity of the human condition. At the time of publication, *Confabulario* was relatively well-received, but over time Arreola's short stories have come to be seen as his strongest work. "The Switchman" in particular has received attention as a piece that is emblematic of the author's mastery of allegory and satire.

Author Biography

Juan José Arreola was born on September 12, 1918, in Ciudad Guzman, in Jalisco, Mexico. The fourth of fourteen children in an intensely religious family, he was forced to leave school at twelve to apprentice with a bookbinder. Although he worked at a series of jobs as a young man, he was drawn to writing and acting from an early age, and in 1939 he enrolled in the Instituto de Bellas Artes in Mexico City to study acting. His acting career took him briefly to France, but the bulk of his professional work consists of the written word.

Arreola began writing when he moved to Mexico City, where he collaborated with other young Mexican writers, including Juan Rulfo, on a literary journal entitled *Pan*. His first story to gain recognition was *Hizo el bien Mientras Vivio*, which was published in 1943. Over the course of the next two decades he would write a play, *La Hora de todos*, which won best play of 1953 by the Mexican National Institute of Fine Arts, and many short stories and prose sketches, most of which were compiled in the collection *Confabulario total*, published in 1962. The year 1963 saw the publication of his chaotically structured novel, *La feria*, which at the time received mostly negative reviews, and in 1971 he published *Palindroma*, a collection including stories and a one-act play. Although he is famous for the broad range of genres in which he writes, Arreola is best known for his short stories, which are markedly philosophical in content and range from satirical animal fables to biographies of historical figures. His best-known works include his *Bestiaro*, in which he satirizes human qualities through a series of animals, and the absurd short story ''The Switchman.'' For the most part, Arreola stopped producing new fiction by the early 1970s, although he remains productive today. Over the years he has worked as an editor, in television, and as a lecturer conducting writers' workshops.

Plot Summary

''The Switchman'' opens at a deserted train station in an unnamed country. The stranger arrives sweaty and out of breath from the effort of carrying his heavy suitcase, and mops his face with his handkerchief. His watch reads the exact time his train is scheduled to depart, but there is no sign of it; he worries that he has missed the train.

Out of nowhere appears an old man who taps him on the shoulder. The man is dressed like a railroader and carries a red lantern that is so small it looks like a toy. The stranger assumes he is affiliated with the railroad, and the implication is that he is the switchman for whom the story is named. The stranger asks the old man if the train has left, and in response the old man asks him if he has not been in the country long, indicating that the question is ridiculous and that the stranger is clearly not familiar with the system. The stranger insists that he must be in T_ by the following day at the latest, and the switchman responds that the stranger obviously doesn't understand the situation. He advises him to procure a room at the inn, ideally by the month. The stranger argues that he doesn't want to stay, and in response the switchman says he should let him work out his problem himself, but instead he will inform him of the situation. Thus begins their dialogue comprised almost solely of the stranger's questions and the switchman's answers.

According to the switchman, ''This country is famous for its railroads.'' Apparently this fame is due to the poor reputation of the railroads, but the switchman insists that the timetables and ticket sales have been greatly improved. In effect, he reports, it has been improved such that by all appearances there is a working rail system linking every town in the country, but in fact the trains do not adhere to the schedules. In the meantime, he insists, everyone is patient with the system out of patriotism. The stranger learns that although rails do pass through the town, the train doesn't necessarily come through it, although a few have been known to do so, and perhaps he might be lucky enough to get one. The stranger asks if the theoretical train will go to his destination, and the switchman treats the question as if he is asking more than is reasonable. The stranger argues that his ticket is for his destination, and the switchman concedes that although most people would agree with his logic, locals cope with the circumstances by purchasing massive amounts of tickets to locations all over the country, and never expect to reach their destination.

The switchman explains that the railroads take the trains through impassable areas in their desire to serve their citizens, and as a result, the trains can take a long time. In fact, he says, people often die in the course of their trip, and as a result funeral coaches are available. He also describes areas in which there is only one rail or none at all, resulting in wrecks, and tells of a town which came into being because of such a wreck. At the stranger's dismay at this news, the old man tries to bolster his courage, relaying a story about a group who found their train at an abyss without a bridge. According to the now-famous story, the group carried the train in pieces across the abyss and a river at its bottom, reassembled it on the other side, and received a discount for their trouble.

In response to these anecdotes, the stranger continues to insist that he must reach his destination by the next day. The switchman applauds his tenacity and suggests he stay at the inn until a train arrives and then take that one. He explains that most people take this course, and it is possible that thousands of people may compete with him to board the train, but it is worth a try. Apparently riots often result from passengers trying to board trains, and a school of railroad etiquette was established to cope with the situation. The switchman also urges the stranger to be vigilant about disboarding at the correct stop, because in an effort to remedy overcrowding, the railroad has built imitation cities inhabited by dummies. People are often tricked into leaving the train and abandoned in such places. The trains are also equipped to project mirages in the windows, to trick passengers into believing the train is moving or that they have reached their destinations. The switchman explains that in hopes of reaching his destination, he must focus on his goal and speak to no one, because the railroads are full of spies who might undermine his efforts and in fact force him to spend the rest of his life in a prison car. According to the switchman, all of this effort on the part of the railroad is designed to convince all passengers to give in to their fates and cease caring about a destination.

At this the stranger asks the old man if he has traveled the rails much, and the old man replies that he is a retired switchman who comes to the station to remember the good old days. In fact he has never traveled, but relies on the stories of others. He relays another story of passengers tricked into disboarding to admire the scenery and then abandoned, and then asks the stranger if he would like to spend the rest of his life in a remote, beautiful spot with a girl. He winks and smiles at the stranger, and then jumps in alarm at the sound of a train whistle. The switchman runs at the train, gesturing wildly with his lantern, and calls back to the stranger, asking again the name of his destination. The stranger replies that it is X_, a different destination from his previous one. This reply coincides with a name or identity change for him; previously called the stranger, he is now called

Juan Jose Arreola

the traveler. At the moment he submits to the ways of the railroad, the old man disappears into the morning, and the train noisily approaches the station.

Characters

The Stranger

The stranger is a man waiting for a train at a deserted station. The first of the two characters in the story, he is a foreigner to the area, as indicated by the switchman's question, ''Haven't you been in this country very long?'' When he is first introduced, the stranger is out of breath and sweating profusely from the effort of carrying his suitcase. He urgently needs to get to the town of T_ by the next day at the latest, and initially he is dejected at the possibility that he has missed his train. He asks the switchman if the train has already left, and when he first hears the story of the rail system in this anonymous country, he is incredulous and horrified. He questions the switchman methodically, insisting upon the logic that he has purchased a ticket, so he must be able to reach his destination. Over the course of the story, however, he comes to accept the switchman's logic, and by the end he has changed the name of his destination to fit the absurdity of the situation, and is identified as a traveler.

The Switchman

The switchman for whom the story is named is actually a retired switchman, who comes to the station to "remember the good old days." He appears out of nowhere, carrying a red lantern so tiny it looks like a toy. When the stranger asks him if the train has come and gone, the switchman advises him to book a room at the inn for as long as possible, suggesting it may be a long time before a train comes through the town. Thus begins his absurd account of the rail system, which he delivers in a matter-of-fact way and without irony. Throughout the dialogue, the switchman is kind and congenial, committed to his bizarre story, and patient with the stranger's protests and questions. He offers the stranger advice and encouragement in a good-natured way, and when the train shows up, he runs at it, gesturing wildly with his lantern, and vanishes into the morning.

Themes

Existentialism

Arreola himself acknowledges that existentialist thought is an influence upon his work, and in particular upon "The Switchman." Existentialism is a philosophy that asserts that life in and of itself is without inherent meaning, and that man projects meaning onto it. When the stranger insists that he must reach his destination, he imparts urgency of purpose and thus meaning into his life. The switchman's stories, by contrast, imply the subjectivity of the stranger's desires. His bizarre tale of the railroad, with its myriad possibilities, suggests that the world—in this case the world of travel—is arbitrary and crazy, and that there is something ludicrous about trying to project set expectations onto it. The world of the rails is wild and unpredictable, without reasonable, rational laws, such as the stranger's logic that a ticket to his destination should take him to it. In this way the switchman's story epitomizes the existential world, in which nothing makes logical sense. In existential literature, characters tend to be identified by their role or function rather than by a name, as they are in "The Switchman." The

stranger is an example of identity through function in that he first called the stranger because he is foreign to the area and to the system, but once he changes his destination and submits to the rail system, he becomes a traveler. When the stranger changes his destination, he ceases asserting his will and submits to the existential world of the railroad.

Absurdity

By definition, absurdity concerns that which is senseless, illogical and untrue. Although there is no school of thought devoted to the absurd, an absurd worldview suggests the meeting of a meaningless world with man's efforts to impart meaning onto that world. The switchman's stories are absurd in that the events are far-fetched and ridiculous. It is out of the question, for example, that passengers would carry a dismantled train down an abyss, across a river, and up the other side to reassemble it. Similarly, it is absurd that the stranger would take these stories as truth and change his plans accordingly. The absurdity of both the stranger's actions and the switchman's tales suggest that the stranger's urgency to reach his destination is absurd. The outcome of the story reflects upon man's role in the world in general, and the absurdity in the rhythms of everyday life.

The Fantastic/Magical Realism

The fantastic in literature involves the use of detail associated with fantasy, or out of bounds of what is considered realistic. The fantastic is closely tied to the genre known as Magical Realism, which generally entails a synthesis of magical or supernatural details with things rational or realistic. "The Switchman" incorporates both these genres in that the very unrealistic conversation between the stranger and switchman is narrated in a very matter of fact, realistic way, which allows the reader to consider the larger implications of the story without focusing on what is bizarre about the story's details. Throughout the story, use of fantastic detail is tied to the sense of the absurd. For example, it is unrealistic that people would spend a life's fortune on train tickets without knowledge of their destination, as the switchman claims. He treats this fantastic suggestion as a matter of fact, and in so doing, draws the stranger into a world in which the fantastic is the norm. In the course of the story, the reader is drawn in such that the story reads as an allegory for everyday life, in which the most basic events are imbued with a sense of the absurd.

Style

Point of View

"The Switchman" is relayed by a third-person narrator, delivered without explicit opinions. The only glimpse into either character's mind is the early description of the stranger as "dejected and thoughtful." Aside from this, any sense for the characters' thoughts and feelings comes from the dialogue, in which the stranger anxiously asks questions, and the old man matter-of-factly delivers answers. This use of a third-person omniscient narrator is typical of existential literature, in particular Kafka, and lends immediacy to the story. Throughout most of the text the reader identifies loosely with the stranger, whose incredulous reactions are appropriate to the ludicrous story he is told. However, when he changes the name of his destination and becomes a traveler at the end of the story, this identification halts. The fact that the character has submitted to the world of the rails leaves the reader suspended and alone to consider the implications of the absurd on his own life.

Construction

The structure of "The Switchman" is dictated by the title; it is a switching back and forth between the two men in conversation. The first paragraph and the last describe the action of the stranger arriving at the station, and of the old man running off into the distance waving his lantern. These two passages aside, the entire text is a dialogue between the two men, comprised mainly of short questions asked by the stranger, and answers delivered by the old man. This structure provides the text with two stories in one; the story that the old man tells about the railroad, and the larger story of the stranger being impacted by the old man's story. Throughout the tale, the reader identifies with the stranger's incredulity because the old man's story is bizarre and unbelievable. The stranger's change of destination on account of the story, however, breaks that identification and amplifies the absurdity of both stories. This construction is in keeping with the style of existentialist authors such as Kafka, whose matter-of-fact deliveries lend themselves to the absurdity of the subject matter.

Symbolism

As the title suggests, the switchman himself operates as a symbol in the story. At first glance it

Topics for Further Study

- Research existentialism, and then discuss how "The Switchman" fits into this school of writing. What evidence of Franz Kafka's influence do you find?

- Critics disagree about the role of Magical Realism in "The Switchman." Research Magical Realism and discuss your opinion. Where do you draw the line between use of the fantastic and Magical Realism?

- Critics offer widely disparate interpretations of "The Switchman." Compare and contrast several of these interpretations, and offer your own interpretation with evidence to back it up.

- To what effect does Arreola use dialogue between his two characters as the bulk of the narrative? Discuss the role of point of view in the story, and use another contrasting work of short fiction as an example.

would appear that the title makes reference to the old man, who, by all appearances looks to be an employee of the railroad. His lantern in particular suggests his occupation, except for the fact that it is "so small it appears to be a toy." The size of the lantern calls into question the man's authority, and use of the word toy suggests that the encounter is a game. By definition a switchman is one who aids in transferring a train from one track to another, essentially a guide at a junction. In effect the old man is a guide for the stranger, indicated by the fact that he carries a light; he educates him about the ins and outs of the rail system, and influences him literally to switch tracks and change his destination. Interestingly, the switchman is not only retired, but has never traveled himself, so his credibility is questionable. This change, however, suggests another interpretation of the word switchman; literally, one who switches, which is what the stranger does in changing his destination. Interpretation of the title calls into question the larger interpretation of the story and forces readers to examine how literally both the old man's story and the larger story should be taken.

As a means of transportation, the rail system is a symbol of travel, forward motion, and progress. Because trains can only move forward and backward, they suggest a limited range of motion and, as such, a limited version of progress. According to the old man, the image of the rail system has been much improved based on ticket sales and timetables. In reality, however, the system is sub-operational; it is only a myth that is possible to travel the country by rail, a story that is maintained by citizens out of patriotism. Obviously the rail system in the story represents public transportation in Mexico, which is famous for being poor. Metaphorically it represents progress and life in general, which is hindered by insistence upon maintaining an image.

Literary Heritage

The whole of Mexican literature is vast, various, and distinguished, characterized by the blend of cultures which have contributed to it. Mexican culture is an intersection of indigenous people, Africans who were brought to Mexico in the slave trade, and the Spanish conquistadors who arrived in 1519 and conquered the Aztec empire. The earliest Mexican works consist of Mayan oral histories; the earliest recorded works are the pre-Columbian *Chilam Balam* and *Popol Vuh*, which chronicle many Mayan myths and legends. Most other early literature is Spanish work on two main topics, missionary writing and documentation by the conquistadors. The writing of the conquistadors documents events, geography and the indigenous people they encountered, in the form of journals, annals and letters home and to the Spanish crown. One of the earliest of these is a collection of letters by Hernan Cortes entitled *Cartas de Relacion*. Spanish missionary writing chronicles the evangelical efforts to convert the native people to Christianity. Notably, almost none of the writing during the first century of colonialism was for pleasure. Poetry emerged before prose in the new Spain; the first poetry recorded from the late 1500s is a collection of Christmas carols, part of the conversion effort. Theater appeared in the late sixteenth century, also as part of religious ceremony. Scholars believe that theater initially involved clergy acting out religious scenarios, but by the seventeenth century both sacred and secular theater had emerged, often performed in the streets by professional actors.

The result of this cultural mix is the mestizo, of mixed blood, who since the end of the nineteenth century have comprised the largest ethnic group of the population; modern Mexican literature reflects this fundamental ethnic blend. What today is popularly known as Magical Realism has its roots in European literature, and is often identified with Kafka's use of the fantastic in a very matter-of-fact way, without explanation, as a part of everyday life resulting in an absurd effect. In the last fifty years, however, Magical Realism has become emblematic of Latin American literature as well. Magical Realism suits Mexican literature, as it does Latin American literature in general, in this blend of the fantastic with everyday life. The drama of Catholic spirituality converges with magic and legends inherent in Native American culture in such an way that the mystical is incorporated into everyday life and, in effect, into literature.

Historical Context

Arreola was born only a year after the end of the Mexican Revolution, which was led by Emiliano Zapata and Pancho Villa. The Revolution called for the transfer of land to peasant farmers and the right of Mexican citizens to elect their leaders. Hence Arreola was raised during a long period of social reform, which entailed new rights for the Mexican people, and redistribution and organization of resources. The new constitution, which was drafted only a year before his birth, provided for radical reforms, including a labor code that gave workers the right to organize and strike. It also put into effect term limits for the president and placed severe limitations on the Roman Catholic Church, which had previously controlled a great deal of land as well as the school system. During the 1920s and 1930s social and land reform continued, including the restoration of communal lands to Native Americans. Despite the progress, however, politics entailed bribery, concessions, and assassinations, and many of the changes were very controversial. In 1926, the Catholic Church conducted a strike, which suspended all religious services, and resulted in the Cristero Rebellion. During the three-year conflict, at least 90,000 Mexicans were killed in battles over secular versus Church power. The 1930s saw continued land reform, including the establishment of

Compare & Contrast

- **1953:** The Mexican President Adolfo Ruiz Cortines makes a constitutional change that gives women the right to vote. This is a tremendous step, as only since the Mexican Revolution have citizens had the right to elect their leaders.

  Today: Everyone has the right to vote in Mexico, although government corruption is such that voting is seen as ineffective.

- **1947:** President Miguel Ameman Valdes, the first Mexican president without a military background since the Revolution, becomes the first Mexican president to visit the U.S. as head of state, in an effort to boost foreign trade.

  1994: Mexico, the U.S., and Canada agree to the NAFTA treaty, a joint trade endeavor aimed at meeting the trade needs of all three nations.

- **1950s:** Postwar Mexico experiences the growth of industry and agriculture. The years after World War II reflect a rise in prosperity similar to that seen in the U.S., resulting in growth of the middle class.

  Today: Mexican society is comprised of a vast lower class; poverty and malnutrition are the rule rather than the exception.

- **1930s and 1940s:** The domestic focus is on redistribution of land to the peasantry for communal farming and production.

  Today: Mexico is infamous for its uncontrolled urbanization, which has resulted in gigantic slums on the outskirts of all urban centers, and massive air and water pollution.

---

communal farms and the seizure of private property for social welfare. It is noteworthy that the topography of Mexico continues to make transportation difficult, particularly between the western coastal plains and the central plateau. The railways were seized and nationalized in 1937 in the course of political reforms, but have never been adequately maintained. As a result, Mexican railroads have been infamous for being poor since then, and serve as an apt metaphor for insufficiently executed reform in the country.

During the years between the Revolution and World War II, most contemporary Mexican literature consisted of either escapist fantasy or strict realism, which documented the changing social structure. The Second World War, however, shifted global consciousness as the world considered man's new powers of destruction. Mexico joined the U.S. war effort against the Axis powers on May 22, 1942, which shifted the national focus from domestic to global reform and gave rise to new literary trends in Mexico. According to Ross Larson in Fantasy and Imagination in the Mexican Narrative, "young writers led by Juan Jose Arreola and later by Carlos

Fuentes were disregarding the powerful Spanish tradition of regionalistic realism and were employing symbolic techniques to express other views of reality." Postwar Mexico, which is the period during which "The Switchman" was written, saw a shift in industrial and agricultural growth, as well as the growth of the middle class. These changes mainly served to widen the gap between rich and poor, and social inequality has grown steadily since then. Social discontent in Mexico in the 1960s resulted in activism similar to that seen in the United States. Population growth and uncontrolled urbanization became a problem during the 1970s, resulting in unemployment and massive malnutrition. Since then political corruption, staggering foreign debt, problems with the oil market, and government links to drug trafficking have plagued Mexico. The quality of life for the majority of Mexicans has continued to decline, and is responsible for the influx of its citizens across U.S. borders for work. The 1990s have been marked by uprisings of the Zapatista Army of National Liberation, demanding economic and political reforms, and the NAFTA trade agreements between Canada, Mexico, and the

U.S., aimed at diminishing trade barriers among the nations.

Critical Overview

When *Confabulario* was released in 1952, it was met with a generally warm reception. A decade later, however, when it was released with the rest of Arreola's published work in *Confabulario total*, it was met with great applause. By the 1960s, Arreola had earned his reputation as a skillful satirist. His fiction tends to lack traditional literary devices such as plot and character development; in these departures from literary convention, Arreola crafts stylistically original pieces grounded in allegory. Ross Larson, in *Fantasy and Imagination in the Mexican Narrative*, cites Arreola as a leader and revolutionary in Mexican literature during the 1950s in his use of ''symbolic techniques to express other views of reality.'' He describes his work as ''concise, ironic parables and satires that aspire to formal perfection.'' Arreola's work is characterized by a sense of the absurd, and the short stories in the collection, particularly ''The Switchman,'' are considered emblematic of his work.

Luis Dávila, in the Twayne's World Authors Series book entitled *Juan José Arreola*, reports that ''Although . . . Arreola is one of the most distinguished writers in Mexico and Spanish America, and is much publicized, actual critical scrutiny of his works is surprisingly scarce.'' However, he asserts, ''The Switchman'' ''is probably Arreola's most famous and most discussed story.'' As ''the one story by Arreola which has been most commented upon by critics. . .'' he reports, ''its commentators differ widely in their interpretations.'' He continues, ''The very fact that the critics' interpretations are so different, and yet all so fitting, says a great deal about Arreola's talent.'' In keeping with the author's stylistic reputation, Dávila asserts ''The only consensus is that the story is not only a satire on Mexico's railroads, although it is at least that.'' He goes on to discuss the skill with which Arreola incorporates the existential into the story, creating bizarre scenarios which resonate with the familiar absurdity of daily life. He writes, ''Even though the story is a fantasy, it accurately simulates the perceived and felt reality in which human beings live.'' Besides his skillful representation of the human condition, however, Dávila admires Arreola's particularly Latin American approach to existentialism and absurdity, which may advocate boarding the train of life without care for the destination. He quotes the switchman, who says, ''While you travel, have faith,'' and suggests that ''even though his words are no license to stretch the story into a manual of hope, they accompany Arreola's readers as they await their next trains for destinations unknown.''

D. Curtis Pulsipher, in his dissertation ''The Use of the Fantastic, Neo-Fantastic, Animals and Humor As Vehicles For Satire in the Works of Juan José Arreola and Murilo Rubiao,'' offers similar praise of the story. He, too, notes that ''The Switchman'' ''is the short story by the Mexican author which has received the most critical acclaim; it is Arreola's single most anthologized piece and has been translated into various foreign languages.'' He continues, ''Critics have seen in this tale the perfect example of the absurd, the forceful stamp of Kafka, and a political satire with a few metaphysical traces; they have even seen in it a paragon of Magic Realism.'' He continues, ''This short story is one of the Mexican author's finest works, and through it he displays his concern with man in the twentieth-century, knee-deep in inexplicable mire in which going forward and going backward only leads him further into the quagmire. The only alternative open to man is to fight with the absurd by embracing it, somehow outdo the absurdity in absurdity.'' Overall, despite the disparity in interpretations of the story, critical consensus is that ''The Switchman'' is a finely crafted work of existentialist fiction, and continues to accumulate critical distinction as time passes.

Criticism

Jennifer Lynch

Lynch is a freelance writer in northern New Mexico. In the following essay, she explores readings of ''The Switchman'' as an existentialist, absurdist work.

Although interpretations of ''The Switchman'' vary, most critics agree that the story is an existentialist work with an emphasis on the absurd. On the most obvious level the story is a satire on the Mexican public railroad, which is famous for being atrocious, and an allegory for Mexican public policy in general. On a deeper level, however, the story concerns man's search for meaning in an absurd world.

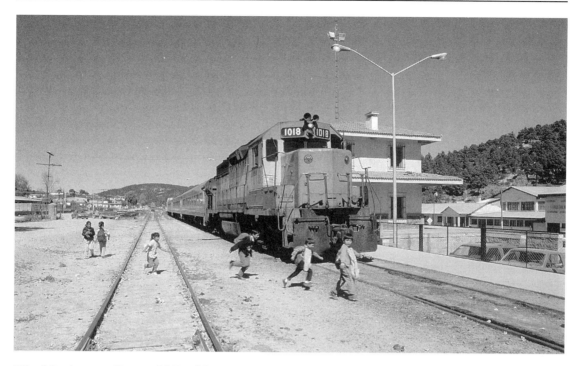

The Mexican railway, Al Pacifico, *runs from the city of Chihuahua through Cooper Canyon to the city of Mochis.*

Despite Arreola's use of the fantastic, the story resonates with familiarity; the reader identifies strongly with the outrage of the stranger who believes in the logic that a train ticket should take him to his destination. Although, as is generally the case in Arreola's fiction, the stranger's character does not necessarily develop, he undergoes a transformation that leaves the reader hanging; without identification aside from oneself, the reader is left to consider the implications of the story on everyday life. Arreola provides the stranger, and hence his readers, with a guide, the switchman, and may offer some unorthodox advice as to how to handle the existentialist crisis. Although his credibility is dubious, the switchman offers encouragement at the very least, and perhaps advocates to the reader, as he does to the stranger, switching tracks when boarding the train of life.

The story opens with the arrival of the stranger at the train station. He is identified only as a stranger, in keeping with the tendency in existentialist literature to identify characters with function, rather than with personal details or names. The stranger wishes to travel by train to the town of T_; in fact he has a ticket for his destination. However, there is no train in sight, and he wonders if it has already come and gone. The stranger encounters an old man, a retired switchman, who reports that travel in this country is an unpredictable, arbitrary experience, and so begins their dialogue, in which the switchman informs the stranger of the perils and idiosyncrasies of the rails.

"This country is famous for its railroads," the switchman begins, and it turns out they are famous for their timetables, ticket sales, and brochures. Actual regular, prescribed train service, however, is the exception rather than the rule. According to the switchman, train travel may just as easily result in getting marooned in the jungle as it may result in death. Fortunately, though, funeral cars are available for embalming purposes in the case of the latter. As was the case throughout Mexico in the 1950s, when the story was written, as well as today, the country's rugged terrain makes for unpredictable service at best. After the Mexican Revolution, the railroads were nationalized in an effort to put public resources in the hands of the people. The result, however well-intentioned, was, and still is, a neglected and sub-operational system rather like the one depicted in "The Switchman." Such a rail system is an apt metaphor for the decline of not only public transportation in Mexico, but public services

What Do I Read Next?

- *Bestiaro* (1958) is Juan José Arreola's most famous work besides *Confabulario and Other Inventions*. It is a collection of short stories, vignettes, and fables using animals to personify human qualities.

- Arreola's best-known work is *Confabulario and Other Inventions* (1964). It contains the sum total of his work through 1961, including his most acclaimed short stories.

- *Where the Air Is Clear* (1971) is Carlos Fuentes' first and best-known novel. The lyrically told story includes members across the social spectrum in post-Revolutionary Mexico.

- *Existence and Being* (1949) is Martin Heidegger's definitive work on existentialist thought.

- Ross Larson's *Fantasy and Imagination in the Mexican Narrative* (1977) is an excellent resource for contextualizing the work of many Mexican authors, including Arreola.

- Juan Rulfo is a contemporary of Arreola, and worked with him on publications in the early 1940s. His *The Burning Plain* (1941) is a collection of evocative, beautifully written stories about life after the Mexican Revolution.

- *Magical Realism: Theory, History, Community* (1995) is an extremely thorough, up-to-date historical and critical discussion of Magical Realism by a variety of authors. Edited and with an introduction by Lois Parkinson Zamora and Wendy B. Faris.

---

in general. Based on the premise of delivering power to the people after the Revolution, the Mexican government consistently turned such properties over to the public through the 1930s and 1940s without plans or resources for maintenance. Neglect and exploitation under the postulate of the good of the people resulted in the train system Mexico sports today: painfully like the switchman's image of the train pressing ahead without a track until, worn down to the axles, it grinds to a halt.

As an allegory for Mexican institutions, "The Switchman" is a grim portrait of the country. As an answer to twentieth-century existentialism, however, the story offers provocative alternative readings. Given that existentialism is based on the premise that life is without inherent meaning, "The Switchman" epitomizes man's attempt to project logic and reason onto life, both from the stranger's point of view and the reader's. The rail system, as an institution run in an arbitrary way by omnipotent management, is a model of the existentialist oppressor. Like Gregor's employers in Kafka's *Metamorphosis,* the management is all-powerful, and as for Gregor, any effort the stranger makes to fight them is hopeless.

His destination is arbitrary despite the fact that he has purchased a ticket, in keeping with general human logic regarding travel, and in fact the goal of the management is to dissuade him of his imperative destination. In the switchman's words, "The hope is that one day the passengers will capitulate to fate, give themselves into the hands of an omnipotent management, and no longer care to know where they are going and where they have come from." It is entirely absurd that this should be the case, just as it is absurd that passengers who encounter a bridgeless abyss should dismantle the train, carry it down the abyss, across a river, and up the other side to reassemble it, only to receive a discount for their trouble.

The switchman delivers these fantastic tales as fact, and in so doing, identifies the reader with the stranger, who resists them as impossible, at least for a while. Although the switchman's matter-of-fact delivery is in keeping with the style of existentialist literature, the reader, like the stranger, contends with the idea that he is not in control of his circumstances; to do otherwise would be to relinquish control of not only his destination, but his destiny.

The switchman, from the beginning of the story, is clearly a guide for the stranger. He carries a lantern, in effect a light, which generally symbolizes knowledge. He also tells the contentious stranger that, "Frankly, I ought to leave you to your fate. But just the same, I'll give you some information." In effect he offers to lead and counsel the stranger, in keeping with his occupation as a switchman, which is essentially a guide for a train at a junction. However, the switchman's credibility is called into question by certain details. The lantern that he carries is tiny and likened to a toy, suggesting that he is not an authority, but a caricature of authority. Also, his lantern is red, which is in keeping with his job as a switchman, but traditionally symbolic of danger or warning. The fact that logic and, consequently, tradition are called into question in the story makes the switchman's role even more a mystery. Above all, however, the switchman's credibility is called into question at the end of the story when he reveals that he is retired and no longer works on the railroad. He reports, "...I just come here now and again to remember the good old days. I've never traveled and I have no desire to. But the travelers tell me stories."

The stories relayed by the switchman would appear to undermine the stranger's imperative, especially by the climax of the story, when the switchman suggests, "Wouldn't you like to end your days in a picturesque unknown spot in the company of a young girl?" According to most of his narrative, he might as well be part of the management, committed to dissuading the public of their projected destinations. However, throughout the text the switchman offers sporadic encouragement, such as "You need to pluck up your courage; perhaps you may even become a hero" and "All right! I'm glad to see you aren't giving up your project. It's plain you are a man of conviction" and "Try it anyway." These affirmations ring contrastingly throughout his discouraging stories, and reach a peak when the train arrives. He breaks into a run for the train and calls back to the stranger, "You are lucky! Tomorrow you will arrive at your famous station." The meaning of this statement is ambiguous, since it is followed by the question, "What did you say its name was?" The stranger replies with a different destination from his original, suggesting that he has, in fact, capitulated to fate.

The stranger's transformation into a traveler is, in keeping with the entire story, ambiguous. On one hand it can be viewed as the ultimate submission to the management, and unwillingness to "At least

> Although his credibility is dubious, the switchman offers encouragement at the very least, and perhaps advocates to the reader, as he does to the stranger, switching tracks when boarding the train of life."

try." On the other hand, the fact that the stranger's name changes to traveler suggests an active role. As reported earlier in the story, "passengers' lives suffer important transformations" and the stranger/traveler is willing to submit to change. The switchman tells the stranger, "While you travel, have faith," suggesting that the author advocates willingness to board the train of life, however meaningless and arbitrary it may be, regardless of destination. As the old man counsels, "Once on the train, your life will indeed take on some direction. What difference does it make whether it's T_ or not?"

Source: Jennifer Lynch, in an essay for *Literature of Developing Nations for Students*, Gale, 2000.

John R. Burt

In the following review on Juan Jose Arreola's El guardagujas, *John R. Burt discusses this allegorical story and its possible ties to a story written by the American author Nathaniel Hawthorne in 1843.*

The well known short story by Juan José Arreola, "El guardagujas" from *Confabulario* (1952) gives pleasure on at least two levels. On the surface it offers a humorous treatment of a literal railroad where almost everything imaginable seems to go wrong regularly. Beneath the surface it possesses a thoughtful allegorical nature which has been widely recognized. The only thing about the allegory for which there is considerable agreement is that more is intended than a mere chronicling of the inadequacies of Mexico's railway system. Interpretations vary greatly, ranging from a Mexican reply to a materialistic view of life (Menton), through an allegory of the lessons taught the soul before birth (Echevarría), to a satire on politics (Bente). Yulan M. Washburn, the most widely known critic of

Arreola's work, ends his discussion of the allegory by admitting that perhaps the only adequate summary is the sweeping declaration "that it has to do with the irregularities of our whole world." (Since all these discussions deal with "allegory" in one way or another, let us understand by the term to mean: "A form of extended metaphor in which objects and persons in a narrative, either in prose or verse, are equated with meanings that lie outside the narrative itself. Thus it represents one thing in the guise of another—an abstraction in that of a concrete image" [Thrall]).

Even though allegorical literature has been with us for centuries (Plato, Prudentius, Dante, Quevedo, Cervantes, Bunyan and many more), the selection of a railroad by Arreola strikes a peculiarly modern note, and seemingly suggests a contemporary, "machine-age" turn of mind.

On the surface the story of "El guardagujas" tells of a weary traveler who has reached a deserted station, exhausted from bearing his heavy baggage which no one would help carry ("su gran valija, que nadie quiso cargar, le había fatigado en extremo"). A little old man, the Switchman, appears as if from nowhere ("salido de quien sabe donde"), and begins conveying a strange set of revelations about the workings of the railroads in the unnamed country where the traveler now finds himself.

The ambiguity of the story lends itself easily to numerous possible interpretations. The traveler can be 'Anyman' journeying through 'life,' and the fact that he has reached a momentary, deserted way station reflects the isolation of the 'moment' (a pause) which we all feel from time to time in life. The baggage for which he is unable to find help is almost certainly his own personal past and concerns. The Switchman is his 'conscience,' or that part of his mind which sees life objectively, as if at a distance. The sections of track alluded to by the switchman are 'paths of life,' and the destinations are the 'careers and goals' reached by other "travelers" before. With these thoughts in mind the following interpretation becomes clearer.

Item in the story Deserted station Heavy luggage Traveler Switchman Inn (fonda) for travelers Tracks New sections of track Track sections lacking 1 rail Trains Tickets Train Company (empresa) Police Spies "T" "F" "X"

Possible meaning [Elements of a "Christian" interpretation are in brackets] A given moment of life/ the present. One's personal past. [sins] Anyone. One's conscience/ unconscious mind. [soul] Momentarily "dwelling" in the present. Life. New careers,

destinations, goals. Some destinies are more difficult for certain people to reach Movement through life. Degrees/training for life's careers. Fate/destiny. [God's will] The protection of the establishment. Spiteful people. A specific goal in life. "Felicidad"— serendipity/ unexpected happiness. Acceptance of fate. [Christ]

The few suggestions above for a tentative (somewhat forced) Christian interpretation (as well as the use by Arreola of the metaphor of the railroad) bring to mind the allegorical presentation of another railroad written almost a century and a half ago by Nathaniel Hawthorne in a story entitled, "The Celestial Railroad" (1843).

In comparing the two stories, one is struck almost at once by the similar, lightly ironic tone of both works (as well as the similar use of the railroad to symbolize the journey through life). One wonders at this point if further investigation might reveal more than the expected surface similarities resulting from their common use of the one central metaphor. To find the answer let us undertake a more detailed comparison.

Because the two works share a good number of qualities, it is possible to compare them schematically:

Hawthorne *"The Celestial Railroad" (1843)* A Christian Allegory in which the traveler tries to choose his fate. Language explicitly contains religious overtones. The railroad makes several stops which are more important than is the act of traveling. The story cites John Bunyan, and in part is a light-hearted continuation of Bunyan's *The Pilgrim's Progress.* The goal for the travelers is the Celestial City, but many stop at Vanity Fair and do not manage to leave again. Two pilgrims on foot reach the Celestial City long before those on the Train do. (Mr. Stick-to-the-right and Mr. Foot-it-to-heaven.) A Major part of the story deals with Vanity Fair and the market which sells illusions and vanities. The whole story is deliberately shown to be a dream—narrator establishes dream state at beginning and end. The purpose clearly is to point out a Christian moral: "Railroads do not constitute an 'easy' way to get to heaven." Mr. Smooth-it-away has an answer for almost every question the traveler can raise. The result of these answers finds the traveler able to see the dichotomy between life's reality and the illusion of the train journey. This is emphasized by the Traveler's relief felt upon awakening at the end of the story. Mr Smooth-it-away is the director of the Railroad corporation and is revealed at the end to be either the devil himself or his agent.

ARREOLA *"El guardaguias" (1952)* An allegory of life in which the traveler learns to accept fate's choice for him. Very little in explicitly religious overtone. Railroad traverses various sections which symbolize paths through life. An acceptance of movement as fate is understood. No previous writer or work is mentioned. Only our traveler has specific goal—"T." Stops are fortuitous or "predestined" by the Company ("empresa"). The only foot travelers mentioned are those who advance the Company over sections not traversed by anyone before. Most of story is a dialog between the Switchman and the traveler over the illusions and realities of travel. The whole story is perhaps an illusion with an ambiguous beginning and an unclear end (unclear as to the intended meaning of the illusion if there is one). The purpose is ambiguous—in the interpretation suggested in this study, a choice is made at the end to accept the vicissitudes of life. The Switchman has an answer for almost every question the traveler can raise. The result of these answers finds the traveler able and willing to accept any destination the train may take. The Switchman is a lifetime employee of the railroad, and is revealed at the end to be (little more than) an inspirational beacon showing the way to where the traveler can rejoin life.

By establishing some of the principal elements of plot and motivation in which the stories seem to agree or disagree, it has been shown that there is a good deal of similarity—much of it plausibly stemming from the use of a common metaphor—the railroad, and from the use of a common technique—a dialogue between an "innocent" traveler and a sophisticated, seasoned veteran of the tracks.

To carry the comparison one step farther it will be useful to compare specific images as well as choices of language.

Hawthorne tells us that his "friendly" guide, Mr. Smooth-it-away, "had never actually visited the Celestial City, yet seemed... well acquainted with its laws, customs, policy, and statistics." Arreola introduces a much simpler character in his Switchman, but one nonetheless who shares Mr. Smooth-it-away's lack of having visited the traveler's destination, "Yo señor, sólo soy guardagujas.... No he viajado nunca, ni tengo ganas de hacerlo."

Both travelers learn about a bridge over a perilous body of water. In the first case, Hawthorne explains, "Our coach rattled out of the city, and at a short distance from its outskirts, passed over a bridge of elegant construction, but somewhat too slight, as I imagined, to sustain any considerable weight. On either side lay an extensive quagmire. ..." The Switchman tells a considerably more heroic tale about a group of travelers who carry on despite the absence of a bridge. "En la ruta faltaba el puente que debía salvar un abismo." The engineer convinced the passengers to continue, and under his direction the train was disassembled and carried to the other side of the "abismo, que todavía

> By drawing the comparison between Hawthorne and Arreola, it has been seen that there are indeed a large number of similarities between their two stories. There seem to be enough to suggest that Arreola may have read Hawthorne's story and was 'inspired' by it."

reservaba la sorpresa de contener en su fondo un río caudaloso." The similarity of the peril is noteworthy even though resolved in very different ways.

Hawthorne comments through the narrator on the quantity of luggage many passengers carry, concluding that he would not care to trust the previously mentioned bridge, "if each passenger were encumbered with as heavy luggage as that gentleman and myself." Arreola discusses luggage only at the beginning of the story when the weary traveler appears at the deserted station, bearing heavy baggage which no one else would help carry. Luggage forms a standard metaphor in many allegories for one's troubled past.

Hawthorne presents the idea of tickets and the ticket office through a comparison with *The Pilgrim's Progress*: "The reader of John Bunyan will be glad to know that Christian's old friend Evangelist, who was accustomed to supply each pilgrim with a mystic roll, now presides at the ticket office." Arreola presents the idea of tickets through the Switchman who agrees with the principle that a ticket to a specific destination should entitle the traveler to passage there, yet despite that, he notes that in the inn, there are people who have purchased numerous tickets for all the main destinations in the land, "podrá usted hablar con personas que han tomado sus precauciones, adquiriendo grandes cantidades de boletos." We all know people who have studied at school or in life preparing themselves for all kinds of futures (which never seem to come—they haven't yet boarded a train). In both stories the tickets are valuable, forming one means of initiating the movement towards one's destiny. They also continue the extended metaphor of railroading.

Hawthorne describes the boarding scene, comparing the moment to one in Bunyan: "A large number of passengers were already at the station house awaiting the departure of the cars. By the aspect and demeanor of these persons, it was easy to judge that the feelings of the community had undergone a very favorable change in reference to the celestial pilgrimage. It would have done Bunyan's heart good to see it." Arreola paints a vastly different moment when the Switchman advises the traveler to grab the first train he can, boarding as early as possible: "Trate de hacerlo cuando menos; mil personas estarán para impedírselo. Al llegar un convoy, los viajeros, irritados por una espera demasiado larga, salen de la fonda en tumulto para invadir ruidosamente la estación." As is often the case, many people try for the same job or career at the same time, and some, having waited a long time are especially irritable. Hawthorne's society seems artificially genteel and Arreola's perhaps just as artificially rude.

Hawthorne frequently speaks of the burden Bunyan's Pilgrim had to bear, and compares the luggage many are traveling with on the train, which "would be delivered to their respective owners at the journey's end." Arreola doesn't speak more of the burden of the luggage, but he does explain through the Switchman that in the event of death, "es motivo de orgullo para los conductores depositar el cadáver de un viajero—lujosamente embalsamado—en los andenes de la estación que prescribe su boleto." In essence the burden of one's past reaches the same destiny as the rest of the traveler.

Hawthorne's traveler is made aware of the propensity of the train to pass through areas replete with illusion, "mere delusions, which I ought to be heartily ashamed of; but all through the Dark Valley I was tormented and pestered, and dolefully bewildered with the same kind of waking dreams." Arreola conveys a similar idea. Once on the train (assuming a path in life towards a goal), even then one is not certain of reaching one's destination, "podriá darse el caso de que usted creyera haber llegado a T., y sólo fuese una illusión." One is often tempted to stop at an illusory goal in life. The Switchman continues the analogy: "Hay estaciones que son pura apariencia: han sido construidas en plena selva y llevan el nombre de alguna ciudad importante." Illusion is an allegorical commonplace (Honig), but noteworthy in the similarity of use by both writers.

Hawthorne's traveler plans to enjoy his next stop—Vanity, "where Vanity Fair is still at the height of prosperity, and exhibits an epitome of whatever is brilliant, gay, and fascinating beneath the sun. As I purposed to make a considerable stay here. . . ." The length of his planned stay reminds us of the Switchman's advice: "Lo que debe hacer ahora mismo es buscar alojamiento en la fonda para viajeros." These rooms are highly sought after, and those who manage to get one dwell here on the long term, knowing that, "le resultará más barato y recibirá mejor atención." By taking lodging as the Switchman suggests, one accepts the present moment and lives entirely in the present. For many travelers through life, this is one way to remove oneself from the constant turmoil of the journey, not mattering whether the stop is in Vanity or simply a deserted station. Those who live on the long term in the present may find better treatment in the present than many of those who just pass through. Yet at the same time, this life style is a kind of imprisonment so that those who dwell here are likely to find themselves in an ashen building that looks and is much like a prison "un extraño edificio ceniciento que más bien parecía un presidio."

Hawthorne's traveler observes the spending behavior of his fellow passengers at Vanity Fair, noting that "some of the purchasers, I thought, made very foolish bargains. For instance, a young man, having inherited a splendid fortune, laid out a considerable portion of it in the purchase of diseases, and finally spent all the rest for a heavy lot of repentance and a suit of rags. In one shop, there were a great many crowns of laurel and myrtle, which soldiers, authors, statesmen, and various other people pressed eagerly to buy; some purchased these paltry wreaths with their lives, others by a toilsome servitude of years, and many sacrificed whatever was most valuable, yet finally slunk away without the crown." Arreola's Switchman speaks of one person who has spent a liftime and a fortune on round trip journeys, an amount great enough so that one whole new section of track is going to be built from the money. In both stories the idea is the same. Be it for glory or vainglory, the purchase may cost one's life.

Hawthorne's traveler comments on how part of the journey passed by as though through a haze. "My recollections of the journey are now, for a little space, dim and confused, inasmuch as a singular drowsiness here overcame me, owing to the fact that we were passing over the enchanted ground, the air of which encourages a disposition to sleep.'' Arreola tells us also of parts of the journey and unusual cars provided by the company, equipped with special slides to project on the windows and creating thus an illusion. The locomotives on those trains are also equipped to provide the sensation of moving even when the train is not doing so. Some times we advance through life while we think we are not moving, and are stationary when we think we are advancing.

Near the end of the story, Hawthorne notes a sudden change in the train in that ''the engine now announced the close vicinity of the final station house by one last and horrible scream, in which there seemed to be distinguishable every kind of wailing and woe, and bitter fierceness of wrath, all mixed up with the wild laughter of a devil or a madman.'' Arreola too tells us that the approaching train is more than merely another train, ''Al fondo del paisaje, la locomotora se acercaba como un ruidoso advenimiento.'' Both trains and their engines are justifiably momentous—they have the power to change the route of one's life forever.

The friendly guide for Hawthorne's traveler is suddenly transformed at the end, ''And then did my excellent friend Mr. Smooth-it-away laugh outright, in the midst of which cachinnation a smoke wreath issued from his mouth and nostrils, while a twinkle of lurid flame darted out of either eye, proving indubitably that his heart was all of a red blaze.'' Arreola's Switchman also changes, but in a much more genial manner: ''El viejecillo sonriente hizo un guiño y se quedó mirando al viajero, lleno de bondad y de picardía.'' This sudden change in the two guides adds to the power of the moment by underlining it as a kind of transfiguration for all.

Whereas Hawthorne's traveler awakens at this moment, exclaiming ''thank Heaven it was a dream!'', Arreola's traveler decides that a change in his destination is appropriate, indicating that the Switchman has convinced him to accept destiny, to accept anything that life brings. That decision enables the Switchman to disappear and the train (a path through life) to appear. At that moment ''el viejecillo se disolvó en la clara mañana. Pero el punto rojo de la linterna siguió corriendo y saltando entre los rieles, imprudentemente, al encuentro del tren.'' The inspiration of the conversation, of the respite, lingers on, signaling a new awareness on the part of the traveler. No longer insistent on going to T., he is now prepared to accept what life offers, and in doing so, will be transported soon to a crossroads, and from there to another, and so on, and perhaps with luck may even wind up at ''F.''

By drawing the comparison between Hawthorne and Arreola, it has been seen that there are indeed a large number of similarities between their two stories. There seem to be enough to suggest that Arreola may have read Hawthorne's story and was ''inspired'' by it. Much of the similarity is undoubtedly due to the similarity of metaphor—once one decides to write an allegory using the railroad as the central metaphor, many of the other elements must accordingly fall into place: bridges, tunnels, tickets, stations, passengers, etc. That one would also choose to make it a dialogue between two men, one a complete stranger to the line, and the other a sophisticated denizen, is a bit less likely. Least likely of all would be a similarity of detail: the same burdensome luggage; a similar tumult at boarding; a canyon with water in the bottom that must be crossed; illusions occurring to all the passengers at the same time; a fools' paradise of vain, hollow people; an engine whose noise brings about an eerie sense of forboding.

Despite the considerable similarities that have been pointed out, the two works are vastly different in their manner of revealing allegorical meaning. For the chatty, deliberately humorous, tongue-in-cheek Hawthorne story, there is only one likely interpretation which all readers are led to recognize immediately. The first paragraph begins, ''Not a great while ago, passing through the gate of dreams, I visited that region of the earth in which lies the famous City of Destruction.'' If the ''gate of dreams'' and ''City of Destruction'' aren't enough to cause recognition of Hawthorne's allegorical intent, he makes it more explicit yet in the first paragraph with the clearly meaningful names ''Celestial City'' and ''Mr. Smooth-it-away.'' Many in his audience would already have read or at least would have been acquainted with *The Pilgrim's Progress*, and hence Hawthorne's deliberate borrowing of the term, ''City of Destruction'' from Bunyan would reinforce his allegorical intent as well as declare his purpose of humorously continuing Bunyan's story. His nineteenth-century audience would have been well-used to lengthy sermons with frequent, heavy-handed allegories, and would have enjoyed thoroughly both the satire and the serious meaning of his story.

On the other hand, for the more surrealistic allegory of Arreola, there are any number of interpretations, witness the possibilities mentioned in Ramírez and Washburn. While Hawthorne's story must be read as an allegory in order to be enjoyed, Arreola's story, with less obvious humor, satisfies on the surface as a dream-like story of a mysterious encounter with a friendly stranger in a land where the railroad behaves with a mind of its own. It satisfies a second time when the subtle hints of allegory cause the reader to recognize some of these possibilities as well. Had Arreola chosen the same heavy-handed technique used by Hawthorne, the story would have lost considerably thereby and might have seemed hopelessly old-fashioned to his twentieth-century audience. Instead, the open-ended nature of ''El guardagujas'' is very suggestive.

In the final analysis Hawthorne seeks to preach (albeit humorously) a Christian moral to his nineteenth-century audience, whereas Arreola intends merely to reveal interesting and amusing possibilities about life and railroading to his twentieth-century audience.

What seems likely after having compared the two stories at length is that Arreola read Hawthorne's story as a young man and saw an idea and a technique in it that he liked very much. After some time, he consciously or unconsciously used its skeleton to flesh out his own allegory, utilizing his own philosophy of life, with the result being the little gem, ''El guardagujas.''

Source: John R. Burt, ''This is no way to run a railroad: Arreola's Allegorical Railroad and a possible source,'' in *Hispania,* Vol. 71, No. 4, December, 1988, p. 806.

George R. McMurray

In the following essay, George R. McMurray outlines the shared insights regarding the twentieth-century experience between Albert Camus' The Myth of Sisphus *and Juan Jose Arreola's* The Switchman *to suggest that Arreola's short story aptly illustrates Camus' definition of the absurd.*

In 1942 Albert Camus published his book of essays entitled *The Myth of Sisyphus* in which he developed his concept of the absurd in an effort to give meaning to human life in a senseless, war-torn world without God. A decade later, in 1952, the Mexican writer Juan José Arreola published ''The Switchman,'' a short story that reveals a philosophical position somewhat similar to that of Camus. This essay attempts to delineate attitudes shared by these two authors, the first a kind of pagan moralist and the second an ironic observer of the human condition.

Arreola is only one of many contemporary writers who have demonstrated a sympathetic response to Camus' assessment of the complex modern environment. An outstanding example of Mexican short fiction, ''The Switchman'' can be read on different levels and perhaps for this reason has never been completely understood. Briefly summarized, it is the tale of a stranger burdened with a large suitcase who arrives at a deserted station at the exact time his train is supposed to leave. As he gazes at the tracks that ''melted away in the distance,'' an old man carrying a tiny red lantern appears from out of nowhere and proceeds to inform the stranger of the hazards of train travel in this country. It seems that, although an elaborate network of railroads has been planned and partially completed, the service is highly unreliable. Therefore the horrified stranger, who keeps indicating that he must arrive at his destination, ''T,'' the next day, is advised to rent a room by the month in a nearby inn, an ash-colored building resembling a jail where many would-be travelers are lodged. The switchman then relates a series of preposterous anecdotes illustrating the numerous difficulties one might encounter in attempting to board the train, and the problems that might arise during any given trip. The stranger is also told that it should make no difference to him whether or not he reaches his destination, ''T,'' that once he is on the train his life will indeed ''take on some direction.'' When asked if he has traveled a great deal, the old man replies that he has never gotten on a train, nor does he have any desire to do so. At this moment a whistle is heard in the distance, indicating the train's arrival. But upon inquiring again where the stranger wants to go, the switchman receives the answer ''X'' instead of ''T.'' In the final lines the old man vanishes as he breaks into a run along the tracks, and only the red lantern remains visible before the noisily approaching engine.

In *The Myth of Sisphus* Camus states that neither man alone nor the world by itself is absurd. Rather the absurd arises from the clash between reasoning, finite man, on the one hand, striving for order, unity and happiness and, on the other, the silent, unreasonable world offering no response to his persistent demands. The absurd man is one who recognizes a kind of void or lack of meaning in life and resolves to commit himself to the conflict between his intentions and the reality he encounters. Like Sisyphus, who was condemned by the gods to roll a huge stone up a hill again and again for eternity and whom Camus considers the epitome of the absurd hero, the absurd man can attain heroic proportions by rebelling against his torment and by demonstrating that the struggle itself gives definition to his existence. The absurd, then, is the metaphysical state of conscious man fully aware of death and nothingness; it is lucid reason pitted against chaos; it is the only certainty linking man with an alien world devoid of absolutes. The feeling of the absurd can come at any moment, but it is most likely to happen when "the stage sets collapse" and the individual, suddenly aware of the seductive rhythm of daily routine, asks himself the crucial question, "Why?" What follows can be a complete awakening to consciousness of the absurd or, if one is not on his guard, a loss of this awareness and a return to the chain of meaningless, repetitive acts. Thus, once man has recognized the absurd, he must keep it alive by maintaining a state of revolt against the certainty of ultimate defeat, this being his only means of achieving self-fulfillment and of transcending the tragedy of his existence.

According to Camus, the concept of the absurd restores man's freedom to live life to the fullest, liberating him from the bonds of preconceived values, and making fate a human and individual matter. The absurd also negates hope for the future and considers action in the Here and Now to be an end in itself. Suicide and faith in God, then, are out of the question because either would represent an escape from the absurd, terminating the necessary state of tension between reasoning man and the unreasonable world. By his emphasis on this state of tension, Camus demonstrates his admiration for reason, but he also recognizes its limits and the impossibility of reducing the unintelligible world to rational principles. As prime examples of the absurd man, he lists the actor, the conqueror, Don Juan, the creator, and, perhaps most important here, the traveler, who is "constantly on the move."

Although the French thinker has defined and illustrated the absurd in lucid, rational language, subsequent practitioners of absurd literature have often relied on fantasy and other antirational devices to present their perceptions of life without purpose. Some of these writers, including Beckett, Ionesco, Borges, Cortázar and Arreola, have attacked reason more forcefully, and probably more effectively, than Camus.

In "The Switchman" the railroad journey could be construed as a metaphor of absurd existence, and

> " Whatever interpretation the reader may choose, it appears likely that Arreola is not only deeply concerned with man's quest for values in a world fraught with uncertainty, but also with the exploration of a reality lying beyond the confines of reason."

the act of boarding the train, as both an awareness of the absurd and an acceptance of its challenges on the part of the passengers who, once on board, realize they may not be taken where they want to go. At the beginning of the story the stranger is a nonabsurd man and, one might add, an amusing victim of irony, because he has complete faith in reason and assumes that because he has purchased a ticket he will arrive at his destination on schedule. The switchman likewise is a nonabsurd man, for while he is fully aware of the absurd, he has never boarded a train, has no intention of doing so, and thus has in no way committed himself to revolt. He is, rather, a passive, ironic observer of life and perhaps the author's persona. The stranger's heavy suitcase would seem to represent the burden of reason he carries around with him, the railroad tracks melting into the distance his uncertain destiny, and the ash-colored inn a kind of jail for all the potential passengers who are still trapped in the mechanical cycle of daily routine and who have yet to pose the Camusian question, "Why?" The elaborate network of uncompleted railroads gives expression to man's fruitless efforts to reduce the unreasonable world to rational principles, an idea reinforced by the switchman's ludicrous allusions to expeditionary trains taking years to complete their runs and the necessity of adding funeral cars in case of deaths along the way. Furthermore, we are told that trains occasionally travel on roadbeds where the rails are missing, resulting in disastrous accidents. One such mishap occurred after the train wheels were worn away to their axels. The stranded passengers met the challenge by founding the town of "F," which became a happy, progressive community "filled with mischievous children playing with rusty vestiges of the train.''

When the stranger exclaims that he has no desire for such adventures, the old man responds, ''You need to pluck up your courage; perhaps you may ever become a hero.'' He then narrates the episode of two hundred passengers on a train that arrived at the edge of an abyss over which the railway builders had failed to construct a bridge. Inspired by the engineer's pep talk, the passengers took the train apart and carried it down an embankment and across a river so that they might continue their journey. The management was so pleased by the results of their ingenuity that plans for building a bridge were abandoned and a discount was offered to passengers willing to repeat the same adventure. In Camusian terms these travelers would represent absurd heroes committed to the principle of living life to the fullest and making action an end in itself. The founding of the town of ''F'' after the accident, moreover, suggests the absurd man's rejection of the antiquated values of the past, symbolized by the rusty vestiges of the wrecked train, and his acceptance of the challenge to forge his own destiny.

The unreasonable, disorderly world encountered by the absurd man is also illustrated by the switchman's references to the violent disputes among ticketholders on the station platform and the schools organized to teach methods of getting on a fast-moving train, if necessary with the aid of armor. To the stranger's question regarding what he can do to assure his arrival at his destination, the switchman advises him to initiate his journey with the firm idea that he is going to ''T,'' although it's hard to tell if it will do any good.'' Furthermore, once on board the train, the stranger should take every possible precaution. It seems there could be spies planted among the travelers to denounce them for their most innocent remarks, leading to their incarceration for life in a prison car. Moreover, in order to deceive the passengers and cause them to get off at the wrong stops, the management has constructed false stations referred to as ''stage sets'' enlivened with realistic dummies. At the same time, to reduce the anxiety of the travelers, the train windows have been provided with ingenious devices to create the illusion of movement through captivating landscapes when, in reality, the train is motionless. As the switchman explains, ''The hope is that one day the passengers will capitulate to fate, give themselves into the hands of an omnipotent management, and no longer care to know where they are going or where they have come from.'' Thus, like

Camus, Arreola seems to suggest the necessity of keeping the absurd alive by recognizing that reality is illusory, that nothing is certain except the absurd, and that only by facing life squarely can one give it meaning and value. This posture of permanent revolt against fate, embodied here in the ''omnipotent management,'' will also prevent the absurd man from being lulled back into his state of unawareness prior to the collapse of the stage sets which triggered his initial encounter with the absurd.

The climax of the story occurs when the train approaches and the switchman asks the stranger to repeat his destination. The latter's reply, ''X,'' indicates his acceptance of the absurd unknown. Moreover, the fact that in these lines for the first time in the story he is called the ''traveler'' instead of the ''stranger'' underscores his newly acquired role as an absurd man with the potential of becoming a hero like the passengers who carried the train across the abyss.

The images set forth in the final lines of the story are also closely related to its thematic content. Immediately after the traveler informs the switchman of his new destination, ''X,'' we are told that ''the little old man dissolved in the clear morning. But the red speck of his lantern kept on running and leaping imprudently between the rails to meet the train. In the distant landscape the train was noisily approaching.'' Thus, the stranger's transformation from a nonabsurd to an absurd man, the disappearance of the switchman, and the train's arrival set the stage for the ensuing absurd journey. It would seem, then, that the tiny lantern confronting the oncoming train symbolizes the absurd clash between limited human reason and the dark forces of destruction.

''The Switchman'' is a tale that lends itself to multiple interpretations, its ambiguities serving to augment its impact. Whatever interpretation the reader may choose, it appears likely that Arreola is not only deeply concerned with man's quest for values in a world fraught with uncertainty, but also with the exploration of a reality lying beyond the confines of reason. The Mexican author is less militant than Camus in his revolt against the human condition, but at the same time he may be less optimistic about man's potential. Whereas Camus' hero Sisyphus constitutes a model for giving meaning to existence, Arreola's anonymous stranger would seem to personify twentieth-century alienation in a world dominated by institutionalized technology, namely the railroad, which has presented man with the illusion of self-determination but, in reality, has merely created a metaphoric labyrinth for his absurd and dangerous odyssey.

On an esthetic level, the symbolic imagery and structural balance of Arreola's tale represent his attempt to give artistic coherence to the elusive reality that he, as an absurd creator, finds unacceptable. Thus, when the tension between the ironic observer (the switchman) and the man of reason (the stranger) is finally dissolved, it is immediately replaced by the confrontation between the traveler (that absurd Camusian hero "constantly on the move") and his uncertain destiny. With this sudden shift from one level of dramatic tension to another, the reader realizes that the title of the story may not refer to a railroad switchman but to a kind of catalyst-agent whose role is to awaken the protagonist to the absurd and "switch" him onto another track. If we accept this premise, the switchman could represent the stranger's alter ego, and the entire story, a metaphor of modern man's awakening to Camus' famous question, "Why?"

In conclusion, there is no proof that Arreola has been directly influenced by Camus' philosophy. Still, it is not unlikely that a voracious reader like Arreola, who studied in France immediately after World War II, was acquainted with *The Myth of Sisyphus* by 1952, the year he published The "Switchman." Camus' essays indicate an ethical direction toward secular, anthropocentric humanism, one of his fundamental principles being that man must oppose the unreasonable universe even though his search for order may make him appear absurd. Arreola seems to share a similar metaphysical stance, although his roguish humor and fantasy set him apart from the more serious-minded Frenchman. Both authors, however, project philosophical insights corresponding closely to the twentieth-century experience. Unlike the naturalists, who envision a Utopian future characterized by man's domination of nature through science, and unlike Dostoevski's underground man, whose contradictions lie within himself, Camus and Arreola believe the human

dilemma stems from the disproportion between lucid intention and chaotic reality. Camus' definition of the absurd, it seems to me, is poetically illustrated by the switchman's internalized journey whether or not Arreola was consciously aware of *The Myth of Sisyphus* at the time he wrote his story.

Source: George R. McMurray, "Albert Camus' Concept of the Absurd and Juan Jose Arreola's 'The Switchman,'" in *Latin American Literary Review,* Vol. VI, No. 11, Fall-Winter, 1977, p.30.

Sources

Arreola, Juan José, *Confabulario and Other Inventions,* translated by George D. Schade, University of Texas Press, 1964, pp.78-85.

Davila, Luis, ed., *Juan José Arreola,* Twayne's World Authors Series, Indiana University, 1983, pp. 49-53.

Larson, Ross, *Fantasy and Imagination in the Mexican Narrative,* Center for Latin American Studies, Arizona State University, 1977, pp. 102-03.

Pulsipher, Curtis D., *The Use of the Fantastic, Neo-Fantastic, Animals and Humor as Vehicles for Satire in the Works of Juan José Arreola and Murilo Rubiao,* University of Illinois at Urbana-Champaign, 1985, pp. 186, 192.

Further Reading

Menton, Seymour, *Magic Realism Rediscovered, 1918-1981,* Art Alliance Press, 1983.
> Menton, an authority on all things Latin American, discusses the way Magical Realism is manifested in twentieth-century Latin American literature.

Pena, Carlo Gonzales, *History of Mexican Literature,* Southern Methodist University Press, 1968.
> A thorough overview of Mexican literature through 1943, including an in-depth discussion of Spanish colonialism on all kinds of Mexican writing.

Washburn, Yulan M., *Juan José Arreola,* Twayne, 1983.
> More criticism and interpretation on the author.

The Time of the Hero

Mario Vargas Llosa

1962

One of the greatest Latin American novelists of the twentieth century, Mario Vargas Llosa belongs to a group of writers who brought Latin American fiction out of the regionalist doldrums of the nineteenth century to the attention of the world. This group includes Jorge Luis Borges, Gabriel García Márquez, Julio Cortazar, and Carlos Fuentes. Vargas Llosa, sometimes referred to as the national conscience of Peru, has made a career out of adapting personal and historical events, without bothering about accuracy, to the novel using highly sophisticated techniques of nonlinearity and multiple viewpoint.

His first novel, winner of the Premio Biblioteca Breve (1962) and Premio de la Critica Espanola (1963), *La ciudad y los perros* (literally ''the city and the dogs'' but published in English as *The Time of the Hero*) made use of his own experience at the Leoncio Prado Academy. The novel was so accurate in its portraiture of the academy that the academy's authorities burned 1000 copies and condemned the book as a plan by Ecuador to denigrate Peru. Such a reception guaranteed the book's sales but its content made it the greatest Latin American novel of adolescence: It is the story of young Peruvian males in their transition to manhood.

The Time of the Hero tells a tale of murder: a squealing cadet must be silenced by a gang called The Circle. The reasons given by The Circle, as well as the rationalization of the authorities to excuse the

death as an accident, reveal the process of forming boys into men in a world dominated by the military. The academy does not teach fundamentals; it teaches boys how to exist in hierarchical command-structures and to never, ever squeal. The main characters suffer through a military academy but minor characters portray a non-military route. Although a microcosm of Peruvian society, the novel's themes are universal: masculinity, secrecy, and the military.

Author Biography

Although born in Arequipa, Peru, in 1936, Vargas Llosa spent his early boyhood with his mother, Dora Llosa Ureta, in Cochabamba, Bolivia, where his grandfather was the Peruvian consul. Vargas Llosa attended a series of schools and led a normal middle-class boy's life until his parents reunited and his father, Ernesto Vargas Maldonaldo, discovered his talent for writing poetry. Fearing for the boy's masculinity, Ernesto moved the family to Lima and sent the boy, in 1950, to attend Leoncio Prado Academy. His two years at the academy formed the basis for a novella as well as his famous first novel, *The Time of the Hero*.

His first work, however, was a three-act play published in 1952 while finishing high school in Piura. For the next few years, Vargas Llosa published short stories in Peruvian literary reviews. He also coedited several journals and attended San Marcos University in Lima where he took courses in literature and law. In 1955, he caused a minor family scandal when he married Julia Urquidi —his aunt. They divorced in 1964.

In 1958, he left for Europe and lived for varying periods in Paris, England, the U.S., and Spain. While in France, Vargas Llosa worked on the manuscript that would become *The Time of the Hero*. This became his first novel in 1962 and won two major awards establishing him as a major Latin American novelist—a stature that would be cemented with his second novel, *The Green House* (1966). During this time, in 1959, he completed a dissertation on Gabriel García Márquez's fiction at the University of Madrid. Also during this time, Vargas Llosa was an intellectual spokesman for revolutionary movements throughout Latin America. This advocacy period ended in 1971 when his criticism

of the censorship of artists in Cuba caused him to be ostracized by the Latin American Left. He married Patricia (a cousin) in 1965 and they had three children: Alvaro, Gonzalo, and Morgana.

Vargas Llosa returned to Peru in 1974 and seven years later, *The War of the End of the World* announced his abandonment of socialism. He began espousing free-market democracy and anti-authoritarian liberalism in Peru. He turned down the post of prime minister in the early 1980s to concentrate on writing but the government's plan to nationalize the banks of Peru in 1987 forced him to stand up for his beliefs and protest the plan. Vargas Llosa quickly gained supporters and the government backed down. Fired by this victory, his supporters formed Fredemo, a political party, to champion the ideas of free-market democracy and individual liberty. Fredemo formed a coalition, Liberty Movement, with two other parties. Together, they nominated Vargas Llosa as their presidential candidate. In 1988, opinion polls showed Vargas Llosa well ahead of his rival, Alberto Fujimori, by more than 2 to 1. However, his support gradually eroded and Vargas Llosa lost. He reflected on this political experience in *A Fish in the Water*.

Not long after the election, Vargas Llosa returned to Spain, where he accepted citizenship. However, he currently spends his time in London.

Plot Summary

The Circle

The Time of the Hero opens at night during a meeting of The Circle—a gang of four cadets in their final year of the Leoncio Prado Academy led by the Jaguar. Their clubhouse is "the windowless latrine" and they are rolling the dice to see who will steal the answers to the chemistry exam. This criminal act sets off a violent chain reaction although The Circle intended only to pass an important exam a mere two months before graduation. Cava, a peasant, rolled the four, meaning he must make arrangements on behalf of The Circle with those cadets on duty to grant him anonymous passage to the academic building. This is easily granted and Cava goes off into the night while Boa and Curly, relieved by the roll of the die, go off to bed.

Later that night, while the Poet and the Slave (forced to take Jaguar's place), who are members of

Mario Vargas Llosa

the same section as The Circle, are on patrol. Cava goes forth to steal the exam. While the Poet engages Lt. Huarina in a strange metaphysical discussion away from his proper post, the Slave observes Cava crossing to the academic building. While breaking into the building, Cava accidentally breaks a windowpane he had just painfully removed. As Boa later says, "You have to be stupid to do that" and scared. Cava, as a peasant, was susceptible to both. Grabbing the exam and scooping the shards of glass into his pocket, Cava runs back to the barracks.

The Slave

When the exam's theft is discovered, those who were on patrol that night are confined to barracks until the responsible party confesses or someone squeals. The Slave, whose life has been "sheer hell" due to the abuse rained on him by the section and particularly The Circle, had rarely been free of confinement. Most recently, he sent the Poet to Teresa's house to make apologies on his behalf for missing a date. Because of the exam theft, the Slave has been confined again. The Slave asks the Poet to write a letter to Teresa but the Poet refuses. The Slave, in desperation, decides to squeal. Among the cadets, squealing is the worst crime to commit against fellow cadets. However, as Jaguar reveals at the end of the novel, squealing can be justified if

done out of revenge for a comrade but not for the sake of getting a pass. The Slave, fed up with being kept from seeing Teresa, reasons that he has everything to gain by squealing on his tormentors. With such motives, the Slave squeals on Cava to Lt. Huarina and receives a pass.

Unknown to the Slave, the Poet—who had written letters to Teresa for the Slave—decides to take Teresa for himself. Too cowardly to admit this to the Slave, he simultaneously befriends the Slave while refusing to write letters for him. The Poet tries to get the Slave to stop being cowardly but the real coward is the Poet. As the Poet tells Teresa, during the Slave's time of anguish "he thought I was his friend" but the Poet was really stealing his girlfriend. However, Teresa makes it quite clear she never viewed the Slave as her boyfriend.

When Cava's court-martial becomes expulsion, the Jaguar "almost went crazy afterward but not on account of the peasant, just himself." Since the Jaguar organized his year against hazing when they were first-years, he had become the undisputed ringleader. Therefore, to squeal on any scheme of his was to betray the Jaguar himself. He therefore gathers with his remaining circle to figure out who squealed. But Jaguar already knows; like an animal, he can smell it. He decides to cleanse his section of its weak element once and for all. His Darwinian act stems from loyalty to the group and himself.

The Cover-Up

While on a training exercise, the Slave—who happens to be directly in front of the Jaguar—is shot. Enraged by this act and feeling guilty at having made a move on the Slave's girl, the Poet spills the beans to Lt. Gamboa—he reveals the way the cadets break rules against drinking, smoking, gambling, and sneaking out as well as his theory that The Circle took its revenge. The Slave, says the Poet, did not accidentally shoot himself as the official story academy officials are telling parents says (the doctors made a strictly medical report and neglected to mention that "there's isn't any question about it, he got shot from behind"), but Jaguar shot him. Lt. Gamboa believes him and raids the barracks of the first section to find evidence to substantiate the Poet's claims about rule infraction but no evidence against the Jaguar.

Angered by all the trouble, the Colonel intercedes in the investigation. During the locker searches, all the pornographic writings of the Poet come to light. With these stories in hand, the Colonel blackmails the Poet; if the Poet will withdraw the charge and be a perfect angel, the writings will be burnt. The Colonel then, by referencing the Poet's fantastic writing, tells him that clearly his imagination ran away with him and he dreamed up the conspiracy. Seeing he has no support and no evidence, the Poet agrees to withdraw the charge. Before being released, he is mistakenly imprisoned with Jaguar. They fight and the Poet gets the worst of it. After being ordered silent by Lt. Gamboa, the cadets return to the barracks. Along the way, the Poet begins to doubt himself because the Jaguar appears genuinely surprised that it was the Slave who squealed on Cava. Thus, everyone can believe the official story which labels the Slave's death accidental.

Useless Objectives

Lt. Gamboa, who acted on the Poet's information and turned the barracks upside down during an investigation of rule infraction, is transferred to an out-of-the-way post. Just before he goes, Jaguar confesses to him. He is motivated by self-revelation—the entire fifth year blames the Jaguar for Lt. Gamboa's crackdown and they shun him. Jaguar accepts this because he refuses to squeal on the Poet, but he realizes how the Slave must have felt. Lt. Gamboa tells him to forget the whole thing because nobody wants to know: to clear up the death of the Slave would be an attempt at a "useless objective." By this Lt. Gamboa means that, just as in war, when an enemy surrenders you do not kill him because that would be bad economics: "it would be easier to bring Arana back to life than to convince the army it's made an error." Jaguar's epiphany includes the realization that the world of loyalty he created among the cadets was a false and fickle one.

The end of the novel is fraught with ambiguity. The cadets graduate and return home to forget all about the academy. At this point, the unidentified fourth narrator reveals himself as the Jaguar: the legitimate suitor of Teresa who struggled on the streets as an orphan. Jaguar marries Teresa and finds a steady job. The Poet, meanwhile, still melancholy about the academy, chooses someone from the middle class. He intends to marry her after he gets an engineering degree in the U.S. In the end, both the Poet and the Jaguar marvel at how normal life went on without them, as if the horror of the academy means nothing. Moreover, although their insight might have led them to change their views of society, each happily resumes his designated place;

the Jaguar becomes a lowly functionary, while the Poet takes his place in the upper class. Worse, the Poet, using a metaphor repeated throughout the novel, "could remember many of the events as if they were a motion picture, and for days at a time he could avoid thinking of the Slave."

Characters

Mr. Arana

Mr. Arana differs from Alberto's father only slightly. He does not treat his wife well, abandons her for stretches of time, and has many girlfriends. He is an absent father to Ricardo, the Slave, and blames his wife for Ricardo's fault. When Ricardo has been shot and lies dying in the hospital, Mr. Arana moans to Alberto about the challenge he has had to face in making Ricardo a man: "It hasn't been easy to make a man out of him. He's my only son." Mr. Arana wants to believe the Academy did him good, that it undid all that his wife and Aunt Adeline did to emasculate young Ricardo. Mr. Arana does everything but consider his role in Ricardo's upbringing, especially his failure to ever appreciate Ricardo. In fact, Mr. Arana constantly insulted Ricardo as if he were not there, saying, "he acts like a girl." Mr. Arana represents the worst kind of father.

Ricardo Arana

Ricardo, in terms of the *machismo* of Peruvian society, is a degenerate. Faced with the bravest boy in grade school, "he was not afraid. . .all he felt was a complete discouragement and resignation." From this moment on, Ricardo adopted a humble and subservient attitude and employed passive-aggressive strategies with his father and other macho performers. This personality wins him the designation of Slave by the Jaguar, who makes use of his natural subservience.

Ricardo's inability to play silly games and to feel fear of his fellow humans as well as his desire to protect his mother from his misogynistic father mark him as someone destined to die. Ricardo makes men aware of the fallibility of their *machismo* behavior. Thus, Ricardo carries incredible symbolic weight and can be interpreted according to many patterns. Ricardo represents the existentialist stranger, the man who speaks the truth in Plato's cave. As in that parable, he must die. Ricardo can be read as a Christ figure who dies for the sins of the boys at the hands of their high priest. His death serves as a possible means of salvation for those willing to reflect. However, Ricardo's death does not bring salvation but allows the boys to continue to play at being men.

Arrospide

Arrospide, a rich white kid from Miraflores (like Alberto), intends to survive the Academy with good marks and in good standing with his peers. Based on these goals, Arrospide willingly accepts the thankless role of Brigadier of the first section for all three years. He allows The Circle liberty and simply goes with the flow. In the end, he leads the coup against the Jaguar with relish. By destroying the Jaguar, whether or not the rumor Curly started is true, Arrospide becomes the leader of the first section in name and spirit just in time for graduation.

The Boa

See Valdivieso

Porfirio Cava

''Cava had been born and brought up in the mountains, cold weather was nothing new to him; it was fear that was giving him goose pimples.'' The fear stalking Cava is the fear of failure both to please the Jaguar and to survive the academy; it is the fear of being unable to handle a situation forced upon him. If he doesn't survive the academy, he is destined to live the life of a peasant. If he does survive, he hopes to climb the social ladder however slightly through a career in the military. Fate is against him in the most iconographic sense—he rolls the dice and lands a ''four.'' ''Get going,'' the Jaguar commands. Cava must steal the answers to the upcoming chemistry exam for the other three members of The Circle and for whoever else wants to buy them.

Cava, an Indian, wins respect by being a part of The Circle. Thus, even an avowed racist like the Boa forgives him for being Indian and befriends him. Cava plays the role of The Circle's peddler in the section. He arranges the selling of items stolen from other cadets in other sections to fellow cadets who want to pass inspection. Cava has a special hatred for the French teacher, Mr. Fontana. Consequently, Cava makes French class hell for Fontana. He thinks Fontana is gay and relentlessly disrupts

class. The Boa and the other cadets both approve of and follow Cava's lead.

Curly

A member of The Circle who partakes in the gang bangs and acts of bestiality described by the Boa. He witnesses the Jaguar's vow, ''if I get screwed, everybody gets screwed.'' Upon this basis, the section labels the Jaguar a squealer when Gamboa ransacks the barracks for misdemeanors.

Alberto Fernandez

One of the protagonists, Alberto, earned his nickname when he began writing letters and pornographic stories for money. The Poet shares his origination from a comfortable white middle-class family in Miraflores with the brigadier, Arrospide. However, inside the academy, such a background does not mean much. Only the esteem of one's fellow cadets brings merit. Along with being a narrator of his own life and contemporary events, the Poet brings about the major event of the novel by underhandedly pursuing his friend's girl. While he does not find Teresa beautiful, the Poet admires her intelligence and enjoys the attention she gives him. It is the attention a poor girl gives to anyone sporting the equipage of a higher station in society.

The Poet, as the most conscious and articulate character, receives the most scrutiny because he is the most revealed. Consequently, the evidence never substantiates his claim on reliability and masculinity. This uncertainty begins with his introduction when he confusingly attempts to mislead and seek advice from a man he does not respect, Lt. Huarina. Again and again, the Poet will behave in a manner that clashes with the code of honor and *machismo* he is supposed to be learning. For example, real men brag about sexual exploits that they actually have. Instead, both in his pornographic writing and when he talks about the prostitute, Golden Toes, ''no one suspected that he knew about [Golden Toes] because he repeated anecdotes he had been told and invented all kinds of lurid stories.'' Pained adolescence and the demands of military *machismo* excuse such lying behavior, but for the Poet they become a habit that spills into civilian life.

At his duplicitous worst, the Poet never corrects the Slave in his idea that the two of them are friends. Instead, the Poet tries to make a man of the Slave and hides the truth about his relations with Teresa. This act of cowardice haunts him when he is forced to console the Slave's father with lies about how great the Slave was. Finally, with such a compromised integrity and tortured by doubt, he cannot challenge Jaguar using truth as an instrument. Indeed, Jaguar easily dupes him with a story just as the Colonel blackmailed the Poet with his pornographic stories. The Poet represents a theory of literature—stories change and make up reality until it is difficult to discern what is real and what is story.

Like the Slave, the Poet exists as an existential stranger. He never entirely bends to the wishes of The Circle and they punish him by denying access to the exam answers. Instead of bending to those around him, the Poet deludes himself and others with his stories and letters. He assumes the role of the fool in Jaguar's court or his Cave. He produces the fantasies that distract and amuse the cadets and, in return, the Poet is unharmed. He serves his purpose but it is without purpose. When Alberto finds purpose—love, friendship, truth—it is too late because he has cried wolf too many times with his stories. In fact, Alberto is not even sure if he believes that Jaguar killed Ricardo.

Lieutenant Gamboa

Lieutenant Gamboa represents the ideal soldier. All the cadets stand in awe of him. He is their role model. His notion of justice and military propriety is based on the book of regulations that he has memorized. His attempt to enforce those regulations when the Poet squeals brings him exile in Juliaca.

Flaco Higueras

Flaco, known as Skinny, is a thief who helps Jaguar help his mother with household expenses. Skinny also teaches Jaguar how to survive in the world of *machismo*.

Lieutenant Remigio Huarina

Among the cadets and officers, Huarina fosters little respect. "He was small and weak, his voice when he gave commands made everyone laugh." In addition, his punishments are arbitrary; Huarina invented "the punishment lottery" by which cadets are randomly punished depending on where they stand in formation. In the black and white world of the military, nobody respects arbitrary gray.

When the Slave decides to stand up to the world, he goes to Huarina and squeals on Cava.

Huarina seizes the information with enthusiasm hoping that he will win some respect. Huarina gains in standing and represents the classic situation of the victory of the undeserving. Gamboa, the man with the most integrity, gains exile—Huarina, a promotion.

The Jaguar

Central and South American ranchers mistakenly view the largest member of the American cat family, the endangered jaguar (once honored as a god among pre-Columbian Peruvians), as a pest. They believe that the jaguar eats their cattle, scientific evidence to the contrary notwithstanding. A forest and savanna creature, the jaguar wears a coat ranging from yellow to rust red with black rosettes. The jaguar is a fitting namesake for the story's most powerful and mysterious personality.

The Jaguar works in the shadows as his stalking of Cava shows from the start. Cava, when returning from his hunt, sees "a dark shape loom[ing] up in front of him." The Jaguar, with "big pale feet with long dirty toenails" and hands "like two white claws," takes Cava's prey, the exam answers. Such characteristic actions prompt Boa to say "the devil must have a face like the Jaguar's, the same kind of smile, the same sharp horns." But it is the Jaguar's laugh that really gets people.

The Jaguar's effort to make men out of his fellow cadets is done, as all evil intentions are, for his own benefit. Therefore, he represents the man-making tool that parents believe resides inside the academy. However, the Jaguar—and the parents behind him—never realize that boys like Alberto and Ricardo must act for themselves, find their own identities and their own manhood. It was the Jaguar's paternal impatience, more than any thing else, that made him confess to being the cause of Ricardo's death. According to the Jaguar, "we" all killed him.

Marcela

Like Helena, the young woman who dumps and humiliates Alberto, Marcela is a member of Alberto's social class. Cementing the idea that Alberto willingly imitates his Don Juan-esque father, Marcela is an anagram for the name of Alberto's mother, Carmela. Marcela signifies that Alberto will occupy an important position in Peruvian society like his parents and his grandparents.

The Negro

See Vallano

The Poet

See Alberto Fernandez

Skinny

See Flaco Higueras

The Slave

See Ricardo Arana

Teresa

Within the masculine discourse of the barracks, there are two types of woman. The first, Golden Toes, is the whore upon whom the aspiring soldier can practice his lust. The other is the virgin. Teresa represents the virgin who is to be protected in times of war and maintained by a proper husband in times of peace. The Slave, the Jaguar, and the Poet compete for the love of Teresa. Thus, although she simply goes to school, works, and cleans house, Teresa is a major moving force in the novel and in the world of boys. Teresa also allows for an examination of class in Peruvian society; the Jaguar wins her hand at the end, thus allowing him to move up the social ladder and occupy a position as a clerk in a bank.

Valdivieso

In South America, the largest of the boa or boidae, the anaconda, are known to measure twenty feet. Legends have grown up about boas and the people of the Amazon basin are wary of the creatures. The character Boa is named for this South American reptile. A snake can also symbolize the phallus. The Boa, who has a "huge body, a deep voice, a shock of greasy hair over a narrow face," embodies the animal nature of young males and their awakening sexual preoccupations. He always wins the puerile physical contests the first section holds to pass the time—especially masturbatory races judged by Paulino. In terms of the novel, the Boa represents the perfect cadet: his irreproachable loyalty and physical abilities makes him an ideal soldier; his lackluster intelligence enables him to follow orders; and his genuine love of life make him a pleasurable person to live with. Even though he is a narrator, beyond the Boa's reflections on life in the Academy he does not move the plot. Instead, he tells readers about previous actions The Circle, of which he is a prominent member, has choreographed and he also recounts the physical exploits of other cadets.

The Boa expresses the racism of Peruvian society through his comments on Indians and peasants. He tells how he had to make an exception for Cava—an Indian from the mountains—with great difficulty. Otherwise, the Boa regards blacks, Indians, or mixed breeds as inferior. The Boa, as his name suggests, is an animal. He has sex with chickens and then roasts them. He cruelly manipulates a dog's affections and even maims the animal for disturbing him during an inspection. Just like a snake, he never quite accepts the Jaguar as his master and often fantasizes about killing him—stealthily as would a snake. However, the Jaguar has tamed him as a charmer tames a snake, using the tune of violence. The Boa, at his most eloquent, recollects the fights The Circle has engaged in with the Jaguar at the lead.

Vallano

Unlike Cava, Vallano, a black cadet, cannot escape the overt racism of the lighter-hued Peruvians. They call him "The Negro" and describe him in stereotypical fashion, saying, "like all Negroes, you can tell it from his eyes, what eyes, what fear, what jumping around" or, the oft-repeated, "who can trust a Negro." With such a name, a physical name not unlike the animal names, it is not surprising that Vallano is a sympathizer of The Circle although he is not a member. Still, they recognize the Negro as the only "real" student. For this reason, the Poet deals with him as often as possible. The Poet, after the Jaguar turns him down, offers a few letters for a certain number of points on the chemistry exam. During the exam, Vallano is the only student described as working through the questions.

Vallano makes a huge contribution to the culture of the Fifth Section when he brings a pornographic story back from town. *Eleodora's Pleasures* becomes the favorite reading of every member of the section. When Vallano started the story out he found himself out of business because the Poet started selling his own stories. From that moment on, pornographic tales become an intrinsic and sophisticated component of life in the barracks.

Themes

Masculinity

According to Lt. Gamboa, half the boys are sent to the academy "so they won't be gangsters. . .and

Topics for Further Study

- The initiation rituals described in the novel are also known by the term "hazing." Research the role of hazing in neighborhoods, gangs, boarding schools, fraternities, or military academies. What is hazing and how does it differ depending on setting, if at all? Why is this traditional practice under scrutiny? What are the legal issues? Do you think hazing is simply a part of growing up and that the death rate is unavoidable?

- How many levels of masculinity are there in the novel? How many levels of race? Compare the multiplicity of hierarchical levels in Peruvian society to the structure of the U.S.

- William Faulkner looms behind the Latin American Boom. Compare Faulkner's *Light in August* to *The Time of the Hero*. How, for example, has Vargas Llosa drawn from Faulkner and with what results?

- Given the preoccupation with sex that the adolescent boys have throughout the novel, reflect on the implications of the opening citation from Sartre on gender.

- Research the debate in America over gays in the military. How has the debate changed perceptions of masculinity?

- Research the role of the U.S. in the manufacturing of military regimes throughout Latin America during the Cold War. For example, why do U.S. and Latin American political activists object to the U.S.'s School of the Americas? What sort of academy is it and what are the most likely accomplishments of its graduates?

---

the other half, so they won't turn out to be fairies. It's their parents' fault." Gamboa's comment leads to a discussion about the difference between soldiers and cadets. Soldiers can be physically beaten until they are so civilized an Indian only appears to be Indian. Cadets, which cannot be so abused, are not quite so accomplished but they do learn one thing: being a man depends on whether a boy is s——— or he s———. In military terms, the ultimate sign of manhood is murder. However, his parents determine the degree of a boy's success either by letting him grow up—like Tico or Skinny—or telling him to become a man. Towards that end, parents send their boys to an academy where the boys must negotiate a paradox. They are expected to be soldier-like men but they are not soldiers, they are not killers.

The Slave does not succeed in becoming a man because the deck is stacked against him. He has a nearly Freudian relationship with his mother, indicated by his awareness of her kissing him on the lips: "Why does she kiss me on the mouth?" He

learns the hard way that his parents are merely separated and suddenly sees "his mother and a man were...kissing." Slave, in undeclared rebellion, refuses to kiss his father. Later, he tries to defend his mother against being beat up. He loses and is unable to fight another man again; he is impotent. Such docility causes his father to send him to the military academy where he hopes they will make "a man out of him." His father blames the mother, declaring, "There's nothing like a woman to ruin a boy's life".

In contrast to the Slave, the Poet does not take his mother's side. He does kiss his father's cheek. Consequently, Poet's father acknowledges him: "He's a man now." Thereafter, Poet imitates his father's attitude toward his mother by neglecting her. The Jaguar is successful because he has no father to compete with and is acknowledged early on as a man. His aunt ensures his success as a man by sleeping with him—s——— other people is an essential component of being a man. Skinny helps by teaching Jaguar how to manipulate others and how to fight. All of this helps Jaguar be the man to teach his fellow cadets how to survive. He has only one more step to take: murder.

The Poet tries to help the Slave overcome his docility but instead reveals that what makes him most manly is fear. "But you're a soldier here whether you like it or not. And the thing in the army is to be real tough, to have guts. . . S——— them first before they s——— you. There isn't any other way. I don't like to be s———." Being s——— can be literal—as with Boa's rape of chickens, dogs, and a first-year named "fatboy." But it is also metaphorical. The Jaguar's enslavement of Slave—the Slave does the Jaguar's work—is a form of emasculation.

Masculinity depends on acknowledgment by older men and women of one's manhood. It also depends on the stature a boy can hold among his fellow gang members. Except for Jaguar, the cadets are in an awkward position. Teresa's aunt echoes the commiseration of Lt. Gamboa: "The Academy!. . .I thought he was a man." However, one can beat that trap since "a man has to accept responsibility for his actions. . ." The recognition of the Jaguar's accomplishment will not come from the gang he formed; it must come from outside. He realizes that and confesses to Gamboa. He is not punished but freed to build a life with Teresa: the surest proof of manhood, the family.

Secrecy

Along with masculinity, secrecy is the most prevalent theme in the novel. From the start, the world of the cadets exists "in the uncertain glow" of a lightbulb. Secrecy is what allows the next generation to form: "The officers don't know anything about what goes on in the barracks." This is natural. Gamboa doesn't seem concerned about his lack of information or about their nicknames even though early in the novel he says, "I know them as if they were my own kids." However, as the Poet continues to tell him what the cadets do in secret and how they exist, this concerns Gamboa. The level of secrecy that marks the culture of the barracks mirrors that of the thieves in Skinny's band. Secrecy maintains the foundation of group loyalty and the foundation of the Academy. Secrecy is supported with physical pressure and taunting.

The Jaguar, the focal point of secrecy, explains all of this to Gamboa. He explains it because he realizes that he no longer needs a group to sustain his personal identity but he does need the under-standing of a very well-respected officer like Gamboa. Jaguar realizes this after Arrospide identifies him as a squealer: "You're a traitor, a coward. . .you don't even deserve to have us beat you up." Jaguar realizes there is no gratitude from the group he created. He tells Gamboa the ultimate secret, that he killed the Slave because the Slave was an insult to masculinity, to the section, and to him personally. In response, the exiled Gamboa—the only officer of integrity—sets Jaguar free. The secret is kept because they both know that if the secret were revealed to the Colonel, the Academy would be destroyed.

Friendship

Because of the masculine discourse wherein a man is the s——— or the s———, the idea of friendship becomes charged with uneasiness and confusion. The intricacies of masculine loyalties betray the finer notions of what being a friend is all about. This begins with Alberto's reminiscences of his childhood. Having been invited to partake in soccer games, his recollections are a series of tales of bravado: broken windows, running from the authorities, having a girlfriend, or negotiating a steep cliff. At the academy, this intensifies. Boa defines friendship by fighting: defending the Jaguar, winning approval, and being tough. The Poet and Slave almost escape this cycle but the Poet, corrupted by barracks discourse, is too homophobic and full of subterfuge. Poet just wants Teresa.

The Slave admits that the Poet has won his confidence: "You're the only friend I've got. . .the only person I like to be with." Such an honest admission makes the Poet uneasy at several levels. Most immediately, it challenges the notions he holds about masculinity: "That sounds like the way a fairy says he's in love with somebody." But the Slave does not allow the discourse of the abusive barracks to intrude. Instead, he continues to be a friend—generous with himself and his cigarettes—and the Poet enjoys responding. Against his will, the Poet enjoys talking with the Slave without needing to perform with all the *machismo* required by Boa or Jaguar. However, the Poet has learned, from the Academy, that friendship must include pain and, perversely, he clings to this by not telling the Slave about stealing Teresa. Ironically, the only one hurt by the secret is the Poet.

Realizing the value of the Slave's gift, the Poet mourns him openly. Jaguar mourns him too, in his own way. Both young men have tasted genuine humanity in the Christ-like Slave. Poet admits all this to Teresa, proclaiming, "He was my friend." Worse than that, the Slave "thought I was his friend and I" was using him in the same way everyone else used him. The Slave gives self-knowledge to the Poet and to Jaguar. As a result, neither is the same nor are they able to run with the crowd.

Style

Narrative

Excepting a few geniuses—like Joanot Martorell and Victor Hugo whose *Les Miserables* Vargas Llosa read while attending the Leoncio Prado Academy—the novel before Flaubert and Faulkner, according to Vargas Llosa, is primitive. The novels of the nineteenth and early twentieth century carried out the project of realism and naturalism too well. They made the novel serve the function of documentation. Conversely, and Vargas Llosa has written on this many times, the modern novelist uses what the primitive novel documents—feelings, events, facts, etc.—to make art. As he says in *The Perpetual Orgy* "everything depends essentially on form, the deciding factor in determining whether a subject is beautiful or ugly, true false. . .the novelist must be above all else an artist, a tireless and incorruptible craftsman of style." The primitive novelist depended on plot and character to create mystery and suspense. The modernist uses narrative techniques like multiple viewpoints, vagueness, and nonlinear weavings of viewpoints to create a literary world.

In *The Time of the Hero*, Vargas Llosa successfully demonstrated his theory by weaving together four narrators into one plotline. By integrating the voices of Boa, Jaguar, Poet, and Slave, a truer representation of life in the academy forms. By complicating the narrative technique, Vargas Llosa enables the structure of the story to bolster the plot. For example, by failing to identify Jaguar as one of the four, the judging of Jaguar remains impossible until he reveals himself to Lt. Gamboa. In other words, the narrative technique contains the power of the narration in the novel instead of giving it to the reader.

The technique of multiple perspectives utilizes the Faulknerian mode of nonlinear presentation. From the beginning, while the drama of the final two months at the academy unfolds, various flashbacks provide depth to the main characters as well

as explanation to the importance of The Circle and the theft of an exam. The Slave has a flashback of moving; the Poet has a similar experience. Then there is a third flashback by an unidentified character which tricks the reader into believing it is either Slave or Poet. This confusion is not cleared up until the end. The confusion disallows an easy judgment of Jaguar. Instead, Jaguar, like Poet and Slave, reflects the environment of his upbringing. Using this technique bolsters the theme of secrecy as well as the confusing labyrinth of information each cadet masters according to the stature they have in their year. Jaguar, as undisputed master, even masters the narrative due to this secrecy as well as the lack of belief about the murder which accompanies his confession. Since the Poet has been favored as nearly a hero throughout the novel, the revelation that the Jaguar is the hero is not believable.

Plundering and Borrowing

In *Temptation of the World*, Efrain Kristal characterizes Vargas Llosa's literary technique "as a kind of amalgam of his own experience, literary works, other genres including cinema, and the research he has done around the world." It is no accident, therefore, that *The Time of the Hero* is rife with allusions and borrowings from other works. For example, a major influence on literature after World War II is existentialism and one novel in particular, *The Stranger* by Albert Camus, had a tremendous impact. Camus' novel concerns a murder committed by a man who found himself in a tense situation, bothered by the sunlight. Similarly, no one who has read Camus can miss the allusion to that famous Algerian murder scene when Jaguar beats a boy up for courting Teresa: "the sun broke into my head." There are obvious differences but the allusion is intentional.

Less recondite, the novel as a whole takes advantage, inexactly, of Vargas Llosa's own life experience. He was actually a student at the same military school. But that is where the resemblance ends. Instead, Vargas Llosa taps into an entire genre of boarding-school literature. Robert Musil's *Young Törless* also has a gang that tortures the weak and ends ambiguously. Another example of borrowing that looms over the entire work is the almost Oedipal family dynamic. Each character succeeds to the extent that he is able to overcome the emasculation his father performs on him. Jaguar's victory depends, in part, on the death of his parents. The Poet has enough personal vitality to negotiate survival in the world outside his mother. The Slave never transitions from the world of the mother to that of the father. This is the source of his slave nature.

Such utilization of other works of art borders on the post-modern. As Vargas Llosa explains in *Perpetual Orgy*, "Imitation in literature is not a moral problem but an artistic one: all writers use, to varying degrees, forms that have been used before, but only those incapable of transforming these plagiarisms into something deserve to be called imitators." The success of the modern novel is its ability to stand on its own while also tapping into literature that is already transcendent of place and time. Camus' *The Stranger* was never confined, as a primitive novel would be, to Algeria and, therefore, allusion to the novel is safe, whereas, allusions to novels read only in Peru would be lost.

Literary Heritage

Colonial Literature and Independence

Although the conquistadors destroyed the libraries of the Inca, intellectuals of Indian and Spanish descent tried to recover as much as possible of pre-Conquest Peruvian literature. The most formidable of such efforts was undertaken by Garcilaso de la Vega—known as El Inca Garcilaso. By his mother's side he was of royal Inca heritage and Spanish by his father. He put together several volumes of Incan legends in Spanish.

When the Spanish finally left Latin America in 1830, writers dabbled with the techniques of Romanticism before adopting the form of the realist novel as the best vehicle for national literatures. These Spanish American novels, the "novelas de la tierra" or Regionalist novels, describe Latin American landscapes and rural life in exhaustive detail. Examples of such novels include *Dona Barbara* by Romul Gallegos or *The Vortex* by Jose Eustasio Rivera. Once this literature began to mix with indigenous myths and Latin American writers learned about the European avant-garde, a uniquely Latin American literature was born. The first generation of modernist Latin American writers created their techniques in Europe and then returned home. While Latin American modernism was forming, the nationalists were winning the culture wars. Nationalists promoted the regionalist style arguing that modernism was inappropriate.

Modernism

In Europe, the first generation of modernists made contact with each other, the European modernists and the avant-garde. Argentinean Jorge Luis Borges, Guatemalan Miguel Angel Asturias, and Cuban Alejo Carpentier studied the Mayan collections at the Sorbonne in Paris and the British Museum in London. In the former, they met the leading surrealists, Andre Breton and Paul Eluard, and in the latter made contact with the Bloomsbury Group. Other Latin American writers would join this nexus until, finally, Gabriel García Márquez, Carlos Fuentes, and the young Mario Vargas Llosa arrived. As a group, they praised William Faulkner, Marcel Proust, John Dos Passos, Franz Kafka, Gustave Flaubert, and Jean-Paul Sartre.

The heritage of the modern Latin American novel, therefore, sees its origins in the realists and not in the varied forms of the Enlightenment or the Romantics. The primitive novel, whether written by Charles Dickens or Victor Hugo, concerned itself with capturing the events of life. Eventually, the modernists—James Joyce and Virginia Woolf—revealed a way out. However, it took Flaubert and Faulkner to make use of the pathway and they inspired the generation of writers known as "El Boom," the greatest period of Spanish-language literature since Spain's seventeenth-century Golden Age.

The Boom

Throughout the 1940s Borges announced to Latin America that, contrary to the belief of the nationalists, literary invention is good. This enabled an awakening of creativity. García Márquez wrote under the influence of Borges and Faulkner. In the 1950s, Vargas Llosa had concluded that writing in the primitive, regionalist manner kept the Latin American novel Latin American. Following Borges and García Márquez, Vargas Llosa decided that the novel could be freed of this confinement when it ceased to be Latin American and began to be a literary world independent of the reader's possession of a Latin American experience. The key was to use the narrator and, through narrative techniques, to realize that authors do not record, but create.

Two forces assisted the new energy in Latin American fiction. First, the tough literary agent Carmen Balcells was on the lookout for Latin American fiction. Seix Barral, the most prestigious Spanish-language publishing firm, listened to Balcell. The American publishing house Harper and Row wanted to cash in on the buzz surrounding Latin

American modernism and they were helped by a superb translator, Gregory Rabassa. The economic forces combined with the creative juices so that by the late 1950s, the boom began and everyone was reading fiction by Latin American authors.

Historical Context

Colonialism and Independence

During the sixteenth and seventeenth centuries, Lima, known to the Spanish as the City of Kings, served as the transition center for silver mined in the Andes and destined for Spain. With the fall of the Spanish Empire and the expiration of easily extractable silver, Lima declined. In the backcountry, the Indians were locked in a cycle of poverty that began with Spanish rule. Even in the 1990s, Indians form the peasant class of Peruvian society and Vargas Llosa notes a few of them in his book of 1962. The Indians are poor, malnourished, and during the 1990s wracked by cholera. Lima was renewed in the late nineteenth century when guano—bird droppings—were in demand due to their high concentrations of nitrogen, which is used in gunpowder. Peru had a huge supply of guano that it mined for the West. Chile, however, took the guano during the War of the Pacific (1879-1884) and Peru had to find other sources of economic sustenance.

Foreign investment helped Peru become a mercantile economy in the first half of the twentieth century. Peru exported copper, sugar, cotton, fishmeal, oil (until that too ran out), and wool. But as an export economy, Peru could not attract investors or create an industrial base. Therefore, much of its natural resources remained untapped; recovering from centuries of colonial exploitation proved impossible. This changed when the Cold War began and the West became interested in Peru. Still, foreign investment and deforestation (a.k.a. economic growth) did not accelerate until the last quarter of the twentieth century.

General Odriá

During World War II, Peru, on the side of the Allies, only declared war against Japan and Germany in 1945 (in order to be a charter member of the United Nations). Peru's willingness to participate in world affairs and the onset of the Cold War brought Peru neo-imperialist attention from the U.S. In 1945, José Luis Bustamante y Rivero won the presidency of Peru representing a coalition of leftist parties including the American Popular Revolutionary Alliance (APRA). Part of their program included land reform for the Indians. This legitimately elected democratic government was not defended by the United Nations or the U.S. when General Manuel Odriá, supported by the oligarchy and military, overthrew them. For eight years, the corrupt and brutal regime of Odriá, who became president in 1950 though his opponent did not appear on the ballot, marginalized the socialist elements and increased defense spending rather than resolve Peru's long-standing problems. During Odriá's reign, university campuses were full of military spies and social mobility was tied to patriotic military service. Odriá's defense spending included an extension of its territorial waters. This move angered the U.S., whose fishing fleet regularly used those waters, but Peru exercised this extension in concert with Chile and Ecuador. The U.S. did little but protest. Peru, under Odriá, also initiated several cooperative pacts with Brazil. It is in this milieu that Vargas Llosa places his novel *The Time of the Hero*.

In 1956, Odriá allowed elections and lost to Manuel Prado y Ugarteche who had been president during World War II. Ostensible democratic rule continued; real power remained the domain of the forty families who formed the oligarchy with the support of the Catholic Church. During the next open elections, Victor Andres Belaunde won by promising economic reforms. In the meantime, the socialist left had been invigorated by the success of Fidel Castro's communist revolution in Cuba in 1959. It seemed possible to repeat Castro's success throughout Latin America. In 1965, tired of waiting for land reform, 300,000 Indians revolted. In response, the military, no longer willing to stand quietly behind the oligarchy, took over the government. By 1968, a military junta under General Juan Velasco Alvarado created a distinct pattern of Peruvian socialism. The military instituted land reforms. By 1975, the landowning elite had been destroyed and 40% of the land had been transferred to cooperative or peasant use. Economic downturns discredited the junta and Belaunde returned as president in 1980. His attempts to reverse the junta's programs led to widespread protests and the rise of the Shining Path.

Peru's Population

As the heartland of the ancient Inca Empire, it is not surprising to find that the most numerous segment of the approximately 25 million Peruvians is

Compare & Contrast

- **1960s:** In response to the Cuban Revolution, a force of U.S. CIA-trained Cuban exiles invade Cuba unsuccessfully in 1961 (an incident known as ''the Bay of Pigs''). The U.S.S.R., to help defend its communist ally, tries to install missiles in Cuba. The U.S. refuses to allow the placement of missiles so close. The tense standoff in the fall of 1962 ends when the U.S. promises not to invade Cuba.

  Today: Although many governments have changed their policies, the U.S. maintains a trade embargo on Cuba. Cuba, meanwhile, has outlived its larger communist ally, the Soviet Union, and has sought trade and reconciliation with anyone, including the Pope.

- **1960s:** Much of Latin America adopts import substitution industrialization (ISI) economic theory after World War I until the 1960s. This protectionist policy encourages domestic production of items otherwise imported. Political instability fostered by the neglect of land reform issues lead to its demise.

  Today: Fujimori, having defeated Shining Path and furthered Belaunde's privatization schemes, has made Peru friendly to foreign (especially Japanese and U.S.) investors. The economy has grown and the disparity between the rich and poor has increased.

- **1960s:** To stem the flow of people to the West, East German soldiers ripped up the streets on the night of April 13, 1961, and the Berlin Wall was born.

  Today: The Berlin Wall has been down since 1989 but the reunification of Germany has proven costly and painful.

- **1960s:** Renegade priests throughout Latin America switched sides and began preaching 'liberation theology.' No longer supporters of the oligarchy, the priests sermonized against oppression of the poor and spoke favorably of Marxist reforms. Meanwhile, Pope John XXIII convened the Second Vatican Council to begin a reform of the Catholic Church.

  Today: Catholicism is still strong in Latin America although as economic conditions improve for more people, its followers are secularizing. Pope John Paul II has made huge strides in reforming the church and in breaking down barriers between Catholicism, the Eastern Orthodox church, other sects of Christianity, Jews, and Muslims.

Native American (45 percent). Mestizos, those of mixed European (mostly Spanish) and Indian heritage, make up the next 37 percent. Those who consider themselves white make up 15 percent of the population, and the rest is split mostly between those of African and Japanese heritage. Because of historical circumstances, 90 percent of the people are Catholic, and Spanish remained the official language until 1975, when Quechua joined Spanish as the official languages of Peru.

Economically, heritage means a great deal in Peru. Those who happen to have more European heritage also happen to claim more academic credentials and occupy the highest-paying jobs. These people make up the cream of Peruvian society and speak Spanish as well as another European language. By contrast, the Indians, who often do not speak Spanish let alone another European language, are relegated to peasant status, which borders on serfdom. They labor in agricultural industries or as sweatshop labor.

Just prior to embarking on his life in Europe, Vargas Llosa went on an anthropological expedition, visiting a tribe in the deep jungles of Peru. He was shocked, according to Rossman: ''I discovered that Peru was not only a country of the twentieth century. . .but that Peru was also part of the Middle Ages and the Stone Age.'' He reflected on this disparity in his widely celebrated second novel, *The Green House*.

Shining Path

The plight of the Indian peasants and their unanswered plea for reform found a new champion in the 1980s in the form of a militant Maoist organization, the Shining Path. They laid siege to the government and in the ensuing conflict, some 15,000 people were "disappeared." Meanwhile, Peru's highland during the 1990s became the number-one production source for cocaine destined for the U.S. Alberto Fujimori, who defeated Vargas Llosa in the 1990 elections, used his popularity to assume emergency powers. Using ruthless military tactics in the face of terrorist acts and reprisals, Fujimori's military—with U.S. aid through the War on Drugs program—routed the forces of Shining Path. By 1992, the leader of Shining Path, Abimael Guzman, was in prison and Fujimori continued to pursue free-market economics.

The Time of the Hero *examines the codes of conduct and secrecy instilled into Peruvian military cadets.*

Critical Overview

After reworking a mammoth 1500-page manuscript, Vargas Llosa found a publisher for *The Time of the Hero* with the most prestigious Hispanic publisher, Seix Barral of Barcelona. When the novel came out in 1963, having already been awarded one literary prize, Vargas Llosa proved that the recent international attention focused on Latin American fiction had not been misplaced. In Latin America, the novel—unlike many internationally acclaimed novels—was an instant bestseller. Critical reception has been wholly enthusiastic and ranges from appreciation for the subtlety of Vargas Llosa's social critique to his ability to utilize modernist techniques and further "El Boom." Some critics credit Vargas Llosa's novel with moving the boom in Latin American literature into its second wave. Carlos Fuentes heralded the boom with his 1958 novel, *Where the Air Is Clear,* and García Márquez's 1967 novel, *One Hundred Years of Solitude,* marked the start of the final wave.

In his acceptance speech for an award for *The Green House* in 1967, Vargas Llosa postulated that the writer is under obligation to help society improve by airing its dirty laundry. He believes that by exposing human failings in fictional form, people can better see what they need to do. As Charles Rossman says in "Mario Vargas Llosa's *The Green*

House: Modernist Novel from Peru," Vargas Llosa has always felt this way but *The Time of the Hero* "neither conveys a simple, didactic message nor recommends an explicit course of action." Still, Vargas Llosa's first novel was a huge success and more than verified his authorial theory: he had exposed military culture and they responded in kind.

"One thousand copies were ceremoniously burned in the patio of the school and several generals attacked it bitterly. One of them said that the book was the work of a 'degenerate mind,' and another, who was more imaginative, claimed that I had undoubtedly been paid by Ecuador to undermine the prestige of the Peruvian Army," Vargas Llosa recalls in a *New York Times* article, "A Passion for Peru." While the military was busy vilifying Vargas Llosa, critics were in raptures over the technical, specifically narrative, sophistication of the work. Jose Miguel Oviedo explores the prescience of Vargas Llosa's insight into the role of the military, showing that the author reveals the way in which military life "reproduce[s] itself, deformed and monstrous, on the other side of the social body. What allowed the military to survive destroyed the essence of civilian life, asphyxiating it under the hateful norms of imposition and supremacy that many times have been singled out as great regulators in the narrative world of Vargas Llosa.'' For Oviedo, the revelation of this insight makes the novel a moral one.

J. J. Armas Marcelo explains how Vargas Llosa uses secrecy as a technique to expose the military hegemony Oviedo sees exposed. Oviedo's two sides of society become, in Marcelo, the world of appearance and the world of secrecy. ''These two worlds are within the same forge of the narrative structure of the work, shaping, to a greater or lesser degree, the symmetry or asymmetry of the elements that constitute the novelistic whole.'' Not only does Vargas Llosa expose military culture but he immerses the reader in that culture by employing secrecy and ambiguity around the central crime in the novel.

Other critics have picked up on the bipolarity of Peruvian society as presented by Vargas Llosa. The novel, writes D. P. Gallagher, ''is never better than when it is showing how for young Peruvians social intercourse presupposes the jettisoning of one's best instincts.'' Raymond Williams says, ''The plot and structure makes inevitable an awareness of Peruvian society and a judgment of the characters' actions.'' Williams adds that Vargas Llosa's techniques successfully force ''adjustments in the reading process to understand. . .temporarily suspending traditional assumptions about'' how novels work. Sara Castro-Klaren notes that Vargas Llosa's characterization technique mimics the chivalric tale where characters ''often act under an assumed name or a disguised identity.'' The disguise, subsequently, turns out to be a truer representation of the character's real self. Thus, we remember Jaguar as the kingpin and not as the kind man offering to help an old friend.

Because of the candid way Vargas Llosa has admitted to being influenced by European existential writers as well as writers of the American South, critics have often attempted to make comparisons. Efrain Kristal compares *The Time of the Hero* to William Faulkner's *Light in August*, one of Vargas Llosa's favorites. Like Faulkner, Vargas Llosa's plot hinges on the revelation of ''a hidden fact at a particularly timely moment.'' R. Z. Sheppard says that García Márquez is Faulkner while Vargas Llosa is ''aesthetically, if not stylistically, [Peru's] Dreiser'' and his first novel ''was a brutal slab of naturalism.''

There were some negative reviews. Luis Harss and Barbara Dohmann characterize *The Time of the Hero* as obsessively ''realist.'' They view the novel as ''a desperate search for wholeness. A sort of vicarious return to the womb of a lost reality.'' Despite this early review, Vargas Llosa enjoys a positive reputation even though his subsequent works have not been ceremoniously burned. John Updike explains this continued favor, noting that ''the Peruvian man of letters, Mario Vargas Llosa, is almost too good to be true; cosmopolitan, handsome, and versatile, he puts a pleasant face on the Latin American revolution in the novel, and. . .makes everybody, even North Americans, feel better about being a writer.''

Criticism

Jeremy W. Hubbell

Hubbell has an M. Litt. from the University of Aberdeen and is currently pursuing a Ph. D. in history at the State University of New York, Stony Brook. In the following essay, he explores the way in which Vargas Llosa exposes the construct of military masculinity as it displaces machismo.

The Time of the Hero, with its militaristic anthem and its critical investigation of masculinity, puts one in mind of those stories which support the warrior code. Many early reviews said that the novel was anti-military but only because it showed the messiness behind the uniforms. In point of fact, the novel takes no position on the military—it simply describes how homosocial networks function within the very hierarchical environment of the military and reflect a preestablished hypocritical ideology surrounding the marriage institution. Each example of parenthood shown to us reveals a fractured state of marriage whose affect on the surviving boys is a further denigration of that institution and of women specifically. Vargas Llosa shows how military constructions of masculinity in mid-twentieth-century Peruvian culture spill over into civilian life and into the lives of young boys. The gender strategy of the novel is very specific: boys become men insofar as they reject feminine sensibilities, reject the mother who is also resented by the father. In such a divisive domestic atmosphere, the authoritarian nature of the military brings order and regulation first to masculinity and then to the household. Before reviewing the novel for the way in which it explores masculinity molded by the mili-

What Do I Read Next?

- In his second novel, *La casa verde* (1966; translation by Gregory Rabassa published as *The Green House* 1968), Vargas Llosa again took experiences from his own life and created a work about the whole of Peru. His visit with an Amazonian tribe as part of an anthropological expedition as well as his experience of a brothel in the town of Piura establish the basis for a meeting of two ends of Peruvian culture that seldom occurs. The novel begins when two nuns and a sergeant with his helpers steal two girls from the Aguaruna tribe but the girls escape.

- Vargas Llosa's acceptance speech in 1967 for an award for *Green House* has been published as *La literatura es fuego* (*Literature Is Fire*). In this speech, Vargas Llosa summarized his view of the writer. He said that the writer has an obligation to assist his society in whatever way he can. For him, this means that the writer must engage in constructive criticism with the society he inhabits.

- *Conversacion en la catedral* (1969; translation by Rabassa published as *Conversation in the Cathedral*, 1975) is the story of Santiago Zavala. Much like Vargas Llosa's other males, Santiago is expected to follow in his father's footsteps. The opposite happens when Santiago chooses to fraternize with the lower class in order to escape the corruption of his father's social group.

- Vargas Llosa underwent an artistic transition which is revealed in his 1973 novel, *Pantaleon y las visitadoras* (published as *Captain Pantoja and the Special Service*, 1978). While the artistic technique differs from the novels of the 1960s, the themes are familiar: the military and corruption. Captain Pantaleon Pantoja has been given special orders to go undercover and establish a prostitution ring to serve soldiers at the front. The army hopes to end rapes on civilian women in this way but they cannot be connected with trafficking in female flesh, so Pantoja cannot tell anybody who he really is.

- Using a bit of his own biography, Vargas Llosa's 1977 novel, *La tia Julia y el escribidor* (translated as *Aunt Julia and the Scriptwriter*, 1982), concerns a novelist who falls in love with his aunt. This novel explores, with humor, the struggles of the creative process.

- One of Vargas Llosa's most recent novels, *Death in the Andes* (1996), involves the Shining Path movement, Dionysian rituals, a witch, human sacrifice, mystery, and Peruvian society. The storyline focuses on the disappearance of three men from a village and the soldiers who investigate. The tale turns into a murder mystery and a panoramic depiction of late-twentieth-century Peru.

- The German academies of the early twentieth century served as the model for such institutions as the Leoncio Prado Academy. Robert Musil's novel *Young Torless* reveals the psychological torment boys inflict on each other in such high-stress academies. Although the protagonists are dismissed as mere boys, their mentality and behavior are not dissimilar from those of the army officers they revere.

- British schoolboys are just as capable of living out male fantasies as German, Peruvian, or American boys. William Golding said as much in his classic novel, *Lord of the Flies*. A nuclear war leads to the evacuation of Britain and a planeload of prep-school boys crashes on an island. Once there, the boys form two gangs and the gang representing primitive nature would have won had the adult rescuers been any later.

- The pressure placed on young men of the upper classes by their fathers is enormous, even in America. In *The Dead Poets Society*, by N. H. Kleinbaum and Stephen Haft (1989), rich boys are schooled in a stuffy atmosphere until a new English teacher, Mr. Keating, turns them on to great poets like Walt Whitman. They are so excited about literature as a result that they begin to break the rules in order to read poetry or to pursue love. Neil Perry would rather kill himself than live in his father's world where everything is serious and being an actor in a Shakespearean drama is outlawed.

tary, it would be instructive to note another highly militaristic culture and its literary component.

One of the major factors that brought about the end of the Great War was the threat of revolution at home. Germany's structural integrity, for example, received a challenge in the form of a working-class colony supported by the remnants of the navy in the north, and various pockets of Polish, Estonian, and Latvian nationalists inspired by Wilson's Fourteen Points and the Russian Revolution. There was also a remaining thread from the Russian Red Army. Chancellor Ebert hired men from the upper class with military training or those who had graduated from military academies and formed the Friekorpsmen to reestablish order—the army was full of the working class and could not be trusted. Their enemies were the disgruntled working classes dissatisfied with the existing order and anyone else who might have caused Germany's defeat. They pursued this goal vigorously from 1918 to 1923 but survived the non-war years to form the core of Hitler's SS. In his 1977 opus, *Male Fantasies,* Klaus Theweleit records his analysis of a cache of novels written for and about the Friekorpsmen in Germany.

The Friekorpsmen were elite soldiers, well trained, and ruthless in their mission. That the German State used force to put itself back together is not the issue but the mentality and identity they created to do this is interesting to anyone seeking to understand military regimes and their impact on gender roles. The Friekorpsmen, as Theweleit finds, are fresh young men (some just out of the academy) "whose 'manhood' was half-brutal and half-comical." They developed a subconscious wherein the communist and socialist women were not to be trusted but assaulted, raped, or just killed. Prostitutes were a tolerated necessity for letting off steam. The women to be revered and left nearly chaste were the "white women"—women of the upper class (oftentimes sisters) who supported the Friekorps mission and served as their nurses. Such sexual tensions fill innumerable novels written for and about Friekorps adventures. The hierarchical sexual taxonomy of the Friekorps melded well with Nazi ideals but the proposition that Theweleit offers showing that militaristic regimes accompany sexual politics helps us to relate the sexual elements in *The Time of the Hero* to the military manhood being formulated in Peru. Where civilian structures break down or appear to weaken and there is a self-regulating institution capable of resorting to force, that militaristic group absorbs civilian society.

Critic Jose Miguel Oviedo, in "On Vargas Llosa's Intellectuals and the Military," notes succinctly that the military "reproduce[s] itself, deformed and monstrous, on the other side of the social body. What allowed the military to survive destroyed the essence of civilian life, asphyxiating it under the hateful norms of imposition and supremacy that many times have been singled out as great regulators in the narrative world of Vargas Llosa." The relationship, as Vargas Llosa shows, is not a simple one. The political and economic disruption wracking Peru during the twentieth century—the loss in war or the weak position it holds on the world stage—lead parents to conclude that their boys are in jeopardy of emasculation. Rich parents send boys to the academy and poor parents hope to give their boys more opportunity. Once there, all the psychological tensions the boys have absorbed from their corrupt households—each of the main boys' parents have enormous marital difficulties—is played out on each other.

As with the Friekorps, the military authorities at the Leonicio Prado Academy feel, on behalf of Peru, that their existence is threatened unless they have a strong military force supporting the state. This goes beyond the Colonel's personal battles over the status of the academy. Rather, the military officers believe that Peru is ill-prepared in military terms because its boys are sissies, civilians run the country, and enemies surround the nation. Such is the discussion between Captain Garrido and Lt. Gamboa as the pivotal wargames are being set up. In sum, "it doesn't mean a damned thing to be a soldier in Peru any more." Little do they know that in a few years the military will run the country; for the moment, however, their efforts are achieving results. As if realizing their frustration, during the exercise a weak element among the cadets is eliminated. The cadet known as the Slave is killed because he failed to be a man. The struggle among the cadets over being able to be identified as a man reflects the larger societal tensions.

The other cadets arrived at the Academy as boys, almost women, and were immediately pounced on by the older boys and initiated. The Jaguar, however, "defended them. . .They were scared to death of the initiations, they trembled like women, and I taught them how to be men." The Jaguar taught them loyalty to the group, how to establish a black market, and how and where to have sex—at Golden Toes' who counts off the number of cadets that day and says, "I must be you guys' mascot." The Jaguar enforces group loyalty through cruelty and The Circle backs him up. A continuous example is made of the Slave who is incapable of profiting from the lessons he is offered in masculinity.

The Slave remembers a formative playground moment which seems to belie the Spanish title of the novel, the city and the dogs. He remembers how the other boys would surround him during recess: "their mouths were like fierce muzzles ready to snap at him." The boys shouted at him to "Go on" and cry. In frustration and fear, he did. Once he tried to fight back but his body refused to oblige and he was beaten. Since then he has given up but he sees in the antics of the cadets in the academy to what extremes such pack-like behavior can go. Boys form gangs just like men form armies. To be an integral member of a gang is to be a man.

Meanwhile, the boys carry their abusive mindset into the city where they meet with the approving glances of women and men. They define themselves first in the relationship where they saw their fathers act as men, by neglecting their mothers. Alberto shows happiness toward his mother when she relays money from his father; "his mother had not seen him naked since he had become a cadet." She had not seen him weak or dependent. He performed masculinity in a simple act of shyness. The mother, in response, ministrates to him. At every turn of the transition from boyhood to manhood there must be a woman to mark the progression. Whether it is the old woman who disapproves of Jaguar beating Teresa's friend, Jaguar's sexual initiation at the hands of his aunt, or Teresa's aunt wishing the man calling on Teresa were a real man, a soldier—old women regulate the definition of manhood. This is ironic given that Mr. Arana assumes it is the military that gives that designation. Thus, the brutalization Ricardo experiences in the academy was unnecessary—he just needed Teresa to love him and he knew that. The world of the dogs will not let him have such an easy life.

A man is formed in the city among the dogs. He becomes a man first to the degree to which he adopts a negative attitude towards his mother and secondly, the degree to which he can adapt and manipulate the politics of whatever group he is in. At first, a boy must master his neighborhood gang. An intensification of this is the military academy. In his interaction with the gang, part of his stature involves the way he interacts with women. On the one hand, he partakes in the traffic of illicit sex so that he can brag about having visited Golden Toes. On the other, he has to have a legitimate love interest. For Jag-

> " The gender strategy of the novel is very specific: boys become men insofar as they reject feminine sensibilities, reject the mother who is also resented by the father."

uar, Slave, and Poet, this interest is the virginal maiden Teresa who is awaiting rescue from her impoverishment. On the topic of Teresa, the sexual dynamics of masculinity are clearly delineated. Jaguar and Poet dream of being with her but not of having sex with her. In fact, to masturbate the cadets use nasty stories and the images of whores, and should Teresa's face appear they grow ashamed and limp. Boa, the most explicit, says intercourse is "more like a game" where the penis simply tries to penetrate chickens, llamas, fatboys, friends, whores, and enemies.

The parallels between the military elements in Peru and Germany are not exact. Every society with a military complex will have some of the components Theweleit sees in the Friekorps and that Vargas Llosa reveals in his tale about a military academy. The degree of infiltration, however, differs. In Peru, the military plays a larger role than it does, say, in America, even during the buildup of the 1980s when every boy aspired to be Rambo. The point is that in Peru, where hypocritical family members obsessed about the masculinity of their boys rather than fix their corrupted marriages, the military academy was viewed as a curative. The academy was seen as a "reform school" to which "half of them are sent here so they won't turn out to be gangsters. . .and the other half, so they won't turn out to be fairies." Instead, they turn out to be brutalized men with strange conceptions of loyalty, friendship, and sex, begging for the rigors and authenticity that men like Lt. Gamboa represent. When military dictatorships take over such societies, men such as Alberto or his father are not oppressed but, like the Friekorpsmen, get what they ask for.

The boom in Latin American literature as well as the political turmoil of twentieth-century Latin

America have been marked by male perspectives and male dictators. The central theme of *The Time of the Hero* is masculinity or how a boy in Peru becomes a man and what that means. Each primary character experiences molding masculine forces and similarly rejects maternal forces. The novel exposes the way in which masculinity works but no decisive criticism is advanced—that is for the reader to do. Masculinity has several operatives. First, although the principle is rife with irony and qualifications, ''a man has to accept the responsibility for his actions.'' He cannot squeal and he must pull his fair share of the group's weight whether that weight is a theft or a brawl. Second, he must be sexually active while preserving the good woman, his chaste wife. He can sleep around so long as he preserves and protects his family and makes his boy into a man.

Source: Jeremy W. Hubbell, in an essay for *Literature of Developing Nations for Students*, Gale, 2000.

Hilda L. Baker

In the following essay on Mario Vargas Llosa's novel The Time of the Hero (La cuidad y los perros), *Hilda L. Baker discusses the engrossment of the reader that the novel engenders, and what impact this has both on narrative structure and within literary theories of reader-writer constructed spaces.*

> *Reading is never a natural and innocent activity. The condition of the reader is to come after, to be constituted as reader by the repertoire of other texts, both literary and nonliterary, which are always already in place and waiting to be displaced by a critical reading. —Jonathan Culler*

In literary critical circles, a contemporary author's reputation customarily rests more on his recent works than on his earlier efforts, however well received they might have been. Too often we critical readers forget our initial enthusiasm for a work in our rush to assess more current pieces. We tend to establish hierarchies of quality across the works of a single author and, once such niches are fashioned, to ignore the works that occupy those artificial categories, concentrating instead on the creative publications as yet uncatalogued.

This, in brief, is the regimen to which all novelists, at least in Latin America, subject themselves as they write and continue to write. However, there are reactions to literature, and there are reactions. Of all of the novels published in Latin America since 1960—during the period called the ''boom''—no work that I know of has engendered more observable reactions than Mario Vargas Llosa's

La ciudad y los perros (*The Time of the Hero*). Outside Peru the novel was well received, was heralded as a literary happening, and was even awarded a literary prize in Spain where it was published. Meanwhile, some Peruvian readers, especially residents of Lima, were aghast to find in that first edition a street map of their capital city (the setting of the action in the novel) together with a photograph of Leoncio Prado Academy (a prestigious paramilitary school that exists to this day in Lima). These two visual aids, along with the vividly portrayed cheating scandal that comprises the central narrative sequence of the novel, were perceived as nothing less than a brash insult to ''the institution.'' Hence, with zeal worthy of any viceregal Inquisitor in colonial Spanish America, the cadets and officials of Lima's Leoncio Prado burned a pile of these ''illustrated'' editions in protest.

Those visceral responses to his work must have delighted Vargas Llosa, who remarked during a round-table discussion dedicated to *The Time of the Hero,* ''I do not admire novelists who keep the reader at a distance.'' Clearly, Vargas Llosa's book-burning readers suffered not from excessive detachment from the created reality, but rather from what Erving Goffman terms *engrossment,* ''the matter of being carried away into something.'' Such total involvement in a fictive world calls to mind that paragon of reader-participants, Don Quixote, who destroyed the puppet theater of Master Pedro (Part II, chapter 26) in his zealous efforts to assist damsels in distress (puppets though they might be). Cervantes' beleaguered knight and Vargas Llosa's incensed readers share a lack of aesthetic distance, that is, ''the reader's awareness that art and reality are separate.'' Yet it is involvement, not aesthetic distance, that is the hallmark of most accomplished narratives. In fact, Vargas Llosa attributes the generic supremacy and the novelist's primary challenge to the possibility of such engrossment: ''the novel is . . . the genre that installs the reader at the very heart of the reality evoked in the book. The author's obligation is to keep him there.''

My memory of the initial reactions to *The Time of the Hero,* together with my encounters with other texts in the intervening years, prompts this revaluation or re-vision of the novel. I want to focus particularly on this engrossment or involvement, to analyze what I perceive to be essential markers within the work that determine the reader's performance. As I begin the description of the reading process, I am reminded of Clifford Geertz's comment that ultimately critical reading is ''not an experimental science in search of law but an interpretive one in search of meaning.''

The primary conceptual vehicle for considering this involvement is the notion of framing. Although ''framing'' is a metaphor appropriated from the pictorial arts, it and its consequences are fundamental to fiction. Boris Uspensky's comments on the frame are useful to our understanding of the organization of a novel and the ways we learn ''how to be'' readers:

> We may say that the frame of a painting (primarily, its real frame) belongs necessarily to the space of the external observer (that is, of the person who views the painting and who occupies a position external to the representation)—and not to that imaginary three-dimensional space represented in the painting. When we mentally enter the imaginary space, we leave the frame behind, just as we no longer notice the wall on which the picture is hung; for that reason, the frame of a painting may possess its own independent decorative elements and ornamental representations. The frame is the borderline between the internal world of the representation and the world external to the representation.

Following this logic, we can say that the boundaries of the narrative world are marked (and thus enclosed) by the narrator of a novel. Indeed, it is the narrating function that provides the reader with a psychological orientation toward the events recounted therein. However, in fiction the narrator is also the nexus between interior and exterior, between the demands of the created reality and the expectations that the reader brings with him to the act of reading. It is the successful structuring of this frame that induces the reader to accept the norms and premises defining the interior coherence of a novel. What is more important, as Goffman points out, ''frame . . . organizes more than meaning; it also organizes involvement.''

Though we virtually take it for granted, the title of a novel is often one of the first clues to the quality and direction of the reader's conceptual involvement and properly should be considered integral to the frame of the work. The ultimate meaning of the title, replete with connotations that the work can lend to it, is necessarily completely perceived only after the reading experience. In the case of Vargas Llosa's novel, however, the title provides an essential clue to one of the primary organizational principles in the work, a clue that is deleted from the frame of the English translation. Conversations with the novelist after the publication of this novel reveal that he debated at length over the title (a fact that confirms, to some extent, the importance of

> " The reader's involvement points out the existence of growing gray areas, actions that defy categorization, social responsibilities that threaten individuality, and individual behaviors that menace the established social order."

even that one line). Initially the work was to be called *La moroda del héroe* (*The Hero's Dwelling*), whence the title for the English translation. Later that was changed to *Los impostores* (*The Imposters*), a more explicitly sarcastic reference to the problems treated in the novel. Finally, the Spanish edition was published with the title *La ciudad y los perros* (*The City and the Dogs*), a phrase, Monegal asserts, that highlights the tension between the characters and their environment (Monegal). Undoubtedly, that is one aspect of the significance of the title. I would suggest that, more than merely communicating a univocal message to the reader, the title as it finally appeared establishes very subtly the basic narrative format of the novel. Spatially, the episodes all occur either in the city or at the academy. The connection between the two major settings (ignoring the subsettings that actually exist within each) is always one of the ''dogs,'' the cadets now in their fifth year who reacted to their third-year initiation into the academy by organizing all manner of subterfuge against the other cadets and the school officials. The term *dog* would normally refer to the third-year cadets, but for the reader it comes to designate the small group of cadets who are involved in the cheating scandal that results in one cadet's death. Essentially, the fictive present includes all of those events that follow chronologically the theft of the chemistry examination (the event that opens the novel), and the central narrative sequence ends with the cadets' departure from the academy. The Epilogue of the novel focuses once more on two of the cadets (Alberto and the Jaguar) after they have left the academy, and affords the only projection into the future, into the lives of the characters beyond the academy.

Not only does the Spanish title circumscribe the spatial aspects of the novel; in its duplicating construction it also hints at the temporal skeleton of the work. In addition to the alternation between those episodes set in the city and those which take place at the academy, there is a corresponding alternation between episodes that advance the central narrative sequence (the cheating scandal) and others that provide social backgrounds for three of the cadets (Alberto Fernández, the Jaguar, and Ricardo Arana). Each of these episodes belongs to a fictive past remote from the central action of the novel. Somehow one expects such background information to provide clues to or causes for the fundamental problems set forth in the novel. But the reader's expectations are not fulfilled, for the details of each cadet's earlier life outside the academy seem to pertain to individuals that hardly resemble those whom we meet inside the academy. Each of the narrations terminates with the youth's decision to enroll at Leoncio Prado: three cadets, and three distinct reasons for subjecting oneself to the discipline and rigors of paramilitary life.

Before I suggest the results of Vargas Llosa's contrapuntal narration, let me specify those units that I am calling *episodes. The Time of the Hero* consists of two lengthy sections, each having eight chapters, and an Epilogue. Heading each of the long sections is an epigraph, which is yet another means of orienting the reader toward the novelistic world. Each chapter in turn is divided into numerous subsections separated from one another by the typographical conventions of blank spaces and (in the Spanish edition) the capitalization of initial words in the following section. Only the last chapter of Part I is of one piece; it recounts the field maneuvers (''war games'') during which Ricardo Arana is killed. Two of the chapters (chapter 4, Part I, and chapter 1, Part II) are divided into ten sections each. This organization into episodic sections within the larger chapter divisions facilitates the movement among multiple temporal and spatial settings.

The principal result of such temporal fragmentation is that the reader experiences a constant interplay between past and present, between actors in the primary setting (the academy) and others in the secondary location (the city). Throughout the novel the central narrative provides an axis around which all other events revolve. Flashbacks to earlier moments in the academic lives of these cadets and regressions to childhood memories both reflect the continuing problems provoked for cadets and officials alike by the theft of the examination. Through

this contrapuntal rhythm the stress is placed on simultaneity, on the shifting center of the fictive present and the confounding effects of such movement. The ultimate result is the blurring of temporal and spatial categories, the interpenetration of time and space. Sharon Spencer's summary of this process is relevant to the narrative organization of Vargas Llosa's novel:

> The spatialization of time in the novel is the process of splintering the events that, in a traditional novel, would appear in a narrative sequence and of arranging them so that past, present and future actions are presented in reversed, or combined, patterns; when this is done, the events of the novel have been ''spatialized,'' for the factor that constitutes their orientation to reality is the place where they occur.

It should be noted that this structural format and its effects are not unique to Vargas Llosa's first novel. In *The Green House* (1966) and *Conversation in The Cathedral* (1969), this technique achieves its fullest development and becomes almost a trademark of Vargas Llosa's narrative style.

Beyond the title, which simultaneously heralds the reader's involvement and, in this novel, initiates that process, there are other markers that shape and determine reader response in *The Time of the Hero.* At least one critic has noted certain resemblances between this novel and the detective story format; in fact, the work is best viewed in the context of one long literary tradition of the riddle or puzzle. Vargas Llosa refracts, even multiplies, the puzzle format until it not only contributes to the structural frame of the work but also affects the conceptual apprehension and ultimate interpretation of the novel. I would point out that this mystery/riddle/puzzle technique has received mixed responses from critical readers. Luis Harss, for one, regards it as bothersome and questions the effectiveness of such ''seductions'' of the reader. Harss goes so far as to assert that ''Vargas Llosa has the bad habit of witholding vital information.'' To his complaint I would reply that this organization and expositional technique is successfully integrated into the system of the narrative world and performs both structural and cognitive functions, both of which contribute to the reader's comprehension of the significance in the novel. In Jonathan Culler's terms, however, my expectations of the work are tempered by a textual repertoire different from that of Harss.

Despite the fact that the initial impetus of the action is a misdemeanor (which the reader ''witnesses'') that results in the death of Ricardo Arana and prompts the investigation that occupies the second half of the novel, the most significant aspects of the puzzle frame relate only tangentially to those events. Structurally, the work draws on detective fiction but in fact moves well beyond the conventions of that genre. It is important to indicate that even in this little novel the conventions of detective stories, since they should be familiar both to reader and author, serve as another orienting device and lead the reader to expect "an ongoing continuity of values." The detective story frame, however, is relegated to the background about midway through the novel. Thereafter the invention of the work takes over, and the reader is guided through a process that (in any good mystery) would lead to the resolution of conflicts, the answers to persistent questions, and a stabilized outcome favorable to most of the characters.

In *The Time of the Hero,* however, ambiguity and paradox remain unresolved. Rather than being lucid sources of illumination for the reader, the narrators in this novel generate conflicting meanings. Instead of one meaning or one truth, the novel provides clues to a range of meanings and possibilities of truth that call attention to the means by which we each arrive at our own personal worldviews. Ultimately, we are reminded in multiple ways that "imaginative truth" is often "a lie which [we] value."

Returning to the puzzle frame, I want to present two examples of the questions that arise within the first two chapters of the novel, answers to which are only revealed in later chapters. The first concerns the identity of one of the characters, not himself a narrator, but rather an optic through which the reader views a sequence of events in the fictive past. After the initial narration of the theft of the examination, the scene changes to Salaverry Avenue in Lima and the childhood of someone named Ricardo. Until that moment the reader has encountered no character by that name. Nor is anyone revealed to be Ricardo in the section that follows. Among the characters we have met, it could be the Boa, the Jaguar, or the Slave, none of whom has been called by his given name up to that point. Before the end of chapter 1 we can eliminate the Boa (we think), since he performs a narrating function of his own utilizing first-person pronouns. The final identification of this Ricardo is made at the end of chapter 2, when the Slave gives his name as Ricardo Arana.

I would underscore the fact that there is one characteristic of that first episode that persists throughout all of the sections devoted to the Slave.

The key to the temporal position of these episodes is to be found in the phrase "El Esclavo ha olvidado" ("The Slave has forgotten") and its variant "El Esclavo no recuerda" ("The Slave doesn't remember"). The latter we find in the section of chapter 1 that details the initiation of the cadets, told indirectly through the eyes of the Slave before the reader can positively identify him as Ricardo Arana. In a world of shifting narrators and settings, the reader begins to search for connections between the episodes, and an observant reader would probably note the similarity between the two phrases. By the time we are certain of his identity at the end of chapter 2, we have already encountered one oblique indication of Ricardo Arana's schoolboy nickname.

Each of the sections concerning Ricardo begins with the phrase "The Slave has forgotten" (my translation), which, by virtue of its recurrence, becomes part of the narrative frame. (In a like manner, those episodes dealing with Alberto's childhood tend to include an early reference to Diego Ferré Street, and thus promote the reader's orientation within the narration.) It is interesting that one element of this framing device does not survive the translation process. Semantically, the frame remains unchanged; syntactically, it is altered. The translator chooses to maintain the narrative past tense in English and thereby deletes the verbal aspect of the phrase. (Compare "The Slave *has* forgotten," my translation, with "The Slave *had* forgotten," copyrighted translation.) What always follows these present-tense assertions by the omniscient narrator is a past-tense account of Ricardo's childhood. What, then, is the vantage of this narrator? There must be something in the fictive present that permits him such statements as preludes to past narrations. The last episode in Ricardo's childhood recounts the day his parents announced their decision to enroll him at Leoncio Prado. That section is in the same chapter (Part II, chapter 1) in which the other cadets learn of the Slave's death. The end of his childhood memories coincides with his premature death at the academy. Therefore, if we maintain the introductory phrase in its present tense, the collective memories take on the repetitive qualities of a litany, a linguistic device that blends with the ongoing narration and still provides reinforcement of the cadet's death.

The second riddle, one which for many readers is unsolved until the Epilogue, is the identity of the narrator who is the friend of Skinny Higueras and is always around Bellavista Plaza. We encounter this first-person narrator in chapter 2, Part I. What we learn about him in this initial section is that he has a brother, that his father is dead, and that he studies with a girl friend named Tere. Again, a process of elimination is put to work, and we recall that, given the characters we have met, this person could be the Boa (unlikely) or the Jaguar. By this stage in the novel, however, it is clear that Alberto is to be one of the principal figures, and certain intuitions (perhaps a desire to give him a voice of his own instead of hearing him through the mediating omniscient narrator) lead us to suspect that these passages may be yet another view of Alberto's childhood. Conflicting information should allow the reader to eliminate this possibility by chapter 5 of Part I. This narrator's father is dead; Alberto's is not. The confusion is promoted by Alberto's involvement with Teresa. Are there two Teresas? Unlike the accounts of Ricardo and Alberto's childhood (both narrated in the third person), this account continues well into Part II of the novel. The final installment in this third series of flashbacks is in chapter 7, Part II. Like the other two, this series also terminates with the narrator's decision to enroll at Leoncio Prado. Still, no positive identification has been confirmed by information available in other sections of the novel. The reader can only surmise who this narrator might be. The Epilogue solves the riddle unequivocally; in fact, the answer is in the very last section of the novel. The Jaguar and Skinny Higueras are once again together, reviewing each other's experiences. This time the narration is third rather than first person, and the Jaguar's name is mentioned near the beginning of the section. The pieces fit; the problem is solved. Yet the solution to the narrator's identity only highlights how little these accounts of childhood experiences actually contribute to our understanding of the cadet's conduct within the academy. The vital information, which in a detective story would set one's mind at rest, only renews—even heightens—the reader's perplexity in *The Time of the Hero.*

For observant readers, however, this narrator's identity should come as no surprise. There are at least four clues lodged in other sections of the novel, minor details which, taken together, establish rather clearly that Skinny Higueras' friend is the Jaguar. First, Alberto admits at one point that he attended La Salle Academy before he came to Leoncio Prado. The first-person narrator reports seeing the La Salle students on the street one day. This narrator could not be a La Salle student, therefore not Alberto. Second, Alberto is from Miraflores (an upper-class suburb of Lima) while the narrator

seems to be from Bellavista. We can thereby eliminate Alberto. (Now the reader's task changes from elimination to confirmation.) Third, the Boa remembers that the Jaguar once said that he was from Bellavista, and in the same breath comments that the Jaguar uses his head and feet to fight. Fourth, the description of the Jaguar during the initiation emphasizes his fighting style (head and feet). The first-person narrator reveals that his brother taught him to use his head and feet to fight.

Such a detailed inventory of clues and counterclues might seem to digress from the central concern of framing and involvement. But it is precisely the presence of the detective-story frame and its operational modes with which the reader is familiar that encourages this quest for clues.

There is at least one more characteristic of the narrative frame in Vargas Llosa's novel that does not survive translation. I present this because I believe that it may be the key (at least *a* key) to the overt reactions to the publication of the novel in 1962. Earlier I mentioned the liturgical opening of all of the sections that recount Ricardo Arana's childhood. Recall that in Spanish the use of the present tense at the beginning of those passages creates a temporal texture that is absent from the passages cast in the narrative past tense in English. Several critics have noted that tense alternation—even indiscriminate usage of verb tenses—is a hallmark of Vargas Llosa's style. In *The Time of the Hero,* Vargas Llosa's tense alternation is not at all random or without purpose. There are, in fact, specific instances of narration in the present tense, passages that describe recurrent scenes (dawn and reveille at the academy, chapter 2, Part I) or present elements of the setting that may exist outside of the novel (the description of Diego Ferré Street). In the following paragraph, which is the translator's version, consider the perceptual effects of substituting the present tense which Vargas Llosa himself used, for each of the italicized past-tense verbs:

> Diego Ferré Street *was* less than three hundred yards long, and a stranger to it would have thought it was an alley with a dead end. In fact, if you *looked* down it from the corner of Larco Avenue, where it *began,* you *could* see a two-story house closing off the other end two blocks away. . . . At a distance, that house *seemed* to end Diego Ferré, but actually it *stood* on a narrow cross street, Porta. (my emphasis)

Induced to accept the immediacy of the scene by the use of the present tense, the reader accompanies the narrator on a walking tour of Diego Ferré Street, not merely a setting for Vargas Llosa's novel, but rather an apparently "real" neighborhood into which one might venture at any time. In the first edition of the novel, this attitude on the reader's part, or the facilitation of this attitude, was reinforced by the inclusion of the city map. This contrast between verbal tenses establishes the transcendence of the setting and, at the same time, endows the events with a presence and presentness that they might not otherwise display.

The product of this narrative technique is a double-edged sword. Clearly, the reader is drawn into the world of the novel because of this strategy. It also enlists the reader's capacities to visualize, thereby rendering the novelistic space more vivid. However, such a technique also leaves open the possibility of some spatial projection beyond the realm of the novel, beyond the covers of the book or the boundaries of the reader's imagination. For the cadets and officials of Leoncio Prado, the implied resemblance (and explicit coincidence) between Vargas Llosa's academy and their own prompted an indignant public reaction designed (I would assume) to deny any such relationship. Their demonstrated disapproval served more to spotlight than to suppress that social critical possibility.

In *The Time of the Hero*, the success of Vargas Llosa's presentation depends, in large measure, on the careful implementation and integration of familiar structural frames that induce the reader into involving himself in the created reality. The narrative stress patterns established by means of the alternating rhythm create an interface, a zone of significance between two poles of meaning. The reality of the novel is not a Manichean world; neither the reader nor the characters are permitted the luxury of all-or-nothing attitudes, of yes-or-no answers. The reader's involvement points out the existence of growing gray areas, actions that defy categorization, social responsibilities that threaten individuality, and individual behaviors that menace the established social order. The moral and social dilemmas that circumscribe the world portrayed in the novel are paralleled in the reader's experience by the subversion of the initial behavioral frame (the detective story, mystery, or puzzle) that was to guide him through the novel. While the frame overtly involves the reader in the novel, it also covertly affords him the experience of implication and deception that are integral to the social drama comprising the work.

Vargas Llosa manages to station both the characters and the reader in an interstitial, interstructural zone in which we struggle to discern the shadows and specters of behavioral demands that will operate within the world of the fictive academy and, perhaps, could extend beyond the experience of this novel. The narrative frame erected in *The Time of the Hero* is sustained by means of multilevel alternation: third-person narration vs. first-person narration, fictive past vs. fictive present, past-tense verbs vs. present-tense verbs, the city vs. the academy. Reading Vargas Llosa's novel becomes a retrogressive procedure in which the reader is required to retreat three steps and retrieve lost pieces of the chain of events in order to advance four steps in pursuit of the accelerating action. Frustrating and puzzling though it be, it is the reader's involvement in and response to the operational modes of the work that permit him to perceive its "configurative meaning." As Wolfgang Iser summarizes, the novel is "the genre in which reader involvement coincides with meaning production."

Source: Hilda L. Baker, "'Of how to be and what to see while you are being': The Reader's Performance in The Time of the Hero," in *Texas Studies in Literature and Language,* Vol. XIX, No. 4, Winter, 1997, p. 396.

Roy A. Kerr

In the following essay, Roy Kerr examines the narrative structure of Mario Vargas Llosa's novel La cuidad y los perros (The Time of the Hero) *by examining Vargas Llosa's use of the character Boa, whose narration combines generalities and specifics to reveal not only the story of the novel, but aspects of the writer himself.*

All narrative has a minimal pair of essential characteristics: "the presence of a story and a story teller". Narrators assume diverse voices and perspectives in telling their tales. A useful distinction in this regard is between narration in which the narrator is present as a character, and that in which the narrator is absent from the tale. When a protagonist narrates a portion of a work of fiction, part of our notion of his character arises from the perception of him in the role of storyteller. Analysis of a fictive narrator's comments may reveal aspects of the character's personality that remain hidden in the accounts of his actions in the novel.

Mario Vargas Llosa's first novel, *La ciudad y los perros* (1963), has been described as a work in which "Few characters are delineated in any great depth." Nevertheless, two figures, Jaguar and Boa, reveal much about themselves in their roles as narrators in the novel. Their commentaries, com-

> **"** Were it not for his monologues, Boa's second self would remain as hidden from the reader as it is from the academy cadets. As a narrator who ostensibly directs his comments only to himself or to his dog, he reveals that he can act responsibly and demonstrate affection."

prising about twenty percent of the work, provide refracted yet substantive self-portraits. In the wealth of critical studies devoted to the novel, the figure of Boa generally has been neglected. A review of the statements that he makes as storyteller reveals a characterologic complexity and diversity that merit critical consideration.

Boa Valdevieso narrates thirteen segments of the novel. Initially his monologues provide the reader with scabrous but factual generalizations about cadet life at the Leoncio Prado Military Academy. In detailing specific incidents, such as Cava's abortive attempt to steal a chemistry exam, and Richi's death while on manoeuvers, Boa's visceral reactions serve as an emotional barometer that reflects his function as "una directa emanación de la masa colegial." Valdevieso's disparate narrations thus reveal a careful structuring that combines generality with specificity in a cohesive story unit.

In addition to contributing significantly to plot development, Boa's monologues reveal much about the teller of the tale. At the novel's outset, he is described from outside the frame of his own narration: "un cuerpo y una voz desmesurados, un plumero de pelos grasientos que corona una cabeza prominente, un rostro diminuto. . . ." Later he is observed in action as a potential buyer of Alberto's pornographic novelettes, and as the lone defender of the beleaguered Jaguar. Almost everything else that the reader learns about his character is gleaned from his own narrative.

For his peers, Boa is epitomized in a word: "bruto." This characterization is corroborated partially by his own testimony. He himself recalls participating in an incident in which cadet Cava rapes and kills a chicken. Later, he confirms his attempt to aid his companions in the sexual assault of a cadet, and reveals that he deliberately broke the leg of his dog.

Boa's worship of the *machismo* code represents another facet of his brutish nature. Although he fears and at times hates Jaguar, he admires him as "un hombre de pelo en pecho." He glories in exertion that causes him to perspire heavily, since "así transpiran los machos." Commenting on the exasperated weeping of his French instructor, Fontana, he reveals that for him, the shedding of tears implies effeminacy: "Y entonces cerró los ojos y cuando los abrió, lloraba. Es un marica." In contrast, instructors who respond forcefully to students, such as Lieutenant Gamboa, are viewed distinctly. After enduring harsh physical punishment ordered by the Lieutenant, the cadet's impression of the officer differs markedly from his view of Fontana: "Gamboa es formidable, ahí nos dimos cuenta de lo formidable que es Gamboa."

Boa's racist commentaries reveal another aspect of his churlish nature. As a *cholo*, he views Whites with scorn: "Los blanquiñosos son pura pinta, cara de hombre y alma de mujer, les falta temple." The *serranos*, Indian mountain peasants, receive even greater abuse. His comments on their attributes form a litany of ignorance and prejudice:

Los serranos son tercos. . . Los serranos son un
    poco brutos
Yo creo que el colegio le contagió las pulgas a la
    perra, las pulgas de los serranos.
Los serranos son bien hipócratas. . . .

The cruelty, *machismo*, and racism that Boa's own musings verify as aspects of his nature appear to paint a sordid portrait of a sadistic personality. Nevertheless, the cadet's own words reveal another side of his character, one that contrasts with, and to some extent ameliorates the brutish element. His cruelty, for example, is mitigated by his ingenuous, puerile nature. In this respect, his narrative has been compared to that of "la voz primaria y anormal del Benjy de *The Sound and the Fury*." Symptomatic of his naïeveté is a fear of spirits and goblins. When plans go awry, he rationalizes that "El diablo se mete siempre en todo con sus cachos peludos." He believes that his dog can protect him from ghosts: "me hubiera gustado tenerla a mi lado en la glorieta, para espantar el miedo: ladra perra, zape a los malos espíritus.'' Additionally, he associates Jaguar's features with a devil: "El diablo debe tener la cara del Jaguar, su misma risa y además los cachos puntiagudos." When causal explanations are lacking, the cadet's reaction is one of superstitious fatalism: "Estaba visto que nadie se salvaba, ha sido cosa de brujería."

Such childlike superstitions and fears are those of an immature or underdeveloped mind that does not always act according to logic or reason. Viewed in this light, Boa's demonstrations of brutality assume a different dimension. He rarely commits premeditated acts of violence; rather, they result from anger, frustration, or from attempts to please other cadets. During the aforementioned attempted rape of a cadet, for example, Boa's monologue reveals that the incident was initiated by Jaguar, Rulos, and Cava. His role, though not laudatory, was limited to the physical restrainment of the victim.

Although he participates in the humilliation of Professor Fontana, his monologues reveal that Jaguar and Cava were the major instigators of these incidents. Boa expresses satisfaction at the baiting, yet feels compassion for the victim: "A veces da compasión, no es mala gente, sólo un poco raro... Es un buen tipo."

When he actively participates in violence, such as the maiming of his pet, Boa accepts responsibility for his actions: "Le di la mala, con intención." He likewise expresses sincere regret for his deed: "Es un animal bien leal, me compadezco de haberla machucado."

Valdevieso's prejudice against *serranos*, outlined above, stems from impressions gained by witnessing the results of a beating inflicted upon his step-brother by Indians: "Será por eso que los serranos siempre me han cído atravesados." Despite an inculcated hatred, Boa comes to respect *el serrano* Cava as a friend. Boa, the oaf presumed idiot, is conscious of this radical change in attitude, and chronicles it in his monologue: "Pobre serrano, no era mala gente, después nos llevamos bien. Al principio me caía mal, por las cosas que le hicieron al Ricardo [su hermanastro]." Ultimately, the *cholo* proposes friendship to the Indian: "Y después yo fui hasta la cama del pobre Cava y le dije: 'oye, quedamos como amigos.' Y él me dijo: 'por supuesto'". At this juncture, the brutish cadet transcends his base nature, forming a bond of human affection based upon personal experience rather than on untested stereotypes.

Like many characters in *La ciudad y los perros*. Boa is not what he appears to be at first glance. His peers view him as a brute whose strength and atavistic cruelty are to be feared, respected, or exploited. Were it not for his monologues, Boa's second self would remain as hidden from the reader as it is from the academy cadets. As a narrator who ostensibly directs his comments only to himself or to his dog, he reveals that he can act responsibly and demonstrate affection. Dramatic irony is achieved through the reader's dual perception of Boa's bestial façade together with a glimpse of the isolated cadet who loves his scraggly pet and who remains loyal to Jaguar and Cava.

Prior to its publication, one of the tentative titles proposed for *La ciudad y los perros* was, *Los impostores*. While Boa's narrative provides essential information with regard to plot, the revelation of aspects of the cadet's own personality that surface in his narration also verifies his need to conceal his inner feelings, his hidden self, and to become yet another imposter in the savage environment of the Leoncio Prado Academy.

Source: Roy A. Kerr, "The Secret Self: Boa in Vargas Llosa's La ciudad y los perros," in *Romance Notes,* Vol. XXIV, No. 2, Winter, 1983, p. 111.

J.J. Armas Marcelo

Constructed on the basis of an apparently chaotic duality of time and space, Mario Vargas Llosa's novel *The Time of the Hero* could be assigned, as José Promis Ojeda correctly has done, to the "long literary tradition characterized by the presence of the 'enigma.';" Generally, the plot of the novel corresponds to the following episodes:

a) Theft of an exam at a military school (the Leoncio Prado).

b) Collective punishment. Weekend leaves are suspended for the cadets in the section in which the robbery occurred until the thief or thieves should be discovered.

c) Denunciation of the thief by a cadet of his section before the military authorities of the school.

d) The informer's violent death during military maneuvers.

e) A new accusation of the presumed assassin by other cadets before the same military authorities.

f) Pertinent investigation is begun.

g) The investigation is suspended. The military authorities determine that the cadet's death was an accident.

> One deduces from this criticism that the author at times loosens the reins of discourse, because the text becomes the master of the situation, because the story itself becomes the agent that forges its own strategy."

But going beyond the simple boundaries of a superficial reading of the plot—in which "the city" and "the school" appear as the central spaces of the narration—other darker, more profound, more functional and more labyrinthine worlds emphasize the ambiguous characteristic of *duplicity* (personal, temporal, conceptual and functional), so that the same characteristic will be the center of contradiction, the grounds for two opposite poles, for two strata that fuse together and split apart simultaneously and constantly during the narrative process. This gives rise to a dual structure which is bipolar, oppositive and presented in a clear process of diminution that will continue fragmenting into two halves, always smaller as conceptual units—those levels that we are discovering and analyzing in the novel.

The *asymmetry* of the formal structure that Vargas Llosa utilizes in the novel has been pointed out with some insistence, as if—on managing as he pleases a great number of technical elements—the arbitrariness of the author exercised complete dominance over it and unbalanced the narrative discourse with marked anarchy. One deduces from this criticism that the author at times loosens the reins of discourse, because the text becomes the master of the situation, because the story itself becomes the agent that forges its own strategy. On the other hand, there are those who point out the constant presence of the author suffocating his creation, the actions of his characters and the way in which episodes and protagonisms are arranged within the novel. Nevertheless, it is here, at this exact point of conceptual confluence, that I see that Mario Vargas Llosa has tried to situate the narrative totality: *between ambiguity and determinism*. This conceptual duality accentuates even more the standard of bipolarity that sums up the novel at whatever level one tries to arrive at analytical dissection. It is quite possible that, during the first phase of creation, Vargas Llosa did not insist rationally on this two-dimensional process, but that the process of creation itself included within its essence the project of rupture with a single, linear dimension.

On one hand, Luis Harss classifies Vargas Llosa as a novelist "stubbornly deterministic and antivisionary," incapable of forcing his characters to overcome those situations which "determine" that his "individuals . . . are lost in the density of their environment. There are no persons, but rather states of consciousness that are manifest only through the situations that define them." In the same vein, Rosa Boldori, determined to analyze the novel through the prism of magical and one-dimensional fate as deus ex machina, catalogues *The Time of the Hero* as a "novel of environmental determinism": chance, accident, fate decide the actions of the characters.

On the other hand, José Miguel Oviedo, one of the most profound critics of the works and literary personality of Mario Vargas Llosa, observes that it is liberty—at times conditioned by the environment or by situations in which social pressure exerts its power, at times dissolving itself nervously in the doubt of the characters—that will make of *The Time of the Hero* an existential novel, one that frames within its interior the humiliating conditioning of rules and collective environments and the irrational rebellion of those who, placed in a determined "situation," dodge the difficulties and freely choose the best personal way to escape the labyrinth. It is, then, in that "mixture of two totally different philosophies: social determinism and existentialism," perceived by McMurray, that the factor is rooted which forces the characters many times to configure as luck or ambiguity (but by their own will) those actions or reactions that function as key elements in *The Time of the Hero*. The same factor, independently of the strings that the author controls through the complicated mechanism of creation, forces each concept in *The Time of the Hero* (attraction or rejection, confinement or dissociation) to provoke its opposite, makes each concept function in the role of its opposite in order to contrast the problematic and maladapted personalities of the protagonists and to define them in bipolarity, in the symbiosis of violence and serenity, of appearance and secrecy, the fusion that marks within the novel the pendulum-like movement taking it from one concept to another, from one pole to its opposite.

We understand that chance is not, then, the key element in the total conformation of *The Time of the Hero,* and that, at the same time, it does not structurally exercise any organizing function in the narrative discourse. Neither is it possible to establish adequate, serious and profound analytical consequences starting from the unidimensional suppositions of deterministic criticism. It would seem much more coherent to examine the structural functionality of a work from the point of conceptual bipolarity of the opposing contexts. In this sense, two distinct worlds move within the novel: the world of appearance and the world of secrecy, areas to which we have referred earlier. These two worlds are within the same forge of the narrative structure of the work, shaping, to a greater or lesser degree, the symmetry or asymmetry of the elements that constitute the novelistic whole.

If we enumerate now, analytically, the characteristics of the first eight chapters of the novel (part one), we will observe that these proportionate, symmetrical, objective characteristics shape an interior world which responds to secret codes, to different readings of the world of appearance. As an inherent consequence of these same characteristics, there flows, in this first part of the novel, a fundamental concept in which criticism has not placed sufficient interest: secrecy. If we examine part two of the novel, the second eight chapters, we will observe in it characteristics opposite to those indicated in the first part of the novel. Here reign subjectivity and spontaneity, that is, the denunciation which wears down the secret passages of the clandestine world of the cadets, a subterranean world with its own laws, with codes of honor created in the image and likeness of their organizers. Critical analysis determines that in the first eight chapters the action is somehow moved along by a personal and collective consciousness which respects to the greatest extent those secret codes that shape the world of the cadets. No other person in *The Time of the Hero* will have access to this clandestine world, because only the cadets have the ability to be absolutely knowledgeable of the rules of their world; only they, within their different personalities, can consent to and complete the secrets which they themselves offer in order to shape and constitute a different world, distant, opposed to that of appearance with rules imposed from without, at first from a familial basis and later from the school's military basis.

Consequently the code of values of the cadets is basically supported by *secrecy:* all the cadets are, to some extent, accomplices of all the clandestine acts of the Circle; they all participate in its benefits and its prejudices. But the cadets, as a group, merit a more profound study, in this case, with respect to their behavior. Without a doubt they are the group of actors that has the most meaning in the work. The world of *The Time of the Hero* is completely tinged by pressure from the cadets who act as the real, the only protagonists in the story. Around them revolve action and relationship; they direct the dynamism of the narrative discourse, marking the point of action and the counterpoint of relationship; they impose their perspective. Other characters in the work, who are many times only excuses to explicate the plot that connects the adolescents, are arranged in relation to the cadets and their behavior; they will be the ones actually responsible for their action, for the choice of their "situation." They are, finally, the authors of a secret code of values, of their secret world, a world closed, blind, without the solution of continuity, a world which connects them with a universe created by themselves, first, in order to escape family pressure, then second, to make fun of military rules. Their vital motives will impose themselves through the course of the narration, and finally they (except the propitiatory victim, the Slave) are the ones capable of fleeing toward maturity, that relative independence of individual liberty (Alberto, Jaguar . . .). They are the ones who arrange and disarrange, who choose and who feel disdain, who keep silent or denounce. The cadets take it upon themselves to emulate their elders (familial and military) upon breaking those binding pacts that demand the internal coherence of the group, and they avoid, up until the moment of denunciation, the conceptual counterpoint of treason. They are the sardonic witnesses of family discord, of which they will take advantage, and the silent accomplices, the mute shapers of the apparently strict world demarcated by military rules. They themselves are responsible for internal disagreements, the victims also (the Slave, for example) of the deeds which individual sentiments end up imposing upon the collective code, upon their apparent and fictitious camaraderie.

Thus, the cadets themselves will dissolve their secret world. After Alberto's denunciation before Lieutenant Gamboa (part two, chapter three) will come the discovery of that clandestine world the cadets have concocted and the consequential dismantling of the values which, for the cadets, constitute manliness: the escapes (*contras*), the cigarettes, the alcoholic drinks, the thefts, "business," the violent sexual world of masturbation and bestialism. That denunciation is based on one of the principal events of the novel: the death of the Slave. Denunciation and vengeance are products of the same youthful strategy. When Alberto denounces the Circle's activity, he emphasizes the secrecy of school life:

> "They drove [the Slave] crazy, they bullied him all the time, and now they've murdered him!" . . . Alberto said. "The officers don't know anything about what goes on in the barracks."
>
> "Everybody in the Academy smokes," Alberto said aggressively . . . "The officers don't know a thing about what goes on."
>
> "Pisco and beer, Lieutenant. Didn't I tell you the officers don't know what's going on? The cadets drink more in the Academy than they do when they're on pass."
>
> "Who killed him?"
>
> "The Jaguar, Sir, the leader. . . ."
>
> "Who is the Jaguar" Gamboa asked. "I don't know the nicknames of the cadets. Tell me their right names."

Furthermore, the cadets, as a collective entity, not only carry out the complicated mechanisms of the content, nor are they limited to manipulating only the functionality of the anecdote: upon analysis, there exists a gradual parallelism between the internal coherence of the cadets' world—which, I repeat, is founded on secrecy—and the proportionality of the formal structure of *The Time of the Hero*. On attending the disintegration of the code of values they secretly invent and sustain in the Academy, we are attending the slow dissolution of the proportionality of the formal structure of the novel, still prevailing in almost all of part one. As long as the collective codes of the adolescents remain intact and their content is respected by the cadets, we can speak of the proportional equilibrium of the novelistic structure; as a counterpoint, it will be from the basis of the dissolution of those codes—which have made possible the union between the cadets and their secret world—that the proportionality, the certain regularity in the structural levels of the novel, disintegrates in order to give way to the formal incoherence of the structure. Thus it can be determined that the concept of secrecy exercises a structural function in *The Time of the Hero*.

When does the regularity, the structural proportionality of the novel, begin to crack? Two episodes mark the boundary of this rupture: first, for personal reasons, Ricardo Arana, "the Slave," denounces the theft of the chemistry test (part one, chapter six). The collective complicity breaks down, and, sec-

ond, the same Arana suffers a fatal accident during military maneuvers (part one, chapter eight). But these are only conjectures, and only the collective complicity has broken down here. The cadets and the reader will not realize, until much later, that those two episodes are marking the beginning of the dissolution of the honor code, precipitating motives and countermotives, accusations and denunciations that finally will bring about the disintegration of the secret world of the adolescents. It will be from the point of the news of the Slave's death (part two, chapter one) that the novel's plot, moving toward its denouement, shows us—to us the readers and to the officials of the school—the secret world of the cadets. Simultaneously that process of conceptual dissolution will influence directly the structural parameter of the work. The irregular behavior of the principal group of actors in the novel leads simultaneously to an irregular structure at formal levels.

This functionality of the concept of secrecy in the formal structure of the novel constitutes, without a doubt, one of the fundamental characteristics and, at the same time, one of the most outstanding stylistic features of *The Time of the Hero*.

Source: J.J. Armas Marcelo, "Secrecy: A Structural Concept of The Time of the Hero," in *World Literature Today*, Vol. 52, No. 1, Winter, 1978, p. 68.

Frank Dauster

In the following essay on Mario Vargas Llosa's novel The Time of the Hero (La cuidad y los perros)*, Frank Dauster discusses the relationships between history and literature and the varying interpretations of reality they may engender.*

The relations between history and literature have concerned man since he first developed what might be called a historical consciousness. Aristotle has said:

> It is, moreover, evident . . . that it is not the function of the poet to relate what has happened, but what may happen—what is possible according to the laws of probability or necessity. The poet and the historian differ not by writing in verse or in prose. The work of Herodotus might be put into verse, and it would still be a species of history with meter no less than without it. The true difference is that one relates what has happened, the other what may happen. Poetry, therefore, is a more philosophical and a higher thing than history: for poetry tends to express the universal, history the particular.

Now certainly no historian would accept Aristotle's hierarchy, nor, probably, his distinction into particular and universal. It is not at all certain that

Aristotle meant this distinction in the bald terms cited. The fact remains, however, that the historian and the social scientist deal in the collection and interpretation of verifiable data, whereas the novelist, poet or dramatist is usually totally unconcerned with such phenomena. How then may these areas be related? In what way is literature valid as source material for non-literary investigations? And, to go a step further, in what way or ways do the literary critic and the historian share an interest in literature?

It is obvious that much criticism and many critics share no such interest at all and would reject such questions as invalid. The New Critics, for example, and formalist criticism in general are remote from such matters. But few of us are exclusively formalists, and nearly all of us sometimes read for other purposes. Usigli's *Corona de sombra* is a most interesting experiment in dramatic form and stage technique; it is also, and this must not be forgotten, an attempt to interpret all Mexican history after the French Intervention in the light of the events of that Intervention and the brief Empire. Clearly, there is here an area of considerable mutual concern.

Corona de sombra has been subjected to criticism by historians because of Usigli's tinkering with verifiable fact. Without resuscitating the old chestnut about how historical is a historical novel, it is fair to say that Usigli commits virtually every sin in the literal-minded historian's catalogue. He alters chronology, attributes invented ideas and speeches to historical figures and, in general, recreates history in a highly idiosyncratic fashion.

> He cometido diversas arbitrariedades e incurrido en anacronismos deliberados, que responden todos a un objeto. Por ejemplo, Pío IX sólo alcanza la aceptación de la infalibilidad pontifical después del 70, y en mi pieza habla de ella en 1866. Vista a la distancia, reducida a las cuatro presurosas y heladas líneas de los mortuarios enciclopédicos, y amplificada por la memoria y la actualidad, la gran acción, la línea maestra de la vida de Pío IX es ésa. Su obra en definitiva es haber contrarrestado en lo posible la pérdida del poder temporal de la iglesia con el reconocimiento de los dogmas. Dudo que pudiera reprocharse a un sonetista el encerrar su tema en catorce versos, y este procedimiento me parece teatralmente intachable. ¿Qué es Pío Nono sino el símbolo original de la infalibilidad del Papa?

The fundamental opposition is made clear in a "Carta crítica" by Marte R. Gómez, published in the same volume, in which Gómez holds the position that literature must at all times be literally faithful to recorded history. Usigli's answer denies this pettyfogging approach and spells out his belief

> **Rather, I suggest that the novel, the play, the short story and the poem may be sources of crucial insights into the complex reality of the world about us."**

in the function of the writer when he speaks of "la historia, que desatiendo en el detalle, pero que interpreto en la trayectoria del tiempo."

Obviously, Usigli's point of view is that the writer is a trustworthy interpretor of reality. This does not seem to me as potentially dangerous a thesis as might at first appear. We do not suggest that the artist is the one source of revealed truth in regard to anything, but certainly his perspective on reality is an important one. Who better than Quevedo makes us shudder at the grim spectacle of a high culture in decline, a great empire falling into ruin? In our own South, long before the nation realized the enormity of racism, Faulkner captured the complex social relations racism produces. These are only two of the giants who have captured the spirit of an epoch or a culture, who have shown reality from an admittedly partial but nonetheless valid point of view, but they illuminate the point. Nor need the works be of such stature; the astonishing plays of the Rosas period would be an invaluable source to the historian of Argentina. If, to return to Aristotle, tragedy is "an imitation of an action that is serious, complete and of a certain magnitude . . . ," is not all art an "imitation" of some portion of the artist's world? Is not literature truly a mirror of the world, if we speak of the giants such as Cervantes or Shakespeare, or at least a partial vision of reality, in the work of any serious artist?

There are important applications of these notions when we deal with the work of such younger writers as Mario Vargas Llosa. Students of his novels repeatedly refer to them as microcosms. It would be a serious error to regard a novel such as *La ciudad y los perros* as some sort of marvelous code which would explain for us the vagaries of things Peruvian, but the book undeniably contains much which is important in this respect: hostility toward the *serranos*, the frivolity of the bourgeoisie, urban poverty, the intransigent self-seeking of much of the military. There are implications for all Latin America: the rigidly defined social classes and inveterate *machismo* are only two examples.

But these are all, to use Aristotle's term, particulars, and it might be argued that there is something in *La ciudad y los perros* which transcends the particular. We may well be appalled at a monstrosity such as the Colegio Leoncio Prado, but it does exist, and its governing officials chose to burn publicly a thousand copies of the novel. But the benighted gentlemen who saw fit to respond in the time-honored fashion of the closed mind to what they considered an attack on their institution, were completely mistaken. Ironically, the real significance of the novel is more drastic still. The arsonists may have been correct when they maintained that it was not literally true; but the literal truth of the Leoncio Prado is secondary to the higher truth which is undeniable, the spiritual horror which no amount of book burning can hide. Whether those responsible were in any way connected with the coup which ousted the government of President Belaúnde Terry is unknown, but when Vargas Llosa portrayed all Lima as a military establishment, he accurately captured the spirit of the city's ruling caste.

It is in this sense that *La ciudad y los perros* speaks of Aristotle's universals. As Emir Rodríguez Monegal has said of "The new novelists," "Their novels are mirrors and, at the same time, anticipations." Lima is, for Vargas Llosa, a regimented inhuman society which forces even its youth into a moral and intellectual straightjacket: "Así, la historia de un grupo de adolescentes se convierte en una radiografía de la crueldad en las relaciones humanas y por extensión de la sociedad que la justifica como parte de su entrenamiento necesario. De un modo u otro se reconoce que los jóvenes deben ser duros porque la vida es dura, implacables porque la sociedad empuja a los débiles y los aplasta." This is, after a fashion, Horatio Alger in reverse; innocence is exploited and the traditional values mocked. It would perhaps not be too exaggerated to see the novel as the destruction of the myth of bourgeois education. Rodríguez Monegal has written eloquently of the falsification of honor which lies at the heart of *La ciudad y los perros,* of the manner in which all the characters are alienated and driven to adopt behavior which is essentially contrary to their natures. He has spoken of the work as an allegory of honor, of "códigos y contracódigos." The moral corruption which permeates the novel speaks to the heart of the problem.

But how may the historian utilize this material? There is the obvious danger that he suffers from misconceptions about the nature of literature. In a recent article in the *New York Times Book Review,* John Lukacs said that

> the novelist's description of certain contemporary scenes is often first-rate historical evidence. I have often thought that Stendhal's . . . description of Waterloo in *The Charterhouse of Parma* ought to be required reading in our military colleges, since it is such a powerful corrective to abstract schemes of battle orders, as well as to the false image of the 19th century battle being one long melee of brightly uniformed soldiers, punctuated by the flashes of bayonets, the sabers of cavalry, and the Beethovenian sound of cannon in the background.

But this is not the point; literature is not some sort of documentation. Lukacs is closer to the mark when he states approvingly that Lampedusa's *The Leopard* "tells us more about the 1860 'revolution' in Sicily . . . than what most liberal historians tell us." But what are we to make of his astonishing assertion that "the artistic task of the historian is greater [than that of the novelist], because his restrictions are greater?"

This is a radical misunderstanding of what literature is all about, a disregard for that which is most characteristic of art, the process of artistic creation. It is not, however, my purpose to debate hierarchies of creative value, whether Aristotelian or Lukacsian. Rather, I suggest that the novel, the play, the short story and the poem may be sources of crucial insights into the complex reality of the world about us. There is probably no better means to understand many of the causes and certainly the fundamental fact of the Mexican Revolution than Yáñez' *Al filo del agua.* Yáñez, Rulfo, Fuentes, Paz and two or three others ought to be required reading for anyone who wishes to study Mexico from any point of view or any discipline, simply because they are enormously illuminating perspectives on the very complicated fabric of Mexican reality. They are not statistics and cannot be substituted for statistics, but it is doubtful that any amount of statistical or archival research will ever give the insight into Mexican reality which we receive from their work.

It would be naive not to recognize that the novelists themselves are cognizant of this aspect of their work; the social commitment of younger Latin American writers is notorious. Vargas Llosa has stated, "Creo que ambos—el intelectual y el creador—deben ocupar un puesto en la lucha pro la liberación nacional, en cuanto ciudadanos." The key words here are ''en cuanto ciudadanos''; Vargas Llosa distinguishes between the artist as artist and the artist as citizen. It would be erroneous to infer that he and his generation are writing political or social tracts. On the contrary; the artist is a perpetual noncomformist who will be critical of *any* social or political organism.

> Es preciso . . . recordar a nuestras sociedades lo que les espera. Advertirles que la literatura es fuego, que ella significa inconformismo y rebelión, que la razón de ser del escritor es la protesta, la contradicción y la crítica. Explicarles que no hay término medio: que la sociedad suprime para siempre esa facultad humana que es la creación artística y elimina de una vez por todas a ese perturbador social que es el escritor, o admite la literatura en su seno y en ese caso no tiene más remedio que aceptar un perpetuo torrente de agresiones, de ironías, de sátiras, que irán de lo adjetivo a lo esencial, de lo pasajero a lo permanente, del vértice a la base de la pirámide social. Las cosas son así y no hay escapatoria: el escritor ha sido, es y seguirá siendo un descontento. Nadie que esté satisfecho es capaz de escribir, nadie que esté de acuerdo, reconciliado con la realidad, comentaría el ambicioso desatino de inventar realidades verbales. La vocación literaria nace del desacuerdo de un hombre con el mundo, de la intuición de deficientias, vacíos y escorias a su alrededor. La literatura es una forma de insurrección permanente y ella no admite las camisas de fuerza. Todas las tentativas destinadas a doblegar su naturaleza airada, díscola, fracasarán. La literatura puede morir pero no será nunca conformista.

But the serious writer does not come easily to this position, nor is he simply a gadfly. Vargas Llosa has given testimony of the internal tensions created by this double vocation.

> Pero entiendo que en el caso del creador se plantea un desgarramiento irremediable, ya que en el creador el elemento determinante no es nunca racional, sino espontáneo, incontrolable, esencialmente intuitivo. Y el escritor no puede poner ese elemento al servicio de nada de una manera premeditada. En cierta forma, el creador se plantea así una verdadera duplicidad, o por lo menos una terrible tensión: quiere ser fiel a una determinada concepción política y al mismo tiempo necesitaser fiel a su vocación. Si ambas coinciden, perfecto, peso si divergen se plantea la tensión, se produce el desgarramiento. No debemos, empero, rehuir ese desgarramiento; debemos, por el contrario, asumirlo plenamente, y de ese mismo desgarramiento hacer literatura, hacer creación. Es una opción difícil, complicada, torturada, si se quiere, pero imprescindible.

I suggest that precisely in this tension, we may find invaluable intuitions about the nature of Latin America today. These intuitions are radically different from those we find in the novels of forty years ago, which are often closer to sociological studies than to literature. As Rodríguez Monegal has pointed out, the new novelists ''han concluido de una vez

por todas con el realismo documental, con la novela de la tierra, con la denuncia social de tipo panfletario, con la escisión maniqueísta del mundo en personajes buenos (los explotados, siempre) y personajes malos, con la mediocre prosa de altas intenciones.''

Again, we must not confuse the perspective on the world which we find in these younger writers with some sort of preachment. No one will ever understand what literature is until he learns the lesson which Kitto points out: ''When therefore we say that the Greek dramatist was an artist, we are not using a tired platitude meaning that he preferred pretty verses and plots to ill-made ones; we mean that he felt, thought and worked like a painter or a musician, not like a philosopher or a teacher.''

The new novelists are just such artists, and their works are artistic wholes. Not only is it ludicrous to attempt to abstract information from the plots while ignoring the fact that these plots form part of a work of art; such a procedure overlooks the fact that in the form, too, there is meaning. Vargas Llosa's predilection for the chivalric novel is little short of notorious. This is not simply a matter of pardonable aberrant criticism, but a vital link in his creative process. His fascination is rooted in the effort to capture the whole of reality:

> Lo que más sorprende al lector en las novelas de caballería, es la habilidad del narrador para capturar la realidad a todos sus niveles. Ahí vemos transcurrir la vida cotidiana de la Edad Media . . . estas novelas, escritas en un lenguaje a veces bárbaro, son como tentativas de abarcar la realidad a todos sus niveles, pretender decirlo todo, quieren abarcarlo todo. Yo creo que las mejores novelas son las que se han acercado a esta posición, es decir, las que expresan las cosas desde todos los puntos de vista que se pueden expresar. . . .

Is this not what *La ciudad y los perros* or *La casa verde* are really all about, a *total experience*? Complexity may be captured only through complexity. Vargas Llosa's use of different techniques for different characters, the intricately interwoven plot strands, the wildly mercurial and almost irrelevant chronology, and the deliberate withholding of crucial pieces of information, may all be literary tricks, but they are tricks which help the reader to capture the spirit of a whole society through the microcosm of the Colegio Leoncio Prado. Vargas Llosa has said that the best novels ''convierten la lectura en una experiencia del mundo.'' This experience of the world, expressed through the artist's capacities, gives us an unrivalled intuitive perception of the reality around us and it is a source of rare insight. This is the real value of literature to the historian of the social scientist: not as documentation, but as a source of intuitions, of revealing insights into the fabric of the writer's world. Insofar as the critic or the historian would perceive the nature of our world, not through a mass of accumulated data but through the revealing perception of which the artist is supremely capable, so they share a common interest, whatever other professional concerns may also lead them to literature. As Joseph Sommers has said so aptly, "the novelist is somehow connected with history, . . . by channels of intuition, psychology or spirit he participates in his times. Paradoxically, however, the extent to which he respects his craft, treating the novel as an autonomous creation, is the degree to which he may convey indirectly a significant interpretive commentary on his times."

Source: Frank Dauster, "Aristotle and Vargas Llosa: Literature, History and the Interpretation of Reality," in *Hispania,* May, 1970, p. 273.

Sources

Castro-Klaren, Sara, *Understanding Mario Vargas Llosa,* University of South Carolina Press, 1990.

Gallagher, D. P., "Mario Vargas Llosa," Oxford University Press, 1973, pp. 122-43.

Gerdes, Dick, "*The Time of the Hero* : Lost Innocence," in *Mario Vargas Llosa,* Twayne Publishers, 1985, pp. 33-52.

Harss, Luis, and Barbara Dohmann, "Mario Vargas Llosa, or The Revolving Door," in their *Into the Mainstream: Conversations with Latin-American Writers,* Harper, 1967, pp. 342-75.

Kristal, Efrain, *Temptation of the Word: The Novels of Mario Vargas Llosa,* Vanderbilt University Press, 1998.

Marcelo, J. J. Armas, "Secrecy: A Structural Concept of *The Time of the Hero,*" in *World Literature Today,* translated by Mary E. Davis, Vol. 52, No. 1, Winter, 1978, pp. 68-70.

Oviedo, Jose Miguel, "The Theme of the Traitor and the Hero: On Vargas Llosa's Intellectuals and the Military," translated by Richard A. Valdes, in *World Literature Today,* Vol. 52, No. 1, Winter, 1978, pp. 16-24.

Rossman, Charles, "Mario Vargas Llosa's *The Green House*: Modernist Novel from Peru," in *The Modernists, Studies in a Literary Phenomenon: Essays in Honor of Harry T. Moore,* edited by Lawrence B. Gamache and Ian S. MacNiven, Farleigh Dickinson University Press, 1987, pp. 261-74.

Sheppard, R. Z., "Caged Condor," in *Time,* February 17, 1975, pp. E3, 84.

Vargas Llosa, Mario, "A Passion for Peru," in *New York Times Magazine,* November 20, 1983, pp. 106, 108.

————, *The Perpetual Orgy: Flaubert and Madame Bovary,* translated by Helen Lane, Farrar, Straus, 1986.

Williams, Raymond Leslie, "The Beginnings," in *Mario Vargas Llosa,* Ungar, 1986, pp. 19-38.

Further Reading

Allende, Isabel, *Of Love and Shadows,* Bantam Books, 1988.
   Allende brings a feminist challenge to both the masculine world of Latin America and the Boom. *Of Love and Shadows* takes place in a Latin American country gripped by a military dictator. A wealthy woman, Irene Beltran, and a Spanish exile's son, Francisco Leal, fall in love but discover a crime which puts their lives at risk.

Bronte, Charlotte, *Jane Eyre,* Scholastic Paperbacks, 1996.
   One of the first novels to investigate the struggles of a youth against circumstances is Bronte's *Jane Eyre* (originally published in 1847). Jane struggles through a boarding-school situation where there is a hint of some of the physical abuses associated with twentieth-century boarding-school stories.

Ehrenreich, Barbara, *Blood Rites: Origins and History of the Passions of War,* Henry Holt, 1998.
   Ehrenreich, who wrote the foreword to the University of Minnesota Press edition of Theweleit's *Male Fantasies,* has been a leading contributor to American histories of sexuality. In *Blood Rites,* Ehrenreich argues that humans developed war to deal with the anxieties of self-consciously being a part of the food chain. This argument is then used as a foundation to explain why modern efforts to achieve peace are so difficult.

Fuentes, Carlos, *Where the Air Is Clear,* Noonday Press, 1971.
   The first novel of El Boom, Fuentes' 1958 story indicts Mexican society by discussing its post-revolutionary reality. An epic of Mexico City urban history, Fuentes weaves together the biographies of zany characters—including an Aztec god—to unlock the Mexican psyche.

García Márquez, Gabriel, *One Hundred Years of Solitude,* Harperperennial Library, 1998.
   Perhaps the most famous novel of the Latin American Boom, García Márquez's 1967 masterpiece perfected the magical realism style. The novel records the history of post-colonial Latin America through the fantastic struggles of the Buendia family.

Gibson, James William, *Warrior Dreams: Violence and Manhood in Post-Vietnam America,* Hill and Wang, 1994.
   Gibson goes undercover to visit gun camps and affiliates of militia groups. He finds military and fascist fantasies lurk in the hidden compounds of these far-right groups even in America.

Oviedo, Jose Miguel, "The Theme of the Traitor and the Hero: On Vargas Llosa's Intellectuals and the Military," translated by Richard A. Valdes, in *World Literature Today*, Vol. 52, No. 1, Winter, 1978, pp. 16-24.

Oviedo discusses the consistency with which Vargas Llosa employs the dichotomy of intellectual and military men in his fiction. The regularity with which this theme occurs leads Oviedo to conclude that this dichotomy is important to Peruvian culture and to Vargas Llosa personally. Somehow, this dichotomy must be resolved peacefully since both are intrinsic to Peru's culture.

Puig, Manuel, *Kiss of the Spider Woman*, edited by Erroll McDonald, translated by Thomas Colchie, Vintage Books, 1991.

Originally published in 1976 as *El beso de la mujer arana*, *Kiss of the Spider Woman* remains the most famous novel by Puig—a member of the Boom generation condemned in his home country of Argentina for his overt homosexuality. Two men are holding a conversation in jail: the first is Molina, an apolitical homosexual; the other is Valentin, a young socialist revolutionary outraged by Molina's sexuality. By the end of the novel, they have fallen in love and switched places and perspectives.

Swanson, Philip, *The New Novel in Latin America*, Manchester University Press, 1995.

Swanson analyzes the Boom in Latin American literature by showing how it came about and who the major figures were. This account takes away the surprise of the Boom by showing who influenced Fuentes, Vargas Llosa, and García Márquez.

Theweleit, Klaus, *Male Fantasies*, Polity Press, 1987.

Theweleit examines the papers and libraries of leading Friekorpsmen to expose the sexual tensions which accompanied their warrior ideology. He places their sexual politics in the context of Fascism and its heritage of the European history of sexuality.

Vargas Llosa, Mario, *Pez, en el agua (A Fish in the Water: A Memoir)*, Farrar Straus & Giroux, 1994.

Vargas Llosa records his experience as a presidential candidate and reflects on his life. He tells of the disgusting nature of back-stabbing that accompanies political campaigning as well as the story of his journey from boy to man.

Valley Song

Athol Fugard
1995

Athol Fugard's *Valley Song* premiered in Johannesburg, South Africa in August, 1995. The playwright himself directed the production and played two of the play's three characters: The Author, a figure modeled on Fugard himself, and Abraam Jonkers, the elderly "coloured" farmer who represents the "old" South Africa. Fugard repeated this theatrical tour de force when the play reached America, in a production by the Manhattan Theatre Club at the McCarter Theatre in Princeton, New Jersey in October, 1995. Both performances were warmly received by audiences and critics, several of whom expressed gratitude that Fugard was still writing intense, meaningful dramas about the lives of ordinary South Africans, even in the post-apartheid era.

Since the playwright had built his career over four decades of writing about the injustices of apartheid and state-mandated racial segregation, there was some concern when apartheid officially ended in 1992, and Nelson Mandela, a black leader, was elected president in 1994, that Fugard may have run out of things to say. However, as Jack Barbera observed in the *Nation,* "*Valley Song* is as timeless as it is timely, a story of the old fearful of change and the young with their hopes and impatience, and of a teller of stories."

Like most of Fugard's plays, the plot of *Valley Song* is quite simple, and less important than the secrets it reveals about its characters are the themes it presents its audience. The play contains two

stories woven into one. In the first, a young, black South African girl decides to leave her elderly grandfather behind on their farm in the Sneeuberg Valley so she can escape to the city and pursue her dreams of becoming a famous singer. The other story concerns an aging white South African playwright who is prepared to leave behind the ''artificial'' world of the theater and urban life and move himself back to his origins in the farmland of the Karoo. His days of planning and dreaming about the ''Glorious Future'' are nearing an end just as the young girl's are beginning, and *Valley Song* is really the tale of the torch of hope passing from one generation to the next—a bold and magnificent gesture by a man whom many critics have dubbed one of the greatest living English-language playwrights.

Author Biography

Athol Harold Lannigan Fugard was born June 11, 1932 in Middelburg, a small village in the semi-desert Karoo region of South Africa. His mother, Elizabeth Magdalena Potgieter Fugard, was an Afrikaner who could trace her ancestry back to the earliest Dutch settlers of 1652. His father, Harold David Fugard, was a South African with English and Irish roots. At his grandmother's request, the boy who would one day become his country's most famous playwright was named Athol after a former British governor of South Africa, the Earl of Athlone.

When he was three years old, Fugard's family moved to Port Elizabeth, where the playwright has since spent most of his life. In his introduction to *Boesman and Lena and Other Plays*, published in 1978, Fugard describes his adopted hometown as ''an almost featureless industrial port on the Indian Ocean. . .assaulted throughout the year by strong southwesterly and easterly winds.'' Port Elizabeth, Fugard explains, is a city of hundreds of thousands of people—blacks, whites, Indians, Chinese and ''Coloured'' (mixed race) citizens who represent every socioeconomic level. Growing up, Fugard witnessed almost daily the injustice of racial segregation under South Africa's cruel policy of apartheid. Despite its featurelessness, harsh weather, and culture clashes, however, Fugard proudly claims,

''I cannot conceive of myself as separate from it,'' and several of his plays are set in and around Port Elizabeth.

Fugard's father, a musician who led a number of jazz bands, had lost a leg in a childhood accident. Shortly after the family relocated, a lifetime of depression and physical ailments overtook him. In Port Elizabeth, the elder Fugard spent much of his time either drinking heavily or sick in bed. Elizabeth Fugard, meanwhile, operated the St. George's Park Tearoom. Fugard described his father in a 1982 interview for *New Yorker* magazine as a man ''full of pointless, unthought-out prejudices.'' He considered his mother, on the other hand, to be completely color-blind. At the Tearoom, she hired a number of black waiters, and one of them, Sam Semela, became Fugard's closest childhood friend and one of the greatest influences on his life and later career.

One night when his mother was away, Fugard received a call from the nearby Central Hotel. His father was passed out drunk on the floor of the hotel's bar. Young Athol asked Sam for his help, and the two went to the hotel to collect his father. The boy had to ask permission for Sam to enter the whites-only bar, and was humiliated as he walked out past the staring eyes of strangers with his drunken father on Sam's back. The incident, along with Sam's kind treatment of Fugard as an innocent white child in a world that abused its black citizens, became the basis for Fugard's 1982 play *Master Harold. . .and the Boys.*

Though Fugard read constantly and wrote occasionally as a boy, he did not become an artist early in life. After elementary school he studied automobile mechanics on a scholarship at Port Elizabeth Technical College, and later attended the University of Cape Town, majoring in philosophy and social anthropology. He dropped out of school before finishing his degree, hitchhiked the length of the African continent, then, penniless, took a position onboard the *S.S. Graigaur* as an apprentice seaman. Two years later Fugard came ashore back home in Port Elizabeth, determined to become a writer. He worked for a while as a journalist, then met and married Sheila Meiring, an actress working in Cape Town.

Fugard and his new wife founded a theater company, the Circle Players in 1957, then moved to

Johannesburg in 1958, where he took a job as a clerk in the Fordsburg Native Commissioner's Court. In the Court, Fugard helped process blacks accused of violating South Africa's "Pass Laws" and witnessed firsthand the terrible atrocities of apartheid. Fugard lamented to the *New Yorker,* "It was just so awful and ugly. We literally disposed of people at the rate of one every two minutes. There was no question of defense—the evidence was rigged. It was like a sausage machine."

Abandoning his clerk's job, Fugard became a stage manager for South Africa's National Theatre Organization and began writing plays in earnest. His first real success was *The Blood Knot* (1961), a play about two South African half-brothers, one black, the other coloured but able to pass for white. Fugard himself starred in the production, something he has done almost continuously ever since.

The Blood Knot set the stage for nearly all of Fugard's later work. Most of his plays are intimate, personal portrayals of tragic events in the lives of two or three characters. Very often his plays contain mixed casts (black, white, and mixed-race characters), and they are all set against the difficult social and political environment of his native South Africa. Plays such as *Hello and Goodbye* (1965), *Boesman and Lena* (1969), *Sizwe Banzi Is Dead* (1972), *A Lesson From Aloes* (1978), *Master Harold. . .and the Boys* (1982), and *My Children! My Africa!* (1989) have won Fugard awards and worldwide recognition and have earned him respect as, in the words of Stephen Gray in *New Theatre Quarterly,* "the greatest active playwright in English."

Because the backdrop, if not the subject, of Fugard's plays for so many years was his country's divisive policies of apartheid, many critics wondered what his future as a playwright would hold once apartheid was abolished and steps were taken toward racial equality. White South African President F. W. de Klerk began the process of dismantling apartheid in 1990 when he ended the ban on the African National Congress, and began releasing political prisoners and repealing the many segregation laws that separated whites and blacks. A few years later, in 1994, Nelson Mandela, the black former leader of the African National Congress who was jailed by the white South African government for twenty-seven years, was inaugurated as South Africa's president, and the long struggle for racial equality in the troubled country began a new chapter.

For his part, Fugard did not end his career as a dramatist when the door finally closed on apartheid. With the help of five young South African women, he assembled a collaborative piece called *My Life* (1996) which revealed their experiences, desires, and fears about the new South Africa. He followed *My Life* with *Valley Song* (1996), a frankly autobiographical play that prompted critics to realize that Fugard's talent extended well beyond political boundaries. As Jack Barbera reported in a review of the play for the *Nation,* "He tells stories, and if the new South Africa has altered the nature of people's problems, it only means there are new challenges, new stories to tell."

Plot Summary

Valley Song opens with The Author, a white man in his sixties representing Fugard himself, showing the audience a handful of "genuine Karoo pumpkin seeds," describing the beauty and richness of the land in the Sneeuberg Mountains of South Africa's great Karoo region, and inviting the onlookers to imagine Abraam Jonkers, a "coloured" (mixed-race) tenant farmer now in his seventies, planting the seeds in the fresh spring earth just after a rain. The images in The Author's opening monologue—seeds, earth, rain, mountains and valleys—are important not only to the setting of *Valley Song,* but to the personalities of the characters and the larger themes at work in the play.

As The Author talks, he turns into Abraam Jonkers, known to everyone in the village of Nieu-Bethesda as "old Buks." Old Buks has lived in the village his entire life, working as a tenant farmer on the same piece of land his father worked on when he was a boy. While the land has been owned by a white family, the Landmans, for generations, Abraam Jonkers and his family have only been allowed to live on the edge of it and farm a few acres. Old Buks has raised the crops for the Landmans, and his wife, before she died, cleaned their house and scrubbed their floors. Now the Landmans are gone, and the property is for sale.

As Buks sings fragments of an old song he once knew and plants pumpkin seeds in the damp soil, his granddaughter, Veronica, arrives with his lunch. She is black, seventeen, filled with youthful energy and tender devotion toward her grandfather, whom she calls ''Oupa.'' As Veronica lays out their lunch— bread with jam and a thermos of tea—Buks tells her he is concerned about a white man who visited that morning looking to buy the house and property. Because Buks does not own the land on which he lives and farms, the owner could tell him to leave, a fate worse than death for the old man. Veronica does not want to see her Oupa displaced, but losing the land, to her, might mean opportunity instead of tragedy. She complains that nothing ever happens in the small valley village, and what she is really seeking now is ''Adventure and Romance!''

More than anything, Veronica wants to be a famous singer. She has a lovely natural voice, and constantly makes up songs to sing to entertain herself and old Buks. She sings him a song she made up that morning called ''Railway Bus O Railway Bus,'' which is about her desire to jump on a fast bus and travel the world, seeing all of the big cities and strange places she has only heard about. The song reminds old Buks of painful memories and prompts him to finally tell Veronica about her mother and her past.

Veronica's mother, Caroline, was Buks' only daughter. When she was still a young girl, she ran away to Johannesburg with her troublemaking boyfriend. A year went by before Buks and his wife, Betty, received a phone call from a hospital in the city. Caroline was quite sick, so Betty went to be with her. When she returned on the ''railway bus'' she brought Veronica, a newborn baby. Caroline had died. Old Buks and Betty raised Veronica, their granddaughter, as if she were their own child. Now Buks' life is changing. Betty died when Veronica was only a few years old, and now, it seems, Veronica wants to run away to the city like her mother did before her. To make matters worse, a white man is asking questions about his land, and he faces an uncertain future.

Later that night, Veronica sneaks off to the village. She is standing on an apple box, pretending she is on TV singing for thousands of people, when The Author steps out of the shadows and surprises her. After an initial fright, Veronica tells The Author about her fantasy of being a famous performer. He warns her about the danger of dreams that are impossible to achieve, but she insists that if people

Athol Fugard (on right, holding cup).

dream ''properly'' and believe hard enough, they can make a dream come true.

The next day Veronica and old Buks receive the news: the white man they have seen around town is going to buy the land on which they live and farm. Veronica suggests they fight against losing their home, perhaps by taking a petition to the government, but Buks is resigned to the situation. He is used to deferring to the white people who own most of the land, and plans to talk to the white man to convince him to let Buks and Veronica stay on to tend the land and clean his house, as their family has done for years.

Buks' suggestion leads to a major confrontation between him and his granddaughter. While Buks is perfectly content to live his few remaining years growing vegetables on the small patch of earth he calls home, with Veronica working as a servant for a new white boss, she has different ideas. She believes there are better opportunities available to her in the new South Africa, now that blacks have equal access to the jobs whites have and can live in the cities like anyone else. Buks, however, interprets Veronica's ambition as ingratitude and a rejection of all of the values he holds dear. For the first time in their lives, he is angry with her, and his anger brings her to tears.

The next Sunday, Buks catches The Author just before he leaves town to return to the city for awhile. He offers the white man a wheelbarrow full of vegetables, and pleads with him to let him stay on the land, and maybe to let his granddaughter keep his house clean. To The Author, who is looking to buy the land as a place to escape from the "make-believe world of theatre," this gesture makes the sale. The character, really Fugard himself in disguise, tells the audience about his desire to get away from the "nonsense from actors and producers and critics," and live for a while in the "real" world. He stops himself short, however, when he realizes the significance of the land to old Buks. Although The Author has the means to simply write out a check and pick up a Title Deed to the property, it is Buks and his family who have worked the soil and grown up with the land for at least two generations. It is only because of South Africa's terrible history of denying equality to its black citizens that Buks must now beg the white man for what may rightfully be his.

As The Author considers the guilt he is feeling, Veronica joins him, and reveals to the audience her hatred for the land the two men love so much. "It gives us food," she says, "but it takes our lives." She thinks of her beloved Oupa as a slave to the land, and is convinced it is fear of being trapped by the land that drove her mother away. Once again the Author tries to warn Veronica about the danger of dreaming too big, but she stubbornly resists him and insists, "You will never see me on my knees scrubbing a white man's floor."

Veronica and Buks' next confrontation arrives with the mail. Although Buks cannot read, he opened a letter Veronica received from a friend in Johannesburg and had a friend read it to him. From its contents, he learned that Veronica is planning to leave the valley and find work in the city so she can pursue her singing career. Faced with the letter, Veronica admits to the plan, and shows Buks some money she has saved by singing for white people on the street in the village. Buks calls her meager savings "Devil's money" and hurls it out into the field. That Sunday, Veronica will not sing in church. The joy in her voice has been crushed by old Buks' treatment of her dreams.

Months pass, and in the middle of winter Veronica comes to her Oupa to tell him that he must let her go. Like the pumpkin seeds he plants and tends

so carefully, she tells him she, too, has grown up. She explains to him that her singing is her life, and she must tend it the way old Buks tends his vegetables. He warns her that it is a bad world outside of their little valley, but she insists that he has helped to make her strong, and the time for her to leave is now. Finally, old Buks gives Veronica his blessing, and she leaves him with a song about the valley that she loves.

On her way out of town, Veronica encounters The Author for the last time. He admits that he understands the ambitions that are driving her onward, and was only testing her resolve earlier when he questioned the seriousness of her dreams. Both of them, the author and the singer, are artists who answer to a mysterious higher calling. They both go where their dreams lead them. The Author, who is nearing the end of his life, is running out of dreams about the "Glorious Future," and in a touching symbolic gesture, he tells Veronica, "The future belongs to you now." Because The Author is actually Fugard, the playwright, the line has a deeper meaning. Fugard has spent his career on the stage "dreaming" about a brighter future for his country. Now, late in life, he is seeing some changes occur, but knows he will not be around to see them reach fruition. It will be up to new artists, black and white, to dream new dreams.

Veronica runs off to the city, leaving behind The Author and old Buks. To keep from ending the play with old Buks "slumped in defeat and misery," however, The Author reaches out to him and entices him back to life in the only way he understands: through the land. The Author tells Buks about the new spring rain that fell the night before, and offers him a handful of pumpkin seeds so he can plant his field and draw new life from the earth once more.

Characters

The Author

The Author in *Valley Song* is just that: Athol Fugard himself, appearing as a character in his own play. He is a white man in his sixties, a successful and prosperous playwright who was born in the

Karoo region of South Africa, but has lived most of his life in Port Elizabeth and traveled the cities of the world. Like the real-life Fugard, The Author has devoted his career to writing hopeful plays about the future of his country, but is now "sick and tired of the madness and desperate scramble of my life in the make-believe world of theatre."

What he wants now is to live in the "real" world, so he has chosen to return to the Karoo and purchase a small house on a piece of farmland, where he can live out the rest of his days writing *prose* ("no more nonsense from actors and producers and critics"), smelling the rich, fertile land, and eating the vegetables that grow in his own patch of the earth. His conscience, however, causes him to be troubled at the plight of Abraam Jonkers, the poor old black man who has lived his entire life on the land The Author is buying, but because of South Africa's racial discrimination, has never been able to own any of it for himself.

The Author also comes to know Jonkers' granddaughter, Veronica. Though he initially seems to challenge Veronica's dreams of one day becoming a famous singer, The Author actually understands the mysterious force that drives the young girl toward her goal, and recognizes that now that his days are coming to an end, the future belongs to her and to her generation.

Abraam Jonkers

Abraam Jonkers is a "Coloured" (mixed-race) South African man in his seventies. Called "old Buks" by everyone in his village and "Oupa" by his granddaughter, Veronica, Abraam has lived his entire life in Nieu-Bethesda, a small village in the Sneeuberg Mountains of South Africa's great Karoo region, except for his short service as a prison guard in the Transvaal during World War II. Both he and his father, Jaap Jonkers, have been tenant farmers on the property of the Landmans, a white family. When he was a boy, his father explained to him that if he grew up to be a good man, then God would make his days sweet as the grapes that grew in their valley. To be a good man, he explained, Abraam must work hard on the land, love everyone who lives in his home and village, and have faith and worship God in the village church.

Since that time, old Buks has tried to live his life just as his father directed. He has experienced many disappointments over the years. He lost his daughter to the city when she ran away to Johannesburg seeking adventure and opportunity and died there, still a young girl. He lost his beloved wife to old age, and buried her beneath the earth he loves so dearly. Now, near death himself, he is afraid of losing the only person he has left, his granddaughter Veronica, to her dreams of becoming a famous singer.

Abraam Jonkers represents the "old" South Africa in the play. He is painfully aware of his racial status and what it has represented in his world—no education, little opportunity, and a constant fear of white society and its dangers. Because he has lived through the worst his country has to offer, he is not as optimistic as Veronica about her chances in the world outside their valley.

Veronica Jonkers

Veronica is a seventeen-year-old black teenager. Though she was born in Johannesburg, her mother died shortly afterward, and she was brought back to Nieu-Bethesda in the Sneeuberg Mountain valley by her grandmother, Betty Jonkers. A few years later, her grandmother also died, and she has been raised since then by her grandfather, Abraam, whom she calls "Oupa." Unlike her grandfather, she barely remembers the injustices and atrocities of apartheid in the "old" South Africa. Because of this, she is freer to dream and to think about life outside the valley than her Oupa seems to be.

Veronica's big dream is to become a famous singer and appear on television. She has a naturally beautiful voice—even old Buks remembers her "singing" when she was just a baby—but her grandfather cannot stand the thought of her leaving him and their farm, so she must choose between the love of her Oupa and the life she has known, or the uncertainty of the world outside and the possibility that her dream might not come true.

Initially The Author challenges her, warning her that unrealistic dreams can lead to bitterness and resentment. Later, though, it is apparent that the old white man and the young black girl are a lot alike, but at different stages in their lives. The Author was once a starry-eyed dreamer, with high hopes for his country, but his days of dreaming are nearing an end. Veronica, on the other hand, is just beginning. She now represents the hopes and dreams of South Africa's future.

Topics for Further Study

- Athol Fugard has spent much of his career as a playwright creating dramas that tell powerful stories about the lives of individual people, while at the same time criticizing South Africa's unjust system of apartheid. Read a Fugard play written before 1990, during the apartheid era, such as *Master Harold . . . and the Boys* or *My Children! My Africa!* How is Fugard's work from this time different from *Valley Song*, a play written for the "new" South Africa? How are the two plays similar? Consider such things as each play's setting, characters, and dominant themes.

- In literature, a *symbol* is something that represents something else, and is often used to communicate deeper levels of meaning. In Nathaniel Hawthorne's famous novel *The Scarlet Letter,* for example, the red letter "A" worn by Hester Prynne is a symbol not only of her supposed crime (adultery), but also of her neighbors' bigotry and her own courageous pride. Like many playwrights who write about important *ideas,* Fugard relies on many symbols in his work to communicate deeper levels of meaning to his audiences. In *Valley Song,* one of the more important symbols is the land in the Sneeuberg Mountain valley where Abraam and Veronica Jonkers live, and where The Author has chosen to retreat in his old age. Examine all the ways the land is viewed by the characters, and explain how it becomes an important symbol in the play.

- The word "apartheid" means "separateness" in the Afrikaans, or Cape Dutch, language of South Africa. Apartheid was used as a social and political tool by the ruling National Party from 1948 to 1994 to divide the races in South Africa and provide separate treatment for each. Research apartheid and how it affected the lives of blacks, whites, "Coloureds," and Asians living in South Africa. How might this system have affected Abraam Jonkers' lot in life as a rural coloured man? What benefits might The Author have received as an urban white man? What challenges is Veronica likely to face in Johannesburg as a young black girl, even though apartheid has officially ended?

- *Dreams* are important in one way or another to each of the characters in *Valley Song.* What do each of the characters dream about? How does each character try to achieve his or her dream? How likely is each characters' dream to come true?

- What are some of the ways *age* and *youth* are important to *Valley Song*? Consider such things as how the young and old characters view things differently, the importance of the past to the events of the play, and how the passage of time is affecting racial politics in South Africa.

Themes

Dreams

Everyone in *Valley Song* is pursuing a dream, and it is the nature of the characters' dreams and how far they are willing to go to achieve them that really defines who they are in the world of the play.

Abraam Jonkers' dream is the simplest of the three. It was handed to him by his father when he

was just a young boy. While working in the fields one day, his father explained to him that if he grew up to be a good man, then God would make his days as sweet as the grapes that grew in their valley. To be a good man, he explained, Abraam must work hard on the land, love everyone who lives in his home and village, and have faith and worship God in the village church. Since that time, everything Abraam has done has been an attempt to live up to his father's directions. He has dedicated himself to the same patch of land, his "akkers," that his father farmed, and is inseparable from the earth, even though he can never own it himself. He has cared for everyone in his home—his daughter, Caroline; his wife, Betty; and now his granddaughter, Veronica—even as they have left him one at a time. And he is devoted to his faith in God, despite the fact that his days have not always been as sweet as the grapes of his valley.

Insofar as Abraam's dream of a simple, honest life on the land is productive and not harmful to others, it seems admirable, but his dream comes with complications as well. It interferes with the aspirations of his daughter and granddaughter, who don't share his love for the land. Abraam's simple dream also seems narrow and outdated with the prospect of a "new" South Africa, where everyone—black, white, and coloured alike—is free to dream bigger dreams.

Veronica represents the spirit of this new South Africa. She has lofty dreams of leaving the valley village and heading off to the big city where she can become a famous singer and one day appear on television. Because she is too young to have experienced the worst of apartheid in the old regime, she does not share the fears of her grandfather that the white world will close the door of opportunity that leads to the fulfillment of her dream. Her energy, enthusiasm, and passion for her dream are enviable and exciting, but they, too, carry danger. As The Author warns her more than once, if dreams are too big they may not come true, and dashed dreams can lead to disappointment and bitterness.

For his part, The Author has had his share of both passionate dreaming with some success and unrealistic dreaming with disappointing results. In his sixty-plus years he has achieved some of the fame and fortune as an artist that Veronica is seeking, but the struggle has taken a toll on him. Where he once had grand dreams about a "Glorious Future" for his country, he now dreams only of escaping the artificial world of cities and the theater and living out his days in the "real" world of the Karoo farmland. He tells Veronica, "The future belongs to you now," and symbolically passes the torch of hope, the ability to keep on dreaming, from his generation to the next.

Cycle of Life

Valley Song begins and ends with The Author presenting the audience with a symbol of fertility: a handful of pumpkin seeds. The seeds represent the cycle of life, an idea that is central to the play and its characters. Just as the seeds are planted in the ground, sprout with the sunshine and rain, grow into vines and "Flat White Boer" pumpkins, then return new seeds to the earth, the characters and the society they live in experience birth, growth, death, and renewal.

Each of the three characters that appear in the play is somehow tied to the land, and therefore directly affected by nature's cycle of life. For Abraam Jonkers, the land has been both his life and his living since he was a boy. Every year he plants the seeds in the earth, tends the sprouts and vines, harvests the vegetables, then retreats indoors for the winter while the land lies dormant. He has been a witness to the complete cycle of life of his daughter, who ran away and died in the city, and his wife, who grew old and died on their farm. In the end, faced with the loss of his granddaughter as well, it is the land that saves Abraam. Instead of allowing him to be left "slumped in defeat and misery," The Author presents him with another handful of pumpkin seeds, and they are the key to Abraam's rejuvenation. Once more old Buks tramps into the fields to plant again, suggesting that the cycle of death and rebirth will continue. Like the pumpkin fields, old Buks will once again come to life.

For Veronica, the land is a trap. She, too, has experienced the cycle of seasons, the planting and harvesting of crops, and feels the rhythm of life in their small village in the valley. But she is part of a new generation that is not satisfied with the life its grandparents and parents led. She requires a different sort of nurturing—a tending of the soul—in order to thrive. At one point she pleads with old Buks, "I am also a living thing, you know. I also want to grow." Her growth, she is convinced, can only occur outside the valley, where new opportunities await young blacks in the cities that once turned them away. "My singing is my life," she tells her grandfather. "I must look after it the way Oupa looks after his vegetables. I know that if I stay here in the Valley it will die."

For The Author, the land is his dream for his twilight years. His cycle of life, like old Abraam's, is nearing an end, and like the seeds in his hand, he wants to return to the earth of the countryside where he was born. For many years he has waited for the world outside, the world of cities he has lived in, to change. He has been desperate for his country to evolve out of its ignorant, blind prejudices and into a free society. Now that the change he has waited for so long is starting to take place, he is ready for others to pick up where he is leaving off. He wants to slow down the pace of his life and live in the valley that is "the unspoilt, innocent little world it was when I first discovered it."

Signs that The Author's dream of a free South Africa is coming true appear throughout *Valley Song*. The country, like its characters, is growing and changing. When old Buks fears losing his "akkers" to the white man who is planning to buy all the land, Veronica urges him to appeal to the government, which has been "taking the land and giving it back to the people," in an attempt to right some of the wrongs committed by the apartheid-era government. As a sign that what she says is true, Veronica relates an experience she had at the post office, when Mrs. Oliphant, the black postal worker, turned away the town's white Brigadier at closing time, telling the infuriated man, "This is no longer the old South Africa, Brigadier." When Veronica's friend, Priscilla, writes her from Johannesburg, she assures her that there are plenty of jobs available, and lots for them to do, a very different situation from the one black South Africans faced only a few years before. In the cycle of life, the playwright seems to be suggesting, his work is nearing an end, and the work of the new generation, rebuilding the country, is just beginning.

Style

Point of View

Every story told has a "point of view," a perspective through which the events of the plot take on additional meaning, depending on who is telling the tale. *Valley Song* presents its audience with three different points of view at different times in the play. Abraam Jonkers, a "Coloured" South African in his seventies; Veronica Jonkers, his seventeen-year-old black granddaughter; and The Author, Fugard himself at sixty, each address the audience directly on occasion, or speak to unseen figures on the stage, and share their individual views of the play's events. Because of the characters' "soliloquies" throughout the play, they reveal more about themselves than they might have in dialogues with other characters. Taken together, they also represent three different voices on a single theme: What is the future of the "new" South Africa?

When Abraam is by himself, he talks to his dead wife, Betty, and tries to work through conflicts he is experiencing. By listening to him describe the anguish he is feeling at seeing his granddaughter grow apart from him, and worrying about what the white man who is going to buy his land might do with him, the audience gains a deeper sympathy for this sometimes stubborn old man. Having lived through the entire apartheid era and seen its devastating effects on his country, Abraam is not as optimistic about the future as Veronica, and far less trusting than she of white society. Abraam's point of view is that of a coloured man from the old South Africa: poor, undereducated, and used to being subservient to whites, but kind-hearted, well-intentioned, and supportive of his family.

Veronica actually addresses the audience directly, and everything about her manner when she does so suggests that she is much stronger and more independent than the quiet, devoted granddaughter image she presents to her "Oupa." She says things she would never say to her grandfather for fear of hurting him. "He's like a slave now to that little piece of land," she raves. "That's all he lives for, and it's not even his. He talks about nothing else, worries about nothing else, prays for nothing else." Hers is the point of view of youth in South Africa. Too young to remember the terrible past, and tired of seeing the weight of it bear down on their parents and grandparents, young black South Africans, Fugard seems to suggest, are ready to offer new hope for the future and demand a role in creating it.

The point of view of The Author, while not necessarily the most important, is certainly the most prominent in the play. Unlike Abraam and Veronica, who are voices from South Africa's historically oppressed and marginalized coloured and black population, The Author speaks from the point of view of privilege. As a white male, he has enjoyed the benefits of a good education, quality housing, access to good employment, and a share in running the government and the economy. In his direct address to the audience, he reveals the guilt he feels at being able to buy old Buks' land out from under him, and he regrets that all of the dreams he had for a changed South Africa will not come true in his lifetime. The Author's point of view is similar to that of many whites at the time of South Africa's radical transformation from a racially segregated society into a free and open democracy: part fear, part exhilaration, and a little bit of guilt and regret along with a sense of pride and accomplishment. As an old, white South African moving out of the way so the next generation of young, black South Africans can build the future, The Author suffers from a sense of nostalgia for the way the world was, but is equally eager to see it evolve into the way he always hoped it would be.

Setting

The setting of a play has a tremendous influence on the effectiveness of its plot, themes, and characters. The location of the action, the time period in which it occurs, and the cultural characteristics of the society in which its characters live all contribute to the full impact a drama has on its audience.

Valley Song is set in the present day in and around Nieu-Bethesda, a small village tucked into a valley of the Sneeuberg Mountains in South Africa's great semi-desert Karoo region. Fugard explains in a prefatory note to his play that, like most rural South African villages, "Nieu-Bethesda is still essentially divided into two areas: the white town and the outlying 'location' populated by coloreds and blacks." In this particular rural village, there are 950 "coloured" (mixed-race) people, and only 65 whites. Despite the great changes that have been overtaking South Africa since the last apartheid laws were officially revoked in 1992, the rich, fertile farmland in the valley is still all owned by whites.

Fugard takes great care in the preface to his play to ensure readers understand that, although the Karoo region is almost entirely desert, and the sun beats down on the hot earth day after day without rain, it is nevertheless breathtaking in its beauty. He quotes Carolyn Slaughter, who said, "This is the Karoo. And for those who have lost their hearts to it, no other place on earth can compare." Seemingly, it is this contrast between nature at its cruelest and tantalizing beauty that both attracts and repels the characters in the play. The Author refers to "a glorious Karoo spring day" just after a rain, when the earth smells rich and alive with the fragrance of roses and pine trees. Although he has lived most of his life at a distance from nature, it is this promise of rebirth and renewal that has brought him back to the "real" world, to a natural setting.

Even in the countryside, however, the characters cannot escape the *time* that they live in, which is as important as the location is to the plot of the play. In the few short years that have passed since South Africa ended apartheid and declared itself a free society, many things seem to have changed. There is the promise of opportunity for blacks in the cities,

and recourse to the government and the law for wrongs committed in the name of racial prejudice. Still, the playing field has not been leveled. The Author is able to drive into Nieu-Bethesda and casually write a check for the land Abraam Jonkers has tended his entire life, but will never be able to own.

Literary Heritage

South Africa is inhabited by a broad range of cultures including Dutch, German and English white settlers, black Africans from many different tribes across the continent, "coloreds" (people of mixed descent) and Asian people (mainly people from India and Pakistan). White colonists were first attracted to the South African coast in the eighteenth century for its abundant resources. Since their arrival, the white minority population has sought to control the black majority population of the region.

When Fugard wrote his play *Boesman and Lena* in 1969, all major black African political organizations had been banned, and blacks in the country were segregated and assigned to Bantustans ("homelands"), restricted from travelling outside these areas (except to work for whites in very limited circumstances). The minority white population by this time controlled over eighty percent of the land, all the government, and the vast majority of natural resources, though black African uprisings against white control were frequent throughout the 1960s and 1970s.

The state of the arts, in particular the theater, were hazardous during this time. Although stage dramas were often less censored than were novels, television and movies (which were often banned before their public release), the laws regarding apartheid made theater production increasingly difficult. Rising international protest against South Africa's apartheid policies caused many countries and playwrights to shun South Africa. At the same time (1965), new apartheid laws were passed prohibiting mixed-race casts and segregating audiences by race. By 1966, British Equity would not allow its performers to act in these conditions. As a consequence, South Africa faced a dearth of plays, performers, and touring companies. While the South African government did provide limited funding for the arts, access to these funds required adherence to the strict apartheid policies governing public performances; because of these restrictions, many artists worked outside subsidized theater.

Some artists, such as Gibson Kent, created all-black touring groups and performed only for black audiences. Other companies (i.e., the Space Theatre and the Market Theatre) devised ways of circumventing the apartheid laws and created works with mixed race casts and occasionally mixed audiences. The segregation laws regarding casts and audiences were not repealed until 1977, during which time several notable playwrights, performers, and writers (including Fugard) had emerged against the turbulent political background. These performers are often credited with helping to raise national and international awareness of South Africa's apartheid policies.

Athol Fugard, who began (and continued) his writing career while South Africa's apartheid policies were in place, was considered by the South African government to be a "political risk." He was often censored and occasionally prevented from travel from and return to his home country. Today, Fugard is recognized in both his own country and internationally as one of the greatest living playwrights in the English language, and is credited with helping to dismantle the unjust system of apartheid through his drama. Fugard's works are characterized by his personal portrayals of tragic events in the lives of two or three characters, often utilizing casts of mixed race characters set against difficult political, social, and economic backgrounds of South Africa. His dramas depict the devastating effects of apartheid, and represent a microcosm of South Africa as a whole.

Historical Context

The most significant historical event surrounding the creation of Fugard's *Valley Song* was the dismantling of apartheid and South Africa's rebirth as a free society just as the play was being produced. "Apartheid," which means "separateness" in the Afrikaans language, was the set of laws used by the white, ruling National Party between 1948 and 1992 to segregate the races in South Africa and provide different rights and privileges to each. Under the apartheid system, there were four official races: white, black, "Coloured" (mixed-race), and Asian. Only whites had complete freedom to travel and

work anywhere they chose, a quality education, and the right to vote. The other races were restricted by "Pass Laws" that required them to live in specially designated "homelands" in townships at the edges of white cities, provided them with minimum education, and few opportunities for employment and improvement of their standard of living.

Apartheid came to an end when F. W. de Klerk succeeded P. W. Botha as South African President in 1989. De Klerk lifted the ban on the African National Congress (ANC), a black rights organization, in 1990, released many longtime political prisoners, including Nelson Mandela, a black ANC leader who had been imprisoned for 27 years, and repealed all of the laws supporting apartheid. In 1993, de Klerk and Mandela were jointly awarded the Nobel Peace Prize for successfully negotiating South Africa's transition to a nondiscriminatory democracy, and in 1994 Mandela himself won an open election to his country's presidency.

Despite the victory of South Africa's majority black population over the unjust system of apartheid, living conditions for most nonwhite citizens of the country at the time that Fugard wrote *Valley Song* were still far from equal to those enjoyed by the former ruling white class. Relatively few nonwhites owned property. Because they had been given a poor education, the blacks and coloureds of South Africa were unable to compete for new jobs, even once they were eligible to apply for them. To complicate matters further, different political factions arose among the nonwhite groups in the country, with each fearing what the other might do if it were to win an election and rewrite the country's constitution.

In the 1994 election, 20 million votes were cast, with 63 percent in favor of Nelson Mandela and the African National Congress Party. Even though it was associated with fifty years of tyranny, the National Party still managed to secure 20 percent of the votes and retain some authority in the new government. When Mandela took over as president, he faced the daunting task of trying to unite South Africa's quarreling racial parties, restructure the entire economy, provide housing and health benefits to millions of people, unite and improve the country's educational system, and provide new employment opportunities and economic benefits to people who had known only poverty and despair.

One of the new government's most difficult tasks, however, was trying to uncover and report all of the human rights violations that had occurred during the terrible apartheid years. In April 1996, the Truth and Reconciliation Commission, headed by Archbishop Desmond Tutu, was formed to investigate allegations of crimes ranging from theft and assault to rape, torture, and murder. The Commission's intent was to consider amnesty for those, both black and white, who confessed their crimes, and to provide recommendations for reparations to the victims. At the same time that the Truth and Reconciliation Commission was meeting, just after *Valley Song* was first produced, South Africa adopted a new constitution that does not allow any form of discrimination based on race, gender, age, or sexual orientation, and attempts to ensure the rights of all of its citizens to a representative voice in government.

The country has a long way to go to recover from years of mishandling. Unemployment remains extremely high—approximately 40 percent of the workforce. The crime rate is terrible—about 57 in every 100,000 citizens are murdered each year, compared to 7 of every 100,000 in the United States. Millions of blacks still do not have adequate housing and, despite merging fourteen separate education departments into one unified, nondiscriminatory system, South Africa still faces a terrible shortage of teachers, textbooks, and classroom space, and a severe lack of funding to pay for improvements. Thabo Mbeki, the new head of the ANC who succeeded Nelson Mandela as president in the 1999 elections, hopes to pick up where his predecessor left off and continue reforming the troubled country.

Critical Overview

Athol Fugard has always been a multitalented theatrical artist, often acting in and occasionally directing his own plays. Never before *Valley Song*, however, did the playwright write so much of his own life into one of his plays, then choose to act two of the parts and direct himself and his co-performer. *Valley Song* premiered in Johannesburg, South Africa in August, 1995 with Fugard directing and playing the parts of The Author and Abraam Jonkers, and Esmeralda Bihl portraying Veronica Jonkers. Several months later, in October, 1995, the play opened in the U.S. at the McCarter Theatre in Princeton, New Jersey. This production, staged in association with the Manhattan Theatre Club, also

listed Fugard in the multiple roles of author, director, and actor of two parts, with Lisa Gay Hamilton as Veronica.

Fugard has long been respected by American audiences and critics as an outspoken voice against his country's unjust apartheid segregation policies, and as the author of several poetic, poignant dramas set against South Africa's tumultuous political scene over the past forty years. His accomplishments, coupled with his tour de force performance in *Valley Song*, earned him praise both at home and abroad. As Robert King reported in the *North American Review*, "He received entrance applause at its American premiere in Princeton's McCarter Theatre, a tribute to his life as well as to his art." Because Fugard the man was obviously the inspiration for The Author in his play, King noted, he received additional response from his audience when he expressed regret at leaving "the real world of the Karoo" for the "make believe world of the theatre."

Beyond Fugard's unique accomplishments as both creator and interpreter of his play, however, critics mostly expressed appreciation for his continued ability to capture the history and mood of his entire country within the struggles of a handful of people. The plight of Veronica and old Buks led several reviewers to draw comparisons between their intergenerational family struggle and the larger conflicts facing the newly liberated and unified South Africa. Reviewing the Arizona Theatre Company's 1997 production for *Arizona Arts Review Online*, Mark Turvin noted, "The transition from apartheid to democracy in South Africa seems to have been a smooth one, but the subsequent new travails for blacks there are only now being discovered. With freedom comes dreams, and with dreams comes responsibility, and some of those dreams may remain unfulfilled. Mr. Fugard has brought these problems across with a positive spirit that gives the work a punctuation to all of his pieces." Critic John Bemrose optimistically wrote in *Maclean's,* "Veronica's troubled longing for the future is also South Africa's. If its determination for a better future is anything as strong as hers, it may well get there yet."

Perhaps most importantly, *Valley Song* seemed to answer a question that ran through the minds of many critics and scholars when F. W. de Klerk ended apartheid between 1990 and 1992 and black leader Nelson Mandela was elected president of South Africa in 1994: What would Fugard write about? He had, after all, built a career around plays

South African President Nelson Mandela and second Deputy President F. W. de Klerk during an inauguration ceremony in 1994.

that directly or indirectly attacked his country's government and policies. Not to worry. John Bemrose reported in *Maclean's,* "*Valley Song* is a watershed play for Fugard—his first since the collapse of apartheid two years ago. Throughout his 40-year career, Fugard has drawn on his outrage at South Africa's institutionalized racism to help power such dramas as *The Road to Mecca* and *My Children! My Africa!* But the mood in *Valley Song* is different. Gone is the shadow of the police state. Freedom is in the air.''

Jack Barbera, reviewing the play for the *Nation,* suggested, "Now we have *Valley Song* to demonstrate the truth of Fugard's claim that the end of apartheid would not put him out of business. He tells stories, and if the new South Africa has altered the nature of people's problems, it only means there are new challenges, new stories to tell.''

The significance of placing himself, a successful white male author, in the center of this particular play's story also led critics to reflect on what the playwright may be thinking about his new role in the new South Africa. King noted, "He suggests a poignant, personal truth—that with a new day dawning for south African blacks, his day may be coming to an end.'' The end, however, is not meant to be

final or disheartening. King continues, "It's time, *Valley Song* argues, for the white male, surely Fugard himself, to step aside, to let the black woman sing her song to the world. That song will be all the more winning for being born on native soil.''

Criticism

Lane A. Glenn

Lane A. Glenn has a Ph. D. specializing in theater history and literature. In this essay he considers Athol Fugard's exploration of what it means to be an artist in Valley Song.

At an early age, Athol Fugard knew he would one day be an artist. In a 1989 interview with director Lloyd Richards in the *Paris Review,* Fugard remembered the importance of music and storytelling in his family. His father was a jazz musician, as well as an avid reader and storyteller, and Fugard recalled dreaming about becoming a composer or concert pianist and writing short stories of his own as a boy. "By eighteen, by the time I went to university, I knew that somehow my life was going to be about putting words on paper,'' he told Richards.

What Do I Read Next?

- Fugard has written nearly two dozen plays. All of them are set in his native South Africa, and many share some of the same qualities: intimate, small-cast, poetic dramas set against the beauty of the South African countryside and the tragedy of its politics. Fugard's first big success, *The Blood Knot* (1961), is about two half-brothers, one black, the other nearly white but technically "colored," and the effects of apartheid on their lives. In *Master Harold. . .and the Boys* (1982), a young white South African boy learns some lessons about family, love, and dignity from the two black servants in his parents' café. *My Children! My Africa!* (1989) explores the devastating effects of anti-apartheid demonstrations and township riots on a black teacher and two of his students, one black, the other white.

- August Wilson's 1985 Pulitzer Prize-winning play *Fences* is set in Pittsburgh in the 1950s, before the Civil Rights movement in the United States provided African Americans greater equality in education, employment, and standards of living. Like *Valley Song*, *Fences* depicts an intergenerational conflict that is rooted in the past and revolves around issues of family loyalty and racial divisions. Troy, a former baseball player in America's "Negro League," refuses to let his son, Cory, take advantage of a college football scholarship, because he doesn't believe white society will give him the opportunity to actually play.

- Susan Glaspell's 1916 play *Trifles* is a murder mystery with a twist. A farmer in rural New England has been strangled to death in his sleep, and the local sheriff and attorney are convinced his wife did it, but they cannot find a motive. While the men poke around the farmhouse looking for clues to the crime, the women remember the wife, Minnie, as she used to be: a pretty young girl who loved people and especially loved to sing. Her husband changed her by keeping her at home, in a cold farmhouse set back off the road away from people. Like Veronica in *Valley Song*, Minnie had a spirit that would not be beaten by people who did not believe in her, and could not be contained in a world that would not let her sing.

- Novelist James A. Michener has written several books of historical fiction, including *Hawaii*, *Alaska*, and *Mexico*. In *The Covenant* (1980), Michener explores the tortuous history of South Africa from the arrival of the first European immigrants in the fifteenth century through the creation of the modern South African nation and the tragedy of apartheid. The saga combines fact with fiction and focuses on Willem van Doorn and ten generations of his descendants as they struggle through the country's colonization, the Great Trek, the Boer War, and other important, defining events in South Africa's history.

- Norman Silver's 1993 collection of stories *An Eye for Color* is narrated by Basil, a Jewish teenager living in Capetown, South Africa. Basil's tales reflect the world around him, organized by apartheid, where common events take on new meaning because of the rigid class structure system and race laws governing his country. In one story, Basil tells his girlfriend about a beating he saw two blacks endure, and she responds that they must have provoked it. Basil sees a young girl get reclassified from being white, with all its attendant privileges, to being black, which means she must move from their neighborhood and attend another school. This collection is particularly aimed at teenage readers.

> ''I know that I am propelled, obsessed, driven to make things. That is all I understand in terms of creative energy. I think that every human being on God's earth has got a spark of that energy.'''

After trying his hand at poetry and considering a novel, Fugard found his calling in the theater at the age of twenty-five, and since that time he has understood that his purpose in life is to create art through drama, to touch people and occasionally effect change through the living art of playwriting. ''I have some sort of creative energy,'' the author revealed in a 1993 speech transcribed in *Twentieth Century Literature*. ''I know that I am propelled, obsessed, driven to make things. That is all I understand in terms of creative energy. I think that every human being on God's earth has got a spark of that energy. Some people have great big conflagrations and furnaces burning away.''

Glimpses of Fugard's own creative furnace—his life and identity as an artist in South Africa—can be found in several of his plays, most notably *Master Harold. . .and the Boys* (1982), a frankly autobiographical work about a family event from his teenage years. Fugard has often appeared onstage in performances of his plays, portraying the light-skinned half-brother Morris in *The Blood Knot* (1961), the angry Coloured outcast Boesman in *Boesman and Lena* (1969), and several more of his creations over the years. But never until *Valley Song* (1995) did the playwright literally insert himself into one of his plays as a character, interacting with and even seeming to control his fictional counterparts.

Like all of Fugard's previous plays, *Valley Song* presents its audience with important ideas about love, loyalty, the beauty of the land, and the importance of dreams. But the appearance of the playwright himself in the form of The Author adds a unique new dimension to the work and allows Fugard to raise whole new questions about art and those who create it. *Valley Song* asks, how is an artist made? What obligation does an artist have to his or her art? What is the value of art to society? What does an artist do when he has outlived his usefulness; when he is running out of creative energy? Through the characters of The Author, an aging white man, and Veronica, a black teenage girl, Fugard contemplates these questions and examines what it means to be an artist in a world that does not always understand the artist's craft.

As The Author, Fugard has spent a lifetime living in Port Elizabeth, South Africa and presenting his make-believe stories about real life to audiences in cities around the world. Now, past sixty years old, he has returned to the land of his birth, South Africa's great Karoo region, to buy a piece of land and experience the ''real'' world for a change. He tells the audience, ''A vision of a new life unfolded before me. I could see myself sitting on my stoop after a good day of writing—all prose now, no more nonsense from actors and producers and critics—sitting there on my stoop watching the sun set and admiring my land, finally at peace with myself.''

Like Fugard himself, The Author is a somewhat self-satisfied white South African male, who has achieved a degree of fame writing plays that criticize the way white society has treated the non-white majority in his country. His success has given him a measure of financial comfort, and he could, if he chose, now turn his back on the troubles of the world. But he has an artist's sensitivity to the plight of other human beings. In his interview with Lloyd Richards, Fugard suggested, ''If you are a true artist, you will have a very finely tuned moral mechanism.'' The Author's moral mechanism causes him to feel guilt at his ability to drive into the little village of Nieu-Bethesda and casually write a check for the land old Abraam Jonkers has spent his life farming, but will never be able to own because of the color of his skin. It is a dilemma he did not expect to face in the ''new,'' post-apartheid South Africa, and it gives him pause. How successful can he really have been as an artist if society has changed so little in his lifetime?

That question has certainly bothered Fugard himself from time to time. Because his plays have always had a political undertone to them, audiences and critics have come to expect him to write dramas that are meant to change the world—a daunting task for anyone, artist or not. He maintains, however, that art continually contributes to the world around us. ''Art has a role,'' he told Richards. ''Art is at work in South Africa. But art works subterraneanly.

It's never the striking, superficial cause and effect people would like to see. Art goes underground into people's dreams and surfaces months later in strange, unexpected actions.''

Besides not expecting to face a moral challenge over an issue of race in Nieu-Bethesda, The Author also did not seem to count on discovering a kindred spirit—another artist—in this sleepy town in the Sneeuberg Mountain valley. Veronica Jonkers, a black teenager, has been a singer since the day she was born. Her grandfather, Abraam, remembers that as a baby she did not even cry so much as she opened her eyes wide, stretched her little mouth open and sang out loud. He tells Veronica, ''Your Ouma always used to say to me: If that child ever stops singing, Abraam Yonkers, then you must know there is something wrong with the world.''

And, sure enough, Veronica has been singing ever since. Like the ''creative energy'' that drives Fugard to write plays, Veronica sings her way through each day, and feels compelled to do whatever it takes to achieve her dream of becoming a famous performer, even though her grandfather doesn't understand why she would want to leave home and face the dangers of the world outside their valley. Veronica experiences the same initial resistance felt by many budding artists. She has a sense of purpose, and a plan for her life is beginning to unfold, but she must convince those around her who do not share her artistic sensibilities that she can overcome the odds and succeed at her craft. She pleads with her grandfather, ''All I know is that when I sing, I'm alive. My singing is my life. I must look after it the way Oupa looks after his vegetables. I know that if I stay here in the Valley it will die.''

Veronica, like The Author and Fugard himself, has been given the artist's *mission:* to go forth into the world, overcome terrible obstacles, and produce the art she is uniquely gifted to create. Her gift is song, while Fugard's, and therefore The Author's, is stories. ''My essential sense of myself is that of a storyteller,'' he revealed in *Twentieth Century Literature.* ''The only safe place I have ever known is when I am in the middle of a story as its teller.''

Of course, in *Valley Song* Fugard is quite literally in the middle of his story, which gives him the opportunity to express his fear that his usefulness as an artist may be nearing an end, even though all his hopes for the future have not yet been realized. ''A lot of my dreams didn't come true and

I saw them very clearly,'' The Author warns Veronica when she shares her dream of stardom with him. But she is unshakable and committed to her dream. Her artistic powers also seem stronger than his. While he is torn between the life he knew in the theater and turning to writing ''simple prose,'' and not doing either one effectively at the moment, she is focused on her most singular talent. With a simple song she is able to bring her old grandfather back to the present when his mind starts to wander and he thinks he is talking to his long-dead wife.

The difference between The Author and Veronica is striking. The Author believes he has ''just about used up all of the 'Glorious Future''' that he once had, but Veronica's future, like the future of young blacks across South Africa in the 1990s, is just beginning. As Robert King noted in the *North American Review,* ''He suggests a poignant, personal truth—that with a new day dawning for South African blacks, his day may be coming to an end.''

Watching your talents fade or your technique become obsolete is not easy for an artist, and, though he has admitted to fearing the day when his ''appointment book is empty'' and he cannot write any more, Fugard's unquenchable optimism keeps him constantly vigilant for the next opportunity his world might have to find redemption through creation. Over the years, he reported in *Twentieth Century Literature,* he has been surprised again and again by the strength of character and the resiliency of South Africa's young blacks, even in the face of terrible treatment under apartheid. ''I have been moved to see the many young men and women who, with an innate instinct for decency and justice which every human being is born with. . .fight free of that system,'' he reported. ''I have had the most unbelievably inspiring encounters over the years, with young men and women who have had every reason to hate, to resent, to be hell-bent on destruction, and who instead turn out to be individuals of love and tolerance and forgiveness.''

So, like any good artist, Fugard borrowed from his surroundings and turned his life into his art. *Valley Song* becomes, in effect, the gesture of The Author, Fugard, the artist, passing the torch from his generation to the next, with every expectation that progress will be made. ''The future belongs to you now,'' The Author tells Veronica, and with those few simple words, the world changes. As King observed, ''It's time, *Valley Song* argues, for the white male, surely Fugard himself, to step aside, to let the black woman sing her song to the world. That song will be all the more winning for being born in native soil.''

Source: Lane A. Glenn, in an essay for *Literature of Developing Nations for Students*, Gale, 2000.

Nelson Pressly

In the following review of the Washington, D.C. production of Athol Fugard's play Valley Song, *Nelson Pressley overviews the play's plotline and calls it a provocative and "often elusive" politically-edged performance, characteristic of Fugard's works.*

South African playwright Athol Fugard, author of *Master Harold . . . and the Boys, Sizwe Banzi Is Dead, Statements After An arrest Under the Immorality Act* and other plays protesting racial conditions in his homeland, doesn't have apartheid to kick around anymore.

Still, *Valley Song* now at the Kennedy Center's Eisenhower Theater in a production directed by and starring the playwright, is typical of Mr. Fugard's works: It is topical, earnest and sometimes movingly lyrical. It is still informed by racial oppression—things don't change overnight, after all. Spiritual repression, the theme of his incandescent *The Road to Mecca,* plays a big part here, too.

But the chief theme is change. At its most basic level, *Valley Song* is about a 17-year-old black girl named Veronica and her grandfather; the young girl is striding toward the future, while the old man is mired in the past.

Veronica is a free spirit who aspires to make it big as a singer. Veronica is a boisterous, fearless, funny character, and Lisa Gay Hamilton gives a very entertaining performance as she banters with the grandfather. Miss Hamilton sings with unembellished joy; her body twists with delight and her arms wave and flutter like twin flags in a happy breeze. Her Veronica comes so alive in her music that it is easy to read her as a sweet emblem of liberation.

In *Valley Song,* it isn't the government that crushes Veronica's dreams. It is Abraam ''Buks'' Jonkers, her grandfather, played by Mr. Fugard. For Buks, apartheid hasn't ended. He still tills the ground on land he doesn't own, and when a white writer—called the Author in the play and also played by Mr. Fugard—comes around to the property where Buks has lived and worked all his life, Buks goes hat in hand to beg to keep his place.

That prompts Veronica to call her grandfather a ''useless old coloured''. Buks can't understand why Veronica wouldn't want to be a domestic for the white Author—it's a living wage, after all, he argues—and their argument crystallizes a generational dispute that is complicated by the new freedoms in South Africa. Buks, whose fears are intensified by family tragedies in the not-too-distant past, simply doesn't think the way Veronica does.

''What's the use of a little dream, eh?'' she asks at one point. That statement defines her, but big dreams terrify Buks. He wants to stick to the narrow world he knows, no matter how precarious it is.

The performances are exquisite. Miss Hamilton's Veronica is radiant, and it's painful to see her light dimmed by Buks. Mr. Fugard is a different sort of actor than the fluid and utterly believable Miss Hamilton. Acting with a storyteller's wily cunning, he switches from playing the Author to Buks by donning a wool cap, slowing his step and pitching his voice slightly higher.

There is a whiff of deliberate artifice to Mr. Fugard's performance that is in keeping with Susan Hilferty's set design, which features an askew curtain behind a largely barren stage.

Having one actor play both parts—the white Author and the black Buks—gives *Valley Song* a provocative and often elusive political edge. Sometimes it goads you to see how close the concerns of the two men are—their feelings for the valley are almost identical—yet there is something subversive about hearing the white man recount the black man's servile appeal to him, stocked as it is with humble, smiling ''Master''s.

At such moments, the lovely, moving ''Valley Song'' takes on a teasing complexity that is wonderful to behold.

Source: Nelson Pressly, ''Play paints picture of pain dreams emerging from 'Valley' of apartheid,'' in *The Washington Times,* May 5, 1997, p. 11.

Jack Barbera

In the following review of the New York production of Athol Fugard's play Valley Song, *Jack Barbera overviews the play's plotline and examines the various ways in which the playwright is catego-rized by reviewers and critical essayists.*

What is clear from Athol Fugard's new play, *Valley Song*, held over at the Manhattan Theatre Club through January 21, is that the only box in which the playwright's work belongs is the stage itself, especially if the set is designed by Susan Hilferty, who has been working with Fugard for fifteen years. She has marked off a rectangular arena for the conflicts in *Valley Song* and painted it the colors of the semi-arid Karoo, where the story takes place. Curtains hanging from horizontal rods at the rear are the same colors, suggesting a low line of hills in the distance and the endless vistas of the region, Where earth and sky seem of a piece. A diagonal rod flashes across the backdrop, suggesting both the divisions between the characters and also the fact that Abraam Jonkers's life is winding down at the same time his granddaughter Veronica's life is starting to take off.

But what about the boxes in which critics and scholars try to place Fugard? Is he a "regional author"? Not in the sense sometimes implied, a category in which authors are put who are mainly of interest because of the region they write about. The fascination, early in Fugard's career, with this brave voice coming out of South Africa obscured to some extent the fact that his work was powerful in its art, and not only in its subject matter. Is he a "political playwright"? Fugard's plays have often depicted life under apartheid, but they are not political pamphlets. The tight sense of Fugard as a political playwright was implied, for example, when reporters in 1990 began peppering him with variations on the question, "Haven't de Klerk and Nelson Mandela put you out of business?"

A different historical coffin in which to bury Fugard was suggested a few years ago by a scholar who concluded that it is the playwright's early collaborative work with black performers that defines his value in the new South Africa, "because it shows how he found the voice of the voiceless," a task presumably no longer needed now that all are free to speak for themselves. No sooner was Fugard placed in that box than South African theatergoers were viewing *My Life,* which he put together with five young South African women of different racial and social backgrounds, helping them to express their experiences, hopes and fears. Critics in South Africa praised him for this "new beginning," but,

> " 'What's the use of a little dream, eh?' she asks at one point. That statement defines her, but big dreams terrify Buks. He wants to stick to the narrow world he knows, no matter how precarious it is."

as Mark Gevisser has pointed out, some considered Fugard's recognition that "he couldn't find his own words for South Africa's new reality" an evasion. Now we have *Valley Song* to demonstrate the truth of Fugard's claim that the end of apartheid would not put him out of business. He tells stories, and if the new South Africa has altered the nature of people's problems, it only means there are new challenges, new stories to tell. By nature Fugard is a minimalist. He said recently, "I need to stay on a very specific focus and trust that the dreaded word "universal" will look after itself." For him, like Faulkner, the universal does look after itself; his characters have a resonance that makes them who they are and more.

Fugard has said that the only safe place in his life is in the middle of a story, because then he knows who he is and why he is. In *Valley Song* he has put himself in the middle of his story as a third character, The Author, who tells us about Jonkers and his granddaughter, and who interacts with each. The Author is a playwright who buys a home in the Karoo, as Fugard has done. He envisions himself at a future time sitting on his porch after a good day of writing—all prose, he says, "no more nonsense from actors and producers and critics." Fugard, too, has expressed a weariness of late with the business of playwriting, and recently published in South Africa a prose work, *Cousins,* which seems to be part of an autobiography in progress. In that memoir Fugard looks back at the influence two cousins had on his development as a playwright. The mysterious and sinister Garth one day delivered to him a confession that explained the "dark aberrations" of his character. That is my real territory as a dramatist," Fugard noted, "the world of secrets, with their powerful effect on human behaviour and the

> For him, like Faulkner, the universal does look after itself; his characters have a resonance that makes them who they are and more."

trauma of their revelation." The moment of revelation in his new play comes when Abraam admits he has opened his granddaughter's letter, and Veronica confesses her desire to move to Johannesburg, where she can take singing lessons and pursue her dream of fame. Fugard's other cousin, Johnnie, had been an accomplished piano player. On lazy Sunday afternoons as he played, images would come to Athol, who would turn diem into stories. "I have come to believe," Fugard wrote, "that those sessions with Johnnie were the first formative experiences that led to my career as a dramatist." Fugard's passion for music is evident in *Valley Song*. He wrote the lyrics of the simple songs that Lisa Gay Hamilton, as Veronica, sings a cappella. (The engaging tunes for those songs were written by a young Afrikaner musician, Didi Kriel.). Hamilton brings to her role all the expressiveness and vitality it requires, along with physical beauty and a lovely voice. Fugard's love of music is also evident in the Afrikaans hymns in the play, and in the majestic King James English of two psalms he recites simply and stirringly as The Author (Fugard also plays the Coloured Abraam).

But the importance of Fugard's having created musical stories with cousin Johnnie is not really about the incorporation of music into his plays, or his feel for the rhythms of language. The importance, Fugard noted, has to do with the ability he developed to organize and control the emotional event of a story in the way a musical composition organizes and controls the flow of thought and feeling in time. Consider, again, *Valley Song*. It opens with The Author showing the audience some Karoo pumpkin seeds and inviting us to imagine them in the hands of old Abraam Jonkers, planting them in, the soil. The Author begins to enact what he describes, and he soon becomes the old man in repartee with his granddaughter about his time as a corporal in the military.

We see their love for each other and Abraam's delight in the simple songs she makes up—but not the song about the railway bus. Years before, the bus had taken Veronica's mother to Johannesburg, where she soon died. But Veronica sees the new South Africa as a world of possibility, where Coloureds can dream big and will not have to beg menial jobs from whites, while Abraam fears the changing future and considers Veronica's singing for money to be begging from whites.

Eventually Veronica leaves. Abraam, who cannot understand her need, is devastated. His daughter died when she left home, his wife has died, he is old and now he will be alone. And yet the ending is surprisingly upbeat, and it is a perfectly believable surprise. Fugard orchestrated it from the start with those seeds. Abraam will not be left "slumped in defeat and misery," The Author tells us. That would be "a dishonourable discharge from life," and Abraam is "an honourable old soldier." His love for the land tempts him to go and plant again, and his rebirth is like the everyday miracle of a dry, hard seed bursting into life.

The conflicts between Abraam and his granddaughter are not a matter of right and wrong but of different perspectives. There is reason to be concerned for Veronica's future: An unrealistically big dream can lead to bitterness. But if she does not pursue her dream she may suffer a death of the spirit. South Africa today is a country filled with people whose situations mirror those of Veronica and Abraam, and whites like The Author, who fears he will become one of the "pale, frightened white faces looking out on a world that doesn't belong to them anymore." The future offers promise and danger. But *Valley Song* is as timeless as it is timely, a story of the old fearful of change and the young with their hopes and impatience, and of a teller of stories, "that most ancient of all the arts," as Fugard notes in *Cousins*. *Valley Song* is a story without a right or wrong, but it has a point of view in seeing its characters with love. That loving gaze, that celebratory presentation, is pure Fugard.

Source: Jack Barbera, "Valley Song," (theatre review) in *The Nation,* Vol. 262, No. 4, January 29, 1996, p. 35.

Robert L. King

In the following review of the production of Athol Fugard's play Valley Song, *Robert L. King, in outlining the plotline, writes that he sees the plot as an allegory for Fugard's own writing career, diminishing now as his role the need for his work decreases.*

Athol Fugard gets four credits in the program for his new play, *Valley Song*–he wrote it, directed it and played two of the three parts. He received entrance applause at its American premiere in Princeton's McCarter Theatre, a tribute to his life as well as to his art. The play, despite Fugard's personal involvement and commitment, ultimately submerges the author's self in an allegory, one in which he passes the creative torch to the first generation to mature after the formal end of apartheid in South Africa. Fugard plays ''The Author, a White man'' and Abraam Jonkers (or Buks) ''an old Coloured tenant farmer''; both men have deep attachments to the land and both see it as fecund, literally so to the farmer and metaphorically to the creative writer. In the latter role, Fugard provoked appreciative chuckles when he said that he left ''the real world of the Karoo'' where there is no ''nonsense'' for the ''make believe world of the theatre.'' Throughout his career, Fugard has worked the resources of that make believe to question and undermine the appearances of civility that authorize discrimination. In his collaborations with John Kani and Winston Ntshona (*Sizwe Bansi is Dead* and *The Island*), in *The Blood Knot* and in *Master Harold*, Fugard displays, through theatrical convention, costume and role-playing, the socially acquired nature of racism, its conventional behavior. Whites learn how to dominate; blacks to accommodate, sometimes preserving a measure of dignity with irony. In *Valley Song*, however, digging, saluting, dancing and other actions are performed more to illustrate the acts themselves than to invite questions about their deeper significance. Similarly, speeches of simple exposition are delivered straight out to the audience. On a basic level of creativity, Fugard forsakes subtlety for clarity while on a higher level, he suggests a poignant, personal truth—that with a new day dawning for South African blacks, his day may be coming to an end.

With the house lights up, Fugard entered carrying pumpkin seeds; he mimed the digging and planting of Buks, the tenant farmer and his alter ego. As Buks, he spoke of hearing the valley sing in its springtime promise of new life. His granddaughter's singing is also a *valley song*; her voice fills the theater several times in the play. She, Veronica, wants to leave the valley to become a singer in Johannesburg; she does not want the job that Buks

> **"** On a basic level of creativity, Fugard forsakes subtlety for clarity while on a higher level, he suggests a poignant, personal truth—that with a new day dawning for South African blacks, his day may be coming to an end."

would have her take, doing housework for the White Author. She hopes for a better future after apartheid: ''Isn't it supposed to be different now?'' So far, though, everything is ''just the same,'' and the young woman's talent is frustrated: ''I am also a living thing, you know. I also want to grow.'' As this kind of clarity is delivered, it completely occupies our attention, while on reflection such lines can be heard in a larger context which deepens their meaning. Fugard himself had blacks technically listed as his house workers so that they could write, act and ''grow.'' As White Author, Fugard would ''own a piece of the Karoo'' even though the tenant farmer has worked that land with his hands and can probably make a stronger moral claim to it. One has title from ''a piece of paper''; the other has the legacy from a father who structured his life on land, house and Church. At the end, the white man invites Buks to plant pumpkin seeds with him; to him, the Karoo's creative potential is sensual and immediate—it smells and feels better than a woman. Now, after apartheid, the two older men are joined by a common enterprise for the first time and can find fulfillment in the Karoo. Veronica, reminiscent of the young Fugard, is being pulled away from it so that she can flourish artistically: ''I'll die if I have to live my whole life here.'' In an echo of The Master Builder, the young woman's enthusiasm prompts the old artist to say that he once had a dream of his own.

At one point, Buks can't quite sing an aria he learned while guarding an Italian prisoner of war; at others, he has no problem with hymns learned in Church. In contrast, Lisa Gay Hamilton sings Veronica's new songs with an exuberance and sincerity that refute the heritage of an imposed culture. It's time, *Valley Song* argues, for the white male, surely Fugard himself, to step aside, to let the black woman sing her song to the world. That song will be all the more winning for being born in native soil.

Source: Robert L. King, ''Valley Song,'' (theatre review) in *The North American Review,* Vol. 281, No. 2, March–April, 1996, p. 45.

Sources

Barbera, Jack, review of *Valley Song*, in *Nation*, January 29, 1996, p. 35.

Bemrose, John, review of *Valley Song*, in *Maclean's*, April 29, 1996, p. 71.

Fugard, Athol, transcript of speech, in *Twentieth Century Literature*, Winter, 1993, p. 381.

———, *Valley Song*, Theatre Communications Group, 1996.

King, Robert L., review of *Valley Song*, in *North American Review*, March-April, 1996, p. 45.

Richards, Lloyd, interview with Athol Fugard, in *Paris Review*, Summer, 1989, pp. 129-151.

Turvin, Mark, article, in *Arizona Arts Review Online*, December, 1997, http://www.mychele.com/aaro/song.html

Further Reading

Brockett, Oscar G., *History of the Theatre*, 8th ed., Allyn and Bacon, 1998.
  Brockett's *History of the Theatre* is a comprehensive volume, covering more than 2,000 years of worldwide theatrical tradition. Of special interest, however, is ''The Theatre of Africa,'' a new chapter the author added with the seventh edition of this highly respected theater sourcebook. In this chapter, Brockett covers the history and performance traditions of Nigeria, Ghana, Kenya, Zaire, and countries all across the African continent, including the Republic of South Africa.

Fugard, Athol, *Notebooks 1960-1977*, A. D. Donker, 1983.
  Fugard began keeping notebooks of his thoughts and experiences in 1959 when he and his wife traveled to Europe. His first entries became the basis for his 1960 play *The Blood Knot*, and ever since the brief sketches and ideas he has recorded in his notebooks have provided him with the characters, plots, and themes of his plays. This collection of Fugard's notebooks covers the first half of his career, from the creation of *The Blood Knot* through a production of *Sizwe Banzi Is Dead* at London's Royal Court Theatre in 1977.

Gray, Stephen, ed., *Athol Fugard*, McGraw-Hill, 1982.
  This collection of scholarship about Athol Fugard is part of the ''South African Literature Series'' and contains a chronology of events in the playwright's life, reviews of his plays, critical essays, interviews with the author, and an extensive bibliography suggesting additional resources for study.

Thompson, Leonard, *A History of South Africa*, Yale University Press, 1996.
  Thompson writes about the entire history of South Africa, from its earliest known inhabitants through the present day, with an emphasis on the black majority population.

Waldmeir, Patti, *Anatomy of a Miracle: The End of Apartheid and the Birth of the New South Africa*, W. W. Norton, 1997.
  Waldmeir is a journalist who became acquainted with Nelson Mandela and F. W. de Klerk, the two men primarily responsible for the dismantling of apartheid, and witnessed the events leading up to the integration of South African society and restoration of political power to that country's black majority. In *Anatomy of a Miracle* she uses interviews and eyewitness accounts to tell the story of the end of apartheid from the unrest of the early 1980s through Mandela's release from prison and inauguration as president in 1994.

The Village Witch Doctor

Amos Tutuola's story "The Village Witch Doctor" was originally published as part of the 1967 novel *Ajaiyi and His Inherited Poverty* and then as the title story in his 1990 collection, *The Village Witch Doctor and Other Stories*. Tutuola is known as the first African writer to gain international recognition. This story is one of many loosely based on Yoruba folktales of the oral tradition, which Tutuola heard as a child. Tutuola's non-standard form of written English, his first language being Yoruba, was controversial for its grammatical incorrectness and apparent lack of sophistication, what Dylan Thomas referred to in a controversial designation as "new English."

"The Village Witch Doctor" is about Aro, a man from a wealthy family, and his friend Osanyin, a witch doctor. After Aro asks Osanyin to help him bury his inherited fortune, the witch doctor goes back to dig up the fortune and buries it in his own shrine. As a result of this theft, which Aro never finds out was perpetrated by his friend the witch doctor, Aro dies in poverty. This "inherited poverty" is passed on to his son, Jaye, and, eventually, to his grandson, Ajaiyi. With each generation, the family becomes increasingly impoverished. In a state of abject poverty, Ajaiyi goes to the witch doctor for advice on how to escape his poverty. Osanyin advises him to place nine rams in nine sacks on his father's grave, as a trade for the return of his fortune by his dead father. The witch doctor then steals the first six rams from the grave and

Amos Tutuola

1967

butchers them for food. Ajaiyi, however, tricks the witch doctor by hiding in one of the last three sacks and jumping out with a machete to demand the return of his family fortune.

This story includes themes of inheritance, wealth, and poverty, as captured by repeated reference to the family's "inherited poverty" and the witch doctor's deceitful insistence that if Ajaiyi follows his advice, he will become "money man!" The theme of deceit and cleverness are also prominent in the story, as the witch doctor first cleverly deceives three generations of men out of their family fortune, and then Ajaiyi cleverly deceives the witch doctor into returning the fortune to its rightful owners.

Author Biography

Amos Tutuola has been described by Bernth Lindfors as "one of the great eccentrics in African literature" who "appears to be the kind of man least likely to win an international reputation as an author." Tutuola was born in Abeokuta, Western Nigeria, in 1920. Ethnically of Yoruba descent, and raised speaking Yoruba, Tutuola wrote, in English, epic adventures and short stories loosely derived from Yoruba myths and folk narratives. Tutuola's family was Christian. His father, Charles, was a cocoa farmer, and his mother's name was Esther. It was not until after his death that his reading public learned his family name was not Tutuola but Odegbami, Tutuola being his father's first name. Throughout his childhood, Tutuola received a checkered education, totaling less than six years, often changing schools due to family and financial circumstances, and working intermittently on his father's farm. Nonetheless, he excelled in school, and several times skipped ahead a grade. Lindfors comments that "considering his cultural background, minimal education, and lack of literary sophistication, it is surprising that he began writing at all and even more astonishing that he chose to write in English rather than in Yoruba, his native tongue." During World War II, Tutuola was enlisted in the Royal Air Force, from 1943 to 1945. In 1947, Tutuola married Victoria Alake, but a lesser known fact is that he had a total of four wives and eleven children. He held several different types of jobs: He was trained as a coppersmith, was employed as a messenger in the Nigerian Government Labor Department, and worked for the Nigerian Broadcasting Corporation. He began writing down stories

traditionally told in the Yoruba oral tradition on pieces of scrap paper as an antidote to boredom at work, and his first manuscript was sent to a London publisher in handwritten form. Upon publication of his first novel, *The Palm-Wine Drinkard* (1952), Tutuola won immediate acclaim in Britain and the United States. To the African literati, however, Tutuola, with his technically "bad" grammar and crudely written narrative style, was an embarrassment. Many African intellectuals felt that the Western world celebrated Tutuola because his writing catered to colonialist perceptions of Africa and Africans as primitive and unsophisticated. His second novel, *My Life in the Bush of Ghosts* (1954), was equally well-received in the West and criticized in Africa. However, as Western readers and critics began to tire of Tutuola's style with subsequent publications, African critics began to appreciate Tutuola as an important writer. By the time of his death, he had published nine novels and two short story collections, including the 1990 *The Village Witch Doctor and Other Stories*. Tutuola died of diabetes and hypertension on June 8, 1997, in poverty and obscurity, having been unable to afford adequate medical attention for his ailments. Both African and Western literary communities were slow to publicly commemorate Tutuola upon his death, but eventually recognized him as the first internationally known African writer and an important contributor to African literature. Oyekan Owomoyela said that Tutuola "died as he had lived, among uncertainties, contradictions, and controversy."

Plot Summary

As the story opens, Aro is a middle-aged man from a rich family. When his father died, he "inherited a large sum of money, farms, and other valuable property." One night, Aro invites his friend Osanyin, the village witch doctor, to help him bury his fortune in two large water pots out in the bush, in order to protect it from theft. Osanyin returns to the spot one midnight a few months later and digs up Aro's fortune, then buries it "in front of his gods which were in the shrine." When Aro goes, a few months later, to retrieve some of the money, he finds that it is gone. He goes to Osanyin for help. Osanyin tells him to go home, and that he, Osanyin, will ask his gods to tell him who took the money. Without actually asking the gods, Osanyin then tells Aro that his gods told him it was Osanyin's dead father who had stolen the inherited money from him. Aro goes with Osanyin to the site where the money had been buried and curses whoever stole it. He swears, "'My money will be recovered in the near or far future from whomsoever has stolen it, by my son, or my son's son, or one of my generation.'" Although maintaining his secret of having stolen the fortune from his friend, Osanyin goes home "worriedly. . .as if it had been revealed to Aro that Osanyin was the person who stole the money." From that point, Aro "started to live in poverty." Finally, "Aro died of poverty and he left poverty for his son Jaye."

Jaye marries "a very wretched lady," and two years later they have a son, Ajaiyi. After his wife dies, and after "several years' hard work," Jaye "became so poor and weary that he could not go and work on the farm any more," and so his son works the farm to support himself and his father. When Ajaiyi turns thirty and wishes to marry, his father cannot afford the marriage, and so Ajaiyi pawns his labor for the money to marry. He marries "a beautiful lady." Several months later, Jaye "fell seriously ill and died within a few days." Upon his death, Jaye's son cannot afford to pay for his funeral, and so must pawn his labor in order to afford the funeral expenses.

Pawned out to two different pawnbrokers, Ajaiyi's entire day is devoted to working for others, and he has only a few hours in the evenings to work his own farm. As a result, "his inherited poverty became even more severe." When he goes to Osanyin, the village witch doctor, for advice, Osanyin advises him to place nine rams in nine sacks on top of his father's grave, in order to trade with his dead father in exchange for the family fortune. Ajaiyi pawns his labor a third time, but can still only afford to buy six rams. He and his wife decide that they will leave the six rams as a first installment to his dead father, and then buy the other three rams with the money which the dead father will supposedly give them in trade. Osanyin then sneaks out to the father's grave at night with his servants and takes the six rams which Ajaiyi has placed there as a first installment. Osanyin takes the rams home and butchers them for food.

When Ajaiyi and his wife learn that placing the six rams on the grave has not brought them wealth, Osanyin advises Ajaiyi to place the remaining three rams on his father's grave. Ajaiyi then hides himself with a machete in one of the three sacks, and, when Osanyin and his servants bring the sacks home,

Ajaiyi jumps out of the third and threatens Osanyin, behaving as if he believes Osanyin is his dead father and demanding the family fortune. Terrified, Osanyin eventually returns the fortune to Ajaiyi.

Characters

Ajaiyi

Ajaiyi is Jaye's son and Aro's grandson. When Jaye becomes too ill and weary to work his own farm, Ajaiyi must work the farm himself in order to support the two of them. When Ajaiyi reaches thirty years of age and wishes to marry, his father cannot afford the marriage, and so Ajaiyi pawns his labor for the money to marry. He marries "a beautiful lady," but when, several months later, his father dies, Ajaiyi again pawns his labor in order to pay for the funeral. Pawned out to two different pawnbrokers, Ajaiyi's entire day is devoted to working for others, and he has only a few hours in the evenings to work his own farm. As a result, "his inherited poverty became even more severe." When he goes to Osanyin, the village witch doctor, for advice, Osanyin advises him to place nine rams in nine sacks on top of his father's grave, in order to trade with his dead father in exchange for the family fortune. Ajaiyi pawns his labor a third time, but can still only afford to buy six rams. He and his wife decide that they will leave the six rams as a first installment to his dead father, and then buy the other three rams with the money which the dead father will supposedly give them in trade. When this does not work, Osanyin advises Ajaiyi to place the remaining three rams on his father's grave. Ajaiyi then hides himself with a machete in one of the three sacks, and, when Osanyin and his servants bring the sacks home, Ajaiyi jumps out of the third and threatens Osanyin, behaving as if he believes Osanyin is his dead father and demanding the family fortune. Terrified, Osanyin eventually returns the fortune to Ajaiyi.

Ajaiyi's Wife

Ajaiyi's wife is described as "a beautiful lady." Ajaiyi pawns his labor in order to afford to marry her. Once they are married, it is she who advises Ajaiyi to go to the village witch doctor for advice on how to end his inherited poverty. When they can only afford six of the nine rams Osanyin has advised them to place on the dead father's grave, it is she who suggests they buy six rams as a first installment to the dead father. When this does

Media Adaptations

- Tutuola's first novel, *The Palm-Wine Drinkard*, was adapted for the stage by Kola Ogunmola.

---

not work, it is Ajaiyi's wife who advises him to go again to the village witch doctor for advice. Ajaiyi carries out each of his wife's wishes only with reluctance.

Aro

Aro is the father of Jaye and the grandfather of Ajaiyi. As the story opens, Aro is a middle-aged man from a rich family. When his father died, he "inherited a large sum of money, farms, and other valuable property." One night, Aro invites his friend Osanyin, the village witch doctor, to help him bury his fortune in two large water pots out in the bush, in order to protect it from theft. When Aro goes, a few months later, to retrieve some of the money, he finds that it is gone. He goes to Osanyin for help. Osanyin tells him to go home, and that he, Osanyin, will ask his gods to tell him who took the money. Osanyin then tells Aro that his gods had told him it was his dead father who had stolen the inherited money from him. Aro goes with Osanyin to the site where the money had been buried and curses whoever stole it. He swears that, "'My money will be recovered in the near or far future from whomsoever has stolen it, by my son, or my son's son, or one of my generation.'" From that point, Aro "started to live in poverty." Finally, "Aro died of poverty and he left poverty for his son Jaye." Nonetheless, Aro's curse of the person who stole his money, and his declaration that the money will be recovered, comes true in the end of the story when his grandson, Ajaiyi, recovers the fortune while terrifying Osanyin, who had stolen it from Aro years before.

Jaye

Jaye is the son of Aro and the father of Ajaiyi. When, after his inherited fortune is stolen, Aro dies of poverty, Jaye inherits his father's poverty. Jaye marries "a very wretched lady," and two years later they have a son, Ajaiyi. After his wife dies, and after "several years' hard work," Jaye "became so poor and weary that he could not go and work on the farm any more," and so his son works the farm to support himself and his father. Several months after his son is married, Jaye "fell seriously ill and died within a few days." Upon his death, Jaye's son cannot afford to pay for his funeral, and so must pawn his labor in order to afford the funeral expenses. Thematically, the business of the funeral further indicates the burden of "inherited poverty" which grows with the passing of each generation of this family.

Jaye's Wife

Jaye's wife is referred to as "a very wretched lady, of whom no one could tell how or from where she had come to the village." Two years later, she and Jaye have a son, Ajaiyi. The family grows "poorer and poorer," and "at last Ajaiyi's mother died suddenly in poverty."

Osanyin

Osanyin is the village witch doctor of the story's title. He "was well known throughout the village and also all other surrounding villages because of his profession." His friend, Aro, invites him one night to help bury his inherited fortune in two large water pots out in the bush under a tree. Osanyin returns to the spot one midnight a few months later and digs up Aro's fortune, then buries it "in front of his gods which were in the shrine." When Aro comes to Osanyin to report that his fortune has been stolen, the village witch doctor deceitfully tells his friend to go home while he asks his gods who took the money. Without asking the gods, Osanyin goes to Aro's home and tells him that the gods said his dead father had taken the money. Aro then goes to where the money had been buried and curses whoever stole it. Although maintaining his secret of having stolen the fortune from his friend, Osanyin goes home "worriedly. . .as if it had been revealed to Aro that Osanyin was the person who stole the money." When Aro's grandson, Ajaiyi, comes to Osanyin years later for advice on how to end his "inherited poverty," Osanyin deceitfully advises him to place nine rams in nine sacks on his father's grave, as a trade for his family fortune. Osanyin then sneaks out to the father's grave at night with his servants and takes the six rams which Ajaiyi has placed there as a first installment. Osanyin takes the rams home and butchers them for food. When Ajaiyi comes to Osanyin for further advice, the witch doctor tells him to place the remaining three rams on his father's grave. Ajaiyi, however, tricks the witch doctor by hiding himself in one of the sacks supposedly containing a ram. When Osanyin brings the three bags home with his servants, Ajaiyi jumps out of the third and threatens Osanyin with a machete until he gives him the family fortune.

Themes

Justice

This story contains the classic theme, or moral, that, in the end, everyone gets what he deserves. In other words, evil is punished and good is rewarded. Furthermore, suffering inflicted by one man upon another is vindicated in the end. The witch doctor, although he successfully deceives three generations of men out of their family fortune, is ultimately punished for his evil deeds. In the world of this story, it seems that fate is at work, to the extent that Osanyin, the witch doctor, becomes the agent of his own undoing. When Aro curses whoever has stolen his buried fortune, Osanyin is compelled to assert that the curse will come true in order to protect his secret. Osanyin is unsettled by the curse, and by having to echo the curse, because he has in effect been cursed, and cursed himself, as a result of this deception. All of Osanyin's lies come back to haunt him in the end. He deceives Ajaiyi, Aro's grandson, by claiming that the gods have told him his "inherited poverty" is due to his dead father having stolen his rightful inheritance from him. Osanyin tells Ajaiyi that he must place nine rams in nine sacks on his father's grave, as a trade for the return of the family fortune. Osanyin then sneaks out to the grave and takes the rams home to be butchered for his food. However, Ajaiyi ultimately tricks Osanyin into returning the fortune when he hides in one of the sacks with a machete and jumps out of the sack once Osanyin has brought it home. Ajaiyi punishes Osanyin for his deceit by terrifying him with the machete. It is Osanyin's lie which comes back to haunt him because Ajaiyi pretends that he believes Osanyin is in fact his dead father who has supposedly stolen the money from him. Thus, Ajaiyi turns Osanyin's own lie against him in order to punish him for the theft. In the end, therefore, the wicked

are punished and the good are rewarded with their rightful inherited wealth.

Family and Inheritance

This story follows three generations of men and their wives through the inheritance, theft, and recovery of the family fortune. Family is thus a central theme of the story. In addition, the inheritance of both wealth and poverty are carried down through a patrilineal line of descent; each man inherits the financial status of his father. The continuation of the line of descent is indicated by Aro's curse upon the person who stole his buried fortune. Aro, standing on his father's grave, declares, "My money will be recovered in the near or far future from whomsoever has stolen it, by my son, or my son's son, or one of my generation!" This projection of revenge by future generations is carried out when Aro's grandson, Ajaiyi, does in fact recover the family fortune from the man who had stolen it. The theme of family is also tied to concerns about pride and status within the village community. Ajaiyi, Jaye's son, must procure the money necessary to obtain a wife, because his father cannot afford to do so; this circumstance is a measure of the family's poverty, as Jaye explains: "According to our tradition, it is a father's duty to make a marriage for his son." And again, when Jaye dies, Ajaiyi must obtain the money for a proper funeral ceremony in order to avoid the "shame" of not being able to afford to bury his own father. Thus, family in this story is central to both the financial and social status of the individual.

Style

The Yoruba Folktale

Tutuola's stories are loosely based on traditional Yoruba folktales, originally told in oral form. African critics pointed out early in Tutuola's writing career that he seemed to have borrowed heavily from the Nigerian writer Fagunwa, who wrote Yoruban folktales in the Yoruban language. Subsequent critics, however, have noted that Tutuola's stories are infused with his own particular style of narrative, and do not include the pointed moralizing which Fagunwa's tales emphasized. In his later writing, however, which would include "The Village Witch Doctor", Tutuola consciously included more specific elements of traditional Yoruba lore into his stories.

Topics for Further Study

- Tutuola has been compared to fellow Nigerian writers Chinua Achebe and Daniel O. Fagunwa. Learn more about one of these authors and his work. Compare his work and literary reputation to that of Tutuola. In what ways is this author's representation of African culture and history different from or similar to that of Tutuola? What themes are of concern to this author? In what ways does his writing style compare to that of Tutuola?

- Tutuola is Nigerian. Learn more about the history of Nigeria during the pre-colonial period, the colonial period, and after national independence. What major historical events and political struggles occurred during these periods in Nigerian history?

- Tutuola was ethnically of Yoruba descent. Learn more about the history, social structure, and culture of the Yoruba people. What different tribal identities exist within the broader category of Yoruba people? What was the effect of colonization on Yoruba culture and social structure? What is the status of the Yoruba people in Africa today?

- Although Tutuola was raised speaking the Yoruba language, he wrote exclusively in English. Learn more about the Yoruba language. In what countries is Yoruba spoken? Why do you suppose Tutuola chose to write in English?

- Tutuola is credited with recording in written English an oral narrative tradition of Yoruba culture and language. Other writers have recorded the traditional oral folktales of their own cultures, for example, *Italian Folktales*, collected by Italo Calvino; *Grimm's Fairy Tales,* a collection of traditional German fairy tales, collected by the Brothers Grimm; and *A Thousand and One Nights* (also called *Arabian Nights*), which is an ancient collection of tales from the Middle East. Read a story from one of these collections. Compare it to Tutuola's tale. In what ways does it contain similar themes and narrative structure to that of Tutuola? In what ways do these folktales differ from each other?

- Tutuola's stories are a liberal rendering of stories told to and by him as a child among his family, friends, and community. What stories have been told to or by you among your own family, friends, or community? Write down a story you have only heard in oral form. What changes occur in the process of translating an oral story to written form? What elements of the story are lost in the process of transcription? Does the process of writing it down add to or embellish the story in any way?

Repetition and Rhythm

Although every culture has its particular style of folktale, critics have found many similarities in folktales across a spectrum of cultures. Italo Calvino, for example, in collecting and transcribing traditional Italian folktales, has noted the "rhythm" and "hard logic" with which these stories are told. Rhythm, according to Calvino, is a function of repetition: "The technique of oral narration in the popular tradition follows functional criteria. It leaves out necessary details but stresses repetition: for example, when a tale consists of a series of the same obstacles to be overcome by different people. A child's pleasure in listening to stories lies partly in waiting for things he expects to be repeated; situations, phrases, formulas. Just as in poems and songs the rhymes help to create rhythm, so in prose narrative there are events that rhyme." "The Village Witch Doctor" is also structured by a rhythm of anticipated repetitions. The male of each generation of the family in the story—Aro, Jaye, and Ajaiyi—follows a similar set of experiences and actions. Both Aro and Ajaiyi go repeatedly to the village witch doctor for advice, and are repeatedly deceived by him. Aro and Jaye, and their wives, each die ''suddenly'' of poverty. Repeated actions are also taken by individual characters. For example, Ajaiyi has no choice but to pawn his labor for money three different times in the story.

Language

Tutuola's stories have been noted for their non-standard use of the English language. These stories, written in English, are loosely based on Yoruba oral folktales. And, while English was not Tutuola's first language, he also received only a minimal formal education. As a result, his early novels and stories were characterized by grammatical errors which the editors chose to leave uncorrected, in order to capture Tutuola's narrative voice. By the time ''The Village Witch Doctor'' was published, late in Tutuola's career, he had made efforts to improve his use of standard English in his writing. As a result, as Oyekan Owomoyela noted, ''If. . .Tutuola's English in the earliest novels approximated that of contemporary secondary class two students, and in the later ones. . .that of secondary class four users. . .certainly by *Witch Doctor* he was writing at a level that compares easily with that of high school certificate holders.'' Harold R. Collins, however, asserts that, despite the increasing standardization of Tutuola's use of English in the later stories, ''the language of the new romance is still pure Tutuolan—unschoolmastered and unedited, robust and sinewy.''

Literary Heritage

Tutuola's short stories, written in English, are derived from the oral tradition of his native African tribe, the Yoruba. Tutuola's literary style is noted for its preservation of the speech patterns characteristic of oral storytelling, which boldly defy the dictates of standard written English. Daniel Fangunwa earlier transcribed similar traditional stories into the Yoruba language, and some critics have denigrated Tutuola for borrowing too heavily from his work, while others note that Tutuola has added his own literary voice to these traditional tales. Tutuola's renditions of stories he heard among his family and fellow members of his tribal village can also be categorized among written works of folklore based on oral traditions, such as *Italian Folktales*, by Italo Calvino, and *Grimm's Fairy tales*, compiled from German folktales by the Brothers Grimm. Tutuola's

fiction also belongs to the category of African fiction written in English which emerged in the latter half of the twentieth century, roughly commensurate with the achievement of national independence among many African nations in the years after World War II. As a Nigerian, Tutuola's work is categorized with other twentieth century West African writers, most notably the Nigerian Chinua Achebe, whose novel *Things Fall Apart* was first published in 1954. Since many African nations remained part of the British Commonwealth, even after independence, Tutuola's work is also part of the broader development of English literature of the British Commonwealth.

Historical Context

Nigeria

Tutuola was born and lived throughout his life in Nigeria, and his life spanned most of twentieth-century Nigerian history. By the beginning of the nineteenth century, the area of West Africa now known as Nigeria was inhabited by various tribal peoples often at war with one another. In the latter half of the nineteenth century, the area came increasingly under the rule of British traders and missionaries, and eventually was politically conquered by the British. In 1894, the two protectorates of Benin and Yorubaland were combined by the British to create the Niger Coast Protectorate. The British government eventually took control of the areas which had been run by the Royal Niger Company. The British re-divided the region into the Protectorate of Northern Nigeria and Southern Nigeria. In 1914, these two territories were merged by the British and renamed the Colony and Protectorate of Nigeria. In the early twentieth century, the British instituted what they called ''indirect rule,'' which was a policy of allowing for native rule at a local level, overseen by a British governmental rule of the colony. Violent rebellion against British rule, resulting in significant casualties, took place in 1906, 1918, and 1929. Throughout the 1950s, pressure for self-rule increased, and new constitutions were adopted several times. In 1960, Nigeria was granted national self-rule. Subsequently, however, internal tensions between various ethnic groups led to national instability. In 1966, a military coup was attempted, in which the prime minister was murdered; however, the military head who came into power as a result of this coup was assassinated that same year. During that year, inter-ethnic tensions erupted into violence. A civil war began in 1967 when several states declared themselves an independent Republic of Biafra. The Biafrans surrendered in 1970. In 1975, a military coup was enacted, and in 1976 the leader of that coup was assassinated. Another military coup took place in 1983. In 1985, Nigeria saw its sixth coup in a period of twenty years. Nigeria's first presidential elections in 1993 were ruled illegitimate, and another military coup resulted.

The Yoruba

Tutuola's ethnic identity was Yoruba. The Yoruba are one of the two most populous tribal identities in Nigeria. Among the more than 24 million Yorubans in Nigeria today, the men are traditionally farmers or craftsmen, and the women, who do not farm, are traditionally shop-owners and tradeswomen. The Yoruba are known for their bronze casting skills, using the ''lost wax'' technique. To this day, the city of Ile-Ife is of great importance to the Yoruba, as it is traditionally considered to be the location of the creation of the earth.

Nigerian Novelists

Tutuola is one among several prominent modern Nigerian novelists. Daniel Fagunwa, a Nigerian, was the first to publish a full-length novel in the Yoruba language. Published in 1938, the novel's title is translated as *The Forest of a Thousand Demons,* and is essentially a collection of traditional Yoruba fairy tales with a clearly stated moral which shows the influence of Christian missionary education. Tutuola has often been criticized as having borrowed rather heavily from his early reading of Fagunwa's work. Chinua Achebe, probably the best known African writer in the Western world and also a Nigerian, is famous for his 1954 novel, *Things Fall Apart,* which idealizes a lost traditional African culture destroyed by colonialism.

Critical Overview

Oyekan Owomoyela, writing in 1999, stated that, while ''Amos Tutuola is the first African author to get international fame,'' he is also ''undoubtedly one of the most controversial of African writers; indeed, many would assert that he is indisputably, and by far, the most controversial.'' Bernth Lindfors has pointed out that Tutuola ''appears to be the kind of man least likely to win an international reputation as an author.'' Lindfors goes on to explain that ''considering his cultural background, minimal education, and lack of literary sophistication, it is surprising that he began writing at all and even more astonishing that he chose to write in English rather than in Yoruba, his native tongue.''

Tutuola, whose life work includes nine novels and two short-story collections, became known for his epic novels loosely based on traditional Yoruba folktales he learned as a child. The most controversial quality of his writing is the nonstandard use of written English, which Western critics found charming and early African critics regarded as disgraceful.

Tutuola's first novel, *The Palm-Wine Drinkard* (1952), gained immediate recognition and generally positive reception in England and the United States. Harold R. Collins notes that, as a result of the publication of Tutuola's first novel, ''Anglo-Nigerian literature was on the world scene, for it was immediately successful.'' Lindfors explains that ''the first reviewers greeted Tutuola's unusual tale with wide-eyed enthusiasm, hailing the author as a primitive genius endowed with amazing originality and charming naivete.'' Lindfors states, ''Tutuola's second book, *My Life in the Bush of Ghosts* (1954), was welcomed with the same mixture of awe, laughter and bewilderment that had greeted his first.'' Collins claims that, with the publication of this second book, Tutuola ''was established as a genuine West African literary bombshell.'' Collins goes on to depict the international breadth of Tutuola's success: ''In England he was a big success; his books got enthusiastic reviews from Dylan Thomas and V. S. Pritchett. In America Grove Press brought out his second romance, and he achieved such fame as to be mentioned in *Vogue.* French, German, Italian, and Yugoslav translations attested to considerable European interest.''

However, upon publication of his third novel, *Simbi and the Satyr of the Dark Jungle* (1955), Western critics began to cool to Tutuola. As Owomoyela pointed out, ''Within the space of a few years. . .some of his early admirers were reversing themselves, proclaiming his diminishing literary powers or expressing irritation with the very qualities and affectations they had earlier applauded.'' Lindfors adds, ''By the time Tutuola's fourth and fifth books. . .appeared. . .his European and American readers were tired of his fantasies and fractured English. They expressed impatience with his inability to develop new themes and techniques and deplored his crippling limitations as a writer." Collins sums up this decline in Western reception of Tutuola's work, stating that "it must be admitted that the Western critics' admiration for Tutuola's work was pretty much a flash in the pan. After *My Life in the Bush of Ghosts* these critics are either silent or patronizingly severe or damningly faint in their praise."

Far from Western critics, the African literati immediately took offense at Tutuola's international recognition. They were both concerned with the image of Africa and Africans that his work promulgated in the West and suspicious of Western motives in praising Tutuola as a primitive and exotic curiosity which was in keeping with a patronizing colonialist view of Africa. Collins noted:

> Many educated Nigerians were simply horrified by the books. They deplored his "crudities," his lack of inhibitions, and the folk tale basis of his romances. . .; they accused poor, shy, diffident Tutuola of encouraging an unprogressive kind of mythical thinking, of leading the West African literature up a blind alley, and, most important, of giving the supercilious, prejudiced westerners an excuse for continuing to patronize the allegedly superstitious Nigerians! The Nigerians' sense of their vulnerability to western scorn seems to give the greatest force to their objections to Tutuola's work.

However, Owomoyela has pointed out that these early criticisms by Africans were not entirely off the mark:

> Dylan Thomas's description of Tutuola's usage as "young English written by a West African" certainly betrayed that subtext, as did V. S. Pritchett's priceless description of Tutuola's voice as "like the beginning of man on earth, man emerging, wounded and growing."

Lindfors similarly sums up the early African critical response to Tutuola, and to the West's adoration of his work:

> Indeed, Nigerians disliked Tutuola for the same reasons that Europeans and Americans treasured him: his subject matter was exotic and his grammar atrocious. Educated Africans suspected that the bizarre narratives of this messenger-turned-author appealed to foreigners because they projected an image of Africa as uncouth, primitive and barbaric—an image which happened to coincide with the foreign stereotype of the "Dark Continent." As a consequence, many of Tutuola's countrymen were convinced he was only being patronized by condescending racists and was really unworthy of serious consideration as a creative writer.

However, in the 1960s and 1970s, having achieved national independence and with greater confidence in the Western world's image of Africa,

A Nigerian shaman, or witch doctor. In Tutuola's story, the village witch doctor tricks a friend out of his family's fortune.

African critics began to warm to Tutuola. Collins has noted that, eventually, "most educated Nigerians are willing to admit that American and English critics may just possibly be right, that Tutuola is in fact a great writer." Lindfors further characterizes this sea change in the response of African critics to Tutuola's stories:

> Africans . . . were just beginning to appreciate his mythical imagination and extravagant sense of humor. In the mid-sixties a number of African literary critics wrote reappraisals of his work, probing his special strengths and weaknesses as a creative artist. By this time most sub-Saharan states had achieved political independence so African intellectuals were less self-conscious about their image abroad. Tutuola's books could therefore be evaluated more objectively than before, and many Africans discovered they liked them despite their oddities and obvious flaws.

Lindfors states that, by 1967, with the publication of *Ajaiyi and His Inherited Poverty*, "Tutuola's reputation was fairly secure both in Africa and abroad." Nonetheless, Collins, writing in 1969, stated that "some Nigerian critics recognized Tutuola's extraordinary talent, but Tutuola has always been 'controversial,' and even now a Westerner's praise for Tutuola will bring a somewhat wary glance from an educated Nigerian.''

Criticism

Liz Brent

Brent has a Ph.D. in American culture, with a specialization in film studies, from the University of Michigan. She is a freelance writer and teaches courses in the history of American cinema. In the following essay, Brent discusses the themes of cleverness and deceit and poverty and wealth in ''The Village Witch Doctor.''

As in many folktales, this story revolves around the themes of cleverness and deceit. Osanyin, the witch doctor, cleverly deceives three generations of men out of their inherited fortune. In the end, however, the grandson of the man whom Osanyin originally deceived is able to successfully use his cleverness in order to deceive Osanyin into returning the family fortune.

Throughout the story, the reader is reminded of the many deceptions, small and large, which the village witch doctor visits upon Aro and his descendants. When Aro first comes to Osanyin to report that his buried family fortune has been stolen, the witch doctor ''pretended to be surprised and innocent'' of the matter. In assuring Aro that he will ask his gods who has stolen the money, Osanyin ''caressed Aro as he deceived him.'' When, without actually consulting his gods, Osanyin reports to Aro that they have told him his own dead father has stolen his inheritance, the witch doctor ''deceitfully'' feigns surprise at this solution to the mystery. Finally, Aro ''believed the faulty explanation'' Osanyin offers him.

Osanyin's deceptions take the form not only of outright lies, but also of the false face he puts on for those he is deceiving. The narration of the story frequently points out to the reader the ways in which the witch doctor pretends to have only his friend's interests in mind, all the while scheming to continue the deception from which he has profited. As the story opens, and Aro explains to Osanyin that he wishes to bury his fortune to keep it safe from thieves, Osanyin's response is one of cheerfully agreeing to help his friend; however, the reader, in retrospect, may detect that this cheerful demeanor on the part of the witch doctor is forced, as he is already scheming to steal his friend's money. When

Aro asks him to help bury the money, and explains why, the witch doctor's response is described in the following manner: '''Oh, yes,' Osanyin replied cheerfully, 'I see your point. Let us carry the money to the bush and bury it there before daybreak!''' His enthusiasm, as indicated by the exclamation point which ends the sentence, indicates the forced nature of his professed interest in protecting his friends' money from theft. And when, several months later, Aro goes to Osanyin to report the theft, the witch doctor goes so far as to pretend he doesn't even understand what Aro has told him: ''The witch doctor pretended to be surprised and innocent by saying, 'Has your money been stolen, or is it you cannot remember what you wanted to tell me?'''

When Aro returns to his father's grave to curse whoever had stolen the money, the witch doctor, in order to maintain his deception, is put in a position of having to ''reluctantly'' reinforce a curse which is in fact aimed at Osanyin himself: ''Then his friend reluctantly said, 'Let your curse come to pass on whoever has stolen your money.''' Ultimately, then, Osanyin is undone by the powers of his own deception. His unease with endorsing Aro's curse is described when ''the witch doctor worriedly returned to his house as if it had been revealed to Aro that Osanyin was the person who stole the money.'' Thus, the witch doctor's layering of deception causes him to bring justice down upon his own head, as the curse is realized by the end of the story.

Osanyin's greed and deception are made ironic by his status as a respected witch doctor, ''well known throughout the village and also all other surrounding villages.'' The hypocrisy practiced by the witch doctor is emphasized by the ways in which he specifically uses his profession as a means of deceiving others. The fact that Aro and each of his descendants go to Osanyin for advice facilitates Osanyin's schemes. Furthermore, the ways in which Osanyin utilizes his sacred profession to further his profane ends is made apparent by the fact that he buries the stolen fortune ''in front of his gods which were in the shrine.'' He further abuses his position by repeatedly claiming to consult his gods in order to help the victims of his theft, and then not consulting the gods at all but only further deceiving them in order to protect his own wealth.

In the end, it is Ajaiyi's cleverness and deceit of Osanyin which wins him back the money that is rightfully his. Osanyin hides himself with a machete in one of the sacks on his father's grave which

What Do I Read Next?

- *The Palm-Wine Drinkard and His Dead Palm-Wine Tapster in the Deads' Town* (1952) is Tutuola's first novel, an epic adventure loosely linking together a number of traditional Yoruba folktales.

- *My Life in the Bush of Ghosts* (1954), Tutuola's second novel, was as enthusiastically received in England and the U.S. as was his first.

- *Ajaiyi and His Inherited Poverty* (1967) is the novel on which the short story "The Village Witch Doctor" is based.

- *Yoruba Folktales* (1986) was compiled and translated by Tutuola.

- *The Village Witch Doctor and Other Stories* (1990) is Tutuola's collection of short stories.

- *The Forest of a Thousand Demons* (1938) by Daniel Fagunwa is a novel based on a collection of traditional Yoruba folktales.

Osanyin believes to hold a ram. When Osanyin steals what he believes are three sacks of rams and brings them back to his shrine to butcher them for food, Ajaiyi jumps out of the third sack, surprising the clever and deceitful witch doctor. Ajaiyi's cleverness and deceit further facilitate his success as he pretends that he thinks Osanyin is in fact his dead father who has supposedly stolen his inheritance from him. By this means, Ajaiyi succeeds in terrifying the witch doctor into returning the fortune. The fortune thus goes to the man who is cleverest in his deceit.

This story also centers on themes of poverty and wealth. The entire story is focused on the theft, and ultimate retrieval, of a family fortune. The fate of these characters, and each new generation of the family, is inextricably linked to the status of their financial situation. Aro, in the opening of the story, is "from a rich family." When his father dies, Aro "inherited a large sum of money, farms, and other valuable property." Fearing that someone may steal his fortune from his home, Aro buries it out in the bush under a tree, believing that "his inherited wealth was safe."

The witch doctor's greed for wealth motivates him to steal the family fortune of a man who is his friend, who trusts him and seeks him out for advice. The lust for money in the witch doctor is thus strong enough to motivate him to betray a trusted friend over a period of several generations.

Wealth is also clearly important to Aro and his descendants. When Aro learns that his buried fortune has been stolen, he "held his head in both hands and burst into tears." As a result of the theft, "Aro started to live in poverty." This poverty, as inherited by Aro's descendants, determines all of the significant events of their lives and even causes their deaths. Having to work hard on his farm as a result of the theft of his inheritance, Aro eventually becomes "so poor and weary that he could not go and work on the farm any more." When Aro's son, Jaye, wishes to marry, he cannot provide the needed money to afford the marriage. This "inherited poverty," as passed on from father to son in a patrilineal society, threatens the pride and status of Aro's descendants, as well as their material conditions. As Aro explains to Jaye: "According to our tradition, it is a father's duty to make a marriage for his son. But as you know I am in great poverty. My poverty is so great that I have not had even a half-kobo for the past four years. So, my dear Ajaiyi, it is a great pity that I have no money with which to pay the dowry for you. I am sorry, indeed." As a result, Jaye must pawn his labor in order to raise the money. When, after Jaye marries, Aro dies, Jaye's poverty again causes him to pawn his labor in order to pay for the funeral. And, as with the marriage, Jaye is obligated

> In the world of this story, financial status is the most important factor in the life of a family, and determines the fate of each individual in that family."

to do so as a matter of tradition and pride, thereby avoiding the shame of his community: "Ajaiyi had no money to spend on the funeral ceremony for his father. Of course, as it was a great shame if he failed to perform the funeral ceremony, Ajaiyi was forced to go and pawn himself to another pawnbroker, who gave him the money which he spent on his father's funeral expenses." Because almost all of his time is committed to working for other people, he has little time to work on his own farm, and "his inherited poverty became even more severe."

The theme of desire for money is expressed in the witch doctor's phrase, "Money man!," which he uses to assure Ajaiyi that he will be able to recover the family fortune. Osanyin tells Ajaiyi, "'Yes, it is sure you will be a rich man. . .And when a person has money, the people call him 'Money man!'" The ecstasy attendant upon wealth is expressed by the way in which "the witch doctor and Ajaiyi shouted together, laughing, 'Money man!'" Ajaiyi's wife also uses this phrase, particularly in pointing out to Ajaiyi the status attendant upon those with money, and the comparative shame of poverty; in urging him to carry out the witch doctor's plan for ending their poverty, she declares, "'Can't you see, when you go here, you see 'Money man!' You go there, you see 'Money man!'"

The primary concern of the story with financial status is summed up through the happy conclusion, in which Ajaiyi and his wife recover "four thousand *naira*" from the witch doctor, upon which they "were free from their poverty and other burdens, as soon as Ajaiyi refunded the money to the three pawnbrokers." In the world of this story, financial status is the most important factor in the life of a family, and determines the fate of each individual in that family.

Source: Liz Brent, in an essay for *Literature of Developing Nations for Students*, Gale, 2000.

Richard Bauerle

In his brief review of Amos Tutuola's new volume of stories, The Village Witch Doctor and Other Stories, *Richard Bauerle still finds delight in Tutuola's tales, which are based on traditional Yoruba embellished with some modern twists.*

Amos Tutuola's new volume contributes eighteen more stories to his already large number, all based on traditional Yoruba folktales. His themes are much like those in his previous books: greed, thievery, betrayal, fraud, et cetera. However, the milieu is in some cases more modern. The major plot device is that of the trickster tricked. The title story is typical though more elaborate than most. The witch doctor keeps tricking his victim in different ways until finally the tables are turned. The characters in the tales include many familiar figures: the tortoise, the jungle drummer, the beetle lady, and people with regular Yoruba names.

Tutuola's manner of telling his stories is, as one would expect, closer to that of his later books than to that of his first and most famous work, *The Palm-Wine Drinkard*. There is more of the writer and less of the talker. Almost gone are such rich expressions as "He said whisperly" and "We took our fear back." Still, one occasionally encounters such fresh phrasing as "The priest lived lonely in the heart of the forest." It is gratifying to see Tutuola at age seventy still busy enriching African literature with his illuminating interpretations.

Source: Richard Bauerle, "Africa & The West Indies," (reviews) in *World Literature Today,* Vol. 64, No. 3, Summer, 1991, p. 539.

John Haynes

In the following brief review, John Haynes discusses Amos Tutuola's book The Village Witch Doctor and Other Stories, *a collection of fables and retellings of old Yoruba folk tales for which Tutuola is widely known.*

Although *The Palm Wine Drinkard* was Amos Tutuola's first published novel, he had written *The Wild Hunter in the Bush of the Ghosts* earlier, in 1948, and sent the exercise-book manuscript to Faber and Faber where it stayed until 1982, when Three Continents Press issued a limited scholars's edition with a facsimile of Tutuola's handwriting. In 1983, while attending the International Writers' Workshop at Iowa, Tutuola was asked to prepare the present edition. In his foreword, Bernth Lindfors writes:

He went through the typescript of the original version carefully, correcting obvious errors and restructuring several episodes. I was asked to lend a hand in the revision and to supervise computerized typesetting of the final text.

Lindfors' phrasing is a little unfortunate in that it may give the impression to some readers, not in possession of the earlier text, that some scholarly tinkering has been going on. We are reassured that "what is being presented here is basically the same old *Wild Hunter* in more modern dress", but all this does sound a little jaunty at a time when African writers and critics are increasingly wary of the role of western scholars and publishers in handling their work. "This transformation" [*sic*], Lindfors concludes, "achieved by means of the latest technological miracles, is very much in keeping with the spirit of the story."

Is it? It is only in a very superficial sense that Tutuola deals in "miracles". His cosmology is one that undermines the western notion of the "miracle" a bizarre deviance from the stable, solid world of western rationalism and literary naturalism.

The Wild Hunter, like *The Palm Wine Drinkard*, challenges this whole cultural scenario and draws on vernacular Yoruba writing. In *The Palm Wine Drinkard* Tutuola carried the challenge into the very structure of his prose by using a non-standard kind of English which, though sometimes taken as a quaint index of semi-literacy, was in fact, as Chinua Achebe has pointed out, a conscious choice. *The Wild Hunter* is in standard English but with tellingly non-standard deployment of the "bureaucratese" of his civil service years. Thus if you want to get into heaven you need the official letter from, of all places, the office of the Devil, who

> would forward the letter to the record office in heaven without delay. . . . The Devil suggested that the person should use two envelopes. He or she should write his or her name and address on the back of one of the two envelopes, and the correct postage stamps should be affixed to it.

Like a good mission-school précis writer he cites exact dates and numbers, but not in quite the clerical spirit. He uses them for ironically precise approximations. A stream is "about seventeen feet wide", in heaven "the yard was about four thousand miles square". The colonial clerk's precision is mocked by being seen, from the clerk's point of view, in its true pointlessness. This is Nigeria. This is the Bush. In a naturalistic story, setting limits the options of the characters. In the Bush anything at all can happen. Tutuola can always produce any situation he wants whatever, at any point. What compels

his reader's interest is neither the "naivety" of the writing, nor the bizarre ghosts he concocts, but his sheer intensity and worry about his hero's spiritual quest.

The Village Witch Doctor and other stories is a collection of fables, also in standard English, [. . .] much slighter than *The Wild Hunter* and more readily [. . .] comfortable western view of African quaintness; as also, more worryingly, to the sentiment that the Zulu poet, Mazisi Kunene, put into the mouth of Shaka: that conquered nations end up with a literature of children's fables about animals. Not all Tutuola's fables are about animals. They deal with tricksters, devious juju-men, often with an explicit moral about the wages of disobedience. The story of Tortoise's degeneration from a promising, handsome young man to an armed robber who sells his own town to an enemy and then foments civil war there will remind Nigerians of the betrayal in high places of the promise that independence seemed once to hold, and the subsequent descent into civil war and poverty.

Source: John Haynes, "Precise Approximations and trickster tales," in *Times Literary Supplement,* May 18–24, 1990, p. 534.

Sources

"Amos Tutuola," in *Dictionary of Literary Biography*, Volume 125: *Twentieth-Century Caribbean and Black African Writers*, second series, edited by Bernth Lindfors and Reinhard Sander, Gale, 1993, p. 332.

Collins, Harold R., *Amos Tutuola*, Twayne, 1969, pp. x, 19-22.

Lindfors, Bernth, ed., *Critical Perspectives on Amos Tutuola*, Three Continents Press, 1975, pp. xiii-xiv, 3, 73.

Owomoyela, Okeyan, *Amos Tutuola Revisited*, Twayne, 1999, p. 143.

Further Reading

Larson, Charles R., ed., *Under African Skies: Modern African Stories*, Farrar, Straus, 1997.
    A collection of short stories by modern African writers such Ngugi wa Thiong'o, Ama Ata Aidoo, and Chinua Achebe. Includes "The Complete Gentleman" by Tutuola.

Owomoyela, Okeyan, *Amos Tutuola Revisited*, Twayne, 1999.
    A reappraisal of Tutuola's works and literary influence in retrospect following his death in 1997.

Quayson, Ato, *Strategic Transformations in Nigerian Writing*, Indiana University Press, 1997.

    Critical analysis of Nigerian novelists Rev. Samuel Johnson, Amos Tutuola, Wole Soyinka, and Ben Okri.

Where the Air Is Clear

Carlos Fuentes

1958

The publication of Carlos Fuentes's debut novel in 1958 created much controversy with its critical and loosely Marxist look at the social strata and history of Mexico City. *Where the Air Is Clear* deals with the issues of Mexican identity and need for self-knowledge, and paints a society torn between its ancient mythology and the contemporary modernity, severely shattered on social, political, economic, and spiritual levels. The novel, often called one of the primary works of the magic realism tradition, also established Fuentes as Mexico's leading contemporary novelist and one of the founders of "El Boom" in Latin American literature.

The thorough blend of myth, history, and modernity in the novel, as in Fuentes's other works, signifies the author's search for the viable identity of his country which would encompass its ancient roots as well as its present society. The characters of *Where the Air Is Clear* present diverse personal experiences as affected by the Mexican Revolution of 1910. From Ixca Cienfuegos, a mysterious embodiment of the Aztec war god, to Federico Robles, a revolutionary turned business tycoon who rejects his Indian heritage, Fuentes examines Mexican history and society through his characters whose names and individual memories comprise the novel's chapters. Vacillating perspectives and montage-like sections compose Fuentes's experimental narrative style, giving it a surreal tone and enabling him to present the vast and self-contrasting spectrum of personal memoirs and lifestyles in Mexico City. The frag-

mentary nature of his fiction reflects the author's vision of his country; Fuentes told John P. Dwyer in an interview, "our political life is fragmented, our history shot through with failure, but our cultural tradition is rich, and I think the time is coming when we will have to look at our faces, our own past."

Author Biography

One of Mexico's premier novelists and its foremost 'ambassador without a portfolio' (someone who utilizes his celebrity status to political ends), Fuentes has been a champion of goodwill for relations between the West and Latin America; good relations between the United States and Mexico has been a particular interest. This agenda shows in his fiction and intellectual enterprises.

Like other prominent members of the intellectual elite in Latin America and key figures of "El Boom," Fuentes comes from the ruling class. His father, Rafael Fuentes Boettiger, was a career diplomat stationed in Panama City in 1928 where his wife, Berta Macias Rivas, gave birth to Fuentes on November 11. Boettiger's career moved the family to Brazil in the early 1930s and then to Washington, DC from 1934 to 1940. While in Brazil, Boettiger served as secretary to Alfonso Reyes—a famous writer himself. Reyes later mentored Fuentes. At elementary school in Washington, DC, Fuentes experienced the tensions existing between the U.S. and Mexico for the first time. The impression stayed with him and became a major theme of his fiction. The family's next stop was Santiago, Chile, where Fuentes attended the Grange school with Jose Donoso, who later became a writer in his own right and who credits Fuentes with starting "El Boom."

Fuentes, after attending high school in Mexico City, stayed in his home country to attend the National University of Mexico. During his university years, Fuentes began writing as a hobby. After graduation, he studied international law in Geneva, Switzerland, as he began to follow in the footsteps of his role models. His career in foreign affairs began in the 1950s and culminated in an ambassadorship to France from 1975 to 1977. Fuentes resigned his ambassadorship when it was revealed that Mexico's current president, Gustavo Diaz Ordaz, ordered the Tlateloco student massacre in 1968.

The publication of *Where the Air Is Clear* in 1958 not only made Fuentes an internationally recognized writer but launched "El Boom," an intense period of international recognition of Latin American literature. Beginning with Fuentes' work of 1958, novels of "El Boom" brought universal themes and sophisticated technique to the literature of Latin America, making the career of novelist viable.

Fuentes married screen actress Rita Macedo in 1959, with whom he had one daughter. They were divorced in 1969. In 1972, Fuentes married Sylvia Lemus, a journalist, and they had two children. Fuentes has won many awards and served as visiting lecture or fellow at many universities, including Cambridge, Princeton, and Harvard. The most notable appointment was his election to the Colegio Nacional in 1972 where the welcoming speech for his appointment was delivered by the Nobel Prizewinning poet Octavio Paz.

President Miguel de la Madrid awarded Fuentes the Mexican Premio Nacional de la Literatura in 1984. Three years later in Madrid, King Juan Carlos awarded him the Spanish Premio Cervantes. During the 1990s, Fuentes has remained active, especially as a writer of Hispanic cultural history and essays encouraging positive Mexican-American relations.

Plot Summary

Ixca and Gladys Garcia

Through a collection of character sketches in Mexico City, Fuentes shows the dynamism of postrevolutionary Mexico in the 1940s and 1950s as it tries to sort itself out. The characters can be seen as deities struggling for control of Mexico. The figure tying them all together, Ixca Cienfuegos, discounts the present and future to believe in the past. He is in fact a doorway for the reemergence of the Aztec gods who want revenge for their overthrow by the Spaniards. In keeping with Aztec mythology, Ixca needs a blood sacrifice to bring about a return to the past and an overthrow of the new gods, the jet set. Ironically, the other figure looming throughout the novel is Gladys Garcia, a verifiable descendant of the Aztecs, a prostitute whom Ixca, in all his wanderings, never meets. But Ixca wanders through the jet-set class and the lower classes as he tries to find a suitable sacrifice.

Navel of the Moon

The jet set gathers at Bobo's party for a night of fun; intellectuals, artists, ambitious beauties, tycoons, old aristocracy and the *nouveau riches* ("newly rich") mingle and exchange social favors at the event. As aged *bon vivants* seduce novices and well-dressed women exchange "class for cash" at Bobo's, in the city's poor neighborhoods a cabdriver takes his family to dinner because he gambled on a horse race and won, and an illegal immigrant worker returns from California with gifts his family can't use because they don't have electricity. At the party, Norma breaks Rodrigo's heart, while her husband Federico "takes care" of Librato, an associate injured at work, in an example of business cruelty. Other characters are introduced in respective loneliness: Federico's mistress Hortensia, Rodrigo's mother Rosenda, and the cabdriver's wife Rosa—whose husband dies in a car crash after their dinner. Ixca scans the party with disgust, noting the social roleplaying that all engage in, because everybody needs favors to maintain their own social status. The morning after the party, Ixca visits his friend Rodrigo who is considering suicide and views the decadence of the de Ovandos family.

Carlos Fuentes

Ixca Shows the Lower Class

Federico Robles tells Ixca about his childhood memories of hardship in rural Mexico, his apprenticeship with the local priest and expulsion when he got involved with his niece, his experiences of fighting in the revolution, and the transition afterward described in terms of progress. Federico becomes a wealthy and powerful banker in the corrupt new economy.

Norma Larragoiti recalls her poor background, her arrival to the city to live with her bourgeois uncle, and the social ambition that made her trade her beauty and elegance for a place at the top, achieved with her marriage to Federico. Her life feels sterile and unhappy.

At the end of Part I, Ixca and Rodrigo Pola walk to a local bar, where the poet dwells in his intellectual identity crisis and recalls his school days and youth, his involvement with the college poets, his failed relationship with Norma, and the unsuccessful life he has now.

Mother Wants a Sacrifice

Part II opens with an anonymous old man showing his grandson where the palaces used to be along the streets of Mexico City before the revolution. Within the "City of Palaces," Federico reviews his marriage as he watches Norma preparing

for another superficial social function; in the meantime, the jet-set members gather for a meeting with a Serbian prince, which turns into a bizarre physical fight when the aristocracy is offended by the opportunist comments about "trade over tradition." Natasha talks to Rodrigo about the marginalism of the Mexican ideological system and culture.

Ixca finds out about Federico's business machinations and crimes from his old acquaintance Librado Ibarra, who became a union lawyer after the revolution, turned to investment capitalism to keep afloat, and got injured in the process. Ibarra reveals more of Mexico's history.

Ixca continues his search for pre-revolution memories, but finds a cool reception at the bottom of the social ladder, with the cabdriver Beto and the immigrant worker Gabriel. Later, Gabriel dines with his father's old friends who fought in the war. He then goes to the poor man's night on the town: a bullfight, a bar, and a whorehouse.

Ixca visits his mother Teodula, who announces that she is waiting to die and asks for a sacrifice. The two perform the death rituals for Teodula's family.

Meanwhile, the widow's neighbor Rosa gets a job in Norma's household; Gabriel gets beat up by a gang.

Ixca Attempts to Select a Sacrifice

Ixca visits Rodrigo's mother, who recalls her marriage, loss of her husband, and ensuing poverty. She dies wishing to see her estranged son. Ixca arranges Rosenda's funeral and sends Teodula to tell Rodrigo, who snubs her. Rodrigo writes about his weakness and indecision in choosing how to live his life; Ixca tells him of his beliefs in the eternal, ancient Mexico of the Indian gods, and proclaims that sacrifice is divine. Unfortunately, despite Ixca's urging, Rodrigo does not kill himself.

Federico and the poet Manuel Zamacona discuss the new society, in a clash of the capitalist and spiritual views. Later, Federico finds peace with Hortensia. Pimpinela refuses to answer Ixca's questions about her life; once alone, she recalls how she adapted to the post-revolution Mexico, trading her class for the money of the opportunists, in an effort to survive.

Ixca Tries to Sacrifice His Love

Ixca questions Norma about her memories; the two are attracted to each other and become lovers. She fears his untouchable, confident social attitude, because her status depends on keeping up appearances. The jet set spreads the rumor about Ixca and Norma; word gets out about Federico's business machinations. Rodrigo decides to pursue financial success as a screenplay writer. Ixca takes Norma out on the boat during a storm and throws her into the water; she swims out, believing he drowned, and goes wild after the close encounter with death.

Non-Ceremonial Sacrifices

Regules arranges Federico's downfall and makes a profit out of it. Ixca returns to Teodula and has a vision of the Robles's destruction. During Ixca's visit, Hortensia remembers her life, hardships, blindness, and love for Federico. Norma refuses to play social games and breaks ties with the jet set; Federico realizes his collapse; Ixca preaches the authentic power of Mexico to Manuel. Federico remembers with guilt the murder of a union worker that he ordered.

During the Independence Day celebration, the jet set parties; Gabriel and his friends get drunk, vent their discontent, and he gets killed; Rosa's child dies; Manuel gets shot for no reason; and a fight between the Robles results in a house fire, in which Norma dies. Teodula accepts her death as sacrifice and tells Ixca to abandon his modern life and stay to live with Rosa.

Mercedes refuses to see Ixca but recalls her life and relationship with Federico years ago in her uncle's house, which resulted in the birth of her son Manuel. After wandering into Gabriel's wake, Federico goes to Hortensia as his last resort for redemption.

Ixca Is Still Trying

Part II opens three years later. Regules's daughter proves the continuance of the jet-set snobbish tradition in her relationships. The new gods will not die. Ixca meets now-successful Rodrigo and almost gets them into a car crash as he reveals that his effort to bring back the Aztec gods has failed. Ixca complains to Rodrigo that his mother forced him to live with Rosa, "that servant girl," and abandon the "authentic" life. Ixca then resumes the narration and invokes the gods and the people, nameless and named, to save Mexico.

Characters

Beto

Beto is a happy-go-lucky cabdriver and Gabriel's friend with a shady past: he spent some time in prison for "knocking off" someone.

Pierre Caseaux

The aging seducer of the upper class, Pierre (the fashionable translation of "Pedro") is a wealthy Epicurean fully aware of the power of his money and status. He frequently "updates" his relationships with always-younger, ambitious beauties.

Hortensia Chacon

Hortensia is another representative of the low social class; an illegitimate daughter of an Indian servant, the girl grows up with poverty and silence in the de Ovando household. Hortensia marries a clerk who gives in to alcoholism, prostitutes, and severe abuse of his silent wife due to his growing discontent with his job and social status. Hortensia finds a job as a typist and leaves him, taking the children along, but the husband blinds her in rage. Her employer Federico Robles visits her at the hospital; the two fall in love. Hortensia is similar to Ixca in her spiritual, wordless connection to the ancient past; her love redeems Federico.

Ixca Cienfuegos

The novel opens and ends with Ixca's narration, a poetic and poignant description of Mexico City's decadence. As a character, Ixca is not very clearly defined; however, he connects the narratives of the other main characters as he visits them and inquires about their life stories. Confident, handsome, mysterious, tall, dark, with black eyes and Indian features, Ixca comes from the spiritually rich background of the ancestral Mexico, embodied in the mystical character of his mother Teodula. His profession and social position is undefined: the jet set believes he is "the brain behind a great banker" as well as a "gigolo and a marijuana addict," but nobody really knows what he does.

Ixca reveals Mexico's social corruption, alienation, and misery in each class, as he asks various characters about their memories. His main agenda, however, is to find a blood sacrifice among the new Mexicans to appease the ancient Indian gods: Ixca tries to push his friend Rodrigo into committing suicide, throws his mistress Norma into the stormy sea, and brings about the political downfall of Norma's husband Federico Robles, one of the country's wealthiest and most powerful men. Ixca pursues the authentic, pre-Hispanic Mexico underneath the layer of the new culture; after Norma's death, he obeys his mother and goes to live in poverty with her Indian widow neighbor; but after three years, he leaves and almost gets Rodrigo into a car crash.

Gabriel

Gabriel is a young man from the city's social underbelly, who illegally works in California during the year to support his family. He is the embodiment of ambition without a venue to succeed, searching for an escape from his circumstances through violence and various ways to make himself feel alive and free. He is killed by a street gang.

Charlotte Garcia

A self-proclaimed international society whore, Charlotte is a beautiful woman who spends her life in affairs with members of the world's jet set.

Gladys Garcia

Gladys is an aging Indian prostitute who appears at the beginning and the end of the novel, symbolizing the unchanging social hopelessness of the lowest class. She has one regular customer and the memory of another, the cabdriver Beto, with whom she had a personal relationship. After a night of work, Gladys retreats to church for spiritual recovery. She envies the *nouveau riches*.

Bobo Gutierrez

The host of the city's wildest jet-set parties, Bobo is a snobbish, flamboyant entertainer who gathers the *crmeè de la crmeè* at his fashionable house and always greets his guests—aristocrats, intellectuals, and "queers"—with the same exclamations.

Librado Ibarra

Librado was a law student and Robles's colleague who became the union attorney in his dream to reinvent Mexico after the revolution—but ended up in prison instead. Once released, Librado becomes an associate at Robles's factory where he works to keep afloat financially, but gets his foot caught in a machine and the company refuses to give him compensation. Librado knows a lot about Robles's criminal business schemes and confides in Ixca.

Junior

A representative example of the post-revolutionary generation, Junior is the son of the *nouveau riche*: a youth who has never earned a penny, but gets his wealth from his conservative father.

Norma Larragoiti de Robles

Norma is an ambitious, extremely beautiful woman in pursuit of wealth and status, who develops impeccable taste and personality to match her jet-set goals; she marries Federico Robles and trades her elegance and high-class skills for his money.

Norma's father, a small businessman, committed suicide when his business collapsed due to the post-revolutionary changes in the national economy. The mother sent Norma to live with her aunt and uncle in Mexico City, where the girl develops high social aspirations. A ruthless social climber, Norma tells her new friends that she also comes from an aristocratic family and throws away the pictures of her family, ashamed of their poverty and low class. She manages to handle occasional pangs of conscience, but the love affair with Ixca and the close encounter with death make her reexamine her life: she abandons the social roleplay with her aristocratic friends and defies Federico. Norma dies in the fire that marks her husband's social downfall.

Teodula Moctezuma

The embodiment of ancient mysticism, Teodula is a character who represents the eternal, mythological world under the rule of blood-thirsty Aztec gods, the spiritual and authentic Mexico before the Spanish conquests. She practices the old traditions, always wears her wedding jewelry, calmly awaits death because she believes in rebirth as the natural cycle of life, and performs death rituals on the skeletons of her husband and children that she keeps buried in her cellar. Ixca relies on her teachings and vows to find a human sacrifice for her, so that the ancient gods may be satisfied. After Norma's death, Teodula makes Ixca renounce the modern world and live with Rosa, her widow neighbor.

Rosa Morales

Rosa becomes a widow when her husband, cabdriver Juan Morales, dies in a car crash. They were returning from a lavish family dinner, a celebration of Juan's win of 800 pesos in a horse race; he plans to turn his life around, get a daytime shift, and spend more time with his family. After the tragedy, Rosa has to support the family and finds a job as a maid in Norma's household. Two of Rosa's children die shortly after.

Natasha

An aging beauty queen, St. Petersburg singer, and "the monarch of Mexico City's international set," Natasha is an occasional advisor to the incoming young women; she instructs them on using their sexuality and elegance to create a place for themselves at the top.

Dona Lorenza Ortiz de Ovando

Pimpinela's old aunt, Dona Lorenza, a member of the old aristocracy that sought exile in the United States and Europe during the turmoil of the revolution, stands as the epitome of the once-ruling decadent class now refusing to accept the changes. She continues to live by the same impossible standards, willing to die rather than join the lower social classes and work for a living. Dona Lorenza returns to Mexico impoverished with her grandson, a spineless, weak, and idiotic man in his twenties reared to live in the past with his grandmother. She is eternally bitter about the opportunistic class that succeeded her at the social peak.

Pichi

Pichi is a beautiful, shallow young woman, an example of "female meat on the market" trying to make it into the highest social class with her looks, meager education, and relationships with upper-class men.

Gervasio Pola

Gervasio is Rodrigo's father but they have never met. At the time of his wife's pregnancy, Gervasio was in the Belen war prison; he escaped with three other prisoners. In their search for a Zapata camp they could join, the fugitives separated; Gervasio was caught first and told his captors where to find his friends, because he didn't want to die alone.

Rodrigo Pola

Rodrigo is an unsuccessful, self-conscious poet who desperately hangs onto the high-class lifestyle. After his father's death in the revolution, Rodrigo grows up in poverty under the tentative eye of his controlling, clinging mother. During his school days, he befriends Roberto Regales who shows him the power of lies and manipulation in achieving one's goals. Shaken by the experience, Rodrigo turns to the idealistic world of poetry and finds a temporary niche among young existentialist poets at the university. However, after the publication of his first book of verses, he is expelled from the group. In the meantime, Rodrigo leaves home after a conflict with his mother, and falls in love with the young Norma, who dates him for a while but rejects him for someone with more money and better prospects.

Rodrigo's self-pity and identity crisis are a reflection of his struggle between conformity and rebellion: he must choose between mastering the modern success of making money, or sticking to his old-fashioned principles and staying poor. Finally, he turns his back on existential ideals and starts to write movie scripts that achieve great commercial success. He marries an impoverished aristocrat, Pimpinela de Ovando, trading his money for her class, and fully joins the jet set.

Prince Vampa

Another cardboard figure in the makeup of the Mexican high class, Prince Vampa gains his prestigious position with lies and the right attitude: he is actually a cook. His success in the group testifies to the new jet set's need to "strengthen" its position with blue blood.

Betina Regules

Betina is the next generation of the Mexican top society; the rich and beautiful daughter of the attorney Regules, she falls in love with a poor poet and law student, Jaime. However, when she brings him to one of Bobo's parties, the other women advise the young girl that he is too provincial for her status and money. Betina's character shows that society doesn't change.

Roberto Regules

Roberto, a powerful lawyer, a political shark, and a social climber, manipulates everybody around him in order to maintain and improve his own social status. As a schoolboy, he destroys a teacher with false accusations; as an adult, he facilitates Robles's collapse and arranges to profit from it. Roberto marries his secretary Sylvia and gives her the prestige of upper-class living, but their marriage is a loveless one.

Federico Robles

An example of rags-to-riches success, Federico, a son of Indian peasants who worked on the land of Don Ignacio de Ovando, has vivid memories of the unbearable living conditions of the low class, the talk of strikes that eventually inspired the revolution, and the hardships and abuse his family had to endure. Young Federico was sent to live and study with the local priest, but was thrown out when the priest caught him sleeping with his niece, Mercedes Zamacona. He ends up joining one of the generals in the revolution and fighting his way across Mexico for years, witnessing countless atrocities of war, and learning about power. Federico becomes a war hero at the battle at Celaya.

In the country ripe for changes after the revolution, Federico enters the competitive field of bourgeois development. He studies law, becomes a provincial attorney, commits ruthless crimes for the post-revolution government, and manages to create great wealth and power through business machinations in a lawless economy, becoming a modern tycoon over night. Because he lacks class, he marries Norma to bring elegance and appropriate social status to his public life; but he finds love with his blind Indian mistress.

Sentimental and cruel at the same time, Federico believes in the self he had created through the revolution and rejects his Indian origins; but when his world crumbles, his identity takes a hard blow in a recognition of corruption. He withdraws from city life and capitalism, marries his mistress, and becomes a cotton farmer in northern Mexico.

Manuel Zamacona

A modern poet and brooding intellectual accepted into the high-class circles, Manuel is Federico Robles's illegitimate son; his writings and conversations exemplify the wave of intellectual identity crisis in the country plagued by social decay. Manuel preaches reverence before life and reconstruction of the Mexican culture; he questions the historical, cultural, and spiritual makeup of Europe, Mexico, and the United States, looking at the various layers of influence and mistakes made along the way. In a talk with Robles, Manuel questions the economic reforms made by entrepreneurs after the revolution, and the foreign models used to restructure the country ending up in thorough corruption. Manuel dies a senseless death at a bar, during the drunken celebration of Independence Day.

Rosenda Zubaran de Pola

Gervasio's wife and Rodrigo's mother, Rosenda is another person profoundly changed by the revolution: a spoiled and naive girl raised on milk candy, Rosenda marries the young colonel Gervasio and spends a year in a household with increasing social standing and wealth, as her husband prospers under President Madero. However, she becomes a widow within a year after the wedding and all the money disappears in the revolution. Pregnant, rejected by her family for losing everything because she married a soldier, Rosenda starts a new life with her son: she earns enough to sustain them and raises Rodrigo as a replacement for the husband who abandoned her. As the son grows, she becomes more depressed with her loss of youth and vitality, and jealous of his other contacts with the world. Upon finding Rodrigo's poetry, Rosenda tears it up and tells him that nobody can choose his or her own way of life, because the world is stronger than the individual. She dies wanting to see her estranged son once again.

Pimpinela de Ovando

One of the socially valuable remnants of Mexican aristocracy, Pimpinela brings blue-blood prestige to the *nouveau riches* (newly rich people) of the new Mexico. While the revolution was gaining momentum, Pimpinela's father made sufficient changes, selling haciendas and buying real estate, to ensure a comfortable life for his family; however, the aristocratic lifestyle is forever changed after the revolution. Pimpinela's mother tries to protect the girl from the ''mixing'' at the top of the social ladder and takes her to Europe.

Upon her return to Mexico, Pimpinela longs to use her status for social connections; she offers the class granted by her company in exchange for financial and business favors, because the family funds are running low. She arranges a dinner to introduce her aged aunt and Norma, so that Norma's husband will give de Ovando's cousin a job at the bank. Eventually, Pimpinela marries Rodrigo, who solves all of her financial problems.

Themes

Culture Clash

One of the most powerful themes of *Where the Air Is Clear* is the sharp division between the social strata of 1950s Mexico City, along the fault lines of income and class, as well as race—with the indigenous Indians placed in the lowest rank, like the prostitute Gladys. Fuentes illustrates the conflict between the old and the new reigning members of the Mexican elite in several scenes, such as the dinner at the impoverished de Ovando household where the social climber Norma Robles meets the bitter aristocratic matriarch Lorenza de Ovando. The event is set up by Lorenza's cousin Pimpinela, an ambitious beauty struggling to retain her family's status and save them from starvation. Pimpinela is an example of the fully adapted social member, who willingly trades ''class for cash'' both in her marriage and at the salon parties. She asks the opportunist wife Norma Robles to use her husband's influence and get her company shares; as soon as she mentions dinner at her aunt's, Norma cannot ''keep her eyes from shining.'' In turn, Pimpinela tells Lorenza that ''an upstart, obnoxious, vulgar'' married to ''a savage from God knows what jungle'' is coming to dinner, and it is necessary for the aunt to welcome her so that her grandson can get a job at the bank.

The old aristocrat's determination to show the *nouveau riche* her place fails, as ''Norma, radiant, wrapped in mink and playing carelessly with her pearls, visibly affirmed the sense of security in this new world, of freedom and belonging, which had used to be [de Ovandos'] own feeling.'' After the dinner, Lorenza and Norma return to their social circles, competing to point out the flaws of the other: one criticizes the lack of grace and presumptuous airs of the ''daughter of some sheepherder''

who dared to take her place at the top of the hierarchy, and the other ridicules the aristocrat's refusal to accept well-deserved defeat. In the meantime, both fragments of the upper class live in denial: Lorenza awaits another revolution to restore her class because her grandson, Benjamin, has no skill beyond his aristocratic European grooming; while Norma tells her fashionable friends that her mother is actually an old servant, and her husband Federico hides his Indian heritage under expensive suits and white facial powder.

Fuentes also shows the sharp contrast between the peak and the bottom of Mexico City's social food chain in one of the book's first chapters, in which the narrative cuts back and forth from the lavish parties of the *nouveau riches* to the filthy slums inhabited by the poor. The lonely morning of the aging prostitute Gladys, after a night of work in a smoky nightclub, stands in stark opposition to the after-party morning of the jet set: some of its members are sleeping, and others preparing for another day of successful transactions (Norma is tanning and pampering herself, and Pimpinela is on the way to collect her shares at the bank). Every once in a while, the narrative jumps from the memories of its wealthy characters to descriptions of the usually nameless members of the poor or working classes, whose everyday activities appear as incredulously different and more burdensome than those of the recently arisen bourgeoisie.

The Supernatural

Part of the elusive identity of Fuentes's 1950s Mexico lies in the suppressed ancient past and the country's pre-Hispanic Indian heritage. The characters of Ixca Cienfuegos and his mother Teodula Moctezuma embody this past, its religion and spirituality, and bring a mysterious and supernatural element into the potpourri of the modern Mexican selfhood. Teodula at first appears to be praying to the Catholic Virgin Mary, but her words of worship, offering of her heart, and the skirt made of serpents show that her goddess is actually Coatlicue—the Aztec earth deity, who daily gives birth to the sun in the morning and swallows it in death in the evening. In Aztec representation, Coatlicue wears a necklace of human skulls and hands; she is a womb and a tomb at once, giving birth to death. Her son, the god of war, kills all of her other children as soon as he is born. Likewise, Teodula has lost all of her children, except Ixca—whom she sends out to find her a blood sacrifice that would redeem the suffering of her people. Deeply engaged in a death cult, Teodula performs rituals over the skeletons of her husband and children. She also calmly speaks of her own death and accepts it as a part the natural life cycle.

Ixca's monologues, at the beginning and the end of the novel, are full of invocations of ancient spirits as the only true and authentic powers over his land. His personality is mystical and undefined throughout the novel: there are speculations about his life and social position, but nobody knows for sure who he is or what he does. A symbolic embodiment of an ancient god of war, Ixca attempts to perform his duty on several occasions: for example, he tries to persuade Rodrigo to kill himself, and pushes Norma overboard into tempestuous waves. When Norma dies in a house fire witnessed by Teodula, the old woman tells her son that the sacrifice is completed and he withdraws from social life. Ixca's identity as a deadly entity appears in allusions: Rosa's son, frightened by Ixca's invitation to take him to eat, bites the man's hand and makes it bleed. The next time the boy is mentioned, he is dead and Rosa is preparing to bury him. When Ixca tastes his own "acrid [and] metallic" blood from the bitten hand, "his head swam with that taste; blood whirled in his ears like two breaths, united by an hour of terror." The boy might have been mysteriously poisoned by Ixca's blood, but the unspoken connection between events remains.

The character of Hortensia, Federico Robles' blind mistress of Indian origins, is another possible mythical embodiment: her connection with the world, especially with her lover, has some supernatural qualities. As opposed to the mysterious forces of Ixca and Teodula, Hortensia represents the nurturing, healing power of ancient Mexico; Federico goes to her to free himself from the pain of his everyday life at the social peak, and returns to her after he loses everything to start a happy and fulfilling life of redemption on a farm. Hortensia feels a certain affinity with Ixca, which further alludes to her possible mythical identity; she senses that they both "come from far away," can "understand without words," and have "faces that frighten us and carry us to the limits of passions, good and evil" and that would cause fear in others, "who would destroy us if we would show our true faces." Also, she speaks of her relationship with Federico as a union outside his social domain, the reality beyond "what life has made him," and declares that "the world which at last will be Federico's and [hers] is right here" and will make itself known once Federico finds his "true face." Like Ixca, Hortensia appears to believe in a true Mexico under-

Topics for Further Study

- Do some research on Mexico's "Day of the Dead" celebration. What was the state of this celebration in the 1950s? How has it become intrinsic to national identity for all Mexicans?

- Mexico City has one of the finest subway systems in the world. What were some of the challenges posed by its construction and how did the artifacts unearthed during construction help answer questions about Mexico's past?

- Fuentes was very keen on astrology. Using evidence from the book, ascribe a sign of the zodiac to each of your favorite characters. Or, use the characters to create a pack of Tarot cards.

- Given the title, *Where the Air Is Clear*, research the problems Mexico City faces today in terms of congestion, smog, and pollution. What can be done to provide clean air and water to every person in a city as populous as Mexico City?

neath the ruling modern one, waiting to emerge after the destruction of the cultural constructs; once that destruction happens in her lover's life, Hortensia embraces him and offers him a new, clean beginning.

Style

Symbolism

The narrative of *Where the Air Is Clear* contains an abundance of symbols, which serve to relate Aztec mythology and contemporary history into a new Mexican identity. Some of the symbols that connect the novel's themes of self as ancient and modern are jewelry, fire, and vision.

Two diametrically opposed characters who rely on jewelry as their symbol of status and self are Teodula and Norma. Teodula proudly wears her wedding jewelry and refuses to take it off, because it symbolizes the ancient life of the Aztec culture;

her last name is a link with the Aztec emperor Moctezuma, who was killed by the Spanish conquistador Cortes. Teodula's persistence in wearing the elaborate jewels signifies that she hangs on to the famous lost treasure of Moctezuma, and expects revenge on the ''newcomers.'' Only when she witnesses an apparent sacrifice of Norma's death in the flames, Teodula throws her jewels into the pyre. Ironically, the fire starts when Federico leaves his house in rage, crashing furniture and throwing burning candles on the floor, angered because Norma refuses to give him her jewelry to sell in a financial crisis. Like Teodula, Norma clings to her beliefs and her idea of self, as well as the jewelry as a visible statement of her status.

Another important symbol in the novel, fire is a recurring element in the Aztec mythology, most clearly evident in Ixca's name: his first name means ''to roast,'' and his last ''a thousand fires.'' Ixca's function is that of an avenger who would burn off the impurity in a sacrificial offering and let the true Mexican identity arise. The imagery of flames appears in many descriptions of the city's panorama, as well as in the imagery of the sun (another powerful Aztec element). The importance of fire as a symbol of self is here present in the name of the individual and his sense of social purpose; Ixca also often sees flames, real or imagined, and uses the imagery of fire to describe his visions of Mexico City.

Vision is a symbol of relation to the true Mexican identity: the contemporary world is often referred to as visible, while the mythological world of Mexico's past is difficult, if not impossible, to see. Ixca tries not to see anything clearly when he first arrives at Bobo's party, yet is himself described rather mystically as being ''everywhere, but no one ever sees him.'' The mystical quality in the vision of Teodula and her son appears in their ''visions'' of the world and the future: Teodula apparently perceives the wishes of the Aztec gods, while Ixca can occasionally ''see'' his ancient land, like on ''a corner where stone broke into shapes of flaming shafts and red skulls and still butterflies: a wall of snakes beneath the twin roofs of rain and fire.'' The insight into the authentic Mexico is granted only to those who look within, and allow themselves to ''see'' their memories: Hortensia's blindness gives her great spiritual ''vision''—she can ''see'' the true Federico beyond his modern personality. Also, Federico can remember his old, real self when he lets ''the heavy curtains inside his eyes slowly rise and reveal the inner pupil of memory, liquid, pinpoint.''

Magical Realism

Cuban novelist Alejo Carpentier first used the term ''magical realism'' in the 1940s to describe the tendency of contemporary Latin American authors to use the elements of folklore, myth, and fantasy in descriptions of their everyday issues, especially to veil the political and historical problems of his day in mystical narration. An exemplary magical realist novel is *One Hundred Years of Solitude* by the Colombian author Gabriel Garcia Marquez; other writers in this tradition are the Brazilian Jorge Amado, the Argentines Julio Cortazar and Jorge Luis Borges, the Chilean Isabel Allende, and Fuentes. This generation of Latin American novelists usually focuses on the major theme of searching for epic and heroic universal ''Truths'' in their works; in the highly symbolic language and narrative shifts from the realistic to the mythological, these authors employ the fantastic in order to illuminate the mundane elements of life.

In *Where the Air Is Clear*, the lack of separation between 1950s Mexico and the mythology of Aztec gods is magical realism. Superstition or witchcraft is not sufficient, rather the fantastic notion that Ixca is the Aztec god of war trying to bring back the pantheon of Aztec gods to avenge their dethronement makes the novel a member of the magical realist genre.

Narrative

The fragmentary technique of Fuentes's writing style in *Where the Air Is Clear* is a modern device adopted from contemporary European and American authors, namely William Faulkner and James Joyce. Many critics have noted that the narrative defies time and space, as the plot flows from one setting and period to another; Fuentes thus presents the city as fluid, its community changing from day to day, but at the same time fragmented and divided across numerous boundaries of social signifiers. Fuentes stated that he wanted to create an affect of omniscient interdependence of all the elements of Mexico City: from its ancient past (Ixca's Aztec visions), to the revolution (memories of violence and change), to the modern day (the everyday lives in the social strata). The narration is thus given a collective voice, as all city's inhabitants become united in the social fabric of the text— through unseen relations among characters, the time and space travel in the metamorphosing Mexico, and the rapid point-of-view changes. Chapters are named after characters whose memories give various perspectives and situate them in the history of

Mexico. Manuel is Federico's son, though neither knows it; Federico's recollections flow from the street into a modern office building and link the top and the bottom of the society; and Lorenza's reality feeds on the country's aristocratic past. The narrative is especially fluid at the novel's end, as Ixca's voice blends with the voices of the whole city and envelops all of the elusive Mexican identity in its equally volatile structure, moving ''over all the city's profiles, over broken dreams and conquests, over old summits of headfeathers and blood.''

Literary Heritage

Mexcio City, founded on top of the ruins of the Aztec capital which the Spanish conquistadors dumped into the lake, became one cultural center of Spanish American dominion (Lima served as the other). Except for a few codices, the libraries of the Aztecs and the Mayans—when they were found— fueled huge bonfires conducted by the Spanish Inquisition. Any information that survived in oral or parchment form, therefore, formed a natural resistance to the colonial overlords.

With Spanish conquest, literature began appearing in the Spanish language about the Mexican Valley. Most notably, Bartolome de las Casas, a Dominican missionary, deplored the treatment of the indigenous at the hands of the Spaniards in *The Devastation of the Indies.* Bernal Diaz del Castillo wrote a three-volume history of the conquest between 1568 and 1580. The most influential writings of the colonial period were those composed by conquistadors in letters and reports back to Spain. These writings formed the basis of culture clash— the Spanish soldiers had no preparation for the sights they encountered in the Aztec capital and no way of understanding Aztec culture.

With the exception of Juan Ruiz de Alarcon y Mendoza who contributed to the Golden Age of Spanish Literature during the seventeenth century, Mexican literature was a vapid imitation of European forms. After the Spanish left, Mexico had to form its own national identity and actively looked to the arts and literature for help. This aid arrived with the Latin American Vanguard; the term is used to designate Latin American modernists who were inspired by late-nineteenth-century French literature. The Vanguard plus the European Avant-Garde would inspire ''El Boom.'' These movements rejected traditional ''imitative'' literature and resuscitated indigenous culture (in part by visiting it in European museums) while performing the role of social critique.

A prominent figure from this period in Mexico was Peruvian Cesar Vallejo. In his *Human Poems* (1939), he investigated the Maya-Quiche myths. These sacred tales had been written down for the first time in the sixteenth century. Vallejo inspired sociopolitical consciousness among writers. Octavio Paz proved even more influential on Latin American literature but especially Mexican literature and identity. He shared Vallejo's theory of political being. He made his first mark on the literary world in the mid-1920s but it was his *Labyrinth of Solitude* that won him the greatest notoriety. This collection of essays described the Mexican character with all its pimples—it angered people but it inspired more honest and uniquely Latin American works of fiction.

Inspired by the European Avant-Garde as well as the Argentinean Jorge Luis Borges and Octavio Paz, Carlos Fuentes launched Latin American literature into the international spotlight and thereby instigated ''El Boom.'' His first novel, *La región más transparente* (*Where the Air Is Clear*) of 1958, fabricated Mexico City using indigenous myths and showing all social classes. The success of this novel inspired other Latin American writers (many of whom had met in Europe) to cease imitation and answer Borges' demand that they create.

Historical Context

The Mexican Revolution

The Mexican Revolution of 1910 was a result of a long line of squelched rebellions in pursuit of independence without tyranny; most of the nineteenth century passed with the country wavering between democracy and dictatorship, with the population rising against the Spanish, the French, and its own rulers. Mexico was one of the few Latin American countries in which mestizos (people of mixed white and native blood) and natives actively participated in the struggle for independence. At the beginning of the twentieth century, Mexico was under the thirty-year autocratic rule of Porfirio Diaz, who let foreign investors take control of much of his land, selling its resources for ridiculously low prices; he also stifled a few industrial strikes with

Compare & Contrast

- **1950s:** The U.S.S.R. beat the U.S. into space with the launching of Sputnik in 1957.

  Today: Russia insists on maintaining the oldest orbiting space station in hopes that tourism will bring revenue to its space agency. Meanwhile, the U.S. has had to pay part of Russia's contribution to the International Space Station to keep work on schedule.

- **1950s:** Six European nations form the European Economic Community (EEC). Between them, the nations abolish mutual tariffs and begin laying the groundwork for a Common Market.

  Today: Canada, Mexico, and the U.S. form a free-trade zone, NAFTA. The European Union more than doubles the number of countries in the EEC, and has its own currency, bureaucracy, and the beginnings of an EU military organization that will be separate from NATO.

- **Mexico:** In 1998, 27 percent of the Mexican population lived below the poverty line and 2.8 percent were unemployed. Its industrial sector remains a mix of outmoded and modern machinery. NAFTA has allowed exports to nearly double to the U.S. and Canada. Living standards are expected to keep rising. The accompanying

  positivism has hid many of the pitfalls—increased environmental problems and rampant consumerism.

  United States: As the new century opens, the U.S. is enjoying its longest running boom economy, its lowest unemployment rates, budget surpluses, and almost zero inflation. Ironically, the U.S. has been unable to solve many of its growing infrastructure problems—crumbling public school buildings, overreliance on automobile transit, and a stockpile of nuclear waste.

- **Mexico:** The Zapatistas rose against the Mexican government in 1994. They are Indians who are still waiting for government and land reforms. They received military attention but little has changed to alleviate their impoverishment.

  United States: During the 1990s, various radical groups challenged the U.S. government. Unfortunately, the clash between U.S. authorities and a religious group in Waco, Texas led to unnecessary deaths. Other standoffs have ended peaceably. Unlike the Zapatistas, these groups were not united in a demand for rational reforms of government based on universal human rights accords.

---

violence. The Mexican Revolution erupted when Diaz was reelected to the presidency in 1910; by 1917, the fight had claimed about one million lives in a struggle, on the one hand, between the middle class and the Diaz government and, on the other, a grass-roots peasant revolt against the owner classes for a share of the wealth. Although the enemy was the same, the two groups did not agree on their revolutionary goals, which caused much confusion and prolonged the bloodshed in the race for political control.

The struggle began when the would-be opponent of Diaz, Francisco Indalecio Madero, called for nullification of the election; Diaz resigned and fled

to France in 1911 because of the riots in Mexico City. Madero, who then assumed the presidency but did not make the expected reforms, was denounced by the peasants' revolts led by Emiliano Zapata and Pancho Villa. Madero was ousted and murdered in 1913 by General Victoriano Huerta, a corrupt dictator eventually driven from power. Zapata and Villa held the presidential seat for a year, until the bloody battle of Celaya in 1915 when Venustiano Carranza and Alvaro Obregon conquered the city and full-scale civil war erupted.

The revolution formally ended in February 1917 with a proclamation of a new constitution: it was a nationalistic, anticlerical document, considered the world's first socialist constitution, which allowed only one-term presidency, in order to prevent the possible Diaz-type dictatorship. It also gave government, rather than the Catholic Church, control over schools; provided for public ownership of land and resources; and ensured basic labor rights. Carranza became president in 1917, but political instability and fighting between various revolutionary groups continued throughout the next decade. The revolutionary hero Zapata was killed in 1919, and both Carranza and Obregon (president 1920-24) were assassinated in military coups.

In 1929, Mexico entered a period of political stability with the formation of an official government party that united most of the social groups that had participated in the revolution; since 1945, it has been called the Institutional Revolutionary Party (Partido Revolucionario Institucional—PRI). Although the business environment improved during the stable years, the mix of socialist leadership, foreign investment, and years of exploitation has had a damaging effect on the national economy.

Post-WWII Mexico

Economic reforms that took place after the Mexican Revolution allowed for the formation of a stable middle class. The leadership of Lazaro Cardenas (1934-40) aimed to realize the socialist goals of the revolution: he orchestrated massive land redistribution, helped establish strong labor unions, extended education to remote areas of the country, and nationalized foreign petroleum holdings, mostly U.S.-owned. Mexico and the U.S. reached a compensation agreement in 1944, when the two were WWII allies.

In the post-war years, the Latin American intellectual world burst forth with a powerful ideological sense of national identity; the "Boom" started once the native intellectuals returned from European universities and applied modern philosophical, literary, and artistic techniques, novelties, and approaches to the state of their countries. In the 1950s, the temporal setting of *Where the Air Is Clear*, Mexico was undergoing a post-revolutionary revival of national identity. In that and the following decade, the country's intellectuals—among them painter Diego Rivera and novelists Octavio Paz and Fuentes—also engaged in this attempt at redefining Mexican nationality. In 1958, when Fuentes' first novel was published, the issue of social class became important to the concept of national identity.

Although the post-war years brought political stability, economic growth, and the formation of the middle classes, the country's poorest population still suffered a low standard of living which differed little from pre-Revolutionary times. The artists working in the tradition of magic realism also recalled their national past, the pre-European Latin America of distinct spirituality, and used it both as a contrast and as a supplement to the discussion of modern-day social issues in their countries.

Critical Overview

Fuentes' debut novel has inspired much criticism with its experimental narrative technique, its combination of history, anthropology, sociology, music, and cinema, and its soul-felt critique of modern Mexico. Some critics recognized the author's imaginative and powerful style as revolutionary in Latin American literature, while others rebuked his storytelling strategies. In a review for the *New Yorker*, Anthony West writes of *Where the Air Is Clear*: "With the bravery of a young man, Senor Fuentes has cleared all ideas of what a novel ought to be from his mind and has decided, quite simply, to put what is it to be Mexican, and all of Mexico, in this book." West further praises the way Fuentes leaves the construction of his "social mosaic" to the reader, despite the author's being "not the most polished and assured of writers." On the other hand, Richard Gilman's article for *Commonweal* describes the novel as a poor "attempt to extricate a living imagination from the entombed, self-devouring realities of Mexican consciousness, forever mourning its sundered past, incessantly projecting its possible future shapes, and torn between its ill-defined authenticity and the directing pressure of more advanced societies." Gilman, after comparing the Mexican and Russian revolutions, further calls Fuentes "neither Turgenev nor a Dostoyevsky" and states that the form and the experience of the novel "don't hold together" in its passionate but stylistically ineffective narration.

However, the majority of criticism recognized the connection between Fuentes' work and the contemporary modern techniques, such as the visual processes employed by John Dos Passos in the *U.S.A. Trilogy* : in "The Guerilla Dandy," by Enrique Krauze, the novel is called "an important

Fuentes's story combines Mexico's ancient past and present, as well as reality and the supernatural. Depicted here, the ancient Aztec temple Teocalli, constructed to worship the rain god, Tlaloc, and the sun god, Huitzilopochtli, the ubiquitous narrator of Where the Air is Clear.

step in Mexican narrative [that] acclimatized the genre of the urban novel.'' Also, many critics have pointed out with Krauze the link between Fuentes and ''that great actor of painting, Diego Rivera''—another author of ''immense texts and murals that proceed more by accumulation and schematic juxtaposition than by imaginative connection.'' According to the creative strengths in this comparison, ''the best of Fuentes is in the verbal avalanche of his prose'' and the almost cinematic composition of his narrative, cutting from one ambient to another in a thorough coverage of the life of Mexico City.

In his chapter in *Carlos Fuentes: A Critical View,* Luis Leal writes that the author follows the distinctive models of William Faulkner, Malcolm Lowry, and Miguel Angel Asturias—authors who utilize mythology in their fiction, ''either as a form or theme in the context of the realistic novel.'' Fuentes elaborates on this model by applying the technique to write ''creative history,'' Leal points

out, in which history and myth keep the novel in equilibrium by balancing each other.

The readings and critical interpretations of the author's voice in his debut novel vary greatly. Saul Maloff, in *Saturday Review,* describes *Where the Air Is Clear* as impressive because Fuentes writes ''always as an artist, never as an ideologist'' about a socially dense scene ''that is so often the undoing of the 'political' novelist.'' On the other hand, Fernanda Eberstadt calls the novel ''marred by authorial self-indulgence and pretentiousness'' that turns the work into ''a highly self-conscious melange of advertising slogans, refrains from popular songs, and overheard fragments of cocktail-party chitchat.'' However, she does praise the novel as energetic storytelling despite Fuentes' ''efforts to smother it in affectation.''

Other theoretical reviews focused on the philosophical concepts present within the novel's thematic motifs. In an article for *Comparative Literature*, Maarten van Delden writes that *Where the Air Is Clear* contains two main philosophical perspectives: first, a view of self derived ''primarily from existentialist ideas found in the works of Andre Gide, Jean-Paul Sartre, and Albert Camus,'' and second, the view of self as part of the communal mythical past. The highly individualist existentialist self is ''discontinuous, contingent, wholly unaffected by any kind of socio-cultural conditioning permanently separated from a stable and enduring core of meaning''; the other self, that of collective consciousness, ''loses all vestiges of autonomy [and] the individual merges entirely with the communal past, specifically with Mexico's Aztec heritage.'' Van Delden points out certain similarities between Fuentes' novel and the works by existentialist authors; he also analyzes the two philosophical views as embodied in the novel's characters, specifically Ixca as the symbol of the communal self-identity and Rodrigo as the existentialist presence. By the end of the novel, both of these characters fail in finding themselves in their respective theoretical niches: Ixca rejects Teodula's domination and the imposed life with Rosa, while Rodrigo, after attempting to embrace an existentialist existence, finally gives into the world and its principles of operation and becomes a successful businessman.

Overall, the criticism of *Where the Air Is Clear* had pointed out the novel's controversial elements, placed the work in perspective of its influences, shown its effects on the development of Latin American and modern literature in general, and recognized Fuentes as a prominent figure in contemporary literature.

Criticism

Jeremy W. Hubbell

Hubbell, with an M.Litt from the University of Aberdeen, currently pursues a Ph.D. in history at the State University of New York, Stony Brook. In the following essay, he examines the narrative value of the characters of Where the Air Is Clear *and their symbolic representation of the various fragments of Mexican society in the 1950s.*

Many elements of Fuentes' writing style have been examined by various critics of *Where the Air Is Clear*, but the most prominent feature of the novel proves to be its characters. Fuentes makes the individual carriers of the story crucial to the plot, which relies on their memories and resulting actions; indeed, the characters' names are used as titles for most of the novel's chapters. Characters are thus labeled as necessary for the flow of the story, but on a deeper level, they also function as symbols for the many parts of the versatile and elusive identity of Mexico City. The symbolism of individual characters serves as an eloquent expression of Fuentes' view of his country's society.

The novel's main character and a thread that connects all the rest, Ixca Cienfuegos is a mysterious avenger of the Aztec gods: he causes destruction in the lives of other characters, in search of a blood sacrifice to appease the ancient deities. Ixca embodies pre-Columbian Mexico and claims that the past holds the key to the nation's authentic, original identity. However, even Ixca has individual problems with his own identity: he decidedly follows his mother's instructions and firmly believes in the ancient spirituality, to the extent that he withdraws to live in poverty with a widow once the sacrifice has been performed. However, Ixca goes through a crisis of faith at the novel's end: he reappears and almost gets himself and Rodrigo killed, shouting and laughing hysterically because his revenge obviously did not cause desired social changes. Ixca is enigmatic, confident, evasive, and difficult to define; other characters most often fear him on an intuitive level and one even compare him to an all-seeing god. He is anything and everything, from business adviser, to go-between, to gigolo; he makes friends, obtains their confessions and memo-

ries, and eventually betrays them, bringing about their ruin. Rosa's son escapes in panic when Ixca offers to buy him dinner; his mistress Norma is afraid of his cool temperament and disregard for the social factors that her life revolves around; and Junior tells his girlfriend Pichi: "Let's see, Cienfuegos, and be careful there. I'll keep him away from you," when they encounter Ixca at a party. Like the deeply buried ancient heritage of the blood-thirsty Aztec gods, Ixca too is to be feared by the descendants of the conquistadors. The scene in which his mother takes the coffins from her basement and paints the skeletons of Ixca's father and siblings in an ancient death ritual is all the more horrific for Ixca's calm acceptance of it; in fact, he seems to be perfectly comfortable only in that ceremonial setting.

Another way in which Ixca functions as a symbol of the pre-Hispanic Mexican culture is presented in his monologues: in the beginning of the book, he introduces himself as a somewhat universal inhabitant of Mexico City; throughout the book, he often serves as a channel for the memories of other characters, even when they refuse to talk to him (like Pimpinela and Mercedes); and at the novel's end, his monologue extends beyond his person to envelop all of the city's history, material and spiritual contents, and people, in a surreal flow of words: "names which could be clotted with blood and gold, rounded names, pointed names, lights of stars, ink-mummied names, names dripping like drops of your unique mascara, that of your anonymity, face flesh hiding fleshed faces, the thousand faces, one mask Acamapichtli, Cortes, Sor Juana, Itzcoatl, Juarez, Tezozomoc, Gante, Ilhuicamina, Madero. . ." This all-inclusive narrative style speaks of another ancient concept, that of a collective voice of the city; Ixca represents the communal sense of self of the distant past. Ixca asks Rodrigo to choose between the then and the now by saying that alienation comes with modernization: "Over here you will be anonymous, a brother to everyone in solitude. Over there you will have your name, and in the crowd nobody will touch you, and you will not touch anybody."

Along with Ixca, the characters of his mother Teodula, the prostitute Gladys, and the blind Hortensia also symbolize the Aztec heritage. Teodula, completely immersed in the world of the past, believes wholeheartedly in the ancient world as everpresent and just waiting to reemerge and overthrow the false modern "gods" of the bourgeoisie. Gladys symbolizes the estranged heritage of the

What Do I Read Next?

- Several of the short stories collected in Fuentes' first book, *Los Dias Enmascarados* (*The Masked Days*) of 1954, are direct antecedents to *Where the Air Is Clear*. Many of the stories in the 1954 work are accessible in English in *Burnt Water* (1980). These short stories introduce the theme of entrance by the ancient gods of the Aztec and Maya into contemporary society to protest material culture.

- In what was dubbed the 'last novel of the Mexican revolution,' Fuentes intended to create a character who could embody Mexico. *The Death of Artemio Cruz* (1962) resulted from the effort. In this novel, Cruz lies on his deathbed as his legacy is created. Supposedly, Cruz was a good, ideal, and true revolutionary but in all honesty he was corrupt, a capitalist, and selfish. Considered Fuentes' finest novel, the work cynically views the aftermath of the Mexican revolutionary impulse.

- The almost postmodern attempt at cultural synthesis, Fuentes' *Zona sagrada* (1967; translated as *Holy Place*) blends Aztec and Greek myth. Tlazolteotl, the Aztec goddess of carnal love and decay, meets Greek and Egyptian cultures for the first time.

- Fuentes has authored a number of essays and historical works. Perhaps the most well-known of the latter category, *Buried Mirror*, accompanied a BBC documentary in 1990. The scope of the work covers all of Spanish-American history from cave drawings to current political wranglings but the illustrations are abundant. The theme of the work hinges on the idea that there exists a Hispanic culture and tradition of shared images and artistic works.

- Octavio Paz had a tremendous impact on Fuentes' generation. For Fuentes' interests in the themes of national identity, Paz' 1950 work *El Laberinto de la soledad* (*The Labyrinth of Solitude*) was an invaluable touchstone. In this work, Paz explores the character of Mexico as an amalgam of politics, history, and myth. He also explored the tensions between the indigenous and the conquistadors; his social criticism earned him fame but also ill will from the rulers of Mexico.

- The mysterious disappearance of famed American writer Ambrose Bierce in 1914, the time of revolution in Mexico, has been a subject of intrigue for Mexican and American audiences. Fuentes has postulated a marvelous explanation in his novel, *Gringo Viejo* (*The Old Gringo*).

- The most recent novel by E. L. Doctorow accentuates the mythical status of New York City. In *City of God: A Novel* (2000), Doctorow shows the world an end-of-the-century portrait of the city that stops just short of magical realism. The theft of a crucifix and its discovery atop the Synagogue for Evolutionary Judaism and the subsequent loss of faith by the detective priest is just the beginning.

- Raymond Leslie Williams, who has written numerous books and articles on literature, explains the evolution of attention on Latin American literature in *The Modern Latin-American Novel* (1998). Williams, along with a chronology of important literary works since 1945, provides an overview of who knew who, where ''El Boom'' derived its inspiration and technique, and the positioning of important Latin American writers in terms of each other and their literary heritage.

---

twentieth-century Aztec descendants, who live in poverty and envy the ''new gods'' of the city's jet set; she also signifies poverty, hopelessness, and fatalistic passivity. Hortensia, unlike Ixca and

Teodula, represents the positive, accepting and nourishing qualities of the Mexican spiritual past; she does not cause Federico's downfall, but patiently awaits it and offers him redemption in her love.

Federico Robles, another major character who embodies a part of Mexican identity as a descendant of the indigenous Indians, rejects his origins and strives to become as modern as possible. After making important government connections during and after the Mexican revolution, Federico establishes himself as a successful businessman through unscrupulous machinations. Once he is catapulted to a prominent position, Federico does everything he can to affirm his new status: he marries Norma to give him elegance and class, has the business headquarters of his industrial empire in an ultramodern (and ultra-tall) building, wears silk ties and expensive suits, and even lightens his features with facial powder. Federico symbolizes the modern Mexico, which, in a desperate effort to distance itself from the origins of poverty and anonymity of peasant life, forgets that the revolution was fought for the freedom and empowerment of the lower classes. The hardships Federico had endured in his youth and during the revolution must be erased if he is to be fully accepted into the social elite; the aristocratic ideal in post-war Mexico still scrutinizes the self-made individual. His character also embodies the corruption of modernization; however, Federico remains connected with his background in his relationship with Hortensia. The actual fragility of his social status, shown in the ease of his financial success and collapse, symbolizes the underlying instability of every social class in the new society.

Other characters in the *nouveau riches* group who reject Mexico's past and fully invest in the future are Federico's wife Norma, the attorney Roberto Regules, and most of the jet set of Bobo's parties. Norma also comes from a poor background, but manages to build herself up for life at the social peak. With her beauty, education, charm, and high-class manners, she manages to marry into the standing she desires, but her life feels empty. Roberto is a version of Federico without scruples, a political and professional shark concerned only with maintaining his own status, increasing his own wealth, and keeping up appearances.

A character embodying the leftover Porfirian elite, Dona Lorenza is a haughty old lady living in expectations of a revolution that would put her class back on top. When Porfirio Diaz fled to Paris, the aristocratic class followed in exile to Europe and the United States, most of them losing all their possessions in Mexico due to socialist reforms. Lorenza's husband had enough foresight to maneuver out of this predicament, and maintain his family in wealth; but after his death, the next generation of de Ovandos

> The symbolism of individual characters serves as an eloquent expression of Fuentes' view of his country's society."

brings about absolute financial collapse and they return to Mexico.

While her niece Pimpinela has managed to adapt to the circumstances and successfully trades "class for cash," Lorenza lives in denial of the new world around her: she raises her grandson exclusively as an aristocrat, without any useful skills, and tries to maintain her prestige when Norma (in her flashing mink and pearls) comes for dinner. The family of de Ovandos is dying out in alcoholism, loneliness, and sterility, except for Pimpinela who marries a *nouveau riche*. The character of Lorenza signifies the destructive lack of flexibility that ruins her social class, as it did their dictator.

Two characters represent the intellectual layer of new Mexico City: Rodrigo Pola, an unsuccessful poet turned successful screenplay writer, and Manuel Zamacona, also a poet and the novel's "intellectual spokesperson," who according to Wendy Faris in *Carlos Fuentes* presents "the ideas of Octavio Paz and other essayists of the post-revolutionary period." Indeed, Paz' *The Labyrinth of Solitude* serves as a kind of pre-text for *Where the Air Is Clear*.

Rodrigo embodies the self-doubt, identity crisis, and a social class in "conflict between conformity and rebellion," as stated by Maarten Van Delden in *Carlos Fuentes, Mexico, and Modernity*. His personality reflects the existentialist beliefs, then prevalent in France, that emphasized the themes of anxiety and superfluity and regarded the essence of human life as unchangeable by its social environment. The selfish individuality of Rodrigo's character shows in his desperate attempts to define his own uniqueness: he leaves his mother because he needs independence of thought, and walks away from the literary group at the university because he feels he has a different destiny. Although Ixca believes that Rodrigo has suicidal tendencies, the poet confesses to himself that he wants to live. Finally, Rodrigo does what is necessary for success: he throws away his existentialist ideals and makes a fortune writing movie scripts. Manuel, on the other hand, maintains his belief system and even manages to touch the conscience of Federico (Manuel does not know that Frederico is his father) in a discussion of the true effects of the revolution and the economic growth afterward. However, Manuel's senseless death symbolizes the fatalistic, destructive nature and future of the new Mexico. His literal and Rodrigo's intellectual death signify the failure of spiritual renewal through philosophical and artistic idealism.

Finally, the identity of the bottom social class exists in the character of Gabriel, a working-class son who spends most of the year in California, working illegally and earning just enough to support his family. Gabriel embodies the always-present anger of the poor, looking for an outlet in drinking and violence. He is the representative of the working class who did not get a slice of the post-revolutionary rags-to-riches dream, like Federico and Norma. Also, like Gladys, Gabriel does not have a way to reach the upper classes except in absurd imitations of their behaviors: he brings his mother a blender from America, but forgets that there is no electricity in his house. In a conversation with a friend, Gabriel compares the inequality in the American social hierarchy to the immobile structure in Mexico: "So what if [Americans] don't let you in their crappy restaurant? You able to get in the Ambassador in Mexico City?" Gabriel wants to find a stable job in the city so he can earn a living and stay with his family, but dies trying. His destiny foreshadows that of Gladys, who cannot get a job at the store and is getting old for prostitution. Both characters embody the hopelessness of Mexico's lowest classes.

As Faris pointed out, Fuentes provides Alejo Carpentier with an urban geography of a Latin American city similar in universal resonance to James Joyce's Dublin through the infrastructure visible and invisible. She considers that the connections occur through characters; however, those connections happen under very precise conditions. Further, the interactions almost always fail to contribute to a sense of national identity sought after by the characters and the author himself. Divided by their beliefs, racial and social origins, philosophies and professions, the inhabitants of Fuentes' Mexico often fail to recognize what they all have in common: a pursuit of an authentic and welcoming city of freedom and honest opportunities for all, and—of course—plenty of clear air.

Source: Jeremy W. Hubbell, in an essay for *Literature of Developing Nations for Students*, Gale, 2000.

Maarten Van Delden

In the following essay, Maarten Van Delden discusses Carlos Fuentes' treatment of the nature of self in his novel La region mas transparente. *Van Delden examines how Fuentes presents the self in two perspectives: on one hand being unaffected or formed by culture and on the other being directly tied to past, culture, and geography and how he seeks to resolve this seeming conflict.*

La Región Más Transparente (1958). Carlos Fuentes's first novel, oscillates between two different perspectives on the nature of the self and its relations to history and the community. On the one hand, the novel outlines a view of the self that derives primarily from existentialist ideas found in the works of André Gide, Jean-Paul Sartre, and Albert Camus. In this view, the self is discontinuous, contingent, wholly unaffected by any kind of socio-cultural conditioning, permanently separated from a stable and enduring core of meaning—and it is precisely for this reason that it possesses an absolute freedom to mold itself into constantly new shapes. On the other hand, the novel proposes a vision in which the self loses all its vestiges of autonomy; the individual merges entirely with the communal past, specifically with Mexico's Aztec heritage. This past is viewed as the origin and ground of an unalterable, culturally determined identity to which the self is inextricably attached. I will proceed to examine the conflict between these two views on a number of textual levels, after which I will conclude by arguing that the rather remarkable final section of the novel constitutes an attempt to resolve this conflict through the aesthetic embodiment of a concept of revolution. Fuentes expresses his vision of revolution by means of an inventive appropriation of the modernist technique of "spatial form." I will also show how the concept of revolution evolves in Fuentes's more recent work.

Toward the end of *La región más tranparente*, Manuel Zamacona, the novel's intellectual spokesman, is senselessly murdered by a man he has never seen before. Afterwards, the killer coolly states that he did not like the way Zamacona had looked at him. The incident is reminiscent of the *acte gratuit* motif as it appears in the works of Gide, Sartre, and Camus. Fuentes himself suggested a link with the existentialist tradition in a 1966 interview with Emir Rodríguez Monegal. In speaking of how the social and cultural realities of Mexico had somehow managed to anticipate certain artistic and philosophical

Modern view of Temple Mayor in Mexico City, site of the ancient Aztec capital, Tenochtitlan.

currents in Europe and the United States, Fuentes made the following observation:

> Hay un existencialismo *avant la lettre*, y muy obvio. México es un país del instante. El mañana es totalmente improbable, peligroso: te pueden matar en una cantina, a la vuelta de una esquina, porque miraste feo, porque comiste un taco. Vives el hoy porque el mañana es improbable. ("Diálogo")

Fuentes's comment can be read as a gloss on the scene of Zamacona's death, which stands, then, as an illustration of the existentialist quality of Mexican life.

However, the existentialist act in *La región* is presented in a manner radically different from similar incidents in the works of Fuentes's French precursors. Lafcadio Wluiki's gratuitous murder of a complete stranger—whom he pushes out of a moving train—in Gide's *Les caves du Vatican* (1914) and Meursault's unmotivated killing of an Arab in Camus's *L'étranger* (1942) are by no means identical actions, but what they have in common is that in each case the perpetrator is at the center of the narrative. The events are related from Lafcadio's and Meursault's points of view. In Fuentes, on the other hand, the perspective is completely inverted: the victim is the protagonist and the killer remains a shadowy, indistinct figure on the margins of the narrative.

The symmetry of this inversion is reinforced by a number of other details connected with Lafcadio's *acte gratuit* in *Les caves du Vatican*. Even before he thrusts his victim out of the train, Lafcadio has been planning to leave Europe for what he calls "un nouveau monde," the islands of Java and Borneo. And as he begins to speculate on the possibility of committing this unusual crime, he reminds himself that, in any case, the next day he will be "en route pour les îles," and so will never be found out. In this way, my two projects, the gratuitous murder and the voyage to a faraway place, become linked together. Both are strategies for asserting one's freedom, for rejecting the old, oppressive ways of Europe. "'Que tout ce qui peut être soit!' C'est comme ça que je m'explique la Création...," Lafcadio exclaims at one point, and throughout the novel he remains intent on demonstrating his love for what he calls "ce qui pourrait être...." The desire to transgress all limits, to expand the realm of the possible, is expressed both in geographical terms, in the plan to flee to the East Indies, and in ethical terms, in the unmotivated murder of a stranger. Both projects are ways of affirming that one is bound by nothing. Or,

"The desire to transgress all limits, to expand the realm of the possible, is expressed both in geographical terms, in the plan to flee to the East Indies, and in ethical terms, in the unmotivated murder of a stranger. Both projects are ways of affirming that one is bound by nothing."

as Camus put it in *L'homme révolté* (1951): "La théorie de l'acte gratuit couronne la revendication de la liberté absolue."

In *La región*, Natasha, an aging singer from St. Petersburg, alerts us to a difference between Mexico and Europe that speaks directly to this question of freedom and the transgression of limits:

> Por lo menos a nosotros nos queda siempre eso: la posibilidad de s'enfuir de buscar el lá-bas. El Dorado fuera de nuestro continente. ¿Pero ustedes? Ustedes no, mon vieux, ustedes no tienen su là-bas, ya están en él, ya están en su límite. Yen él tienen que escoger, vero?

In Gide, the idea of the limit depends on a more fundamental conceptual division of the world into a center (Europe) and a periphery (the non-European parts of the globe). From the perspective of the center, the existence of the periphery guarantees the possibility of freedom and escape. From the periphery itself, however, things look very different. If one's existence is perceived as already being at the limit, then the possibility of further displacement is eliminated. The result is the undoing of the very concept of the limit, and the collapse of the chain of analogies whereby a writer such as Gide links the notion of the limit to the ideas of the escape to a new world, the *acte gratuit*, and freedom. This emerges very clearly in the case of Zamacona's death. Fuentes does not use the incident to demonstrate the absolute nature of individual freedom. Instead, with the focus now on the victim, the scene evokes the old Latin American theme of a violent and hostile environment from which there is no escape. And even if we were to extract from this episode a different kind of existentialist motif—such as the notion of the absurd—such elements would exist in a state of tension with the larger narrative pattern into which the episode is absorbed. For Zamacona is only one of many of the novel's characters who suffer a violent death on Independence Day, and this juxtaposition of death and celebration is clearly designed to recall the ancient Aztec belief that human sacrifices are necessary to ensure the continuity of life. The series of deaths at the end of the novel hints at the persistence of these mythical patterns beneath the surface of modern Mexico and at the fragility of the individual in the face of such forces.

This reading of Zamacona's death is at odds with the interpretation Fuentes himself offers in the interview with Rodríguez Monegal, where he proposes that we regard it as evidence of the instantaneousness of Mexican life, and not, as I have just suggested, of the continued power of ancient cosmogonies beneath the country's veneer of modernity. In fact, Fuentes never wholly eliminates either of these two possible readings. Two details in the scene of Zamacona's death indicate how Fuentes tries to hold together these alternative interpretations. First, when Zamacona gets out from his car and approaches the cantina, he recites a line from Nerval to himself: "et c'est toujours la seule—ou c'est le seul moment. . .". Nerval's idea that each moment in time is unique anticipates the existentialist conception of time, in which every instant is a new creation, disconnected from past and future. This notion of temporality is a focal point of Sartre's well-known analysis of Camus's *L'étranger*. Sartre describes Meursault as a man for whom "Seul le présent compte, le concret" (*Situations, I*). He links this vision of time to Camus's absurdist world-view in which God is dead and death is everything: "La présence de la mort au bout de notre route a dissipé notre avenir en fumée, notre vie est 'sans lendemain,' c'est une succession de présents." Fuentes's use of the quotation from Nerval seems designed to allude to such ideas about time, and thus to prepare us for the sudden, inexplicable flare-up of violence that leaves Zamacona dead.

But if this leads to a view of Zamacona's death as an absurd, meaningless event, another feature of this episode suggests a quite different point of view: the emphasis on the eyes and on the act of seeing. Zamacona's killer, as I observed earlier, justifies his deed by saying that he did not like the way Zamacona had looked at him. Furthermore, the only mention of the murderer's appearance is of his eyes:

Uno de los hombres le dio la cara a Manuel Zamacona; desprendido como un trompo de la barra de madera, con los ojos redondos y sumergidos de canica, disparó su pistola dos, tres, cinco veces sobre el cuerpo de Zamacona.

The killer's submerged and marble-like eyes link him to the realm of the invisible, subsisting beneath the surface existence of Fuentes's Mexico. Invisibility is generally associated in *La región* with Mexico's origins in its pre-Hispanic past, a connection captured most vividly in the figure of Hortensia Chacón, the blind woman who leads the powerful self-made banker Federico Robles back to his indigenous roots. Hortensia represents the beneficent side of the dark world beneath the country's semblance of progress and modernity. The killer, on the other hand, represents the violent, menacing side of this world: figuratively blind where Hortensia is literally so, this anonymous figure wishes to punish Zamacona for the look in his eyes, that is, for his location within the visible world of modern Mexico. Wanting to blind him as much as to kill him, he demonstrates the enduring power of Mexico's past.

There can be little doubt that the manner of Zamacona's death reveals the persistence of an atavistic violence lurking beneath the country's surface life. The question that remains unanswered, however, is whether this violence remains integrated with ancient cosmological rhythms, or whether it has lost its connection with ritual and has been expelled into a world of existential absurdity. This ambiguity is sustained in the development of the novel's plot after Zamacona's death.

It is difficult to ignore the connection between Ixca Cienfuegos's search, at his mother's behest, for a sacrificial victim with which to propitiate the gods, and the series of deaths that occur toward the end of the novel. But we can never be entirely sure that the sacrifices really are sacrifices, nor that they are responsible for a renewal of the life-cycle. Ixca's mother, Teódula Moctezuma, for her part, does not question the significance of these events. After Norma Larragoiti dies in the fire that burns down her house, Teódula tells Ixca that she believes the sacrifice has now been fulfilled, and that the normal course of life will be resumed. At the same moment, as if to confirm Teódula's vision of life's rebirth, the sun begins to rise.

Fuentes does not always represent this idea of cyclical return with such solemnity. While Part Two of the novel concludes with the destruction or downfall of many of the central characters, Part Three resumes three years later with the description of a young couple falling in love. But both Jaime Ceballos and Betina Régules have such stale and conventional natures that we inevitably sense an element of the parodic in this vision of life's regeneration. The effect is reinforced when the scene shifts again to a party hosted by Bobó Gutiérrez, whom we observe greeting his guests with the exact same words he had used approximately three years earlier, near the beginning of the novel: ''¡Caros! Entren a aprehender las eternas verdades.'' Bobó's eternal truths are clearly a mockery. We recognize here not return and renewal, but paralysis and decay.

Fuentes leaves his readers suspended between a world ruled by profound mythological rhythms, and an alternative, modern world of drift and contingency. He never fully decides which of these two pictures is finally truer to the reality of Mexico. This same conflict shapes the meditation on identity and authenticity that receives novelistic form through the contrasting careers of Ixca Cienfuegos and Rodrigo Pola. Although two other characters, Federico Robles and Manuel Zamacona, are also central to the development of this theme, I shall focus on Ixca and Rodrigo, since their confrontation after Bobó's last party effectively brings the plot of the novel to a close, thus suggesting the importance of these two figures to Fuentes's articulation of the problem of subjectivity.

Rodrigo Pola is an emblematic modern personality—a type toward the definition of which the existentialists made a significant contribution. Rodrigo's connection with this tradition of the modern self is clear from the first words he speaks. Into a discussion about the social function of art, he interjects the following observation: ''No todos tenemos que ser el cochino hombre de la calle o, por oposición, *un homme révolté* . . . .'' While Rodrigo appears to reject the opposition he posits here, these words in fact encapsulate the defining axis of his personality, a conflict between conformity and rebellion. The allusion to Camus is clearly meant to recall the existentialist emphasis on subjectivity, on the need for individuals to create their own values without reference to a realm of *a priori* truths or to society's received notions. Initially, Rodrigo's actions are guided by a similar search for authentic self-definition.

As he grows up, Rodrigo—who wants to be a writer—has to struggle against the oppressive demands of his mother, Rosenda, who, having lost her husband during the Mexican Revolution, cannot bear the thought of her son also escaping from her grip. The conflict between Rodrigo and his mother revolves around the question of who creates the self and thus has power over it. Rosenda wishes the moment in which she gave birth to her son to be prolonged forever. She wants always to be the mother, the child owing its existence to her alone. Rodrigo speaks with horror of "ese deseo de beberme entero, de apresarme entre sus piernas y estar siempre, hasta la consumación de nuestras tres vidas, dándome a luz sin descanso, en un larguísimo parto de noches y días y años . . . ." To this idea of the enduring power derived from the act of giving birth to a child, Rodrigo opposes a notion of figurative birth in which the self engenders itself: "me sentí. . . hijo, más que de mis padres, de mi propia, breve, sí, pero para mi única, incanjeable experiencia. . . ." In this, he appears to be heeding the existentialist exhortation to free oneself from all forms of external conditioning.

It is worth recalling, however, that there were different phases within the tradition of French existentialism. While the earlier work of Sartre and Camus tended to emphasize the absolute nature of individual freedom and favored the themes of anxiety, absurdity, and superfluousness, their later work sought to establish a more affirmative view of existentialist philosophy. In *L'existentialisme est un humanisme* (1946), for example, Sartre sought to demonstrate that existentialism provides a philosophical basis for an attitude of engagement with the world and commitment to one's fellow human beings. Camus's *L'homme révolté* interprets the act of rebellion against an intolerable situation not as an individualistic gesture, but as a sign of the fundamental truth of human solidarity. Rebellion, according to Camus, is always potentially an act of self-sacrifice, and so implies the existence of values that transcend the individual. Camus himself regarded the shift in his work from a concern with the absurd to a concern with rebellion as the sign of a new focus on the group instead of the individual: "Dans l'expérience absurde, la souffrance est individuelle. A partir du mouvement de révolte, elle a conscience d'être collective, elle est l'aventure de tous" (*L'homme révolté*).

Rodrigo, by opposing "l'homme révolté" to man in the mass ("el cochino hombre de la calle"), evokes the more strictly individualistic side of existentialist thought. But in the course of the novel, Rodrigo's efforts to assert his own uniqueness become increasingly fruitless. This failure implies a critique of the early version of existentialism, with its one-sided emphasis on self-creation and self-

renewal as the path to authentic selfhood, and its neglect of the social dimension of human life. Rodrigo's pursuit of a total freedom from all external constraints leads first to feelings of alienation and inauthenticity, and eventually to a complete turnaround, an unconditional surrender to society's norms of success.

In one episode, we see Rodrigo making faces at himself in the mirror, rapidly shifting expressions, "hasta sentir que su rostro y el reflejado eran dos, distintos, y tan alejados entre sí como la luna verdadera que nadie conoce y su reflejo quebrado en un estanque." This scene recalls a similar moment in *La nausée* where Roquentin studies his reflection in a mirror and is struck by the incomprehensible, alien appearance of his own face Fuentes's adaptation of this motif suggests a similar perspective on the impossibility of discovering a stable, continuous identity, and the consequent susceptibility of the self to being constantly remolded into new shapes. For a moment, Rodrigo seems to recoil from his performance; he feels an urge to sit down and write, to leave what he calls "una sola constancia verdadera." Ironically enough, the text he produces articulates a theory of the self as a mask, a form of play. Everything becomes arbitrary and gratuitous. The self is cast loose from any serious attachment, even from that most fundamental attachment, the body itself. Thus, Rodrigo is at one point led to assert that it is a matter of indifference whether one's face is, in actual fact, ugly or beautiful; the act of self-creation can apply even to one's physical appearance. The material world, even in its most primary manifestation, is fully subject to the individual will: "El problema consiste en saber cómo se imagina uno su propia cara. Que la cara sea, en realidad, espantosa o bella, no importa. Todo es imaginarse la propia cara interesante, fuerte, definida, o bien imaginarla ridícula, tonta y fea."

If the theory of the mask is initially designed to free the self from all forms of predetermination, then Rodrigo's radical application of this principle appears to produce the opposite result. Rodrigo himself eventually recognizes that the histrionic self-display into which he has fallen effectively obliterates the possibility of achieving genuine freedom; he admits that he has become a captive of his own game: "Se vuelve uno esclavo de su propio juego, el movimiento supera y condena a la persona que lo inició, y entonces sólo importa el movimiento; uno es llevado y traído por él, más que agente, elemento."

A few pages later, the description of a thunderstorm dramatizes the extent of Rodrigo's estrangement from the world:

> La tormenta lo envolvía en una percusión líquida, implacable. Arriba, el espacio se canjeaba a sí mismo estruendos, luz sombría: todos los mitos y símbolos fundados en la aparición de la naturaleza se concentraban en el cielo potente, ensamblador de un poderío oculto. Resonaba el firmamento con una tristeza ajena a cualquier circunstancia: no gratuita, sino suficiente.

Fuentes's conception of the natural world, as it emerges from this passage, has important implications for his view of the status of the perceiving subject. The storm's concentrated, implacable power, its relation to the deep, continuous rhythms of nature, and its aura of timelessness are at the farthest possible remove from the inconsequentiality and arbitrariness that define Rodrigo's relations to himself and to the world. The implications of this contrast for Fuentes's larger view of the self can perhaps be sensed most clearly through a comparison with certain passages in Sartre's *La nausée* that deal with the same issues.

Fuentes's use of the pathetic fallacy encourages a view of the realms of the human and the nonhuman as deeply interrelated. The reference to the sky's occult powers may appear to lift the natural world to a position that transcends the human, but it also implies that nature is pregnant with meanings that are of great consequence to human life. The use of the verb "envolver" defines the exact nature of the relationship: it is impossible to think of human beings as separate from the universe in which they live. Roquentin, in *La nausée,* recognizes this human inclination to search for connections between ourselves and the physical world, to treat it, for example, as a text waiting for its meaning to be unveiled. At one point he describes a priest walking along the seaside as he reads from his breviary: "Par instants il léve la téte et regarde la mer d'un air approbateur: la mer aussi est un bréviaire, elle parle de Dieu." But Roquentin furiously rejects this attempt at humanization: "La *vraie* mer est froide et noire, pleine de bêtes; elle rampe sous cette mince pellicule verte qui est faite pour tromper les gens." In *La nausée* the world of objects and natural processes does not envelop the human world in a transcendent, protective manner; instead, it is conceived as a realm of brute, unredeemable fact from which a lucid consciousness will recoil in horror.

If Rodrigo is a failed existentialist, part of the explanation may lie in the way Fuentes has stacked the deck against him. In a world where natural phenomena exude such a compelling and inscrutable sense of purpose and power, the individual can hardly presume to play God with his own existence. Fuentes has created a character with existentialist features, but has placed him in a setting entirely different from the kind that would have been envisioned by the existentialists themselves. As a result, the existentialist project is effectively invalidated.

Ixca Cienfuegos represents, on the level of character, the same mythical forces which Fuentes evokes through his description of the thunderstorm. Ixca, whose first name derives from the Nahuatl word for bake, or cook, and whose last name alludes to the original time in Aztec mythology when fires lit up the universe, is a shadowy yet central presence in the novel. One character compares him to God because of his seeming omnipresence. Ixca's search for a sacrificial victim is part of an attempt to reintegrate Mexican society into a sacred, cosmic order, and thus to overcome the kind of self-division and self-estrangement suffered by a typical product of the modern world such as Rodrigo. The contrast between the two men emerges clearly in the description of an early evening walk they take along the Paseo de la Reforma:

> Rodrigo miraba como el polvo se acumulaba en los zapatos amarillos. Se sentía consciente de todos sus movimientos nerviosos. Y Cienfuegos como si no caminara, como si lo fuera empujando la leve brisa de verano, como si no tuviera esas piernas, esas manos que tanto estorbaban a Rodrigo.

While Rodrigo is severely afflicted with the modern disease of self-consciousness, Ixca is entirely at ease, in possession of an unfissured consciousness that exists in harmony with the natural world. Ixca does not search for an increasingly intense awareness of his own separateness from others. He is deeply at odds with the idea of a unique, individual personality waiting to be liberated from external oppression. Fuentes shows him in an intense, sometimes conflictive relationship with his mother, in which he submits to her wishes instead of rebelling, as Rodrigo does. Ixca advocates self-forgetfulness rather than self-regard: "Olvidarse de sí, clave de las felicidades, que es olvidarse de los demás; no liberarse a sí: sojuzgar a los demás." His vision ultimately evolves out of his belief in the absolute nature of the nation's origins, and the priority of these origins over the claims of contemporary individuals. Mexico, he claims, "es algo fijado para siempre, incapaz de evolución. Una roca inconmovible que todo lo tolera. Todos los limos pueden crecer sobre esa roca, pero la roca en sí no cambia, es la misma, para siempre.'' At one point, Ixca urges Rodrigo to choose between the two Mexicos, the ancient and the modern: ''Acá serás anónimo, hermano de todos en la soledad. Allá tendrás tu nombre, y en la muchedumbre nadie te tocará, no tocarás a nadie.'' The possession of a name becomes an emblem of the barren, atomistic individualism that rules over the contemporary world. In the mythical world Ixca believes in, the individual is absorbed into a larger order of fraternal belonging.

Neither Rodrigo nor Ixca offers a satisfying solution to the problem of authenticity. Rodrigo's inner restlessness seems so gratuitous and self-indulgent that it comes as no surprise to see him eventually give up his rebellion against the world. If each new mask is the result of an arbitrary choice, then why not choose the mask that will bring success and prosperity? By the end of the novel, Rodrigo has become a successful writer of screenplays for the movie industry, a hack who has cynically mastered a simple formula for success.

But if Rodrigo's cult of individuality ultimately proves fruitless and self-defeating, Ixca's violent attack on the notion of a personal life does not seem much more appealing. His behavior becomes increasingly menacing, at times literally poisonous. We may note, for example, the terror he inspires in little Jorgito Morales when he meets him outside the Cathedral and offers to buy him some candy. In order to escape from Ixca's grip, Jorgito bites his hand, drawing blood. But the next time we see him, over a hundred pages later, the boy is dead. Since it is never clear that the regeneration Ixca is after actually takes place, we are left simply with the image of a man who goes around causing havoc in the lives of others. If Rodrigo's emptiness is that of a life lived without reference to the transcendent, then Ixca displays the perhaps more sinister emptiness of someone who has voided himself of all human emotions: ''en realidad Ixca se sustentaba sobre un imenso vacío, un vacío en el que ni la piedad, ni el amor, ni siquiera el odio de los demás era admitido.''

The final confrontation between Ixca and Rodrigo, three years after the main events of the novel, brings the plot to a close, and seems designed to show that while their respective destinies are diametrically opposed, they are equally stunted and unfulfilled. While Rodrigo scales the heights of social success, Ixca disappears from Mexico City altogether, living in obscurity with Rosa Morales, the cleaning lady, and her remaining children. On the surface, Rodrigo has been transformed into a new person, yet he is haunted by the past: ''¿Crees que porque estoy aquí ya no estoy allá?... ¿Crees que una nueva vida destruye a la antigua, la cancela?'' Ixca, on the other hand, while having apparently reconciled himself to the demands of the mythical past, now finds himself abandoned in the present, divided from the very past he thought he was embracing. He describes his condition in the same plaintive tones as Rodrigo:¿Crees que recuerdo mi propia cara? Mi vida comienza todos los días . . . y nunca tengo el recuerdo de lo que pasó antes . . . .''

Wendy Faris has drawn attention to Fuentes's fondness for the rhetorical figure of the chiasmus, which he employs not only at the level of individual sentences but also at the level of plot-structures. The paths followed by Rodrigo and Ixca trace a chiastic design. If at the beginning of the novel Rodrigo represents the present-oriented pole, and Ixca the past-oriented, then the final confrontation between the two men constitutes a complete reversal of this relationship. By the end of the novel, Rodrigo can no longer escape the past, while Ixca lives his life as though it were starting anew at every instant.

The result of this chiastic pattern is to lead the novel into an impasse. The plot of *La región* offers no clear resolution to the problems of authenticity and national identity which the novel articulates. Fuentes rejects the existentialist project of liberating the self from the past, of investing life with value simply through the agency of free individual choice, but he also rejects the attempt to provoke a return to the cultural origins of Mexico. Both these approaches to the problems of subjectivity and community are shown to be fruitless, even self-cancelling.

The novel, however, does not end with the conversation between Rodrigo and Ixca. After the two friends separate, the text undergoes a series of unusual transformations. Ixca gradually sheds his corporeality, and little by little absorbs the different facets of the surrounding city, until eventually he and the city become a single entity. In a subsequent transformation, Ixca becomes the characters of the novel itself, so that finally Ixca, the city, and the book become metaphors for one another, in an operation that may be understood as an attempt to lift the novel onto a plane distinct from ordinary narrativity. In a final transition, Ixca disappears into his own voice, but the voice that speaks in the novel's concluding chapter is one no longer tied to a particular space or time; it is a voice that aims to give a total and instantaneous vision of Mexico, as well as of the novel Fuentes has written about it. This final chapter, entitled "La región más transparente del aire," suggests an attempt to recapitulate and condense the novel; it is a mélange of densely metaphorical descriptions of the Mexican people, scenes from Mexican history, and echoes of the main narrative of the novel itself.

The guiding conception behind this remarkable novelistic flight is the attempt to escape from linear time, to propose and embody an alternative vision of temporality in which, as Fuentes writes, "todo vive al mismo tiempo." Among writers of the present century, Fuentes clearly does not stand alone in his fascination with the break with linear time. For Octavio Paz, for example, the idea of a zone of pure time, beyond chronology, provides the very basis for his definition of poetry: "El poema es mediación: por gracia suya, el tiempo original, padre de los tiempos, encarna en un instante. La sucesión se convierte en presente puro, manantial que se alimenta a sí mismo y trasmuta al hombre" (*El arco y la lira*). In the area of the novel, one of the most influential codifications of the modernist aesthetic is Joseph Frank's 1945 essay "Spatial Form in Modern Literature"; it centers precisely on this attempt to create forms that are not dependent on linear, chronological methods of organization. Frank's essay, particularly his discussion of the basic features of spatial form, and the type of content it conveys, clarifies Fuentes's relationship to modernist writing. It also contributes to an understanding of the function of the novel's final chapter, in which the techniques of spatial form are most emphatically deployed and appear to constitute an effort to escape from the impasse with which the actual plot of the novel concludes.

According to Frank, in the works of poets such as Eliot and Pound, and novelists such as Joyce, Proust, and Djuna Barnes, the normal temporal unfolding of the text is repeatedly interrupted, with the result that the unity of these works is no longer located in a continuous narrative progression, but in the reflexive references and cross-references relating different points in the text to one another. The reader, in reconstructing these patterns, must ignore the aspects of temporal flow and external reference that are fundamental to more conventional works of literature. The reconstructed patterns must be perceived simultaneously, as a configuration in space. Frank goes on to argue that the most important consequence of the deployment of spatial form in literature is the erasure of a sense of historical depth. Different moments in time become locked together in a timeless unity that evokes the world of myth rather than history.

Clearly, numerous objections could be made to the concept of spatial form, in particular to the term itself, which may seem inappropriately metaphorical. My interest here, however, is not in the accuracy of the term itself, but in the narrative techniques the term was designed to describe, and in the revolt against linear, progressive time implied by the use of these techniques.

Fuentes's attempt, in *La región,* to disrupt the straightforward temporal flow of the novel is not restricted to the final chapter. To the extent that the novel as a whole constitutes an attempt—along the lines of James Joyce's *Ulysses* (1992) and John Dos Passos's *Manhattan Transfer* (1925)—to recreate the life of a city within its pages, the rejection of a sequential organization of the text appears entirely fitting. What Frank would call the "spatializing" technique of the juxtaposition of unrelated textual fragments corresponds to the essentially spatial entity being represented. A typical instance of this technique occurs near the beginning of Fuentes's novel, where the narrator, in a decidedly small-scale imitation of the "Wandering Rocks" chapter of *Ulysses,* traces the simultaneous activities in different parts of the city of various characters on the morning after one of Bobó's parties. The revolt against linear time is also apparent in those moments in the text when past and present are conflated within the mind of an individual character. This device is used most strikingly in the case of Federico Robles, who, as a firm believer in economic progress and a builder of post-Revolutionary Mexico, represents the attachment to the singularity of chronological time in one of its most powerful forms. Although he rejects the past, Robles nevertheless, at Ixca's urging, undertakes the perilous journey inward, and is eventually led to an almost Proustian apprehension of pure time freed from the habitual constraints of consecutiveness. In one scene, while making love to Hortensia, Robles bites the woman's hair, an act that suddenly evokes an image from the day he fought at the battle of Celaya during the Mexican Revolution, and bit the reins of his horse as he rode into the fray. The merging of past and present is underscored by the paratactic arrangement of the following two sentences: "Llano ensangrentado de Celaya. Cuerpo húmedo y abierto de Hortensia." Robles's vision is particularly significant since it seems to be at least partly responsible for his decision to abandon his public role as a powerful financier in the nation's capital and return to his obscure roots in the country. His decision constitutes an explicit rejection of the rigorously linear time of economic progress.

The important question is whether, as Frank would argue, the disruption of a continuous temporal progression within a narrative necessarily implies a return to the timeless world of myth. It seems doubtful, if only because it is not altogether clear why we should be locked into a binary opposition between history conceived purely in a linear fashion, on the one hand, and myth as the eternal repetition of the same, on the other. The question, then, is what purpose does Fuentes's use of these techniques serve? In answering, I want to focus in particular on the relationship between the main body of the narrative and the poetic finale with which it concludes. One of the most remarkable features of *La región* is that while most of the devices Frank enumerates in his article on spatial form are in evidence throughout the novel, they are most spectacularly exploited at the end, in a manner without real equivalent in the texts Frank discusses. This does not mean, however, that the reader is now truly transported into the realm of myth. I would suggest, instead, that the final section of the novel ought to be read as an attempt to lift the text onto a completely different level, in the hope of offering a resolution to the ambiguities with which the plot concludes. Since these ambiguities center on the opposition between the mythical and the existential views of life, it seems unlikely that such a resolution would take the form of a more determined affirmation of the mythical, a move that would simply eliminate one of the poles of the opposition.

We can begin measuring Fuentes's distance from the mythical approach by looking at the principal features of Frank's definition of myth. Frank quotes Mircea Eliade, who identifies myth as a realm of "eternal repetition," where time becomes "cosmic, cyclical and infinite" (*The Widening Gyre*). Frank discovers a similar emphasis on repetition and uniformity in the works of modernists such as Joyce, Eliot, and Pound, whose techniques of juxtaposition and allusion he believes underline the fundamental sameness of the human condition through the ages. Octavio Paz, in his discussion of the poetic technique of *simultaneísmo* (which we may regard as another term for spatial form), reaches a similar conclusion: he argues that Pound and Eliot developed their experimental poetic in order to "reconquistar la tradición de la Divina Comedia, es

decir, la tradición de Occidente" (*Los hijos del limo*). Both projects, the return to myth and the recapture of tradition, are driven by a search for cultural coherence and identity.

Fuentes has frequently discussed the notion that different temporal planes may have a simultaneous existence, but he has a very different understanding of the implications of this fact. When he discusses "la simultaneidad de los tiempos mexicanos" ("Kierkegaard en la Zona Rosa") which he opposes to the linearity of European time, he does not mean that the juxtaposition of these different temporal levels would reveal an underlying continuity between the various phases of Mexican history. Nor is this the effect he pursues at the end of *La región*. The torrent of images, names, and historical episodes he unleashes here evokes a tumultuous, unrestrained multiplicity. In the same essay Fuentes writes that Mexican time "se divierte con nosotros, se revierte contra nosotros, se invierte en nosotros, se subvierte desde nosotros, se convierte en nombre nuestro." These verbs describe not continuity and coherence, but an unceasing process of metamorphosis. He argues that the simultaneous existence in Mexico of all historical levels results from a decision of the land and its people to maintain alive all of time, for the simple reason that "ningún tiempo se ha cumplido aún" Fuentes's Mexican past, in other words, is profoundly different from the past to which the Anglo-American modernists wished to return. It offers not the fullness of an established tradition, but a variety of unfinished projects. Fuentes attacks the proponents of modernization in Mexico, with their cult of the present and of progress, for having suppressed this feature of Mexican time. To return to the cultural and historical multiplicity of Mexico constitutes an act of liberation, a rebellion against the enslaving prejudices of modernity. Fuentes believes that such a rebellion in fact took place during the Mexican Revolution:

> Sólo la Revolución—y por eso, a pesar de todo, merece una R mayúscula—hizo presente todos los pasados de México. Lo hizo instantáneamente, como si supiera que no sobraría tiempo para esta fiesta de encarnaciones. ("Kierkegaard")

This view of the Mexican Revolution is explicitly expressed in *La región* by Manuel Zamacona, who declares at one point that "La Revolución nos descubre la totalidad de la historia de México," a statement that exactly replicates statements Fuentes has made elsewhere in his own name. It is an idea that can be traced to Octavio Paz, who in *El laberinto de la soledad* described the Mexican Revolution as "un movimiento tendiente a reconquistar nuestro pasado, asimilarlo y hacerlo vivo en el presente." My argument is that at the end of *La región,* Fuentes tries to reproduce on the aesthetic level this revolutionary resuscitation of Mexico's many-sided past. He creates a textual model of ferment, upheaval, and open-endedness. This vision of the simultaneous coexistence of all times overturns the linear approach to time represented by Rodrigo Pola, and by the new Mexican bourgeoisie's deification of progress. But the constant process of change and dispersal implied by this vision of time as "fiesta" also subverts the obsession with the unity and singularity of origins expressed in the figure of Ixca Cienfuegos. Fuentes's alternative is his concept of revolutionary time, a vision of simultaneity that promises freedom and possibility, but does not dispense with a strong sense of the shaping powers of the past. This paradoxical fusion of freedom and necessity, of futurity and pastness, is made possible by an ambiguity in the word "revolution" itself, which generally refers to a clean break with the past, a drastic change in the social order, but, in an older version of the word, which Fuentes clearly wants his readers to recall, indicates a process of cyclical return. In the imaginative space Fuentes creates at the end of *La región*, these two meanings are held together in an ultimately utopian gesture.

A utopian vision of revolution has been a consistent element in Fuentes's work. In the 1980s, Fuentes has continued to discuss revolutions, in Mexico and elsewhere, in the same terms he used in the 1950s. In his 1983 Harvard commencement speech, for example, he declared that the Mexican Revolution had brought to light "the totality of our history and the possibility of a culture" (*Myself with Others*). He went on to connect the Mexican experience with that of other countries now passing through revolutionary phases:

> Paz himself, Diego Rivera and Carlos Chávez, Mariano Azuela and José Clemente Orozco, Juan Rulfo and Rufino Tamayo: we all work and exist because of the revolutionary experience of our country. How can we stand by as this experience is denied, through ignorance and arrogance, to other people, our brothers, in Central America and the Caribbean?

In *Gringo viejo* (1985), Fuentes once again explores his ideas about the Mexican Revolution. At one point in the novel, the soldiers in the rebel army of Pancho Villa occupy the mansion of a wealthy family that has fled the country. When the soldiers enter the ballroom, with its huge mirrors, they are astonished at the sight of their own reflections; for the first time in their lives they are seeing their own bodies in their entirety. In this way, the Revolution has finally allowed these men and women to discover who they really are. A similar notion is articulated in the broad opposition the narrative constructs between Mexico before and Mexico during the Revolution. Before the Revolution the country was merely an aggregate of static, isolated communities. The Revolution sets the country in motion; the people leave their villages and towns and finally begin to discover the common purpose that binds the nation together as a whole. The Revolution, in this view, constitutes an explosive moment of self-recognition in the nation's history.

Fuentes's most recent novel, *Cristóbal Nonato* (1987), however, reveals a distinct shift in perspective: revolutions, both past and present, are now seen in a far less sanguine light. The spirit of the Mexican Revolution is recreated in a mocking, though affectionate, manner in the figure of General Rigoberto Palomar, who owes his high military rank to a somewhat unusual feat: at the age of eighteen he was elevated in one stroke from trumpeter to general for having recovered the arm General Alvaro Obregón lost during the battle of Celaya. In the novel's present, at the age of ninety-one, General Palomar is the last survivor of the Revolution, in which he maintains an irrational faith premised on two contradictory assumptions: "1) la Revolución no había terminado y 2) la Revolución había triunfado y cumplido todas sus promesas." This discrediting of the concept of revolution takes on a less light-hearted form when it comes to a depiction of the revolutionary spirit of the late twentieth century. The embodiment of this spirit is Matamoros Moreno, whose leadership of the revolutionary forces of Mexico is both absurd, in that it grows out of the resentments of a frustrated writer, and somewhat sinister, in that his name, the "Ayatollah," links him to a reactionary religious fanaticism. In this way, the belief in the possible emergence of a new, more benign, order is severely attenuated.

A final element in Fuentes's revised view of the nature of revolution consists of his rethinking the relationship between the erotic and the political. Wendy Faris has observed that in much of Fuentes's work "love and revolution are allied, the physical upheaval and implied freedom of eroticism often serving as analogues for social liberation, both moving us toward some kind of utopia" ("Desire and Power"). In *Cristóbal Nonato,* however, the personal and the political are no longer so easily reconciled; the relationship between these two dimensions of existence turns out to be fraught with difficulties. When young Angel Palomar abandons his wife in the middle of her pregnancy in order to pursue an infatuation with the vain and superficial daughter of one of Mexico's richest men, he manages to convince himself that he is doing it in order to keep alive his iconoclastic and rebellious spirit. He is, in other words, chasing Penny López for the right ideological reasons. But Angel is not entirely convinced by his own attempt at self-justification; he continues to be perplexed by "la contradicción entre sus ideas y su práctica" and he is finally unable to find the correct adjustment between his sex life and his politics: "Su sexualidad renaciente, era progresista o reaccionaria? Su actividad política, debía conducirlo a la monogamía o al harén?" The only possible conclusion is that these two realms are in some sense incommensurable: "ante un buen acostón se estrellan todas las ideologías." In this way, revolution, deprived of a clear basis in personal experience, becomes a far more complex, baffling and even improbable event. Whether *Cristóbal Nonato* signals a major shift in Fuentes's work it is too early to say. What is clear, however, is that it is precisely Fuentes's persistent engagement with the question of the interrelations between the private and the public, between the individual self and its historical circumstances, that constitutes his most powerful claim on our interest.

Source: Maarten Van Delden, "Myth, Contingency, and Revolution in Carlos Fuentes's La region mas transparente," in *Comparative Literature,* Vol. 43, No. 4, Fall, 1991, p. 326.

Sean French

In the following essay, Sean French reviews Carlos Fuentes' novel The Old Gringo, *an historical fiction dramatizing the life of Ambrose Bierce and seeking to capture the history and breadth of his adopted country, Mexico.*

Ambrose Bierce was a misanthrope, a nihilist, and America's most celebrated journalist. At the end of his career he decided not to fade away. In 1913, a bitter and beaten seventy-one-year-old, he lit out for Mexico and disappeared. Rumour has it that he joined Pancho Villa's revolutionary army and died in action the following year. Where history stops, the novel can begin. Carlos Fuentes's *The Old Gringo* takes up Bierce's story from the moment he crosses the Rio Grande with a suitcase containing two of his own books, a copy of *Don Quixote* and a Colt .44.

Fuentes clearly has only the most perfunctory interest in creating a plausible version of what might have happened. The "old gringo" (Bierce is never named: it is only through hints, allusions or reading the dustjacket that we find out the truth) rides across the desert and stumbles on a revolutionary detachment in Chihuahua commanded by the self-styled General Tomás Arroyo. He has led a rising on the estate where he was born and brought up as a virtual slave. The landowners have fled, but Harriet Winslow, the prim American school-teacher they had hired, remains stubbornly behind. The general refuses to accept Bierce as a recruit until the old gringo demonstrates improbable skill with his revolver.

This novel is crammed with incident, much of it of the most melodramatic kind. We are told frequently that the old gringo has come to Mexico to die. He rides into battle with Arroyo's troops and performs acts of astonishing bravery, but he is not killed. Meanwhile Harriet Winslow is cured of her inhibitions in the course of a love affair with the virile General Arroyo. The tale reaches a predictably violent conclusion, and as in many a western only the woman survives to return to civilization.

But what is the book really about? Bierce wonders himself: "Was he here to die or to write a novel about a Mexican general and an old gringo and a Washington schoolteacher lost in the deserts of northern Mexico?" *The Old Gringo* is about Ambrose Bierce the man, but it also makes sophisticated use of his literary and political career. The form of the novel alludes to Bierce's celebrated short story, "An Occurrence at Owl Creek Bridge", about a Confederate soldier being hanged from a bridge during the American Civil War. He feels the rope break and the story details his escape and journey across country. Finally he reaches home, but as he runs towards his wife everything goes black and he dies, swinging from the bridge. The whole story has taken place in his mind at the moment of his death.

Fuentes hints that this novel may be taking place in similar fashion in Bierce's mind as he dies. To complicate matters; the story is also unfolding in the confused memory of Harriet Winslow, reliving the events many years later in her Washington, DC, walk-up apartment. He is in her dream, but she is in his dream as well.

For the Mexicans, their country is all too real, and there are vivid evocations in this book of desert, heat and smells. But Mexico is also present as a state of mind, a subject of fantasy. Harriet Winslow and Bierce both enter Mexico as carefully delineated representatives of imperialism, with disdain for this primitive, chaotic country in the United States' back yard. Much in *The Old Gringo* is muddy, even on a second reading, but the anti-Americanism is clear enough. As Bierce put it to Harriet, with the author's obvious approval,

> remember how we killed our Redskins and never had the courage to fornicate with the squaws and at least create a half-breed nation. We are caught in the business of forever killing people whose skin is of a different color. Mexico is the proof of what we could have been, so keep your eyes wide open.

This is a curious novel, alternately whimsical and immensely impressive. The vitality and virtuosity of Fuentes's narrative - in this superb translation, something like Jack London rewritten by Borges—are breathtaking. This is a story composed of fragments: moments of violence, passion or revelation, captured in memories and dreams. In other hands the effect could have been diffuse and boring, but Fuentes gives it the strange solidity of a fable. Yet much of the characterization—the demure schoolteacher, the macho rebel leader with "his uneasy sex, never restful"—is crude caricature. And the real subject of the novel, Mexico itself, which, we are told, redeems Bierce (compensating him "with a life: the life of his senses, awakened from lethargy by his proximity to death"), remains in the background.

It's only when one turns to Fuentes's first book, *Where the Air is Clear* (first published in 1960 but appearing now in English for the first time), that we see fully what Mexico means to him. And if *The Old Gringo* seems starved of characters, perhaps it's because Fuentes used a career's worth of them in his first novel, a prodigious attempt to give Mexico its *Comédie Humaine* and *Ulysses* between the covers of one book. He tells the story of family after family—bankers, revolutionaries, artists, prostitutes, socialites—and, with flamboyant dexterity, weaves them together. At the heart of the book are two young men, Ixca Cienfuegos and Rodrigo Pola, who are on a troubled quest to discover how they can live in this violent, impoverished country, a country which destroyed Rodrigo's father, Gervasio, a revolutionary, executed during the 1913 civil war (an event that obsesses Fuentes). Fuentes portrays much of his country with loathing: the squalor of Mexico City, the corruption, the political oppression. The novel's most troubling, complicated character is Federico Robles, once a revolutionary comrade of Gervasios's and now a successful banker. "Here

there is only one choice", he tells the two young radicals, "we make the nation prosperous, or we starve." And if that means putting Mexico under the economic control of the United States, he is willing to pay that price.

Where the Air is Clear (again, in an excellent translation) lacks the formal discipline of *The Old Gringo*, but it is attempting something more difficult and interesting, which is to embrace all sides of a country, ranging from the old Spanish Empire to the Aztec culture of the sun the Spanish found when they arrived, from capitalism to revolutionary socialism: "Mexico is the only world radically cut off from Europe which has to accept the fatality of Europe's complete penetration and use the European words for both life and death, although the being of her life and faith are of a different language."

Of course, all this proves difficult to resolve and the novel ends in a sort of mystical trance of affirmation and reconciliation. It does have its moments of shrillness, over-insistence or sentimentality but is nevertheless a very exciting book, partly because it is written out of excitement for a great new subject. As one character puts it: "One does not explain Mexico. One believes in Mexico, with fury, with passion, and in alienation."

Source: Sean French, "Shouting from the Backyard," in *Times Literary Supplement,* July 4, 1986, p. 733.

Luis Leal

In the following essay, author Luis Leal reviews Carlos Fuentes' novel Where the Air is Clear *and his unique use of combining myth and fiction to create a synthesized biography of Mexico City.*

Gabriel García Márquez, in his Nobel lecture, stated that Latin American reality is a reality not of paper, "but one that lives within us and determines each instant of our countless daily deaths, and that nourishes creativity, full of sorrow and beauty.... Poets and beggars, musicians and prophets, warriors and scoundrels, all creatures of that unbridled reality, we have had to ask but little of imagination, for our crucial problem has been a lack of conventional means to render our lives believable."

Latin American writers, truly more than any other group, have rendered those lives believable by means of their creative works, especially their novels. Alongside the names of García Márquez and other prominent Latin American authors we find that of Carlos Fuentes, whose novels have given us an inside picture of Mexico's reality, a picture

> "Although *Where the Air Is Clear* reflects an experimental technique, Fuentes succeeded in creating a picture of Mexico City never before attempted by a novelist. He not only created a new language and preserved the secrets, the miseries, and the hopes of the City, but went beyond to dramatize the nature of the struggle between two cultures, Western and non-Western."

which would be difficult to duplicate in history books, and which has not been duplicated by other writers. To accomplish this he has made use not only of history, but also of the living myths— ancient and modern—that have had so much influence in shaping the nation's destiny. With these materials he has produced, under the guise of fiction, one of the most penetrating visions of Mexico and its inhabitants. This he has done in most of his works, but especially in the novels *Where the Air Is Clear, The Death of Artemio Cruz,* and, more recently, in *Distant Relations,* as well as in his collection of essays, *Tiempo mexicano* (*Mexican Time*).

García Márquez and Carlos Fuentes have been instrumental in perfecting a type of fiction that another Latin American Nobel prize winner, Miguel Angel Asturias, had made known earlier. Like Asturias, García Márquez and Fuentes have combined two narrative modes, the realistic (historical) and the mythical. As has been observed by Northrop Frye, the combination of these two dissimilar modes of fiction creates technical problems for making the narrative plausible. Latin American novelists, however, have been successful in solving this problem, which Frye calls *displacement.*

Carlos Fuentes has been successful in giving us a mythified vision of Mexican history. Although his fiction is essentially realistic, he has abandoned the traditional forms in order to embrace a new type of

realism, a realism based on the utilization of mythical themes and structures combined with realistic characteres, scenes, and dialogues, as practiced by Juan Rulfo, García Márquez, and other contemporary writers.

In Fuentes the change has not been abrupt. The title of his first book, *Los días enmascarados* (''Masked Days''), published in 1954, already referred to the Aztec myth of the five days at the end of the year when time stopped in readiness for the new life, the rebirth, the eternal return. The relation between myth and reality is best expressed in his story ''Chac Mool'' a story inspired by an event that took place in 1952, an exhibition of Mexican art in Europe which included the statue of the prehispanic god of rain, the god whose mere presence brought on a deluge of rain, according to the Mexican newspaper account read by Fuentes. In 1964, in an interview, he said that ''the data from the sensational, journalistic account of the art exhibit focused my attention on a fact evident to all Mexicans: the living presence of old cosmological forms from a Mexico lost forever but which, nevertheless, refuses to die and manifests itself from time to time through a mystery, an apparition, a reflection.''

In that short story Fuentes recreates the myth of the eternal return by the illusory transformation of a statue of a god, Chac Mool, which the protagonist has bought and placed in the basement of his house, where it comes back to life with the coming of the rains. The importance of the past upon the present is given expression by having the ancient god control its owner, finally driving him to suicide.

The novels of Fuentes, with some exceptions, can be considered as mythical approaches to history, or creative history. His success as a novelist is due in great part to this use of myth to interpret history, for history, as Ernst Cassirer has observed, is determined by the mythology of the people. ''In the relation between myth and history,'' he wrote, ''myth proves to be the primary, history the secondary and derived factor. It is not by its history that the mythology of a nation is determined, but, conversely, its history is determined by its mythology—or rather, the mythology of a people does not *determine* but *is* its fate, its destiny as decreed from the very beginning.'' This idea of the determination of the fate of a people from the very beginning appears in *Where the Air is Clear* and is expressed by one of the central characters, Ixca Cienfuegos, who symbolizes the mythical nature of Mexico City. He says, ''Today is born of that very origin which, without knowing it, controls us, who have always lived within it.''

In an interview Fuentes said that in *Where the Air Is Clear* he tried, among other things, to write a personal biography of Mexico City, ''its silhouettes, its secrets, a city which I love and hate at the same time because in it are presented with the greatest brutality the miseries and hopes of all my country. I tried to produce a synthesis of present-day Mexico: conflicts, aspirations, rancors.''

In the novel the miseries are described realistically, and the hopes and aspirations are projected into the future. The miseries are present day, the hopes are for a brighter tomorrow. These hopes he placed on the younger generation, who in 1951, the year in which most of the action in the novel takes place, was sweeping away the old remnants of the past in a search for better ways. He himself contributed with his literary works, in which he created a new language. Fuentes firmly believes in the importance of language in any interpretation of reality. The relationship between language and reality is, indeed, at the bottom of all his creations, for it is through language, he tells us, that Latin American reality has been distorted, ''Much before television was invented,'' he wrote, ''reality was already disguised by a false language. The Renaissance language of the Conquest hides the Medieval kernel of the colonizing enterprise, like the Laws of the Indies that of the *Encomienda*. The illuminist language of the Independence hide the remaining feudalism, and the positivist 19th century language of liberalism the sell-out to financial imperialism. . . . The language of the Revolution hides the reality of the counter revolution.''

For us, *Where the Air Is Clear* is much more than a biography of Mexico City, an expose of its true reality, or the creation of a new language. It is a metaphor expressing the confrontation between two universal cultures, two different ways of life, those of the West and those of indigenous America. All the characters, all the scenes, all the dialogues, and the ideas, concepts, and opinions, all the imagery, all the motives, all the popular elements are nothing but examples of that struggle, a struggle that was the subject of the novel *The Plumed Serpent* (1926) by D. H. Lawrence.

Since Mexico was one of the first non-Western countries to receive the impact of the West, it became a laboratory for the study of the consequences of the conquest of one civilization by another. The historian Arnold Toynbee, expert in the study of this phenomenum, wrote in 1939, in his *A Study of History*, that in Mexico the movement of revolt had not been a reaction against the civilization of the West. The Mexicans, he said,

> have not been seeking to extricate themselves from the Western toils in which the civilization of their forebears was caught and bound, four hundred years ago, by Cortés and his fellow *conquistadores*. On the contrary, the Mexicans have been seeking in our generation to take a fabulous Western kingdom of Heaven by storm. . . . On this showing, we may pronounce that the *ci-devant* Central American civilization, as well as the *ci-devant* Andean civilization, has now been completely incorporated into our Western body social.

Fifteen years later, however, Toynbee modified his statement, as a result, we assume, of his visit to Mexico in 1953. He made the observation that the Indian culture had really not been absorbed by Western civilization. He wrote in 1954, ''The Mexican Revolution of A.D. 1821, which might thus have appeared to have completed the incorporation of the Central American into the Western World, had been followed by the Revolution of A.D. 1910, in which the buried but hibernating indigenous society had suddenly bestirred itself, raised its head, and broken through the crust of culture deposited by officious Castilian hands on the grave into which the conquistadores had thrust a body that they believed themselves to have slain'' (VII, 1954).

Among the intellectuals active in Mexico during the early fifties, the years when the action of *Where the Air is Clear* takes place and also when Toynbee was invited to address them on the subject of the relations between the West and the rest of the world, the nature of Mexican life and culture was a subject very much in vogue. Octavio Paz wrote at length about it in his seminal book, *The Labyrinth of Solitude*, the first edition of which appeared in 1950. Four years before Toynbee published his last remarks about Mexico, Paz had said, ''The Revolution was a sudden immersion of Mexico in her own being, from which she brought back up, almost blindly, the essentials of a new kind of state. In addition, it was a return to the past, a reuniting of the ties broken by the Reform and the Diaz dictatorship, a search for our own selves, and a return to the maternal womb.''

Paz, however, went beyond Toynbee to postulate that there was now only one civilization. ''All of today's civilizations,'' he says in his revised edition of *The Labyrinth of Solitude* (1959), ''derive from that of the Western world, which has assimilated or crushed its rivals. . . . The contemporary crisis is not a struggle between two diverse cultures, as the conservatives would have us believe, but rather an internal quarrel in a civilization that no longer has any rivals, a civilization whose future is the future of the whole world.'' Toynbee's idea of conflict between different cultures and not Paz' concept of internal struggle within Western culture is the one presented by Fuentes in his novel.

No less important than the influence of Octavio Paz upon Fuentes' conception of the world in his novel was that of the intellectuals who in 1947–1948 formed the group *Hiperión,* led by the philosopher Leopoldo Zea. The main preoccupation of these young thinkers was the definition of the psyche of the Mexican and the destiny of Mexico as a nation. The name *Hiperión* was selected because Hiperión, the child of heaven and earth, symbolized for them the study of Mexico's life and culture in the context of the universal and the concrete, the national and the Western. The group, which was active until 1952, is represented in the novel by Zamacona, whose tragic death is symbolic of the lack of communication between members of different social classes, as well as the disregard with which intellectuals are treated in Mexico.

In Fuentes' novel the most important characters that symbolize the struggle between Western and non-Western cultures are Federico Robles, his wife Norma, Manuel Zamacona, Rodrigo Pola, Ixca Cienfuegos, and his mother Teódula Moctezuma. Robles and Ixca represent the two extremes, Robles the total acceptance and Ixca the total rejection of Western culture. It is ironic that Robles, an old Indian revolutionary but now a prosperous and powerful industrialist, should be the representative of Western culture. This fact, from the perspective of narrative technique, is important because the author does not want to give a Manichean interpretation of Mexican reality by presenting all Indians as opposed to Western culture.

Robles is a realist and believes that Mexico's only way out is to adopt the West's economic system in order to raise the standard of living of the people by creating industry and a middle class. The creation of a stable middle class is essential, he says, because it is ''the surest protection against tyranny and unrest.'' For him there is only one truth; he says, ''We make the nation prosperous or we starve.'' He wants to forget Mexico's past and look to tomorrow. ''Here in Mexico,'' he says to Zamacona, ''we can't give ourselves the luxury of intellectualism. Here we have to look to the future.'' He rejects not only the past, but men of letters as well. ''Poets,'' he says, ''are of the past. . .the past is done with, forever.'' He stops at nothing to have what he calls progress, that is, material progress. He wants, like President Miguel Alemán, who was then ruling Mexico, to increase tourism and to attract foreign capital. To reach his goal, he says, he has the right ''to stomp on whomever we care to.''

At the other extreme we find Ixca Cienfuegos and his mother Teódula who, like Don Ramiro and Cipriano in *The Plumed Serpent,* want to substitute Western culture with the native cultures of Mexico. Unlike Robles, who thought that a stable middle class should predominate, Ixca and Teódula want the anonymous masses to prevail. Ixca tells Zamacona: ''You think his [Robles'] cheap marketplace power which lacks all greatness is better than a power which at least had the imagination to ally itself with the great forces, permanent and inviolable, of the cosmos? With the sun itself?

Ixca's philosophy is based on the myth of the return to the origins, since everything, according to him, was determined at that moment. In Mexico, he says, nothing is indispensable, since sooner or later an anonymous secret force floods and transforms everything. ''A force that is older than all our memories . . . the beginning, the origin. All the rest is masquerade. There, in our origin, Mexico still exists . . . And what Mexico is, is fixed forever, incapable of evolution.''

Teódula Moctezuma, with her dead ancestors buried under the floor of her house, her magic jewelry, and her desire for a sacrifice to the gods in order to start a new cycle of life, also symbolizes Mexico's past, a mythical Mexico part of which still survives, and which still believes in rituals and in sacrifices as the only way for man to redeem himself. The Mexican people have been chosen by the gods to feed the sun and keep it moving so that mankind can survive. Without sacrifices this would be impossible. When Teódula achieves her goal of having a sacrifice—she believes that the death of Norma, Robles' wife, was caused by Ixca—she feels that her mission has been accomplished. As an offering to the gods she throws her jewelry into the fire where Norma's body is, and later says to Ixca: ''Now we can return to being what we are, my son. Now we have no reason to pretend. You will come back to your own here, with me. . . . Each of us must be what he is, and you know it.''

Ixca questions whether the present is better than the mythical past. In a confrontation between

Ixca and Zamacona, who represents not the mythical but the historical past, as well as the present/future, Ixca says:

> Salvation for the whole world depends upon this anonymous people who are at the world's center, the very navel of the star. Mexico's people, the only people who are contemporaneous with the world itself, the only ones who live with their teeth biting into the original breast. . . . Today is born of that very origin which, without knowing it, controls us, who have always lived within it.

During the dialogue, Ixca was thinking that if

> Mexicans are not saved, no one will be saved. If here in this land . . . the gift is not possible, the gift that is asked for, grace and love, then it is not possible anywhere for anyone. Either Mexicans are saved, or not a single being in all creation is saved.

Zamacona, who stands for the individual, rejects the idea of sacrifice and insists on making every one who commits a crime responsible for his own actions. "For every Mexican who dies in vain, sacrified," he says, "there is another Mexican who is guilty; for this death not to have been in vain, someone must assume guilt for it. Guilt for every aborigine who was crushed, for every starving mother . . . But who will assume the guilt for Mexico, Ixca, who?"

The confrontation between Zamacona and Robles, unlike that with Ixca, is on a different level. The questions that preoccupy Robles, who is really Zamacona's father, a fact unknown to both, are not guilt and salvation, but the elimination of the remnants of the past which, according to Robles, only hinder Mexico's road to progress and prosperity. When Zamacona tells Robles that Mexico has always tried to imitate foreign models, Robles replies, "And what do you want friend? Shall we wear feathers and eat human flesh again?". Zamacona answers with a speech that constitutes the central message of the novel:

> That's exactly what I don't want, Licenciado. I want our sleep to lose those shadows. I want to understand what it means to wear feathers in order not to wear them and in order to be myself. I don't want us to take pleasure in mourning our past, but to penetrate the past and understand it, reduce it to reason, cancel what is dead, save what is living, and know at last what Mexico really is and what may be done with her.

The problem with Mexico, according to Zamacona, is that, since the Conquest, it has never been itself. In all aspects of life and culture the country has tried to imitate either the European or the American way of life. This idea was first examined by the Mexican philosopher Samuel Ramos, who in 1934, in his slender book, *Profile of Man and*

Culture in Mexico, for the first time dared to peek behind Mexico's mask. For him, the problem with the country was the tendency to imitate European culture superficially, without ever digesting it and making it a part of the national psyche. The solution for him, as for Zamacona and his group in the novel, was to adopt the best that Europe and the United States could offer, and integrate it with the best that the indigenous cultures had preserved. Zamacona tells Robles:

> We've always tried to imitate models that were foreign to us, to wear clothes that could not fit, to disguise our faces to conceal the fact that we are different, by definition different, with nothing in common with anyone . . . Don't you see Mexico wounding herself by trying to become Europe and the United States? . . . Everything, monarchy, reform, liberalism, centralism, has always been a mummery?

Zamacona's observation that Mexico is forever imitating foreign models sounds like an echo of Octavio Paz in his book *The Labyrinth of Solitude*, a copy of which Zamacona was carrying when he met Ixca and Robles. In that book, Paz summarizes the nature of Mexico's history and the Mexican's plight: his search for identity and his desire to end his isolation and once again participate in the events that shape the destiny of the world. Paz says:

> The history of Mexico is the history of a man seeking his parentage, his origins. He has been influenced at one time or another by France, Spain, the United States and the militant indigenists of his own country, and he crosses history like a jade comet, now and then giving off flashes of lightning. What is he pursuing in his eccentric course? He wants to go back beyond the catastrophe he suffered: he wants to be a sun again, to return to the center of that life from which he was seperated one day. (Was that day the Conquest? Independence?). Our solitude has the same roots as religious feelings. It is a form of orphanhood, an obscure awareness that we have been torn from the All, and an ardent search: a flight and a return, an effort to re-establish the bonds that unite us with the universe.

Paz wrote those words in 1950. Fuentes published his novel in 1958, and García Márquez gave expression to the same idea in 1966, in his famous novel, *One Hundred Years of Solitude*.

The deaths of both Norma and Zamacona are interpreted as sacrifices. This revelation of the mythical nature of Mexican history is accomplished by the use of image and metaphor. The characters, the descriptions of the city, the action, and the plot are all expressed by uniting two worlds, that of the remote past and that of the present. The interaction between the characters representing each culture becomes the central technique of displacement.

Mythical episodes are used by Fuentes to give his work a pure, literary quality. History and myth balance each other to give the novel equilibrium. The introduction, spoken by Ixca, offers the key to the structure of the novel. Mexico City, as the modern version of ancient Tenochtitlán, is the center of the world, El ombligo del mundo (the navel of the world), a sacred city. According to Mircea Eliade, the center ''is pre-eminently the zone of the sacred, the zone of absolute reality.''

The image of the eagle and the serpent, related to the myth of the founding of Mexico City, implies another myth: that Mexicans must forego Western civilization and return to their origins in order to survive. A similar myth is the one mentioned by Ixca regarding the creation of the sun. The god that became the sun was a humble god, a leprous god, ''a leper, yes, a leper, who first leaped into the brazier of original creation in order to feed that flame. He was reborn, changed into a star. A motionless star. One sacrifice by itself, even one like that, isn't enough. Daily sacrifice is needed, daily feeding so that the sun will give light, and in turn feed us.'' In the realistic world of the novel, the sacrificial victims. Norma, Zamacona, Feliciano Sánchez, Froilán Reyero, Gabriel, and the boy Jorge, come from all social classes and represent all philosophies.

The two solutions proposed to save Mexico, that is, the adoption of foreign models and the return to the origins, are rejected. Both Robles and Ixca Cienfuegos finally realize that they have been wrong and both lose faith in their ideas, Robles after losing his wife and all his material possessions, and Ixca after his mother's death. After he is bankrupt and disgraced, dethroned like an old king by a younger one, Robles begins to assume the guilt which Zamacona preaches. Thinking about what he had done to the labor leader Feliciano Sánchez and his employee Froilán Reyero, ''two names that were a way of naming all the anonymous dead, enslaved starving, . . . Robles felt that the sadness and desolation of every Mexican life.'' Ixca also realizes that his mother was wrong. He tells Rodrigo Pola during the reckless car ride at the end of the novel, ''It was all a terrible game, that's all, a game of forgotten rites and signs and dead words . . . she believed that Norma's death was a necessary sacrifice, and that once the sacrifice was given, we could return and bury ourselves in lives of poverty, mumble hysterical words over our [dead], play with humility!''

In the novel a relationship exists between the three ideological positions taken by Robles, who stands for material progress; Ixca, who stands for *indigenismo*; and Zamacona, who stands for a fusion of the two, and the three narrative elements, that of reality, myth, and prophecy. There is also a relationship of these ideological positions and the narrative elements to the concept of time. The present in the novel, Robles' Mexico, is a precise historical circumstance: the state of Mexican society in the year 1951; the past, Ixca's Mexico, is the mythical origin of the city; and the future, Zamacona's Mexico, the prophecy as to its destiny. Other characters in the novel also represent either the past, the present, or the future, and Fuentes' genius lies in his creation of characters who are symbolic of the social world in which they move, whether they live, culturally, in the mythical past, the realistic present, or the illusory future.

In his essay, *Cervantes o la crítica de la lectura* (*Cervantes or the Criticism of Reading*), Fuentes says that ''Utopia is to become a reality not in the nihilistic storm that forces us to begin from zero every time, but in the fusion of the values we have received from the past with the values we are to create in the present.'' Also, that ''the present in itself is not enough: to be a present in the full sense of the word requires a sense of the past and a capacity to imagine the future.'' This is precisely what Fuentes has done in his novels and short stories. In *Where the Air Is Clear* he has taken the mythical past of Mexico City, fused it with a reconstruction of life during the early fifties and, from this, projected a vision of the future through three characters, Robles, Ixca, and Zamacona. For Robles, Mexicans will not survive if the country is not industrialized. Ixca, on the other hand, believes that the world will be saved by the anonymous mass of Mexican people, and if Mexico cannot be saved, human beings can be saved. Zamacona believes that Mexico's salvation depends on grace, and love, and if grace and love are banished by the restoration of sacrifices or the pursuit of a materialistic way of life, the country is doomed.

Although *Where the Air Is Clear* reflects an experimental technique, Fuentes succeeded in creating a picture of Mexico City never before attempted by a novelist. He not only created a new language and preserved the secrets, the miseries, and the hopes of the City, but went beyond to dramatize the nature of the struggle between two cultures, Western and non-Western. Through dramatic interaction between the characters he was able to symbolize that struggle, a struggle which results in the rejection of both foreign and native models in favor of a synthesis of the two out of which will grow the Mexican culture of the future, a prophecy that is yet to be fulfilled.

Source: Luis Leal, ''Realism, Myth, and Prophecy in Fuentes' Where the Air is Clear,'' in *Confluencia,* Vol. 1, No. 1, Fall, 1985, p. 75.

Richard M. Reeve

In the following review, Richard M. Reeve deconstructs the unusually expansive period author Carlos Fuentes took to compose and rework his panoramic novel La región más transparente *and examines how Fuentes' detailed efforts allowed the book to retain its relevancy over several decades.*

It is the practice of some authors, especially poets, to rework and polish their writings over a period of many years while continuing to make additions and corrections to future editions. Not so with Carlos Fuentes, who seems to produce a literary work and to leave it immediately in the hands of the reader and critic, while moving on to his next endeavor. Thus the case of the composition and reworking of *La región más transparente* over a period of a quarter of a century is an anomaly worthy of close examination. It is relatively easy to establish the concluding date of this process, 1974, which saw the publication of the novel in the Aguilar edition of his *Obras completas* with its apparent final revisions. But my choice of 1949 as the year when Fuentes began the novel is much more arbitrary.

The inspiration for a panoramic novel about life in the modern metropolis no doubt arose in Carlos Fuentes' mind with his experiences as a child moving from one large city to another: Washington, D.C.; Rio de Janeiro; Santiago, Chile; Buenos Aires; and finally to Mexico City. Also, by the age of fifteen he had read John Dos Passos' *Manhattan Transfer*, marveling at its style and structure. The year 1949 is decisive, however, since it marks the beginning of Fuentes' active publishing career and includes among other key but little known writings a short story set in New York City and a series of articles about the cultural milieu of the Mexican capital. Finally, a later date in the mid-1950s might also be defended. With the publication of his collection of short stories, *Los días enmascarados* (1954) Fuentes could dedicate himself in earnest to his novel, and indeed fragments of the work began appearing in magazines and newspapers in the years 1955 and 1956. Beginning in the fall of 1956, Fuentes, as the fortunate recipient of a fellowship from the Rockefeller-sponsored Centro Mexicano de Escritores, was able to devote himself full time to *La región más transparente*. The novel itself, after much speculation and controversy, finally appeared in the spring of 1958.

Mexico in the 1950s

Carlos' father, Rafael Fuentes Boettiger, embarked upon a long and distinguished career as a diplomat in the 1920s and served with every president of Mexico from the Revolution to the 1950s. The main action of *La región más transparente* transpires in the years 1951 and 1953, during the presidency of Miguel Alemán, Mexico's 58th president and the first civilian since Juárez to hold the office for a full term. Mexico was passing through a period of unprecedented change and growth. Alemán, who was known as the businessman's president, remains to this day the center of impassioned controversy, but during the fifties his dynamic personality and colossal enterprises seemed to bedazzle the multitude. Skyscrapers began dotting the skyline, the magnificent new campus of the National University rose up on a former lava bed, and North American tourists arrived in increasing numbers. Mexico was becoming more international with the influx of Spanish refugees in the late thirties and other European nationals in the forties.

During the decade of the fifties the country was governed in the main by two presidents named Adolfo: Ruiz Cortines and López Mateos. Fuentes has characterized them as belonging to the faceless center; neither radical like Cárdenas nor rightist like Alemán. *La región más transparente* was published in 1958, an election year. The 6th of July elections were characterized as the quietest in history; women voted for a president for the first time. López Mateos received 6,767,754 votes; Luis Alvarez, his PAN opponent, obtained 705,303, while Miguel Menéndez López, the presidential candidate for the Communist Party, received fewer write-in votes than comic actor Cantinflas.

Mexico's population continued to spiral at the astonishing and alarming rate of 3 percent annually. The capital city was estimated to have 5,448,218 inhabitants. Classroom and teacher shortages were so severe that only 41 percent of school-age children could attend school. Illiteracy was estimated at 50 percent.

In cultural achievements, 1958 saw increasing literary activity. It was labeled the year of the novel and *La región más transparente* the novel of the year. Poetry was less fortunate and only Octavio

Paz's excellent *La estación violenta* mitigated a disastrous year for the genre. José Luis Martínez published the important but controversial *Antología del ensayo mexicano*. Critics lamented the decline of the theater in Mexico although attendance was higher than ever. Of the eighty plays presented during the year only twelve were written by Mexican playwrights. During 1958 Luis G. Basurto's *Cada quien su vida* would reach one thousand consecutive representations and actress Rita Macedo (Fuentes' fiancée) and Ernest Alonso combined to produce *Intermezzo* by Jean Giraudoux. Emmanuel Carballo counted forty-one books of fiction published in the country during 1958. He believed Fuentes to be the best of the new writers and Martín Luis Guzmán, who had just published *Muertes históricas*, to be the best of the veterans. Luis Spota's *Casi el paraíso* remained the best seller of the year with its third and fourth printings and a total of 21,000 copies in three years, a very sizable figure for a Latin American novel in those days.

Foreshadowing of La región más transparente in Fuentes' Early Writings

In contrast to many Mexican writers of the early part of this century, Carlos Fuentes did not grow up nor spend any appreciable time in the rural countryside. Those authors, most of whom were eventually drawn to the city (Azuela, Yáñez, Rulfo), had rural experiences from their childhood and youth to draw upon. Others (Martín Luis Guzmán) would live in the interior during the emotion-filled years of the Revolution and would often return to this unique occurrence in their fiction.

Not so with Fuentes, who in fact seldom resided in Mexico. By the time he was a teenager, he had spent more time in the United States than in any Latin country. At this crucial period of his life Fuentes was almost to the point of losing his native language, thus motivating his parents to send him to summer school in Mexico. Consequently Fuentes was above all a man with a vision of the big city, or rather of many big cities. He also enjoyed the unique advantage of being able to compare his own Mexican metropolis with most of the major ones in this hemisphere. This fascination with cities would burgeon until, not surprisingly, his first published writings would focus on the novelty of Mexico City, eventually culminating in his masterful portrait of the Mexican capital in his first novel.

Although Fuentes composed several unpublished works of fiction during his teenage years, his first known published short story, "Pastel rancio," appeared in the November 1949 issue of *Mañana*. Surprisingly, the piece is set in New York City rather than the Distrito Federal de México. Fuentes had visited Manhattan on numerous occasions and had sailed to South America from there in 1941. The main events of the story revolve around the disembarking of transoceanic passengers and would thus disqualify the nonport cities of Washington, D.C., and Mexico City that Fuentes might logically have chosen as his setting. The description of New York is brief—the principal action is the arrival of a displaced person from war-torn Europe. The European refugee will become a popular character in *La región más transparente* and again is prominent in *Cambio de piel* (1967). Even the Jewish race of the main character foreshadows protagonists in later works. The Jew is much less numerous in Mexico City than other major Latin American metropolises and seldom appears in Mexican fiction.

Carlos Fuentes did not publish another piece of fiction for five years, but the numerous essays which were beginning to appear anticipate topics of importance which would surface in his novel, still almost a decade away from publication. During the fall of 1949 José Pagés Llergo invited him to collaborate in the Mexican weekly *Hoy*. Fuentes had not yet turned twenty-one. His first article, "Fue al infierno de visita pero lo vio tan mal que decidió regresar a México," was not of a caliber to make Fuentes immortal. It consisted of an interview with Leonardo Alcalá who claimed to be the third incarnation of God. Even so, the statements on reincarnation would show up in later writings, and the setting, an impoverished "barrio" of Mexico City, is not too distant from that of the "pelado" group in *La región más transparente*. Other articles by Fuentes published in *Hoy* during the following months treated "basfumismo," existentialism, and the Mexican cinema, most of which we will examine in more detail in later sections.

The most important of these articles carried the long but significant title, "Descubriendo al México de 1950: México es la única gran ciudad mestiza que existe en el mundo." In spite of the piece's supreme importance in foreshadowing themes in Fuentes' first novel, it has surprisingly not yet been analyzed by the critics. The essay begins with the author labeling the Mexican capital a "metropolis and large village." Perhaps in his earlier residence in Argentina Fuentes recalled Lucio V. López using the term "la gran aldea" in a novel of the same title to refer to Buenos Aires. In any case it is a logical slogan for a city experiencing rapid growth and changing its character. Fuentes next focuses on the contrasts: "New and old city, beautiful and ugly owing to its decadence and newness." Another unique feature is the lack of ghettos. Next comes a comparison with other famous metropolitan centers in which Fuentes had lived: "Río de Janeiro has what God has given her, New York what man gave her, and Mexico has God, man and tourists." The theme of the unrelenting past which resurfaces to haunt the present is later developed in many of Fuentes' short stories and novels, but is anticipated in these lines from the essay: "Upon the pyramids still stinking with thick and black blood are raised the elaborate walls of the Cathedral; upon the vestibules and moldy patios are built the 'Pepe Bars''; who knows what will be constructed tomorrow. No one knows and no one cares. Variety makes everything more interesting."

Fuentes next passes to "México Abajo" and begins by listing a number of cantinas and brothels. One announces "English Spoken" and another "paint me red and blue and call me Superman." The latter phrase is used word for word in a cocktail party scene in the first novel. Another fascinating facet of the lower depths of Mexico City, according to Fuentes, is the enormous number of witches and wizards. A few names are given including that of Leonardo Alcalá, the New Messiah of Canal de Norte about whom Fuentes had previously written.

Several paragraphs are subsequently devoted to "Mexico Arriba," a class Fuentes knew much more intimately, as we shall see a bit later. Among the city's aristocracy he lists: "New rich, the pseudopopoffs and other social climbers." Each will be pictured in detail in his novel. He then asks the question: "And the aristocracy of the day before yesterday? They're the only ones who don't count; they make up the bourgeoisie of today." The same phrase appears almost intact in the novel, where, to the identical question asked by Príncipe Vampa, Charlotte García responds: "They're the only ones who don't count, at least not in Mexico, they're the petite bourgeoisie of today" (*Región*). A major percentage of the Mexican aristocracy is made up of foreigners: "A curious phenomenon on the Mexican social scene are the 'Internationals Incorporated'; false aristocratic titles, eccentric poses, people who don't do anything because it would take up too much of their time." The above-mentioned falsetitled gentry are extremely important and Fuentes referred in not too oblique a fashion to a recent scandal in Mexico City which would serve as novelistic material for both Fuentes and Luis Spota.

Fuentes further pictures his capital, Mexico City, as the "one place on earth so pliable, eccentric, and uncivilized that 'snobbism' and 'esnobismo' embrace fraternally." After a lengthy quotation from Eça de Queiroz, Fuentes concludes with "enough of the new 'grandezas mexicanas,'" recalling the famous poem by Balbuena which also is cited at a cocktail party in *La región más transparente*.

Now let us look briefly at nine short stories published between the years 1954 and 1956 containing themes which surface in the novel. "Pantera en jazz" was printed in the short-lived and little-known magazine *Ideas de México*. It is practically unknown to the public and Fuentes has never chosen to include it in any of his anthologies. The plot follows a student who fears that a panther has found its way into his bathroom. Never willing to look and unable to call the police, the protagonist eventually loses his mind. Only a few months later Fuentes treats the subject in almost identical fashion in his famous short story "Chac Mool." In the latter instance the presence from the past which destroys modern man is a statue of a Mayan rain god. In the same *Los días enmascarados* anthology, published in November of 1954, the author repeats the theme in "Por boca de los dioses" and "Tlactocatzine, del Jardín de Flandes." In the first an Aztec goddess kills a contemporary Mexican and in the second it is the ghost of nineteenth-century Carlota of Hapsburg who accomplishes the deed. In each case they anticipate the semi-mythical figures of Ixca Cienfuegos and Teódula Moctezuma in *La región más transparente*. The latter is constantly pleading for her disciple to provide a sacrifice. Ixca will defend his philosophy of returning to the past to save Mexico in a spirited debate with intellectual Manuel Zamacona (spokesman for the future) and banker Federico Robles (man of the present).

The conflict between the present and the past so prominent in the above-cited stories is treated in a more universal fashion in the science fiction story "El que inventó la pólvora," also found in *Los días enmascarados*. Here modern technology is the villain which brings about the end of civilization. Another story in the volume, "Letanía de la orquídea," takes place in Panama. The dual worlds of Panama and the Canal Zone, which Fuentes had just visited in September 1954, personify the Spanish-and-English-speaking "aristocracy" of the

"International Set" pictured in *La región más transparente,* but to a broader degree mirror the dual background of Fuentes himself. The final story in the volume is "En defensa de la Trigolibia," an essay-like work which has been little studied. Perhaps more than any of his early publications this brief linguistic *tour de force* demonstrates Fuentes' remarkable ear for language which can be observed in all of his writings.

In March and September of 1956, just two years before the appearance of *La región más transparente,* Fuentes issued two more stories which have not been collected in anthologies. The first, "El muñeco," follows the madness of Empress Carlota on her return to Europe in a vain attempt to save Maximilian's crumbling empire. Whole passages from the story describing the execution of the emperor and the embalming of his body are quoted verbatim in the final sixteen-page monologue which concludes the novel. "Trigo errante," the second story, has a setting in modern-day Israel and includes as protagonist Lazarus, who still remains alive after the miracle of his raising by Jesus. The themes of immortality and reincarnation so central to later novels such as *Cambio de piel* and *Cumpleaños* make a curious early appearance in *La región más transparente* . In a debate between Robles, Cienfuegos, and Zamacona, the role of Lazarus becomes pivotal in the latter's argument.

> "The only one who can never be saved is he who is resurrected, because he can neither commit crime nor feel guilt. He has known death and come back from it."
>
> "Lazarus?" said Cienfuegos.
>
> "Lazarus. In the unconscious background of his spirit palpitates the conviction that every time he dies, he will be brought back to life. He may be grasping and treacherous, he may commit all crimes with the certainty that on the day of death he will return to commit new crimes. No one may hold him to account. Lazarus cannot die on earth. But he is dead forever in heaven. The resurrected man may not save himself because he cannot renounce anything, because he isn't free, because he can't sin." (*Región*)

Before concluding we should mention that as a student at the National University Carlos Fuentes was on the staff of the school's journal, *Revista de la Universidad de México.* In this capacity he wrote more than a dozen book and motion picture reviews. The book reviews help us to understand Fuentes' contemporaneous reading habits, but have little use for the purposes of this essay. Such is not the case of the motion picture reviews, which will be discussed in another section.

Real Life Sources

Many events from Fuentes' personal life as a young man growing up in Mexico City at mid-century are no doubt reflected in *La región más transparente.* Some are known and a few can be deduced, but it is the broader panorama of the national intellectual, political and cultural scene which will now be our principal focus.

We have previously discussed the Alemán era in our introductory remarks and will not repeat these observations. Suffice it to say that the period represented a time of substantial change and growth which has seldom been duplicated in Mexican history. Carlos Fuentes' family belonged to the social and political elite. As a handsome, articulate, wealthy and extroverted organizer he was not simply a witness of the changing face of Mexico, but a participant in its inner circle. Two of his acquaintances, Pablo Palomino and Daniel Dueñas, have documented this period, and their articles plus occasional notices in the society pages furnish us with considerable information on these years. Carlos excelled in organizing parties, and his presence was particularly sought after at such gatherings where he was "a magnificent participant with his gaiety and facility for mimicry." Dueñas recalls: "We still recall him at Ricardo de Villar's house pretending to be an Uruguayan anarchist or interpreting oriental operas with a gong and showing only the whites of his eyes." His playful nature can be seen in other accounts of the time: "We all celebrated his success as a blind beggar wandering up and down Madero and San Juan de Letrán streets alongside Enrique Creel de la Barra." And a brief note from the society page of June 1949: "Carlitos Fuentes related his most recent nocturnal adventures and combats with cabdrivers. Doña Berta, his mother, is somewhat disturbed over the turbulent life of her precocious offspring." As a regular at the literary *tertulias* held at the home of Cristina Moya, Carlos played the role of the *enfant terrible* "reading short stories savoring of simultaneism, dadaism, and . . . snobbism" (Dueñas).

Perhaps Fuentes' most controversial and sensational activity at the time was his participation in the founding of an exclusive social circle called "Vasfumistas." Attempts were made at that period and in later years to give Vasfumismo (also spelled Basfumismo and Vhazfumismo) the status of a philosophical orientation similar to the European vanguard groups of the twenties and thirties, but in reality it was more of a tight-knit social group. Pablo Palomino recalls that they had viewed some silent film classics and decided to try something similar: "Something which was totally new, without any precedents." They possessed the means among themselves to produce the film; one of their close friends had practical filming experience, and they would be the actors. Later it was decided that Fuentes and Creel de la Barra would write a play rather than a film script. Ernesto de la Peña put forth a name for the group, "Basfumismo," which suggested also their slogan: "por el humo, al ser" ("through smoke to being").

Huge parties were held which were outstandingly successful; plans for the play and film were dropped for the time being. The society columns buzzed with rumors of their mysterious doings. Under the title of "Definición para el basfumismo" they were described as: "All geniuses, all frustrated, touched in the head but not locked up, harmless crazies (except Valentín Saldaña, Ruggiero Asta and Carlitos Fuentes) plus more than a little extraordinary." Even Carlos published an article with the intriguing title of "¡Pero usted no sabe aún lo que es el basfumismo!" which instead of clarifying the issues only clouded them more.

Because of the exclusive nature of the group, jealous outsiders began spreading rumors about the practice of nefarious rites and prohibited cults. A wealthy owner of a bakery even contributed funds to help eradicate this social evil. Certain politicians anxious to exploit the basfumista publicity sought discussions with its members. But by the end of 1949 the movement had run its course; one of its members was married and Fuentes was on his way to Europe for graduate studies.

Although "Basfumismo" died a quiet death, its memory lingered on in later fiction. Many of the cocktail parties in *La región más transparente* would seem to be recreations of basfumista entertainments. Probably a good number of the fictional party goers were modeled on real people, and Bobo Gutiérrez, the irrepressible festivity organizer in the novel, is not too much different from Fuentes himself. Pablo Palomino, the previously mentioned chronicler of the movement and friend of Fuentes, has also left us a fictional view of the time in his little-known novel *Autopsia*.

Palomino's *Autopsia* precedes *La región más transparente* by almost three years, having been published in August of 1955. It had a small one-time printing of 1,000 copies and except for one known review the novel seems to have been (and continues to be) totally ignored. Although it is much briefer

(164 pages) and less ambitious than Fuentes' novel, the two works share a number of characteristics. Both are urban novels set in contemporary Mexico City. One of Palomino's characters agonizes about having children in the Atomic Age. Another main character is a foreigner (Italian) living in Mexico and there is even a lesbian. Palomino presents several cocktail party scenes with snatches of conversation on a variety of political and cultural topics: those of Fuentes, however, are infinitely more dynamic and demonstrate a much greater artistic skill. The psychological insights in *Autopsia* are the traditional author-narrator interpretation while Fuentes makes greater use of the stream-of-consciousness technique. In one chapter Palomino has a character frequent the lower class night life of Mexico City anticipating in skeletal fashion Fuentes' more consummately drawn *pelado* sections. Both would appear to be based on basfumista nocturnal escapades of the two youthful authors.

On the intellectual-artistic scene only the writers-philosophers are in evidence in *La región más transparente*. Strangely enough, painters are missing as are actors and actresses. This is hard to explain since Fuentes' good friend and neighbor is none other than famed painter José Luis Cuevas, and his fiancée, Rita Macedo, had starred in Buñuel films. These fields of endeavor were certainly not unknown to Fuentes and would be used in later fiction.

Two groups of writers make their appearance in the novel, one led by Tomás Mediana and a looser grouping represented by, but not necessarily directed by, Manuel Zamacona. Mediana is not an active participant in *La región más transparente* but is recalled in a flashback by Rodrigo Pola. Mediana's group flourished in the decades of the twenties and thirties. They wished to renovate Mexican literature by producing a new journal which would translate innovative European writers. Tomás subscribes to the *Nouvelle Revue Française* and wants Mexico to become acquainted with Proust. In many ways this group seems to describe the "Contemporáneos" movement which became active shortly before Fuentes' birth but some of whose members he would probably know through his father's government service (Torres Bodet) or in the journalistic field (Novo).

It is the second grouping of writers, which flourished in the late forties and early fifties, precisely the exact time period of *La región más transparente*, which most interests us. Its principal representative, Manuel Zamacona, is primarily a poet, a profession which banker Federico Robles considers a luxury in an underdeveloped country. Although Zamacona first appears in the novel at a cocktail party, it is the following day as Zamacona is writing an essay on Mexico that we come to know him. Fuentes actually includes the entire nine-page text of the essay! Among Zamacona's reading materials are *El laberinto de la soledad* and volumes by Guardini, Alfonso Reyes and Nerval. In one scene he has just returned from a series of formal discussions.

> A round-table discussion of Mexican literature. It is necessary to mention the serapes of Saltillo, was Franz Kafka the tool of Wall Street, is social literature anything more than the eternal triangle between two Stajanovitches and a tractor, if we are not the more universal the more Mexican we are, and vice versa, should we write like Marxists or like Buddhists. Many prescriptions, zero books. (*Región*)

In an interview, Fuentes has described Zamacona as a "composite portrait of many Mexican intellectuals. Many recognized themselves in him. They protested, they attacked me in the street, they tried to set my house on fire. So there must be some truth to the portrait. Because at the bottom, in the whole 'Mexicanist' movement, there was that redemptorist attitude."

To better comprehend the above statement it will be useful to review the intellectual climate in Mexico City during the early fifties. In the late forties there emerged the Grupo Filosófico Hiperión, headed by Leopoldo Zea and including in its membership Jorge Portilla, Joaquín Macgregor, Emilio Uranga, Luis Villoro, Ricardo Guerra, Salvador Reyes Nevares, and Fausto Vega. "Hiperión" was the name selected because it symbolized the union between heaven and earth and was to demonstrate the group's preoccupation with both universal and national answers to the dilemmas facing their country. Round table discussions and a series of more than a dozen publications followed in the next few years. The series entitled "México y lo Mexicano" consisted of studies by philosophers, historians, economists, sociologists, scientists, psychologists, and literary figures. Foreigners who had visited Mexico or written about it also contributed: Mariano Picón Salas, José Gaos and José Moreno Villas. One name strangely missing is that of Octavio Paz, who was apparently in Europe most of this time although his famous *El laberinto de la soledad* was published in 1950. The following year *El perfil del hombre y la cultura en México* by Samuel Ramos, which first appeared in 1934, was reprinted in an inexpensive edition.

Another source of fictional material which Fuentes was to take from real life was the large foreign population which comprised both an important and a highly visible element of Mexican society, especially among the upper classes. They were labeled the "International Set," and as we have already seen, Fuentes alluded to them in his early essay on Mexico City. It seems somewhat strange that in spite of his long years of residence in the United States, Fuentes in interviews mentions no friends among this group and the only North Americans in his fiction tend to be caricatures of the simple-minded tourist or the money-grabbing businessman-investor.

The Spaniard, on the other hand, is viewed much differently. Mexico was profoundly affected by the Spanish Civil War, and its sympathies were so strongly in favor of the Republic that it has only recently renewed diplomatic relations with the post-Franco government. Refugees from the peninsula found a welcome home in Mexico, and Spanish intellectuals played significant roles in the university and the publishing world. Fuentes studied with one of these exiles, Manuel Martínez Pedroso, and paid homage to him in an article in the *Revista de la Universidad de México* in the summer of 1958. Pedroso, who translated *Das Kapital*, had been rector at the Universidad de Salamanca and *diputado* at the Cortes of 1936. Later he served the Republic in Warsaw and Moscow before coming to Mexico. Salvador Novo writes of the professor's fondness for Fuentes: "He also spoke to me about Carlos Fuentes of whom he is very fond, a paternal fondness. He is alarmed about the premature fervor of the Fondo publicists who are proclaiming him Mexico's best writer."

In *La región más transparente* Fuentes includes a sympathetic episode in which Spanish exiles recall their escape from Fascist Spain; the incident is brief and does not form a part of the novel's plot. Four years later Fuentes would return to the subject in *La muerte de Artemio Cruz* and follow Lorenzo Cruz on his idealistic crusade to Spain to carry on what he felt were his father's revolutionary goals.

A considerably more negative view is offered in *La región más transparente* of the exiled European nobility who come to Mexican shores. Among them: Contessa Aspacuccoli, Conde Lemini, Natasha, the Serbian Prince "Pinky," and Príncipe Vampa.

At least one has bought his title, and even worse, another turns out to be a fraud. In real life Fuentes would often mingle with the nobility at their parties. A note from a society page in 1950 states: "Carlitos Fuentes invited everyone present to Prince Bernard of Holland's ball." Fuentes was not in the country in the fall of 1941 when King Carol, recently exiled from the throne of Romania, would arrive in Mexico with a female traveling companion and a reported $7,000,000 to "set up court." It was the social event of the year. Fuentes very definitely was in Mexico in 1949 for the much publicized Otto Wilhelm von Hohenzollern escapade. Otto, supposedly the little known son of the Kaiser by a second marriage, was feted by an adoring Mexican upper society, interviewed frequently and even invited to write a series of articles on the world situation for the weekly *Mañana*. The prince turned out to be the adventurer Rico David Tancous, wanted by several governments including the U.S. for bigamy, false impersonation, and robbery.

Within a decade two best-selling novels in Mexico would treat the bogus prince theme—*La región más transparente* was one of them. The other was by journalist Luis Spota who authored many popular books based on current events. His novel, *Casi el paraíso*, used the imposter as the central character, and since the public saw it as a roman á clef, it was an immediate success, going through six editions in four years. Spota's prince turns out to be the illegitimate son of a poor Italian prostitute. Before he can wed the daughter of a Mexican millionaire he is discovered and arrested by Mexican immigration officials and the FBI.

For Fuentes the imposter prince becomes only a minor episode, who although discovered is not arrested. One character recalls the scandal:

> "And what news is there of the imposter Vampa?" Charlotte raised a hand to her heart. "Ay! Don't remind me of that fatal blow. I don't know how to breathe afterward. Just think how he fooled us!"

> Bobo's face wrinkled in pain. "His only title was to a pizza show in 'Frisco. He was a cook there."

> "And we treated him as a blue blood! Don't remind me Bobo, I die of anger . . . and imagine, Pierre Caseaux gave him a job in his kitchen. Every time I eat there, I have the feeling the macaroni knows all my secrets."

Since Spota had already beaten Fuentes to the punch by two years it is an interesting speculation as to whether the latter might not have planned to do more with the episode. Both novels also share other similar characters: the party organizer, Charlotte García in *La región más transparente* and Carmen Pérez Mendiola in *Casi el paraíso*. Others are the wealthy bankers who have risen from poverty to power through their participation in the Revolution. Spota's Alonso Ronia states: "Thirty years ago I was out in the provinces plowing behind a team of mules." Fuentes' Federico Robles' father did the same on a plot of ground in Uruapan.

One final area of Mexican cultural life which Fuentes utilizes to create his fictional world is the Mexican motion picture industry. From his early youth Fuentes has been a fan of the cinema. Many of his characters talk about the movies and screen stars. His first wife, Rita Macedo, had worked in several Buñuel films, and *La región más transparente* is dedicated to her. Fuentes, himself, has written several admiring articles on Buñuel plus a review of the latter's *El ángel exterminador*. He is also the author of a number of film scripts, the most important being *Los caifanes*, which won a prize at Cannes, and *Pedro Páramo*, based on Juan Rulfo's famous novel. In 1953 and 1954 Fuentes regularly reviewed films, among them *Beat the Devil* with Humphrey Bogart and Marlon Brando's *The Wild One*, for the *Revista de la Universidad de México*.

In *La región más transparente* Fuentes' vision of the Mexican motion picture industry is anything but favorable. In fact his presentation of the producers and script writers crosses the line to caricature. Rodrigo Pola, a frustrated poet, finally finds fame and fortune turning out potboiler scripts. What began as a daring treatment of social taboos is "adapted" by the producers to the public taste, to the actresses they already have in mind and to previously chosen sites—all combined with some religion and ranchero music! The delighted producers tell Pola to write up the script in the following week and two weeks later the film will be shot and completed. If all this seems too farcical we can only cite an article which appeared almost as if by coincidence in a Mexico City daily a few months after Fuentes' novel came out. In it Benito Alazraki, once the great hope of Mexico with prestigious films such as *Raices*, stated: "I prefer to make B movies and drive a Cadillac than artistic cinema and ride the city buses."

Pre-Publication Fragments of *La región más transparente*

Some three years before *La región más transparente* would appear in the bookstores of Mexico City, fragments of the novel were beginning to be published in local newspapers and magazines. Some of the selections show only moderate stylistic changes from the 1958 version, but others contain major changes in characters and plots. These fragments furnish a most fascinating insight into the evolution of the novel before it reached its final form.

The earliest of the four known fragments was published in the March 28, 1955 issue of *Revista de la Universidad de México*. It is three pages long and carries the title "Los restos." The novel version in smaller format has a length of nine pages and is titled "Los de Ovando." Essentially they are of identical length with most of the changes consisting of stylistic polishing. All of the same characters appear and all carry the same names: Pimpinela de Ovando, Doña Lorenza, Juaquinito, Don Francisco, Fernanda, Benjamin, Norma Larragoiti, and Federico Robles. The selection follows the self-imposed exile of the wealthy de Ovando family with the fall of Porfirio Díaz and their subsequent return to Mexico City. Most of the changes are of the word substitution variety: for example: "tenía apuntados" becomes in the novel "estaban apuntados," "recámara" changes to "alcoba," "escenas pastoriles" later becomes "escenas bucólicas," "azotea alquilada" is modified to "azotea arrendada," and "¿no?" is replaced by "¿verdad?" Federico Robles' bank is called "Banco Internacional de Crédito Industrial S.A." in the 1955 version, but in the novel it is "Banco de Ahorro Mexicano S.A." Another change throughout the novel version is the italicizing of several French words. One phrase eliminated from the novel describes the infantile Benjamín: "Luego se sentaba en el suelo a jugar al águila o sol; dos águilas, perdía y entonces quedaba prohibido comer postre."

Our next pre-novel fragment was published in the November-December 1955 issue of *Revista Mexicana de Literatura*, the second number of a journal Fuentes cofounded. Here the title is "La línea de la vida"; in the novel it is the name of the principal character in the chapter, "Gervasio Pola." Once more the majority of the changes are word substitutions: "supurando" becomes in the novel "supurantes," "yo y Pedro" is reversed to "Pedro y yo," the same with "ya acercándose" to "acercándose ya," "el pino" to "un pino," and "a las llamas" to "al fuego." There are two examples of "las plantas" clarified to "las plantas del pie." Another expansion is "la madrugada" to "el principio de la madrugada." Other stylistic changes seen in the novel will be the use of italics

to call attention to the occurrence of stream of consciousness.

Some significant additions can be noted toward the end of the episode. Whereas the federal officer in charge of the execution is simply called "el capitán rubio," in the novel he is named and described more fully: "Captain Zamacona, blond and slender, with a carefully waxed mustache." He will appear several more times in the book and his sister, Mercedes Zamacona, is the center of one of the main episodes. All of which seems to indicate that while Fuentes may have had his main episodes already in mind or on paper by 1955, he still was working out relationships between characters and events. This is evident in another addition. In the fragment at the moment of Gervasio Pola's execution, he is thinking only of "mujeres" and "padres." In contrast, the novel includes the significant line: "to your wife, to your unknown son." This wife and unseen son also play major roles in the novel. One other new line in the final version is "¡Viva Madero!—gritó Froilán en el instante de la descarga." The 1955 fragment omits mention of the shot; only their falling to the ground is described.

The third novel fragment also appeared in Fuentes' journal *Revista Mexicana de Literatura*, this time in the sixth number dated July-August 1956. Both have the same title, "Maccualli," the Nahuatl word for commoners. The action follows a typical Sunday afternoon of several lower class "pelados" as they attend the bullfights and then visit some cantinas. The journal selection is shorter, omitting the first five and a half pages in which the pelados converse with Ixca Cienfuegos and the last five pages as one of them unexpectedly meets a former girlfriend in a brothel.

Of the four selections we are examining, this one is closest to the final 1958 rendering. "El domingo" changes to "El domingo siguiente," the cantina "Los amores de Cúpido" becomes Mexicanized to "Los amores de Cuauhtémoc," "tennis" is spelled "tenis," the same with "zipper" to "ziper," "¡Si quieres ver cogidas . . ." is finalized as "Si quieres cogidas . . . ," and "los expendios de libros pornográficos" is toned down to "puestos de revistas." Also the next-to-last line in the magazine version, which did not seem to make sense and was probably a typographical error, is removed from the novel.

"Calavera del quince" is the title of one of the chapters in *La región más transparente*; it is called the same in the final fragment we shall examine.

Apparently it is the same selection which was printed in the June 26, 1955, Sunday supplement of *Novedades*, but I have been unable to examine it and have therefore used the version published by Emmanuel Carballo in his *Cuentos mexicanos modernos* (1956). Of all the four selections we have studied, this seems to differ the most from what eventually appeared in the novel. Each version contains about twenty scenes, but only half are duplicates. The anthology selection devotes considerable space to Tomás Mediana, who is dropped from the novel. The jailing of labor agitator, Feliciano Sánchez, also appears but in the novel is placed in the preceding chapter. A nameless Indian on a pilgrimage whose story is told in five short fragments receives but one paragraph in the novel version.

On the other hand, the novel account adds scenes of Robles working in his office, Zamacona taking leave of Cienfuegos, Bobo and the international set traveling to Cuernavaca, Zamacona's death, Robles recalling his childhood, Robles telling his wife that they are ruined, Teódula throwing her jewels into Robles' burning house, Ixca by Rosa Morales' side after the death of her son, and Teódula's statement to Ixca that his mission is completed. One final difference we will discuss in a moment is the changes of names given to three characters.

Perhaps the most striking alteration in the two accounts is the complete dropping of the character of Tomás Mediana. In the novel he never makes an appearance, but is part of Rodrigo Pola's past recalled in a conversation with Ixca. Mediana, as we have stated earlier, was head of a writer's group which wanted to introduce the innovative European movements to Mexican readers. In the 1955 selection we see a more personal side of his character, and told from his point of view. His father has returned unexpectedly and is working as a humble waiter in a café. Tomás had hardly known him, was not even sure his parents had ever married, since his father was such a carefree Don Juan. For years he had told everyone that his father had died in France in the battle of the Marne. In later scenes Mediana reflects upon his literary career. It would appear likely that Fuentes had originally intended to make Tomás one of his major characters but in the end reduced his importance since the novel already included two other writers, Rodrigo Pola and Manuel Zamacona.

The scene describing the death of Doña Zenaida's son also shows considerable reworking. In the novel Ixca Cienfuegos stands by her side

comforting her. Fuentes gives her the more mundane name of Rosa Morales, possibly in order not to distract from the high priestess of the primitive religion whom he dubs with the exotic sobriquet of Teódula Moctezuma. Rosa Morales is probably more fitting as a name symbolizing her plebeian status; her husband, a taxi driver, is Juan Morales.

The most interesting metamorphosis to observe in these two versions is that of the pelados. The novel follows four, maybe five. In the fragment there are only two and their names are changed; Fifo is called Gabriel in the novel, but there will also be a pelado by the name of Fifo. Nacho will be converted to Beto. In the novel Gabriel has worked as a bracero and frequently includes English words in his speech. The early account has him say: "Ya tan temprano" while Fuentes changes this in the novel to "ya tan erly." On the same page a phrase with the word "suit" is added (meaning "dulce" not "traje"). Fuentes in the novel also seems more intent on capturing their authentic slang usage: "para" becomes "pa'," "tomen de la botella" changes to "empínense la botella," and "no juegues con la muerte" is "hoy me la pela la mera muerte calaca." "Si no fuera por los amigos" changes to "Si no fuera por los cuates" and "¡Se me hace lo que el aire a Juárez!" becomes "le viene más guango que el aire a Juárez, mano." Several songs are changed in the two accounts. The words from the famous corrido by José A. Jiménez, "no vale nada, la vida, la vida no vale nada," are not found in *La región más transparente* but curiously enough surface in 1962 on the title page of *La muerte de Artemio Cruz*.

Probably the most interesting modification is what Fuentes has done with the violent murder of one of the pelados. In the early version an unknown "gordo" comes up to Fifo in a cantina and after stabbing him says: "A mí nadie me mira así" ("Nobody looks at me like that"). The novel has Gabriel (previously called Fifo in the fragment) stabbed by a "thin man with a slouch hat" who runs into the pelado unexpectedly. The murderer's words this time are "I told you, buddy, you wouldn't catch me twice . . . you can't treat me like this. . . ." However, the words "Nobody looks at me like that" are not forgotten but utilized earlier by Fuentes in the novel's chapter by a "marble-eyed man" when he unexpectedly stabs Manuel Zamacona, who has stopped in a small town for gasoline.

First Reactions to the Novel

La región más transparente appeared in the stores of Mexico City on Monday, April 7, 1958.

The previous day Elena Poniatowska had published a lengthy interview with Fuentes in the Sunday cultural supplement of the newspaper *Novedades*. Apparently, she had read a pre-publication copy of the novel. Emmanuel Carballo writing eleven years later states that the book was published on the 29th of March. Most likely he was consulting the printing information on the last page of the novel. These are always estimates and may vary by several weeks or more. The date given by Poniatowska at the time of the event seems much more likely. Numerous reviews were printed in various Mexico City newspapers during the months of April, May, and June. Opinions vary on how quickly the novel sold out; some reports say a week, others suggest several months. A second printing is dated November 18, 1958. The April printing was 4,000 copies and the one in November numbered 5,000; both respectable amounts for the time. The November edition remained available for several years and was purchased by the author of this study in Mexico City in the summer of 1960. Of the Mexican novels of that period it seems likely that only *Casi el paraíso* had sold in greater numbers over a short span.

The title of the novel dates all the way back to 1917, coming from Alfonso Reyes' famous epigraph introducing a chapter of *Visión de Anáhuac*: "Viajero: has llegado a la región más transparente del aire." It is probable that at first Fuentes intended to use the whole phrase since that is the one given with the fragments published in 1955 and 1956. In the end, however, he dropped the last part, "del aire." No one would accuse Fuentes of plagiarizing his title; it had long since become a popular designation for the Valley of Mexico. The choice was a fortuitous one; it was easily identified with Mexico City, but offered intriguing possibilities for irony since the novel pictured the capital city as anything but clear and beautiful. Some confusion has arisen about the originality of the phrase with Alfonso Reyes. It seems that Rodolfo, his brother, had been quoted that it came from Alexander Humbolt's description of New Spain. Alfonso says that this is not the case; he had thought up the phrase himself.

The controversy surrounding *La región más transparente* did not begin in 1958, but actually several years earlier with the publication of the novel fragments. An anonymous note commenting on the "de Ovando" chapter suggested "if the whole resembles the sample, Carlos Fuentes without doubt will be recognized as one of Mexico's outstanding novelists." The "Línea de vida" episode in *Revista Mexicana de Literatura* produced

four very favorable reviews. On the other hand, Fernando Benitez, director of the "México en la Cultura" supplement of *Novedades* was called on the carpet for printing some of the controversial material of the young novelist. One thing about Fuentes' writings, they were never ignored!

In the spring of 1958 there were complaints that *La región más transparente* was launched on the market as if it were a new laundry detergent, a comment almost identical to what had been said in 1954 about *Los días enmascarados*. As a matter of fact, there may have been considerable truth in the allegation. An anonymous note about this time is typical of the abundance of publicity given the book: "They say that Emmanuel Carballo doesn't begin his television program anymore by greeting the public from the 'región más transparente del aire,' but rather from the 'región más Carlos-fuentes.'"

Most of the earlier reviewers were personally acquainted with Fuentes, and thus their prejudices either for or against him naturally come to the surface. Of approximately two dozen reviews published in the first few months, five were openly hostile, another dozen extremely laudatory and the rest fairly neutral. In somewhat of an understatement J. M. García Ascot portrayed *La región más transparente* as "a book which has produced some controversy." Enrique González Rojo observed, "This novel inaugurates, in our opinion, a new cycle in the twentieth century Mexican novel." José Emilio Pacheco commented enthusiastically: "Many of the pages of *La región más transparente* will go down in history as some of the finest prose writing ever produced in Mexico." Rafael Solana, an important author in his own right, believed that Fuentes may have been overly ambitious, "but the presence of a great writer can be detected in each page." For Luis Cardoza y Aragón it was "one of the most significant books published in Mexico in recent years."

On the other side of the coin, Arturo Martínez Cáceres was less than generous:

> The first impression that the novel produces is of a torpid, almost unnecessary, complexity. The influence of Faulkner, undigested let alone assimilated, can be detected, amen to some pseudomodernist techniques whose origin even the novice reader will immediately recognize as Proustian, Woolfian, Joycean and Huxlean; all of which give the book a respectable size which certainly is not the least of its defects.

Journalist Rubén Salazar Mallén, whose own novels in the forties were considered forerunners for their experimental techniques, called *La región más transparente* "nothing but a pastiche." This word would be widely repeated by future reviewers. He goes on to say: "Carlos Fuentes has made an ingenious transplant of James Joyce's *Ulysses*, but he is thirty-five years late." He nevertheless felt that Fuentes had talent if he would close his ears to the blind adulation of friends. Salazar Mallén's review of *Las buenas conciencias* the following year was very positive.

One surprising source of negative criticism came from playwright and novelist Elena Garro, wife of Fuentes' good friend Octavio Paz. She had her doubts even about the book's genre:

> It is true that Fuentes piles on one apparent novelistic element after another; piling on words, names, actions; loading more images on top of the already inundated ones. Fuentes gets carried away: carried away with the sound of his portable Remington. He beats on it so loud that the reader can't escape from the deafening noise of keys pounded on for hours on end. One must put the book aside, rest from the noise and the confusion which grow by the minute.

She concludes: "The evaluation of this book, in spite of the good laugh that it gave us, is tragic. It is a book by someone who has only partially found himself and who is struggling desperately to find others." As a result of her ferocious utterances she would be nicknamed "the claw" by the local writing community.

The most vicious attack on the novel did not surface until three years later and appeared in the letters to the editor of the Mexico City newspaper, *Excélsior*. Apparently it began as a protest against Fuentes and his colleagues who were accused of using the National University facilities, in particular the radio station, to disseminate Communist propaganda. Licenciado Eulogio Cervantes (the name is suspect!) accuses Fuentes of blatant plagiarism: "*La región más transparente* is the product of a series of 'expropriations' as ferocious as those realized in Cuba by Castro." He calls the novel a "pastiche" using the techniques of Joyce, Dos Passos, Baroja and Cela, and adds, "We shouldn't condemn him for imitating Cela or Joice [*sic*], only for doing it so badly." Señor Cervantes then lists some sixty pages of the novel which are taken from Paz's *El laberinto de la soledad*, several major characters from Michael Valbeck's *Caídos del cielo* (*Headlong from Heaven* in its original English version), parts from Jorge Portillas' *Fenomenología del relajo* and Eunice Odio's long poem, *El tránsito del fuego*.

We have already discussed the portrayal of, but certainly not the plagiarism of, the Hiperión group—Octavio Paz and other intellectuals of the early fifties who were concerned with defining Mexico's past, present, and future. Perhaps a few words are in order regarding Valbeck's *Headlong from Heaven*. This South African novel was translated into Spanish in the late 1950s and José Vázquez Amaral, reviewing *La región más transparente* for *Saturday Review*, first called attention to what he felt was a similarity between the two books. In reality the kinship is very superficial. Valbeck tells of a wealthy but ugly businessman married to a beautiful woman, a plot which has occurred hundreds of times in fiction and probably millions of times in real life. The rest of the novel develops along the lines of a "who done it." Finally, I have examined with considerable care Odio's long poem, *El tránsito del fuego*, and can find absolutely no points of comparison.

As might be expected, the reaction of fellow novelists, especially those outside of Mexico, tended to be very favorable. On September 7, 1958, Julio Cortázar sent congratulations from Paris and enclosed a lengthy and perceptive analysis of *La región más transparente* which is published in the Aguilar edition of Fuentes' *Obras completas*. While well aware that many of the allusions to Mexican customs and history passed over his head, he nonetheless saw many typical character types (Rodrigo Pola, Norma, Gabriel) which "are very similar to certain Argentine types which appear in Europe with considerable modification." On the negative side he found the introductory chapters slow moving and confused; also the characterization of the motion picture people as too "stereotyped and caricatured at the same time." The chapters on Gervasio Pola and Rodrigo he believed to be particularly well done as were those on Robles and the pelados: "Your dialogues are real dialogues, not that strange product that so many novelists invent (I'm thinking of Mallea, for example); as if they had never spoken to their lover or even their banker."

The Cuban novelist and poet, José Lezama Lima, was equally laudatory: "I have read your novel *La región más transparente* and have found it powerful and desirable, vibrating in its symbols and masks." He admonishes Fuentes not to worry about those who try to find influences in every paragraph: "They found influences in Proust and Joyce; and they invented many others. But if we are found to have them . . . we must be beheaded." He concludes by observing: "I don't believe there have been written in Mexico, or in any other part of America, very many novels better than yours.''

Writing from Uruguay Mario Benedetti concluded that *La región más transparente* offered an honest portrait of many Latin American problems. Upon the first reading of several of Fuentes' novels he had made critical notes in the margins, but: ''the second time I decided to just enjoy each novel.'' Peruvian Mario Vargas Llosa saw the novel as ''a seething crowded mural of Mexico City, an attempt to capture in fiction all the layers of that pyramid from the indigenous base with its ceremonial rites to its pinnacle made up of a cosmopolitan and snobbish oligarchy whose appetites, fashions and impudences are borrowed from New York and Paris.''

Of particular interest are Carlos Fuentes' own observations given in a variety of interviews over the years in which he has proffered his own analysis of the strengths and weaknesses of *La región más transparente*. In speaking to Luis Harss he called it, ''A biography of a city . . . a synthesis of present day Mexico.'' To a French reporter he commented, ''In my first novel I tried, among other things, to write a personal biography about that species of whale anchored in our high valley, Mexico City: its silhouettes, its secrets, a city which I love and hate at the same time because in it are presented with the greatest brutality the miseries and hopes of all my country. I tried to produce a synthesis of present-day Mexico: conflicts, aspirations, rancors.''

Fuentes also answered Emmanuel Carballo in much the same vein: ''It began as an elementary observation of Mexico City and the necessity of being a witness to what was happening to it. I wanted to offer a testimony of its life, rediscovered by the imagination.'' In a letter to the *Saturday Review* Carlos suggested: *''Where the Air Is Clear* is the first of a series of novels designed to give an extensive and interwoven panorama of Mexican life. It depicts the black part of Mexico, a Mexico that is now dying and being swept away by a vigorous younger generation.''

In December 1958 during an interview with Elena Poniatowska, Fuentes was anxious to talk about his next novel, but agreed to comment a bit further on his first. Among the defects which he now perceived in *La región más transparente* were: ''The incapacity of reducing to a unity an excess of material. Symbols piled upon characters without letting them evolve more naturally. Too many contortions, a continuous verbal exaltation which detracts from the rest of the novel, a lack of love, superficialities.'' In response to Poniatowska's assessment of the characters as almost caricatures, he answers: ''But they really are caricatures! It would have been a lie to give them human dimension. All these puppets of the cocktail parties, the Jockey Club, the International Set, showers and bankers conventions are cardboard paper-dolls. How can a newly arrived bourgeoisie be human?'' Asked what he feels are the strengths of the novel, Fuentes answers: ''Objectively, one thing. I swear that I wrote it from beginning to end with all the honesty I was capable of at that time. In any case, when I wrote *La región más transparente* I promised myself never to lie. I lived inside that world.''

Translations and Critical Reaction from Abroad

The first reactions to *La región más transparente* from abroad came not from journalists, but from professors of Spanish literature who were working with the Spanish edition. In the fall of 1958 the first two reviews of the novel were published in the United States. George Wing, then a young professor at the University of California at Berkeley, wrote a short review in the fall issue of *Books Abroad*. He saw Fuentes as an angry young man who felt deeply ''the betrayal of the ideals of the Revolution.'' Wing made comparisons with Dos Passos' writings and concluded by calling *La región más transparente* the best Mexican novel since *Al filo del agua*. In November of 1958 Jefferson Rea Spell, a long-time observer of the Latin American novel and professor at the University of Texas, published a brief review in *The Hispanic American Historical Review* in which he observed: ''This novel, which reveals acquaintance with and sympathy for certain new techniques in fiction writing, will repay the effort expended in its reading.''

The following year, Luis Andrés Murrillo produced for *Revista Iberoamericana* the most extensive review of the novel printed in the United States up to that time. He labeled the work ''panorámico-histórico'' and ''realista-simbélico.'' After some perceptive comments on characterization and structure he concluded with these remarks on the style: ''Many lines of the book are genuine prose poems. The final section in which the symbol-city comes together contains pages composed with extraordinary virtuosity.'' In the winter of 1964 University of Connecticut professor Robert G. Mead, Jr., a keen student of Latin American literature who follows the literary movements but also monitors the publishing industry and social environment, brought out the first of his two major studies on Carlos Fuentes. The earlier one in *Books Abroad* (1964) examined Fuentes as part of the contemporary Mexican scene. Mead had the advantage of five years of perspective and was thoroughly acquainted with the criticism on *La región más transparente* previously published in Mexico City. He saw the three types of reactions that the novel produced as a mirror of current Mexican literary criticism.

By the time Mead's article was in circulation the English translation of *La región más transparente* was out and many newspaper and magazine reviews had appeared in the U.S.A. No exact publication date of this version is known although the first review was printed in September 1960 with most of the others appearing in November and December of that year; a few followed in the early months of 1961.

The English title chosen was *Where the Air Is Clear*, the publisher was Ivan Obolensky in New York, and the translator was Sam Hileman. Hileman had first met Fuentes in Mexico City during the mid-1950s when the two enjoyed fellowships at the Centro Mexicano de Escritores. Hileman, himself a writer, lived in later years in Los Angeles where he did graduate work in English at U.C.L.A. During the next decade he subsequently translated three other novels by Fuentes: *Las buenas conciencias, La muerte de Artemio Cruz* and *Cambio de piel. Where the Air Is Clear* sold quite well in the bookstores. A second printing of the novel was made that same year and in 1971 Obolensky brought out a paperback edition under the Noonday label which is still available.

Where the Air Is Clear was reviewed by a variety of publications in the United States and Great Britain. Major newspapers in all sections of the country recognized it: in New York the *Times*, the *Herald Tribune*, and the *World Telegram and Sun*; in the Midwest the *Chicago Tribune*, the *Columbus Dispatch*, and the *Kansas City Star*; and elsewhere papers in San Francisco, St. Petersburg, Raleigh, Abilene, El Paso, and New Orleans. Magazines which reviewed the novel ranged from religious (*Catholic World*) to Marxist (*People's World, Mainstream*) in addition to such prestigious publications as the *New Yorker, Commonweal*, the *National Guardian*, and the *Saturday Review*.

Anthony West in the *New Yorker* and Selden Rodman in the *New York Times* were the most enthusiastic. Rodman had met Fuentes several years earlier in Mexico, although he did not mention the fact in his review. He saw the work as "the most ambitious and skillful novel to come out of Mexico in a long time, and by all odds the most 'modern.'" West also lauded the work while recognizing the "many errors of taste and simple beginner's mistakes." Speaking of Fuentes he observed: "he creates his people wholesale and marches them off by battalions, lavishly equipped with life stories, to take their place in his full-scale social panorama." He concluded: "If Señor Fuentes is not the most polished and assured writer, and if some of his episodes are coarsely imagined and hasty, he is at any rate endowed with the courage and the power to attempt and to achieve a really big thing."

On the more negative side are the observations of Richard Gilman in *Commonweal* and José Vázquez Amaral in the *Saturday Review*. While admiring some parts of the novel, Gilman observed: "But it doesn't really come off. The form and experience don't quite hold together. . . . It steps into a solipsistic world of manifestos, occult reveries, private myth-making and over-literary hymns to life that never attain the verbal originality and imaginative coherence that might justify them." Vázquez Amaral pointed out many possible influences and borrowings and saw the work as a roman á clef. (His attempts to identify the characters brought an angry letter from Fuentes which was published in a later number of the magazine.) His conclusion is that *Where the Air Is Clear* is an ambitious "pastiche," but does not give credit to Salazar Mallén who had used the word two years earlier. Vázquez Amaral is one of the few critics to mention the language of the translation which he feels is much too free. "It is not fair to quarrel with the translator's difficulties with slang. But it is hard to justify inaccurate interpretations of standard Spanish."

Perhaps a few words would be appropriate regarding the translation, especially since we have a unique situation in a contemporary work of the existence of two translations into English. Almost a year before the novel was published Lysander Kemp included an English version of a chapter in *Evergreen Review*. Interestingly enough, Kemp translated Fuentes' novelette, *Aura*, six years later.

Both translations are quite free; perhaps Kemp's reads a bit smoother, but Hileman may capture Fuentes' unique style better. Both take liberties in translating and both make mistakes. In the first paragraph of the "Gervasio Pola" chapter Hileman erroneously translates "botines de cuero" as "leather buttons," while Kemp omits to mention that Islas is "calvo." A page later the "puertas" of a garbage cart is called "cover" by Hileman. He also expands "cúmulo de basura" to read, "rotted vegetables and excrement," while Kemp keeps it as "load of garbage." For "Gervasio, al pie de la sierra, aflojú los muslos," Hileman reads: "At the foot of the mountain, Gervasio dropped," and Kemp: "Gervasio slackened his pace at the foot of the sierra."

Through the years additional translations have been made of *La región más transparente*; into French (1964), Czech (1966), Polish (1972) and German (1973). The French edition done by Robert Marrast includes a prologue by Miguel Angel Asturias. Marrast also translated the French version of *La muerte de Artemio Cruz*. Also noteworthy in the French edition of *La región más transparente* is the inclusion of a chronology of Mexican history combined with events from the lives of characters in the novel. For example, under the date of 1909 we read in the first column that Federico Robles goes to live in Morelia with a priest; the second column states that Francisco I. Madero declares himself a candidate for president of Mexico. Another first is a list of characters in the novel. Some eight members of the de Ovando family are cataloged, seven Zamaconas, and three Polas. Other listings are: the Bourgeoisie, Foreigners, Intellectuals, Lower Class, and Revolutionaries. These listings and descriptions make reading the novel much less confusing, especially in the initial chapters when so many characters are introduced. Occasionally we are given background information that does not appear in the novel. Dardo Morratto is an Argentine writer, but we now discover (perhaps in jest) that he has been secretary to Victoria Ocampo and a proofreader for Jorge Luis Borges. Also for the first time we discover that Tomás Mediana, about whom we have spoken several times, dies tragically in 1950.

La región más transparente *Today*

In spite of the almost universal recognition of *La muerte de Artemio Cruz* as Fuentes' masterpiece and the publicity surrounding each new publication, *La región más transparente* continues to reach a substantial body of new and appreciative readers each year. At most recent count it had gone through more than a dozen Spanish printings and has been continually available in English.

Perhaps the most significant publishing event of the seventies regarding the book was its inclusion in the 1,414 page *Obras completas*, volume I, done by Aguilar in 1974. The pages have been reset in a sightly larger format which is easier to read, although each continues to contain thirty-six lines. The newer version also includes the useful "Cuadro Cronológico" and the list of "personajes" which had first appeared in the French edition.

There seems to be only a very slight revision of the text. A few typographical errors are corrected and most foreign words are now in italics ("blue-jeans," "Handicap," "claxon," "Jockey," "kaputt," "pedigree," "very fain"). A few words change: "hilos de gomina" (Fondo version) becomes "Hilo de gomina" (Aguilar version). A period does not end a paragraph of stream of consciousness in the Fondo edition, "profesa" (Fondo) is capitalized by Aguilar. The incorrect date, 1857, for the execution of Maximilian (Fondo) is printed in long form and corrected by Aguilar: "mil ochocientos sesenta y siete."

With the passage of time *La región más transparente* has grown in stature among the Mexican critics. The occasion of its fourth printing, exactly a decade after the first, produced an uncommonly large number of reviews, apparently by younger critics. The shock of technique and exposé had worn off and the book's style no longer seemed out of place in Latin American fiction. Several reviewers commented upon the volume's historical importance as a "novel which breaks barriers." Rigoberto Lasso Tizareño observed: "This novel in our opinion opens a new cycle in the Mexican novel of our century." Vilma Fuentes (no relation) stated: ". . . for a new generation different and far removed, *La región más transparente* is enlightening in its chaos, while it appears fantastic and unbelievable in its historical background. Fuentes' book has grown but not aged."

Perhaps Emmanuel Carballo, who collaborated with Fuentes in a number of literary activities in the fifties, has best summed up the novel's importance: "For me the most important event of that year (1958) was the publication of *La región más transparente*, a work which closes the cycle of the rural-provincial novel and opens that of the post-revolutionary and metropolitan novel, fiercely critical. With this book Carlos Fuentes is converted into the style dictator of Mexican prose."

Source: Richard M. Reeve, "The Making of *La region mas transparente*," in *Carlos Fuentes, A Critical View,* edited by Robert Brody and Charles Rossman, University of Texas Press, 1982, pp. 34–63.

Sources

Dwyer, John P., "Conversation with a Blue Novelist," in *Review*, Vol. 12, Fall, 1974, pp. 54–8.

Gilman, Richard, "The Self-Conscious Culture of Modern Mexico," in *Commonweal*, 1961, pp. 510–11.

Krauze, Enrique, "The Guerilla Dandy," in *The New Republic*, Vol. 198, No. 26, June 27, 1988, pp. 28–34, 36–38.

Leal, Luis, "History and Myth in the Narrative of Carlos Fuentes," in *Carlos Fuentes: A Critical View*, edited by Robert Brody and Charles Rossman, University of Texas Press, 1982, pp. 3–17.

Maloff, Saul, "Growing Pains of a Bourgeois," in *Saturday Review*, Vol. XLIV, No. 50, December 16, 1961, pp. 20–1.

van Delden, Maarten, "Myth, Contingency, and Revolution in Carlos Fuentes's *La region mas transparente*," in *Comparative Literature*, Vol. 43, No. 4, Fall, 1991, pp. 326–45.

West, Anthony, "The Whole Life," in *the New Yorker*, March 4, 1961, pp. 123–25.

Further Reading

Cortazar, Julia, *Hopscotch*, translated by Gregory Rabassa, Pantheon Books, 1987.

> Originally published as *Rayuela* in 1963, Cortazar's book of "El Boom" soon transcended his generation. The work is a rare example of the truly innovative surviving the moment of its publication. According to a plan Cortazar sets forth, the reader must arrange the pieces of this open-ended novel into a whole.

van Delden, Maarten, *Carlos Fuentes, Mexico, and Modernity*, Vanderbilt University Press, 1998.

> Van Delden discusses the various modernist philosophies reflected upon throughout Fuentes' fiction. These include Fuentes' use of existentialism as well as his utilization of theories of national identity construction.

Faris, Wendy, "The Development of a Collective Voice: *Where the Air Is Clear*," in *Carlos Fuentes*, Frederick Ungar Publishing Co., 1983.

> Faris explores the ways in which Fuentes' *Where the Air Is Clear* builds communication between his characters through memory, myth, and personal and national identity.

Fuentes, Carlos, *A New Time for Mexico*, translated by Marina G. Gutman, University of California Press, 1997.

> At the end of the twentieth century, Fuentes looks back on Mexico's history since the Mexican Revolution of 1910. From that moment of liberation, Fuentes argues, Mexico has stumbled along a path toward authoritarianism that resulted in the long rule of the PRI. This reflection includes Fuentes' conversation with the Zapatista spokesman, Subcommander Marcos.

Fuentes, Carlos, *The Crystal Frontier: A Novel in Nine Stories*, translated by Alfred J. Mac Adam and Alfred M. Adam, Farrar, Straus, 1997.

> This recent work by Fuentes weaves together nine stories to show the state of tension and space that exists between Mexico and the U.S. The work is a meditation on border relations suggesting that crystalline walls, not razor wire, separate gringos and Mexicans. This is a shame since the two are destined to live together.

Krauze, Enrique, *Mexico: Biography of Power: A History of Modern Mexico, 1810-1996*, translated by Hank Heifetz, Harperperennial Library, 1998.

> This new history of Mexico uses the biographies of men who controlled or struggled for control of that nation during the past two centuries. The most interesting aspect of Krauze's work is his argument that the caudilloa leader had a tremendous influence on Mexican history. Men's fortunes rose and fell depending on their proper use of this role.

Poniatowska, Elena, *Massacre in Mexico*, translated by Helen R. Lane, University of Missouri Press, 1992.

> Originally published as *La noche de Tlatelolco* in 1971 and containing an introduction by Octavio Paz, this work has been since claimed as a masterpiece of documentary work. Poniatowska recounts the events of the 1968 massacre using information gathered through interviews. The work and the author have created controversy on both sides of the political aisle ever since.

Reeve, Richard M., "The Making of *La region mas transparente*: 1949-1974," in *Carlos Fuentes, A Critical View*, edited by Robert Brody and Charles Rossman, University of Texas Press, 1982.

> Fuentes' novel aroused some controversy for a number of years after publication because it seemed to describe real people and real events. Reeve discusses the making of the book as a reflection of the events of the time period and Fuentes' biography.

Silko, Leslie Marmon, *Almanac of the Dead: A Novel*, Penguin, 1992.

> Partially responsible for the boom in fiction by indigenous people of the U.S., Silko's monster novel, *Almanac of the Dead,* follows magical realism more closely than *Ceremony* (1977). The novel centers on Tucson but involves illegal border crossing, drug dealing, prophecy, and the historical consciousness that the American Southwest is not American. In fact, the illegality of activities along the border merely continues 500 years of struggle against the European invaders.

Wide Sargasso Sea

Jean Rhys
1966

When *Wide Sargasso Sea* was published in 1966 it helped to rescue its author, Jean Rhys, from the obscurity into which she had fallen. Her previous novels and short stories, published between the two world wars, were out of print. Rhys, who had succumbed to an alcohol addiction, lived an isolated life in a remote village in England, a country she had always despised. *Wide Sargasso Sea* caught the immediate attention of critics, won the prestigious W. H. Smith Award and Heinemann Award, and earned Rhys a place in the literary canon. The unique novel seeks to recreate the true story of Bertha Mason, the Jamaican mad wife of Edward Rochester in Charlotte Bronte's *Jane Eyre*. In telling Bertha's story (known in *Wide Sargasso Sea* as Antoinette Cosway), Rhys explores the complex relations between white and black West Indians, and between the old slaveholding West Indian families and the new English settlers in the post-emancipation Caribbean. Set mainly in Jamaica and Dominica, the country of Rhys's birth, the novel describes how Antoinette became mad. In Bronte's novel, Bertha/Antoinette is a monster, described as violent, insane, and promiscuous. Rhys creates instead a sympathetic and vulnerable young woman who seeks, unsuccessfully, to belong. The themes explored in the novel, especially the status of women and the race relations between newly freed slaves and their former owners, have drawn the attention of critics. Other critics debate the merits of the novel, saying that it relies too closely on *Jane Eyre*

and cannot stand alone. Certainly, Rhys's novel forces readers to reexamine Bronte's novel and consider the significance of race in the nineteenth-century English novel.

Author Biography

Set in mid-1800s Jamaica, *Wide Sargasso Sea* is the least overtly autobiographical of Rhys's fiction. However, critics have noticed some connections between Rhys's life and family history and that of her doomed protagonist, Antoinette Cosway. Born Ella Gwendolyn Rees Williams in 1890, Rhys was the third child of a Creole mother and a Welsh doctor. She grew up in Dominica, one of the Windward Islands, and, like her heroine, moved from the Caribbean to England while still a teenager. Rhys's ancestors on her mother's side had been slaveholders in Dominica, and their plantation house was burned down by freed slaves soon after emancipation. Antoinette witnesses a similar scene in *Wide Sargasso Sea*. Like Antoinette, Rhys was educated at a convent school. Rhys left the Caribbean when her parents discovered her relationship with a part-black man. In *Wide Sargasso Sea*, Antoinette's husband shuttles her off to England after hearing rumors of her illicit affair with her "mulatto" cousin Sandi. Tragically, Antoinette's insanity was also mirrored in Rhys's bouts with depression and occasional confinements in mental institutions.

Moving to England in 1907, Rhys tried her hand at acting. Finding work as a chorus girl, Rhys eventually became the kept mistress of an older man. This relationship, and many subsequent ones, ended unhappily. In 1917, Rhys married Willem Lenglet, a Dutch writer. After the couple moved to Paris in 1924, Rhys began publishing her short stories under the patronage of the English novelist Ford Madox Ford. Her first novel, *Quartet*, published in 1928, was a thinly veiled fictional account of her love affair with Ford. Rhys eventually returned to England, where she continued to write stories and novels featuring female protagonists on the margins of society. In 1939, Rhys disappeared from the public eye for a number of years. She had married Leslie Tilden-Smith, her literary agent, in 1937. Two years after his death in 1945, she married his cousin Max Hamer. In 1948, Rhys was briefly institutionalized at the Holloway Prison Hospital. Her alcoholic assault on her neighbors led the authorities to question her sanity. Around this time,

the British radio actress Selma Vas Dias began to search for Rhys, hoping to do a radio broadcast of Rhys's 1939 novel *Good Morning Midnight*. Vas Dias and many others had assumed Rhys was dead.

With new public interest in her writing, Rhys secured a contract for the novel that would become *Wide Sargasso Sea*. Still drinking to excess, caring for her ailing third husband, and hampered by poor health, Rhys did not complete the novel until 1966. In a letter, Rhys explained that she had "brooded over *Jane Eyre* for years" and that she "was vexed at [Bronte's] portrait of the 'paper tiger' lunatic, the all wrong creole scenes, and above all by the real cruelty of Mr. Rochester." Her re-reading of Charlotte Bronte's *Jane Eyre* inspired her to write the "true story" of Bertha Mason, whom Rhys renamed Antoinette Cosway. *Wide Sargasso Sea* was an instant success, winning the W. H. Smith Award for writers and the Heinemann Award of the Royal Society of Literature. Rhys followed this novel with two more collections of short stories. She was working on her autobiography, *Smile Please*, when she died at the age of 88 in 1979.

Plot Summary

Part I

Jean Rhys's *Wide Sargasso Sea* attempts to fill in the blanks of a fictional character's life story. Here Rhys creates a biography for Bertha Mason, the insane wife of Edward Rochester in Charlotte Bronte's novel *Jane Eyre*. As Rhys's novel begins, Bertha Mason, known through most of the narrative as Antoinette Cosway, is a child living on the overgrown and impoverished Coulibri Estate in Jamaica.

The story begins in 1839, six years after slavery was abolished in the British Empire, of which Jamaica was part. Antoinette, the young narrator of Part I, describes both her family's isolation and poverty in the wake of emancipation. She lives alone with her mother Annette, her brother Pierre, and three black servants, Christophine, Godfrey, and Sass, on the sprawling, but crumbling Cosway family plantation. No neighbors visit the family because Annette Cosway, who was born on Martinique, is considered an outsider. The family's only friend, Mr. Luttrell, kills himself on the novel's opening page. Antoinette believes he was tired of waiting for the world of former slaveowners to improve. Soon after, Annette's horse is poisoned,

Jean Rhys

presumably by former slaves. Voicing the precariousness of their position, Annette remarks, "Now we are marooned."

Antoinette is even more isolated than her mother. Her mother devotes her time and attention to Pierre, who is mentally retarded, and repels Antoinette's affectionate advances. Black children taunt Antoinette, calling her a "white cockroach." When she finally does make friends with Tia, a black girl, the friendship soon ends. After Antoinette calls Tia a "nigger," Tia retaliates by saying that Antoinette and her family are "white niggers," not like the "real white people" who have money and position. Tia then steals Antoinette's clothes, forcing Antoinette to dress herself in Tia's rags. Just at this moment, Antoinette meets some "real white people," new friends of her mother's. Her mother is embarrassed that Antoinette is so unpresentable. Believing that her mother is ashamed of her, Antoinette decides that what Tia said must be true. She fears that she can never belong to white or black people.

Selling the last of her jewelry, Annette Cosway is able to dress well and attend the parties of the white elite. She soon has a wealthy Englishman, Mr. Mason, fall in love with her. Gossiping women whisper that perhaps Annette literally bewitched him. After all, she has in her employ Christophine, a known practitioner of obeah, a type of voodoo. Antoinette is distressed when she overhears these rumors at her mother's wedding to Mr. Mason. The rumors signal to her how far from really belonging she and her family are.

Soon after the wedding, the family, including Antoinette's Aunt Cora, return to Coulibri. Mr. Mason is able to fix up the plantation and hire many more servants. Aunt Cora and Annette fear that their new wealth may leave them even more vulnerable than they were in their poverty. Aunt Cora warns Mr. Mason not to speak of replacing the black laborers with East Indian "coolies" in front of the black servants. Mr. Mason laughs off such warnings, saying that blacks are like children and not to be feared. He thinks that if no one molested the Cosway family when they were poor and defenceless, surely no one will harm them now. Annette pleads with him to leave Coulibri, but he accuses her of being irrational. Antoinette, who remains silent through these debates, agrees with Mr. Mason that they should stay at the plantation. It is the only place where she feels safe.

Aunt Cora and Annette are proved right, however, when black laborers burn down Coulibri. The fire begins in Pierre's room after his black nurse abandons him. As the family tries to escape the fire, they realize that an angry mob awaits them outside. In the chaos that ensues, Annette runs back into the house to try to save her parrot, Coco. She fails, and Coco, all afire, falls from the house into the crowd. Taking this as a bad omen, the mob disperses. Before she can be taken away, Antoinette spies her old friend Tia in the distance. She runs toward her, "for she was all that was left of my life as it had been. We had eaten the same food, slept side by side, bathed in the same river. As I ran, I thought, I will live with Tia and I will be like her. Not to leave Coulibri. Not to go." But Tia interrupts this reverie by throwing a rock at Antoinette. As the blood trickles down Antoinette's face, she looks at Tia: "We stared at each other, blood on my face, tears on hers. It was as if I saw myself. Like in a looking glass."

When the narrative resumes, Antoinette has just woken up from a long illness. She learns that Pierre died from the injuries he sustained in the fire. She further learns that her mother has gone insane.

In her madness, Annette attempted to kill Mr. Mason. Relative peace follows these revelations. Antoinette attends a convent school where she feels safe and at peace. Her stepfather, Mr. Mason, often visits her there. As Part I comes to a close, Antoinette learns that Mr. Mason wants her to leave the convent. She fears returning to the outside world, and her sleep is troubled by nightmares.

Part II

The narrator of Part II is Edward Rochester, the hero of Charlotte Bronte's *Jane Eyre.* He is never named in Rhys's novel, but the details he gives of his life make it clear to the reader that he is a younger version of Bronte's character. The narration of Part II begins several months after Antoinette voiced her fears of leaving the sanctuary of the convent for the outside world. In that time, Mr. Mason has died and his son, Richard, has arranged the marriage of Antoinette to Rochester. Put ashore in the town of Massacre, Dominica with his new bride, Rochester thinks to himself, ''So it was all over.'' He has gone through with a marriage arranged primarily for financial reasons and has now come to the ''honeymoon-house,'' a property Antoinette inherited from her mother.

Almost immediately, Rochester begins to doubt his wife. He questions her racial purity: ''Creole of pure English descent she may be, but [her eyes] are not English or European either.'' He also questions what he has been told about her: ''The girl is thought to be beautiful, she is beautiful. And yet. . .'' As he muses on his marriage, he thinks frequently of his father and brother back in England. As a younger son, Edward is not guaranteed an inheritance. To make his way in the world, he has come to the West Indies. His father has enjoined him to marry a Caribbean heiress to secure a fortune. Rochester wonders, though, whether he has sold his soul to fulfill his family's ambitions.

Despite the strong physical attraction Rochester feels toward Antoinette, he still questions their relationship. When he receives a letter from a man claiming to be her half-brother, Rochester finds it easy to believe the worst of her. His correspondent, Daniel Cosway, tells Rochester of Annette Cosway's insanity and promiscuity and suggests that Antoinette has engaged in an illicit sexual relationship with her black cousin Sandi Cosway. Armed with this information, Rochester believes he has been deceived by Richard Mason, his own father, and by Antoinette. He thinks they purposely hid the fact of Antoinette's promiscuity and her propensity for madness. He spurns the sexual advances of his affectionate wife, and begins to sleep alone.

At this point, Rochester's narrative is interrupted, and Antoinette begins to tell her own story. She has fallen deeply in love with Rochester and is hurt by his coldness. She seeks out her old nurse, Christophine, and asks for a magic potion to make Edward love her again. Edward then resumes the narration. Antoinette drugs his wine with the love potion Christophine made. The drug works: Rochester makes love to Antoinette. When he awakes, he is angered by what his wife has done. In an act of revenge, he has sex with Amelie, the ''half-caste'' serving girl who reminds Rochester of Antoinette. Antoinette hears the two making love, and becomes very bitter. She tells her husband that he has destroyed the one place where she felt free and happy. Christophine believes that Rochester's actions will break Antoinette. She needs Rochester to return her passionate love. Rochester says that he will always take care of Antoinette, but it is clear that he will never love her. When he looks at her, he sees only her ''blank lovely eyes.'' He decides that the eyes are mad, and that his wife is insane. He declares that he will never touch her again, and that he'll lock her away from the caresses of others. As Part II comes to a close, Antoinette and Rochester leave the honeymoon-house, and Rochester determines to sell the property.

Part III

Grace Poole, another character from Bronte's *Jane Eyre,* begins the narration of Part III. In Bronte's novel, Grace is the woman hired to care for Bertha/Antoinette when she is locked in the attic of Thornfield Hall, Rochester's home in England. In Rhys's novel, Grace tells of how Rochester's father and brother have died and how Edward has become very wealthy. He has instructed his housekeeper to hire Grace at extremely high wages to look out for the mad woman, Antoinette. Grace calls her ''that girl who lives in her own darkness.'' She describes Antoinette as ''still fierce,'' and notes that she needs to be watched carefully.

Antoinette resumes narration of the story, and through her cloudy recollections of how she has come to live in this cold English attic, she reveals what happened to her after she and Rochester left the honeymoon house. Rochester kept her in a house in the countryside and seldom visited her. Alone, she was often visited by her cousin Sandi, and the two became lovers. Enraged by this news, Rochester took his wife to England.

It is unclear how long Antoinette has been confined in the attic. Grace tells her that she has attacked her brother, Richard Mason. But Antoinette has a hard time distinguishing between reality and her nightmares. She envisions herself time and again burning down Thornfield Hall. She imagines jumping from the roof to the cold stones below and ending her life. In her dreams, this fire gets mixed up with the one that destroyed Coulibri. She sees the dying burning parrot, and hears her husband screaming her name, Bertha. In her imagination, she sees her old friend Tia beckoning her to swim in the pool where they once played. As the novel ends, Antoinette declares, ''I know why I was brought here and what I must do.'' She grabs a candle in preparation for burning down Thornfield, just as Bertha Mason finally does in Bronte's *Jane Eyre*.

Characters

Amelie

Amelie is a ''half-caste'' servant at Rochester and Antoinette's ''honeymoon-house'' in Dominica. Amelie mocks Antoinette, calling her a ''white cockroach.'' Rochester, who thinks Amelie resembles Antoinette, has sex with Amelie within earshot of Antoinette. Afterwards, Amelie, who has often said that she feels sorry for Rochester, remarks ''I find it in my heart to be sorry for [Antoinette] too.'' Amelie seems to have planned her seduction of Rochester in order to get money to leave the island.

Baptiste

A black servant at the ''honeymoon house'' on Dominica, Baptiste does not hide his disdain of Rochester.

Daniel Boyd

See Daniel Cosway

Aunt Cora

The widow of a slave owner, Aunt Cora takes care of Antoinette after her mother goes insane. Aunt Cora and Mr. Mason do not get along. He blames her for not helping out the Cosway family when they were poor and isolated. Aunt Cora believes that Mr. Mason's treatment of his black workers will endanger the Cosway/Mason family. Later, Aunt Cora blames Richard Mason for arranging an unsuitable marriage for Antoinette: ''It's disgraceful. . .It's shameful. You are handing over everything the child owns to a perfect stranger. Your father would have never allowed it. She should be protected, legally.'' Aunt Cora is afraid that the marriage settlements leave Antoinette vulnerable, but is powerless to change them.

Annette Cosway

The daughter and wife of slave owners, Annette Cosway leads a precarious existence as a young widow with two children in post-emancipation Jamaica. A native of Martinique, Annette is considered an outsider by Jamaican society. She is an unresponsive mother to Antoinette who craves her mother's attention. She does lavish time and energy on her mentally retarded and physically disabled son, Pierre. Fearing for the future and hoping to end her impoverishment, Annette gets the rich Mr. Mason to fall in love with her. The local gossips believe that she used the powers of her voodoo-practicing servant Christophine to entrap her second husband. After the fire at Coulibri, Annette goes insane, unable to face the deaths of her son and pet parrot. In her madness, she attacks Mr. Mason and tries to kill him. When Antoinette visits her in her confinement, Annette has become the sexual plaything of her black caregiver.

Antoinette Cosway

A monster in Charlotte Bronte's *Jane Eyre*, Antoinette Cosway, otherwise known as Bertha Mason, is the heroine of Rhys's novel. A sensitive child as the novel begins, Antoinette narrates the story of her life. Isolated from society and hungry for her mother's attention, Antoinette tries to find her rightful place in the world. The local blacks taunt her, calling her a ''white cockroach,'' and white women speak of her strangeness. In post-emancipation Jamaica, former slaves hate her because her father was a slave owner. Emancipation left the Cosways impoverished, and their poverty isolates them from white society. Antoinette seeks solace in the wild ruins of the family's formerly grand plantation, Coulibri. She feels a kinship toward the vibrant colors and lushness of the overgrown grounds. But Antoinette is banished from this Garden of Eden. After her mother, Annette, marries the wealthy Mr. Mason, she is supposed to take her place in a more ordered and orderly world. The wild Caribbean plantation is remodeled as an English country estate. This paradise is finally lost when disgruntled black servants burn Coulibri to the ground. As she watches it burn, Antoinette knows that she has lost her home forever. Later, Antoinette finds solace in a convent school where she is protected from the outside world. Antoinette loses this haven when her stepfather, Mr. Mason, arranges her marriage to Edward Rochester. Falling passionately in love with her husband, Antoinette hopes that their "honeymoon house" can become a true home. Her husband, however, spurns her advances, much as her mother did. This final rejection, coupled with her earlier isolation, leads Antoinette to the brink of insanity. Eventually imprisoned in Rochester's English house, Thornfield Hall, Antoinette plots to burn it down and to take a suicide leap from its roof. In a dream vision, she imagines that she can jump back to Coulibri and into the beckoning arms of her black childhood friend, Tia. In death she hopes to find a place to belong.

Daniel Cosway

DanielCosway, who is part black, claims to be Antoinette's illegitimate half-brother. He writes Rochester a letter explaining that Antoinette's mother went mad and that Antoinette has led a promiscuous life. His actions destroy all possibilities that Antoinette and Rochester will be happy in marriage. Antoinette says that Daniel is not really her brother, and that he has caused this misery out of his hatred for all white people.

Pierre Cosway

Pierre Cosway, described as an "idiot" by the local gossips, is Antoinette's younger brother. His physical and mental disabilities serve to further isolate the Cosways in the years before Annette Cosway's marriage to Mr. Mason. Pierre dies as a result of injuries sustained in the fire that destroys Coulibri. Remorse over his death is one of the main

Media Adaptations

- *Wide Sargasso Sea* was adapted as a film in 1993 by Carol Angier, John Dugian, and Jan Sharpe. The Australian film stars Karina Lombard, Rachel Ward, Michael York, Nathaniel Parker, and Naomi Watts. The sexually explicit nature of the film earned it an NC-17 rating, but an edited R-rated version is also available through New Line Home Video.

- The composer Gordon Crosse wrote a musical score called *Memories of Morning: A Monodrama for Mezzo-soprano and Orchestra* in 1973 that is loosely based on Rhys's novel. The score is available through Oxford University Press.

- In 1996, Australian composer Brian Howard adapted *Wide Sargasso Sea* into a chamber opera.

causes of his mother's subsequent insanity. Pierre's mental disabilities also add to Rochester's suspicion that Antoinette is hereditarily predisposed to mental illness.

Sandi Cosway

Sandi, the black grandson of Antoinette's father, appears fleetingly in the novel as a kind man who tries to protect Antoinette. He scares off the black children who taunt her on her way to school. Years later, his kindness makes him the subject of rumors: Daniel tells Rochester that Antoinette and Sandi were involved sexually. Locked in Thornfield Hall, Antoinette recalls Sandi's frequent visits to her after her marriage and remembers their last kiss. After her marriage to Rochester was effectively dissolved, Sandi and Antoinette did become lovers. He had offered to protect her from Rochester and had wanted to run away with her. Enraged by news of their affair, Rochester takes Antoinette to England.

Christophine Dubois

Christophine, an obeah (voodoo) practitioner from Martinique, is one of three black servants to stay with the Cosway family after emancipation. A formidable character, Christophine's obeah powers are legendary among both the Jamaican blacks and whites. Christophine frightens the local black women into helping her in the Cosway kitchen. White women assume that Christophine used black magic to help Annette ''catch'' her second husband, Mr. Mason. Though Antoinette is also somewhat frightened of Christophine, Christophine acts as a mother figure to her. After silently noticing Antoinette's loneliness, Christophine arranges for Tia to be Antoinette's companion. Christophine also tells Annette that she is neglecting her daughter: ''She run wild, she grow up worthless. And nobody care.'' After Antoinette grows up and gets married, Christophine is still the only person who looks out for her welfare. Unhappy that her husband has stopped loving her, Antoinette turns to Christophine for advice. Christophine tells her to leave her husband: ''When man don't love you, more you try, more he hate you, man like that.'' Refusing to listen, Antoinette begs Christophine for a magical cure. Christophine relents and provides her with a drug to seduce Rochester. As Christophine predicts, however, the drug ultimately makes Rochester hate Antoinette. Just as she tried to get Antoinette's mother to care for her child, Christophine attempts (and fails) to persuade Rochester to love his wife, if only a little.

Godfrey

Godfrey is one of three black servants who remain with the Cosway family after emancipation. However, Annette does not trust him; she believes he is complicit in the poisoning of her horse. During the fire at Coulibri, Godfrey does not try to help the white family.

Josephine

See Christophine Dubois

Mannie

Mannie, the black groom who comes to Coulibri after Mr. Mason marries Annette Cosway, is the only new servant whom Antoinette likes. He is one of three servants to stay loyal to the Cosway/Mason family during the plantation fire. He tries to put out the fire and fearlessly confronts those who set it: ''What all you are, eh? Brute beasts?'' Shouting back, the crowd calls him a ''black Englishman.''

Annette Mason

See Annette Cosway

Bertha Mason

See Antoinette Cosway

Mr. Mason

Mr. Mason, Annette Cosway's second husband, is a rich Englishman who has recently come to Jamaica. Local gossip has it that he could have married any woman he wanted. The white Spanish Town ladies are surprised that he chose Annette, an impoverished widow with a disabled son and a strange daughter. Mr. Mason restores the Cosway home, Coulibri, to its former grandeur. As an Englishman, he seems ignorant of the racial politics on Jamaica. He plans to replace his black laborers with East Indian ''coolies,'' and doesn't realize the extent to which his workers will resent this change. The fire at Coulibri takes him unawares, despite the constant warnings of Aunt Cora that black animosity toward the rich white family runs high. Mr. Mason also holds very stereotypical views about blacks: he believes that they are like harmless children. He is not comfortable with the close relations the Cosways have with their black relatives. Antoinette and Pierre have many black half-siblings—their father was a notorious womanizer—and Annette has always befriended these children. Mr. Mason demands that these ties be cut. Trying to endow Coulibri with specifically English values, Mr. Mason fills the house with English art and orders the cook to prepare English dishes. Ultimately, Mr. Mason can control neither Coulibri nor his wife. His English possessions burn in the fire and his wife goes insane. Still trying to control the fate of the Cosway family, he plans Antoinette's marriage to Rochester before he dies. But Rochester, like Mr. Mason, is unable to anglicize either Antoinette or her Caribbean possessions.

Richard Mason

Richard Mason, Antoinette Cosway's (Bertha Mason's) stepbrother, is one of the characters who also appear in Charlotte Bronte's *Jane Eyre*. Richard is responsible for arranging the marriage of Antoinette to Edward Rochester. Christophine and Aunt Cora each worry that the marriage settlements leave Antoinette vulnerable and dependent upon

Rochester, a man the family barely knows. In both novels, Rochester blames Richard for keeping the secret of Annette Cosway/Mason's insanity and believes that Richard purposely hid evidence of Antoinette's madness and promiscuity. Antoinette/Bertha violently attacks Richard when he visits her in her confinement in England. While he appears infrequently in Rhys's novel, Richard's actions have a profound effect on the novel's heroine.

Myra

Myra, a black servant, comes to Coulibri after Mr. Mason marries Annette Cosway. Aunt Cora warns Mr. Mason that Myra cannot be trusted and that he should not discuss his plans to fire the black workers in front of her. Mr. Mason laughs off these concerns, saying that Myra and all blacks are "children" who are "too damn lazy to be dangerous." Aunt Cora's fears are later confirmed. When the black workers set fire to the estate, Myra is mysteriously absent. The fire begins in Pierre's room, where Myra was supposed to be watching the child.

Grace Poole

Grace Poole, who narrates a short section of Part Three, is Antoinette/Bertha's nurse in England. She appears as a character also in *Jane Eyre*. Grace feels protected by the isolation of her position—she's alone in a large mansion with an insane woman and just two other servants. She is also glad to have the money. Her alcohol problem, which is described in some detail in *Jane Eyre*, is alluded to here. She is afraid of Antoinette "when her eyes have that look" and knows that despite her confinement, Antoinette is "still fierce."

Edward Rochester

Antoinette's husband, and the narrator of Part Two, is clearly meant to be a young Edward Rochester, the hero of Bronte's *Jane Eyre*. However, Rhys never gives a name to this character in *Wide Sargasso Sea*. As a younger son with no prospects of inheritance, Rochester has come to Jamaica to make his fortune. He feels coerced by his father and by Antoinette's family into marrying Antoinette for her money. In a letter to his father, Rochester writes: "I have sold my soul or you have sold it, and after all the girl is thought to be beautiful, she is beautiful. And yet. . ." Despite Antoinette's beauty, Roches-

ter has serious reservations about her. She seems foreign and unfamiliar and, like the West Indies themselves, possibly threatening. Rochester becomes obsessed with her purity, even questioning whether she is really white. He notes her "dark alien eyes" and concludes that while "of pure English descent she may be," her eyes "are not English or European either." After receiving a letter from Daniel Cosway, who claims to be Antoinette's half-brother, Rochester decides—erroneously—that Antoinette, like her mother, is promiscuous and insane. He trusts her even less after she drugs his wine in an attempt to make him love her. Punishing her for this transgression, Rochester has sex with the black servant Amelie within earshot of Antoinette. Rochester had earlier commented that Amelie looked like Antoinette and had speculated that they might be sisters. In substituting the black "sister" for the white, Rochester shows what he thinks of Antoinette: that she is alien, foreign, and "other." Rochester comes across as racist in these scenes, repulsed by and distrustful of blacks. As Rochester and Antoinette leave their honeymoon house, he blames her for destroying his future: "Above all I hated her. For she belonged to the magic and the loveliness. She had left me thirsty and all my life would be thirst and longing for what I had lost before I found it." Out of desperation and anger, Rochester isolates his wife, withdrawing his physical affection. After he hears rumors of her affair with her black cousin, Sandi, he takes Antoinette to England. Deciding that she is insane, he locks her in the attic. Her eventual insanity becomes the confirmation of all his fears. Throughout his narration in Part Two, Rochester presents himself as a helpless victim of circumstance. In his bitterness, he lashes out at Antoinette, spurning her love and destroying her potential for happiness as well as his own.

Sass

Sass is one of three black servants to stay with the Cosways after emancipation. He helps to protect the Cosway/Mason family during the fire at Coulibri.

Disastrous Thomas
See Sass

Tia

Tia is Antoinette's first friend. The two swim and play together, and, for a brief while, are happy.

The friendship ends after Antoinette calls Tia a "nigger." Tia retaliates by calling Antoinette a "white nigger" and by stealing her clothes. During the fire at Coulibri, Antoinette hopes that Tia and her mother will let her live with them. As she starts running toward Tia, Tia throws a rock at Antoinette. Staring at each other, the blood trickles down Antoinette's face while the tears fall down Tia's. Their racial difference divides them even as they feel for each other. Years later, before she goes to burn down Thornfield Hall, Antoinette imagines that Tia is beckoning her and that the two can be friends again.

Themes

Race Relations and Prejudice

How people of different races get along and what prejudices they hold are major themes in this book. As the book opens, the former slaveowners and the newly freed slaves await compensation from the British government. In this time of change— the novel begins in 1839, five years after slavery had ended and one year after the apprenticeship system of forced black labor had ended—the relations between black and white West Indians were tense. This tension erupts as the fire at Coulibri. The black workers burn the symbol of white oppression, the plantation house. Further, the newly arriving English colonists—represented in the book by Mr. Mason and Edward Rochester—are prejudiced against blacks. Mr. Mason calls them children and believes blacks make bad workers. Rochester describes blacks through racist characterizations. Both Mr. Mason and Rochester want Antoinette to disown her black half-siblings and other relatives. This prejudice is also evident in their fears of miscegenation. Rochester is disgusted with himself after he sleeps with a half-black woman, and he questions Antoinette's racial heritage. Antoinette's presumably sexual relationship with her black cousin Sandi causes Rochester to declare her insane and lock her in the attic at Thornfield Hall. Likewise, Annette Cosway's sexual liaison with a black caretaker is the mark of her insanity. In her dream at the end of the novel, Antoinette envisions a harmony between blacks and whites that has eluded her in life. By burning down Thornfield Hall, the symbol of her oppression in marriage, she imaginatively aligns herself with the blacks who burned down their symbol of oppression, Coulibri. Such alignment, however, seems only possible in the imagination. Antoinette's early friendship with the black child Tia is marred by the racial slurs each uses to describe the other. Years later, locked in the attic, Antoinette dreams of a reconciliation with Tia. However, as many West Indian critics have pointed out, such a possibility remains illusory, a mad woman's fantasy.

Isolation

Throughout the novel, the isolation of its major characters is a major theme. Characters are variously isolated by geography, social position, race, and insanity. At the beginning of the novel, the Cosway family is isolated by living at Coulibri, a plantation far from Spanish Town, the center of white civilization on Jamaica. This geographic isolation is highlighted by the death of Annette's horse. Without transportation, the Cosway family is, in the words of Annette, "marooned." As white former slaveowners, the Cosways are further isolated. Former slaves have abandoned the family, and the recently freed blacks despise their old oppressors. Later, Edward Rochester feels as though he has been exiled from England. Feeling no affinity for the lush Caribbean surroundings, he feels alone, even in marriage. Antoinette experiences a similar alienation when she is locked in the attic of Rochester's English home. These feelings of isolation are emotional as well as geographical. Antoinette tries to find love— from her mother, from Tia, and from Rochester— but time and again her advances are spurned. Rochester similarly feels locked out from his father's affection. As a child, Antoinette is a social outcast; her family's poverty separates them from other white families on Jamaica. Called a "white nigger" she seems to belong neither to black or white society. Her mother, as a native of Martinique, finds no friends among white Jamaican society. The black servant Christophine is held at bay by other black servants. From Martinique like her mistress, Christophine's ways seem foreign and frightening to the Jamaicans. The extent to which Antoinette and her mother feel isolated is finally manifested in their insanity. Locked away from society, Antoinette and Annette are marked as outcasts. Unaware of the passage of time or how they came to be imprisoned, both face the ultimate isolation of being unable to communicate at all.

Doubles

The novel presents many black and white doubles. This doubling ties back into the theme of racial difference and prejudice, as the novel explores both what brings women of different races together and what separates them. As young girls, Tia and Antoinette are doubles. They play together like sisters, but they also seem to be mirror reflections of the other. This is especially apparent when Tia dons Antoinette's dress and leaves her own ragged outfit for Antoinette. Dressed in the black girl's clothes, Antoinette becomes the "white nigger" that Tia has called her. Wearing Tia's dress, Antoinette is rejected by her mother and white society as an outsider, much as white society would reject Tia because of her race. Later, when Tia throws a rock at Antoinette, the blood streaming down Antoinette's face is a reflection of the tears streaming down Tia's. They each hurt because of the racial gulf that separates them. In Part II, Rochester sees Amelie as a black reflection of Antoinette. He notes that the two could be sisters. By sleeping with Amelie, he then symbolically trades one sister for the other. In many ways, Amelie is the embodiment of the blackness he sees in Antoinette. Rochester does not quite trust that Antoinette is all white. The repulsion he feels upon waking up in Amelie's arms is matched by the repulsion he felt toward his wife when she seduced him with "black" magic. Antoinette and her mother Annette are another example of black and white doubles. Annette's blackness is metaphorical; as an insane and "impure" woman (she engages in a miscegenational relationship with her black caretaker), she has lost her claims on white society. The similarity of their names and fates links Annette to Antoinette. Rochester tries to erase this doubleness by changing Antoinette's name to Bertha. He is afraid that Annette's promiscuity and insanity, which have "blackened" her name, will taint her daughter. In many ways, Antoinette can only become close to her mother by following a similar life path, ultimately leading to her own affair with a black man and her eventual insanity.

Style

Point of View

The novel is divided into three parts. In the first, Antoinette is the only narrator. In the second part,

Topics for Further Study

- Rhys based her character Antoinette Cosway on Bertha Mason, the madwoman in Charlotte Bronte's *Jane Eyre*. Compare the depictions of the two women.

- In *Wide Sargasso Sea* the black servants set fire to Coulibri after they learn that Mr. Mason is planning on importing workers from the East Indies. How did the diverse working population—Indian, Chinese, African-Caribbean, white Creole, and European—interact in the nineteenth-century Caribbean?

- Investigate the care of the mentally ill in the nineteenth century and compare their treatment to the way in which Annette Cosway Mason and Antoinette Cosway are treated.

- Research the living conditions of emancipated slaves in Jamaica and/or Dominica. How accurately does Rhys describe their lives?

Rochester takes over, but his narrative is interrupted briefly by Antoinette. In the third part, the English nurse Grace Poole is the narrator until Antoinette regains the narrative voice. This first-person narration is significant because it lets the reader see the world through the subjective gaze of flawed characters. In Parts I and II, Antoinette reveals her own naivety by relating her story. She so obviously does not understand the world she has been born into. Why her mother rejects her, why Tia will refuse to shelter her in the midst of the riot at Coulibri, and why Rochester will reject the gift of her love are all mysteries to this uneducated, ignorant, and yet sympathetic heroine. Watching Antoinette struggle to belong and witnessing her repeated rejections through her eyes, the reader cannot help but pity the fragility of Antoinette's position. However, when Rochester takes over the narration, as Sanford Sternlicht argues in his chapter on the novel, "It is as if the author is allowing the accused to convict himself on his own testimony." As the "villain" of the novel, the man who eventually causes Antoinette's insanity and locks her away, Rochester is ostensibly an unsympathetic character. He unwittingly reveals his racism by recording his reactions to the black people he meets. His greed, his lack of respect for his wife and her culture, his willingness to blame anyone and everyone for his life's disappointments become apparent as he tries to portray himself as a victim of circumstance. Despite this, in his narration Rochester reveals himself to be a passionate man, who, blinded by prejudice, is denying his own happiness as well as his wife's. Grace Poole, the alcoholic nurse hired to care for Antoinette in England, is an equally subjective narrator. So caught up in her desire to escape the pressures of the outside world, she cannot comprehend the tragedy of Antoinette's imprisonment. When Antoinette once again takes over, Rhys succeeds in presenting the world through a madwoman's eyes. In a letter, Rhys had noted, ''A mad girl speaking all the time is too much!'' In splitting the narrative, though, Rhys shows how all perspectives are limited, if not by madness then by prejudice, self interest, and ignorance.

Setting

The setting of *Wide Sargasso Sea* is a very important factor in the novel. The Sargasso Sea evokes both fear and tranquillity. Rachel Carson describes how the Sargasso holds ''legendary terrors for sailing ships'' but also how its skies are ''seldom clouded.'' In the novel, the Caribbean seems to be both paradisiacal and threatening. The lush growth, the vibrant colors, make Antoinette feel as though she is growing up in the Garden of Eden, but that the Garden has ''gone wild.'' The wildness seems to encroach on the inroads civilization has made. Rochester imagines that the ''honeymoon-house'' is being invaded by the ever-growing forest. The heat and color of Jamaica and Dominica are also contrasted to the cold grayness of England. The time setting of the novel is another crucial factor. Though Rhys decided to write the ''true story'' of Charlotte Bronte's character, Bertha Mason, Rhys broke from Bronte by moving the time setting from the late 1700s to the 1840s. This shift allows her to depict a volatile time period. Slavery had recently been abolished in the Caribbean, and the economic repercussions of emancipation changed Caribbean society. This is evident in both the decay of Coulibri, a once-rich plantation, as well as in the riot staged by black workers afraid that they will soon be replaced by East Indian laborers.

Symbolism

Wide Sargasso Sea is filled with recurring symbols. Coulibri, the big plantation house that is burned to the ground by black laborers, is a symbol of slavery and oppression. Thornfield Hall, Rochester's English estate, is equally a symbol of oppression, but of a different sort. Locked in the attic, Antoinette sees Thornfield Hall as the symbol of her husband's power over her. Burning it down, she symbolically reaches out to the blacks who burned down her childhood home. Clothes are also important symbols in the novel. When Antoinette puts on Tia's dress, she feels as though she has put on Tia's skin. Antoinette imagines that her white mother and their white neighbors see her as a ''white nigger.'' Later in life, Antoinette wears the white dress that Rochester likes in an attempt to make him love her. But Rochester, noting that the dress does not fit Antoinette correctly, sees this as yet another way that his wife is different and doesn't fit into his English ideals. After she has gone insane, Antoinette asks her keeper again and again to let her wear her red dress. The red dress symbolizes both her infidelity—she wore a similar dress when her lover Sandi visited her—and the fire and warmth of the Caribbean. She imagines, as she sees the dress on the floor, that it is a fire spreading across the room. This reminder of the Caribbean inspires her finally to burn down Thornfield Hall and to figuratively return to the place of her youth.

Literary Heritage

Critics argue about which literary heritage Rhys draws upon in her novel Wide Sargasso Sea. Some, like Sandra Drake, argue that Rhys uses a particularly Afro-Caribbean tradition in her novel: ''This reading is sustained by the centrally Afro-Caribbean structure of the novel, by the quintessentially Afro-Caribbean figure of the zombi, and by the Africa-derived beliefs about the relations between the living and the dead that the concept of the zombi—the living-dead—incorporates.'' Drake believes that the novel favors an Afro-Caribbean worldview over a European one, and that Rhys challenges her readers to reject the Western idea that African beliefs are ''foolish.'' Others see Rhys, who left Dominica as a teenager and only returned for one brief visit, as belonging to the European Modernist tradition. Mary Lou Emery finds, however, that such categories ''limit our understanding of her work.'' She argues instead that the modernist writer, the West Indian writer, and the woman writer can be seen as complimentary categories that help shape each other. The power of European influence on Rhys's novel can certainly not be denied. She did, after all, choose to write the ''true story'' of a character she borrowed from one of the best known nineteenth-century English novels, *Jane Eyre*. The mixture of African and English elements seems finally to best represent the literary heritage of the West Indies, where so many different cultures intermingled over centuries of colonization.

Historical Context

Rhys wrote *Wide Sargasso Sea* between 1945 and 1966. Critic Elizabeth Nunez-Harrell writes in ''The Paradoxes of Belonging: The White West Indian Woman in Fiction,'' that the novel is a ''response to the nationalistic mood in [the West Indies] of the late 1950s and 1960s.'' During this time period Jamaica became independent of Britain (in 1962). Dominica, the country of Rhys's birth and the setting for Part II, did not become independent until 1978. In these times of change, which also saw a large influx of West Indian immigrants into England, the relations between whites and blacks were often tense, erupting sometimes into violence. Not addressing these questions directly, Rhys chose to set her novel between 1839 and 1845. Slavery had ended in the British colonies in 1833, so these years were also ones of change.

In deciding to tell the ''true story'' of Bertha Mason, the Creole madwoman in Charlotte Bronte's *Jane Eyre*, Rhys confronted directly English stereotypes about the Caribbean and also how white and black West Indians viewed the English. Interestingly, Rhys changed the time setting. Bronte's novel is set in the late 1700s, before the abolition of slavery in the British colonies. By moving the setting, Rhys places her characters in a much more volatile time period. The West Indian planters who had made their fortunes cultivating sugar with slave laborers were impoverished by abolition. Their property

values plummeted, and they found it difficult to secure a labor force to work their declining estates. White West Indians had threatened secession from England over the question of emancipation. In his history of West Indian slavery, *Capitalism and Slavery*, Eric Williams quotes one Jamaican planter as saying, ''We owe no more allegiance to the inhabitants of Great Britain than we owe our brother colonists in Canada. . .We do not for a moment acknowledge that Jamaica can be cited to the bar of English opinion to defend her laws and customs.'' In other words, white Jamaicans did not want to accept British sovereignty, and felt that England had no right to abolish slavery in their land. Meanwhile, new English colonists were able to make a fortune buying up devalued West Indian estates. As is apparent in Mr. Mason's and Edward Rochester's attitudes toward the former slave owners in the novel, the new arrivals felt morally superior to the West Indian whites who had supported a system of human bondage. However, as the former slave Christophine notes in *Wide Sargasso Sea*, abolition and the new colonists did not bring blacks complete freedom: ''No more slavery! She had to laugh! ''These new ones have Letter of the Law. Same thing. They got magistrate. They got fine. They got jail house and chain gang. They got tread machine to mash up people's feet. New ones worse than old ones—more cunning, that's all.''' In fact, immediately following emancipation, the British put an apprenticeship system into effect. The freed slaves were forced to stay with their former masters and accept whatever wages the masters chose to pay. Steep fines and imprisonment awaited those blacks who sought greater freedom. The new white colonists tried to create a greater divide between blacks and whites. In Rhys's novel, Antoinette and Pierre have many part-black half-siblings, children of their father's frequent liaisons with black women. Their mother Annette welcomes these children and accepts them into her home. Mr. Mason, however, tries to put a stop to this interaction. Antoinette recalls that Mr. Mason tried to instill in her shame for having black relatives. Similarly, Rochester is repulsed after he sleeps with a black servant. Having sex with her, he feels, puts him on the same level as the immoral old slave owners.

These three distinct groups—white West Indians, black West Indians, and English colonists— uneasily inhabited the small islands of the English-speaking Caribbean. In the years following abolition, black rebellions frequently erupted, and the white governors were often accused of treating their black subjects too harshly. Rhys's ancestors watched their plantation burn down shortly after emancipation. Rhys, too, would have been aware of the debate surrounding what was known as the Governor Eyre controversy. In 1865, Jamaican Governor Eyre quelled a black rebellion using an extreme amount of force. Eminent English writers immediately began debating over what was the correct way to protect the white minority interests in the overwhelmingly black Caribbean. Novelist Charles Dickens supported Eyre, believing that any white violence was justified for fear of potential black violence. Scientist Charles Darwin, on the other hand, believed that Eyre's barbarity could never be justified. What is important to remember is that Jamaica and other far-flung British colonies were significant in England. The English discussed how best to govern these colonies and theorized about the racial differences of their inhabitants. One thing that Rhys contends with in her novel is how the Caribbean is perceived through various forms of English discourse. In deciding to tell the "true story" of a Creole subject whom readers knew only through Charlotte Bronte's eyes, Rhys lets the colonials talk back.

Critical Overview

Wide Sargasso Sea was an immediate critical success. The book won for its author two prestigious awards, the W. H. Smith Literary Award and the Heinemann Award of the Royal Society for Literature. Critics were attracted to Rhys's imaginative retelling of the story of the madwoman Bertha Mason from Charlotte Bronte's beloved novel, *Jane Eyre*. The tie to Bronte that probably brought *Wide Sargasso Sea* its wide readership also brought its share of controversy. Early reviewer Walter Allen declared that the book could "not exist in its own right" and only works as an interesting appendage to Bronte's better novel. Others disagree. Michael Thorpe believes that *Wide Sargasso Sea* actually forces readers to see *Jane Eyre* as a flawed, "more 'dated' work, marred by stereotyping and crude imaginings."

Critical attention to Jean Rhys and her last novel is ever growing. As Judith L. Raiskin writes in her introduction to the novel, "*Wide Sargasso Sea* has served as a touchstone text for critics interested in modernism, feminism, and post-colonial theory." If feminists have, in the words of Raiskin, "been challenged by a novel that rewrites an English classic [*Jane Eyre*] long touted for its feminist vision," they have come to see how "the issues of race and slavery raised in *Wide Sargasso Sea* complicate not only many evaluations of *Jane Eyre* but also the readings of Rhys's 'European fiction' that analyze exploitation in terms of gender only." In other words, feminist critics have been forced to understand both how women are simultaneously united by gender and divided by racial and class difference in their assessments of Rhys's novel.

But *Wide Sargasso Sea* has not only challenged feminist critics to reexamine Rhys's other works. Pierrette M. Frickey states that not until the publication of this last novel did Rhys become "known as a West Indian writer." Critics try to trace the significance of Rhys's Caribbean childhood in the structure and imagery of the novel. Sandra Drake argues that Rhys draws on a particularly Afro-Caribbean literary tradition, and that she uses her knowledge of voodoo and zombies to make an anti-European statement in *Wide Sargasso Sea*. Kenneth Ramchand, however, is quick to point out that not all West Indian writers and critics want to claim Rhys as one of their own. He quotes poet Edward Brathwaite who believes that "white Creoles in the English and French West Indies have separated themselves by too wide a gulf and have contributed too little culturally. . .to give credence to the notion that they can. . .meaningfully identify or be identified with the spiritual world on this side of the Sargasso Sea." But many find it hard to argue with the West Indian feeling of Rhys's last novel. Indeed recent critics point, with humor, to the 1974 assessment of A. Alvarez that Rhys was "the best living English novelist." In her indictment of English imperialism and in her evocation of a Caribbean landscape and culture, Jean Rhys is a powerful and gifted novelist, but certainly not English.

Criticism

Kimberly Lutz

Lutz is an instructor at New York University and has written for a wide variety of educational

A scene from the 1993 film adaption of Wide Sargasso Sea.

publishers. In the following essay, she discusses racial identity and ambiguity in Wide Sargasso Sea.

In her unfinished autobiography, *Smile Please*, Jean Rhys records her childhood longing to be black: "[My mother] loved babies, any babies. Once I heard her say that black babies were prettier than white ones. Was this the reason why I prayed so ardently to be black, and would run to the looking-glass in the morning to see if the miracle had happened? And though it never had, I tried again. Dear God, let me be black." In an unpublished manuscript entitled "Black Exercise Book," Rhys

suggests that she can boast a distant black ancestor: "My great grandfather and his beautiful Spanish wife. Spanish? I wonder." In questioning the ethnic heritage of this presumably darker skinned woman, Rhys questions the stories her family has told about their ethnicity. On at least one occasion, in "The Bible Is Modern," Rhys called herself "black" to imply her alienation from English culture. As Judith L. Raiskin writes, "While Rhys did not identify herself racially as other than white Creole, her self-identification as. . .'black' is a political stance meant to position her in opposition to the metropolitan colonizing culture." In desiring to be black, in

What Do I Read Next?

- In Charlotte Bronte's 1847 novel *Jane Eyre*, Rhys found the inspiration for *Wide Sargasso Sea*. *Jane Eyre* traces the travails of a poor English governess. In this novel, Bertha Antoinetta Mason appears fleetingly as a crazed Creole madwoman who threatens Jane Eyre's happiness.

- *The Wonderful Adventures of Mrs. Seacole in Many Lands*, Mary Seacole's 1857 autobiography. The Jamaican-born Seacole relates her life as a nurse in the West Indies, Central America, England, and the Crimea. This woman of mixed Scottish and African ancestry describes her rise to fame as a celebrated nurse as well as the racial prejudice she encountered along the way.

- In her 1934 novel, *Voyage in the Dark*, Rhys tells the story of Anna Morgan, a white West Indian woman who lives in England. Often dreaming of home and feeling alienated by life in England, Anna becomes an alcoholic prostitute.

- In her posthumously published *Smile Please: An Unfinished Autobiography* (1979), Rhys recollects her Dominican childhood and reflects on the tensions that divided blacks from whites.

- ''Jean Rhys'' is Caribbean writer Derek Walcott's 1981 poetic tribute to the author. Walcott imaginatively recreates how Rhys came to write *Wide Sargasso Sea* in this short poem.

- In *The Female Malady: Women, Madness, and English Culture, 1830-1980* (1985), Elaine Showalter discusses the diagnosis and treatment of mentally ill women in England. She includes an analysis of *Jane Eyre*'s Bertha Mason, and describes the historical background of such a character.

---

searching for a black ancestor, and in aligning herself with black West Indians, Rhys complicated the boundaries between black and white so stark in her time, and even starker in the mid-nineteenth century, the timeframe of her best-known novel, *Wide Sargasso Sea*.

Certainly race and racial difference are complicated categories in a novel set just after the emancipation of slavery in the British colonies. The heroine of the novel, Antoinette Cosway, otherwise known as Bertha Mason, is called at one point a ''white nigger.'' Similarly, the Cosway/Mason family's servant Mannie is called a ''black Englishman.'' Held up as opposites, pairing the categories of ''white'' with ''nigger'' and ''black'' with ''Englishman'' seems to be paradoxical. As Lee Erwin argues in his article '''Like in a Looking Glass': History and Narrative in *Wide Sargasso Sea*,'' such terms indicate an ''interchangeability of racial positions.'' What becomes apparent, however, is that these words have meaning beyond simple racial

designations, and really speak to the competing meanings attached to race throughout the novel. What it means to be black or white in *Wide Sargasso Sea* depends on who's telling the story. Racial difference takes on widely different meanings as the novel is narrated variously by Antoinette and Edward Rochester. Erwin suggests that Rochester ''interprets racial difference in moral and sexual terms,'' that blackness implies sexual and moral perversion, while whiteness stands for purity. Meanwhile, Erwin says that Antoinette views race ''in terms of historically specific shifts in class and economic power.'' Feeling neither black nor white, Antoinette is torn between the discourses of what race means.

Antoinette's main desire in this novel is to belong—whether with her mother, with her first (and only) friend Tia, or with her husband Edward Rochester. She is, in turn, rejected by each one. Time and again this rejection is coded as a rejection based on racial difference. Rejected alike by her white Creole mother, by her black friend, and by her

English husband, to what racial and ethnic category does Antoinette belong? As a child, Antoinette sees the gulf emerge between her and Tia. Angry at her friend, Antoinette calls Tia a ''nigger.'' This racial slur immediately shifts the meaning of their petty argument. Antoinette does not need to prove that she is right because she is white. Designating Tia as a ''cheating nigger,'' Antoinette reduces her friend to a stereotype. Tia counters by calling Antoinette a ''white nigger.'' At this moment Antoinette is forced to literally put on Tia's dress (Tia has stolen Antoinette's) and to figuratively put on the dress of the racial stereotype. As a ''white nigger'' Antoinette is, in Tia's words, not ''real white people.'' Without money, Antoinette and her family have lost position. Whiteness, in Tia's definition, signals power and wealth, and to be a ''black nigger is better than white nigger.'' To be a ''white nigger'' is to be reduced to living like one's former slaves, eating their food and wearing their clothes.

In Tia's dress and weighed down by Tia's slur, Antoinette returns home where her mother is entertaining their new English neighbors. The ragged dress contrasts with the visitors' ''beautiful clothes.'' Antoinette cannot bring herself to speak to these people who seem so different from her. When later her mother refuses to speak or look at her, Antoinette thinks to herself, ''what Tia said is true.'' As a ''white nigger'' Antoinette is further separated from a mother who has already spurned the advances of her affectionate daughter. Later, after her mother has married the English Mr. Mason, Antoinette realizes that no one would mistake her mother for English. To Antoinette, Englishness is epitomized by Mr. Mason's painting of ''The Miller's Daughter'' which depicts ''a lovely English girl with brown curls and blue eyes and a dress slipping off her shoulders'' and by Mr. Mason himself, ''so sure of himself, so without a doubt English.'' Her Creole mother is ''so without a doubt not English, but no white nigger either. Not my mother. Never had been. Never could be.'' Antoinette believes that her mother would have died if Mr. Mason had not been able to restore to her the standing and wealth of her former position. But Antoinette cannot be restored to a position she never held. She feels alienated from her mother and stepfather's position. Instead of embracing Mr. Mason as a father, Antoinette can only call him her ''white pappy,'' indicating again her distance from his whiteness and his power. For as Judith Raiskin explains in a footnote to the novel, ''big Pappy'' was a term used by Jamaican slaves to refer to their masters. In many ways, even

> ''In desiring to be black, in searching for a black ancestor, and in aligning herself with black West Indians, Rhys complicated the boundaries between black and white. . .''

though newly enriched, Antoinette is still clothed in Tia's dress.

Antoinette recognizes her affinity with Tia on her last day at Coulibri. The plantation burning, the Cosway/Mason family struggles to escape both the rising flames and the rising anger of the black mob seeking to destroy their white oppressors. At this moment, Antoinette realizes that more than Coulibri is her home. She belongs to the land and the people who inhabit it. Seeing Tia in the distance, Antoinette runs to her ''for she was all that was left of my life that had been. We had eaten the same food, slept side by side, bathed in the same river.'' This is what kinship means; this is what it means to belong. But almost at the same moment that Antoinette decides ''I will live with Tia and I will be like her,'' the hope is dashed by the rock Tia throws at her. Tia's action makes her cry as she watches the blood run down Antoinette's face. Love and friendship cannot bridge the gulf of racial difference in nineteenth-century Jamaica.

Years afterward, her mother and stepfather both dead, Antoinette follows in her mother's footsteps by marrying an Englishman, Edward Rochester. Rochester has been told that his wife is ''Creole of pure English descent.'' In the section he narrates, however, Rochester questions this heritage. When he ultimately rejects his wife, Rochester does so because he has designated her as ''black.'' Antoinette's physical features (''dark alien eyes''), fellowship with black servants, and sexual desire for her husband first make Rochester suspicious of her racial and sexual purity. Later, when he knows that she has employed the power of obeah—black magic—to seduce him, learns that she has many black half-siblings, and hears rumors of her sexual relationship with her black relative Sandi, Rochester is convinced of Antoinette's otherness. His greatest fear, as he feels simultaneously attracted to and repulsed by the exotic Caribbean, is that he is vulnerable, that he can become as alienated from Europe as Antoinette. After all, Rochester has come to Jamaica because England cannot support him. His only chance for wealth, he and his family believe, is for him to marry a Creole heiress. But what if instead of anglicizing his wife—as he tries to do by renaming her Bertha—she contaminates him? The house with the English furnishings and books in which they live on Dominica is in danger of becoming engulfed by the forest. Rochester imagines as he leaves that the house cries out: "Save me from destruction, ruin and desolation. . .But what are you doing here you folly? So near the forest. Don't you know that the forest is a dangerous place? And that the dark forest always wins? Always. If you don't, you soon will, and I can do nothing to help you." To stay English, to stay white, Rochester must reject the wild Caribbean and his wife who is of it. To him, Jamaica, Dominica, and his wife's sensuality are a dream from which he must awake. He hates what he cannot control or understand: "I hated the mountains and the hills, the rivers and the rain. I hated the sunsets of whatever colour, I hated its beauty and its magic and the secret I would never know. I hated its indifference and the cruelty which was part of its loveliness. Above all I hated her. For she belonged to the magic and the loveliness."

As the novel ends, far from the "honeymoon-house" on Dominica, and instead inside a cold attic in Thornfield Hall, Rochester's English estate, Antoinette has been banished once more from her home. Coulibri has been long in ashes, and locked up as a madwoman in England, the Caribbean exists to Antoinette only as a dream. Known now as Bertha Mason, she is glimpsed fleetingly by the readers of Charlotte Bronte's *Jane Eyre*. The madwoman in the attic, Antoinette appears, in Bronte's words, as "a discoloured face. . .a savage face. . .purple: the lips were swelled and dark; the brow furrowed; the black eyebrows raised over the bloodshot eyes." In *Jane Eyre*, Bertha *is* Rochester's Caribbean nightmare, and she is described through racialized language that connects her to the savage. Ironically, in *Wide Sargasso Sea*, it is to the European conception of the savage that Antoinette wishes to belong. Critics of Rhys's last novel notice both Antoinette Cosway's desire to be black and her political solidarity with the oppressed black workers at Coulibri. When, for instance, Antoinette hopes to live with Tia and her mother after black workers have burned down Coulibri, Erwin argues that An-

toinette "will try to be black." Despite the failure of her efforts, at the end of the novel Antoinette dreams that Tia is beckoning her, that she can finally find a home with her former friend. Sandra Drake argues in "'All that Foolishness/That All Foolishness': Race and Caribbean Culture as Thematics of Liberation in Jean Rhys' *Wide Sargasso Sea*" that when Antoinette decides to burn down Thornfield Hall, she aligns herself with the black workers who burned down Coulibri. Together they stand against imperialism and a European worldview. In Charlotte Bronte's and Edward Rochester's minds, Antoinette/Bertha is the dark Other, a woman whose Caribbean heritage, insanity, and sexual impurity mark her as black, not white. Antoinette accepts this designation to the extent that she knows she doesn't belong in cold England. However, her dream vision, her desire to "try to be black," seems as doomed as her childhood attempt. In the vision fueled by her madness, Antoinette chooses to jump to Tia and away from Rochester. But it seems that Antoinette, who has never been able to be black or white, will find the hard pavestones that greet her suicide leap as jarring as Tia's rock.

Source: Kimberly Lutz, in an essay for *Literature of Developing Nations for Students*, Gale, 2000.

Maria Olaussen

In the following essay on Jean Rhys's novel, Wide Sargasso Sea, *Maria Olaussen examines the author's narrative structure to show the construction of Rhy's own racial identity both in the context of the novel and in a larger, political context.*

Jean Rhys, while reluctantly trying to settle in England as a white West Indian, started working on her novel *Wide Sargasso Sea* with the primary intention of describing the Dominica of her childhood. In 1956, she wrote in a letter: "I still work but write mostly about the vanished West Indies of my childhood. Seems to me that wants doing badly—for never was anything more vanished or forgotten. Or lovely" (*Letters*). This preoccupation with the lost island of her childhood came very early on to be tied to another concern, that of "rescuing" the white Creole madwoman from the denigrating descriptions of her found in *Jane Eyre*. The choice of *Jane Eyre* as a starting point is important to Rhys. In one of her letters, she writes about her work on the novel: "it might be possible to unhitch the whole thing from Charlotte Brontë's novel, but I don't want to do that. It is that particular mad Creole I want to write about, not any of the other mad

Creoles'' (*Letters*). This connection to one of Britain's most well-known women writers puts Rhys's exploration of the construction of her own racial identity into a larger political context. Rhys shows awareness of the fact that the meaning of who she is as a white West Indian woman cannot be understood separately from the way this identity has been constructed in the dominant Anglo-Saxon cultural context.

Rhys worked on the novel during the 1950s and 1960s, a period of increasing West Indian immigration to Britain and of a growing awareness of the issues involved in struggles for independence in colonized countries. She sets her novel in a time that was crucial in the development of colonial history: the time just following the passing of the Abolition of Slavery Act in 1833. She focuses on the experience of the white plutocracy, people born in the West Indies who derived their wealth, status, and identity from the system of slavery. In the mid-nineteenth century, the colonies were no longer economically important for Britain. Planters often pocketed their compensation money, sold their estates, and left the island. The freed slaves bought land where they could or squatted on the estates. Estate owners who decided to stay on, therefore, were faced with a process of considerable restructuring which left many of them destitute (Williams). Rhys's primary concern was the fate of a woman belonging to a group that no longer has a place, or in John Hearne's words, ''a marginal community run over and abandoned by History.''

An important part of the exploration of the white colonial experience is an understanding of the consequences of the division between black and white. Rhys remembers a fierce longing to be part of the black community, something she expected to happen through a miracle: ''Dear God, let me be black'' (*Smile*), she used to pray. She often describes black women in contrast to white women: ''They were stronger than we were, they could walk a long way without getting tired, carry heavy weights with ease . . . Also there wasn't for them as there was for us, what I thought of as the worry of getting married . . . Black girls . . . seemed to be perfectly free'' (*Smile*). Rhys's clearly expressed longing for blackness in her letters, in her autobiography, and in her fiction has caused critics to draw the conclusion that she was concerned with issues of racial justice and that she had taken the side of black people. Lucy Wilson, for instance, looks at Rhys's black characters Christophine in *Wide Sargasso Sea* and Selina in the short story ''Let Them Call it Jazz'' and

Charlotte Brontë, pictured here, wrote Jane Eyre, *the novel upon which Rhys based* Wide Sargasso Sea.

comments on the contrast to the white characters. She sees Rhys's description of both strong and assertive black women and the weak and dependent white women as a way of fighting for justice. According to Wilson, Rhys simply describes two ways of being victimized and two ways of non-cooperation with oppressive structures. Selma James similarly sees the ending of *Wide Sargasso Sea* as a reconciliation between black and white:

> Many years before she had said, ''I will live with Tia and I will be like her.'' But first she had to let Tia know the terms on which she planned for them to be together. All she had offered Tia before was the domination of her white skin. But as Antoinette burns down the Great House which imprisons her—as Tia had burnt down the Great House which was the centre of her exploitation—Tia welcomes her home.

Elizabeth Nunez-Harrell reads Rhys's autobiographical comments on her childhood preference for a black doll over a white one as an indication of her ''sense of kinship with her black compatriots.'' Carole Angier in her biography of Rhys draws similar conclusions from Rhys's own statements about her relations to black people. Although Angier analyzes Rhys's fiction carefully, her analyses do not include a critical approach to Rhys's professed

> The specific limitations and complications connected with white womanhood did not apply to black women, and therefore Rhys sees them as 'perfectly free.'"

preference for black over white people. On the contrary, this is one of the rare instances where Angier takes Rhys's own view and hands it on unexamined.

Rhys's rather complicated attitude towards black people should be looked at in the context of her enterprise of writing the Creole madwoman's part of the story. It is the "worrying of getting married" that for her defines womanhood. The specific limitations and complications connected with white womanhood did not apply to black women, and therefore Rhys sees them as "perfectly free." Needless to say, this is not an accurate description of black women's lives but a construction which functions to define the dilemma of the white woman as a biological necessity. For a white woman, blackness as freedom means that the only way for her to be free is by miraculously changing the colour of her skin; biological determinism is thus not limited to sex alone.

This clinging to biological determinism can be understood within the context of Rhys's own lack of a clearly defined identity. Lee Erwin argues that although in *Wide Sargasso Sea* Rhys takes up her West Indian past, she cannot be said to articulate West Indian nationalism. "The novel seems rather to inhabit a limbo *between* nationalisms; it exists as a response to the loss, rather than the recovery, of a 'place-to-be-from.'" Mary Lou Emery describes Jean Rhys asking: "Am I an expatriate? Expatriate from where?" In this way, Rhys articulates the connection between place and identity which Houston A. Baker describes as follows:

> For place to be recognized by one as actually PLACE, as a personally valued locale, one must set and maintain the boundaries. If one, however, is constituted and maintained by and within boundaries set by a dominating authority, then one is not a setter of place but a prisoner of another's desire. Under the displac-

ing impress of authority even what one calls and, perhaps, feels is one's *own place* is, from the perspective of human agency, *placeless*. Bereft of determinative control of boundaries, the occupant of authorized boundaries would not be secure in his or her own eulogized world but maximally secured by another, a prisoner of interlocking, institutional arrangements of power.

In *Wide Sargasso Sea*, the starting point is this placelessness. Although Rhys's novel starts with Antoinette's childhood in Coulibri, its boundaries lie outside the novel in another woman's text. In *Jane Eyre* we have the madwoman Bertha locked up in the attic of Thornfield Hall. We know the ending of the story and thus the restrictions placed on both the narrative and the main character. The significant title "Wide Sargasso Sea" refers to the dangers of the sea voyage. Rochester first crosses the Atlantic alone to a place which threatens to destroy him, then once more, bringing his new wife to England. Both Rochester and Antoinette are transformed through this passage. Rochester gives Antoinette a new name, Bertha, and in England she finally is locked up as mad. Rhys finds her own place in *Jane Eyre*, "a prisoner of another's desire." She sets out to describe that place and, in doing that, she redefines it as her own. In her challenge to *Jane Eyre*, Rhys draws on the collective experience of black people as sought out, uprooted, and transported across the Middle Passage and finally locked up and brutally exploited for economic gain. She uses this experience and the black forms of resistance as modes through which the madwoman in *Jane Eyre* is recreated.

Another white Dominican novelist, Phyllis Shand Allfrey, also makes her white protagonists use black ways of resistance in her novel *The Orchid House*, first published in 1952. In distinction to Shand Allfrey, Rhys constructs black womanhood as exactly that which is desirable and lacking in the white woman's position. Here many critics actually repeat Rhys's wishful thinking, equating British colonial rule over all inhabitants of the colonies with the specific situation of slavery. Emery writes: "The protagonist of *Wide Sargasso Sea*, Antoinette (Bertha) Cosway Mason (Rochester), undergoes sexual and class enslavement as a white Creole woman." Such a definition of slavery disregards the actual, historical institution of slavery as experienced by black people under the domination of their white owners. That these white slave owners could also be oppressed and excluded by metropolitan politics and the fact that patriarchal oppression took on a specific meaning for a white Creole woman still did not make her share the experience of slavery. Rhys does not suggest such a "women and blacks" equation; instead, she moves within the shifting boundaries of constructed racial identities desperately trying to find her own place. Her descriptions of black women serve this purpose.

With the imprisoned madwoman in Thornfield as both starting point and end, Rhys starts her own narrative. The narrator is the madwoman but her tale is the young Antoinette's. The theme is the fear and the possibility of losing one's whiteness. The very first sentences of the novel set the tone: "They say when trouble comes close ranks, and so the white people did. But we were not in their ranks." Also the black people point out that they now lack real whiteness: "Real white people, they got gold money. They didn't look at us, nobody see them come near us. Old time white people nothing but white nigger now, and black nigger better than white nigger."

The lack of real whiteness gains increasing significance when Antoinette grows up. The meaning of her sexual identity is what ultimately determines her racial identity and vice versa. Antoinette recollects an incident where she returned home in her black friend Tia's dress to find that they had beautifully dressed white visitors. Antoinette's appearance in a black girl's torn and dirty dress causes a great deal of disturbance; it shows that she is not part of the real white people. The black servant Christophine is the one who points to the necessity for change when she says: "She run wild, she grow up worthless." Tia's dress has to be burned, and Antoinette's mother comes out of her passive state and tries to provide Antoinette with new clothes. Antoinette remembers this change in her mother: "it was my fault that she started to plan and work in a frenzy, in a fever to change our lives." Here Antoinette has a dream which is then repeated three times in the novel, each time with more clarity and detail:

> I dreamed that I was walking in the forest. Not alone. Someone who hated me was with me, out of sight. I could hear heavy footsteps coming closer and though I struggled and screamed I could not move.

This dream suggests fear of sexual violation. Antoinette fears her future when it becomes clear that she cannot grow up like Tia.

The real change, however, comes with Mr Mason, Antoinette's mother's second husband. He sees himself as a liberator; he "rescues" Antoinette from growing up worthless, from being a "white

nigger." This he does by reestablishing the black-white dichotomy, reintroducing the connection of white with wealth and domination, and the connection to England. For Antoinette the meaning of being a woman is firmly placed within a colonial context. Growing up worthless, on the other hand, is the result of a situation where the black-white dichotomy no longer exists.

The most important black character in *Wide Sargasso Sea* is the servant Christophine. She is the first character to speak within Antoinette's narrative and her voice is used to explain the behaviour of the white people. "The Jamaican ladies had never approved of my mother, 'because she pretty like pretty self' Christophine said." A description of Christophine, again, is given by Antoinette's mother Annette. Antoinette wants to know who Christophine is, her origin and her age. Annette tells her that Christophine was a wedding present from her first husband; she knows that Christophine comes from Martinique, but she doesn't know her age. Annette says:

> I don't know how old she was when they brought her to Jamaica, quite young. I don't know how old she is now. Does it matter? Why do you pester and bother me about all these things that happened long ago? Christophine stayed with me because she wanted to stay. She had her own very good reasons you may be sure. I dare say we would have died if she'd turned against us and that would have been a better fate.

Christophine's most important function as a powerful protector and nursing mother-figure is thus introduced against the backdrop of the information that she was a wedding gift. The life of the white family is now in the hands of a person who once was part of their property. The reasons for staying are Christophine's own, her age is unknown, her origin on another island. She is thus outside the sphere of what can be controlled and understood by the white family once slavery has ended.

Christophine is mentioned in her relation to Antoinette at a point in the narrative where Antoinette most clearly describes the indifference of her mother to herself: "she pushed me away, . . . without a word, as if she had decided once and for all that I was useless to her." When her own mother pushes her away and finds her 'useless,' Antoinette turns to Christophine for the mothering she needs. It is Antoinette who finds Christophine useful. "So I spent most of my time in the kitchen which was in an outbuilding some way off. Christophine slept in the little room next to it." Antoinette's mother, the white lady, develops only her feminine qualities in spite of their distressing situation. These qualities, such as beauty, fragility, dependence, and passivity, make it impossible for her to change actively their situation. They also make her unable to care for her daughter or to perform the most necessary household tasks. Antoinette's mother concentrates her energies on survival in a feminine way in that she does everything to get a new husband.

Christophine's function in the novel has to be understood within the overall context of the white woman's tale. Antoinette's narrative in Part One is a reminiscence of her childhood which carries within it an awareness of the loss of place and identity which, for her, is the meaning of womanhood. Christophine belongs to her childhood, to a period of time which is lost even before the narrative begins. Gayatri Chakravorty Spivak writes about Christophine:

> Christophine is tangential to this narrative. She cannot be contained by a novel which rewrites a canonical English text within the European novelistic tradition in the interest of the white Creole rather than the native. No perspective *critical* of imperialism can turn the Other into a self, because the project of imperialism has always already historically refracted what might have been the absolutely Other into a domesticated Other that consolidates the imperialist self.

Black feminist critics in the United States have studied black female characters in texts by white authors and pointed to the way in which these characters are constructed to fit a view of history which mystifies the oppression of black people. Although there are important differences between the American South and the Caribbean, they have the history of slavery in common. Hazel Carby argues that stereotypes about black women have their origin in slavery and furthermore that these stereotypes do not exist in isolation but should be understood in connection with dominant ideas about white women. "The dominating ideology to define the boundaries of acceptable female behavior from the 1820s until the Civil War was the 'cult of true womanhood.'" This ideology defined white women as physically delicate and saw this as an outward sign of chastity, sensitivity, and refinement; it also defined the black woman but in different terms. Here the physical strength and endurance necessary for the work required of black women were seen as signs of moral and spiritual depravity. The function of these stereotypes becomes clear only when the situation of the white slave-owning man is seen as the determining instance, the centre around which female identities were constructed. Carby writes:

The effect of black female sexuality on the white male was represented in an entirely different form from that of the figurative power of while female sexuality. Confronted by the black woman, the white man behaved in a manner that was considered to be entirely untempered by any virtuous qualities: the white male, in fact, was represented as being merely prey to the rampant sexuality of his female slaves. A basic assumption underlying the cult of true womanhood was the necessity for the white female to "civilize" the basic instincts of man. But in the face of what was constructed as the overt sexuality of the black female, excluded as she was from the parameters of virtuous possibilities, these baser male instincts were entirely uncontrolled.

In contrast to the stereotype of the black woman as a "whore," another stereotype emerged, that of the "mammy." Barbara Christian points out that also this stereotyped role has to be looked at in the context of the role of the white woman. "The mammy figure, Aunt Jemima, the most prominent black female figure in southern white literature, is in direct contrast to the ideal white woman, though both images are dependent on each other for their effectiveness." The mammy is the house slave or domestic servant, who is represented as being loyal to the white family and who has no ties to the black community; the needs of her own family do not interfere with her work for the white family. She is harmless or benevolent and can therefore be trusted with a great deal of responsibility when it comes to taking care of the white children. In this way the contradiction of considering black people less than human and at the same time entrusting the care of one's children to them is to some extent made less apparent. Christian argues that the mammy, the whore, and the conjure woman as stereotypical roles for the black woman are based on a fear of female sexuality and spiritual power. In the oral tradition of the slaves the mammy is still present as a stereotype:

> She is there as cook, housekeeper, nursemaid, seamstress, always nurturing and caring for her folk. But unlike the white southern image of mammy, she is cunning, prone to poisoning her master, and not at all content with her lot.

The complexity of Christophine as a character does not challenge these stereotypes. Christophine's relations to her own children and to the rest of the community are made to fit the needs of the white family without making Christophine's own situation seem overly oppressive. Only one of her children survived and he is now grown. She does not have a husband having chosen to be independent. Although the family unit takes on different forms because of the situation of slavery, there is ample evidence to show that such units existed and were maintained and recognized as families by the black community (Klein). Similarly, the fact that black women could have children on their own, and thus were not subject to the same rules as white settler women, does not mean that most black women did not, sooner or later, live together with men. According to Herbert S. Klein, it was common during slavery for black women in the Caribbean ''to engage in pre-marital intercourse on a rather free basis. This continued until the birth of the first child. At this point in time a woman usually settled down into a relationship which might or might not be with the child's father.'' As Hortense J. Spillers has written in an analysis of the meaning of black American kinship systems as determined by slavery,

> ''kinship'' loses meaning, *since it can be invaded at any given and arbitrary moment by the property relations*. I certainly do not mean to say that African peoples in the New World did not maintain the powerful ties of sympathy that bind blood-relations in a network of feeling, of continuity. It is precisely *that* relationship—not customarily recognized by the code of slavery—that historians have long identified as the inviolable ''Black Family.''

Rhys works within an ideological framework where property relations are given the meaning of blood-relations for black people. By describing Christophine as perfectly free of social ties and responsibilities, she makes her primary attachment to the white family seem natural. Being a white Creole woman implies the necessity of securing a husband by clinging to a definition of womanhood which makes that husband necessary in the first place. The black woman is, however, free to work and support herself. She is furthermore in a position to help the white woman in distress until the husband is found. She is not able to prevent the ultimate disaster where the white woman is victimized precisely through her womanhood, but she herself is saved because as a black woman she is excluded from that definition of womanhood.

Black feminist critics claim that it is the mystification of sexual relations between white men and black women that has given rise to the stereotype of the black whore. We find two important incidents of this kind in *Wide Sargasso Sea*. Antoinette's father is said to have had several children by his black slaves; one of these children, Daniel Cosway, approaches Rochester with fatal information about the Cosway family. This he does in revenge for not having received proper recognition as one of the family. Daniel's mother is described as a liar, some-

one who tempted Mr Cosway and then tried to trick him into taking responsibility for her son.

The second incident concerns Rochester and the servant girl Amélie on the honeymoon island. Amélie destroys what is left between Rochester and Antoinette by seducing Rochester at a crucial moment. She is scheming and finally manages to take advantage of the white man so that she can start a new life with the money she gets from him; at the same time, it is the ''white cockroach'' that she is willing to harm most ruthlessly. Thus we have the white mistress, victimized by the white servant woman who takes advantage of the white master and husband. Christophine takes the side of the white mistress when she tells Rochester, '''Why you don't take that worthless good-for-nothing girl somewhere else? But she love money like you love money—must be why you come together. Like goes to like.'''

In both these incidents the victim is the white wife. The first incident causes suffering for Antoinette's mother and later destroys Antoinette's life; the second incident brings a great deal of pain to Antoinette and constitutes a turning point in her life. The black women are not seen to suffer; even the white men are to some extent victims of their own confusion caused by the cunning of the black women. The mammy turns against the whore in defending the white mistress. The identification of black with sexual power and white with innocent confusion is further underlined through the description of Antoinette's mother: mad and abandoned, being sexually abused by her black warden while his female mate watches them, smiling maliciously.

Significantly, Rochester is the narrator of Part Two of the novel, which describes his encounters with Daniel Cosway and Amélie. In this way his confusion and fear of the island, his desire for black women, and his guilt are all narrated from his point of view. This narrative also contains the possibility of blackness for Antoinette but here blackness is given an entirely new meaning. When Daniel Cosway visits Rochester he makes a clear link between sexual promiscuity and blackness: '''Give my love to your wife—my sister,' he called after me venomously. 'You are not the first to kiss her pretty face. Pretty face, soft skin, pretty colour-not yellow like me. But my sister just the same.''' Shortly afterwards, Rochester looks at Antoinette and thinks that she looks very much like Amélie. As Lee Erwin points out,

[i]f Antoinette's racial imagination is metaphoric, based upon the wished-for substitution of one term for another, Rochester's is metonymic, constantly expressing itself as a perception of contamination from contiguity, one racial term slipping or "leaking" into another through sheer proximity, obsessively perceived as sexual.

Antoinette's own wish to be part of the black people is thus supported by Rochester's fears. Rochester's narrative gives the British point of view. This point of view starts in *Jane Eyre* and we know that what really happens next is that Antoinette goes mad and has to be incarcerated in the attic of Thornfield Hall. We also know that she will set fire to the house, kill herself, and blind Rochester. By giving Rochester a voice in the narrative, Rhys shows that this is only his perception of events. If we complement the black feminist insight about race and gender construction with analyses of nineteenth-century British definitions of womanhood, we find that sexual desire and womanhood are defined as mutually exclusive. Furthermore, Victorian psychiatrists established a link between mental illness in women and the female reproductive system. Elaine Showalter has studied these discussions and concludes that

> [i]n contrast to the rather vague and uncertain concepts of insanity in general which Victorian psychiatry produced, theories of female insanity were specifically and confidentially linked to the biological crises of the female life cyle—puberty, pregnancy, childbirth, menopause—during which the mind would be weakened and the symptoms of insanity might emerge.

In Victorian discussions, female sexuality exists as a symptom of mental illness. In 1857, William Acton found sexual desire in women only among low and immoral women whom he encountered in the divorce courts and the lunatic asylum (Hellerstein). Not surprisingly, Charlotte Brontë describes her madwoman very much in accordance with the beliefs and attitudes of her time. *Jane Eyre* provides clear indications that Rochester fears Bertha's sexuality: "Bertha Mason, the true daugther of an infamous mother, dragged me through all the hideous and degrading agonies which must attend a man bound to a wife at once intemperate and unchaste." In *Wide Sargasso Sea*, Rhys takes up this element but places it within Rochester's narrative. His encounters with the island, Amélie, Daniel Cosway, and finally Christophine's love-potion are described as a powerful illicit force, at once tempting and dangerous. The only escape is to project all the forbidden feelings onto Antoinette and define her as mad because of these feelings: "She'll loosen her black hair, and laugh and coax and flatter (a mad girl. She'll not care who she's loving.) She'll moan and cry and give herself as no sane woman would— or could. *Or could*." Rochester experiences only a brief conflict about the reality of his vision. He is aware of all that he has to give up in order to keep his view of the world intact.

> I shall never understand why, suddenly, bewilderingly, I was certain that everything I had imagined to be truth was false. False. Only the magic and the dream are true—all the rest's a lie. Let it go. Here is the secret. Here.

In Antoinette's narrative, which continues in Part Three and gives the final meaning to the events taking place in Part One, the alternative vision is expressed. The vision can only exist if the reality of England and the meaning of being a white woman in that context is denied. An identification with blackness is established as the only possible escape. In Part One, the burning of the great house at Coulibri is a final and clear manifestation of the hostility of the black people towards their oppressors. Antoinette's narrative is shaped around this event, in that everything that took place before it is reinterpreted and thus turns into premonitions. Everything that happened after the event is seen as resulting from this. The dead horse, poisoned by the black people, is one of the first signs of hostility. "Now we are marooned." is the reaction of Antoinette's mother. Mary Lou Emery argues that this term, referring to the Maroon communities of escaped slaves, might suggest for Antoinette a possible way out of the necessity of getting married and living the life of a white lady.

> Inadvertently Annette alludes to places in the island's history that Antoinette might inhabit and the wild unexplored parts of the island that may help her to survive. And she suggests possible kinship with Christophine, who, as an obeah woman, practices a magic that enables survival in dangerous and hostile environments.

When the black people burn the house and it becomes clear that white and black are irreconcilable, Antoinette chooses sides: she runs back to her black friend Tia.

> As I ran, I thought, I will live with Tia and I will be like her. Not to leave Coulibri. Not to go. Not. When I was close I saw the jagged stone in her hand but I did not see her throw it.

Here Antoinette still believes that her racial identity is simply a matter of choice, that through an act of will she can make herself belong to the black community. The rejection by Tia places Antoinette firmly within the white community and thus secures her white female identity. Significantly, Antoinette's

Aunt Cora later refers to the wound inflicted by Tia in this way: "That is healing very nicely. It won't spoil you on your wedding day." The wound inflicted through the separation of white from black did not only not spoil her on her wedding day, it was in fact a necessary prerequisite for her wedding with a British gentleman. Without that separation she would not have been able to escape the risk of 'growing up worthless.'

The feeling of impending danger is momentarily relieved at the convent. The convent represents a world where definitions of womanhood are suspended and where the necessity of counteracting black hostility and fighting for a place among the black people is no longer present. As soon as Antoinette is visited by Mr Mason the security vanishes.

> It may have been the way he smiled, but again a feeling of dismay, sadness, loss, almost choked me. This time I did not let him see it.

> It was like that morning when I found the dead horse. Say nothing and it may not be true.

> But they all knew at the convent. The girls were very curious but I would not answer their questions and for the first time I resented the nuns' cheerful faces.

> They are safe. How can they know what it can be like *outside*?

Here Antoinette has her dream for the second time. This time the dream contains even more clearly the fear of sexual violation but also an active determination not to fight or try to escape. It is significant that the visit by Mr Mason is a premonition equal to the incident of the dead horse. In this way, fear of sexual violation is linked to the rejection by Tia: Antoinette is not a black person; thus she cannot escape what lies in store for all white women.

The theme of the burning of the Great House is repeated in the third part of the novel when Antoinette in a dream sets fire to Rochester's mansion in England. This dream is described by Antoinette when she has already lost her sanity and her ability to communicate her view of the world to other people. We arrive, then, back at *Jane Eyre*, from a world of relative clarity and sanity to a world of madness. This is the result of the passage across the Sargasso Sea and the other side of *Jane Eyre*. Rhys thus invites a comparison between Antoinette's situation and that of the slaves. Antoinette is captured, sold, given a new name, transported across the sea, and locked up. She does, however, offer passive resistance; the love-potion prepared by Christophine makes Rochester think he has been poisoned. Antoinette also resists in that she refuses her new identity. In *Wide Sargasso Sea*, Bertha remains Antoinette. For her to keep this identify she is compelled to remember and to perform an important task, something which she has seen coming to her ever since the house at Coulibri was burned.

> There is no looking glass here and I don't know what I am like now. I remember watching myself brush my hair and how my eyes looked back at me. The girl I saw was myself yet not quite myself. Long ago when I was a child and very lonely I tried to kiss her. But the glass was between us—hard, cold and misted over with my breath. Now they have taken everything away. What am I doing in this place and who am I?

Shortly afterwards, Antoinette has her dream for the third time. Now the dream is clear; she knows why she was brought to England. Antoinette is far from a passive victim. She is determined to fulfil her mission even though its significance lies entirely in the West Indies of her childhood. The confrontation with her mirror image in the hall brings her great confusion, and it is only by escaping that image that she can hold on to the significance of her dream. She calls to Christophine for help and miraculously escapes "the ghost" in the mirror.

The struggle for "Antoinette" against "Bertha" continues through the last part of the novel. "Antoinette" is connected to the island and the power of Christophine's obeah, whereas Rochester's attempts to turn her into a Victorian woman is in Part Two rejected by Antoinette as just another form of obeah. In the dream, Antoinette sees the Coulibri of her childhood in the red sky:

> I saw my doll's house and the books and the picture of the Miller's Daughter. I heard the parrot call as he did when he saw a stranger, *Qui est là? Qui est là?* and the man who hated me was calling too, Bertha! Bertha! The wind caught my hair and it streamed out like wings. It might bear me up, I thought, if I jumped to those hard stones. But when I looked over the edge I saw the pool at Coulibri. Tia was there. She beckoned to me and when I hesitated, she laughed. I heard her say, You frightened? And I heard the man's voice, Bertha! Bertha! All this I saw and heard in a fraction of a second. And the sky so red. Someone screamed and I thought, *Why did I scream?* I called "Tia!" and jumped and woke.

The dream finally shows her what she is supposed to do: "Now at last I know why I was brought here and what I have to do." The second burning implies liberation and fulfillment and this meaning it derives by refusing the English context. At the event at Coulibri the whole family was saved by their parrot, which frightened the superstitious black people when it was falling off the railing with its clipped wings alight. Antoinette embodies the burning parrot when she jumps down from the battlement at Thornfield Hall, her hair aflame. As Wilson Harris suggests, Rhys here evokes the black legend of flying to freedom. In Virginia Hamilton's retelling of the legend ''The People Could Fly'' some slaves knew how to fly already in Africa but had to shed their wings on the slave ship. They thus looked the same as all other slaves but owned the secret knowledge and flew away to freedom when the situation in the fields became unbearable. The Master ''said it was a lie, a trick of the light'' (Hamilton). Rhys similarly invokes a secret knowledge which changes the meaning of her actions, a mission which will give her a new identity outside of that prescribed for her by patriarchal demands. The Master will always have his own interpretation of events, but within this frame Antoinette creates her own alternative.

It is finally the combination of both Rochester's and Antoinette's narratives that points towards blackness as the escape from white femininity. Lee Erwin sees Rochester's narrative as determinate in this respect: ''The impossible desire evident in Antoinette's narrative, that is, to occupy a racial position not open to her, can only realize itself in the gaze of the Other, in an attempt to perform the impossible feat of seeing herself from the place from which she is seen.'' Antoinette's use of black strategies of resistance reinforces the meaning of blackness as freedom. In exploring the construction of a particular white female identity, Rhys denies the existence of systematic oppression of black women. They, in turn, become ''prisoners of another's desire'' as the white Creole madwoman is set free.

Source: Maria Olaussen, ''Jean Rhys's Construction of Blackness as Escape from White Femininity in 'Wide Sargasso Sea,''' in *ARIEL,* Vol. 24, No. 2, April, 1993, pp. 65–82.

Drake, Sandra, '''All that Foolishness/That All Foolishness': Race and Caribbean Culture as Thematics of Liberation in Jean Rhys' *Wide Sargasso Sea*,'' *Critica*, Vol. 2, No. 2, Fall, 1990, pp. 97-112.

Emery, Mary Lou, ''Modernist Crosscurrents,'' in her *Jean Rhys at World's End: Novels of Colonial and Sexual Exile*, University of Texas Press, 1990, pp. 7-20.

Erwin, Lee, '''Like in a Looking Glass': History and Narrative in *Wide Sargasso Sea*,'' *Novel*, Vol. 22, No. 2, Winter, 1989, pp. 143-58.

Frickey, Pierette M., ''Introduction,'' in *Critical Perspectives on Jean Rhys*, edited by Pierrette M. Frickey, Three Continents Press, 1990, pp. 1-13.

Nunez-Harrell, Elizabeth, ''The Paradoxes of Belonging: The White West Indian Woman in Fiction,'' in *Modern Fiction Studies*, Vol. 31, No. 2, Summer, 1985, pp. 281-93.

Raiskin, Judith L., ''Notes,'' in her *Wide Sargasso Sea: Backgrounds, Criticisms*, by Jean Rhys, edited by Judith L. Raiskin, W.W. Norton and Company, 1999, pp. 20, 149.

———, ''Preface,'' in her *Wide Sargasso Sea: Backgrounds, Criticisms*, by Jean Rhys, edited by Judith L. Raiskin, W. W. Norton and Company, 1999, pp. ix-xii.

Ramchand, Kenneth, *An Introduction to the Study of West Indian Literature*, Thomas Nelson and Sons, 1976, pp. 91-107.

Rhys, Jean, ''The Bible Is Modern,'' in *Wide Sargasso Sea: Backgrounds, Criticisms*, edited by Judith L. Raiskin, W. W. Norton and Company, 1999, pp. 148-49.

———, ''Black Exercise Book,'' in *Wide Sargasso Sea: Backgrounds, Criticisms*, edited by Judith L. Raiskin, W. W. Norton and Company, 1999, pp. 155-56.

———, ''Selected Letters,'' in *Wide Sargasso Sea: Backgrounds, Criticisms*, edited by Judith L. Raiskin, W. W. Norton and Company, 1999, pp. 132-45.

———, *Smile Please: An Unfinished Autobiography*, Harper and Row, 1979.

Sternlicht, Sanford, ''*Wide Sargasso Sea*,'' in his *Jean Rhys*, Twayne, 1997.

Thorpe, Michael, '''The Other Side': *Wide Sargasso Sea* and *Jane Eyre*,'' in *Ariel*, Vol. 8, No. 3, July, 1977, pp. 99-110.

Williams, Eric, ''The Slaves and Slavery,'' in his *Capitalism and Slavery*, The University of North Carolina Press, 1994, pp. 197-208.

Sources

Allen, Walter, review, in *New York Times Book Review*, June 18, 1967, p. 5.

Alvarez, A., ''The Best Living English Novelist,'' in *New York Times Book Review*, March 17, 1974, pp. 6-7.

Bronte, Charlotte, *Jane Eyre*, Penguin Classics, 1985.

Carson, Rachel, ''The Sargasso Sea,'' in *Wide Sargasso Sea: Backgrounds, Criticisms*, edited by Judith L. Raiskin, W. W. Norton and Company, 1999, pp. 117-19.

Further Reading

Ramchand, Kenneth, ''*Wide Sargasso Sea*,'' in *Critical Perspectives on Jean Rhys*, edited by Pierrette M. Frickey, Three Continents Press, 1990.

Ramchand argues that *Wide Sargasso Sea* truly is a West Indian novel. However, he believes that ''to say a novel is West Indian is not to deny its accessibility to a non-West Indian, nor indeed to deny the validity of a non-West Indian's reading.''

Sternlicht, Sanford, *Jean Rhys*, Twayne, 1997.
This critical biography of Jean Rhys provides information on Rhys's life as well as an analysis of each of her works. The chapter on *Wide Sargasso Sea* describes the novel's major themes.

Thomas, Sue, *The Worlding of Jean Rhys*, Greenwood Press, 1999.
In this book, Thomas explains that she "wanted to begin to understand Rhys's locations, the manner in which she situates her authorial and narrative voices politically and ethically in relation to the worlds of her fiction and autobiographical writing."

Glossary of Literary Terms

A

Aestheticism: A literary and artistic movement of the nineteenth century. Followers of the movement believed that art should not be mixed with social, political, or moral teaching. The statement "art for art's sake" is a good summary of aestheticism. The movement had its roots in France, but it gained widespread importance in England in the last half of the nineteenth century, where it helped change the Victorian practice of including moral lessons in literature. Edgar Allan Poe is one of the best-known American "aesthetes."

Allegory: A narrative technique in which characters representing things or abstract ideas are used to convey a message or teach a lesson. Allegory is typically used to teach moral, ethical, or religious lessons but is sometimes used for satiric or political purposes. Many fairy tales are allegories.

Allusion: A reference to a familiar literary or historical person or event, used to make an idea more easily understood. Joyce Carol Oates's story "Where Are You Going, Where Have You Been?" exhibits several allusions to popular music.

Analogy: A comparison of two things made to explain something unfamiliar through its similarities to something familiar, or to prove one point based on the acceptance of another. Similes and metaphors are types of analogies.

Antagonist: The major character in a narrative or drama who works against the hero or protagonist. The Misfit in Flannery O'Connor's story "A Good Man Is Hard to Find" serves as the antagonist for the Grandmother.

Anthology: A collection of similar works of literature, art, or music. Zora Neale Hurston's "The Eatonville Anthology" is a collection of stories that take place in the same town.

Anthropomorphism: The presentation of animals or objects in human shape or with human characteristics. The term is derived from the Greek word for "human form." The fur necklet in Katherine Mansfield's story "Miss Brill" has anthropomorphic characteristics.

Anti-hero: A central character in a work of literature who lacks traditional heroic qualities such as courage, physical prowess, and fortitude. Anti-heroes typically distrust conventional values and are unable to commit themselves to any ideals. They generally feel helpless in a world over which they have no control. Anti-heroes usually accept, and often celebrate, their positions as social outcasts. A well-known anti-hero is Walter Mitty in James Thurber's story "The Secret Life of Walter Mitty."

Archetype: The word archetype is commonly used to describe an original pattern or model from which all other things of the same kind are made. Archetypes are the literary images that grow out of the "collective unconscious,'' a theory proposed by psychologist Carl Jung. They appear in literature as incidents and plots that repeat basic patterns of life. They may also appear as stereotyped characters. The ''schlemiel'' of Yiddish literature is an archetype.

Autobiography: A narrative in which an individual tells his or her life story. Examples include Benjamin Franklin's *Autobiography* and Amy Hempel's story ''In the Cemetery Where Al Jolson Is Buried,'' which has autobiographical characteristics even though it is a work of fiction.

Avant-garde: A literary term that describes new writing that rejects traditional approaches to literature in favor of innovations in style or content. Twentieth-century examples of the literary *avant-garde* include the modernists and the minimalists.

B

Belles-lettres: A French term meaning ''fine letters'' or ''beautiful writing.'' It is often used as a synonym for literature, typically referring to imaginative and artistic rather than scientific or expository writing. Current usage sometimes restricts the meaning to light or humorous writing and appreciative essays about literature. Lewis Carroll's *Alice in Wonderland* epitomizes the realm of belles-lettres.

Bildungsroman: A German word meaning ''novel of development.'' The *bildungsroman* is a study of the maturation of a youthful character, typically brought about through a series of social or sexual encounters that lead to self-awareness. J. D. Salinger's *Catcher in the Rye* is a *bildungsroman*, and Doris Lessing's story ''Through the Tunnel'' exhibits characteristics of a *bildungsroman* as well.

Black Aesthetic Movement: A period of artistic and literary development among African Americans in the 1960s and early 1970s. This was the first major African-American artistic movement since the Harlem Renaissance and was closely paralleled by the civil rights and black power movements. The black aesthetic writers attempted to produce works of art that would be meaningful to the black masses. Key figures in black aesthetics included one of its founders, poet and playwright Amiri Baraka, formerly known as LeRoi Jones; poet and essayist Haki R. Madhubuti, formerly Don L. Lee; poet and playwright Sonia Sanchez; and dramatist Ed Bullins. Works representative of the Black Aesthetic Movement include Amiri Baraka's play *Dutchman,* a 1964 Obie award-winner.

Black Humor: Writing that places grotesque elements side by side with humorous ones in an attempt to shock the reader, forcing him or her to laugh at the horrifying reality of a disordered world. ''Lamb to the Slaughter,'' by Roald Dahl, in which a placid housewife murders her husband and serves the murder weapon to the investigating policemen, is an example of black humor.

C

Catharsis: The release or purging of unwanted emotions—specifically fear and pity—brought about by exposure to art. The term was first used by the Greek philosopher Aristotle in his *Poetics* to refer to the desired effect of tragedy on spectators.

Character: Broadly speaking, a person in a literary work. The actions of characters are what constitute the plot of a story, novel, or poem. There are numerous types of characters, ranging from simple, stereotypical figures to intricate, multifaceted ones. ''Characterization'' is the process by which an author creates vivid, believable characters in a work of art. This may be done in a variety of ways, including (1) direct description of the character by the narrator; (2) the direct presentation of the speech, thoughts, or actions of the character; and (3) the responses of other characters to the character. The term ''character'' also refers to a form originated by the ancient Greek writer Theophrastus that later became popular in the seventeenth and eighteenth centuries. It is a short essay or sketch of a person who prominently displays a specific attribute or quality, such as miserliness or ambition. ''Miss Brill,'' a story by Katherine Mansfield, is an example of a character sketch.

Classical: In its strictest definition in literary criticism, classicism refers to works of ancient Greek or Roman literature. The term may also be used to describe a literary work of recognized importance (a ''classic'') from any time period or literature that exhibits the traits of classicism. Examples of later works and authors now described as classical include French literature of the seventeenth century, Western novels of the nineteenth century, and American fiction of the mid-nineteenth century such as that written by James Fenimore Cooper and Mark Twain.

Climax: The turning point in a narrative, the moment when the conflict is at its most intense. Typically, the structure of stories, novels, and plays is one of rising action, in which tension builds to the climax, followed by falling action, in which tension lessens as the story moves to its conclusion.

Comedy: One of two major types of drama, the other being tragedy. Its aim is to amuse, and it typically ends happily. Comedy assumes many forms, such as farce and burlesque, and uses a variety of techniques, from parody to satire. In a restricted sense the term comedy refers only to dramatic presentations, but in general usage it is commonly applied to nondramatic works as well.

Comic Relief: The use of humor to lighten the mood of a serious or tragic story, especially in plays. The technique is very common in Elizabethan works, and can be an integral part of the plot or simply a brief event designed to break the tension of the scene.

Conflict: The conflict in a work of fiction is the issue to be resolved in the story. It usually occurs between two characters, the protagonist and the antagonist, or between the protagonist and society or the protagonist and himself or herself. The conflict in Washington Irving's story "The Devil and Tom Walker" is that the Devil wants Tom Walker's soul but Tom does not want to go to hell.

Criticism: The systematic study and evaluation of literary works, usually based on a specific method or set of principles. An important part of literary studies since ancient times, the practice of criticism has given rise to numerous theories, methods, and "schools," sometimes producing conflicting, even contradictory, interpretations of literature in general as well as of individual works. Even such basic issues as what constitutes a poem or a novel have been the subject of much criticism over the centuries. Seminal texts of literary criticism include Plato's *Republic,* Aristotle's *Poetics,* Sir Philip Sidney's *The Defence of Poesie,* and John Dryden's *Of Dramatic Poesie.* Contemporary schools of criticism include deconstruction, feminist, psychoanalytic, poststructuralist, new historicist, postcolonialist, and reader-response.

D

Deconstruction: A method of literary criticism characterized by multiple conflicting interpretations of a given work. Deconstructionists consider the impact of the language of a work and suggest that the true meaning of the work is not necessarily the meaning that the author intended.

Deduction: The process of reaching a conclusion through reasoning from general premises to a specific premise. Arthur Conan Doyle's character Sherlock Holmes often used deductive reasoning to solve mysteries.

Denotation: The definition of a word, apart from the impressions or feelings it creates in the reader. The word "apartheid" denotes a political and economic policy of segregation by race, but its connotations—oppression, slavery, inequality—are numerous.

Denouement: A French word meaning "the unknotting." In literature, it denotes the resolution of conflict in fiction or drama. The *denouement* follows the climax and provides an outcome to the primary plot situation as well as an explanation of secondary plot complications. A well-known example of *denouement* is the last scene of the play *As You Like It* by William Shakespeare, in which couples are married, an evildoer repents, the identities of two disguised characters are revealed, and a ruler is restored to power. Also known as "falling action."

Detective Story: A narrative about the solution of a mystery or the identification of a criminal. The conventions of the detective story include the detective's scrupulous use of logic in solving the mystery; incompetent or ineffectual police; a suspect who appears guilty at first but is later proved innocent; and the detective's friend or confidant—often the narrator—whose slowness in interpreting clues emphasizes by contrast the detective's brilliance. Edgar Allan Poe's "Murders in the Rue Morgue" is commonly regarded as the earliest example of this type of story. Other practitioners are Arthur Conan Doyle, Dashiell Hammett, and Agatha Christie.

Dialogue: Dialogue is conversation between people in a literary work. In its most restricted sense, it refers specifically to the speech of characters in a drama. As a specific literary genre, a "dialogue" is a composition in which characters debate an issue or idea.

Didactic: A term used to describe works of literature that aim to teach a moral, religious, political, or practical lesson. Although didactic elements are often found in artistically pleasing works, the term "didactic" usually refers to literature in which the message is more important than the form. The term may also be used to criticize a work that the critic finds "overly didactic," that is, heavy-handed in its delivery of a lesson. An example of didactic literature is John Bunyan's *Pilgrim's Progress.*

Dramatic Irony: Occurs when the reader of a work of literature knows something that a character in the work itself does not know. The irony is in the contrast between the intended meaning of the statements or actions of a character and the additional information understood by the audience.

Dystopia: An imaginary place in a work of fiction where the characters lead dehumanized, fearful lives. **George Orwell's** *Nineteen Eighty-four,* and Margaret Atwood's *Handmaid's Tale* portray versions of dystopia.

E

Edwardian: Describes cultural conventions identified with the period of the reign of Edward VII of England (1901-1910). Writers of the Edwardian Age typically displayed a strong reaction against the propriety and conservatism of the Victorian Age. Their work often exhibits distrust of authority in religion, politics, and art and expresses strong doubts about the soundness of conventional values. Writers of this era include E. M. Forster, H. G. Wells, and Joseph Conrad.

Empathy: A sense of shared experience, including emotional and physical feelings, with someone or something other than oneself. Empathy is often used to describe the response of a reader to a literary character.

Epilogue: A concluding statement or section of a literary work. In dramas, particularly those of the seventeenth and eighteenth centuries, the epilogue is a closing speech, often in verse, delivered by an actor at the end of a play and spoken directly to the audience.

Epiphany: A sudden revelation of truth inspired by a seemingly trivial incident. The term was widely used by James Joyce in his critical writings, and the stories in Joyce's *Dubliners* are commonly called "epiphanies."

Epistolary Novel: A novel in the form of letters. The form was particularly popular in the eighteenth century. The form can also be applied to short stories, as in Edwidge Danticat's "Children of the Sea."

Epithet: A word or phrase, often disparaging or abusive, that expresses a character trait of someone or something. "The Napoleon of crime" is an epithet applied to Professor Moriarty, arch-rival of Sherlock Holmes in Arthur Conan Doyle's series of detective stories.

Existentialism: A predominantly twentieth-century philosophy concerned with the nature and perception of human existence. There are two major strains of existentialist thought: atheistic and Christian. Followers of atheistic existentialism believe that the individual is alone in a godless universe and that the basic human condition is one of suffering and loneliness. Nevertheless, because there are no fixed values, individuals can create their own characters—indeed, they can shape themselves—through the exercise of free will. The atheistic strain culminates in and is popularly associated with the works of Jean-Paul Sartre. The Christian existentialists, on the other hand, believe that only in God may people find freedom from life's anguish. The two strains hold certain beliefs in common: that existence cannot be fully understood or described through empirical effort; that anguish is a universal element of life; that individuals must bear responsibility for their actions; and that there is no common standard of behavior or perception for religious and ethical matters. Existentialist thought figures prominently in the works of such authors as Franz Kafka, Fyodor Dostoyevsky, and Albert Camus.

Expatriatism: The practice of leaving one's country to live for an extended period in another country. Literary expatriates include Irish author James Joyce who moved to Italy and France, American writers James Baldwin, Ernest Hemingway, Gertrude Stein, and F. Scott Fitzgerald who lived and wrote in Paris, and Polish novelist Joseph Conrad in England.

Exposition: Writing intended to explain the nature of an idea, thing, or theme. Expository writing is often combined with description, narration, or argument.

Expressionism: An indistinct literary term, originally used to describe an early twentieth-century school of German painting. The term applies to almost any mode of unconventional, highly subjective writing that distorts reality in some way. Advocates of Expressionism include Federico Garcia Lorca, Eugene O'Neill, Franz Kafka, and James Joyce.

F

Fable: A prose or verse narrative intended to convey a moral. Animals or inanimate objects with human characteristics often serve as characters in fables. A famous fable is Aesop's "The Tortoise and the Hare."

Fantasy: A literary form related to mythology and folklore. Fantasy literature is typically set in non-existent realms and features supernatural beings. Notable examples of literature with elements of fantasy are Gabriel Garcia Marquez's story "The Handsomest Drowned Man in the World" and Ursula K. LeGuin's "The Ones Who Walk Away from Omelas."

Farce: A type of comedy characterized by broad humor, outlandish incidents, and often vulgar subject matter. Much of the comedy in film and television could more accurately be described as farce.

Fiction: Any story that is the product of imagination rather than a documentation of fact. Characters and events in such narratives may be based in real life but their ultimate form and configuration is a creation of the author.

Figurative Language: A technique in which an author uses figures of speech such as hyperbole, irony, metaphor, or simile for a particular effect. Figurative language is the opposite of literal language, in which every word is truthful, accurate, and free of exaggeration or embellishment.

Flashback: A device used in literature to present action that occurred before the beginning of the story. Flashbacks are often introduced as the dreams or recollections of one or more characters.

Foil: A character in a work of literature whose physical or psychological qualities contrast strongly with, and therefore highlight, the corresponding qualities of another character. In his Sherlock Holmes stories, Arthur Conan Doyle portrayed Dr. Watson as a man of normal habits and intelligence, making him a foil for the eccentric and unusually perceptive Sherlock Holmes.

Folklore: Traditions and myths preserved in a culture or group of people. Typically, these are passed on by word of mouth in various forms—such as legends, songs, and proverbs—or preserved in customs and ceremonies. Washington Irving, in "The Devil and Tom Walker" and many of his other stories, incorporates many elements of the folklore of New England and Germany.

Folktale: A story originating in oral tradition. Folktales fall into a variety of categories, including legends, ghost stories, fairy tales, fables, and anecdotes based on historical figures and events.

Foreshadowing: A device used in literature to create expectation or to set up an explanation of later developments. Edgar Allan Poe uses foreshadowing to create suspense in "The Fall of the House of Usher" when the narrator comments on the crumbling state of disrepair in which he finds the house.

G

Genre: A category of literary work. Genre may refer to both the content of a given work—tragedy, comedy, horror, science fiction—and to its form, such as poetry, novel, or drama.

Gilded Age: A period in American history during the 1870s and after characterized by political corruption and materialism. A number of important novels of social and political criticism were written during this time. Henry James and Kate Chopin are two writers who were prominent during the Gilded Age.

Gothicism: In literature, works characterized by a taste for medieval or morbid characters and situations. A gothic novel prominently features elements of horror, the supernatural, gloom, and violence: clanking chains, terror, ghosts, medieval castles, and unexplained phenomena. The term "gothic novel" is also applied to novels that lack elements of the traditional Gothic setting but that create a similar atmosphere of terror or dread. The term can also be applied to stories, plays, and poems. Mary Shelley's *Frankenstein* and Joyce Carol Oates's *Bellefleur* are both gothic novels.

Grotesque: In literature, a work that is characterized by exaggeration, deformity, freakishness, and disorder. The grotesque often includes an element of comic absurdity. Examples of the grotesque can be found in the works of Edgar Allan Poe, Flannery O'Connor, Joseph Heller, and Shirley Jackson.

H

Harlem Renaissance: The Harlem Renaissance of the 1920s is generally considered the first significant movement of black writers and artists in the United States. During this period, new and established black writers, many of whom lived in the region of New York City known as Harlem, published more fiction and poetry than ever before, the first influential black literary journals were established, and black authors and artists received their first widespread recognition and serious critical appraisal. Among the major writers associated with this period are Countee Cullen, Langston Hughes, Arna Bontemps, and Zora Neale Hurston.

Hero/Heroine: The principal sympathetic character in a literary work. Heroes and heroines typically exhibit admirable traits: idealism, courage, and integrity, for example. Famous heroes and heroines of literature include Charles Dickens's Oliver Twist, Margaret Mitchell's Scarlett O'Hara, and the anonymous narrator in Ralph Ellison's *Invisible Man*.

Hyperbole: Deliberate exaggeration used to achieve an effect. In William Shakespeare's *Macbeth,* Lady Macbeth hyperbolizes when she says, "All the perfumes of Arabia could not sweeten this little hand."

I

Image: A concrete representation of an object or sensory experience. Typically, such a representation helps evoke the feelings associated with the object or experience itself. Images are either "literal" or "figurative." Literal images are especially concrete and involve little or no extension of the obvious meaning of the words used to express them. Figurative images do not follow the literal meaning of the words exactly. Images in literature are usually visual, but the term "image" can also refer to the representation of any sensory experience.

Imagery: The array of images in a literary work. Also used to convey the author's overall use of figurative language in a work.

In medias res: A Latin term meaning "in the middle of things." It refers to the technique of beginning a story at its midpoint and then using various flashback devices to reveal previous action. This technique originated in such epics as Virgil's *Aeneid.*

Interior Monologue: A narrative technique in which characters' thoughts are revealed in a way that appears to be uncontrolled by the author. The interior monologue typically aims to reveal the inner self of a character. It portrays emotional experiences as they occur at both a conscious and unconscious level. One of the best-known interior monologues in English is the Molly Bloom section at the close of James Joyce's *Ulysses.* Katherine Anne Porter's "The Jilting of Granny Weatherall" is also told in the form of an interior monologue.

Irony: In literary criticism, the effect of language in which the intended meaning is the opposite of what is stated. The title of Jonathan Swift's "A Modest Proposal" is ironic because what Swift proposes in this essay is cannibalism—hardly "modest."

J

Jargon: Language that is used or understood only by a select group of people. Jargon may refer to terminology used in a certain profession, such as computer jargon, or it may refer to any nonsensical language that is not understood by most people. Anthony Burgess's *A Clockwork Orange* and James Thurber's "The Secret Life of Walter Mitty" both use jargon.

K

Knickerbocker Group: An indistinct group of New York writers of the first half of the nineteenth century. Members of the group were linked only by location and a common theme: New York life. Two famous members of the Knickerbocker Group were Washington Irving and William Cullen Bryant. The group's name derives from Irving's *Knickerbocker's History of New York.*

L

Literal Language: An author uses literal language when he or she writes without exaggerating or embellishing the subject matter and without any tools of figurative language. To say "He ran very quickly down the street" is to use literal language, whereas to say "He ran like a hare down the street" would be using figurative language.

Literature: Literature is broadly defined as any written or spoken material, but the term most often refers to creative works. Literature includes poetry, drama, fiction, and many kinds of nonfiction writing, as well as oral, dramatic, and broadcast compositions not necessarily preserved in a written format, such as films and television programs.

Lost Generation: A term first used by Gertrude Stein to describe the post-World War I generation of American writers: men and women haunted by a sense of betrayal and emptiness brought about by the destructiveness of the war. The term is commonly applied to Hart Crane, Ernest Hemingway, F. Scott Fitzgerald, and others.

M

Magic Realism: A form of literature that incorporates fantasy elements or supernatural occurrences into the narrative and accepts them as truth. Gabriel Garcia Marquez and Laura Esquivel are two writers known for their works of magic realism.

Metaphor: A figure of speech that expresses an idea through the image of another object. Metaphors suggest the essence of the first object by identifying it with certain qualities of the second object. An example is "But soft, what light through yonder window breaks?/ It is the east, and Juliet is the sun" in William Shakespeare's *Romeo and Juliet.* Here, Juliet, the first object, is identified with qualities of the second object, the sun.

Minimalism: A literary style characterized by spare, simple prose with few elaborations. In minimalism, the main theme of the work is often never discussed directly. Amy Hempel and Ernest Hemingway are two writers known for their works of minimalism.

Modernism: Modern literary practices. Also, the principles of a literary school that lasted from roughly the beginning of the twentieth century until the end of World War II. Modernism is defined by its rejection of the literary conventions of the nineteenth century and by its opposition to conventional morality, taste, traditions, and economic values. Many writers are associated with the concepts of modernism, including Albert Camus, D. H. Lawrence, Ernest Hemingway, William Faulkner, Eugene O'Neill, and James Joyce.

Monologue: A composition, written or oral, by a single individual. More specifically, a speech given by a single individual in a drama or other public entertainment. It has no set length, although it is usually several or more lines long. "I Stand Here Ironing" by Tillie Olsen is an example of a story written in the form of a monologue.

Mood: The prevailing emotions of a work or of the author in his or her creation of the work. The mood of a work is not always what might be expected based on its subject matter.

Motif: A theme, character type, image, metaphor, or other verbal element that recurs throughout a single work of literature or occurs in a number of different works over a period of time. For example, the color white in Herman Melville's *Moby Dick* is a "specific" *motif,* while the trials of star-crossed lovers is a "conventional" *motif* from the literature of all periods.

N

Narration: The telling of a series of events, real or invented. A narration may be either a simple narrative, in which the events are recounted chronologically, or a narrative with a plot, in which the account is given in a style reflecting the author's artistic concept of the story. Narration is sometimes used as a synonym for "storyline."

Narrative: A verse or prose accounting of an event or sequence of events, real or invented. The term is also used as an adjective in the sense "method of narration." For example, in literary criticism, the expression "narrative technique" usually refers to the way the author structures and presents his or her story. Different narrative forms include diaries, travelogues, novels, ballads, epics, short stories, and other fictional forms.

Narrator: The teller of a story. The narrator may be the author or a character in the story through whom the author speaks. Huckleberry Finn is the narrator of Mark Twain's *The Adventures of Huckleberry Finn.*

Novella: An Italian term meaning "story." This term has been especially used to describe fourteenth-century Italian tales, but it also refers to modern short novels. Modern novellas include Leo Tolstoy's *The Death of Ivan Ilich,* Fyodor Dostoyevsky's *Notes from the Underground,* and Joseph Conrad's *Heart of Darkness.*

O

Oedipus Complex: A son's romantic obsession with his mother. The phrase is derived from the story of the ancient Theban hero Oedipus, who unknowingly killed his father and married his mother, and was popularized by Sigmund Freud's theory of psychoanalysis. Literary occurrences of the Oedipus complex include Sophocles' *Oedipus Rex* and D. H. Lawrence's "The Rocking-Horse Winner."

Onomatopoeia: The use of words whose sounds express or suggest their meaning. In its simplest sense, onomatopoeia may be represented by words that mimic the sounds they denote such as "hiss" or "meow." At a more subtle level, the pattern and rhythm of sounds and rhymes of a line or poem may be onomatopoeic.

Oral Tradition: A process by which songs, ballads, folklore, and other material are transmitted by word of mouth. The tradition of oral transmission predates the written record systems of literate society.

Oral transmission preserves material sometimes over generations, although often with variations. Memory plays a large part in the recitation and preservation of orally transmitted material. Native American myths and legends, and African folktales told by plantation slaves are examples of orally transmitted literature.

P

Parable: A story intended to teach a moral lesson or answer an ethical question. Examples of parables are the stories told by Jesus Christ in the New Testament, notably ''The Prodigal Son,'' but parables also are used in Sufism, rabbinic literature, Hasidism, and Zen Buddhism. Isaac Bashevis Singer's story ''Gimpel the Fool'' exhibits characteristics of a parable.

Paradox: A statement that appears illogical or contradictory at first, but may actually point to an underlying truth. A literary example of a paradox is George Orwell's statement ''All animals are equal, but some animals are more equal than others'' in *Animal Farm.*

Parody: In literature, this term refers to an imitation of a serious literary work or the signature style of a particular author in a ridiculous manner. A typical parody adopts the style of the original and applies it to an inappropriate subject for humorous effect. Parody is a form of satire and could be considered the literary equivalent of a caricature or cartoon. Henry Fielding's *Shamela* is a parody of Samuel Richardson's *Pamela.*

Persona: A Latin term meaning ''mask.'' Personae are the characters in a fictional work of literature. The persona generally functions as a mask through which the author tells a story in a voice other than his or her own. A persona is usually either a character in a story who acts as a narrator or an ''implied author,'' a voice created by the author to act as the narrator for himself or herself. The persona in Charlotte Perkins Gilman's story ''The Yellow Wallpaper'' is the unnamed young mother experiencing a mental breakdown.

Personification: A figure of speech that gives human qualities to abstract ideas, animals, and inanimate objects. To say that ''the sun is smiling'' is to personify the sun.

Plot: The pattern of events in a narrative or drama. In its simplest sense, the plot guides the author in composing the work and helps the reader follow the work. Typically, plots exhibit causality and unity and have a beginning, a middle, and an end. Sometimes, however, a plot may consist of a series of disconnected events, in which case it is known as an ''episodic plot.''

Poetic Justice: An outcome in a literary work, not necessarily a poem, in which the good are rewarded and the evil are punished, especially in ways that particularly fit their virtues or crimes. For example, a murderer may himself be murdered, or a thief will find himself penniless.

Poetic License: Distortions of fact and literary convention made by a writer—not always a poet— for the sake of the effect gained. Poetic license is closely related to the concept of ''artistic freedom.'' An author exercises poetic license by saying that a pile of money ''reaches as high as a mountain'' when the pile is actually only a foot or two high.

Point of View: The narrative perspective from which a literary work is presented to the reader. There are four traditional points of view. The ''third person omniscient'' gives the reader a ''godlike'' perspective, unrestricted by time or place, from which to see actions and look into the minds of characters. This allows the author to comment openly on characters and events in the work. The ''third person'' point of view presents the events of the story from outside of any single character's perception, much like the omniscient point of view, but the reader must understand the action as it takes place and without any special insight into characters' minds or motivations. The ''first person'' or ''personal'' point of view relates events as they are perceived by a single character. The main character ''tells'' the story and may offer opinions about the action and characters which differ from those of the author. Much less common than omniscient, third person, and first person is the ''second person'' point of view, wherein the author tells the story as if it is happening to the reader. James Thurber employs the omniscient point of view in his short story ''The Secret Life of Walter Mitty.'' Ernest Hemingway's ''A Clean, Well-Lighted Place'' is a short story told from the third person point of view. Mark Twain's novel *Huckleberry Finn* is presented from the first person viewpoint. Jay McInerney's *Bright Lights, Big City* is an example of a novel which uses the second person point of view.

Pornography: Writing intended to provoke feelings of lust in the reader. Such works are often condemned by critics and teachers, but those which can be shown to have literary value are viewed less harshly. Literary works that have been described as pornographic include D. H. Lawrence's *Lady Chatterley's Lover* and James Joyce's *Ulysses.*

Post-Aesthetic Movement: An artistic response made by African Americans to the black aesthetic movement of the 1960s and early 1970s. Writers since that time have adopted a somewhat different tone in their work, with less emphasis placed on the disparity between black and white in the United States. In the words of post-aesthetic authors such as Toni Morrison, John Edgar Wideman, and Kristin Hunter, African Americans are portrayed as looking inward for answers to their own questions, rather than always looking to the outside world. Two well-known examples of works produced as part of the post-aesthetic movement are the Pulitzer Prize-winning novels *The Color Purple* by Alice Walker and *Beloved* by Toni Morrison.

Postmodernism: Writing from the 1960s forward characterized by experimentation and application of modernist elements, which include existentialism and alienation. Postmodernists have gone a step further in the rejection of tradition begun with the modernists by also rejecting traditional forms, preferring the anti-novel over the novel and the anti-hero over the hero. Postmodern writers include Thomas Pynchon, Margaret Drabble, and Gabriel Garcia Marquez.

Prologue: An introductory section of a literary work. It often contains information establishing the situation of the characters or presents information about the setting, time period, or action. In drama, the prologue is spoken by a chorus or by one of the principal characters.

Prose: A literary medium that attempts to mirror the language of everyday speech. It is distinguished from poetry by its use of unmetered, unrhymed language consisting of logically related sentences. Prose is usually grouped into paragraphs that form a cohesive whole such as an essay or a novel. The term is sometimes used to mean an author's general writing.

Protagonist: The central character of a story who serves as a focus for its themes and incidents and as the principal rationale for its development. The protagonist is sometimes referred to in discussions of modern literature as the hero or anti-hero. Well-known protagonists are Hamlet in William Shakespeare's *Hamlet* and Jay Gatsby in F. Scott Fitzgerald's *The Great Gatsby.*

R

Realism: A nineteenth-century European literary movement that sought to portray familiar characters, situations, and settings in a realistic manner. This was done primarily by using an objective narrative point of view and through the buildup of accurate detail. The standard for success of any realistic work depends on how faithfully it transfers common experience into fictional forms. The realistic method may be altered or extended, as in stream of consciousness writing, to record highly subjective experience. Contemporary authors who often write in a realistic way include Nadine Gordimer and Grace Paley.

Resolution: The portion of a story following the climax, in which the conflict is resolved. The resolution of Jane Austen's *Northanger Abbey* is neatly summed up in the following sentence: ''Henry and Catherine were married, the bells rang and every body smiled.''

Rising Action: The part of a drama where the plot becomes increasingly complicated. Rising action leads up to the climax, or turning point, of a drama. The final ''chase scene'' of an action film is generally the rising action which culminates in the film's climax.

Roman a clef: A French phrase meaning ''novel with a key.'' It refers to a narrative in which real persons are portrayed under fictitious names. Jack Kerouac, for example, portrayed various his friends under fictitious names in the novel *On the Road.* D. H. Lawrence based ''The Rocking-Horse Winner'' on a family he knew.

Romanticism: This term has two widely accepted meanings. In historical criticism, it refers to a European intellectual and artistic movement of the late eighteenth and early nineteenth centuries that sought greater freedom of personal expression than that allowed by the strict rules of literary form and logic of the eighteenth-century neoclassicists. The Romantics preferred emotional and imaginative expression to rational analysis. They considered the individual to be at the center of all experience and so placed him or her at the center of their art. The Romantics believed that the creative imagination reveals nobler truths—unique feelings and attitudes—than those that could be discovered by logic or by scientific examination. ''Romanticism'' is also used as a general term to refer to a type of sensibility found in all periods of literary history and usually considered to be in opposition to the principles of classicism. In this sense, Romanticism signifies any work or philosophy in which the exotic or dreamlike figure strongly, or that is devoted to individualistic expression, self-analysis, or a pursuit of a higher realm of knowledge than can be discovered by human reason. Prominent Romantics include Jean-Jacques Rousseau, William Wordsworth, John Keats, Lord Byron, and Johann Wolfgang von Goethe.

S

Satire: A work that uses ridicule, humor, and wit to criticize and provoke change in human nature and institutions. Voltaire's novella *Candide* and Jonathan Swift's essay "A Modest Proposal" are both satires. Flannery O'Connor's portrayal of the family in "A Good Man Is Hard to Find" is a satire of a modern, Southern, American family.

Science Fiction: A type of narrative based upon real or imagined scientific theories and technology. Science fiction is often peopled with alien creatures and set on other planets or in different dimensions. Popular writers of science fiction are Isaac Asimov, Karel Capek, Ray Bradbury, and Ursula K. Le Guin.

Setting: The time, place, and culture in which the action of a narrative takes place. The elements of setting may include geographic location, characters's physical and mental environments, prevailing cultural attitudes, or the historical time in which the action takes place.

Short Story: A fictional prose narrative shorter and more focused than a novella. The short story usually deals with a single episode and often a single character. The "tone," the author's attitude toward his or her subject and audience, is uniform throughout. The short story frequently also lacks *denouement*, ending instead at its climax.

Signifying Monkey: A popular trickster figure in black folklore, with hundreds of tales about this character documented since the 19th century. Henry Louis Gates Jr. examines the history of the signifying monkey in *The Signifying Monkey: Towards a Theory of Afro-American Literary Criticism,* published in 1988.

Simile: A comparison, usually using "like" or "as," of two essentially dissimilar things, as in "coffee as cold as ice" or "He sounded like a broken record." The title of Ernest Hemingway's "Hills Like White Elephants" contains a simile.

Social Realism: The Socialist Realism school of literary theory was proposed by Maxim Gorky and established as a dogma by the first Soviet Congress of Writers. It demanded adherence to a communist worldview in works of literature. Its doctrines required an objective viewpoint comprehensible to the working classes and themes of social struggle featuring strong proletarian heroes. Gabriel Garcia Marquez's stories exhibit some characteristics of Socialist Realism.

Stereotype: A stereotype was originally the name for a duplication made during the printing process; this led to its modern definition as a person or thing that is (or is assumed to be) the same as all others of its type. Common stereotypical characters include the absent-minded professor, the nagging wife, the troublemaking teenager, and the kindhearted grandmother.

Stream of Consciousness: A narrative technique for rendering the inward experience of a character. This technique is designed to give the impression of an ever-changing series of thoughts, emotions, images, and memories in the spontaneous and seemingly illogical order that they occur in life. The textbook example of stream of consciousness is the last section of James Joyce's *Ulysses*.

Structure: The form taken by a piece of literature. The structure may be made obvious for ease of understanding, as in nonfiction works, or may be obscured for artistic purposes, as in some poetry or seemingly "unstructured" prose.

Style: A writer's distinctive manner of arranging words to suit his or her ideas and purpose in writing. The unique imprint of the author's personality upon his or her writing, style is the product of an author's way of arranging ideas and his or her use of diction, different sentence structures, rhythm, figures of speech, rhetorical principles, and other elements of composition.

Suspense: A literary device in which the author maintains the audience's attention through the build-up of events, the outcome of which will soon be revealed. Suspense in William Shakespeare's *Hamlet* is sustained throughout by the question of whether or not the Prince will achieve what he has been instructed to do and of what he intends to do.

Symbol: Something that suggests or stands for something else without losing its original identity. In literature, symbols combine their literal meaning with the suggestion of an abstract concept. Literary symbols are of two types: those that carry complex associations of meaning no matter what their contexts, and those that derive their suggestive meaning from their functions in specific literary works. Examples of symbols are sunshine suggesting happiness, rain suggesting sorrow, and storm clouds suggesting despair.

T

Tale: A story told by a narrator with a simple plot and little character development. Tales are usually relatively short and often carry a simple message. Examples of tales can be found in the works of Saki, Anton Chekhov, Guy de Maupassant, and O. Henry.

Tall Tale: A humorous tale told in a straightforward, credible tone but relating absolutely impossible events or feats of the characters. Such tales were commonly told of frontier adventures during the settlement of the west in the United States. Literary use of tall tales can be found in Washington Irving's *History of New York,* Mark Twain's *Life on the Mississippi,* and in the German R. F. Raspe's *Baron Munchausen's Narratives of His Marvellous Travels and Campaigns in Russia.*

Theme: The main point of a work of literature. The term is used interchangeably with thesis. Many works have multiple themes. One of the themes of Nathaniel Hawthorne's "Young Goodman Brown" is loss of faith.

Tone: The author's attitude toward his or her audience may be deduced from the tone of the work. A formal tone may create distance or convey politeness, while an informal tone may encourage a friendly, intimate, or intrusive feeling in the reader. The author's attitude toward his or her subject matter may also be deduced from the tone of the words he or she uses in discussing it. The tone of John F. Kennedy's speech which included the appeal to "ask not what your country can do for you" was intended to instill feelings of camaraderie and national pride in listeners.

Tragedy: A drama in prose or poetry about a noble, courageous hero of excellent character who, because of some tragic character flaw, brings ruin upon him- or herself. Tragedy treats its subjects in a dignified and serious manner, using poetic language to help evoke pity and fear and bring about catharsis, a purging of these emotions. The tragic form was practiced extensively by the ancient Greeks. The classical form of tragedy was revived in the sixteenth century; it flourished especially on the Elizabethan stage. In modern times, dramatists have attempted to adapt the form to the needs of modern society by drawing their heroes from the ranks of ordinary men and women and defining the nobility of these heroes in terms of spirit rather than exalted social standing. Some contemporary works that are thought of as tragedies include *The Great Gatsby* by F. Scott Fitzgerald, and *The Sound and the Fury* by William Faulkner.

Tragic Flaw: In a tragedy, the quality within the hero or heroine which leads to his or her downfall. Examples of the tragic flaw include Othello's jealousy and Hamlet's indecisiveness, although most great tragedies defy such simple interpretation.

U

Utopia: A fictional perfect place, such as "paradise" or "heaven." An early literary utopia was described in Plato's *Republic,* and in modern literature, Ursula K. Le Guin depicts a utopia in "The Ones Who Walk Away from Omelas."

V

Victorian: Refers broadly to the reign of Queen Victoria of England (1837-1901) and to anything with qualities typical of that era. For example, the qualities of smug narrow-mindedness, bourgeois materialism, faith in social progress, and priggish morality are often considered Victorian. In literature, the Victorian Period was the great age of the English novel, and the latter part of the era saw the rise of movements such as decadence and symbolism.

Cumulative Author/Title Index

A

Achebe, Chinua
  Anthills of the Savannah: V1
The Agüero Sisters (Garcia): V1
Aidoo, Ama Ata
  Anowa: V1
  No Sweetness Here: V2
Allende, Isabel
  Aphrodite: V1
  The House of the Spirits: V1
Among the Volcanoes
  (Castañeda): V1
An Astrologer's Day (Narayan): V1
Annie John (Kincaid): V1
Anowa (Aidoo): V1
Anthills of the Savannah
  (Achebe): V1
Aphrodite (Allende): V1
Arreola, Juan José
  The Switchman: V2

B

Bâ, Mariama
  So Long a Letter: V2
Bad Influence (Ortiz Cofer): V1
Bernardo, José Raúl
  Silent Wing: V2
Boesman and Lena (Fugard): V1
Borges, Jorge Luis
  The Garden of Forking Paths: V1
Breath, Eyes, Memory (Danticat): V1
Business (Cruz): V1

C

Castañeda, Omar S.
  Among the Volcanoes: V1
Castillo, Ana
  So Far From God: V2
Clarke, Austin C.
  Leaving This Island Place: V2
Cruz, Victor Hernández
  Business: V1

D

Danticat, Edwidge
  Breath, Eyes, Memory: V1
  The Farming of Bones: V1
Desai, Anita
  Studies in the Park: V2
Dream on Monkey Mountain
  (Walcott): V1

E

Esquivel, Laura
  The Law of Love: V2
  Like Water for Chocolate: V2

F

Fable (Paz): V1
Family Ties (Lispector): V1
A Far Cry from Africa (Walcott): V1
The Farming of Bones (Danticat): V1
Fear (Mistral): V1
The Friends (Guy): V1
Fuentes, Carlos
  Where the Air Is Clear: V2

Fugard, Athol
  Boesman and Lena: V1
  Valley Song: V2

G

Garcia, Cristina
  The Agüero Sisters: V1
García Márquez, Gabriel
  *The Handsomest Drowned
    Man*: V1
  *One Hundred Years of
    Solitude*: V2
The Garden of Forking Paths
  (Borges): V1
Girl (Kincaid): V1
The Glass of Milk (Rojas): V1
Guy, Rosa
  The Friends: V1

H

The Handsomest Drowned Man
  (García Márquez): V1
The House of the Spirits
  (Allende): V1
Hyppolite, Joanne
  Seth and Samona: V2

I

I, Rigoberta Menchú (Menchú): V1

J

Jasmine (Mukherjee): V1

K

Kincaid, Jamaica
  Annie John: V1
The Kiss of the Spider Woman
  (Puig): V1

L

The Latin Deli (Ortiz Cofer): V2
The Law of Love (Esquivel): V2
Leaving This Island Place
  (Clarke): V2
Like Water for Chocolate
  (Esquivel): V2
Lispector, Clarice
  Family Ties: V1

M

The Management of Grief
  (Mukherjee): V2
The Martyr (wa Thiong'o): V2
Mehta, Gita
  A River Sutra: V2
Menchú, Rigoberta
  I, Rigoberta Menchú: V1
The Middleman (Mukherjee): V2
Mistral, Gabriela
  Fear: V1
Mukherjee, Bharati
  Jasmine: V1

N

Narayan, R. K.
  An Astrologer's Day: V1

Neruda, Pablo
  Ode to My Socks: V2
Ngugi wa Thiong'o,
  Petals of Blood: V2
No Sweetness Here (Aidoo): V2

O

Ode to My Socks (Neruda): V2
One Hundred Years of Solitude
  (García Márquez): V2
Ortiz Cofer, Judith
  Bad Influence: V1
  The Latin Deli: V2

P

Paz, Octavio
  Fable: V1
Petals of Blood (Ngugi wa
  Thiong'o): V2
*Pierre Menard, Author of the
  Quixote* (Borges): V2
Prayer to the Masks (Senghor): V2
Puig, Manuel
  *The Kiss of the Spider
  Woman*: V1

R

Rhys, Jean
  Wide Sargasso Sea: V2
A River Sutra (Mehta): V2
Rojas, Manuel
  The Glass of Milk: V1

S

Senghor, Léopold Sédar
  Prayer to the Masks: V2
Seth and Samona (Hyppolite): V2
Silent Wing (Bernardo): V2
So Far From God (Castillo): V2
So Long a Letter (Bâ): V2
Studies in the Park (Desai): V2
The Switchman (Arreola): V2

T

The Time of the Hero (Vargas
  Llosa): V2
Tutuola, Amos
  The Village Witch Doctor: V2

V

Valley Song (Fugard): V2
Vargas Llosa, Mario
  The Time of the Hero: V2
The Village Witch Doctor
  (Tutuola): V2

W

wa Thiong'o, Ngugi
  The Martyr: V2
Walcott, Derek
  Dream on Monkey Mountain: V1
  A Far Cry from Africa: V1
Where the Air Is Clear (Fuentes): V2
Wide Sargasso Sea (Rhys): V2

Nationality/Ethnicity Index

African American
Kincaid, Jamaica
Annie John: V1

American
Castillo, Ana
So Far From God: V2
Danticat, Edwidge
Breath, Eyes, Memory: V1
The Farming of Bones: V1
Hyppolite, Joanne
Seth and Samona: V2
Kincaid, Jamaica
Annie John: V1

Antiguan
Kincaid, Jamaica
Girl: V1

Argentine
Borges, Jorge Luis
The Garden of Forking Paths: V1
*Pierre Menard, Author of the
Quixote*: V2
Puig, Manuel
*The Kiss of the Spider
Woman*: V1
Rojas, Manuel
The Glass of Milk: V1

Black
Achebe, Chinua
Anthills of the Savannah: V1

Clarke, Austin C.
Leaving This Island Place: V2
Danticat, Edwidge
Breath, Eyes, Memory: V1
The Farming of Bones: V1
Guy, Rosa
The Friends: V1
Ngugi wa Thiong'o,
Petals of Blood: V2
Tutuola, Amos
The Village Witch Doctor: V2
Walcott, Derek
Dream on Monkey Mountain: V1
A Far Cry from Africa: V1

Brazilian
Lispector, Clarice
Family Ties: V1

Canadian
Clarke, Austin C.
Leaving This Island Place: V2

Chilean
Mistral, Gabriela
Fear: V1
Neruda, Pablo
Ode to My Socks: V2

Columbian
García Márquez, Gabriel
*The Handsomest Drowned
Man*: V1

*One Hundred Years of
Solitude*: V2

Cuban-American
Bernardo, José Raúl
Silent Wing: V2
Garcia, Cristina
The Agüero Sisters: V1

English
Rhys, Jean
Wide Sargasso Sea: V2

Ghanian
Aidoo, Ama Ata
Anowa: V1
No Sweetness Here: V2

Guatemalan
Castañeda, Omar S.
Among the Volcanoes: V1

Hispanic
Allende, Isabel
Aphrodite: V1
The House of the Spirits: V1
Arreola, Juan José
The Switchman: V2
Castillo, Ana
So Far From God: V2
Cruz, Victor Hernández
Business: V1

Fuentes, Carlos
   Where the Air Is Clear: V2
García Márquez, Gabriel
   *The Handsomest Drowned
      Man*: V1
   *One Hundred Years of
      Solitude*: V2
Lispector, Clarice
   Family Ties: V1
Neruda, Pablo
   Ode to My Socks: V2
Ortiz Cofer, Judith
   The Latin Deli: V2
Puig, Manuel
   *The Kiss of the Spider
      Woman*: V1
Rojas, Manuel
   The Glass of Milk: V1
Vargas Llosa, Mario
   The Time of the Hero: V2

Indian

Desai, Anita
   Studies in the Park: V2
Mukherjee, Bharati
   The Management of Grief: V2
   The Middleman: V2
Narayan, R. K.
   An Astrologer's Day: V1

Indian-American

Mehta, Gita
   A River Sutra: V2

Indian; American

Mukherjee, Bharati
   Jasmine: V1

Kenyan

Ngugi wa Thiong'o,
   Petals of Blood: V2
wa Thiong'o, Ngugi
   The Martyr: V2

Mexican

Arreola, Juan José
   The Switchman: V2
Esquivel, Laura
   The Law of Love: V2
   Like Water for Chocolate: V2
Fuentes, Carlos
   Where the Air Is Clear: V2
Paz, Octavio
   Fable: V1

Native American (Quiche)

Menchú, Rigoberta
   I, Rigoberta Menchú: V1

Nigerian

Achebe, Chinua
   Anthills of the Savannah: V1
Tutuola, Amos
   The Village Witch Doctor: V2

Peruvian

Vargas Llosa, Mario
   The Time of the Hero: V2

Peruvian; Chilean

Allende, Isabel
   Aphrodite: V1

The House of the Spirits: V1

Puerto Rican

Cruz, Victor Hernández
   Business: V1
Ortiz Cofer, Judith
   Bad Influence: V1
   The Latin Deli: V2

Senegalese

Bâ, Mariama
   So Long a Letter: V2
Senghor, Léopold Sédar
   Prayer to the Masks: V2

South African

Fugard, Athol
   Boesman and Lena: V1
   Valley Song: V2

St. Lucian

Walcott, Derek
   Dream on Monkey Mountain: V1
   A Far Cry from Africa: V1

Trinidadian-American

Guy, Rosa
   The Friends: V1

West Indian

Kincaid, Jamaica
   Annie John: V1
Walcott, Derek
   Dream on Monkey Mountain: V1
   A Far Cry from Africa: V1

Subject/Theme Index

*Boldface terms appear as subheads in Themes section.

1950s
  Where the Air Is Clear: 506, 512, 514, 517, 539, 543-544, 551-552

A

Abandonment
  Leaving This Island Place: 30-32, 37
  Like Water for Chocolate: 60, 63
  The Martyr: 104-105
  No Sweetness Here: 124-125
  Pierre Menard, Author of the Quixote: 254, 256
  A River Sutra: 284-285
  So Far From God: 336, 339-340
  So Long a Letter: 376, 378, 380-382, 387-390, 395-396
  The Time of the Hero: 443, 448
  Where the Air Is Clear: 526, 528, 530, 532
Abstinence
  Petals of Blood: 233
Absurdity
  The Switchman: 420
Absurdity
  The Management of Grief: 78-80
  Pierre Menard, Author of the Quixote: 255-257, 261-262
  The Switchman: 420-422, 432-435
  Where the Air Is Clear: 524-526
Adulthood
  Studies in the Park: 413, 415

Adventure and Exploration
  One Hundred Years of Solitude: 181, 185-186, 191, 193-196
  So Far From God: 358-359
  The Switchman: 433-434
  Where the Air Is Clear: 543, 545, 547
Africa
  The Martyr: 84-85, 90-93, 96-99, 102, 104-105
  No Sweetness Here: 129, 133-134
  Petals of Blood: 203-206, 210-216, 222-223, 231, 234
  Prayer to the Masks: 265, 267-268, 271-273, 277-279
  So Long a Letter: 376-378, 394, 397-399
  Valley Song: 472-474, 478-482, 485, 487-488
  The Village Witch Doctor: 498-499
Alcoholism, Drugs, and Drug Addiction
  One Hundred Years of Solitude: 171-172
Alienation of the Land
  Petals of Blood: 209
Alienation
  No Sweetness Here: 131-133
  Where the Air Is Clear: 527, 529-530
  Wide Sargasso Sea: 568-570
Allegory
  One Hundred Years of Solitude: 183
  Petals of Blood: 220, 223

  The Switchman: 417, 420, 424, 427-432
Ambiguity
  Pierre Menard, Author of the Quixote: 241-242
  So Long a Letter: 397
Ambition
  One Hundred Years of Solitude: 190, 193, 195
  Where the Air Is Clear: 543, 548, 550-551
American Northeast
  Where the Air Is Clear: 539-541, 551
American South
  One Hundred Years of Solitude: 191, 193-194
American Southwest
  So Far From God: 358, 360-361
Americanization, Capitalism, and Immigrant Identity
  The Middleman: 110
Angels
  Petals of Blood: 221-222
Anger and Hatred
  The Law of Love: 18
Anger
  The Law of Love: 18-19, 23-24
  Like Water for Chocolate: 41, 44, 46, 50
  So Far From God: 347-348, 352
  So Long a Letter: 389-391
  Where the Air Is Clear: 508, 514-515
Apartheid
  Valley Song: 470, 477-482

Apathy
    A River Sutra: 297-298
Appearance Vs. Reality
    The Village Witch Doctor: 500
Art and Experience
    The Latin Deli: An Ars Poetica: 4
Arthurian Legend
    The Management of Grief: 76
Atonement and Forgiveness
    The Law of Love: 18
Atonement
    Petals of Blood: 232-234
    A River Sutra: 299-302
    Where the Air Is Clear: 512-513

B

Beauty
    The Middleman: 120-124
    No Sweetness Here: 131, 133
    Ode to My Socks: 139, 141-144,
        148, 151-153
    One Hundred Years of Solitude:
        170-171, 176-177, 194-195
    Seth and Samona: 309, 311, 313
    So Long a Letter: 393-395
    Studies in the Park: 402-403, 408
    Wide Sargasso Sea: 567, 569-570
Betrayal
    The Martyr: 93-95
Bildungsroman
    Studies in the Park: 413, 415

C

Capitalism
    The Middleman: 107, 110, 112
    Petals of Blood: 202, 209-
        212, 230-232
Central America
    The Middleman: 117-118
    Silent Wing: 321-322, 326-330
Change and Transformation
    The Law of Love: 18
Charity
    The Martyr: 89
Childhood
    Leaving This Island Place:
        27-28, 35
    So Long a Letter: 386, 388-389
    The Time of the Hero: 456-458
    Wide Sargasso Sea: 571-574
Christianity
    Petals of Blood: 210
Christianity
    The Martyr: 85, 89, 91-92
    Petals of Blood: 205, 210,
        221-223
    So Far From God: 361
    The Switchman: 428-429
City Life
    The Latin Deli: An Ars Poetica:
        1, 4-6

    Where the Air Is Clear:
        541, 543, 552
Colonialism
    The Martyr: 87
Colonialism
    The Martyr: 85, 87, 89-90, 105
    One Hundred Years of Solitude:
        178-181, 184, 186, 188
    Prayer to the Masks: 265,
        270, 272
Communism
    Ode to My Socks: 139, 145-147
Connection to the Land
    Prayer to the Masks: 268
Contrast of Africa and Europe
    Prayer to the Masks: 268
Courage
    The Middleman: 114, 117-119
    Petals of Blood: 210, 216, 226-
        227, 231, 234
    Silent Wing: 328-329
    So Long a Letter: 390-391
    The Switchman: 434
Creativity and Imagination
    Like Water for Chocolate: 45
Creativity
    Like Water for Chocolate: 45-47,
        50-51, 61-64
    *Pierre Menard, Author of the
        Quixote:* 260-261
    Prayer to the Masks: 267-268
    Valley Song: 484-485
Crime and Criminals
    One Hundred Years of Solitude:
        161-162, 172
    Petals of Blood: 205, 211-212
    A River Sutra: 301
    The Time of the Hero: 437-439,
        444-445, 461, 463-464
    The Village Witch Doctor: 492-
        493, 500-501
    Where the Air Is Clear: 545, 549
Critique of Capitalism
    Petals of Blood: 209
Cruelty and Violence
    Like Water for Chocolate: 44
Cruelty
    Like Water for Chocolate: 44, 46
    No Sweetness Here: 129-130
    One Hundred Years of Solitude:
        192, 195-196
    Petals of Blood: 211, 213-216
    So Far From God: 350-
        351, 361-363
    The Time of the Hero: 447, 450,
        452-453, 461
    Where the Air Is Clear: 524-525
    Wide Sargasso Sea: 554, 565-566
Culture Clash
    The Latin Deli: An Ars Poetica: 3
    The Management of Grief: 70
    Seth and Samona: 309
    Where the Air Is Clear: 512

Curiosity
    Where the Air Is Clear:
        540-542, 547
Cycle of Life
    Valley Song: 477
Cynicism
    The Middleman: 112-113

D

Dance
    Prayer to the Masks: 267-
        268, 279-280
Death
    Seth and Samona: 309
Death in Life, Life in Death
    Studies in the Park: 403
Death
    The Law of Love: 15-16
    Leaving This Island Place:
        27-33, 36-37
    Like Water for Chocolate: 40-
        41, 45, 60-61
    The Management of Grief:
        67-68, 72
    The Martyr: 85-86, 89, 91-93
    No Sweetness Here: 123-
        124, 127, 130
    One Hundred Years of Solitude:
        161-162, 170, 172, 174-177,
        185, 187, 190, 192-193,
        198-199
    Petals of Blood: 205-206,
        215, 231-234
    Prayer to the Masks: 268,
        270-271, 280
    A River Sutra: 282-284
    Seth and Samona: 305-306,
        311-313
    Silent Wing: 327-330
    So Far From God: 335-342, 348-
        351, 354, 356-360, 364-365
    So Long a Letter: 371, 376-378,
        387-391, 395-399
    Studies in the Park: 403, 405
    The Time of the Hero: 437,
        439, 445, 448
    Valley Song: 472-473, 478
    The Village Witch Doctor: 491-
        493, 497, 500-502
    Where the Air Is Clear: 508, 512-
        514, 523-525, 532-538, 543,
        545, 547, 550, 552
    Wide Sargasso Sea: 556-558, 564
Deceit
    The Village Witch Doctor:
        500-501
Depression and Melancholy
    So Long a Letter: 393-395
Description
    *The Latin Deli: An Ars
        Poetica:* 2-3

One Hundred Years of Solitude:
182, 184
Petals of Blood: 226-227
So Far From God: 362, 364-365
Studies in the Park: 407-411
The Time of the Hero: 458
Where the Air Is Clear: 525, 527
Wide Sargasso Sea: 571-573

Despair
One Hundred Years of Solitude:
190, 192-193
Prayer to the Masks: 267-
268, 273

Detective Fiction
The Time of the Hero: 456-459

Dialect
The Middleman: 116
Studies in the Park: 405-406

Dialogue
The Martyr: 102, 104
No Sweetness Here: 127, 129
The Switchman: 417-418
Where the Air Is Clear: 534-535

Difference
Seth and Samona: 309

Disease
One Hundred Years of Solitude:
179, 182-188

Divorce
No Sweetness Here: 123-127
So Far From God: 342
So Long a Letter: 392-395

Doubles
Wide Sargasso Sea: 563

Drama
The Martyr: 95-97, 101
Valley Song: 470-471, 477,
479-482

Dreams
Valley Song: 476

Dreams and Visions
One Hundred Years of Solitude:
181, 184, 186, 190-191,
195-196
Silent Wing: 321-322, 326-330
So Far From God: 347, 349-351
Studies in the Park: 400, 402-404
The Switchman: 428, 430-432
Valley Song: 473-474, 477-478,
482, 484-485
Where the Air Is Clear: 508, 513-
515, 524-525, 529, 531
Wide Sargasso Sea: 570,
573, 576-577

Duty and Responsibility
Like Water for Chocolate: 44

Duty and Responsibility
Like Water for Chocolate: 44, 46

E

Education
Petals of Blood: 211

Emotions
The Latin Deli: An Ars Poetica:
3, 5, 9-10
The Law of Love: 23
Like Water for Chocolate: 45-46,
50, 52, 55-57
The Management of Grief:
78, 80-81
The Middleman: 121
No Sweetness Here: 130, 135
Ode to My Socks: 142
Petals of Blood: 234
*Pierre Menard, Author of the
Quixote:* 254
A River Sutra: 295
Silent Wing: 321, 327
So Far From God: 339,
348, 357, 364
So Long a Letter: 376, 388
Studies in the Park: 408, 414
Valley Song: 488
Where the Air Is Clear: 528, 540
Wide Sargasso Sea: 562

Epic
One Hundred Years of Solitude:
190-191, 194-196

Error
*Pierre Menard, Author of the
Quixote:* 251, 254, 257,
259-260, 263

Essay
*The Latin Deli: An Ars
Poetica:* 12
One Hundred Years of Solitude:
178, 180
*Pierre Menard, Author of the
Quixote:* 236, 238, 240-245
Where the Air Is Clear: 541-542

Eternity
One Hundred Years of Solitude:
190, 193, 195-196
So Long a Letter: 394
Where the Air Is Clear: 508, 517,
525-527, 530, 534, 536-537

Europe
The Management of Grief:
67, 72-73
The Martyr: 85-86, 91, 96-98
Ode to My Socks: 145-147
One Hundred Years of Solitude:
169, 171, 173, 190-191
Petals of Blood: 204, 214, 216
*Pierre Menard, Author of the
Quixote:* 242-244, 256,
259-260
Prayer to the Masks: 267-268,
271-273, 277-278
The Time of the Hero: 447-449
Where the Air Is Clear: 516,
523-524, 537, 540, 542-
545, 548-549
Wide Sargasso Sea: 554, 557-
558, 564-566, 571-573, 577

European vs. African Traditions
So Long a Letter: 375

Evil
The Martyr: 99
*One Hundred Years of
Solitude:* 193
Petals of Blood: 212, 215-
216, 231, 233
A River Sutra: 300-301
So Far From God: 363
So Long a Letter: 393-394
Where the Air Is Clear: 513,
541, 543, 550

Execution
Where the Air Is Clear: 542,
546, 549, 552

Exile
The Martyr: 97, 99
Ode to My Socks: 145-148
Seth and Samona: 311-312

Existentialism
The Switchman: 420

Existentialism
The Switchman: 420-421,
425-426
Where the Air Is Clear: 522-528

Exploitation of Women
So Far From God: 338

Exploitation
The Martyr: 98-99
Petals of Blood: 205, 210-
212, 230, 234
Prayer to the Masks: 267-268
So Far From God: 339, 355,
360, 362, 365

Expressionism
*One Hundred Years of
Solitude:* 178

F

Family
*One Hundred Years of
Solitude:* 169
Studies in the Park: 402

Family and Inheritance
The Village Witch Doctor: 495

Family and Paternity
Leaving This Island Place: 30

Family Life
Leaving This Island Place: 31
Like Water for Chocolate: 40,
59, 61, 63-64
So Far From God: 341, 347-348

Family Space
So Far From God: 339

Farm and Rural Life
No Sweetness Here: 136-137
Petals of Blood: 209-210, 213-
215, 228-229, 234
Prayer to the Masks: 274-275
So Far From God: 360-361
The Switchman: 423

Valley Song: 470-474, 479, 482, 489-490

The Village Witch Doctor: 493, 498

Fate and Chance

Like Water for Chocolate: 60-63

One Hundred Years of Solitude: 178, 180, 183-185, 192-193

Pierre Menard, Author of the Quixote: 252, 254-255, 263

So Long a Letter: 369, 371, 377, 392-396, 399

The Switchman: 428-431, 434-435

The Time of the Hero: 463

Where the Air Is Clear: 534, 536-538

Fear and Terror

Seth and Samona: 306, 309, 311

So Far From God: 348-350

Valley Song: 473-474, 482

Wide Sargasso Sea: 556, 563-564, 571, 573-575

Femininity

Wide Sargasso Sea: 572, 574-578

Feminism

No Sweetness Here: 128-130

So Far From God: 341, 354, 356, 362, 365

So Long a Letter: 369, 375, 378, 392, 396-398

Film

Like Water for Chocolate: 38, 48, 53, 55

Where the Air Is Clear: 540, 542-543, 549

Flesh vs. Spirit

The Law of Love: 18

Folklore

The Management of Grief: 75

One Hundred Years of Solitude: 170, 182-185, 189, 191-192, 195-196

So Far From God: 355

The Village Witch Doctor: 491, 497-499

Foreshadowing

Silent Wing: 329

Forgiveness

The Law of Love: 14, 16, 18-20

So Far From God: 353

Free Will Vs. Determinism

The Time of the Hero: 462-463

Freedom and Slavery

Silent Wing: 326

Freedom

The Middleman: 119-120

So Long a Letter: 398

Where the Air Is Clear: 522-524, 531

Friendship

The Time of the Hero: 444

G

Gender and Beauty Standards

No Sweetness Here: 126

Gender Roles

No Sweetness Here: 126, 131, 133

So Far From God: 346

The Time of the Hero: 452

Generosity

The Martyr: 84-85, 88-89

Ghost

Like Water for Chocolate: 45-46

Prayer to the Masks: 267-268, 275-277

God

One Hundred Years of Solitude: 197-199

A River Sutra: 292

So Far From God: 346, 351-353

Where the Air Is Clear: 512-514, 534, 538

Grief and Sorrow

The Management of Grief: 66, 68, 70-72, 77-82

No Sweetness Here: 124, 127

Seth and Samona: 305-306

So Far From God: 357, 362, 365-366

So Long a Letter: 372, 375, 377-378, 388, 390

Guilt

Leaving This Island Place: 35-37

So Long a Letter: 396

Where the Air Is Clear: 537-538

H

Happiness and Gaiety

So Long a Letter: 370-372, 392-398

The Village Witch Doctor: 502

Hatred

The Law of Love: 14-16, 19

Like Water for Chocolate: 48

Petals of Blood: 224

So Far From God: 360-361

So Long a Letter: 390-392, 396-397

Studies in the Park: 410

Where the Air Is Clear: 524

Wide Sargasso Sea: 570, 573, 575-577

Heaven

One Hundred Years of Solitude: 175

Petals of Blood: 222

The Switchman: 428-429

Where the Air Is Clear: 535-536

Hell

So Far From God: 349, 352-353

Heritage and Ancestry

The Latin Deli: An Ars Poetica: 1-4, 7-8

Prayer to the Masks: 267-268, 273-278

So Far From God: 359, 361-363

The Time of the Hero: 448

Heroism

The Management of Grief: 75-76

The Middleman: 116

One Hundred Years of Solitude: 189-190

Petals of Blood: 227-228, 231-232

Silent Wing: 328

So Long a Letter: 386-388, 393, 395-397

The Switchman: 434-435

Historical Periods

One Hundred Years of Solitude: 185

History

Leaving This Island Place: 30, 32-33

The Management of Grief: 73

The Martyr: 85, 89-91

Ode to My Socks: 145, 147, 154-157

One Hundred Years of Solitude: 179-182, 185-186, 189-190, 194-197

Petals of Blood: 223-224, 227-231

Pierre Menard, Author of the Quixote: 240-241, 252-253, 258-260

Prayer to the Masks: 267, 270, 272

Seth and Samona: 311-312

So Far From God: 355-359, 362, 366

Studies in the Park: 405-406

The Time of the Hero: 464-466

Valley Song: 474, 480-481

Where the Air Is Clear: 506-507, 514-515, 518, 534-535, 538-539, 544, 548-549

Homelessness

So Far From God: 354-355, 359-360, 366

Where the Air Is Clear: 512, 515

Honor

Silent Wing: 319, 321, 325-326, 329-330

So Far From God: 336, 340, 365

The Time of the Hero: 444

Hope

The Management of Grief: 68, 71, 74-78

Petals of Blood: 228-232, 235

Silent Wing: 321, 325-327

Valley Song: 471, 477-479

Where the Air Is Clear: 534-535

Human Condition

Where the Air Is Clear: 530

Humor
   The Law of Love: 20-21
   One Hundred Years of Solitude:
      192, 194-195
   Pierre Menard, Author of the
      Quixote: 259, 261
   So Far From God: 333, 340
   The Switchman: 427, 431-432

I

Identity
   The Latin Deli: An Ars Poetica: 4
Ignorance
   One Hundred Years of Solitude:
      189, 193-194
   So Long a Letter: 394, 396
   Where the Air Is Clear: 539, 541,
      543, 546-547
Illegitimacy
   Leaving This Island Place:
      27-28, 32
Imagery and Symbolism
   The Latin Deli: An Ars Poetica:
      2-3, 9-10
   Leaving This Island Place:
      30, 35-36
   Like Water for Chocolate: 46,
      53, 55-56, 64
   The Martyr: 85, 89, 93-94
   Ode to My Socks: 145,
      150, 153-155
   One Hundred Years of Solitude:
      161, 170-171, 176-179,
      183-187
   Petals of Blood: 221-223,
      227-229
   Pierre Menard, Author of the
      Quixote: 240, 242-244, 252
   Prayer to the Masks: 267-268
   So Far From God: 359-360
   Studies in the Park: 403-
      404, 413-414
   The Switchman: 424-425, 428-
      431, 434-435
   Where the Air Is Clear: 514, 519,
      521-522, 529, 534-538
   Wide Sargasso Sea: 564, 566
Imagination
   One Hundred Years of Solitude:
      174-177
   Pierre Menard, Author of the
      Quixote: 256
Imagism
   Ode to My Socks: 148
Immigrants and Immigration
   The Latin Deli: An Ars
      Poetica: 1-8
   Leaving This Island Place: 32-34
   The Management of Grief:
      67, 72-75, 78
   The Middleman: 107, 110-
      114, 118-122

Imperialism
   The Martyr: 96, 98-99
   One Hundred Years of Solitude:
      183-188
Insanity
   Wide Sargasso Sea: 554-557,
      563-564, 577
Irony
   The Middleman: 112-113, 121
   No Sweetness Here: 136-137
   Pierre Menard, Author of the
      Quixote: 252-253, 256-257,
      260-263
   So Far From God: 349
   The Switchman: 432-433
Islamism
   A River Sutra: 281-283, 292
   So Long a Letter: 370-372,
      378-382, 388
   Studies in the Park: 405
Isolation
   A River Sutra: 290
   Wide Sargasso Sea: 562

J

Justice
   The Village Witch Doctor: 495

K

Killers and Killing
   The Law of Love: 15-16, 20
   The Management of Grief:
      66-68, 73
   The Martyr: 84, 86, 88-89, 95
   One Hundred Years of Solitude:
      161, 171-172, 183, 187-
      188, 195-196
   Petals of Blood: 212, 233-234
   A River Sutra: 284, 292
   So Far From God: 336-339
   The Time of the Hero: 443-444
   Where the Air Is Clear: 512-514,
      517, 522-525, 543
Knowledge
   No Sweetness Here: 132
   One Hundred Years of Solitude:
      182-184, 189-190, 196-200
   A River Sutra: 299
   So Far From God: 354-356,
      361-362, 366
   So Long a Letter: 371

L

Landscape
   Ode to My Socks: 153-155
   One Hundred Years of Solitude:
      170-171, 191, 193-194
   Petals of Blood: 209, 211-213,
      225-228, 231-232

   A River Sutra: 281-285, 290-
      296, 299-301
   Silent Wing: 322, 326-327
   So Far From God: 356, 359-360
   Valley Song: 471-474, 477-479
   Where the Air Is Clear: 544,
      547-548, 552
   Wide Sargasso Sea: 569-570
Law and Order
   The Law of Love: 14, 16, 18-20
   The Martyr: 98-100
   The Middleman: 108, 110-112
   One Hundred Years of Solitude:
      172, 178, 180-181, 188
   Petals of Blood: 202-205, 211,
      213-215, 221, 223
   So Long a Letter: 370-371, 376-
      377, 393, 396-397
   Valley Song: 479-482
   The Village Witch Doctor: 500
   Where the Air Is Clear: 541, 545
Leaving
   Leaving This Island Place: 30
Limitations and Opportunities
   One Hundred Years of Solitude:
      179-180, 184, 189
   Valley Song: 473, 477, 479-480
   Where the Air Is Clear: 524
Literary Criticism
   Ode to My Socks: 139, 148
   One Hundred Years of Solitude:
      173, 175
   Pierre Menard, Author of the
      Quixote: 240, 248-249
   The Time of the Hero: 454, 465
   The Village Witch Doctor: 499
   Where the Air Is Clear: 551
Literary Terms
   One Hundred Years of
      Solitude: 197
Loneliness
   Leaving This Island Place: 37
   The Martyr: 96
   The Middleman: 119-122
   No Sweetness Here: 126, 136-137
   One Hundred Years of
      Solitude: 183
   A River Sutra: 283, 290
   So Far From God: 363-364
   So Long a Letter: 389, 391
   Where the Air Is Clear: 531
   Wide Sargasso Sea: 554-556
Love
   A River Sutra: 289
Love and Honor
   Silent Wing: 325
Love and Passion
   Like Water for Chocolate: 44
Love and Passion
   The Latin Deli: An Ars
      Poetica: 3-5
   The Law of Love: 14-16, 19-26

Like Water for Chocolate: 40-41, 45-46, 49-58, 61, 63
The Middleman: 119-121
Ode to My Socks: 156-157
Petals of Blood: 225, 229, 232-234
A River Sutra: 282-284, 290-293, 297-301
Silent Wing: 321-322, 327-331
So Far From God: 336, 338, 347-349, 359-360, 363-364
So Long a Letter: 371-372, 379-382, 390-391, 394-399
The Time of the Hero: 443-445
Valley Song: 474, 476-477
Where the Air Is Clear: 507-508, 517, 523, 525, 528-529, 532, 545, 547, 549-550
Wide Sargasso Sea: 557-558, 563-564, 575-577
Lower Class
The Martyr: 102-105
Petals of Blood: 204-206, 210-214
So Long a Letter: 392-393
The Time of the Hero: 437-438, 448-449
Wide Sargasso Sea: 564-565
Loyalty
The Management of Grief: 71
The Martyr: 93-95
The Middleman: 112
Ode to My Socks: 139, 145
Pierre Menard, Author of the Quixote: 256, 261-262
A River Sutra: 300-301
So Far From God: 358-361
So Long a Letter: 392-393
The Time of the Hero: 439, 444, 452-453
Valley Song: 477-478
Where the Air Is Clear: 541, 547

M

Magic Realism
The Latin Deli: An Ars Poetica: 3, 5
The Law of Love: 15, 19-22
Like Water for Chocolate: 38, 46-49, 57-58
One Hundred Years of Solitude: 170-171, 174-176, 179-189
The Switchman: 422, 424
Where the Air Is Clear: 505, 514, 517
Magic
One Hundred Years of Solitude: 180-181, 185, 187, 194-195
The Village Witch Doctor: 495, 500
Wide Sargasso Sea: 556-557, 566, 569-570

Marriage and Tradition
No Sweetness Here: 125
Marriage
Like Water for Chocolate: 39-41, 46, 49-50, 58-63
The Middleman: 122-125
A River Sutra: 284, 290
So Far From God: 333-336, 347, 349-352
So Long a Letter: 370-371, 377-383, 386-398
Where the Air Is Clear: 508, 512-513
Wide Sargasso Sea: 557, 562, 573, 575, 577
Martyr
The Martyr: 85, 89, 91-92
Masculinity
The Time of the Hero: 442
Masculinity
The Time of the Hero: 436-437, 444, 450, 452-454
Maternal Love
No Sweetness Here: 126
Meaning and Interpretation
Pierre Menard, Author of the Quixote: 240
Meaning of Life
The Law of Love: 18
Memory
Pierre Menard, Author of the Quixote: 239
Memory and Reminiscence
One Hundred Years of Solitude: 179, 182-184
Petals of Blood: 224-226
Pierre Menard, Author of the Quixote: 238-240
Where the Air Is Clear: 507-508, 514
Mental Instability
Wide Sargasso Sea: 576
Middle Class
So Long a Letter: 393, 395-398
Middle East
The Management of Grief: 66, 68, 70-77
The Middleman: 113, 117-118
A River Sutra: 283-284, 291-296
Studies in the Park: 404-407
Modernism
One Hundred Years of Solitude: 159, 172, 178-180, 186-187
Pierre Menard, Author of the Quixote: 243-244
The Time of the Hero: 446-447
Where the Air Is Clear: 522, 529-530
Wide Sargasso Sea: 566
Monarchy
One Hundred Years of Solitude: 184-185

Where the Air Is Clear: 544-545
Money and Economics
Petals of Blood: 202, 205, 209-213
Seth and Samona: 312
So Far From God: 354, 356, 358-359, 366
So Long a Letter: 395, 397, 399
The Time of the Hero: 439, 446-449
The Village Witch Doctor: 493, 495, 497, 500-502
Where the Air Is Clear: 507-508, 515-517, 522, 541, 544-546, 551
Wide Sargasso Sea: 556, 564, 571-573
Monologue
Studies in the Park: 401, 403-404
The Time of the Hero: 460-461
Mood
The Management of Grief: 75, 77
Morals and Morality
The Law of Love: 20
Leaving This Island Place: 36
The Martyr: 99, 101
Ode to My Socks: 141-143
One Hundred Years of Solitude: 194
Petals of Blood: 206, 210-212, 216, 224-225, 229-232
Pierre Menard, Author of the Quixote: 260-261
So Far From God: 350, 359-361
So Long a Letter: 369, 371-372, 376-378, 396, 398
The Time of the Hero: 436, 446, 450
Murder
The Law of Love: 15-16
The Martyr: 84-85, 88, 93-95
Petals of Blood: 203-205, 212, 214, 233-234
The Time of the Hero: 443-445
Where the Air Is Clear: 523-524
Music
The Law of Love: 24-25
The Martyr: 90
Petals of Blood: 204-205, 213, 220, 222
Prayer to the Masks: 265, 267-270
A River Sutra: 281, 283-285, 290-291, 299-301
Valley Song: 471-474, 482, 485-490
Where the Air Is Clear: 545, 547, 551
Mystery and Intrigue
Like Water for Chocolate: 58-61
A River Sutra: 282-284, 290-291

The Time of the Hero: 437,
444-445, 449-450, 457-
459, 462-464
Where the Air Is Clear: 535-538
Myths and Legends
The Management of Grief: 75-77
One Hundred Years of Solitude:
170-172, 175-176, 190,
194, 196-200
Prayer to the Masks: 266, 268,
270, 274-275
A River Sutra: 284-285,
292, 299-300
So Far From God: 352,
355, 357-358
Where the Air Is Clear: 505-
506, 514-515, 524-525, 528-
530, 536-538

N

Narration
The Latin Deli: An Ars Poetica:
10-12
The Law of Love: 21-24
Leaving This Island Place:
28-33, 36-37
Like Water for Chocolate: 41, 45,
47, 49-50, 55-56, 60-64
The Management of Grief: 75, 77
The Martyr: 87-90
The Middleman: 108, 110-
112, 115-116
No Sweetness Here: 123-
131, 135-137
One Hundred Years of Solitude:
179-190, 194-195
Petals of Blood: 210-211,
216-220, 229
*Pierre Menard, Author of the
Quixote:* 236-238, 241-242,
246-254, 257-263
A River Sutra: 282-285, 290-292,
295-298, 301-302
Seth and Samona: 310, 313
Silent Wing: 320, 326, 328
So Far From God: 340, 354-355,
358, 362-363
So Long a Letter: 377-378, 388-
391, 394-398
Studies in the Park: 401, 403-404
The Switchman: 421, 423,
428-429
The Time of the Hero: 445-446,
450, 454-463
The Village Witch Doctor:
496-497
Where the Air Is Clear: 505, 508,
512-515, 518, 523-524, 530-
531, 536, 538
Wide Sargasso Sea: 555-557,
564, 572-576

Nationalism and Patriotism
One Hundred Years of Solitude:
190-191, 194
Nature
The Middleman: 117
Ode to My Socks: 139, 141-142,
147, 154-156
One Hundred Years of Solitude:
170, 183, 189, 191-192
Petals of Blood: 209, 224,
229-234
*Pierre Menard, Author of the
Quixote:* 254-255, 259-262
Prayer to the Masks: 268, 273
A River Sutra: 290-291, 301
So Far From God: 350,
352, 354, 360
So Long a Letter: 394-397
The Time of the Hero: 460-461
Valley Song: 477, 479, 482
Where the Air Is Clear: 522,
524, 526-527, 534-535,
538, 542-543
Nihilism
*Pierre Menard, Author of the
Quixote:* 260-261
North America
The Latin Deli: An Ars Poetica:
2-5, 9
The Law of Love: 14-16, 19-21
Leaving This Island Place: 28-34
Like Water for Chocolate: 39,
45, 47, 53-55
The Management of Grief:
68, 72-78, 81
The Middleman: 111, 113-114
Ode to My Socks: 146-147
One Hundred Years of Solitude:
172-173, 191, 194-195
Seth and Samona: 304-306,
312-313
Silent Wing: 320-322, 327-
328, 331
The Switchman: 422-424
The Time of the Hero: 448
Where the Air Is Clear: 505-508,
513-519, 522-525, 528-552
Novel
The Law of Love: 14-15, 19-26
Leaving This Island Place: 34
Like Water for Chocolate: 38-39,
45-51, 54-64
The Martyr: 90-92, 97, 99-104
No Sweetness Here: 129
One Hundred Years of Solitude:
159, 161, 169-170, 173,
197-200
Petals of Blood: 203-205, 210-
213, 216-220, 224-228,
231, 233, 235
*Pierre Menard, Author of the
Quixote:* 250, 252-253,
260-261

A River Sutra: 285, 290-
293, 297-301
Seth and Samona: 311, 313
Silent Wing: 319-320, 326-328
So Far From God: 334, 336,
338-342, 346-350, 353-
363, 366-372
So Long a Letter: 376-398
Studies in the Park: 405-408
The Time of the Hero: 437-439,
445-447, 450, 452-468
The Village Witch Doctor:
497-498
Where the Air Is Clear: 506, 513-
515, 518, 522-552
Wide Sargasso Sea: 555, 557-
558, 563-566, 569-575
Nurturance
*The Latin Deli: An Ars
Poetica:* 4-5
Like Water for Chocolate: 52-53
So Far From God: 362

O

Obedience
Like Water for Chocolate: 44
Ode
Ode to My Socks: 139, 141-148,
151-154, 157
Old Age
Studies in the Park: 414-415
The Switchman: 419, 421-
422, 434
Valley Song: 470-471, 477-478
Oppression
Petals of Blood: 210

P

Parody
Like Water for Chocolate: 51-54
*Pierre Menard, Author of the
Quixote:* 245, 248, 250-
251, 260-262
So Far From God: 368
Patriarchy
So Long a Letter: 386, 388, 391
Perception
The Switchman: 433, 435
The Time of the Hero: 454-
455, 465-468
Wide Sargasso Sea: 574, 576
Permanence
*One Hundred Years of
Solitude:* 191
So Long a Letter: 392, 397-398
Where the Air Is Clear: 518,
522, 525-526
Persecution
Like Water for Chocolate: 44
Petals of Blood: 230
So Far From God: 349, 352-
353, 357, 364

So Long a Letter: 383-385, 388-
    390, 393-398
Where the Air Is Clear: 524-525
Wide Sargasso Sea: 571,
    575, 577
Perseverance
    One Hundred Years of Solitude:
        190-193
Personal Identity
    *The Latin Deli: An Ars
        Poetica:* 1-5
    Petals of Blood: 232, 234
    So Far From God: 354,
        356, 360, 362
    Where the Air Is Clear: 505, 507,
        512-515, 518-519, 522
    Wide Sargasso Sea: 571-574,
        577-578
Personification
    One Hundred Years of Solitude:
        176-177
    Where the Air Is Clear: 512-513,
        519, 521-522, 531
Philosophical Ideas
    One Hundred Years of Solitude:
        170, 191, 195
    *Pierre Menard, Author of the
        Quixote:* 236, 240-241, 250-
        251, 254-263
    The Switchman: 420, 424,
        432-433
    The Time of the Hero: 462
    Where the Air Is Clear: 517-518,
        526, 536-538
Pleasure
    Ode to My Socks: 142-143
Plot
    The Law of Love: 22
    Like Water for Chocolate: 60-61
    The Time of the Hero: 445,
        450, 461-464
    Valley Song: 478-479
    Where the Air Is Clear: 528-
        530, 544-545
Poetry
    *The Latin Deli: An Ars
        Poetica:* 1-10
    Ode to My Socks: 140-157
    *Pierre Menard, Author of the
        Quixote:* 240-243, 252-253
    Prayer to the Masks: 266-
        271, 275-278
    Silent Wing: 320, 325, 327-329
    The Time of the Hero: 438-439,
        444-445, 465-466
    Where the Air Is Clear:
        541, 544-545
Point of View
    No Sweetness Here: 127, 129
    *One Hundred Years of
        Solitude:* 198
    Petals of Blood: 211, 213,
        217-219

A River Sutra: 299-300
Studies in the Park: 401, 403
The Time of the Hero: 465-466
Wide Sargasso Sea: 575-576
Politicians
    The Martyr: 90-91
    The Middleman: 118
    Ode to My Socks: 141, 145-147
    Prayer to the Masks: 271, 273
    The Switchman: 422-423
    The Time of the Hero: 447
    Valley Song: 470, 480-482
    Where the Air Is Clear: 545, 552
Politics
    The Management of Grief:
        67-68, 73-74
    The Martyr: 88, 90-92, 96-102
    The Middleman: 108, 110-
        112, 116
    Ode to My Socks: 139, 144-
        148, 154-157
    One Hundred Years of Solitude:
        161-162, 172-173, 180-184,
        187-192, 195-196
    Petals of Blood: 203-204,
        210, 213-223
    *Pierre Menard, Author of the
        Quixote:* 243-245
    Prayer to the Masks: 267,
        270-273
    A River Sutra: 284, 290, 292
    Seth and Samona: 311-312
    Silent Wing: 321, 327-328
    So Far From God: 340-341,
        347, 349, 351, 354-359,
        362, 364-366
    So Long a Letter: 378, 386-388
    Studies in the Park: 404-405
    The Switchman: 423-424,
        429-431
    The Time of the Hero: 448-449,
        453, 465-467
    Valley Song: 473, 478-482
    Where the Air Is Clear: 506,
        514-518, 525-529, 532, 539-
        540, 543-546
Postcolonialism
    One Hundred Years of Solitude:
        178-189
Postmodernism
    Like Water for Chocolate: 51-52
    One Hundred Years of Solitude:
        179-180, 183-184, 188-189
    *Pierre Menard, Author of the
        Quixote:* 242-245, 250
Poverty
    Seth and Samona: 311-312
    The Village Witch Doctor: 492-
        493, 497, 501-502
Pragmatism
    *Pierre Menard, Author of the
        Quixote:* 258-259

Pride
    So Long a Letter: 392-393, 398
    The Switchman: 428, 430-431
Prostitution
    Petals of Blood: 205, 210-
        211, 229-234
    A River Sutra: 290-291, 299, 301
    Where the Air Is Clear: 506-508,
        515, 519, 521-522
Psychology and the Human Mind
    *The Latin Deli: An Ars
        Poetica:* 3, 6
    One Hundred Years of Solitude:
        184-185
    *Pierre Menard, Author of the
        Quixote:* 239-240, 253-254,
        263
    A River Sutra: 300
    So Far From God: 361
    So Long a Letter: 387, 391, 393-
        394, 397, 399
    The Time of the Hero:
        443, 455-456
Public Opinion
    The Martyr: 87
Punishment
    The Village Witch Doctor: 495

R

Race Relations and Prejudice
    Wide Sargasso Sea: 562
Race
    The Management of Grief: 74
    Prayer to the Masks: 266-267,
        272, 278-280
    So Far From God: 349, 352, 354-
        358, 361, 363-364
    Valley Song: 470, 472-473,
        478-482
    Wide Sargasso Sea: 554-557,
        563-571, 576, 578
Racism
    Seth and Samona: 309
Racism and Prejudice
    Prayer to the Masks: 271-272
    Valley Song: 477-482
    Wide Sargasso Sea: 563-565
Realism
    Like Water for Chocolate: 58
    One Hundred Years of Solitude:
        170-171, 181
Relation to the Ancestors
    Prayer to the Masks: 268
Relationships among Women
    So Long a Letter: 375
Religion
    The Management of Grief: 70
    So Far From God: 339
Religion and Religious Thought
    The Law of Love: 14-15, 20
    The Management of Grief: 70, 73
    The Martyr: 92, 96, 101

One Hundred Years of Solitude:
170, 175-176, 190, 196, 199
Petals of Blood: 205, 210,
221, 225-227
Prayer to the Masks: 278-279
A River Sutra: 285, 290-295
Silent Wing: 320-322, 328-330
So Far From God: 339, 341, 348,
350-351, 355-362
So Long a Letter: 369, 377-379
Studies in the Park: 405-406
The Switchman: 428
The Time of the Hero: 448
Where the Air Is Clear: 506,
508, 512, 514, 516, 536-
537, 547, 551
Religious Works
So Long a Letter: 379-380
Renunciation
A River Sutra: 290
Revenge
The Law of Love: 22-23
Like Water for Chocolate: 50
Petals of Blood: 232-233
So Long a Letter: 395-396
Roman Catholicism
So Far From God: 354-355,
358, 361-362
The Time of the Hero: 447-448

S

Sacrifice for the Greater Good
Silent Wing: 326
Saints
One Hundred Years of Solitude:
176-177
So Far From God: 359-360
Salvation
Where the Air Is Clear: 537-538
Sanity and Insanity
Like Water for Chocolate: 45
Satire
Petals of Blood: 220-221
The Switchman: 417, 424
Science and Technology
One Hundred Years of Solitude:
192, 195-200
Prayer to the Masks: 268,
270, 272, 279
A River Sutra: 297-300
Sculpture
Silent Wing: 328-330
Sea and Sea Adventures
Leaving This Island Place:
29-30, 36-37
The Management of Grief:
68, 71-73
One Hundred Years of Solitude:
194-196
Wide Sargasso Sea: 577
Search For Knowledge
No Sweetness Here: 131-133, 137

Petals of Blood: 211-212,
220-222
So Long a Letter: 376-378
Valley Song: 480-481
Search for Self
The Management of Grief: 71
Secrecy
The Time of the Hero: 444
Self-confidence
*One Hundred Years of
Solitude:* 191
Self-realization
A River Sutra: 282, 285, 290-
292, 298-301
Selfishness
The Management of Grief: 71-72
Sentimentality
*The Latin Deli: An Ars
Poetica:* 9-10
Setting
The Management of Grief: 72
The Middleman: 107, 111
The Time of the Hero: 454-459
Valley Song: 479
Where the Air Is Clear: 540, 542
Wide Sargasso Sea: 564-565
Sex and Sexuality
The Law of Love: 18
The Middleman: 107-108, 112
One Hundred Years of Solitude:
159, 161-162, 173
Petals of Blood: 204-205,
211, 231, 233
A River Sutra: 284, 290-291
So Far From God: 334-336, 346,
348, 350, 352
The Time of the Hero:
450, 452-454
Wide Sargasso Sea: 554, 557,
562-563, 572-577
Sex Roles
Like Water for Chocolate: 44
Sexism
Seth and Samona: 316-317
Sexual Abuse
The Law of Love: 15-16, 22-23
Sickness
One Hundred Years of Solitude:
183-185, 188
Sin
The Martyr: 99
One Hundred Years of Solitude:
182-183, 187-188, 194-195
Petals of Blood: 205, 210, 216,
230, 232-233
So Far From God: 348, 351
So Long a Letter: 372, 375, 378
Where the Air Is Clear: 507, 516
Slavery
Seth and Samona: 312-313
So Long a Letter: 395
The Time of the Hero: 437-439,
444-446, 463-464

Wide Sargasso Sea: 555-556,
564-566, 572-578
Social Climbing
Leaving This Island Place: 30
Social Order
Leaving This Island Place: 27
The Martyr: 98-99, 103-105
Petals of Blood: 210, 230
So Long a Letter: 392-393
Where the Air Is Clear: 515,
517, 521-522
Wide Sargasso Sea: 557
Socialism
Petals of Blood: 203, 210-211,
216, 220-222
The Time of the Hero: 448
Where the Air Is Clear: 505, 517
Solitude
*One Hundred Years of
Solitude:* 169
Solitude
One Hundred Years of Solitude:
161, 169, 177, 194, 196
So Long a Letter: 370, 376, 382,
384, 394-396
Soul
The Law of Love: 14-16, 20-21
South America
Ode to My Socks: 144-147
One Hundred Years of Solitude:
172-173
*Pierre Menard, Author of the
Quixote:* 242-244
The Time of the Hero: 446-450,
453-454, 458
Where the Air Is Clear:
539-540, 550
Space Exploration and Study
The Law of Love: 14, 16, 19, 21
Spiritual Leaders
One Hundred Years of Solitude:
161-162, 170, 190-192
Petals of Blood: 220-221
Seth and Samona: 311-312
So Far From God: 360-362
Spiritual vs. Physical
So Far From God: 339
Spirituality
Prayer to the Masks: 265-
268, 278-279
So Far From God: 339, 341, 346-
348, 351-362
Sports and the Sporting Life
Leaving This Island Place: 27-30
The Middleman: 117-118
Storms and Weather Conditions
Ode to My Socks: 155-156
Petals of Blood: 227-228
Stream of Consciousness
Studies in the Park: 401,
404, 407-408
Where the Air Is Clear: 546, 552

Structure
    Like Water for Chocolate:
        45, 47-48
    The Management of Grief: 76-77
    Ode to My Socks: 144
    So Far From God: 334, 340
    So Long a Letter: 386-388
    The Switchman: 423
    The Time of the Hero: 445,
        450, 462-464
Success and Failure
    Leaving This Island Place:
        28, 30-31
Supernatural
    Like Water for Chocolate: 45
Supernatural
    Like Water for Chocolate: 45-46
    One Hundred Years of
        Solitude: 171
Surrealism
    The Law of Love: 19-20
    One Hundred Years of
        Solitude: 178

T

The Beauty of Utility
    Ode to My Socks: 142
The Extraordinary in the Ordinary
    Ode to My Socks: 142
The Fantastic/Magical Realism
    The Switchman: 420
The Individual and Society
    The Middleman: 114, 117
The Middleman
    The Middleman: 110
The Pen and the Sword
    Silent Wing: 325
The Struggle for Independence
    Petals of Blood: 210
The Supernatural
    Where the Air Is Clear: 512
The Synthesis of African and
    European Culture
Prayer to the Masks: 268Time
    and Change
    The Law of Love: 14, 16, 18-19
    Petals of Blood: 204-205, 210-
        212, 230-233
    So Far From God: 356, 362-363
    So Long a Letter: 397

Where the Air Is Clear: 514, 525,
        528, 530, 534, 536
Tone
    The Martyr: 88-89
    The Middleman: 113
    Ode to My Socks: 154, 156-157
    One Hundred Years of
        Solitude: 173
    Pierre Menard, Author of the
        Quixote: 250-251, 261-262

U

Ugliness
    The Latin Deli: An Ars Poetica:
        1, 3, 6-10
    A River Sutra: 290, 292
    Silent Wing: 328, 330
Uncertainty
    One Hundred Years of Solitude:
        189-191, 197
    So Long a Letter: 392,
        394-395, 399
Understanding
    The Management of Grief: 78-79
    Pierre Menard, Author of the
        Quixote: 247-248, 257,
        259, 263
    A River Sutra: 297, 299
    The Time of the Hero: 455-456
Upper Class
    Where the Air Is Clear: 507, 512,
        515, 541, 545
Utopianism
    One Hundred Years of Solitude:
        190-191, 196

V

Victim and Victimization
    Like Water for Chocolate: 44
Village versus City
    Petals of Blood: 210

W

War, the Military, and Soldier Life
    The Management of Grief:
        66, 72-75
    The Martyr: 98-101
    The Middleman: 108, 110-
        113, 116

Ode to My Socks: 144-147
One Hundred Years of Solitude:
    162, 169-174, 185-187
Prayer to the Masks: 268,
    270-272
So Far From God: 347, 349,
    353-355, 365
Studies in the Park: 405
The Time of the Hero: 437-439,
    444-450, 453, 461, 463-464
The Village Witch Doctor:
    497-498
Where the Air Is Clear:
    507, 512-517
Wealth
    Petals of Blood: 202, 209-
        211, 215
    The Village Witch Doctor:
        500-502
Western Hemisphere
    Ode to My Socks: 146
    Seth and Samona: 311-312
Wildlife
    Ode to My Socks: 141-144,
        149-150
    One Hundred Years of Solitude:
        195-196
    Prayer to the Masks: 268,
        270, 277-278
    So Far From God: 350-351
    The Time of the Hero: 438-
        439, 444-445, 450, 452-
        453, 456-461
Wisdom
    One Hundred Years of Solitude:
        198-199
    A River Sutra: 298, 300-301
Witch
    The Village Witch Doctor: 491-
        493, 497, 499-502
Woman as Daughter, Wife,
    and Mother
    So Far From God: 338
World War II
    Pierre Menard, Author of the
        Quixote: 243-244
    Prayer to the Masks: 272-273

Y

Yearning
    The Latin Deli: An Ars Poetica: 9